Contents

Welcome to the 46th edition of the AA's bestselling *Caravan and Camping Guide* – over 900 fully inspected and independently graded camping parks across England, Scotland, Wales Northern Ireland and the Republic of Ireland.

Who's in the Guide?

Within these pages you'll find simple rural campsites, beautifully landscaped parks with top quality toilet facilities and excellent customer care, and self-contained Holiday Centres that offer a wide range of sport, leisure and entertainment facilities. All have touring facilities for caravanners and campers. We also include Holiday Home Parks offering holiday caravans and lodges for hire. The sites pay an annual fee for the inspection, the recognition and rating.

AA Pennant Classification

Campsites apply for AA recognition and they receive an unannounced visit each year by one of the AA's qualified Campsite Inspectors. Touring pitches, facilities and hospitality are fully checked and campsites are graded for 1 to 5 Pennants, or rated as a Holiday Centre, using fixed criteria for each Pennant rating. A qualitative assessment score is also given to each campsite. For 2014 we have introduced Gold Pennants to identify the top quality parks that score 90% and above within the 2 to 5 Pennant ratings.

AA Campsites of the Year

Following nominations by our inspectors we award an overall winner from three national finalists, five regional winners and a Holiday Centre winner – all are selected for their outstanding overall quality and high levels of customer care. Our two special awards recognise the best small campsite, a new award for 2014, and the most improved campsite. Polmanter Touring Park, St Ives is the worthy overall winner. See page 100 for details.

An In-depth Look

This year we reveal more about the inspection process and how our inspectors award a Pennant rating and the quality % score in the AA Guide to Pennants (page 12). Our second feature explores farm diversification from cattle to camping at Sumners Ponds Fishery & Campsite in West Sussex, revealing the costs of developing a 4-Pennant site (with a 86% score) from a 5-caravan site over a 10-year period (page 28).

Campsites – Best For...

Our quick reference list highlights the inspector's favourite campsites for stunning views, waterside pitches, on-site fishing, great places to stay with your children, good restaurants on site, those that are eco-friendly and even where the toilets are really top-notch. Then there's sites where you can glamp it up and stay in a fully equipped yurt, wooden pod, wigwam, safari tent or shepherd's hut.

Camping Card Scheme

Use the money-saving Camping Card (see inside the back cover) for reduced rates if you book in advance at campsites that have signed up for the scheme. Look for the highlighted AA Camping Card Site banner on the individual campsite entries or view the quick reference list by county on page 469.

How to Use the Guide

1 LOCATION

Place names are listed alphabetically within each county.

2 MAP REFERENCE

Each site is given a map reference for use in conjunction with the atlas section at the back of the guide. The map reference comprises the guide map page number, the National Grid location square and a two-figure map location reference.

For example: **Map 15 SJ52**.

15 refers to the page number of the map section at the back of the guide.

SJ is the National Grid lettered square (representing 100,000sq metres) in which the location will be found.

5 is the figure reading across the top or bottom of the map page.

2 is the figure reading down each side of the map page.

3 PLACES TO VISIT

Suggestions of nearby places to visit for adults and children.

4 AA CAMPING CARD SCHEME

See explanation on page 9.

5 RATING & SITE NAME

Campsites are listed in descending order of their Pennant Quality rating. Sites are rated from one to five Pennants and are also awarded a score ranging from 50%-100% according to how they compare with other parks within the same Pennant rating. Some sites are given a Holiday Centre grading. For a fuller explanation see pages 12-17. A category for parks catering only for recreational vehicles (**RV**) has been created (no toilet facilities are provided at these sites).

NEW indicates that the site is new in the guide this year. Where the name appears in *italic* type the information that follows has not been confirmed by the campsite for 2014.

6 SIX-FIGURE MAP REFERENCE

Each entry also includes a six-figure National Grid reference as many sites are in remote locations. Use the reference alongside the relevant Ordnance Survey map and in conjunction with the atlas at the back of this guide to help you find the precise location.

7 CONTACT DETAILS

---

1 **MODBURY**   **Map 3 SX65** **2**

3 **Places to visit**

Overbeck's, SALCOMBE, TQ8 8LW, 01548 842893 www.nationaltrust.org.uk

4 **AA CAMPING CARD SITE** **18**

5 ►►► 81% Pennymoor **17**
Camping & Caravan Park

(SX685516) **6** **16**

PL21 0SB

7 ☎ 01548 830542

e-mail: enquiries@pennymoor-camping.co.uk
dir: *Exit A38 at Wrangaton Cross. Left & straight over x-rds. 4m, pass petrol station, 2nd left. Site 1.5m on right* **8**

9 * 🚐 £10-£18 🚐 £10-£18 Å £10-£18

15

10 Open 15 Mar-15 Nov (rs 15 Mar-mid May one toilet & shower block only open)

Last arrival 20.00hrs Last departure 10.00hrs

11 A well-established rural park on part level, part gently sloping grass with good views over distant Dartmoor and the countryside in between. The park has been owned and run by the same family since 1935, and is very carefully tended, with clean, well-maintained toilets and a relaxing atmosphere. 12.5 acre site. 119 touring pitches. 3 hardstandings. Caravan pitches. Motorhome pitches. Tent pitches. 76 statics.

12 **AA Pubs & Restaurants nearby:** California Country Inn, MODBURY, PL21 0SG, 01548 821449

Leisure: ⚙

13 **Facilities:** 🕯️ ☉ 🏳️ ✳️ ⚒️ 🛗 🛁 📶 ♻️ ❶

Services: 🔌 ⬜ 🛢️ ⊘ 🚽 🛒 ⌄

Within 3 miles: ⚓ 🛍️

14 **Notes:** No skateboards or scooters, no noise after 22.00hrs. Dogs must be kept on leads.

8 DIRECTIONS

Brief directions from a recognisable point, such as a main road, are included in each entry. Please contact the individual site for more detailed directions or try AA Route Planner at **theAA.com**, and enter the postcode.

9 PRICES

Rates are given after each appropriate symbol (🚐 Caravan, 🚌 Campervan, ⛺ Tent) and are the overnight cost for one caravan or tent, one car and two adults, or one motorhome and two adults. The prices vary according to the number of people in the party, but some parks have a fixed fee per pitch regardless of the number of people. Please note that some sites charge separately for certain facilities, including showers; and some sites charge a different rate for pitches with or without electricity. Prices are supplied to us in good faith by the site operators and are as accurate as possible. They are, however, only a guide and are subject to change during the currency of this publication.
* If this symbol appears before the prices, it indicates that the site has not advised us of the prices for 2014; they relate to 2013.

10 OPENING, ARRIVAL & DEPARTURE TIMES

Parks are not necessarily open all year and while most sites permit arrivals at any time, checking beforehand is advised (see page 18).

11 DESCRIPTION

Descriptions are based on information supplied by the AA inspector at the time of the last visit.
Please note: The AA Pennant classification is based on the touring pitches and the facilities only. AA inspectors do not visit or report on statics or chalets for hire under the AA Caravan & Camping quality standards scheme. However the AA has introduced the category of Holiday Homes 🏠 and these static caravan, chalet or lodge-only parks are inspected.
For sites other than those marked with 🏠 we only include the number of static caravan pitches in order to give an indication of the nature and size of the site.

12 AA PUBS & RESTAURANTS

An entry may include suggestions for nearby pubs and/or restaurants recognised by the AA. Some of these establishments will have been awarded Rosettes for food excellence. To find out the distance by road between the campsite and the pub or restaurant, enter both postcodes into a Sat Nav or the AA Route Planner at **theAA.com**.

13 SYMBOLS & ABBREVIATIONS

These are divided into Leisure, Facilities, Services and Within 3 miles sections. A guide to abbreviations and symbols can be found on pages 10 and 11 and at the bottom of the pages throughout the guide.

14 NOTES

This includes information about additional facilities and any restrictions the site would like their visitors to be aware of.
🚫 As most sites now accept credit and debit cards, we have only indicated those that don't accept cards.

15 PHOTOGRAPH

Optional photograph/s supplied by the campsite.

16 COUNTRYSIDE DISCOVERY

 A small group of family-run parks that have fewer than 150 pitches, each sharing a common theme of tranquillity. **www.countryside-discovery.co.uk**

17 BEST OF BRITISH

 A group of over 50 parks, both large and small, which focus on high quality facilities and amenities.
www.bob.org.uk

18 DAVID BELLAMY AWARDS

Many AA recognised sites are also recipients of a David Bellamy Award for Conservation. The awards are graded Gold, Silver and Bronze. The symbols we show indicate the 2012/13 winners as this was the most up-to-date information at the time of going to press. For the 2013/14 winners please contact:
**British Holiday & Homes Parks Association
Tel: 01452 526911   www.bellamyparks.co.uk**

Facilities for disabled guests

The Equality Act 2010 provides legal rights for disabled people including access to goods, services and facilities, and means that service providers may have to consider making adjustments to their premises. For more information about the Act see:
www.gov.uk/definition-of-disability-under-equality-act-2010
If a site has told us that they provide facilities for disabled visitors their entry in the guide will include the following symbol: ♿. The sites in this guide should be aware of their responsibilities under the Act. However, we recommend that you always telephone in advance to ensure the site you have chosen has facilities to suit your needs.

See your
kids smiling
on your **seaside** escape

Save up to
50%*
on **2014** holidays

You can't beat a good touring or camping seaside holiday

- **23** UK touring and camping holiday parks
- Choice of **6 pitch types** – from basic grass to fully serviced hard-standing
- Modern shower blocks and amenities
- Pets welcome for only **£1*** a night
- Splash around in our heated pools - some with flumes and slides

- Be adventurous - try out our many sports activities and facilities
- Dazzling family entertainment and fun packed kids' clubs
- There's tasty food and drink on the menu at all our parks
- Most of our parks are right beside the sea - **so don't forget your buckets and spades**

We welcome

To find out more, order a brochure and to book

Call: **0843 658 6450**   Quote: **TO_AA**

Calls cost 5p per minute plus network extras.
Open 7 days a week, 9am – 9pm

Haven touring
+camping

Britain's Favourite Seaside Holiday

Go online at **www.haventouring.com/toaa**

AA Camping Card Scheme

In this edition of the *AA Caravan & Camping Guide* you will find some sites highlighted with the **AA CAMPING CARD SITE** banner. This indicates that the site has signed up to the AA Camping Card Scheme, and means they have agreed to offer reduced rates to campers who book in advance, citing the AA Camping Card, and show the card on arrival at the site. The offers are provided by and are available entirely at the discretion of participating campsites. Offers may include, for example, reduced pitch prices at certain times of the week or year. These discounts will only be available to those booking in advance, stating at the time of booking that an AA Camping Card is being used, and showing the card on arrival. Scheme terms and campsite terms of booking will apply. You'll need to contact the site to find out what they are offering. We hope this will encourage you to visit sites and explore parts of the country you may not have considered before.

For a list of sites that accept this card please see page 469

Terms and conditions

This card may be used at any campsite specified as accepting the AA Camping Card within the *AA Caravan & Camping Guide 2014* and is valid for and may be applied to stays that expire before 31.1.2015.

To make use of the benefits of the AA Camping Card Scheme you must notify any participating campsite that you are a cardholder at your time of advance booking and provide details. Scheme Cards are issued and enclosed with your copy of the *AA Caravan & Camping Guide 2014* at the point of initial purchase.

The card entitles the bearer to any discount or other benefits being offered by the campsite under the scheme at the time of making an advance booking. Participating campsites may formulate, provide, vary or withdraw offers at their discretion. Offers may vary from campsite to campsite. Acceptance by you of any offer made by a campsite is an agreement between you and the campsite. Offers are subject to availability at time of booking and presentation of the booker person's AA Camping Card on arrival. Photocopies will not be accepted. Campsite terms and conditions will apply.

Only one card per person or party accepted. No change given. This card is valid during the period(s) specified by the campsites concerned, and will not be valid after 31.1.2015. This card cannot be used in conjunction with any other discount voucher or special offer. No cash alternative available. This scheme will be governed by English law.

Symbols & Abbreviations

Facilities

- 🛁 Bath
- 🚿 Shower
- ⊙ Electric Shaver
- Hairdryer
- ❄ Ice Pack Facility
- ♿ Disabled Facilities
- ℂ Public Telephone
- 💲 Shop on Site or within 200yds
- 🛒 Mobile Shop (calling at least 5 days per week)
- BBQ Area
- ⊼ Picnic Area
- Wi-fi Wi-fi Access
- Internet Access
- ♻ Recycling Facilities
- 𝒊 Tourist Information
- 🐕 Dog Exercise Area

Leisure

- Indoor Swimming Pool
- Outdoor Swimming Pool
- Tennis Court

Services

- T Toilet Fluid
- 🍽 Café or Restaurant
- Fast Food/Takeaway
- Baby Care
- Electric Hook Up
- Motorvan Service Point
- Launderette
- Licensed Bar

- 🔍 Games Room
- 𝕄 Children's Playground
- ✋ Kid's Club
- ∪ Stables & Horse Riding
- 9/18-hole Golf Course
- Boats for Hire
- Cinema
- ♫ Entertainment
- Fishing
- ◎ Mini Golf
- Watersports
- Gym
- ⚽ Sports Field
- Spa Spa
- Separate TV room

Abbreviations

- Calor Gas
- Camping Gaz
- Battery Charging

BH Bank Holiday/s
Etr Easter
Spring BH Spring Bank Holiday (Whitsun)
dep departure
fr from
hrs hours
m mile
mdnt midnight
rdbt roundabout
rs restricted service
RV Recreational Vehicles
U rating not confirmed
wk week
wknd weekend

- ⊗ no dogs
- no credit or debit cards
- children of all ages accepted

Guide to AA Pennants

AA Campsite Inspectors are often asked how they actually inspect and grade a campsite. How do we arrive at a particular Pennant rating and what does the Quality Score mean? Senior Inspector Colin Church unravels the mystery and explains the AA Pennant Grading Scheme.

All AA Campsite Inspectors have enjoyed many years of caravanning or camping as a pastime, so they are very experienced and knowledgeable about the industry and what makes a good camping site or park. Each inspector owns a caravan, a motorhome or a tent which they use during the summer inspection season; an inspector books and stays anonymously on a park.

Campsite inspectors are no different to any other caravanners or campers in that they all have our own likes and dislikes when it comes to choosing a campsite. So, to correctly assess a campsite, it is very important that they look closely at fixed criteria within the AA Pennant Scheme to grade each site, and not take their own opinions into account.

The AA Pennant Scheme is very similar to the scheme the AA uses to assess hotels and B&Bs. Parks are classified on a 5-point scale according to their style and the range of facilities they offer. As the number of Pennants increases so the quality and variety of facilities is generally greater. There is also a separate category for holiday centres which provide full day and evening holiday entertainment as well as offering complete touring facilities for campers and caravanners.

It is important to point out that, regardless of grade, we do expect that all AA parks meet a minimum standard - they should be clean, well maintained and welcoming. They must also have a local authority licence and satisfy fire regulations. Pennant criteria is explained on pages 15-16.

The Inspection and Report

When a campsite owner applies for AA recognition, the site receives an unannounced visit each year by one of the AA's qualified inspectors. The site pays an annual fee for the inspection, the recognition and grading, and receives an entry in the *AA Caravan & Camping Guide*, as well as **theAA.com** and the Caravan & Camping app. During a visit the inspector will apply detailed criteria for each Pennant rating, identifying where changes or improvements have been made or where action needs to be taken to correct or improve things.

At the end of the visit the inspector will inform the site owner of the Pennant grading he will be recommending as well as discussing any areas where improvements need to be made. The inspection process and subsequent dialogue with the owner will form the basis of a detailed report, which is subsequently sent to the owner.

Quality Score

As well as listing the Pennant grading beside each entry in the Caravan & Camping Guide, we also include a percentage score.

Several years ago the AA inspection team recognised that although a campsite ticked all the criteria boxes for a particular grade there could be some real differences between sites awarded the same grade. So, a method and scoring system was developed to identify the key differences within each grade in order to give both owners and guide users a measure of a campsite's overall quality.

For example, there could be a small 2-Pennant campsite with a quality score of 89%, which indicates that although it is a fairly basic site it has really good facilities and spacious pitches. Conversely, a 4-Pennant park with a quality score of 82% reflects slightly lower quality despite the fact that the park ticked all the boxes for a 4-Pennant grade; reasons for this could be smaller pitch sizes, lack of hardstandings or fewer private facilities in the toilet blocks. The percentage score is a qualitative assessment of the following eight categories:

- Levels of customer care
- Quality of toilet and shower facilities
- Cleanliness and maintenance of toilet and shower facilities
- Numbers of cubicled or en suite facilities including disabled facilities
- Public areas such as laundry; reception; tourist information room
- Other site facilities such as a café, swimming pool, restaurant and entertainment
- Size and layout of the pitches, ease of access and proximity to services
- Landscaping and ground maintenance including outbuildings

What does this all mean for the campers? These quality standards, and in particular the AA Pennant scheme, give the customer peace of mind when

choosing or visiting a particular campsite, as all sites have been independently assessed to a very detailed set of criteria. These standards have been fine tuned over the many years of inspecting sites and also by listening to what campers expect when choosing a site.

The AA Pennant scheme is very different to popular 'campsite reviews' found on many websites. Although both have their place, the Pennant Scheme avoids personal likes and dislikes when assessing a site, and instead provides a more objective consideration of campsite facilities.

The Pennant Criteria

One Pennant Parks

 These parks offer a fairly simple standard of facilities including:

- No more than 30 pitches per acre
- At least 5% of the total pitches allocated to touring caravans
- An adequate drinking water supply and reasonable drainage
- Washroom with flush toilets and toilet paper provided, unless no sanitary facilities are provided in which case this should be clearly stated
- Chemical disposal arrangements, ideally with running water, unless tents only
- Adequate refuse disposal arrangements that are clearly signed
- Well-drained ground and have some level pitches
- Entrance and access roads of adequate width and surface
- Location of emergency telephone clearly signed
- Emergency telephone numbers fully displayed

Two Pennant Parks

 Parks in this category should meet all of the above requirements, but offer an increased level of facilities, services, customer care, security and ground maintenance. They should include the following:

- Separate washrooms, including at least two male and two female WCs and wash basins per 30 pitches
- Hot and cold water direct to each basin
- Externally lit toilet blocks
- Warden available during day, times to be indicated
- Shop/chemist is clearly signed
- Dish-washing facilities, covered and lit
- Basic security (i.e. lockable gate and/or CCTV)
- Reception area

Three Pennant Parks

Many parks come within this rating and the range of facilities is wide. All parks will be of a very good standard and will meet the following minimum criteria:

- Facilities, services and park grounds are clean and well maintained, with buildings in good repair and attention paid to customer care and park security
- Evenly surfaced roads and paths
- Clean modern toilet blocks with all-night lighting and containing toilet seats in good condition, soap and hand dryers or paper towels, mirrors, shelves and hooks, shaver & hairdryer points, and lidded waste bins in female toilets
- Modern shower cubicles with sufficient hot water and attached, private changing space
- Electric hook-ups
- Some hardstanding/wheel runs/firm, level ground
- Laundry with automatic washing and drying facilities, separate from toilets

- Children's playground with safe equipment
- 24-hour public telephone on site or nearby where mobile reception is poor
- Warden availability and 24-hour contact number clearly signed

Four Pennant Parks

These parks have achieved an excellent standard in all areas, including landscaping of grounds, natural screening and attractive park buildings, and customer care and park security. Toilets are smart, modern and immaculately maintained, and generally offer the following facilities:

- Spacious vanitory-style washbasins, at least two male and two female per 25 pitches
- Fully-tiled shower cubicles with doors, dry areas, shelves and hooks, at least one male and one female per 30 pitches
- Availability of washbasins in lockable cubicles, or combined toilet/washing cubicles, or a private/family room with shower/toilet/washbasin

Other requirements are:
- Baby changing facilities
- A shop on site, or within reasonable distance
- Warden available 24 hours
- Reception area open during the day, with tourist information available
- Internal roads, paths and toilet blocks lit at night
- Maximum 25 pitches per campable acre
- Toilet blocks heated October to Easter
- Approximately 50% of pitches with electric hook-ups
- Approximately 10% of pitches have hardstandings
- Late arrivals enclosure
- Security barrier and/or CCTV

Five Pennant Premier Parks

 Premier parks are of an extremely high standard, set in attractive surroundings with superb mature landscaping. Facilities, security and customer care are of an exceptional quality. As well as the above they will also offer:

- First-class toilet facilities including several designated self-contained cubicles, ideally with WC, washbasin and shower.
- Ideally electric hook-ups to 75% of pitches
- Approximately 20% of pitches have hardstandings
- Some fully-serviced 'super' pitches: of larger size, with water & electricity supplies connected
- A motorhome service point
- Toilet block/s should be heated
- Excellent security - coded barrier or number plate recognition & CCTV

Many Premier Parks will also provide:

- Heated swimming pool
- Well-equipped shop
- Café or restaurant and bar
- A designated walking area for dogs (if accepted)

Gold Pennants ▶ ▶ ▶ ▶ ▶

AA Gold Pennants are awarded to the very best camping parks with a Quality Score of 90% and above within the 2, 3, 4 and 5 Pennant ratings.

Holiday Centres

In this category we distinguish parks which cater for all holiday needs including cooked meals and entertainment. They provide:

- A wide range of on-site sports, leisure and recreational facilities
- Supervision and security at a very high level

- A choice of eating outlets
- Facilities for touring caravans that equal those available to rented holiday accommodation
- A maximum density of 25 pitches per acre
- Clubhouse with entertainment
- Laundry with automatic washing machines

Holiday Home Parks

 Parks in this category are static only parks offering holiday caravans, chalets or lodges for hire and catering for all holiday needs. They provide:

- Quality holiday hire caravans and chalets or luxurious lodges
- A wide range of on-site sports, leisure and recreational facilities
- Supervision and security at a very high level
- A choice of eating outlets
- Clubhouse with entertainment

Beecraigs Caravan & Camping Site, Linlithgow

Useful Information

Booking Information

It is advisable to book in advance during peak holiday seasons and in school or public holidays. It is also wise to check whether or not a reservation entitles you to a particular pitch. It does not necessarily follow that an early booking will secure the best pitch; you may simply have the choice of what is available at the time you check in.

Some parks may require a deposit on booking which may be non-returnable if you have to cancel your holiday. If you do have to cancel, notify the proprietor at once because you may be held legally responsible for partial or full payment unless the pitch can be re-let. Consider taking out insurance such as AA Travel Insurance, tel: 0800 085 7240 or visit: **theAA.com** for details about how to cover a lost deposit or compensation. Some parks will not accept overnight bookings unless payment for the full minimum period (e.g. two or three days) is made.

Last Arrival – Unless otherwise stated, parks will usually accept arrivals at any time of the day or night, but some have a special 'late arrivals' enclosure where you have to make temporary camp to avoid disturbing other people on the park. Please note that on some parks access to the toilet block is by key or pass card only, so if you know you will be late, do check what arrangements can be made.

Last Departure – Most parks will specify their overnight period – e.g. noon to noon. If you overstay the departure time you can be charged for an extra day.

Chemical Closet Disposal Point

You will usually find one on every park, except those catering only for tents. It must be a specially constructed unit, or a WC permanently set aside for the purpose of chemical disposal and with adjacent rinsing and soak-away facilities. However, some local authorities are concerned about the effect of chemicals on bacteria in cesspools etc, and may prohibit or restrict provision of chemical closet disposal points in their areas.

Complaints

If you have any complaints speak to the park proprietor or supervisor immediately, so that the matter can be sorted out on the spot. If this personal approach fails you may decide, if the matter is serious, to approach the local authority or tourist board. AA guide users may also write to:

The Co-ordinator,
AA Caravan & Camping Scheme,
AA Lifestyle Guides,
13th floor, Fanum House,
Basing View,
Basingstoke, RG21 4EA

The AA may at its sole discretion investigate any complaints received from guide users for the purpose of making any necessary amendments to the guide. The AA will not in any circumstances act as representative or negotiator or undertake to obtain compensation or enter into further correspondence or deal with the matter in any other way whatsoever. The AA will not guarantee to take any specific action.

Dogs

Dogs may or may not be accepted at parks; this is entirely at the owner's or warden's discretion (assistance dogs should be accepted). Even when the park states that they accept dogs, it is still discretionary, and certain breeds may not be considered as suitable, so we strongly advise that you check when you book.* Dogs should always be kept on a lead and under control, and letting them sleep in cars is not encouraged.

*Some sites have told us they do not accept dangerous breeds.
The following breeds are covered under the Dangerous Dogs Act 1991 –
Pit Bull Terrier, Japanese Tosa, Dogo Argentino and Fila Brazilerio.

Electric Hook-Up

This is becoming more generally available at parks with three or more Pennants, but if it is important to you, you should check before booking. The voltage is generally 240v AC, 50 cycles, although variations between 200v and 250v may still be found. All parks in the AA scheme which provide electric hook-ups do so in accordance with International Electrotechnical Commission regulations. Outlets are coloured blue and take the form of a lidded plug with recessed contacts, making it impossible to touch a live point by accident. They are also waterproof. A similar plug, but with protruding contacts which hook into the recessed plug, is on the end of the cable which connects the caravan to the source of supply, and is dead. This equipment can usually be hired on site, or a plug connector supplied to fit your own cable. You should ask for the male plug; the female plug is the one already fixed to the power supply. This supply is rated for either 5, 10 or 16 amps and this is usually displayed on a triangular yellow plate attached to source of supply. If it is not, be sure to check at the site reception. This is important because if you overload the circuit, the trip switch will operate to cut off the power supply. The trip switch can only be reset by a park official, who will first have to go round all the hook-ups on park to find the cause of the trip. This can take a long time and will make the culprit distinctly unpopular with all the other caravanners deprived of power, to say nothing of the park official. Tents and trailer tents are recommended to have a Residual Circuit Device (RCD) for safety reasons and to avoid overloading the circuit. It is a relatively simple matter to calculate whether your appliances will overload the circuit. The amperage used by an appliance depends on its wattage and the total amperage used is the total of all the appliances in use at any one time. If you are not sure whether your camping or caravanning equipment can be used at a park, check beforehand.

Average amperage

Portable black & white TV 50 watts approx.	0.2 amp
Small colour TV 90 watts approx.	0.4 amp
Small fan heater 1000 watts (1kW) approx.	4.2 amp
One-bar electric fire NB each extra bar rates	
1000 watts (1kW)	4.2 amp
60 watt table lamp approx.	0.25 amp
100 watt light bulb approx.	0.4 amp
Battery charger 100 watts approx.	0.4 amp
Small fridge 125 watts approx.	0.4 amp
Domestic microwave 600 watts approx.	2.5 amp

Motor Caravans

At some parks motor caravans are only accepted if they remain static throughout the stay. Also check that there are suitable level pitches at the parks where you plan to stay.

Overflow Pitches

Campsites are legally entitled to use an overflow field which is not a normal part of their camping area for up to 28 days in any one year as an emergency method of coping with additional numbers at busy periods. When this 28 day rule is being invoked site owners should increase the numbers of sanitary facilities accordingly. In these circumstances the extra facilities are sometimes no more than temporary portacabins.

Parking

Some park operators insist that cars be put in a parking area separate from the pitches; others will not allow more than one car for each caravan or tent.

Park Restrictions

Many parks in our guide are selective about the categories of people they will accept on their parks. In the caravan and camping world there are many restrictions and some categories of visitor are banned altogether. Where a park has told us of a restriction/s this is included in notes in their entry.

On many parks in this guide, unaccompanied young people, single-sex groups, single adults, and motorcycle groups will not be accepted. The AA takes no stance in this matter, basing its Pennant classification on facilities, quality and maintenance. On the other hand, some parks cater well for teenagers and offer magnificent sporting and leisure facilities as well as discos; others have only very simple amenities. A small number of parks in our guide exclude all children in order to create an environment aimed at holiday makers in search of total peace and quiet (see page 41).

Pets Travel Scheme

The importation of animals into the UK is subject to strict controls. Penalties for trying to avoid these controls are severe. However, the Pet Travel Scheme (PETS) allows cats, dogs, ferrets and certain other pets coming from the EU and certain other countries to enter the UK without quarantine provided the appropriate conditions are met. For details:
www.gov.uk/take-pet-abroad
PETS HELPLINE on 0870 241 1710
E-mail: pettravel@ahvla.gsi.gov.uk
Pets resident in the British Isles (UK, Republic of Ireland, Isle of Man and Channel Islands) are not subject to any quarantine or PETS rules when travelling within the British Isles.

Seasonal Touring Pitches

Some park operators allocate a number of their hardstanding pitches for long-term seasonal caravans. These pitches can be reserved for the whole period the campsite is open, generally between Easter and September, and a fixed fee is charged for keeping the caravan on the park for the season. These pitches are in great demand, especially in popular tourist areas, so enquire well in advance if you wish to book one.

Shops

The range of food and equipment in shops is usually in proportion to the size of the park. As far as our Pennant requirements are concerned, a mobile shop calling several times a week, or a general store within easy walking distance of the park is acceptable.

Unisex Toilet Facilities

An ever-increasing number of parks now offer unisex toilet facilities instead of (or sometimes as well as) separate units for men and women. If the type of toilet facility is important to you, please check what the park has to offer at the time of booking.

Island Camping

Channel Islands

Tight controls are operated because of the narrow width of the mainly rural roads. On all of the islands tents can be hired on recognised campsites.

Alderney

Neither caravans nor motor caravans are allowed, and campers must have a confirmed booking on the one official campsite before they arrive.

Guernsey

Only islanders may own and use towed caravans, but a limited number of motor caravans are now permitted on the island. The motor caravan, used for overnight accommodation, must be not more than 6.9mtrs long, must be booked into an authorised site (Fauxquets Valley Campsite, La Bailloterie or Le Vaugrat Camp Site) and must obtain a permit from the site operator before embarking on a ferry for Guernsey - Condor Ferries will not accept motor caravans without this permit. A window sticker must be displayed, motor caravans must return to the site each night, and the visits are limited to a maximum of one month. Permission is not required to bring a trailer tent to the island. For further details see www.visitguernsey.com

Herm and Sark

These two small islands are traffic free. Herm has a small campsite for tents, and these can also be hired. Sark has two campsites. New arrivals are met off the boat by a tractor which carries people and luggage up the steep hill from the harbour. All travel is by foot, on bicycle, or by horse and cart.

Jersey

Visiting caravans are allowed into Jersey, provided they are to be used as holiday accommodation only. Caravans will require a permit for travelling to and from the port and campsite on their arrival and departure days only. Motorvans may travel around the island on a daily basis, but must return to the campsite each night. Bookings should be made through the chosen campsite, who will also arrange for a permit. Early booking is strongly recommended during July and August.

Isle of Man

Motor caravans may enter with prior permission. Trailer caravans are not allowed on the island without a permit. Written application for permission should be made to the Secretary, Planning Committee, Department of Infrastructure, Murray House, Mount Havelock, Douglas IM1 2SF. The shipping line cannot accept caravans without this written permission.

Isles of Scilly

Caravans and motor caravans are not allowed, and campers must stay at official sites. Booking is advisable on all sites, especially during school holidays.

Scottish Islands

Inner Isles (including Inner Hebrides)

Skye is accessible to caravans and motor caravans, and has official camping sites, but its sister isles of **Rhum** and **Eigg** have no car ferries, and take only backpackers. On the **Isle of Bute** only official camping is allowed. The islands of **Mull**, **Islay**, **Coll** and **Arran** have official campsites, and welcome caravans, motor caravans and tenters; offsite camping is also allowed with the usual permission. **Iona**, a backpacker's paradise, does not permit non-residents' vehicles. Wild camping is permitted on **Tiree** in accordance with the Scottish Outdoor Access Code (see www.isleoftiree.com). Prior arrangements must be made if you wish to camp with a motor vehicle, or go wild camping on **Colonsay** or **Cumbrae** (see www.colonsay.org.uk) and **Great Cumbrae** does not permit caravanning or camping, although organized groups may stay with official permission. **Jura & Gigha** have small, designated areas, and **Lismore** bans caravans but permits camping, although there are no official sites and few suitable places.

Orkney

There are no camping and caravanning restrictions, and plenty of beauty spots in which to pitch camp.

Shetland

There are seven official campsites on the Shetlands, but visitors can camp anywhere with prior permission. Caravans and motor caravans must stick to the main roads. Camping 'böds' offer budget accommodation in unisex dormitories for campers with their own bed rolls and sleeping bags. There is a campsite on **Fetler** (see www.fetler.org), but no camping or caravanning is permitted on **Noss** and **Fair Isle**.

Western Isles (Outer Hebrides)

There are official campsites on these islands, but wild camping is allowed within reason, and with the landowner's prior permission.

AA Campsites of the Year

96% POLMANTER TOURING PARK

ST IVES, CORNWALL page 100

From the moment you pass through the gate at Polmanter Touring Park you know you have arrived at a top quality park. You will immediately be impressed by the smart and welcoming entrance, the ample parking for booking in, the beautiful landscaping across the park, the smooth road surfaces, and the reception area, where the staff are professional and courteous, making you feel relaxed and very welcome after a long drive. In fact, everyone, including the maintenance staff, are polite, helpful and welcoming. The ultra-modern toilet facilities are top quality and kept spotlessly clean, and include first-class, fully-serviced shower rooms and baby bathrooms. You can expect the pitches, grass, shrubs, hedges, play areas, swimming pool and the bar and restaurant areas to be immaculately maintained - even the smallest details are not overlooked. Facilities include tennis courts, pitch-and-putt, arcade games and a poplar bar and restaurant which offers entertainment in season and overlooks the outdoor pool. Excellent, ongoing improvements year on year have seen an increase in the number of hardstanding pitches, refurbishment of the bar area and effective changes to the landscaping of the park. Even when full, the park doesn't feel overcrowded with its spacious pitches that offer optimum privacy for campers. The commitment shown by the owners, management and staff to ensure that holidaymakers have a great experience at Polmanter is commendable. A worthy overall winner.

SCOTLAND

92% CAIRNSMILL HOLIDAY PARK

ST ANDREWS, FIFE page 377

Cairnsmill Holiday Park is located on a hillside just outside St Andrews, with great views over the countryside and only a short walk or drive into the town, although a regular bus service passes the site entrance. It is a perfect base to explore Fife and its many traditional fishing villages, plus it is only a short drive to Dundee. This family-owned park has been tastefully developed over the years and now has mature landscaping in the grounds, including a private fishing lochan. The 54 caravan pitches are large, have hardstanding and are sheltered by large well-tended hedges; there are 12 individual grass pitches for campers, all served by modern, spotlessly-maintained washrooms and amenity blocks. There are also modern static caravans and smart bunkhouse-type accommodation available for hire. The social hub of the park is the newly refurbished entertainment complex, and the sparkling swimming pool is housed in a new, state-of-the-art building with excellent facilities, including a redeveloped lounge and club area. The owners are continually improving the facilities, with free Wi-fi access, new outdoor play areas for children, a new laundry room and improved security, which clearly indicates they are keeping abreast of customer expectations.

WALES

►►►►► 87% TYDDYN ISAF CARAVAN PARK

DULAS, ISLE OF ANGLESEY page 400

Surely there can't be a more ideally located park than Tyddyn Isaf, which benefits from direct access to an award-winning beach. The pitch density is excellent, and major groundworks in recent years has created large level areas, many fully serviced, on sloping fields to ensure that the stunning coastal views are enjoyed by all - the sunsets are particularly spectacular! The park has been in the same family for many years, and Beverley and Arthur Mount were joined two years ago by their daughter Haley and her husband Simon, so that the family tradition of excellent hospitality and service continues. The touring and level camping areas have neat, lush grass and are surrounded by shrubs and wild flowers, the result of a dedicated planting programme, in order to attract an amazing variety of wildlife; the only sounds to be heard are birdsong and the waves as they break on the sandy beach. The amenities blocks are equipped with modern fixtures and fittings and even the camping unit benefits from under-floor heating and power showers. The licensed bar and bistro, replete with a large alfresco area and stunning sea views, is at the top of the park and is a great place to relax at the end of the day.

AA Campsites of the Year – Regional Award Winners

SOUTH WEST ENGLAND

►►►►► 87% WOODOVIS PARK

TAVISTOCK, DEVON page 170

Peacefully located at the end of private, half-mile, tree-lined drive, Woodovis Park is a well-kept and beautifully landscaped park in a remote woodland setting on the edge of the Tamar Valley. It offers superb on-site facilities and high levels of customer care from hands-on owners, John and Dorothy Lewis, and their hard-working team, and makes a top quality base for exploring the attractions of Dartmoor, Plymouth and the South Ham coast and countryside. If you want to know what to do and where to go in the area, just check out the high-tech interactive touch screen system in the information/games room – it's brilliant. Woodovis is well laid out and maintained to the highest level, with well-appointed and spotlessly clean facilities. The toilets are immaculate and pitches are spacious and include excellent hardstandings and 13 fully-serviced pitches. There's a good fenced play area, an open space for ball games and a decent games room to keep children amused, plus an indoor swimming pool and, for adults, a sauna. There are also luxury camping pods, well-appointed static homes and a self-catering cottage for hire. Customer care initiatives include free foraging tours, story-telling evenings, and a weekly and very popular hog roast in main season, which brings campers together for an informal evening. Guests can be assured of a warm welcome at this lovely park.

SOUTH EAST ENGLAND

►►►►► 87% SWISS FARM TOURING & CAMPING

HENLEY-ON-THAMES, OXFORDSHIRE page 257

The progress that this campsite has made over the past few years has been quite remarkable – it has been transformed from a very mediocre site to a top 5-pennant park, and full credit must go to owner Joseph Bolase and his enthusiastic team. Swiss Farm occupies an enviable location within walking distance of Henley-on-Thames, a beautiful town beside the River Thames and famous for the annual Henley Regatta, when booking is essential for a stay on the park. The site offers excellent facilities throughout, including spacious pitches, many of which have hardstandings, electric and waste water. There are two modern and well-appointed toilet and shower blocks plus an excellent outdoor swimming pool, as well as a very tasteful bar area. There is also a peaceful fishing lake for the keen angler to enjoy. The whole park is well landscaped and makes for a peaceful and relaxing camping environment, the attention to detail across the park is excellent and campers are guaranteed a warm welcome from the whole team. Further exciting improvements are planned and the park is now a member of the prodigious Best of British group of campsites, which underlines its overall quality.

HEART OF ENGLAND

▶▶▶▶▶ 83% FIELDS END WATER CARAVAN PARK & FISHERY

DODDINGTON, CAMBRIDGESHIRE page 46

Owner Charlie Broughton has invested considerable time, energy and money in transforming this former small Certified Location site for five caravans into a top quality 5-pennant park. What's more amazing is that he has achieved it all in just six years! Thorough research and careful attention to detail has seen this excellent park evolve and rise out of the flat Fenland landscape. Situated on a bank of clay above the surrounding countryside, skilful use of natural contours resulted in the construction of three wide terraces accommodating 38 fully serviced pitches, each with very spacious gravel hardstandings and fringed by varied and colourful shrubs. For tents, there is a separate lush grassy paddock and all pitches here have electric. The entrance and interior roads are of deep, well-managed gravel and all the buildings, including the stunning reception building, the modern, pristinely kept toilet block and the owner's residence, are smartly clad in dark stained timber, which combine with the excellent landscaping to create a park with huge visual appeal. The two large fishing lakes are well stocked with a wide variety of species and five acres of woodland offer good opportunities for gentle walks. The most recent development has been the construction of three swish timber lodges, all luxuriously furnished and equipped with log burners; two have hot tubs.

NORTH WEST ENGLAND

▶▶▶▶▶ 85% WOODCLOSE CARAVAN PARK

KIRKBY LONSDALE, CUMBRIA page 123

A warm welcome is assured at this ideally located park that is situated between the Yorkshire Dales and the Lake District National Park, in the Lune Valley. Set in nine acres, with stunning rural views, this mature, well-equipped park that has been upgraded after major investment to ensure a memorable holiday experience. The beautifully landscaped grounds attract a large variety of wildlife and the generous pitch density ensures optimum privacy. On arrival, customers are greeted by a stunning display of seasonal flowers, neat, lush grass and scented shrubs that create an excellent first impression. Additional wigwams of various sizes have been introduced to create a separate Wigwam Village amongst mature trees, and this area benefits from its own top-notch toilets and showers. Touring areas, located on tiered fields, shielded by trees and flora are serviced by the main amenities block; these offer excellent standards and privacy options with unisex shower rooms that also contain a toilet and wash basin. There is no need to leave the park for exercise, as extensive woodland walks from the park ensure a 'back to nature' experience, and the well-stocked shop provides both essentials and locally sourced and reared produce.

AA Campsites of the Year *continued*

NORTH EAST ENGLAND

▶▶▶▶▶ **87% SOUTH MEADOWS CARAVAN PARK**

BELFORD, NORTHUMBERLAND page 250

Set in 40 acres of beautiful Northumbrian countryside, a short drive from unspoilt beaches and magnificent Bamburgh Castle, South Meadows has been transformed in recent years and is now a top quality touring and holiday park. Joining the AA Pennant Scheme for the first time in 2014, and achieving an excellent 5-Pennant 87% rating, the park is extremely spacious and no expense has been spared in its landscaping and development. Tree planting on a grand scale has been carried out, grassy areas are beautifully mown and most of the generous hardstanding touring pitches are fully serviced. The new solar heated amenity block is ultra modern and has definite 'wow' factor, with quality fittings, unisex fully-serviced cubicles, and smart family rooms (with double-headed showers), and everywhere is spotlessly clean, fresh and well maintained. Key additions in the last year included a stunning children's adventure playground, complete with a zip-wire, an excellent motorhome service point and free Wi-fi across the park. Campers can expect high levels of customer care from owner Simon Dunham and his professional team in the swish reception building and across the park. Dogs are very welcome too and they have two walking areas, one in a glorious bluebell wood. South Meadows is the perfect base to explore Holy Island, the Farne Islands and the Scottish Borders, and Belford which is just a five-minute walk from the park.

HOLIDAY CENTRE OF THE YEAR

  87% HAFAN Y MOR HOLIDAY PARK

PWLLHELI, GWYNEDD page 417

Ideally located on the unspoilt Lleyn Peninsula, near the attractions of Caernarfon, Portmerion and Abersoch, this popular holiday destination has been transformed by massive investment in recent years into a must-do location for an away-from-it-all experience. The beautifully landscaped grounds guarantee colour at all times of the year and include stunning displays of indigenous flora that attracts a wide variety of wildlife. The all-weather attractions include a pool complex with slides and flumes, an indoor sports area for fitness and enjoyment, and lively entertainment is provided in the show bars. For the more adventurous, climbing walls with abseiling, the Leap of Faith and zip wires test both nerves and stamina, and perhaps the roller disco might appeal in order to wind down. In addition to a large lake, the park has the great benefit of direct access to coastal paths and a beach. Great eating options include the Mash & Barrel, Pappa John's Pizza, Starbucks, Burger King and a traditional fish and chip takeaway. The touring park, with its own dedicated wardens and underfloor-heated amenities block, features 75 fully-serviced Euro pitches, each with electric and TV hook-up, water and waste water disposal.

ROGER ALMOND MOST IMPROVED CAMPSITE

SMALL CAMPSITE OF THE YEAR

▶▶▶▶ 85% GROUSE HILL CARAVAN PARK

ROBIN'S HOOD BAY, NORTH YORKSHIRE page 343

True to his word owner Andrew Butterfield has poured money into improving this stunningly located park, which is set on a sunny south-facing slope overlooking a wooded valley and the heather-covered moorland of the North Yorkshire Moors National Park. From a typical 3-Pennant park, Andrew has transformed it into a top 4-Pennant park with a high quality score of 85%. After completely landscaping the sloping park to create attractive, level, tiered terraces for tourers which make the most of the gorgeous view, he refurbished all three amenity blocks with modern fixtures and fittings, including excellent privacy cubicles and a unisex, fully serviced shower room and bathroom. Also, at great expense, he has installed a water treatment plant to improve the drinking water across the park, built a disposal point for the growing number of motorhomes that visit the park, and improved the security on the park by adding coded barriers and CCTV. The most recent development on park has been the addition of eight Big Chief Wigwams (wooden camping pods) which sleep up to five people and are fully equipped with fridge, microwave, kettle, toaster, heating, electric lights and a bed. Each one has a decked seating area with views across rolling hills. Grouse Hill, with Whitby and Scarborough close by, is now the perfect base for walking, cycling and touring.

96% GREENACRES CAMPING

SHEPTON MALLET, SOMERSET page 277

Within sight of the famous Glastonbury Tor, this small, family orientated campsite is mainly suited to tents and small motorhomes, and offers a very traditional away-from-it-all camping experience, with plenty of space and a very safe environment for children to explore and enjoy themselves. Greenacres is a very level site surrounded by lovely open countryside, a good network of footpaths and quiet country lanes for enjoyable cycling. The small facility block is excellent, well appointed and spotlessly clean. There are a few electric hook-ups available for the larger family tents and motorhomes. Enthusiastic owner, Duncan Forrester ensures his guests receive a warm welcome and have an enjoyable and pleasant stay. He even organises a 'glow worm safari' at certain times of the year, which both children and their parents really enjoy. The site is well positioned for visiting nearby Glastonbury, the beautiful city of Wells and its cathedral, plus other attractions such as Wookey Hole, Cheddar Gorge and the city of Bath. There are many small campsites across the country which provide this simpler, more traditional style of camping loved by families, and Greenacres is an excellent example and a worthy winner of this new award.

Pod beside Sumners Lake

Developing a Campsite

From cattle to camping, David Hancock discovers how one family transformed their farm into a thriving fishery and campsite, and the costs they incurred over a ten-year period.

Many farmers in Britain today are finding it hard to make a living. Livestock farmers, for example, have seen their animals struck down with diseases such as Bluetongue, Foot and Mouth and Bovine TB in recent years, plus slashed subsidies and policy reforms over the past two decades have contributed to a business environment in which they increasingly compete with global suppliers.

The result is that farmers have had to think laterally to survive. Farm diversification – where the farmer develops new money-making activities away from, or in addition to, his traditional farming pursuits – has become more and more commonplace. Diversification can make better use of the farm's physical resources, help integrate farm businesses into the wider rural economy, bring revenue into the area, creating employment and stimulating spin-off business opportunities.

Today, over 50% of farms in Britain supplement income through diversification, with many branching out and innovating within the tourism sector.

A Case Study

One such farming family that has embraced diversification in order for their farm to survive and the family to succeed are the Smiths. Over the past decade they have transformed Slaughterford Farm in Barns Green, West Sussex into a thriving fishery and campsite, now called Sumners Ponds Fishery & Campsite.

Bryon Smith, a fourth generation farmer, bought the 100-acre farm in 1969 and maintained a dairy herd of 115 cows until 1984 when the milk quota system was introduced; this capped the amount of milk that a farmer could sell each year without paying a levy. Feeling heavily penalised, like many dairy farmers with small herds, Bryon gave up milking in favour of rearing beef cattle, and the farm still has a herd of 40 today.

Fishing Focus

Having always been a progressive, forward-thinking farmer, Bryon began diversifying and introducing other activities on the farm as early as 1988, with the dredging and extension of the pond (Farm Pond) for fishing. At the same time the family developed an agricultural plant-contracting business, which specialised in pond and lake creation and renovation on farms, and son, Simon Smith took over the management of this side of the business.

The decision to focus more heavily on fishing was taken 1992 with the development of Sumners Lake and it was a year later that Bryon opened one of the paddocks as a Certified Location (CL) for five caravans, primarily aimed at the fishing fraternity. However, cattle and caravans don't really mix, certainly in the same paddock, and the upheaval of moving the cattle when caravans arrived nearly resulted in the Smiths giving up the CL Site. A decision was made to move the caravans to a beautiful spot beside Sumners Lake.

As the popularity of fishing grew as a leisure activity during the late 1990s, the demand on the limited number of caravan pitches was proving difficult to manage, especially as the set up and organisation of the CL site was a little chaotic. No bookings were taken and it was often a free-for-all situation, with far more caravans parked at the lakeside than were really permitted. In 2003 the family decided to expand both the camping and the fishing – Simon gave up contracting to concentrate on developing these businesses on the farm.

Early Development

With the help of an EU grant work began in April 2004 on developing Bluebell Park, the first proper camping area, on land beside a bluebell wood. Small, sheltered and intimate, with just 34 pitches (17 hardstandings), all with electric hook-ups, a good toilet block, children's play area and warden's accommodation, it is particularly

Reception, café and terrace

suitable for families. The total cost of this development was roughly £5,000 per pitch. Having completed Bluebell Park, the Smith family created undercover storage for 60 caravans in a former barn, and they offer a popular caravan pull-out and pitch service when owners wish to stay on the park, rather than have occupied seasonal pitches.

At the same time permission was granted to transform the CL Site beside Sumners Pond into a defined camping area with 27 pitches. Electric hook-ups and hardstandings, and portacabin toilets were installed in 2005, with 11 premium lakeside pitches more suited, and nearly always, fully booked by those wishing to fish. This area was further developed in 2009, with the installation of two smart lakeside cabins, replete with decking and dedicated 'swim areas'.

The year 2004 also saw the creation of a third, 3.5 acre, landscaped fishing lake (Match Lake), set well away from the campsite. As its names suggests it is primarily designed for the match fisherman and provides prolific opportunities with barbell, chub, carp, tench and roach. Sumners Lake is stocked with carp up to 34lbs and pike to 15lbs, among other fish, so it's no wonder that the Smith's property soon became known as a favoured destination for avid anglers.

Ribbon Park

Ribbon Park is the third and final camping area to be developed at Sumners Pond. Work started in 2010 following the development of the 2-acre Ribbon Lake that occupies former paddocks between Bluebell Park and Farm Pond.

Ribbon Lake cost £33,000 to construct and is stocked with £25,000 worth of fish, including tench, chub, barbell and

Digging Farm Pond, 1988

Overlooking the café and Sumners Lake

bream. The meandering ribbon of water has islands to fish from and is popular with match fishermen as well as beginners or parent-and-child teams.

The camping area is located below the lake and has 36 pitches, with a good mix of hardstandings and grass tent pitches, plus four wooden camping pods which

have been a very popular addition to the park. There are six camping pods in total (two beside Sumners Lake) and six extra hardstandings, created over the 2012/13 winter, each at a cost of around £6,000.

Work on the new toilet block for Sumners Lake started of the 2012 season and it is a top quality facility, with

Camping pods on Ribbon Park

cubicled washbasins, a fully equipped family room and new laundry room. Simon would like to have built a totally eco-friendly block with photovoltaic panels to convert sunlight into electricity and a solar thermal heating system, but the costs were prohibitive. However, the infrastructure can be adapted to include his eco ideas at a future date.

The landscaping, installation of drainage and electricity, the new toilet block, the camping pods and the construction of a road and pedestrian bridge at the edge of Farm Pond cost a total of £460,000.

Café Culture

In 2003 Simon had a shed on skids that could slide across the field to a position close to Sumners Lake. It was manned for a few hours a day to meet and greet fisherman and campers and, with a kettle, microwave and three-ring stove, it was possible to offer them tea, coffee and bacon sandwiches.

Since 2005, following several extensions, this shed has morphed into a permanent structure, combining a proper reception with a tackle shop and a full-blown licensed café offering good food all day. Outside decking and a small floating pontoon on the lake have since been added and it is now the hub of the park, serving fishermen, campers, visiting locals, walkers and cyclists alike. Close to £150,000 has been spent on developing this facility.

A Family Affair

Since Simon took over the reigns in 2003, the management, development and expansion of Sumners Ponds has become a real family business, with sister Jenny managing the bookings, and sons George and Harry actively involved in the day-to-day running of the park. During the summer months they employ 40 people and use local cleaners and tradesmen. Where possible, much of lake digging and groundwork (drainage/electricity) on the camping areas are undertaken by Simon, his sons and the permanent staff, which ensures everyone is fully employed over the winter period.

A Decade of Development

Sumners Ponds remains a working farm with its small beef herd. However, of the 100 acres, camping and fishing now occupy 40 acres, with a further 40 acres rented by the Smiths in order to produce hay and straw for cattle feed. Woodland takes up a further 15 acres and these have recently been improved through thinning and coppicing to encourage the growth of bluebells and other wild flowers, and footpaths have been created for campers to explore. The remaining land supports the beef herd, and meat from the calves that they rear to maturity appears on the café menus.

Since 2009 most of their money has been invested in improving the fishing and camping facilities and making the woodland and farm accessible to all through a network of footpaths and tracks. Today, fishing equates to 25% of turnover and provides the best margins per pound spent, while camping equates to 50% and is the most profitable activity. The final 25% comes from the café's revenue which is the trickiest to make money from due to the high labour and food costs.

The future looks bright and plans for winter 2013/14 include digging another fishing lake, moving the camping/fishing reception away from the café area and closer to the farm entrance, and adding improved security with a coded barrier.

For the Smith family day-to-day life revolves around fishing and camping and on summer weekends there can be over 600 people on the farm. Sacrificing their privacy and diversifying into the leisure industry has secured the future of the farm for the next generation.

Sumners Ponds, Fishery & Campsite, Chapel Road, Barns Green, West Sussex, RH13 OPR
Tel 01403 732539
See entry on page 301

Café area

Best for…

The AA thinks these are the best sites for…

…waterside pitches

ENGLAND

SOUTH END CARAVAN PARK,
Barrow-in-Furness, Cumbria
SLENINGFORD WATERMILL CC PARK,
North Stainley, North Yorkshire
SWALE VIEW CARAVAN PARK,
Richmond, North Yorkshire

SCOTLAND

INVER MILL FARM CARAVAN PARK,
Dunkeld, Perth & Kinross
SKYE C&C CLUB SITE,
Edinbane, Isle of Skye

WALES

RIVERSIDE CAMPING,
Caernarfon, Gwynedd

NORTHERN IRELAND

**DRUMAHEGLIS MARINA & CARAVAN
PARK,** Ballymoney, Co Antrim

…stunning views

ENGLAND

TRISTRAM C&C PARK,
Polzeath, Cornwall
TROUTBECK C&C CLUB SITE,
Troutbeck, Cumbria
SYKESIDE CAMPING PARK,
Patterdale, Cumbria
GALMPTON TOURING PARK,
Brixham, Devon
HIGHLANDS END HOLIDAY PARK,
Bridport, Dorset
NEW HALL FARM TOURING PARK,
Southwell, Nottinghamshire
WIMBLEBALL LAKE,
Dulverton, Somerset
HOWGILL LODGE,
Bolton Abbey, North Yorkshire
WOLDS WAY CARAVAN & CAMPING,
West Knapton, North Yorkshire

CHANNEL ISLANDS

ROZEL CAMPING PARK,
St Martin, Jersey

SCOTLAND

OBAN C&C PARK, Oban,
Argyll & Bute
LINNHE LOCHSIDE HOLIDAYS,
Corpach, Highland
INVERCOE C&C PARK,
Glencoe, Highland
JOHN O'GROATS CARAVAN SITE,
John O'Groats, Highland

WALES

ST DAVID'S PARK,
Pentraeth, Isle of Anglesey
BRON-Y-WENDON CARAVAN PARK,
Llanddulas, Conwy
BODNANT CARAVAN PARK,
Llanwrst, Conwy
HENDWR COUNTRY PARK,
Llandrillo, Denbighshire
BEACH VIEW CARAVAN PARK,
Abersoch, Gwynedd
TYN-Y-MUR TOURING & CAMPING
Abersoch, Gwynedd
TRAWSDIR TOURING C&C PARK,
Barmouth, Gwynedd
EISTEDDFA, Criccieth, Gwynedd
BARCDY TOURING C&C PARK,
Talsarnau, Gwynedd
FISHGUARD BAY C&C PARK,
Fishguard, Pembrokeshire
CARREGLWYD C&C PARK,
Port Einon, Swansea

…good on-site restaurants

ENGLAND

STROUD HILL PARK,
St Ives, Cambridgeshire
TRISTRAM C&C PARK,
Polzeath, Cornwall
BINGHAM GRANGE T&C PARK,
Bridport, Dorset
HIGHLANDS END HOLIDAY PARK,
Bridport, Dorset
BAY VIEW HOLIDAY PARK,
Bolton-Le-Sands, Lancashire
THE OLD BRICK KILNS,
Barney, Norfolk
**BEACONSFIELD FARM CARAVAN
PARK,** Shrewsbury, Shropshire

CHANNEL ISLANDS

BEUVELANDE CAMP SITE,
St Martin, Jersey

SCOTLAND

GLEN NEVIS C&C PARK,
Fort William, Highland

WALES

ST DAVID'S PARK,
Pentraeth, Isle of Anglesey

…top toilets

ENGLAND

CARNON DOWNS C&C PARK,
Truro, Cornwall
BEECH CROFT FARM,
Buxton, Derbyshire
RIVERSIDE C&C PARK,
South Molton, Devon
SHAMBA HOLIDAYS,
St Leonards, Dorset
TEVERSAL C&C CLUB SITE,
Teversal, Nottinghamshire
DELL TOURING PARK,
Bury St Edmunds, Suffolk
MOON & SIXPENCE,
Woodbridge, Suffolk
RIVERSIDE CARAVAN PARK,
High Bentham, North Yorkshire
WAYSIDE HOLIDAY PARK,
Pickering, North Yorkshire
MOOR LODGE PARK,
Leeds, West Yorkshire

SCOTLAND

SKYE C&C CLUB SITE,
Edinbane, Isle of Skye
BEECRAIGS C&C SITE,
Linlithgow, West Lothian

…on-site fishing

ENGLAND

FIELDS END WATER CP, & FISHERY
Doddington, Cambridgeshire
BACK OF BEYOND TOURING PARK,
St Leonards, Dorset
BLACKMORE VALE C&C PARK,
Shaftesbury, Dorset

WOODLAND WATERS,
Ancaster, Lincolnshire
**LAKESIDE CARAVAN PARK &
FISHERIES,** Downham Market,
Norfolk
THORNEY LAKES CARAVAN PARK,
Langport, Somerset
**MARSH FARM CARAVAN SITE, &
CARLTON MERES COUNTRY PARK**
Saxmundham, Suffolk
**SUMNERS PONDS FISHERY &
CAMPSITE,** Barns Green,
West Sussex

SCOTLAND

HODDOM CASTLE CARAVAN PARK,
Ecclefechan, Dumfries & Galloway
MILTON OF FONAB CARAVAN SITE,
Pitlochry, Perth & Kinross
GART CARAVAN PARK, Callander,
Stirling

WALES

AFON TEIFI C&C PARK,
Newcastle Emlyn, Carmarthenshire
YNYSYMAENGWYN CARAVAN PARK,
Tywyn, Gwynedd

...the kids

ENGLAND

TREVORNICK HOLIDAY PARK,
Holywell Bay, Cornwall
EDEN VALLEY HOLIDAY PARK,
Lostwithiel, Cornwall
GOLDEN VALLEY C&C PARK,
Ripley, Derbyshire
**FRESHWATER BEACH HOLIDAY
PARK,** Bridport, Dorset
SANDY BALLS HOLIDAY CENTRE,
Fordingbridge, Hampshire
HEATHLAND BEACH HOLIDAY PARK,
Kessingland, Suffolk
GOLDEN SQUARE TOURING PARK,
Helmsley, North Yorkshire
RIVERSIDE CARAVAN PARK,
High Bentham, North Yorkshire
GOOSEWOOD CARAVAN PARK,
Sutton-on-the-Forest, North Yorkshire

SCOTLAND

BLAIR CASTLE CARAVAN PARK,
Blair Atholl, Perth & Kinross

WALES

HOME FARM CARAVAN PARK,
Marian-Glas, Isle of Anglesey
**HENDRE MYNACH TOURING C&C
PARK,** Barmouth, Gwynedd
**TRAWSDIR TOURING C&C PARK,
BARMOUTH,** Gwynedd

...being eco-friendly

ENGLAND

SOUTH PENQUITE FARM,
Blisland, Cornwall
RIVER DART COUNTRY PARK,
Ashburton, Devon
BROOK LODGE FARM C&C PARK,
Cowslip Green, Somerset

SCOTLAND

SHIELING HOLIDAYS,
Craignure, Isle of Mull

WALES

**CAERFAI BAY CARAVAN & TENT
PARK,** St Davids, Pembrokeshire

...glamping it up
and staying in a pod or wigwam

ENGLAND

TREGOAD PARK, Looe, Cornwall
RUTHERN VALLEY HOLIDAYS,
Ruthernbridge, Cornwall
**LOW WRAY NATIONAL TRUST
CAMPSITE,** Ambleside, Cumbria
WILD ROSE PARK,
Appleby-in-Westmorland,
Cumbria (wigwams)
ESKDALE C&C CLUB SITE,
Boot, Cumbria
**GREAT LANGDALE NATIONAL TRUST
CAMPSITE,** Great Langdale, Cumbria
WOODCLOSE CARAVAN PARK,
Kirkby Lonsdale, Cumbria (wigwams)
**WASDALE HEAD NATIONAL TRUST
CAMPSITE,** Wasdale Head, Cumbria
THE QUIET SITE, Watermillock,
Cumbria
LEE VALLEY CAMPSITE, London E4
BELLINGHAM C&C CLUB SITE,
Bellingham, Northumberland
COTSWOLD VIEW TOURING PARK,
Charlbury, Oxfordshire

SCOTLAND

LINWATER CARAVAN PARK,
East Calder, West Lothian

...or staying in a yurt

ENGLAND

SOUTH PENQUITE FARM,
Blisland, Cornwall
TREVELLA TOURIST PARK,
Crantock, Cornwall
**GREAT LANGDALE NATIONAL TRUST
CAMPSITE,** Great Langdale, Cumbria
BLACKMORE VALE C&C PARK,
Shaftesbury, Dorset
**ACTON FIELD CAMPING SITE &
HERSTON C&C PARK,** Swanage,
Dorset

...or staying in a tipi

ENGLAND

**LOW WRAY NATIONAL TRUST
CAMPSITE,** Ambleside, Cumbria
SYKESIDE CAMPING PARK,
Patterdale, Cumbria
BLACKMORE VALE C&C PARK,
Shaftesbury, Dorset
SANDY BALLS HOLIDAY CENTRE,
Fordingbridge, Hampshire
**ROEBECK CAMPING & CARAVAN
PARK,** Ryde, Isle of Wight

WALES

EISTEDDFA, Criccieth, Gwynedd

...or staying in a safari tent

ENGLAND

TREVELLA TOURIST PARK,
Crantock, Cornwall
**BURNHAM-ON-SEA HOLIDAY
VILLAGE,** Burnham-on-Sea, Somerset

...or staying in a shepherd's hut

ENGLAND

HARFORD BRIDGE HOLIDAY PARK,
Tavistock, Devon
BLACKMORE VALE C&C PARK,
Shaftesbury, Dorset

AA Holiday Centres

ENGLAND

CORNWALL
BUDE
Sandymouth Holiday Park
HAYLE
St Ives Bay Holiday Park
HOLYWELL BAY
Holywell Bay Holiday Park
Trevornick Holiday Park
LOOE
Tencreek Holiday Park
MULLION
Mullion Holiday Park
NEWQUAY
Newquay Holiday Park
PERRANPORTH
Perran Sands Holiday Park
ST MERRYN
Harlyn Sands Holiday Park
WIDEMOUTH BAY
Widemouth Bay Caravan Park

CUMBRIA
FLOOKBURGH
Lakeland Leisure Park
POOLEY BRIDGE
Park Foot Caravan & Camping Park
SILLOTH
Stanwix Park Holiday Centre

DEVON
CROYDE BAY
Ruda Holiday Park
DAWLISH
Lady's Mile Holiday Park
EXMOUTH
Devon Cliffs Holiday Park
MORTEHOE
Twitchen House Holiday Village
SHALDON
Coast View Holiday Park
WOOLACOMBE
Golden Coast Holiday Village
Woolacombe Bay Holiday Village
Woolacombe Sands Holiday Park

DORSET
BRIDPORT
Freshwater Beach Holiday Park
West Bay Holiday Park
HOLTON HEATH
Sandford Holiday Park
POOLE
Rockley Park
WEYMOUTH
Littlesea Holiday Park
Seaview Holiday Park

DURHAM, COUNTY
BLACKHALL COLLIERY
Crimdon Dene

ESSEX
CLACTON-ON-SEA
Highfield Grange
Martello Beach Holiday Park
MERSEA ISLAND
Waldegraves Holiday Park
ST LAWRENCE
Waterside St Lawrence Bay
ST OSYTH
The Orchards Holiday Park
WALTON ON THE NAZE
Naze Marine

KENT
EASTCHURCH
Warden Springs Caravan Park

LANCASHIRE
BLACKPOOL
Marton Mere Holiday Village

LINCOLNSHIRE
CLEETHORPES
Thorpe Park Holiday Centre
MABLETHORPE
Golden Sands Holiday Park

SALTFLEET
Sunnydale
SKEGNESS
Southview Leisure Park

MERSEYSIDE
SOUTHPORT
Riverside Holiday Park

NORFOLK
BELTON
Wild Duck Holiday Park
BURGH CASTLE
Breydon Water
CAISTER-ON-SEA
Caister Holiday Park
GREAT YARMOUTH
Vauxhall Holiday Park
HUNSTANTON
Manor Park Holiday Village
Searles Leisure Resort

NORTHUMBERLAND
BERWICK-UPON-TWEED
Haggerston Castle
NORTH SEATON
Sandy Bay

SOMERSET
BREAN
Holiday Resort Unity
Warren Farm Holiday Centre
BRIDGWATER
Mill Farm Caravan & Camping Park
BURNHAM-ON-SEA
Burnham-on-Sea Holiday Village
CHEDDAR
Cheddar Woods Holiday Park

SUFFOLK
KESSINGLAND
Kessingland Beach Holiday Park

SUSSEX, EAST
CAMBER
Camber Sands

SUSSEX, WEST
SELSEY
Warner Farm Touring Park

WIGHT, ISLE OF
COWES
Thorness Bay Holiday Park
ST HELENS
Nodes Point Holiday Park
SHANKLIN
Lower Hyde Holiday Park
WHITECLIFF BAY
Whitecliff Bay Holiday Park

YORKSHIRE, EAST RIDING OF
SKIPSEA
Skipsea Sands
Skirlington Leisure Park
TUNSTALL
Sand le Mere Holiday Village

YORKSHIRE, NORTH
FILEY
Blue Dolphin Holiday Park
Flower of May Holiday Park
Primrose Valley Holiday Park
Reighton Sands Holiday Park

YORKSHIRE, EAST RIDING OF
WITHERNSEA
Withernsea Sands

SCOTLAND

DUMFRIES & GALLOWAY
GATEHOUSE OF FLEET
Auchenlarie Holiday Park
SOUTHERNESS
Southerness Holiday Village

EAST LOTHIAN
LONGNIDDRY
Seton Sands Holiday Village

HIGHLAND
DORNOCH
Grannie's Heilan Hame Holiday Park
NAIRN
Nairn Lochloy Holiday Park

NORTH AYRSHIRE
SALTCOATS
Sandylands

PERTH & KINROSS
TUMMEL BRIDGE
Tummel Valley Holiday Park

SCOTTISH BORDERS
EYEMOUTH
Eyemouth

SOUTH AYRSHIRE
AYR
Craig Tara Holiday Park
COYLTON
Sundrum Castle Holiday Park

WALES

CEREDIGION
BORTH
Brynowen Holiday Park

CONWY
TOWYN
Ty Mawr Holiday Park

DENBIGHSHIRE
PRESTATYN
Presthaven Sands Holiday Park

GWYNEDD
PORTHMADOG
Greenacres Holiday Park
PWLLHELI
Hafan Y Mor Holiday Park

PEMBROKESHIRE
TENBY
Kiln Park Holiday Centre

SWANSEA
SWANSEA
Riverside Caravan Park

Premier Parks ►►►►►

5 GOLD PENNANTS

ENGLAND

CAMBRIDGESHIRE
ST IVES
Stroud Hill Park

CHESHIRE
WHITEGATE
Lamb Cottage Caravan Park

CORNWALL
BUDE
Wooda Farm Holiday Park
MEVAGISSEY
Seaview International Holiday Park
PADSTOW
Padstow Touring Park
ST IVES
Polmanter Touring Park
ST JUST-IN-ROSELAND
Trethem Mill Touring Park
TRURO
Carnon Downs Caravan & Camping Park

DEVON
DARTMOUTH
Woodlands Grove Caravan & Camping Park
NEWTON ABBOT
Dornafield
Ross Park
SIDMOUTH
Oakdown Country Holiday Park

DORSET
BRIDPORT
Highlands End Holiday Park
CHARMOUTH
Wood Farm Caravan & Camping Park
LYTCHETT MINSTER
South Lytchett Manor C&C Park
WAREHAM
Wareham Forest Tourist Park

LANCASHIRE
SILVERDALE
Silverdale Caravan Park

NORFOLK
CLIPPESBY
Clippesby Hall

OXFORDSHIRE
STANDLAKE
Lincoln Farm Park Oxfordshire

SOMERSET
BISHOP SUTTON
Bath Chew Valley Caravan Park
GLASTONBURY
The Old Oaks Touring Park

SUFFOLK
WOODBRIDGE
Moon & Sixpence

WIGHT, ISLE OF
NEWBRIDGE
The Orchards Holiday Caravan Park
RYDE
Whitefield Forest Touring Park

SCOTLAND

FIFE
ST ANDREWS
Craigtoun Meadows Holiday Park
Cairnsmill Holiday Park

WALES

ANGLESEY, ISLE OF
MARIAN-GLAS
Home Farm Caravan Park

GWYNEDD
BARMOUTH
Trawsdir Touring Caravans & Camping Park

WREXHAM
EYTON
The Plassey Leisure Park

5 BLACK PENNANTS

ENGLAND

BERKSHIRE
HURLEY
Hurley Riverside Park
CAMBRIDGESHIRE
DODDINGTON
Fields End Water Caravan Park & Fishery

CHESHIRE
CODDINGTON
Manor Wood Country Caravan Park

CORNWALL
CARLYON BAY
Carlyon Bay Caravan & Camping Park
CRANTOCK
Trevella Tourist Park
GOONHAVERN
Silverbow Park
LANDRAKE
Dolbeare Park Caravan and Camping
LEEDSTOWN
Calloose Caravan & Camping Park
LOSTWITHIEL
Eden Valley Holiday Park
NEWQUAY
Hendra Holiday Park
PENTEWAN
Sun Valley Holiday Park
REDRUTH
Globe Vale Holiday Park
REJERRAH
Newperran Holiday Park
ST AUSTELL
River Valley Holiday Park
ST IVES
Ayr Holiday Park
ST MERRYN
Atlantic Bays Holiday Park
ST MINVER
Gunvenna Caravan Park
TRURO
Cosawes Park
Truro Caravan and Camping Park
WATERGATE BAY
Watergate Bay Touring Park

CUMBRIA
AMBLESIDE
Skelwith Fold Caravan Park
APPLEBY-IN-WESTMORLAND
Wild Rose Park
BOOT
Eskdale Camping & Caravanning Club Site

KESWICK
Castlerigg Hall Caravan & Camping Park
KIRKBY LONSDALE
Woodclose Caravan Park
PENRITH
Lowther Holiday Park
TROUTBECK [NEAR KESWICK]
Troutbeck C&C Club Site
ULVERSTON
Bardsea Leisure Park
WINDERMERE
Fallbarrow Park
Park Cliffe Camping & Caravan Estate

DEVON
BRAUNTON
Hidden Valley Park
CLYST ST MARY
Crealy Meadows C&C Park
COMBE MARTIN
Newberry Valley Park
DAWLISH
Cofton Country Holidays
DREWSTEIGNTON
Woodland Springs Adult Touring Park
KINGSBRIDGE
Parkland Caravan and Camping Site
PAIGNTON
Beverley Parks Caravan & Camping Park
SAMPFORD PEVERELL
Minnows Touring Park
TAVISTOCK
Langstone Manor Camping & Caravan Park
Woodovis Park
BRIDPORT
Bingham Grange Touring & Camping Park
CHARMOUTH
Newlands Caravan & Camping Park
CHRISTCHURCH
Meadowbank Holidays

ST LEONARDS
Shamba Holidays
SWANAGE
Ulwell Cottage Caravan Park
WEYMOUTH
East Fleet Farm Touring Park
WIMBORNE MINSTER
Merley Court
Wilksworth Farm Caravan Park

HAMPSHIRE
FORDINGBRIDGE
Sandy Balls Holiday Village
ROMSEY
Hill Farm Caravan Park

HEREFORDSHIRE
PEMBRIDGE
Townsend Touring Park

KENT
ASHFORD
Broadhembury Caravan & Camping Park
MARDEN
Tanner Farm Touring C&C Park

LANCASHIRE
THORNTON
Kneps Farm Holiday Park

LINCOLNSHIRE
WOODHALL SPA
Woodhall Country Park

NORFOLK
BARNEY
The Old Brick Kilns
BELTON
Rose Farm Touring & Camping Park
NORTH WALSHAM
Two Mills Touring Park

NORTHUMBERLAND
BELFORD
South Meadows Caravan Park
BELLINGHAM
Bellingham C&C Club Site
BERWICK-UPON-TWEED
Ord House Country Park

NOTTINGHAMSHIRE
TEVERSAL
Teversal C&C Club Site

OXFORDSHIRE
HENLEY-ON-THAMES
Swiss Farm Touring & Camping

SHROPSHIRE
BRIDGNORTH
Stanmore Hall Touring Park
SHREWSBURY
Beaconsfield Farm Caravan Park
Oxon Hall Touring Park
TELFORD
Severn Gorge Park
WHEATHILL
Wheathill Touring Park

SOMERSET
CROWCOMBE
Quantock Orchard Caravan Park
PORLOCK
Porlock Caravan Park
WELLS
Wells Holiday Park
WIVELISCOMBE
Waterrow Touring Park

STAFFORDSHIRE
LONGNOR
Longnor Wood Holiday Park

SUSSEX, EAST
BEXHILL
Kloofs Caravan Park

WIGHT, ISLE OF
WROXALL
Appuldurcombe Gardens Holiday Park

WORCESTERSHIRE
HONEYBOURNE
Ranch Caravan Park

YORKSHIRE, NORTH
ALLERSTON
Vale of Pickering Caravan Park
ALNE
Alders Caravan Park

Premier Parks ►►►►► *continued*

HARROGATE
Rudding Holiday Park
Ripley Caravan Park
HELMSLEY
Golden Square Touring Caravan Park
HIGH BENTHAM
Riverside Caravan Park
OSMOTHERLEY
Cote Ghyll Caravan & Camping Park
RIPON
Riverside Meadows Country Caravan Park
SCARBOROUGH
Jacobs Mount Caravan Park
SUTTON-ON-THE-FOREST
Goosewood Caravan Park
WYKEHAM
St Helens Caravan Park

CHANNEL ISLANDS

JERSEY
ST MARTIN
Beuvelande Camp Site

SCOTLAND

ABERDEENSHIRE
HUNTLY
Huntly Castle Caravan Park

DUMFRIES & GALLOWAY
BRIGHOUSE BAY
Brighouse Bay Holiday Park
CREETOWN
Castle Cary Holiday Park
ECCLEFECHAN
Hoddom Castle Caravan Park

EAST LOTHIAN
DUNBAR
Thurston Manor Leisure Park

HIGHLAND
CORPACH
Linnhe Lochside Holidays

PERTH & KINROSS
BLAIR ATHOLL
Blair Castle Caravan Park
River Tilt Caravan Park

STIRLING
ABERFOYLE
Trossachs Holiday Park

WEST DUNBARTONSHIRE
BALLOCH
Lomond Woods Holiday Park

WALES

ANGLESEY, ISLE OF
DULAS
Tyddyn Isaf Caravan Park

CARMARTHENSHIRE
LLANDOVERY
Erwlon Caravan & Camping Park
NEWCASTLE EMLYN
Cenarth Falls Holiday Park

CONWY
LLANDDULAS
Bron-Y-Wendon Caravan Park
LLANRWST
Bron Derw Touring Caravan Park

GWYNEDD
BARMOUTH
Hendre Mynach Touring Caravan &
Camping Park
TAL-Y-BONT
Islawrffordd Caravan Park

MONMOUTHSHIRE
USK
Pont Kemys Caravan & Camping Park

PEMBROKESHIRE
ST DAVIDS
Caerfai Bay Caravan & Tent Park

POWYS
BRECON
Pencelli Castle Caravan & Camping Park
CHURCHSTOKE
Daisy Bank Caravan Park

SWANSEA
PONTARDDULAIS
River View Touring Park

NORTHERN IRELAND

CO ANTRIM
BALLYMONEY
Drumaheglis Marina & Caravan Park
BUSHMILLS
Ballyness Caravan Park

CO FERMANAGH
BELCOO
Rushin House Caravan Park

Adults – No Children Parks

Over 50 of the parks in the AA pennant rating scheme have opted to provide facilities for adults only, and do not accept children. The minimum age for individual parks may be 18, or 21, while one or two pitch the limit even higher. For more information please contact the individual parks.

ENGLAND

CAMBRIDGESHIRE
Fields End Water Caravan Park & Fishery, Doddington
Stroud Hill Park, St Ives

CHESHIRE
New Farm Caravan Park, Wettenhall
Lamb Cottage Caravan Park, Whitegate

CORNWALL
Killiwerris Touring Park, Chacewater
Wayfarers Caravan & Camping Park, St Hilary

CUMBRIA
Green Acres Caravan Park, Carlisle
Larches Caravan Park, Mealsgate

DERBYSHIRE
Clover Fields Touring Caravan Park, Buxton

DEVON
Woodland Springs Adult Touring Park, Drewsteignton
Zeacombe House Caravan Park, East Anstey
Widdicombe Farm Touring Park, Torquay

DORSET
Bingham Grange Touring & Camping Park, Bridport
Fillybrook Farm Touring Park, Hurn
Back of Beyond Touring Park, St Leonards

ESSEX
Golden Grove, Great Saling

HEREFORDSHIRE
Cuckoo's Corner Campsite, Moreton on Lugg

LANCASHIRE
Manor House Caravan Park, Blackpool

LINCOLNSHIRE
Long Acres Touring Park, Boston
Orchard Park, Boston

NORFOLK
Two Mills Touring Park, North Walsham
Lowe Caravan Park, Saham Hills
The Rickels Caravan & Camping Park, Stanhoe
Breckland Meadows Touring Park, Swaffham
Lode Hall Holiday Park, Three Holes

NOTTINGHAMSHIRE
New Hall Farm Touring Park, Southwell

OXFORDSHIRE
Wysdom Touring Park, Burford

SHROPSHIRE
Beaconsfield Farm Caravan Park, Shrewsbury
Severn Gorge Park, Telford
Wheathill Touring Park, Wheathill

SOMERSET
Bath Chew Valley Caravan Park, Bishop Sutton
Exe Valley Caravan Site, Bridgetown
Cheddar Bridge Touring Park, Cheddar
The Old Oaks Touring Park, Glastonbury
Long Hazel Park, Sparkford
Greenacres Touring Park, Wellington
Homestead Park, Wells
Wells Holiday Park, Wells
Waterrow Touring Park, Wiveliscombe

STAFFORDSHIRE
Longnor Wood Holiday Park, Longnor

SUFFOLK
Moat Barn Touring Caravan Park, Woodbridge

WEST MIDLANDS
Somers Wood Caravan Park, Meriden

WIGHT, ISLE OF
Riverside Paddock Camp Site, Newport

YORKSHIRE, EAST RIDING OF
Blue Rose Caravan Country Park, Brandesburton

YORKSHIRE, NORTH
Shaws Trailer Park, Harrogate
Foxholme Caravan Park, Helmsley

YORKSHIRE, WEST
Moor Lodge Park, Leeds
St Helena's Caravan Park, Leeds

SCOTLAND

ABERDEENSHIRE
Aden Caravan and Camping Park, Mintlaw

WALES

MONMOUTHSHIRE
Wernddu Caravan Park, Abergavenny

POWYS
Daisy Bank Caravan Park, Churchstoke
Riverside Caravan & Camping Park, Crickhowell
Dalmore Camping & Caravanning Park, Llandrindod Wells

WREXHAM
The Trotting Mare, Overton

England

Low Tide at Clovelly

ISLE OF - Places incorporating the words 'Isle' or 'Isle of' will be found under the actual name, eg Isle of Wight is listed under Wight, Isle of. Channel Islands and Isle of Man, however, are listed between England and Scotland, and there is also a section in the guide for Scottish Islands.

BERKSHIRE

FINCHAMPSTEAD — Map 5 SU76

Places to visit

West Green House Gardens, HARTLEY WINTNEY, RG27 8JB, 01252 844611 www.westgreenhouse.co.uk

Museum of English Rural Life, READING, RG1 5EX, 0118 378 8660 www.merl.org.uk

Great for kids: The Look Out Discovery Centre, BRACKNELL, RG12 7QW, 01344 354400 www.bracknell-forest.gov.uk/be

▶▶▶ 80% California Chalet & Touring Park (SU788651)

Nine Mile Ride RG40 4HU
☎ 0118 973 3928 & 07447 475833
e-mail: enquiries@californiapark.co.uk
dir: *From A321 (S of Wokingham), right onto B3016 to Finchampstead. Follow Country Park signs on Nine Mile Ride*

* ⊞ £21-£24 ⊞ £21-£24 ▲ £18-£45

Open all year

Last arrival flexible Last departure noon

A simple, peaceful woodland site with secluded pitches among the trees, adjacent to the country park. Several pitches have a prime position beside the lake with their own fishing area. Three new large hardstandings have been created, with more planned for 2014; the chalet accommodation has been upgraded and the toilet block revamped with quality vanity units and fully tiled showers. Trees have now been thinned to allow more sunshine onto pitches, and future investment plans are very positive for this well located park. 5.5 acre site. 44 touring pitches. 44 hardstandings. Caravan pitches. Motorhome pitches. Tent pitches.

AA Pubs & Restaurants nearby: The Broad Street Tavern, WOKINGHAM, RG40 1AU, 0118 977 3706

L'ortolan, SHINFIELD, RG2 9BY, 0118 988 8500

Facilities: 📷⊙☞🕭🚿🛁🚽 ♻ ❶

Services: 🚰🔌 ▌🎁 ⬛🛒↯

Within 3 miles: 🎣🐎🚣◎🛁🛒∪

Notes: No ground fires, no washing of caravans. Dogs must be kept on leads.

HURLEY

Places to visit

Cliveden, CLIVEDEN, SL6 0JA, 01628 605069 www.nationaltrust.org.uk/cliveden

The Hell-Fire Caves, WEST WYCOMBE, HP14 3AJ, 01494 524411 (office) www.hellfirecaves.co.uk

Great for kids: Bekonscot Model Village and Railway, BEACONSFIELD, HP9 2PL, 01494 672919 www.bekonscot.co.uk

HURLEY — Map 5 SU88

PREMIER PARK

▶▶▶▶▶ 83% Hurley Riverside Park (SU826839)

Park Office SL6 5NE
☎ 01628 824493 & 823501
e-mail: info@hurleyriversidepark.co.uk
dir: *Signed on A4130 (Henley to Maidenhead road), just W of Hurley*

* ⊞ £15-£28 ⊞ £15-£28 ▲ £13-£25

Open Mar-Oct

Last arrival 20.00hrs Last departure noon

A large Thames-side site with a good touring area close to the river. A quality park with three beautifully appointed toilet blocks, one of which houses excellent, fully serviced unisex facilities. Level grassy pitches are sited in small, sectioned areas, and this is a generally peaceful setting. There are furnished tents for hire. 15 acre site. 200 touring pitches. 18 hardstandings. Caravan pitches. Motorhome pitches. Tent pitches. 290 statics.

LEISURE: 🏊 Indoor swimming pool 🏊 Outdoor swimming pool 🎢 Children's playground 🧒 Kid's club 🎾 Tennis court 🎱 Games room 📺 Separate TV room ⛳ 9/18 hole golf course 🚣 Boats for hire 🎬 Cinema 🎵 Entertainment 🎣 Fishing ◎ Mini golf 🏄 Watersports 💪 Gym 🏟 Sports field **Spa** ∪ Stables

FACILITIES: 🛁 Bath 🚿 Shower ⊙ Electric shaver 💇 Hairdryer ❄ Ice Pack Facility ♿ Disabled facilities 📞 Public telephone 🛒 Shop on site or within 200yds 🚚 Mobile shop (calls at least 5 days a week) 🍖 BBQ area 🪑 Picnic area 📶 Wi-fi 🖥 Internet access ♻ Recycling ❶ Tourist info 🐕 Dog exercise area

AA Pubs & Restaurants nearby: Black Boys Inn, HURLEY, SL6 5NQ, 01628 824212

Hotel du Vin Henley-on-Thames, HENLEY-ON-THAMES, RG9 2BP, 01491 848400

Hurley Riverside Park

Leisure: ⚄ ✪
Facilities: ⋔ ☉ �📷 ⚡ ⚙ 🕓 🚿 🚽 ⌕ WI-FI ♻ 🛈
Services: 🔌 📶 🔋 ⊘ T ↯
Within 3 miles: ↓ ⚑ ⛱ ℘ 🔒 📶

Notes: No unsupervised children, no young groups, no commercial vehicles, no fires or fire pits. Quiet park policy. Max 2 dogs per pitch. Dogs must be kept on leads. Fishing in season, slipway, nature trail, riverside picnic grounds.

see advert on opposite page

Places to visit

Highclere Castle & Gardens, HIGHCLERE, RG20 9RN, 01635 253210 www.highclerecastle.co.uk

West Berkshire Museum, NEWBURY, RG14 5AS, 01635 519231 www.westberkshiremuseum.org.uk

Great for kids: The Living Rainforest, HAMPSTEAD NORREYS, RG18 0TN, 01635 202444 www.livingrainforest.org

►►► 80% *Bishops Green Farm Camp Site* (SU502630)

Bishops Green RG20 4JP
☎ 01635 268365
dir: *Exit A339 (opposite New Greenham Park) towards Bishops Green & Ecchinswell. Site on left, approx 0.5m by barn*

🚐 ⚏ ▲

Open Apr-Oct

Last arrival 21.30hrs

A sheltered and secluded meadowland park close to the Hampshire/Berkshire border, offering very clean and well-maintained facilities, including a toilet block with a disabled/family room. There are woodland and riverside walks to be enjoyed around the farm, and coarse fishing is also available. The site is very convenient for visiting the nearby market town of Newbury with its attractive canal in the town centre. 1.5 acre site. 30 touring pitches. 6 hardstandings. Caravan pitches. Motorhome pitches. Tent pitches.

Facilities: ⋔ ☉ ⚙ 🚽
Services: 🔌 📶 ↯
Within 3 miles: ↓ ℘ 🔒
Notes: ⊘ Dogs must be kept on leads.

Places to visit

Basildon Park, LOWER BASILDON, RG8 9NR, 0118 984 3040 www.nationaltrust.org.uk/basildonpark

Mapledurham House, MAPLEDURHAM, RG4 7TR, 0118 972 3350 www.mapledurham.co.uk

Great for kids: Beale Park, LOWER BASILDON, RG8 9NH, 0844 826 1761 www.bealepark.co.uk

---

►►► 85% Wellington Country Park

(SU728628)

Odiham Rd RG7 1SP
☎ 0118 932 6444
e-mail: info@wellington-country-park.co.uk
web: www.wellington-country-park.co.uk
dir: *M4 junct 11, A33 S towards Basingstoke. Or M3 junct 5, B3349 N towards Reading*

🚐 ⚏ ▲

Open Mar-Nov

Last arrival 17.30hrs (16.30hrs in low season). Last departure noon

A peaceful woodland site, popular with families, set within an extensive country park, which comes complete with lakes and nature trails; these are accessible to campers after the country park closes. The park offers good facilities that include a new laundry. There's also a herd of Red and Fallow deer that roam the meadow area. This site is ideal for those travelling on the M4. 80 acre site. 72 touring pitches. 10 hardstandings. Caravan pitches. Motorhome pitches. Tent pitches.

AA Pubs & Restaurants nearby: The George & Dragon, SWALLOWFIELD, RG7 1TJ, 0118 988 4432

Leisure: ⚄ ♫
Facilities: ⋔ ☉ 📷 ⚡ ⚙ 🕓 🚿 ⌕ WI-FI ♻ 🛈
Services: 🔌 📶 🔋 ⏀ ☕ 🍴
Within 3 miles: ↓ ◎ ⛱ 🔒 📶 ∪

Notes: No open fires, Dogs must be kept on leads. Miniature railway, crazy golf, maze, animal corner. Access to Wellington Country Park.

BRISTOL

BRISTOL

See Cowslip Green (Somerset)

CAMBRIDGESHIRE

COMBERTON Map 12 TL35

Places to visit

Imperial War Museums, Duxford, DUXFORD, CB22 4QR, 01223 835000 www.iwm.org.uk

Audley End House & Gardens, AUDLEY END, CB11 4JF, 01799 522842 www.english-heritage.org.uk/daysout/properties/audley-end-house-and-gardens

Great for kids: Linton Zoological Gardens, LINTON, CB21 4NT, 01223 891308 www.lintonzoo.co.uk

►►►► **91% Highfield Farm Touring Park** *(TL389572)*

Best of British

Long Rd CB23 7DG
☎ 01223 262308
e-mail: enquiries@highfieldfarmtouringpark.co.uk
dir: *M11 junct 12, A603 (Sandy). 0.5m, right onto B1046 to Comberton*

🚐 🚙 ⛺

Open Apr-Oct

Last arrival 22.00hrs Last departure 14.00hrs

Run by a very efficient and friendly family, the park is on a well-sheltered hilltop, with spacious pitches including a cosy backpackers/cyclists' area, and separate sections for couples and families. There is a one and a half mile marked walk around the family farm, that has stunning views. 8 acre site. 120 touring pitches. 52 hardstandings. Caravan pitches. Motorhome pitches. Tent pitches.

AA Pubs & Restaurants nearby: The Three Horseshoes, MADINGLEY, CB23 8AB, 01954 210221

Restaurant 22, CAMBRIDGE, CB4 3AX, 01223 351880

Leisure: 🛝

Facilities: 🚿 ⊙ 💨 ✲ ✆ [S] 🐕 [Wi-fi] ⓘ

Services: 🗨 ▣ 🔒 🍃 [T] 🍴 ⚓

Within 3 miles: ⛳ 🎣 [S] ▣ ∪

Notes: ⊗ Dogs must be kept on leads. Postbox.

DODDINGTON

Places to visit

WWT Welney Wetland Centre, WELNEY, PE14 9TN, 01353 860711 www.wwt.org.uk

Flag Fen Archaeology Park, PETERBOROUGH, PE6 7QJ, 01733 313414 www.vivacity-peterborough.com/museums-and-heritage/flag-fen

DODDINGTON Map 12 TL49

REGIONAL WINNER - HEART OF ENGLAND AA CAMPSITE OF THE YEAR 2014

PREMIER PARK

►►►►► **83% Fields End Water Caravan Park & Fishery** *(TL378908)*

Benwick Rd PE15 0TY
☎ 01354 740199
e-mail: info@fieldsendfishing.co.uk
dir: *Exit A141, follow signs to Doddington. At clock tower in Doddington turn right into Benwick Rd. Site 1.5m on right after sharp bends*

* 🚐 £16.50-£20 🚙 £16.50-£20 ⛺ £14-£15

Open all year

Last arrival 20.30hrs Last departure noon

This meticulously planned and executed park makes excellent use of its slightly elevated position in The Fens. The 33 fully serviced pitches, all with very generous hardstandings, are on smart terraces with sweeping views of the countryside. The two toilet blocks contain several combined cubicle spaces, and there are shady walks through mature deciduous woodland adjacent to two large and appealingly landscaped fishing lakes. Three high quality pine lodges are now available as holiday lets. 20 acre site. 52 touring pitches. 17 hardstandings. Caravan pitches. Motorhome pitches. Tent pitches.

AA Pubs & Restaurants nearby: The Crown Inn, BROUGHTON, PE28 3AY, 01487 824428

The Old Bridge Hotel, HUNTINGDON, PE29 3TQ, 01480 424300

Facilities: 🚿 ⊙ 💨 ✲ ♿ [S] 🐕 [Wi-fi] ♻ ⓘ

Services: 🗨 ▣ 🔒 [T]

Within 3 miles: ⛳ 🎣 ◎ [S] ▣

Notes: Adults only. Dogs must be kept on leads.

HEMINGFORD ABBOTS — Map 12 TL27

►►► 79% Quiet Waters Caravan Park (TL283712)

PE28 9AJ
☎ **01480 463405**
e-mail: quietwaters.park@btopenworld.com
web: www.quietwaterscaravanpark.co.uk
dir: *Follow village signs from A14 junct 25, E of Huntingdon, site in village centre*

* ☐ £15.50-£19.50 ☐ £15.50-£19.50
Å £15.50-£19.50

Open Apr-Oct

Last arrival 20.00hrs Last departure noon

This is an attractive little site on the banks of the Great Ouse that has been in the same family ownership for over 80 years. It is found in a really charming village just a mile from the A14, making an ideal centre from which to tour the Cambridgeshire area. There are fishing opportunities, rowing boats for hire and many walks and cycling routes directly from the park. There are holiday statics for hire. 1 acre site. 20 touring pitches. 18 hardstandings. Caravan pitches. Motorhome pitches. Tent pitches. 40 statics.

AA Pubs & Restaurants nearby: The Cock Pub and Restaurant, HEMINGFORD GREY, PE28 9BJ, 01480 463609

The Old Bridge Hotel, HUNTINGDON, PE29 3TQ, 01480 424300

Facilities: ℝ ☉ ℙ ✳ ᨣ ◷ ᴡ-ꜰ ❶
Services: ☐ ☐ ☐ ∅
Within 3 miles: ⌿ ≄ ⵍ ℓ ☐ ☐ ∪
Notes: Dogs must be kept on leads.

HUNTINGDON — Map 12 TL27

Places to visit
Ramsey Abbey Gatehouse, RAMSEY, PE26 1DG, 01480 301494 www.nationaltrust.org.uk
Fitzwilliam Museum, CAMBRIDGE, CB2 1RB, 01223 332900 www.fitzmuseum.cam.ac.uk
Great for kids: The Raptor Foundation, WOODHURST, PE28 3BT, 01487 741140 www.raptorfoundation.org.uk

►►► 80% Huntingdon Boathaven & Caravan Park (TL249706)

The Avenue, Godmanchester PE29 2AF
☎ **01480 411977**
e-mail: boathaven.hunts@virgin.net
dir: *S of town. Exit A14 at Godmanchester junct, through Godmanchester on B1043 to site (on left by River Ouse)*

☐ ☐ Å

Open all year (rs Winter open subject to weather)

Last arrival 21.00hrs

A small, well laid out site overlooking a boat marina and the River Ouse, set close to the A14 and within walking distance of Huntingdon town centre. The toilets are clean and well kept. A pretty area has been created for tents beside the marina, with wide views across the Ouse Valley. Weekend family activities are organised throughout the season. 2 acre site. 24 touring pitches. 18 hardstandings. Caravan pitches. Motorhome pitches. Tent pitches.

AA Pubs & Restaurants nearby: The Old Bridge Hotel, HUNTINGDON, PE29 3TQ, 01480 424300

King William IV, FENSTANTON, PE28 9JF, 01480 462467

Facilities: ℝ ☉ ℙ ✳ ᨣ ᴙ ᨤ ᴡ-ꜰ ❶
Services: ☐ ☐ ☐ ∅ ☐ ☐
Within 3 miles: ⌿ ≄ ⵍ ℓ ≄ ☐
Notes: No cars by tents. Dogs must be kept on leads.

►►► 79% The Willows Caravan Park (TL224708)

Bromholme Ln, Brampton PE28 4NE
☎ **01480 437566**
e-mail: willows@willows33.freeserve.co.uk
dir: *Exit A14/A1 signed Brampton, follow Huntingdon signs. Site on right near Brampton Mill pub*

☐ ☐ Å

Open all year

Last arrival 20.00hrs Last departure noon

A small, friendly site in a pleasant setting beside the River Ouse, on the Ouse Valley Walk. Bay areas have been provided for caravans and motorhomes, and planting for screening is gradually maturing. There are launching facilities and free river fishing. 4 acre site. 50 touring pitches. 10 hardstandings. 10 seasonal pitches. Caravan pitches. Motorhome pitches. Tent pitches.

AA Pubs & Restaurants nearby: The Old Bridge Hotel, HUNTINGDON, PE29 3TQ, 01480 424300

Leisure: ⚠ ✿
Facilities: ℝ ☉ ✳ ᨣ ᴡ-ꜰ ❶
Services: ☐ ☐ ☐
Within 3 miles: ⌿ ≄ ⵍ ℓ ☐
Notes: ⊗ No cars by tents. 5mph one-way system, no generators, no groundsheets. Ball games allowed on field only. Dogs must be kept on leads. Free book lending/exchange.

ST IVES
Map 12 TL37

Places to visit

The Farmland Museum and Denny Abbey, WATERBEACH, CB25 9PQ, 01223 860988 www.english-heritage.org.uk/daysout/ properties/denny-abbey-and-the-farmland-museum

Oliver Cromwell's House, ELY, CB7 4HF, 01353 662062 www.visitely.org.uk

PREMIER PARK

▶▶▶▶▶ **95% Stroud Hill Park** *(TL335787)*

Best of British

Fen Rd PE28 3DE
☎ **01487 741333**
e-mail: stroudhillpark@btconnect.com
dir: *Exit B1040 in Pidley follow signs for Lakeside Lodge Complex, into Fen Rd, site on right*

Open all year

Last arrival 20.00hrs Last departure noon

A superb adults-only caravan park designed to a very high specification in a secluded and sheltered spot not far from St Ives. A modern timber-framed barn houses the exceptional facilities. These include the beautifully tiled toilets with spacious cubicles, each containing a shower, washbasin and toilet. A bar and café, AA-rosette restaurant (Marcello @ the barn), small licensed shop, tennis court and coarse fishing are among the attractions. There are three pay-as-you-go golf courses plus ten-pin bowling nearby. 6 acre site. 60 touring pitches. 44 hardstandings. Caravan pitches. Motorhome pitches. Tent pitches.

AA Pubs & Restaurants nearby: The Old Ferryboat Inn, HOLYWELL, PE27 4TG, 01480 463227

The Lazy Otter, STRETHAM, CB6 3LU, 01353 649780

Leisure: ⟋
Facilities: ⟋⊙⟋✳⟋⟋⟋⟋⟋⟋ ♻ ⟋
Services: ⟋⟋⟋⟋⟋⟋⟋⟋
Within 3 miles: ⟋⟋⟋⊙⟋⟋⟋⟋

Notes: Adults only. No large motorhomes. Dogs must be kept on leads.

WISBECH
Map 12 TF40

Places to visit

Peckover House & Garden, WISBECH, PE13 1JR, 01945 583463 www.nationaltrust.org.uk/peckover

Sandringham House, Gardens & Museum, SANDRINGHAM, PE35 6EN, 01485 545408 www.sandringhamestate.co.uk

Great for kids: Butterfly & Wildlife Park, SPALDING, PE12 9LE, 01406 363833 www.butterflyandwildlifepark.co.uk

▶▶▶ **85% Little Ranch Leisure** *(TF456062)*

Begdale, Elm PE14 0AZ
☎ **01945 860066**
dir: *From rdbt on A47 (SW of Wisbech) take Redmoor Lane to Begdale*

⟋ £12-£17 ⟋ £12-£17 ⟋ £12-£17

Open all year

A friendly family site set in an apple orchard, with 25 fully serviced pitches and a beautifully designed, spacious toilet block. Now enlarged, with an extra 15 lakeside pitches, the site overlooks two fishing lakes; the famous horticultural auctions at Wisbech are nearby. 10 acre site. 40 touring pitches. 40 hardstandings. Caravan pitches. Motorhome pitches. Tent pitches.

AA Pubs & Restaurants nearby: Crown Lodge Hotel, WISBECH, PE14 8SE, 01945 773391

The Hare Arms, STOW BARDOLPH, PE34 3HT, 01366 382229

Facilities: ⟋⊙⟋✳⟋⟋ ♻ ⟋
Services: ⟋⟋⟋
Within 3 miles: ⟋⟋
Notes: ⟋ Dogs must be kept on leads.

CHESHIRE

CODDINGTON
Map 15 SJ45

Places to visit

Cholmondeley Castle Gardens, CHOLMONDELEY, SY14 8AH, 01829 720383 www.cholmondeleycastle.com

Hack Green Secret Nuclear Bunker, NANTWICH, CW5 8AP, 01270 629219 www.hackgreen.co.uk

Great for kids: Dewa Roman Experience, CHESTER, CH1 1NL, 01244 343407 www.dewaromanexperience.co.uk

PREMIER PARK

▶▶▶▶▶ **89% Manor Wood Country Caravan Park** *(SJ453553)*

GOLD

Manor Wood CH3 9EN
☎ **01829 782990 & 07762 817827**
e-mail: info@manorwoodcaravans.co.uk
dir: *From A534 at Barton, turn opposite Cock O'Barton pub signed Coddington. Left in 100yds. Site 0.5m on left*

* ⟋ £13.50-£24 ⟋ £13.50-£24 ⟋ £13.50-£24

Open all year (rs Oct-May swimming pool closed)

Last arrival 19.00hrs Last departure 11.00hrs

A secluded landscaped park in a tranquil country setting with extensive views towards the Welsh Hills across the Cheshire Plain. The park offers fully serviced pitches, a heated outdoor swimming pool and all-weather tennis courts. Wildlife is encouraged and there is a fishing lake; country walks and nearby pubs as added attractions. The generous pitch density provides optimum privacy and the superb amenities block has excellent decor, under-floor heating and smart modern facilities with very

LEISURE: ⟋ Indoor swimming pool ⟋ Outdoor swimming pool ⟋ Children's playground ⟋ Kid's club ⟋ Tennis court ⟋ Games room ⟋ Separate TV room ⟋ 9/18 hole golf course ⟋ Boats for hire ⟋ Cinema ⟋ Entertainment ⟋ Fishing ⟋ Mini golf ⟋ Watersports ⟋ Gym ⟋ Sports field Spa ⟋ Stables
FACILITIES: ⟋ Bath ⟋ Shower ⟋ Electric shaver ⟋ Hairdryer ⟋ Ice Pack Facility ⟋ Disabled facilities ⟋ Public telephone ⟋ Shop on site or within 200yds ⟋ Mobile shop (calls at least 5 days a week) ⟋ BBQ area ⟋ Picnic area ⟋ Wi-fi ⟋ Internet access ⟋ Recycling ⟋ Tourist info ⟋ Dog exercise area

good privacy options. 8 acre site. 45 touring pitches. 38 hardstandings. 30 seasonal pitches. Caravan pitches. Motorhome pitches. Tent pitches. 18 statics.

AA Pubs & Restaurants nearby: The Calveley Arms, HANDLEY, CH3 9DT, 01829 770619

1851 Restaurant at Peckforton Castle, PECKFORTON, CW6 9TN, 01829 260930

Leisure: ⚓ Ⅿ ⚽ ◎ 🎣

Facilities: 🍴 ⊙ 🎱 ✳ ⅙ 🔥 🛒 📶 🖥 ♻ ❶

Services: 🔌 🗄 ⚓

Within 3 miles: 🎣 ✏ 🏧 🗄

Notes: No cars by caravans. No cycles, no noise after 23.00hrs. Dogs must be kept on leads.

DELAMERE   Map 15 SJ56

Places to visit

Jodrell Bank Discovery Centre, JODRELL BANK, SK11 9DL, 01477 571766 www.jodrellbank.net

Little Moreton Hall, CONGLETON, CW12 4SD, 01260 272018 www.nationaltrust.org.uk

Great for kids: Chester Zoo, CHESTER, CH2 1LH, 01244 380280 www.chesterzoo.org

---

AA CAMPING CARD SITE

▶▶▶▶ **83% Fishpool Farm Caravan Park** *(SJ567672)*

Fishpool Rd CW8 2HP
☎ **01606 883970 & 07501 506583**
e-mail: enquiries@fishpoolfarmcaravanpark.co.uk
dir: *From Tarporley take A49 towards Cuddington. Left onto B5152. Continue on B5152 (Fishpool Rd). Site on right*

🚐 �335 Ⓐ

Open 15 Feb-15 Jan

Last arrival 19.00hrs Last departure noon

Developed on a former hay field on the owner's farm, this excellent park has a shop/reception, a superb purpose-built toilet block with laundry facilities, a picnic area, and 50 spacious pitches, all with electric hook-up. There is a lakeside lodge, coarse fishing and a nature walk. 5.5 acre site. 50 touring pitches. 14 hardstandings. Caravan pitches. Motorhome pitches. Tent pitches. 1 static.

AA Pubs & Restaurants nearby: The Dysart Arms, BUNBURY, CW6 9PH, 01829 260183

Alvanley Arms Inn, TARPORLEY, CW6 9DS, 01829 760200

Leisure: Ⅿ ◎ 🎣 ▭

Facilities: 🍴 ⊙ 🎱 ✳ ⅙ 🔥 🛒 📶 ♻ ❶

Services: 🔌 🗄 ⚓ ⚓

Within 3 miles: 🎣 ✏ ◎ 🏊 🏧 🗄 ∪

Notes: Dogs must be kept on leads. Dog walks. Fresh eggs from own hens.

KNUTSFORD   Map 15 SJ77

Places to visit

Tabley House, KNUTSFORD, WA16 0HB, 01565 750151 www.tableyhouse.co.uk

Great for kids: Jodrell Bank Discovery Centre, JODRELL BANK, SK11 9DL, 01477 571766 www.jodrellbank.net

---

▶▶▶ **77% Woodlands Park** *(SJ743710)*

Wash Ln, Allostock WA16 9LG
☎ **01565 723429 & 01332 810818**
dir: *M6 junct 18 take A50 N to Holmes Chapel for 3m, turn into Wash Ln by Boundary Water Park. Site 0.25m on left*

🚐 �335 Ⓐ

Open Mar-6 Jan

Last arrival 21.00hrs Last departure 11.00hrs

A very tranquil and attractive park in the heart of rural Cheshire, and set in 16 acres of mature woodland where in spring the rhododendrons look stunning. Tourers are located in three separate wooded areas that teem with wildlife and you will wake up to the sound of birdsong. This park is just five miles from Jodrell Bank. 16 acre site. 40 touring pitches. Caravan pitches. Motorhome pitches. Tent pitches. 140 statics.

AA Pubs & Restaurants nearby: The Dog Inn, KNUTSFORD, WA16 8UP, 01625 861421

The Duke of Portland, LACH DENNIS, CW9 7SY, 01606 46264

Facilities: 🍴 ⊙ ⅙

Services: 🔌 🗄

Within 3 miles: 🎣 ✏ 🏧 🗄

Notes: ⊗ No skateboards or rollerblades. Dogs must be kept on leads.

SIDDINGTON   Map 15 SJ87

Places to visit

Capesthorne Hall, CAPESTHORNE, SK11 9JY, 01625 861221 www.capesthorne.com

Gawsworth Hall, GAWSWORTH, SK11 9RN, 01260 223456 www.gawsworthhall.com

Great for kids: Jodrell Bank Discovery Centre, JODRELL BANK, SK11 9DL, 01477 571766 www.jodrellbank.net

---

▶▶▶▶ **87% Capesthorne Hall**
(SJ841727)

Congleton Rd SK11 9JY
☎ **01625 861221**
e-mail: info@capesthorne.com
dir: *Exit A34. Telephone site for detailed directions*

✳ 🚐 fr £25 �335 fr £25

Open Apr-Oct

Last arrival 22.00hrs Last departure noon

Located within the grounds of the notable Jacobean Capesthorne Hall, this lush, all level site provides generously sized pitches, all with electricity and most with hardstandings. The Scandanavian-style amenities block has a smart, quality, modern interior and very good privacy levels. Guests also have the opportunity to visit the award-winning gardens on certain days and there are many extensive walking opportunities directly from the camping areas. 5 acre site. 50 touring pitches. 30 hardstandings. Caravan pitches. Motorhome pitches.

AA Pubs & Restaurants nearby: The Wizard Inn, NETHER ALDERLEY, SK10 4UB, 01625 584000

Facilities: 🍴 ⅙ ⊙ 🔥 📶 ♻ ❶

Services: 🔌 🗄 🍴

Within 3 miles: 🎣 ◎ 🗄

Notes: Minimum 3 night stay on BH wknds. No motorised scooters or skateboards. Only gas BBQs permitted. Dogs must be kept on leads. Access to Capesthorne Hall & Gardens (additional cost for hall only).

WETTENHALL Map 15 SJ66

►►► 85% New Farm Caravan Park

(SJ613608)

Long Ln CW7 4DW
☎ 01270 528213 & 07970 221112
e-mail: info@newfarmcheshire.com
dir: *M6 junct 16, A500 towards Nantwich, right onto Nantwich bypass (A51). At lights turn right, follow A51 Caster & Tarporely signs. After Calveley right into Long Ln (follow site sign). Site in 2m*

🚐 🚐

Open all year

Last arrival 20.00hrs Last departure noon

Diversification at New Farm led to the development of four fishing lakes, quality AA-listed B&B accommodation in a converted milking parlour, and the creation of a peaceful small touring park. The proprietors provide a very welcome touring destination within this peaceful part of Cheshire. Expect good landscaping, generous hardstanding pitches, a spotless toilet block, and good attention to detail throughout. Please note there is no laundry. 40 acre site. 24 touring pitches. 17 hardstandings. 6 seasonal pitches. Caravan pitches. Motorhome pitches.

AA Pubs & Restaurants nearby: The Nags Head, HAUGHTON MOSS, CW6 9RN, 01829 260265

Crewe Hall, CREWE, CW1 6UZ, 01270 253333

Facilities: 🏕 🔫 ☼ 🛏 🐕 WiFi
Services: 🔌 🚰 🖤 ↴
Within 3 miles: 🎣 ⛳ 🛍 🅿 🛒 🔁 U

Notes: Adults only. Dogs must be kept on leads.

WHITEGATE Map 15 SJ66

Places to visit

The Cheshire Military Museum, CHESTER, CH1 2DN, 01244 327617
www.cheshiremilitarymuseum.co.uk

Chester Cathedral, CHESTER, CH1 2HU, 01244 500961 www.chestercathedral.com

PREMIER PARK

►►►►► 91% Lamb Cottage Caravan Park *(SJ613692)*

Dalefords Ln CW8 2BN
☎ 01606 882302
e-mail: info@lambcottage.co.uk
dir: *From A556 turn at Sandiway lights into Dalefords Ln, signed Winsford. Site 1m on right*

* 🚐 £23-£27 🚐 £22-£26

Open Mar-Oct

Last arrival 20.00hrs Last departure noon

A secluded and attractively landscaped adults-only park in a glorious location where the emphasis is on peace and relaxation. The serviced pitches are spacious with wide grass borders for sitting out and the high quality toilet block is spotlessly clean and immaculately maintained. A good central base for exploring this area, with access to nearby woodland walks and cycle trails. 6 acre site. 45 touring pitches. 45 hardstandings. 14 seasonal pitches. Caravan pitches. Motorhome pitches. 26 statics.

AA Pubs & Restaurants nearby: The Bear's Paw, WARMINGHAM, CW11 3QN, 01270 526317

Facilities: 🏕 ⊙ 🔫 ♿ 🕐 🛏 WiFi ♻ 🛈
Services: 🔌 🖾 🔒
Within 3 miles: 🎣 🅿 🛒 U

Notes: Adults only. No tents (except trailer tents), no commercial vehicles. Dogs must be kept on leads.

LEISURE: 🏊 Indoor swimming pool 🏊 Outdoor swimming pool 🛝 Children's playground 🙌 Kid's club 🎾 Tennis court 🎱 Games room 📺 Separate TV room
⛳ 9/18 hole golf course ⛵ Boats for hire 🎬 Cinema 🎭 Entertainment 🎣 Fishing ⛳ Mini golf 🏄 Watersports 🏋 Gym 🏟 Sports field Spa U Stables
FACILITIES: 🛁 Bath 🚿 Shower ⊙ Electric shaver 🎯 Hairdryer ❄ Ice Pack Facility ♿ Disabled facilities 🕐 Public telephone 🛍 Shop on site or within 200yds
🏪 Mobile shop (calls at least 5 days a week) 🍖 BBQ area 🌲 Picnic area WiFi Wi-fi 💻 Internet access ♻ Recycling 🛈 Tourist info 🐕 Dog exercise area

SERVICES: 🔌 Electric hook up 🔲 Launderette 🍷 Licensed bar 🔋 Calor Gas 🔥 Camping Gaz T Toilet fluid 🍽 Café/Restaurant 🍔 Fast Food/Takeaway
🔋 Battery charging 🍼 Baby care ⚓ Motorvan service point ABBREVIATIONS: BH/bank hols-bank holidays Etr-Easter Spring BH-Spring Bank Holiday dep-departure
fr-from hrs-hours m-mile mdnt-midnight rdbt-roundabout rs-restricted service wk-week wknd-weekend x-rds-cross roads 🚫 No credit cards 🚫 No dogs
👫 Children of all ages accepted See page 9 for details of the AA Camping Card Scheme

Cornwall

Known for its wild moorland landscapes, glorious river valleys, quaint towns and outstanding coastline, Cornwall is one of the country's most popular holiday destinations. Boasting the mildest and sunniest climate in the United Kingdom, as a result of its southerly latitude and the influence of the Gulf Stream, the county benefits from more than 1,500 hours of sunshine each year.

St Ives

Bordered to the north and west by the Atlantic and to the south by the English Channel, the county boasts prehistoric sites, colourful mythology, a wealth of ancient traditions, a legacy of tin mining and impressive cultural diversity. Cornwall is acknowledged as one of the Celtic nations by many locals and use of the revived Cornish language has increased.

St Piran's flag is regarded by many as the national flag of Cornwall and an emblem of the Cornish people. It is said that St Piran, who is alleged to have discovered tin, adopted the flag's two colours – a white cross on a black background – after spotting the white tin amongst the black coals and ashes.

The coast
The Cornish coastline offers miles of breath-takingly beautiful scenery. The northern coast is open and exposed; the 735-ft High Cliff, between Boscastle and St Gennys, represents the highest sheer drop cliff in the county. In contrast are long stretches of golden sandy beaches, including those at St Ives, and Newquay, now an internationally renowned surfing destination.

▶

The Lizard, at Cornwall's most southerly point, is a geological masterpiece of towering cliffs, stacks and arches as is Land's End, on the county's south-west corner. The legendary 603-mile (970km) walk from this point to John O'Groats at the northern tip of Scotland creates a daunting challenge that numerous people, including sportsmen and TV personalities, have tackled with varying degrees of success over the years.

Truro is Cornwall's great cathedral city, with a wealth of Georgian buildings, quaint alleyways and historic streets adding to its charm. Compared to many cathedrals throughout the country, Truro's is relatively young; the foundation stones were laid in 1880 and the western towers were finally dedicated some thirty years later.

● St Michael's Mount

Inspirational Cornwall

Mysterious Bodmin Moor lies at the heart of Cornwall. In 1930 the writer Daphne du Maurier spent a night at Jamaica Inn in Bolventor, which inspired the famous novel of the same name; *Menabilly*, her home near Fowey, on Cornwall's south coast, was the inspiration for '*Manderley*', the house in *Rebecca*, almost certainly her best-known and best-loved book. It is said that one day while out walking she spotted a flock of seagulls diving and wheeling above a newly ploughed field, which gave her the idea for the short story *The Birds*, which Alfred Hitchcock memorably turned into a horror film.

Walking and Cycling

Naturally, walking and cycling are very popular pursuits in Cornwall. The South West Coast Path offers many miles of rugged coastal grandeur and stunning views, while inland there is the chance to combine this most simple of outdoor pursuits with suitably green and environmentally friendly train travel. Tourist information centres provide leaflets showing a variety of linear or circular walks incorporating branch line stations; easy-to-follow maps are included. One popular route involves taking the train along the scenic Atlantic Coast line to Luxulyan, then cutting across country on foot for 2.5 miles (4km) to reach the Eden Project.

Festivals and Events

- The Newlyn Fish Festival takes place on August Bank Holiday Monday.
- Penzance hosts the Golowan Festival and Mazey Day for two weeks in mid-June.
- St Ives has its Feast Day in early February and the St Ives Festival of Music and the Arts for two weeks in early September.
- The Rock Oyster Festival, a celebration of food, music and art, takes place at Dinham House near Wadebridge in June.

● Porth Moina, Land's End

● Newquay beach

CORNWALL & ISLES OF SCILLY

ASHTON Map 2 SW62

Places to visit

Poldark Mine and Heritage Complex, WENDRON, TR13 0ER, 01326 573173 www.poldark-mine.com

Great for kids: The Flambards Theme Park, HELSTON, TR13 0QA, 01326 573404 www.flambards.co.uk

AA CAMPING CARD SITE

►►► 78% Boscrege Caravan & Camping Park *(SW595305)*

TR13 9TG

☎ 01736 762231

e-mail: enquiries@caravanparkcornwall.com

dir: *A394 from Helston signed Penzance. In Ashton (Lion & Lamb pub on right) right into Higher Lane, approx 1.5m (thatched cottage on right) left at site sign. NB for recommended towing route contact the park*

* 🚐 £13-£20 🚘 £13-£20 ⛺ £13-£20

Open Mar-Nov (rs Jan-Nov statics open)

Last arrival 22.00hrs Last departure 11.00hrs

A quiet and bright little touring park divided into small paddocks with hedges, that offers plenty of open spaces for children to play in. This family-owned park has clean, well-painted toilet facilities and neatly trimmed grass. By an Area of Outstanding Natural Beauty at the foot of Tregonning Hill, this site makes an ideal base for touring the southern tip of Cornwall; Penzance, Land's End, St Ives and the beaches in between are all within easy reach. 14 acre site. 50 touring pitches. 10 seasonal pitches. Caravan pitches. Motorhome pitches. Tent pitches. 38 statics.

AA Pubs & Restaurants nearby: The Victoria Inn, PERRANUTHNOE, TR20 9NP, 01736 710309

New Yard Restaurant, HELSTON, TR12 6AF, 01326 221595

Leisure: 🛝 ⚽

Facilities: 🚿 ⊙ 💨 ❄ ☎ 🧺 🐕 [Wi-fi] ♻ ℹ

Services: 🚐 ▣ ■ 🍃 [T] ▬

Within 3 miles: ⛳ ⛵ 🎣 ◎ 🌊 🛒 ▣ 🐎

Notes: No fires, no noise after 23.00hrs. Dogs must be kept on leads. Microwave & freezer available, nature trail.

BLACKWATER Map 2 SW74

Places to visit

Royal Cornwall Museum, TRURO, TR1 2SJ, 01872 272205 www.royalcornwallmuseum.org.uk

East Pool Mine, POOL, TR15 3NP, 01209 315027 www.nationaltrust.org.uk

►►►► 83% Chiverton Park *(SW743468)*

East Hill TR4 8HS

☎ 01872 560667 & 07789 377169

e-mail: chivertonpark@btopenworld.com

dir: *Exit A30 at Chiverton rdbt (Starbucks) onto unclassified road signed Blackwater (3rd exit). 1st right, site 300mtrs on right*

🚐 🚘 ⛺

Open Mar-end Oct

Last arrival 19.00hrs Last departure noon

A small, well-maintained site with some mature hedges dividing pitches, sited midway between Truro and St Agnes. Facilities include a good toilet block and a steam room, sauna and gym. All touring pitches are fully serviced. There is a games room with pool table, and the children's outside play equipment proves popular with families. 4 acre site. 12 touring pitches. 10 hardstandings. Caravan pitches. Motorhome pitches. Tent pitches. 50 statics.

Leisure: 🏋 🛝 🏓 **Spa** **Facilities:** 🚿 ⊙ 💨 ❄ ♿ 🧺 [Wi-fi] ♻ ℹ **Services:** 🚐 ▣ ⩊

Within 3 miles: ⛳ 🎬 🎣 🌊 🛒 ▣ 🐎

Notes: No ball games. Dogs must be kept on leads. Drying lines.

►►►► 82% *Trevarth Holiday Park*

(SW744468)

TR4 8HR

☎ 01872 560266

e-mail: trevarth@btconnect.com

web: www.trevarth.co.uk

dir: *Exit A30 at Chiverton rdbt onto B3277 signed St Agnes. At next rdbt take road signed Blackwater. Site on right in 200mtrs*

🚐 🚘 ⛺

Open Apr-Oct

Last arrival 22.00hrs Last departure 11.30hrs

A neat and compact park with touring pitches laid out on attractive, well-screened high ground adjacent to the A30 and A39 junction. This pleasant little park is centrally located for touring, and is maintained to a very good standard. There is a large grassed area for children to play on which is away from all tents. 4 acre site. 30 touring pitches. 10 hardstandings. 2 seasonal pitches. Caravan pitches. Motorhome pitches. Tent pitches. 20 statics.

AA Pubs & Restaurants nearby: Driftwood Spars, ST AGNES, TR5 0RT, 01872 552428

Leisure: 🛝 🏓

Facilities: 🚿 ⊙ 💨 ❄ ☎ [Wi-fi] ♻ ℹ

Services: 🚐 ▣ ■ 🍃 ▬

Within 3 miles: 🎣 🌊 🛒 🐎

Notes: Dogs must be kept on leads.

LEISURE: 🏊 Indoor swimming pool ≋ Outdoor swimming pool 🛝 Children's playground ✋ Kid's club 🎾 Tennis court 🏓 Games room 📺 Separate TV room ⛳ 9/18 hole golf course ⛵ Boats for hire 🎬 Cinema ♫ Entertainment 🎣 Fishing ◎ Mini golf 🌊 Watersports 🏋 Gym ⚽ Sports field **Spa** 🐎 Stables
FACILITIES: 🛁 Bath 🚿 Shower ⊙ Electric shaver 💨 Hairdryer ❄ Ice Pack Facility ♿ Disabled facilities ☎ Public telephone 🛒 Shop on site or within 200yds 🚚 Mobile shop (calls at least 5 days a week) 🍖 BBQ area 🧺 Picnic area [Wi-fi] Wi-fi 💻 Internet access ♻ Recycling ℹ Tourist info 🐕 Dog exercise area

BLISLAND
Map 2 SX17

Places to visit

Tintagel Old Post Office, TINTAGEL, PL34 0DB, 01840 770024 www.nationaltrust.org.uk/main/w-tintageloldpostoffice

►►► 85% South Penquite Farm
(SX108751)

South Penquite PL30 4LH
☎ 01208 850491
e-mail: thefarm@bodminmoor.co.uk
dir: *From Exeter on A30 exit at 1st sign to St Breward on right, (from Bodmin 2nd sign on left). Follow narrow road across Bodmin Moor. Ignore left & right turns until South Penquite Farm Lane on right in 2m*

🚐 Å £16

Open May-Oct

Last arrival dusk Last departure 14.00hrs

This genuine 'back to nature' site is situated high on Bodmin Moor on a farm committed to organic agriculture. As well as camping there are facilities for adults and children to learn about conservation, organic farming and the local environment, including a fascinating and informative farm trail (pick up a leaflet); there is also a Geocaching trail. Toilet facilities are enhanced by a timber building with quality showers and a good disabled facility. The site has designated areas where fires may be lit. Organic home-reared lamb burgers and sausages are for sale, and one field contains four Mongolian yurts, available for holiday let. 4 acre site. 40 touring pitches. Motorhome pitches. Tent pitches. 4 bell tents/yurts.

AA Pubs & Restaurants nearby: The Blisland Inn, BLISLAND, PL30 4JF, 01208 850739

The Old Inn & Restaurant, ST BREWARD, PL30 4PP, 01208 850711

Leisure: 🅰 🔍
Facilities: 🌰 ⊙ 🏳 ✳ ⅄ 🕭 🛒 ♻ ℹ
Services: 🗐 **Within 3 miles:** ↯ 🖉 ⅃ 🛆 🗐 ∪
Notes: 🚫 No caravans, no pets.

BODMIN
Map 2 SX06

Places to visit

Wick Heritage Museum, WICK, KW1 5EY, 01955 605393 www.wickheritage.org

Great for kids: Eden Project, ST AUSTELL, PL24 2SG, 01726 811911 www.edenproject.com

►►►► 79% Mena Caravan & Camping Park *(SW041626)*

PL30 5HW
☎ 01208 831845
e-mail: mena@campsitesincornwall.co.uk
dir: *Exit A30 onto A389 N signed Lanivet & Wadebridge. In 0.5m 1st right & pass under A30. 1st left signed Lostwithiel & Fowey. In 0.25m right at top of hill. 0.5m then 1st right. Entrance 100yds on right*

🚐 🚐 Å

Open all year

Last arrival 22.00hrs Last departure noon

This grassy site is about four miles from the Eden Project and midway between the north and south Cornish coasts. Set in a secluded, elevated position with high hedges for shelter, it offers plenty of peace and quiet. There is a small coarse fishing lake on site, hardstanding pitches, a shop and a café, with a new alfresco decking area, where breakfasts, cream teas and takeaway food can be purchased. The site is on the Saint's Way, and nearby is the neolithic hill fort of Helman Tor, the highest point on Bodmin Moor. There is a fish and chip restaurant in Lanivet (approximately one mile) - from here there is a bus service to Bodmin. 15 acre site. 25 touring pitches. 4 hardstandings. Caravan pitches. Motorhome pitches. Tent pitches. 2 statics.

AA Pubs & Restaurants nearby: The Borough Arms, DUNMERE, PL31 2RD, 01208 73118

Trehellas House Hotel & Restaurant, BODMIN, PL30 3AD, 01208 72700

Leisure: 🅰 🔍
Facilities: 🌰 ⊙ 🏳 ✳ ⅄ 🕭 🛒 🛒 ♻ ℹ
Services: 🗐 🗐 🛢 🗐 T 🍽 🍴
Within 3 miles: ↯ 🖉 ⅃ 🛆 🗐 ∪

BOSCASTLE
Map 2 SX09

Places to visit

Tintagel Castle, TINTAGEL, PL34 0HE, 01840 770328 www.english-heritage.org.uk/daysout/properties/tintagel-castle

Tintagel Old Post Office, TINTAGEL, PL34 0DB, 01840 770024 www.nationaltrust.org.uk/main/w-tintageloldpostoffice

Great for kids: The Milky Way Adventure Park, CLOVELLY, EX39 5RY, 01237 431255 www.themilkyway.co.uk

►► 80% Lower Pennycrocker Farm
(SX125927)

PL35 0BY
☎ 01840 250613
e-mail: karyn.heard@yahoo.com
dir: *Exit A39 at Marshgate onto B3263 towards Boscastle, site signed in 2m*

✳ 🚐 fr £12 🚐 fr £12 Å fr £12

Open Etr-Oct

Last arrival 20.30hrs Last departure anytime

Mature Cornish hedges provide shelter for this small, family-run site on a dairy farm. Spectacular scenery and the nearby coastal footpath are among the many attractions, along with fresh eggs, milk and home-made clotted cream for sale. The excellent toilets and showers enhance this site's facilities. Two traditional Cornish cottages are available to let. 6 acre site. 40 touring pitches. Caravan pitches. Motorhome pitches. Tent pitches. 1 wooden pod.

AA Pubs & Restaurants nearby: The Port William, TREBARWITH, PL34 0HB, 01840 770230

The Wellington Hotel, BOSCASTLE, PL35 0AQ, 01840 250202

Facilities: 🌰 ⊙ ✳ ⅄ 🕭 🛒 🛒
Services: 🗐 🛢 ⅃
Within 3 miles: ⅃ 🗓 🖉 🗐 ∪
Notes: 🚫 No noise after 22.00hrs. Dogs must be kept on leads.

BRYHER (ISLES OF SCILLY) Map 2 SV81

▶▶▶ 80% Bryher Camp Site

(SV880155)

TR23 0PR
☎ 01720 422559
e-mail: relax@bryhercampsite.co.uk
web: www.bryhercampsite.co.uk
dir: *Accessed by boat from main island of St Mary's*

⚠

Open Apr-Oct

Set on the smallest inhabited Scilly Isle with spectacular scenery and white beaches, this tent-only site is in a sheltered valley surrounded by hedges. Pitches are located in paddocks at the northern end of the island which is only a short walk from the quay. There is a good, modern toilet block, and plenty of peace and quiet. Although located in a very quiet area, the Fraggle Rock Bar and Restaurant and a well-equipped shop are within easy reach. There is easy boat access to all the other islands. 2.25 acre site. 38 touring pitches. Tent pitches.

AA Pubs & Restaurants nearby: Hell Bay, BRYHER, TR23 0PR, 01720 422947

Leisure: ⚽
Facilities: ♪⊙ℙ⚹♻ ❶
Services: ⬛ 🛢 🖉 ⬚
Within 3 miles: ⚓⚑ℙ◎⬚ 🏠🛢 U
Notes: No cars by tents. No pets.

BUDE Map 2 SS20

See also Kilkhampton, Holsworthy (Devon) & Bridgerule (Devon)

🏖 86% *Sandymouth Holiday Park*

(SS214104)

Sandymouth Bay EX23 9HW
☎ 08442 729530
e-mail: enquiries@sandymouthbay.co.uk
web: www.sandymouthbay.co.uk
dir: *Signed from A39 approx 0.5m S of Kilkhampton, 4m N of Bude*

🚐🚙⚠

Open Mar-26 Nov (rs 16 May-9 Jul (excl half term week) closed for private booking)

Last arrival 21.00hrs Last departure 10.00hrs

A bright and friendly holiday park with glorious and extensive sea views from all areas. The park offers modern and well-maintained touring facilities, alongside excellent leisure and entertainment facilities, notably the eye-catching pirate galleon in the fabulous children's play area. 24 acre site. 22 touring pitches. 22 hardstandings. Caravan pitches. Motorhome pitches. Tent pitches.

AA Pubs & Restaurants nearby: The Bush Inn, MORWENSTOW, EX23 9SR, 01288 331242

The Castle Restaurant, BUDE, EX23 8LG, 01288 350543

Leisure: 🏊⚠⬇⚽🎱🎵
Facilities: ♪⊙ℙ⚹🕐🛢🖥♻ ❶
Services: 🚐⬛ 🍴🎽🅣🍽⬚
Within 3 miles: ⚓⚑ℙ◎⬚ 🏠🛢 U
Notes: Dogs must be kept on leads. Sauna.

PREMIER PARK

▶▶▶▶▶ 91% Wooda Farm Holiday Park

Best of British
GOLD

(SS229080)

Poughill EX23 9HJ
☎ 01288 352069
e-mail: enquiries@wooda.co.uk
web: www.wooda.co.uk
dir: *2m E. From A39 at outskirts of Stratton follow unclassified road signed Poughill*

* 🚐 £18-£32 🚙 £14-£32 ⚠ £14-£27

Open Apr-Oct (rs Apr-May & mid Sep-Oct shop hours limited, bar & takeaway)

Last arrival 20.00hrs Last departure 10.30hrs

An attractive park set on raised ground overlooking Bude Bay, with lovely sea views. The park is divided into paddocks by hedges and mature trees, and offers high quality facilities in extensive colourful gardens. A variety of activities is provided by way of the large sports hall and hard tennis court, and there's a super children's playground. There are holiday static caravans for hire. At the time of our last inspection the site was planning to install a fully interactive information screen in the reception area, which will be for customer use. 50 acre site. 200 touring pitches. 80 hardstandings. Caravan pitches. Motorhome pitches. Tent pitches. 55 statics.

AA Pubs & Restaurants nearby: The Bush Inn, MORWENSTOW, EX23 9SR, 01288 331242

The Castle Restaurant, BUDE, EX23 8LG, 01288 350543

Leisure: ⛳⚠🎾⚽🎱🖵
Facilities: 🛁♪⊙ℙ⚹🕐🛢🖥🎽📻⬚ ♻ ❶
Services: 🚐⬛ 🍴🛢🖉🅣🍽⬚🛢⬇
Within 3 miles: ⚓⚑🎪ℙ◎⬚ 🏠🛢 U
Notes: Restrictions on certain dog breeds, skateboards, rollerblades & scooters. Dogs must be kept on leads. Coarse fishing, clay pigeon shooting, pets' corner, woodland walks.

see advert on opposite page

▶▶▶▶ 87% Budemeadows Touring Park (SS215012)

Widemouth Bay EX23 0NA
☎ 01288 361646
e-mail: holiday@budemeadows.com
dir: *3m S of Bude on A39. Follow signs after turn to Widemouth Bay. Site accessed via layby from A39*

* ⬛ £16-£28.50 ⬛ £16-£28.50 ▲ £16-£28.50

Open all year (rs Sep-late May shop, bar & pool closed)

Last arrival 21.00hrs Last departure 11.00hrs

This is a very well-kept site of distinction, with good quality facilities, hardstandings and eight fully serviced pitches. Budemeadows is set on a gentle sheltered slope in nine acres of naturally landscaped parkland, surrounded by mature hedges. The internal doors in the facility block have all been painted in pastel colours to resemble beach huts. The site is just one mile from Widemouth Bay, and three miles from the unspoilt resort of Bude. 9 acre site. 145 touring pitches. 24 hardstandings. 4 seasonal pitches. Caravan pitches. Motorhome pitches. Tent pitches.

AA Pubs & Restaurants nearby: Bay View Inn, WIDEMOUTH BAY, EX23 0AW, 01288 361273

The Castle Restaurant, BUDE, EX23 8LG, 01288 350543

Budemeadows Touring Park

Leisure: ⬛ ⬛ ⬛ ⬛
Facilities: ⬛ ⬛ ⬛ ⬛ ⬛ ⬛ ⬛ ⬛ ⬛ ⬛ ⬛ ⬛ ⬛ ⬛ ⬛ ⬛
Services: ⬛ ⬛ ⬛ ⬛ ⬛ ⬛ ⬛ ⬛ ⬛
Within 3 miles: ⬛ ⬛ ⬛ ⬛ ⬛ ⬛ ⬛ ⬛ ⬛ ⬛

Notes: No noise after 23.00hrs, breathable groundsheets only. Dogs must be kept on leads. Table tennis, giant chess, baby changing facility.

▶▶▶▶ 86% Widemouth Fields Caravan & Camping Park (SS215010)

Park Farm, Poundstock EX23 0NA
☎ 01288 361351 & 01489 781256
e-mail: enquiries@widemouthbaytouring.co.uk
dir: *M5 junct 27 (signed Barnstaple). A361 to rdbt before Barnstaple. Take A39 signed Bideford & Bude. (NB do not exit A39 at Stratton). S for 3m, follow sign just past x-rds to Widemouth Bay. Into lay-by, entrance on left*

⬛ £16.50-£28 ⬛ £16.50-£28 ▲ £14.50-£19.50

Open Apr-Sep

Last arrival dusk Last departure noon

In a quiet location with far reaching views over rolling countryside, this site is only one mile from the golden beach at Widemouth Bay, and just three miles from the resort of Bude. The park has a well-stocked shop, many hardstanding pitches and a new, cosy bar that offers takeaway breakfasts. The toilets are of outstanding quality with a many combined fully serviced cubicles. All the buildings resemble log cabins which certainly adds to the appeal of the site. There is a courtesy shuttle bus into Bude and to the Widemouth Bay Holiday Village, where the facilities can be used by the touring campers. 15 acre site. 156 touring pitches. 156 hardstandings. 20 seasonal pitches. Caravan pitches. Motorhome pitches. Tent pitches. 5 statics.

continued

SERVICES: ⬛ Electric hook up ⬛ Launderette ⬛ Licensed bar ⬛ Calor Gas ⬛ Camping Gaz ⬛ Toilet fluid ⬛ Café/Restaurant ⬛ Fast Food/Takeaway
⬛ Battery charging ⬛ Baby care ⬛ Motorvan service point **ABBREVIATIONS:** ⬛ BH/bank hols-bank holidays Etr-Easter Spring BH-Spring Bank Holiday dep-departure
fr-from hrs-hours m-mile mdnt-midnight rdbt-roundabout rs-restricted service wk-week wknd-weekend x-rds-cross roads ⬛ No credit cards ⬛ No dogs
⬛ Children of all ages accepted See page 9 for details of the AA Camping Card Scheme

BUDE *continued*

AA Pubs & Restaurants nearby: Bay View Inn, WIDEMOUTH BAY, EX23 0AW, 01288 361273

Leisure: 🅰 ☉ ⬜

Facilities: ⬤ 🔥 ☉ ℙ ✳ ❤ ⓢ ⬚ 🗕 ⭙ ⅏ ♻ ❶

Services: ☺ ⬚ ⬚ ⬚ 🍽 ⬚ ⬆ ⬇

Within 3 miles: ⬚ ⬚ ⬚ ⬚ ☉ ⬚ ⬚ ⬚ ∪

Notes: Entry to site by swipecard only, deposit taken at time of check in.

▶▶▶▶ 85% Pentire Haven Holiday Park *(SS246111)*

Stibb Rd, Kilkhampton EX23 9QY
☎ **01288 321601**
e-mail: holidays@pentirehaven.co.uk
dir: *A39 from Bude towards Bideford, in 3m turn left signed Sandymouth Bay*

✱ 🚐 £9.95-£27 🚐 £9.95-£27 ⛺ £9.95-£27

Open 31 Mar-3 Nov

Last arrival 23.30hrs Last departure 10.30hrs

A very open grass site handy for many beautiful beaches, but in particular the surfing beach of Bude only four miles away. New management and enthusiastic staff continue to make a real impression on this improving park. There are excellent toilet facilities in addition to a very good children's playground and a small swimming pool, which is open during the busy season. There is a new rally field and holiday static caravans are available for hire or to buy. 23 acre site. 120 touring pitches. 46 hardstandings. 40 seasonal pitches. Caravan pitches. Motorhome pitches. Tent pitches.

AA Pubs & Restaurants nearby: Bay View Inn, WIDEMOUTH BAY, EX23 0AW, 01288 361273

The Castle Restaurant, BUDE, EX23 8LG, 01288 350543

Leisure: ⬚ 🅰 ☉ ☉ ⬤ 🎵

Facilities: 🔥 ℙ ✳ ❤ ⓢ ⭙ ⅏ ♻ ❶

Services: ☺ ⬚ ⬚ ⬚ ⬚ 🍽 ⬚ ⬚ ⬆ ⬇

Within 3 miles: ⬚ ⬚ ⬚ ⬚ ⬚ ⬚ ∪

Notes: No fires. Dogs must be kept on leads.

see advert below

▶▶▶▶ 80% Willow Valley Holiday Park *(SS236078)*

Bush EX23 9LB
☎ **01288 353104**
e-mail: willowvalley@talk21.com
dir: *On A39, 0.5m N of junct with A3072 at Stratton*

🚐 🚐 ⛺

Open Mar-end Oct

Last arrival 21.00hrs Last departure 11.00hrs

A small sheltered park in the Strat Valley with level grassy pitches and a stream running through it. The friendly family owners have improved all areas of this attractive park, including a smart toilet block and an excellent reception/shop. The park has direct access from the A39, and is only two miles from the sandy beaches at Bude. There are four pine lodges for holiday hire. 4 acre site. 41 touring pitches. Caravan pitches. Motorhome pitches. Tent pitches. 4 statics.

AA Pubs & Restaurants nearby: The Bickford Arms, HOLSWORTHY, EX22 7XY, 01409 221318

The Castle Restaurant, BUDE, EX23 8LG, 01288 350543

Leisure: 🅰

Facilities: 🔥 ☉ ℙ ✳ ❤ ⓢ ⬚ ⅏ ♻ ❶

Services: ☺ ⬚ ⬚ 🍽 ⬚ ⬚

Within 3 miles: ⬚ ⬚ ⬚ ☉ ⬚ ⬚ ⬚ ∪

Notes: ☺ Dogs must be kept on leads.

▶▶▶ 85% Upper Lynstone Caravan Park *(SS205053)*

Lynstone EX23 0LP
☎ **01288 352017**
e-mail: reception@upperlynstone.co.uk
dir: *0.75m S of Bude on coastal road to Widemouth Bay*

🚐 🚐 ⛺

Open Apr-Oct

Last arrival 22.00hrs Last departure 10.00hrs

There are extensive views over Bude to be enjoyed from this quiet, sheltered family-run park, a terraced grass site suitable for all units. A new, spotlessly clean and top quality toilet block was built for the 2013 season, plus there is a children's playground and a reception with a shop that sells basic food supplies and camping

---

LEISURE: 🏊 Indoor swimming pool 🏊 Outdoor swimming pool 🅰 Children's playground 🙌 Kid's club ☉ Tennis court ⬤ Games room ⬜ Separate TV room ⬚ 9/18 hole golf course ⬚ Boats for hire 🎬 Cinema 🎵 Entertainment 🎣 Fishing ◎ Mini golf 🏄 Watersports 💪 Gym ☉ Sports field Spa ∪ Stables
FACILITIES: ⬤ Bath 🔥 Shower ☉ Electric shaver ℙ Hairdryer ✳ Ice Pack Facility ❤ Disabled facilities ⓢ Public telephone ⬚ Shop on site or within 200yds ⬚ Mobile shop (calls at least 5 days a week) ⬚ BBQ area 🗕 Picnic area ⅏ Wi-fi ⬚ Internet access ♻ Recycling ❶ Tourist info 🐕 Dog exercise area

spares. Static caravans for holiday hire. A path leads directly to the coastal footpath with its stunning sea views, and the old Bude Canal is just a stroll away. 6 acre site. 65 touring pitches. Caravan pitches. Motorhome pitches. Tent pitches. 41 statics.

AA Pubs & Restaurants nearby: The Castle Restaurant, BUDE, EX23 8LG, 01288 350543

Leisure: ⚓

Facilities: ⌂ ⊙ ⬚ ✳ ⛲ ⛻ ♻ ❶

Services: ⊡ ⊡ ⬛ ⊘ T ⬛

Within 3 miles: ⤵ ⬚ ❒ ❷ ⊙ ⬚ ⬚ U

Notes: No groups. Baby changing room.

▶▶▶▶ 85% *Juliot's Well Holiday Park* (SX095829)

PL32 9RF
☎ **01840 213302**
e-mail: holidays@juliotswell.com
web: www.juliotswell.com
dir: *Through Camelford, A39 at Valley Truckle turn right onto B3266, 1st left signed Lanteglos, site 300yds on right*

⊞ ⬚ ⊼

Open all year

Last arrival 20.00hrs Last departure 11.00hrs

Set in the wooded grounds of an old manor house, this quiet site enjoys lovely and extensive views across the countryside. A rustic inn on site offers occasional entertainment, and there is plenty to do, both on the park and in the vicinity. The superb, fully serviced toilet facilities are very impressive. There are also self-catering pine lodges, static caravans and five cottages for hire. 33 acre site. 39 touring pitches. Caravan pitches. Motorhome pitches. Tent pitches. 82 statics.

AA Pubs & Restaurants nearby: The Mill House Inn, TREBARWITH, PL34 0HD, 01840 770200

Leisure: ⚓ ⚓ ⬚

Facilities: ⬚ ⌂ ⬚ ⬚ ⊙ ⬚ ⛻ ⬚ W-fi

Services: ⊡ ⊡ ⬚ ⊙ ⬚

Within 3 miles: ⤵ ❒ ⊙ ⬚ U

Notes: Complimentary use of cots & high chairs.

▶▶▶ 78% *Lakefield Caravan Park* (SX095853)

Lower Pendavey Farm PL32 9TX
☎ **01840 213279**
e-mail: lakefieldcaravanpark@btconnect.com
dir: *From A39 in Camelford onto B3266, right at T-junct, site 1.5m on left*

⊞ ⬚ ⊼

Open Etr or Apr-Sep

Last arrival 22.00hrs Last departure 11.00hrs

Set in a rural location, this friendly park is part of a specialist equestrian centre, and offers good quality services. All the facilities are immaculate and spotlessly clean. Riding lessons and hacks always available, with a BHS qualified instructor. Newquay, Padstow and Bude are all easily accessed from this site. 5 acre site. 40 touring pitches. Caravan pitches. Motorhome pitches. Tent pitches.

AA Pubs & Restaurants nearby: The Old Inn & Restaurant, ST BREWARD, PL30 4PP, 01208 850711

Facilities: ⌂ ⊙ ⬚ ✳ ⛻ ❶

Services: ⊡ ⬚ ⊘ T ⬚ ⬛

Within 3 miles: ⤵ ❒ ⬚ U

Notes: Dogs must be kept on leads. On-site lake.

Places to visit

Charlestown Shipwreck & Heritage Centre, ST AUSTELL, PL25 3NJ, 01726 69897 www.shipwreckcharlestown.com

Eden Project, ST AUSTELL, PL24 2SG, 01726 811911 www.edenproject.com

Great for kids: Wheal Martyn Museum & Country Park, ST AUSTELL, PL26 8XG, 01726 850362 www.wheal-martyn.com

---

PREMIER PARK

▶▶▶▶▶ 89% Carlyon Bay Caravan & Camping Park (SX052526)

Bethesda, Cypress Av PL25 3RE
☎ **01726 812735**
e-mail: holidays@carlyonbay.net
dir: *Exit A390 W of St Blazey, left onto A3092 for Par, right in 0.5m. On private road to Carlyon Bay*

* ⊞ £16-£29 ⬚ £16-£29 ⊼ £13-£26

Open Etr-28 Sep (rs Etr-mid May & mid-end Sep swimming pool, takeaway & shop closed)

Last arrival 21.00hrs Last departure 11.00hrs

An attractive, secluded site set amongst a belt of trees with background woodland. The spacious grassy park is beautifully landscaped and offers quality toilet and shower facilities and plenty of on-site attractions, including a well-equipped games room, TV room, café, an inviting swimming pool, and occasional family entertainment. It is less than half a mile from a sandy beach and the Eden Project is only two miles away. 35 acre site. 180 touring pitches. 12 hardstandings. Caravan pitches. Motorhome pitches. Tent pitches.

AA Pubs & Restaurants nearby: Austells, ST AUSTELL, PL25 3PH, 01726 813888

Leisure: ⚓ ⚓ ⬚ ⬚ ⬚ ⬚

Facilities: ⌂ ⊙ ⬚ ✳ ⬚ ⊙ ⬚ ⬚ W-fi ♻ ❶

Services: ⊡ ⊡ ⬚ ⊘ T ⬚ ⬛ ⬛ ⬚

Within 3 miles: ⤵ ⬚ ⬚ ❒ ⊙ ⬚ ⬚ ⬚ U

Notes: No noise after 23.00hrs. Dogs must be kept on leads. Crazy golf. Children's entertainment in Jul-Aug only.

see advert on page 62

SERVICES: ⊡ Electric hook up ⬚ Launderette ⬚ Licensed bar ⬛ Calor Gas ⊘ Camping Gaz T Toilet fluid ⬚ Café/Restaurant ⬛ Fast Food/Takeaway ⬚ Battery charging ⬚ Baby care ⬚ Motorvan service point **ABBREVIATIONS:** BH/bank hols-bank holidays Etr-Easter Spring BH-Spring Bank Holiday dep-departure fr-from hrs-hours m-mile mdnt-midnight rdbt-roundabout rs-restricted service wk-week wknd-weekend x-rds-cross roads ⊗ No credit cards ⊗ No dogs ⬚ Children of all ages accepted See page 9 for details of the AA Camping Card Scheme

CARLYON BAY *continued*

▶▶▶▶ 80% *East Crinnis Camping & Caravan Park* (SX062528)

Lantyan, East Crinnis PL24 2SQ
☎ 01726 813023 & 07950 614780
e-mail: eastcrinnis@btconnect.com
dir: *From A390 (Lostwithiel to St Austell) take A3082 signed Fowey at rdbt by Britannia Inn, site on left*

⊞ ⊞ Å

Open Etr-Oct

Last arrival 21.00hrs Last departure 11.00hrs

A small rural park with spacious pitches set in individual bays about one mile from the beaches at Carlyon Bay, and just two miles from the Eden Project. The friendly owners keep the site very clean and well maintained, and also offer three self-catering holiday lodges and two yurts for hire. It is a short walk to Par where restaurant food can be found. 2 acre site. 25 touring pitches. 6 hardstandings. Caravan pitches. Motorhome pitches. Tent pitches. 2 bell tents/yurts.

AA Pubs & Restaurants nearby: The Britannia Inn & Restaurant, PAR, PL24 2SL, 01726 812889

The Rashleigh Inn, POLKERRIS, PL24 2TL, 01726 813991

Austells, ST AUSTELL, PL25 3PH, 01726 813888

Leisure: ⚒ ✈
Facilities: ⌂ ⊙ ℗ ✳ ⅙ 🕾 🛱 🚻 WiFi 🖳 ♻ 🛈
Services: 🗩 🖬
Within 3 miles: ↓ ⚓ 🗓 ℘ ⊚ 🛶 🏦 🗄 U
Notes: Dogs must be kept on leads. Coarse fishing, wildlife & pond area with dog walk.

NEW ▶▶▶▶ 80% Killiwerris Touring Park (SW753454)

Penstraze TR4 8PF
☎ 01872 561356 & 07734 053593
e-mail: killiwerris@aol.com
dir: *Telephone for directions*

* ⊞ £20-£24 ⊞ £20-£24

Open all year

Last arrival 21.00hrs Last departure 11.00hrs

A small, adults-only, family-run touring park, just five miles from Truro and four miles from the coastal village of St Agnes, making it an ideal base for exploring west Cornwall. The site has a sunny aspect yet is sheltered by mature trees giving it a very private feel. The facilities are of an exceptionally high standard and include a modern and smart amenities block. It is a peaceful spot in which to relax and get away from the crowds. 2.2 acre site. 20 touring pitches. 17 hardstandings. Caravan pitches. Motorhome pitches.

Notes: Adults only. 🐾

▶▶▶ 80% Little Trevothan Caravan & Camping Park (SW772179)

Trevothan TR12 6SD
☎ 01326 280260
e-mail: sales@littletrevothan.co.uk
web: www.littletrevothan.co.uk
dir: *A3083 onto B3293 signed Coverack, approx 2m after Goonhilly ESS, right at Zoar Garage onto unclassified road. Approx 1m, 3rd left. Site 0.5m on left*

* ⊞ £13-£16 ⊞ £13-£16 Å £13-£16

Open Mar-Oct

Last arrival 21.00hrs Last departure noon

LEISURE: ☁ Indoor swimming pool   ≋ Outdoor swimming pool   🎠 Children's playground   ⚓ Kid's club   🎾 Tennis court   🎱 Games room   🖵 Separate TV room   ⚑ 9/18 hole golf course   ⚓ Boats for hire   🎬 Cinema   🎵 Entertainment   ℘ Fishing   ⊚ Mini golf   🛶 Watersports   ☗ Gym   ⊕ Sports field   **Spa**   U Stables
FACILITIES: 🛁 Bath   🚿 Shower   ⊙ Electric shaver   ℗ Hairdryer   ✳ Ice Pack Facility   ⅙ Disabled facilities   ☎ Public telephone   🖻 Shop on site or within 200yds   🖾 Mobile shop (calls at least 5 days a week)   🍖 BBQ area   🛱 Picnic area   WiFi Wi-fi   🖳 Internet access   ♻ Recycling   🛈 Tourist info   🐾 Dog exercise area

A secluded site, with excellent facilities, near the unspoilt fishing village of Coverack, with a large recreation area and good play equipment for children. The nearby sandy beach has lots of rock pools for children to play in, and the many walks both from the park and the village offer stunning scenery. 10.5 acre site. 70 touring pitches. 10 hardstandings. 9 seasonal pitches. Caravan pitches. Motorhome pitches. Tent pitches. 22 statics.

AA Pubs & Restaurants nearby: The New Inn, MANACCAN, TR12 6HA, 01326 231323

Leisure: ⚠ ☺ ✎ ☐

Facilities: 📵 ⊙ ☎ ✳ ☺ 🖐 ♿ ↻ ❶

Services: 🔌 🗄 🔋 ⊘ 🚽 ☕

Within 3 miles: ✎ ⛵ 🏧 🛒

Notes: ⊘ No noise between 22.00hrs-08.30hrs. Dogs must be kept on leads.

CRANTOCK (NEAR NEWQUAY)   Map 2 SW76

PREMIER PARK

►►►►► 89% Trevella Tourist Park *(SW801599)*

GOLD

TR8 5EW
☎ **01637 830308**
e-mail: holidays@trevella.co.uk
dir: Between Crantock & A3075

🚐 🚍 🛆

Open Etr-Oct (rs Etr-mid May & mid Sep-Oct pool closed)

Last arrival 21.00hrs Last departure 10.00hrs

A well-established and very well-run family site, with outstanding floral displays. Set in a rural area close to Newquay, this stunning park boasts three teeming fishing lakes for the both experienced and novice angler, and a superb outdoor swimming pool and paddling area. The toilet facilities include excellent en suite wet rooms. All areas are neat and clean and the whole park looks stunning. Yurts, Eurotents and safari tents are available for hire. 15 acre site. 200 touring pitches. 64 hardstandings. Caravan pitches. Motorhome pitches. Tent pitches. 116 statics.

AA Pubs & Restaurants nearby: The Smugglers' Den Inn, CUBERT, TR8 5PY, 01637 830209

The Lewinnick Lodge Bar & Restaurant, NEWQUAY, TR7 1NX, 01637 878117

Leisure: ⛵ ⚠ ✎ ☐

Facilities: 📵 ⊙ ☎ ✳ ☺ 🖐 ♿ 🗄 ➕ 🚰 📶 ↻ ❶

Services: 🔌 🗄 🔋 ⊘ 🚽 ☕ 🍴 🛒 🚿 ↯ ⛽

Within 3 miles: ✎ ⛳ 🏊 ⚓ 🏧 🛒 🏌 ⛵

Notes: Families & couples. Dogs must be kept on leads. Crazy golf, safari & ready tents (8 of each), charge for Wi-fi.

see advert on page 85

►►►► 85% Treago Farm Caravan Site *(SW782601)*

TR8 5QS
☎ **01637 830277**
e-mail: info@treagofarm.co.uk
dir: From A3075 (W of Newquay) turn right for Crantock. Site signed beyond village

🚐 🚍 🛆

Open mid May-mid Sep

Last arrival 22.00hrs Last departure 18.00hrs

A grass site in open farmland in a south-facing sheltered valley with a fishing lake. This friendly family park has spotless toilet facilities, which include three excellent heated family rooms, a good shop and bar with takeaway food, and it has direct access to Crantock and Polly Joke beaches, National Trust land and many natural beauty spots. 5 acre site. 90 touring pitches. Caravan pitches. Motorhome pitches. Tent pitches. 10 statics.

AA Pubs & Restaurants nearby: The Smugglers' Den Inn, CUBERT, TR8 5PY, 01637 830209

The Lewinnick Lodge Bar & Restaurant, NEWQUAY, TR7 1NX, 01637 878117

Leisure: ✎ ☐

Facilities: 📵 ⊙ ☎ ✳ ☺ 🗄 ➕ 🚰 ↻ ❶

Services: 🔌 🗄 🍴 🔋 ⊘ 🚽 ☕

Within 3 miles: ✎ ⛵ ✎ ⚓ 🏊 🏧 🛒 ⛵

Notes: Dogs must be kept on leads.

►►► 82% Quarryfield Holiday Park

(SW793608)

TR8 5RJ
☎ **01637 872792 & 830338**
e-mail: quarryfield@crantockcaravans. orangehome.co.uk
dir: From A3075 (Newquay-Redruth road) follow Crantock signs. Site signed

* 🚐 £14-£20 🚍 £14-£20 🛆 £14-£20

Open Etr to end Oct (rs May-Oct pool open)

Last arrival 23.00hrs Last departure 10.00hrs

This park has a private path down to the dunes and golden sands of Crantock Beach, about ten minutes away, and it is within easy reach of all that Newquay has to offer, particularly for families. The park has very modern facilities, and provides plenty of amenities including a great swimming pool. Extensive improvements have been made to the bar and the children's play area. 10 acre site. 145 touring pitches. Caravan pitches. Motorhome pitches. Tent pitches. 43 statics.

AA Pubs & Restaurants nearby: The Smugglers' Den Inn, CUBERT, TR8 5PY, 01637 830209

The Lewinnick Lodge Bar & Restaurant, NEWQUAY, TR7 1NX, 01637 878117

Leisure: ⛵ ⚠ ✎

Facilities: 📵 ⊙ ☎ ✳ ☺ 🖐 ☺ 🗄 ➕ 🚰 ↻

Services: 🔌 🗄 🔋 🔋 ⊘ 🍴 🛒 🚿 ⛽

Within 3 miles: ✎ ⛵ 🏧 🏊 ⚓ 🏧 🛒 ⛵

Notes: No campfires, quiet after 22.30hrs. Dogs must be kept on leads.

CRANTOCK (NEAR NEWQUAY) *continued*

►►► 81% Crantock Plains Touring Park *(SW805589)*

GOLD

TR8 5PH
☎ 01637 830955 & 07837 534964
e-mail: crantockp@btconnect.com
dir: Exit Newquay on A3075, 2nd right signed to park & Crantock. Site on left in 0.75m on narrow road

Open mid Apr-end Sep

Last arrival 22.00hrs Last departure noon

A small rural park with pitches on either side of a narrow lane, surrounded by mature trees for shelter. This spacious, family-run park has good modern toilet facilities and is ideal for campers who appreciate peace and quiet; it is situated approximately 1.2 miles from pretty Crantock, and Newquay is within easy reach. 6 acre site. 60 touring pitches. 20 seasonal pitches. Caravan pitches. Motorhome pitches. Tent pitches.

AA Pubs & Restaurants nearby: The Smugglers' Den Inn, CUBERT, TR8 5PY, 01637 830209

The Lewinnick Lodge Bar & Restaurant, NEWQUAY, TR7 1NX, 01637 878117

Leisure: ⋀ ✪ ◣
Facilities: ⬧ ☉ ☞ ✳ ⬥ ⬤ ⓢ ☛ ❼
Services: ☎ ⓦ ▤
Within 3 miles: ♨ ✦ ☷ ⌯ ☇ ⟲ ⓢ ⟳ ∪

Notes: No skateboards. Dogs must be kept on leads.

CUBERT
Map 2 SW75

Places to visit

Blue Reef Aquarium, TYNEMOUTH, NE30 4JF, 0191 258 1031 www.bluereefaquarium.co.uk

Trerice, TRERICE, TR8 4PG, 01637 875404 www.nationaltrust.org.uk

Great for kids: Dairy Land Farm World, NEWQUAY, TR8 5AA, 01872 510246 www.dairylandfarmworld.com

►►► 81% Cottage Farm Touring Park *(SW786589)*

Treworgans TR8 5HH
☎ 01637 831083
e-mail: info@cottagefarmpark.co.uk
web: www.cottagefarmpark.co.uk
dir: From A392 towards Newquay, left onto A3075 towards Redruth. In 2m right signed Cubert, right again in 1.5m signed Crantock, left in 0.5m

* ⬤ £12-£16 ⬛ £12-£16 ⋀ £12-£16

Open Apr-Sep

Last arrival 22.30hrs Last departure noon

A small grassy touring park nestling in the tiny hamlet of Treworgans, in sheltered open countryside close to a lovely beach at Holywell Bay. This quiet family-run park boasts very good quality facilities including a new fenced playground for children, with a climbing frame, swings, slides etc. 2 acre site. 45 touring pitches. 2 hardstandings. Caravan pitches. Motorhome pitches. Tent pitches. 1 static.

AA Pubs & Restaurants nearby: The Smugglers' Den Inn, CUBERT, TR8 5PY, 01637 830209

The Plume of Feathers, MITCHELL, TR8 5AX, 01872 510387

Facilities: ⬧ ☉ ☞ ✳ ⟲ ❼
Services: ☎ ⓦ ▤ ⟿
Within 3 miles: ♨ ✦ ☷ ⌯ ◎ ☇ ⟲ ⓢ ⟳ ∪

Notes: No noise after 23.00hrs. Dogs must be kept on leads.

EDGCUMBE
Map 2 SW73

Places to visit

Poldark Mine and Heritage Complex, WENDRON, TR13 0ER, 01326 573173 www.poldark-mine.com

Trevarno Estate Garden & Museum of Gardening, HELSTON, TR13 0RU, 01326 574274 www.trevarno.co.uk

Great for kids: Cornish Seal Sanctuary, GWEEK, TR12 6UG, 01326 221361 www.sealsanctuary.com

The Flambards Theme Park, HELSTON, TR13 0QA, 01326 573404 www.flambards.co.uk

►►► 81% *Retanna Holiday Park* *(SW711327)*

TR13 0EJ
☎ 01326 340643
e-mail: retannaholpark@btconnect.com
web: www.retanna.co.uk
dir: On A394 towards Helston, site signed on right. Site in 100mtrs

⬤ ⋀

Open Apr-Oct

Last arrival 21.00hrs Last departure noon

A small family-owned and run park in a rural location midway between Falmouth and Helston, and only about eight miles from Redruth. Its well-sheltered grassy pitches make this an ideal location for visiting the lovely beaches and towns nearby. For a fun day out the Flambards Experience is only a short drive away, and for sailing enthusiasts, Stithians Lake is on the doorstep. 8 acre site. 24 touring pitches. Caravan pitches. Tent pitches. 23 statics.

AA Pubs & Restaurants nearby: Trengilly Wartha Inn, CONSTANTINE, TR11 5RP, 01326 340332

Leisure: ⋀ ✪ ◣ ⟋
Facilities: ⬧ ☉ ✳ ⬥ ⓢ ⓢ ☴ ⟲ ⬀ ⬛ ⟲ ❼
Services: ☎ ⓦ ⬧ ⟋ Ⓣ ▤
Within 3 miles: ♨ ✦ ⌯ ◎ ☇ ⓢ ⟳ ∪

Notes: No pets, no disposable BBQs, no open fires. Free use of fridge/freezer in laundry room, free air bed inflation, free mobile phone charging.

FALMOUTH — Map 2 SW83

Places to visit

Pendennis Castle, FALMOUTH, TR11 4LP, 01326 316594 www.english-heritage.org.uk/daysout/properties/pendennis-castle

Trebah Garden, MAWNAN SMITH, TR11 5JZ, 01326 252200 www.trebah-garden.co.uk

Great for kids: National Maritime Museum Cornwall, FALMOUTH, TR11 3QY, 01326 313388 www.nmmc.co.uk

AA CAMPING CARD SITE

▶▶▶ **74% Pennance Mill Farm Touring Park** (SW792307)

Maenporth TR11 5HJ
☎ 01326 317431
dir: From A39 (Truro to Falmouth road) follow brown camping signs towards Maenporth Beach. At Hill Head rdbt take 2nd exit for Maenporth Beach

* 🚐 £20-£23 🚙 £20-£23 ▲ £20-£23

Open Etr-Nov

Last arrival 22.00hrs Last departure 10.00hrs

The safe, sandy bay at Maenporth, just half a mile away, can be accessed via a private woodland walk and cycle ride directly from this park. It is a mainly level, grassy park in a rural location sheltered by mature trees and shrubs and divided into three meadows. It has a modern toilet block. 6 acre site. 75 touring pitches. 12 hardstandings. Caravan pitches. Motorhome pitches. Tent pitches. 4 statics.

AA Pubs & Restaurants nearby: Trengilly Wartha Inn, CONSTANTINE, TR11 5RP, 01326 340332

Budock Vean - The Hotel on the River, MAWNAN SMITH, TR11 5LG, 01326 252100

Leisure: 🏔 🏊 🔍
Facilities: 📶 ☉ ✲ 🕐 🚰 🛒 🚻 ♻ ✚
Services: 🔌 🗄 🔋 🥡 🍴 🚽 🛠
Within 3 miles: ⬇ 🚴 🎯 💪 🏌 ◎ ≽ 🏬 🗄 ♻ ⛳
Notes: 🐕 No noise after 23.00hrs.

▶▶ **81% Tregedna Farm Touring Caravan & Tent Park** (SW785305)

Maenporth TR11 5HL
☎ 01326 250529
e-mail: enquiries@tregednafarmholidays.co.uk
dir: Take A39 from Truro to Falmouth. Turn right at Hill Head rdbt. Site 2.5m on right

🚐 🚙 ▲

Open Apr-Sep

Last arrival 22.00hrs Last departure 13.00hrs

Set in the picturesque Maen Valley, this gently-sloping, south-facing park is part of a 100-acre farm. It is surrounded by beautiful wooded countryside just minutes from the beach, with spacious pitches and well-kept facilities. 12 acre site. 40 touring pitches. Caravan pitches. Motorhome pitches. Tent pitches.

AA Pubs & Restaurants nearby: Trengilly Wartha Inn, CONSTANTINE, TR11 5RP, 01326 340332

Budock Vean - The Hotel on the River, MAWNAN SMITH, TR11 5LG, 01326 252100

Leisure: 🏔
Facilities: 📶 ☉ ✲ 🕐 🚰 🚻 ♻ ✚
Services: 🔌 🗄 🥡
Within 3 miles: ⬇ 🏌 🎯 ◎ ≽ 🗄 🏬
Notes: 🐕 Only 1 dog per pitch. Dogs must be kept on leads.

FOWEY — Map 2 SX15

Places to visit

St Catherine's Castle, FOWEY, 0870 333 1181 www.english-heritage.org.uk/daysout/properties/st-catherines-castle

Restormel Castle, RESTORMEL, PL22 0EE, 01208 872687 www.english-heritage.org.uk/daysout/properties/restormel-castle

Great for kids: Wheal Martyn Museum & Country Park, ST AUSTELL, PL26 8XG, 01726 850362 www.wheal-martyn.com

▶▶▶ **83% Penmarlam Caravan & Camping Park** (SX134526)

Bodinnick PL23 1LZ
☎ 01726 870088
e-mail: info@penmarlampark.co.uk
dir: From A390 at East Taphouse take B3359 signed Looe & Polperro. Follow signs for Bodinnick & Fowey, via ferry. Site on right at entrance to Bodinnick

* 🚐 £15.50-£26.50 🚙 £15.50-£26.50 ▲ £15.50-£26.50

Open Apr-Oct

Last departure noon

This tranquil park set above the Fowey Estuary in an Area of Outstanding Natural Beauty, with access to the water, continues to improve. Pitches are level, and sheltered by trees and bushes in two paddocks, while the toilets are spotlessly clean and well maintained. The shop is licensed and sells local and other Cornish produce. Good walks surrounding the site include one to the Penruan passenger ferry, and one to the Bodinnick car ferry giving easy access to Fowey. 4 acre site. 63 touring pitches. 20 seasonal pitches. Caravan pitches. Motorhome pitches. Tent pitches.

AA Pubs & Restaurants nearby: The Ship Inn, FOWEY, PL23 1AZ, 01726 832230

The Fowey Hotel, FOWEY, PL23 1HX, 01726 832551

Facilities: 📶 ☉ 🅿 ✲ ♿ 🚰 🚻 🛒 📶 💻 ♻ ✚
Services: 🔌 🗄 🔋 🥡 🚽 🍴
Within 3 miles: ⬇ 🚴 🎯 💪 🏌 ≽ 🗄 🏬 ⛳
Notes: Dogs must be kept on leads. Private slipway, small boat storage.

GOONHAVERN
Map 2 SW75

See also Rejerrah

Places to visit
Trerice, TRERICE, TR8 4PG, 01637 875404
www.nationaltrust.org.uk

Blue Reef Aquarium, NEWQUAY, TR7 1DU,
01637 878134 www.bluereefaquarium.co.uk

Great for kids: Dairy Land Farm World,
NEWQUAY, TR8 5AA, 01872 510246
www.dairylandfarmworld.com

PREMIER PARK

►►►►► 84% Silverbow Park (SW782531)
GOLD

Perranwell TR4 9NX
☎ 01872 572347
e-mail: silverbowhols@btconnect.com
dir: Adjacent to A3075, 0.5m S of village

🚐 🚃 Å

Open May-end Sep

Last arrival 22.00hrs Last departure 10.30hrs

This park, on the main road to Newquay, has a quiet garden atmosphere, and appeals to families with young children. The superb landscaped grounds and good quality toilet facilities, housed in an attractive chalet-style building, including four family rooms, are maintained to a very high standard with attention paid to detail. Leisure facilities include two inviting swimming pools (outdoor and indoor), a bowling green, and a nature walk around small lakes, with a summer house where children can take part in a number of nature activities. 14 acre site. 100 touring pitches. 2 hardstandings. 24 seasonal pitches. Caravan pitches. Motorhome pitches. Tent pitches. 15 statics.

AA Pubs & Restaurants nearby: The Smugglers' Den Inn, CUBERT, TR8 5PY, 01637 830209

The Plume of Feathers, MITCHELL, TR8 5AX, 01872 510387

Silverbow Park

Leisure: 🏊 🏊 ⛳ 🎾 🎱

Facilities: 🛁 🍴 ⚡ 🪒 ✂ ♿ 🔥 🛒 WiFi 🌀 ℹ

Services: 🔌 🚿 🚽 🛢 🗑

Within 3 miles: 🎣 ⛳ 🚲 🐴 🛶 🎢 🎮 🛍 Ů

Notes: 🐕 No cycling, no skateboards, no noise after 21.00hrs. Short mat bowls rink, conservation/information area, indoor/outdoor table tennis.

see advert on opposite page

►►►► 86% Penrose Holiday Park
(SW795534)

TR4 9QF
☎ 01872 573185
e-mail: info@penroseholidaypark.com
web: www.penroseholidaypark.com
dir: From Exeter take A30, past Bodmin & Indian Queens. Just after Wind Farm take B3285 towards Perranporth, site on left on entering Goonhavern

🚐 🚃 Å

Open Apr-Oct

Last arrival 21.30hrs Last departure 10.00hrs

A quiet sheltered park set in five paddocks divided by hedges and shrubs, only a short walk from the village. Lovely floral displays enhance the park's appearance, and the grass and hedges are neatly trimmed. Four cubicle family rooms are very popular, and there is a good laundry, a smart reception building, and an internet café. 9 acre site. 110 touring pitches. 48 hardstandings. Caravan pitches. Motorhome pitches. Tent pitches. 24 statics.

AA Pubs & Restaurants nearby: The Smugglers' Den Inn, CUBERT, TR8 5PY, 01637 830209

The Plume of Feathers, MITCHELL, TR8 5AX, 01872 510387

Leisure: 🅰

Facilities: 🛁 🍴 🏷 ⚡ 🪒 ✂ ♿ 🔥 🛒 WiFi 💻 🌀 ℹ

Services: 🔌 🚿 🚽 🛢 🗑 📺 🍴 🛒 🗑

Within 3 miles: 🎣 🚲 ⛳ 🎢 🛶 🎮 🛍 Ů

Notes: Families & couples only. Dogs must be kept on leads. Campers' kitchen.

►►► 80% Little Treamble Farm Touring Park (SW785560)

Rose TR4 9PR
☎ 01872 573823 & 07971 070760
e-mail: info@treamble.co.uk
dir: A30 onto B3285 signed Perranporth. Approx 0.5m right into Scotland Rd signed Newquay. Approx 2m to T-junct, right onto A3075 signed Newquay. 0.25m left at Rejerrah sign. Site signed 0.75m on right

🚐 🚃 Å

Open all year

Last departure noon

This site, within easy reach of Padstow, Newquay and St Ives, is set in a quiet rural location with extensive countryside views across an undulating valley. There is a small toilet block with a disabled facility and a well-stocked shop. This working farm is adjacent to a Caravan Club site. 1.5 acre site. 20 touring pitches. Caravan pitches. Motorhome pitches. Tent pitches.

AA Pubs & Restaurants nearby: The Smugglers' Den Inn, CUBERT, TR8 5PY, 01637 830209

The Plume of Feathers, MITCHELL, TR8 5AX, 01872 510387

Facilities: 🍴 🏷 ✂ 🛒 🌀 ℹ

Services: 🔌 🚿 📺 🛒

Within 3 miles: 🎣 ⛳ 🎮 🛍 Ů

▶▶▶ **78%** *Sunny Meadows Tourist Park* (SW782542)

Rosehill TR4 9JT
☎ **01872 571333**
dir: *From A30 onto B3285 signed Perranporth. At Goonhavern turn left at T-junct, then right at rdbt to Perranporth. Site on left*

⌂ ⌂ Å

Open Etr-Oct

Last arrival 22.30hrs Last departure 10.30hrs

A gently-sloping park in a peaceful, rural location, with mostly level pitches set into three small hedge-lined paddocks. Run by a friendly family, the park is just two miles from the long sandy beach at Perranporth; Newquay is only a 20-minute drive away. 14.5 acre site. 100 touring pitches. 1 hardstanding. Caravan pitches. Motorhome pitches. Tent pitches. 4 statics.

AA Pubs & Restaurants nearby: The Smugglers' Den Inn, CUBERT, TR8 5PY, 01637 830209

The Plume of Feathers, MITCHELL, TR8 5AX, 01872 510387

Leisure: 𝔸
Facilities: 🅿☉✳&🛒♻
Services: 🔌🔒🚿T🍴
Within 3 miles: ↨🚲🛒🎣U

Notes: 🚗 One car per pitch. Dogs must be kept on leads. Pool table & family TV room; washing machine & tumble dryer.

GORRAN	Map 2 SW94

Places to visit

Caerhays Castle Gardens, GORRAN, PL26 6LY, 01872 501310 www.caerhays.co.uk

The Lost Gardens of Heligan, PENTEWAN, PL26 6EN, 01726 845100 www.heligan.com

Great for kids: Wheal Martyn Museum & Country Park, ST AUSTELL, PL26 8XG, 01726 850362 www.wheal-martyn.com

▶▶▶ **80%** *Treveague Farm Caravan & Camping Site* (SX002410)

PL26 6NY
☎ **01726 842295**
e-mail: treveague@btconnect.com
web: www.treveaguefarm.co.uk
dir: *B3273 from St Austell towards Mevagissey, pass Pentewan at top of hill, right signed Gorran. Past Heligan Gardens towards Gorran Churchtown. Follow brown tourist signs from fork in road. (NB roads to site are single lane & very narrow. It is advisable to follow guide directions & not Sat Nav)*

⌂ £9-£22 ⌂ £9-£22 Å £9-£22

Open Apr-Sep

Last arrival 21.00hrs Last departure noon

Spectacular panoramic coastal views can be enjoyed from this rural park, which is set on an organic farm and well equipped with modern facilities. A stone-faced toilet block with a Cornish slate roof is an attractive and welcome feature, as is the building that houses the smart reception, café and shop, which sells meat produced on the farm. There is an aviary with exotic birds, and also chinchillas. A footpath leads to the fishing village of Gorran Haven in one direction, and the secluded sandy Vault Beach in the other. The site is close to a bus route. 4 acre site. 46 touring pitches. Caravan pitches. Motorhome pitches. Tent pitches.

AA Pubs & Restaurants nearby: The Ship Inn, MEVAGISSEY, PL26 6UQ, 01726 843324

The Crown Inn, ST EWE, PL26 6EY, 01726 843322

Leisure: 𝔸 ☸
Facilities: 🅿☉🅿✳&🅂🛒🚿WiFi💻♻𝒊
Services: 🔌🔒T🍴🍴🛒🛒🚮
Within 3 miles: ↨🚲🛒🛒
Notes: Bird & animal hide with wide-screen monitors.

GORRAN *continued*

▶▶▶ 80% Treveor Farm Caravan & Camping Site *(SW988418)*

PL26 6LW
☎ **01726 842387**
e-mail: info@treveorfarm.co.uk
web: www.treveorfarm.co.uk
dir: *From St Austell bypass left onto B3273 for Mevagissey. On hilltop before descent to village turn right on unclassified road for Gorran. Right in 5m, site on right*

🚐 🚑 ▲

Open Apr-Oct

Last arrival 20.00hrs Last departure 11.00hrs

A small family-run camping park set on a working farm, with grassy pitches backing onto mature hedging. This quiet site, with good facilities, is close to beaches and offers a large coarse fishing lake. 4 acre site. 50 touring pitches. Caravan pitches. Motorhome pitches. Tent pitches.

AA Pubs & Restaurants nearby: The Ship Inn, MEVAGISSEY, PL26 6UQ, 01726 843324

The Crown Inn, ST EWE, PL26 6EY, 01726 843322

Leisure: ⚠

Facilities: 🏕☉🍴✳♻ **ⓘ**

Services: 🔌🗑

Within 3 miles: 🎣 ⛵ ⑤

Notes: No hard balls, kites or frizbees. Dogs must be kept on leads.

GORRAN HAVEN   Map 2 SX04

Places to visit

Caerhays Castle Gardens, GORRAN, PL26 6LY, 01872 501310 www.caerhays.co.uk

The Lost Gardens of Heligan, PENTEWAN, PL26 6EN, 01726 845100 www.heligan.com

Great for kids: Wheal Martyn Museum & Country Park, ST AUSTELL, PL26 8XG, 01726 850362 www.wheal-martyn.com

▶▶ 74% Trelispen Caravan & Camping Park *(SX008421)*

PL26 6NT
☎ **01726 843501**
e-mail: trelispen@care4free.net
dir: *B3273 from St Austell towards Mevagissey, on hilltop before descent into Mevagissey turn right on unclassified road to Gorran. Through village, 2nd right towards Gorran Haven, site signed on left in 250mtrs (NB it is advisable to use guide directions not Sat Nav)*

🚐 🚑 ▲

Open Etr & Apr-Oct

Last arrival 22.00hrs Last departure noon

A quiet rural site set in three paddocks, and sheltered by mature trees and hedges. The simple toilets have plenty of hot water, and there is a small laundry. Sandy beaches, pubs and shops are nearby, and Mevagissey is two miles away. There is a bus stop 100yds from the site with a regular service to Mevagissey and St Austell. 2 acre site. 40 touring pitches. Caravan pitches. Motorhome pitches. Tent pitches.

AA Pubs & Restaurants nearby: The Ship Inn, MEVAGISSEY, PL26 6UQ, 01726 843324

The Crown Inn, ST EWE, PL26 6EY, 01726 843322

Leisure: ⚠

Facilities: 🏕☉✳

Services: 🔌🗑

Within 3 miles: 🎣 ⛵ ⑤🗑

Notes: ☺ 30-acre nature reserve.

GWITHIAN   Map 2 SW54

Places to visit

East Pool Mine, POOL, TR15 3NP, 01209 315027 www.nationaltrust.org.uk

▶▶▶▶ 90% Gwithian Farm Campsite *(SW586412)*

Gwithian Farm TR27 5BX
☎ **01736 753127**
e-mail: camping@gwithianfarm.co.uk
dir: *Exit A30 at Hayle rdbt, 4th exit signed Hayle, 100mtrs. At 1st mini-rdbt right onto B3301 signed Portreath. Site 2m on left on entering village*

🚐 £18-£29 🚑 £18-£29 ▲ £14-£25

Open 31 Mar-1 Oct

Last arrival 21.00hrs Last departure 17.00hrs

An unspoilt site located behind the sand dunes of Gwithian's golden beach, which can be reached by footpath directly from the site, making this an ideal location for surfers. The site boasts stunning floral displays, a superb toilet block with excellent facilities, including a bathroom and baby-changing unit, and first-class hardstanding pitches. Each attractive pitch has been screened by hedge planting. There is a good pub opposite. 7.5 acre site. 87 touring pitches. 31 hardstandings. Caravan pitches. Motorhome pitches. Tent pitches.

AA Pubs & Restaurants nearby: Basset Arms, PORTREATH, TR16 4NG, 01209 842077

Porthminster Beach Restaurant, ST IVES, TR26 2EB, 01736 795352

Leisure: ☺

Facilities: 🏕☉🍴✳♿⑤🚿🗑🏠 ᴍ♻ **ⓘ**

Services: 🔌🗑🛢🚿Ⓣ🧺↯

Within 3 miles: ⬇⛵◎🎣⑤🗑∪

Notes: No ball games after 21.00hrs, no noise after 22.30hrs. Debit cards (no credit cards) accepted. Dogs must be kept on leads. Surf board & wet suit hire, table tennis.

LEISURE: 🏊 Indoor swimming pool 🏊 Outdoor swimming pool ⚠ Children's playground 🧒 Kid's club ⚲ Tennis court 🎱 Games room ▭ Separate TV room ⛳ 9/18 hole golf course ⛵ Boats for hire 🎬 Cinema 🎵 Entertainment 🎣 Fishing ◎ Mini golf 🌊 Watersports 🏋 Gym ✪ Sports field **Spa** ∪ Stables
FACILITIES: 🛁 Bath 🏕 Shower ☉ Electric shaver 🍴 Hairdryer ✳ Ice Pack Facility ♿ Disabled facilities 🕿 Public telephone ⑤ Shop on site or within 200yds 🗑 Mobile shop (calls at least 5 days a week) 🍖 BBQ area 🏠 Picnic area ᴍ Wi-fi 🖥 Internet access ♻ Recycling ⓘ Tourist info 🐕 Dog exercise area

HAYLE Map 2 SW53

Places to visit

Tate St Ives, ST IVES, TR26 1TG, 01736 796226
www.tate.org.uk/stives

Barbara Hepworth Museum & Sculpture
Garden, ST IVES, TR26 1AD, 01736 796226
www.tate.org.uk/stives

89% *St Ives Bay Holiday Park*
(SW577398)

73 Loggans Rd, Upton Towans TR27 5BH
☎ **01736 752274**
e-mail: stivesbay@btconnect.com
web: www.stivesbay.co.uk
dir: *Exit A30 at Hayle then immediate right onto B3301 at mini-rdbts. Site entrance 0.5m on left*

Open Etr-1 Oct

Last arrival 21.00hrs Last departure 09.00hrs

An extremely well-maintained holiday park with a relaxed atmosphere situated adjacent to a three mile beach. The various camping fields are set in hollows amongst the sand dunes and are very tastefully laid out, with the high camping fields enjoying stunning views over St Ives Bay. The touring sections are in a number of separate locations around the extensive site. The park is specially geared for families and couples, and as well as the large indoor swimming pool there are two pubs with seasonal entertainment. 90 acre site. 240 touring pitches. Caravan pitches. Motorhome pitches. Tent pitches. 250 statics.

AA Pubs & Restaurants nearby: White Hart, LUDGVAN, TR20 8EY, 01736 740574

Porthminster Beach Restaurant, ST IVES, TR26 2EB, 01736 795352

Leisure: 🏊 ⛰ 🎱 🎣 🎮 🎵
Facilities: 🚿 ☉ 🅿 ☀ ♿ 🕐 ⓢ 🏧 WiFi 🔌 ♻ ❶
Services: 🔌 ⓢ 🍷 🛢 ⌀ Ⓣ 🍴 🔋 🏧 ⚓
Within 3 miles: ✔ 🏌 ◎ ⓢ ⓢ ∪
Notes: No pets. Crazy golf, video room.

►►► 85% Atlantic Coast Caravan Park *(NW580400)*

53 Upton Towans, Gwithian TR27 5BL
☎ **01736 752071**
e-mail: enquiries@atlanticcoastpark.co.uk
dir: *From A30 into Hayle, turn right at double rdbt. Site 1.5m on left*

Open Mar-early Jan

Last arrival 20.00hrs Last departure 11.00hrs

Fringed by the sand-dunes of St Ives Bay and close to the golden sands of Gwithian Beach, the small, friendly touring area offers fully serviced pitches. There's freshly baked bread, a takeaway and a bar next door. This park is ideally situated for visitors to enjoy the natural coastal beauty and attractions of south-west Cornwall. The entrance and exit roads to the touring park have been widened to improve the access. Static caravans for holiday hire. 4.5 acre site. 15 touring pitches. 5 seasonal pitches. Caravan pitches. Motorhome pitches. Tent pitches. 50 statics.

AA Pubs & Restaurants nearby: White Hart, LUDGVAN, TR20 8EY, 01736 740574

Porthminster Beach Restaurant, ST IVES, TR26 2EB, 01736 795352

Facilities: 🚿 ☉ 🅿 ☀ ♿ 🕐 ⓢ WiFi ♻ ❶
Services: 🔌 ⓢ Ⓣ 🍴 🔋
Within 3 miles: ✔ 🏌 ◎ ⚓ ⓢ ⓢ ∪
Notes: No commercial vehicles, gazebos or day tents. Dogs must be kept on leads.

►►► 84% Higher Trevaskis Caravan & Camping Park *(SW611381)*

Gwinear Rd, Connor Downs TR27 5JQ
☎ **01209 831736**
dir: *On A30 at Hayle rdbt take exit signed Connor Downs, in 1m right signed Carnhell Green. Site 0.75m just after level crossing*

✱ 🚐 £12-£20 🚌 £12-£20 ⛺ £12-£20

Open mid Apr-Sep

Last arrival 20.00hrs Last departure 10.30hrs

An attractive paddocked and terraced park in a sheltered rural position on a valley side with views towards St Ives. The terrace areas are divided by hedges. This secluded park is personally run by owners who keep it quiet and welcoming. Three unisex showers are a great hit with visitors. Fluent German is spoken. 6.5 acre site. 82 touring pitches. 3 hardstandings. Caravan pitches. Motorhome pitches. Tent pitches.

AA Pubs & Restaurants nearby: White Hart, LUDGVAN, TR20 8EY, 01736 740574

Porthminster Beach Restaurant, ST IVES, TR26 2EB, 01736 795352

Leisure: ⛰ ✿
Facilities: 🚿 ☉ 🅿 ☀ 🕐 ⓢ ♻ ❶
Services: 🔌 ⓢ 🛢 ⌀ Ⓣ ⚓
Within 3 miles: ✔ 🏌 ◎ ⚓ ⓢ ⓢ
Notes: 🚫 Max speed 5mph, balls permitted on field only. Max 2 dogs, no dangerous dogs. Dogs must be kept on leads.

HAYLE ***continued***

►►► 81% Treglisson Touring Park
(SW581367)

Wheal Alfred Rd TR27 5JT
☎ 01736 753141
e-mail: enquiries@treglisson.co.uk
dir: *4th exit off rdbt on A30 at Hayle. 100mtrs, left at 1st mini-rdbt. Approx 1.5m past golf course, site sign on left*

🚐 £11-£18.50 🚙 £11-£18.50 ⛺ £11-£18.50

Open Etr-Sep

Last arrival 20.00hrs Last departure 11.00hrs

A small secluded site in a peaceful wooded meadow and a former apple and pear orchard. This quiet rural site has level grass pitches and a well-planned modern toilet block, and is just two miles from the glorious beach at Hayle with its vast stretch of golden sand. 3 acre site. 26 touring pitches. 6 hardstandings. Caravan pitches. Motorhome pitches. Tent pitches.

AA Pubs & Restaurants nearby: White Hart, LUDGVAN, TR20 8EY, 01736 740574

Porthminster Beach Restaurant, ST IVES, TR26 2EB, 01736 795352

Leisure: 🛝

Facilities: 🚿 ⊙ 💇 ❄ ♿ 🐕 [Wi-fi] ♻ ℹ

Services: 🔌 🧺 🛏

Within 3 miles: ⛳ 🎣 🏄 [S] 🧺

Notes: Max 6 people per pitch. Dogs must be kept on leads.

82% Riviere Sands Holiday Park *(SW556386)*

GOLD

Riviere Towans TR27 5AX
☎ 01736 752132
e-mail: rivieresands@haven.com
web: www.haven.com/rivieresands
dir: *A30 towards Redruth. Follow signs into Hayle, cross double mini rdbt. Turn right opposite petrol station towards Towans and beaches. Park 1m on right*

Open Mar-Oct

Close to St Ives and with direct access to a safe, white-sand beach, Riviere Sands is an exciting holiday park with much to offer families. Children can enjoy the crazy golf, amusements, swimming pool complex, and the beach of course; evening entertainment for adults is extensive and lively. There are a good range of holiday caravans and apartments.

Change over day: Mon, Fri, Sat **Arrival and departure times:** Please contact the site

Statics 295 Sleeps 6-8 Bedrms 2-3 Bathrms 1-2 Toilets 1-2 Freezer TV Sky/FTV Elec inc Gas inc Grass area

Children 👪 Cots Highchair

Leisure 🏊 🌊 👋 🛝

HELSTON

See also Ashton

Places to visit

Trevarno Estate Garden & Museum of Gardening, HELSTON, TR13 0RU, 01326 574274 www.trevarno.co.uk

Goonhilly Satellite Earth Station Experience, HELSTON, TR12 6LQ, 0800 679593 www.goonhilly.bt.com

Great for kids: The Flambards Theme Park, HELSTON, TR13 0QA, 01326 573404 www.flambards.co.uk

HELSTON — Map 2 SW62

►►►► 86% *Lower Polladras Touring Park* *(SW617308)*

GOLD

Carleen, Breage TR13 9NX
☎ 01736 762220
e-mail: lowerpolladras@btinternet.com
web: www.lower-polladras.co.uk
dir: *From Helston take A394 then B3302 (Hayle road) at Ward Garage, 2nd left to Carleen, site 2m on right*

🚐 🚙 ⛺

Open Apr-Jan

Last arrival 22.00hrs Last departure noon

An attractive rural park with extensive views of surrounding fields, appealing to families who enjoy the countryside. The planted trees and shrubs are maturing, and help to divide the area into paddocks with spacious grassy pitches. The site has a dish-washing area, a games room, a dog and nature walk, two fully serviced family rooms and Wi-fi. Plans include building a campers' kitchen. 4 acre site. 39 touring pitches. 23 hardstandings. Caravan pitches. Motorhome pitches. Tent pitches. 3 statics.

AA Pubs & Restaurants nearby: The Ship Inn, PORTHLEVEN, TR13 9JS, 01326 564204

Kota Restaurant with Rooms, PORTHLEVEN, TR13 9JA, 01326 562407

New Yard Restaurant, HELSTON, TR12 6AF, 01326 221595

Leisure: 🛝 ♠

Facilities: 🚿 ⊙ 💇 ❄ ♿ [S] 🪑 🐕 [Wi-fi]

Services: 🔌 🧺 🔒 🌿 [T] 🛏 ⚓

Within 3 miles: ⛳ ⛵ 🎬 🎣 ◎ 🏄 [S] 🧺 🐎

Notes: 🅿 Caravan storage area.

LEISURE: 🏊 Indoor swimming pool 🌊 Outdoor swimming pool 🛝 Children's playground 👋 Kid's club 🎾 Tennis court ♠ Games room 📺 Separate TV room ⛳ 9/18 hole golf course ⛵ Boats for hire 🎬 Cinema 🎵 Entertainment 🎣 Fishing ◎ Mini golf 🏄 Watersports 🏋 Gym ⚽ Sports field **Spa** 🐎 Stables
FACILITIES: 🛁 Bath 🚿 Shower ⊙ Electric shaver 💇 Hairdryer ❄ Ice Pack Facility ♿ Disabled facilities ☎ Public telephone [S] Shop on site or within 200yds 🚚 Mobile shop (calls at least 5 days a week) 🍖 BBQ area 🪑 Picnic area [Wi-fi] Wi-fi 💻 Internet access ♻ Recycling ℹ Tourist info 🐕 Dog exercise area

AA CAMPING CARD SITE

►►► 78% Poldown Caravan Park

(SW629298)

Poldown, Carleen TR13 9NN
☎ 01326 574560
e-mail: stay@poldown.co.uk
dir: *From Helston follow Penzance signs for 1m, right onto B3302 to Hayle, 2nd left to Carleen, 0.5m to site*

* 🚐 £11.50-£17 🚐 £11.50-£17 ▲ £11.50-£17

Open Apr-Sep

Last arrival 21.00hrs Last departure noon

Ideally located for visiting the towns of Helston, Penzance and St Ives, this small, quiet site is set in attractive countryside. The park is sheltered by mature trees and shrubs. All the level grass pitches have electricity, and there are toilet facilities. 2 acre site. 13 touring pitches. 2 hardstandings. Caravan pitches. Motorhome pitches. Tent pitches. 7 statics. 2 bell tents/yurts.

AA Pubs & Restaurants nearby: The Ship Inn, PORTHLEVEN, TR13 9JS, 01326 564204

Kota Restaurant with Rooms, PORTHLEVEN, TR13 9JA, 01326 562407

New Yard Restaurant, HELSTON, TR12 6AF, 01326 221595

Leisure: 🅰
Facilities: 🌂☉🅿✳️🅰️🔥💧🐕🚽 Wi-Fi 🔳♻️ℹ️
Services: 🔌🅾️🛒✉️⚡
Within 3 miles: ↓🎣🏇🅿️🛒◎⛴️🛍️🎪♈️

Notes: Debit cards (not credit cards) accepted. Dogs must be kept on leads. Table tennis.

►►► 76% Skyburriowe Farm

(SW698227)

Garras TR12 6LR
☎ 01326 221646
e-mail: bkbenney@hotmail.co.uk
web: www.skyburriowefarm.co.uk
dir: *From Helston A3083 to The Lizard. After Culdrose Naval Airbase continue straight at rdbt, in 1m left at Skyburriowe Ln sign. In 0.5m right at Skyburriowe B&B/Campsite sign. Pass bungalow to farmhouse. Site on left*

🚐 £12-£20 🚐 £12-£20 ▲ £12-£20

Skyburriowe Farm

Open Apr-Oct

Last arrival 22.00hrs Last departure 11.00hrs

A leafy no-through road leads to this picturesque farm park in a rural location on the Lizard Peninsula. The toilet block offers excellent quality facilities, and most pitches have electric hook-ups. There are some beautiful coves and beaches nearby, and for a great day out Flambards Experience is also close by. Under the supervision of the owner, children are permitted to watch his herd of Friesian cows being milked. 4 acre site. 30 touring pitches. 4 hardstandings. Caravan pitches. Motorhome pitches. Tent pitches.

AA Pubs & Restaurants nearby: The Ship Inn, PORTHLEVEN, TR13 9JS, 01326 564204

Kota Restaurant with Rooms, PORTHLEVEN, TR13 9JA, 01326 562407

New Yard Restaurant, HELSTON, TR12 6AF, 01326 221595

Skyburriowe Farm

Facilities: 🌂☉✳️🅰️🔥♻️ℹ️
Services: 🔌✉️
Within 3 miles: ↓🅿️🛒⛴️🛍️♈️

Notes: 🚭 Quiet after 23.00hrs. Dogs must be kept on leads.

HOLYWELL BAY   Map 2 SW75

Places to visit
Trerice, TRERICE, TR8 4PG, 01637 875404
www.nationaltrust.org.uk
Blue Reef Aquarium, NEWQUAY, TR7 1DU, 01637 878134 www.bluereefaquarium.co.uk
Great for kids: Newquay Zoo, NEWQUAY, TR7 2LZ, 0844 474 2244
www.newquayzoo.org.uk

94% Trevornick Holiday Park

(SW776586)

TR8 5PW
☎ 01637 830531
e-mail: info@trevornick.co.uk
web: www.trevornick.co.uk
dir: *3m from Newquay exit A3075 towards Redruth. Follow Cubert & Holywell Bay signs*

🚐 🚐 ▲

Open Etr & mid May-mid Sep

Last arrival 21.00hrs Last departure 10.00hrs

A large seaside holiday complex with excellent facilities and amenities. There is plenty of entertainment including a children's club and an evening cabaret, adding up to a full holiday experience for all the family. A sandy beach is just a 15-minute footpath walk away. The park has 68 ready-erected tents for hire. 20 acre site. 688 touring pitches. 53 hardstandings. 8 seasonal pitches. Caravan pitches. Motorhome pitches. Tent pitches.

AA Pubs & Restaurants nearby: The Smugglers' Den Inn, CUBERT, TR8 5PY, 01637 830209

Leisure: 🏊🅰🟡◎🎾🎵 Spa
Facilities: 🐾🌂☉🅿️✳️🅰️🔥💧🐕🚽 Wi-Fi ♻️ℹ️
Services: 🔌🅾️🍴🛢️✏️🚽🍽️✉️🍟
Within 3 miles: ↓🎣🏇🅿️🛒◎⛴️🛍️♈️

Notes: Families & couples only. Dogs must be kept on leads. Fishing, golf course, entertainment, fun park, Eurotents.

SERVICES: 🔌 Electric hook up 🅾️ Launderette 🍺 Licensed bar 🛢️ Calor Gas 🚿 Camping Gaz 🚽 Toilet fluid 🍴 Café/Restaurant 🍟 Fast Food/Takeaway ✉️ Battery charging 🍼 Baby care ⚡ Motorvan service point **ABBREVIATIONS:** BH/bank hols-bank holidays Etr-Easter Spring BH-Spring Bank Holiday dep-departure fr-from hrs-hours m-mile mdnt-midnight rdbt-roundabout rs-restricted service wk-week wknd-weekend x-rds-cross roads 🚭 No credit cards 🚫 No dogs 👶 Children of all ages accepted See page 9 for details of the AA Camping Card Scheme

HOLYWELL BAY *continued*

79% Holywell Bay Holiday Park *(SW773582)*

GOLD

TR8 5PR
☎ 0844 335 3756
e-mail: touringandcamping@parkdeanholidays.com
web: www.parkdeantouring.com
dir: *Exit A30 onto A392, take A3075 signed Redruth, right in 2m signed Holywell/Cubert. Through Cubert past Trevornick to site on left*

* ⬛ £11-£44 ⬛ £11-£44 ▲ £8-£38

Open Apr-Oct (rs 3 May-22 Sep pool open)

Last arrival 23.00hrs Last departure 10.00hrs

Close to lovely beaches in a rural location, this level grassy park borders on National Trust land, and is only a short distance from the Cornish Coastal Path. The touring area is at the rear in a very quiet and flat area. The park provides a popular entertainment programme for the whole family (including evening entertainment), and there is an outdoor pool with a water slide and children's clubs. Newquay is just a few miles away. 16 acre site. 39 touring pitches. Caravan pitches. Motorhome pitches. Tent pitches. 156 statics.

AA Pubs & Restaurants nearby: The Smugglers' Den Inn, CUBERT, TR8 5PY, 01637 830209

Leisure: ⬛ ⬛ ⬛ ⬛ ⬛

Facilities: ⬛ ⬛ ⬛ ⬛ ⬛ ⬛

Services: ⬛ ⬛ ⬛ ⬛ ⬛ ⬛ ⬛

Within 3 miles: ⬛ ⬛ ⬛ ⬛ ⬛ ⬛ ⬛

Notes: Dogs must be kept on leads. Surf school & hire shop.

INDIAN QUEENS

Places to visit

Lanhydrock, LANHYDROCK, PL30 5AD, 01208 265950 www.nationaltrust.org.uk

Charlestown Shipwreck & Heritage Centre, ST AUSTELL, PL25 3NJ, 01726 69897 www.shipwreckcharlestown.com

Great for kids: Eden Project, ST AUSTELL, PL24 2SG, 01726 811911 www.edenproject.com

INDIAN QUEENS
Map 2 SW95

▶▶▶ 76% *Gnome World Caravan & Camping Park (SW890599)*

Moorland Rd TR9 6HN
☎ 01726 860812 & 860101
e-mail: gnomesworld@btconnect.com
dir: *Signed from slip road at A30 & A39 rdbt in village of Indian Queens - site on old A30, now unclassified road*

⬛ ⬛ ▲

Open Mar-Dec

Last arrival 22.00hrs Last departure noon

Set in open countryside, this spacious park is set on level grassy land only half a mile from the A30 (Cornwall's main arterial route) and in a central holiday location for touring the county, and accessing the sandy beaches on the north Cornwall coast. Please note that there are no narrow lanes to negotiate. 4.5 acre site. 50 touring pitches. 25 hardstandings. Caravan pitches. Motorhome pitches. Tent pitches. 60 statics.

LEISURE: 🏊 Indoor swimming pool 🏊 Outdoor swimming pool ⛰ Children's playground 🪁 Kid's club 🎾 Tennis court 🎱 Games room ⬛ Separate TV room ⛳ 9/18 hole golf course ⛵ Boats for hire 🎬 Cinema 🎭 Entertainment 🎣 Fishing ◎ Mini golf 🏄 Watersports 🏋 Gym 🏈 Sports field **Spa** ⬛ Stables
FACILITIES: 🛁 Bath 🚿 Shower ⊙ Electric shaver 🔥 Hairdryer ❄ Ice Pack Facility ♿ Disabled facilities 📞 Public telephone 🏪 Shop on site or within 200yds 🏪 Mobile shop (calls at least 5 days a week) ⬛ BBQ area 🍴 Picnic area **Wi-Fi** Wi-fi ⬛ Internet access ♻ Recycling ❼ Tourist info 🐕 Dog exercise area

AA Pubs & Restaurants nearby: The Plume of Feathers, MITCHELL, TR8 5AX, 01872 510387

Gnome World Caravan & Camping Park

Leisure: ⚐

Facilities: ↖☺🅿✳&🚿🛗

Services: 🔌🗑🛢

Within 3 miles: 🛴🎣🛒U

Notes: Dogs must be kept on leads. Nature trail.

see advert on opposite page

see advert on opposite page

JACOBSTOW   Map 2 SX19

Places to visit

Launceston Castle, LAUNCESTON, PL15 7DR, 01566 772365 www.english-heritage.org.uk/daysout/properties/launceston-castle

Tamar Otter & Wildlife Centre, LAUNCESTON, PL15 8GW, 01566 785646 www.tamarotters.co.uk

Great for kids: Launceston Steam Railway, LAUNCESTON, PL15 8DA, 01566 775665 www.launcestonsr.co.uk

►►► 78% Edmore Tourist Park

(SX184955)

Edgar Rd, Wainhouse Corner EX23 0BJ

☎ **01840 230467**

e-mail: enquiries@cornwallvisited.co.uk

dir: *Exit A39 at Wainhouse Corner onto Edgar Rd, site signed on right in 200yds*

* 🚐 £14-£16 🚗 £14-£16 ▲ £14-£16

Open 1 wk before Etr-Oct

Last arrival 21.00hrs Last departure noon

A quiet family-owned site in a rural location with extensive views, set close to the sandy surfing beaches of Bude, and the unspoilt sandy beach and rock pools at Crackington Haven. The friendly owners keep all facilities in a very good condition including the lovely grounds, and the site has hardstanding pitches and gravel access roads. There is an excellent children's play area. The site

is handy for bus routes as it is close to the A39. 3 acre site. 28 touring pitches. 2 hardstandings. 2 seasonal pitches. Caravan pitches. Motorhome pitches. Tent pitches. 2 statics.

AA Pubs & Restaurants nearby: Bay View Inn, WIDEMOUTH BAY, EX23 0AW, 01288 361273

Leisure: ⚐

Facilities: ↖☺🅿✳©🏊

Services: 🔌🗑🛢🍴

Within 3 miles: 🛒

Notes: 🐕 Dogs must be kept on leads.

KENNACK SANDS   Map 2 SW71

Places to visit

Cornish Seal Sanctuary, GWEEK, TR12 6UG, 01326 221361 www.sealsanctuary.com

Trevarno Estate Garden & Museum of Gardening, HELSTON, TR13 0RU, 01326 574274 www.trevarno.co.uk

Great for kids: Goonhilly Satellite Earth Station Experience, HELSTON, TR12 6LQ, 0800 679593 www.goonhilly.bt.com

The Flambards Theme Park, HELSTON, TR13 0QA, 01326 573404 www.flambards.co.uk

►►►► 87% *Chy Carne Holiday Park*

(SW725164)

Kuggar, Ruan Minor TR12 7LX

☎ **01326 290200 & 291161**

e-mail: enquiries@camping-cornwall.com

web: www.chycarne.co.uk

dir: *From A3083 onto B3293 after Culdrose Naval Air Station. At Goonhilly ESS right onto unclassified road signed Kennack Sands. Left in 3m at junct*

🚐🚗▲

Open Etr-Oct

Last arrival dusk

This spacious 12-acre park is in a quiet rural location and has excellent family facilities. There are extensive sea and coastal views over the sandy beach at Kennack Sands, less than half a mile away. Food is available from the site takeaway, or the local hostelry is not far away in the village. 12 acre site. 30 touring pitches. 4 hardstandings. Caravan pitches. Motorhome pitches. Tent pitches. 18 statics.

AA Pubs & Restaurants nearby: Cadgwith Cove Inn, CADGWITH, TR12 7JX, 01326 290513

Leisure: ⚐🏊

Facilities: ↖☺🅿✳&🖥🚿🛗WiFi

Services: 🔌🗑🛢🍴🎮🛒♿

Within 3 miles: 🛴🎣🏇🚣©🛒🗑U

►►► 85% Silver Sands Holiday Park *(SW727166)*

Gwendreath TR12 7LZ

☎ **01326 290631**

e-mail: info@silversandsholidaypark.co.uk

dir: *From Helston follow signs to St Keverne. After BT Goonhilly Station turn right at x-rds signed Kennack Sands, 1.5m, left at Gwendreath sign, site 1m (NB it is recommended that guide directions are followed not Sat Nav)*

🚐 £15-£22 🚗 £15-£22 ▲ £13-£22

Open 21 Mar-2 Nov

Last arrival 21.00hrs Last departure 11.00hrs

A small, family-owned park in a remote location, with individually screened pitches providing sheltered suntraps. The owners continue to upgrade the park, improving the landscaping, access roads and toilets; lovely floral displays greet you on arrival. A footpath through the woods leads to the beach and the local pub. One of the nearby beaches is the historic Mullion Cove, and for the children a short car ride will ensure a great day out at the Flambards Experience. 9 acre site. 35 touring pitches. Caravan pitches. Motorhome pitches. Tent pitches. 17 statics.

AA Pubs & Restaurants nearby: Cadgwith Cove Inn, CADGWITH, TR12 7JX, 01326 290513

Leisure: ⚐☺▢

Facilities: ↖☺🅿✳©🚿🛗WiFi♻🎮

Services: 🔌🗑🛢🎮

Within 3 miles: 🏇🛒🗑U

Notes: No noise after 23.00hrs. Dogs must be kept on leads.

KILKHAMPTON — Map 2 SS21

Places to visit

Dartington Crystal, GREAT TORRINGTON, EX38 7AN, 01805 626242 www.dartington.co.uk

RHS Garden Rosemoor, GREAT TORRINGTON, EX38 8PH, 01805 624067 www.rhs.org.uk/rosemoor

Great for kids: The Milky Way Adventure Park, CLOVELLY, EX39 5RY, 01237 431255 www.themilkyway.co.uk

►► 75% Upper Tamar Lake (SS288118)

Upper Tamar Lake EX23 9SB
☎ 01288 321712
e-mail: info@swlakestrust.org.uk
dir: From A39 at Kilkhampton onto B3254, left in 0.5m onto unclassified road, follow signs approx 4m to site

* ⛺ £13-£16 ⛺ £13-£16 ▲ £13-£16

Open Apr-Oct

Last departure 10.00hrs

A well-trimmed, slightly sloping site overlooking the lake and surrounding countryside, with several signed walks. The site benefits from the excellent facilities provided for the watersports centre and coarse anglers, with a rescue launch on the lake when the flags are flying. A good family site, with Bude's beaches and surfing waves only eight miles away. 2 acre site. 28 touring pitches. 2 hardstandings. Caravan pitches. Motorhome pitches. Tent pitches. 3 wooden pods.

AA Pubs & Restaurants nearby: The Bush Inn, MORWENSTOW, EX23 9SR, 01288 331242

Leisure: ⅍

Facilities: ⌐ ⌑ ⌓ ⌔ ⌕ ⌖ ⌗ ⌘ ⌙

Services: ⌚ ⌛ ⌜

Within 3 miles: ⌝ ⌞ ⌟ ⌠ ⌡ ⌢ ⌣

Notes: No open fires. Off-ground BBQs only. No swimming in lake. Dogs must be kept on leads. Canoeing, sailing, windsurfing, cycle hire.

LANDRAKE — Map 3 SX36

Places to visit

Cotehele, CALSTOCK, PL12 6TA, 01579 351346 www.nationaltrust.org.uk

Mount Edgcumbe House & Country Park, TORPOINT, PL10 1HZ, 01752 822236 www.mountedgcumbe.gov.uk

Great for kids: The Monkey Sanctuary, LOOE, PL13 1NZ, 01503 262532 www.monkeysanctuary.org

PREMIER PARK

►►►►► 85%

Dolbeare Park Caravan and Camping (SX363616)

Best of British GOLD

St Ive Rd PL12 5AF
☎ 01752 851332
e-mail: reception@dolbeare.co.uk
web: www.dolbeare.co.uk
dir: A38 to Landrake, 4m W of Saltash. At footbridge over A38 turn right, follow signs to site (0.75m from A38)

⛺ ⛺ ▲

Open all year

Last arrival 18.00hrs Last departure noon

Set in meadowland close to the A38 and the Devon/Cornwall border, this attractive touring park is run by innovative, forward-thinking owners, who have adopted a very 'green' approach to running the park. The smart toilet block is very eco-friendly - electronic sensor showers, an on-demand boiler system, flow control valves on the taps, and low-energy lighting, as well as an impressive family room. The park is extremely well presented, with excellent hardstanding pitches, a good tenting field, offering spacious pitches, and good provision for children with a separate ball games paddock and nature trail. Expect high levels of customer care and cleanliness. The on-site shop sells fresh bread and local produce. One pre-erected, fully equipped Eurotent is available for hire. 9 acre site. 60 touring pitches. 54 hardstandings. 12 seasonal pitches. Caravan pitches. Motorhome pitches. Tent pitches.

AA Pubs & Restaurants nearby: The Crooked Inn, SALTASH, PL12 4RZ, 01752 848177

Leisure: ⅍ ⌾

Facilities: ⌐ ⌑ ⌓ ⌔ ⌕ ⌖ ⌗ ⌘ ⌙ ⌚ ⌛ ⌜ ⌝

Services: ⌞ ⌟ ⌠ ⌡ ⌢ ⌣ ⌤ ⌥ ⌦

Within 3 miles: ⌧ ⌨ ⌫ ⌬ ⌭ ⌮ ⌯

Notes: No cycling, no kite flying, late arrival fee payable after 18.00hrs. Dogs must be kept on leads. Off-licence, free use of fridge & freezer.

see advert on opposite page

LEEDSTOWN (NEAR HAYLE) — Map 2 SW63

Places to visit

East Pool Mine, POOL, TR15 3NP, 01209 315027 www.nationaltrust.org.uk

Godolphin House, GODOLPHIN CROSS, TR13 9RE, 01736 763194 www.nationaltrust.org.uk/godolphin

PREMIER PARK

►►►►► 82% Calloose Caravan & Camping Park (SW597352)

TR27 5ET
☎ 01736 850431 & 0800 328 7589
e-mail: calloose@hotmail.com
dir: From Hayle take B3302 to Leedstown, turn left opposite village hall before entering village. Site 0.5m on left at bottom of hill

⛺ ⛺ ▲

Open all year

Last arrival 22.00hrs Last departure 11.00hrs

A comprehensively equipped leisure park in a remote rural setting in a small river valley. This very good park is busy and bustling, and offers bright, clean toilet facilities, an excellent games room, an inviting pool, a good children's play area, and log cabins and static caravans for holiday hire. 12.5 acre site. 109 touring pitches. 29 hardstandings. Caravan pitches. Motorhome pitches. Tent pitches. 25 statics.

AA Pubs & Restaurants nearby: Mount Haven Hotel & Restaurant, MARAZION, TR17 0DQ, 01736 710249

Leisure: ⚓ ⛰ 👤 🎣 ⬜

Facilities: 🚿 ⊙ 📷 ⚒ ✻ ⚿ ⦿ 📶 🛗

Services: 🔌 ▣ 🍺 🧴 ⏍ T ⑩ 🔋 🐦

Within 3 miles: 📍 ▣ ▣

Notes: No noise after mdnt, no pets in statics or lodges. Crazy golf, skittle alley.

LOOE

Places to visit

Antony House, TORPOINT, PL11 2QA, 01752 812191
www.nationaltrust.org.uk/antony

Mount Edgcumbe House & Country Park, TORPOINT, PL10 1HZ, 01752 822236
www.mountedgcumbe.gov.uk

Great for kids: The Monkey Sanctuary, LOOE, PL13 1NZ, 01503 262532
www.monkeysanctuary.org

| LOOE | Map 2 SX25 |

AA CAMPING CARD SITE

81% Tencreek Holiday Park
(SX233525)

Polperro Rd PL13 2JR
☎ **01503 262447**
e-mail: reception@tencreek.co.uk
web: www.dolphinholidays.co.uk
dir: *Take A387 1.25m from Looe. Site on left*

∗ 🚐 £12-£22 🚎 £12-£22 ▲ £12-£22

Open all year

Last arrival 23.00hrs Last departure 10.00hrs

Occupying a lovely position with extensive countryside and sea views, this holiday centre is in a rural spot but close to Looe and Polperro. There is a full family entertainment programme, with indoor and outdoor swimming pools, an adventure playground and an exciting children's club. The superb amenities blocks include several private family shower rooms with WC and washbasin. 24 acre site. 254 touring pitches. 12 hardstandings. 120 seasonal pitches. Caravan pitches. Motorhome pitches. Tent pitches. 101 statics.

AA Pubs & Restaurants nearby: Barclay House, LOOE, PL13 1LP, 01503 262929

Trelaske Hotel & Restaurant, LOOE, PL13 2JS, 01503 262159

Tencreek Holiday Park

Leisure: ⚓ ⛰ 👤 🎣 ⚽ 🐦 🎵

Facilities: 🚿 ⊙ 📷 ✻ ⚿ ⦿ 📷 📶 WI-FI 💻 ♻ 🅰

Services: 🔌 ▣ 🍺 🧴 ⏍ T ⑩ 🔋 🐦 🚐 ⚕

Within 3 miles: ⬇ ⬆ 🏇 📍 ⊙ ⬇ ▣ ▣ ⟳

Notes: Families & couples only. Dogs must be kept on leads.

see advert on page 76

SERVICES: 🔌 Electric hook up ▣ Launderette 🍺 Licensed bar 🅰 Calor Gas ⊘ Camping Gaz T Toilet fluid ⑩ Café/Restaurant 🍟 Fast Food/Takeaway 🔋 Battery charging 🐦 Baby care ⚕ Motorvan service point **ABBREVIATIONS:** BH/bank hols-bank holidays Etr-Easter Spring BH-Spring Bank Holiday dep-departure fr-from hrs-hours m-mile mdnt-midnight rdbt-roundabout rs-restricted service wk-week wknd-weekend x-rds-cross roads 🈺 No credit cards ⊗ No dogs 🧒 Children of all ages accepted See page 9 for details of the AA Camping Card Scheme

LOOE *continued*

▶▶▶▶ 83% Polborder House Caravan & Camping Park *(SX283557)*

Bucklawren Rd, St Martin PL13 1NZ
☎ 01503 240265
e-mail: reception@polborderhouse.co.uk
dir: *Approach Looe from E on A387, follow B3253 for 1m, left at Polborder & Monkey Sanctuary sign. Site 0.5m on right*

Open all year

Last arrival 22.00hrs Last departure 11.00hrs

A very neat and well-kept small grassy site on high ground above Looe in a peaceful rural setting. Friendly and enthusiastic owners continue to invest in the park. The toilet facilities have upmarket fittings (note the infra-red operated taps and under floor heating). A bus stops at the bottom of the lane, but you must flag down the driver. A coastal walk runs by the site, and it is a 20-minute walk to the beach at Looe. 3.3 acre site. 31 touring pitches. 19 hardstandings. Caravan pitches. Motorhome pitches. Tent pitches. 5 statics.

AA Pubs & Restaurants nearby: Barclay House, LOOE, PL13 1LP, 01503 262929

Trelaske Hotel & Restaurant, LOOE, PL13 2JS, 01503 262159

Leisure:
Facilities:
Services:
Within 3 miles:
Notes: Dogs must be kept on leads.

▶▶▶▶ 81% Camping Caradon Touring Park *(SX218539)*

Trelawne PL13 2NA
☎ 01503 272388
e-mail: enquiries@campingcaradon.co.uk
dir: *Site signed from junct of A387 & B3359, between Looe & Polperro. Take B3359 towards Pelynt & Lanreath. Site on right*

Open all year (rs Nov-Mar by booking only)

Last arrival 21.00hrs Last departure noon

Set in a quiet rural location between the popular coastal resorts of Looe and Polperro, this family-run and developing eco-friendly park is just one and half miles from the beach at Talland Bay. The site caters for both families and couples. The owners take great pride in the site and offer some quality facilities and service to their campers throughout their stay; their constant aim is to provide a carefree and relaxing holiday. The local bus stops inside the park entrance. 3.5 acre site. 75 touring pitches. 23 hardstandings. Caravan pitches. Motorhome pitches. Tent pitches.

AA Pubs & Restaurants nearby: Old Mill House Inn, POLPERRO, PL13 2RP, 01503 272362

Barclay House, LOOE, PL13 1LP, 01503 262929

Leisure:
Facilities:
Services:
Within 3 miles:
Notes: Quiet hours 23.00hrs-07.00hrs & barrier not operational. Dogs must be kept on leads. Family room with TV, undercover washing up area, RCD lead hire, rallies welcome.

▶▶▶▶ 81% *Tregoad Park* *(SX272560)*

St Martin PL13 1PB
☎ 01503 262718
e-mail: info@tregoadpark.co.uk
web: www.tregoadpark.co.uk
dir: *Signed with direct access from B3253, or from E on A387 follow B3253 for 1.75m towards Looe. Site on left*

Open all year (rs low season bistro closed)

Last arrival 20.00hrs Last departure 11.00hrs

Investment continues at this smart, terraced park with extensive sea and rural views, about a mile and a half from Looe. All pitches are level. The facilities are well maintained and spotlessly clean, and there is a swimming pool with adjacent jacuzzi and sun patio, and a licensed bar where

LEISURE: 🏊 Indoor swimming pool 🏊 Outdoor swimming pool ⚲ Children's playground 🏑 Kid's club 🎾 Tennis court 🎱 Games room 📺 Separate TV room 🏌 9/18 hole golf course ⛵ Boats for hire 🎬 Cinema 🎵 Entertainment 🎣 Fishing ◎ Mini golf 🏄 Watersports 🏋 Gym 🏉 Sports field **Spa** ♨ Stables
FACILITIES: 🛁 Bath 🚿 Shower ⊙ Electric shaver 🩱 Hairdryer ❄ Ice Pack Facility ♿ Disabled facilities ☎ Public telephone 🛒 Shop on site or within 200yds 🚚 Mobile shop (calls at least 5 days a week) 🍖 BBQ area 🍴 Picnic area 📶 Wi-fi 🖥 Internet access ♻ Recycling ❶ Tourist info 🐕 Dog exercise area

bar meals are served in the conservatory. The site has fishing lakes stocked with carp, tench and roach. There is a bus stop at the bottom of the drive for the Plymouth and Truro routes. Static caravans, holiday cottages and two camping pods are available for holiday hire. 55 acre site. 200 touring pitches. 60 hardstandings. Caravan pitches. Motorhome pitches. Tent pitches. 7 statics.

AA Pubs & Restaurants nearby: Barclay House, LOOE, PL13 1LP, 01503 262929

Trelaske Hotel & Restaurant, LOOE, PL13 2JS, 01503 262159

Leisure: 🏊 ⚑ 🎣 💻

Facilities: 🛏 🌂 ⊙ 🄿 ✳ ✖ 🔥 🐕 ᴡɪꜰɪ

Services: 🔌 🗑 🍴 💳 ⊘ Ⓣ 🍽 🔋 ⚒ 🛢

Within 3 miles: ⚓ ⛳ 🎣 🚴 ◎ ⛵ 🛒 🎯 U

Notes: Dogs must be kept on leads. Crazy golf, ball sports area.

►►► 82% Trelay Farmpark (SX210544)

Pelynt PL13 2JX
☎ 01503 220900
e-mail: stay@trelay.co.uk
dir: *From A390 at East Taphouse, take B3359 S towards Looe. After Pelynt, site 0.5m on left (NB due to single track roads it is advisable to follow guide directions not Sat Nav)*

🚐 🚗 Å

Open Dec-Oct

Last arrival 21.00hrs Last departure 11.00hrs

A small site with a friendly atmosphere set in a pretty rural area with extensive views. The good-size grass pitches are on slightly-sloping ground, and the toilets are immaculately kept, as is the excellent washing-up room. Looe and Polperro are just three miles away. 4.5 acre site. 66 touring pitches. 3 hardstandings. 7 seasonal pitches. Caravan pitches. Motorhome pitches. Tent pitches. 54 statics.

AA Pubs & Restaurants nearby: Old Mill House Inn, POLPERRO, PL13 2RP, 01503 272362

Barclay House, LOOE, PL13 1LP, 01503 262929

Leisure: ⚑

Facilities: 🌂 ⊙ 🄿 ✳ ✖ 🔥 ᴡɪꜰɪ ♻ ❶

Services: 🔌 🗑 🍴 ⊘ Ⓣ 🔋 🛢

Within 3 miles: ⛳ 🎣 🛒 🎯 U

Notes: No skateboards, ball games or kites. Dogs must be kept on leads. Fridge & freezer.

LOSTWITHIEL   Map 2 SX15

Places to visit

Restormel Castle, RESTORMEL, PL22 0EE, 01208 872687 www.english-heritage.org.uk/daysout/properties/restormel-castle

Eden Project, ST AUSTELL, PL24 2SG, 01726 811911 www.edenproject.com

AA CAMPING CARD SITE

PREMIER PARK

►►►►► 82% Eden Valley Holiday Park (SX083593)

PL30 5BU
☎ 01208 872277
e-mail: enquiries@edenvalleyholidaypark.co.uk
dir: *1.5m SW of Lostwithiel on A390 turn right at brown/white sign in 400mtrs (NB it is advisable to follow guide directions not Sat Nav)*

🚐 £13-£17   🚗 £13-£17   Å £13-£17

Open Etr or Apr-Oct

Last arrival 22.00hrs Last departure 11.30hrs

A grassy park set in attractive paddocks with mature trees. A gradual upgrading of facilities continues, and both buildings and grounds are carefully maintained and contain an impressive children's play area. This park is ideally located for visiting the Eden Project, the nearby golden beaches and sailing at Fowey. There are also two self-catering lodges. 12 acre site. 56 touring pitches. 40 hardstandings. 20 seasonal pitches. Caravan pitches. Motorhome pitches. Tent pitches. 38 statics.

AA Pubs & Restaurants nearby: The Crown Inn, LANLIVERY, PL30 5BT, 01208 872707

Leisure: ⚑ ☺ 🎣

Facilities: 🌂 ⊙ 🄿 ✳ ✖ 🔥 ☺ 🔥 ᴡɪꜰɪ ♻ ❶

Services: 🔌 🗑 🍴 ⊘ Ⓣ 🔋 🛢

Within 3 miles: ⛳ 🎣 🚴 ◎ ⛵ 🛒 🎯 U

Notes: Dogs must be kept on leads. Table football, pool, table tennis, football.

LUXULYAN   Map 2 SX05

Places to visit

Restormel Castle, RESTORMEL, PL22 0EE, 01208 872687 www.english-heritage.org.uk/daysout/properties/restormel-castle

Eden Project, ST AUSTELL, PL24 2SG, 01726 811911 www.edenproject.com

►►► 78% *Croft Farm Holiday Park* (SX044568)

PL30 5EQ
☎ 01726 850228
e-mail: enquiries@croftfarm.co.uk
dir: *Exit A30 at Bodmin onto A391 towards St Austell. In 7m left at double rdbt onto unclassified road towards Luxulyan/Eden Project, continue to rdbt at Eden, left signed Luxulyan. Site 1m on left. (NB do not approach any other way as roads are very narrow)*

🚐 🚗 Å

Open 21 Mar-21 Jan

Last arrival 18.00hrs Last departure 11.00hrs

A peaceful, picturesque setting at the edge of a wooded valley, and only one mile from The Eden Project. Facilities include a well-maintained toilet block, a well-equipped dishwashing area, replete with freezer and microwave, and a revamped children's play area reached via an attractive woodland trail. There is a good bus service to St Austell and Luxulyan (the bus stop is at the site's entrance) and trains run to Newquay. 10.5 acre site. 52 touring pitches. 42 hardstandings. 32 seasonal pitches. Caravan pitches. Motorhome pitches. Tent pitches. 45 statics.

AA Pubs & Restaurants nearby: The Crown Inn, LANLIVERY, PL30 5BT, 01208 872707

Leisure: ⚑ 🎣

Facilities: 🛏 🌂 ⊙ 🄿 ✳ ✖ ☺ 🔥 🐕 ᴡɪꜰɪ ♻ ❶

Services: 🔌 🗑 🍴 ⊘ Ⓣ 🔋

Within 3 miles: ⚓ ⛳ 🎣 🚴 🛒 🎯

Notes: No skateboarding, ball games only in playing field, quiet between 23.00hrs-07.00hrs. Woodland walk, information room.

MARAZION   Map 2 SW53

See also St Hilary

Places to visit

St Michael's Mount, MARAZION, TR17 0HT, 01736 710507 www.stmichaelsmount.co.uk

Trengwainton Garden, PENZANCE, TR20 8RZ, 01736 363148 www.nationaltrust.org.uk/trengwainton

►►► 82% Wheal Rodney Holiday Park *(SW525315)*

Gwallon Ln TR17 0HL
☎ **01736 710605**
e-mail: reception@whealrodney.co.uk
dir: *Exit A30 at Crowlas, signed Rospeath. Site 1.5m on right. From Marazion centre turn opposite Fire Engine Inn, site 500mtrs on left*

🚐 🚍 Å

Open Etr-Oct

Last arrival 20.00hrs Last departure 11.00hrs

Set in a quiet rural location surrounded by farmland, with level grass pitches and well-kept facilities. Within half a mile are the beach at Marazion and the causeway or ferry to St Michael's Mount. A cycle route is within 400 yards; Penzance is only a short car or cycle ride away. 2.5 acre site. 30 touring pitches. Caravan pitches. Motorhome pitches. Tent pitches.

AA Pubs & Restaurants nearby: Godolphin Arms, MARAZION, TR17 0EN, 01736 710202

Mount Haven Hotel & Restaurant, MARAZION, TR17 0DQ, 01736 710249

Leisure: 🌊

Facilities: 🍳 ⊙ 🍳 ✳ 🕙 🛈 🗑 WiFi ♻ 🛈

Services: 🔌 🗑 🚰

Within 3 miles: ⬇ 🎣 ◎ 🌊 ⬇ 🗑 🗑 ∪

Notes: Quiet after 22.00hrs. Dogs must be kept on leads.

MAWGAN PORTH   Map 2 SW86

►►►► 81% Sun Haven Valley Holiday Park *(SW861669)*

TR8 4BQ
☎ **01637 860373**
e-mail: sunhaven@sunhavenvalley.com
dir: *Exit A30 at Highgate Hill junct for Newquay; follow signs for airport. At T-junct turn right. At beach level in Mawgan Porth take only road inland, then 0.25m. Site 0.5m beyond S bend*

* 🚐 £15-£37 🚍 £15-£37 Å £11-£37

Open Apr-Oct

Last arrival 22.00hrs Last departure 10.30hrs

An attractive site with level pitches on the side of a river valley; being just off the B3276 this makes an ideal base for touring the Padstow and Newquay areas. The very high quality facilities include a TV lounge and a games room in a Swedish-style chalet, and a well-kept adventure playground. Trees and hedges fringe the park, and the ground is well drained. 5 acre site. 109 touring pitches. 11 hardstandings. Caravan pitches. Motorhome pitches. Tent pitches. 38 statics.

AA Pubs & Restaurants nearby: The Falcon Inn, ST MAWGAN, TR8 4EP, 01637 860225

The Scarlet Hotel, MAWGAN PORTH, TR8 4DQ, 01637 861800

Leisure: 🎡 🔍 🖵

Facilities: 🛁 🍳 ⊙ 🍳 ✳ 🕙 🛈 WiFi 🖥 ♻ 🛈

Services: 🔌 🗑 🔒 🗑 🆃

Within 3 miles: ⬇ 🎣 ◎ 🗑 🗑 ∪

Notes: Families & couples only. Dogs must be kept on leads.

►►► 80% *Trevarrian Holiday Park* *(SW853661)*

TR8 4AQ
☎ **01637 860381 & 0845 2255910**
e-mail: holiday@trevarrian.co.uk
dir: *From A39 at St Columb rdbt turn right onto A3059 towards Newquay. Fork right in approx 2m for St Mawgan onto B3276. Turn right, site on left*

🚐 🚍 Å

Open all year

Last arrival 22.00hrs Last departure 11.00hrs

A well-established and well-run holiday park overlooking Mawgan Porth beach. This park has a wide range of attractions including a free entertainment programme in peak season and a 10-pin bowling alley with licensed bar. It is only a short drive to Newquay and approximately 20 minutes to Padstow. 7 acre site. 185 touring pitches. 10 hardstandings. Caravan pitches. Motorhome pitches. Tent pitches.

AA Pubs & Restaurants nearby: The Falcon Inn, ST MAWGAN, TR8 4EP, 01637 860225

Leisure: 🎡 🎢 ⚽ 🔍 🖵 🎵

Facilities: 🛁 🍳 ⊙ 🍳 ✳ 🕙 🛈 🗑 🆃 WiFi ♻ 🛈

Services: 🔌 🗑 🍴 🗑 🆃 🍽 🚰 🛒 ⛟

Within 3 miles: ⬇ ⬇ 🗑 🎣 ◎ 🗑 🗑 ∪

Notes: No noise after mdnt. Dogs must be kept on leads. Crazy golf.

MEVAGISSEY   Map 2 SX04

See also Gorran & Pentewan

AA CAMPING CARD SITE

PREMIER PARK

►►►►► 93% Seaview International Holiday Park *(SW990412)*

Boswinger PL26 6LL
☎ **01726 843425**
e-mail: holidays@seaviewinternational.com
web: www.seaviewinternational.com
dir: *From St Austell take B3273 signed Mevagissey. Turn right before entering village. Follow brown tourist signs to site (NB very narrow lanes to this site; it is advisable to follow guide directions not Sat Nav)*

* 🚐 £9-£45 🚍 £9-£45 Å £9-£45

LEISURE: 🌊 Indoor swimming pool 🌊 Outdoor swimming pool 🎡 Children's playground 🖐 Kid's club 🎾 Tennis court 🔍 Games room 🖵 Separate TV room ⬇ 9/18 hole golf course 🚣 Boats for hire 🎬 Cinema 🎵 Entertainment 🎣 Fishing ◎ Mini golf 🌊 Watersports 💪 Gym ⚽ Sports field **Spa** ∪ Stables
FACILITIES: 🛁 Bath 🍳 Shower ⊙ Electric shaver 🍳 Hairdryer ✳ Ice Pack Facility 🕙 Disabled facilities 🕙 Public telephone 🗑 Shop on site or within 200yds 🗑 Mobile shop (calls at least 5 days a week) 🍴 BBQ area 🎋 Picnic area WiFi Wi-fi 🖥 Internet access ♻ Recycling 🛈 Tourist info 🐾 Dog exercise area

Seaview International Holiday Park

Open Mar-end Sep (rs mid Sep-end May swimming pool closed)

Last arrival 20.00hrs Last departure 10.00hrs

An attractive holiday park set in a beautiful environment overlooking Veryan Bay, with colourful landscaping, including attractive flowers and shrubs. It continues to offer an outstanding holiday experience, with its luxury family pitches, super toilet facilities, takeaway, shop and an alfresco eating area complete with a TV screen. The beach is just half a mile away. There is also an 'off the lead' dog walk, and a 'ring and ride' bus service to Truro, St Austell and Plymouth stops at the park gate. Static caravans are available for holiday hire. 28 acre site. 201 touring pitches. 29 hardstandings. 15 seasonal pitches. Caravan pitches. Motorhome pitches. Tent pitches. 39 statics.

AA Pubs & Restaurants nearby: The Ship Inn, MEVAGISSEY, PL26 6UQ, 01726 843324

Leisure: 🏄 🎿 🏊 ⚽

Facilities: 🚿 ♻ ⊙ 🅿 ✳ ♿ Ⓢ 🛒 🪑 WiFi 🖥 ♻ ❶

Services: 🔌 ⭕ 🔋 ⌀ Ⓣ 🍽 🍴 🛒 ↓

Within 3 miles: ⤢ ∕ ◎ ⛵ 🛒

Notes: Restrictions on certain dog breeds. Dogs must be kept on leads. Crazy golf, volleyball, badminton, scuba diving, boules.

see advert below

SERVICES: 🔌 Electric hook up 🅾 Launderette 🍸 Licensed bar 🔋 Calor Gas ⌀ Camping Gaz Ⓣ Toilet fluid 🍽 Café/Restaurant 🛒 Fast Food/Takeaway 🔋 Battery charging 🍼 Baby care ↓ Motorvan service point **ABBREVIATIONS:** BH/bank hols-bank holidays Etr-Easter Spring BH-Spring Bank Holiday dep-departure fr-from hrs-hours m-mile mdnt-midnight rdbt-roundabout rs-restricted service wk-week wknd-weekend x-rds-cross roads 🚫 No credit cards 🚫 No dogs 👶 Children of all ages accepted See page 9 for details of the AA Camping Card Scheme

MULLION
Map 2 SW61

Places to visit

Trevarno Estate Garden & Museum of Gardening, HELSTON, TR13 0RU, 01326 574274 www.trevarno.co.uk

Goonhilly Satellite Earth Station Experience, HELSTON, TR12 6LQ, 0800 679593 www.goonhilly.bt.com

Great for kids: Cornish Seal Sanctuary, GWEEK, TR12 6UG, 01326 221361 www.sealsanctuary.com

The Flambards Theme Park, HELSTON, TR13 0QA, 01326 573404 www.flambards.co.uk

 78% Mullion Holiday Park (SW699182)

SILVER

Ruan Minor TR12 7LJ
☎ 0844 335 3756 & 01326 240428
e-mail: touringandcamping@parkdeanholidays.com
web: www.parkdeantouring.com
dir: A30 onto A39 through Truro towards Falmouth. A394 to Helston, A3083 for The Lizard. Site 7m on left

* 🚐 £9-£29 🚜 £9-£29 ▲ £7-£25

Mullion Holiday Park

Open Apr-Oct (rs 3 May-22 Sep outdoor pool open)

Last arrival 22.00hrs Last departure 10.00hrs

A comprehensively-equipped leisure park geared mainly for self-catering holidays, and set close to the sandy beaches, coves and fishing villages on The Lizard peninsula. There is plenty of on-site entertainment for all ages, with indoor and outdoor swimming pools and a bar and grill. 49 acre site. 105 touring pitches. 9 hardstandings. Caravan pitches. Motorhome pitches. Tent pitches. 305 statics.

AA Pubs & Restaurants nearby: The Halzephron Inn, GUNWALLOE, TR12 7QB, 01326 240406

Leisure: 🏊⛱🎪⚽✋🔍⌨🎵

Facilities: 🎣⊙📷✳❤⚲🕐💲🚿♨ WI-FI 🖥 ♻ ❶

Services: 🔌🗑🚰🍴🛒🚙

Within 3 miles: ↕🏌◎⛷🚲♨🎣↻

Notes: Dogs must be kept on leads. Scuba diving, football pitch, surf & cycle hire, multi-sports court.

AA CAMPING CARD SITE

▶▶▶ **77% Franchis Holiday Park** (SW698203)

BRONZE

Cury Cross Lanes TR12 7AZ
☎ 01326 240301
e-mail: enquiries@franchis.co.uk
web: www.franchis.co.uk
dir: Exit A3083 on left 0.5m past Wheel Inn PH, between Helston & The Lizard

* 🚐 £13-£18 🚜 £13-£18 ▲ £11-£18

Open Apr-Oct

Last arrival 20.00hrs Last departure 10.30hrs

A mainly grassy site surrounded by hedges and trees, located on Goonhilly Downs and in an ideal position for exploring the Lizard Peninsula. The site is divided into two paddocks for tourers, and the pitches are a mix of level and slightly sloping. There are good facilities for families, and for a fun-filled family day out Flambards Experience is less than 20 minutes' drive away in Helston. 16 acre site. 57 touring pitches. 14 seasonal pitches. Caravan pitches. Motorhome pitches. Tent pitches. 12 statics.

LEISURE: 🏊 Indoor swimming pool ⛱ Outdoor swimming pool 🎪 Children's playground ✋ Kid's club 🎾 Tennis court 🎱 Games room 📺 Separate TV room ⛳ 9/18 hole golf course ⛵ Boats for hire 🎬 Cinema 🎵 Entertainment 🎣 Fishing ◎ Mini golf 🏄 Watersports 🏋 Gym ⚽ Sports field **Spa** ♨ ↻ Stables
FACILITIES: 🛁 Bath 🚿 Shower ⊙ Electric shaver ✳ Hairdryer ❄ Ice Pack Facility ♿ Disabled facilities 🕐 Public telephone 💲 Shop on site or within 200yds 🚐 Mobile shop (calls at least 5 days a week) 🍴 BBQ area 🌲 Picnic area **WI-FI** Wi-fi 🖥 Internet access ♻ Recycling ❶ Tourist info 🐕 Dog exercise area

AA Pubs & Restaurants nearby: The Halzephron Inn, GUNWALLOE, TR12 7QB, 01326 240406

Franchis Holiday Park

Facilities: ⚓☉☀ 🖪 ⌁ WIFI ♻ ❼

Services: ⚡🖥 🍴⌀ T 🛒

Within 3 miles: ⌕ ✈ 🕭 🗐 🗑 ↺

Notes: Dogs must be kept on leads.

see advert on opposite page

NEWQUAY
Map 2 SW86

See also Rejerrah

Places to visit

Blue Reef Aquarium, NEWQUAY, TR7 1DU, 01637 878134 www.bluereefaquarium.co.uk

Newquay Zoo, NEWQUAY, TR7 2LZ, 0844 474 2244 www.newquayzoo.org.uk

Great for kids: Dairy Land Farm World, NEWQUAY, TR8 5AA, 01872 510246 www.dairylandfarmworld.com

81% Newquay Holiday Park *(SW853626)*

TR8 4HS
☎ 0844 335 3756
e-mail: touringandcamping@parkdeanholidays.com
web: www.parkdeantouring.com
dir: *From Bodmin on A30, under low bridge, right towards RAF St Mawgan. Take A3059 towards Newquay, site past Treloy Golf Club*

✻ 🚐 £8-£43 🚃 £8-£43 ▲ £8-£43

Open Apr-Oct (rs 3 May-22 Sep outdoor pool complex open)

Last arrival 21.00hrs Last departure 10.00hrs

A well-maintained park with a wide range of indoor and outdoor activities. A children's playground and bar and grill enhance the facilities, and the club and bars offer quality entertainment. Three heated outdoor pools and a giant waterslide are very popular. 60 acre site. 53 touring pitches. 10 hardstandings. Caravan pitches. Motorhome pitches. Tent pitches. 312 statics.

AA Pubs & Restaurants nearby: The Lewinnick Lodge Bar & Restaurant, NEWQUAY, TR7 1NX, 01637 878117

Leisure: ⚏ ⋒ ♨ ⚲ ⛶ ♫

Facilities: ⚓☉🍴☀🖪 ⌁🗑 WIFI

Services: ⚡🖥 🍴⌀ T 🍴🛒 🛒

Within 3 miles: ⌕ ✈ 🕭 ◎ 🗑 🗑 ↺

Notes: Dogs must be kept on leads.

PREMIER PARK

▶▶▶▶▶ 84% Hendra Holiday Park *(SW833601)*

TR8 4NY
☎ 01637 875778
e-mail: enquiries@hendra-holidays.com
dir: *A30 onto A392 signed Newquay. At Quintrell Downs over rdbt, signed Lane, site 0.5m on left*

✻ 🚐 £12.55-£22 🚃 £12.55-£22 ▲ £12.55-£22

Open 25 Mar-4 Nov (rs Apr-Spring BH & Sep-Oct outdoor pool closed)

Last arrival dusk Last departure 10.00hrs

A large complex with holiday statics and superb facilities including an indoor fun pool and an outdoor pool. There is a children's club for the over 6s, evening entertainment during high season, a skateboard park, fish and chip shop and a fantastic coffee shop. The touring pitches are set amongst mature trees and shrubs, and some have fully serviced facilities. All amenities are open to the public. This site generates most of its own electricity from a 1.5 megawatt solar farm. There are camping pods available for hire. 80 acre site. 548 touring pitches. 28 hardstandings. Caravan pitches. Motorhome pitches. Tent pitches. 307 statics. 6 wooden pods.

AA Pubs & Restaurants nearby: The Lewinnick Lodge Bar & Restaurant, NEWQUAY, TR7 1NX, 01637 878117

Leisure: ⚏ ⚐ ♈ ⋒ ♨ ⚲ ⚲ ⛶ ♫
Facilities: ⚓☉🍴☀🖪 ⌁🗑 🗑 🍴 WIFI 🖥
♻ ❼

Services: ⚡🖥 🍴⌀ 🖊 T 🍴🛒 🛒 🛒

Within 3 miles: ⌕ ✈ 🕭 🗑 🗑 ↺

Notes: Families & couples only. Dogs must be kept on leads. Solarium, train rides, skate & scooter park.

see advert on page 83

▶▶▶▶ 85% Trencreek Holiday Park *(SW828609)*

Hillcrest, Higher Trencreek TR8 4NS
☎ 01637 874210
e-mail: trencreek@btconnect.com
dir: *A392 to Quintrell Downs, right towards Newquay, left at 2 mini-rdbts into Trevenson Rd to site*

✻ 🚐 £11.30-£18.50 🚃 £11.30-£18.50
▲ £11.30-£18.50

Open Spring BH-mid Sep

Last arrival 22.00hrs Last departure noon

An attractively landscaped park in the village of Trencreek, with modern toilet facilities of a very high standard. Two well-stocked fishing lakes, and evening entertainment in the licensed clubhouse, are extra draws. Located about two miles from Newquay with its beaches and surfing. 10 acre site. 194 touring pitches. 8 hardstandings. Caravan pitches. Motorhome pitches. Tent pitches. 6 statics.

AA Pubs & Restaurants nearby: The Lewinnick Lodge Bar & Restaurant, NEWQUAY, TR7 1NX, 01637 878117

Leisure: ⚏ ⋒ ⚲ ⛶

Facilities: ⚓☉🍴☀🖪 ⌁🗑 🗑 ❼

Services: ⚡🖥 🍴⌀ T 🍴🛒 🛒

Within 3 miles: ⌕ ✈ 🕭 🗑 ◎ 🗑 🗑 ↺

Notes: ⊗ Families & couples only.

SERVICES: ⚡ Electric hook up 🖥 Launderette 🍴 Licensed bar 🪨 Calor Gas ⌀ Camping Gaz T Toilet fluid 🍴 Café/Restaurant 🛒 Fast Food/Takeaway 🔋 Battery charging 🚼 Baby care ⚓ Motorvan service point **ABBREVIATIONS:** BH/bank hols-bank holidays Etr-Easter Spring BH-Spring Bank Holiday dep-departure fr-from hrs-hours m-mile mdnt-midnight rdbt-roundabout rs-restricted service wk-week wknd-weekend x-rds-cross roads 🚫 No credit cards ⊗ No dogs 🌢 Children of all ages accepted See page 9 for details of the AA Camping Card Scheme

NEWQUAY *continued*

▶▶▶▶ **80% Porth Beach Tourist Park** *(SW834629)*

Porth TR7 3NH
☎ 01637 876531
e-mail: info@porthbeach.co.uk
dir: *1m NE off B3276 towards Padstow*

* 🚐 £16-£36 🚐 £16-£36 ▲ £14-£41

Open Mar-Nov

Last arrival 18.00hrs Last departure 10.00hrs

This attractive, popular park offers level, grassy pitches in neat and tidy surroundings. It is a well-run site set in meadowland in a glorious location adjacent to Porth Beach's excellent sands. 6 acre site. 200 touring pitches. 19 hardstandings. Caravan pitches. Motorhome pitches. Tent pitches. 18 statics.

AA Pubs & Restaurants nearby: The Lewinnick Lodge Bar & Restaurant, NEWQUAY, TR7 1NX, 01637 878117

Leisure: 🅐

Facilities: 🏪⊙♿🛍️ℹ️♻️ℹ️

Services: 🚐🔌🛢️🧹🛒🚽

Within 3 miles: ↧🎣🎡🐎🟥◎♨️🎱🏪♻️U

Notes: Families & couples only. Dogs must be kept on leads.

see advert on page 84

AA CAMPING CARD SITE

▶▶▶▶ **80% Treloy Touring Park** *(SW858625)*

TR8 4JN
☎ 01637 872063 & 876279
e-mail: stay@treloy.co.uk
web: www.treloy.co.uk
dir: *On A3059 (St Columb Major-Newquay road)*

🚐🚐▲

Open Etr or Apr-Sep (rs Sep pool, takeaway, shop & bar)

Last arrival 21.00hrs Last departure 10.00hrs

An attractive site with fine countryside views, that is within easy reach of resorts and beaches. The pitches are set in four paddocks with mainly level but some slightly sloping grassy areas. Maintenance and cleanliness are very high. There is a very nice swimming pool. 18 acre site. 223 touring pitches. 30 hardstandings. 15 seasonal pitches. Caravan pitches. Motorhome pitches. Tent pitches.

AA Pubs & Restaurants nearby: The Lewinnick Lodge Bar & Restaurant, NEWQUAY, TR7 1NX, 01637 878117

Leisure: 🏊🅐🎣⚽🎱♣️♫

Facilities: 🏪⊙♿✳️♿🛍️ℹ️🐕️ℹ️♻️ℹ️

Services: 🚐🔌🍽️🛢️🧹🅣🍴🛒🚽

Within 3 miles: ↧🎣🎡🐎◎♨️🎱🏪U

Notes: Concessionary green fees for golf.

see advert below

▶▶▶ **80% Trethiggey Touring Park** *(SW846596)*

Quintrell Downs TR8 4QR
☎ 01637 877672
e-mail: enquiries@trethiggey.co.uk
dir: *A30 onto A392 signed Newquay at Quintrell Downs rdbt, left onto A3058, pass Newquay Pearl centre. Site 0.5m on left*

🚐🚐▲

Open Mar-Dec

Last arrival 22.00hrs Last departure 10.30hrs

A family-owned park in a rural setting that is ideal for touring this part of Cornwall. It is pleasantly divided into paddocks with maturing trees and shrubs, and offers coarse fishing and tackle hire. This site has a car park for campers as the camping fields are set in a car-free zone for children's safety. 15 acre site. 200 touring pitches. 35 hardstandings. 12 seasonal pitches. Caravan pitches. Motorhome pitches. Tent pitches. 12 statics.

AA Pubs & Restaurants nearby: The Lewinnick Lodge Bar & Restaurant, NEWQUAY, TR7 1NX, 01637 878117

Leisure: 🅐🎣🖵

Facilities: 🛁🏪⊙✳️♿🛍️🅣🐕️ℹ️🖥️♻️ℹ️

Services: 🚐🔌🍽️🛢️🧹🅣🍴🛒🚽

Within 3 miles: ↧🎣🎡🐎◎♨️🎱🏪U

Notes: No noise after mdnt. Dogs must be kept on leads. Off-licence, recreation field.

see advert on page 84

LEISURE: 🅐 Indoor swimming pool 🅐 Outdoor swimming pool 🅐 Children's playground 🖐️ Kid's club 🎾 Tennis court 🎱 Games room 🖵 Separate TV room ↧ 9/18 hole golf course 🚤 Boats for hire 🎬 Cinema ♫ Entertainment 🎣 Fishing ◎ Mini golf 🏄 Watersports 💪 Gym ♨️ Sports field Spa U Stables
FACILITIES: 🛁 Bath 🏪 Shower ⊙ Electric shaver ✳️ Hairdryer ✳️ Ice Pack Facility ♿ Disabled facilities 🕿 Public telephone 🛍️ Shop on site or within 200yds 🅖 Mobile shop (calls at least 5 days a week) 🍴 BBQ area 🅟 Picnic area ℹ️ Wi-fi 🖥️ Internet access ♻️ Recycling ℹ️ Tourist info 🐕️ Dog exercise area

A park for all seasons

Trethiggey Holiday Park

Quintrell Downs, Newquay, Cornwall TR8 4QR

Set in beautiful countryside, Trethiggey is an award-winning touring park just minutes from Cornwall's "Coast of Dreams" and some of the finest beaches in Europe.

Centrally positioned for top attractions including the Eden Project, we're only seven miles from Newquay International Airport.

AA

Tel: 01637 877672   E-mail: enquiries@trethiggey.co.uk   Online booking: www.trethiggey.co.uk

5★ FAMILY TOURING & CAMPING BREAKS St IVES EXPLORE EVERYTHING CORNWALL

POLMANTER TOURING PARK

Call: +44 (0)1736 795640
reception@polmanter.co.uk

Polmanter Touring Park
St Ives, Cornwall TR26 3LX

www.polmanter.co.uk

PorthBeach tourist park

LOO OF THE YEAR Awards   Club WiFi   AA

Only 100m from the beach!

Call: 01637 876531
or book online at
www.porthbeach.co.uk

Porth, Newquay,
Cornwall, TR7 3NH

follow us...

independent, top graded parks, offering fabulous facilities, superb locations and superior service – especially for families and couples – choose a great holiday from cornwall's finest quality parks

www.cornwallfinestparks.co.uk

cornwall's finest parks

NEWQUAY *continued*

►►►► 77% Trenance Holiday Park

(SW818612)

Edgcumbe Av TR7 2JY
☎ 01637 873447
e-mail: enquiries@trenanceholidaypark.co.uk
dir: *Exit A3075 near viaduct. Site by boating lake rdbt*

🚐 🚌 ⛺

Open 21 Apr-22 Sep

Last arrival 22.00hrs Last departure 10.00hrs

A mainly static park popular with tenters, close to Newquay's vibrant nightlife, and serving excellent breakfasts and takeaways. Set on high ground in an urban area of town, with cheerful owners and clean facilities. The local bus stops at the site entrance. 12 acre site. 50 touring pitches. Caravan pitches. Motorhome pitches. Tent pitches. 190 statics.

AA Pubs & Restaurants nearby: The Lewinnick Lodge Bar & Restaurant, NEWQUAY, TR7 1NX, 01637 878117

Leisure: 🏓

Facilities: 🚿 ⊙ 💨 ❄ ♿ 📞 🏪 [Wi-fi] 💻 ♻ ℹ

Services: 🔌 🌀 🛢 🔥 [T] 🍽 🍔 🔋 🚼

Within 3 miles: ⛳ 🚣 🎬 🎣 ◎ 🏄 🏪 🌀 🐴

Notes: No pets.

►►► 83% *Trebellan Park* *(SW790571)*

Cubert TR8 5PY
☎ 01637 830522
e-mail: enquiries@trebellan.co.uk
dir: *4m S of Newquay, turn W off A3075 at Cubert sign. Left in 0.75m onto unclassified road*

🚐 🚌 ⛺

Open May-Oct

Last arrival 21.00hrs Last departure 10.00hrs

A terraced grassy rural park within a picturesque valley with views of Cubert Common, and adjacent to the Smuggler's Den, a 16th-century thatched inn. This park has a very inviting swimming pool and three well-stocked coarse fishing lakes. 8 acre site. 150 touring pitches. Caravan pitches. Motorhome pitches. Tent pitches. 7 statics.

AA Pubs & Restaurants nearby: The Lewinnick Lodge Bar & Restaurant, NEWQUAY, TR7 1NX, 01637 878117

Leisure: 🌊 🛝 📺

Facilities: 🚿 ⊙ 💨 ❄ ♿ 📞 🧺

Services: 🔌 🌀 🍔

Within 3 miles: ⛳ 🎣 ◎ 🏄 🏪 🌀 🐴

Notes: Families & couples only. Dogs must be kept on leads.

►►► 79% Riverside Holiday Park

(SW829592)

Gwills Ln TR8 4PE
☎ 01637 873617
e-mail: info@riversideholidaypark.co.uk
web: www.riversideholidaypark.co.uk
dir: *A30 onto A392 signed Newquay. At Quintrell Downs cross rdbt signed Lane. 2nd left in 0.5m onto unclassified road signed Gwills. Site in 400yds*

* 🚐 £14-£19 🚌 £14-£19 ⛺ £14-£19

Open Mar-Oct

Last arrival 22.00hrs Last departure 10.00hrs

A sheltered valley beside a river in a quiet location is the idyllic setting for this lightly wooded park that caters for families and couples only; the site is well placed for exploring Newquay and Padstow. There is a lovely swimming pool. The site is close to the wide variety of attractions offered by this major resort. Self-catering lodges, cabins and static vans are for hire. 11 acre site. 65 touring pitches. Caravan pitches. Motorhome pitches. Tent pitches. 65 statics.

AA Pubs & Restaurants nearby: The Lewinnick Lodge Bar & Restaurant, NEWQUAY, TR7 1NX, 01637 878117

Leisure: 🏊 🛝 🏓 📺

Facilities: 🚿 ⊙ 💨 ❄ ♿ 📞 🏪 [Wi-fi] ♻ ℹ

Services: 🔌 🌀 🍷 🛢 🔥 [T] 🍔 🔋

Within 3 miles: ⛳ 🚣 🎬 🎣 ◎ 🏄 🏪 🌀 🐴

Notes: Families & couples only. Dogs must be kept on leads.

OTTERHAM — Map 2 SX19

Places to visit

Launceston Castle, LAUNCESTON, PL15 7DR, 01566 772365 www.english-heritage.org.uk/daysout/properties/launceston-castle

Launceston Steam Railway, LAUNCESTON, PL15 8DA, 01566 775665 www.launcestonsr.co.uk

Great for kids: Tamar Otter & Wildlife Centre, LAUNCESTON, PL15 8GW, 01566 785646 www.tamarotters.co.uk

►►► 83% *St Tinney Farm Holidays* *(SX169906)*

GOLD

PL32 9TA
☎ 01840 261274
e-mail: info@st-tinney.co.uk
dir: *From A39 follow Otterham sign onto unclassified road. Then follow site signs*

🚐 🚌 ⛺

Open Etr-Oct

Last arrival 21.00hrs Last departure 10.00hrs

A family-run farm site in a rural area with nature trails, lakes, valleys and offering complete seclusion. Visitors are free to walk around the farmland lakes and lose themselves in the countryside. 34 acre site. 20 touring pitches. Caravan pitches. Motorhome pitches. Tent pitches. 6 statics.

AA Pubs & Restaurants nearby: The Wellington Hotel, BOSCASTLE, PL35 0AQ, 01840 250202

Leisure: 🌊 🛝 🏓

Facilities: 🚿 ⊙ 💨 ❄ 🐕 [Wi-fi] ♻ ℹ

Services: 🔌 🌀 🍷 🛢 🔥 [T] 🍽 🔋

Within 3 miles: 🎣 🏪

Notes: No open fires, noise restrictions. Dogs must be kept on leads. Coarse fishing.

LEISURE: 🏊 Indoor swimming pool 🌊 Outdoor swimming pool 🛝 Children's playground ✋ Kid's club 🎾 Tennis court 🏓 Games room 📺 Separate TV room ⛳ 9/18 hole golf course 🚣 Boats for hire 🎬 Cinema 🎵 Entertainment 🎣 Fishing ◎ Mini golf 🏄 Watersports 🏋 Gym ⚽ Sports field **Spa** 🐴 Stables
FACILITIES: 🛁 Bath 🚿 Shower ⊙ Electric shaver 💨 Hairdryer ❄ Ice Pack Facility ♿ Disabled facilities 📞 Public telephone 🏪 Shop on site or within 200yds 🚚 Mobile shop (calls at least 5 days a week) 🍖 BBQ area 🧺 Picnic area [Wi-fi] Wi-fi 💻 Internet access ♻ Recycling ℹ Tourist info 🐕 Dog exercise area

PADSTOW
Map 2 SW97

See also Rumford

Places to visit

Prideaux Place, PADSTOW, PL28 8RP,
01841 532411 www.prideauxplace.co.uk

PREMIER PARK

▶▶▶▶▶ 95% Padstow
Touring Park (SW913738)

GOLD

PL28 8LE

☎ 01841 532061

e-mail: bookings@padstowtouringpark.co.uk

dir: 1m S of Padstow, on E side of A389
(Padstow to Wadebridge road)

* ➡ £16-£28.50 ➡ £12-£28.50 ▲ £12-£28.50

Open all year

Last arrival 21.00hrs Last departure 11.00hrs

Improvements continue at this popular park set
in open countryside above the quaint fishing
town of Padstow, which can be approached by
footpath directly from the park. It is divided
into paddocks by maturing bushes and hedges
that create a peaceful and relaxing holiday
atmosphere. 13.5 acre site. 150 touring
pitches. 39 hardstandings. Caravan pitches.
Motorhome pitches. Tent pitches. 12 statics.

AA Pubs & Restaurants nearby: The Seafood
Restaurant, PADSTOW, PL28 8BY,
01841 532700

Paul Ainsworth at No. 6, PADSTOW, PL28 8AP,
01841 532093

Leisure: /🄰

Facilities: 🌂⊙🄿☀️⚅🖫🖳 🗑 ⬛ ♻ 𝟎

Services: 🔌🅕 🛢⌀Ⓣ🝀🚾♿

Within 3 miles: ↕🕏 🄿◎♨🖾🖳U

Notes: No groups, no noise after 22.00hrs.
Dogs must be kept on leads. Coffee shop.

▶▶▶ 74% Padstow Holiday
Park (SW009073)

BRONZE

Cliffdowne PL28 8LB

☎ 01841 532289

e-mail: mail@padstowholidaypark.co.uk

dir: Exit A39 onto either A389 or B3274 to
Padstow. Site signed 1.5m before Padstow

🚐🚙▲

Open Mar-Dec

Last arrival 17.00hrs Last departure noon

An excellent and quiet site of exceptional quality
within a mile of Padstow which can be reached via
a footpath. It is mainly a static park with some
touring pitches in a small paddock and others in
an open field. Three holiday letting caravans are
available. 5.5 acre site. 27 touring pitches.
Caravan pitches. Motorhome pitches. Tent pitches.
74 statics.

AA Pubs & Restaurants nearby: The Seafood
Restaurant, PADSTOW, PL28 8BY, 01841 532700

Leisure: /🄰

Facilities: 🌂⊙🄿☀️⚅🖫🚾 ♻ 𝟎

Services: 🔌🅕 🛢⌀Ⓣ

Within 3 miles: ↕🕏 🗄🄿◎♨🖾🖳U

Notes: 🚫

PENTEWAN
Map 2 SX04

Places to visit

The Lost Gardens of Heligan, PENTEWAN,
PL26 6EN, 01726 845100 www.heligan.com

Charlestown Shipwreck & Heritage Centre,
ST AUSTELL, PL25 3NJ, 01726 69897
www.shipwreckcharlestown.com

Great for kids: Eden Project, ST AUSTELL,
PL24 2SG, 01726 811911 www.edenproject.com

PREMIER PARK

▶▶▶▶▶ 84% Sun Valley
Holiday Park (SX005486)

GOLD

Pentewan Rd PL26 6DJ

☎ 01726 843266 & 844393

e-mail: reception@sunvalleyholidays.co.uk

dir: From St Austell take B3273 towards
Mevagissey. Site 2m on right

* ➡ £15-£32.50 ➡ £15-£32.50 ▲ £15-£32.50

Open all year (rs Winter pool, restaurant &
touring field)

Last arrival 22.00hrs Last departure 10.30hrs

In a picturesque wooded valley, this neat park
is kept to a high standard. The extensive
amenities include tennis courts, indoor
swimming pool, takeaway, licensed clubhouse
and restaurant. The sea is just a mile away,
and can be accessed via a footpath and cycle
path along the river bank. Bicycles can be hired
on site. A public bus stops at the site entrance.

20 acre site. 29 touring pitches. 13
hardstandings. Caravan pitches. Motorhome
pitches. Tent pitches. 75 statics.

AA Pubs & Restaurants nearby: The Crown Inn,
ST EWE, PL26 6EY, 01726 843322

Leisure: 🏊/🄰🏓🎣🎵

Facilities: 🌂⊙🄿☀️⚅🖫🖳🗑🚾 ♻ 𝟎

Services: 🔌🅕 🍴🛢⌀🝀🚾♿

Within 3 miles: ↕🕏 🗄🄿♨🖾🖳U

Notes: No motorised scooters, skateboards or
bikes at night. Certain pet restrictions apply,
please contact the site for details. Dogs must
be kept on leads. Pets' corner, outdoor & indoor
play areas.

▶▶▶ 83% Heligan Woods (SW998470)

PL26 6BT

☎ 01726 842714 & 844414

e-mail: info@pentewan.co.uk

dir: From A390 take B3273 for Mevagissey at
x-roads signed 'No caravans beyond this point'.
Right onto unclassified road towards Gorran, site
0.75m on left

🚐🚙▲

Open 16 Jan-26 Nov (rs 9-11am & 5-6pm
Reception open)

Last arrival 22.00hrs Last departure 10.30hrs

A pleasant peaceful park adjacent to the Lost
Gardens of Heligan, with views over St Austell Bay
and well-maintained facilities. Guests can also
use the extensive amenities at the sister park,
Pentewan Sands, and there's a footpath with
direct access to Heligan Gardens. 12 acre site. 89
touring pitches. 24 hardstandings. 3 seasonal
pitches. Caravan pitches. Motorhome pitches. Tent
pitches. 17 statics.

AA Pubs & Restaurants nearby: Austells,
ST AUSTELL, PL25 3PH, 01726 813888

Leisure: /🄰

Facilities: 🝀🌂⊙🄿🕙🖫🚾

Services: 🔌🅕 🛢⌀🝀♿

Within 3 miles: ↕🕏 🗄🄿♨🖾🖳U

SERVICES: 🔌 Electric hook up 🅕 Launderette 🍴 Licensed bar 🛢 Calor Gas ⌀ Camping Gaz Ⓣ Toilet fluid 🍴 Café/Restaurant 🝀 Fast Food/Takeaway
🛒 Battery charging 🚼 Baby care ♿ Motorvan service point **ABBREVIATIONS:** BH/bank hols-bank holidays Etr-Easter Spring BH-Spring Bank Holiday dep-departure
fr-from hrs-hours m-mile mdnt-midnight rdbt-roundabout rs-restricted service wk-week wknd-weekend x-rds-cross roads 🚫 No credit cards 🚫 No dogs
👪 Children of all ages accepted See page 9 for details of the AA Camping Card Scheme

PENTEWAN *continued*

NEW ▶▶▶ 83% Little Winnick Touring Park *(SX007482)*

PL26 6DL
☎ 01726 843687
e-mail: mail@littlewinnick.co.uk
dir: *A390 to St Austell, then B3273 towards Mevagissey, site in 3m on left*

* ⛺ £6-£25 ⛟ £6-£25 ▲ £6-£25

Open Etr-end Oct

Last arrival 21.00hrs Last departure noon

A small, well maintained rural site within walking distance of Pentewan and its beautiful beach. It has neat level pitches, including some hardstanding pitches, an excellent children's play area, and quality toilet and facility blocks. It borders the River Winnick and also the Pentewan cycle trail from St Austell to Pentewan, and The Lost Gardens of Heligan and Mevagissey are nearby. There is a bus stop outside the park to Mevagissey and Gorran Haven or St Austell (Asda) Charlestown and Fowey. 14 acre site. 90 touring pitches. 28 hardstandings. 2 seasonal pitches. Caravan pitches. Motorhome pitches. Tent pitches.

AA Pubs & Restaurants nearby: The Ship Inn, MEVAGISSEY, PL26 6UQ, 01726 843324

The Crown Inn, ST EWE, PL26 6EY, 01726 843322

Leisure: ⋀ ⚽

Facilities: ⚡ ⊙ ⚑ ⚒ ⓢ ⊞ ⚹ Wi-fi ▭ ♻ ❶

Services: ⚡ ⑤ ⚒ ⚓

Within 3 miles: ⚓ ⚑ ⊞ ⚑ ⚑ ⓢ ⑤

Notes: No noise 22.00hrs-07.00hrs. Dogs must be kept on leads.

PENZANCE   Map 2 SW43

See also Rosudgeon

Places to visit
Trengwainton Garden, PENZANCE, TR20 8RZ, 01736 363148
www.nationaltrust.org.uk/trengwainton

St Michael's Mount, MARAZION, TR17 0HT, 01736 710507 www.stmichaelsmount.co.uk

▶▶▶ 78% Bone Valley Caravan & Camping Park *(SW472316)*

Heamoor TR20 8UJ
☎ 01736 360313
e-mail: wardmandie@yahoo.co.uk
dir: *Exit A30 at Heamoor/Madron rdbt. 4th on right into Josephs Ln. 800yds left into Bone Valley. Entrance 200yds on left*

* ⛺ £17.50-£18.50 ⛟ £17.50-£18.50 ▲ £13.50-£18.50

Open all year

Last arrival 22.00hrs Last departure 10.00hrs

A compact grassy park on the outskirts of Penzance with well-maintained facilities. It is divided into paddocks by mature hedges, and a small stream runs alongside. 1 acre site. 17 touring pitches. 8 hardstandings. Caravan pitches. Motorhome pitches. Tent pitches. 3 statics.

AA Pubs & Restaurants nearby: Dolphin Tavern, PENZANCE, TR18 4BD, 01736 364106

Harris's Restaurant, PENZANCE, TR18 2LZ, 01736 364408

Leisure: ▭

Facilities: ⚡ ⚑ ⊙ ⚑ ⚹ ⚒ ⓢ ⊞ Wi-fi

Services: ⚡ ⑤ ∅ ⓣ

Within 3 miles: ⚓ ⊞ ⓢ ⑤ ∪

Notes: No noise after mdnt. Dogs must be kept on leads. Campers' lounge, kitchen & laundry room.

PERRANPORTH   Map 2 SW75

See also Rejerrah

Places to visit
Royal Cornwall Museum, TRURO, TR1 2SJ, 01872 272205
www.royalcornwallmuseum.org.uk

Trerice, TRERICE, TR8 4PG, 01637 875404
www.nationaltrust.org.uk

Great for kids: Blue Reef Aquarium, NEWQUAY, TR7 1DU, 01637 878134
www.bluereefaquarium.co.uk

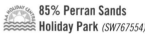

85% Perran Sands Holiday Park *(SW767554)*

TR6 0AQ
☎ 0871 231 0871
e-mail: perransands@haven.com
web: www.haven.com/perransands
dir: *A30 onto B3285 towards Perranporth. Site on right before descent on hill into Perranporth*

⛺ ⛟ ▲

Open mid Mar-end Oct (rs mid Mar-May & Sep-Oct some facilities may be reduced)

Last arrival 22.00hrs Last departure 10.00hrs

Situated amid 500 acres of protected dune grassland, and with a footpath through to the surf and three miles of golden sandy beach, this lively park is set in a large village-style complex. It offers a complete range of on-site facilities and entertainment for all the family, which makes it an extremely popular park. There are two top-of-the-range facility blocks. 550 acre site. 363 touring pitches. Caravan pitches. Motorhome pitches. Tent pitches. 600 statics.

AA Pubs & Restaurants nearby: Driftwood Spars, ST AGNES, TR5 0RT, 01872 552428

Leisure: ⚓ ⚓ ⋀ ⚓ ⚽ ♫

Facilities: ⚡ ⚑ ⚑ ⚹ ⚒ ⊙ ⓢ Wi-fi ♻ ❶

Services: ⚡ ⑤ ⚑ ⚓ ∅ ⓣ ⚑ ⚒

Within 3 miles: ⚓ ⚑ ⊙ ⚑ ⓢ ⑤ ∪

Notes: No commercial vehicles, no bookings by persons under 21yrs unless a family booking. Max 2 dogs per booking, certain dog breeds banned. Dogs must be kept on leads.

►►►► 82% Tollgate Farm Caravan & Camping Park (SW768547)

Budnick Hill TR6 0AD
☎ 01872 572130
e-mail: enquiries@tollgatefarm.co.uk
dir: Exit A30 onto B3285 to Perranporth. Site on right 1.5m after Goonhavern

Open Etr-Sep

Last arrival 20.00hrs Last departure 11.00hrs

A quiet site in a rural location with spectacular coastal views. Pitches are divided into four paddocks sheltered and screened by mature hedges. Children will like the play equipment and pets' corner, while adults can enjoy the food at the Farm Kitchen, which is open daily. The three miles of sand at Perran Bay are just a walk away through the sand dunes, or by car it is a three-quarter mile drive. There are now five camping pods for hire. 10 acre site. 102 touring pitches. 10 hardstandings. 12 seasonal pitches. Caravan pitches. Motorhome pitches. Tent pitches. 5 wooden pods.

AA Pubs & Restaurants nearby: Driftwood Spars, ST AGNES, TR5 0RT, 01872 552428

Tollgate Farm Caravan & Camping Park

Leisure: ⚙ ☺
Facilities: ⌐ ☺ ♉ ✳ ⅍ ☒ ⓢ ㉆ ㎡ ⒲ ♻ ❶
Services: ⊡ ⓢ 🛢 ⊘ Ⓣ 📦 ⛟ ⍒
Within 3 miles: ↧ ⸙ 🎱 ♪ ◎ ⍨ ⓢ ⓢ ∪
Notes: No large groups. Dogs must be kept on leads.

see advert below

►►► 82% Higher Golla Touring & Caravan Park (SW756514)

Penhallow TR4 9LZ
☎ 01872 573963 & 07800 558407
e-mail: trevor.knibb@gmail.com
web: www.highergollatouringpark.co.uk
dir: A30 onto B3284 towards Perranporth (straight on at junct with A3075). Approx 2m. Site signed on right

🚐 £14-£20 🚃 £14-£20 Å £10-£20

Higher Golla Touring & Caravan Park

Open Etr-end Sep (rs Spring BH wk & peak season shop open)

Last arrival 20.00hrs Last departure 10.30hrs

This peacefully located park is just two miles from Perranporth and its stunning beach, and extensive country views can be enjoyed from all pitches. It has high quality and immaculate toilet facilities, and every pitch has electricity and a water tap. 2 acre site. 18 touring pitches. 2 hardstandings. 4 seasonal pitches. Caravan pitches. Motorhome pitches. Tent pitches. 2 statics.

AA Pubs & Restaurants nearby: Driftwood Spars, ST AGNES, TR5 0RT, 01872 552428

Facilities: ⌐ ☺ ♉ ✳ ⓢ ㉆ ㎡ ⒲ ♻ ❶
Services: ⊡ ⓢ Ⓣ ⍒
Within 3 miles: ↧ ♪ ◎ ⍨ ⓢ ⓢ ∪
Notes: No kite flying, quiet between 21.00hrs-08.00hrs. Dogs must be kept on leads.

SERVICES: ⊡ Electric hook up ⓢ Launderette ⛾ Licensed bar ♉ Calor Gas ⊘ Camping Gaz Ⓣ Toilet fluid ⍖ Café/Restaurant ⛟ Fast Food/Takeaway 📦 Battery charging 🛒 Baby care ⍒ Motorvan service point **ABBREVIATIONS:** BH/bank hols-bank holidays Etr-Easter Spring BH-Spring Bank Holiday dep-departure fr-from hrs-hours m-mile mdnt-midnight rdbt-roundabout rs-restricted service wk-week wknd-weekend x-rds-cross roads ⊛ No credit cards ⊗ No dogs ⨯ Children of all ages accepted See page 9 for details of the AA Camping Card Scheme

PERRANPORTH *continued*

▶▶▶ 70% *Perranporth Camping & Touring Park* (SW768542)

Budnick Rd TR6 0DB
☎ 01872 572174
dir: *0.5m E off B3285*

🚐 🚍 🛆

Open Spring BH-Sep (rs Etr & end Sep shop, swimming pool & club facilities closed)

Last arrival 23.00hrs Last departure noon

A pleasant site, great for families and just a five-minute, easy walk to Perranporth's beautiful beach and less than ten minutes to the shops and restaurants in the town centre. There is a clubhouse/bar and heated swimming pool for the sole use of those staying on the site. There is also a takeaway food outlet and small shop. 9 static caravans for holiday hire. 6 acre site. 120 touring pitches. 4 hardstandings. Caravan pitches. Motorhome pitches. Tent pitches. 9 statics.

AA Pubs & Restaurants nearby: Driftwood Spars, ST AGNES, TR5 0RT, 01872 552428

Perranporth Camping & Touring Park

Leisure: 🏊 ⚠ 🔍 🖵
Facilities: 🛁 🏠 ⊙ 🖤 ✳ ⚟ 🖻 🖵 🛒 🤚 ❶
Services: 🔌 🖻 🛢 🍴 🛢 ⌀ 🔲 🚌
Within 3 miles: ⚓ 🛶 🎣 ◎ 🍴 🛒 🖻 🖵 ↻

Notes: No noise after 23.00hrs. Dogs must be kept on leads.

see advert below

POLPERRO
Map 2 SX25

▶▶ 77% Great Kellow Farm Caravan & Camping Site (SX201522)

Lansallos PL13 2QL
☎ 01503 272387
e-mail: kellow.farm@virgin.net
dir: *From Looe to Pelynt. In Pelynt left at church follow Lansallos sign. Left at x-rds, 0.75m. At staggered x-rds left, follow site signs. (NB access is via single track lanes. It is advisable to follow guide directions not Sat Nav)*

✽ 🚐 £10-£12 🚍 £10-£12 🛆 £10-£12

Open Mar-3 Jan

Last arrival 22.00hrs Last departure noon

Set on a high level grassy paddock with extensive views of Polperro Bay, this attractive site is on a working dairy and beef farm, and close to National Trust properties and gardens. It is situated in a very peaceful location close to the fishing village of Polperro. 3 acre site. 30 touring pitches. 25 seasonal pitches. Caravan pitches. Motorhome pitches. Tent pitches. 10 statics.

AA Pubs & Restaurants nearby: Old Mill House Inn, POLPERRO, PL13 2RP, 01503 272362

Barclay House, LOOE, PL13 1LP, 01503 262929

Facilities: 🏠 ⊙ ✳ 🤚 ♻ ❶
Services: 🔌
Within 3 miles: 🛶 🎣 🖻

Notes: 🐕 No noise after 23.00hrs. Dogs must be kept on leads.

LEISURE: 🏊 Indoor swimming pool 🏊 Outdoor swimming pool ⚠ Children's playground 🤚 Kid's club 🎾 Tennis court 🎱 Games room 🖵 Separate TV room ⛳ 9/18 hole golf course 🚣 Boats for hire 🎬 Cinema 🎵 Entertainment 🎣 Fishing ◎ Mini golf 🏄 Watersports 🏋 Gym 🏟 Sports field **Spa** ↻ Stables
FACILITIES: 🛁 Bath 🚿 Shower ⊙ Electric shaver 🖤 Hairdryer ✳ Ice Pack Facility ⚟ Disabled facilities 🕾 Public telephone 🖻 Shop on site or within 200yds 🏪 Mobile shop (calls at least 5 days a week) 🍴 BBQ area 🪑 Picnic area 📶 Wi-fi 💻 Internet access ♻ Recycling ❶ Tourist info 🐕 Dog exercise area

POLRUAN Map 2 SX15

Places to visit

Restormel Castle, RESTORMEL, PL22 0EE, 01208 872687 www.english-heritage.org.uk/daysout/properties/restormel-castle

Great for kids: The Monkey Sanctuary, LOOE, PL13 1NZ, 01503 262532 www.monkeysanctuary.org

►►► 88% Polruan Holidays-Camping & Caravanning (SX133509)

Polruan-by-Fowey PL23 1QH
☎ 01726 870263
e-mail: polholiday@aol.com
web: www.polruanholidays.co.uk
dir: A38 to Dobwalls, left onto A390 to East Taphouse. Left onto B3359. Right in 4.5m signed Polruan

Open Etr-Oct

Last arrival 21.00hrs Last departure noon

A very rural and quiet site in a lovely elevated position above the village, with good views of the sea. The River Fowey passenger ferry is close by, and the site has a good shop, and barbecues to borrow. The bus for Polperro and Looe stops outside the gate, and the foot ferry to Fowey, which runs until 11pm, is only a 10-minute walk away. 3 acre site. 47 touring pitches. 7 hardstandings. Caravan pitches. Motorhome pitches. Tent pitches. 10 statics.

AA Pubs & Restaurants nearby: The Ship Inn, FOWEY, PL23 1AZ, 01726 832230

The Fowey Hotel, FOWEY, PL23 1HX, 01726 832551

Leisure: ⚙

Facilities: ⚙⊙⌒✳⚙⛽⚙ 📺 ♻ 𝟢

Services: ⚙⚙🔋⚙🚽⚙🚽

Within 3 miles: ✿⚓♨🚤⚓♿⊙

Notes: No skateboards, rollerskates, bikes, water pistols or water bombs. Dogs must be kept on leads.

POLZEATH Map 2 SW97

►►► 87% South Winds Caravan & Camping Park (SW948790)

Polzeath Rd PL27 6QU
☎ 01208 863267 & 862215
e-mail: info@southwindscamping.co.uk
web: www.polzeathcamping.co.uk
dir: Exit B3314 onto unclassified road signed Polzeath, site on right just past turn to New Polzeath

Open May-mid Sep

Last arrival 21.00hrs Last departure 10.30hrs

A peaceful site with beautiful sea and panoramic rural views, within walking distance of a golf complex, and just three quarters of a mile from beach and village. There's an impressive reception building, replete with tourist information, TV, settees and a range of camping spares. 16 acre site. 165 touring pitches. Caravan pitches. Motorhome pitches. Tent pitches.

AA Pubs & Restaurants nearby: Restaurant Nathan Outlaw, ROCK, PL27 6LA, 01208 863394

Facilities: ⚙⊙⌒✳⚙⊙⛽🐾📶 ♻ 𝟢

Services: ⚙⚙🔋⚙🚽⚙🚽

Within 3 miles: ⚓♨🇭♿⊙⚓♿⊙

Notes: Families & couples only, no disposable BBQs, no noise 23.00hrs-07.00hrs. Dogs must be kept on leads. Restaurant & farm shop adjacent, Stepper Field open mid Jul-Aug.

see advert on page 92

►►► 87% Tristram Caravan & Camping Park (SW936790)

PL27 6TP
☎ 01208 862215
e-mail: info@tristramcampsite.co.uk
web: www.polzeathcamping.co.uk
dir: From B3314 onto unclassified road signed Polzeath. Through village, up hill, site 2nd right

Open Mar-Nov (rs mid Sep reseeding the site)

Last arrival 21.00hrs Last departure 10.00hrs

An ideal family site, positioned on a gently sloping cliff with grassy pitches and glorious sea views, which are best enjoyed from the terraced premier pitches, or over lunch or dinner at the Café India adjacent to the reception overlooking the beach. There is direct, gated access to the beach, where surfing is very popular, and the park has a holiday bungalow for rent. The local amenities of the village are only a few hundred yards away. 10 acre site. 100 touring pitches. Caravan pitches. Motorhome pitches. Tent pitches.

AA Pubs & Restaurants nearby: Restaurant Nathan Outlaw, ROCK, PL27 6LA, 01208 863394

Facilities: ⚙⊙⌒✳⚙⊙⛽📶 ♻ 𝟢

Services: ⚙⚙🔋⚙🚽🍴📺

Within 3 miles: ⚓♨🇭♿⊙⚓♿⊙

Notes: No ball games, no disposable BBQs, no noise between 23.00hrs-07.00hrs. Dogs must be kept on leads. Surf equipment hire.

see advert on page 92

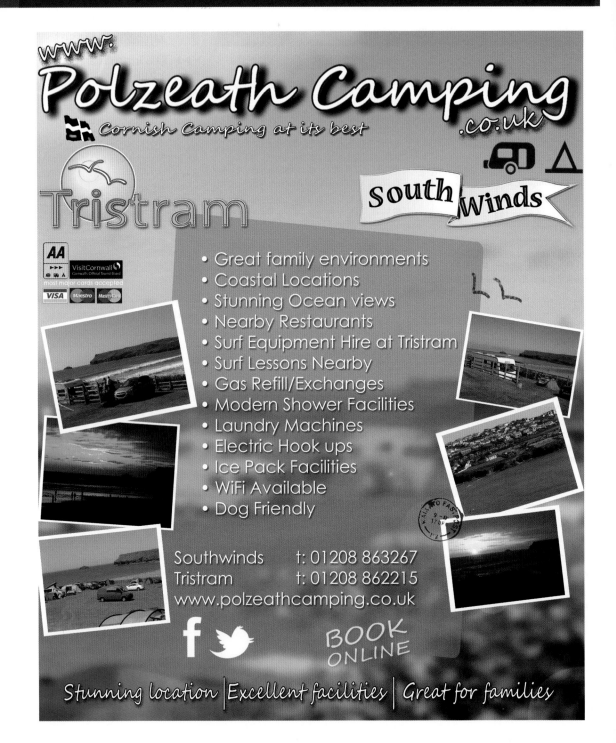

LEISURE: 🏊 Indoor swimming pool 🏊 Outdoor swimming pool 🛝 Children's playground 🖐 Kid's club 🎾 Tennis court 🎱 Games room 📺 Separate TV room
⛳ 9/18 hole golf course ⛵ Boats for hire 🎬 Cinema 🎵 Entertainment 🎣 Fishing ⛳ Mini golf 🏄 Watersports 💪 Gym ✪ Sports field Spa ♨ Stables
FACILITIES: 🛁 Bath 🚿 Shower ⊙ Electric shaver 💈 Hairdryer ❄ Ice Pack Facility ♿ Disabled facilities 📞 Public telephone 🛒 Shop on site or within 200yds
🏪 Mobile shop (calls at least 5 days a week) 🍴 BBQ area 🌲 Picnic area WiFi Wi-fi 💻 Internet access ♻ Recycling 🛈 Tourist info 🐕 Dog exercise area

PORTHTOWAN
Map 2 SW64

►► ►► **94%**
Porthtowan Tourist Park
(SW693473)

Mile Hill TR4 8TY
☎ **01209 890256**
e-mail: admin@porthtowantouristpark.co.uk
web: www.porthtowantouristpark.co.uk
dir: *Exit A30 at junct signed Redruth/Porthtowan. Take 3rd exit at rdbt. 2m, right at T-junct. Site on left at top of hill*

* ◘ £10-£18 ◘ £10-£18 ▲ £10-£18

Open Apr-Sep

Last arrival 21.30hrs Last departure 11.00hrs

A neat, level grassy site on high ground above Porthtowan, with plenty of shelter from mature trees and shrubs. The superb toilet facilities considerably enhance the appeal of this peaceful rural park, which is almost midway between the small seaside resorts of Portreath and Porthtowan, with their beaches and surfing. There is a purpose-built games/meeting room with a good library where tourist information leaflets are available. 5 acre site. 80 touring pitches. 11 hardstandings. 8 seasonal pitches. Caravan pitches. Motorhome pitches. Tent pitches.

AA Pubs & Restaurants nearby: Driftwood Spars, ST AGNES, TR5 0RT, 01872 552428

Leisure: ⚠ ☺ ♦
Facilities: ⛫ ☺ ⌷ ✻ ♿ ☺ 🔊 ⌂ ⛺ ᴡᴵ-ʜ ♻ ❼
Services: ◘ ⓢ ⌷ ⌀ ⊤ ⛟
Within 3 miles: ↓日 ⚓ ⚲ ⓢ ⓢ ⓢ ∪

Notes: No bikes or skateboards in Jul & Aug. Dogs must be kept on leads.

AA CAMPING CARD SITE

► ►► ► **72% Wheal Rose Caravan & Camping Park** *(SW717449)*

Wheal Rose TR16 5DD
☎ **01209 891496**
e-mail: whealrose@aol.com
dir: *Exit A30 at Scorrier sign, follow signs to Wheal Rose. Site 0.5m on left (Wheal Rose to Porthtowan road)*

* ◘ £14-£18 ◘ £14-£18 ▲ £14-£18

Open Mar-Dec

Last arrival 21.00hrs Last departure 11.00hrs

A quiet, peaceful park in a secluded valley setting, which is well placed for visiting both the lovely countryside and the surfing beaches of Porthtowan (two miles away). The friendly owners work hard to keep this park in immaculate condition, with a bright toilet block and well-trimmed pitches. There is a swimming pool and a games room. 6 acre site. 50 touring pitches. 6 hardstandings. Caravan pitches. Motorhome pitches. Tent pitches. 3 statics.

AA Pubs & Restaurants nearby: Basset Arms, PORTREATH, TR16 4NG, 01209 842077

Leisure: ⚐ ⚠ ☺ ♦
Facilities: ⛫ ☺ ⌷ ✻ ♿ ☺ 🔊 ⌂ ᴡᴵ-ʜ ▭ ♻ ❼
Services: ◘ ⓢ ⌷ ⌀ ⊤ ⛟
Within 3 miles: ↓日 ⚲ ⚓ ⓢ ⓢ ∪

Notes: 5mph speed limit, minimum noise after 23.00hrs, gates locked 23.00hrs. Dogs must be kept on leads.

PORTREATH
Map 2 SW64

Places to visit
East Pool Mine, POOL, TR15 3NP, 01209 315027
www.nationaltrust.org.uk

AA CAMPING CARD SITE

► ►► ► **84% Tehidy Holiday Park** *(SW682432)*

Harris Mill, Illogan TR16 4JQ
☎ **01209 216489**
e-mail: holiday@tehidy.co.uk
web: www.tehidy.co.uk
dir: *Exit A30 at Redruth/Portreath junct onto A3047 to 1st rdbt. Left onto B3300. At junct straight over signed Tehidy Holiday Park. Past Cornish Arms pub, site 800yds at bottom of hill on left*

* ◘ £12-£21 ◘ £12-£21 ▲ £12-£21

Open all year (rs Nov-Mar part of shower block & shop closed)

Last arrival 20.00hrs Last departure 10.00hrs

An attractive wooded location in a quiet rural area only two and a half miles from popular beaches. Mostly level pitches on tiered ground, and the toilet facilities are bright and modern. Holiday static caravans for hire. 4.5 acre site. 18 touring pitches. 11 hardstandings. 4 seasonal pitches. Caravan pitches. Motorhome pitches. Tent pitches. 32 statics. 2 wooden pods.

AA Pubs & Restaurants nearby: Basset Arms, PORTREATH, TR16 4NG, 01209 842077

Leisure: ⚠ ☺ ♦ ⊐
Facilities: ⛫ ☺ ⌷ ✻ ♿ ☺ 🔊 ⌂ ᴡᴵ-ʜ ♻ ❼
Services: ◘ ⓢ ⌀ ⊤ ⛟ ⛟
Within 3 miles: ↓ ‡ 日 ⚲ ⊚ ⓢ ⓢ ⓢ ∪

Notes: No pets, no noise after 23.00hrs. Trampoline, off-licence, cooking shelter.

see advert on page 85

SERVICES: ◘ Electric hook up ⓢ Launderette ⓟ Licensed bar ⌷ Calor Gas ⌀ Camping Gaz ⊤ Toilet fluid ⓘⓞⓘ Café/Restaurant ⛟ Fast Food/Takeaway ⛟ Battery charging ⛟ Baby care ⛟ Motorvan service point **ABBREVIATIONS:** ⌇ BH/bank hols-bank holidays Etr-Easter Spring BH-Spring Bank Holiday dep-departure fr-from hrs-hours m-mile mdnt-midnight rdbt-roundabout rs-restricted service wk-week wknd-weekend x-rds-cross roads ⊗ No credit cards ⊗ No dogs ⛟ Children of all ages accepted See page 9 for details of the AA Camping Card Scheme

PORTSCATHO — Map 2 SW83

Places to visit

St Mawes Castle, ST MAWES, TR2 3AA, 01326 270526 www.english-heritage.org.uk/daysout/properties/st-mawes-castle

Trelissick Garden, TRELISSICK GARDEN, TR3 6QL, 01872 862090 www.nationaltrust.org.uk/trelissick

▶▶▶ 80% Trewince Farm Touring Park (SW868339)

TR2 5ET
☎ 01872 580430
e-mail: info@trewincefarm.co.uk
dir: *From St Austell take A390 towards Truro. Left on B3287 to Tregony, following signs to St Mawes. At Trewithian, turn left to St Anthony. Site 0.75m past church*

Open May-Sep

Last arrival 23.00hrs Last departure 11.00hrs

A site on a working farm with spectacular sea views from its elevated position. There are many quiet golden sandy beaches close by, and boat launching facilities and mooring can be arranged at the nearby Percuil River Boatyard. The village of Portscatho with shops and pubs and attractive harbour is approximately one mile away. 3 acre site. 25 touring pitches. Caravan pitches. Motorhome pitches. Tent pitches.

AA Pubs & Restaurants nearby: The New Inn, VERYAN, TR2 5QA, 01872 501362

The Quarterdeck at the Nare, VERYAN, TR2 5PF, 01872 500000

Facilities: ⬚⬚⬚⬚⬚⬚⬚⬚
Services: ⬚⬚⬚⬚
Within 3 miles: ⬚⬚⬚⬚
Notes: Dogs must be kept on leads.

REDRUTH — Map 2 SW64

Places to visit

East Pool Mine, POOL, TR15 3NP, 01209 315027 www.nationaltrust.org.uk

Pendennis Castle, FALMOUTH, TR11 4LP, 01326 316594 www.english-heritage.org.uk/daysout/properties/pendennis-castle

Great for kids: National Maritime Museum Cornwall, FALMOUTH, TR11 3QY, 01326 313388 www.nmmc.co.uk

PREMIER PARK

▶▶▶▶▶ 86% Globe Vale Holiday Park (SW708447)

Radnor TR16 4BH
☎ 01209 891183
e-mail: info@globevale.co.uk
dir: *A30 take Redruth/Porthtowan exit then Portreath/North Country exit from rdbt, right at x-rds into Radnor Rd, left after 0.5m, site on left after 0.5m*

* ⬚ £13-£24 ⬚ £13-£24 Å £13-£24

Open all year

Last arrival 20.00hrs Last departure 10.00hrs

A family owned and run park set in a quiet rural location yet close to some stunning beaches and coastline. The park's touring area has a number of full facility hardstanding pitches, a high quality toilet block, a comfortable lounge bar serving bar meals, and holiday static caravans. 13 acre site. 138 touring pitches. 19 hardstandings. Caravan pitches. Motorhome pitches. Tent pitches. 10 statics.

AA Pubs & Restaurants nearby: Basset Arms, PORTREATH, TR16 4NG, 01209 842077

Leisure: ⬚⬚
Facilities: ⬚⬚⬚⬚⬚⬚⬚⬚
Services: ⬚⬚⬚⬚⬚⬚⬚⬚⬚⬚
Within 3 miles: ⬚⬚⬚⬚⬚
Notes: Dogs must be kept on leads. Shower block heated in winter.

see advert on page 85

▶▶▶▶ 80% Lanyon Holiday Park (SW684387)

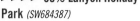

Loscombe Ln, Four Lanes TR16 6LP
☎ 01209 313474
e-mail: info@lanyonholidaypark.co.uk
dir: *Signed 0.5m off B2397 on Helston side of Four Lanes village*

* ⬚ £10-£24 ⬚ £10-£24 Å £10-£24

Open Mar-Oct

Last arrival 21.00hrs Last departure noon

Small, friendly rural park in an elevated position with fine views to distant St Ives Bay. This family owned and run park continues to be upgraded in all areas, and is close to a cycling trail. There is a well-stocked bar and a very inviting swimming pool. Stithians Reservoir for fishing, sailing and windsurfing is two miles away. Two holiday cottages are available. 14 acre site. 25 touring pitches. Caravan pitches. Motorhome pitches. Tent pitches. 49 statics.

AA Pubs & Restaurants nearby: Basset Arms, PORTREATH, TR16 4NG, 01209 842077

Leisure: ⬚⬚⬚⬚⬚
Facilities: ⬚⬚⬚⬚⬚⬚⬚⬚⬚⬚⬚⬚
Services: ⬚⬚⬚⬚⬚⬚
Within 3 miles: ⬚⬚⬚⬚⬚⬚⬚⬚⬚
Notes: Families only. Take-away service, all-day games room.

see advert on page 83

▶▶▶ 79% Cambrose Touring Park (SW684453)

Portreath Rd TR16 4HT
☎ 01209 890747
e-mail: cambrosetouringpark@supanet.com
dir: *A30 onto B3300 towards Portreath. Approx 0.75m at 1st rdbt right onto B3300. Take unclassified road on right signed Porthtowan. Site 200yds on left*

* ⬚ £10-£17.50 ⬚ £10-£17.50 Å £10-£17.50

Open Apr-Oct

Last arrival 22.00hrs Last departure 11.30hrs

Situated in a rural setting surrounded by trees and shrubs, this park is divided into grassy paddocks. It is about two miles from the harbour village of Portreath. The site has an excellent swimming pool with a sun bathing area. 6 acre site. 60 touring pitches. Caravan pitches. Motorhome pitches. Tent pitches.

LEISURE: 🏊 Indoor swimming pool 🏊 Outdoor swimming pool 🎠 Children's playground 🎯 Kid's club 🎾 Tennis court 🎱 Games room 📺 Separate TV room ⛳ 9/18 hole golf course 🚣 Boats for hire 🎬 Cinema 🎵 Entertainment 🎣 Fishing ⛳ Mini golf 🏄 Watersports 💪 Gym 🏟 Sports field ♨ Spa ♻ Stables
FACILITIES: 🛁 Bath 🚿 Shower ⚡ Electric shaver 💇 Hairdryer ❄ Ice Pack Facility ♿ Disabled facilities 📞 Public telephone 🏪 Shop on site or within 200yds 🚐 Mobile shop (calls at least 5 days a week) 🍖 BBQ area 🍽 Picnic area 📶 Wi-fi 💻 Internet access ♻ Recycling ℹ Tourist info 🐕 Dog exercise area

AA Pubs & Restaurants nearby: Basset Arms, PORTREATH, TR16 4NG, 01209 842077

Leisure: 🚣 /🛝 😊 🎣

Facilities: 🏪 ⊙ 🍴 ※ ⚿ 🕒 🗑 🚻 📶 ▤ ♻ 🛈

Services: 🔌 🗑 ▣ 🍴 T 🚮 🐾

Within 3 miles: ⅃ 🎡 🔗 ◎ 🖢 🎱 🛒 U

Notes: No noise after 23.30hrs. Dogs must be kept on leads. Mini football pitch.

AA CAMPING CARD SITE

►►► 73% Stithians Lake Country Park *(SW705369)*

Stithians Lake, Menherion TR16 6NW
☎ **01209 860301**
e-mail: stithianswatersports@swlakestrust.org.uk
dir: *From Redruth take B3297 towards Helston. Follow brown tourist signs to Stithians Lake, entrance by Golden Lion Inn*

* 🚐 £13-£20 🚛 £13-£20 ▲ £13-£20

Open all year

Last arrival 17.30hrs Last departure noon

This simple campsite is a two-acre field situated adjacent to the Watersports Centre, which forms part of a large activity complex beside Stithians Lake. Campers are required to use the functional toilet and shower facilities at the centre, and there is an excellent waterside café that also serves breakfasts. This is the perfect campsite for watersport enthusiasts. 2.1 acre site. 40 touring pitches. Caravan pitches. Motorhome pitches. Tent pitches.

AA Pubs & Restaurants nearby: Basset Arms, PORTREATH, TR16 4NG, 01209 842077

Leisure: /🛝

Facilities: 🏪 ※ ⚿ 🗑 📶 ♻ 🛈

Services: 🔌 🗑 🍴

Within 3 miles: 🎡 🔗 🖢 🎱 🛒 U

Notes: Dogs must be kept on leads.

REJERRAH Map 2 SW75

Places to visit

Trerice, TRERICE, TR8 4PG, 01637 875404 www.nationaltrust.org.uk

Blue Reef Aquarium, NEWQUAY, TR7 1DU, 01637 878134 www.bluereefaquarium.co.uk

Great for kids: Newquay Zoo, NEWQUAY, TR7 2LZ, 0844 474 2244 www.newquayzoo.org.uk

PREMIER PARK

►►►►► 87% Newperran Holiday Park *(SW801555)*

TR8 5QJ
☎ **01872 572407**
e-mail: holidays@newperran.co.uk
dir: *4m SE of Newquay & 1m S of Rejerrah on A3075. Or A30 (Redruth), exit B3275 Perranporth, at 1st T-junct right onto A3075 towards Newquay, site 300mtrs on left*

🚐 🚛 ▲

Open Etr-Oct

Last arrival mdnt Last departure 10.00hrs

A family site in a lovely rural position near several beaches and bays. This airy park offers screening to some pitches, which are set in paddocks on level ground. High season entertainment is available in the park's high quality country inn, and the café has an extensive menu. There is also a swimming pool with a separate toddlers' paddling area. 25 acre site. 357 touring pitches. 20 hardstandings. Caravan pitches. Motorhome pitches. Tent pitches. 16 statics.

AA Pubs & Restaurants nearby: The Smugglers' Den Inn, CUBERT, TR8 5PY, 01637 830209

Leisure: 🏊 /🛝 😊 🎣 🎵

Facilities: 🏪 ⊙ 🍴 ※ ⚿ 🕒 🗑 🚻 📶 ♻ 🛈

Services: 🔌 🗑 🍴 ▣ 🍴 ⊘ T 🍴 🚮 🍔 🛒

Within 3 miles: ⅃ 🎡 🔗 ◎ 🖢 🎱 🛒 U

Notes: Families & couples only. Dogs must be kept on leads.

see advert on page 83

ROSUDGEON Map 2 SW52

Places to visit

Trengwainton Garden, PENZANCE, TR20 8RZ, 01736 363148 www.nationaltrust.org.uk/trengwainton

Goonhilly Satellite Earth Station Experience, HELSTON, TR12 6LQ, 0800 679593 www.goonhilly.bt.com

Great for kids: The Flambards Theme Park, HELSTON, TR13 0QA, 01326 573404 www.flambards.co.uk

►►►► 87% Kenneggy Cove Holiday Park *(SW562287)*

Higher Kenneggy TR20 9AU
☎ **01736 763453**
e-mail: enquiries@kenneggycove.co.uk
web: www.kenneggycove.co.uk
dir: *On A394 between Penzance & Helston, turn S into signed lane to site & Higher Kenneggy*

* 🚐 £17-£26 🚛 £17-£26 ▲ £17-£26

Open 12 May-Sep

Last arrival 21.00hrs Last departure 11.00hrs

Set in an Area of Outstanding Natural Beauty with spectacular sea views, this family-owned park is quiet and well kept, with a well-equipped children's play area, superb toilets, and a takeaway food facility offering home-cooked meals. A short walk along a country footpath leads to the Cornish Coastal Path, and on to the golden sandy beach at Kenneggy Cove. It's a half mile walk to the main road to pick up the local bus which goes to Penzance or Helston, with many pretty Cornish coves en route. There is a fish and chip shop and Chinese restaurant with takeaway a short drive away. 4 acre site. 45 touring pitches. Caravan pitches. Motorhome pitches. Tent pitches. 7 statics.

continued

ROSUDGEON *continued*

AA Pubs & Restaurants nearby: The Victoria Inn, PERRANUTHNOE, TR20 9NP, 01736 710309

The Ship Inn, PORTHLEVEN, TR13 9JS, 01326 564204

Leisure: ⋀ ⊕

Facilities: ↾ ⊙ ⌦ ✳ ⑤ 🚾 ♻ ❶

Services: 🔌 ⑤ 🔨 ⬛ ∅ T ➜ ⬇

Within 3 miles: ↓ ⬦ ⋆ ℓ ⬦ ⑤ ⑤ ∪

Notes: ⊛ No large groups, no noise after 22.00hrs. Dogs must be kept on leads. Fresh bakery items, breakfasts.

RUMFORD   Map 2 SW87

Places to visit

Prideaux Place, PADSTOW, PL28 8RP, 01841 532411 www.prideauxplace.co.uk

---

▶▶▶ **80% Music Water Touring Park**
(SW906685)

PL27 7SJ
☎ **01841 540257**
dir: *A39 at Winnards Perch rdbt onto B3274 signed Padstow. Left in 2m onto unclassified road signed Rumford & St Eval. Site 500mtrs on right*

🚐 £11-£16 ⛺ £11-£16 ▲ £11-£16

Open Apr-Oct

Last arrival 23.00hrs Last departure 10.30hrs

Set in a peaceful location yet only a short drive to the pretty fishing town of Padstow, and many sandy beaches and coves. This family owned and run park has grassy paddocks, and there is a quiet lounge bar and a separate children's games room. 8 acre site. 55 touring pitches. 2 hardstandings. Caravan pitches. Motorhome pitches. Tent pitches. 2 statics.

AA Pubs & Restaurants nearby: The Seafood Restaurant, PADSTOW, PL28 8BY, 01841 532700

Leisure: ⬟ ⋀ ⬤

Facilities: ↾ ⊙ ⌦ ✳ ⤒ ✈ ♻ ❶

Services: 🔌 ⑤ 🍴 🔨 ∅ ♻

Within 3 miles: ☰ ℓ ⬦ ⑤ ⑤ ∪

Notes: ⊛ One tent per pitch, maximum 2 dogs per pitch. Dogs must be kept on leads. Pets' corner (ponies, chickens).

RUTHERNBRIDGE   Map 2 SX06

Places to visit

Prideaux Place, PADSTOW, PL28 8RP, 01841 532411 www.prideauxplace.co.uk

Cornwall's Regimental Museum, BODMIN, PL31 1EG, 01208 72810

Great for kids: Pencarrow, BODMIN, PL30 3AG, 01208 841369 www.pencarrow.co.uk

---

▶▶▶ **79% Ruthern Valley Holidays** *(SX014665)*

GOLD

PL30 5LU
☎ **01208 831395**
e-mail: camping@ruthernvalley.com
web: www.ruthernvalley.com
dir: *A389 through Bodmin, follow St Austell signs, then Lanivet signs. At top of hill right onto unclassified road signed Ruthernbridge. Follow signs*

* 🚐 £16-£20 ⛺ £16-£20 ▲ £12.50-£17

Open all year

Last arrival 20.30hrs Last departure noon

An attractive woodland site peacefully located in a small river valley west of Bodmin Moor. This away-from-it-all park is ideal for those wanting a quiet holiday, and the informal pitches are spread in four natural areas, with plenty of sheltered space. There are also 12 lodges, heated wooden wigwams, camping pods, and static holiday vans for hire. 7.5 acre site. 26 touring pitches. 2 hardstandings. Caravan pitches. Motorhome pitches. Tent pitches. 3 statics. 3 tipis. 3 wooden pods.

AA Pubs & Restaurants nearby: The Swan Hotel, WADEBRIDGE, PL27 7DD, 01208 812526

Trehellas House Hotel & Restaurant, BODMIN, PL30 3AD, 01208 72700

Leisure: ⋀

Facilities: ↾ ⊙ ✳ ⊙ ⑤ ✈ 🚾 ▭ ❶

Services: 🔌 ⑤ ∅ T ➜

Within 3 miles: ↓ ℓ ⑤ ⑤ ∪

Notes: ⊘ No noise 22.30hrs-07.00hrs, no fires. Woodland area, farm animals.

ST AGNES   Map 2 SW75

Places to visit

Royal Cornwall Museum, TRURO, TR1 2SJ, 01872 272205 www.royalcornwallmuseum.org.uk

Trerice, TRERICE, TR8 4PG, 01637 875404 www.nationaltrust.org.uk

---

AA CAMPING CARD SITE

▶▶▶▶ **79% Beacon Cottage Farm Touring Park** *(SW705502)*

Beacon Dr TR5 0NU
☎ **01872 552347 & 07879 413862**
e-mail: beaconcottagefarm@lineone.net
web: www.beaconcottagefarmholidays.co.uk
dir: *From A30 at Threeburrows rdbt take B3277 to St Agnes, left into Goonvrea Rd, right into Beacon Drive, follow brown sign to site*

🚐 £17-£23 ⛺ £17-£23 ▲ £17-£23

Open Apr-Oct

Last arrival 20.00hrs Last departure noon

A neat and compact site on a working farm, utilizing a cottage and outhouses, an old orchard and adjoining walled paddock. The unique location on a headland looking north-east along the coast comes with stunning views towards St Ives, and the keen friendly family owners keep all areas very well maintained. 5 acre site. 70 touring pitches. 2 seasonal pitches. Caravan pitches. Motorhome pitches. Tent pitches.

AA Pubs & Restaurants nearby: Driftwood Spars, ST AGNES, TR5 0RT, 01872 552428

Leisure: ⋀ ⊕

Facilities: ↾ ⊙ ⌦ ✳ ⑤ ▭ ✈ 🚾 ♻ ❶

Services: 🔌 ⑤ ∅ ➜ ⬇

Within 3 miles: ↓ ⬦ ℓ ⊙ ⬦ ⑤ ⑤ ∪

Notes: No large groups. Dogs must be kept on leads. Secure year-round caravan storage.

▶▶▶ **82% Presingoll Farm Caravan & Camping Park** *(SW721494)*

TR5 0PB
☎ **01872 552333**
e-mail: pam@presingollfarm.co.uk
dir: *From A30 Chiverton rdbt take B3277 towards St Agnes. Site 3m on right*

* 🚐 fr £14 ⛺ fr £14 ▲ fr £14

Presingoll Farm Caravan & Camping Park

Open Etr & Apr-Oct

Last departure 10.00hrs

An attractive rural park adjoining farmland, with extensive views of the coast beyond. Family owned and run, with level grass pitches, and a modernised toilet block in smart converted farm buildings. There is also a campers' room with microwave, freezer, kettle and free coffee and tea, and a children's play area. This is an ideal base for touring the Newquay and St Ives areas. 5 acre site. 90 touring pitches. 6 hardstandings. Caravan pitches. Motorhome pitches. Tent pitches.

AA Pubs & Restaurants nearby: Driftwood Spars, ST AGNES, TR5 0RT, 01872 552428

Leisure: ⚲

Facilities: ⚲⊙☔︎❉⚲☉⚲⚲⚲♲ ❶

Services: ⚲⚲⚲ **Within 3 miles:** ⚲⚲⚲

Notes: ⊗ No large groups. Dogs must be kept on leads.

ST ALLEN   Map 2 SW85

Places to visit

Royal Cornwall Museum, TRURO, TR1 2SJ, 01872 272205
www.royalcornwallmuseum.org.uk

Trerice, TRERICE, TR8 4PG, 01637 875404
www.nationaltrust.org.uk

Great for kids: Dairy Land Farm World, NEWQUAY, TR8 5AA, 01872 510246
www.dairylandfarmworld.com

►►► 82% Tolcarne Campsite

(SW826513)

Tolcarne Bungalow TR4 9QX
☎ 01872 540652 & 07881 965477
e-mail: dianemcd@talktalk.net
dir: *A30 towards Redruth. Approx 1m W of Carland Cross rdbt 2nd left to St Allen. 1m, 3rd left to site*

⚲⚲⚲

Open all year

Last arrival 22.00hrs Last departure noon

A rural site with fantastic countryside views from the terraced pitches. Expect level, beautifully mown pitches and a spotlessly clean and purpose-built facilities block with bathrooms and a fully-equipped laundry room. Tenters have use of a campers' kitchen. 1 acre site. 10 touring pitches. 5 seasonal pitches. Caravan pitches. Motorhome pitches. Tent pitches.

AA Pubs & Restaurants nearby: The Plume of Feathers, MITCHELL, TR8 5AX, 01872 510387

Facilities: ⚲⊙❉⚲☉⚲⚲ ❶

Services: ⚲⚲⚲

Within 3 miles: ⚲⚲⚲

Notes: ⊗ No noise after 22.30hrs. Dogs must be kept on leads.

ST AUSTELL   Map 2 SX05

See also Carlyon Bay

Places to visit

Charlestown Shipwreck & Heritage Centre, ST AUSTELL, PL25 3NJ, 01726 69897
www.shipwreckcharlestown.com

Eden Project, ST AUSTELL, PL24 2SG, 01726 811911 www.edenproject.com

Great for kids: Wheal Martyn Museum & Country Park, ST AUSTELL, PL26 8XG, 01726 850362 www.wheal-martyn.com

PREMIER PARK

►►►►► 84% River Valley Holiday Park *(SX010503)*

London Apprentice PL26 7AP
☎ 01726 73533
e-mail: mail@cornwall-holidays.co.uk
web: www.rivervalleyholidaypark.co.uk
dir: *Take B3273 from St Austell to London Apprentice. Site signed, direct access to site from B3273*

* ⚲ £13-£32 ⚲ £13-£32 ⚲ £13-£32

River Valley Holiday Park

Open Apr-end Sep

Last arrival 21.00hrs Last departure 11.00hrs

A neat, well-maintained family-run park set in a pleasant river valley. The quality toilet block and attractively landscaped grounds make this a delightful base for a holiday. All pitches are hardstanding, mostly divided by low fencing and neatly trimmed hedges, and the park offers a good range of leisure facilities, including an inviting swimming pool, a games room, an internet room, and an excellent children's play area. There is direct access to river walks and an off-road cycle trail to the beach at Pentewan. The site is on the bus route to St Austell. 2 acre site. 45 touring pitches. 45 hardstandings. Caravan pitches. Motorhome pitches. Tent pitches. 40 statics.

AA Pubs & Restaurants nearby: Austells, ST AUSTELL, PL25 3PH, 01726 813888

Leisure: ⚲⚲⚲

Facilities: ⚲⊙☔︎❉⚲☉⚲⚲⚲⚲ ♲ ❶

Services: ⚲⚲

Within 3 miles: ⚲⚲⚲⚲⚲⚲⚲⚲

Notes: Dogs must be kept on leads.

see advert on page 98

SERVICES: ⚲ Electric hook up ⚲ Launderette ⚲ Licensed bar ⚲ Calor Gas ⚲ Camping Gaz ⚲ Toilet fluid ⚲ Café/Restaurant ⚲ Fast Food/Takeaway ⚲ Battery charging ⚲ Baby care ⚲ Motorvan service point **ABBREVIATIONS:** BH/bank hols-bank holidays Etr-Easter Spring BH-Spring Bank Holiday dep-departure fr-from hrs-hours m-mile mdnt-midnight rdbt-roundabout rs-restricted service wk-week wknd-weekend x-rds-cross roads ⊗ No credit cards ⊗ No dogs ⚲ Children of all ages accepted See page 9 for details of the AA Camping Card Scheme

ST AUSTELL *continued*

AA CAMPING CARD SITE

▶▶▶▶ 81% Meadow Lakes *(SW966485)*

Hewas Water PL26 7JG

☎ 01726 882540

e-mail: info@meadow-lakes.co.uk

web: www.meadow-lakes.co.uk

dir: *From A390 4m SW of St Austell onto B3287, Tregony. 1m, site on left*

* ⊞ £8-£26.50 ⇌ £8-£26.50 ▲ £8-£26.50

Open mid Mar-end Oct

Last arrival 20.00hrs

Set in a quiet rural area, this extensive park is divided into paddocks with mature hedges and trees, and has its own coarse fishing lakes. This friendly, family park has enthusiastic and hands-on owners - all facilities are immaculate and spotlessly clean. The park offers organised indoor and outdoor activities for children in the summer holidays (there is a play barn for when the weather is unsuitable for using the two outdoor play areas), and at other times caters for adult breaks. There are animals in pens which children can enter. Self-catering lodges, static caravans and nine bungalows are also found at this site. The bus to Truro and St Austell stops within half a mile of the site. 56 acre site. 200 touring pitches. 11 hardstandings. 30 seasonal pitches. Caravan pitches. Motorhome pitches. Tent pitches. 35 statics. 4 wooden pods.

AA Pubs & Restaurants nearby: Austells, ST AUSTELL, PL25 3PH, 01726 813888

Leisure: ⇌ ⋔ ⚽ ☺ ⚲ ⬜

Facilities: ⊯ ⋔ ☞ ✳ ⚅ 🖫 🛦 ⛱ 🛏 Wi-Fi 🖥 ♻ 🛈

Services: 🖲 🛢 🔒 ⬛

Within 3 miles: ⌿ ✈ ☷ ℓ ⚓ 🛢 🛢 U

Notes: Dogs must be kept on leads. Table tennis, tots' TV room.

▶▶▶ 78% Court Farm Holidays

(SW953524)

St Stephen PL26 7LE

☎ 01726 823684

e-mail: info@courtfarmcornwall.co.uk

dir: *From St Austell take A3058 towards Newquay. Through St Stephen (pass Peugeot garage). Right at St Stephen/Coombe Hay/Langreth/Industrial site sign. 400yds, site on right*

* ⊞ £11-£21.50 ⇌ £11-£21.50 ▲ £8-£18

Open Apr-Sep

Last arrival by dark Last departure 11.00hrs

Set in a peaceful rural location, this large camping field offers plenty of space, and is handy for the Eden Project and the Lost Gardens of Heligan. Coarse fishing, and star-gazing facilities at the Roseland Observatory are among the on-site attractions. It is a five-minute walk to a Co-op store, and also to the bus stop on the Newquay to St Austell route. 4 acre site. 20 touring pitches. 5 hardstandings. Caravan pitches. Motorhome pitches. Tent pitches.

AA Pubs & Restaurants nearby: Austells, ST AUSTELL, PL25 3PH, 01726 813888

Leisure: ⋔

Facilities: ⋔ ☺ ✳ ⛱ 🛏 Wi-Fi

Services: 🖲 🛒

Within 3 miles: ⌿ ☷ ℓ 🛢 🛢 U

Notes: No noise after dark. Astronomy lectures.

ST BLAZEY GATE   Map 2 SX05

Places to visit

Eden Project, ST AUSTELL, PL24 2SG, 01726 811911 www.edenproject.com

St Catherine's Castle, FOWEY, 0870 333 1181 www.english-heritage.org.uk/daysout/properties/st-catherines-castle

Great for kids: Wheal Martyn Museum & Country Park, ST AUSTELL, PL26 8XG, 01726 850362 www.wheal-martyn.com

▶▶▶ 84% Doubletrees Farm

(SX060540)

Luxulyan Rd PL24 2EH

☎ 01726 812266

e-mail: doubletrees@eids.co.uk

dir: *On A390 at Blazey Gate. Turn by Leek Seed Chapel, almost opposite BP filling station. After approx 300yds turn right by public bench into site*

* ⊞ £15 ⇌ £15 ▲ £15

Open all year

Last arrival 22.30hrs Last departure 11.30hrs

A popular park with terraced pitches offering superb sea and coastal views. Close to beaches, and the nearest park to the Eden Project (a

---

LEISURE: 🏊 Indoor swimming pool   ⇌ Outdoor swimming pool   ⋔ Children's playground   🙌 Kid's club   🎾 Tennis court   ⚲ Games room   ⬜ Separate TV room   ⌿ 9/18 hole golf course   ✈ Boats for hire   ☷ Cinema   ♫ Entertainment   ℓ Fishing   ☺ Mini golf   ⚓ Watersports   🏋 Gym   ☺ Sports field   Spa   U Stables

FACILITIES: ⊯ Bath   ⋔ Shower   ☺ Electric shaver   ☞ Hairdryer   ✳ Ice Pack Facility   ⚅ Disabled facilities   ☎ Public telephone   🖫 Shop on site or within 200yds   🛦 Mobile shop (calls at least 5 days a week)   ⛱ BBQ area   🛏 Picnic area   Wi-Fi Wi-fi   🖥 Internet access   ♻ Recycling   🛈 Tourist info   ⛱ Dog exercise area

20-minute walk), it is very well maintained by friendly owners. There is a Chinese restaurant, a fish and chip shop and bus stop in St Blazey Gate within 300 yards of the entrance. 1.57 acre site. 32 touring pitches. 6 hardstandings. Caravan pitches. Motorhome pitches. Tent pitches.

AA Pubs & Restaurants nearby: Austells, ST AUSTELL, PL25 3PH, 01726 813888

Facilities: 🅿️☉✳️👶🛁♿️🎾🚰

Services: 📧🗑️🔋

Within 3 miles: ⬇️🏇✎☉♨️🗑️🛒U

Notes: ⊗ No noise after mdnt. Dogs must be kept on leads.

ST BURYAN   Map 2 SW42

►►► 87% Treverven Touring Caravan & Camping Park (SW410237)

Treverven Farm TR19 6DL
☎ 01736 810200 & 810318
e-mail: info@treverventouringpark.co.uk
dir: A30 onto B3283 1.5m after St Buryan, left onto B3315. Site on right in 1m

🚐🚎🅰️

Open Etr-Oct

Last departure noon

Situated in a quiet Area of Outstanding Natural Beauty, with panoramic sea and country views, this family-owned site is located off a traffic-free lane leading directly to the coastal path. The toilet facilities are very good, and Treverven is ideally placed for exploring west Cornwall. There is an excellent takeaway facility on site. 6 acre site. 115 touring pitches. Caravan pitches. Motorhome pitches. Tent pitches.

AA Pubs & Restaurants nearby: The Old Success Inn, SENNEN, TR19 7DG, 01736 871232

Leisure: 🅰️

Facilities: 🅿️☉🅿️✳️👶🛁☉🛁🎾🚰📶♻️ℹ️

Services: 📧🗑️🔋🚿Ⓣ🍴🔋♻️

Within 3 miles: 🏇✎♨️🗑️🛒

Notes: No noise after 22.00hrs. Dogs must be kept on leads. Toaster & kettle available.

ST COLUMB MAJOR   Map 2 SW96

Places to visit

Prideaux Place, PADSTOW, PL28 8RP, 01841 532411 www.prideauxplace.co.uk

Cornwall's Regimental Museum, BODMIN, PL31 1EG, 01208 72810

Great for kids: Pencarrow, BODMIN, PL30 3AG, 01208 841369 www.pencarrow.co.uk

---

AA CAMPING CARD SITE

►►►► 79% Trewan Hall

(SW911646)

TR9 6DB
☎ 01637 880261 & 07900 677397
e-mail: enquiries@trewan-hall.co.uk
dir: From A39 N of St Columb Major (do not enter town) turn left signed Talskiddy & St Eval. Site 1m on left

* 🚐 £12-£19.60 🚎 £12-£19.60 🅰️ £12-£19.60

Open 11 May-17 Sep (rs Low season shop open shorter hours)

Last arrival 22.00hrs Last departure noon

Trewan Hall lies at the centre of a Cornish estate amid 36 acres of wooded grounds. The site's extensive amenities include an excellent new toilet block, extra hook-ups and improved security, plus a 25-metre swimming pool, and a free, live theatre in a stone barn throughout July and August. The campsite shop stocks everything from groceries to camping equipment. The site also has fine gardens, four acres of woods for dog walking and a field available for ball games. St Columb is just a short walk away. 14.27 acre site. 200 touring pitches. Caravan pitches. Motorhome pitches. Tent pitches.

AA Pubs & Restaurants nearby: The Falcon Inn, ST MAWGAN, TR8 4EP, 01637 860225

Leisure: 🛶🏊🅰️☉🎾🎵

Facilities: 🛏️🅿️☉🅿️✳️👶🛁🎾🚰📶♻️ℹ️

Services: 📧🗑️🔋🚿Ⓣ🔋♻️

Within 3 miles: ⬇️🏇☉♨️🗑️🛒U

Notes: Families & couples only. No cycling, no driving on fields from mdnt-08.00hrs, no noise after mdnt. Dogs must be kept on leads. Library, billiard room.

►►► 87% Southleigh Manor Naturist Park (SW918623)

TR9 6HY
☎ 01637 880938
e-mail: enquiries@southleigh-manor.com
dir: Exit A30 at junct with A39 signed Wadebridge. At Highgate Hill rdbt take A39. At Halloon rdbt take A39. At Trekenning rdbt take 4th exit signed RSPCA & Springfield Centre. Site 500mtrs on right

* 🚐 £17-£23.50 🚎 £17-£23.50 🅰️ £17-£23.50

Open Etr-Oct

Last arrival 20.00hrs Last departure 10.30hrs

A very well maintained, naturist park in the heart of the Cornish countryside, catering for families and couples only. Seclusion and security are very well planned, and the lovely gardens provide a calm setting. There are two lodges and static caravans for holiday hire. A bus stop at the entrance gate gives easy access to Newquay, Padstow or St Ives. 4 acre site. 50 touring pitches. Caravan pitches. Motorhome pitches. Tent pitches.

AA Pubs & Restaurants nearby: The Falcon Inn, ST MAWGAN, TR8 4EP, 01637 860225

Leisure: 🏊🅰️

Facilities: 🅿️☉🅿️✳️☉🎾🚰📶♻️ℹ️

Services: 📧🗑️🔋🚿🔋Ⓣ🍴🔋

Within 3 miles: ⬇️✎🗑️🛒U

Notes: ⊗ Dogs to remain beside pitch/caravan except when exercising off site. Sauna, spa bath, pool table, putting green.

SERVICES: 📧 Electric hook up 🗑️ Launderette 🍺 Licensed bar 🔋 Calor Gas ⊘ Camping Gaz Ⓣ Toilet fluid 🍴 Café/Restaurant 🔋 Fast Food/Takeaway 🔋 Battery charging 🚼 Baby care 🚐 Motorvan service point **ABBREVIATIONS:** BH/bank hols-bank holidays Etr-Easter Spring BH-Spring Bank Holiday dep-departure fr-from hrs-hours m-mile mdnt-midnight rdbt-roundabout rs-restricted service wk-week wknd-weekend x-rds-cross roads ⊗ No credit cards ⊗ No dogs 👶 Children of all ages accepted See page 9 for details of the AA Camping Card Scheme

ST GILES-ON-THE-HEATH

See Chapmans Well (Devon)

ST HILARY
Map 2 SW53

Places to visit

Godolphin House, GODOLPHIN CROSS, TR13 9RE, 01736 763194
www.nationaltrust.org.uk/godolphin

Great for kids: The Flambards Theme Park, HELSTON, TR13 0QA, 01326 573404
www.flambards.co.uk

AA CAMPING CARD SITE

►►►► 84% Wayfarers Caravan & Camping Park *(SW558314)*

Relubbus Ln TR20 9EF
☎ 01736 763326
e-mail: elaine@wayfarerspark.co.uk
dir: *Exit A30 onto A394 towards Helston. Left at rdbt onto B3280 after 2m. Site 1.5m on left on bend*

🚐 £19.50-£26 🚐 £19.50-£26 ▲ £17-£23

Open May-Sep

Last arrival 19.00hrs Last departure 11.00hrs

Located in the centre of St Hilary, two and half miles from St Michael's Mount, this is a quiet sheltered park in a peaceful rural setting. It offers spacious, well-drained pitches and very well cared for facilities. It has a separate car park for campers which makes the camping area safer. 4.8 acre site. 39 touring pitches. 25 hardstandings. Caravan pitches. Motorhome pitches. Tent pitches. 3 statics.

AA Pubs & Restaurants nearby: Godolphin Arms, MARAZION, TR17 0EN, 01736 710202

Facilities: 🏕️ 🕈 🇵 ✳️ 🕭 🔌 🖳 🛒 🔄 ❶
Services: 🔌 📶 🛢️ 🖎 🕭 ▣ 🗑️ 🛒
Within 3 miles: 🕃 ➕ 🎣 🔘 🏊 🏧 🗗 U
Notes: Adults only. 🐾 No pets.

►►► 77% Trevair Touring Park
(SW548326)

South Treveneague TR20 9BY
☎ 01736 740647
e-mail: info@trevairtouringpark.co.uk
dir: *A30 onto A394 signed Helston. 2m to rdbt, left onto B3280. Through Goldsithney. Left at brown site sign. Through 20mph zone to site, 1m on right*

🚐 🚐 ▲

Open Etr-Nov

Last arrival 22.00hrs Last departure 11.00hrs

Set in a rural location adjacent to woodland, this park is level and secluded, with grassy pitches. Marazion's beaches and the famous St Michael's Mount are just three miles away. The friendly owners live at the farmhouse on the park. 3.5 acre site. 40 touring pitches. Caravan pitches. Motorhome pitches. Tent pitches. 2 statics.

AA Pubs & Restaurants nearby: Godolphin Arms, MARAZION, TR17 0EN, 01736 710202

Facilities: 🏕️ 🕈 ☀️ 🔄 🔌 ❶
Services: 🔌 📶 🛒
Within 3 miles: 🕃 🔘 🏊 🗗 🗗 U
Notes: 🐾 No noise after 23.00hrs. Dogs must be kept on leads.

ST IVES

Places to visit

Barbara Hepworth Museum & Sculpture Garden, ST IVES, TR26 1AD, 01736 796226
www.tate.org.uk/stives

Tate St Ives, ST IVES, TR26 1TG, 01736 796226
www.tate.org.uk/stives

ST IVES
Map 2 SW54

ENGLAND AND OVERALL WINNER OF THE AA CAMPSITE OF THE YEAR 2014

PREMIER PARK

►►►►► 96% Polmanter Touring Park *(SW510388)*

Best of British

Halsetown TR26 3LX
☎ 01736 795640
e-mail: reception@polmanter.com
dir: *Signed from B3311 at Halsetown*

🚐 🚐 ▲

Open Spring BH-10 Sep (rs Spring BH shop, pool, bar & takeaway food closed, bus does not run)

Last arrival 21.00hrs Last departure 10.00hrs

A well-developed touring park on high ground, Polmanter is an excellent choice for family holidays and offers high quality in all areas, from the immaculate modern toilet blocks to the outdoor swimming pool and hard tennis courts. Pitches are individually marked and sited in meadows, and the park has been tastefully landscaped, which includes a field with full-facility hardstanding pitches to accommodate larger caravans and motorhomes. The fishing port and beaches of St Ives are just a mile and a half away, and there is a bus service in high season. 20 acre site. 270 touring pitches. 60 hardstandings. Caravan pitches. Motorhome pitches. Tent pitches.

AA Pubs & Restaurants nearby: The Tinners Arms, ZENNOR, TR26 3BY, 01736 796927

Leisure: 🏊 🎢 🎾 ⚽ 🎱
Facilities: 🏕️ 🕈 🇵 ✳️ 🕭 🔌 🖳 🛒 📶 🖳 🔄 ❶
Services: 🔌 📶 🔧 🛢️ 🖎 ▣ 🍴 🛒 🚿 🛒 🗑️
Within 3 miles: 🕃 ➕ 🗓️ 🎣 🔘 🏊 🏧 🗗 🗗 U
Notes: Family camping only. No skateboards, roller blades or heelys. Dogs must be kept on leads. Putting green.

see advert on page 84

LEISURE: 🏊 Indoor swimming pool 🏊 Outdoor swimming pool 🎢 Children's playground 🪁 Kid's club 🎾 Tennis court 🎱 Games room 🖵 Separate TV room 🏌️ 9/18 hole golf course 🚣 Boats for hire 🎬 Cinema 🎵 Entertainment 🎣 Fishing 🔘 Mini golf 🏄 Watersports 🏋️ Gym 🟢 Sports field **Spa** U Stables
FACILITIES: 🛁 Bath 🚿 Shower 🔌 Electric shaver 💨 Hairdryer ✳️ Ice Pack Facility 🕭 Disabled facilities 📶 Public telephone 🛒 Shop on site or within 200yds 🏪 Mobile shop (calls at least 5 days a week) 🍖 BBQ area 🛋️ Picnic area 📶 Wi-fi 🖳 Internet access 🔄 Recycling ❶ Tourist info 🐾 Dog exercise area

PREMIER PARK

►►►►► 86% Ayr Holiday Park *(SW509408)*

TR26 1EJ
☎ **01736 795855**
e-mail: recept@ayrholidaypark.co.uk
dir: *From A30 follow St Ives 'large vehicles' route via B3311 through Halsetown onto B3306. Site signed towards St Ives town centre*

* 🚐 £17-£35 🚏 £17-£35 🛖 £17-£35

Open all year
Last arrival 22.00hrs Last departure 10.00hrs

A well-established park on a cliff side overlooking St Ives Bay, with a heated toilet block that makes winter holidaying more attractive. There are stunning views from most pitches, and the town centre, harbour and beach are only half a mile away, with direct access to the coastal footpath. This makes an excellent base for surfing enthusiasts. Please note that it is advisable not to follow Sat Nav; use guide directions and avoid the town centre. 4 acre site. 40 touring pitches. 20 hardstandings. Caravan pitches. Motorhome pitches. Tent pitches.

AA Pubs & Restaurants nearby: The Watermill, ST IVES, TR27 6LQ, 01736 757912

Leisure: 🎦 🎣
Facilities: 🛁 🅿 ⊙ 🍽 ✳ ♿ 🕐 🗑 🛁 🐕 🅆🄸🄵🄸 💻 ♻ ❼
Services: 🔌 🛢 🏪 ⊘ 🔵 🅃 🚮 ⚡
Within 3 miles: 🚶 ⛳ 🎣 ◎ 🔥 🐘 🛒 ∪
Notes: No disposable BBQs. Dogs must be kept on leads.

►►►► 81% *Penderleath Caravan & Camping Park (SW496375)*

Towednack TR26 3AF
☎ **01736 798403 & 07840 208542**
e-mail: holidays@penderleath.co.uk
dir: *From A30 take A3074 towards St Ives. Left at 2nd mini-rdbt, approx 3m to T-junct. Left then immediately right. Next left*

🚐 🚏 🛖

Open Etr-Oct
Last arrival 21.30hrs Last departure 10.30hrs

Set in a rugged rural location, this tranquil park has extensive views towards St Ives Bay and the north coast. Facilities are all housed in modernised granite barns, and include spotless toilets with fully serviced shower rooms, and there's a quiet licensed bar with beer garden, a food takeaway, breakfast room and bar meals. The owners are welcoming and helpful. 10 acre site. 75 touring pitches. Caravan pitches. Motorhome pitches. Tent pitches.

AA Pubs & Restaurants nearby: The Watermill, ST IVES, TR27 6LQ, 01736 757912

Leisure: 🎦 🎣
Facilities: 🅿 ⊙ 🍽 ✳ ♿ 🕐 🗑 🐕 ♻ ❼
Services: 🔌 🛢 🏪 🍽 ⊘ 🅃 🍽 🚮 ⚡
Within 3 miles: 🚶 ⛳ 🎣 ◎ 🔥 🐘 🛒 ∪
Notes: No campfires, no noise after 23.00hrs, dogs must be well behaved. Dogs must be kept on leads. Bus to St Ives in high season.

►►►► 80% *Trevalgan Touring Park (SW490402)*

Trevalgan TR26 3BJ
☎ **01736 791892**
e-mail: reception@trevalgantouringpark.co.uk
dir: *From A30 follow holiday route to St Ives. B3311 through Halsetown to B3306. Left towards Land's End. Site signed 0.5m on right*

* 🚐 £19-£26 🚏 £19-£26 🛖 £19-£26

Open Spring BH-Sep
Last arrival 21.30hrs Last departure 11.00hrs

An open park next to a working farm in a rural area on the coastal road from St Ives to Zennor. The park is surrounded by mature hedges, but there are extensive views over the sea. There are very good toilet facilities including family rooms, and a large TV lounge and recreation room with drinks machine. There is a safari tent with tables and chairs so that campers can eat outside during inclement weather. 9 acre site. 120 touring pitches. Caravan pitches. Motorhome pitches. Tent pitches.

Notes: ⊗

►► 87% Balnoon Camping Site *(SW509382)*

Halsetown TR26 3JA
☎ **01736 795431 & 07751 600555**
e-mail: nat@balnoon.fsnet.co.uk
dir: *From A30 take A3074, at 2nd mini-rdbt 1st left signed Tate/St Ives. In 3m turn right after The Lodge at Balnoon*

* 🚐 £11.50-£15.50 🚏 £11.50-£15.50 🛖 £11.50-£15.50

Open Etr-Oct
Last arrival 20.00hrs Last departure 11.00hrs

Small, quiet and friendly, this sheltered site offers superb views of the adjacent rolling hills. The two paddocks are surrounded by mature hedges, and the toilet facilities are kept spotlessly clean. The beaches of Carbis Bay and St Ives are about two miles away. 1 acre site. 23 touring pitches. Caravan pitches. Motorhome pitches. Tent pitches.

AA Pubs & Restaurants nearby: The Tinners Arms, ZENNOR, TR26 3BY, 01736 796927

Facilities: 🅿 ⊙ 🍽 ✳ ♻
Services: 🔌 ⊘ 🅃 🍽
Within 3 miles: 🚶 ⛳ 🎣 ◎ 🔥 🐘 🛒 ∪
Notes: ⊗ No noise between 23.00hrs-07.30hrs. Dogs must be kept on leads. Provisions available to buy during peak season.

SERVICES: 🔌 Electric hook up 🛢 Launderette 🏪 Licensed bar 🅰 Calor Gas ⊘ Camping Gaz 🅃 Toilet fluid 🍽 Café/Restaurant 🍟 Fast Food/Takeaway 🔋 Battery charging 🍼 Baby care ⚡ Motorvan service point **ABBREVIATIONS:** BH/bank hols-bank holidays Etr-Easter Spring BH-Spring Bank Holiday dep-departure fr-from hrs-hours m-mile mdnt-midnight rdbt-roundabout rs-restricted service wk-week wknd-weekend x-rds-cross roads ⊗ No credit cards ⊗ No dogs 👶 Children of all ages accepted See page 9 for details of the AA Camping Card Scheme

ST JUST (NEAR LAND'S END)   Map 2 SW33

Places to visit

Geevor Tin Mine, PENDEEN, TR19 7EW, 01736 788662 www.geevor.com

Carn Euny Ancient Village, SANCREED, 0870 333 1181 www.english-heritage.org.uk/daysout/properties/carn-euny-ancient-village

AA CAMPING CARD SITE

►►► 84% Roselands Caravan and Camping Park *(SW387305)*

Dowran TR19 7RS
☎ **01736 788571 & 07718 745065**
e-mail: info@roselands.co.uk
dir: *From A30 Penzance bypass turn right for St Just on A3071. 5m, turn left at sign after tin mine chimney, follow signs to site*

🚐 £10-£18.50 🚍 £10-£18.50 ▲ £10-£18.50

Open Mar-Oct

Last arrival 21.00hrs Last departure 11.00hrs

A small, friendly park in a sheltered rural setting, an ideal location for a quiet family holiday. The owners continue to upgrade the park, and in addition to the attractive little bar there is an indoor games room, children's playground and good toilet facilities. 4 acre site. 35 touring pitches. 5 seasonal pitches. Caravan pitches. Motorhome pitches. Tent pitches. 15 statics.

AA Pubs & Restaurants nearby: The Wellington, ST JUST [NEAR LAND'S END], TR19 7HD, 01736 787319

Harris's Restaurant, PENZANCE, TR18 2LZ, 01736 364408

The Navy Inn, PENZANCE, TR18 4DE, 01736 333232

Leisure: 🏔 🔍 ☐
Facilities: 🍴⊙℉⚡☉🛁🔥🚽🏧💻⚽❤️ⓘ
Services: 🔌🅿️🚽🛒🔩⊘Ⓣ🍽️🚮🛒
Within 3 miles: ↓🚴⛵🅂🛁🔄U

Notes: Dogs must be kept on leads. Dog walks on moors.

►►► 81% *Trevaylor Caravan & Camping Park (SW368222)*

Botallack TR19 7PU
☎ **01736 787016 & 07816 992519**
e-mail: trevaylor@cornishcamping.co.uk
dir: *On B3306 (St Just-St Ives road), site on right 0.75m from St Just*

🚐 🚍 ▲

Open Mar-Oct

Last arrival 21.00hrs Last departure 11.00hrs

A sheltered grassy site located off the beaten track in a peaceful location at the western tip of Cornwall; it makes an ideal base for discovering Penzance and Land's End. The dramatic coastline and the pretty villages nearby are truly unspoilt. Clean, well-maintained facilities and a good shop are offered along with a bar serving meals. For 2013 the enthusiastic owners increased the number of electric hook ups, installed heating in the shower block and refurbished the bar. An open-top bus stops at the entrance to the site. 6 acre site. 50 touring pitches. Caravan pitches. Motorhome pitches. Tent pitches. 5 statics.

AA Pubs & Restaurants nearby: The Wellington, ST JUST [NEAR LAND'S END], TR19 7HD, 01736 787319

Harris's Restaurant, PENZANCE, TR18 2LZ, 01736 364408

The Navy Inn, PENZANCE, TR18 4DE, 01736 333232

Leisure: 🏔 🔍 ☐
Facilities: 🍴℉⚡☉🛁💻 ♻️ ⓘ
Services: 🔌🅿️🚽🔩⊘Ⓣ🍽️🛒🛒
Within 3 miles: ↓🚴⛵🅂🛁🔄U

Notes: Quiet after 22.00hrs. Dogs must be kept on leads.

AA CAMPING CARD SITE

►►► 80% Kelynack Caravan & Camping Park *(SW374301)*

Kelynack TR19 7RE
☎ **01736 787633**
e-mail: kelynackholidays@tiscali.co.uk
dir: *1m S of St Just, 5m N of Land's End on B3306*

🚐 🚍 ▲

Open all year

Last arrival 22.00hrs Last departure 10.00hrs

A small secluded park that sits alongside a stream in an unspoilt rural location. The level grass pitches are in two areas. The park is within reach of Land's End, Sennen Cove, Minack Theatre and Penzance. 3 acre site. 28 touring pitches. 3 hardstandings. Caravan pitches. Motorhome pitches. Tent pitches. 13 statics.

AA Pubs & Restaurants nearby: The Wellington, ST JUST [NEAR LAND'S END], TR19 7HD, 01736 787319

Harris's Restaurant, PENZANCE, TR18 2LZ, 01736 364408

The Navy Inn, PENZANCE, TR18 4DE, 01736 333232

Leisure: 🏔 🔍
Facilities: 🍴⊙℉⚡☉🛁🔥🚽💻 ♻️ ⓘ
Services: 🔌🅿️🚽🔩⊘Ⓣ🛒🛒
Within 3 miles: ↓🚴⛵🅂🛁U

Notes: Dogs must be kept on leads. Dining & cooking shelter.

LEISURE: 🏊 Indoor swimming pool 🏊 Outdoor swimming pool 🏔 Children's playground 🪁 Kid's club 🎾 Tennis court 🔍 Games room ☐ Separate TV room
↓ 9/18 hole golf course ⛵ Boats for hire 🎬 Cinema 🎵 Entertainment 🎣 Fishing ◎ Mini golf 🌊 Watersports 💪 Gym ❤️ Sports field **Spa** U Stables
FACILITIES: 🛁 Bath 🚿 Shower ⊙ Electric shaver ℉ Hairdryer ☀️ Ice Pack Facility 👨‍🦽 Disabled facilities ☎ Public telephone 🛒 Shop on site or within 200yds
🏪 Mobile shop (calls at least 5 days a week) 🍖 BBQ area 🪵 Picnic area 💻 Wi-fi 💻 Internet access ♻️ Recycling ⓘ Tourist info 🐕 Dog exercise area

AA CAMPING CARD SITE

►►► 77% Secret Garden Caravan & Camping Park *(SW370305)*

Bosavern House TR19 7RD
☎ **01736 788301**
e-mail: mail@bosavern.com
web: www.secretbosavern.com
dir: *Exit A3071 near St Just onto B3306 (Land's End road). Site 0.5m on left*

🚐 🚐 Å

Open Mar-Oct

Last arrival 22.00hrs Last departure noon

A neat little site in a walled garden behind a guest house, where visitors can enjoy breakfast, and snacks in the bar in the evening. This site is in a fairly sheltered location with all grassy pitches. Please note that there is no children's playground. 1.5 acre site. 12 touring pitches. Caravan pitches. Motorhome pitches. Tent pitches.

AA Pubs & Restaurants nearby: The Wellington, ST JUST [NEAR LAND'S END], TR19 7HD, 01736 787319

Harris's Restaurant, PENZANCE, TR18 2LZ, 01736 364408

The Navy Inn, PENZANCE, TR18 4DE, 01736 333232

Leisure: 🖵
Facilities: 🐾 ⊙ ⚹ ⓒ Wi-fi 💻 ♻ 🔁
Services: 🔌 🔟 🍴 🛒 💧 🛁
Within 3 miles: ↓ 🟢 🥾 🔟
Notes: No pets.

ST JUST-IN-ROSELAND   Map 2 SW83

Places to visit

St Mawes Castle, ST MAWES, TR2 3AA, 01326 270526 www.english-heritage.org.uk/ daysout/properties/st-mawes-castle

Trelissick Garden, TRELISSICK GARDEN, TR3 6QL, 01872 862090 www.nationaltrust.org.uk/trelissick

---

PREMIER PARK

►►►►►► 90% Trethem Mill Touring Park *(SW860365)*

Best of British GOLD

TR2 5JF
☎ **01872 580504**
e-mail: reception@trethem.com
dir: *From Tregony on A3078 to St Mawes. 2m after Trewithian, follow signs to site*

* 🚐 £18-£26 🚐 £18-£26 Å £18-£26

Open Apr-mid Oct

Last arrival 20.00hrs Last departure 11.00hrs

A quality park in all areas, with upgraded amenities including a reception, shop, laundry, and disabled/family room. This carefully-tended and sheltered park is in a lovely rural setting, with spacious pitches separated by young trees and shrubs. The very keen family who own the site are continually looking for ways to enhance its facilities. 11 acre site. 84 touring pitches. 61 hardstandings. Caravan pitches. Motorhome pitches. Tent pitches.

AA Pubs & Restaurants nearby: The Victory Inn, ST MAWES, TR2 5DQ, 01326 270324

Hotel Tresanton, ST MAWES, TR2 5DR, 01326 270055

Driftwood, PORTSCATHO, TR2 5EW, 01872 580644

Leisure: 🅰 ⊙
Facilities: 🐾 ⊙ 🏳 ⚹ ⓒ 🔟 🛗 Wi-fi ♻ 🔁
Services: 🔌 🔟 🍴 🛒 T 💧 🛁
Within 3 miles: 🥾 🟢 🥾 🔟 🔟
Notes: No skateboards or rollerblades. Dogs must be kept on leads. Information centre.

ST MARY'S (ISLES OF SCILLY)   Map 2 SV91

Places to visit

Isles of Scilly Museum, ST MARY'S, TR21 0JT, 01720 422337 www.iosmuseum.org

---

►►► 80% Garrison Campsite *(SV897104)*

Tower Cottage, The Garrison TR21 0LS
☎ **01720 422670**
e-mail: info@garrisonholidays.com
dir: *10 mins' walk from quay to site*

* Å £17.10-£22

Open Etr-Oct

Last arrival 20.00hrs Last departure 19.00hrs

Set on the top of an old fort with superb views, this park offers tent-only pitches in a choice of well-sheltered paddocks. There are modern toilet facilities (with powerful showers), a superb children's play area and a good shop at this attractive site, which is only ten minutes from the town, the quay and the nearest beaches. There is easy access to the other islands via the direct boat service from the Hugh Town quay; the campsite owners will transport all luggage, camping equipment etc to and from the quay. Good food is available in the many hostelries in the main town. 9.5 acre site. 120 touring pitches. Tent pitches.

Facilities: 🐾 ⊙ 🏳 ⚹ ⓒ 🔟 Wi-fi ♻ 🔁
Services: 🔌 🔟 🍴 🛒 🛁
Within 3 miles: ↓ 🥾 🟢 🥾 🔟 🔟 U
Notes: No cars on site, no open fires, no pets.

SERVICES: 🔌 Electric hook up 🔟 Launderette 🍴 Licensed bar 🔋 Calor Gas 🚗 Camping Gaz T Toilet fluid 🍴 Café/Restaurant 🍟 Fast Food/Takeaway 🛁 Battery charging 🍼 Baby care 🛵 Motorvan service point **ABBREVIATIONS:** BH/bank hols-bank holidays Etr-Easter Spring BH-Spring Bank Holiday dep-departure fr-from hrs-hours m-mile mdnt-midnight rdbt-roundabout rs-restricted service wk-week wknd-weekend x-rds-cross roads 🔟 No credit cards 🚫 No dogs 👶 Children of all ages accepted See page 9 for details of the AA Camping Card Scheme

ST MERRYN (NEAR PADSTOW) Map 2 SW87

Places to visit

Prideaux Place, PADSTOW, PL28 8RP, 01841 532411 www.prideauxplace.co.uk

81% *Harlyn Sands Holiday Park* (SW873752)

Lighthouse Rd, Trevose Head PL28 8SQ
☎ 01841 520720 & 01752 841485
e-mail: enquiries@harlynsands.co.uk
web: www.harlynsands.co.uk
dir: *Exit B3276 in St Merryn centre onto unclassified road towards Constantine Bay & Trevose Golf Club. Through golf club, left to site*

Open Etr-end Oct

Last arrival 22.00hrs Last departure 10.00hrs

A family park for 'bucket and spade' holidays, surrounded by seven bays each with its own sandy beach. The on-site entertainment for children and adults is extensive, and there is an indoor swimming pool complex, excellent restaurant and takeaway, and a quiet over-30s lounge bar. 21 acre site. 160 touring pitches. 6 hardstandings. 60 seasonal pitches. Caravan pitches. Motorhome pitches. Tent pitches. 350 statics.

AA Pubs & Restaurants nearby: The Seafood Restaurant, PADSTOW, PL28 8BY, 01841 532700

Leisure:

Facilities:

Services:

Within 3 miles:

Notes: Families only. Dogs must be kept on leads. Arcade, clubhouse, chip shop.

PREMIER PARK

►►►►► 85% Atlantic Bays Holiday Park (SW890717)

St Merryn PL28 8PY
☎ 01841 520855
e-mail: info@atlanticbaysholidaypark.co.uk
dir: *From A30 SW of Bodmin take exit signed Victoria/Roche, 1st exit at rdbt. At Trekenning rdbt 4th exit signed A39/Wadebridge. At Winnards Perch rdbt left B3274 signed Padstow. Left in 3m, follow signs*

Open Mar-2 Jan

Last arrival 21.00hrs Last departure noon

Atlantic Bays has a mix of hardstanding and grass pitches, a high quality toilet/shower block and a comfortable bar/restaurant. The park is set in a rural area yet only two miles from the coast and beautiful sandy beaches, and within easy reach of the quaint fishing village of Padstow, and Newquay for fantastic surfing. 27 acre site. 70 touring pitches. 50 hardstandings. Caravan pitches. Motorhome pitches. Tent pitches. 171 statics.

AA Pubs & Restaurants nearby: The Seafood Restaurant, PADSTOW, PL28 8BY, 01841 532700

Leisure:

Facilities:

Services:

Within 3 miles:

Notes: Dogs must be kept on leads.

►►►► 82% Carnevas Holiday Park & Farm Cottages (SW862728)

Carnevas Farm PL28 8PN
☎ 01841 520230 & 521209
e-mail: carnevascampsite@aol.com
dir: *From St Merryn on B3276 towards Porthcothan Bay. Approx 2m turn right at site sign onto unclassified road opposite Tredrea Inn. Site 0.25m on right*

* £10.50-£18 £10.50-£18 £10.50-£18

Open Apr-Oct (rs Apr-Spring BH & mid Sep-Oct shop, bar & restaurant closed)

A family-run park on a working farm, divided into four paddocks on slightly sloping grass. The toilets are central to all areas, and there is a small licensed bar serving bar meals. An ideal base for exploring the fishing town of Padstow or the surfing beach at Newquay. 8 acre site. 195 touring pitches. Caravan pitches. Motorhome pitches. Tent pitches. 14 statics.

AA Pubs & Restaurants nearby: The Seafood Restaurant, PADSTOW, PL28 8BY, 01841 532700

Leisure:

Facilities:

Services:

Within 3 miles:

Notes: No skateboards, no supermarket deliveries. Dogs must be kept on leads.

►►► 80% Trevean Caravan & Camping Park (SW875724)

Trevean Ln PL28 8PR
☎ 01841 520772
e-mail: trevean.info@virgin.net
dir: *From St Merryn take B3276 to Newquay for 1m. Turn left for Rumford. Site 0.25m on right*

£10-£14 £10-£14 £10-£14

LEISURE: Indoor swimming pool, Outdoor swimming pool, Children's playground, Kid's club, Tennis court, Games room, Separate TV room, 9/18 hole golf course, Boats for hire, Cinema, Entertainment, Fishing, Mini golf, Watersports, Gym, Sports field, **Spa**, Stables
FACILITIES: Bath, Shower, Electric shaver, Hairdryer, Ice Pack Facility, Disabled facilities, Public telephone, Shop on site or within 200yds, Mobile shop (calls at least 5 days a week), BBQ area, Picnic area, Wi-fi, Internet access, Recycling, Tourist info, Dog exercise area

Trevean Caravan & Camping Park

Open Apr-Oct (rs Spring BH-Sep shop open)

Last arrival 22.00hrs Last departure 11.00hrs

A small working farm site with level grassy pitches in open countryside. The toilet facilities are clean and well kept, and there is a laundry and good children's playground. 1.5 acre site. 68 touring pitches. 35 seasonal pitches. Caravan pitches. Motorhome pitches. Tent pitches. 3 statics.

AA Pubs & Restaurants nearby: The Seafood Restaurant, PADSTOW, PL28 8BY, 01841 532700

Leisure: ⚲ ⚙

Facilities: ⚲⊙⌇✳⚲⚙⚙🚿⚲🚽 ʍ﹣ ♻ 🆔

Services: ⚲⚙ 🔋⚗🛗

Within 3 miles: ⚲✳⚙⊙🛗⚙🚽∪

Notes: Dogs must be kept on leads.

►► 80% Tregavone Touring Park
(SW898732)

Tregavone Farm PL28 8JZ
☎ 01841 520148
e-mail: info@tregavone.co.uk
dir: *From A389 towards Padstow, right after Little Petherick. In 1m just beyond Padstow Holiday Park turn left into unclassified road signed Tregavone. Site on left, approx 1m*

* ⚲ £10-£12 ⚲ Å

Open Mar-Oct

Situated on a working farm with unspoilt country views, this spacious grassy park, run by friendly family owners, makes an ideal base for exploring the north Cornish coast and the seven local golden beaches with surfing areas, or for enjoying quiet country walks from the park. 3 acre site. 40 touring pitches. Caravan pitches. Motorhome pitches. Tent pitches.

AA Pubs & Restaurants nearby: The Seafood Restaurant, PADSTOW, PL28 8BY, 01841 532700

Facilities: ⚲⊙✳🚽

Services: ⚲⚙🛗

Within 3 miles: ⚲✳⊟⚙⊙🛗⚙🚽∪

Notes:

ST MINVER
Map 2 SW97

AA CAMPING CARD SITE

PREMIER PARK

►►►►► 82% Gunvenna Caravan Park *(SW969782)*

PL27 6QN
☎ 01208 862405
e-mail: gunvenna.bookings@gmail.com
dir: *From A39 N of Wadebridge take B3314 (Port Isaac road), site 4m on right*

⚲ ⚲ Å

Open Etr-Oct

Last arrival 20.30hrs Last departure 11.00hrs

An attractive park with extensive rural views in a quiet country location, yet within three miles of Polzeath. This popular park is family owned and run, and provides good facilities in an ideal position for touring north Cornwall. The park has excellent hardstanding pitches, maturing landscaping and a beautiful indoor swimming pool with a glass roof. Two wooden mini glamping lodges, a holiday cottage and static caravans are for hire. The beach at Polzeath is very popular with the surfers. 10 acre site. 75 touring pitches. 23 hardstandings. 15 seasonal pitches. Caravan pitches. Motorhome pitches. Tent pitches. 44 statics. 2 wooden pods.

AA Pubs & Restaurants nearby: The Swan Hotel, WADEBRIDGE, PL27 7DD, 01208 812526

Restaurant Nathan Outlaw, ROCK, PL27 6LA, 01208 863394

Leisure: ⚲ ⚲ ⚲

Facilities: ⚲⚲⊙⌇✳⚙⚙⊙🚿⚲🚽 ʍ﹣ ♻ 🆔

Services: ⚲⚙🔋⚗⎯🛗⚲⚱

Within 3 miles: ⚲✳⚙🛗⚙🚽∪

Notes: No under 16yrs in pool unless accompanied by an adult. Owners must clear up after their dogs. Dogs must be kept on leads.

SENNEN
Map 2 SW32

Places to visit

Geevor Tin Mine, PENDEEN, TR19 7EW, 01736 788662 www.geevor.com

Carn Euny Ancient Village, SANCREED, 0870 333 1181 www.english-heritage.org.uk/daysout/properties/carn-euny-ancient-village

►►► 83% Trevedra Farm Caravan & Camping Site *(SW368276)*

TR19 7BE
☎ 01736 871818 & 871835
e-mail: trevedra@btconnect.com
dir: *Take A30 towards Land's End. After junct with B3306 turn right into farm lane. (NB Sat Nav directs beyond site entrance to next lane which is unsuitable for caravans)*

⚲ ⚲ Å

Open Etr or Apr-Oct

Last arrival 19.00hrs Last departure 10.30hrs

A working farm with dramatic sea views over to the Scilly Isles, just a mile from Land's End. This popular campsite offers well-appointed toilets, a well-stocked shop, and a cooked breakfast or evening meal from the food bar. There is direct access to the coastal footpath, and two beautiful beaches are a short walk away. 8 acre site. 100 touring pitches. Caravan pitches. Motorhome pitches. Tent pitches.

AA Pubs & Restaurants nearby: The Old Success Inn, SENNEN, TR19 7DG, 01736 871232

Facilities: ⚲⊙⌇✳⚙🛗 ʍ﹣ ♻ 🆔

Services: ⚲⚙🔋⚗⎯🍽🛗⚲⚱

Within 3 miles: ⚲⚙🛗⚙

Notes: No open fires, no noise 22.00hrs-08.00hrs. Dogs must be kept on leads.

SUMMERCOURT — Map 2 SW85

Places to visit

Trerice, TRERICE, TR8 4PG, 01637 875404 www.nationaltrust.org.uk

Blue Reef Aquarium, NEWQUAY, TR7 1DU, 01637 878134 www.bluereefaquarium.co.uk

Great for kids: Dairy Land Farm World, NEWQUAY, TR8 5AA, 01872 510246 www.dairylandfarmworld.com

RV ►►►► 95% Carvynick Country Club (SW878564)

TR8 5AF
☎ 01872 510716
e-mail: info@carvynick.co.uk
web: www.carvynick.co.uk
dir: *Accessed from A3058*

£18-£27 £18-£30

Open all year (rs Jan-early Feb restricted leisure facilities)

Set within the gardens of an attractive country estate, this spacious, dedicated American RV Park (also home to the 'Itchy Feet' retail company) provides full facility pitches on hardstandings. The extensive on-site amenities, shared by the high-quality time share village, include an indoor leisure area with swimming pool, fitness suite, badminton court and a new bar and restaurant serving good food. 47 touring pitches. Caravan pitches. Motorhome pitches.

AA Pubs & Restaurants nearby: The Plume of Feathers, MITCHELL, TR8 5AX, 01872 510387

Leisure:

Facilities:

Services:

Within 3 miles:

Notes: Dogs must be exercised off site & kept on leads.

TINTAGEL — Map 2 SX08

See also Camelford

Places to visit

Tintagel Castle, TINTAGEL, PL34 0HE, 01840 770328 www.english-heritage.org.uk/daysout/properties/tintagel-castle

Tintagel Old Post Office, TINTAGEL, PL34 0DB, 01840 770024 www.nationaltrust.org.uk/main/w-tintageloldpostoffice

Great for kids: Tamar Otter & Wildlife Centre, LAUNCESTON, PL15 8GW, 01566 785646 www.tamarotters.co.uk

►►► 76% *Headland Caravan & Camping Park* (SX056887)

Atlantic Rd PL34 0DE
☎ 01840 770239
e-mail: headland.caravan@talktalkbusiness.net
dir: *From B3263 follow brown tourist signs through village to Headland*

Open Etr-Oct

Last arrival 21.00hrs

A peaceful family-run site in the mystical village of Tintagel, close to the ruins of King Arthur's Castle. There are two well-terraced camping areas with sea and countryside views, immaculately clean toilet facilities, and good, colourful planting across the park. The Cornish coastal path and the spectacular scenery are just two of the attractions here, and there are safe bathing beaches nearby. There are holiday statics for hire. 5 acre site. 62 touring pitches. Caravan pitches. Motorhome pitches. Tent pitches. 28 statics.

AA Pubs & Restaurants nearby: The Port William, TREBARWITH, PL34 0HB, 01840 770230

Leisure:

Facilities:

Services:

Within 3 miles:

Notes: Quiet after 23.00hrs. Dogs must be exercised off site & kept on leads.

TORPOINT — Map 3 SX45

Places to visit

Antony House, TORPOINT, PL11 2QA, 01752 812191 www.nationaltrust.org.uk/antony

Mount Edgcumbe House & Country Park, TORPOINT, PL10 1HZ, 01752 822236 www.mountedgcumbe.gov.uk

Great for kids: The Monkey Sanctuary, LOOE, PL13 1NZ, 01503 262532 www.monkeysanctuary.org

AA CAMPING CARD SITE

►►►► 76% Whitsand Bay Lodge & Touring Park (SX410515)

Millbrook PL10 1JZ
☎ 01752 822597
e-mail: enquiries@whitsandbayholidays.co.uk
dir: *From Torpoint take A374, turn left at Anthony onto B3247 for 1.25m to T-junct. Turn left, 0.25m, right into Cliff Rd. Site 2m on left*

* £15-£30 £15-£30 £12.50

Open all year (rs Sep-Mar opening hours at shop, pool & bar restricted)

Last arrival 19.00hrs Last departure 10.00hrs

A very well-equipped park with panoramic coastal, sea and countryside views from its terraced pitches. A quality park with upmarket toilet facilities and other amenities. There is a guided historic walk around The Battery most Sundays, and a bus stop close by. 27 acre site. 49 touring pitches. 30 hardstandings. 15 seasonal pitches. Caravan pitches. Motorhome pitches. Tent pitches. 5 statics.

AA Pubs & Restaurants nearby: The Halfway House Inn, KINGSAND, PL10 1NA, 01752 822279

Leisure:

Facilities:

Services:

Within 3 miles:

Notes: Families & couples only. Dogs must be kept on leads. Putting green, chapel, library, amusement arcade.

LEISURE: Indoor swimming pool Outdoor swimming pool Children's playground Kid's club Tennis court Games room Separate TV room 9/18 hole golf course Boats for hire Cinema Entertainment Fishing Mini golf Watersports Gym Sports field Stables
FACILITIES: Bath Shower Electric shaver Hairdryer Ice Pack Facility Disabled facilities Public telephone Shop on site or within 200yds Mobile shop (calls at least 5 days a week) BBQ area Picnic area Wi-fi Internet access Recycling Tourist info Dog exercise area

TRURO
Map 2 SW84

See also Portscatho

Places to visit

Royal Cornwall Museum, TRURO, TR1 2SJ, 01872 272205 www.royalcornwallmuseum.org.uk

Trewithen Gardens, PROBUS, TR2 4DD, 01726 883647 www.trewithengardens.co.uk

Great for kids: Pencarrow, BODMIN, PL30 3AG, 01208 841369 www.pencarrow.co.uk

PREMIER PARK

►►►►► 94% Carnon Downs Caravan & Camping Park

(SW805406)

Carnon Downs TR3 6JJ
☎ 01872 862283
e-mail: info@carnon-downs-caravanpark.co.uk
dir: *Take A39 from Truro towards Falmouth. Site just off main Carnon Downs rdbt, on left*

* ➡ £21-£30 ➡ £21-£30 ▲ £21-£30

Open all year

Last arrival 22.00hrs Last departure 11.00hrs

A beautifully mature park set in meadowland and woodland close to the village amenities of Carnon Downs. The four toilet blocks provide exceptional facilities in bright modern surroundings. An extensive landscaping programme has been carried out to give more spacious pitch sizes, and there is an exciting children's playground with modern equipment, plus a football pitch. 33 acre site. 150 touring pitches. 80 hardstandings. Caravan pitches. Motorhome pitches. Tent pitches. 2 statics.

AA Pubs & Restaurants nearby: The Pandora Inn, MYLOR BRIDGE, TR11 5ST, 01326 372678

Tabb's, TRURO, TR1 3BZ, 01872 262110

Leisure: 🎬 ▢

Facilities: 🛏 🐾 ☉ ☝ ✳ ⚅ ⟳ 🕁 ♻ ✪

Services: 🔌 ▢ 🔋 ∅ 🅣 ▄ ⚒

Within 3 miles: ↧ ⚘ 日 ⋒ ≋ 🅑 🅑 ∪

Notes: No children's bikes in Jul & Aug. Baby & child bathroom.

PREMIER PARK

►►►►► 82% Truro Caravan and Camping Park *(SW772452)*

TR4 8QN
☎ 01872 560274
e-mail: info@trurocaravanandcampingpark.co.uk
dir: *Exit A390 at Threemilestone rdbt onto unclassified road towards Chacewater. Site signed on right in 0.5m*

➡ £20-£30 ➡ £20-£30 ▲ £20-£30

Open all year

Last arrival 19.00hrs Last departure 10.30hrs

An attractive south-facing and well-laid out park with spacious pitches, including good hardstandings, and quality modern toilets that are kept spotlessly clean. It is situated on the edge of the City of Truro yet close to many beaches, with St Agnes just ten minutes away by car. It is equidistant from both the rugged north coast and the calmer south coastal areas. There is a good bus service from the gate of the park to Truro. 8.5 acre site. 51 touring pitches. 26 hardstandings. Caravan pitches. Motorhome pitches. Tent pitches. 49 statics.

AA Pubs & Restaurants nearby: The Wig & Pen, TRURO, TR1 3DP, 01872 273028

Probus Lamplighter Restaurant, TRURO, TR2 4JL, 01726 882453

Facilities: 🛏 🐾 ☉ ☝ ✳ ⚅ ⟳ 🕁 ⟦WiFi⟧ 🖥 ♻ ✪

Services: 🔌 ▢ 🔋 ∅ 🅣 ▄ ⚒

Within 3 miles: ↧ 日 ⋒ ⟳ ≋ 🅑 🅑 ∪

Notes: Dogs must be kept on leads.

PREMIER PARK

►►►►► 81% Cosawes Park *(SW768376)*

Perranarworthal TR3 7QS
☎ 01872 863724
e-mail: info@cosawes.com
dir: *Exit A39 midway between Truro & Falmouth. Direct access at site sign after Perranarworthal*

* ➡ £15-£23 ➡ £15-£23 ▲ £13-£17

Open all year

Last arrival 21.00hrs Last departure 10.00hrs

A small touring park, close to Perranarworthal, in a peaceful wooded valley, midway between Truro and Falmouth, with a two-acre touring area. There are spotless toilet facilities that include two smart family rooms. Its stunning location is ideal for visiting the many nearby hamlets and villages close to the Carrick Roads, a stretch of tidal water, which is a centre for sailing and other boats. 2 acre site. 59 touring pitches. 25 hardstandings. 15 seasonal pitches. Caravan pitches. Motorhome pitches. Tent pitches.

AA Pubs & Restaurants nearby: The Pandora Inn, MYLOR BRIDGE, TR11 5ST, 01326 372678

Facilities: 🐾 ☉ ☝ ✳ ⚅ ⟳ 🕁 ⟦WiFi⟧ ♻ ✪

Services: 🔌 ▢ 🔋 🅣 ▄ ⚒

Within 3 miles: ↧ ⚘ 日 ⋒ ⟳ ≋ 🅑 🅑 ∪

Notes: Dogs must be kept on leads. Underfloor heating, vanity cubicles. Fish & chips every Thursday evening.

SERVICES: 🔌 Electric hook up ▢ Launderette 🍸 Licensed bar 🔋 Calor Gas ∅ Camping Gaz 🅣 Toilet fluid 🍽 Café/Restaurant 🍔 Fast Food/Takeaway ▄ Battery charging 🚼 Baby care ⚒ Motorvan service point **ABBREVIATIONS:** BH/bank hols-bank holidays Etr-Easter Spring BH-Spring Bank Holiday dep-departure fr-from hrs-hours m-mile mdnt-midnight rdbt-roundabout rs-restricted service wk-week wknd-weekend x-rds-cross roads ⊗ No credit cards ⊗ No dogs 👶 Children of all ages accepted See page 9 for details of the AA Camping Card Scheme

TRURO *continued*

▶▶▶ 80% Summer Valley *(SW800479)*

Shortlanesend TR4 9DW
☎ 01872 277878
e-mail: res@summervalley.co.uk
dir: *3m NW off B3284*

* 🚐 £12-£19 🚎 £12-£19 ▲ £12-£19

Open Apr-Oct

Last arrival 20.00hrs Last departure 11.00hrs

A very attractive and secluded site in a rural setting midway between the A30 and the cathedral city of Truro. The keen owners maintain the facilities to a good standard. 3 acre site. 60 touring pitches. Caravan pitches. Motorhome pitches. Tent pitches.

AA Pubs & Restaurants nearby: Old Ale House, TRURO, TR1 2HD, 01872 271122

Bustophers Bar Bistro, TRURO, TR1 2PN, 01872 279029

Leisure: /🄰

Facilities: 🏹⊙🖤☀🕓🖻🚻📶♻🅸

Services: 🔌🖲🔒🖉🆃🛒

Within 3 miles: ⚓🎋🖉◎🖻🚩∪

Notes: Dogs must be kept on leads. Campers' lounge.

WADEBRIDGE Map 2 SW97

Places to visit

Prideaux Place, PADSTOW, PL28 8RP, 01841 532411 www.prideauxplace.co.uk

Cornwall's Regimental Museum, BODMIN, PL31 1EG, 01208 72810

Great for kids: Pencarrow, BODMIN, PL30 3AG, 01208 841369 www.pencarrow.co.uk

---

▷▷▷▷ 90% St Mabyn Holiday Park *(SX055733)*

GOLD

Longstone Rd, St Mabyn PL30 3BY
☎ 01208 841677
e-mail: info@stmabyn.co.uk
web: www.stmabynholidaypark.co.uk
dir: *S of Camelford on A39, left after BP garage onto B3266 to Bodmin, 6m to Longstone, right at x-rds to St Mabyn, site approx 400mtrs on right*

🚐🚎▲

Open 15 Mar-Oct (rs 15 Mar-Spring BH & mid Sep-Oct swimming pool may be closed)

Last arrival 22.00hrs Last departure noon

A family-run site situated close to the picturesque market town of Wadebridge and within easy reach of Bodmin; it is centrally located for exploring both the north and south coasts of Cornwall. The park offers peace and tranquillity in a country setting and at the same time provides plenty of on-site activities including a swimming pool and children's play areas. Holiday chalets and fully-equipped holiday homes are available to rent, along with a choice of pitches. 12 acre site. 120 touring pitches. 49 hardstandings. Caravan pitches. Motorhome pitches. Tent pitches. 20 statics. 1 wooden pod.

AA Pubs & Restaurants nearby: The Swan Hotel, WADEBRIDGE, PL27 7DD, 01208 812526

The Borough Arms, DUNMERE, PL31 2RD, 01208 73118

Leisure: 🛶/🄰🎱🖵

Facilities: 🏹⊙🖤☀🕭♿🕓🖻🚻📶🖥♻🅸

Services: 🔌🖲🔒🖉🆃🛒🚐

Within 3 miles: ⚓🖉🖻🚩∪

Notes: Quiet from 23.00hrs-07.00hrs, information book given on arrival. Small animal area (goats).

▶▶▶▶ 89% The Laurels Holiday Park *(SW957715)*

Padstow Rd, Whitecross PL27 7JQ
☎ 01209 313474
e-mail: info@thelaurelsholidaypark.co.uk
dir: *A39 onto A389 signed Padstow, follow signs. Site entrance 1st right*

* 🚐 £10-£24 🚎 £10-£24 ▲ £10-£24

Open Etr or Apr-Oct

Last arrival 20.00hrs Last departure 11.00hrs

A very smart and well-equipped park with individual pitches screened by hedges and young shrubs. The enclosed dog walk is of great benefit to pet owners, and the Camel (cycle) Trail and Padstow are not far away. An excellent base if visiting the Royal Cornwall Showground. 2.2 acre site. 30 touring pitches. 2 hardstandings. Caravan pitches. Motorhome pitches. Tent pitches.

AA Pubs & Restaurants nearby: The Swan Hotel, WADEBRIDGE, PL27 7DD, 01208 812526

Leisure: /🄰

Facilities: 🏹⊙🖤☀🕭🕵🚻📶🖥♻🅸

Services: 🔌🖲🛒

Within 3 miles: ⚓🎋🖉🖻🚩∪

Notes: Family park. No group bookings. Dogs must be kept on leads. Wet suit dunking bath & drying area.

▶▶▶ 84% Little Bodieve Holiday Park *(SW995734)*

Bodieve Rd PL27 6EG
☎ 01208 812323
e-mail: info@littlebodieve.co.uk
dir: *From A39 rdbt on Wadebridge by-pass take B3314 signed Rock/Port Isaac, site 0.25m on right*

🚐🚎▲

Open Apr-Oct (rs Early & late season pool, shop & clubhouse closed)

Last arrival 21.00hrs Last departure 11.00hrs

Rurally located with pitches in three large grassy paddocks, this family park is close to the Camel Estuary. The licensed clubhouse provides bar meals, with an entertainment programme in high season, and there is a swimming pool with sun terrace plus a separate waterslide and splash pool. This makes a good base from which to visit the Royal Cornwall Showground. 22 acre site. 195 touring pitches. Caravan pitches. Motorhome pitches. Tent pitches. 75 statics.

AA Pubs & Restaurants nearby: The Swan Hotel, WADEBRIDGE, PL27 7DD, 01208 812526

Leisure: 🛶/🄰🎱🎵

Facilities: 🛁🏹⊙🖤☀🕭♿🕓🖻🚻📶🖥♻🅸

Services: 🔌🖲🖤🖉🆃🍴🛒🏧

Within 3 miles: ⚓🎋🖉◎🖻🚩∪

Notes: Families & couples only. Dogs must be kept on leads. Crazy golf.

WATERGATE BAY
Map 2 SW86

AA CAMPING CARD SITE

PREMIER PARK

▶▶▶▶▶ **86% Watergate Bay Touring Park** *(SW850653)*

SILVER

TR8 4AD
☎ 01637 860387
e-mail: email@watergatebaytouringpark.co.uk
web: www.watergatebaytouringpark.co.uk
dir: *From Bodmin on A30 follow Newquay airport signs. Continue past airport, left at T-junct, site 0.5m on right. (NB for Sat Nav use TR8 4AE)*

* ⊞ £11-£22 ⊞ £11-£22 ▲ £11-£22

Open Mar-Nov (rs Mar-Spring BH & Sep-Oct restricted bar, café, shop & pool)

Last arrival 22.00hrs Last departure noon

A well-established park above Watergate Bay, where acres of golden sand, rock pools and surf are seen as a holidaymakers' paradise. The toilet facilities are appointed to a high standard, and there is a well-stocked shop and café, an inviting swimming pool, and a wide range of activities including tennis courts and other outdoor facilities for all ages, plus regular entertainment in the clubhouse. 30 acre site. 171 touring pitches. 14 hardstandings. Caravan pitches. Motorhome pitches. Tent pitches. 2 statics.

AA Pubs & Restaurants nearby: Fifteen Cornwall, WATERGATE BAY, TR8 4AA, 01637 861000

Watergate Bay Touring Park

Leisure: ☜ ☜ ⋀ 🖐 ⌣ ☉ ☍ ⌂ 🎵
Facilities: ☚ ☝ ☉ ☡ ☀ ⚸ ☺ ☺ ☷ ☞ 🛁 ▣ ♲ ❼
Services: ☒ ⓢ ☷ 🔒 ⬚ T ⫿ 🔜 ▦ ➿ ⬇
Within 3 miles: ↯ ✐ ◎ ≋ ⬚ ⬚

Notes: Dogs must be kept on leads. Free minibus to beach during main school holidays.

see advert below

WIDEMOUTH BAY
Map 2 SS20

72% Widemouth Bay Caravan Park *(SS199008)*

EX23 0DF
☎ 01271 866766
e-mail: bookings@jfhols.co.uk
dir: *From A39 take Widemouth Bay coastal road, turn left. Site on left*

⊞ ⊞ ▲

Open Etr-Oct

Last arrival dusk Last departure 10.00hrs

A partly sloping rural site set in countryside overlooking the sea and one of Cornwall's finest beaches. There's nightly entertainment in the high season with an emphasis on children's and family club programmes. This park is located less than half a mile from the sandy beaches of Widemouth Bay. A superb base for surfing. 58 acre site. 220 touring pitches. 90 hardstandings. Caravan pitches. Motorhome pitches. Tent pitches. 200 statics.

AA Pubs & Restaurants nearby: Bay View Inn, WIDEMOUTH BAY, EX23 0AW, 01288 361273

The Castle Restaurant, BUDE, EX23 8LG, 01288 350543

Leisure: ☜ ⋀ 🖐 ☍ 🎵
Facilities: ☚ ☉ ☡ ☀ ⚸ ☺ ☷ ☞ 🛁 ▣
Services: ☒ ⓢ ☷ ⫿ ▦
Within 3 miles: ↯ ≒ ☶ ✐ ◎ ≋ ⬚ ⬚ ⬚ ∪

Notes: Crazy golf.

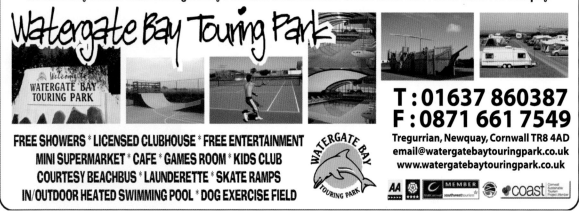

SERVICES: ☒ Electric hook up ⓢ Launderette ☷ Licensed bar ⬚ Calor Gas ⌀ Camping Gaz T Toilet fluid ⫿ Café/Restaurant ▦ Fast Food/Takeaway 🔜 Battery charging ➿ Baby care ⬇ Motorvan service point **ABBREVIATIONS:** BH/bank hols-bank holidays Etr-Easter Spring BH-Spring Bank Holiday dep-departure fr-from hrs-hours m-mile mdnt-midnight rdbt-roundabout rs-restricted service wk-week wknd-weekend x-rds-cross roads ◎ No credit cards ⊗ No dogs 👣 Children of all ages accepted See page 9 for details of the AA Camping Card Scheme

WIDEMOUTH BAY ***continued***

►►► 79% Cornish Coasts Caravan & Camping Park *(SS202981)*

Middle Penlean, Poundstock, Bude EX23 0EE
☎ 01288 361380
e-mail: enquiries5@cornishcoasts.co.uk
dir: *5m S of Bude on A39, 0.5m S of Rebel Cinema on right*

* 🚐 £12-£16 🚌 £12-£16 ⛺ £7-£16

Open Apr-Oct

Last arrival 22.00hrs Last departure 10.30hrs

Situated on the A39 midway between Padstow and the beautiful surfing beaches of Bude and Widemouth Bay, this is a quiet park with lovely terraced pitches that make the most of the stunning views over the countryside to the sea. The reception is in a 13th-century cottage, and the park is well equipped and tidy, with the well maintained and quirky toilet facilities (note the mosaic vanity units) housed in a freshly painted older-style building. 3.5 acre site. 46 touring pitches. 8 hardstandings. Caravan pitches. Motorhome pitches. Tent pitches. 4 statics.

AA Pubs & Restaurants nearby: Bay View Inn, WIDEMOUTH BAY, EX23 0AW, 01288 361273

The Castle Restaurant, BUDE, EX23 8LG, 01288 350543

Leisure: 🛝

Facilities: 🚿 ⊙ 💨 ❄ ♿ 🏪 ♻ ℹ

Services: 🔌 🧺 🛢 🧊 [T] 🛏

Within 3 miles: ⛵ 🎣 ◎ 🏄 🏪 🧺 🐴

Notes: Quiet after 22.00hrs. Dogs must be kept on leads. Post office.

►►► 75% Penhalt Farm Holiday Park *(SS194003)*

EX23 0DG
☎ 01288 361210
e-mail: denandjennie@penhaltfarm.fsnet.co.uk
web: www.penhaltfarm.co.uk
dir: *From Bude on A39 take 2nd right to Widemouth Bay road, left at end by Widemouth Manor signed Millook onto coastal road. Site 0.75m on left*

🚐 🚌 ⛺

Open Etr-Oct

Splendid views of the sea and coast can be enjoyed from all pitches on this sloping but partly level site, set in a lovely rural area on a working farm. About one mile away is one of Cornwall's finest beaches which proves popular with all the family as well as surfers. 8 acre site. 100 touring pitches. 12 hardstandings. Caravan pitches. Motorhome pitches. Tent pitches. 1 static.

AA Pubs & Restaurants nearby: Bay View Inn, WIDEMOUTH BAY, EX23 0AW, 01288 361273

The Castle Restaurant, BUDE, EX23 8LG, 01288 350543

Leisure: 🛝 🎱

Facilities: 🚿 ⊙ 💨 ❄ ♿ ☎ 🏪 🐕

Services: 🔌 🧺 🧊 🛏

Within 3 miles: ⛳ ⛵ 🎬 🎣 🏄 🏪 🐴

Notes: Dogs must be kept on leads. Pool table, netball & football posts, air hockey & table tennis.

LEISURE: 🏊 Indoor swimming pool 🏊 Outdoor swimming pool 🛝 Children's playground ✋ Kid's club 🎾 Tennis court 🎱 Games room 📺 Separate TV room ⛳ 9/18 hole golf course ⛵ Boats for hire 🎬 Cinema 🎵 Entertainment 🎣 Fishing ◎ Mini golf 🏄 Watersports 🏋 Gym ⚽ Sports field **Spa** 🐴 Stables
FACILITIES: 🛁 Bath 🚿 Shower ⊙ Electric shaver 💨 Hairdryer ❄ Ice Pack Facility ♿ Disabled facilities ☎ Public telephone 🏪 Shop on site or within 200yds 🚚 Mobile shop (calls at least 5 days a week) 🍖 BBQ area 🪑 Picnic area [Wi-fi] Wi-fi 💻 Internet access ♻ Recycling ℹ Tourist info 🐕 Dog exercise area

Cumbria

Think of Cumbria and you immediately picture a rumpled
landscape of magical lakes and mountains and high green
fells. For sheer natural beauty and grandeur, the English
Lake District is hard to beat, and despite traffic congestion
and high visitor numbers, this enchanting corner of the
country manages to retain its unique individuality and
sense of otherness.

● Loweswater

Even on a glorious summer's day, you can still escape the 'madding crowd' and discover Lakeland's true heart and face. It is a fascinating place, characterised by ever changing moods and a timeless air of mystery. By applying a little effort and leaving the tourist hotspots and the busy roads far behind, you can reach and appreciate the Lake District that inspired William Wordsworth, Samuel Taylor Coleridge, Arthur Ransome and Robert Southey.

Derwent Water – the 'Queen of the English Lakes' is one of the most popular lakes in the region and certainly the widest. Shelley described it as 'smooth and dark as a plain of polished jet.' Windermere, to the south, is the largest lake and the town of the same name is a popular tourist base; this is one of the few places in the Lake District that has a railway. Away from the lakes and the various watersports are miles of country for the adventurous to explore. The towering summits of Helvellyn, Scafell, Scafell Pike and Great Gable are the highest peaks in England.

Along the eastern edge of the 866-square mile National Park and handy for the West Coast main line and the M6 are several well-known towns – Kendal and Penrith. ▶

● Rosthwaite

● Wordworth's Dove Cottage, Grasmere

To the north is the ancient and historic city of Carlisle; once a Roman camp – its wall still runs north of the city – it was captured during the Jacobean rising of 1745. The cathedral dates back to the early 12th century.

The southern half of Cumbria is often bypassed and overlooked in favour of the more obvious attractions of the Lake District. Visitors who do journey beyond the park boundaries are usually impressed and inspired in equal measure by its wealth of delights. The Lune Valley, for example, remains as lovely as it was when Turner came here to paint, and the 19th-century writer John Ruskin described the view from 'The Brow,' a walk running behind Kirkby Lonsdale's parish church, as 'one of the loveliest scenes in England.'

Walking and Cycling

Walkers are spoilt for choice in Cumbria and the Lake District. Numerous paths and trails crisscross this rugged mountain landscape. That is part of its appeal – the chance to get up close and personal with Mother Nature. For something even more ambitious and adventurous, there are several long-distance trails.

The 70-mile (112km) Cumbria Way follows the valley floors rather than the mountain summits, while the 190-mile (305km) Coast to Coast has just about every kind of landscape and terrain imaginable. The route, pioneered by the well-known walker and writer, Alfred Wainwright, cuts across the Lake District, the Yorkshire Dales and the North York Moors, spanning the width of England between St Bees on the Cumbrian west coast, and Robin Hood's Bay on the North Yorkshire and Cleveland Heritage Coast.

The region also offers a walk with a difference and one which brings a true sense of drama and adventure. At the extreme southern end of Cumbria, in the reassuring company of official guide Cedric Robinson, MBE, you can cross the treacherous, deceptively beautiful sands of Morecambe Bay on foot. The bay, which is Britain's largest continuous intertidal area, is renowned for its quick sand and shifting channels. Many lives have been lost here over the years but in Cedric's expert hands, it is safe to cross.

The region is also popular with cyclists with lots of cycle hire outlets and plenty of routes to choose from. The 12-mile Wast Water to Santon Bridge cycle route passes England's deepest lake and is reputed to offer the finest view of the Lake District. It's quite a tough challenge and not suitable for under-11s.

There are also waymarked bike trails in Grizedale Forest and Whinlatter Forest.

Festivals and Events

Cumbria offers something in the region of 500 festivals and events throughout the year. The choice includes:

- Ambleside Daffodil and Spring Flower Festival in late March.
- Ulverston Walking Festival at the end of April and beginning of May.
- In July there is the Coniston Water Festival, famous for its Duck Race at Church Bridge; the Carlisle Festival of Nations; the Carlisle Summer Classical Music Festival at the cathedral.
- The Westmorland County Show takes place at Crooklands, near Kendal, in early September while the Dickensian Festival is staged in Ulverston in late November.
- Model Railway and Transport Exhibition at Barrow-in-Furness, in October.
- There are winter lighting events along Hadrian's Wall in November and December; and Christmas at the Castle at Muncaster Castle, Ravenglass.

● Derwent Water

CUMBRIA

AMBLESIDE   Map 18 NY30

Places to visit

The Armitt Museum & Library, AMBLESIDE, LA22 9BL, 015394 31212 www.armitt.com

Beatrix Potter Gallery, HAWKSHEAD, LA22 0NS, 015394 36269 www.nationaltrust.org.uk

Great for kids: Lakes Aquarium, LAKESIDE, LA12 8AS, 015395 30153 www.lakesaquarium.co.uk

PREMIER PARK

▶▶▶▶▶ 87% Skelwith Fold Caravan Park (NY355029)

GOLD

LA22 0HX
☎ 015394 32277
e-mail: info@skelwith.com
dir: *From Ambleside on A593 towards Coniston, left at Clappersgate onto B5286 (Hawkshead road). Site 1m on right*

* ☎ £21-£33.50 ☎ £21-£33.50

Open Mar-15 Nov

Last arrival dusk Last departure noon

In the grounds of a former mansion, this park is in a beautiful setting close to Lake Windermere. Touring areas are dotted in paddocks around the extensively wooded grounds, and the all-weather pitches are set close to the many facility buildings. The premium pitches are quite superb. There is a five-acre family recreation area, which has spectacular views of Loughrigg Fell. 130 acre site. 150 touring pitches. 130 hardstandings. 30 seasonal pitches. Caravan pitches. Motorhome pitches. 320 statics.

AA Pubs & Restaurants nearby: Wateredge Inn, AMBLESIDE, LA22 0EP, 015394 32332

Drunken Duck Inn, AMBLESIDE, LA22 0NG, 015394 36347

Leisure: ⋔ ⌔ ✤
Facilities: ⋔ ⊙ ℱ ✷ ⅋ Ⓢ ⓢ ⊞ ⅋ ⊞ 🖥 ♻
Services: ⊞ ⓢ ⬟ ⅋ ⌴ 🛆 ⅋
Within 3 miles: ⅋ ⅋ ⊟ ⅋ ⊚ ⅋ ⓢ ⓢ ⥀
Notes: Dogs must be kept on leads.

▶▶▶▶ 80% The Croft Caravan & Campsite (SD352981)

North Lonsdale Rd, Hawkshead LA22 0NX
☎ 015394 36374
e-mail: enquiries@hawkshead-croft.com
dir: *From B5285 in Hawkshead turn into site opposite main public car & coach park*

* ☎ £23-£28.50 ☎ £23-£28.50 ▲ £17-£28.50

Open Mar-Jan

Last arrival 21.30hrs Last departure noon

In the historic village of Hawkshead, which is now a popular destination for Beatrix Potter fans, this former working farm has a large tent and touring field, bordering a beck and the sound of running water and birdsong are welcome distractions. Most pitches are fully serviced with water, electricity, TV hook-up and waste water disposal. The smart amenities block provides family bathrooms. In an adjoining field there are stylish wood-clad lodges. 5 acre site. 75 touring pitches. 26 hardstandings. Caravan pitches. Motorhome pitches. Tent pitches. 20 statics.

AA Pubs & Restaurants nearby: The Queen's Head Inn & Restaurant, HAWKSHEAD, LA22 0NS, 015394 36271

Kings Arms, HAWKSHEAD, LA22 0NZ, 015394 36372

Leisure: ⚲
Facilities: ⛭ ⋔ ⊙ ℱ ✷ ⅋ Ⓢ ⓢ ⅋ ⊞ ♻ ❶
Services: ⊞ ⓢ ⬟
Within 3 miles: ⅋ ⓢ ⓢ
Notes: No noise 23.00hrs-07.00hrs. Dogs must be kept on leads.

▶▶▶ 78% Low Wray National Trust Campsite (NY372013)

Low Wray LA22 0JA
☎ 015394 32733 & 32039
e-mail: campsite.bookings@nationaltrust.org.uk
dir: *3m SW of Ambleside on A593 to Clappersgate, then B5286. Approx 1m left at Wray sign. Site approx 1m on left*

☎ ▲

Open wk before Etr-Oct

Last arrival variable Last departure 11.00hrs

Picturesquely set on the wooded shores of Lake Windermere, this site is a favourite with tenters and watersport enthusiasts. The toilet facilities are housed in wooden cabins, and tents can be pitched in wooded glades with lake views or open grassland; here there are wooden camping pods, and a mini-reservation of tipis and solar-heated bell tents. In partnership with Quest 4 Adventure, many outdoor activities are available for families (bookable during school holidays). Fresh bread is now baked daily on site in addition to visits from the hot-food van in season. 10 acre site. 140 touring pitches. Motorhome pitches. Tent pitches. 10 wooden pods.

AA Pubs & Restaurants nearby: Wateredge Inn, AMBLESIDE, LA22 0EP, 015394 32332

Drunken Duck Inn, AMBLESIDE, LA22 0NG, 015394 36347

Kings Arms, HAWKSHEAD, LA22 0NZ, 015394 36372

Leisure: ⋔
Facilities: ⛭ ⊙ ℱ ✷ ⅋ Ⓢ ⓢ ⅋ ♻ ❶
Services: ⊞ 🛆 ⅋
Within 3 miles: ⅋ ⊟ ⅋ ⊚ ⅋ ⓢ ⓢ
Notes: No cars by tents. No groups of more than 4 unless a family group with children, no noise between 23.00hrs-07.00hrs. Dogs must be kept on leads. Launching area for sailing craft, orienteering course, bike hire.

▶▶▶ 77% Hawkshead Hall Farm (SD349988)

Hawkshead LA22 0NN
☎ 015394 36221
e-mail: enquiries@hawksheadhall-campsite.com
dir: *From Ambleside take A593 signed Coniston, then B5286 signed Hawkshead. Site signed on left just before Hawkshead. Or from Coniston take B5285 to T-junct. Left, then 1st right into site*

* ☎ £17-£20 ☎ £17-£20 ▲ £16.50-£20

Open Mar-Oct

Last arrival 21.00hrs Last departure noon

A mainly camping site a few minutes' walk from village centre in a landscape of gentle rolling hills. The pitch sizes are generous and there's a very well-equipped, purpose-built amenities block. Surrounded by unspoiled countryside, the adjoining fields are a delight for families, especially during the lambing season. 55 touring pitches. Caravan pitches. Motorhome pitches. Tent pitches.

LEISURE: 🏊 Indoor swimming pool 🏊 Outdoor swimming pool ⋔ Children's playground 🏌 Kid's club ⛹ Tennis court ⚲ Games room ⬜ Separate TV room ⛳ 9/18 hole golf course ⛵ Boats for hire 🎬 Cinema 🎵 Entertainment ⅋ Fishing ⊚ Mini golf ⛵ Watersports 🏋 Gym ⊕ Sports field **Spa** ⥀ Stables
FACILITIES: ⛭ Bath ⋔ Shower ⊙ Electric shaver ℱ Hairdryer ✷ Ice Pack Facility ⅋ Disabled facilities Ⓒ Public telephone Ⓢ Shop on site or within 200yds ⓢ Mobile shop (calls at least 5 days a week) 🍖 BBQ area ⅋ Picnic area 📶 Wi-fi 🖥 Internet access ♻ Recycling ❶ Tourist info 🐕 Dog exercise area

AA Pubs & Restaurants nearby: The Queen's Head Inn & Restaurant, HAWKSHEAD, LA22 0NS, 015394 36271

Kings Arms, HAWKSHEAD, LA22 0NZ, 015394 36372

Facilities: 🔌⊙🖨☀🔥♻ 🛈

Services: 🚽

Within 3 miles: 🎣🏊🛶💲💷🎣∪

Notes: No noise 23.00hrs-07.00hrs.

APPLEBY-IN-WESTMORLAND　　Map 18 NY62

Places to visit

Brougham Castle, BROUGHAM, CA10 2AA, 01768 862488 www.english-heritage.org.uk/ daysout/properties/brougham-castle

Acorn Bank Garden and Watermill, TEMPLE SOWERBY, CA10 1SP, 017683 61893 www.nationaltrust.org.uk

Great for kids: Wetheriggs Animal Rescue & Conservation Centre, PENRITH, CA10 2DH, 01768 866657 www.wetheriggsanimalrescue.co.uk

---

PREMIER PARK

▶▶▶▶▶ **88%** *Wild Rose Park* (NY698165)

Ormside CA16 6EJ
☎ 017683 51077
e-mail: reception@wildrose.co.uk
web: www.wildrose.co.uk
dir: *Signed on unclassified road to Great Ormside, off B6260*

🚐🚃Å

Open all year (rs Nov-Mar shop closed, restaurant rs, pool closed 6 Sep-27 May)

Last arrival 22.00hrs Last departure noon

Situated in the Eden Valley, this large leisure group-run park has been carefully landscaped and offers superb facilities maintained to an extremely high standard, including four wooden wigwams for hire. There are several individual pitches, and extensive views from most areas of the park. Traditional stone walls and the planting of lots of indigenous trees help it to blend into the environment, and wildlife is actively encouraged. New for 2014 - a stylish new reception with adjacent internet café, the Ferret and Firkin bar with slate floor and pub games (and where dogs are welcome) and a

choice of adults-only and family entertainment rooms. 85 acre site. 226 touring pitches. 140 hardstandings. Caravan pitches. Motorhome pitches. Tent pitches. 273 statics. 4 tipis.

AA Pubs & Restaurants nearby: The Royal Oak Appleby, APPLEBY-IN-WESTMORLAND, CA16 6UN, 017683 51463

Tufton Arms Hotel, APPLEBY-IN-WESTMORLAND, CA16 6XA, 017683 51593

Leisure: 🌊⛰🎣♣♫

Facilities: 🔌⊙🖨☀♿💲🛒🅿🍴📺 ♻ 🛈

Services: 🚽🗑🍺📶🌭T🍴🛒♻🚐

Within 3 miles: 🎣♣⊙💲💷

Notes: No unaccompanied teenagers, no group bookings, no noise after 22.30hrs, no dangerous dogs. Dogs must be kept on leads. Pitch & putt, fishing.

BARROW-IN-FURNESS

Places to visit

The Dock Museum, BARROW-IN-FURNESS, LA14 2PW, 01229 876400 www.dockmuseum.org.uk

Furness Abbey, BARROW-IN-FURNESS, LA13 0PJ, 01229 823420 www.english-heritage.org.uk/ daysout/properties/furness-abbey

Great for kids: South Lakes Wild Animal Park, DALTON-IN-FURNESS, LA15 8JR, 01229 466086 www.wildanimalpark.co.uk

---

BARROW-IN-FURNESS　　Map 18 SD26

▶▶▶ **84% South End Caravan Park**
(SD208628)

Walney Island LA14 3YQ
☎ 01229 472823 & 471556
e-mail: enquiries@secp.co.uk
web: www.walneyislandcaravanpark.co.uk
dir: *M6 junct 36, A590 to Barrow, follow signs for Walney Island. Cross bridge, turn left. Site 6m south*

* 🚐 £16.50-£22.50 🚃 £16.50-£22.50

Open Mar-Oct (rs Mar-Etr & Oct pool closed)

Last arrival 22.00hrs Last departure noon

A friendly family-owned and run park next to the sea and close to a nature reserve, on the southern end of Walney Island. It offers an extensive range of quality amenities including an adult lounge, and high standards of cleanliness and maintenance. 7 acre site. 50 touring pitches. 15 hardstandings. 34 seasonal pitches. Caravan pitches. Motorhome pitches. 250 statics.

AA Pubs & Restaurants nearby: The Stan Laurel Inn, ULVERSTON, LA12 0AB, 01229 582814

Leisure: 🌊⛰🎣♣☐

Facilities: 🔌⊙☀♿🅿🍴📶📺♻

Services: 🚽🗑🍺📶🌭🛒♻🚐

Within 3 miles: 🎣♣💲💷∪

Notes: Dogs must be kept on leads. Bowling green, snooker table.

SERVICES: 🔌 Electric hook up 🗑 Launderette 🍺 Licensed bar 🔥 Calor Gas ⊘ Camping Gaz T Toilet fluid 🍴 Café/Restaurant 🍟 Fast Food/Takeaway 🔋 Battery charging 🍼 Baby care 🚐 Motorvan service point **ABBREVIATIONS:** BH/bank hols-bank holidays Etr-Easter Spring BH-Spring Bank Holiday dep-departure fr-from hrs-hours m-mile mdnt-midnight rdbt-roundabout rs-restricted service wk-week wknd-weekend x-rds-cross roads 🚫 No credit cards 🚫 No dogs 👶 Children of all ages accepted See page 9 for details of the AA Camping Card Scheme

BASSENTHWAITE LAKE

See map for locations of sites in the vicinity

BOOT
Map 18 NY10

Places to visit

Steam Yacht Gondola, CONISTON, LA21 8AJ, 015394 41962 www.nationaltrust.org.uk/gondola

The Ruskin Museum, CONISTON, LA21 8DU, 015394 41164 www.ruskinmuseum.com

Great for kids: Ravenglass & Eskdale Railway, RAVENGLASS, CA18 1SW, 01229 717171 www.ravenglass-railway.co.uk

PREMIER PARK

►►►►► 84% Eskdale Camping & Caravanning Club Site *(NY179011)*

CA19 1TH

☎ 019467 23253 & 0845 130 7633

e-mail: eskdale.site@thefriendlyclub.co.uk

dir: *Exit A595 at Gosforth or Holmrook to Eskdale Green, then signs for Boot. Site on left towards Hardknott Pass after railway, 150mtrs after Brook House Inn*

🚐 Å

Open Mar-14 Jan

Last arrival 20.00hrs Last departure noon

Stunningly located in Eskdale, a feeling of peace and tranquillity prevails at this top quality campsite, with the sounds of running water and birdsong the only welcome distractions. Although mainly geared to campers, the facilities here are very impressive, with a smart amenities block, equipped with efficient modern facilities including an excellent fully serviced wet room-style, family room with power shower. The surrounding mountains, and the mature trees and shrubs create a wonderful 'back to nature' feeling. There's a nest of camping pods under the trees, with gravel access paths and barbecues, a super backpackers' field and a self-catering camping barn. Expect great attention to detail and a high level of customer care. The park is only a quarter of a mile from Boot station on the Ravenglass/Eskdale railway (La'al Ratty). 8 acre site. 100 touring pitches. Motorhome pitches. Tent pitches. 10 wooden pods.

AA Pubs & Restaurants nearby: Brook House Inn, BOOT, CA19 1TG, 019467 23288

Leisure: 🅰 🅯

Facilities: 🌂 ☉ ℘ ✳ 🕃 🕘 🖫 🖮 🚐 ♻ 🅸

Services: 🖭 🖻 🖿 ⌀ 🅣 🛒 🚽 ⛟

Within 3 miles: 🚶 ℘ ⑤ 🖫 🆄

Notes: Site gates closed & no noise 23.00hrs-07.00hrs, no open fires. Dogs must be kept on leads. Camping barn, free drying room, hot & cold drinks station, toast & hot snacks.

BOWNESS-ON-WINDERMERE

Sites are listed under Windermere

CARLISLE
Map 18 NY35

Places to visit

Carlisle Castle, CARLISLE, CA3 8UR, 01228 591992 www.english-heritage.org.uk/daysout/properties/carlisle-castle

Tullie House Museum & Art Gallery Trust, CARLISLE, CA3 8TP, 01228 618718 www.tulliehouse.co.uk

Great for kids: Trotters World of Animals, BASSENTHWAITE, CA12 4RD, 017687 76239 www.trottersworld.com

►►►► 84% Green Acres Caravan Park *(NY416614)*

High Knells, Houghton CA6 4JW

☎ 01228 675418 & 07720 343820

e-mail: info@caravanpark-cumbria.com

dir: *M6 junct 44, A689 E towards Brampton for 1m. Left at Scaleby sign. Site 1m on left*

✱ 🚐 £15-£17 🚐 £15-£17 Å £10-£14

Open Apr-Oct

Last arrival 21.00hrs Last departure noon

A small, adults-only touring park in rural surroundings close to the M6 with distant views of the fells. A convenient stopover, this pretty park is run by keen, friendly owners who maintain high standards throughout. The site has a caravan and motorhome pressure-washer area, a field and woodland dog walk and two superb unisex shower rooms which include toilet and wash basin. 3 acre site. 30 touring pitches. 30 hardstandings. 12 seasonal pitches. Caravan pitches. Motorhome pitches. Tent pitches.

Leisure: 🅯

Facilities: 🌂 ☉ ℘ ✳ 🖮 🚐 ♻ 🅸

Services: 🖭 🖻

Within 3 miles: 🚶 🖻

Notes: Adults only. 🐕 Dogs must be kept on leads.

►►► 86% Dandy Dinmont Caravan & Camping Park *(NY399620)*

Blackford CA6 4EA

☎ 01228 674611

e-mail: dandydinmont@btopenworld.com

dir: *M6 junct 44, A7 N. Site 1.5m on right after Blackford sign*

🚐 £16 🚐 £16 Å £14-£15

Open Mar-Oct

Last arrival 21.00hrs Last departure noon

A sheltered, rural site, screened on two sides by hedgerows and only one mile from the M6 and Carlisle. The grass pitches are immaculately kept, and there are some larger hardstandings for motor homes. This park attracts mainly adults; please note that cycling and ball games are not allowed. Touring customers are invited to view the private award-winning garden. 4.5 acre site. 47 touring pitches. 14 hardstandings. Caravan pitches. Motorhome pitches. Tent pitches. 15 statics.

Facilities: 🌂 ☉ ℘ ✳ 🖮 ♻ 🅸

Services: 🖭 🖻 🖿

Within 3 miles: 🚶 ℘ ◎ ⑤ 🖫 🆄

Notes: Children's activities are restricted. Dogs must be exercised off site & kept on leads. Covered dishwashing area.

CARTMEL

Places to visit

Holker Hall & Gardens, HOLKER, LA11 7PL, 015395 58328 www.holker.co.uk

Hill Top, NEAR SAWREY, LA22 0LF, 015394 36269 www.nationaltrust.org.uk/hilltop

Great for kids: Lakes Aquarium, LAKESIDE, LA12 8AS, 015395 30153 www.lakesaquarium.co.uk

LEISURE: 🏊 Indoor swimming pool 🏊 Outdoor swimming pool 🅰 Children's playground 🅙 Kid's club 🎾 Tennis court 🎱 Games room 🖵 Separate TV room 🏌 9/18 hole golf course 🚣 Boats for hire 🎬 Cinema 🎵 Entertainment 🎣 Fishing ◎ Mini golf 🏄 Watersports 🏋 Gym 🅯 Sports field **Spa** 🆄 Stables **FACILITIES:** 🛁 Bath 🌂 Shower ☉ Electric shaver ℘ Hairdryer ✳ Ice Pack Facility 🕃 Disabled facilities 🕘 Public telephone ⑤ Shop on site or within 200yds 🖾 Mobile shop (calls at least 5 days a week) 🍴 BBQ area 🖮 Picnic area 🖬 Wi-fi 🖳 Internet access ♻ Recycling 🅸 Tourist info 🅃 Dog exercise area

CARTMEL Map 18 SD37

►►► 78% Greaves Farm Caravan Park (SD391823)

Field Broughton LA11 6HR
☎ 015395 36587 & 36329
dir: M6 junct 36, A590 signed Barrow. Approx 1m before Newby Bridge, turn left at x-rds signed Cartmel/Staveley. Site 2m on left just before church

* 🚐 £16-£18 🚏 £16-£18 ▲ £14-£18

Open Mar-Oct

Last arrival 21.00hrs Last departure noon

A small family-owned park close to a working farm in a peaceful rural area. Motorhomes are parked in a paddock which has spacious hardstandings, and there is a large field for tents and caravans. This simple park is carefully maintained, offers electric pitches (6amp), and there is always a sparkle to the toilet facilities. Static holiday caravans for hire. 3 acre site. 20 touring pitches. 9 hardstandings. Caravan pitches. Motorhome pitches. Tent pitches. 20 statics.

AA Pubs & Restaurants nearby: The Cavendish Arms, CARTMEL, LA11 6QA, 015395 36240

The Masons Arms, CARTMEL, LA11 6NW, 015395 68486

Rogan & Company Restaurant, CARTMEL, LA11 6QD, 015395 35917

Facilities: 🅿️ ☉ 🅿️ ✳ ⊕ 🗮 ♻ 🅘

Services: 🔌 🛢

Within 3 miles: ⌗ ⌇ 🖊 ⋛ 🖻 ∪

Notes: 🐕 Couples & families only, no noise after 23.00hrs, no open fires. Dogs must be kept on leads. Separate chalet for dishwashing. Small freezer & fridge available.

CROOKLANDS Map 18 SD58

Places to visit

Levens Hall, LEVENS, LA8 0PD, 015395 60321 www.levenshall.co.uk

RSPB Leighton Moss Nature Reserve, SILVERDALE, LA5 0SW, 01524 701601 www.rspb.org.uk/leightonmoss

Great for kids: South Lakes Wild Animal Park, DALTON-IN-FURNESS, LA15 8JR, 01229 466086 www.wildanimalpark.co.uk

►►►► 82% Waters Edge Caravan Park (SD533838)

LA7 7NN
☎ 015395 67708 & 67527
e-mail: info@watersedgecaravanpark.co.uk
dir: M6 junct 36, A65 towards Kirkby Lonsdale, at 2nd rdbt follow signs for Crooklands/Endmoor. Site 1m on right at Crooklands garage, just beyond 40mph limit

* 🚐 fr £16.50 🚏 fr £16.50 ▲ fr £10

Open Mar-14 Nov (rs Low season bar not always open on wkdays)

Last arrival 22.00hrs Last departure noon

A peaceful, well-run park close to the M6, pleasantly bordered by streams and woodland. A Lakeland-style building houses a shop and bar, and the attractive toilet block is clean and modern. This is ideal either as a stopover or for longer stays. 3 acre site. 26 touring pitches. 26 hardstandings. 8 seasonal pitches. Caravan pitches. Motorhome pitches. Tent pitches. 20 statics.

AA Pubs & Restaurants nearby: The Plough Inn Lupton, LUPTON, LA6 1PJ, 015395 67700

Leisure: 🎣 ▭

Facilities: 🅿️ ☉ 🅿️ ✳ ⊕ 🗮 🅘

Services: 🔌 🗐 🍴 🛢 ⊘ 🆃

Within 3 miles: 🖊 🖻 ∪

Notes: No cars by tents. Dogs must be kept on leads.

CUMWHITTON Map 18 NY55

Places to visit

Nenthead Mines, ALSTON, CA9 3PD, 01434 382294 www.npht.com/nentheadmines

Lanercost Priory, BRAMPTON, CA8 2HQ, 01697 73030 www.english-heritage.org.uk/daysout/properties/lanercost-priory

►►► 69% Cairndale Caravan Park (NY518523)

CA8 9BZ
☎ 01768 896280
dir: Exit A69 at Warwick Bridge on unclassified road through Great Corby to Cumwhitton, left at village sign, site 1m

* 🚐 £10-£12 🚏 £10-£12

Open Mar-Oct

Last arrival 22.00hrs

Lovely grass site set in the tranquil Eden Valley with good views to distant hills. The all-weather touring pitches have electricity, and are located close to the immaculately maintained toilet facilities. Static holiday caravans for hire. 2 acre site. 5 touring pitches. 5 hardstandings. Caravan pitches. Motorhome pitches. 15 statics.

AA Pubs & Restaurants nearby: The String of Horses Inn, FAUGH, CA8 9EG, 01228 670297

Facilities: 🅿️ ☉ ✳ ♻

Services: 🔌 🛢 🗮

Within 3 miles: ⌗ ⌇ 🖊 ⋛

Notes: 🐕

SERVICES: 🔌 Electric hook up 🗐 Launderette 🍴 Licensed bar 🛢 Calor Gas ⊘ Camping Gaz 🆃 Toilet fluid 🍴 Café/Restaurant 🗮 Fast Food/Takeaway 🗮 Battery charging 🍼 Baby care 🚐 Motorvan service point **ABBREVIATIONS:** BH/bank hols-bank holidays Etr-Easter Spring BH-Spring Bank Holiday dep-departure fr-from hrs-hours m-mile mdnt-midnight rdbt-roundabout rs-restricted service wk-week wknd-weekend x-rds-cross roads 🅒 No credit cards 🅧 No dogs 🅘 Children of all ages accepted See page 9 for details of the AA Camping Card Scheme

FLOOKBURGH Map 18 SD37

Places to visit

Holker Hall & Gardens, HOLKER, LA11 7PL, 015395 58328 www.holker.co.uk

Hill Top, NEAR SAWREY, LA22 0LF, 015394 36269 www.nationaltrust.org.uk/hilltop

Great for kids: Lakes Aquarium, LAKESIDE, LA12 8AS, 015395 30153 www.lakesaquarium.co.uk

 82% Lakeland Leisure Park *(SD372743)*

Moor Ln LA11 7LT
☎ **0871 231 0883**
e-mail: lakeland@haven.com
web: www.haven.com/lakeland
dir: *On B5277 through Grange-over-Sands to Flookburgh. Left at village square, site 1m*

Open mid Mar-end Oct (rs mid Mar-May & Sep-Oct reduced activities, outdoor pool closed)

Last arrival anytime Last departure 10.00hrs

A complete leisure park with full range of activities and entertainments, making this flat, grassy site ideal for families. The touring area, which includes 24 fully serviced pitches, is quietly situated away from the main amenities, but the swimming pools, all-weather bowling green and evening entertainment are just a short stroll away. A new lake featuring water sporting opportunities opened in 2013. 105 acre site. 185 touring pitches. Caravan pitches. Motorhome pitches. Tent pitches. 800 statics.

AA Pubs & Restaurants nearby: The Cavendish Arms, CARTMEL, LA11 6QA, 015395 36240

The Masons Arms, CARTMEL, LA11 6NW, 015395 68486

Rogan & Company Restaurant, CARTMEL, LA11 6QD, 015395 35917

Leisure: 🏊 ⛵ 🎠 ✋ ⚽ 🎵
Facilities: 🛁 ⊙ 🔌 🚿 🔋 📶 🖥 ♻ ❗
Services: 🚽 🗑 🍴 🛒 T 🍽 ♨ 🛒
Within 3 miles: ⤢ 🎣 ◎ ⛵ 🏌 🛒 🐴 ∪

Notes: No cars by caravans or tents. No commercial vehicles. Family park, no bookings by persons under 21yrs unless a family booking. Max 2 dogs per booking, certain dog breeds banned. Dogs must be kept on leads.

see advert below

GRANGE-OVER-SANDS Map 18 SD47

See also Cartmel

Places to visit

Dove Cottage and The Wordsworth Museum, GRASMERE, LA22 9SH, 015394 35544 www.wordsworth.org.uk

Honister Slate Mine, BORROWDALE, CA12 5XN, 01768 777230 www.honister-slate-mine.co.uk

▶▶▶ **78% Oak Head Caravan Park**
(SD389839)

Ayside LA11 6JA
☎ **015395 31475**
web: www.oakheadcaravanpark.co.uk
dir: *M6 junct 36, A590 towards Newby Bridge, 14m. From A590 bypass follow signs for Ayside*

* 🚐 fr £20 🚐 fr £20 ▲ £18-£20

Open Mar-Oct

Last arrival 20.00hrs Last departure noon

Three miles from Grange-over-Sands and with direct access from A590 south of Newby Bridge, this is a pleasant terraced site with two separate areas - grass for tents and all gravel pitches for caravans and motorhomes. The site is enclosed within mature woodland and surrounded by hills; it is located in a less busy area but convenient for all the Lake District attractions. 10 acre site. 60 touring pitches. 30 hardstandings. Caravan pitches. Motorhome pitches. Tent pitches. 71 statics.

LEISURE: 🏊 Indoor swimming pool ⛲ Outdoor swimming pool 🎢 Children's playground ✋ Kid's club 🎾 Tennis court 🎱 Games room 📺 Separate TV room ⛳ 9/18 hole golf course ⛵ Boats for hire 🎬 Cinema 🎭 Entertainment 🎣 Fishing ◎ Mini golf 🏄 Watersports 💪 Gym ⚽ Sports field Spa ∪ Stables
FACILITIES: 🛁 Bath 🚿 Shower ⊙ Electric shaver ✂ Hairdryer ❄ Ice Pack Facility ♿ Disabled facilities 📞 Public telephone 🛒 Shop on site or within 200yds 🛒 Mobile shop (calls at least 5 days a week) 🍴 BBQ area 🌲 Picnic area 📶 Wi-fi 🖥 Internet access ♻ Recycling ❗ Tourist info 🐕 Dog exercise area

AA Pubs & Restaurants nearby: The Cavendish Arms, CARTMEL, LA11 6QA, 015395 36240

The Masons Arms, CARTMEL, LA11 6NW, 015395 68486

Rogan & Company Restaurant, CARTMEL, LA11 6QD, 015395 35917

Leisure: ◎

Facilities: ♠⊙🅿☀🌡☏

Services: 🔌🗑🛢🧹🔋

Within 3 miles: ⚓🚣🎣🚴🏇🛶

Notes: ⊛ No open fires, no noise after 23.00hrs. Dogs must be kept on leads.

GREAT LANGDALE — Map 18 NY20

Places to visit

Dove Cottage and The Wordsworth Museum, GRASMERE, LA22 9SH, 015394 35544 www.wordsworth.org.uk

Honister Slate Mine, BORROWDALE, CA12 5XN, 01768 777230 www.honister-slate-mine.co.uk

▶▶▶ 77% Great Langdale National Trust Campsite (NY286059)

LA22 9JU
☎ 015394 63862 & 32733
e-mail: campsite.bookings@nationaltrust.org.uk
web: www.ntlakescampsites.org.uk
dir: From Ambleside, A593 to Skelwith Bridge, right onto B5343, approx 5m to New Dungeon Ghyll Hotel. Site on left just before hotel

🚐🚕Å

Open all year

Last departure 11.00hrs

Nestling in a green valley, sheltered by mature trees and surrounded by stunning fell views, this site is an ideal base for campers, climbers and fell walkers. The large grass tent area has some gravel parking for cars, and there is a separate area for groups, and one for families with a children's play area. Attractive wooden cabins house the toilets, the reception and shop (selling fresh baked bread and pastries), and drying rooms, and there are wooden camping pods and two yurts for hire. Additionally, it is a gentle ten-minute walk to The Sticklebarn Tavern, the only National Trust run pub. 9 acre site. 220 touring pitches. Motorhome pitches. Tent pitches. 3 wooden pods.

AA Pubs & Restaurants nearby: The New Dungeon Ghyll Hotel, GREAT LANGDALE, LA22 9JX, 015394 37213

The Britannia Inn, ELTERWATER, LA22 9HP, 015394 37210

Langdale Hotel & Spa, ELTERWATER, LA22 9JD, 015394 37302

Leisure: 🛝

Facilities: ♠⊙☀🌡☏🎱♻

Services: 🗑🛢🧹

Within 3 miles: 🎣🛢

Notes: No cars by tents. No noise between 23.00hrs-07.00hrs, no groups of 4 or more unless a family with children. Dogs must be kept on leads.

HOLMROOK — Map 18 SD09

Places to visit

The Beacon, WHITEHAVEN, CA28 7LY, 01946 592302 www.thebeacon-whitehaven.co.uk

The Rum Story, WHITEHAVEN, CA28 7DN, 01946 592933 www.rumstory.co.uk

Great for kids: Ravenglass & Eskdale Railway, RAVENGLASS, CA18 1SW, 01229 717171 www.ravenglass-railway.co.uk

▶▶▶ 75% Seven Acres Caravan Park (NY078014)

CA19 1YD
☎ 01946 822777
e-mail: reception@seacote.com
dir: Site signed on A595 between Holmrook & Gosforth

🚐🚕Å

Open Mar-15 Jan

Last arrival 21.00hrs Last departure 10.30hrs

This sheltered park is close to quiet west Cumbrian coastal villages and beaches, and also handy for Eskdale and Wasdale. There is a good choice of pitches, some with hedged bays for privacy and some with coastal views. The park has a heated toilet block. 7 acre site. 37 touring pitches. 20 hardstandings. Caravan pitches. Motorhome pitches. Tent pitches. 16 statics.

AA Pubs & Restaurants nearby: Bower House Inn, ESKDALE GREEN, CA19 1TD, 019467 23244

Facilities: ♠⊙🅿☀🌡🛏♻🛈

Services: 🔌🗑🛠

Within 3 miles: ⚓🎣🎱🛢🛶

Notes: Dogs must be kept on leads.

KESWICK — Map 18 NY22

Places to visit

Cumberland Pencil Museum, KESWICK, CA12 5NG, 017687 73626 www.pencilmuseum.co.uk

Honister Slate Mine, BORROWDALE, CA12 5XN, 01768 777230 www.honister-slate-mine.co.uk

Great for kids: Mirehouse, KESWICK, CA12 4QE, 017687 72287 www.mirehouse.com

PREMIER PARK

▶▶▶▶▶ 87% Castlerigg Hall Caravan & Camping Park (NY282227)

Castlerigg Hall CA12 4TE
☎ 017687 74499
e-mail: info@castlerigg.co.uk
dir: 1.5m SE of Keswick on A591, turn right at sign. Site 200mtrs on right past Heights Hotel

🚐🚕Å

Open mid Mar-7 Nov

Last arrival 21.00hrs Last departure 11.30hrs

Spectacular views over Derwent Water to the mountains beyond are among the many attractions at this lovely Lakeland park. Old farm buildings have been tastefully converted into excellent toilets with private washing cubicles and a family bathroom, reception and a well-equipped shop, and there is a kitchen/dining area for campers, and a restaurant/takeaway. There is a superb toilet block, and wooden camping pods and a further ten all-weather pitches are located in the tent field. 8 acre site. 48 touring pitches.

continued

SERVICES: 🔌 Electric hook up 🗑 Launderette 🍽 Licensed bar 🛢 Calor Gas 🧹 Camping Gaz 🅃 Toilet fluid 🍴 Café/Restaurant 🍟 Fast Food/Takeaway 🔋 Battery charging 🍼 Baby care 🚐 Motorvan service point ABBREVIATIONS: BH/bank hols-bank holidays Etr-Easter Spring BH-Spring Bank Holiday dep-departure fr-from hrs-hours m-mile mdnt-midnight rdbt-roundabout rs-restricted service wk-week wknd-weekend x-rds-cross roads ⊛ No credit cards ⊗ No dogs 🧒 Children of all ages accepted See page 9 for details of the AA Camping Card Scheme

KESWICK *continued*

48 hardstandings. Caravan pitches. Motorhome pitches. Tent pitches. 30 statics.

AA Pubs & Restaurants nearby: The Kings Head, KESWICK, CA12 4TN, 017687 72393

Castlerigg Hall Caravan & Camping Park

Leisure: 📺

Facilities: 🛁 🚿 🪒 💨 ❄ ♿ 📞 🛒 🐕 [Wi-fi]

Services: 🧺 🗄 🔒 🍃 [T] 🍴 🥡 🛍 ⛽

Within 3 miles: ⛳ ⛵ 🎬 🎣 ◎ 🏄 🛒 🗄 🐴

Notes: Dogs must be kept on leads & not left unattended. Campers' kitchen, sitting room.

see advert below

►►►► 78% *Gill Head Farm Caravan & Camping Park* (NY380269)

Troutbeck CA11 0ST
☎ 017687 79652
e-mail: enquiries@gillheadfarm.co.uk
web: www.gillheadfarm.co.uk
dir: *M6 junct 40, A66, A5091 towards Troutbeck. Right after 100yds, then right again*

🚐 🚙 ⛺

Open Apr-Oct

Last arrival 22.00hrs Last departure noon

A family-run park on a working hill farm with a wide variety of trees and shrubs in addition to pretty, seasonal floral displays; the site has lovely fell views. It has level touring pitches, and a log cabin dining room that is popular with families. Tent pitches are gently sloping in a separate field with glorious views towards Keswick. 5.5 acre site. 42 touring pitches. 21 hardstandings. Caravan pitches. Motorhome pitches. Tent pitches. 17 statics.

AA Pubs & Restaurants nearby: The George, KESWICK, CA12 5AZ, 017687 72076

Leisure: 🛝 📺

Facilities: 🚿 🪒 💨 ❄ 📞 🛒 🪑 🐕

Services: 🧺 🗄 🔒 🍃

Within 3 miles: ⛳ ⛵ 🎣 🏄 🛒 🐴

Notes: No fires.

►►► 77% Burns Farm Caravan Park (NY307244)

St Johns in the Vale CA12 4RR
☎ 017687 79225 & 79112
e-mail: linda@burns-farm.co.uk
dir: *Exit A66 signed Castlerigg Stone Circle/Youth Centre/Burns Farm. Site on right in 0.5m*

🚐 🚙 ⛺

Open Mar-4 Nov

Last departure noon

Lovely views of Blencathra and Skiddaw can be enjoyed from this secluded park, set on a working farm which extends a warm welcome to families. This is a good choice for exploring the beautiful and interesting countryside. Food can be found in the pub at Threlkeld. 2.5 acre site. 32 touring pitches. Caravan pitches. Motorhome pitches. Tent pitches.

AA Pubs & Restaurants nearby: Farmers Arms, KESWICK, CA12 5RN, 017687 72322

Facilities: 🚿 🪒 ❄ ♿ 📞 [Wi-fi] ♻

Services: 🧺 🗄 🔒 🥡

Within 3 miles: ⛳ ⛵ 🎬 🎣 ◎ 🏄 🛒 🗄 🐴

Notes: 🚫 No noise after mdnt.

LEISURE: 🏊 Indoor swimming pool 🌊 Outdoor swimming pool 🛝 Children's playground ✋ Kid's club 🎾 Tennis court ♠ Games room 📺 Separate TV room ⛳ 9/18 hole golf course ⛵ Boats for hire 🎬 Cinema 🎵 Entertainment 🎣 Fishing ◎ Mini golf 🏄 Watersports 🏋 Gym ⚽ Sports field **Spa** 🐴 Stables
FACILITIES: 🛁 Bath 🚿 Shower 🪒 Electric shaver 💨 Hairdryer ❄ Ice Pack Facility ♿ Disabled facilities 📞 Public telephone 🛒 Shop on site or within 200yds 🚚 Mobile shop (calls at least 5 days a week) 🍖 BBQ area 🪑 Picnic area [Wi-fi] Wi-fi 💻 Internet access ♻ Recycling ℹ Tourist info 🐕 Dog exercise area

KIRKBY LONSDALE
Map 18 SD67

Places to visit

Sizergh Castle & Garden, SIZERGH, LA8 8AE, 015395 60951 www.nationaltrust.org.uk

Kendal Museum, KENDAL, LA9 6BT, 01539 815597 www.kendalmuseum.org.uk

Great for kids: Dales Countryside Museum & National Park Centre, HAWES, DL8 3NT, 01969 666210 www.yorkshiredales.org.uk/dcm

REGIONAL WINNER - NORTH WEST ENGLAND AA CAMPSITE OF THE YEAR 2014

PREMIER PARK

▶▶▶▶▶ 85% Woodclose Caravan Park *(SD618786)*

GOLD

High Casterton LA6 2SE
☎ 015242 71597
e-mail: info@woodclosepark.com
web: www.woodclosepark.com
dir: *On A65, 0.25m after Kirkby Lonsdale towards Skipton, park on left*

🚐 🚚 Å

Open Mar-Oct

Last arrival 21.00hrs (no arrivals before 13.00hrs). Last departure noon

A peaceful, well-managed park set in idyllic countryside within the beautiful Lune Valley, and centrally located for exploring the Lakes and Dales. Ideal for that 'back to nature' experience, with riverside walks, on-site woodland walks for both families and dogs, and top notch amenities blocks with fully serviced cubicles with one allocated for the 'Wigwam' pod village and camping field. The generous pitches are surrounded by mature trees and seasonal planting. Parts of the site are havens for wildlife. 9 acre site. 29 touring pitches. 28 hardstandings. Caravan pitches. Motorhome pitches. Tent pitches. 65 statics. 11 wooden pods.

AA Pubs & Restaurants nearby: The Sun Inn, KIRKBY LONSDALE, LA6 2AU, 015242 71965

The Whoop Hall, KIRKBY LONSDALE, LA6 2HP, 015242 71284

The Pheasant Inn, KIRKBY LONSDALE, LA6 2RX, 015242 71230

Leisure: 🎱 ⚽

Facilities: 🅿 ⊙ 🌮 ⚒ ⚙ 🕐 🔲 🚰 🐕 Wi-Fi 🖥 ♻ ❽

Services: 🔌 🔲 🔋 ⊘

Within 3 miles: 🎣 🚵 🏪 🔲 ⛷

Notes: Dogs must be kept on leads. Cycle hire, crock boxes for hire.

▶▶▶▶ 79% New House Caravan Park *(SD628774)*

LA6 2HR
☎ 015242 71590
e-mail: colinpreece9@aol.com
dir: *1m SE of Kirkby Lonsdale on A65, turn right into site entrance 300yds past Whoop Hall Inn*

* 🚐 £17.50 🚚 £17.50

Open Mar-Oct

Last arrival 20.00hrs

Colourful floral displays greet new arrivals, creating an excellent first impression at this former farm, which has been carefully changed to provide well-spaced pitches, with hardstandings sheltered by surrounding mature trees and shrubs. An ideal base for exploring the Yorkshire Dales and the Lake District. 3 acre site. 50 touring pitches. 50 hardstandings. Caravan pitches. Motorhome pitches.

AA Pubs & Restaurants nearby: The Sun Inn, KIRKBY LONSDALE, LA6 2AU, 015242 71965

The Whoop Hall, KIRKBY LONSDALE, LA6 2HP, 015242 71284

The Pheasant Inn, KIRKBY LONSDALE, LA6 2RX, 015242 71230

Facilities: 🅿 ⊙ 🌮 ⚒ ⚙ 🕐 🚰 🐕 Wi-Fi 🖥 ♻ ❽

Services: 🔌 🔲 🔋 ⊘ T 🚂 ⛟

Within 3 miles: 🎣 🚵 🏪 🔲

Notes: ⊗ No cycling. Dogs must be kept on leads.

LONGTOWN
Map 21 NY36

Places to visit

Carlisle Castle, CARLISLE, CA3 8UR, 01228 591992 www.english-heritage.org.uk/daysout/properties/carlisle-castle

Tullie House Museum & Art Gallery Trust, CARLISLE, CA3 8TP, 01228 618718 www.tulliehouse.co.uk

▶▶ 75% Camelot Caravan Park *(NY391666)*

CA6 5SZ
☎ 01228 791248
dir: *M6 junct 44, A7, site 5m N & 1m S of Longtown*

🚐 🚚 Å

Open Mar-Oct

Last arrival 20.00hrs Last departure noon

A very pleasant level grassy site in a wooded setting near the M6, with direct access from the A7, and simple, clean toilet facilities. The park is an ideal stopover site. 1.5 acre site. 20 touring pitches. Caravan pitches. Motorhome pitches. Tent pitches. 2 statics.

Facilities: 🅿 ⊙ ⚒ 🚰 ❽ **Services:** 🔌

Within 3 miles: 🚵 🔲 ⛷ **Notes:** ⊗

SERVICES: 🔌 Electric hook up   🔲 Launderette   🍺 Licensed bar   🔋 Calor Gas   ⊘ Camping Gaz   T Toilet fluid   🍽 Café/Restaurant   🍟 Fast Food/Takeaway   🔋 Battery charging   🚼 Baby care   ⛟ Motorvan service point   **ABBREVIATIONS:** BH/bank hols-bank holidays   Etr-Easter   Spring BH-Spring Bank Holiday   dep-departure   fr-from   hrs-hours   m-mile   mdnt-midnight   rdbt-roundabout   rs-restricted service   wk-week   wknd-weekend   x-rds-cross roads   ⊗ No credit cards   ⊗ No dogs   👶 Children of all ages accepted   See page 9 for details of the AA Camping Card Scheme

MEALSGATE Map 18 NY24

Places to visit

Jennings Brewery Tour and Shop, COCKERMOUTH, CA13 9NE, 0845 129 7190 www.jenningsbrewery.co.uk

Wordsworth House and Garden, COCKERMOUTH, CA13 9RX, 01900 824805 www.nationaltrust.org.uk/wordsworthhouse

►►►► 80% Larches Caravan Park

(NY205415)

CA7 1LQ
☎ 016973 71379 & 71803
dir: *On A595 (Carlisle to Cockermouth road)*

🚐 🚌 ⛺

Open Mar-Oct (rs Early & late season)

Last arrival 21.30hrs Last departure noon

This over 18s-only park is set in wooded rural surroundings on the fringe of the Lake District National Park. Touring units are spread out over two sections. The friendly family-run park offers constantly improving facilities, including a small swimming pool, and a well-stocked shop that also provides a very good range of camping and caravanning spares. 20 acre site. 35 touring pitches. 30 hardstandings. Caravan pitches. Motorhome pitches. Tent pitches.

AA Pubs & Restaurants nearby: Oddfellows Arms, CALDBECK, CA7 8EA, 016974 78227

Facilities: 🚿 🪒 💨 ❄ ♿ 📞 [$] 🐕

Services: 🚏 👕 🛢 🍃 [T] 🛏

Within 3 miles: ⛳ 🎣 👕 🐴

Notes: Adults only. 🚫 Indoor pool opens mid 2014.

MILNTHORPE Map 18 SD48

Places to visit

Levens Hall, LEVENS, LA8 0PD, 015395 60321 www.levenshall.co.uk

RSPB Leighton Moss Nature Reserve, SILVERDALE, LA5 0SW, 01524 701601 www.rspb.org.uk/leightonmoss

Great for kids: Lakes Aquarium, LAKESIDE, LA12 8AS, 015395 30153 www.lakesaquarium.co.uk

►►►► 75% *Hall More Caravan Park* *(SD502771)*

GOLD

Hale LA7 7BP
☎ 01524 781453
e-mail: enquiries@pureleisure-holidays.co.uk
dir: *M6 junct 35, A6 towards Milnthorpe for 4m. Left at Lakeland Wildlife Oasis, follow brown signs*

🚐 🚌 ⛺

Open Mar-Jan

Last arrival 22.00hrs Last departure 10.00hrs

Set on former meadowland and surrounded by mature trees, this constantly improving rural park provides neat, well-spaced pitches with colourful hedged areas enhanced by pretty seasonal flowers. The site is adjacent to a fishery where fly fishing for trout is possible, and near a farm with stables offering pony trekking. There are seven wooden camping pods for hire. 4 acre site. 44 touring pitches. 7 hardstandings. Caravan pitches. Motorhome pitches. Tent pitches. 60 statics.

AA Pubs & Restaurants nearby: The Wheatsheaf at Beetham, BEETHAM, LA7 7AL, 015395 62123

Facilities: 🚿 🪒 💨 ❄ 📞 🐕

Services: 🚏 👕 🛢 🍃 ⚡

Within 3 miles: ⛳ 🎣 [$] 👕 🐴

PATTERDALE Map 18 NY31

►►► 78% Sykeside Camping Park

(NY403119)

Brotherswater CA11 0NZ
☎ 017684 82239
e-mail: info@sykeside.co.uk
dir: *Direct access from A592 (Windermere to Ullswater road) at foot of Kirkstone Pass*

* 🚐 £22.50-£25 🚌 £22.50-£25 ⛺ £13.50-£20.50

Open all year

Last arrival 22.30hrs Last departure 14.00hrs

A camper's delight, this family-run park is sited at the foot of Kirkstone Pass, under the 2,000ft Hartsop Dodd in a spectacular area with breathtaking views. The park has mainly grass pitches with a few hardstandings, an area with tipis for hire, and for those campers without a tent there is bunkhouse accommodation. There's a small campers' kitchen and the bar serves breakfast and bar meals. There is abundant wildlife. 10 acre site. 86 touring pitches. 5 hardstandings. Caravan pitches. Motorhome pitches. Tent pitches.

AA Pubs & Restaurants nearby: Queen's Head, TROUTBECK, LA23 1PW, 015394 32174

The Inn on the Lake, GLENRIDDING, CA11 0PE, 017684 82444

Leisure: 🛝

Facilities: 🚿 🪒 💨 ❄ 📞 [$] 🧺 🐕 💻 ♻ ℹ

Services: 🚏 👕 🍷 🛢 🍃 [T] 🍴 🛏 🍟

Within 3 miles: ⛵ 🎣 🏄 [$] 👕

Notes: No noise after 23.00hrs. Laundry & drying room.

PENRITH

Places to visit

Dalemain Mansion & Historic Gardens, DALEMAIN, CA11 0HB, 017684 86450 www.dalemain.com

Shap Abbey, SHAP, CA10 3NB, 0870 333 1181 www.english-heritage.org.uk/daysout/properties/shap-abbey

Great for kids: The Rheged Centre, PENRITH, CA11 0DQ, 01768 868000 www.rheged.com

PENRITH

Map 18 NY53

PREMIER PARK

▶▶▶▶▶ 85% Lowther
Holiday Park (NY527265)

GOLD

Eamont Bridge CA10 2JB
☎ **01768 863631**
e-mail: alan@lowther-holidaypark.co.uk
web: www.lowther-holidaypark.co.uk
dir: *3m S of Penrith on A6*

* ⊕ £20-£33 ⊕ £20-£33 ▲ £20-£33

Open mid Mar-mid Nov

Last arrival 22.00hrs Last departure 22.00hrs

A secluded natural woodland site with lovely riverside walks and glorious countryside surroundings. The park is home to a rare colony of red squirrels, and trout fishing is available on the two-mile stretch of the River Lowther which runs through it. A birdwatch scheme with a coloured brochure has been introduced, inviting guests to spot some of the 30 different species that can be seen on the park. 50 acre site. 180 touring pitches. 50 hardstandings. 80 seasonal pitches. Caravan pitches. Motorhome pitches. Tent pitches. 403 statics. 2 wooden pods.

AA Pubs & Restaurants nearby: The Yanwath Gate Inn, YANWATH, CA10 2LF, 01768 862386

Queen's Head Inn, TIRRIL, CA10 2JF, 01768 863219

Cross Keys Inn, PENRITH, CA11 8TP, 01768 865588

Lowther Holiday Park

Leisure: 🎬 ⊙ 🔍 ♫

Facilities: ♿ ⚓ ⊙ ℗ ⚒ ⚙ 🚿 📶 💻 ♻ ❔

Services: 🔌 🔲 🛢 💧 ⊘ Ⓣ 🍴 🛒 🍔 ♿ ⚡

Within 3 miles: ⚓ 🎣 ℗ ◎ ⛵ 🏇 ⛳ ∪

Notes: Families only, no commercial vehicles, no cats, rollerblades or skateboards. Dogs must be kept on leads.

see advert below

Lowther

HOLIDAY PARK
THE LAKE DISTRICT

TOURING • CAMPING • PODS • HOLIDAY HOME SALES

Set in 50 acres of natural wooded parkland on the banks of the River Lowther, our David Bellamy Award Winning Park makes the ideal choice for your touring and camping holiday.

Holiday Homes for Hire
Holiday Homes for Sale
Timber Lodges
Touring & Camping
PODS

T: 01768 863631 E: info@lowther-holidaypark.co.uk
www.lowther-holidaypark.co.uk

PENRITH ***continued***

►►►► 83% Flusco Wood

(NY345529)

GOLD

Flusco CA11 0JB
☎ 01768 480020 & 07818 552931
e-mail: info@fluscowood.co.uk
dir: *From Penrith to Keswick on A66 turn right signed Flusco. Approx 800mtrs, up short incline to right. Site on left*

* 🚐 £20-£23 🚌 £20-£23

Open 22 Mar-Oct

Last arrival 20.00hrs Last departure noon

Flusco Wood is set in mixed woodland with outstanding views towards Blencathra and the fells around Keswick. It combines two distinct areas, one of which has been designed specifically for touring caravans in neat glades with hardstandings, all within close proximity of the excellent log cabin-style toilet facilities. 24 acre site. 36 touring pitches. 36 hardstandings. 20 seasonal pitches. Caravan pitches. Motorhome pitches.

AA Pubs & Restaurants nearby: The Yanwath Gate Inn, YANWATH, CA10 2LF, 01768 862386

Queen's Head Inn, TIRRIL, CA10 2JF, 01768 863219

Cross Keys Inn, PENRITH, CA11 8TP, 01768 865588

Leisure: 🛝

Facilities: 🚿 ⊙ 💨 ✱ ♿ ✆ [S] 🧺 🐕 💻 ♻ ℹ

Services: 🔌 ▣ 🔒 [T]

Within 3 miles: 🎬

Notes: Quiet site, not suitable for large groups. Dogs must be kept on leads.

PENRUDDOCK — Map 18 NY42

►►► 80% *Beckses Caravan Park*

(NY419278)

CA11 0RX
☎ 01768 483224
dir: *M6 junct 40, A66 towards Keswick. Approx 6m, at caravan park sign turn right onto B5288. Site on right in 0.25m*

🚐 🚌 ⛺

Open Etr-Oct

Last arrival 20.00hrs Last departure 11.00hrs

A small, pleasant site on sloping ground with level pitches and views of distant fells, on the edge of the National Park. This sheltered park is in a good location for touring the north lakes. 4 acre site. 23 touring pitches. Caravan pitches. Motorhome pitches. Tent pitches. 18 statics.

AA Pubs & Restaurants nearby: Queen's Head, TROUTBECK, LA23 1PW, 015394 32174

Facilities: 🚿 ⊙ 💨 🐕 ♻

Services: 🔌 🔒 🔥 [T] 🛒

Within 3 miles: 🎣 🐴

Notes: No noise after 23.00hrs.

PENTON — Map 21 NY47

►►► 76% Twin Willows *(NY449771)*

The Beeches CA6 5QD
☎ 01228 577313 & 07850 713958
e-mail: davidson_b@btconnect.com
dir: *M6 junct 44, A7 signed Longtown, right into Netherby St, 6m to Bridge Inn pub. Right then 1st left, site 300yds on right*

🚐 £20-£28 🚌 £20-£28 ⛺ £15

Open all year

Last arrival 22.00hrs Last departure 10.00hrs

Twin Willows is a spacious park in a rural location on a ridge overlooking the Scottish border. All facilities, including all-weather pitches, are of a high quality. The park is suited to those who enjoy being away-from-it-all yet at the same time like to explore the area's rich history. A seasonal marquee is erected to hold regular barbecue and hog roast parties. 3 acre site. 16 touring pitches. 16 hardstandings. 10 seasonal pitches. Caravan pitches. Motorhome pitches. Tent pitches. 1 static. 1 wooden pod.

Leisure: 🏊 🏋 🛝 ⚽

Facilities: 🚿 ⊙ 💨 ✱ ♿ ✆ [S] 🧺 🐕 [Wi-fi] 💻 ♻ ℹ

Services: 🔌 ▣ 🔒 🔥 [T] 🍴 🛒 🍔 ⛽

Within 3 miles: 🎣 [S] ▣ 🐴

Notes: 🚫 Dogs must be kept on leads.

POOLEY BRIDGE — Map 18 NY42

AA CAMPING CARD SITE

85% Park Foot Caravan & Camping Park *(NY469235)*

Howtown Rd CA10 2NA
☎ 017684 86309
e-mail: holidays@parkfootullswater.co.uk
web: www.parkfootullswater.co.uk
dir: *M6 junct 40, A66 towards Keswick, then A592 to Ullswater. Turn left for Pooley Bridge, right at church, right at x-rds signed Howtown*

* 🚐 £21-£39 🚌 £14-£39 ⛺ £14-£34

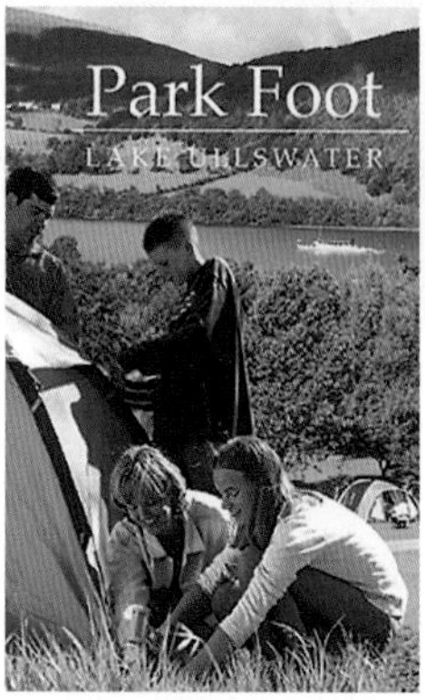

Open Mar-Oct (rs Mar-Apr & mid Sep-Oct clubhouse open wknds only)

Last arrival 22.00hrs Last departure noon

A lively park with good outdoor sports facilities, and boats can be launched directly onto Lake Ullswater. The attractive, mainly tenting, park has many mature trees, lovely views across the lake, and a superb amenities block in the family-only field. The Country Club bar and restaurant provides good meals, as well as discos, live music and entertainment in a glorious location. There are lodges and static caravans for holiday hire. 40 acre site. 323 touring pitches. 32 hardstandings. Caravan pitches. Motorhome pitches. Tent pitches. 131 statics.

AA Pubs & Restaurants nearby: The Yanwath Gate Inn, YANWATH, CA10 2LF, 01768 862386

Queen's Head Inn, TIRRIL, CA10 2JF, 01768 863219

LEISURE: 🏊 Indoor swimming pool 🏊 Outdoor swimming pool 🛝 Children's playground 👋 Kid's club 🎾 Tennis court 🎱 Games room 📺 Separate TV room ⛳ 9/18 hole golf course ⛵ Boats for hire 🎬 Cinema 🎭 Entertainment 🎣 Fishing ◎ Mini golf 🌊 Watersports 🏋 Gym ⚽ Sports field **Spa** 🐴 Stables
FACILITIES: 🛁 Bath 🚿 Shower ⊙ Electric shaver 💨 Hairdryer ✱ Ice Pack Facility ♿ Disabled facilities ✆ Public telephone [S] Shop on site or within 200yds 🚚 Mobile shop (calls at least 5 days a week) 🍖 BBQ area 🧺 Picnic area [Wi-fi] Wi-fi 💻 Internet access ♻ Recycling ℹ Tourist info 🐕 Dog exercise area

Leisure: 🅰️ 🐾 🎱 🎣 ⊐ 🎵 🕹️

Facilities: 🅵 ⊙ 🅵 ✳️ ♿ 🕐 🖄 🅸 🐴 🕊️ WiFi 🖥️ ♻️ 🛈

Services: 🔌 🅐 🍴 🔥 ∅ Ⓣ 🍴 🛒 🚮 ⚡ ↓

Within 3 miles: ⚡ ✎ ⅃ 🏊 🅐 🅐 U

Notes: Families & couples only. Dogs must be kept on leads. Boat launch, pony trekking, pool table, table tennis, bike hire, kids' club in summer holidays.

▶▶▶ 82% Waterfoot Caravan Park (NY462246)

GOLD

CA11 0JF

☎ 017684 86302

e-mail: enquiries@waterfootpark.co.uk

web: www.waterfootpark.co.uk

dir: *M6 junct 40, A66 for 1m, A592 for 4m, site on right before lake. (NB do not leave A592 until site entrance; Sat Nav not compatible)*

🚐 🚙

Open Mar-14 Nov

Last arrival 21.30hrs Last departure noon

A quality touring park with neat, hardstanding pitches in a grassy glade within the wooded grounds of an elegant Georgian mansion. Toilet facilities are clean and well maintained, and the lounge bar with a separate family room enjoys lake views, and there is a path to Ullswater. Aira Force waterfall, Dalemain House and Gardens and Pooley Bridge are all close by. Please note that there is no access via Dacre. 22 acre site. 34 touring pitches. 30 hardstandings. Caravan pitches. Motorhome pitches. 146 statics. 2 wooden pods.

AA Pubs & Restaurants nearby: The Yanwath Gate Inn, YANWATH, CA10 2LF, 01768 862386

Queen's Head Inn, TIRRIL, CA10 2JF, 01768 863219

Leisure: 🅰️ ⊙ 🎣 🎵

Facilities: 🛏️ 🅵 ⊙ 🅵 ✳️ ♿ 🕐 🖄 🅸 🐴 🕊️ WiFi 🖥️ ♻️ 🛈

Services: 🔌 🅐 🍴 🔥 ∅ Ⓣ 🛒 ↓

Within 3 miles: ⅃ ⚡ ⍝ ✎ ◎ 🏊 🅐 🅐 U

Notes: No tents. Dogs must be kept on leads.

SANTON BRIDGE
Map 18 NY10

Places to visit

Brantwood, CONISTON, LA21 8AD, 015394 41396
www.brantwood.org.uk

▶▶▶ 78% The Old Post Office Campsite (NY110016)

CA19 1UY

☎ 01946 726286 & 01785 822866

e-mail: enquiries@theoldpostofficecampsite.co.uk

dir: *From A595 at Holmrook follow Santon Bridge signs, at T-junct left, site on right before river (NB Sat Nav may suggest a route via Wrynose & Hardknott Passes which may not be suitable for your vehicle at night or in bad weather)*

🚐 🚙 🅰️

Open all year

Last departure noon

A family-run campsite in a delightful riverside setting, beside an attractive stone bridge, that has very pretty pitches. The enthusiastic owner is steadily upgrading the park. Permits for salmon, sea and brown trout fishing are available, and there is an adjacent pub. Five camping pods are available for hire. 2.2 acre site. 40 touring pitches. 5 hardstandings. Caravan pitches. Motorhome pitches. Tent pitches. 5 wooden pods.

AA Pubs & Restaurants nearby: Bridge Inn, SANTON BRIDGE, CA19 1UX, 019467 26221

Bower House Inn, ESKDALE GREEN, CA19 1TD, 019467 23244

Wasdale Head Inn, WASDALE HEAD, CA20 1EX, 019467 26229

Leisure: 🅰️

Facilities: 🅵 ⊙ 🅵 ✳️ ♿ 🅸 🐴

Services: 🔌 🅐 ↓

Within 3 miles: ✎ 🅐 U

Notes: Dogs must be kept on leads.

SILLOTH
Map 18 NY15

90% Stanwix Park Holiday Centre (NY108527)

Greenrow CA7 4HH

☎ 016973 32666

e-mail: enquiries@stanwix.com

dir: *1m SW on B5300. From A596 (Wigton bypass), follow signs to Silloth on B5302. In Silloth follow signs to site, approx 1m on B5300*

🚐 🚙 🅰️

Open all year (rs Nov-Feb (ex New Year) no entertainment, shop closed)

Last arrival 21.00hrs Last departure 11.00hrs

A large well-run family park within easy reach of the Lake District. Attractively laid out, with lots of amenities to ensure a lively holiday, including a 4-lane automatic, 10-pin bowling alley. Excellent touring areas with hardstandings, one in a peaceful glade well away from the main leisure complex, and there's a campers' kitchen and clean, well-maintained toilet facilities. 4 acre site. 121 touring pitches. 100 hardstandings. Caravan pitches. Motorhome pitches. Tent pitches. 212 statics.

Leisure: 🏊 🚣 ✝️ 🅰️ 🐾 🎱 🎣 ⊐ 🎵 Spa

Facilities: 🛏️ 🅵 ⊙ 🅵 ✳️ ♿ 🕐 🖄 WiFi ♻️ 🛈

Services: 🔌 🅐 🍴 🔥 Ⓣ 🍴 🛒 ↓

Within 3 miles: ⅃ ✎ ◎ 🅐 🅐

Notes: Families only. Dogs must be kept on leads. Amusement arcade.

see advert on page 128

SERVICES: 🔌 Electric hook up 🅐 Launderette 🍴 Licensed bar 🔥 Calor Gas ∅ Camping Gaz Ⓣ Toilet fluid 🍴 Café/Restaurant 🛒 Fast Food/Takeaway 🔋 Battery charging 🚼 Baby care ↓ Motorvan service point **ABBREVIATIONS:** BH/bank hols-bank holidays Etr-Easter Spring BH-Spring Bank Holiday dep-departure fr-from hrs-hours m-mile mdnt-midnight rdbt-roundabout rs-restricted service wk-week wknd-weekend x-rds-cross roads 🅐 No credit cards 🚫 No dogs 👶 Children of all ages accepted See page 9 for details of the AA Camping Card Scheme

SILLOTH *continued*

AA CAMPING CARD SITE

►►►► 88% Hylton Caravan Park

(NY113533)

Eden St CA7 4AY
☎ 016973 31707 & 32666
e-mail: enquiries@stanwix.com
dir: *On entering Silloth on B5302 follow signs for site, approx 0.5m on left, (at end of Eden St)*

* ⊡ £21.40-£23.40 ⊞ £21.40-£23.40
Å £21.40-£23.40

Open Mar-15 Nov

Last arrival 21.00hrs Last departure 11.00hrs

A smart, modern touring park with excellent toilet facilities including several bathrooms. This high quality park is a sister site to Stanwix Park, which is just a mile away and offers all the amenities of a holiday centre, which are available to Hylton tourers. 18 acre site. 90 touring pitches. Caravan pitches. Motorhome pitches. Tent pitches. 213 statics.

Leisure: ⚑
Facilities: ⊯ ⚑ ⊙ ⚑ ⊱
Services: ⊡ ⊙ ⊟ ⚑ ⊔
Within 3 miles: ⊥ ⚑ ⊚ ⊟ ⊟
Notes: Families only. Dogs must be kept on leads.

►►► 77% *Westmorland Caravan Park* *(NY609060)*

Orton CA10 3SB
☎ 01539 711322
e-mail: caravans@westmorland.com
web: www.westmorland.com/caravan
dir: *Exit M6 at Westmorland Services, 1m from junct 38. Site accessed through service area from either N'bound or S'bound carriageways. Follow park signs*

⊞ ⊞

Open Mar-Nov

Last arrival anytime Last departure noon

An ideal stopover site adjacent to the Tebay service station on the M6, and handy for touring the Lake District. The park is screened by high grass banks, bushes and trees, and is within walking distance of the excellent farm shop and restaurant within the services complex, where caravan park customers enjoy a 10% discount. 4 acre site. 70 touring pitches. 70 hardstandings. 43 seasonal pitches. Caravan pitches. Motorhome pitches. 7 statics.

LEISURE: 🏊 Indoor swimming pool 🏊 Outdoor swimming pool ⚑ Children's playground ✋ Kid's club 🎾 Tennis court 🎱 Games room 📺 Separate TV room ⛳ 9/18 hole golf course ⛵ Boats for hire 🎬 Cinema 🎵 Entertainment 🎣 Fishing ⛳ Mini golf 🏄 Watersports 💪 Gym ⚽ Sports field Spa 🐴 Stables
FACILITIES: 🛁 Bath 🚿 Shower ⊙ Electric shaver ✂ Hairdryer ❄ Ice Pack Facility ♿ Disabled facilities 📞 Public telephone 🏪 Shop on site or within 200yds 🛒 Mobile shop (calls at least 5 days a week) 🍖 BBQ area 🪑 Picnic area 📶 Wi-fi 💻 Internet access ♻ Recycling ℹ Tourist info 🐕 Dog exercise area

AA Pubs & Restaurants nearby: The Fat Lamb Country Inn, RAVENSTONEDALE, CA17 4LL, 015396 23242

The Black Swan, RAVENSTONEDALE, CA17 4NG, 015396 23204

Facilities: ⬡☉☂☀⬡⬡⬡⬡⬡⬡⬡ 𝟎

Services: ⬡⬡ ⬡⬡⬡⬡⬡⬡

Within 3 miles: ⬡⬡⬡

TROUTBECK (NEAR KESWICK)　　Map 18 NY32

PREMIER PARK

▶▶▶▶▶ 81% **Troutbeck Camping and Caravanning Club Site** (NY365271)

Hutton Moor End CA11 0SX
☎ 017687 79149
dir: M6 junct 40, A66 towards Keswick. In 9.5m sharp left for Wallthwaite. Site 0.5m on left

* ⬡ £11.10-£23.40　⬡ £11.10-£23.40
⬡ £11.10-£23.40

Open 9 Mar-11 Nov & 26 Dec-2 Jan

Last arrival 20.00hrs Last departure noon

Beautifully situated between Penrith and Keswick, this quiet, well-managed Lakeland campsite offers two immaculate touring areas, one a sheltered paddock for caravans and motorhomes, with serviced hardstanding pitches, and a maturing lower field, which has spacious hardstanding pitches and a superb and very popular small tenting area that enjoys stunning and extensive views of the surrounding fells. The toilet block is appointed to a very high standard and includes two family cubicles, and the log cabin reception/shop stocks local and organic produce. A luxury caravan, sleeping six, is available for hire. The enthusiastic franchisees offer high levels of customer care and are constantly improving the park, which is well-placed for visited Keswick, Ullswater and the north lakes. Non-members are also very welcome. 5 acre site. 54 touring pitches. 36 hardstandings. Caravan pitches. Motorhome pitches. Tent pitches. 20 statics.

Leisure: ⬡

Facilities: ⬡☉☂☀⬡⬡⬡⬡⬡ ⬡ 𝟎

Services: ⬡⬡⬡⬡⬡⬡⬡⬡⬡

Within 3 miles: ⬡⬡⬡

Notes: Site gates closed 23.00hrs-07.00hrs. Dogs must be kept on leads. Dog walk.

ULVERSTON　　Map 18 SD27

Places to visit

The Dock Museum, BARROW-IN-FURNESS, LA14 2PW, 01229 876400
www.dockmuseum.org.uk

Furness Abbey, BARROW-IN-FURNESS, LA13 0PJ, 01229 823420 www.english-heritage.org.uk/daysout/properties/furness-abbey

Great for kids: South Lakes Wild Animal Park, DALTON-IN-FURNESS, LA15 8JR, 01229 466086 www.wildanimalpark.co.uk

PREMIER PARK

▶▶▶▶▶ 87% **Bardsea Leisure Park** (SD292765)

Priory Rd LA12 9QE
☎ 01229 584712 & 484363
e-mail: reception@bardsealeisure.co.uk
dir: M6 junct 36, A590 towards Barrow. At Ulverston take A5087, site 1m on right

⬡ ⬡

Open all year

Last arrival 21.00hrs Last departure 18.00hrs

An attractively landscaped former quarry, making a quiet and very sheltered site. Many of the generously-sized pitches offer all-weather full hook-ups, and a luxury toilet block provides plenty of fully serviced cubicles. Set on the southern edge of the town, it is convenient for both the coast and the Lake District and there's an excellent caravan accessories shop on site. Please note that this site does not accept tents. 5 acre site. 83 touring pitches. 83 hardstandings. 50 seasonal pitches. Caravan pitches. Motorhome pitches. 88 statics.

AA Pubs & Restaurants nearby: Farmers Arms Hotel, ULVERSTON, LA12 7BA, 01229 584469

Leisure: ⬡⬡

Facilities: ⬡☉☂☀⬡⬡⬡⬡⬡⬡⬡ ⬡

Services: ⬡⬡⬡⬡⬡⬡⬡⬡⬡

Within 3 miles: ⬡⬡⬡⬡⬡⬡

Notes: No noise after 22.30hrs. Dogs must be kept on leads.

WASDALE HEAD　　Map 18 NY10

▶▶▶ 76% *Wasdale Head National Trust Campsite* (NY183076)

CA20 1EX
☎ 015394 63862 & 32733
e-mail: campsite.bookings@nationaltrust.org.uk
web: www.ntlakescampsites.org.uk
dir: From A595(N) left at Gosforth; from A595(S) right at Holmrook for Santon Bridge, follow signs to Wasdale Head

⬡ ⬡

Open all year (rs Wknds Nov-Feb shop open)

Last departure 11.00hrs

Set in a remote and beautiful spot at Wasdale Head, under the stunning Scafell peaks at the head of the deepest lake in England. Clean, well-kept facilities are set centrally amongst open grass pitches and trees, where camping pods are also located. There are eight hardstandings for motorhomes and eight electric hook-ups for tents. The renowned Wasdale Head Inn is close by. 5 acre site. 120 touring pitches. 6 hardstandings. Motorhome pitches. Tent pitches. 3 wooden pods.

AA Pubs & Restaurants nearby: Wasdale Head Inn, WASDALE HEAD, CA20 1EX, 019467 26229

Facilities: ⬡☉☂☀⬡⬡⬡⬡⬡

Services: ⬡⬡⬡

Notes: No cars by tents. No groups of more than 4 unless a family with children. Dogs must be kept on leads.

WATERMILLOCK Map 18 NY42

►►►► 87% The Quiet Site

(NY431236)

Ullswater CA11 0LS
☎ **07768 727016**
e-mail: info@thequietsite.co.uk
dir: *M6 junct 40, A592 towards Ullswater. Right at lake junct, then right at Brackenrigg Hotel. Site 1.5m on right*

Open all year (rs Low season bar open some wkdays only)

Last arrival 22.00hrs Last departure noon

A well-maintained site in a lovely, peaceful location, with good terraced pitches offering great fells views, very good toilet facilities including family bathrooms, and a charming 'olde-worlde' bar. Their policy of green sustainability is commendable, with solar panels and a bio mass boiler delivering heating and hot water to the amenity blocks, even when the site is busy. There are 13 wooden camping pods and a self-catering stone cottage for hire. 10 acre site. 100 touring pitches. 60 hardstandings. Caravan pitches. Motorhome pitches. Tent pitches. 23 statics. 13 wooden pods.

AA Pubs & Restaurants nearby: Macdonald Leeming House, WATERMILLOCK, CA11 0JJ, 0844 879 9142

Rampsbeck Country House Hotel, WATERMILLOCK, CA11 0LP, 017684 86442

Leisure:
Facilities:
Services:
Within 3 miles:

Notes: Quiet from 22.00hrs. Pool table, soft play area for toddlers, caravan storage.

AA CAMPING CARD SITE

►►►► 81% Cove Caravan & Camping Park *(NY431236)*

Ullswater CA11 0LS
☎ **017684 86549**
e-mail: info@cove-park.co.uk
dir: *M6 junct 40, A592 for Ullswater. Right at lake junct, then right at Brackenrigg Inn. Site 1.5m on left*

* ⊕ £20-£34 ⊕ £20-£34 ▲ £15-£30

Open Mar-Oct

Last arrival 21.00hrs Last departure noon

A peaceful family site in an attractive and elevated position with extensive fell views and glimpses of Ullswater Lake. Extensive ground works have been carried out in order to provide spacious, mostly level pitches. Pretty, seasonal flowers are planted amid the wide variety of mature trees and shrubs. 3 acre site. 50 touring pitches. 27 hardstandings. 10 seasonal pitches. Caravan pitches. Motorhome pitches. Tent pitches. 39 statics.

AA Pubs & Restaurants nearby: Macdonald Leeming House, WATERMILLOCK, CA11 0JJ, 0844 879 9142

Rampsbeck Country House Hotel, WATERMILLOCK, CA11 0LP, 017684 86442

Cove Caravan & Camping Park

Leisure:
Facilities:
Services:
Within 3 miles:

Notes: No open fires, no noise after 22.30hrs. Dogs must be kept on leads.

see advert below

LEISURE: 🏊 Indoor swimming pool 🏊 Outdoor swimming pool 🎠 Children's playground Kid's club 🎾 Tennis court Games room Separate TV room 9/18 hole golf course Boats for hire Cinema Entertainment Fishing Mini golf Watersports Gym Sports field Spa Stables
FACILITIES: Bath Shower Electric shaver Hairdryer Ice Pack Facility Disabled facilities Public telephone Shop on site or within 200yds Mobile shop (calls at least 5 days a week) BBQ area Picnic area Wi-fi Internet access Recycling Tourist info Dog exercise area

►►►► 81% Ullswater Caravan, Camping & Marine Park *(NY438232)*

High Longthwaite CA11 0LR
☎ 017684 86666
e-mail: info@ullswatercaravanpark.co.uk
web: www.ullswatercaravanpark.co.uk
dir: *M6 junct 40, A592, W towards Ullswater for 5m. Right, alongside Ullswater for 2m, right at phone box. Site 0.5m on right*

* 🚃 £14.50-£27.50 🚌 £14.50-£27.50 ⛺ £14.50-£27.50

Open Mar-Nov (rs Low season bar open wknds only)

Last arrival 21.00hrs Last departure noon

A pleasant rural site with its own nearby boat launching and marine storage facility, making it ideal for sailors. The family-owned and run park enjoys fell and lake views, and there is a bar, café and shop on site. Many of the pitches are fully serviced and there are wooden cabins with barbecues. Please note that the Marine Park is one mile from the camping area. 12 acre site. 160 touring pitches. 58 hardstandings. Caravan pitches. Motorhome pitches. Tent pitches. 55 statics. 4 wooden pods.

AA Pubs & Restaurants nearby: Macdonald Leeming House, WATERMILLOCK, CA11 0JJ, 0844 879 9142

Rampsbeck Country House Hotel, WATERMILLOCK, CA11 0LP, 017684 86442

Leisure: 🛝 🔍
Facilities: 🚿 🔘 💨 ❄ ♿ 🛍 🐕 [Wi-Fi] ♻
Services: 🔌 🧺 🍷 🛢 🍃 [T] 🔋
Within 3 miles: ⛵ 🎣 🏊 🛍 🧺 🐴
Notes: No open fires, no noise after 23.30hrs. Dogs must be kept on leads. Boat launching & moorings 1m.

WINDERMERE

Places to visit

Holehird Gardens, WINDERMERE, LA23 1NP, 015394 46008 www.holehirdgardens.org.uk

Blackwell The Arts & Crafts House, BOWNESS-ON-WINDERMERE, LA23 3JT, 015394 46139 www.blackwell.org.uk

Great for kids: Lake District Visitor Centre at Brockhole, WINDERMERE, LA23 1LJ, 015394 46601 www.brockhole.co.uk

WINDERMERE Map 18 SD49

PREMIER PARK

►►►►► 87% Park Cliffe Camping & Caravan Estate *(SD391912)*

Best of British — David Bellamy Conservation Award GOLD

Birks Rd, Tower Wood LA23 3PG
☎ 01539 531344
e-mail: info@parkcliffe.co.uk
dir: *M6 junct 36, A590. Right at Newby Bridge onto A592. 3.6m right into site. (NB due to difficult access from main road this is the only advised direction for approaching the site)*

* 🚃 £26-£31 🚌 £26-£31 ⛺ £20.50-£35.50

Open Mar-9 Nov (rs Wknds & school hols facilities open fully)

Last arrival 22.00hrs Last departure noon

A lovely hillside park set in 25 secluded acres of fell land. The camping area is sloping and uneven in places, but well drained and sheltered; some pitches have spectacular views of Lake Windermere and the Langdales. The park offers a high level of customer care and is very well equipped for families (family bathrooms), and there is an attractive bar and brasserie restaurant serving quality food; three static holiday caravans are for hire. 25 acre site. 60 touring pitches. 60 hardstandings. 25 seasonal pitches. Caravan pitches. Motorhome pitches. Tent pitches. 56 statics. 5 wooden pods.

AA Pubs & Restaurants nearby: Eagle & Child Inn, WINDERMERE, LA8 9LP, 01539 821320

Jerichos, WINDERMERE, LA23 1BX, 015394 42522

Leisure: 🛝 🔍
Facilities: 🚿 🔘 💨 ❄ ♿ ☎ 🛍 🪑 🐕 [Wi-Fi] ♻ ℹ
Services: 🔌 🧺 🍷 🛢 🍃 [T] 🍴 🍔 🍼 ⛛
Within 3 miles: ⛳ ⛵ 🎬 🎣 🎯 🏊 🛍 🧺 🐴
Notes: No noise 23.00hrs-07.30hrs. Dogs must be kept on leads. Off-licence.

PREMIER PARK

►►►►► 84% Fallbarrow Park *(SD401973)*

David Bellamy Conservation Award GOLD

Rayrigg Rd LA23 3DL
☎ 015395 69835
e-mail: enquiries@southlakelandparks.co.uk
dir: *0.5m N of Windermere on A591. At mini-rdbt turn left to Bowness Bay & the Lake. Site 1.3m on right*

* 🚃 £18.50-£35 🚌 £18.50-£35

Open Mar-mid Nov

Last arrival 22.00hrs Last departure 12.00hrs

A park set in impressive surroundings just a few minutes' walk from Bowness on the shore of Lake Windermere. There is direct access to the lake through the park. The site has good, hedged, fully serviced pitches, quality toilet facilities, a deli and café serving meals using locally sourced produce, and a comfortable lounge bar for adults only with a wood burning stove. The site has 30 holiday hire statics. 32 acre site. 26 touring pitches. 26 hardstandings. Caravan pitches. Motorhome pitches. 269 statics.

AA Pubs & Restaurants nearby: Eagle & Child Inn, WINDERMERE, LA8 9LP, 01539 821320

Jerichos, WINDERMERE, LA23 1BX, 015394 42522

Leisure: 🛝 🔍 📺
Facilities: 🚿 🔘 💨 ❄ ♿ ☎ 🛍 🪑 🐕 [Wi-Fi] 💻 ♻ ℹ
Services: 🔌 🧺 🍷 🛢 🍴 🍔 ⛛
Within 3 miles: ⛳ ⛵ 🎬 🎣 🎯 🏊 🛍 🧺 🐴
Notes: No tents, no cycling, no scooters. Dogs must be kept on leads. Boat launching.

WINDERMERE *continued*

►►►► 84% Hill of Oaks & Blakeholme *(SD386899)*

LA12 8NR

☎ 015395 31578

e-mail: enquiries@hillofoaks.co.uk

web: www.hillofoaks.co.uk

dir: *M6 junct 36, A590 towards Barrow. At rdbt signed Bowness turn right onto A592. Site approx 3m on left*

* 🚐 £17-£37 🚎 £17-£37

Open Mar-14 Nov

Last departure noon

A secluded, heavily wooded park on the shores of Lake Windermere. Pretty lakeside picnic areas, woodland walks and a play area make this a delightful park for families, with excellent serviced pitches, a licensed shop and a heated toilet block. Watersports include sailing and canoeing, with private jetties for boat launching. 31 acre site. 43 touring pitches. 43 hardstandings. Caravan pitches. Motorhome pitches. 215 statics.

AA Pubs & Restaurants nearby: Eagle & Child Inn, WINDERMERE, LA8 9LP, 01539 821320

Jerichos, WINDERMERE, LA23 1BX, 015394 42522

Leisure: ⚠ ⚽

Facilities: 🐕 ⊙ 🎯 ✳ ♿ 🕐 🛒 🚿 🛏 WI-FI 🖥 🛁 ❂

Services: 🔌 🛢 🚽 T ⚓

Within 3 miles: 🚴 ⚓ 🎣 ◎ ⛵ 🛒 🐴 ∪

Notes: No tents (except trailer tents), no groups. Dogs must be kept on leads.

SERVICES: 🔌 Electric hook up 🔃 Launderette 🍺 Licensed bar 🛢 Calor Gas 🔥 Camping Gaz Ⓣ Toilet fluid 🍽 Café/Restaurant 🍔 Fast Food/Takeaway
🔋 Battery charging 🚼 Baby care ⚓ Motorvan service point **ABBREVIATIONS:** BH/bank hols-bank holidays Etr-Easter Spring BH-Spring Bank Holiday dep-departure
fr-from hrs-hours m-mile mdnt-midnight rdbt-roundabout rs-restricted service wk-week wknd-weekend x-rds-cross roads 🚫 No credit cards 🚫 No dogs
👶 Children of all ages accepted See page 9 for details of the AA Camping Card Scheme

Derbyshire

Think of Derbyshire and you instantly think of
the Peak District, the first of Britain's glorious and
much-loved National Parks and still the most popular.
This is where the rugged, sometimes inhospitable
landscape of north England meets the gentler beauty
of the Midland counties.

● Mam Tor, near Castleton

Within the National Park lies the upland country of the Dark Peak, shaped over the centuries by silt from the region's great rivers, and where gritstone outcrops act as monuments to the splendour and magic of geology. History was made in this corner of Derbyshire in 1932 when 500 ramblers spilled on to Kinder Scout to argue for the right of public access to the countryside.

Southern landscape

To the south is the White Peak, different in both character and appearance. This is a land of limestone, of deep wooded gorges, underground caves and high pastures crisscrossed by traditional drystone walls. There are dales, too – the most famous among them being Dovedale, the haunt of countless writers and artists over the years. Not surprisingly, Wordsworth and Tennyson sought inspiration here and much of it retains a rare, magical quality.

Fine buildings

Look in and around the Peak District National Park and you'll find an impressive range of fine

▶

buildings. Calke Abbey (NT) is not an abbey at all but a magnificent baroque mansion dating back to the beginning of the 18th century.

World-famous Chatsworth, the palatial home of the Duke of Devonshire, is one of Derbyshire's most cherished visitor attractions. Work began on the original building in 1549 and the house has been substantially altered and enlarged over the years. The 1,000-acre park is the jewel in Chatsworth's crown; designed by 'Capability' Brown, it includes rare trees, a maze and the highest gravity-fed fountain in the world.

Towns and villages

As well as the county's palatial houses, there is an impressive array of quaint villages and historic towns. Chesterfield is known for the crooked spire of its church, while Buxton is acknowledged as one of the country's loveliest spa towns. Bakewell introduced the tradition of the Bakewell Pudding and the villagers of Tissington still maintain the old custom of well dressing on Ascension Day.

● Midland Railway Centre, Ripley

Walking and Cycling

Derbyshire is just the place for exhilarating walking where almost every person you pass is pleasant and friendly. The Peak District offers more demanding and adventurous routes, including the High Peak Trail, which runs from Hurdlow to Cromford, and the Monsal Trail, which extends from Haddon Park to Topley Pike. There is also the 26-mile (42km) Limestone Way from Matlock to Castleton and the 35-mile (56km) Gritstone Trail from Disley to Kidsgrove. Derbyshire's most famous walk is undoubtedly the Pennine Way, which starts at Edale in the Peak District and runs north for 251 miles (404km) to Kirk Yetholm in Scotland.

In common with other parts of the country, the Peak District includes a number of disused railway tracks that have been adapted to user-friendly cycle trails. Among many popular cycle trails are several family routes around Derwent reservoir, where 617 Squadron, 'The Dambusters', famously practised low-level flying during the Second World War.

Festivals and Events

Among many fixtures are the following:
- The Ashbourne Shrovetide Football on Shrove Tuesday and Ash Wednesday.
- The Bamford Sheep Dog Trials, the Chatsworth Horse Trials and the Castleton Garland Ceremony in May.
- In July there is the Bakewell Carnival, the Padley Pilgrimage and the Buxton Festival.
- September sees the Matlock Bath Illuminations and Firework Display and December the Castleton Christmas Lights and the Boxing Day Raft Race at Matlock Bath.

Waterfall on Bonsall Brook, near Cromford

DERBYSHIRE

ASHBOURNE — Map 10 SK14

Places to visit

Kedleston Hall, KEDLESTON HALL, DE22 5JH, 01332 842191 www.nationaltrust.org.uk

Wirksworth Heritage Centre, WIRKSWORTH, DE4 4ET, 01629 825225 www.storyofwirksworth.co.uk

Great for kids: Crich Tramway Village, CRICH, DE4 5DP, 01773 854321 www.tramway.co.uk

AA CAMPING CARD SITE

►►► 79% Carsington Fields Caravan Park *(SK251493)*

Millfields Ln, Nr Carsington Water DE6 3JS
☎ **01335 372872 & 07546 210956**
e-mail: bookings@carsingtoncaravaning.co.uk
dir: *From Belper towards Ashbourne on A517, right approx 0.25m past Hulland Ward into Dog Ln. 0.75m right at x-rds signed Carsington. Site on right approx 0.75m*

🚐 🚕 Å

Open Mar-Oct

Last arrival 21.00hrs Last departure 18.00hrs

A very well-presented and spacious park with a good toilet block, open views and a large fenced pond that attracts plenty of wildlife. The popular tourist attraction of Carsington Water is a short stroll away, with its variety of leisure facilities including fishing, sailing, windsurfing and children's play area. The park is also a good base for walkers. 6 acre site. 58 touring pitches. 19 hardstandings. 8 seasonal pitches. Caravan pitches. Motorhome pitches. Tent pitches.

AA Pubs & Restaurants nearby: The Coach and Horses Inn, FENNY BENTLEY, DE6 1LB, 01335 350246

Bentley Brook Inn, FENNY BENTLEY, DE6 1LF, 01335 350278

Facilities: 🅟 ⊙ ⴵ ☀ ⅋ 🚿 ⚲ ⛟ WiFi ♻ ❶
Services: 🔌 ⛟
Within 3 miles: ⅌ ⅌ ⤳ 🛍 ↻

Notes: No large groups or group bookings, no noise after 23.00hrs. Dogs must be kept on leads. Fish & chip meals to order between 17.00hrs-20.00hrs, Indian takeaway free delivery to site.

BAKEWELL — Map 16 SK26

Places to visit

Chatsworth, CHATSWORTH, DE45 1PP, 01246 565300 www.chatsworth.org

Chesterfield Museum and Art Gallery, CHESTERFIELD, S41 7TD, 01246 345727 www.visitchesterfield.info

►►► 81% Greenhills Holiday Park *(SK202693)*

Crowhill Ln DE45 1PX
☎ **01629 813052 & 813467**
e-mail: info@greenhillsholidaypark.co.uk
web: www.greenhillsholidaypark.co.uk
dir: *1m NW of Bakewell on A6. Signed before Ashford-in-the-Water, onto along unclassified road on right*

🚐 🚕 Å

Open Feb-Nov (rs Feb-Apr & Oct-Nov bar & shop closed)

Last arrival 22.00hrs Last departure noon

A well-established park set in lovely countryside within the Peak District National Park. Many pitches enjoy uninterrupted views, and there is easy accessibility to all facilities. A clubhouse, shop and children's playground are popular features. 8 acre site. 172 touring pitches. 30 hardstandings. Caravan pitches. Motorhome pitches. Tent pitches. 73 statics.

AA Pubs & Restaurants nearby: The Bull's Head, BAKEWELL, DE45 1QB, 01629 812931

Piedaniel's, BAKEWELL, DE45 1BX, 01629 812687

Leisure: Ⓐ ⚽ ⅃
Facilities: 🅟 ⊙ ⅋ ☀ & ⓢ 🚿 WiFi 🖥 ♻ ❶
Services: 🔌 ⛟ ⬛ 🚿 ⌀ Ⓣ ⅋ ⤳ ⅂
Within 3 miles: ⅌ ⅌ ◎ 🛍 ⅂ ↻

BIRCHOVER — Map 16 SK26

Places to visit

Haddon Hall, HADDON HALL, DE45 1LA, 01629 812855 www.haddonhall.co.uk

The Heights of Abraham Cable Cars, Caverns & Hilltop Park, MATLOCK BATH, DE4 3PD, 01629 582365 www.heightsofabraham.com

►►►► 82% Barn Farm Campsite *(SK238621)*

Barn Farm DE4 2BL
☎ **01629 650245**
e-mail: gilberthh@msn.com
dir: *From A6 take B5056 towards Ashbourne. Follow brown signs to site*

🚐 £22 🚕 £22 Å £10-£15

Open Etr-Oct

Last arrival 21.00hrs Last departure 11.00hrs

An interesting park on a former dairy farm with the many and varied facilities housed in high quality conversions of old farm buildings. Three large and well-maintained touring fields offer sweeping views across the Peak National Park. There is an excellent choice in the provision of privacy cubicles, including shower and wash basin cubicles and even a shower and sauna. There are five stylish, camping barns, for hire. 15 acre site. 62 touring pitches. 3 hardstandings. Caravan pitches. Motorhome pitches. Tent pitches.

AA Pubs & Restaurants nearby: The Druid Inn, BIRCHOVER, DE4 2BL, 01629 653836

The Peacock at Rowsley, ROWSLEY, DE4 2EB, 01629 733518

Leisure: Ⓐ ☺ ⚲ ⏷
Facilities: 🅟 ⊙ ⅋ ☀ & ⓢ 🚿 ⤳ 🖥 ♻ ❶
Services: 🔌 ⛟ 🚿 ⌀ Ⓣ
Within 3 miles: ⅌ ⅌ ⅌ ◎ ⤳ 🛍 ⅂ ↻

Notes: No music after 22.30hrs, minimum noise 22.30hrs-07.00hrs. Dogs must be kept on leads. Vending machines.

BUXTON

Places to visit

Eyam Hall, EYAM, S32 5QW, 01433 631976 www.eyamhall.com

Poole's Cavern (Buxton Country Park), BUXTON, SK17 9DH, 01298 26978 www.poolescavern.co.uk

---

LEISURE: 🏊 Indoor swimming pool 🏊 Outdoor swimming pool Ⓐ Children's playground 🪁 Kid's club ☺ Tennis court ⚲ Games room ⏷ Separate TV room ⅃ 9/18 hole golf course ⛵ Boats for hire 🎬 Cinema ⅃ Entertainment 🎣 Fishing ◎ Mini golf 🏄 Watersports 💪 Gym ☺ Sports field Spa ↻ Stables
FACILITIES: 🛁 Bath 🚿 Shower ⊙ Electric shaver ⅋ Hairdryer ☀ Ice Pack Facility & Disabled facilities Ⓢ Public telephone 🛍 Shop on site or within 200yds 🛒 Mobile shop (calls at least 5 days a week) 🍖 BBQ area ⤳ Picnic area WiFi Wi-fi 🖥 Internet access ♻ Recycling ❶ Tourist info ⤳ Dog exercise area

BUXTON
Map 16 SK07

AA CAMPING CARD SITE

▶▶▶▶ 84% Lime Tree Park (SK070725)

Dukes Dr SK17 9RP
☎ 01298 22988
e-mail: info@limetreeparkbuxton.com
dir: *1m S of Buxton, between A515 & A6*

* ⚌ £18-£22 ⚌ Å £15-£22

Open Mar-Oct

Last arrival 20.00hrs Last departure noon

A most attractive and well-designed site, set on the side of a narrow valley in an elevated location, with separate, neatly landscaped areas for statics, tents, touring caravans and motorhomes. There's good attention to detail throughout including the clean toilets and showers. Its backdrop of a magnificent old railway viaduct and views over Buxton and the surrounding hills, make this a sought-after destination. There are eight static caravans, a pine lodge and two apartments available for holiday lets. 10.5 acre site. 106 touring pitches. 22 hardstandings. Caravan pitches. Motorhome pitches. Tent pitches. 43 statics.

AA Pubs & Restaurants nearby: The Queen Anne Inn, GREAT HUCKLOW, SK17 8RF, 01298 871246

Leisure: ⚑ ⚊ ☐
Facilities: ⚐ ☉ ⚐ ✳ ⚐ ☉ ⚐ ⚐ ▤ ♻ **❶**
Services: ⚐ ⚐ ⚐ ☐ ☐ ▵ ⚌
Within 3 miles: ⚐ ☺ ⚐ ⚐ ⚐ ∪

Notes: No noise after 22.00hrs, no fires. Dogs must be kept on leads.

▶▶▶▶ 81% Beech Croft Farm
(SK122720)

GOLD

Beech Croft, Blackwell in the Peak SK17 9TQ
☎ 01298 85330
e-mail: mail@beechcroftfarm.co.uk
dir: *Exit A6 midway between Buxton & Bakewell. Site signed*

* ⚌ £18-£22 ⚌ £18-£22 Å £13.50-£16

Beech Croft Farm

Open all year (rs Nov-Feb not open for tents)

Last arrival 21.30hrs

A small terraced farm site with lovely Peak District views. There's a fine stone-built toilet block with ultra-modern fittings, under-floor heating and additional unisex facilities, 31 fully-serviced hardstanding pitches (11 in the camping field), gravel roads, a campers' shelter, and a super tarmac pathway leading from the camping field to the toilet block. This makes an ideal site for those touring or walking in the Peak District. 3 acre site. 30 touring pitches. 30 hardstandings. Caravan pitches. Motorhome pitches. Tent pitches.

AA Pubs & Restaurants nearby: The Queen Anne Inn, GREAT HUCKLOW, SK17 8RF, 01298 871246

Facilities: ⚐ ☉ ✳ ⚐ ⚐ ▤ ⚑ ⚌ ▥ ♻ **❶**
Services: ⚐ ⚐ ⚐ ☐ ☐

Notes: No noise after 22.00hrs. Dogs must be kept on leads.

▶▶▶ 89% Clover Fields Touring Caravan Park (SK075704)

1 Heath View, Harpur Hill SK17 9PU
☎ 01298 78731
e-mail: cloverfields@tiscali.co.uk
dir: *A515, B5053, then immediately right. Site 0.5m on left*

⚌ £24-£25 ⚌ £24-£25 Å £24-£25

Open all year

Last arrival 20.00hrs Last departure 18.00hrs

A developing and spacious adults-only park, just over a mile from the attractions of Buxton, with very good facilities, including an upmarket, timber chalet-style toilet block. All pitches are fully serviced and have individual barbecues, and are set out on terraces, each with extensive views over the countryside. Swathes of natural meadow grasses and flowers cloak the terraces and surrounding fields. 12 acre site. 25 touring pitches. 25 hardstandings. Caravan pitches. Motorhome pitches. Tent pitches.

AA Pubs & Restaurants nearby: The Queen Anne Inn, GREAT HUCKLOW, SK17 8RF, 01298 871246

Facilities: ⚐ ☉ ✳ ⚐ ☉ ⚐ ⚑ ♻ **❶**
Services: ⚐ ⚐ ⚐ ☐ ⚌
Within 3 miles: ⚐ ⚐ ⚐ ⚐ ∪

Notes: Adults only. No commercial vehicles. Dogs must be kept on leads. Small fishing pond, boules area.

HOPE
Map 16 SK18

Places to visit

Speedwell Cavern, CASTLETON, S33 8WA, 01433 620512 www.speedwellcavern.co.uk

Peveril Castle, CASTLETON, S33 8WQ, 01433 620613 www.english-heritage.org.uk/daysout/properties/peveril-castle

▶▶▶ 77% Pindale Farm Outdoor Centre (SK163825)

Pindale Rd S33 6RN
☎ 01433 620111
e-mail: pindalefarm@btconnect.com
dir: *From A6187 in Hope follow Pindale sign between church & Woodroffe Arms. Site 1m on left*

Å

Open Mar-Oct

Set around a 13th-century farmhouse and a former lead mine pump house (now converted to a self-contained bunkhouse for up to 60 people), this simple, off-the-beaten-track site is an ideal base for walking, climbing, caving and various outdoor pursuits. Around the farm are several deeply wooded areas available for tents, and old stone buildings that have been well converted to house modern toilet facilities. 4 acre site. 60 touring pitches. Tent pitches.

AA Pubs & Restaurants nearby: Cheshire Cheese Inn, HOPE, S33 6ZF, 01433 620381

Ye Olde Nags Head, CASTLETON, S33 8WH, 01433 620248

The Peaks Inn, CASTLETON, S33 8WJ, 01433 620247

Facilities: ⚐ ☉ ✳ ▥
Services: ⚐ ⚐
Within 3 miles: ⚐ ∪

Notes: No anti-social behaviour, noise must be kept to minimum after 21.00hrs, no fires. Charge for Wi-fi. Dogs must be kept on leads.

SERVICES: ⚐ Electric hook up ⚐ Launderette ⚐ Licensed bar ⚐ Calor Gas ⚐ Camping Gaz ☐ Toilet fluid ⚐ Café/Restaurant ⚌ Fast Food/Takeaway ⚌ Battery charging ⚌ Baby care ⚌ Motorvan service point **ABBREVIATIONS:** BH/bank hols-bank holidays Etr-Easter Spring BH-Spring Bank Holiday dep-departure fr-from hrs-hours m-mile mdnt-midnight rdbt-roundabout rs-restricted service wk-week wknd-weekend x-rds-cross roads ⚐ No credit cards ⚐ No dogs ⚐ Children of all ages accepted See page 9 for details of the AA Camping Card Scheme

MATLOCK · Map 16 SK35

Places to visit

Peak District Mining Museum, MATLOCK BATH, DE4 3NR, 01629 583834 www.peakmines.co.uk

Haddon Hall, HADDON HALL, DE45 1LA, 01629 812855 www.haddonhall.co.uk

Great for kids: The Heights of Abraham Cable Cars, Caverns & Hilltop Park, MATLOCK BATH, DE4 3PD, 01629 582365 www.heightsofabraham.com

►►►► 84% Lickpenny Caravan Site

(SK339597)

Lickpenny Ln, Tansley DE4 5GF
☎ **01629 583040**
e-mail: lickpennycp@btinternet.com
dir: *From Matlock take A615 towards Alfreton for 3m. Site signed to left, into Lickpenny Ln, right into site near end of road*

* 🚐 £15-£26 🚏 £15-£26

Open all year

Last arrival 20.00hrs Last departure noon (late departure until 18.00hrs for a fee).

A picturesque site in the grounds of an old plant nursery with areas broken up and screened by a variety of shrubs, and with spectacular views, which are best enjoyed from the upper terraced areas. Pitches, several fully serviced, are spacious, well screened and well marked, and facilities are kept to a very good standard. The bistro/coffee shop is popular with visitors. 16 acre site. 80 touring pitches. 80 hardstandings. 20 seasonal pitches. Caravan pitches. Motorhome pitches.

AA Pubs & Restaurants nearby: The Red Lion, MATLOCK, DE4 3BT, 01629 584888

Stones Restaurant, MATLOCK, DE4 3LT, 01629 56061

Leisure: ⚊

Facilities: 🌣⊙℉🔥🕒🛢🛒🚿ᴡɪꜰɪ🖥♻🛈

Services: 🚰🛢🔋🇹🍴🛗

Within 3 miles: ↨✦⌖◎🛢🛍∪

Notes: No noise after 23.00hrs, 1 car per pitch. Dogs must be kept on leads. Child bath available.

NEWHAVEN · Map 16 SK16

Places to visit

Middleton Top Engine House, MIDDLETON, DE4 4LS, 01629 823204 www.derbyshire.gov.uk/countryside

Peak District Mining Museum, MATLOCK BATH, DE4 3NR, 01629 583834 www.peakmines.co.uk

AA CAMPING CARD SITE

►►►► 81% Newhaven Caravan & Camping Park *(SK167602)*

SK17 0DT
☎ **01298 84300**
e-mail: newhavencaravanpark@btconnect.com
web: www.newhavencaravanpark.co.uk
dir: *Between Ashbourne & Buxton at A515 & A5012 junct*

* 🚐 £11-£18.75 🚏 £11-£18.75 ⚊ £11-£18.75

Open Mar-Oct

Last arrival 21.00hrs

Pleasantly situated within the Peak District National Park, this park has mature trees screening the three touring areas. Very good toilet facilities cater for touring vans and a large tent field, and there's a restaurant adjacent to the site. 30 acre site. 125 touring pitches. 60 hardstandings. 40 seasonal pitches. Caravan pitches. Motorhome pitches. Tent pitches. 73 statics.

AA Pubs & Restaurants nearby: Red Lion Inn, BIRCHOVER, DE4 2BN, 01629 650363

The Druid Inn, BIRCHOVER, DE4 2BL, 01629 653836

Leisure: ⚊ ♣

Facilities: 🌣⊙℉🔆🛢🚿🛒♻🛈

Services: 🚰🛢🔋🛗🇹🛍

Within 3 miles: ✦🛢🍴∪

Notes: No noise after 23.00hrs. Dogs must be kept on leads.

RIPLEY · Map 16 SK35

Places to visit

Midland Railway Butterley, RIPLEY, DE5 3QZ, 01773 747674 www.midlandrailwaycentre.co.uk

Denby Pottery Visitor Centre, DENBY, DE5 8NX, 01773 740799 www.denbyvisitorcentre.co.uk

►►►► 84% Golden Valley Caravan & Camping Park *(SK408513)*

Coach Rd DE55 4ES
☎ **01773 513881 & 746786**
e-mail: enquiries@goldenvalleycaravanpark.co.uk
web: www.goldenvalleycaravanpark.co.uk
dir: *M1 junct 26, A610 to Codnor. Right at lights. Right into Alfreton Rd. In 1m left into Coach Rd, park on left. (NB it is advised that Sat Nav is ignored for last few miles & guide directions are followed)*

🚐🚏⚊

Open all year (rs Wknds only in low season bar & café open, children's activities)

Last arrival 21.00hrs Last departure noon

This superbly landscaped park is set within 30 acres of woodland in the Amber Valley. The fully serviced pitches are set out in informal groups in clearings amongst the trees. The park has a cosy bar and bistro with outside patio, a fully stocked fishing lake, an innovative and well-equipped play area, an on-site jacuzzi and fully equipped fitness suite. There is also a wildlife pond and a nature trail. 30 acre site. 45 touring pitches. 45 hardstandings. Caravan pitches. Motorhome pitches. Tent pitches. 1 static.

AA Pubs & Restaurants nearby: Santo's Higham Farm Hotel, HIGHAM, DE55 6EH, 01773 833812

Leisure: ♣⚊🎱📺

Facilities: 🛁🌣⊙℉🔆🛢🚿🛒ᴡɪꜰɪ🖥♻🛈

Services: 🚰🛢🔋🛗🇹🍴🛍🛗

Within 3 miles: ↨⊟🛢🛍∪

Notes: No vehicles on grass, no open fires or disposable BBQs, no noise after 22.30hrs. Dogs must be kept on leads. Zip slide, donkey rides, tractor train, water walking balls, log flume ride.

ROSLISTON — Map 10 SK21

Places to visit

Sudbury Hall and Museum of Childhood, SUDBURY, DE6 5HT, 01283 585305 www.nationaltrust.org.uk

Ashby-de-la-Zouch Castle, ASHBY-DE-LA-ZOUCH, LE65 1BR, 01530 413343 www.english-heritage.org.uk/daysout/ properties/ashby-de-la-zouch-castle

Great for kids: Conkers, MOIRA, DE12 6GA, 01283 216633 www.visitconkers.com

►►►► 80% Beehive Woodland Lakes

(SK249161)

DE12 8HZ

☎ **01283 763981**

e-mail: info@beehivefarm-woodlandlakes.co.uk

dir: *From A444 in Castle Gresley into Mount Pleasant Rd, follow Rosliston signs for 3.5m through Linton to T-junct. Left signed Beehive Farms*

🚐 🚛 Å

Open all year

Last arrival 20.00hrs (18.00hrs low season). Last departure noon

A small, informal and rapidly developing caravan area secluded from an extensive woodland park in the heart of the National Forest National Park. Toilet facilities include four family rooms. Young children will enjoy the on-site animal farm and playground, whilst anglers will appreciate fishing the three lakes within the park; bikes can be hired. There is an adults-only area and camping pods were added in 2013. The Honey Pot tearoom provides snacks and is open most days. 2.5 acre site. 46 touring pitches. 46 hardstandings. Caravan pitches. Motorhome pitches. Tent pitches. Wooden pods.

AA Pubs & Restaurants nearby: The Waterfront, BARTON-UNDER-NEEDWOOD, DE13 8DZ, 01283 711500

Leisure: ⚓

Facilities: 🦽⊙ℱ⚒☆♿🖎⌂📶 ❼

Services: 🔌🗑🔋📬

Within 3 miles: 🚴🎡℘⊙🖎

Notes: Dogs must be kept on leads. Takeaway food delivered to site.

ROWSLEY — Map 16 SK26

Places to visit

Hardwick Hall, HARDWICK HALL, S44 5QJ, 01246 850430 www.english-heritage.org.uk/daysout/ properties/hardwick-old-hall

Temple Mine, MATLOCK BATH, DE4 3NR, 01629 583834 www.peakmines.co.uk

Great for kids: The Heights of Abraham Cable Cars, Caverns & Hilltop Park, MATLOCK BATH, DE4 3PD, 01629 582365 www.heightsofabraham.com

►►► 73% *Grouse & Claret* *(SK258660)*

Station Rd DE4 2EB

☎ **01629 733233**

e-mail: grouseandclaret.matlock@marstons.co.uk

dir: *M1 junct 29. Site on A6, 5m from Matlock & 3m from Bakewell*

🚐 🚛 Å

Open all year

Last arrival 20.00hrs Last departure noon

A well-designed, purpose-built park at the rear of an eating house on the A6 between Bakewell and Chatsworth, and adjacent to the New Peak Shopping Village. The park comprises a level grassy area running down to the river, and all pitches have hardstandings and electric hook-ups. 2.5 acre site. 26 touring pitches. 26 hardstandings. Caravan pitches. Motorhome pitches. Tent pitches.

AA Pubs & Restaurants nearby: The Peacock at Rowsley, ROWSLEY, DE4 2EB, 01629 733518

Leisure: ⚓

Facilities: 🦽⊙⌂📶

Services: 🔌🍽🖎🏧⚓

Within 3 miles: 🚴℘🖎

Notes: No cars by tents. Dogs must be kept on leads.

SHARDLOW — Map 11 SK43

Places to visit

Melbourne Hall & Gardens, MELBOURNE, DE73 8EN, 01332 862502 www.melbournehall.com

►►► 67% Shardlow Marina Caravan Park *(SK444303)*

London Rd DE72 2GL

☎ **01332 792832**

e-mail: admin@shardlowmarina.co.uk

dir: *M1 junct 24a, A50 signed Derby. Exit junct 1 at rdbt signed Shardlow. Site 1m on right*

* 🚐 £13.50-£17.50 🚛 £13.50-£17.50 Å £13.50-£21.50

Open Mar-Jan (rs Mar-Jan office closed between 13.00hrs-14.00hrs)

Last arrival 17.00hrs Last departure noon

A large marina site with restaurant facilities, situated on the Trent/Merseyside Canal. Pitches are on grass surrounded by mature trees, and for the keen angler, the site offers fishing within the marina. The attractive grass touring area overlooks the marina. 25 acre site. 35 touring pitches. 26 hardstandings. 10 seasonal pitches. Caravan pitches. Motorhome pitches. Tent pitches. 73 statics.

AA Pubs & Restaurants nearby: The Old Crown Inn, SHARDLOW, DE72 2HL, 01332 792392

The Priest House Hotel, CASTLE DONINGTON, DE74 2RR, 0845 072 7502

Facilities: 🦽⊙⚒♿🖎 ❼

Services: 🔌🗑🍽📬⊘🅃🍽🏧⚓

Within 3 miles: 🚴🎡🗓℘🖎🗑⊙

Notes: Max 1 child & 2 dogs per unit. Dogs must not be left unattended or tied up outside. Dogs must be kept on leads.

SERVICES: 🔌 Electric hook up 🗑 Launderette 🍽 Licensed bar 🔋 Calor Gas ⊘ Camping Gaz 🅃 Toilet fluid 🍽 Café/Restaurant 🏧 Fast Food/Takeaway ⚓ Battery charging 🚼 Baby care ⚒ Motorvan service point **ABBREVIATIONS:** BH/bank hols-bank holidays Etr-Easter Spring BH-Spring Bank Holiday dep-departure fr-from hrs-hours m-mile mdnt-midnight rdbt-roundabout rs-restricted service wk-week wknd-weekend x-rds-cross roads 🈁 No credit cards 🚫 No dogs
🚼 Children of all ages accepted See page 9 for details of the AA Camping Card Scheme

Devon

With two magnificent coastlines, two historic
cities and a world-famous national park, Devon
sums up all that is best about the British landscape.
For centuries it has been a fashionable and much-loved
holiday destination – especially south Devon's glorious
English Riviera.

● Kingsbridge Estuary

The largest and most famous seaside resort on the southern coast is Torquay, created in the 19th century and still retaining a tangible air of Victorian charm mixed with a pleasing hint of the Mediterranean. Palm trees grace the bustling harbour where colourful yachts and cabin cruisers vie for space and the weather is pleasantly warm and sunny for long hours in the summer.

In and around Torquay

In recent years television and literature have helped to boost Torquay's holiday image. The hotel that was the inspiration for *Fawlty Towers*, starring the incomparable John Cleese, is located in the town, while Agatha Christie, the Queen of Crime, was born and raised in Torquay. A bust of her, unveiled in 1990 to mark the centenary of her birth, stands near the harbour and tourist information centre.

Greenway, Christie's splendid holiday home, now managed by the National Trust and open to the public, lies outside the town, overlooking a glorious sweep of the River Dart. By taking a nostalgic ride on the Paignton and Dartmouth

▶

Steam Railway you can wallow in the world of Poirot and Miss Marple, Christie's famous sleuths, passing close to the house and its glorious grounds.

Dartmoor

One of Agatha Christie's favourite Devon landscapes was Dartmoor. The National Park which contains it covers 365 square miles and includes vast moorland stretches, isolated granite tors and two summits exceeding 2,000 feet. This bleak and brooding landscape is the largest tract of open wilderness left in southern England. More than 100 years ago Sir Arthur Conan Doyle gave Dartmoor something of a boost when he set his classic and most famous Sherlock Holmes' story, *The Hound of the Baskervilles*, in this romantic and adventurous area.

South Devon

Plymouth lies in Devon's south-west corner and is a fine city and naval port with a wide range of visitor attractions, including the Plymouth Mayflower, overlooking Sutton Harbour, an interactive exhibition explaining the city's history. There is particular emphasis on the Spanish Armada and the voyage of the Pilgrim Fathers to America. Exeter can also occupy many hours of sightseeing. As well as the famous cathedral with its Norman twin towers, there is the Guildhall, which includes a Mayor's Parlour with five original Tudor windows, and the Quay House Visitor Centre where the history of the city is illustrated.

Walking and Cycling

The beauty of Devon, of course, is also appreciated on foot. The Dart Valley Trail offers views of the river at its best, while at Dartmouth you can join the South West Coast Path, renowned for its stunning views and breezy cliff-top walking. The trail heads along the coast to South Hams, a rural farming district where gently rolling hills sweep down to the majestic coastline. One of the area's great landmarks is Salcombe, a bustling fishing port with a magnificent natural harbour.

Another popular trail is the 103-mile (164km) Two Moors Way which begins at Ivybridge and crosses Dartmoor before passing through the delightful hidden landscape of R.D.Blackmoor's classic novel *Lorna Doone* to reach Exmoor, which straddles the Devon/Somerset border. On reaching picturesque Lynton and Lynmouth you can link up with the South West Coast Path again to explore north Devon's stunning coastline. Don't miss the Valley of Rocks, an extraordinary collection of peaks and outcrops which add a wonderful sense of drama to this stretch of coast.

There are various leaflets and booklets on cycling available from tourist information centres throughout the county. The Dartmoor Way is a great introduction to the National Park with a choice of off-road cycle routes; there is also a range of cycle trails in the Exmoor National Park.

Festivals and Events

- The Ashburton Carnival takes place at Ashburton in early July.
- Chagford has an Agricultural and Flower show in August.
- During July, Honiton hosts a Fair with the Hot Pennies ceremony; in August there is an Agricultural Show and in October a carnival.

● Salcombe

DEVON

ASHBURTON
Map 3 SX77

Places to visit

Compton Castle, COMPTON, TQ3 1TA,
01803 842382
www.nationaltrust.org.uk/comptoncastle

Tuckers Maltings, NEWTON ABBOT, TQ12 4AA,
01626 334734 www.tuckersmaltings.com

Great for kids: Prickly Ball Farm and
Hedgehog Hospital, NEWTON ABBOT, TQ12 6BZ,
01626 362319 www.pricklyballfarm.com

►►►► 85% River Dart Country Park
(SX734700)

Holne Park TQ13 7NP
☎ 01364 652511
e-mail: info@riverdart.co.uk
web: www.riverdart.co.uk
dir: M5 junct 31, A38 towards Plymouth. In
Ashburton at Peartree junct follow brown site
signs. Site 1m on left. (NB Peartree junct is 2nd
exit at Ashburton - do not exit at Linhay junct as
narrow roads are unsuitable for caravans)

🚐 £14-£31.50 🚎 £14-£31.50 ▲ £14-£31.50

Open Apr-Sep (rs Low season café bar restricted
opening hours)

Last arrival 21.00hrs Last departure 11.00hrs

Set in 90 acres of magnificent parkland that was
once part of a Victorian estate, with many
specimen and exotic trees, this peaceful, hidden-
away touring park occupies several camping
areas, all served with good quality toilet facilities.
In spring the park is a blaze of colour from the
many azaleas and rhododendrons. There are
numerous outdoor activities for all ages including
abseiling, caving and canoeing, plus high quality,
well-maintained facilities. The open moorland of
Dartmoor is only a few minutes away. 90 acre site.
170 touring pitches. 23 hardstandings. Caravan
pitches. Motorhome pitches. Tent pitches.

AA Pubs & Restaurants nearby: Dartbridge Inn,
BUCKFASTLEIGH, TQ11 0JR, 01364 642214

Agaric, ASHBURTON, TQ13 7QD, 01364 654478

Leisure: ⚙ 🏊 🔍
Facilities: 🛁 📞 ☉ 🍴 ✳ & ⓒ 🛍 🎪 🐕 WI-FI ♻ ❶
Services: 🔌 🗑 🍴 🛢 ⌀ Ⓣ 🍴 🛒 🏪 ⛽
Within 3 miles: ⚓ 🎣 🛍 ⌂

Notes: Dogs must be kept on leads. Adventure
playground.

►►►► 84% Parkers Farm Holiday
Park (SX779713)

Higher Mead Farm TQ13 7LJ
☎ 01364 654869
e-mail: parkersfarm@btconnect.com
dir: From Exeter on A38, 2nd left after
Plymouth/29m sign, signed Woodland & Denbury.
From Plymouth on A38 take A383 Newton Abbot
exit, turn right across bridge, rejoin A38, then as
above

* 🚐 £12-£25 🚎 £12-£25 ▲ £10-£20

Open Etr-end Oct (rs Out of season bar &
restaurant open wknds only)

Last arrival 22.00hrs Last departure 10.00hrs

A well-developed site terraced into rising ground
with stunning views across rolling countryside to
the Dartmoor tors. Part of a working farm, this
park offers excellent fully serviced hardstanding
pitches, which make the most of the fine views; it
is beautifully maintained and has good quality
toilet facilities, a popular games room and a bar/
restaurant that serves excellent meals. Large
family rooms with two shower cubicles, a large
sink and a toilet are especially appreciated by
families with small children. There are regular
farm walks when all the family can meet and feed
the various animals. 25 acre site. 100 touring
pitches. 20 hardstandings. Caravan pitches.
Motorhome pitches. Tent pitches. 18 statics.

AA Pubs & Restaurants nearby: Dartbridge Inn,
BUCKFASTLEIGH, TQ11 0JR, 01364 642214

Agaric, ASHBURTON, TQ13 7QD, 01364 654478

Leisure: ⚙ 🕹 ☉ 🔍 ⌂ 🎵
Facilities: 📞 ☉ ✳ & ⓒ 🛍 🎪 🐕 WI-FI ♻ ❶
Services: 🔌 🗑 🍴 🛢 ⌀ Ⓣ 🍴 🏪 ⛽
Within 3 miles: 🎣 🛍 ⌂

Notes: Dogs must be kept on leads. Large field for
dog walking.

AXMINSTER
Map 4 SY29

Places to visit

Branscombe - The Old Bakery, Manor Mill and
Forge, BRANSCOMBE, EX12 3DB, 01752 346585
www.nationaltrust.org.uk

Allhallows Museum, HONITON, EX14 1PG,
01404 44966 www.honitonmuseum.co.uk

Great for kids: Pecorama Pleasure Gardens,
BEER, EX12 3NA, 01297 21542
www.pecorama.info

►►►► 85% Andrewshayes
Holiday Park (ST248088)

Dalwood EX13 7DY
☎ 01404 831225
e-mail: info@andrewshayes.co.uk
web: www.andrewshayes.co.uk
dir: 3m from Axminster (towards Honiton) on
A35, right at Taunton Cross signed Dalwood &
Stockland. Site 150mtrs on right

🚐 £15-£32 🚎 £15-£32 ▲ £15-£27

Open Jul-Aug & wknds (rs Off-peak shop, bar
hours, takeaway limited)

Last arrival 22.00hrs Last departure 11.00hrs

An attractive family park within easy reach of
Lyme Regis, Seaton, Branscombe and Sidmouth in
an ideal touring location. This popular park offers
modern toilet facilities, an outdoor swimming pool
and a quiet, cosy bar with a wide-screen TV. 12
acre site. 150 touring pitches. 105 hardstandings.
100 seasonal pitches. Caravan pitches.
Motorhome pitches. Tent pitches. 80 statics.

Leisure: 🏊 ⚙ ☉ 🔍 ⌂
Facilities: 📞 ☉ 🍴 ✳ & ⓒ 🛍 🎪 🐕 WI-FI ♻ ❶
Services: 🔌 🗑 🍴 🛢 ⌀ 🏪 ⛽
Within 3 miles: 🎣 🛍 ⌂

Notes: Dogs must be kept on leads.

LEISURE: 🏊 Indoor swimming pool ⚽ Outdoor swimming pool Ⓐ Children's playground 🕹 Kid's club 🎾 Tennis court 🔍 Games room 🖵 Separate TV room
⛳ 9/18 hole golf course 🚤 Boats for hire 🎦 Cinema 🎵 Entertainment 🎣 Fishing ⊙ Mini golf ⚓ Watersports 🏋 Gym 🏟 Sports field **Spa** ⌂ Stables
FACILITIES: 🛁 Bath 📷 Shower ⊙ Electric shaver 🎩 Hairdryer ✳ Ice Pack Facility & Disabled facilities ⓒ Public telephone 🛍 Shop on site or within 200yds
📱 Mobile shop (calls at least 5 days a week) 🍴 BBQ area 🎪 Picnic area WI-FI Wi-fi 🖳 Internet access ♻ Recycling ❶ Tourist info 🐕 Dog exercise area

►►► 81% Hawkchurch Country Park

(SY344985)

Hawkchurch EX13 5UL
☎ 08442 729502
e-mail: enquiries@hawkchurchpark.co.uk
dir: *From Axminster towards Charmouth on A35 left onto B3165. Left into Wareham Rd, site on left, follow signs. (NB the lanes near Hawkchurch are narrow)*

🚐 £15-£35 🚏 £15-£35 ▲ £5-£30

Open 15 Feb-4 Jan

Last arrival 21.00hrs Last departure 10.00hrs

This peaceful park is set in mature woodlands right on the Devon and Dorset border, with easy access to the Jurassic Coast Heritage Site, Lyme Regis, Charmouth and West Bay. The site has huge potential, with hardstandings plus tent and rally fields. 30 acre site. 369 touring pitches. 225 hardstandings. Caravan pitches. Motorhome pitches. Tent pitches.

AA Pubs & Restaurants nearby: Fairwater Head Hotel, AXMINSTER, EX13 5TX, 01297 678349

The Mariners, LYME REGIS, DT7 3HS, 01297 442753

Pilot Boat Inn, LYME REGIS, DT7 3QA, 01297 443157

Leisure: 🅰 🎣 🎵
Facilities: 📡⊙📠❄️♿🔌🛁🛒🏧ℹ️
Services: 🔌🅖🍴🔋🗑️🚽🍴
Within 3 miles: ⛳🎠🏇🐾◎🛥️🎯🛒🎣

Notes: Quiet period 22.00hrs-08.00hrs. Dogs must be kept on leads.

BERRYNARBOR   Map 3 SS54

Places to visit
Arlington Court, ARLINGTON, EX31 4LP, 01271 850296
www.nationaltrust.org.uk/arlington-court

Exmoor Zoological Park, BLACKMOOR GATE, EX31 4SG, 01598 763352 www.exmoorzoo.co.uk

Great for kids: Combe Martin Wildlife Park & Dinosaur Park, COMBE MARTIN, EX34 0NG, 01271 882486 www.wildlifedinosaurpark.co.uk

►►► 84% Mill Park Touring Site

(SS559471)

Mill Ln EX34 9SH
☎ 01271 882647
e-mail: millparkdevon@btconnect.com
dir: *M5 junct 27, A361 towards Barnstaple. Right onto A399 towards Combe Martin. At Sawmills Inn take turn opposite Berrynarbor sign*

🚐 🚏 ▲

Open Mar-30 Oct (rs Low season on-site facilities closed)

Last arrival 22.00hrs Last departure 10.00hrs

This family-owned and run park is set in an attractive wooded valley with a stream running into a lake where coarse fishing is available. There is a quiet bar/restaurant with a family room, and the park has two lakeside cocoons and a four-bedroom apartment to let. The park is two miles from Combe Martin and Ilfracombe and just a stroll across the road from the small harbour at Watermouth. 23 acre site. 178 touring pitches. 20 hardstandings. Caravan pitches. Motorhome pitches. Tent pitches. 2 wooden pods.

AA Pubs & Restaurants nearby: The George & Dragon, ILFRACOMBE, EX34 9ED, 01271 863851

11 The Quay, ILFRACOMBE, EX34 9EQ, 01271 868090

Leisure: 🅰 🎣
Facilities: 📡⊙📠❄️♿🔌🛁🏧🛒🏧 WiFi 🖥️ ♻️ ℹ️
Services: 🔌🅖🍴🔋🗑️🚽🍴🍔
Within 3 miles: ⛳🎣🎠🐾◎🛥️🎯🛒🎣⛵

Notes: No large groups. Beauty therapy room.

BICKINGTON (NEAR ASHBURTON)   Map 3 SX87

Places to visit
Bradley Manor, NEWTON ABBOT, TQ12 6BN, 01803 843235
www.nationaltrust.org.uk/devoncornwall

Great for kids: Living Coasts, TORQUAY, TQ1 2BG, 01803 202470
www.livingcoasts.org.uk

►►►► 81% Lemonford Caravan Park *(SX793723)*

TQ12 6JR
☎ 01626 821242
e-mail: info@lemonford.co.uk
web: www.lemonford.co.uk
dir: *From Exeter on A38 take A382, 3rd exit at rdbt, follow Bickington signs*

* 🚐 £13.50-£23 🚏 £13.50-£23 ▲ £13.50-£23

Open all year

Last arrival 22.00hrs Last departure 11.00hrs

Small, secluded and well-maintained park with a good mixture of attractively laid out pitches. The friendly owners pay a great deal of attention to detail, and the toilets in particular are kept spotlessly clean. This good touring base is only one mile from Dartmoor and ten miles from the seaside at Torbay. The bus to Exeter, Plymouth and Torbay stops outside the park. 7 acre site. 82 touring pitches. 55 hardstandings. Caravan pitches. Motorhome pitches. Tent pitches. 44 statics.

AA Pubs & Restaurants nearby: The Wild Goose Inn, NEWTON ABBOT, TQ12 4RA, 01626 872241

Agaric, ASHBURTON, TQ13 7QD, 01364 654478

continued

BICKINGTON (NEAR ASHBURTON) *continued*

Lemonford Caravan Park

Leisure: ⚐

Facilities: ⛟♟⦿☝✳♿⑤🛢♻ ❶

Services: ◉⑤🛢⌀🚽🛒↯

Within 3 miles: ⌖🚲⑤⑤∪

Notes: No noise after 23.00hrs. Dogs must be kept on leads. Clothes-drying area.

see advert below

BRAUNTON

Places to visit

Marwood Hill Gardens, BARNSTAPLE, EX31 4EB, 01271 342528 www.marwoodhillgarden.co.uk

Great for kids: Combe Martin Wildlife Park & Dinosaur Park, COMBE MARTIN, EX34 0NG, 01271 882486 www.wildlifedinosaurpark.co.uk

---

BRAUNTON   Map 3 SS43

PREMIER PARK

▶▶▶▶▶ **85% Hidden Valley Park** *(SS499408)*   Best of British

West Down EX34 8NU

☎ 01271 813837

dir: *Direct access from A361, 8m from Barnstaple & 2m from Mullacott Cross*

🚐 £10-£37 🚃 £10-£37 ▲ £10-£40

Open all year

Last arrival 21.00hrs Last departure 10.30hrs

A delightful, well-appointed family site set in a wooded valley, with superb facilities and a café. The park is set in a very rural, natural location not far from the beautiful coastline around Ilfracombe. The woodland is home to nesting buzzards and woodpeckers, and otters have taken up residence by the lake. Wi-fi is available. There are three fully equipped timber cabins for hire. 32 acre site. 100 touring pitches. 50 hardstandings. 15 seasonal pitches. Caravan pitches. Motorhome pitches. Tent pitches. 3 statics.

AA Pubs & Restaurants nearby: The Williams Arms, BRAUNTON, EX33 2DE, 01271 812360

Leisure: ⚐

Facilities: ⛟♟⦿☝✳♿⑤🐾 📶🖥 ♻ ❶

Services: ◉⑤🛢⌀🚽🍴↯

Within 3 miles: ⌖🚲🎣◉⟰⑤⑤∪

▶▶▶ **80% Lobb Fields Caravan & Camping Park** *(SS475378)*

Saunton Rd EX33 1HG

☎ 01271 812090

e-mail: info@lobbfields.com

dir: *At x-rds in Braunton take B3231 to Croyde. Site signed on right leaving Braunton*

* 🚐 £11-£29 🚃 £11-£29 ▲ £10-£24

Open 28 Mar-2 Nov

Last arrival 22.00hrs Last departure 10.30hrs

A bright, tree-lined park with gently-sloping grass pitches divided into two open areas and a camping field in August. Braunton is an easy walk away, and the golden beaches of Saunton Sands and Croyde are within easy reach. 14 acre site. 180 touring pitches. 11 hardstandings. Caravan pitches. Motorhome pitches. Tent pitches.

AA Pubs & Restaurants nearby: The Williams Arms, BRAUNTON, EX33 2DE, 01271 812360

LEISURE: 🏊 Indoor swimming pool ⚴ Outdoor swimming pool ⚐ Children's playground 🎣 Kid's club ⚲ Tennis court 🎯 Games room ▢ Separate TV room ⌖ 9/18 hole golf course ⚓ Boats for hire 🎬 Cinema 🎵 Entertainment 🎣 Fishing ◎ Mini golf ⟰ Watersports 🏋 Gym 🏟 Sports field Spa ∪ Stables

FACILITIES: ⛟ Bath ♟ Shower ⦿ Electric shaver ☝ Hairdryer ✳ Ice Pack Facility ♿ Disabled facilities ☎ Public telephone ⑤ Shop on site or within 200yds ⑤ Mobile shop (calls at least 5 days a week) 🍴 BBQ area 🐾 Picnic area 📶 Wi-fi 🖥 Internet access ♻ Recycling ❶ Tourist info 🐕 Dog exercise area

Leisure: /A

Facilities: ⁅Ⓞ⌒✻&Ⓛ◐🛏Wi-Fi ♻ 𝒊

Services: ⚡🔲🔒⌀🚽🍴🛒⌄

Within 3 miles: ↓╱🚴🥾🛒🚢U

Notes: No under 18s unless accompanied by an adult. Dogs must be kept on leads. Surfing, boards & wet suits for hire, wet suit washing areas.

BRIDESTOWE — Map 3 SX58

Places to visit

Lydford Castle and Saxon Town, LYDFORD, EX20 4BH, 0870 333 1181 www.english-heritage.org.uk/daysout/ properties/lydford-castle-and-saxon-town

Museum of Dartmoor Life, OKEHAMPTON, EX20 1HQ, 01837 52295 www.museumofdartmoorlife.co.uk

Great for kids: Tamar Otter & Wildlife Centre, LAUNCESTON, PL15 8GW, 01566 785646 www.tamarotters.co.uk

---

►►► 75% Bridestowe Caravan Park

(SX519893)

EX20 4ER

☎ **01837 861261**

e-mail: ali.young53@btinternet.com

dir: *Exit A30 at A386/Sourton Cross junct, follow B3278 signed Bridestowe, left in 3m. In village centre, left onto unclassified road for 0.5m*

* 🚐 £13-£18 🚗 £13-£18 ⛺ £10-£15

Open Mar-Dec

Last arrival 22.30hrs Last departure noon

A small, well-established park in a rural setting close to Dartmoor National Park. This mainly static park has a small, peaceful touring space, and there are many activities to enjoy in the area including fishing and riding. Part of the National Cycle Route 27 - the Devon coast to coast - passes close to this park. 1 acre site. 13 touring pitches. 3 hardstandings. Caravan pitches. Motorhome pitches. Tent pitches. 40 statics.

AA Pubs & Restaurants nearby: The Highwayman Inn, SOURTON, EX20 4HN, 01837 861243

Lewtrenchard Manor, LEWDOWN, EX20 4PN, 01566 783222

Leisure: /A 🎣 Facilities: ⁅Ⓞ✻🆂♻ 𝒊

Services: ⚡🔲🔒⌀🚽🛒

Within 3 miles: ╱🆂🔲

Notes: ⊗ Dogs must be kept on leads.

BRIDGERULE — Map 2 SS20

AA CAMPING CARD SITE

►►► 82% Hedleywood Caravan & Camping Park *(SS262013)*

EX22 7ED

☎ **01288 381404**

e-mail: alan@hedleywood.co.uk

dir: *From Exeter, A30 to Launceston, B3254 towards Bude. Left into Tackbear Rd signed Marhamchurch & Widemouth (at Devon/Cornwall border). Site on right*

🚐 🚗 ⛺

Open all year (rs Main hols bar & restaurant open)

Last arrival anytime Last departure anytime

Set in a very rural location about four miles from Bude, this relaxed family-owned site has a peaceful, easy-going atmosphere. Pitches are in separate paddocks, some with extensive views, and this wooded park is quite sheltered in the lower areas. The restaurant/club house is a popular place to relax. 16.5 acre site. 120 touring pitches. 30 hardstandings. 27 seasonal pitches. Caravan pitches. Motorhome pitches. Tent pitches. 16 statics.

AA Pubs & Restaurants nearby: The Bickford Arms, HOLSWORTHY, EX22 7XY, 01409 221318

Bay View Inn, WIDEMOUTH BAY, EX23 0AW, 01288 361273

Hedleywood Caravan & Camping Park

Leisure: /A 🎣 □

Facilities: ⁅Ⓞ⌒✻&Ⓛ🆂🏸🛏Wi-Fi 🖥 ♻ 𝒊

Services: ⚡🔲🔳🔒⌀Ⓣ🍴🛒⌄

Within 3 miles: ↓╱🆂🔲U

Notes: ⊗ Dogs must be kept on leads. Dog kennels, dog walk & nature trail, caravan storage.

►► 89% *Highfield House Camping & Caravanning* *(SS279035)*

Holsworthy EX22 7EE

☎ **01288 381480**

e-mail: njt@btinternet.com

dir: *Exit A3072 at Red Post x-rds onto B3254 towards Launceston. Direct access just over Devon border on right*

🚐 🚗 ⛺

Open all year

Set in a quiet and peaceful rural location, this park has extensive views over the valley to the sea at Bude, five miles away. The friendly owners, with children of their own, offer a relaxing holiday for families, with the simple facilities carefully looked after. 4 acre site. 20 touring pitches. Caravan pitches. Motorhome pitches. Tent pitches. 8 statics.

AA Pubs & Restaurants nearby: The Bickford Arms, HOLSWORTHY, EX22 7XY, 01409 221318

Bay View Inn, WIDEMOUTH BAY, EX23 0AW, 01288 361273

Facilities: ⁅Ⓞ✻&🏸♻

Services: ⚡🔲

Within 3 miles: ↓🚴🎣╱◎🚢🆂🔲U

Notes: ⊗ Dogs must be kept on leads.

BRIXHAM
Map 3 SX95

Places to visit

Greenway, CHURSTON FERRERS, TQ5 0ES, 01803 842382 www.nationaltrust.org.uk/devoncornwall

Great for kids: Paignton Zoo Environmental Park, PAIGNTON, TQ4 7EU, 0844 474 2222 www.paigntonzoo.org.uk

►►►► 80% *Galmpton Touring Park*
(SX885558)

Greenway Rd TQ5 0EP
☎ 01803 842066
e-mail: enquiries@galmptontouringpark.co.uk
dir: *Signed from A3022 (Torbay to Brixham road) at Churston*

🚐 🚐 Å

Open May-Sep

Last arrival 21.00hrs (late arrival times require prior notice). Last departure 11.00hrs

A stunningly located site, set on high ground overlooking the River Dart and with outstanding views of the creek and anchorage. The park looks smart, and pitches are set on level terraces; the toilet facilities has been upgraded to provide good quality amenities. 10 acre site. 120 touring pitches. 15 hardstandings. Caravan pitches. Motorhome pitches. Tent pitches.

Leisure: ⚠

Facilities: 🅟⊙🅟✳&🅢🖈♻🅘🅞

Services: 🅠🅢🔒⊘🅣↯

Within 3 miles: ⚡🛶🎯🅟◎🛒🅢🅢

Notes: Families & couples only, no dogs during peak season. Dogs must be kept on leads. Bathroom for under 5s (charges apply).

BROADWOODWIDGER
Map 3 SX48

Places to visit

Museum of Dartmoor Life, OKEHAMPTON, EX20 1HQ, 01837 52295 www.museumofdartmoorlife.co.uk

Finch Foundry, STICKLEPATH, EX20 2NW, 01837 840046 www.nationaltrust.org.uk

►►► 79% Roadford Lake *(SX421900)*

Lower Goodacre PL16 0JL
☎ 01409 211507
e-mail: info@swlakestrust.org.uk
dir: *Exit A30 between Okehampton & Launceston at Roadford Lake signs, cross dam wall, site 0.25m on right*

* 🚐 £13-£16 🚐 £13-£16 Å £13-£16

Open Apr-Oct

Last arrival 17.30hrs (late arrival times available if pre-booked). Last departure 11.00hrs

Located right at the edge of Devon's largest inland water, this popular rural park is well screened by mature trees and shrubs. There is an excellent watersports school for sailing, windsurfing, rowing and kayaking, with hire and day launch facilities. This is an ideal location for brown trout fly fishing. One yurt is available for hire. 1.5 acre site. 50 touring pitches. 6 hardstandings. Caravan pitches. Motorhome pitches. Tent pitches.

AA Pubs & Restaurants nearby: Arundell Arms, LIFTON, PL16 0AA, 01566 784666

Facilities: 🅟⊙🅟✳&🚐♻🅘🅞

Services: 🅠🅢🍴

Within 3 miles: ⚡🎯🛒🅢

Notes: Off-ground BBQs only, no open fires. Dogs must be kept on leads. Climbing wall, archery.

BUCKFASTLEIGH
Map 3 SX76

Places to visit

Buckfast Abbey, BUCKFASTLEIGH, TQ11 0EE, 01364 645500 www.buckfast.org.uk

Great for kids: Buckfast Butterfly Farm & Dartmoor Otter Sanctuary, BUCKFASTLEIGH, TQ11 0DZ, 01364 642916 www.ottersandbutterflies.co.uk

► 88% Churchill Farm Campsite
(SX743664)

TQ11 0EZ
☎ 01364 642844 & 07977 113175
e-mail: apedrick@btinternet.com
dir: *From A38 Dart Bridge exit for Buckfastleigh/ Totnes towards Buckfast Abbey. Pass Abbey entrance, up hill, left at x-rds to site opposite Holy Trinity Church*

* 🚐 £12-£15 🚐 £12-£15 Å £12-£15

Open Etr-Sep

Last arrival 22.00hrs

A working family farm in a relaxed and peaceful setting, with keen, friendly owners. Set on the hills above Buckfast Abbey, this attractive park is maintained to a good standard. The spacious pitches in the neatly trimmed paddock enjoy extensive country views towards Dartmoor, and the clean, simple toilet facilities include smart showers. This is a hidden gem for those who love traditional camping. Close to a local bus service and within walking distance of Buckfastleigh, the Abbey and the South Devon Steam Railway. 3 acre site. 25 touring pitches. Caravan pitches. Motorhome pitches. Tent pitches.

AA Pubs & Restaurants nearby: Dartbridge Inn, BUCKFASTLEIGH, TQ11 0JR, 01364 642214

Facilities: 🅟⊙✳&♻🅘🅞

Services: 🅠🖥

Within 3 miles: 🅢

Notes: 🚫 No ball games. Dogs must be kept on leads. Within a Site of Special Scientific Interest.

LEISURE: 🏊 Indoor swimming pool 🏊 Outdoor swimming pool ⚠ Children's playground 🧒 Kid's club 🎾 Tennis court 🎱 Games room 📺 Separate TV room ⛳ 9/18 hole golf course 🚤 Boats for hire 🎬 Cinema 🎵 Entertainment 🎣 Fishing ⛳ Mini golf 🏄 Watersports 🏋 Gym 🏟 Sports field Spa ♨ Stables **FACILITIES:** 🛁 Bath 🚿 Shower ⊙ Electric shaver 🅟 Hairdryer ✳ Ice Pack Facility & Disabled facilities 📞 Public telephone 🅢 Shop on site or within 200yds � Mobile shop (calls at least 5 days a week) 🍖 BBQ area 🎍 Picnic area 📶 Wi-fi 🖥 Internet access ♻ Recycling 🅘 Tourist info 🖈 Dog exercise area

► 84% Beara Farm Caravan & Camping Site *(SX751645)*

Colston Rd TQ11 OLW
☎ 01364 642234
dir: *From Exeter take Buckfastleigh exit at Dart Bridge, follow South Devon Steam Railway/ Butterfly Farm signs. 200mtrs past entrance to South Devon Steam Railway 1st left into Old Totnes Rd, 0.5m right at red brick cottages signed Beara Farm. Approx 1m to site*

* 🚐 fr £11 🚌 fr £11 ⛺ fr £11

Open all year

Last arrival 21.00hrs Last departure anytime

A very good farm park, with clean unisex facilities, run by very keen and friendly owners. A well-trimmed camping field offers peace and quiet. Close to the River Dart and the Dart Valley Steam Railway line, within easy reach of the sea and moors. Please note that the approach to the site is narrow, with passing places, and care needs to be taken. 3.63 acre site. 30 touring pitches. 1 hardstanding. Caravan pitches. Motorhome pitches. Tent pitches.

AA Pubs & Restaurants nearby: Dartbridge Inn, BUCKFASTLEIGH, TQ11 0JR, 01364 642214

Facilities: 🚿 ☉ ✲ 🪑 🐕 ♻ ℹ

Services: 🔋

Within 3 miles: ⛳ [S]

Notes: 🚫💳 No noise after 22.30hrs. Dogs must be kept on leads.

BUDLEIGH SALTERTON Map 3 SY08

Places to visit

Otterton Mill, OTTERTON, EX9 7HG, 01395 568521 www.ottertonmill.com

Great for kids: Bicton Park Botanical Gardens, BICTON, EX9 7BJ, 01395 568465 www.bictongardens.co.uk

►►► 81% Pooh Cottage Holiday Park *(SY053831)*

Bear Ln EX9 7AQ
☎ 01395 442354 & 07875 685595
e-mail: bookings@poohcottage.co.uk
web: www.poohcottage.co.uk
dir: *M5 junct 30, A376 towards Exmouth. Left onto B3179 towards Woodbury & Budleigh Salterton. Left into Knowle onto B3178. Through village, at brow of hill take sharp left into Bear Lane. Site 200yds*

🚐 🚌 ⛺

Open 15 Mar-Oct

Last arrival 21.00hrs Last departure 11.30hrs

A rural park with wide views of the sea and surrounding peaceful countryside. Expect a friendly welcome to this attractive site, with its lovely play area, and easy access to plenty of walks, as well as the Buzzard Cycle Way. On site cycle hire, and there's a bus stop within walking distance. 8 acre site. 16 touring pitches. 45 seasonal pitches. Caravan pitches. Motorhome pitches. Tent pitches. 3 statics.

AA Pubs & Restaurants nearby: Blue Ball Inn, SIDMOUTH, EX10 9QL, 01395 514062

The Salty Monk, SIDMOUTH, EX10 9QP, 01395 513174

Leisure: 🛝

Facilities: 🚿 ☉ ✲ ♿ 🪑 [Wi-fi] ♻ ℹ

Services: 🔌 [▣] 🛢 🍃 [T]

Within 3 miles: ⛳ 🚣 🏋 ⛳ ◎ 🏊 [S] [▣] Ʊ

Notes: No gazebos, 5mph speed limit. Dogs must be kept on leads.

CHAPMANS WELL Map 3 SX39

Places to visit

Launceston Steam Railway, LAUNCESTON, PL15 8DA, 01566 775665 www.launcestonsr.co.uk

Launceston Castle, LAUNCESTON, PL15 7DR, 01566 772365 www.english-heritage.org.uk/daysout/properties/launceston-castle

Great for kids: Tamar Otter & Wildlife Centre, LAUNCESTON, PL15 8GW, 01566 785646 www.tamarotters.co.uk

AA CAMPING CARD SITE

►►► 84% Chapmanswell Caravan Park *(SX354931)*

St Giles-on-the-Heath PL15 9SG
☎ 01409 211382
e-mail: george@chapmanswellcaravanpark.co.uk
web: www.chapmanswellcaravanpark.co.uk
dir: *A338 from Launceston towards Holsworthy, 6m. Site on left at Chapmans Well*

* 🚐 £13.50-£18 🚌 £13.50-£18 ⛺ £10.50-£25.50

Open all year

Last arrival anytime by prior arrangement Last departure anytime by prior arrangement

Set on the borders of Devon and Cornwall in peaceful countryside, this park is just waiting to be discovered. It enjoys extensive views towards Dartmoor from level pitches, and is within easy driving distance of Launceston (7 miles) and the golden beaches at Bude (14 miles). 10 acre site. 50 touring pitches. 35 hardstandings. 32 seasonal pitches. Caravan pitches. Motorhome pitches. Tent pitches. 50 statics.

AA Pubs & Restaurants nearby: The Bickford Arms, HOLSWORTHY, EX22 7XY, 01409 221318

Leisure: 🛝 ♫

Facilities: 🚿 ☉ ✲ ♿ [S] [Wi-fi] ♻ ℹ

Services: 🔌 [▣] 🍺 🛢 🍃 [T] 🍴 🔋 🍔 ⛛

Within 3 miles: ⛳ 🚣 ⛳ 🏊 [S] [▣] Ʊ

Notes: Dogs must be kept on leads.

CHUDLEIGH — Map 3 SX87

Places to visit

Canonteign Falls, CHUDLEIGH, EX6 7NT, 01647 252434 www.canonteignfalls.co.uk

Exeter's Underground Passages, EXETER, EX1 1GA, 01392 665887 www.exeter.gov.uk/passages

Great for kids: Prickly Ball Farm and Hedgehog Hospital, NEWTON ABBOT, TQ12 6BZ, 01626 362319 www.pricklyballfarm.com

▶▶▶ 85% Holmans Wood Holiday Park (SX881812)

Harcombe Cross TQ13 0DZ
☎ **01626 853785**
e-mail: enquiries@holmanswood.co.uk
dir: *M5 junct 31, A38. After racecourse at top of Haldon Hill left at BP petrol station signed Chudleigh, site entrance on left of slip road*

✱ 🚐 £19-£25 🚐 £19-£25 ▲ £14-£16

Open mid Mar-end Oct

Last arrival 22.00hrs Last departure 11.00hrs

A delightful small park set back from the A38 in a secluded wooded area, handy for touring Dartmoor National Park, and the lanes and beaches of south Devon. The facilities are bright and clean, and the grounds are attractively landscaped. 12 acre site. 73 touring pitches. 71 hardstandings. Caravan pitches. Motorhome pitches. Tent pitches. 34 statics.

AA Pubs & Restaurants nearby: Cridford Inn, TRUSHAM, TQ13 0NR, 01626 853694

Leisure: 🏔

Facilities: 🏕🚿♿❄🔌🕭🚻📶🖥️ℹ️

Services: 🔌🗑️🔧💧🧺

Within 3 miles: 🛒🛍️U

Notes: No cycling or skateboards. Pets only allowed at the management's discretion. Dogs must be kept on leads.

CLYST ST MARY — Map 3 SX99

Places to visit

Exeter Cathedral, EXETER, EX1 1HS, 01392 285983 www.exeter-cathedral.org.uk

Exeter's Underground Passages, EXETER, EX1 1GA, 01392 665887 www.exeter.gov.uk/passages

Great for kids: Crealy Adventure Park, CLYST ST MARY, EX5 1DR, 01395 233200 www.crealy.co.uk

The World of Country Life, EXMOUTH, EX8 5BU, 01395 274533 www.worldofcountrylife.co.uk

AA CAMPING CARD SITE

PREMIER PARK

▶▶▶▶▶ 83% Crealy Meadows Caravan and Camping Park

(SY001906)

Sidmouth Rd EX5 1DR
☎ **01395 234888**
e-mail: stay@crealymeadows.co.uk
dir: *M5 junct 30, A3052 signed Exmouth. At rdbt take A3052 signed Seaton. Follow brown Crealy Great Adventure Park signs. Turn right*

🚐 £20-£32.50 🚐 £20-£32.50 ▲ £20-£32.50

Open Mar-Oct

Last arrival 20.00hrs Last departure 10.00hrs

A quality park with excellent toilet facilities, spacious fully serviced pitches and good security, adjacent to the popular Crealy Adventure Park, with free or discounted entry available for all campers. The park is within a short drive of Exeter and the seaside attractions at Sidmouth. Free Wi-fi is available and free kennels can be used on request. Pre-erected luxury safari tents are for hire, and also in the Camelot Village there are medieval pavillion tents for a real glamping experience. For children there is a unique 'own pony' experience. 14.65 acre site. 120 touring pitches. 21 hardstandings. Caravan pitches. Motorhome pitches. Tent pitches. 18 bell tents/yurts.

AA Pubs & Restaurants nearby: The Black Horse Inn, SOWTON, EX5 2AN, 01392 366649

Bridge Inn, TOPSHAM, EX3 0QQ, 01392 873862

Leisure: 🏔🐾🎵

Facilities: 🏕🚿♿❄🔌🕭🚻📶🖥️💻❤️ℹ️

Services: 🔌🗑️🔧💧🚽🍽️💈🛒

Within 3 miles: 🚣🛍️🛒

Notes: Dogs must be kept on leads.

COMBE MARTIN — Map 3 SS54

See also Berrynarbor

Places to visit

Arlington Court, ARLINGTON, EX31 4LP, 01271 850296 www.nationaltrust.org.uk/arlington-court

Great for kids: Combe Martin Wildlife Park & Dinosaur Park, COMBE MARTIN, EX34 0NG, 01271 882486 www.wildlifedinosaurpark.co.uk

PREMIER PARK

▶▶▶▶▶ 85% Newberry Valley Park (SS576473)

Woodlands EX34 0AT
☎ **01271 882334**
e-mail: relax@newberryvalleypark.co.uk
dir: *M5 junct 27, A361 towards Barnstaple. Right at North Aller rdbt onto A399, through Combe Martin to sea. Left into site*

✱ 🚐 £15-£38 🚐 £15-£38 ▲ £14-£38

Open 15 Mar-Oct

Last arrival 20.45hrs (dusk in winter). Last departure 11.00hrs

A family owned and run touring park on the edge of Combe Martin, with all its amenities just a five-minute walk away. The park is set in a wooded valley with its own coarse fishing lake and has a stunning toilet block with underfloor heating and excellent unisex privacy cubicles. The safe beaches of Newberry and Combe Martin are reached by a short footpath opposite the park entrance, where the South West Coast Path is located. 20 acre site. 120 touring pitches. 25 hardstandings. 20 seasonal pitches. Caravan pitches. Motorhome pitches. Tent pitches.

LEISURE: 🏊 Indoor swimming pool 🏊 Outdoor swimming pool 🏔 Children's playground 🧒 Kid's club 🎾 Tennis court 🎱 Games room 📺 Separate TV room 🏌 9/18 hole golf course ⛵ Boats for hire 🎬 Cinema 🎵 Entertainment 🎣 Fishing ◉ Mini golf 🏄 Watersports 🏋 Gym 🏟 Sports field **Spa** U Stables
FACILITIES: 🛁 Bath 🚿 Shower ⊙ Electric shaver 🖤 Hairdryer ❄ Ice Pack Facility ♿ Disabled facilities 🕭 Public telephone 🛒 Shop on site or within 200yds 🛍 Mobile shop (calls at least 5 days a week) 🍖 BBQ area 🛋 Picnic area 📶 Wi-fi 💻 Internet access ♻ Recycling ℹ️ Tourist info 🐾 Dog exercise area

AA Pubs & Restaurants nearby: The George & Dragon, ILFRACOMBE, EX34 9ED, 01271 863851

The Fox & Goose, PARRACOMBE, EX31 4PE, 01598 763239

11 The Quay, ILFRACOMBE, EX34 9EQ, 01271 868090

Leisure: ⚿

Facilities: ⌕ ❢ ☉ ◗ ☀ ⚿ ❹ ◷ ⌥ 🛒 ☵ 🚽 ⚿ ♻ ❼

Services: ⚡ ⬜ ⊤ ☵

Within 3 miles: ⚿ ✐ 🗻 ⬜ ⓪ ∪

Notes: No camp fires. Dogs must be kept on leads.

▶▶▶▶ 88% Stowford Farm Meadows *(SS560427)*

Berry Down EX34 0PW
☎ **01271 882476**
e-mail: enquiries@stowford.co.uk
dir: M5 junct 27, A361 to Barnstaple. Take A39 from town centre towards Lynton, in 1m left onto B3230. Right at garage at Lynton Cross onto A3123, site 1.5m on right

🚐 🚛 ▲

Open all year (rs Winter at certain times bars closed & catering not available).

Last arrival 20.00hrs Last departure 10.00hrs

Very gently sloping, grassy, sheltered and south-facing site approached down a wide, well-kept driveway. This large farm park is set in 500 acres, and offers many quality amenities including a large swimming pool, horse riding and crazy golf. A 60-acre wooded nature trail is an added attraction, as is the mini zoo with its stock of friendly animals. 100 acre site. 700 touring pitches. 115 hardstandings. Caravan pitches. Motorhome pitches. Tent pitches.

AA Pubs & Restaurants nearby: The George & Dragon, ILFRACOMBE, EX34 9ED, 01271 863851

The Fox & Goose, PARRACOMBE, EX31 4PE, 01598 763239

11 The Quay, ILFRACOMBE, EX34 9EQ, 01271 868090

Leisure: ⚿ ⚽ ☉ ⚲ ♫

Facilities: ⌕ ❢ ☉ ◗ ☀ ⚿ ❹ ◷ ⌥ 🛒 🚽 ⚿ ♻ ❼

Services: ⚡ ⬜ ⊤ 🍴 ☵ 🛒 🚐 🚽

Within 3 miles: ⚿ ✐ ◎ ⬜ ⓪ ∪

Notes: Dogs must be kept on leads. Caravan accessory shop, storage, workshop & sales.

CROYDE · Map 3 SS43

Places to visit

Marwood Hill Gardens, BARNSTAPLE, EX31 4EB, 01271 342528 www.marwoodhillgarden.co.uk

Great for kids: Watermouth Castle & Family Theme Park, ILFRACOMBE, EX34 9SL, 01271 863879 www.watermouthcastle.com

---

▶▶▶ 82% Bay View Farm Caravan & Camping Park *(SS443388)*

EX33 1PN
☎ **01271 890501**
dir: M5 junct 27, A361, through Barnstaple to Braunton, left onto B3231. Site at entrance to Croyde

🚐 🚛 ▲

Open Mar-Oct

Last arrival 21.30hrs Last departure 11.00hrs

A very busy and popular park close to surfing beaches and rock pools, with a public footpath leading directly to the sea. Set in a stunning location with views out over the Atlantic to Lundy Island, it is just a short stroll from Croyde. Facilities are clean and well maintained; a family bathroom is available. There is a fish and chip shop on site. Please note that no dogs are allowed. 10 acre site. 70 touring pitches. 38 hardstandings. 10 seasonal pitches. Caravan pitches. Motorhome pitches. Tent pitches. 3 statics.

AA Pubs & Restaurants nearby: The Williams Arms, BRAUNTON, EX33 2DE, 01271 812360

The George & Dragon, ILFRACOMBE, EX34 9ED, 01271 863851

11 The Quay, ILFRACOMBE, EX34 9EQ, 01271 868090

Leisure: ⚿

Facilities: ⌕ ❢ ☉ ◗ ☀ ⚿ ❹ ⓪ 🛒 ♻ ❼

Services: ⚡ ⬜ 🍴 🚐 ⊤ 🍴 ☵ 🚽

Within 3 miles: ⚿ ⧗ ✐ ◎ 🗻 ⬜ ⓪ ∪

Notes: ⊗

CROYDE BAY · Map 3 SS43

86% Ruda Holiday Park *(SS438397)*

EX33 1NY
☎ **0844 335 3756**
e-mail: touringandcamping@parkdeanholidays.com
web: www.parkdeantouring.com
dir: M5 junct 27, A361 to Braunton. Left at main lights, follow Croyde signs

* 🚐 £16-£48 🚛 £16-£48 ▲ £13-£45

Open mid Mar-Oct

Last arrival 21.00hrs Last departure 10.00hrs

A spacious, well-managed park with its own glorious award-winning sandy beach, a surfer's paradise. Set in well-landscaped grounds, it offers a full leisure programme plus daytime and evening entertainment for all the family. The Cascades Tropical Adventure Pool and the entertainment lounge are very popular features. A new summer activity programme has been introduced to suit all age groups. The local bus stops outside the park. 220 acre site. 312 touring pitches. Caravan pitches. Motorhome pitches. Tent pitches. 312 statics.

AA Pubs & Restaurants nearby: The Williams Arms, BRAUNTON, EX33 2DE, 01271 812360

The George & Dragon, ILFRACOMBE, EX34 9ED, 01271 863851

11 The Quay, ILFRACOMBE, EX34 9EQ, 01271 868090

Leisure: ⚿ ⚿ ⚲ 🏊 ☉ ⚲ ⚲ 🗖 ♫

Facilities: ⌕ ❢ ☉ ◗ ☀ ⚿ ❹ ◷ 🛒 ♻

Services: ⚡ ⬜ 🍴 🚐 🍴 ⊘ ⊤ 🍴 ☵ 🚐 🚽

Within 3 miles: ✐ 🗻 ⬜ ∪

Notes: No pets. Coast Bar & Kitchen.

SERVICES: ⚡ Electric hook up ⬜ Launderette 🍴 Licensed bar ▮ Calor Gas ⊘ Camping Gaz ⊤ Toilet fluid 🍴 Café/Restaurant 🚐 Fast Food/Takeaway ☵ Battery charging 🚼 Baby care 🚽 Motorvan service point **ABBREVIATIONS:** BH/bank hols-bank holidays Etr-Easter Spring BH-Spring Bank Holiday dep-departure fr-from hrs-hours m-mile mdnt-midnight rdbt-roundabout rs-restricted service wk-week wknd-weekend x-rds-cross roads ⊛ No credit cards ⊗ No dogs ⬥ Children of all ages accepted See page 9 for details of the AA Camping Card Scheme

CULLOMPTON

See Kentisbeare

DARTMOUTH
Map 3 SX85

Places to visit

Dartmouth Castle, DARTMOUTH, TQ6 0JN, 01803 833588 www.english-heritage.org.uk/daysout/properties/dartmouth-castle

Coleton Fishacre House & Garden, KINGSWEAR, TQ6 0EQ, 01803 752466 www.nationaltrust.org.uk/coleton-fishacre

Great for kids: Woodlands Family Theme Park, DARTMOUTH, TQ9 7DQ, 01803 712598 www.woodlandspark.com

AA CAMPING CARD SITE

PREMIER PARK

▶▶▶▶▶ **90% Woodlands Grove Caravan & Camping Park** (SX813522)

Blackawton TQ9 7DQ
☎ **01803 712598**
e-mail: holiday@woodlandsgrove.com
web: www.woodlands-caravanpark.com
dir: From Dartmouth take A3122, 4m. Or from A38 take A385 to Totnes. Then A381 towards Salcombe, after Halwell take A3122 towards Dartmouth, site signed (brown tourist signs)

Open 28 Mar-2 Nov

Last arrival 22.00hrs Last departure 11.00hrs

A quality caravan and tent park with smart toilet facilities (including excellent family rooms), spacious pitches, including decent hardstandings, and good attention to detail throughout, all set in an extensive woodland environment with a terraced grass camping area. Free entry to the adjoining Woodlands Theme Park (for stays over two nights or more)

makes an excellent package holiday for families, but also good for adults travelling without children who are perhaps seeking a low season break. 16 acre site. 350 touring pitches. 129 hardstandings. Caravan pitches. Motorhome pitches. Tent pitches.

AA Pubs & Restaurants nearby: The Seahorse, DARTMOUTH, TQ6 9BH, 01803 835147

Woodlands Grove Caravan & Camping Park

Leisure: 🅰 🏊 ⛴ 🎡 🎱

Facilities: 🛁 📷 ⊙ 🕭 ✂ ⚷ ⓢ 🔥 ⛱ 📶 💻 ♻ ❶

Services: 🔌 🔄 🔥 💧 🚽 🍴 🛒 ⛺ 🍺

Within 3 miles: ⚓ ◎ 🛒 🛍

Notes: No open fires, fire pits or chimeneas, quiet 22.30hrs-08.00hrs. Dogs must be kept on leads. Falconry centre, woodland walk, mini golf, zoo, farm, dog kennels, bus stop at entrance.

▶▶▶▶ **84% Little Cotton Caravan Park** (SX858508)

Little Cotton TQ6 0LB
☎ **01803 832558**
e-mail: enquiries@littlecotton.co.uk
dir: Exit A38 at Buckfastleigh, A384 to Totnes, A381 to Halwell, take A3122 (Dartmouth Rd), site on right at entrance to town

Open 15 Mar-Oct

Last arrival 22.00hrs Last departure 11.00hrs

A very good grassy touring park set on high ground above Dartmouth, with quality facilities, and park-and-ride to the town from the gate. The immaculate toilet blocks are heated and superbly maintained. Spacious hardstandings are available. The friendly owners offer high levels of customer care and are happy to offer advice on touring in this pretty area. Excellent base for visiting Totnes, Slapton Sands and Kingsbridge. 7.5 acre site. 95 touring pitches. 42

hardstandings. Caravan pitches. Motorhome pitches. Tent pitches.

AA Pubs & Restaurants nearby: The Seahorse, DARTMOUTH, TQ6 9BH, 01803 835147

Facilities: 📷 ⊙ 🕭 ✂ ⚷ ⓢ 🔥 ⛱ 📶 ♻ ❶

Services: 🔌 🔄 🔥 💧 🚽 ⛺

Within 3 miles: ⚓ 🚤 ⛳ 🎣 ◎ 🏄 🛒 🛍

Notes: No noise after 22.30hrs, no footballs. Dogs must be kept on leads.

DAWLISH
Map 3 SX97

Places to visit

Kents Cavern, TORQUAY, TQ1 2JF, 01803 215136 www.kents-cavern.co.uk

Powderham Castle, POWDERHAM, EX6 8JQ, 01626 890243 www.powderham.co.uk

Great for kids: Babbacombe Model Village, TORQUAY, TQ1 3LA, 01803 315315 www.model-village.co.uk

 **84% Lady's Mile Holiday Park** (SX968784)

EX7 0LX
☎ **01626 863411**
e-mail: info@ladysmile.co.uk
dir: 1m N of Dawlish on A379

Open all year (rs Facilities open 23 Mar-Oct)

Last arrival 20.00hrs Last departure 11.00hrs

A holiday site with a wide variety of touring pitches, including some that are fully serviced. There are plenty of activities for everyone, including two swimming pools with waterslides, a children's splash pool, a well-equipped gym, a sauna in the main season, a large adventure playground, and a bar with entertainment in high season. Facilities are kept very clean, and the surrounding beaches are easily accessed. Holiday homes and two, high quality glamping pods are also available. 18 acre site. 570 touring pitches. 30 hardstandings. 70 seasonal pitches. Caravan pitches. Motorhome pitches. Tent pitches. 100 statics. 2 wooden pods.

AA Pubs & Restaurants nearby: The Elizabethan Inn, LUTON (NEAR CHUDLEIGH), TQ13 0BL, 01626 775425

The Anchor Inn, COCKWOOD, EX6 8RA, 01626 890203

LEISURE: 🏊 Indoor swimming pool 🏊 Outdoor swimming pool 🅰 Children's playground 🪁 Kid's club 🎾 Tennis court 🎱 Games room 📺 Separate TV room ⛳ 9/18 hole golf course ⛴ Boats for hire 🎬 Cinema 🎵 Entertainment 🎣 Fishing ◎ Mini golf 🏄 Watersports 💪 Gym ⚽ Sports field **Spa** ♨ Stables
FACILITIES: 🛁 Bath 📷 Shower ⊙ Electric shaver 🕭 Hairdryer ✂ Ice Pack Facility ⚷ Disabled facilities 📞 Public telephone ⓢ Shop on site or within 200yds 🛒 Mobile shop (calls at least 5 days a week) 🔥 BBQ area 🍴 Picnic area 📶 Wi-fi 💻 Internet access ♻ Recycling ❶ Tourist info ⛱ Dog exercise area

Leisure:

Facilities:

Services:

Within 3 miles:

Notes: No noise after mdnt. Dogs must be kept on leads. Bowling alley.

AA CAMPING CARD SITE

PREMIER PARK

▶▶▶▶▶ 85% **Cofton Country Holidays** *(SX967801)*

Starcross EX6 8RP

☎ 01626 890111 & 0800 085 8649

e-mail: info@coftonholidays.co.uk

dir: *On A379 (Exeter to Dawlish road), 3m from Dawlish*

* £13.50-£38.50 £13.50-£38.50
£13.50-£31

Cofton Country Holidays

Open all year (rs Spring BH-mid Sep pool open Etr-end Oct bar & shop open)

Last arrival 20.00hrs Last departure 11.00hrs

This park is set in a rural location surrounded by spacious open grassland, with plenty of well-kept flowerbeds throughout. Most pitches overlook either the swimming pool complex or the coarse fishing lakes and woodlands. A purpose-built toilet block offers smart modern facilities and the on-site pub serves drinks, meals and snacks for all the family, and a mini-market caters for most shopping needs. 45 acre site. 450 touring pitches. 30 hardstandings. 110 seasonal pitches. Caravan pitches. Motorhome pitches. Tent pitches. 76 statics.

AA Pubs & Restaurants nearby: The Elizabethan Inn, LUTON (near Chudleigh), TQ13 0BL, 01626 775425

The Anchor Inn, COCKWOOD, EX6 8RA, 01626 890203

Cofton Country Holidays

Leisure:

Facilities:

Services:

Within 3 miles:

Notes: Dogs must be kept on leads. Soft play area, sauna & steam room.

see advert below

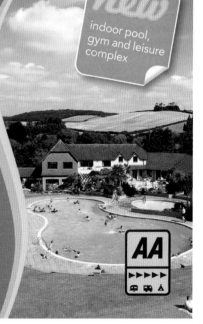

SERVICES: Electric hook up Launderette Licensed bar Calor Gas Camping Gaz Toilet fluid Café/Restaurant Fast Food/Takeaway Battery charging Baby care Motorvan service point **ABBREVIATIONS:** BH-bank hols-bank holidays Etr-Easter Spring BH-Spring Bank Holiday dep-departure fr-from hrs-hours m-mile mdnt-midnight rdbt-roundabout rs-restricted service wk-week wknd-weekend x-rds-cross roads No credit cards No dogs Children of all ages accepted See page 9 for details of the AA Camping Card Scheme

DAWLISH *continued*

AA CAMPING CARD SITE

▶▶▶ 81% Leadstone Camping

(SX974782)

Warren Rd EX7 0NG
☎ 01626 864411
e-mail: info@leadstonecamping.co.uk
web: www.leadstonecamping.co.uk
dir: *M5 junct 30, A379 to Dawlish. Before village turn left on brow of hill, signed Dawlish Warren. Site 0.5m on right*

* 🚐 £19-£24 🚏 £15-£20 ▲ £15-£20

Open 23 May-Aug

Last arrival 22.00hrs Last departure noon

A traditional, mainly level, grassy camping park approximately a half-mile walk from the sands and dunes at Dawlish Warren - a nature reserve and Blue Flag beach. This mainly tented park has been run by the same friendly family for many years, and is an ideal base for touring south Devon. A regular bus service from outside the gate takes in a wide area. The smart, well-equipped timber cabin toilet facility includes some privacy cubicles. There is a pub a short walk away. 8 acre site. 137 touring pitches. 14 seasonal pitches. Caravan pitches. Motorhome pitches. Tent pitches.

AA Pubs & Restaurants nearby: The Elizabethan Inn, LUTON (NEAR CHUDLEIGH), TQ13 0BL, 01626 775425

The Anchor Inn, COCKWOOD, EX6 8RA, 01626 890203

Leisure: ⚑
Facilities: ⚘ ☺ ⚐ ☀ ⚹ ⏰ 🅂 📶 ♻ 🛈
Services: 🔌 🔲 🛢 ⚗ 🛒 ⚗
Within 3 miles: ⚡ ⚓ ◎ 🅂 🅂
Notes: No noise after 23.00hrs. Portable/disposable BBQs allowed. Dogs must be kept on leads.

DREWSTEIGNTON   Map 3 SX79

Places to visit

Castle Drogo, DREWSTEIGNTON, EX6 6PB, 01647 433306
www.nationaltrust.org.uk/castle-drogo

Finch Foundry, STICKLEPATH, EX20 2NW, 01837 840046 www.nationaltrust.org.uk

PREMIER PARK

▶▶▶▶▶ 81% Woodland Springs Adult Touring Park *(SX695912)*

Venton EX6 6PG
☎ 01647 231695
e-mail: enquiries@woodlandsprings.co.uk
web: www.woodlandsprings.co.uk
dir: *Exit A30 at Whiddon Down junct onto A382 towards Moretonhampstead. Site 1.5m on left*

🚐 £20-£26 🚏 £20-£26 ▲ £17-£20

Open all year

Last arrival 20.00hrs Last departure 11.00hrs

An attractive park in a rural area within Dartmoor National Park. This site is surrounded by woodland and farmland, and is very peaceful. The toilet block offers superb facilities, including some for disabled visitors. There is a caravan available to hire. Please note that children are not accepted. 4 acre site. 81 touring pitches. 48 hardstandings. 19 seasonal pitches. Caravan pitches. Motorhome pitches. Tent pitches.

AA Pubs & Restaurants nearby: The Old Inn, DREWSTEIGNTON, EX6 6QR, 01647 281276

Facilities: ⚘ ☺ ⚐ ☀ ⚹ 🅂 ⚑ 🐕 📶 ♻ 🛈
Services: 🔌 🔲 🛢 ⚗ 🅃 🛒 ⚗
Within 3 miles: ⚓ 🅂
Notes: Adults only. No fires, no noise 23.00hrs-08.00hrs. Dogs must be kept on leads. Day kennels, freezer, coffee vending machine.

EAST ALLINGTON   Map 3 SX74

Places to visit

Coleton Fishacre House & Garden, KINGSWEAR, TQ6 0EQ, 01803 752466
www.nationaltrust.org.uk/coleton-fishacre

Kingsbridge Cookworthy Museum, KINGSBRIDGE, TQ7 1AW, 01548 853235
www.kingsbridgemuseum.org.uk

Great for kids: Woodlands Family Theme Park, DARTMOUTH, TQ9 7DQ, 01803 712598
www.woodlandspark.com

▶▶▶ 75% Mounts Farm Touring Park

(SX757488)

The Mounts TQ9 7QJ
☎ 01548 521591
e-mail: mounts.farm@lineone.net
web: www.mountsfarm.co.uk
dir: *A381 from Totnes towards Kingsbridge (NB ignore signs for East Allington). At 'Mounts', site 0.5m on left*

* 🚐 £10-£25 🚏 £10-£25 ▲ £10-£25

Open Mar-Nov

Last arrival 22.00hrs Last departure 16.00hrs

A neat, grassy park divided into four paddocks by mature natural hedges. Three of the paddocks are for the tourers and campers, and the fourth is a children's play area. The laundry, upgraded toilets and well-stocked little shop are in converted farm buildings. There's an on-site snack bar and Calor Gaz retailer. 7 acre site. 50 touring pitches. 10 seasonal pitches. Caravan pitches. Motorhome pitches. Tent pitches.

Leisure: ⚑ ⚽
Facilities: ⚘ ☺ ⚐ ☀ 🅂 ♻ 🛈
Services: 🔌 🔲 🛢 ⚗ 🅃 🛒
Within 3 miles: ⚓ 🅂 ⚡ ♨ 🅂 🅂 ∪
Notes: Dogs must be kept on leads. Camping accessories shop on site.

LEISURE: 🏊 Indoor swimming pool 🏊 Outdoor swimming pool ⚑ Children's playground 🏕 Kid's club 🎾 Tennis court 🎱 Games room 📺 Separate TV room ⛳ 9/18 hole golf course 🚣 Boats for hire 🎬 Cinema 🎵 Entertainment 🎣 Fishing ◎ Mini golf 🏄 Watersports 🏋 Gym ⚽ Sports field **Spa** ∪ Stables
FACILITIES: 🛁 Bath 🚿 Shower ☺ Electric shaver ⚐ Hairdryer ☀ Ice Pack Facility ⚹ Disabled facilities 🕻 Public telephone 🅂 Shop on site or within 200yds 🚐 Mobile shop (calls at least 5 days a week) 🍖 BBQ area 🧺 Picnic area 📶 Wi-fi 💻 Internet access ♻ Recycling 🛈 Tourist info 🐕 Dog exercise area

EAST ANSTEY
Map 3 SS82

Places to visit
Quince Honey Farm, SOUTH MOLTON, EX36 3AZ, 01769 572401 www.quincehoney.com

Tiverton Museum of Mid Devon Life, TIVERTON, EX16 6PJ, 01884 256295 www.tivertonmuseum.org.uk

AA CAMPING CARD SITE

▶▶▶▶ 86% Zeacombe House Caravan Park *(SS860240)*

Blackerton Cross EX16 9JU
☎ **01398 341279**
e-mail: enquiries@zeacombeadultretreat.co.uk
dir: *M5 junct 27, A361 signed Barnstaple, right at next rdbt onto A396 signed Dulverton & Minehead. In 5m at Exeter Inn left, 1.5m, at Black Cat junct left onto B3227 towards South Molton, site 7m on left*

🚐 🚃 Å

Open 7 Mar-Oct

Last arrival 21.00hrs Last departure noon

Set on the southern fringes of Exmoor National Park, this sheltered, adult-only, 'garden' park is nicely landscaped in a tranquil location and enjoys panoramic views towards Exmoor. There is a choice of grass or hardstanding pitches and a unique restaurant-style meal service allowing you to eat a home-cooked evening meal in the comfort of your own unit. 5 acre site. 50 touring pitches. 12 hardstandings. Caravan pitches. Motorhome pitches. Tent pitches.

AA Pubs & Restaurants nearby: The Masons Arms, KNOWSTONE, EX36 4RY, 01398 341231

Woods Bar & Dining Room, DULVERTON, TA22 9BU, 01398 324007

Facilities: ⛽☉🅿❄️🚿🐕🔧❓

Services: 🔌🗑️🛁🚿🚽♨️♿

Within 3 miles: 🎣💲🛒🎣🎯

Notes: Adults only. No awning ground sheets. Dogs must be kept on leads. Caravan store & stay system.

EAST WORLINGTON
Map 3 SS71

▶▶▶▶ 82% *Yeatheridge Farm Caravan Park (SS768110)*

EX17 4TN
☎ **01884 860330**
e-mail: yeatheridge@talk21.com
dir: *M5 junct 27, A361, at 1st rdbt at Tiverton take B3137 for 9m towards Witheridge. Fork left 1m past Nomansland onto B3042. Site on left in 3.5m. (NB do not enter East Worlington)*

🚐 🚃 Å

Open 15 Mar-end Sep

Last arrival 22.00hrs Last departure 10.00hrs

A well-kept park in a remote woodland setting on the edge of the Tamar Valley. It is peacefully located at the end of a private, half-mile, tree-lined drive; it offers superb on-site facilities and high levels of customer care from hands-on owners. The toilets are immaculate and well maintained, plus there is an indoor swimming pool, sauna and a good information and games room, all in a friendly atmosphere. 9 acre site. 85 touring pitches. Caravan pitches. Motorhome pitches. Tent pitches. 12 statics.

AA Pubs & Restaurants nearby: The Grove Inn, KINGS NYMPTON, EX37 9ST, 01769 580406

Leisure: 🏊⛰️⚽🎱🔍

Facilities: 🍴🔥☉🅿✳️🔥♿🅾️🔧⛺🚽♿❓

Services: 🔌🗑️🛁🛁🚿🚽♨️⛽♿

Within 3 miles: 🎣💲🛒🎯

Notes: Dogs must be kept on leads. Fishing, pool table.

EXETER

See Kennford

EXMOUTH

See also Woodbury Salterton

Places to visit
A la Ronde, EXMOUTH, EX8 5BD, 01395 265514 www.nationaltrust.org.uk/alaronde

Bicton Park Botanical Gardens, BICTON, EX9 7BJ, 01395 568465 www.bictongardens.co.uk

Great for kids: The World of Country Life, EXMOUTH, EX8 5BU, 01395 274533 www.worldofcountrylife.co.uk

EXMOUTH
Map 3 SY08

90% Devon Cliffs Holiday Park *(SY036807)*

Sandy Bay EX8 5BT
☎ **0871 231 0870**
e-mail: devoncliffs@haven.com
web: www.haven.com/devoncliffs
dir: *M5 junct 30, A376 towards Exmouth, follow brown signs to Sandy Bay*

🚐 🚃

Open mid Mar-end Oct (rs mid Mar-May & Sep-Oct some facilities may be reduced)

Last arrival anytime Last departure 10.00hrs

A large and exciting holiday park on a hillside setting close to Exmouth, with spectacular views across Sandy Bay. This all-action park offers a superb entertainment programme for all ages throughout the day, with very modern sports and leisure facilities available for everyone. An internet café is just one of the quality amenities, and though some visitors may enjoy relaxing and watching others play, the temptation to join in is overwhelming. South Beach Café, which overlooks the sea, is well worth a visit. Please note that this park does not accept tents. 163 acre site. 43 touring pitches. 43 hardstandings. Caravan pitches. Motorhome pitches. 1800 statics.

AA Pubs & Restaurants nearby: The Globe Inn, LYMPSTONE, EX8 5EY, 01395 263166

Les Saveurs, EXMOUTH, EX8 1NT, 01395 269459

Leisure: 🏊⛰️🎾⚽🏐🎵 Spa

Facilities: 🍴🔥☉🅿♿🅾️🔥♿🚿 🔌 ♻️❓

Services: 🔌🗑️🛁🛁🍴⛽♿

Within 3 miles: ⛳🚴🎣◎⛵💲🛒🎯

Notes: No commercial vehicles, no bookings by persons under 21yrs unless a family booking. Max 2 dogs per booking, certain dog breeds banned, no dogs on beach May-Sep. Dogs must be kept on leads. Crazy golf, fencing, archery, bungee trampoline, aqua jets.

see advert on page 158

SERVICES: 🔌 Electric hook up 🗑️ Launderette 🛁 Licensed bar 🛢️ Calor Gas 🚿 Camping Gaz 🚽 Toilet fluid 🍴 Café/Restaurant ♨️ Fast Food/Takeaway 🔋 Battery charging 🚼 Baby care ♿ Motorvan service point **ABBREVIATIONS:** BH/bank hols-bank holidays Etr-Easter Spring BH-Spring Bank Holiday dep-departure fr-from hrs-hours m-mile mdnt-midnight rdbt-roundabout rs-restricted service wk-week wknd-weekend x-rds-cross roads 🚫 No credit cards ⊗ No dogs 👶 Children of all ages accepted See page 9 for details of the AA Camping Card Scheme

HOLSWORTHY — Map 3 SS30

Places to visit

Dartington Crystal, GREAT TORRINGTON, EX38 7AN, 01805 626242 www.dartington.co.uk

RHS Garden Rosemoor, GREAT TORRINGTON, EX38 8PH, 01805 624067 www.rhs.org.uk/rosemoor

Great for kids: The Milky Way Adventure Park, CLOVELLY, EX39 5RY, 01237 431255 www.themilkyway.co.uk

►►► 79% Headon Farm Caravan Site (SS367023)

Headon Farm, Hollacombe EX22 6NN
☎ 01409 254477
e-mail: reader@headonfarm.co.uk
dir: *From Holsworthy A388 signed Launceston. 0.5m, at hill brow left into Staddon Rd. 1m, (follow site signs) right signed Ashwater. 0.5m, left at hill brow. Site 25yds*

* ₽ £14-£16 ₽ £14-£16 Å £14-£16

Open all year

Last arrival 19.00hrs Last departure noon

Set on a working farm in a quiet rural location. All pitches have extensive views of the Devon countryside, yet the park is only two and a half miles from the market town of Holsworthy, and within easy reach of roads to the coast and beaches of north Cornwall. 2 acre site. 19 touring pitches. 5 hardstandings. Caravan pitches. Motorhome pitches. Tent pitches.

AA Pubs & Restaurants nearby: The Bickford Arms, HOLSWORTHY, EX22 7XY, 01409 221318

Leisure: ⚙ ⚽

Facilities: ╒ ⊙ ✳ ฅ ฅ ♻ ❶

Services: ♥ 🚮

Within 3 miles: ↨ ⌀ 🗄 🛒 ∪

Notes: Breathable groundsheets only. Dogs must be kept on leads. Caravan & motorhome storage.

AA CAMPING CARD SITE

►► 77% Tamarstone Farm (SS286056)

Bude Rd, Pancrasweek EX22 7JT
☎ 01288 381734
e-mail: camping@tamarstone.co.uk
dir: *A30 to Launceston, B3254 towards Bude, approx 14m. Right onto A3072 towards Holsworthy, approx 1.5m, site on left*

* ₽ £10-£13 ₽ £10-£13 Å £10-£13

Open Etr-end Oct

Last arrival 22.00hrs Last departure noon

Four acres of river-bordered meadow and woodland providing a wildlife haven for those who enjoy peace and seclusion. The wide, sandy beaches of Bude are just five miles away, and free coarse fishing is provided on site for visitors. 1 acre site. 16 touring pitches. Caravan pitches. Motorhome pitches. Tent pitches. 1 static.

AA Pubs & Restaurants nearby: The Bickford Arms, HOLSWORTHY, EX22 7XY, 01409 221318

Leisure: ➴

Facilities: ╒ ⊙ ✳ ฅ ฅ ♻ ❶

Services: ♥

Within 3 miles: ↨ ⌀ 🗄 🛒

Notes: ⊗ No noise after mdnt. Pitch must be kept clean & tidy. Dogs must be kept on leads.

►► 75% Noteworthy Farm Caravan and Campsite (SS303052)

Noteworthy, Bude Rd EX22 7JB
☎ 01409 253731 & 07811 000071
e-mail: enquiries@noteworthy-devon.co.uk
dir: *On A3072 between Holsworthy & Bude. 3m from Holsworthy on right*

* ₽ £13-£15 ₽ £13-£15 Å £13-£15

Open all year

Last departure 11.00hrs

This campsite is owned by a friendly young couple with their own children. There are good views from the quiet rural location, and simple toilet facilities. The local bus stops outside the gate on request. 5 acre site. 5 touring pitches. Caravan pitches. Motorhome pitches. Tent pitches. 3 statics.

AA Pubs & Restaurants nearby: The Bickford Arms, HOLSWORTHY, EX22 7XY, 01409 221318

Leisure: ⚙

Facilities: ╒ ⊙ ✳ ℂ ฅ ♻ ⚙

Services: ♥

Within 3 miles: ↨ ⌀ ➴ 🗄 🛒 ∪

Notes: ⊗ No open fires, no noise after 22.30hrs. Dogs must be kept on leads. Dog grooming.

LEISURE: 🏊 Indoor swimming pool 🏊 Outdoor swimming pool 🎠 Children's playground 🧒 Kid's club 🎾 Tennis court 🎱 Games room 📺 Separate TV room ⛳ 9/18 hole golf course 🚣 Boats for hire 🎬 Cinema 🎵 Entertainment 🎣 Fishing ⛳ Mini golf 🏄 Watersports 💪 Gym 🏟 Sports field Spa ∪ Stables

FACILITIES: 🛁 Bath 🚿 Shower ⊙ Electric shaver 🎀 Hairdryer ✳ Ice Pack Facility 👨‍🦽 Disabled facilities 📞 Public telephone 🗄 Shop on site or within 200yds 🛒 Mobile shop (calls at least 5 days a week) 🍖 BBQ area 🎪 Picnic area WiFi Wi-fi 💻 Internet access ♻ Recycling ❶ Tourist info 🐕 Dog exercise area

ILFRACOMBE
Map 3 SS54

See also Berrynarbor

Places to visit

Arlington Court, ARLINGTON, EX31 4LP,
01271 850296
www.nationaltrust.org.uk/arlington-court

Exmoor Zoological Park, BLACKMOOR GATE,
EX31 4SG, 01598 763352 www.exmoorzoo.co.uk

Great for kids: Watermouth Castle & Family
Theme Park, ILFRACOMBE, EX34 9SL,
01271 863879 www.watermouthcastle.com

AA CAMPING CARD SITE

▶▶▶▶ 85% Hele Valley
Holiday Park (SS533472)

Hele Bay EX34 9RD
☎ 01271 862460
e-mail: holidays@helevalley.co.uk
dir: M5 junct 27, A361, through Barnstaple &
Braunton to Ilfracombe. Take A399 towards Combe
Martin. Follow brown Hele Valley signs. In 400mtrs
sharp right to T-junct. Park on left

* ⬤ £16-£35 ⬤ £16-£35 ▲ £16-£35

Open Etr-Oct

Last arrival 21.00hrs Last departure 11.00hrs

A deceptively spacious park set in a picturesque
valley with glorious tree-lined hilly views from
most pitches. High quality toilet facilities are
provided, and the park is within walking distance
of a lovely beach and on a regular bus route.
Camping pods were added to the park in 2013.
The harbour and other attractions of Ilfracombe
are just a mile away. 17 acre site. 55 touring
pitches. 18 hardstandings. Caravan pitches.
Motorhome pitches. Tent pitches. 80 statics. 3
wooden pods.

AA Pubs & Restaurants nearby: The George &
Dragon, ILFRACOMBE, EX34 9ED, 01271 863851

11 The Quay, ILFRACOMBE, EX34 9EQ,
01271 868090

Leisure: ⚲ Spa

Facilities: ⬤⬤⬤⬤⬤⬤⬤⬤⬤⬤⬤⬤

Services: ⬤⬤⬤⬤⬤⬤⬤

Within 3 miles: ⬤⬤⬤⬤⬤⬤⬤⬤⬤

Notes: Groups, motorhomes & tourers by
arrangement only. Dogs must be kept on leads.
Nature trail. Postal collection.

KENNFORD
Map 3 SX98

Places to visit

St Nicholas Priory, EXETER, EX4 3BL,
01392 665858 www.exeter.gov.uk/priory

Quay House Visitor Centre, EXETER, EX2 4AN,
01392 271611 www.exeter.gov.uk/quayhouse

Great for kids: Crealy Adventure Park,
CLYST ST MARY, EX5 1DR, 01395 233200
www.crealy.co.uk

▶▶▶▶ 80% Kennford International
Caravan Park (SX912857)

EX6 7YN
☎ 01392 833046
e-mail: ian@kennfordinternational.com
web: www.kennfordinternational.co.uk
dir: At end of M5 take A38, site signed at Kennford
slip road

* ⬤ £16-£19 ⬤ £16-£19 ▲ £16-£19

Open all year (rs Winter arrival times change)

Last arrival 21.00hrs Last departure 11.00hrs

Screened from the A38 by trees and shrubs, this
park offers many pitches divided by hedging for
privacy. A high quality toilet block complements
the park's facilities. A good, centrally-located
base for touring the coast and countryside of
Devon, and Exeter is easily accessible via buses
that stop nearby. 15 acre site. 22 touring pitches.
4 hardstandings. Caravan pitches. Motorhome
pitches. Tent pitches. 65 statics.

AA Pubs & Restaurants nearby: Bridge Inn,
TOPSHAM, EX3 0QQ, 01392 873862

Leisure: ⚲⚲

Facilities: ⬤⬤⬤⬤⬤⬤⬤⬤⬤⬤

Services: ⬤⬤⬤⬤⬤⬤⬤⬤⬤

Within 3 miles: ⬤⬤⬤⬤⬤⬤⬤⬤⬤

Notes: Dogs must be kept on leads.

KENTISBEARE

Places to visit

Killerton House & Garden, KILLERTON, EX5 3LE,
01392 881345 www.nationaltrust.org.uk

Allhallows Museum, HONITON, EX14 1PG,
01404 44966 www.honitonmuseum.co.uk

Great for kids: Diggerland, CULLOMPTON,
EX15 2PE, 0871 227 7007 www.diggerland.com

KENTISBEARE
Map 3 ST00

AA CAMPING CARD SITE

▶▶▶▶ 80% Forest
Glade Holiday Park

(ST101073)

EX15 2DT ☎ 01404 841381
e-mail: enquiries@forest-glade.co.uk
dir: Tent traffic: from A373 turn left past
Keepers Cottage Inn (2.5m E of M5 junct 28).
(NB due to narrow roads, touring caravans &
larger motorhomes must approach from Honiton
direction. Please phone for access details)

⬤ £16-£22 ⬤ £16-£22 ▲ £14-£21

Open mid Mar-end Oct (rs Low season limited
shop hours)

Last arrival 21.00hrs Last departure noon

A quiet, attractive park in a forest clearing with
well-kept gardens and beech hedge screening;
new camping pods were added in 2013. One of the
main attractions is the site's immediate proximity
to the forest which offers magnificent hillside
walks with surprising views over the valleys.
Please note that because the roads are narrow
around the site, it is best to phone the site for
suitable route details. 15 acre site. 80 touring
pitches. 40 hardstandings. 28 seasonal pitches.
Caravan pitches. Motorhome pitches. Tent pitches.
57 statics. 2 wooden pods.

AA Pubs & Restaurants nearby: The Blacksmiths
Arms, PLYMTREE, EX15 2JU, 01884 277474

Leisure: ⬤⬤⬤⬤⬤

continued

SERVICES: ⬤ Electric hook up ⬤ Launderette ⬤ Licensed bar ⬤ Calor Gas ⬤ Camping Gaz ⬤ Toilet fluid ⬤ Café/Restaurant ⬤ Fast Food/Takeaway
⬤ Battery charging ⬤ Baby care ⬤ Motorvan service point **ABBREVIATIONS:** BH/bank hols-bank holidays Etr-Easter Spring BH-Spring Bank Holiday dep-departure
fr-from hrs-hours m-mile mdnt-midnight rdbt-roundabout rs-restricted service wk-week wknd-weekend x-rds-cross roads ⬤ No credit cards ⬤ No dogs
⬤ Children of all ages accepted See page 9 for details of the AA Camping Card Scheme

KENTISBEARE ***continued***

Facilities: 🚿 🪒 💨 ❄ ♿ ☎ 🛒 🧺 🐕 📶 ♻ ℹ

Services: 🗨 ▣ 🔒 🌿 🅃 🍴 🚚 ⚓

Within 3 miles: 🎣 🛒 🐴

Notes: Families & couples only. Dogs must be kept on leads. Adventure & soft play area, wildlife information room, paddling pool.

see advert below

KINGSBRIDGE **Map 3 SX74**

Places to visit

Kingsbridge Cookworthy Museum, KINGSBRIDGE, TQ7 1AW, 01548 853235 www.kingsbridgemuseum.org.uk

Overbeck's, SALCOMBE, TQ8 8LW, 01548 842893 www.nationaltrust.org.uk

AA CAMPING CARD SITE

PREMIER PARK

►►►►► 75% Parkland Caravan and Camping Site *(SX728462)*

Sorley Green Cross TQ7 4AF
☎ 01548 852723 & 07968 222008
e-mail: enquiries@parklandsite.co.uk
dir: *A384 to Totnes, A381 towards Kingsbridge. 12m, at Stumpy Post Cross rdbt turn right, 1m. Site 200yds on left after Sorley Green Cross*

🚐 £15-£24.50 🚌 £15-£24.50 ⛺ £15-£24.50

Open all year

Last arrival 22.00hrs Last departure 11.30hrs

Expect a high level of customer care at this family-run park set in the glorious South Hams countryside; it has panoramic views over Salcombe and the rolling countryside towards Dartmoor. The immaculately maintained grounds offer generous grass pitches, hardstandings and super pitches. The seasonal on-site shop sells local produce and pre-ordered hampers; the upgraded toilet facilities feature quality, fully serviced cubicles, family washrooms, a bathroom and a fully fitted disabled suite. Babysitting is available by arrangement. A bus stops close to the site entrance, which is handy for exploring the local towns and villages. 3 acre site. 50 touring pitches. 30 hardstandings. 15 seasonal pitches. Caravan pitches. Motorhome pitches. Tent pitches.

AA Pubs & Restaurants nearby: The Fortescue Arms, EAST ALLINGTON, TQ9 7RA, 01548 521215

The Crabshell Inn, KINGSBRIDGE, TQ7 1JZ, 01548 852345

Leisure: 🛝 ♟

Facilities: 🛁 🚿 🪒 💨 ❄ ♿ 🛒 🧺 📶 💻 ♻ ℹ

Services: 🗨 ▣ 🔒 🌿 🅃 🍴 🚚 ⚓

Within 3 miles: ⛳ ⛵ 🎬 🎣 🏄 🛒 ▣ 🐴

Notes: 🚫 🚫 No camp fires, no noise after 23.00hrs, children to be accompanied by an adult when using facilities. Fridge freezers, storage facility.

NEW ►►►► 74% Island Lodge Caravan & Camping Site *(SX738470)*

Stumpy Post Cross TQ7 4BL
☎ 01548 852956 & 07968 222007
e-mail: enquiries@islandlodgesite.co.uk
dir: *A38 S, A384, A381 signed Kingsbridge. 12m, at rdbt at Stumpy Cross turn right, 300mtrs, left, site signed*

🚐 £15-£20 🚌 £15-£20 ⛺ £15-£20

Open all year

Last arrival 20.30hrs Last departure noon

A small, peaceful and well-established park, with extensive views over the South Hams, which has been run by the same family for many years. The toilet facilities are newly refurbished and of good quality; food orders can delivered by arrangement. A scenic two-mile walk will take you to Kingsbridge, or the Kingsbridge bus stops close to the site. There are several dog-friendly beaches nearby. 2 acre site. 30 touring pitches. 15 seasonal pitches. Caravan pitches. Motorhome pitches. Tent pitches.

AA Pubs & Restaurants nearby: The Fortescue Arms, EAST ALLINGTON, TQ9 7RA, 01548 521215

The Crabshell Inn, KINGSBRIDGE, TQ7 1JZ, 01548 852345

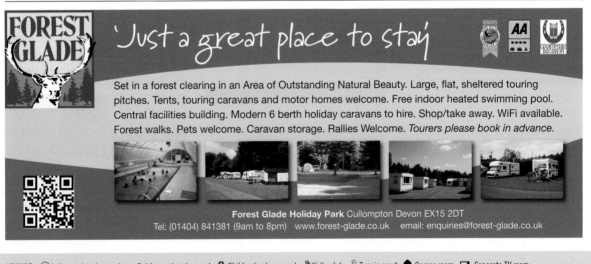

LEISURE: 🏊 Indoor swimming pool 🏊 Outdoor swimming pool 🛝 Children's playground 👋 Kid's club 🎾 Tennis court ♟ Games room 📺 Separate TV room ⛳ 9/18 hole golf course ⛵ Boats for hire 🎬 Cinema 🎵 Entertainment 🎣 Fishing ◎ Mini golf 🏄 Watersports 🏋 Gym ⚽ Sports field **Spa** 🐴 Stables
FACILITIES: 🛁 Bath 🚿 Shower 🪒 Electric shaver 💨 Hairdryer ❄ Ice Pack Facility ♿ Disabled facilities ☎ Public telephone 🛒 Shop on site or within 200yds 🚚 Mobile shop (calls at least 5 days a week) 🍖 BBQ area 🧺 Picnic area 📶 Wi-fi 💻 Internet access ♻ Recycling ℹ Tourist info 🐕 Dog exercise area

Leisure:

Facilities: 🔥⊙🅿☀️&🚿🛒♿ 💻 ♻ ❶

Services: 🔌🚮🛢🧺🚽🛒⬇️

Within 3 miles: ⚡🏃🎯🎣🏌️◎⛴🛥🎿🚤♻

Notes: ◉ Restrictions on certain dog breeds, no generators, play area open 09.00hrs-21.00hrs. Dogs must be kept on leads. Secure caravan storage yard, boat park.

LYNTON   Map 3 SS74

See also Oare (Somerset)

Places to visit

Arlington Court, ARLINGTON, EX31 4LP, 01271 850296
www.nationaltrust.org.uk/arlington-court

Great for kids: Exmoor Zoological Park, BLACKMOOR GATE, EX31 4SG, 01598 763352
www.exmoorzoo.co.uk

►►►► 71% Channel View Caravan and Camping Park

(SS724482)

GOLD

Manor Farm EX35 6LD
☎ 01598 753349
e-mail: relax@channel-view.co.uk
web: www.channel-view.co.uk
dir: *A39 E for 0.5m on left past Barbrook*

* 🚐 £12-£20 🚛 £12-£20 ▲ £12-£20

Open 15 Mar-15 Nov

Last arrival 22.00hrs Last departure noon

On the top of the cliffs overlooking the Bristol Channel, a well-maintained park on the edge of Exmoor, and close to both Lynton and Lynmouth. Pitches can be selected from either those in a hidden hedged area or those with panoramic views over the coast. 6 acre site. 76 touring pitches. 15 hardstandings. Caravan pitches. Motorhome pitches. Tent pitches. 31 statics.

AA Pubs & Restaurants nearby: Rising Sun Hotel, LYNMOUTH, EX35 6EG, 01598 753223

Rockford Inn, BRENDON, EX35 6PT, 01598 741214

Leisure:

Facilities: ➡🏠🔥⊙🅿☀️&🚿◎🛒♿🛒 ♻ ❶

Services: 🔌🚮🛢🧺🚽🛒⬇️

Within 3 miles: 🎣🎿◎⛴🛥🚤♻

Notes: Groups by prior arrangement only. Dogs must be kept on leads. Parent & baby room.

►►► 76% Sunny Lyn Holiday Park

(SS719486)

Lynbridge EX35 6NS
☎ 01598 753384
e-mail: info@caravandevon.co.uk
web: www.caravandevon.co.uk
dir: *M5 junct 27, A361 to South Molton. Right onto A399 to Blackmoor Gate, right onto A39, left onto B3234 towards Lynmouth. Site 1m on right*

🚐 £15.50-£17.50 🚛 £15.50-£17.50
▲ £14.50-£16.50

Open Mar-Oct

Last arrival 20.00hrs Last departure 11.00hrs

Set in a sheltered riverside location in a wooded combe within a mile of the sea, in Exmoor National Park. This family-run park offers good facilities including an excellent café. 4.5 acre site. 9 touring pitches. 5 hardstandings. Caravan pitches. Motorhome pitches. Tent pitches. 7 statics.

AA Pubs & Restaurants nearby: Rising Sun Hotel, LYNMOUTH, EX35 6EG, 01598 753223

Rockford Inn, BRENDON, EX35 6PT, 01598 741214

Facilities: 🔥⊙🅿☀️&🕙🚿🛒 💻 ♻ ❶

Services: 🔌🚮🛢🧺🍴🛒🍺

Within 3 miles: 🎿◎🛥🚤♻

Notes: No cars by tents. No wood fires, quiet after 22.30hrs. Dogs must be kept on leads.

MODBURY

Places to visit

Kingsbridge Cookworthy Museum, KINGSBRIDGE, TQ7 1AW, 01548 853235
www.kingsbridgemuseum.org.uk

Overbeck's, SALCOMBE, TQ8 8LW, 01548 842893
www.nationaltrust.org.uk

Great for kids: National Marine Aquarium, PLYMOUTH, PL4 0LF, 01752 275200
www.national-aquarium.co.uk

MODBURY   Map 3 SX65

AA CAMPING CARD SITE

►►► 81% Pennymoor Camping & Caravan Park (SX685516)

PL21 0SB
☎ 01548 830542
e-mail: enquiries@pennymoor-camping.co.uk
dir: *Exit A38 at Wrangaton Cross. Left & straight over x-rds. 4m, pass petrol station, 2nd left. Site 1.5m on right*

* 🚐 £10-£18 🚛 £10-£18 ▲ £10-£18

Open 15 Mar-15 Nov (rs 15 Mar-mid May one toilet & shower block only open)

Last arrival 20.00hrs Last departure 10.00hrs

A well-established rural park on part level, part gently sloping grass with good views over distant Dartmoor and the countryside in between. The park has been owned and run by the same family since 1935, and is very carefully tended, with clean, well-maintained toilets and a relaxing atmosphere. 12.5 acre site. 119 touring pitches. 3 hardstandings. Caravan pitches. Motorhome pitches. Tent pitches. 76 statics.

AA Pubs & Restaurants nearby: California Country Inn, MODBURY, PL21 0SG, 01548 821449

Rose & Crown, YEALMPTON, PL8 2EB, 01752 880223

Leisure:

Facilities: 🔥⊙🅿☀️&🚿🛒🛒 ♻ ❶

Services: 🔌🚮🛢🧺🚽🛒⬇️

Within 3 miles: ⚡🚿

Notes: No skateboards or scooters, no noise after 22.00hrs. Dogs must be kept on leads.

MOLLAND
Map 3 SS82

Places to visit

Quince Honey Farm, SOUTH MOLTON, EX36 3AZ, 01769 572401 www.quincehoney.com

Cobbaton Combat Collection, CHITTLEHAMPTON, EX37 9RZ, 01769 540740 www.cobbatoncombat.co.uk

►►► 75% *Yeo Valley Holiday Park* (SS788265)

The Blackcock Inn EX36 3NW
☎ 01769 550297
e-mail: info@yeovalleyholidays.co.uk
dir: *From A361 onto B3227 towards Bampton. Follow brown signs for Blackcock Inn. Site opposite*

Open Mar-Nov

Last arrival 20.30hrs Last departure 10.30hrs

Set in a beautiful secluded valley on the edge of Exmoor National Park, this family-run park has easy access to both the moors and the north Devon coastline. The park is adjacent to the Blackcock Inn, which is under the same ownership and serves a variety of locally sourced meals, including breakfast to order. The pub also has a good heated indoor swimming pool and there is fishing close by. 8 acre site. 36 touring pitches. 16 hardstandings. Caravan pitches. Motorhome pitches. Tent pitches. 5 statics.

Leisure:
Facilities:
Services:
Within 3 miles:
Notes: Dogs must be kept on leads.

MORTEHOE
Map 3 SS44

See also Woolacombe

Places to visit

Marwood Hill Gardens, BARNSTAPLE, EX31 4EB, 01271 342528 www.marwoodhillgarden.co.uk

Great for kids: Watermouth Castle & Family Theme Park, ILFRACOMBE, EX34 9SL, 01271 863879 www.watermouthcastle.com

85% **Twitchen House Holiday Village** (SS465447)

Mortehoe Station Rd EX34 7ES
☎ 01271 870848
e-mail: goodtimes@woolacombe.com
dir: *From Mullacott Cross rdbt take B3343 (Woolacombe road) to Turnpike Cross junct. Take right fork, site 1.5m on left*

Open Mar-Oct (rs mar-mid May & mid Sep-Oct outdoor pool closed)

Last arrival mdnt Last departure 10.00hrs

A very attractive park with good leisure facilities. Visitors can use the amenities at all three of Woolacombe Bay holiday parks and a bus service connects them all with the beach. The touring area features pitches (many fully serviced, including 80 for tents) with either sea views or a woodland countryside outlook. A planned £2.5 million development for 2014 will include new restaurants, improved shopping facilities and top notch outdoor leisure attractions. 45 acre site. 334 touring pitches. 110 hardstandings. Caravan pitches. Motorhome pitches. Tent pitches. 278 statics.

AA Pubs & Restaurants nearby: The George & Dragon, ILFRACOMBE, EX34 9ED, 01271 863851

11 The Quay, ILFRACOMBE, EX34 9EQ, 01271 868090

Leisure:
Facilities:
Services:
Within 3 miles:
Notes: Table tennis, sauna, swimming & surfing lessons, climbing wall, bungee trampoline.

►►►► 83% North Morte Farm Caravan & Camping Park (SS462455)

North Morte Rd EX34 7EG
☎ 01271 870381
e-mail: info@northmortefarm.co.uk
dir: *From B3343 into Mortehoe, right at post office. Site 500yds on left*

* ⬛ £15.50-£20.50 ⬛ £12-£20.50 ▲ £12-£18.50

Open Apr-Oct

Last arrival 22.00hrs Last departure noon

Set in spectacular coastal countryside close to National Trust land and 500 yards from Rockham Beach. This attractive park is very well run and maintained by friendly family owners, and the quaint village of Mortehoe with its cafés, shops and pubs, is just a five-minute walk away. 22 acre site. 180 touring pitches. 25 hardstandings. Caravan pitches. Motorhome pitches. Tent pitches. 73 statics.

AA Pubs & Restaurants nearby: The George & Dragon, ILFRACOMBE, EX34 9ED, 01271 863851

11 The Quay, ILFRACOMBE, EX34 9EQ, 01271 868090

Leisure:
Facilities:
Services:
Within 3 miles:
Notes: No large groups. Dogs must be kept on leads.

LEISURE: 🏊 Indoor swimming pool 🏊 Outdoor swimming pool ⋀ Children's playground 🎣 Kid's club ⚲ Tennis court 🎱 Games room ▢ Separate TV room ⛳ 9/18 hole golf course ⛵ Boats for hire 🎬 Cinema 🎵 Entertainment 🎣 Fishing ◉ Mini golf 🏄 Watersports 🏋 Gym 🎯 Sports field ♉ Stables
FACILITIES: 🛁 Bath 🚿 Shower ⊙ Electric shaver 🪒 Hairdryer ✳ Ice Pack Facility ♿ Disabled facilities 🕿 Public telephone 🛒 Shop on site or within 200yds 🛒 Mobile shop (calls at least 5 days a week) 🍖 BBQ area 🏕 Picnic area 📶 Wi-fi 🖥 Internet access ♻ Recycling 🛈 Tourist info 🦮 Dog exercise area

►►►► 83% *Warcombe Farm Caravan & Camping Park* *(SS478445)*

GOLD

Station Rd EX34 7EJ
☎ 01271 870690
e-mail: info@warcombefarm.co.uk
web: www.warcombefarm.co.uk
dir: *On B3343 towards Woolacombe turn right towards Mortehoe. Site less than 1m on right*

🚐 🚙 ⛺

Open 15 Mar-Oct

Last arrival 21.00hrs Last departure 11.00hrs

Extensive views over the Bristol Channel can be enjoyed from the open areas of this attractive park, while other pitches are sheltered in paddocks with maturing trees. The site has 14 excellent super pitches with hardstandings. The superb sandy, Blue Flag beach at Woolacombe Bay is only a mile and a half away, and there is a fishing lake with direct access from some pitches. The local bus stops outside the park entrance. 19 acre site. 250 touring pitches. 10 hardstandings. Caravan pitches. Motorhome pitches. Tent pitches.

AA Pubs & Restaurants nearby: The George & Dragon, ILFRACOMBE, EX34 9ED, 01271 863851

11 The Quay, ILFRACOMBE, EX34 9EQ, 01271 868090

Leisure: 🎠

Facilities: 🍼 🚿 ⊙ 💨 ❄ ♿ 🛒 🪑 🐕 [Wi-fi] 💻 ♻ ℹ

Services: 🔌 🧺 🛢 🔥 [T] 🍴 🔋 🍔 ⬇

Within 3 miles: ⛳ 🏄 🎣 🎯 🛒 🧺 🐴

Notes: No groups unless booked in advance. Dogs must be kept on leads.

►►► 82% Easewell Farm Holiday Village *(SS465455)*

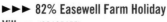

Mortehoe Station Rd EX34 7EH
☎ 01271 871400
e-mail: goodtimes@woolacombe.com
dir: *B3343 to Mortehoe. Turn right at fork, site 2m on right*

🚐 🚙 ⛺

Open Mar-Nov (rs Etr)

Last arrival 22.00hrs Last departure 10.00hrs

A peaceful cliff-top park with full facility pitches for caravans and motorhomes, and superb views. The park offers a range of activities including indoor bowling, snooker and a 9-hole golf course, and all the facilities at the three other nearby holiday centres within this group are open to everyone. 17 acre site. 302 touring pitches. 50 hardstandings. Caravan pitches. Motorhome pitches. Tent pitches. 1 static.

AA Pubs & Restaurants nearby: The George & Dragon, ILFRACOMBE, EX34 9ED, 01271 863851

11 The Quay, ILFRACOMBE, EX34 9EQ, 01271 868090

Leisure: 🏊 🎠 ✋ 🎱 🎵

Facilities: 🚿 ⊙ 💨 ❄ ♿ ☎ 🛒 🪑 🐕 💻 ♻

Services: 🔌 🧺 🍷 🔥 [T] 🍴 🔋 🍔

Within 3 miles: ⛳ ⛵ 🏄 🎣 🎯 🌊 🛒 🧺 🐴

NEWTON ABBOT

See also Bickington

Places to visit

Tuckers Maltings, NEWTON ABBOT, TQ12 4AA, 01626 334734 www.tuckersmaltings.com

Bradley Manor, NEWTON ABBOT, TQ12 6BN, 01803 843235 www.nationaltrust.org.uk/devoncornwall

Great for kids: Prickly Ball Farm and Hedgehog Hospital, NEWTON ABBOT, TQ12 6BZ, 01626 362319 www.pricklyballfarm.com

NEWTON ABBOT — Map 3 SX87

AA CAMPING CARD SITE

PREMIER PARK

►►►►► 96% Ross Park *(SX845671)*

Best of British — GOLD

Park Hill Farm, Ipplepen TQ12 5TT
☎ 01803 812983
e-mail: enquiries@rossparkcaravanpark.co.uk
web: www.rossparkcaravanpark.co.uk
dir: *N of Ipplepen on A381 follow brown site signs & sign for Woodland opposite Texaco garage*

* 🚐 £15.50-£28.50 🚙 £15.50-£28.50 ⛺ fr £14.50

Open Mar-2 Jan (rs Nov-Jan & 1st 3 wks in Mar restaurant/bar closed (ex Xmas/New Year))

Last arrival 21.00hrs Last departure 11.00hrs

A top-class park in every way, with large secluded pitches, high quality toilet facilities (which include excellent family rooms) and colourful flower displays throughout - note the wonderful floral walk to the toilets. The beautiful tropical conservatory also offers a breathtaking show of colour. There's a conservation walk through glorious wild flower meadows, replete with nature trail, a dog shower/grooming area, and six fully serviced pitches. This very rural park enjoys superb views of Dartmoor, and good quality meals to suit all tastes and pockets are served in the restaurant. Expect high levels of customer care - this park gets better each year. Home-grown produce and honey are sold in the shop. A bus, which stops close to the entrance, runs to Totnes and Newton Abbot. 32 acre site. 110 touring pitches. 101 hardstandings. Caravan pitches. Motorhome pitches. Tent pitches.

continued

NEWTON ABBOT *continued*

AA Pubs & Restaurants nearby: The Church House Inn, MARLDON, TQ3 1SL, 01803 558279

The Union Inn, DENBURY, TQ12 6DQ, 01803 812595

Leisure: 🅰 ⊕ ⚑ ⊡
Facilities: 📻 ⊙ 🅿 ✱ ♿ ⓒ 🖥 🎋 🛒 W⋅Fi ♻ ❶
Services: 🔌🛢 🍴🧺⚗️ⓉⓄ🛒⬆️
Within 3 miles: ⤒🅷🖋🛒🅖🛶♈

Notes: Bikes, skateboards/scooters allowed only on leisure field. Snooker, table tennis, badminton.

▶▶▶▶▶ **94%**

Dornafield *(SX838683)*

Bestof British GOLD

Dornafield Farm, Two Mile Oak
TQ12 6DD
☎ **01803 812732**
e-mail: enquiries@dornafield.com
web: www.dornafield.com
dir: *From Newton Abbot take A381 signed Totnes for 2m. At Two Mile Oak Inn right, left at x-rds in 0.5m. Site on right*

* 🚐 £16-£32 🚍 £16-£32 ▲ £14.80-£26

Open 13 Mar-3 Jan

Last arrival 22.00hrs Last departure 11.00hrs

An immaculately kept park in a tranquil wooded valley between Dartmoor and Torbay, divided into three areas. At the heart of the 30-acre site is Dornafield, a 14th-century farmhouse, adapted for campers' use but still retaining much charm. The friendly family owners are always available for help or to give advice. The site has superb facilities in two ultra modern toilet blocks. On-site there is the Quarry Café which provides takeaway fish and chips or jacket potatoes daily. This is a quiet and peaceful location convenient for Torbay, Dartmoor and the charming coastal villages of

---

the South Hams. A bus service to Totnes or Newton Abbot runs nearby. 30 acre site. 135 touring pitches. 119 hardstandings. 13 seasonal pitches. Caravan pitches. Motorhome pitches. Tent pitches.

AA Pubs & Restaurants nearby: The Church House Inn, MARLDON, TQ3 1SL, 01803 558279

The Union Inn, DENBURY, TQ12 6DQ, 01803 812595

Leisure: 🅰 ⚓ ⚑
Facilities: 📻 ⊙ 🅿 ✱ ♿ ⓒ 🖥 🎋 W⋅Fi 🖥 ♻ ❶
Services: 🔌🛢 ⚗️Ⓣ🛒⬆️⬆️
Within 3 miles: ⤒🅷🖋🅖🛒

Notes: Dogs must be kept on leads. Caravan storage (all year).

▶▶▶ **78% Twelve Oaks Farm Caravan Park** *(SX852737)*

Teigngrace TQ12 6QT
☎ **01626 335015**
e-mail: info@twelveoaksfarm.co.uk
dir: *A38 from Exeter left signed Teigngrace (only), 0.25m before Drumbridges rdbt. 1.5m, through village, site on left. Or from Plymouth pass Drumbridges rdbt, take slip road for Chudleigh Knighton. Right over bridge, rejoin A38 towards Plymouth. Left for Teigngrace (only), then as above*

* 🚐 £10-£17.50 🚍 £10-£17.50 ▲ £10-£17.50

Open all year

Last arrival 21.00hrs Last departure 10.30hrs

An attractive small park on a working farm close to Dartmoor National Park, and bordered by the River Teign. The tidy pitches are located amongst trees and shrubs, and the modern facilities are very well maintained. There are two well-stocked fishing lakes and children will enjoy visiting all the farm animals. Close by is Stover Country Park and also the popular Templar Way walking route. 2 acre site. 50 touring pitches. 25 hardstandings.

---

15 seasonal pitches. Caravan pitches. Motorhome pitches. Tent pitches.

AA Pubs & Restaurants nearby: The Elizabethan Inn, LUTON (NEAR CHUDLEIGH), TQ13 0BL, 01626 775425

The Union Inn, DENBURY, TQ12 6DQ, 01803 812595

Leisure: ⚓ 🅰
Facilities: 📻 ⊙ 🅿 ✱ ♿ ⓒ 🖥 🎋 W⋅Fi ♻ ❶
Services: 🔌🛢 ⓉⓄ⬆️
Within 3 miles: ⤒🅷🖋 ⊚ 🛶🅖🛒♈

Notes: No noise after 23.00hrs. Dogs must be kept on leads.

PAIGNTON Map 3 SX86

Places to visit

Dartmouth Steam Railway & River Boat Company, PAIGNTON, TQ4 6AF, 01803 555872 www.dartmouthrailriver.co.uk

Kents Cavern, TORQUAY, TQ1 2JF, 01803 215136 www.kents-cavern.co.uk

Great for kids: Paignton Zoo Environmental Park, PAIGNTON, TQ4 7EU, 0844 474 2222 www.paigntonzoo.org.uk

---

AA CAMPING CARD SITE

▶▶▶▶▶ **86% Beverley Parks Caravan & Camping Park** *(SX886582)*

Bestof British

Goodrington Rd TQ14 7JE
☎ **01803 661979**
e-mail: info@beverley-holidays.co.uk
dir: *On A380, A3022, 2m S of Paignton left into Goodrington Rd. Beverley Park on right*

* 🚐 £17.20-£41.30 🚍 £17.20-£41.30 ▲ £14-£34.10

Open all year

Last arrival 21.00hrs Last departure 10.00hrs

A high quality family-run park with extensive views of the bay and plenty of on-site amenities. The park boasts indoor and outdoor heated swimming pools, plus good bars and restaurants. The toilet facilities are modern and very clean and include excellent fully serviced family rooms. The park complex is attractively laid out with the touring areas divided into nicely screened areas. 12 acre site. 172 touring pitches. 49 hardstandings. Caravan pitches. Motorhome pitches. Tent pitches.

AA Pubs & Restaurants nearby: The Church House Inn, MARLDON, TQ3 1SL, 01803 558279

The Cary Arms, TORQUAY, TQ1 3LX, 01803 327110

The Elephant Restaurant and Brasserie, TORQUAY, TQ1 2BH, 01803 200044

Leisure: 🏊🎱🏐⛰️⛵🎣 ♫ Spa

Facilities: 🚐🔭☉📷☀️🔥🛁🔥 wifi 🖥️ ♻️ ❶

Services: 🔌🛢️🍽️🛒🚰🚻🍴♨️➡️♿

Within 3 miles: 🚶🎣🏇🎠📍◎🏌️🛍️🛒↻

Notes: No pets. Table tennis, sauna, crazy golf, letter box trail.

►►►► 79% *Widend Touring Park* (SX852619)

SILVER

Berry Pomeroy Rd, Marldon TQ3 1RT
☎ **01803 550116**
dir: *Signed from A380 (Torquay ring road) through Marldon. Site approx 1.5m on right*

🚐🚍🛖

Open Apr-end Sep (rs Apr-mid May & mid-end Sep swimming pool & club house closed)

Last arrival 20.00hrs Last departure 10.00hrs

A terraced grass park divided into paddocks and screened on high ground overlooking Torbay with views of Dartmoor. This attractive park is well laid out, divided up by mature trees and bushes but with plenty of open grassy areas. Facilities are of a high standard and offer a heated outdoor swimming pool with sunbathing area, a small lounge bar and a well-stocked shop. A local bus service to Torquay or Totnes runs from end of drive and a railway station is just two miles away. 22 acre site. 207 touring pitches. 6 hardstandings. Caravan pitches. Motorhome pitches. Tent pitches. 16 statics.

AA Pubs & Restaurants nearby: The Church House Inn, MARLDON, TQ3 1SL, 01803 558279

The Cary Arms, TORQUAY, TQ1 3LX, 01803 327110

The Elephant Restaurant and Brasserie, TORQUAY, TQ1 2BH, 01803 200044

Leisure: 🏊⛰️🎣

Facilities: 🔭☉☀️🔥🛁🔥🎣

Services: 🔌🛢️🍽️🛒🚰🚻🔥➡️

Within 3 miles: 🚶🎣🏇🎠📍◎🏌️🛍️🛒↻

Notes: No dogs mid Jul-Aug.

►►► 85% **Whitehill Country Park** (SX857588)

GOLD

Stoke Rd TQ4 7PF
☎ **01803 782338**
e-mail: info@whitehill-park.co.uk
dir: *A385 through Totnes towards Paignton. Turn right by Parkers Arms into Stoke Rd towards Stoke Gabriel. Site on left after approx 1.5m*

* 🚐 £16.10-£31.40 🚍 £16.10-£31.40
🛖 £14-£29.70

Open Etr-Sep

Last arrival 21.00hrs Last departure 10.00hrs

A family-owned and run park set in rolling countryside, with many scenic beaches just a short drive away. This extensive country park covers 40 acres with woodland walks, plenty of flora and fauna and an excellent outdoor swimming pool, a café, plus a bar/restaurant with summer entertainment. It offers ideal facilities, including luxury lodges and camping pods, for an excellent holiday. 40 acre site. 260 touring pitches. Caravan pitches. Motorhome pitches. Tent pitches. 60 statics. 5 wooden pods.

AA Pubs & Restaurants nearby: The Church House Inn, MARLDON, TQ3 1SL, 01803 558279

The Cary Arms, TORQUAY, TQ1 3LX, 01803 327110

The Elephant Restaurant and Brasserie, TORQUAY, TQ1 2BH, 01803 200044

Leisure: 🏊⛰️🎣🖥️

Facilities: 🔭🎣☀️🔥🛁🔥🎣 wifi 🖥️ ♻️ ❶

Services: 🔌🛢️🍽️🛒🚰🍴🔥➡️♿

Within 3 miles: 🚶🎣🏇🎠📍◎🏌️🛍️🛒↻

Notes: Dogs only allowed 28 Mar-23 May, 3 Jun-19 Jul & 2-27 Sep. Dogs must be kept on leads. Walking & cycling trails, letter box trail, craft room, table tennis.

PLYMOUTH Map 3 SX45

Places to visit

Plymouth City Museum & Art Gallery, PLYMOUTH, PL4 8AJ, 01752 304774
www.plymouthmuseum.gov.uk

The Elizabethan House, PLYMOUTH, PL1 2NA, 01752 304774 www.plymouth.gov.uk/museums

Great for kids: National Marine Aquarium, PLYMOUTH, PL4 0LF, 01752 275200
www.national-aquarium.co.uk

►►►► 83% *Riverside Caravan Park* (SX515575)

Leigham Manor Dr PL6 8LL
☎ **01752 344122**
e-mail: office@riversidecaravanpark.com
dir: *A38 follow signs at Marsh Mills rdbt, take 3rd exit, then left. 400yds turn right (keep River Plym on right) to site*

🚐🚍🛖

Open all year (rs Oct-Etr bar, restaurant, takeaway & pool closed)

Last arrival 22.00hrs Last departure 10.00hrs

A well-groomed site on the outskirts of Plymouth on the banks of the River Plym, in a surprisingly peaceful location surrounded by woodland. The toilet facilities are appointed to a very good standard, and include private cubicles, plus there's a good games room and bar/restaurant serving food. This park is an ideal stopover for the ferries to France and Spain, and makes an excellent base for touring Dartmoor and the coast. The local bus stop is just a ten-minute walk from the site. 11 acre site. 259 touring pitches.

continued

PLYMOUTH *continued*

Caravan pitches. Motorhome pitches. Tent pitches. 22 statics.

AA Pubs & Restaurants nearby: The Fishermans Arms, PLYMOUTH, PL1 2NN, 01752 661457

Tanners Restaurant, PLYMOUTH, PL1 2AE, 01752 252001

Artillery Tower Restaurant, PLYMOUTH, PL1 3QR, 01752 257610

Leisure: ⚓ 🎢 🎱 ▭

Facilities: ⚡☉🄿☀♿🕐🛒🚿🔧♻🄘

Services: 🔌🗑🛢🚽🚿🚰🅣🍴🛒🪣⛽

Within 3 miles: ⌕🎯🗓🎣◎⛵🛒🔵⛱◡

Notes: Dogs must be kept on leads.

SALCOMBE
Map 3 SX73

Places to visit

Overbeck's, SALCOMBE, TQ8 8LW, 01548 842893 www.nationaltrust.org.uk

Kingsbridge Cookworthy Museum, KINGSBRIDGE, TQ7 1AW, 01548 853235 www.kingsbridgemuseum.org.uk

---

▶▶▶▶ 78% Karrageen Caravan & Camping Park *(SX686395)*

Bolberry, Malborough TQ7 3EN
☎ 01548 561230
e-mail: phil@karrageen.co.uk
dir: *At Malborough on A381, sharp right through village, in 0.6m right again, 0.9m, site on right*

🚐 £15-£25 🚍 £15-£25 ▲ £15-£30

Open Etr-Sep

Last arrival 21.00hrs Last departure 11.30hrs

A small friendly, family-run park with secluded hidden dells for tents and terraced grass pitches giving extensive sea and country views. There is a well-stocked shop and an excellent, refurbished toilet block that has two cubicled units; one suitable for families and for less able visitors. This park is just one mile from the beach and pretty hamlet of Hope Cove and is a really peaceful park from which to explore the South Hams coast. 7.5 acre site. 70 touring pitches. Caravan pitches. Motorhome pitches. Tent pitches. 25 statics.

AA Pubs & Restaurants nearby: The Victoria Inn, SALCOMBE, TQ8 8BU, 01548 842604

Soar Mill Cove Hotel, SALCOMBE, TQ7 3DS, 01548 561566

Facilities: ⚡☉🄿☀♿🕐🛒🚿📶♻🄘

Services: 🔌🗑🛢🚽🅣🛒🪣

Within 3 miles: ⌕🎯🎣🛒🔵

Notes: 🐕 Dogs must be kept on leads.

▶▶▶ 80% Higher Rew Caravan & Camping Park *(SX714383)*

Higher Rew, Malborough TQ7 3BW
☎ 01548 842681
e-mail: enquiries@higherrew.co.uk
dir: *A381 to Malborough. Right at Townsend Cross, follow signs to Soar for 1m. Left at Rew Cross*

* 🚐 £14-£21 🚍 £14-£21 ▲ £13-£19

Open Etr-Oct

Last arrival 22.00hrs Last departure noon

A long-established park in a remote location within sight of the sea. The spacious, open touring field has some tiered pitches in the sloping grass, and there are lovely countryside or sea views from every pitch. Friendly family owners are continually improving the facilities. 5 acre site. 90 touring pitches. Caravan pitches. Motorhome pitches. Tent pitches.

AA Pubs & Restaurants nearby: The Victoria Inn, SALCOMBE, TQ8 8BU, 01548 842604

Soar Mill Cove Hotel, SALCOMBE, TQ7 3DS, 01548 561566

Leisure: 🎱🎱

Facilities: ⚡☉🄿☀🕐🛒🚿🖥

Services: 🔌🗑🛢🚽🅣🛒

Within 3 miles: 🎯🎣🛒🔵

Notes: 🐕 Minimum noise after 23.00hrs. Tennis court, play barn.

▶▶▶ 78% *Bolberry House Farm Caravan & Camping Park (SX687395)*

Bolberry TQ7 3DY
☎ 01548 561251
e-mail: enquiries@bolberryparks.co.uk
dir: *At Malborough on A381 turn right signed Hope Cove & Bolberry. Take left fork after village signed Soar & Bolberry. Right in 0.6m. Site signed in 0.5m*

🚐 🚍 ▲

Open Etr-Oct

Last arrival 20.00hrs Last departure 11.30hrs

A very popular park in a peaceful setting on a coastal farm with sea views, fine cliff walks and nearby beaches. Customers are assured of a warm welcome and the nicely tucked-away portaloo facilities are smart and beautifully maintained. Wi-fi and ten hardstandings were added for 2013. A mobile fish and chip van calls weekly in high season. There's a super dog-walking area. 6 acre site. 70 touring pitches. Caravan pitches. Motorhome pitches. Tent pitches. 10 statics.

AA Pubs & Restaurants nearby: The Victoria Inn, SALCOMBE, TQ8 8BU, 01548 842604

Soar Mill Cove Hotel, SALCOMBE, TQ7 3DS, 01548 561566

Leisure: 🎢

Facilities: ⚡☉🄿☀🕐🛒♻🄘

Services: 🔌🗑🛒

Within 3 miles: ⌕🎯🗓🎣◎⛵🛒🔵⛱◡

Notes: 🐕

LEISURE: 🏊 Indoor swimming pool 🏊 Outdoor swimming pool 🎢 Children's playground 🎣 Kid's club 🎾 Tennis court 🎱 Games room ▭ Separate TV room ⌕ 9/18 hole golf course ⛵ Boats for hire 🎦 Cinema 🎵 Entertainment 🎣 Fishing ◎ Mini golf ⛵ Watersports 🏋 Gym ♻ Sports field Spa ◡ Stables
FACILITIES: 🛁 Bath 🚿 Shower ☉ Electric shaver 🄿 Hairdryer ☀ Ice Pack Facility ♿ Disabled facilities 🕐 Public telephone 🛒 Shop on site or within 200yds 🏪 Mobile shop (calls at least 5 days a week) 🍴 BBQ area 🪑 Picnic area 📶 Wi-fi 🖥 Internet access ♻ Recycling 🄘 Tourist info 🐕 Dog exercise area

AA CAMPING CARD SITE

►► 69% Alston Camping and Caravan Site (SX716406)

Malborough, Kingsbridge TQ7 3BJ
☎ 01548 561260 & 0780 803 0921
e-mail: info@alstoncampsite.co.uk
dir: *1.5m W of town off A381 towards Malborough*

* 🚐 £12-£20 🚙 £11-£20 ▲ £11-£20

Open 15 Mar-Oct

An established farm site in a rural location adjacent to the Kingsbridge/Salcombe estuary. The site is well sheltered and screened, and approached down a long, well-surfaced narrow farm lane with passing places. The toilet facilities are basic. 16 acre site. 90 touring pitches. Caravan pitches. Motorhome pitches. Tent pitches. 58 statics.

AA Pubs & Restaurants nearby: The Victoria Inn, SALCOMBE, TQ8 8BU, 01548 842604

Soar Mill Cove Hotel, SALCOMBE, TQ7 3DS, 01548 561566

Leisure: 🅰

Facilities: 🌾 ⊙ 🖉 ⚒ ⚙ ⊛ 🗑 ⛇ WIFI ♻ ❶

Services: 🔌 🗑 🏪 ⊘ T ♨

Within 3 miles: ⚓ ⚘ 🎿 ⚕ ✐ 🛒 🗑 ⊡

Notes: Dogs must be kept on leads.

SAMPFORD PEVERELL   Map 3 ST01

Places to visit

Tiverton Castle, TIVERTON, EX16 6RP, 01884 253200 www.tivertoncastle.com

Tiverton Museum of Mid Devon Life, TIVERTON, EX16 6PJ, 01884 256295 www.tivertonmuseum.org.uk

Great for kids: Diggerland, CULLOMPTON, EX15 2PE, 0871 227 7007 www.diggerland.com

PREMIER PARK

►►►►► 81% Minnows Touring Park (SS042148)

Holbrook Ln EX16 7EN
☎ 01884 821770
e-mail: admin@minnowstouringpark.co.uk
dir: *M5 junct 27, A361 signed Tiverton & Barnstaple. In 600yds take 1st slip road, right over bridge, site ahead*

🚐 £14.50-£26.95 🚙 £14.50-£26.95 ▲

Open 3 Mar-3 Nov

Last arrival 20.00hrs Last departure noon

A small, well-sheltered park, peacefully located amidst fields and mature trees. The toilet facilities are of a high quality in keeping with the rest of the park, and there is a good laundry. The park has direct gated access to the canal towpath; a brisk 20-minute walk and there is a choice of pubs and a farm shop, and the bus stop is 15 minutes away. All pitches are hardstanding with some large enough for American RVs; fully serviced pitches are also available. The park has Wi-fi. 5.5 acre site. 59 touring pitches. 59 hardstandings. Caravan pitches. Motorhome pitches. Tent pitches. 1 static.

AA Pubs & Restaurants nearby: The Butterleigh Inn, BUTTERLEIGH, EX15 1PN, 01884 855433

Leisure: 🅰

Facilities: 🌾 ⊙ 🖉 ⚒ ⚙ ⊛ 🗑 ⛁ WIFI ♻ ❶

Services: 🔌 🗑 🏪 ⊘ T ♨

Within 3 miles: ⚓ ✐ 🛒 🗑

Notes: No cycling, no groundsheets on grass. Dogs must be kept on leads. RVs welcome, caravan storage.

SHALDON   Map 3 SX97

Places to visit

Bradley Manor, NEWTON ABBOT, TQ12 6BN, 01803 843235 www.nationaltrust.org.uk/devoncornwall

'Bygones', TORQUAY, TQ1 4PR, 01803 326108 www.bygones.co.uk

Great for kids: Babbacombe Model Village, TORQUAY, TQ1 3LA, 01803 315315 www.model-village.co.uk

77% Coast View Holiday Park (SX935716)

Torquay Rd TQ14 0BG
☎ 01626 818350
e-mail: holidays@coastview.co.uk
dir: *M5 junct 31, A38 then A380 towards Torquay. A381 towards Teignmouth. Right in 4m at lights, over Shaldon Bridge. 0.75m, up hill, site on right*

* 🚐 £22-£40 🚙 £16-£40 ▲ £16-£30

Open mid Mar-end Oct

Last arrival 20.00hrs Last departure 10.00hrs

This park has stunning sea views from its spacious pitches. The family-run park has a full entertainment programme every night for all the family, plus outdoor and indoor activities for children; this site will certainly appeal to lively families. 30 acre site. 38 touring pitches. 6 hardstandings. 21 seasonal pitches. Caravan pitches. Motorhome pitches. Tent pitches. 27 statics.

AA Pubs & Restaurants nearby: ODE dining, SHALDON, TQ14 0DE, 01626 873977

Leisure: 🏊 🅰 🎣 🎵

Facilities: 🌾 ⊙ 🖉 ⚒ ⚙ ⊛ 🗑 ⛏ WIFI 🖥 ♻ ❶

Services: 🔌 🗑 🏪 🏪 ⊘ 🍽 ♨ ⛟ ♨

Within 3 miles: ⚓ ⚘ 🎿 ⚕ ✐ ◉ 🛒 🗑 ⊡

Notes: No noise after 23.00hrs. Dogs must be kept on leads.

SIDMOUTH
Map 3 SY18

Places to visit

Branscombe - The Old Bakery, Manor Mill and Forge, BRANSCOMBE, EX12 3DB, 01752 346585
www.nationaltrust.org.uk

Otterton Mill, OTTERTON, EX9 7HG, 01395 568521
www.ottertonmill.com

Great for kids: Pecorama Pleasure Gardens, BEER, EX12 3NA, 01297 21542
www.pecorama.info

AA CAMPING CARD SITE

PREMIER PARK

▶▶▶▶▶ 92%

Oakdown Country Holiday Park (SY167902)

Gatedown Ln, Weston EX10 0PT
☎ 01297 680387
e-mail: enquiries@oakdown.co.uk
web: www.oakdown.co.uk
dir: Exit A3052, 2.5m E of junct with A375

* 🚐 £14.35-£29.35 🚃 £14.35-£29.35
Å £12.05-£23.50

Open Apr-Oct

Last arrival 22.00hrs Last departure 10.30hrs

A quality, friendly, well-maintained park with good landscaping and plenty of maturing trees that make it well screened from the A3052. Pitches are grouped in groves surrounded by shrubs, with a 50-pitch development replete with an upmarket toilet block. The park has excellent facilities including a 9-hole par 3 golf course and a good shop and café. The park's conservation areas, with their natural flora and fauna, offer attractive walks, and there is a hide by the Victorian reed bed for both casual and dedicated bird watchers. A delightful park in every respect. 16 acre site. 150 touring pitches. 90 hardstandings. Caravan pitches. Motorhome pitches. Tent pitches. 62 statics.

AA Pubs & Restaurants nearby: Blue Ball Inn, SIDMOUTH, EX10 9QL, 01395 514062

The Salty Monk, SIDMOUTH, EX10 9QP, 01395 513174

Dukes, SIDMOUTH, EX10 8AR, 01395 513320

Leisure: 🎱 🔍 💻

Facilities: 🛁 🚿 ⊙ 🌀 ✳ ⚿ ⓒ 💲 🐕 Wi-fi 💻 ♻ ⓘ

Services: 🔌 🔋 🔧 🚰 T 🍴 🛒 ⚒

Within 3 miles: ♨ ⛳ 🎣 🍴 ◎ ⚓ 💲 🏇 ∪

Notes: No bikes, skateboards or kite flying. Dogs must be kept on leads. Use of microwave. Field trail to donkey sanctuary.

AA CAMPING CARD SITE

▶▶▶ 85% **Salcombe Regis Caravan & Camping Park** (SY153892)

Salcombe Regis EX10 0JH
☎ 01395 514303
e-mail: contact@salcombe-regis.co.uk
web: www.salcombe-regis.co.uk
dir: Exit A3052 1m E of junct with A375. From opposite direction turn left past Donkey Sanctuary

* 🚐 £12.25-£22.85 🚃 £12.25-£22.85
Å £12.25-£22.85

Open Etr-end Oct

Last arrival 20.15hrs Last departure 10.30hrs

Set in quiet countryside with glorious views, this spacious park has well-maintained facilities, and a good mix of grass and hardstanding pitches. A footpath runs from the park to the coastal path and the beach. There is a self-catering holiday cottage and static caravans for hire. 16 acre site. 100 touring pitches. 40 hardstandings. 26 seasonal pitches. Caravan pitches. Motorhome pitches. Tent pitches. 10 statics.

AA Pubs & Restaurants nearby: Blue Ball Inn, SIDMOUTH, EX10 9QL, 01395 514062

The Salty Monk, SIDMOUTH, EX10 9QP, 01395 513174

Dukes, SIDMOUTH, EX10 8AR, 01395 513320

Salcombe Regis Caravan & Camping Park

Leisure: ⚤

Facilities: 🖴 🌂 ⊙ 🄵 ✳ ☉ 🛢 🚻 WiFi ♻ ❗

Services: 🔌 🔄 🛢 ⊘ 🅃 ☳ ⚒

Within 3 miles: ↨ 🚴 🎱 🄿 ◎ ⛵ 🄑 🄢 ∪

Notes: Quiet 22.00hrs, no noise 23.00hrs. Dogs must be kept on leads. Putting green.

▶▶▶ 77% Kings Down Tail Caravan & Camping Park *(SY173907)*

Salcombe Regis EX10 0PD
☎ **01297 680313**
e-mail: info@kingsdowntail.co.uk
dir: *Exit A3052 3m E of junct with A375*

* 🚐 £15-£20 🚐 £15-£20 ▲ £15-£20

Open 15 Mar-15 Nov

Last arrival 22.00hrs Last departure noon

A well-kept site on level ground in a tree-sheltered spot on the side of the Sid Valley. This neat family-run park makes a good base for exploring the east Devon coast. 5 acre site. 102 touring pitches. 65 hardstandings. Caravan pitches. Motorhome pitches. Tent pitches.

AA Pubs & Restaurants nearby: Blue Ball Inn, SIDMOUTH, EX10 9QL, 01395 514062

The Salty Monk, SIDMOUTH, EX10 9QP, 01395 513174

Dukes, SIDMOUTH, EX10 8AR, 01395 513320

Kings Down Tail Caravan & Camping Park

Leisure: ⚤ 🎣

Facilities: 🌂 ⊙ 🄵 ✳ ☉ 🛢 🚻 ♻ ❗

Services: 🔌 🔄 🛢 ⊘ 🅃 ☳

Within 3 miles: ↨ 🚴 🄷 🄿 🄑 🄢 ∪

Notes: Dogs must be kept on leads.

see advert on opposite page

SOURTON CROSS — Map 3 SX59

Places to visit

Lydford Gorge, LYDFORD, EX20 4BH, 01822 820320 www.nationaltrust.org.uk/lydfordgorge

Okehampton Castle, OKEHAMPTON, EX20 1JB, 01837 52844 www.english-heritage.org.uk/daysout/properties/okehampton-castle

Great for kids: Tamar Otter & Wildlife Centre, LAUNCESTON, PL15 8GW, 01566 785646 www.tamarotters.co.uk

▶▶▶ 80% Bundu Camping & Caravan Park *(SX546916)*

EX20 4HT
☎ **01837 861747 & 861611**
e-mail: bundu@btconnect.com
dir: *W on A30, past Okehampton. Take A386 to Tavistock. Take 1st left & left again*

* 🚐 £13-£18 🚐 £13-£18 ▲ £12-£18

Open all year

Last arrival 22.30hrs Last departure noon

Welcoming, friendly owners set the tone for this well-maintained site, ideally positioned on the border of the Dartmoor National Park. Along with fine views, well-maintained toilet facilities and level grassy pitches, the Granite Way cycle track

from Lydford to Okehampton that runs along the old railway line (part of the Devon Coast to Coast cycle trail) passes the edge of the park. There is a bus stop and cycle hire a few minutes' walk away. Dogs are accepted. 4.5 acre site. 38 touring pitches. 11 hardstandings. Caravan pitches. Motorhome pitches. Tent pitches.

AA Pubs & Restaurants nearby: The Highwayman Inn, SOURTON, EX20 4HN, 01837 861243

Facilities: 🌂 ⊙ 🄵 ✳ ☉ 🛢 🚻 WiFi 💻 ♻ ❗

Services: 🔌 🔄 🛢 ⊘ 🅃 ☳

Within 3 miles: ↨ 🄷 🄿 🄑 🄢

Notes: Dogs must be kept on leads.

SOUTH MOLTON — Map 3 SS72

Places to visit

Quince Honey Farm, SOUTH MOLTON, EX36 3AZ, 01769 572401 www.quincehoney.com

Cobbaton Combat Collection, CHITTLEHAMPTON, EX37 9RZ, 01769 540740 www.cobbatoncombat.co.uk

Great for kids: Exmoor Zoological Park, BLACKMOOR GATE, EX31 4SG, 01598 763352 www.exmoorzoo.co.uk

---

AA CAMPING CARD SITE

▶▶▶▶ 90% Riverside Caravan & Camping Park *(SS723274)*

Marsh Ln, North Molton Rd EX36 3HQ
☎ **01769 579269**
e-mail: relax@exmoorriverside.co.uk
web: www.exmoorriverside.co.uk
dir: *M5 junct 27, A361 towards Barnstaple. Site signed 1m before South Molton on right*

🚐 £18-£25 🚐 £18-£25 ▲ £10-£24

Open all year

Last arrival 22.00hrs Last departure 11.00hrs

A family-run park, set alongside the River Mole, where supervised children can play, and fishing is

continued

SOUTH MOLTON *continued*

available. This is an ideal base for exploring Exmoor, as well as north Devon's golden beaches. There's on-site entertainment during the school holidays and on Bank Holidays. The site has an award for the excellence of the toilets. The local bus stops at park entrance. 40 acre site. 42 touring pitches. 42 hardstandings. Caravan pitches. Motorhome pitches. Tent pitches. 2 statics.

Leisure: ⚑ ☺ ♫

Facilities: ↴ ⊙ ☞ ✳ ⅃ ⓛ ⓢ ⨍ ⨗ Wi-fi ♻ ❶

Services: ⬛ ⓢ ⬛ ❗ ⌀ ⊤ ⓘ♨ ⬛ ⬗

Within 3 miles: ⅃ �𝄞 ⌀ ☺ ⓢ ⓢ ♈

Notes: Dogs must be kept on leads.

STARCROSS

See Dawlish

STOKE GABRIEL   Map 3 SX85

Places to visit
Berry Pomeroy Castle, TOTNES, TQ9 6NJ, 01803 866618 www.english-heritage.org.uk/daysout/properties/berry-pomeroy-castle

Totnes Museum, TOTNES, TQ9 5RU, 01803 863821 www.devonmuseums.net/totnes

Great for kids: Paignton Zoo Environmental Park, PAIGNTON, TQ4 7EU, 0844 474 2222 www.paigntonzoo.org.uk

▶▶▶ 84% Higher Well Farm Holiday Park *(SX857577)*

Waddeton Rd TQ9 6RN
☎ 01803 782289
e-mail: higherwell@talk21.com
dir: *From Exeter A380 to Torbay, turn right onto A385 for Totnes, in 0.5m left for Stoke Gabriel, follow signs*

⊞ £12-£19.50 ⊞ £12-£19.50 ▲ £12-£19.50

Open 5 Apr-2 Nov

Last arrival 22.00hrs Last departure 10.00hrs

Set on a quiet farm yet only four miles from Paignton, this rural holiday park is on the outskirts of the picturesque village of Stoke Gabriel. A toilet block, with some en suite facilities, is an excellent amenity, and tourers are housed in an open field with very good views. 10 acre site. 80 touring pitches. 3 hardstandings.

Caravan pitches. Motorhome pitches. Tent pitches. 19 statics.

AA Pubs & Restaurants nearby: The Durant Arms, TOTNES, TQ9 7UP, 01803 732240

Steam Packet Inn, TOTNES, TQ9 5EW, 01803 863880

The White Hart Bar & Restaurant, TOTNES, TQ9 6EL, 01803 847111

Facilities: ↴ ⊙ ☞ ✳ ⅃ ⓛ ⓢ ⨍ ♻ ❶

Services: ⬛ ⓢ ⬛ ⌀ ⊤ ⬛ ⬗

Within 3 miles: ⅃ ⌀ ⓢ ⓢ

Notes: No commercial vehicles, pets must not be left unattended in caravans. Dogs must be kept on leads.

▶▶▶ 80% *Broadleigh Farm Park* *(SX851587)*

Coombe House Ln, Aish TQ9 6PU
☎ 01803 782422
e-mail: enquiries@broadleighfarm.co.uk
web: www.broadleighfarm.co.uk
dir: *From Exeter on A38 then A380 towards Torbay. Right onto A385 for Totnes. In 0.5m right at Whitehill Country Park. Site approx 0.75m on left*

⊞ ⊞ ▲

Open Mar-Oct

Last arrival 21.00hrs Last departure 11.30hrs

Set in a very rural location on a working farm bordering Paignton and Stoke Gabriel. The large sloping field with a timber-clad toilet block in the centre is sheltered and peaceful, surrounded by rolling countryside but handy for the beaches. There is also an excellent rally field with good toilets and showers. 7 acre site. 80 touring pitches. Caravan pitches. Motorhome pitches. Tent pitches.

AA Pubs & Restaurants nearby: Rumour, TOTNES, TQ9 5RY, 01803 864682

Royal Seven Stars Hotel, TOTNES, TQ9 5DD, 01803 862125

Facilities: ↴ ⊙ ☞ ✳ ⅃ ♻ ❶

Services: ⬛ ⓢ ⬛

Within 3 miles: ⅃ ⌂ ⌀ ☺ ⓢ ⓢ

Notes: ⊛ Dogs must be kept on leads.

TAVISTOCK   Map 3 SX47

Places to visit
Morwellham Quay, MORWELLHAM, PL19 8JL, 01822 832766 www.morwellham-quay.co.uk

Great for kids: National Marine Aquarium, PLYMOUTH, PL4 0LF, 01752 275200 www.national-aquarium.co.uk

REGIONAL WINNER - SOUTH WEST ENGLAND AA CAMPSITE OF THE YEAR 2014

AA CAMPING CARD SITE

PREMIER PARK

▶▶▶▶▶ 87%
Woodovis Park *(SX431745)*

Gulworthy PL19 8NY
☎ 01822 832968
e-mail: info@woodovis.com
dir: *A390 from Tavistock signed Callington & Gunnislake. At hill top right at rdbt signed Lamerton & Chipshop. Site 1m on left*

* ⊞ £17-£38 ⊞ £17-£38 ▲ £17-£38

Open 22 Mar-1 Nov

Last arrival 20.00hrs Last departure 11.00hrs

A well-kept park in a remote woodland setting on the edge of the Tamar Valley. A peacefully located park at the end of a private, half-mile, tree-lined drive, it offers superb on-site facilities and high levels of customer care from hands-on owners. The toilets are immaculate and well maintained, plus there is an indoor swimming pool, sauna and a good information/games room, all in a friendly atmosphere. 14.5 acre site. 50 touring pitches. 33 hardstandings. 8 seasonal pitches. Caravan pitches. Motorhome pitches. Tent pitches. 35 statics. 3 wooden pods.

AA Pubs & Restaurants nearby: Dartmoor Inn, LYDFORD, EX20 4AY, 01822 820221

Leisure: ⌧ ⚑ ☺ ♜

Facilities: ⬌ ↴ ⊙ ☞ ✳ ⅃ ⓢ ⨍ ⨗ Wi-fi ⬛ ♻ ❶

Services: ⬛ ⓢ ⬛ ⌀ ⊤ ⬛ ⬗ ⬗

Within 3 miles: ⅃ ⌂ ⌀ ☺ ⓢ ⓢ ♈

Notes: Dogs must be kept on leads. Archery, water-walking, physiotherm infra-red therapy cabin, petanque court, outdoor table tennis.

LEISURE: ⌧ Indoor swimming pool ⌦ Outdoor swimming pool ⌐ Children's playground ♣ Kid's club ⌘ Tennis court ♜ Games room ⌑ Separate TV room ⌁ 9/18 hole golf course ⛵ Boats for hire ⌗ Cinema ♫ Entertainment ⌂ Fishing ⊕ Mini golf ⌒ Watersports ⌙ Gym ☺ Sports field **Spa** ♈ Stables
FACILITIES: ⬌ Bath ↴ Shower ⊙ Electric shaver ☞ Hairdryer ✳ Ice Pack Facility ⅃ Disabled facilities ⓛ Public telephone ⓢ Shop on site or within 200yds ⌾ Mobile shop (calls at least 5 days a week) ⨍ BBQ area ⨗ Picnic area Wi-fi Wi-fi ⬛ Internet access ♻ Recycling ❶ Tourist info ⨗ Dog exercise area

AA CAMPING CARD SITE

PREMIER PARK

▶▶▶▶▶ 80% Langstone Manor Camping & Caravan Park *(SX524738)*

Moortown PL19 9JZ
☎ **01822 613371**
e-mail: jane@langstone-manor.co.uk
web: www.langstone-manor.co.uk
dir: *B3357 from Tavistock to Princetown. 1.5m right at x-rds, follow signs. Over bridge, cattle grid, up hill, left at sign. Left to park*

* 🚐 £14-£19 �caravan £14-£19 ▲ £14-£19

Open 15 Mar-Oct (rs 15 Mar-Oct bar & restaurant closed weekdays (excl BH & school hols))

Last arrival 22.00hrs Last departure 11.00hrs

A secluded and very peaceful site set in the well-maintained grounds of a manor house in Dartmoor National Park. Many attractive mature trees provide screening within the park, yet the west-facing terraced pitches on the main park enjoy the superb summer sunsets. There are excellent refurbished toilet facilities, a popular lounge bar with an excellent menu of reasonably priced evening meals. Plenty of activities and places of interest can be found within the surrounding moorland. Dogs are accepted. 6.5 acre site. 40 touring pitches. 10 hardstandings. 5 seasonal pitches. Caravan pitches. Motorhome pitches. Tent pitches. 25 statics. 5 wooden pods.

Leisure: 🏞 🔍

Facilities: 🚿 ⬅ ☉ ⬛ ✳ 🔥 🕐 🚻 wifi ♻ ⊕

Services: 🔌 ☐ 🗄 🚿 ⊘ Ⓣ 🍽 🛒 🚐 ♿

Within 3 miles: ↓ Ħ 🔍 ◎ ⛵ 🛍 🛢 ⛳

Notes: Dogs must be kept on leads. Baguettes, croissants etc available.

▶▶▶▶ 80% *Harford Bridge Holiday Park* *(SX504767)*

Peter Tavy PL19 9LS
☎ **01822 810349 & 07773 251457**
e-mail: stay@harfordbridge.co.uk
web: www.harfordbridge.co.uk
dir: *2m N of Tavistock, off A386 Okehampton Rd, take Peter Tavy turn, entrance 200yds on right*

🚐 �caravan ▲

GOLD

Open all year (rs Nov-Mar statics only & 5 hardstandings)

Last arrival 21.00hrs Last departure noon

This beautiful spacious park is set beside the River Tavy in the Dartmoor National Park. Pitches are located beside the river and around the copses, and the park is very well equipped for the holidaymaker. An adventure playground and games room entertain children, and there is fly-fishing and a free tennis court. A lovely, authentic shepherd's hut complete with furniture, fridge and woodburner is available to let. 16 acre site. 120 touring pitches. 5 hardstandings. 5 seasonal pitches. Caravan pitches. Motorhome pitches. Tent pitches. 80 statics.

AA Pubs & Restaurants nearby: Peter Tavy Inn, TAVISTOCK, PL19 9NN, 01822 810348

Leisure: 🏞 ⚽ 🔍 ▢

Facilities: 🚿 ☉ ⬛ ✳ 🔥 🕐 🚻 🚻 wifi ♻ ⊕

Services: 🔌 ☐ 🗄 ⊘ Ⓣ 🛒 ♿

Within 3 miles: ↓ ⅊ Ħ 🔍 ⛵ 🛍 🛢 ⛳

Notes: Expedition groups welcome by prior arrangement. Dogs must be kept on leads. Baguettes, croissants, snacks, sweets available.

AA CAMPING CARD SITE

▶▶▶▶ 82% Springfield Holiday Park *(SX788935)*

EX6 6EW
☎ **01647 24242**
e-mail: enquiries@springfieldholidaypark.co.uk
dir: *M5 junct 31, A30 towards Okehampton, exit at junct, signed to Cheriton Bishop. Follow brown tourist signs to site. (NB for Sat Nav use postcode EX6 6JN)*

🚐 £15-£20 �caravan £15-£20 ▲ £10-£15

Open 15 Mar-15 Nov

Last arrival 22.00hrs Last departure noon

Set in a quiet rural location with countryside views, this park continues to be upgraded to a smart standard. There is a very inviting heated outdoor swimming pool. It has the advantage of being close to Dartmoor National Park, with village pubs and stores less than a mile away. 9 acre site. 48 touring pitches. 38 hardstandings. 25 seasonal pitches. Caravan pitches. Motorhome pitches. Tent pitches. 49 statics.

AA Pubs & Restaurants nearby: The Old Inn, DREWSTEIGNTON, EX6 6QR, 01647 281276

Leisure: 🏊 🏞 🔍

Facilities: 🚿 ☉ ✳ 🔥 🕐 wifi 🖥 ♻ ⊕

Services: 🔌 ☐ 🗄 ⊘ ♿

Within 3 miles: ↓ 🔍 🛍 🛢

Notes: Dogs must be kept on leads.

Escape to North Devon...

Set within North Devon's breathtaking countryside next to Woolacombe's three miles of golden sandy beach

LEVEL PITCHES & EASY ACCESS

400 ALL WEATHER PITCHES

16 AMP ELECTRIC HOOKUPS

PITCHES FROM JUST £6 per night

- Four award winning Holiday Parks
- Grass and hard standing pitches
- Outstanding leisure facilities
- Sea view touring & super pitches
- Modern amenity blocks
- Activities for all ages

WOOLACOMBE BAY
HOLIDAY PARKS

Call **0844 7700 365**
or visit **woolacombe.com/aac**

We're here

LEISURE: Indoor swimming pool Outdoor swimming pool Children's playground Kid's club Tennis court Games room Separate TV room 9/18 hole golf course Boats for hire Cinema Entertainment Fishing Mini golf Watersports Gym Sports field **Spa** Stables
FACILITIES: Bath Shower Electric shaver Hairdryer Ice Pack Facility Disabled facilities Public telephone Shop on site or within 200yds Mobile shop (calls at least 5 days a week) BBQ area Picnic area **Wi-fi** Wi-fi Internet access Recycling Tourist info Dog exercise area

TIVERTON

See East Worlington

TORQUAY Map 3 SX96

See also Newton Abbot

Places to visit

Torre Abbey, TORQUAY, TQ2 5JE, 01803 293593 www.torre-abbey.org.uk

'Bygones', TORQUAY, TQ1 4PR, 01803 326108 www.bygones.co.uk

AA CAMPING CARD SITE

►►►► 83% Widdicombe Farm Touring Park *(SX876643)*

Marldon TQ3 1ST
☎ 01803 558325
e-mail: info@widdicombefarm.co.uk
dir: *On A380, midway between Torquay & Paignton ring road*

* 🚐 £12.50-£25.50 🚌 £12.50-£25.50 ⛺ £9-£25.50

Open mid Mar-end Oct

Last arrival 20.00hrs Last departure 11.00hrs

A friendly family-run park on a working farm with good quality facilities, extensive views and easy access as there are no narrow roads. The level pitches are terraced to take advantage of the views towards the coast and Dartmoor. This is the only adult touring park within Torquay, and is also handy for Paignton and Brixham. There's a bus service from the park to the local shopping centre and Torquay's harbour. It has a small shop, a restaurant and a lounge bar with entertainment from Easter to the end of September. Club Wi-fi is available throughout the park and The Nippy Chippy van now calls regularly. 8 acre site. 180 touring pitches. 180 hardstandings. 20 seasonal pitches. Caravan pitches. Motorhome pitches. Tent pitches. 3 statics.

AA Pubs & Restaurants nearby: The Church House Inn, MARLDON, TQ3 1SL, 01803 558279

The Cary Arms, TORQUAY, TQ1 3LX, 01803 327110

The Elephant Restaurant and Brasserie, TORQUAY, TQ1 2BH, 01803 200044

Leisure: ♫

Facilities: 🚿 ☺ 🛁 ✱ ♿ 🛒 🐕 Wi-fi ♻ ⓘ

Services: 🔌 🧺 🍷 🔥 ⛽ [T] 🍴 🔋 🍔 ⚓

Within 3 miles: ⛳ 🐎 🏨 🎣 ◎ 🏊 🛒 🧺

Notes: Adults only. No groups, most dog breeds accepted. Dogs must be kept on leads.

WOODBURY SALTERTON Map 3 SY08

Places to visit

The World of Country Life, EXMOUTH, EX8 5BU, 01395 274533 www.worldofcountrylife.co.uk

A la Ronde, EXMOUTH, EX8 5BD, 01395 265514 www.nationaltrust.org.uk/alaronde

Great for kids: Crealy Adventure Park, CLYST ST MARY, EX5 1DR, 01395 233200 www.crealy.co.uk

►►► 87% Browns Farm Caravan Park *(SY016885)*

Browns Farm EX5 1PS
☎ 01395 232895
dir: *M5 junct 30, A3052 for 3.7m. Right at White Horse Inn, follow sign to Woodbury. At junct with Village Rd turn right, site on left*

* 🚐 £12-£15.50 🚌 £12-£15.50 ⛺ £12-£14.50

Open all year

Last departure 11.00hrs

A small farm park adjoining a 14th-century thatched farmhouse, and located in a quiet village. Pitches back onto hedgerows, and the friendly owners keep the excellent facilities very clean. The tourist information and games room, with table tennis, chess etc, is housed in a purpose-built building. The park is just a mile from the historic heathland of Woodbury Common with its superb views. The local bus to Exeter and Exmouth stops at site entrance. 2.5 acre site. 29 touring pitches. 24 hardstandings. Caravan pitches. Motorhome pitches. Tent pitches.

AA Pubs & Restaurants nearby: The Digger's Rest, WOODBURY SALTERTON, EX5 1PQ, 01395 232375

The Golden Lion Inn, TIPTON ST JOHN, EX10 0AA, 01404 812881

Leisure: ♠ ▭

Facilities: 🚿 ☺ 🛁 ✱ ♿ ☎ ⓘ

Services: 🔌 🧺 🔥 ⛽ 🔋

Within 3 miles: ⛳ 🎣 🛒 U

Notes: 💳 No ground sheets in awnings, no music. Dogs must be kept on leads. Hardstandings for winter period, caravan storage.

WOOLACOMBE Map 3 SS44

See also Mortehoe

Places to visit

Arlington Court, ARLINGTON, EX31 4LP, 01271 850296 www.nationaltrust.org.uk/arlington-court

Great for kids: Watermouth Castle & Family Theme Park, ILFRACOMBE, EX34 9SL, 01271 863879 www.watermouthcastle.com

82% Woolacombe Bay Holiday Village *(SS465442)*

Sandy Ln EX34 7AH
☎ 01271 870221
e-mail: goodtimes@woolacombe.com
dir: *From Mullacott Cross rdbt take B3343 (Woolacombe road) to Turnpike Cross junct. Right towards Mortehoe, site approx 1m on left*

🚐 🚌 ⛺

Open Mar-Oct (rs Mar-mid May & mid Sep-Oct no touring, camping only available)

Last arrival mdnt Last departure 10.00hrs

A well-developed touring section in a holiday complex with a full entertainment and leisure programme. This park offers excellent facilities including a steam room and sauna, and an excellent outdoor sports area which includes a new circular Ocean Bar. For a small charge, a bus takes holidaymakers to the other Woolacombe Bay holiday centres where they can take part in any of the activities offered, and there is also a bus to the beach. 8.5 acre site. 180 touring pitches. Caravan pitches. Motorhome pitches. Tent pitches. 237 statics.

continued

WOOLACOMBE *continued*

AA Pubs & Restaurants nearby: The George & Dragon, ILFRACOMBE, EX34 9ED, 01271 863851

11 The Quay, ILFRACOMBE, EX34 9EQ, 01271 868090

The Williams Arms, BRAUNTON, EX33 2DE, 01271 812360

Leisure: 🏊🏖️⛰️🚣🎣⚽🎱📺🎵 Spa
Facilities: 📞⊙☀✳&⊙🚿🛋️🚪📶📺♻
Services: 🔌🔋🍴🍳🍽️🛒🚽
Within 3 miles: ⛳🚤📅⛳◎🏌🏂🎱⛺U

Notes: Health suite, adventure golf, climbing wall, bungee trampoline, surfing & swimming lessons.

see advert on page 172

80% Golden Coast Holiday Village *(SS482436)*

Station Rd EX34 7HW
☎ 01271 872000
e-mail: goodtimes@woolacombe.com
dir: *From Mullacott Cross towards Woolacombe Bay, site 1.5m on left*

🚐 🚗 🅰

Open Feb-Dec (rs mid Sep-May outdoor water park closed)

Last arrival mdnt Last departure 10.00hrs

A holiday village offering excellent leisure facilities together with the amenities available at the other Woolacombe Bay holiday parks. There is a neat touring area with a unisex toilet block, maintained to a high standard. Ten-pin bowling, high ropes course, climbing wall, surfing simulator and adventure golf are just a few of the many activities on offer. 10 acre site. 91 touring pitches. 53 hardstandings. Caravan pitches. Motorhome pitches. Tent pitches. 444 statics.

AA Pubs & Restaurants nearby: The George & Dragon, ILFRACOMBE, EX34 9ED, 01271 863851

11 The Quay, ILFRACOMBE, EX34 9EQ, 01271 868090

The Williams Arms, BRAUNTON, EX33 2DE, 01271 812360

Leisure: 🏊🏖️⛰️🚣🎣⚽🎱📺🎵
Facilities: 📞⊙☀✳&⊙🚿🛋️🚪📶📺
Services: 🔌🔋🍴🍳🍽️🛒🚽
Within 3 miles: ⛳🚤📅⛳◎🏌🏂🎱⛺U

Notes: No pets on touring pitches. Sauna, solarium, fishing, snooker, cinema, bungee trampoline, swimming & surfing lessons.

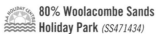

AA CAMPING CARD SITE

80% Woolacombe Sands Holiday Park *(SS471434)*

Beach Rd EX34 7AF
☎ 01271 870569
e-mail: lifesabeach@woolacombe-sands.co.uk
dir: *M5 junct 27, A361 to Barnstaple. Follow Ilfracombe signs to Mullacott Cross. Left onto B3343 to Woolacombe. Site on left*

*🚐 🚗 £5-£17 🅰

Open Mar-Nov

Last arrival 22.00hrs Last departure 10.00hrs

Set in rolling countryside with grass and hardstanding terraced pitches, most with spectacular views overlooking the sea at Woolacombe. The lovely Blue Flag beach can be accessed directly by footpath in 10-15 minutes, and there is a full entertainment programme for all the family in high season. 20 acre site. 200 touring pitches. 75 hardstandings. 50 seasonal pitches. Caravan pitches. Motorhome pitches. Tent pitches. 80 statics.

AA Pubs & Restaurants nearby: The George & Dragon, ILFRACOMBE, EX34 9ED, 01271 863851

11 The Quay, ILFRACOMBE, EX34 9EQ, 01271 868090

The Williams Arms, BRAUNTON, EX33 2DE, 01271 812360

Leisure: 🏊🏖️⛰️🚣🎣⚽🎱📺🎵
Facilities: 📞⊙☀✳&⊙🚿🛋️🚪📶📺♻ ⓘ
Services: 🔌🔋🍴🔒🍳🍽️🍴🛒🚽🚽
Within 3 miles: ⛳🚤📅⛳◎🏌🏂🎱⛺U

Notes: Crazy golf, woodland walk.

►►► 77% *Europa Park* *(SS475435)*

Beach Rd EX34 7AN
☎ 01271 871425
e-mail: europaparkwoolacombe@yahoo.co.uk
dir: *M5 junct 27, A361 through Barnstaple to Mullacott Cross. Left onto B3343 signed Woolacombe. Site on right at Spa shop/garage*

🚐 🚗 🅰

Open all year

Last arrival 23.00hrs Last departure 10.00hrs

A very lively family-run site handy for the beach at Woolacombe, and catering well for surfers but maybe not suitable for a quieter type of stay (please make sure the site is suitable for you before making your booking). Set in a stunning location high above the bay, it provides a wide range of accommodation including surf cabins, surf pods, a yurt and generous touring pitches. Visitors can enjoy the indoor pool and sauna, games room, restaurant/café/bar and clubhouse. 16 acre site. 200 touring pitches. 20 hardstandings. Caravan pitches. Motorhome pitches. Tent pitches. 22 statics. 1 bell tent/yurt.

AA Pubs & Restaurants nearby: The George & Dragon, ILFRACOMBE, EX34 9ED, 01271 863851

11 The Quay, ILFRACOMBE, EX34 9EQ, 01271 868090

The Williams Arms, BRAUNTON, EX33 2DE, 01271 812360

Leisure: 🏊⛰️🎱📺
Facilities: 📞⊙☀⊙🚿
Services: 🔌🔋🍴🍳🍽️🛒🚽🚽
Within 3 miles: ⛳📅⛳◎🏌🏂🎱⛺U

Notes: Beer deck, off licence, pub, big-screen TV.

SERVICES: 🔌 Electric hook up 🧺 Launderette 🍷 Licensed bar 🔥 Calor Gas 🔥 Camping Gaz ⊤ Toilet fluid 🍴 Café/Restaurant 🍔 Fast Food/Takeaway
🔋 Battery charging 🛒 Baby care ⚱ Motorvan service point **ABBREVIATIONS:** BH/bank hols-bank holidays Etr-Easter Spring BH-Spring Bank Holiday dep-departure
fr-from hrs-hours m-mile mdnt-midnight rdbt-roundabout rs-restricted service wk-week wknd-weekend x-rds-cross roads 🚫 No credit cards 🚫 No dogs
👪 Children of all ages accepted See page 9 for details of the AA Camping Card Scheme

Dorset

Dorset means rugged varied coastline and high chalk downland,
with more than a hint of Thomas Hardy, its most famous son.
The coastal grandeur is breathtaking with two famous local
landmarks, Lulworth Cove and Durdle Door, shaped and sculpted
to perfection by the elements. Squeezed in among the cliffs
and set amid some of Britain's most beautiful scenery is a chain
of picturesque villages and occasionally seaside towns.

● Durdle Door

Most prominent among these seaside towns is Lyme Regis, with its sturdy breakwater, known as the Cobb, made famous by Jane Austen in *Persuasion*, and John Fowles in *The French Lieutenant's Woman*. It's the sort of place where Georgian houses and quaint cottages jostle with historic pubs and independently run shops. With its blend of architectural styles and old world charm, Lyme looks very much like a film set, and fans of Austen and Fowles and the big-screen adaptations of their work flock to point their cameras and enjoy its beauty. Before the era of sea-bathing and Victorian respectability, the town was a haunt of smugglers.

Chesil Beach

In sharp contrast to Lyme's steep streets and dramatic inclines is Chesil Beach, a long shingle reef extending for 10 miles (16.1km) between Abbotsbury and Portland. The beach is covered by a vast wall of shingle resulting from centuries of violent weather-influenced activity along the Devon and Dorset coastline. The award-winning novelist Ian McEwan chose this setting for his novel *On Chesil Beach*.

▶

Thomas Hardy

Rural Dorset is where you can be 'far from the madding crowd'- to quote Thomas Hardy. For fans of this popular and much-admired writer there is the chance to visit two National Trust properties - the cob-and-thatch cottage in Higher Bockhampton where he was born and lived until the age of 34, and Max Gate in Dorchester, his home for 40 years and where he wrote some of his best-known works.

Walking and Cycling

For the true walker, however, there is nowhere to beat the magnificent Dorset coastline, particularly in the vicinity of Charmouth and Bridport where the domed Golden Cap stands tall and proud amid the cliffs. At 619ft it is the highest cliff on the south coast. Getting there, however, involves about 0.75 mile (1.2km) of steep walking. The Golden Cap is part of Dorset's spectacular Jurassic Coast, a World Heritage Site. This designated coastline stretches to East Devon.

The South West Coast Path, one of Britain's great walks, extends the length of the Dorset coast, from Lyme Regis to Studland Bay and Poole Harbour, and offers constant uninterrupted views of the coast and the Channel. Away from the sea there are miles of rolling downland walks which are no less impressive than the coastal stretches. The Purbeck Hills, between Weymouth and Poole Harbour, are great for exploring on foot. Cranborne Chase, to the north of Blandford Forum and once a royal forest, is a remote, rural backwater where the walker can feel totally at home.

The National Cycle Network offers the chance to ride from Dorchester through the heart of Dorset to Lyme Regis or north to Sherborne, taking in some of the county's most picturesque villages. There is also the chance to tour the ancient hill forts of Pilsdon Pen, Coneys Castle and Lamberts Castle around Charmouth and the Marshwood Vale – among a wide choice of Dorset cycle routes.

Festivals and Events

- Among numerous live shows, exhibitions, flower festivals and craft fairs, is the Great Dorset Steam Fair in September. This famous event draws many visitors who come to look at vintage and classic vehicles. There are also heavy horse shows and rural crafts.
- Also in September is the two-day Dorset County Show which includes over 450 trade stands, exciting main ring attractions and thousands of animals.
- For something a bit more light-hearted – but perhaps a little uncomfortable - there is the annual Nettle Eating Contest in June, which attracts fans from all over Europe.

Weymouth

Chesil Beach

DORSET

ALDERHOLT   Map 5 SU11

Places to visit

Furzey Gardens, MINSTEAD, SO43 7GL,
023 8081 2464 www.furzey-gardens.org

Breamore House & Countryside Museum,
BREAMORE, SP6 2DF, 01725 512468
www.breamorehouse.com

Great for kids: Rockbourne Roman Villa,
ROCKBOURNE, SP6 3PG, 0845 603 5635
www.hants.gov.uk/rockbourne-roman-villa

PREMIER PARK

►►►►► 80% Hill Cottage
Farm Camping and Caravan
Park (SU119133)

Sandleheath Rd SP6 3EG
☎ 01425 650513 & 07714 648690
e-mail: hillcottagefarmcaravansite@supanet.
com
dir: Take B3078 W of Fordingbridge. Exit at
Alderholt, site 0.25m on left after railway
bridge

* ⚐ £18-£27 ⚐ £18-£27 ▲ £14-£31

Open Mar-Oct

Last arrival 20.00hrs Last departure 11.00hrs

Set within extensive grounds this rural and
beautifully landscaped park offers fully
serviced pitches set in individual hardstanding
bays with mature dividing hedges that give
adequate pitch privacy. The modern toilet block
is kept immaculately clean, and there's a good
range of leisure facilities. In high season there
is an area available for tents. Rallies are very
welcome. A function room with skittle alley is
available, and there is a fully-equipped
shepherd's hut for hire. 40 acre site. 95 touring
pitches. 35 hardstandings. Caravan pitches.
Motorhome pitches. Tent pitches.

AA Pubs & Restaurants nearby: The Augustus
John, FORDINGBRIDGE, SP6 1DG,
01425 652098

Leisure: ⚐ ⚐
Facilities: ⚐⚐⚐⚐⚐⚐⚐⚐⚐⚐⚐ ⚐
⚐ ⚐
Services: ⚐⚐⚐⚐⚐⚐
Within 3 miles: ⚐⚐⚐⚐⚐⚐
Notes: No noise after 22.30hrs. Dogs must be
kept on leads.

BERE REGIS   Map 4 SY89

Places to visit

Kingston Lacy, WIMBORNE, BH21 4EA,
01202 883402 (Mon-Fri)
www.nationaltrust.org.uk

Priest's House Museum and Garden, WIMBORNE,
BH21 1HR, 01202 882533
www.priest-house.co.uk

Great for kids: Monkey World-Ape Rescue
Centre, WOOL, BH20 6HH, 01929 462537
www.monkeyworld.org

AA CAMPING CARD SITE

►►► 82% Rowlands
Wait Touring Park
(SY842933)

Rye Hill BH20 7LP
☎ 01929 472727
e-mail: enquiries@rowlandswait.co.uk
web: www.rowlandswait.co.uk
dir: On approach to Bere Regis follow signs to
Bovington Tank Museum. At top of Rye Hill, 0.75m
from village turn right. 200yds to site

* ⚐ £17-£22.50 ⚐ £17-£22.50 ▲ £15-£19.50

Open mid Mar-Oct (winter by arrangement) (rs
Nov-Feb own facilities required)

Last arrival 21.00hrs Last departure noon

This park lies in a really attractive setting
overlooking Bere Regis and the Dorset countryside,
set amongst undulating areas of trees and
shrubs. The toilet facilities include two family
rooms. Located within a few miles of the Tank
Museum with its mock battles, and is also very
convenient for visiting the Dorchester, Poole and
Swanage areas. 8 acre site. 71 touring pitches. 2
hardstandings. 23 seasonal pitches. Caravan
pitches. Motorhome pitches. Tent pitches.

AA Pubs & Restaurants nearby: Botany Bay Inne,
WINTERBORNE ZELSTON, DT11 9ET, 01929 459227

Leisure: ⚐ ⚐
Facilities: ⚐⚐⚐⚐⚐⚐⚐⚐⚐⚐ ⚐
Services: ⚐⚐⚐⚐⚐⚐⚐
Within 3 miles: ⚐⚐⚐⚐⚐⚐
Notes: No open fires. Dogs must be kept on leads.

BLANDFORD FORUM   Map 4 ST80

Places to visit

Kingston Lacy, WIMBORNE, BH21 4EA,
01202 883402 (Mon-Fri)
www.nationaltrust.org.uk

Old Wardour Castle, TISBURY, SP3 6RR,
01747 870487 www.english-heritage.org.uk/
daysout/properties/old-wardour-castle

Great for kids: Monkey World-Ape Rescue
Centre, WOOL, BH20 6HH, 01929 462537
www.monkeyworld.org

►►►► 81% The Inside Park
(ST869046)

Down House Estate DT11 9AD
☎ 01258 453719
e-mail: mail@theinsidepark.co.uk
dir: From town, over River Stour, follow
Winterborne Stickland signs. Site in 1.5m

⚐ £17.50-£25.45 ⚐ £17.50-£25.45
▲ £17.50-£25.45

Open Etr-Oct

Last arrival 22.00hrs Last departure noon

An attractive, well-sheltered and quiet park, half a
mile off a country lane in a wooded valley.
Spacious pitches are divided by mature trees and
shrubs, and amenities are housed in an
18th-century coach house and stables. There are

some lovely woodland walks within the park, an excellent fenced play area for children and a dog-free area. 12 acre site. 125 touring pitches. Caravan pitches. Motorhome pitches. Tent pitches.

AA Pubs & Restaurants nearby: The Anvil Inn, BLANDFORD FORUM, DT11 8UQ, 01258 453431

Leisure: ⏃ ✎

Facilities: ⬅ ⊙ ⥀ ✳ ⚷ ⊗ ⓢ ⌱ ⊡ ♨ ❂

Services: ⊡ ⓢ ⬛ ⊘ ⊺ ☷

Within 3 miles: ↓ ⅌ ⓢ ⓢ ∪

Notes: Dogs must be kept on leads. Kennels for hire.

BRIDPORT   Map 4 SY49

Places to visit

Forde Abbey, CHARD, TA20 4LU, 01460 221290 www.fordeabbey.co.uk

Dorset County Museum, DORCHESTER, DT1 1XA, 01305 262735 www.dorsetcountymuseum.org

Great for kids: Abbotsbury Swannery, ABBOTSBURY, DT3 4JG, 01305 871858 www.abbotsbury-tourism.co.uk

---

91% Freshwater Beach Holiday Park (SY493892)

Burton Bradstock DT6 4PT
☎ 01308 897317
e-mail: office@freshwaterbeach.co.uk
web: www.freshwaterbeach.co.uk
dir: Take B3157 from Bridport towards Burton Bradstock. Site 1.5m from Crown rdbt on right

* ⛺ £16-£42 ⛟ £16-£42 ⛺ £16-£42

Open mid Mar-mid Nov

Last arrival 22.00hrs Last departure 10.00hrs

A family holiday centre sheltered by a sand bank and enjoying its own private beach. The park offers a wide variety of leisure and entertainment programmes for all the family, plus the Jurassic Fun Centre with indoor pool, gym, 6-lane bowling alley, restaurant and bar is excellent. The park is well placed at one end of the Weymouth/Bridport coast with spectacular views of Chesil Beach. There are three immaculate toilet blocks, with excellent private rooms. 40 acre site. 500 touring pitches. 25 hardstandings. Caravan pitches. Motorhome pitches. Tent pitches. 250 statics.

AA Pubs & Restaurants nearby: The Shave Cross Inn, BRIDPORT, DT6 6HW, 01308 868358

Riverside Restaurant, BRIDPORT, DT6 4EZ, 01308 422011

The Anchor Inn, CHIDEOCK, DT6 6JU, 01297 489215

Freshwater Beach Holiday Park

Leisure: ⎙ ✎ ⚑ ⏃ ⚽ ❂ ✎ ♫ Spa

Facilities: ⬅ ⊙ ⥀ ✳ ⚷ ⊗ ⓢ ⌱ ⊡ 🖵 ❂

Services: ⊡ ⓢ ⬛ ⬛ ⊘ ⊺ ⓘ ☷ ☷

Within 3 miles: ↓ ⅃ ⒣ ⅌ ⊚ ⓢ ⓢ ∪

Notes: Families & couples only. Dogs must be kept on leads. Large TV, kids' club in high season & BH.

see advert on page 182

84% West Bay Holiday Park (SY461906)

West Bay DT6 4HB
☎ 0844 335 3756
e-mail: touringandcamping@parkdeanholidays.com
web: www.parkdeantouring.com
dir: From A35 (Dorchester road), W towards Bridport, take 1st exit at 1st rdbt, 2nd exit at 2nd rdbt into West Bay, site on right

* ⛺ £12-£42 ⛟ £12-£42 ⛺ £12-£42

Open mid Mar-Oct

Last arrival 23.00hrs Last departure 10.00hrs

Overlooking the pretty little harbour at West Bay, and close to the shingle beach, this park offers a full entertainment programme for all ages. There are children's clubs and an indoor pool with flume for all the family, and plenty of evening fun with shows and cabaret etc. The large adventure playground is very popular. The terraced touring section, with its own reception and warden, offers excellent sea views and has hardstandings and super pitches. 6 acre site. 116 touring pitches. Caravan pitches. Motorhome pitches. Tent pitches. 298 statics.

AA Pubs & Restaurants nearby: The West Bay, BRIDPORT, DT6 4EW, 01308 422157

Riverside Restaurant, BRIDPORT, DT6 4EZ, 01308 422011

Leisure: ⎙ ⏃ ✋ ✎

Facilities: ⬅ ⬅ ⊙ ⥀ ✳ ⚷ ⊗ ⓢ ⌱ ⊡

Services: ⊡ ⓢ ⬛ ⬛ ⊘ ⊺ ⓘ ☷ ☷ ⬛ ⬆

Within 3 miles: ↓ ⅃ ⅌ ⊚ ⓢ ⓢ ∪

Notes: No skateboards.

LEISURE: Indoor swimming pool Outdoor swimming pool Children's playground Kid's club Tennis court Games room Separate TV room 9/18 hole golf course Boats for hire Cinema Entertainment Fishing Mini golf Watersports Gym Sports field **Spa** Stables
FACILITIES: Bath Shower Electric shaver Hairdryer Ice Pack Facility Disabled facilities Public telephone Shop on site or within 200yds Mobile shop (calls at least 5 days a week) BBQ area Picnic area **Wi-fi** Wi-fi Internet access Recycling Tourist info Dog exercise area

BRIDPORT *continued*

PREMIER PARK

▷▷▷▷▷ **90%**
Highlands End Holiday Park (SY454913)

Best of British
GOLD

Eype DT6 6AR
☎ 01308 422139 & 426947
e-mail: holidays@wdlh.co.uk
dir: *1m W of Bridport on A35, turn south for Eype. Site signed*

* 🚐 £15.90-£34 🚐 £15.90-£34 Å £13.70-£26

Open 21 Mar-1 Nov

Last arrival 22.00hrs Last departure 11.00hrs

A well-screened site with magnificent cliff-top views over the Channel and the Dorset coast, adjacent to National Trust land and overlooking Lyme Bay. The pitches are mostly sheltered by hedging and well spaced on hardstandings. The excellent facilities include a tasteful bar and restaurant, indoor pool, leisure centre and

The Cowshed, a very good coffee shop. There is a mixture of statics and tourers, but the tourers enjoy the best cliff-top positions. 9 acre site. 195 touring pitches. 45 hardstandings. Caravan pitches. Motorhome pitches. Tent pitches. 160 statics.

AA Pubs & Restaurants nearby: The Shave Cross Inn, BRIDPORT, DT6 6HW, 01308 868358

Riverside Restaurant, BRIDPORT, DT6 4EZ, 01308 422011

The Anchor Inn, CHIDEOCK, DT6 6JU, 01297 489215

Highlands End Holiday Park

Leisure: 🏊 ⛳ 🎱 🎯 😊 🎣 🎵
Facilities: 📷 ⊙ 🍴 ✳ ⚠ ⚲ 🅂 🛒 🚿 🚻 ♻ ❶
Services: 🔌 🔲 🍴 🚽 📶 🍴 🛒 🚰 ↓
Within 3 miles: ↓ ⚲ 🏌 🔲

Notes: Dogs must be kept on leads. Steam room, sauna, pitch & putt.

see advert below

PREMIER PARK

▷▷▷▷▷ **87% Bingham Grange Touring & Camping Park** (SY478963)

Melplash DT6 3TT
☎ 01308 488234
e-mail: enquiries@binghamgrange.co.uk
dir: *From A35 at Bridport take A3066 N towards Beaminster. Site on left in 3m*

🚐 🚐 Å

Open 16 Mar-end Oct (rs Wed (all year), Tue (mid-low season) restaurant & bar closed)

Set in a quiet rural location but only five miles from the Jurassic Coast, this adults-only park enjoys views over the west Dorset countryside. The mostly level pitches are attractively set amongst shrub beds and ornamental trees. There is an excellent restaurant with lounge bar and takeaway, and all facilities are of a high quality. This is a very dog-friendly site. 20 acre site. 150 touring pitches. 85 hardstandings. 50 seasonal pitches. Caravan pitches. Motorhome pitches. Tent pitches.

AA Pubs & Restaurants nearby: The West Bay, BRIDPORT, DT6 4EW, 01308 422157

The Shave Cross Inn, BRIDPORT, DT6 6HW, 01308 868358

Riverside Restaurant, BRIDPORT, DT6 4EZ, 01308 422011

continued

BRIDPORT *continued*

Facilities: 🏠⊙☂✻👆🕐🖥🚿📶♻️ℹ️

Services: 🔌🅿️🚗🔒🛒🚽🍽️♿

Within 3 miles: 🎣🎠✏️🛒🛍️🛥️∪

Notes: Adults only. No under 18s may stay or visit, no noise after 23.00hrs. Dogs must be kept on leads. Woodland walks.

NEW ▶▶▶ 80% Graston Copse Holiday Park *(SY497899)*

GOLD

Annings Ln, Burton Bradstock DT6 4QP
☎ 01308 897361
dir: *Telephone for directions*

* 🚐 £15-£25 🚚 £15-£25 ▲ £12.50-£23

Open 21 Mar-2 Nov

Last departure 11.00hrs

This small, peaceful site is located near the village of Burton Bradstock making it a perfect base for visiting the stunning cliffs and beaches along the Jurassic coastline. The facilities are modern and spotlessly clean. Please note, care is needed if driving through Burton Bradstock to the site. 6.98 acre site. 78 touring pitches. Caravan pitches. Motorhome pitches. Tent pitches. 90 statics.

CERNE ABBAS   Map 4 ST60

Places to visit

Athelhampton House & Gardens, ATHELHAMPTON, DT2 7LG, 01305 848363 www.athelhampton.co.uk

Hardy's Cottage, DORCHESTER, DT2 8QJ, 01305 262366 www.nationaltrust.org.uk

Great for kids: Maiden Castle, DORCHESTER, DT2 9PP, 0870 333 1181 www.english-heritage. org.uk/daysout/properties/maiden-castle

---

▶▶▶ 90% Lyons Gate Caravan and Camping Park *(ST660062)*

Lyons Gate DT2 7AZ
☎ 01300 345260
e-mail: info@lyons-gate.co.uk
dir: *Signed with direct access from A352, 3m N of Cerne Abbas*

🚐 fr £14 🚚 fr £14 ▲ fr £14

Open all year

Last arrival 20.00hrs Last departure 11.30hrs

A peaceful park with pitches set out around the four attractive coarse fishing lakes. It is surrounded by mature woodland, with many footpaths and bridleways. Other easily accessible attractions include the Cerne Giant carved into the hills, the old market town of Dorchester, and the superb sandy beach at Weymouth. Holiday homes are now available for sale. 10 acre site. 90 touring pitches. 24 hardstandings. Caravan pitches. Motorhome pitches. Tent pitches. 14 statics.

AA Pubs & Restaurants nearby: The Piddle Inn, PIDDLETRENTHIDE, DT2 7QF, 01300 348468

The Poachers Inn, PIDDLETRENTHIDE, DT2 7QX, 01300 348358

Leisure: 🎱🎣📺🖥

Facilities: 🏠⊙☂✻👆🕐🖥🚿📶ℹ️

Services: 🔌🅿️🍽️♿

Within 3 miles: 🎣✏️🛍️∪

Notes: Dogs must be kept on leads.

▶▶ 75% Giants Head Caravan & Camping Park *(ST675029)*

Giants Head Farm, Old Sherborne Rd DT2 7TR
☎ 01300 341242
e-mail: holidays@giantshead.co.uk
dir: *From Dorchester into town avoiding by-pass, at Top O'Town rdbt take A352 (Sherborne road), in 500yds right fork at BP (Loder's) garage, site signed*

* 🚐 £8-£18 🚚 £8-£18 ▲ £8-£18

Open Etr-Oct (rs Etr shop & bar closed)

Last arrival anytime Last departure 13.00hrs

A pleasant, though rather basic, park set in Dorset downland near the Cerne Giant (the famous landmark figure cut into the chalk) with stunning views and a newly refurbished toilet block. This is a good stopover site especially for tenters and backpackers on The Ridgeway National Trail. Holiday chalets are available to let. 4 acre site. 50 touring pitches. Caravan pitches. Motorhome pitches. Tent pitches.

AA Pubs & Restaurants nearby: The Greyhound Inn, SYDLING ST NICHOLAS, DT2 9PD, 01300 341303

Facilities: 🏠⊙☂✻🚿♻️ℹ️

Services: 🔌🅿️🍽️♿🛒

Within 3 miles: ✏️🛍️🛍️

Notes: ♿ Dogs must be kept on leads.

CHARMOUTH   Map 4 SY39

Places to visit

Forde Abbey, CHARD, TA20 4LU, 01460 221290 www.fordeabbey.co.uk

Dorset County Museum, DORCHESTER, DT1 1XA, 01305 262735 www.dorsetcountymuseum.org

Great for kids: Abbotsbury Swannery, ABBOTSBURY, DT3 4JG, 01305 871858 www.abbotsbury-tourism.co.uk

---

PREMIER PARK

▶▶▶▶▶ 91% Wood Farm Caravan & Camping Park *(SY356940)*

Best of British

Axminster Rd DT6 6BT
☎ 01297 560697
e-mail: holidays@woodfarm.co.uk
web: www.woodfarm.co.uk
dir: *Accessed directly from A35 rdbt, on Axminster side of Charmouth*

🚐 🚚 ▲

Open Etr-Oct

Last arrival 19.00hrs Last departure noon

This top quality park, the perfect place to relax, is set amongst mature native trees with the various levels of the site falling away into a beautiful valley below. The park offers excellent facilities including family rooms and fully serviced pitches. The facilities throughout the park are spotless. At the bottom end of the park there is an excellent indoor swimming pool and leisure complex, plus the licensed, conservatory-style Offshore Café. There's a good children's play room in addition to tennis courts and a well-stocked, coarse-fishing lake. The park is well positioned on the Heritage Coast near Lyme Regis. Static holiday homes are also available for hire. 13 acre site. 175 touring pitches. 175 hardstandings. 20 seasonal pitches. Caravan pitches. Motorhome pitches. Tent pitches. 92 statics.

Leisure: 🏊⛰️🎾🎱🖥

Facilities: 🚿🏠⊙☂✻👆🕐🖥🚿📶🖥 ♻️ℹ️

Services: 🔌🅿️🔒🍽️🚽🖥⬆️🔌

Within 3 miles: 🎣🚴🎠✏️◎🚣🛍️🛍️∪

Notes: No bikes, skateboards, scooters or roller skates. Dogs must be kept on leads.

PREMIER PARK

▶▶▶▶▶ 81% *Newlands Caravan & Camping Park* (SY374935)

DT6 6RB
☎ 01297 560259
e-mail: enq@newlandsholidays.co.uk
web: www.newlandsholidays.co.uk
dir: *4m W of Bridport on A35*

🚐 🚠 ⛺

Open 10 Mar-4 Nov

Last arrival 21.00hrs Last departure 10.00hrs

A very smart site with excellent touring facilities, set on gently sloping ground in hilly countryside near the sea. The park offers a full cabaret and entertainment programme for all ages, and boasts an indoor swimming pool and an outdoor pool with water slide. Lodges, apartments and motel rooms are available. 23 acre site. 240 touring pitches. 52 hardstandings. Caravan pitches. Motorhome pitches. Tent pitches. 86 statics.

AA Pubs & Restaurants nearby: Pilot Boat Inn, LYME REGIS, DT7 3QA, 01297 443157

Leisure: ❋ ❋ 🛝 ↘ ♦ ⬜ 🎵

Facilities: 🔦 ☉ 🝙 ✳ 🔥 🔵 🕒 🗊 🚻 ♨ WiFi 🖥 ♻ ℹ

Services: 🔌 🗊 🍽 🔋 📦 🚽 🍴 🚰 ⛽

Within 3 miles: ↕ ✈ 📅 🧭 ◎ 🏌 🗊 🗊 U

Notes: Dogs must be kept on leads. Kids' club only during school holidays.

AA CAMPING CARD SITE

▷▷▷ 90% Manor Farm Holiday Centre (SY368937)

Manor Farm Holiday Centre DT6 6QL
☎ 01297 560226
e-mail: enquiries@manorfarmholidaycentre.co.uk
dir: *W on A35 to Charmouth, site 0.75m on right*

* 🚐 £14-£28 🚠 £14-£28 ⛺ £14-£28

Open all year (rs open all year round statics only)

Last arrival 20.00hrs Last departure 10.00hrs

Set just a short walk from the safe sand and shingle beach at Charmouth, this popular family park offers a good range of facilities. There is now an indoor/outdoor swimming pool plus café, a fully-equipped gym and sauna. Children enjoy the activity area and the park also offers a lively programme in the extensive bar and entertainment complex. In addition there are 16 luxury cottages available to let. 30 acre site. 400 touring pitches. 80 hardstandings. 100 seasonal pitches. Caravan pitches. Motorhome pitches. Tent pitches. 29 statics.

AA Pubs & Restaurants nearby: Pilot Boat Inn, LYME REGIS, DT7 3QA, 01297 443157

Leisure: ❋ ❋ 🍴 🛝 ♦ 🎵 Spa

Facilities: 🔦 ☉ 🝙 ✳ 🔥 🔵 🕒 🗊 WiFi ♻ ℹ

Services: 🔌 🗊 🍽 🔋 📦 🚽 🍴 ♨ ⛽

Within 3 miles: ↕ ✈ 📅 🧭 ◎ 🏌 🗊 🗊 U

Notes: ⊘ No skateboards.

CHIDEOCK — Map 4 SY49

Places to visit

Branscombe - The Old Bakery, Manor Mill and Forge, BRANSCOMBE, EX12 3DB, 01752 346585
www.nationaltrust.org.uk

Mapperton, BEAMINSTER, DT8 3NR, 01308 862645
www.mapperton.com

Great for kids: Pecorama Pleasure Gardens, BEER, EX12 3NA, 01297 21542
www.pecorama.info

▶▶▶▶ 85% Golden Cap Holiday Park (SY422919)

Seatown DT6 6JX
☎ 01308 422139 & 426947
e-mail: holidays@wdlh.co.uk
dir: *On A35, in Chideock follow Seatown signs, site signed*

* 🚐 £16-£40 🚠 £16-£40 ⛺ £16-£30.50

Open 21 Mar-2 Nov

Last arrival 22.00hrs Last departure 11.00hrs

A grassy site, overlooking sea and beach and surrounded by National Trust parkland. This uniquely placed park slopes down to the sea, although pitches are generally level. A slight dip hides the view of the beach from the back of the park, but this area benefits from having trees, scrub and meadows, unlike the barer areas closer to the sea which do have a spectacular outlook. This makes an ideal base for touring Dorset and Devon. Lake fishing is possible (a licence can be obtained locally). 11 acre site. 108 touring pitches. 24 hardstandings. Caravan pitches. Motorhome pitches. Tent pitches. 234 statics. 2 wooden pods.

AA Pubs & Restaurants nearby: The West Bay, BRIDPORT, DT6 4EW, 01308 422157

Riverside Restaurant, BRIDPORT, DT6 4EZ, 01308 422011

Leisure: 🛝

Facilities: 🔦 ☉ 🝙 ✳ 🔥 🔵 🕒 🗊 🚻 ♨ WiFi ♻ ℹ

Services: 🔌 🗊 📦 🚽 🍴 🚰 ⛽

Within 3 miles: ↕ 🧭 🗊 🗊

Notes: Dogs must be kept on leads.

SERVICES: 🔌 Electric hook up   🗊 Launderette   🍽 Licensed bar   🔋 Calor Gas   📦 Camping Gaz   🚽 Toilet fluid   🍴 Café/Restaurant   🚰 Fast Food/Takeaway
🔌 Battery charging   🚼 Baby care   ⛽ Motorvan service point   **ABBREVIATIONS:** BH/bank hols-bank holidays   Etr-Easter   Spring BH-Spring Bank Holiday   dep-departure
fr-from   hrs-hours   m-mile   mdnt-midnight   rdbt-roundabout   rs-restricted service   wk-week   wknd-weekend   x-rds-cross roads   ⊛ No credit cards   ⊘ No dogs
🚶 Children of all ages accepted   See page 9 for details of the AA Camping Card Scheme

CHRISTCHURCH   Map 5 SZ19

Places to visit

Red House Museum & Gardens, CHRISTCHURCH, BH23 1BU, 01202 482860 www.hants.gov.uk/museum/redhouse

Hurst Castle, HURST CASTLE, SO41 0TR, 01590 642344 www.english-heritage.org.uk/daysout/properties/hurst-castle

Great for kids: Oceanarium, BOURNEMOUTH, BH2 5AA, 01202 311993 www.oceanarium.co.uk

PREMIER PARK

►►►►► **85% Meadowbank Holidays** *(SZ136946)*

Stour Way BH23 2PQ
☎ **01202 483597**
e-mail: enquiries@meadowbank-holidays.co.uk
web: www.meadowbank-holidays.co.uk
dir: *A31 onto A338 towards Bournemouth. Take 1st exit after 5m then left towards Christchurch on B3073. Right at 1st rdbt into St Catherine's Way/River Way. Stour Way 3rd right, site at end of road*

✻ ⊟ £10-£32 ⇌ £10-£32

Open Mar-Oct

Last arrival 21.00hrs Last departure noon

A very smart park on the banks of the River Stour, with a colourful display of hanging baskets and flower-filled tubs placed around the superb reception area. The facility block is excellent. Visitors can choose between the different pitch sizes, including luxury fully serviced ones. There is also an excellent play area, a good shop on site and coarse fishing on site. Statics are available for hire. 2 acre site. 41 touring pitches. 22 hardstandings. Caravan pitches. Motorhome pitches. 180 statics.

AA Pubs & Restaurants nearby: The Ship In Distress, CHRISTCHURCH, BH23 3NA, 01202 485123

Splinters Restaurant, CHRISTCHURCH, BH23 1BW, 01202 483454

Leisure: ⚠ ⚓

Facilities: ⇌ ⚲ ☺ ℱ ⚿ ⚹ Ⓛ ⚶ ⏲ ᵂᶦᶠᶦ ⊟ ♻ ⚹

Services: ⚡ ⚶ ⚿ ⚯ ⊤ ⚱ ⚙

Within 3 miles: ⚹ ⚓ ⊟ ℱ ⚹ ♨ ⚶ ⚶ ⚶ ∪

Notes: No pets.

CORFE CASTLE   Map 4 SY98

Places to visit

Corfe Castle, CORFE CASTLE, BH20 5EZ, 01929 481294 www.nationaltrust.org.uk

Brownsea Island, BROWNSEA ISLAND, BH13 7EE, 01202 707744 www.nationaltrust.org.uk/brownsea

Great for kids: Swanage Railway, SWANAGE, BH19 1HB, 01929 425800 www.swanagerailway.co.uk

►►►► **89% Corfe Castle Camping & Caravanning Club Site** *(SY953818)*

Bucknowle BH20 5PQ
☎ **01929 480280 & 0845 130 7633**
dir: *A351 from Wareham towards Swanage. In 4m right at foot of Corfe Castle signed Church Knowle. 0.75m right to site on left at top of lane*

⊟ ⇌ Å

Open Mar-Oct

Last arrival 20.00hrs Last departure noon

This lovely campsite, where non-members are also very welcome, is set in woodland near to famous Corfe Castle at the foot of the Purbeck Hills. It has a stone reception building, on-site shop and modern toilet and shower facilities, which are spotless. Although the site is sloping, pitches are level and include spacious hardstandings. The site is perfect for visiting the many attractions of the Purbeck area, including the award-winning beaches at Studland and Swanage, and the seaside towns of Poole, Bournemouth and Weymouth. There is also a station at Corfe for the Swanage Steam Railway. The site is pet friendly. 6 acre site. 80 touring pitches. 33 hardstandings. Caravan pitches. Motorhome pitches. Tent pitches.

AA Pubs & Restaurants nearby: The Greyhound Inn, CORFE CASTLE, BH20 5EZ, 01929 480205

The New Inn, CHURCH KNOWLE, BH20 5NQ, 01929 480357

Leisure: ⚠

Facilities: ⚲ ☺ ℱ ⚹ ⚶ Ⓛ ⚶ ⚶ ♻ ⚶

Services: ⚡ ⚶ ⚿ ⚯ ⊤ ⚱ ⚙

Within 3 miles: ⚹ ⚓ ⊟ ℱ ⚹ ♨ ⚶ ⚶ ⚶ ∪

Notes: Site gates closed 23.00hrs-07.00hrs, arrival after 20.00hrs by prior arrangement only. Dogs must be kept on leads.

►►► **80% Woodyhyde Camp Site** *(SY974804)*

Valley Rd BH20 5HT
☎ **01929 480274**
e-mail: camp@woodyhyde.co.uk
dir: *From Corfe Castle towards Swanage on A351, site approx 1m on right*

✻ ⇌ £14 Å £14

Open Mar-Oct

A large grassy campsite in a sheltered location for tents and motorhomes only, set into three paddocks - one is dog free. There is a well-stocked shop on site, a modern toilet and shower block, and a regular bus service that stops near the site entrance. Electric hook-ups and some hardstandings are available. This site offers traditional camping in a great location. 13 acre site. 150 touring pitches. Motorhome pitches. Tent pitches.

AA Pubs & Restaurants nearby: The Greyhound Inn, CORFE CASTLE, BH20 5EZ, 01929 480205

The New Inn, CHURCH KNOWLE, BH20 5NQ, 01929 480357

Facilities: ⚲ ☺ ℱ ⚹ ⚶ ⚶ ♻

Services: ⚡ ⚿ ⚯

Within 3 miles: ⚶ ⚶

Notes: No noise after 23.00hrs, no open fires. Dogs must be kept on leads.

DORCHESTER

See Cerne Abbas

DRIMPTON Map 4 ST40

Places to visit

Forde Abbey, CHARD, TA20 4LU, 01460 221290 www.fordeabbey.co.uk

Mapperton, BEAMINSTER, DT8 3NR, 01308 862645 www.mapperton.com

►►►► 82% *Oathill Farm Touring and Camping Site* *(ST404055)*

Oathill TA18 8PZ
☎ 01460 30234
e-mail: oathillfarm@btconnect.com
dir: *From Crewkerne take B3165. Site on left just after Clapton*

🚐 🚌 ⛺

Open all year

Last arrival 20.00hrs Last departure noon

This small peaceful park borders Somerset and Devon, with the Jurassic Coast at Lyme Regis, Charmouth and Bridport only a short drive away. The modern facilities are spotless and there are hardstandings and fully serviced pitches available. Lucy's Tea Room serves breakfast and meals. Well-stocked, landscaped fishing ponds are now open. Three luxury lodges are available for hire. 10 acre site. 13 touring pitches. 13 hardstandings. 3 seasonal pitches. Caravan pitches. Motorhome pitches. Tent pitches. 3 statics.

AA Pubs & Restaurants nearby: The Wild Garlic, BEAMINSTER, DT8 3AS, 01308 861446

Leisure: ⚽

Facilities: 🚿 ⊙ 💨 ❄ [$] ⛩ 🐕 [WiFi] 💻 ♻ ⓘ

Services: 🔌 🧺 🍷 🔥 ⛽ [T] 🍴 🔋 🍔 🚰

Within 3 miles: ⛳ 🎣 [$] 🧺 U

Notes: No washing lines, no quad bikes, no noise after 23.00hrs. Separate recreational areas.

FERNDOWN Map 5 SU00

Places to visit

Poole Museum, POOLE, BH15 1BW, 01202 262600 www.boroughofpoole.com/museums

Kingston Lacy, WIMBORNE, BH21 4EA, 01202 883402 (Mon-Fri) www.nationaltrust.org.uk

Great for kids: Oceanarium, BOURNEMOUTH, BH2 5AA, 01202 311993 www.oceanarium.co.uk

►►► 78% St Leonards Farm Caravan & Camping Park *(SU093014)*

Ringwood Rd, West Moors BH22 0AQ
☎ 01202 872637
e-mail: enquiries_stleonards@yahoo.co.uk
web: www.stleonardsfarm.biz
dir: *From Ringwood on A31 (dual carriageway) towards Ferndown exit left into slip road at site sign. From Wimborne Minster on A31 at rdbt (junct of A31 & A347) follow signs for Ringwood (A31) (pass Texaco garage on left) to next rdbt. 3rd exit (ie double back towards Ferndown) exit at slip road for site*

* 🚐 £11-£22 🚌 £11-£22 ⛺ £11-£22

Open Apr-Sep

Last departure 14.00hrs

A private road off the A31 leads to this well-screened park divided into paddocks, with spacious pitches; the site now has a children's play fort. This is one of the nearest parks to Bournemouth which has many holiday amenities. 12 acre site. 151 touring pitches. 30 seasonal pitches. Caravan pitches. Motorhome pitches. Tent pitches. 6 statics.

AA Pubs & Restaurants nearby: Les Bouviers Restaurant with Rooms, WIMBORNE MINSTER, BH21 3BD, 01202 889555

Leisure: 🛝

Facilities: 🚿 ⊙ 💨 ❄ ♿ ⛩ ⓘ

Services: 🔌 🧺 🔥 ⛽

Within 3 miles: ⛳ 🎣 [$] 🧺

Notes: No large groups, no noise after 23.00hrs, no disposable BBQs, no gazebos. Dogs must be kept on leads.

HOLTON HEATH Map 4 SY99

Places to visit

Royal Signals Museum, BLANDFORD FORUM, DT11 8RH, 01258 482248 www.royalsignalsmuseum.com

Larmer Tree Gardens, TOLLARD ROYAL, SP5 5PT, 01725 516971 www.larmertreegardens.co.uk

Great for kids: Moors Valley Country Park, RINGWOOD, BH24 2ET, 01425 470721 www.moors-valley.co.uk

85% Sandford Holiday Park *(SY939916)*

Organford Rd BH16 6JZ
☎ 0844 335 3756 & 01202 631600
e-mail: touringandcamping@parkdeanholidays.com
web: www.parkdeantouring.com
dir: *A35 from Poole towards Dorchester, at lights onto A351 towards Wareham. Right at Holton Heath. Site 100yds on left*

* 🚐 £15.50-£42 🚌 £15.50-£42 ⛺ £12.50-£39

Open Mar-Oct (rs 3 May-22 Sep outdoor pool open)

Last arrival 20.00hrs Last departure 10.00hrs

With touring pitches set individually in 20 acres surrounded by woodland, this park offers a full range of leisure activities and entertainment for the whole family. The touring area, situated at the far end of the park, is neat and well maintained, and there are children's clubs in the daytime and nightly entertainment. A reception area with lounge, bar, café and restaurant creates an

continued

HOLTON HEATH *continued*

excellent and attractive entrance, with a covered area outside with tables and chairs and well-landscaped gardens. Static holiday homes are available for hire or purchase. 64 acre site. 353 touring pitches. 20 hardstandings. 78 seasonal pitches. Caravan pitches. Motorhome pitches. Tent pitches. 344 statics.

AA Pubs & Restaurants nearby: Kemps Country House, WAREHAM, BH20 6AL, 0845 8620315

The Greyhound Inn, CORFE CASTLE, BH20 5EZ, 01929 480205

The New Inn, CHURCH KNOWLE, BH20 5NQ, 01929 480357

Leisure: 🏊🏊🎠👣🎾🎱🎵

Facilities: 🛁🏕☀📻☀🔌♿🔥🎪🍴📶🖥️♻🛈

Services: 🔌🛒🍴🔒🧹🚿🚽🏧🧺🚐⛽

Within 3 miles: ⚓🐟♨️🎡⛳◎🛥️🛒🛍️⛵

Notes: No noise after 23.00hrs, no motorised scooters or carts, max 2 dogs per pitch. Dogs must be kept on leads. Bowling, crazy golf, bike hire.

HURN	Map 5 SZ19

Places to visit

Red House Museum & Gardens, CHRISTCHURCH, BH23 1BU, 01202 482860 www.hants.gov.uk/museum/redhouse

Oceanarium, BOURNEMOUTH, BH2 5AA, 01202 311993 www.oceanarium.co.uk

▶▶ **85% Fillybrook Farm Touring Park** *(SZ128997)*

Matchams Ln BH23 6AW
☎ **01202 478266**
e-mail: enquiries@fillybrookfarm.co.uk
web: www.fillybrookfarm.co.uk
dir: M27 junct 1, A31 to Ringwood. Continue towards Poole, left immediately after Texaco Garage signed Verwood & B3081, left into Hurn Ln signed Matchams. Site on right in 4m

🚐🚌🏕

Open Etr-Oct

Last arrival 20.00hrs Last departure 11.00hrs

A small adults-only park well located on the edge of Hurn Forest, with Bournemouth, Christchurch, Poole and the New Forest within easy reach. The facilities are both modern and very clean. A dry-ski slope, with an adjoining restaurant and small

bar, is a short walk from the site. There is also a separate rally field. 1 acre site. 18 touring pitches. Caravan pitches. Motorhome pitches. Tent pitches.

AA Pubs & Restaurants nearby: The Three Tuns, BRANSGORE, BH23 8JH, 01425 672232

Facilities: 🏕☀📻☀♿🔥🐕♻🛈

Services: 🔌🛒🧹🚿

Within 3 miles: ⚓🐟🛒🛍️⛵

Notes: Adults only. 🐕 No large groups, no commercial vehicles. Dogs must be kept on leads.

LYME REGIS	Map 4 SY39

See also Charmouth

Places to visit

Marwood Hill Gardens, BARNSTAPLE, EX31 4EB, 01271 342528 www.marwoodhillgarden.co.uk

Pecorama Pleasure Gardens, BEER, EX12 3NA, 01297 21542 www.pecorama.info

Great for kids: The World of Country Life, EXMOUTH, EX8 5BU, 01395 274533 www.worldofcountrylife.co.uk

▶▶▶▶ **87% Shrubbery Touring Park** *(SY300914)*

Rousdon DT7 3XW
☎ **01297 442227**
e-mail: info@shrubberypark.co.uk
web: www.shrubberypark.co.uk
dir: 3m W of Lyme Regis on A3052 (coast road)

🚐🚌🏕

Open 22 Mar-Oct

Last arrival 21.00hrs Last departure 11.00hrs

Mature trees enclose this peaceful park, which has distant views of the lovely countryside. The modern facilities are well kept, the hardstanding pitches are spacious, and there is plenty of space for children to play in the grounds. This park is right on the Jurassic Coast bus route, which is popular with visitors to this area. 23 acre site. 120

touring pitches. 23 hardstandings. Caravan pitches. Motorhome pitches. Tent pitches.

AA Pubs & Restaurants nearby: Pilot Boat Inn, LYME REGIS, DT7 3QA, 01297 443157

Leisure: 🅿

Facilities: 🏕☀📻☀♿🔥🔌♻🛈

Services: 🔌🛒🧹⛽🚽

Within 3 miles: ⚓♨️🎡🐟◎🛥️🛒🛍️

Notes: No groups (except rallies). No motor scooters, roller skates or skateboards. Dogs must be kept on leads. Crazy golf.

AA CAMPING CARD SITE

▶▶▶ **84% Hook Farm Caravan & Camping Park** *(SY323930)*

Gore Ln, Uplyme DT7 3UU
☎ **01297 442801**
e-mail: information@hookfarm-uplyme.co.uk
dir: A35 onto B3165 towards Lyme Regis & Uplyme at Hunters Lodge pub. In 2m right into Gore Ln, site 400yds on right

🚐 £12-£30 🚌 £12-£30 🏕 £10-£30

Open 15 Mar-Oct (rs Low season shop closed)

Last arrival 20.00hrs Last departure 11.00hrs

Set in a peaceful and very rural location, this popular farm site enjoys lovely views of Lym Valley and is just a mile from the seaside at Lyme Regis. There are modern toilet facilities and good on-site amenities. Most pitches are level due to excellent terracing - a great site for tents but is also suited to motorhomes and caravans. Please note, it is advised that if arriving by motorhome or if towing a caravan that Sat Nav is not used; there are many narrow roads that have few passing places. 5.5 acre site. 100 touring pitches. 4 hardstandings. Caravan pitches. Motorhome pitches. Tent pitches. 17 statics.

AA Pubs & Restaurants nearby: Pilot Boat Inn, LYME REGIS, DT7 3QA, 01297 443157

Leisure: 🅿

Facilities: 🏕☀📻☀♿🕐🛒🔥

Services: 🔌🛒🧹🏧

Within 3 miles: ⚓♨️🎡🐟◎🛥️🛒🛍️⛵

Notes: 🐕 No groups of 6 adults or more, no dangerous dog breeds.

LYTCHETT MATRAVERS
Map 4 SY99

Places to visit

Brownsea Island, BROWNSEA ISLAND, BH13 7EE, 01202 707744
www.nationaltrust.org.uk/brownsea

Poole Museum, POOLE, BH15 1BW, 01202 262600
www.boroughofpoole.com/museums

Great for kids: Swanage Railway, SWANAGE, BH19 1HB, 01929 425800
www.swanagerailway.co.uk

►►► 79% Huntick Farm Caravan Park (SY955947)

Huntick Rd BH16 6BB
☎ 01202 622222
e-mail: huntickcaravans@btconnect.com
dir: *Between Lytchett Minster & Lytchett Matravers. From A31 take A350 towards Poole. Follow Lytchett Minster signs, then Lytchett Matravers signs. Huntick Rd by Rose & Crown pub*

* ⊞ £14.50-£23 ⊞ £14.50-£23 ▲ £14.50-£23

Open Apr-Oct

Last arrival 21.00hrs Last departure noon

A really attractive little park nestling in rural surroundings edged by woodland, a mile from the village amenities of Lytchett Matravers. This neat grassy park is divided into three paddocks offering a peaceful location, yet it is close to the attractions of Poole and Bournemouth. 4 acre site. 30 touring pitches. Caravan pitches. Motorhome pitches. Tent pitches.

AA Pubs & Restaurants nearby: Botany Bay Inne, WINTERBORNE ZELSTON, DT11 9ET, 01929 459227

Leisure: ⚐ ◉

Facilities: ⚑ ⊙ ✳ ☏ ➤ WiFi ♻ ❶

Services: ⚑ ➊ ❚

Within 3 miles: ⚐ ⊞ ∪

Notes: No ball games on site. Dogs must be kept on leads.

LYTCHETT MINSTER
Map 4 SY99

Places to visit

Clouds Hill, BOVINGTON CAMP, BH20 7NQ, 01929 405616 www.nationaltrust.org.uk

Poole Museum, POOLE, BH15 1BW, 01202 262600
www.boroughofpoole.com/museums

Great for kids: Monkey World-Ape Rescue Centre, WOOL, BH20 6HH, 01929 462537
www.monkeyworld.org

AA CAMPING CARD SITE

PREMIER PARK

►►►►► 92% South Lytchett Manor Caravan & Camping Park (SY954926)

Bestof British

Dorchester Rd BH16 6JB
☎ 01202 622577
e-mail: info@southlytchettmanor.co.uk
dir: *Exit A35 onto B3067, 1m E of Lytchett Minster, 600yds on right after village*

⊞ £16.50-£32 ⊞ £16.50-£32 ▲ £32

Open Mar-2 Jan

Last arrival 21.00hrs Last departure 11.00hrs

Situated in the grounds of a historic manor house the park has modern facilities, which are spotless and well maintained. A warm and friendly welcome awaits at this lovely park which is well located for visiting Poole and Bournemouth; the Jurassic X53 bus route (Exeter to Poole) has a stop just outside the park. This park continues to improve each year and there are plans to develop a new area for 2014. 22 acre site. 150 touring pitches. 85 hardstandings. Caravan pitches. Motorhome pitches. Tent pitches.

AA Pubs & Restaurants nearby: The Rising Sun, POOLE, BH15 1NZ, 01202 771246

The Guildhall Tavern, POOLE, BH15 1NB, 01202 671717

Leisure: ⚐ ◉ ☏ ⊡

Facilities: ⚑ ⊙ ☏ ✳ ⚐ ⊙ ⑤ ➤ ➤ WiFi ▣ ♻ ❶

Services: ⚑ ⑤ ➊ ∥ T ☲ ⚐

Within 3 miles: ⚐ ⊞ ∥ ⚐ ⊞ ⑤ ∪

Notes: No camp fires or Chinese lanterns. Dogs must be kept on leads. TV hook-up on all pitches.

ORGANFORD
Map 4 SY99

Places to visit

Tolpuddle Martyrs Museum, TOLPUDDLE, DT2 7EH, 01305 848237 www.tolpuddlemartyrs.org.uk

Kingston Lacy, WIMBORNE, BH21 4EA, 01202 883402 (Mon-Fri)
www.nationaltrust.org.uk

Great for kids: Farmer Palmer's Farm Park, ORGANFORD, BH16 6EU, 01202 622022
www.farmerpalmers.co.uk

►►►► 85% Pear Tree Holiday Park (SY938915)

Organford Rd, Holton Heath BH16 6LA
☎ 01202 622434
e-mail: enquiries@peartreepark.co.uk
web: www.peartreepark.co.uk
dir: *From Poole take A35 towards Dorchester, onto A351 towards Wareham, at 1st lights turn right, site 300yds on left*

⊞ ⊞ ▲

Open Mar-Oct

Last arrival 19.00hrs Last departure 11.00hrs

A quiet, sheltered country park with many colourful flowerbeds, and toilet facilities that offer quality and comfort. The touring area is divided into terraces with mature hedges for screening, with a separate level tenting area on the edge of woodland. The friendly atmosphere at this attractive park helps to ensure a relaxing holiday. A bridle path leads into Wareham Forest. 9 acre site. 154 touring pitches. 82 hardstandings. Caravan pitches. Motorhome pitches. Tent pitches. 40 statics.

AA Pubs & Restaurants nearby: Botany Bay Inne, WINTERBORNE ZELSTON, DT11 9ET, 01929 459227

Leisure: ⚐

Facilities: ⚑ ⊙ ☏ ✳ ⚐ ⊙ ⑤ ➤ WiFi ♻ ❶

Services: ⚑ ⑤ ➊ ∥ T ☲

Within 3 miles: ◉

Notes: No noise after 22.30hrs. Dogs must be kept on leads.

SERVICES: ⚑ Electric hook up ⑤ Launderette ⚑ Licensed bar ➊ Calor Gas ⚐ Camping Gaz T Toilet fluid ⑩ Café/Restaurant ⚏ Fast Food/Takeaway ☲ Battery charging ⚑ Baby care ⚐ Motorvan service point **ABBREVIATIONS:** BH/bank hols-bank holidays Etr-Easter Spring BH-Spring Bank Holiday dep-departure fr-from hrs-hours m-mile mdnt-midnight rdbt-roundabout rs-restricted service wk-week wknd-weekend x-rds-cross roads ⊗ No credit cards ⊗ No dogs ⚑ Children of all ages accepted See page 9 for details of the AA Camping Card Scheme

OWERMOIGNE — Map 4 SY78

Places to visit

RSPB Nature Reserve Radipole Lake, WEYMOUTH, DT4 7TZ, 01305 778313 www.rspb.org.uk

Clouds Hill, BOVINGTON CAMP, BH20 7NQ, 01929 405616 www.nationaltrust.org.uk

Great for kids: Weymouth Sea Life Adventure Park & Marine Sanctuary, WEYMOUTH, DT4 7SX, 0871 423 2110 www.sealifeeurope.com

►►► 80% Sandyholme Holiday Park *(SY768863)*

Moreton Rd DT2 8HZ
☎ **01308 422139 & 426947**
e-mail: holidays@wdlh.co.uk
web: www.wdlh.co.uk
dir: *From A352 (Wareham to Dorchester road) turn right to Owermoigne for 1m. Site on left*

* ⊞ £14.95-£22.55 ⇌ £14.95-£22.55
Å £12-£17.50

Open 21 Mar-2 Nov (rs Etr)

Last arrival 22.00hrs Last departure 11.00hrs

A pleasant quiet site surrounded by trees and within easy reach of the coast at Lulworth Cove, and handy for several seaside resorts, including Weymouth, Portland, Purbeck and Swanage. The facilities are good, including a children's play area, small football pitch, a shop and tourist information. 6 acre site. 46 touring pitches. 20 seasonal pitches. Caravan pitches. Motorhome pitches. Tent pitches. 52 statics.

AA Pubs & Restaurants nearby: The Smugglers Inn, OSMINGTON MILLS, DT3 6HF, 01305 833125

Lulworth Cove Inn, WEST LULWORTH, BH20 5RQ, 01929 400333

The Castle Inn, WEST LULWORTH, BH20 5RN, 01929 400311

Leisure: ⚲ ⬟ ◕ ❧

Facilities: ⌢ ☞ ✳ ⛬ ◐ 🖻 ⊟ ⚑ Wi-Fi ♻ ❶

Services: ⬙🖻 🖻 🗑 ⊘ ⊤ ⬛⬛ 🗘

Within 3 miles: ✐ 🖻🖻

Notes: Dogs must be kept on leads. Table tennis, wildlife lake.

POOLE

See also Lytchett Minster, Organford & Wimborne Minster

Places to visit

Compton Acres Gardens, CANFORD CLIFFS, BH13 7ES, 01202 700778 www.comptonacres.co.uk

Brownsea Island, BROWNSEA ISLAND, BH13 7EE, 01202 707744 www.nationaltrust.org.uk/brownsea

Great for kids: Oceanarium, BOURNEMOUTH, BH2 5AA, 01202 311993 www.oceanarium.co.uk

POOLE — Map 4 SZ09

88% Rockley Park *(SY982909)*

Hamworthy BH15 4LZ
☎ **0871 231 0880**
e-mail: rockleypark@haven.com
web: www.haven.com/rockleypark
dir: *M27 junct 1, A31 to Poole centre, then follow signs to site*

⊞ ⇌ Å

Open mid Mar-end Oct (rs mid Mar-May & Sep-Oct some facilities may be reduced)

Last departure 10.00hrs

A complete holiday experience, including a wide range of day and night entertainment, and plenty of sports and leisure activities, notably watersports. There is also mooring and launching from the park. The touring area has 60 fully serviced pitches and an excellent toilet and shower block. A great base for all the family set in a good location to explore Poole or Bournemouth. 105 holiday homes are available for hire. 90 acre site. 60 touring pitches. 60 hardstandings.

LEISURE: 🏊 Indoor swimming pool 🏊 Outdoor swimming pool ⚲ Children's playground 🎏 Kid's club 🎾 Tennis court 🎱 Games room ▭ Separate TV room ♣ 9/18 hole golf course ⛵ Boats for hire 🎬 Cinema 🎵 Entertainment ✐ Fishing ◉ Mini golf 🏄 Watersports ❧ Gym ◕ Sports field Spa ∪ Stables
FACILITIES: 🛁 Bath ☂ Shower ◉ Electric shaver ☞ Hairdryer ✳ Ice Pack Facility ⛬ Disabled facilities ◐ Public telephone 🖻 Shop on site or within 200yds 🖾 Mobile shop (calls at least 5 days a week) ⬛ BBQ area 🏔 Picnic area Wi-Fi Wi-fi ⬛ Internet access ♻ Recycling ❶ Tourist info ⚑ Dog exercise area

Caravan pitches. Motorhome pitches. Tent pitches. 1077 statics.

AA Pubs & Restaurants nearby: The Rising Sun, POOLE, BH15 1NZ, 01202 771246

The Guildhall Tavern, POOLE, BH15 1NB, 01202 671717

Leisure: Spa

Facilities:

Services:

Within 3 miles:

Notes: No commercial vehicles, no bookings by persons under 21yrs unless a family booking. Max 2 dogs per booking, certain dog breeds banned. Dogs must be kept on leads. Sailing school.

see advert on opposite page

►►► 75% *Beacon Hill Touring Park* *(SY977945)*

Blandford Road North BH16 6AB
☎ 01202 631631
e-mail: bookings@beaconhilltouringpark.co.uk
dir: *On A350, 0.25m N of junct with A35, 3m NW of Poole*

Open Etr-end Oct (rs Low & mid season some services closed/restricted opening)

Last arrival 23.00hrs Last departure 11.00hrs

Set in an attractive, wooded area with conservation very much in mind. There are two large ponds for coarse fishing within the grounds, and the terraced pitches, with fine views, are informally sited so that visitors can choose their favourite spot. The outdoor swimming pool and tennis court are popular during the summer period. 30 acre site. 170 touring pitches. 10 hardstandings. Caravan pitches. Motorhome pitches. Tent pitches.

AA Pubs & Restaurants nearby: The Rising Sun, POOLE, BH15 1NZ, 01202 771246

The Guildhall Tavern, POOLE, BH15 1NB, 01202 671717

Leisure:

Facilities:

Services:

Within 3 miles:

Notes: Groups of young people not accepted during high season.

PORTESHAM — Map 4 SY68

Places to visit

Tutankhamun Exhibition, DORCHESTER, DT1 1UW, 01305 269571 www.tutankhamun-exhibition.co.uk

Maiden Castle, DORCHESTER, DT2 9PP, 0870 333 1181 www.english-heritage.org.uk/daysout/properties/maiden-castle

Great for kids: Teddy Bear Museum, DORCHESTER, DT1 1JU, 01305 266040 www.teddybearmuseum.co.uk

►►►► 80% Portesham Dairy Farm Campsite *(SY602854)*

Weymouth DT3 4HG
☎ 01305 871297
e-mail: info@porteshamdairyfarm.co.uk
dir: *From Dorchester on A35 towards Bridport. In 5m left at Winterbourne Abbas, follow Portesham signs. Through village, left at Kings Arms pub, site 350yds on right*

* £12-£24 £12-£24 £12-£24

Open Apr-Sep

Last arrival 18.30hrs Last departure 11.00hrs

Located at the edge of the picturesque village of Portesham close to the Dorset coast. This family-run, level park is part of a small working farm in a quiet rural location. Fully serviced and seasonal pitches are available. Near the site entrance is a pub where meals are served, and it has a garden for children to play in. 8 acre site. 90 touring pitches. 61 hardstandings. Caravan pitches. Motorhome pitches. Tent pitches.

AA Pubs & Restaurants nearby: The Manor Hotel, WEST BEXINGTON, DT2 9DF, 01308 897660

Leisure:

Facilities:

Services:

Within 3 miles:

Notes: No commercial vehicles, no groups, no camp fires, minimal noise after 22.00hrs. Dogs must be kept on leads. Caravan storage.

PUNCKNOWLE — Map 4 SY58

Places to visit

Dinosaur Museum, DORCHESTER, DT1 1EW, 01305 269880 www.thedinosaurmuseum.com

Hardy's Cottage, DORCHESTER, DT2 8QJ, 01305 262366 www.nationaltrust.org.uk

Great for kids: Abbotsbury Swannery, ABBOTSBURY, DT3 4JG, 01305 871858 www.abbotsbury-tourism.co.uk

►► 86% Home Farm Caravan and Campsite *(SY535887)*

Home Farm, Rectory Ln DT2 9BW
☎ 01308 897258
dir: *From Dorchester towards Bridport on A35, left at start of dual carriageway, at hill bottom right to Litton Cheney. Through village, 2nd left to Puncknowle (Hazel Ln). Left at T-junct, left at phone box. Site 150mtrs on right. Caravan route: approach via A35 Bridport, then Swyre on B3157, continue to Swyre Lane & Rectory Lane*

Open Apr-Oct

Last arrival 21.00hrs (late arrival time by prior arrangement). Last departure noon

This quiet site hidden away on the edge of a little hamlet is an excellent place to camp. It offers sweeping views of the Dorset countryside from most pitches, and is just five miles from Abbotsbury, and one and a half miles from the South West Coast Path. A really good base from which to tour this attractive area. 6.5 acre site. 47 touring pitches. 14 seasonal pitches. Caravan pitches. Motorhome pitches. Tent pitches.

AA Pubs & Restaurants nearby: The Crown Inn, PUNCKNOWLE, DT2 9BN, 01308 897711

The Manor Hotel, WEST BEXINGTON, DT2 9DF, 01308 897660

Facilities:

Services:

Within 3 miles:

Notes: No cats. No wood-burning fires, skateboards, rollerblades, motorised toys or loud music. Dogs must be kept on leads. Calor gas exchange.

ST LEONARDS Map 5 SU10

Places to visit

Rockbourne Roman Villa, ROCKBOURNE, SP6 3PG, 0845 603 5635
www.hants.gov.uk/rockbourne-roman-villa

Red House Museum & Gardens, CHRISTCHURCH, BH23 1BU, 01202 482860
www.hants.gov.uk/museum/redhouse

Great for kids: Moors Valley Country Park, RINGWOOD, BH24 2ET, 01425 470721
www.moors-valley.co.uk

PREMIER PARK

▶▶▶▶▶ 85% Shamba Holidays *(SU105029)*

Best of British GOLD

230 Ringwood Rd BH24 2SB
☎ 01202 873302
e-mail: enquiries@shambaholidays.co.uk
web: www.shambaholidays.co.uk
dir: *From Poole on A31, pass Woodman Pub on left, straight on at rdbt (keep in left lane), immediately left into East Moors Ln. Site 1m on right*

* ☐ £22-£32 ☐ £22-£32 ▲ £22-£32

Shamba Holidays

Open Mar-Oct (rs Low season some facilities open only at wknds)

Last arrival 20.00hrs (late arrivals by prior arrangement only). Last departure 11.00hrs

This top quality park has excellent modern facilities particularly suited to families. You can be certain of a warm welcome from the friendly staff. There is a really good indoor/outdoor heated pool, plus a tasteful bar supplying a good range of meals. The park is well located for visiting the south coast, which is just a short drive away, and also for the New Forest National Park. 7 acre site. 150 touring pitches. 40 seasonal pitches. Caravan pitches. Motorhome pitches. Tent pitches.

AA Pubs & Restaurants nearby: Old Beams Inn, IBSLEY, BH24 3PP, 01425 473387

Leisure: 🏊 🏊 🎢 ⚽ 🔍
Facilities: 🛁 🚿 ⊙ 🖤 ✂ ⚒ 🕐 🛒 🛒 Wi-fi ♻ 🅹
Services: 🅟 🛢 🍴 🚮 🔌 🅣 🍴 🎍 ⛟
Within 3 miles: 🎣 ⛳ 🛒 🅹 🐎

Notes: No large groups or commercial vehicles, no noise after 23.00hrs, . Dogs must be kept on leads. Phone card top-up facility.

see advert below

LEISURE: 🏊 Indoor swimming pool 🏊 Outdoor swimming pool 🎢 Children's playground 👦 Kid's club 🎾 Tennis court 🔍 Games room 📺 Separate TV room 🏌 9/18 hole golf course ⛵ Boats for hire 🎬 Cinema 🎵 Entertainment 🎣 Fishing ◎ Mini golf 🏄 Watersports 🏋 Gym 🅸 Sports field **Spa** ⛎ Stables
FACILITIES: 🛁 Bath 🚿 Shower ⊙ Electric shaver 🖤 Hairdryer ✳ Ice Pack Facility 🚿 Disabled facilities 🕐 Public telephone 🛒 Shop on site or within 200yds 🛒 Mobile shop (calls at least 5 days a week) 🍴 BBQ area 🎍 Picnic area Wi-fi Wi-fi 🖥 Internet access ♻ Recycling 🅹 Tourist info 🐕 Dog exercise area

▶▶▶▶ 83% Back of Beyond Touring Park (SU103034)

234 Ringwood Rd BH24 2SB
☎ 01202 876968
e-mail: melandsuepike@aol.com
web: www.backofbeyondtouringpark.co.uk
dir: *From E: on A31 over Little Chef rdbt, pass St Leonard's Hotel, at next rdbt U-turn into lane immediately left. Site at end of lane. From W: on A31 pass Texaco garage & Woodman Inn, immediately left to site*

* 🚐 £19-£28 🚎 £19-£28 ▲ £19-£28

Open Mar-Oct

Last arrival 19.00hrs Last departure noon

Set well off the beaten track in natural woodland surroundings, with its own river and lake, yet close to many attractions. This tranquil park is run by keen, friendly owners, and the quality facilities are for adults only. There is river and lake fishing, a 9-hole pitch and putt course, boules and many woodland walks. This park is a haven for wildlife. 28 acre site. 80 touring pitches. 40 seasonal pitches. Caravan pitches. Motorhome pitches. Tent pitches.

AA Pubs & Restaurants nearby: Old Beams Inn, IBSLEY, BH24 3PP, 01425 473387

Facilities: ⬤⊙🅟✳☂☖🗗🛒♲ ❶

Services: 🔌🔲🛢⌀🅃🎫🔼

Within 3 miles: ↕🎣⊚🔟🔟ᚹ

Notes: Adults only. No commercial vehicles.

▶▶▶ 79% Forest Edge Touring Park (SU104024)

229 Ringwood Rd BH24 2SD
☎ 01590 648331
e-mail: holidays@shorefield.co.uk
dir: *From E: on A31 over 1st rdbt (Little Chef), pass St Leonards Hotel, left at next rdbt into Boundary Ln, site 100yds on left. From W: on A31 pass Texaco garage & Woodman Inn, right at rdbt into Boundary Ln*

* 🚐 £12.50-£40.50 🚎 £12.50-£40.50
▲ £10.50-£40.50

Open Feb-3 Jan (rs School & summer hols pool open)

Last arrival 21.00hrs Last departure 10.00hrs

A tree-lined park set in grassland with plenty of excellent amenities for all the family, including an outdoor heated swimming pool and toddlers' pool, an adventure playground and two launderettes. Visitors are invited to use the superb leisure club plus all amenities and entertainment at the sister site of Oakdene Forest Park, which is less than a mile away. Holiday homes are available for hire. 9 acre site. 72 touring pitches. 29 seasonal pitches. Caravan pitches. Motorhome pitches. Tent pitches. 30 statics.

AA Pubs & Restaurants nearby: Old Beams Inn, IBSLEY, BH24 3PP, 01425 473387

Leisure: ⚓ ⚙ 🔍

Facilities: ⬤⊙🅟✳🕒🔟♲ ❶

Services: 🔌🔲🛢⌀🅃

Within 3 miles: ↕🎣⊚🔟🔟ᚹ

Notes: Families & couples only, rallies welcome. 1 car & 1 dog per pitch, no gazebos, no noise after 22.00hrs. Dogs must be kept on leads.

see advert on page 203

SHAFTESBURY Map 4 ST82

Places to visit

Shaftesbury Abbey Museum & Garden, SHAFTESBURY, SP7 8JR, 01747 852910
www.shaftesburyabbey.org.uk

Royal Signals Museum, BLANDFORD FORUM, DT11 8RH, 01258 482248
www.royalsignalsmuseum.com

Great for kids: Sherborne Castle, SHERBORNE, DT9 5NR, 01935 812072
www.sherbornecastle.com

▶▶▶▶ 78% *Blackmore Vale Caravan & Camping Park* (ST835233)

Sherborne Causeway SP7 9PX
☎ 01747 851523 & 01225 290924
e-mail: info@dche.co.uk
dir: *From Shaftesbury's Ivy Cross rdbt take A30 signed Sherborne. Site 2m on right*

🚐🚎▲

Open all year

Last arrival 21.00hrs

This developing touring park now has a refurbished toilet and shower block, a fishing lake and a gym, plus an excellent and growing glamping section which includes tipis, yurts, shepherd huts, bell tents and a camping pod. Special activities take place such as wine tasting, paint balling etc. There are also static homes for hire. 5 acre site. 26 touring pitches. 6 hardstandings. Caravan pitches. Motorhome pitches. Tent pitches. 20 statics. 6 tipis. 8 bell tents/yurts. 1 wooden pod.

AA Pubs & Restaurants nearby: The Kings Arms Inn, GILLINGHAM, SP8 5NB, 01747 838325

The Coppleridge Inn, MOTCOMBE, SP7 9HW, 01747 851980

Leisure: 🏌

Facilities: ⬤⊙🅟✳☖🕒🔟🗗🛒♲ ❶

Services: 🔌🔲🛢⌀🅃🎫🏪

Within 3 miles: 🎣🔟ᚹ

Notes: No noise after mdnt. Dogs must be kept on leads. Caravan sales & accessories.

SERVICES: 🔌 Electric hook up 🔲 Launderette 🍺 Licensed bar 🛢 Calor Gas ⌀ Camping Gaz 🅃 Toilet fluid 🍽 Café/Restaurant 🏪 Fast Food/Takeaway 🔼 Battery charging 🍼 Baby care 🚿 Motorvan service point **ABBREVIATIONS:** BH/bank hols-bank holidays Etr-Easter Spring BH-Spring Bank Holiday dep-departure fr-from hrs-hours m-mile mdnt-midnight rdbt-roundabout rs-restricted service wk-week wknd-weekend x-rds-cross roads 🏧 No credit cards 🚫 No dogs 👶 Children of all ages accepted See page 9 for details of the AA Camping Card Scheme

SIXPENNY HANDLEY · Map 4 ST91

Places to visit

Larmer Tree Gardens, TOLLARD ROYAL, SP5 5PT, 01725 516971 www.larmertreegardens.co.uk

Shaftesbury Abbey Museum & Garden, SHAFTESBURY, SP7 8JR, 01747 852910 www.shaftesburyabbey.org.uk

Great for kids: Moors Valley Country Park, RINGWOOD, BH24 2ET, 01425 470721 www.moors-valley.co.uk

►►►► 85% Church Farm Caravan & Camping Park (ST994173)

The Bungalow, Church Farm, High St SP5 5ND
☎ 01725 552563 & 07766 677525
e-mail: churchfarmcandcpark@yahoo.co.uk
dir: 1m S of Handley Hill rdbt. Exit for Sixpenny Handley, right by school, site 300yds by church

* ⬜ £16-£19 ⬜ £16-£19 ▲ £16-£19

Open all year (rs Nov-Mar 10 vans max)

Last arrival 21.00hrs Last departure 11.00hrs

A spacious park located within the Cranborne Chase Area of Outstanding Natural Beauty; the site is split into several camping areas including one for adults only. There is a first-class facility block with good private facilities and an excellent café/restaurant. The pretty village of Sixpenny Handley with all its amenities is just 200 yards away, and the site is well positioned for visiting the New Forest National Park, Bournemouth, Poole and Stonehenge. 10 acre site. 35 touring pitches. 4 hardstandings. 5 seasonal pitches. Caravan pitches. Motorhome pitches. Tent pitches. 2 statics.

AA Pubs & Restaurants nearby: The Museum Inn, FARNHAM, DT11 8DE, 01725 516261

The Drovers Inn, GUSSAGE ALL SAINTS, BH21 5ET, 01258 840084

Leisure: 🅰
Facilities: 🌣⊙✳⬡⬚🚿📶♻🛈
Services: ⬜⬜⬜⬜⬜⬜⬜⬜⬜⬜⬜
Within 3 miles: ⬜⬜

Notes: Quiet after 23.00hrs. Dogs must be kept on leads. Use of fridge/freezer & microwave.

SWANAGE · Map 5 SZ07

Places to visit

Corfe Castle, CORFE CASTLE, BH20 5EZ, 01929 481294 www.nationaltrust.org.uk

Brownsea Island, BROWNSEA ISLAND, BH13 7EE, 01202 707744 www.nationaltrust.org.uk/brownsea

Great for kids: Swanage Railway, SWANAGE, BH19 1HB, 01929 425800 www.swanagerailway.co.uk

PREMIER PARK

►►►►► 81% *Ulwell Cottage Caravan Park* (SZ019809)

Ulwell Cottage, Ulwell BH19 3DG
☎ 01929 422823
e-mail: enq@ulwellcottagepark.co.uk
web: www.ulwellcottagepark.co.uk
dir: From Swanage N for 2m on unclassified road towards Studland

⬜⬜▲

Open Mar-7 Jan (rs Mar-Spring BH & mid Sep-early Jan takeaway closed, shop open variable hrs)

Last arrival 22.00hrs Last departure 11.00hrs

Nestling under the Purbeck Hills and surrounded by scenic walks, this park is only two miles from the beach. This is a family-run park that caters well for families and couples, and offers a toilet and shower block complete with good family rooms, all appointed to a high standard. There are new fully serviced pitches, a good indoor swimming pool and the village inn offers a good range of meals. 13 acre site. 77 touring pitches. 19 hardstandings. Caravan pitches. Motorhome pitches. Tent pitches. 140 statics.

AA Pubs & Restaurants nearby: The Bankes Arms Hotel, STUDLAND, BH19 3AU, 01929 450225

The Square and Compass, WORTH MATRAVERS, BH19 3LF, 01929 439229

Leisure: 🅰🅰🅰
Facilities: 🌣⊙📺✳⬚🚿🛒📶♻🛈
Services: ⬜⬜⬜⬜⬜⬜⬜⬜
Within 3 miles: ⬜⬜⬜⬜⬜⊙⬜⬜⬜⬜

Notes: No bonfires or fireworks. Dogs must be kept on leads.

►►► 77% Herston Caravan & Camping Park (SZ018785)

Washpond Ln BH19 3DJ
☎ 01929 422932
e-mail: office@herstonleisure.co.uk
dir: From Wareham on A351 towards Swanage. Washpond Ln on left just after 'Welcome to Swanage' sign

* ⬜ £25-£45 ⬜ £20-£45 ▲ £15-£42

Open all year

Set in a rural area, with extensive views of the Purbecks, this tree-lined park has fully serviced pitches plus large camping areas. Herston Halt is within walking distance, a stop for the famous Swanage steam railway between the town centre and Corfe Castle. There are also yurts available for hire. 10 acre site. 100 touring pitches. 71 hardstandings. Caravan pitches. Motorhome pitches. Tent pitches. 5 statics. 6 bell tents/yurts.

AA Pubs & Restaurants nearby: The Bankes Arms Hotel, STUDLAND, BH19 3AU, 01929 450225

The Square and Compass, WORTH MATRAVERS, BH19 3LF, 01929 439229

Leisure: 🅰
Facilities: 🌣⊙📺✳⬚🚿📶♻🛈
Services: ⬜⬜⬜⬜⬜⬜⬜⬜⬜
Within 3 miles: ⬜⬜⬜⬜⊙⬜⬜⬜⬜

Notes: No noise after 23.00hrs. Dogs must be kept on leads.

LEISURE: 🅰 Indoor swimming pool 🅰 Outdoor swimming pool 🅰 Children's playground 🅰 Kid's club 🅰 Tennis court 🅰 Games room 🅰 Separate TV room 🅰 9/18 hole golf course 🅰 Boats for hire 🅰 Cinema 🅰 Entertainment 🅰 Fishing 🅰 Mini golf 🅰 Watersports 🅰 Gym 🅰 Sports field Spa 🅰 Stables
FACILITIES: 🅰 Bath 🅰 Shower ⊙ Electric shaver 🅰 Hairdryer ✳ Ice Pack Facility 🅰 Disabled facilities 🅰 Public telephone 🅰 Shop on site or within 200yds 🅰 Mobile shop (calls at least 5 days a week) 🅰 BBQ area 🅰 Picnic area 📶 Wi-fi 🅰 Internet access ♻ Recycling 🛈 Tourist info 🅰 Dog exercise area

▶▶ 74% Acton Field Camping Site

(SY991785)

Acton Field, Langton Matravers BH19 3HS
☎ 01929 424184 & 439424
e-mail: enquiries@actonfieldcampsite.co.uk
dir: *From A351 right after Corfe Castle onto B3069 to Langton Matravers, 2nd right after village sign (bridleway)*

⊞ £14 ⊞ £14 ▲ £8-£14

Open mid Jul-early Sep (rs Apr-Oct open for organised groups)

Last arrival 22.00hrs Last departure noon

The informal campsite, bordered by farmland on the outskirts of Langton Matravers, with good upgraded toilet facilities. There are superb views of the Purbeck Hills and towards the Isle of Wight, and a footpath leads to the coastal path. The site occupies what was once a stone quarry so rock pegs may be required. 7 acre site. 80 touring pitches. Caravan pitches. Motorhome pitches. Tent pitches.

AA Pubs & Restaurants nearby: The Bankes Arms Hotel, STUDLAND, BH19 3AU, 01929 450225

The Square and Compass, WORTH MATRAVERS, BH19 3LF, 01929 439229

Acton Field Camping Site

Facilities: ⬏ ☉ ✱ ⦿ ♻

Services: ⬛

Within 3 miles: ⬇ ⇞ ↗ ◎ ⩪ 🏠 ⬚ ∪

Notes: ⊘ No open fires, no noise after mdnt. Dogs must be kept on leads.

THREE LEGGED CROSS

Places to visit

Portland Castle, PORTLAND, DT5 1AZ, 01305 820539 www.english-heritage.org.uk/daysout/properties/portland-castle

Moors Valley Country Park, RINGWOOD, BH24 2ET, 01425 470721 www.moors-valley.co.uk

Great for kids: Monkey World-Ape Rescue Centre, WOOL, BH20 6HH, 01929 462537 www.monkeyworld.org

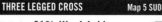

THREE LEGGED CROSS   Map 5 SU00

▶▶▶▶ 81% *Woolsbridge Manor Farm Caravan Park*

(SU099052)

BH21 6RA
☎ 01202 826369
e-mail: woolsbridge@btconnect.com
web: www.woolsbridgemanorcaravanpark.co.uk
dir: *From Ringwood take A31 westward. Approx 1m follow signs for Three Legged Cross & Horton. Site 2m on right*

⊞ ⊞ ▲

Open Mar-Oct

Last arrival 20.00hrs Last departure 10.30hrs

A small farm site with spacious pitches on a level field. This quiet site is an excellent central base

continued

Woolsbridge Manor Farm Caravan Park is modern and well-equipped, with all the facilities expected in a first-rate caravan park including:
● toilets
● showers and basins with hot and cold water
● a baby changing/washing area plus hair dryer
● a separate show/basin/toilet room for disabled use, which may also be used by families.
● laundry room with washing machine, deep sink, and iron
● washing-up room
The cleanliness of these facilities is a priority for the team.

THREE LEGGED CROSS *continued*

for touring the New Forest, Salisbury and the south coast, and is close to Moors Valley Country Park for outdoor family activities. Facilities are good and very clean and there are excellent family rooms available. 6.75 acre site. 60 touring pitches. Caravan pitches. Motorhome pitches. Tent pitches.

AA Pubs & Restaurants nearby: Old Beams Inn, IBSLEY, BH24 3PP, 01425 473387

Woolsbridge Manor Farm Caravan Park

Leisure: /Λ\
Facilities: ☊ ☉ ℙ ☼ ♿ ⓢ 🏛 🚑 ♻ ❶
Services: ⊡ ⓢ ⬚ ∅ 🆃 ⛽
Within 3 miles: ↧ ℙ 🆂 🆂 ∪
Notes: Dogs must be kept on leads.

see advert on page 195

WAREHAM   Map 4 SY98

Places to visit
Compton Acres Gardens, CANFORD CLIFFS, BH13 7ES, 01202 700778
www.comptonacres.co.uk

Brownsea Island, BROWNSEA ISLAND, BH13 7EE, 01202 707744
www.nationaltrust.org.uk/brownsea

Great for kids: Oceanarium, BOURNEMOUTH, BH2 5AA, 01202 311993 www.oceanarium.co.uk

---

PREMIER PARK

►►►►►► 93%
Wareham Forest Tourist Park *(SY894912)*

North Trigon BH20 7NZ
☎ 01929 551393
e-mail: holiday@warehamforest.co.uk
dir: *From A35 between Bere Regis & Lytchett Minster follow Wareham sign into Sugar Hill. Site on left*

🚐 🚗 ▲

Open all year (rs Off-peak season limited services)

Last arrival 21.00hrs Last departure 11.00hrs

A woodland park within the tranquil Wareham Forest, with its many walks and proximity to Poole, Dorchester and the Purbeck coast. Two luxury blocks, with combined washbasin and toilets for total privacy, are maintained to a high standard of cleanliness. A heated outdoor swimming pool, off licence, shop and games room add to the pleasure of a stay on this top quality park. 55 acre site. 200 touring pitches. 70 hardstandings. 70 seasonal pitches. Caravan pitches. Motorhome pitches. Tent pitches.

AA Pubs & Restaurants nearby: Kemps Country House, WAREHAM, BH20 6AL, 0845 8620315

The Greyhound Inn, CORFE CASTLE, BH20 5EZ, 01929 480205

The New Inn, CHURCH KNOWLE, BH20 5NQ, 01929 480357

Leisure: ♨ /Λ\ ☖
Facilities: ☊ ☉ ℙ ☼ ♿ ⓢ 🏛 🚑 📶 ♻ ❶
Services: ⊡ ⓢ ⬚ ∅ 🆃 ⛽ ⛽
Within 3 miles: ↧ ⅏ 日 ℙ 🆂 🆂 ∪

Notes: Families & couples only, no group bookings. Dogs must be kept on leads.

LEISURE: ☜ Indoor swimming pool ☜ Outdoor swimming pool /Λ\ Children's playground ☝ Kid's club ☖ Tennis court ☖ Games room ☐ Separate TV room ↧ 9/18 hole golf course ☜ Boats for hire 目 Cinema ♫ Entertainment ℙ Fishing ◎ Mini golf ☜ Watersports ☝ Gym ☖ Sports field **Spa** ∪ Stables
FACILITIES: ☝ Bath ☊ Shower ☉ Electric shaver ℙ Hairdryer ☼ Ice Pack Facility ♿ Disabled facilities ☍ Public telephone 🏛 Shop on site or within 200yds 🛒 Mobile shop (calls at least 5 days a week) ▦ BBQ area 🚑 Picnic area 📶 Wi-fi 目 Internet access ♻ Recycling ❶ Tourist info 🐾 Dog exercise area

►►►► 80% Birchwood Tourist Park

(SY896905)

Bere Rd, Coldharbour BH20 7PA
☎ **01929 554763**
e-mail: birchwoodtouristpark@hotmail.com
dir: From Poole (A351) or Dorchester (A352) on N side of railway line at Wareham, follow Bere Regis signs (unclassified). 2nd park after 2.25m

Open 13 Dec-23 Nov (rs 31 Oct-1 Mar shop/reception open for 2-3 hrs daily)

Last arrival 21.00hrs Last departure 11.30hrs

Set in 50 acres of parkland located within Wareham Forest, this site offers direct access into ideal areas for walking, mountain biking, and horse and pony riding. This is a spacious open park with plenty of room for young people to play games or football. The modern facilities are in two central locations and are very clean. There is a good security barrier system. 25 acre site. 175 touring pitches. 25 hardstandings. Caravan pitches. Motorhome pitches. Tent pitches.

AA Pubs & Restaurants nearby: Kemps Country House, WAREHAM, BH20 6AL, 0845 8620315

The Greyhound Inn, CORFE CASTLE, BH20 5EZ, 01929 480205

The New Inn, CHURCH KNOWLE, BH20 5NQ, 01929 480357

Leisure: 🅰 😊 🔍
Facilities: 🌂 ☉ ℱ ☀ ☺ ⓢ 🎏 📶 ♻ ❶
Services: 🔌 ⓢ 🔋 ⊘ Ⓣ 🛒 ⛽

Within 3 miles: ⌶ ☇ 日 ℒ ⓢ

Notes: No groups on BH. No generators or camp fires. Dogs must be kept on leads. Pitch & putt, paddling pool.

see advert on opposite page

►►► 86% Lookout Holiday Park

(SY927858)

Stoborough BH20 5AZ
☎ **01929 552546**
e-mail: enquiries@caravan-sites.co.uk
web: www.thelookoutholidaypark.co.uk
dir: Take A351 through Wareham, after crossing River Frome & through Stoborough, site signed on left

Open Mar-Dec (No touring/camping 4 Jan-22 Mar)

Last arrival 22.00hrs Last departure noon

Divided into two paddocks and set well back from the Swanage road, this touring park is separated from the static part of the operation (32 static holiday homes are for hire). There are very good facilities including a newly refurbished toilet block and three new camping pods, while a superb children's playground and plenty of other attractions make this an ideal centre for families. The site is very convenient for visiting Corfe and Swanage. 15 acre site. 150 touring pitches. 99 hardstandings. Caravan pitches. Motorhome pitches. Tent pitches. 89 statics. Wooden pods.

AA Pubs & Restaurants nearby: Kemps Country House, WAREHAM, BH20 6AL, 0845 8620315

The Greyhound Inn, CORFE CASTLE, BH20 5EZ, 01929 480205

The New Inn, CHURCH KNOWLE, BH20 5NQ, 01929 480357

Lookout Holiday Park

Leisure: 🅰 🔍
Facilities: 🌂 ☉ ℱ ☀ ⓢ ⓢ 📶 ♻ ❶
Services: 🔌 ⓢ 🔋 ⊘ Ⓣ ⛽ 🍴 🛒
Within 3 miles: ⌶ ☇ 日 ℒ ⓢ ⓢ ∪

Notes: No pets.

see advert on page 198

NEW ►►► 85% Norden Farm Touring Caravan and Camping Site

(SY950828)

Norden Farm, Corfe Castle BH20 5DS
☎ **01929 480098 & 07790 612426**
e-mail: campsite@nordenfarm.com
dir: On A351 Wareham to Swanage Road, 0.75m before Corfe Castle, 3.5m from Wareham

* 🚐 £14-£20.50 🚌 £14-£20.50 ⛺ £9.50-£13.50

Open Mar-Oct

Last arrival 22.00hrs Last departure 11.00hrs

This delightful farm site offers traditional camping but with excellent toilet and shower facilities. It is a very dog-friendly site and is ideally suited for those who enjoy country pursuits. Its location very close to Corfe Castle also makes it very convenient for visiting Swanage or the Isle of Purbeck. There is also an excellent AA listed Bed & Breakfast operation (with a restaurant – open to all), plus a holiday cottage for hire. 10 acre site. 140 touring pitches. variable seasonal pitches. Caravan pitches. Motorhome pitches. Tent pitches.

AA Pubs & Restaurants nearby: Kemps Country House, WAREHAM, BH20 6AL, 0845 8620315

Leisure: 🅰
Facilities: 🌂 ☉ ℱ ☀ ☺ ⓢ 📶 ♻ ❶
Services: 🔌 ⓢ 🔋 ⊘ Ⓣ 🍴 🛒 ⛽
Within 3 miles: ⌶ ☇ 日 ℒ ⓢ ⓢ

Notes: Strict speed limit of 10mph on site, no noise after 23.00hrs. Dogs must be kept on leads. Hot shower washroom for dogs.

SERVICES: 🔌 Electric hook up ⓢ Launderette 🍺 Licensed bar 🔋 Calor Gas ⊘ Camping Gaz Ⓣ Toilet fluid 🍴 Café/Restaurant 🍟 Fast Food/Takeaway 🛒 Battery charging 👶 Baby care ⛽ Motorvan service point **ABBREVIATIONS:** BH/bank hols-bank holidays Etr-Easter Spring BH-Spring Bank Holiday dep-departure fr-from hrs-hours m-mile mdnt-midnight rdbt-roundabout rs-restricted service wk-week wknd-weekend x-rds-cross roads No credit cards No dogs Children of all ages accepted See page 9 for details of the AA Camping Card Scheme

WAREHAM *continued*

►►► 82% East Creech Farm Campsite *(SY928827)*

East Creech Farm, East Creech BH20 5AP
☎ **01929 480519 & 481312**
e-mail: east.creech@virgin.net
dir: *From Wareham on A351 S towards Swanage. On bypass at 3rd rdbt take Furzebrook/Blue Pool Rd exit, approx 2m site on right*

* 🚐 £12-£19.50 🚐 £12-£19.50 Å £12-£19.50

Open Apr-Oct

Last arrival 20.00hrs Last departure noon

A grassy park set in a peaceful location beneath the Purbeck Hills, with extensive views towards Poole and Brownsea Island. The park boasts a woodland play area, bright, clean toilet facilities and a farm shop selling milk, eggs and bread. There are also three coarse fishing lakes teeming with fish. The park is close to Norden Station on the Swanage to Norden steam railway, and is well located for visiting Corfe Castle, Swanage and the Purbeck coast. 4 acre site. 80 touring pitches. Caravan pitches. Motorhome pitches. Tent pitches.

AA Pubs & Restaurants nearby: Kemps Country House, WAREHAM, BH20 6AL, 0845 8620315

The Greyhound Inn, CORFE CASTLE, BH20 5EZ, 01929 480205

The New Inn, CHURCH KNOWLE, BH20 5NQ, 01929 480357

Leisure: ⚠
Facilities: ⌐⊙☞✳♻ *ℹ*
Services: 🚐🔯
Within 3 miles: ⌁≗日⌒🔯🔯
Notes: No camp fires, no loud noise. Dogs must be kept on leads.

►►► 78% *Ridge Farm Camping & Caravan Park (SY939868)*

Barnhill Rd, Ridge BH20 5BG
☎ **01929 556444**
e-mail: info@ridgefarm.co.uk
web: www.ridgefarm.co.uk
dir: *From Wareham take B3075 towards Corfe Castle, cross river to Stoborough, then left to Ridge. Follow site signs for 1.5m*

🚐 🚐 Å

Open Etr-Sep

Last arrival 21.00hrs Last departure noon

A quiet rural park, adjacent to a working farm and surrounded by trees and bushes. This away-from-it-all park is ideally located for touring this part of Dorset, and especially for birdwatchers, or those who enjoy walking and cycling. This site is perfect for visiting the Arne Nature Reserve. 3.47 acre site. 60 touring pitches. 2 hardstandings. Caravan pitches. Motorhome pitches. Tent pitches.

AA Pubs & Restaurants nearby: Kemps Country House, WAREHAM, BH20 6AL, 0845 8620315

The Greyhound Inn, CORFE CASTLE, BH20 5EZ, 01929 480205

The New Inn, CHURCH KNOWLE, BH20 5NQ, 01929 480357

Facilities: ⌐⊙☞✳🕔🔯♻ *ℹ*
Services: 🚐🔯🔋⌀🔲🎪
Within 3 miles: ⌁≗日⌒🔯🔯U
Notes: 🚫 No dogs Jul-Aug. Dogs must be kept on leads.

WEYMOUTH

Places to visit

RSPB Nature Reserve Radipole Lake, WEYMOUTH, DT4 7TZ, 01305 778313 www.rspb.org.uk

Portland Castle, PORTLAND, DT5 1AZ, 01305 820539 www.english-heritage.org.uk/daysout/properties/portland-castle

Great for kids: Weymouth Sea Life Adventure Park & Marine Sanctuary, WEYMOUTH, DT4 7SX, 0871 423 2110 www.sealifeeurope.com

---

LEISURE: 🏊 Indoor swimming pool 🏊 Outdoor swimming pool ⚠ Children's playground 🎣 Kid's club 🎾 Tennis court ⚫ Games room ☐ Separate TV room ⌁ 9/18 hole golf course ⚓ Boats for hire 🎬 Cinema 🎵 Entertainment 🎣 Fishing ⚫ Mini golf 🏄 Watersports 🏋 Gym ⚽ Sports field **Spa** U Stables **FACILITIES:** 🛁 Bath ⌐ Shower ⊙ Electric shaver ☞ Hairdryer ✳ Ice Pack Facility ♿ Disabled facilities 🕔 Public telephone 🔯 Shop on site or within 200yds 🔯 Mobile shop (calls at least 5 days a week) 🍖 BBQ area 🎪 Picnic area **Wi-fi** Wi-fi 🌐 Internet access ♻ Recycling *ℹ* Tourist info 🐕 Dog exercise area

WEYMOUTH   Map 4 SY67

86% Littlesea Holiday Park (SY654783)

Lynch Ln DT4 9DT

☎ 0871 231 0879

e-mail: littlesea@haven.com

web: www.haven.com/littlesea

dir: *A35 onto A354 signed Weymouth. Right at 1st rdbt, 3rd exit at 2nd rdbt towards Chickerell. Left into Lynch Lane after lights. Site at far end of road*

Open end Mar-end Oct (rs end Mar-May & Sep-Oct facilities may be reduced)

Last arrival mdnt Last departure 10.00hrs

Just three miles from Weymouth with its lovely beaches and many attractions, Littlesea has a cheerful family atmosphere and fantastic facilities. Indoor and outdoor entertainment and activities are on offer for all the family, and the toilet facilities on the touring park are of a good quality. The touring section of this holiday complex is at the far end of the site adjacent to the South West Coast Path in a perfect location. 100 acre site. 120 touring pitches. Caravan pitches. Motorhome pitches. Tent pitches. 720 statics.

AA Pubs & Restaurants nearby: The Old Ship Inn, WEYMOUTH, DT3 5QQ, 01305 812522

Leisure: 🏊 ⛱ ♨ 🏑 ♨ 🎯 🎣 🎵

Facilities: 🔦 ⚙ 🅿 ✳ ⚙ 🔥 🚿 🛒 🔥 🛒 WiFi ♻ ❶

Services: 🔌 🔄 🍽 💧 🚽 🍴 🏪 🚮

Within 3 miles: ⚓ ✈ 🎱 🎣 ⚙ ◎ 🚴 🏌 U

Notes: No commercial vehicles, no bookings by persons under 21yrs unless a family booking, no boats. Max 2 dogs per booking, certain dog breeds banned.

see advert below

83% Seaview Holiday Park (SY707830)

Preston DT3 6DZ

☎ 0871 231 0877

e-mail: seaview@haven.com

web: www.haven.com/seaview

dir: *A354 to Weymouth, follow signs for Preston/ Wareham onto A353. Site 3m on right just after Weymouth Bay Holiday Park*

Open mid Mar-end Oct (rs mid Mar-May & Sep-Oct facilities may be reduced)

Last arrival mdnt Last departure 10.00hrs

A fun-packed holiday centre for all the family, with plenty of activities and entertainment during the day and evening. Terraced pitches are provided for caravans, and there is a separate field for tents. The park is close to Weymouth and other coastal attractions. There's a smart toilet and shower block, plus fully serviced hardstanding pitches. Holiday homes available for hire. 20 acre site. 87 touring pitches. 24 hardstandings. Caravan pitches. Motorhome pitches. Tent pitches. 259 statics.

AA Pubs & Restaurants nearby: The Old Ship Inn, WEYMOUTH, DT3 5QQ, 01305 812522

The Smugglers Inn, OSMINGTON MILLS, DT3 6HF, 01305 833125

Leisure: 🏊 ⛱ ♨ ⚽ 🎯 🎵

Facilities: 🚿 🔦 ⚙ 🅿 ⚙ 🔥 🚿 🛒 🔥 WiFi ♻ ❶

Services: 🔌 🔄 🍽 💧 🍴 🏪 🚮

Within 3 miles: ⚓ ✈ 🎱 🎣 ⚙ ◎ 🚴 🏌 U

Notes: No commercial vehicles, no bookings by persons under 21yrs unless a family booking. Max 2 dogs per booking, certain dog breeds banned. Dogs must be kept on leads.

see advert on page 200

SERVICES: 🔌 Electric hook up 🔄 Launderette 🍽 Licensed bar 🔥 Calor Gas ⚗ Camping Gaz 🚽 Toilet fluid 🍴 Café/Restaurant 🏪 Fast Food/Takeaway 🔋 Battery charging 🚮 Baby care 🚐 Motorvan service point **ABBREVIATIONS:** BH/bank hols-bank holidays Etr-Easter Spring BH-Spring Bank Holiday dep-departure fr-from hrs-hours m-mile mdnt-midnight rdbt-roundabout rs-restricted service wk-week wknd-weekend x-rds-cross roads ⓝ No credit cards ⊗ No dogs 👶 Children of all ages accepted See page 9 for details of the AA Camping Card Scheme

WEYMOUTH *continued*

PREMIER PARK

▶▶▶▶▶ 88% **East Fleet Farm Touring Park** *(SY640797)*

Chickerell DT3 4DW
☎ 01305 785768
e-mail: enquiries@eastfleet.co.uk
dir: *On B3157 (Weymouth to Bridport road), 3m from Weymouth*

* ⊕ £17-£25 ⊕ £17-£25 ▲ £17-£25

Open 16 Mar-Oct

Last arrival 22.00hrs Last departure 10.30hrs

Set on a working organic farm overlooking Fleet Lagoon and Chesil Beach, with a wide range of amenities and quality toilet facilities, with family rooms, housed in a Scandinavian log cabin and facility block. The friendly owners, over 25 years at the park, are welcoming and helpful, and their family bar serving meals and takeaway food is open from Easter and has glorious views from the patio area. There is also a good accessory shop. 21 acre site. 400 touring pitches. 90 hardstandings. 40 seasonal pitches. Caravan pitches. Motorhome pitches. Tent pitches.

AA Pubs & Restaurants nearby: The Old Ship Inn, WEYMOUTH, DT3 5QQ, 01305 812522

Leisure: ⚠ ⚙ 🔍
Facilities: 🖤 🏕 ⊙ 🅿 ✲ 🔥 🕙 🖇 🚿 🚻 WiFi 🖥 ♻ 🔋
Services: 🔋🔼 🍴🔟🍽 🚮 ⬇
Within 3 miles: ♪ ⛷ ⚲ 🦶 ◎ ⛤ 🛒🔋 ∪
Notes: Dogs must be kept on leads.

▶▶▶▶ 85% **Bagwell Farm Touring Park** *(SY627816)*

Knights in the Bottom, Chickerell DT3 4EA
☎ 01305 782575
e-mail: aa@bagwellfarm.co.uk
web: www.bagwellfarm.co.uk
dir: *From A354 follow signs for Weymouth town centre, then B3157 to Chickerell & Abbotsbury, 1m past Chickerell left into site 500yds after Victoria Inn*

⊕ 🚐 ▲

Open all year (rs Winter bar closed)

Last arrival 21.00hrs Last departure 11.00hrs

This well located park is set in a small valley with access to the South West Coast Path and is very convenient for visiting Weymouth and Portland. It has excellent facilities including a good shop, pets' corner, children's play area plus the Red Barn bar and restaurant. 14 acre site. 320 touring pitches. 25 hardstandings. 70 seasonal pitches. Caravan pitches. Motorhome pitches. Tent pitches.

AA Pubs & Restaurants nearby: The Old Ship Inn, WEYMOUTH, DT3 5QQ, 01305 812522

Leisure: ⚠
Facilities: 🖤 🏕 ⊙ 🅿 ✲ 🔥 🕙 🖇 🚿 🚻 WiFi ♻ 🔋
Services: 🔋🔼 🍴🔟🍽 🚮 ⬇
Within 3 miles: 🔋🔋∪
Notes: Families & couples only, no noise after 23.00hrs. Dogs must be kept on leads. Wet suit shower, campers' shelter.

▶▶▶ 90% **West Fleet Holiday Farm** *(SY625811)*

Fleet DT3 4EF
☎ 01305 782218
e-mail: aa@westfleetholidays.co.uk
web: www.westfleetholidays.co.uk
dir: *From Weymouth take B3157 towards Abbotsbury for 3m. Past Chickerell turn left at mini-rdbt to Fleet, site 1m on right*

* ⊕ £13-£23 ⊕ £13-£23 ▲ £13-£23

Open Etr-Sep (rs May-Sep clubhouse & pool available daily)

Last arrival 21.00hrs Last departure 11.00hrs

A spacious farm site with both level and sloping pitches divided into paddocks and screened by hedges. This site has good views of the Dorset countryside, and is a relaxing place for a family holiday. There is a spacious clubhouse with bar, restaurant and entertainment area. Wi-fi is also available. 12 acre site. 250 touring pitches. Caravan pitches. Motorhome pitches. Tent pitches.

AA Pubs & Restaurants nearby: The Old Ship Inn, WEYMOUTH, DT3 5QQ, 01305 812522

LEISURE: 🏊 Indoor swimming pool 🏊 Outdoor swimming pool ⚠ Children's playground 🎣 Kid's club 🎾 Tennis court 🎱 Games room 📺 Separate TV room ⛳ 9/18 hole golf course ⛵ Boats for hire 🎬 Cinema 🎭 Entertainment 🎣 Fishing ◎ Mini golf 🏄 Watersports 💪 Gym ⚙ Sports field Spa ∪ Stables
FACILITIES: 🛁 Bath 🚿 Shower ⊙ Electric shaver 🅿 Hairdryer ✲ Ice Pack Facility 🔥 Disabled facilities 🕙 Public telephone 🖇 Shop on site or within 200yds 🛒 Mobile shop (calls at least 5 days a week) 🍴 BBQ area 🍽 Picnic area WiFi Wi-fi ▬ Internet access ♻ Recycling 🔋 Tourist info 🚻 Dog exercise area

Leisure: 🏊 🛝 ⚽ 🎵
Facilities: 🛁 🚿 ⊙ 💨 ❄ ♿ [S] [Wi-fi] ♻ ℹ
Services: 🔌 🧺 🍷 🛢 ⛽ 🍴 🔋 🍔 ⚓
Within 3 miles: ⛳ [S] 🐎
Notes: Non-family groups by arrangement only, dogs restricted to certain areas. Dogs must be kept on leads.

►►► 86% Pebble Bank Caravan Park

(SY659775)

Camp Rd, Wyke Regis DT4 9HF
☎ 01305 774844
e-mail: info@pebblebank.co.uk
dir: *From Weymouth take Portland road. At last rdbt turn right, then 1st left to Army Tent Camp. Site opposite*

* 🚐 £15.50-£28.50 🚌 £15.50-£28.50 ⛺ £10-£26

Open Etr-mid Oct (rs High season & wknds only bar open)

Last arrival 18.00hrs Last departure 11.00hrs

This site, although only one and a half miles from Weymouth, is in a peaceful location overlooking Chesil Beach and the Fleet. There is a friendly little bar, which offers even better views. The toilet and shower block is very modern and spotlessly clean. 4 acre site. 40 touring pitches. Caravan pitches. Motorhome pitches. Tent pitches. 80 statics.

AA Pubs & Restaurants nearby: The Old Ship Inn, WEYMOUTH, DT3 5QQ, 01305 812522

Leisure: 🛝
Facilities: 🚿 ⊙ 💨 ❄ ♿ [Wi-fi] ℹ
Services: 🔌 🧺 🍷 🛢 ⛽ 🔋
Within 3 miles: ⛳ 🏃 🏋 🎣 ◎ 🚤 [S] 🧺 🐎
Notes: Dogs must be kept on leads.

►►► 80% Rosewall Camping

(SY736820)

East Farm Dairy, Osmington Mills DT3 6HA
☎ 01305 832248
e-mail: holidays@weymouthcamping.com
dir: *Take A353 towards Weymouth. At Osmington Mills sign (opposite garage) turn left, 0.25m, site on 1st right*

🚌 ⛺

Open Etr-Oct (rs Apr-May & Oct shop opening times)

Last arrival 22.00hrs Last departure 10.00hrs

This well positioned, sloping tent site is close to the coast and the South West Coast Path and has great views of Weymouth Bay. There are good toilet and shower blocks at the top and bottom of the site, and also a good shop. This site is a spacious place to camp and very suitable for families. 13 acre site. 225 touring pitches. Motorhome pitches. Tent pitches.

AA Pubs & Restaurants nearby: The Old Ship Inn, WEYMOUTH, DT3 5QQ, 01305 812522

The Smugglers Inn, OSMINGTON MILLS, DT3 6HF, 01305 833125

Leisure: 🛝 **Facilities:** 🚿 ⊙ ❄ ♿ [S] ♻ ℹ
Services: 🧺 🛢 ⛽ 🔋
Within 3 miles: 🏋 🎣 🚤 [S] 🧺 🐎
Notes: Families & couples only, no noise after 23.00hrs. Dogs must be kept on leads. Riding stables & coarse fishing.

►►► 80% Sea Barn Farm *(SY625807)*

Fleet DT3 4ED
☎ 01305 782218
e-mail: aa@seabarnfarm.co.uk
web: www.seabarnfarm.co.uk
dir: *From Weymouth take B3157 towards Abbotsbury for 3m. Past Chickerell turn left at mini-rdbt towards Fleet. Site 1m on left*

* 🚌 £12-£22 ⛺ £12-£22

Open 15 Mar-Oct (rs Mar-Jun & Sep-Oct use of facilities at West Fleet)

Last arrival 21.00hrs Last departure 11.00hrs

This site is set high on the Dorset coast and has spectacular views over Chesil Beach, The Fleet and Lyme Bay, and it is also on the South West Coast Path. Optional use of the clubhouse and swimming pool at West Fleet Holiday Farm is available. Pitches are sheltered by hedging, and there is an excellent toilet facility block, and plenty of space for games. 12 acre site. 250 touring pitches. Motorhome pitches. Tent pitches. 1 static.

AA Pubs & Restaurants nearby: The Old Ship Inn, WEYMOUTH, DT3 5QQ, 01305 812522

Leisure: 🛝
Facilities: 🛁 🚿 ⊙ 💨 ❄ ♿ [S] 🐕 [Wi-fi] ♻ ℹ
Services: 🔌 🧺 🛢 ⛽ [T] 🔋
Within 3 miles: ⛳ [S] 🐎
Notes: Non-family groups by prior arrangement only. Dogs must be kept on leads.

hh 90% Weymouth Bay Holiday Park *(SY705830)*

David Bellamy Conservation Award SILVER

Preston DT3 6BQ
☎ 01305 832271
e-mail: weymouthbay@haven.com
web: www.haven.com/weymouthbay
dir: *From A35 towards Dorchester take A354 signed Weymouth. Follow towards Preston signs onto A353. At Chalbury rdbt 1st left into Preston Rd. Park on right*

Open Mar-Oct

This well-located holiday park, just a short drive away from Weymouth beach, offers the complete holiday experience for the whole family. It has excellent indoor and outdoor pools complete with a 'Lazy River' attraction. There is an excellent choice of eating outlets as well as a full entertainment programme for all. The holiday homes are well appointed throughout. The park is conveniently placed for visiting Portland Bill, Lulworth Cove and Chesil Beach.

Change over day: Mon, Fri, Sat **Arrival and departure times:** Please contact the site

Statics 83 Sleeps 6-8 Bedrms 2-3 Bathrms 1-2 Toilets 1-2 Freezer TV Sky/FTV Elec inc Gas inc Grass area

Children 👪 Cots Highchair **Dogs** 2 on leads No dangerous dogs

Leisure 🏊 🏊 ✋ 🛝

SERVICES: 🔌 Electric hook up 🧺 Launderette 🍷 Licensed bar 🛢 Calor Gas ⛽ Camping Gaz [T] Toilet fluid 🍴 Café/Restaurant 🍔 Fast Food/Takeaway 🔋 Battery charging 🚼 Baby care ⚓ Motorvan service point **ABBREVIATIONS:** BH/bank hols-bank holidays Etr-Easter Spring BH-Spring Bank Holiday dep-departure fr-from hrs-hours m-mile mdnt-midnight rdbt-roundabout rs-restricted service wk-week wknd-weekend x-rds-cross roads 🚫 No credit cards 🚫 No dogs 👪 Children of all ages accepted See page 9 for details of the AA Camping Card Scheme

WIMBORNE MINSTER Map 5 SZ09

Places to visit

Kingston Lacy, WIMBORNE, BH21 4EA,
01202 883402 (Mon-Fri)
www.nationaltrust.org.uk

Priest's House Museum and Garden, WIMBORNE,
BH21 1HR, 01202 882533
www.priest-house.co.uk

Great for kids: Moors Valley Country Park,
RINGWOOD, BH24 2ET, 01425 470721
www.moors-valley.co.uk

PREMIER PARK

►►►►► 86% Merley Court

(SZ008984)

Merley BH21 3AA
☎ 01590 648331
e-mail: holidays@shorefield.co.uk
dir: Site signed on A31, Wimborne by-pass &
Poole junct rdbt

* ⊞ £15.25-£44.50 ⊟ £15.25-£44.50
Å £15.25-£38.75

Open 6 Feb-2 Jan (rs Low season pool closed &
bar, shop open limited hrs)

Last arrival 21.00hrs Last departure 10.00hrs

A superb site in a quiet rural position on the
edge of Wimborne, with woodland on two sides
and good access roads. The park is well
landscaped and offers generous individual
pitches in sheltered grassland. There are plenty
of amenities for all the family, including a
heated outdoor pool, tennis court and
adventure playground plus a tastefully
refurbished bar and restaurant. This park tends
to get busy in summer and therefore advance
booking is advised. Two Eurotents are available
for hire. 20 acre site. 160 touring pitches. 50
hardstandings. Caravan pitches. Motorhome
pitches. Tent pitches. 6 statics. 2 bell tents/
yurts.

AA Pubs & Restaurants nearby: Les Bouviers
Restaurant with Rooms, WIMBORNE MINSTER,
BH21 3BD, 01202 889555

Botany Bay Inne, WINTERBORNE ZELSTON,
DT11 9ET, 01929 459227

Leisure: ⚽ 𝌆 🎱 ☺ 🎯

Facilities: 🛁 🚿 ☺ 🖋 ✳ ⛄ 🅿 ⏲ 🏧 📺 ♻ ❶

Services: 🔌 🗄 🎪 🛢 ⊘ 🚰 🍴 🧺 💧 ⚡

Within 3 miles: 🏌 ⛵ 🎬 🎣 ◎ 🛒 🎱 ∪

Notes: Families & couples only, no noise after
22.00hrs, rallies welcome. Dogs must be kept
on leads. Use of facilities at Oakdene Forest
Park (7m).

see advert on opposite page

PREMIER PARK

►►►►► 85% Wilksworth Farm Caravan Park (SU004018)

Cranborne Rd BH21 4HW
☎ 01202 885467
e-mail: rayandwendy@
wilksworthfarmcaravanpark.co.uk
web: www.wilksworthfarmcaravanpark.co.uk
dir: 1m N of Wimborne on B3078

⊞ £16-£32 ⊟ £16-£32 Å £16-£32

Open Apr-Oct (rs Oct no shop)

Last arrival 20.00hrs Last departure 11.00hrs

A popular and attractive park peacefully set in
the grounds of a listed house in the heart of
rural Dorset. The spacious site has much to
offer visitors, including an excellent heated
swimming pool, takeaway and café, a bar and
restaurant plus a games room. The modern
toilet facilities contain en suite rooms and good
family rooms. 11 acre site. 85 touring pitches.
20 hardstandings. Caravan pitches. Motorhome
pitches. Tent pitches. 77 statics.

AA Pubs & Restaurants nearby: Les Bouviers
Restaurant with Rooms, WIMBORNE MINSTER,
BH21 3BD, 01202 889555

Botany Bay Inne, WINTERBORNE ZELSTON,
DT11 9ET, 01929 459227

Leisure: ⚽ 𝌆 🎱 ☺ 🎯

Facilities: 🛁 🚿 ☺ 🖋 ✳ ⛄ 🅿 ⏲ 🏧 🐕 📶 🖥 ♻ ❶

Services: 🔌 🗄 ⊘ 🚰 🍴 🧺 💧 ⚡

Within 3 miles: 🏌 🎬 🎣 🛒 🎱

Notes: Max 2 dogs per pitch. Dogs must be
kept on leads. Paddling pool, volley ball, mini
football pitch.

►►► 83% Springfield Touring Park

(SY987989)

Candys Ln, Corfe Mullen BH21 3EF
☎ 01202 881719
e-mail: john.clark18@btconnect.com
dir: From Wimborne on Wimborne by-pass (A31)
at W end turn left after Caravan Sales, follow
brown sign

* ⊞ £18-£22 ⊟ £18-£22 Å £10-£22

Open Apr-14 Oct

Last arrival 21.00hrs Last departure 11.00hrs

A small touring park with extensive views over the
Stour Valley and a quiet and friendly atmosphere.
It is well positioned for visiting Poole,
Bournemouth or the really lovely town of
Wimborne. The park is maintained immaculately,
and has a well-stocked shop. 3.5 acre site. 45
touring pitches. 30 hardstandings. Caravan
pitches. Motorhome pitches. Tent pitches.

AA Pubs & Restaurants nearby: Les Bouviers
Restaurant with Rooms, WIMBORNE MINSTER,
BH21 3BD, 01202 889555

Botany Bay Inne, WINTERBORNE ZELSTON,
DT11 9ET, 01929 459227

Leisure: 𝌆

Facilities: 🚿 ☺ 🖋 ✳ ⛄ 🅿 ♻ ❶

Services: 🔌 🗄 🛢 🧺

Within 3 miles: 🏌 🎬 🎣 🛒 🎱 ∪

Notes: ⊘ No skateboards. Dogs must be kept on
leads.

LEISURE: 🏊 Indoor swimming pool 🏊 Outdoor swimming pool 𝌆 Children's playground 🖐 Kid's club 🎾 Tennis court 🎱 Games room 📺 Separate TV room
🏌 9/18 hole golf course ⛵ Boats for hire 🎬 Cinema 🎵 Entertainment 🎣 Fishing ◎ Mini golf 🏄 Watersports 🏋 Gym 🏟 Sports field Spa ∪ Stables
FACILITIES: 🛁 Bath 🚿 Shower ☺ Electric shaver 🖋 Hairdryer ✳ Ice Pack Facility ⛄ Disabled facilities 📞 Public telephone 🛒 Shop on site or within 200yds
🚐 Mobile shop (calls at least 5 days a week) 🍴 BBQ area 🏖 Picnic area 📶 Wi-fi 🖥 Internet access ♻ Recycling ❶ Tourist info 🐕 Dog exercise area

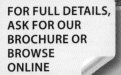

SERVICES: Electric hook up Launderette Licensed bar Calor Gas Camping Gaz Toilet fluid Café/Restaurant Fast Food/Takeaway Battery charging Baby care Motorvan service point **ABBREVIATIONS:** BH/bank hols-bank holidays Etr-Easter Spring BH-Spring Bank Holiday dep-departure fr-from hrs-hours m-mile mdnt-midnight rdbt-roundabout rs-restricted service wk-week wknd-weekend x-rds-cross roads No credit cards No dogs Children of all ages accepted See page 9 for details of the AA Camping Card Scheme

WIMBORNE MINSTER *continued*

AA CAMPING CARD SITE

▶▶▶ 81% Charris Camping & Caravan Park (SY992988)

Candy's Ln, Corfe Mullen BH21 3EF
☎ **01202 885970**
e-mail: bookings@charris.co.uk
web: www.charris.co.uk
dir: *From E, exit Wimborne bypass (A31) W end. 300yds after Caravan Sales, follow brown sign. From W on A31, over A350 rdbt, take next turn after B3074, follow brown signs*

🚐 £14.50-£19.25 🚐 £14.50-£19.25
▲ £13.50-£19.25

Open all year

Last arrival 21.00hrs (earliest arrival time 11.00hrs). Last departure 11.00hrs

A sheltered park of grassland lined with trees on the edge of the Stour Valley. The owners are friendly and welcoming, and they maintain the park facilities to a good standard. Social get-togethers are held for customers including barbecues which are very popular. 3.5 acre site. 45 touring pitches. 12 hardstandings. 10 seasonal pitches. Caravan pitches. Motorhome pitches. Tent pitches.

AA Pubs & Restaurants nearby: Les Bouviers Restaurant with Rooms, WIMBORNE MINSTER, BH21 3BD, 01202 889555

Botany Bay Inne, WINTERBORNE ZELSTON, DT11 9ET, 01929 459227

Facilities: 🅿️☉📻🌂ⓢ📶 ♻ ❶
Services: 🖭🔌🔋🧹Ⓣ♻
Within 3 miles: ↓🏌️ⓢ🔟U

Notes: Dogs must be kept on leads.

WOOL
Map 4 SY88

Places to visit

The Tank Museum, BOVINGTON CAMP, BH20 6JG, 01929 405096 www.tankmuseum.org

Clouds Hill, BOVINGTON CAMP, BH20 7NQ, 01929 405616 www.nationaltrust.org.uk

Great for kids: Monkey World-Ape Rescue Centre, WOOL, BH20 6HH, 01929 462537 www.monkeyworld.org

▶▶▶▶ 81% Whitemead Caravan Park (SY841869)

East Burton Rd BH20 6HG
☎ **01929 462241**
e-mail: whitemeadcp@aol.com
dir: *Signed from A352 at level crossing on Wareham side of Wool*

* 🚐 £15-£22.50 🚐 £15-£22.50 ▲ £12-£19.50

Open mid Mar-Oct

Last arrival 22.00hrs Last departure noon

A well laid-out site in the valley of the River Frome, close to the village of Wool, and surrounded by woodland. A shop and games room enhance the facilities here, and the spotless, modern toilets are heated, providing an excellent amenity. Only a short walk away are the shops and pubs, plus the main bus route and mainline station to Poole, Bournemouth and Weymouth. 5 acre site. 95 touring pitches. 20 seasonal pitches. Caravan pitches. Motorhome pitches. Tent pitches.

AA Pubs & Restaurants nearby: The New Inn, CHURCH KNOWLE, BH20 5NQ, 01929 480357

Leisure: 🎮 🔍
Facilities: 🅿️☉📻🌂♿ⓢ🔥📶 ♻ ❶
Services: 🖭🔌🔋🧹Ⓣ🚌
Within 3 miles: ↓🏌️ⓢ🔟U

Notes: Dogs must be kept on leads.

CO DURHAM

BARNARD CASTLE
Map 19 NZ01

Places to visit

Barnard Castle, BARNARD CASTLE, DL12 8PR, 01833 638212 www.english-heritage.org.uk/daysout/properties/barnard-castle

The Bowes Museum, BARNARD CASTLE, DL12 8NP, 01833 690606 www.thebowesmuseum.org.uk

Great for kids: Raby Castle, STAINDROP, DL2 3AH, 01833 660202 www.rabycastle.com

▶▶▶ 79% Pecknell Farm Caravan Park (NZ028178)

Lartington DL12 9DF
☎ **01833 638357**
dir: *1.5m from Barnard Castle. From A66 take B6277. Site on right 1.5m from junct with A67*

🚐 £12-£19 🚐 £12-£19

Open Apr-Oct

Last arrival 20.00hrs Last departure noon

A small well laid out site on a working farm in beautiful rural meadowland, with spacious marked pitches on level ground. There are many walking opportunities that start directly from this friendly site. 1.5 acre site. 20 touring pitches. 5 hardstandings. Caravan pitches. Motorhome pitches.

AA Pubs & Restaurants nearby: The Fox and Hounds, COTHERSTONE, DL12 9PF, 01833 650241

The Morritt Arms Hotel, BARNARD CASTLE, DL12 9SE, 01833 627232

Rose & Crown Hotel, ROMALDKIRK, DL12 9EB, 01833 650213

Facilities: 🅿️☉📻🔟 ♻ ❶
Services: 🖭🚌
Within 3 miles: ↓🏌️◎ⓢ🔟U

Notes: ⓐ No noise after 22.30hrs. Maximum 2 dogs. Dogs must be kept on leads.

LEISURE: 🏊 Indoor swimming pool 🏊 Outdoor swimming pool 🎮 Children's playground 👦 Kid's club 🎾 Tennis court 🔍 Games room 📺 Separate TV room ⛳ 9/18 hole golf course 🚣 Boats for hire 🎬 Cinema 🎭 Entertainment 🎣 Fishing ◎ Mini golf 🏄 Watersports 🏋 Gym 🏟 Sports field **Spa** U Stables
FACILITIES: 🛁 Bath 🅿️ Shower ☉ Electric shaver 📻 Hairdryer 🌂 Ice Pack Facility ♿ Disabled facilities 🕿 Public telephone ⓢ Shop on site or within 200yds 🚐 Mobile shop (calls at least 5 days a week) 🍖 BBQ area 🌲 Picnic area 📶 Wi-fi 💻 Internet access ♻ Recycling ❶ Tourist info 🐕 Dog exercise area

BEAMISH Map 19 NZ25

Places to visit

Tanfield Railway, TANFIELD, NE16 5ET, 0191 388 7545 www.tanfieldrailway.co.uk

Beamish Museum, BEAMISH, DH9 0RG, 0191 370 4000 www.beamish.org.uk

Great for kids: Diggerland, LANGLEY PARK, DH7 9TT, 0871 227 7007 www.diggerland.com

►►► 78% Bobby Shafto Caravan Park *(NZ232545)*

Cranberry Plantation DH9 0RY
☎ 0191 370 1776
dir: *From A693 signed Beamish to sign for Beamish Museum. Take approach road, turn right immediately before museum, left at pub to site 1m on right*

🚐 🚌 ⛺

Open Mar-Oct

Last arrival 23.00hrs Last departure 11.00hrs

A tranquil rural park surrounded by trees, with very clean and well organised facilities. The suntrap touring area has plenty of attractive hanging baskets, and there is a clubhouse with bar, TV and pool. The hardstandings and the 28 fully serviced pitches enhance the amenities. 9 acre site. 83 touring pitches. 47 hardstandings. Caravan pitches. Motorhome pitches. Tent pitches. 54 statics.

AA Pubs & Restaurants nearby: The Stables Pub and Restaurant, STANLEY, DH9 0YB, 01207 288750

Leisure: ⛹ 🎱 📺

Facilities: 🚿 ⊙ ✱ ♿ ☎ [S] Wi-fi

Services: 🔌 🧺 🍷 🔥 🍃 [T] 🔋

Within 3 miles: ⛳ ⛵ 🏊 🎣 🧺 🐴

BLACKHALL COLLIERY Map 19 NZ43

Places to visit

Hartlepool's Maritime Experience, HARTLEPOOL, TS24 0XZ, 01429 860077 www.hartlepoolsmaritimeexperience.com

Auckland Castle, BISHOP AUCKLAND, DL14 7NR, 01388 743750 www.english-heritage.org.uk/daysout/properties/auckland-castle-deer-house

Great for kids: Captain Cook Birthplace Museum, MIDDLESBROUGH, TS7 8AT, 01642 311211 www.captcook-ne.co.uk

80% *Crimdon Dene* *(NZ477378)*

Coast Rd TS27 4BN
☎ 0871 664 9737
e-mail: crimdon.dene@park-resorts.com
web: www.park-resorts.com
dir: *From A19 just S of Peterlee, take B1281 signed Blackhall. Through Castle Eden, left in 0.5m signed Blackhall. Approx 3m right at T-junct onto A1086 towards Crimdon. Site in 1m signed on left, by Seagull pub*

🚐 🚌

Open Apr-Oct

Last arrival 23.00hrs Last departure 10.00hrs

A large, popular coastal holiday park, handily placed for access to Teeside, Durham and Newcastle. The park contains a full range of holiday centre facilities for both children and their parents. Touring facilities are appointed to a very good standard. 44 touring pitches. 44 hardstandings. 12 seasonal pitches. Caravan pitches. Motorhome pitches. 586 statics.

Leisure: 🏊 ⛹ ✋ 🎱 ♫

Facilities: 🚿 ⊙ ✱ ☎ [S] 🪑 Wi-fi ♻ ℹ

Services: 🔌 🧺 🍷 🍴 🍔

Within 3 miles: ⛳ 🏊 🎣 [S] 🧺 🐴

Notes: No cars by caravans. No quad bikes. Dogs must be kept on leads.

CONSETT Map 19 NZ15

Places to visit

Beamish Museum, BEAMISH, DH9 0RG, 0191 370 4000 www.beamish.org.uk

Tanfield Railway, TANFIELD, NE16 5ET, 0191 388 7545 www.tanfieldrailway.co.uk

Great for kids: Gibside, ROWLANDS GILL, NE16 6BG, 01207 541820 www.nationaltrust.org.uk/gibside

►►► 77% Byreside Caravan Site *(NZ122560)*

Hamsterley NE17 7RT
☎ 01207 560280
dir: *From A694 onto B6310 & follow signs*

🚐 fr £15 🚌 fr £15 ⛺ fr £15

Open all year

Last arrival 22.00hrs Last departure noon

A small, secluded family-run site on a working farm, with well-maintained facilities. It is immediately adjacent to the coast-to-coast cycle track so makes an ideal location for walkers and cyclists. Handy for Newcastle and Durham; the Roman Wall and Northumberland National Park are within an hour's drive. 1.5 acre site. 31 touring pitches. 29 hardstandings. Caravan pitches. Motorhome pitches. Tent pitches.

AA Pubs & Restaurants nearby: The Manor House Inn, CARTERWAY HEADS, DH8 9LX, 01207 255268

Facilities: 🚿 ⊙ ✱ ♿ [S] 🐕 ♻ ℹ

Services: 🔌 🔥 [T] 🔋

Within 3 miles: ⛳ 🏊 [S] 🧺

Notes: No ball games. Dogs must be kept on leads. Caravan storage.

ESSEX

CLACTON-ON-SEA — Map 7 TM11

Places to visit

Harwich Redoubt Fort, HARWICH, CO12 3TE, 01255 503429 www.harwich-society.com

The Beth Chatto Gardens, COLCHESTER, CO7 7DB, 01206 822007 www.bethchatto.co.uk

Great for kids: Colchester Zoo, COLCHESTER, CO3 0SL, 01206 331292 www.colchesterzoo.org

 78% Highfield Grange (TM173175)

London Rd CO16 9QY
☎ 0871 664 9746
e-mail: highfield.grange@park-resorts.com
web: www.park-resorts.com
dir: A12 to Colchester, A120 (Harwich), A133 to Clacton-on-Sea. Site on B1441 clearly signed on left

Open Apr-Oct

Last arrival mdnt Last departure 10.00hrs

The modern leisure facilities at this attractively planned park make it an ideal base for a lively family holiday. The swimming complex with both indoor and outdoor pools and a huge water shoot is especially popular. There are fully serviced touring pitches, each with its own hardstanding, located at the heart of the park. The nearby resorts of Walton on the Naze, Frinton and Clacton all offer excellent beaches and a wide range of popular seaside attractions. 30 acre site. 43 touring pitches. 43 hardstandings. Caravan pitches. Motorhome pitches. 509 statics.

AA Pubs & Restaurants nearby: The Rose & Crown Hotel, COLCHESTER, CO1 2TZ, 01206 866677

The Whalebone, FINGRINGHOE, CO5 7BG, 01206 729307

Leisure: 🏊 🏊 🅰 ⚽ 🎱 🎵
Facilities: 🛁 ☉ 🔌 ♿ 🕐 ⓢ 🎪 📶 💻
Services: 🚐 🗑 🔧 🍴 🏪
Within 3 miles: 🚶 ⛳ 🚤 📍 ◉ 🎣 ⓢ 🔵 ↻
Notes: No fold-in campers or trailer tents.

 75% Martello Beach Holiday Park (TM136128)

Belsize Av, Jaywick CO15 2LF
☎ 0871 664 9782 & 01442 830100
e-mail: martello.beach@park-resorts.com
web: www.park-resorts.com
dir: Telephone for directions

Open Apr-Oct

Last arrival 21.30hrs Last departure 10.00hrs

Direct access to a seven-mile long Blue Flag beach is an undoubted attraction at this holiday park. The touring area is next to the leisure complex, where an indoor and outdoor swimming pool, shops, cafés and bars and evening entertainment are all provided. 40 acre site. 100 touring pitches. Caravan pitches. Motorhome pitches. Tent pitches. 294 statics.

AA Pubs & Restaurants nearby: The Rose & Crown Hotel, COLCHESTER, CO1 2TZ, 01206 866677

The Whalebone, FINGRINGHOE, CO5 7BG, 01206 729307

Leisure: 🏊 🏊 🅰 ⚽ 🎱 🎵
Facilities: 🛁 ☉ 🔌 ✳ ♿ 🕐 ⓢ 📶 💻
Services: 🚐 🗑 🔧 🖊 🍴 🏪
Within 3 miles: 🚶 📍 🔵 ⓢ 🔵 ↻
Notes: ⊗ Watersports.

GREAT SALING — Map 12 TL72

Places to visit

Paycocke's, COGGESHALL, CO6 1NS, 01376 561305 www.nationaltrust.org.uk

AA CAMPING CARD SITE

NEW ► 78% Golden Grove (TL704252)

Piccotts Ln CM7 5DW
☎ 07917 592310
e-mail: louise@salinggrove.com
dir: M11 junct 8A, A120 (Colchester). S of Dunmow take B1256 towards Braintree. After 8m left signed Great Saling. Enter village, right into Piccotts Lane

* 🚐 fr £12 🚐 fr £12 ⚑ fr £10

Open all year

Last arrival 18.00hrs Last departure noon

This site has now been extended to nine pitches and enjoys a peaceful and secluded location behind a large country house, screened by a high line of trees and with a wide expanse of meadow to the front. The all-electric pitches are set out on a wide swathe of gravel and a timber chalet houses a single unisex cubicle with wash basins and WC, a small lounge and library. The whole setting is very rural and abounds with wildlife. 6 acre site. 9 touring pitches. 9 hardstandings. Caravan pitches. Motorhome pitches. Tent pitches.

Facilities: 🐕 ♻ ❶
Services: 🚐 🅣 🖊
Within 3 miles: ⓢ
Notes: Adults only. ⊗ No noise after 22.00hrs. Dogs must be kept on leads.

MERSEA ISLAND　　Map 7 TM01

Places to visit

Layer Marney Tower, LAYER MARNEY, CO5 9US, 01206 330784 www.layermarneytower.co.uk

80% Waldegraves Holiday Park *(TM033133)*

CO5 8SE
☎ 01206 382898
e-mail: holidays@waldegraves.co.uk
web: www.waldegraves.co.uk
dir: *A12 junct 26, B1025 to Mersea Island across The Strood. Left to East Mersea, 2nd right, follow tourist signs to site*

🚐 £18-£27　🚐 £18-£27　▲ £18-£27

Open Mar-Nov (rs Mar-Jun & Sep-Nov (excl BH & school half terms) pool, shop & clubhouse reduced opening hrs, pool open May-Sep weather permitting)

Last arrival 22.00hrs Last departure 15.00hrs

A spacious and pleasant site located between farmland and its own private beach on the Blackwater Estuary. The facilities include two freshwater fishing lakes, a heated swimming pool, café, club, amusements and golf; there is generally good provision for families. 25 holiday static caravans for hire. 25 acre site. 60 touring pitches. 30 seasonal pitches. Caravan pitches. Motorhome pitches. Tent pitches. 250 statics.

AA Pubs & Restaurants nearby: The Peldon Rose, PELDON, CO5 7QJ, 01206 735248

Waldegraves Holiday Park

Leisure: 🏊 🎱 👐 ⚽ 🎣 🎵
Facilities: 🖍 ⊙ 🥤 ✳ ⚷ 🛁 🚿 🚮 🐕 📶 ♻ ❓
Services: 🔌 🗑 🍴 🛢 🚐 🚽 🍴 🎒 🧹
Within 3 miles: ⬇ 🎣 ◎ 🏊 🛒 🛒

Notes: No groups of under 21s. Dogs must be kept on leads. Boating/slipway, pitch & putt, driving range.

see advert below

NEW ►►►► 80% Fen Farm Caravan Site *(TM059143)*

Moore Ln, East Mersea CO5 8FE
☎ 01206 383275
e-mail: havefun@fenfarm.co.uk
dir: *From Colchester B1025 to Mersea Island, left signed East Mersea. 1st right after Dog & Pheasant pub into Moore Lane (road is tidal please check tide times)*

* 🚐 £18-£30　🚐 £18-£30　▲ £18-£30

Open Mar-Oct

The first tents were pitched at Fen Farm in 1923 and over the years the farm gave way entirely to becoming a caravan park. Enjoying an enviable location beside the Blackwater estuary, it has unique atmosphere with a mixture of meadow, woodland and marine shore, and varied wildlife to match each environment. There two excellent solar-heated toilet blocks, which include three family rooms and privacy cubicles, with the newest block constructed in the local style of black clapboard and a red tile roof. There is a woodland dog walk and two well-equipped play areas, while crabbing in the beach pools is also a popular pastime. 65 touring pitches. 3 hardstandings. 65 seasonal pitches. Caravan pitches. Motorhome pitches. Tent pitches. 90 statics.

Leisure: 🎱 🔆
Facilities: 🖍 🥤 ✳ ⚷ 🕐 🛁 🚮 📶 ♻ ❓
Services: 🔌 🗑 🛢 🛒 🚽 🛗
Within 3 miles: 🎣 ◎ 🛒 🛒

Notes: No open fires, no noise after 23.00hrs. Dogs must be kept on leads.

MERSEA ISLAND *continued*

▶▶▶ 79% Seaview Holiday Park

(TM025125)

Seaview Av, West Mersea CO5 8DA
☎ **01206 382534**
e-mail: seaviewholidaypark@googlemail.com
dir: *From A12 (Colchester) onto B1025 (Mersea Island), cross causeway, left towards East Mersea, 1st right, follow signs*

* 🚐 £19-£25 🚐 £19-£25

Open Apr-Oct

Last arrival 18.00hrs (phone site if late arrival expected). Last departure noon

With sweeping views across the Blackwater estuary, this interesting, well-established park has its own private beach, complete with boat slipway and photogenic beach cabins, a modern shop, café and a stylish clubhouse which offers evening meals and drinks in a quiet family atmosphere. The touring area is well maintained and has 40 fully serviced pitches. 30 acre site. 106 touring pitches. 40 hardstandings. 30 seasonal pitches. Caravan pitches. Motorhome pitches. 240 statics.

AA Pubs & Restaurants nearby: The Peldon Rose, PELDON, CO5 7QJ, 01206 735248

Facilities: �🆃 & 🕓 🖻 🛏 🚮

Services: 🔌 🖬 🗑 🍴 🖿 ⛟

Within 3 miles: ⌗ 🚴 🖼 📷 🛍 U

Notes: No noise after mdnt, no boats or jet skis. Dogs must be kept on leads. Private beach.

▶▶▶ 79% Riverside Village Holiday Park

(TQ929951)

Creeksea Ferry Rd, Wallasea Island, Canewdon SS4 2EY
☎ **01702 258297**
e-mail: riversidevillage@tiscali.co.uk
dir: *M25 junct 29, A127 towards Southend-on-Sea. Take B1013 towards Rochford. Follow signs for Wallasea Island & Baltic Wharf*

🚐 🚐 Å

Open Mar-Oct

Situated next to a nature reserve beside the River Crouch, this holiday park is surrounded by wetlands but only eight miles from Southend. A modern toilet block, with disabled facilities, is provided for tourers and there's a handsome

---

reception area. The park has several fishing lakes for site guests (permits available at reception). Several restaurants and pubs are within a short distance. 25 acre site. 60 touring pitches. Caravan pitches. Motorhome pitches. Tent pitches. 159 statics.

Leisure: /Å

Facilities: ⌐ ⊙ ℱ ✳ & 🕓 🖻 🛏 🚮 📶 ♻ ❶

Services: 🔌 🖬 🗑 🖢 📧

Within 3 miles: ⌗ 🖼 📷 🛍 U

Notes: No dogs in tents. Dogs must be kept on leads. Mobile newspaper vendor Sun & BHs.

Places to visit

RHS Garden Hyde Hall, CHELMSFORD, CM3 8AT, 01245 402006 www.rhs.org.uk/hydehall

Kelvedon Hatch Secret Nuclear Bunker, BRENTWOOD, CM14 5TL, 01277 364883 www.secretnuclearbunker.com

Great for kids: Hadleigh Castle, HADLEIGH, 01760 755161 www.english-heritage.org.uk/daysout/properties/hadleigh-castle

79% Waterside St Lawrence Bay *(TL953056)*

Main Rd CM0 7LY
☎ **0871 664 9794**
e-mail: waterside@park-resorts.com
web: www.park-resorts.com
dir: *A12 towards Chelmsford, A414 signed Maldon. Follow B1010 & signs to Latchingdon, then signs for Mayland/Steeple/St Lawrence. Left towards St Lawrence. Site on right*

🚐 🚐 Å

Open Apr-Oct (rs Wknds)

Last arrival 22.00hrs Last departure 10.00hrs

Waterside occupies a scenic location overlooking the Blackwater estuary. In addition to the range of on-site leisure facilities there are opportunities for beautiful coastal walks and visits to the attractions of Southend. Tents are welcome on this expansive site, which has some touring pitches with electricity and good toilet facilities. The park has its own boat storage and slipway onto the Blackwater. 72 touring pitches. Caravan pitches. Motorhome pitches. Tent pitches. 271 statics.

AA Pubs & Restaurants nearby: Ye Olde White Harte Hotel, BURNHAM-ON-CROUCH, CM0 8AS, 01621 782106

The Ferry Boat Inn, NORTH FAMBRIDGE, CM3 6LR, 01621 740208

Leisure: 🏊 /Å 🛶 🎱 🎵

Facilities: ⌐ ℱ & 🕓 🖻 🛏 🚮 📶 🖥

Services: 🔌 🖬 🗑 🍴 ⛟

Within 3 miles: 🖼 📷 🛍

Notes: Sauna, spa pool.

Places to visit

Harwich Redoubt Fort, HARWICH, CO12 3TE, 01255 503429 www.harwich-society.com

Colchester Castle Museum, COLCHESTER, CO1 1TJ, 01206 282939 www.colchestermuseums.org.uk

Great for kids: Colchester Zoo, COLCHESTER, CO3 0SL, 01206 331292 www.colchesterzoo.org

79% The Orchards Holiday Park *(TM125155)*

CO16 8LJ
☎ **0871 231 0861**
e-mail: theorchards@haven.com
web: www.haven.com/theorchards
dir: *From Clacton-on-Sea B1027 towards Colchester. Left after petrol station, straight on at x-rds in St Osyth. Follow signs to Point Clear. Park in 3m*

🚐 Å

Open end Mar-end Oct (rs end Mar-May & Sep-end Oct some facilities may be reduced)

Last arrival anytime Last departure 10.00hrs

The Orchards offers good touring facilities with a quality toilet block which includes a laundry, play area and two very spacious family rooms. The touring pitches are generously sized. There's also direct access to all the leisure, entertainment and dining outlets available on this large popular holiday park on the Essex coast. 140 acre site. 69 touring pitches. Caravan pitches. Tent pitches. 1000 statics.

AA Pubs & Restaurants nearby: The Rose & Crown Hotel, COLCHESTER, CO1 2TZ, 01206 866677

The Whalebone, FINGRINGHOE, CO5 7BG, 01206 729307

LEISURE: 🏊 Indoor swimming pool 🏊 Outdoor swimming pool /Å Children's playground 🧒 Kid's club 🎾 Tennis court 🎱 Games room 📺 Separate TV room 🏌 9/18 hole golf course ⛵ Boats for hire 🎦 Cinema 🎵 Entertainment 🎣 Fishing ⛳ Mini golf 🏄 Watersports 🏋 Gym 🏐 Sports field **Spa** U Stables
FACILITIES: 🛁 Bath 🚿 Shower ⊙ Electric shaver ℱ Hairdryer ✳ Ice Pack Facility & Disabled facilities 🕓 Public telephone 🖻 Shop on site or within 200yds 🏪 Mobile shop (calls at least 5 days a week) 🛏 BBQ area 🍴 Picnic area 📶 Wi-fi 🖥 Internet access ♻ Recycling ❶ Tourist info 🚮 Dog exercise area

Leisure: 🏊 🌊 🛝 🎵

Facilities: 🚿 ⊙ 💨 ♿ 📞 [S] [Wi-fi] 💻 ♻ ℹ

Services: 🔌 🧺 🍷 🛢 🍴 🍔 👶

Within 3 miles: ⛳ 🎣 🎯 🚤 [S] 🧺 🐎

Notes: No cars by tents. No commercial vehicles, no bookings by persons under 21yrs unless a family booking. Max 2 dogs per booking, certain dog breeds banned.

WALTON ON THE NAZE — Map 7 TM22

Places to visit

Ipswich Museum, IPSWICH, IP1 3QH, 01473 433550 www.ipswich.gov.uk

Harwich Redoubt Fort, HARWICH, CO12 3TE, 01255 503429 www.harwich-society.com

73% *Naze Marine* (TM255226)

AA HOLIDAY CENTRE — DAVID BELLAMY CONSERVATION AWARD GOLD

Hall Ln CO14 8HL
☎ 0871 664 9755
e-mail: naze.marine@park-resorts.com
web: www.park-resorts.com
dir: *A12 to Colchester. Then A120 (Harwich road) then A133 to Weeley. Take B1033 to Walton on the Naze seafront. Site on left*

🚌 🚐

Open Apr-Oct

Last arrival anytime Last departure 10.00hrs

With its modern indoor swimming pool, show bar, bar/restaurant and amusements, this park offers a variety of on-site attractions. The park is within easy access of the beaches and attractions of Walton on the Naze, Frinton and Clacton, and the more historic places of interest inland. Please note that this site does not cater for tents. 46 acre site. 41 touring pitches. Caravan pitches. Motorhome pitches. 540 statics.

Leisure: 🏊 🛝 ✋ 🎵

Facilities: 🚿 ⊙ ♿ 📞 [S] 🪑 [Wi-fi] 💻

Services: 🔌 🧺 🍷 🍴 🍔

Within 3 miles: ⛳ 🎣 🚤 [S] 🧺

Notes: Dogs must be kept on leads. Nature walk, natural meadowland.

GLOUCESTERSHIRE

BERKELEY — Map 4 ST69

Places to visit

Dr Jenner's House, BERKELEY, GL13 9BN, 01453 810631 www.jennermuseum.com

WWT Slimbridge, SLIMBRIDGE, GL2 7BT, 01453 891900 www.wwt.org.uk

Great for kids: Berkeley Castle & Butterfly House, BERKELEY, GL13 9BQ, 01453 810303 www.berkeley-castle.com

►►► 77% Hogsdown Farm Caravan & Camping Park *(ST710974)*

Hogsdown Farm, Lower Wick GL11 6DD
☎ 01453 810224
dir: *M5 junct 14 (Falfield), take A38 towards Gloucester. Through Stone & Woodford. After Newport turn right signed Lower Wick*

🚌 🚐 ⛺

Open all year

Last arrival 21.00hrs Last departure 16.00hrs

A pleasant site with good toilet facilities, located between Bristol and Gloucester. It is well positioned for visiting Berkeley Castle and the Cotswolds, and makes an excellent overnight stop when travelling to or from the West Country. 5 acre site. 45 touring pitches. 12 hardstandings. Caravan pitches. Motorhome pitches. Tent pitches.

AA Pubs & Restaurants nearby: The Malt House, BERKELEY, GL13 9BA, 01453 511177

The Anchor Inn, OLDBURY-ON-SEVERN, BS35 1QA, 01454 413331

Leisure: 🛝

Facilities: 🚿 ⊙ ❄ ♻ ℹ

Services: 🔌 🧺 🔋

Within 3 miles: ⛳ 🎣 [S] 🧺 🐎

Notes: No skateboards or bicycles. Dogs must be kept on leads.

CHELTENHAM — Map 10 SO92

Places to visit

Holst Birthplace Museum, CHELTENHAM, GL52 2AY, 01242 524846 www.holstmuseum.org.uk

Sudeley Castle, Gardens & Exhibitions, WINCHCOMBE, GL54 5JD, 01242 602308 www.sudeleycastle.co.uk

Great for kids: Gloucester City Museum & Art Gallery, GLOUCESTER, GL1 1HP, 01452 396131 www.gloucester.gov.uk/citymuseum

►►►► 80% Briarfields Motel & Touring Park *(SO909218)*

Gloucester Rd GL51 0SX
☎ 01242 235324
e-mail: briarfields@hotmail.co.uk
dir: *M5 junct 11, A40 towards Cheltenham. At rdbt left onto B4063, site 200mtrs on left*

* 🚌 £15-£18 🚐 £15-£18 ⛺ £11-£15

Open all year

Last arrival 21.00hrs Last departure noon

A well-designed level park, with a motel, where the facilities are modern and very clean. The park is well-positioned between Cheltenham and Gloucester, with easy access to the Cotswolds. And, being close to the M5, it makes a perfect overnight stopping point. 5 acre site. 72 touring pitches. 72 hardstandings. Caravan pitches. Motorhome pitches. Tent pitches.

AA Pubs & Restaurants nearby: The Gloucester Old Spot, CHELTENHAM, GL51 9SY, 01242 680321

The Royal Oak Inn, CHELTENHAM, GL52 3DL, 01242 522344

Facilities: 🚿 ⊙ 💨 ❄ ♿ [Wi-fi] ♻ ℹ

Services: 🔌 🧺 🚰

Within 3 miles: ⛳ ✈ 🎬 🎣 [S] 🧺 🐎

Notes: No noise after 22.00hrs. Dogs must be kept on leads.

SERVICES: 🔌 Electric hook up 🧺 Launderette 🍷 Licensed bar 🛢 Calor Gas 🔥 Camping Gaz [T] Toilet fluid 🍴 Café/Restaurant 🍔 Fast Food/Takeaway 🔋 Battery charging 👶 Baby care 🚰 Motorvan service point **ABBREVIATIONS:** BH/bank hols-bank holidays Etr-Easter Spring BH-Spring Bank Holiday dep-departure fr-from hrs-hours m-mile mdnt-midnight rdbt-roundabout rs-restricted service wk-week wknd-weekend x-rds-cross roads 💳 No credit cards 🚫 No dogs 👪 Children of all ages accepted See page 9 for details of the AA Camping Card Scheme

CIRENCESTER
Map 5 SP00

Places to visit

Corinium Museum, CIRENCESTER, GL7 2BX, 01285 655611 www.coriniummuseum.cotswold.gov.uk

Chedworth Roman Villa, CHEDWORTH, GL54 3LJ, 01242 890256 www.nationaltrust.org.uk/chedworth

Great for kids: Prinknash Abbey, CRANHAM, GL4 8EX, 01452 812066 www.prinknashabbey.org.uk

►►►► 80% Mayfield Touring Park

(SP020055)

Cheltenham Rd GL7 7BH
☎ **01285 831301**
e-mail: mayfield-park@cirencester.fsbusiness.co.uk
dir: *In Cirencester at rdbt junct of A429 & A417, take A417 signed Cheltenham & A435. Right onto A435, follow brown camping signs to site on left*

* 🚐 £15-£23 🚚 £15-£23 ▲ £13-£21

Open all year

Last arrival 20.00hrs Last departure noon

A gently sloping park on the edge of the Cotswolds, with level pitches and a warm welcome. Popular with couples and families, it offers a good licensed shop selling a wide selection of home-cooked takeaway food. This lovely park makes an ideal base for exploring the Cotswolds and its many attractions, and for walking the nearby Monarch's Way and the Cotswold Way long-distance paths. 12 acre site. 72 touring pitches. 31 hardstandings. 10 seasonal pitches. Caravan pitches. Motorhome pitches. Tent pitches. 33 statics.

AA Pubs & Restaurants nearby: The Crown of Crucis, CIRENCESTER, GL7 5RS, 01285 851806

Hare & Hounds, CHEDWORTH, GL54 4NN, 01285 720288

Facilities: 🌂 ☉ ℉ ⚙ ⛄ 🚿 ⑨ 𝓢 🐾 🚾 ♻ ❶
Services: 🔌 ⊠ 🛢 ⊘ T 🚮
Within 3 miles: 🚲 💲 ⊠

Notes: No cycles or skateboards. Dogs only by prior arrangement. Dogs must be kept on leads.

GLOUCESTER
Map 10 SO81

Places to visit

Gloucester Folk Museum, GLOUCESTER, GL1 2PG, 01452 396868 www.gloucester.gov.uk/folkmuseum

Nature in Art, GLOUCESTER, GL2 9PA, 01452 731422 www.nature-in-art.org.uk

Great for kids: The National Waterways Museum, GLOUCESTER, GL1 2EH, 01452 318200 www.nwm.org.uk

►►► 74% Red Lion Caravan & Camping Park *(SO849258)*

Wainlode Hill, Norton GL2 9LW
☎ **01452 731810 & 01299 400787**
dir: *Exit A38 at Norton, follow road to river*

🚐 🚚 ▲

Open all year

Last arrival 22.00hrs Last departure 11.00hrs

An attractive meadowland park, adjacent to a traditional pub, with the River Severn just across a country lane. There is a private lake for freshwater fishing. This makes an ideal touring base. 24 acre site. 60 touring pitches. 10 hardstandings. 60 seasonal pitches. Caravan pitches. Motorhome pitches. Tent pitches. 85 statics.

AA Pubs & Restaurants nearby: Queens Head, GLOUCESTER, GL2 9EJ, 01452 301882

The Queens Arms, ASHLEWORTH, GL19 4HT, 01452 700395

Leisure: 𝄃
Facilities: 🌂 ☉ ℉ ⚙ ⛄ ⑨ 𝓢 🚻 🐾
Services: 🔌 ⊠ 🛢 ⊘ T 🍽
Within 3 miles: 🚲 ℘ 💲 ∪

NEWENT
Map 10 SO72

Places to visit

Odda's Chapel, DEERHURST, 0870 333 1181 www.english-heritage.org.uk/daysout/properties/oddas-chapel

Westbury Court Garden, WESTBURY-ON-SEVERN, GL14 1PD, 01452 760461 www.nationaltrust.org.uk

Great for kids: International Centre for Birds of Prey, NEWENT, GL18 1JJ, 01531 820286 www.icbp.org

►►► 82% Pelerine Caravan and Camping *(SO645183)*

Ford House Rd GL18 1LQ
☎ **01531 822761**
e-mail: pelerine@hotmail.com
dir: *1m from Newent*

🚐 🚚 ▲

Open Mar-Nov

Last arrival 22.00hrs Last departure 16.00hrs

A pleasant, French-themed site divided into separate areas (Rue de Pelerine and Avenue des Families), plus one for adults-only; there are some hardstandings and electric hook-ups in each area. Facilities are very good, especially for families. It is close to several vineyards, and well positioned in the north of the Forest of Dean with Tewkesbury, Cheltenham and Ross-on-Wye within easy reach. 5 acre site. 35 touring pitches. 2 hardstandings. Caravan pitches. Motorhome pitches. Tent pitches.

AA Pubs & Restaurants nearby: The Yew Tree, CLIFFORD'S MESNE, GL18 1JS, 01531 820719

Three Choirs Vineyards, NEWENT, GL18 1LS, 01531 890223

Facilities: 🌂 ☉ ℉ ⚙ ⛄ 🚾 ♻ ❶
Services: 🔌 ⊠ 🛢 ☕ 🚮
Within 3 miles: 🚲 𝄃 ℘ 💲 ⊠ ∪

Notes: 🐾 Dogs must be kept on leads. Woodburners, chimneas, burning pits available.

LEISURE: 🏊 Indoor swimming pool ⛱ Outdoor swimming pool 𝄃 Children's playground 🪁 Kid's club 🎾 Tennis court ♣ Games room ☐ Separate TV room 🚲 9/18 hole golf course 🚤 Boats for hire 🎬 Cinema 🎵 Entertainment ℘ Fishing ◎ Mini golf 🏄 Watersports 🏋 Gym 🏟 Sports field **Spa** ∪ Stables
FACILITIES: 🛁 Bath 🚿 Shower ☉ Electric shaver ℉ Hairdryer ⚙ Ice Pack Facility ⛄ Disabled facilities 🕭 Public telephone 💲 Shop on site or within 200yds 🏪 Mobile shop (calls at least 5 days a week) 🍖 BBQ area 🧺 Picnic area 🚾 Wi-fi 🖥 Internet access ♻ Recycling ❶ Tourist info 🐾 Dog exercise area

SLIMBRIDGE Map 4 SO70

Places to visit

Dean Forest Railway, LYDNEY, GL15 4ET, 01594 845840 www.dfr.co.uk

Berkeley Castle & Butterfly House, BERKELEY, GL13 9BQ, 01453 810303 www.berkeley-castle.com

Great for kids: WWT Slimbridge, SLIMBRIDGE, GL2 7BT, 01453 891900 www.wwt.org.uk

►►►► 87% Tudor Caravan & Camping *(SO728040)*

GOLD

Shepherds Patch GL2 7BP
☎ 01453 890483
e-mail: aa@tudorcaravanpark.co.uk
web: www.tudorcaravanpark.com
dir: *M5 juncts 13 & 14 follow WWT Wetlands Wildlife Centre-Slimbridge signs. Site at rear of Tudor Arms pub*

🚐 🚌 ⛺

Open all year

Last arrival 20.00hrs Last departure 11.00hrs

This park benefits from one of the best locations in the county, situated right alongside the Sharpness to Gloucester canal and just a short walk from the famous Wildfowl & Wetlands Trust at Slimbridge. The site has two areas, one for adults only, and a more open area with a facility block. There are both grass and gravel pitches complete with electric hook-ups. Being next to the canal, there are excellent walks plus the National Cycle Network route 41 can be accessed from the site. There is a pub and restaurant adjacent to the site. 8 acre site. 75 touring pitches. 48 hardstandings. Caravan pitches. Motorhome pitches. Tent pitches.

Facilities: 🚿 ⊙ ✲ ♿ [S] 🪑 🐕 Wi-fi ♻ ℹ

Services: 🔌 🧺 🍺 🛢 🍃 [T] 🍴 🔋 ⛛

Within 3 miles: ⛵ 🎣 [S] 🧺 🐎

Notes: 🚫💳 Debit cards only (credit cards not accepted). Dogs must be kept on leads.

STONEHOUSE Map 4 SO80

Places to visit

Painswick Rococo Garden, PAINSWICK, GL6 6TH, 01452 813204 www.rococogarden.org.uk

WWT Slimbridge, SLIMBRIDGE, GL2 7BT, 01453 891900 www.wwt.org.uk

►►►► 86% *Apple Tree Park Caravan and Camping Site* *(SO766063)*

A38, Claypits GL10 3AL
☎ 01452 742362 & 07708 221457
e-mail: appletreepark@hotmail.co.uk
dir: *M5 junct 13, A38. Take 1st exit at rdbt. Site 0.7m on left, 400mtrs beyond filling station*

🚐 🚌 ⛺

Open Feb-Nov

Last arrival 21.00hrs Last departure noon

This is a family-owned park conveniently located on the A38, not far from the M5. A peaceful site with glorious views of the Cotswolds, it offers modern and spotlessly clean toilet facilities with under-floor heating. The park is well located for visiting Slimbridge Wildfowl & Wetlands Trust and makes an excellent stopover for M5 travellers. There is a bus stop directly outside the park which is handy for those with motorhomes who wish to visit nearby Gloucester and Cheltenham. This hidden gem is now under new and enthusiastic ownership. 6.5 acre site. 65 touring pitches. 14 hardstandings. 10 seasonal pitches. Caravan pitches. Motorhome pitches. Tent pitches.

Leisure: ⚽

Facilities: 🚿 ⊙ 💨 ✲ ♿ [S] 🐕 Wi-fi 💻 ♻ ℹ

Services: 🔌 🛢 🍃 [T] ⛛

Within 3 miles: ⛵ 🎣 🌊 [S]

Notes: Minimum noise after 22.30hrs. Dogs must be kept on leads.

GREATER MANCHESTER

LITTLEBOROUGH Map 16 SD91

Places to visit

Imperial War Museum North, MANCHESTER, M17 1TZ, 0161 836 4000 www.iwm.org.uk

Manchester Art Gallery, MANCHESTER, M2 3JL, 0161 235 8888 www.manchestergalleries.org

Great for kids: Heaton Park, PRESTWICH, M25 2SW, 0161 773 1085 www.heatonpark.org.uk

►►► 70% Hollingworth Lake Caravan Park *(SD943146)*

Round House Farm, Rakewood Rd, Rakewood OL15 0AT
☎ 01706 378661 & 373919
dir: *From Littleborough or Milnrow (M62 junct 21), follow Hollingworth Lake Country Park signs to Fishermans Inn/The Wine Press. Take 'No Through Road' to Rakewood, then 2nd right*

* 🚐 £14-£16 🚌 £14-£20 ⛺ £8-£20

Open all year

Last arrival 20.00hrs Last departure noon

A popular park adjacent to Hollingworth Lake, at the foot of the Pennines, within easy reach of many local attractions. Backpackers walking the Pennine Way are welcome at this family-run park, and there are also large rally fields. A new amenities block with shop and reception is planned for the 2014 season. 5 acre site. 50 touring pitches. 25 hardstandings. Caravan pitches. Motorhome pitches. Tent pitches. 53 statics.

AA Pubs & Restaurants nearby: The White House, LITTLEBOROUGH, OL15 0LG, 01706 378456

Facilities: 🚿 ⊙ ✲ ♿ ✆ [S] ℹ

Services: 🔌 🧺 🛢 🍃 [T] 🔋 ⛛

Within 3 miles: ⛳ ⛵ 🎣 🌊 [S] 🧺 🐎

Notes: 🚫💳 🚫🐕 Family groups only. Pony trekking.

SERVICES: 🔌 Electric hook up 🧺 Launderette 🍺 Licensed bar 🛢 Calor Gas 🍃 Camping Gaz [T] Toilet fluid 🍴 Café/Restaurant 🥡 Fast Food/Takeaway 🔋 Battery charging 👶 Baby care ⛛ Motorvan service point **ABBREVIATIONS:** BH/bank hols-bank holidays Etr-Easter Spring BH-Spring Bank Holiday dep-departure fr-from hrs-hours m-mile mdnt-midnight rdbt-roundabout rs-restricted service wk-week wknd-weekend x-rds-cross roads 🚫💳 No credit cards 🚫🐕 No dogs 👪 Children of all ages accepted See page 9 for details of the AA Camping Card Scheme

HAMPSHIRE

BRANSGORE — Map 5 SZ19

Places to visit

Sammy Miller Motorcycle Museum, NEW MILTON, BH25 5SZ, 01425 620777 www.sammymiller.co.uk

Red House Museum & Gardens, CHRISTCHURCH, BH23 1BU, 01202 482860 www.hants.gov.uk/museum/redhouse

Great for kids: Moors Valley Country Park, RINGWOOD, BH24 2ET, 01425 470721 www.moors-valley.co.uk

►►► 85% Harrow Wood Farm Caravan Park (SZ194978)

Harrow Wood Farm, Poplar Ln BH23 8JE
☎ **01425 672487**
e-mail: harrowwood@caravan-sites.co.uk
dir: From Ringwood take B3347 towards Christchurch. At Sopley, left for Bransgore, to T-junct. Turn right. Straight on at x-rds. Left in 400yds (just after garage) into Poplar Lane

Open Mar-6 Jan

Last arrival 22.00hrs Last departure noon

A well laid-out, well-drained and spacious site in a pleasant rural position adjoining woodland and fields. Free on-site coarse fishing is available at this peaceful park. Well located for visiting Christchurch, the New Forest National Park and the south coast. 6 acre site. 60 touring pitches. 60 hardstandings. Caravan pitches. Motorhome pitches. Tent pitches. 14 bell tents/yurts.

AA Pubs & Restaurants nearby: The Three Tuns, BRANSGORE, BH23 8JH, 01425 672232

Facilities: 🖕⊙📷✻🕭🕒 Wi-Fi 🚻

Services: 🔌🗑 📦🛒↯

Within 3 miles: 🐟 🛒

Notes: ⊗ No open fires.

FORDINGBRIDGE — Map 5 SU11

Places to visit

Rockbourne Roman Villa, ROCKBOURNE, SP6 3PG, 0845 603 5635 www.hants.gov.uk/rockbourne-roman-villa

Breamore House & Countryside Museum, BREAMORE, SP6 2DF, 01725 512468 www.breamorehouse.com

Great for kids: Moors Valley Country Park, RINGWOOD, BH24 2ET, 01425 470721 www.moors-valley.co.uk

AA CAMPING CARD SITE

PREMIER PARK

►►►►► 88% Sandy Balls Holiday Village (SU167148)

Sandy Balls Estate Ltd, Godshill SP6 2JZ
☎ **0844 693 1336**
e-mail: post@sandyballs.co.uk
web: www.sandyballs.co.uk
dir: M27 junct 1, B3078, B3079, 8m to Godshill. Site 0.25m after cattle grid

* 🚐 £10-£60 � £10-£60 ⚠ £10-£60

Open all year (rs Nov-Feb pitches reduced, no activities)

Last arrival 21.00hrs Last departure 11.00hrs

A large, mostly wooded New Forest holiday complex with good provision of touring facilities on terraced, well laid-out fields. Pitches are fully serviced with shingle bases, and groups can be sited beside the river and away from the main site. There are excellent sporting, leisure and entertainment facilities for the whole family including a jacuzzi, sauna, beauty therapy, horse riding and children's activities. There's also a bistro, information centre and ready-erected tents and lodges for hire. 120 acre site. 225 touring pitches. 225 hardstandings. Caravan pitches. Motorhome pitches. Tent pitches. 37 statics.

AA Pubs & Restaurants nearby: The Augustus John, FORDINGBRIDGE, SP6 1DG, 01425 652098

Leisure: 🏊🏊‍♂️⛱🎠🎯🔍♫ Spa
Facilities: 🖕📷⊙📷✻🕭🕒🛉🎒🚻 Wi-Fi
♻ 🛈
Services: 🔌🗑 🍳🔒🛢📞🛒🏧🚮↯
Within 3 miles: 🐟🏊🛒🛍️🐎

Notes: Groups only by arrangement, no gazebos, no noise after 23.00hrs. Dogs must be kept on leads.

HAMBLE-LE-RICE — Map 5 SU40

Places to visit

Royal Armouries Fort Nelson, FAREHAM, PO17 6AN, 01329 233734 www.royalarmouries.org

Southampton City Art Gallery, SOUTHAMPTON, SO14 7LP, 023 8083 2277 www.southampton.gov.uk/art

Great for kids: Southampton Maritime Museum, SOUTHAMPTON, SO14 2AR, 023 8022 3941 www.southampton.gov.uk/leisure

►►►► 80% Riverside Holidays (SU481081)

**21 Compass Point, Ensign Way
SO31 4RA**
☎ **023 8045 3220**
e-mail: enquiries@riversideholidays.co.uk
web: www.riversideholidays.co.uk
dir: M27 junct 8, follow signs to Hamble on B3397. Left into Satchell Lane, site in 1m

Open Mar-Oct

Last arrival 22.00hrs Last departure 11.00hrs

A small, peaceful park next to the marina, and close to the pretty village of Hamble. The park is neatly kept, and there are two toilet and shower blocks complete with good family rooms. A pub and restaurant are very close by and there are good river walks alongside the Hamble. Lodges and static caravans are available for hire. 6 acre

LEISURE: 🏊 Indoor swimming pool 🏊‍♂️ Outdoor swimming pool 🎢 Children's playground 🪁 Kid's club 🎾 Tennis court 🔍 Games room 📺 Separate TV room
🏌 9/18 hole golf course ⛵ Boats for hire 🎬 Cinema ♫ Entertainment 🎣 Fishing ◎ Mini golf 🏄 Watersports 🏋 Gym 🏐 Sports field **Spa** 🐎 Stables
FACILITIES: 🖕 Bath 🚿 Shower ⊙ Electric shaver 📷 Hairdryer ✻ Ice Pack Facility 🕭 Disabled facilities 🕒 Public telephone 🛒 Shop on site or within 200yds
🛍️ Mobile shop (calls at least 5 days a week) 🍖 BBQ area 🎍 Picnic area Wi-Fi Wi-Fi 🖥 Internet access ♻ Recycling 🛈 Tourist info 🐕 Dog exercise area

site. 77 touring pitches. Caravan pitches. Motorhome pitches. Tent pitches. 45 statics.

AA Pubs & Restaurants nearby: The Bugle, HAMBLE-LE-RICE, SO31 4HA, 023 8045 3000

Riverside Holidays

Facilities: ♿🏁☉🅿✳♿🛁🛈

Services: 🔌🖥️🍴🍼

Within 3 miles: 🎣🛶🚲⛵🛁🛒⛴️

Notes: Dogs must be kept on leads. Bike hire, baby-changing facilities.

see advert below

LINWOOD — Map 5 SU10

►►► 84% Red Shoot Camping Park
(SU187094)

BH24 3QT
☎ 01425 473789
e-mail: enquiries@redshoot-campingpark.com
dir: *A31 onto A338 towards Fordingbridge & Salisbury. Right at brown signs for caravan park towards Linwood on unclassified roads, site signed*

🚐 🚙 ⛺

Open Mar-Oct

Last arrival 19.30hrs Last departure 13.00hrs

Located behind the Red Shoot Inn in one of the most attractive parts of the New Forest, this park is in an ideal spot for nature lovers and walkers. It is personally supervised by friendly owners, and offers many amenities including a children's play area. There are modern and spotless facilities plus a smart reception and shop. 3.5 acre site. 130 touring pitches. Caravan pitches. Motorhome pitches. Tent pitches.

AA Pubs & Restaurants nearby: The High Corner Inn, LINWOOD, BH24 3QY, 01425 473973

Leisure: 🅰

Facilities: 🏁☉🅿✳♿🕐🛁♻

Services: 🔌🖥️🍴🍼♿🍽️🚰

Within 3 miles: 🛶⛵🛁🛒⛴️

Notes: Quiet after 22.30hrs. Dogs must be kept on leads.

MILFORD ON SEA — Map 5 SZ29

►►►► 85% Lytton Lawn Touring Park *(SZ293937)*

Lymore Ln SO41 0TX
☎ 01590 648331
e-mail: holidays@shorefield.co.uk
dir: *From Lymington A337 to Christchurch for 2.5m to Everton. Left onto B3058 to Milford on Sea. 0.25m, left into Lymore Lane*

* 🚐 £12.50-£41.50 🚙 £12.50-£41.50
⛺ £12.50-£37.75

Open 6 Feb-2 Jan (rs Low season shop/reception limited hrs, no grass pitches)

Last arrival 21.00hrs Last departure 10.00hrs

A pleasant well-run park with good facilities, located near the coast. The park is peaceful and quiet, but the facilities of a sister park 2.5 miles away are available to campers, including swimming pool, tennis courts, bistro and bar/carvery, and large club with family entertainment. Fully serviced pitches provide good screening, and standard pitches are on gently-sloping grass. 8 acre site. 136 touring pitches. 53 hardstandings. Caravan pitches. Motorhome pitches. Tent pitches.

continued

MILFORD ON SEA *continued*

AA Pubs & Restaurants nearby: The Royal Oak, DOWNTON, SO41 0LA, 01590 644999

Leisure: ⚙ ☺ ✎

Facilities: ⚡ ☉ ☂ ✻ ⚟ ⚟ ⚟ ⚟ ⚟ ⚟ wifi ♻ 🄸

Services: ⚟ ⚟ ⚟ ⚟ ⚟ ⚟

Within 3 miles: ⚟ ⚟ ⚟ ⚟ ⚟ ⚟ ⚟ ⚟ ⚟ ∪

Notes: Families & couples only, no noise after 22.00hrs, rallies welcome. Dogs must be kept on leads.

see advert on page 203

RINGWOOD

See St Leonards (Dorset)

ROMSEY
Map 5 SU32

Places to visit

The Sir Harold Hillier Gardens, AMPFIELD, SO51 0QA, 01794 369318 www.hilliergardens.org.uk

Avington Park, AVINGTON, SO21 1DB, 01962 779260 www.avingtonpark.co.uk

Great for kids: Longdown Activity Farm, ASHURST, SO40 7EH, 023 8029 2837 www.longdownfarm.co.uk

PREMIER PARK

▶▶▶▶▶ 84% Hill Farm Caravan Park *(SU287238)*

Branches Ln, Sherfield English SO51 6FH
☎ 01794 340402
e-mail: gjb@hillfarmpark.com
dir: *Signed from A27 (Salisbury to Romsey road) in Sherfield English. 4m NW of Romsey & M27 junct 2*

⚟ ⚟ 🛆

Open Mar-Oct

Last arrival 20.00hrs Last departure noon

A small, well-sheltered park peacefully located amidst mature trees and meadows. The two toilet blocks offer smart unisex showers as well as a fully en suite family/disabled room and plenty of privacy in the washrooms. Bramleys, a good café/restaurant, with an outside patio, serves a wide range of snacks and meals. This attractive park is well placed for visiting Salisbury and the New Forest National Park, and the south coast is only a short drive away,

making it an appealing holiday location. 10.5 acre site. 100 touring pitches. 60 hardstandings. Caravan pitches. Motorhome pitches. Tent pitches. 6 statics.

AA Pubs & Restaurants nearby: The Cromwell Arms, ROMSEY, SO51 8HG, 01794 519515

The Three Tuns, ROMSEY, SO51 8HL, 01794 512639

Leisure: ⚙ ☺

Facilities: ⚡ ☉ ☂ ✻ ⚟ ⚟ ⚟ ⚟ ⚟ wifi 🖥 ♻ 🄸

Services: ⚟ ⚟ ⚟ ⚟ ⚟ ⚟ ⚟ ⚟

Within 3 miles: ⚟ ⚟ ⚟ ⚟ ⚟ ⚟ ⚟ ∪

Notes: Minimum noise at all times & no noise after 23.00hrs, one unit per pitch. Site unsuitable for teenagers. 9-hole pitch & putt.

▶▶▶ 82% Green Pastures Farm Camping & Touring Park *(SU321158)*

Ower SO51 6AJ
☎ 023 8081 4444
e-mail: enquiries@greenpasturesfarm.com
dir: *M27 junct 2. Follow Salisbury signs for 0.5m, then brown tourist signs for Green Pastures. Also signed from A36 & A3090 at Ower*

⚟ ⚟ 🛆

Open 13 Mar-Oct

Last arrival 20.30hrs Last departure 11.00hrs

In their first year the new owners have improved this pleasant site by adding a roadway through the park and extra electric hook-ups and by installing a code-access security barrier. The site is well located for visiting Paultons Theme Park, Southampton and the New Forest National Park, and being close to the M27 it is convenient for overnight stops. There are kennels where dogs can be left while you visit the theme park or go shopping. 6 acre site. 53 touring pitches. 6 hardstandings. Caravan pitches. Motorhome pitches. Tent pitches.

AA Pubs & Restaurants nearby: Sir John Barleycorn, CADNAM, SO40 2NP, 023 8081 2236

Facilities: ⚡ ✻ ⚟ ⚟ ⚟ ♻ 🄸

Services: ⚟ ⚟ ⚟ ⚟ ⚟ ⚟

Within 3 miles: ⚟ ⚟ ⚟ ⚟

Notes: No water games, off-ground BBQs only. Dogs must be kept on leads.

WARSASH
Map 5 SU40

Places to visit

Explosion Museum of Naval Firepower, GOSPORT, PO12 4LE, 023 9250 5600 www.explosion.org.uk

Portchester Castle, PORTCHESTER, PO16 9QW, 023 9237 8291 www.english-heritage.org.uk/daysout/properties/portchester-castle

Great for kids: Blue Reef Aquarium, PORTSMOUTH, PO5 3PB, 023 9287 5222 www.bluereefaquarium.co.uk

▶▶▶▶ 84% Dibles Park *(SU505060)*

Dibles Rd SO31 9SA
☎ 01489 575232
e-mail: dibles.park@btconnect.com
dir: *M27 junct 9, at rdbt 5th exit (Parkgate A27), 3rd rdbt 1st exit, 4th rdbt 2nd exit. Site 500yds on left. Or M27 junct 8, at rdbt 1st exit (Parkgate), next rdbt 3rd exit (Brook Ln), 4th rdbt 2nd exit. Site 500yds on left*

⚟ ⚟ 🛆

Open all year

Last arrival 20.30hrs Last departure 11.00hrs

A small peaceful touring park adjacent to a private residential park. The facilities are excellent and spotlessly clean. A warm welcome awaits visitors to this well-managed park, which is very convenient for the Hamble, the Solent and the cross-channel ferries. Excellent information on local walks from the site is available. 0.75 acre site. 14 touring pitches. 14 hardstandings. Caravan pitches. Motorhome pitches. Tent pitches. 46 statics.

AA Pubs & Restaurants nearby: The Jolly Farmer Country Inn, WARSASH, SO31 9JH, 01489 572500

Facilities: ⚡ ☉ ☂ ✻ ⚟ ⚟ ♻ 🄸

Services: ⚟ ⚟ ⚟ ⚟

Within 3 miles: ⚟ ⚟ ⚟ ⚟ ⚟ ⚟ ∪

Notes: Dogs must be kept on leads.

LEISURE: 🏊 Indoor swimming pool 🏊 Outdoor swimming pool ⚙ Children's playground 🛝 Kid's club ⚟ Tennis court ⚟ Games room ⬚ Separate TV room ⚟ 9/18 hole golf course ⚟ Boats for hire ⬚ Cinema ⚟ Entertainment ⚟ Fishing ◎ Mini golf ⚟ Watersports ⚟ Gym ⚟ Sports field **Spa** ∪ Stables
FACILITIES: ⚟ Bath ⚟ Shower ☉ Electric shaver ☂ Hairdryer ✻ Ice Pack Facility ⚟ Disabled facilities ⚟ Public telephone ⚟ Shop on site or within 200yds ⚟ Mobile shop (calls at least 5 days a week) ⚟ BBQ area ⚟ Picnic area wifi Wi-fi 🖥 Internet access ♻ Recycling 🄸 Tourist info ⚟ Dog exercise area

HEREFORDSHIRE

EARDISLAND Map 9 SO45

Places to visit

Berrington Hall, ASHTON, HR6 0DW, 01568 615721 www.nationaltrust.org.uk/berringtonhall

Hergest Croft Gardens, KINGTON, HR5 3EG, 01544 230160 www.hergest.co.uk

Great for kids: Croft Castle & Parkland, CROFT, HR6 9PW, 01568 780246 www.nationaltrust.org.uk/main/w-croftcastle

AA CAMPING CARD SITE

►►► 89% Arrow Bank Holiday Park

(SO419588)

Nun House Farm HR6 9BG
☎ 01544 388312
e-mail: enquiries@arrowbankholidaypark.co.uk
dir: *From Leominster A44 towards Rhayader. Right to Eardisland, follow signs*

* 🚐 £18-£22 🚌 £18-£22 ⛺ £15-£19

Open Mar-7 Jan

Last arrival 21.00hrs Last departure 11.30hrs

This peaceful park is set in the beautiful 'Black and White' village of Eardisland with its free exhibitions, tea rooms and heritage centre. The park is well positioned for visiting the many local attractions, as well as those further afield such as Ludlow Castle, Ross-on-Wye, Shrewsbury and Wales. The modern toilet facilities are spotlessly clean. 65 acre site. 38 touring pitches. 38 hardstandings. 16 seasonal pitches. Caravan pitches. Motorhome pitches. Tent pitches. 60 statics. 4 bell tents/yurts.

AA Pubs & Restaurants nearby: New Inn, PEMBRIDGE, HR6 9DZ, 01544 388427

The Stagg Inn and Restaurant, KINGTON, HR5 3RL, 01544 230221

Facilities: 🚿 ⊙ 💨 ♿ ✆ 🐕 [Wi-fi] ℹ

Services: 🔌 🧺 🛢 ⛽ [T] 🔋

Within 3 miles: ⛳ [S] 🧺

Notes: No ball games, skateboards or cycles. Dogs must be kept on leads.

HEREFORD Map 10 SO53

Places to visit

Cider Museum, HEREFORD, HR4 0LW, 01432 354207 www.cidermuseum.co.uk

Great for kids: Goodrich Castle, GOODRICH, HR9 6HY, 01600 890538 www.english-heritage.org.uk/daysout/properties/goodrich-castle

► 69% Ridge Hill Caravan and Campsite *(SO509355)*

HR2 8AG
☎ 01432 351293
e-mail: ridgehill@fsmail.net
dir: *From Hereford on A49, take B4399 signed Rotherwas. At 1st rdbt follow Dinedor/Little Dewchurch signs, in 1m signed Ridge Hill/Twyford turn right. Right at phone box, 200yds, site on right*

* 🚐 £7 🚌 £7 ⛺ £6-£7

Open Mar-Oct

Last departure noon

A simple, basic site set high on Ridge Hill a few miles south of Hereford. This peaceful site offers outstanding views over the countryside. It does not have toilets or showers, and therefore own facilities are essential, although toilet tents can be supplied on request at certain times of the year. (NB Please do not rely on Sat Nav directions to this site - guidebook directions should be used for caravans and motorhomes). 1.3 acre site. 5 touring pitches. Caravan pitches. Motorhome pitches. Tent pitches.

AA Pubs & Restaurants nearby: Castle House, HEREFORD, HR1 2NW, 01432 356321

Facilities: ♻ ℹ

Within 3 miles: 🏊 ⛳ [S] 🧺

Notes: 💳 Dogs must be kept on leads.

MORETON ON LUGG Map 10 SO54

Places to visit

The Weir Gardens, SWAINSHILL, HR4 7QF, 01981 590509 www.nationaltrust.org.uk

Brockhampton Estate, BROCKHAMPTON, WR6 5TB, 01885 482077 www.nationaltrust.org.uk/brockhampton

►►► 80% Cuckoo's Corner Campsite

(SO501456)

Cuckoo's Corner HR4 8AH
☎ 01432 760234
e-mail: cuckooscorner@gmail.com
dir: *Direct access from A49. From Hereford 2nd left after Moreton on Lugg sign. From Leominster 1st right (non gated road) after brown sign. Right just before island*

🚐 🚌 ⛺

Open all year

Last arrival 21.00hrs Last departure 13.00hrs

This small adults-only site is well positioned just north of Hereford, with easy access to the city. The site has two areas and offers hardstandings and some electric pitches. It is an ideal spot for an overnight stop or for longer stay in order to visit the attractions of the area. For 2014 - the installation of two new unisex rooms with shower, wash basin and toilet. There's a bus stop just outside the site and a full timetable is available from the reception office. 3 acre site. 19 touring pitches. 15 hardstandings. Caravan pitches. Motorhome pitches. Tent pitches.

AA Pubs & Restaurants nearby: England's Gate Inn, BODENHAM, HR1 3HU, 01568 797286

The Wellington, WELLINGTON, HR4 8AT, 01432 830367

Facilities: 🚿 ⊙ ✲ 🐕 [Wi-fi] 💻 ♻ ℹ

Services: 🔌 🧺 🍟

Within 3 miles: 🏊 ⛳ [S]

Notes: Adults only. 💳 No large groups, no noise after 22.30hrs. Dogs must be kept on leads. DVD library, books & magazines.

SERVICES: 🔌 Electric hook up 🧺 Launderette 🍷 Licensed bar 🛢 Calor Gas ⛽ Camping Gaz [T] Toilet fluid 🍴 Café/Restaurant 🍟 Fast Food/Takeaway 🔋 Battery charging 🍼 Baby care 🚰 Motorvan service point **ABBREVIATIONS:** BH/bank hols-bank holidays Etr-Easter Spring BH-Spring Bank Holiday dep-departure fr-from hrs-hours m-mile mdnt-midnight rdbt-roundabout rs-restricted service wk-week wknd-weekend x-rds-cross roads 💳 No credit cards 🚫 No dogs 👪 Children of all ages accepted See page 9 for details of the AA Camping Card Scheme

PEMBRIDGE   Map 9 SO35

Places to visit

The Weir Gardens, SWAINSHILL, HR4 7QF, 01981 590509 www.nationaltrust.org.uk

Brockhampton Estate, BROCKHAMPTON, WR6 5TB, 01885 482077 www.nationaltrust.org.uk/brockhampton

PREMIER PARK

▶▶▶▶▶ 88% *Townsend Touring Park* (SO395583)

Best of British

Townsend Farm HR6 9HB
☎ 01544 388527
e-mail: info@townsend-farm.co.uk
dir: A44 through Pembridge. Site 40mtrs from 30mph on E side of village

🚐 🚙 👤

Open Mar-mid Jan

Last arrival 22.00hrs Last departure noon

This outstanding park is spaciously located on the edge of one of Herefordshire's most beautiful Black and White villages. The park offers excellent facilities, and all hardstanding pitches are fully serviced, and it has its own award-winning farm shop and butchery. Coarse fishing is possible on the site's lake. It also makes an excellent base from which to explore the area, including Ludlow Castle and Ironbridge. There are four camping pods available for hire. 12 acre site. 60 touring pitches. 23 hardstandings. Caravan pitches. Motorhome pitches. Tent pitches.

AA Pubs & Restaurants nearby: New Inn, PEMBRIDGE, HR6 9DZ, 01544 388427

The Stagg Inn and Restaurant, KINGTON, HR5 3RL, 01544 230221

Leisure: ⚿

Facilities: 🛁 🚿 ⊙ 📷 ♿ ⚲ 🔥 ↺ 🐕

Services: 🔌 📶 🛒 ⚱

Within 3 miles: 🏬 📶 ↻

STANFORD BISHOP   Map 10 SO65

▶▶▶ 82% **Boyce Caravan Park**
(SO692528)

WR6 5UB
☎ 01886 884248
e-mail: enquiries@boyceholidaypark.co.uk
web: www.boyceholidaypark.co.uk
dir: A44 onto B4220. In Stanford Bishop 1st left signed Linley Green, 1st right into private driveway

* 🚐 £20-£24 🚙 £20-£24 👤 £20

Open Feb-Dec (static) (rs Mar-Oct (touring))

Last arrival 18.00hrs Last departure noon

A friendly and peaceful park with access allowed onto the 100 acres of farmland. Coarse fishing is also available in the grounds, and there are extensive views over the Malvern and Suckley Hills. There are many farm walks to be enjoyed. 10 acre site. 14 touring pitches. 3 hardstandings. 18 seasonal pitches. Caravan pitches. Motorhome pitches. Tent pitches. 200 statics.

AA Pubs & Restaurants nearby: Live and Let Live, BRINGSTY COMMON, WR6 5UW, 01886 821462

Leisure: ⚿ ⚽

Facilities: 🛁 ⊙ 📷 ✳ ♿ ↺ 🔥 🐕 ❶

Services: 🔌 📶 🛒 ⚱

Within 3 miles: 📶 🏬 📶

Notes: Certain dog breeds are not accepted (call site for details). Dogs must be kept on leads.

SYMONDS YAT (WEST)   Map 10 SO51

Places to visit

The Nelson Museum & Local History Centre, MONMOUTH, NP25 3XA, 01600 710630

Great for kids: Goodrich Castle, GOODRICH, HR9 6HY, 01600 890538 www.english-heritage.org.uk/daysout/properties/goodrich-castle

▶▶▶ 85% **Doward Park Camp Site**
(SO539167)

Great Doward HR9 6BP
☎ 01600 890438
e-mail: enquiries@dowardpark.co.uk
dir: A40 from Monmouth towards Ross-on-Wye. In 2m left signed Crockers Ash, Ganarew & The Doward. Cross over A40, 1st left at T-junct, in 0.5m 1st right signed The Doward. Follow park signs up hill (NB it is advised that Sat Nav is not used for end of journey)

🚙 👤

Open Mar-Oct

Last arrival 20.00hrs Last departure 11.30hrs

This delightful little park is set in peaceful woodlands on the hillside above the Wye Valley. It is ideal for campers and motorhomes but not caravans due to the narrow, twisting approach roads. A warm welcome awaits and the facilities are kept spotless. The Bluebell Wood children's play area is a great place for imaginative games. 1.5 acre site. 28 touring pitches. 6 seasonal pitches. Motorhome pitches. Tent pitches.

AA Pubs & Restaurants nearby: The Mill Race, WALFORD, HR9 5QS, 01989 562891

Leisure: ⚿

Facilities: 🛁 ⊙ 📷 ✳ ♿ 🛒 📶 ❶

Services: 🔌 📶 🛒 🔥 ⚱

Within 3 miles: ↓ ⚲ 📷 ◎ ⚓ 🏬 📶

Notes: No fires, quiet after 22.00hrs. Dogs must be kept on leads.

HERTFORDSHIRE

HODDESDON
Map 6 TL30

AA CAMPING CARD SITE

NEW ►►► 77% Lee Valley Caravan Park Dobbs Weir *(TL382080)*

Charlton Meadows, Essex Rd EN11 0AS
☎ 0845 677 0609
e-mail: dobbsweircampsite@leevalleypark.org.uk
dir: *From A10 follow Hoddesdon signs, at 2nd rdbt left signed Dobbs Weir. At next rdbt 3rd exit. 1m to site on right*

* 🚐 £13.50-£19.20 🚛 £13.50-£19.20
▲ £13.50-£19.20

Open Mar-Jan

Last arrival 21.00hrs Last departure noon

After several years of speculation about its future, Dobbs Weir finally reopened as a touring park in 2013 and provides much needed extra camping facilities close to London. Situated on level ground beside the River Lee, the smallest of the three London Authority parks has an extensively refurbished toilet block with modern facilities, a new large timber chalet housing the reception and shop, and an extremely innovative motorhome service point has been constructed. Plans include adding holiday static caravans and camping pods. On site fishing available. 11 acre site. 158 touring pitches. 15 hardstandings. Caravan pitches. Motorhome pitches. Tent pitches. 24 statics.

AA Pubs & Restaurants nearby: The Fox and Hounds, HUNSDON, SG12 8NH, 01279 843999

Leisure: ⚲

Facilities: ⬥⌂♤⚘☂⚐♨♿

Services: ⬢⚐🔋⚗️Ⓣ⚓

Within 3 miles: ♨⚓⚓⚐⚐

Notes: Dogs must be kept on leads.

see advert on page 234

KENT

ASHFORD
Map 7 TR04

Places to visit

Leeds Castle, MAIDSTONE, ME17 1PL, 01622 765400 www.leeds-castle.com

Great for kids: Thorpe Park, CHERTSEY, KT16 8PN, 0870 444 4466 www.thorpepark.com

PREMIER PARK

►►►►► 87%

Broadhembury Caravan & Camping Park *(TR009387)*

Best of British

Steeds Ln, Kingsnorth TN26 1NQ
☎ 01233 620859
e-mail: holidaypark@broadhembury.co.uk
web: www.broadhembury.co.uk
dir: *M20 junct 10, A2070 towards Brenzett. Straight on at 1st rdbt. Left at 2nd rdbt (avoid fork left). Straight on at next rdbt. Left at 2nd x-rds in village*

* 🚐 £17-£30 🚛 £17-£30 ▲ £15-£25

Open all year

Last arrival 22.00hrs Last departure noon

A well-run and well-maintained small family park surrounded by open pasture; it is neatly landscaped with pitches sheltered by mature hedges. There is a well-equipped campers' kitchen adjacent to the spotless toilet facilities and children will love the play areas, games room and football pitch. The adults-only area, close to the excellent reception building, includes popular fully serviced hardstanding pitches; this area has its own first-class, solar heated toilet block. 10 acre site. 110 touring pitches. 20 hardstandings. Caravan pitches. Motorhome pitches. Tent pitches. 25 statics.

AA Pubs & Restaurants nearby: The Wife of Bath, ASHFORD, TN25 5AF, 01233 812232

The New Flying Horse, WYE, TN25 5AN, 01233 812297

Leisure: ⚲◉♣▭

Facilities: ⬥⌂◉♤♨⚘♿⚐🔋⚓WiFi 🖥🔄♨

Services: ⬢🔋🔋⚗️Ⓣ⚓⚓

Within 3 miles: ♨⌂♤◉🔋⚐∪

Notes: No noise after 22.00hrs. Dogs must be kept on leads.

BIRCHINGTON
Map 7 TR36

Places to visit

Reculver Towers & Roman Fort, RECULVER, CT6 6SU, 01227 740676 www.english-heritage.org.uk/daysout/properties/reculver-towers-and-roman-fort

Great for kids: Richborough Roman Fort & Amphitheatre, RICHBOROUGH, CT13 9JW, 01304 612013 www.english-heritage.org.uk/daysout/properties/richborough-roman-fort-and-amphitheatre

AA CAMPING CARD SITE

►►► 83% Two Chimneys Caravan Park *(TR320684)*

Shottendane Rd CT7 0HD
☎ 01843 841068 & 843157
e-mail: info@twochimneys.co.uk
dir: *From A28 to Birchington Sq right into Park Lane (B2048). Left at Manston Rd (B2050), 1st left*

* 🚐 £15.50-£31.50 🚛 £15.50-£31.50
▲ £15.50-£28.50

Open all year (rs Off peak - shop, bar, pool & diner restricted)

Last arrival 22.00hrs Last departure 11.00hrs

continued

SERVICES: ⬢ Electric hook up ⬜ Launderette 🍷 Licensed bar 🔋 Calor Gas 🔋 Camping Gaz Ⓣ Toilet fluid 🍴 Café/Restaurant 🍔 Fast Food/Takeaway 🔋 Battery charging 🍼 Baby care ⚓ Motorvan service point **ABBREVIATIONS:** BH/bank hols-bank holidays Etr-Easter Spring BH-Spring Bank Holiday dep-departure fr-from hrs-hours m-mile mdnt-midnight rdbt-roundabout rs-restricted service wk-week wknd-weekend x-rds-cross roads ㉒ No credit cards ⊗ No dogs ♦♦ Children of all ages accepted See page 9 for details of the AA Camping Card Scheme

BIRCHINGTON *continued*

An impressive entrance leads into this busy, family-run site, which boasts two swimming pools, a fully-licensed clubhouse, crazy golf, an amusement arcade and a café/bistro. Other attractions include a tennis court and children's play area. The immaculately clean toilet facilities fully meet the needs of visitors at this popular family park. 60 acre site. 250 touring pitches. 5 hardstandings. 20 seasonal pitches. Caravan pitches. Motorhome pitches. Tent pitches. 200 statics.

AA Pubs & Restaurants nearby: The Ambrette, MARGATE, CT9 1QE, 01843 231504

Leisure: 🌊 🛝 ✋ 🎵

Facilities: 🚿 ⊙ 💨 ❄ ♿ ☎ 🏪 [Wi-fi] ♻ ℹ

Services: 🚰 🧺 🍷 🍃 [T] 🍴 🍔 🛒 👶

Within 3 miles: ⛳ ⛵ 🎬 🎣 ◎ 🏄 🏪 🧺 🐴

Notes: 🚫 No gazebos, no noise between 23.00hrs-07.00hrs, no bikes after dusk. Bus service.

►►► 81% Quex Caravan Park *(TR321685)*

GOLD

Park Rd CT7 0BL
☎ 01843 841273
e-mail: quex@keatfarm.co.uk
dir: *From Birchington (A28) turn SE into Park Rd to site in 1m*

🚃 🚐

Open Mar-Nov

Last arrival 18.00hrs Last departure noon

A small parkland site in a quiet and secluded woodland glade, with a very clean toilet block, an excellent café and informative boards around the site describing the wildlife to be seen. This picturesque, well-managed site is just one mile from the village of Birchington, while Ramsgate, Margate and Broadstairs are all within easy reach. 11 acre site. 48 touring pitches. Caravan pitches. Motorhome pitches. 180 statics.

AA Pubs & Restaurants nearby: The Ambrette, MARGATE, CT9 1QE, 01843 231504

Leisure: 🛝 ⚽

Facilities: 🚿 ⊙ 💨 ❄ ☎ 🏪 [Wi-fi] 💻 ♻ ℹ

Services: 🚰 🧺 🔥 🍃 [T] 🍴 🍔 🛒

Within 3 miles: ⛳ ⛵ 🎬 🎣 ◎ 🏄 🏪 🧺 🐴

Notes: Dogs must be kept on leads.

DOVER Map 7 TR34

Places to visit

The White Cliffs of Dover, DOVER, CT16 1HJ, 01304 202756 www.nationaltrust.org.uk

Walmer Castle & Gardens, DEAL, CT14 7LJ, 01304 364288 www.english-heritage.org.uk/daysout/properties/walmer-castle-and-gardens

Great for kids: Dover Castle & Secret Wartime Tunnels, DOVER, CT16 1HU, 01304 211067 www.english-heritage.org.uk/daysout/properties/dover-castle

►►►► 81% Hawthorn Farm Caravan Park *(TR342464)*

GOLD

Station Rd, Martin Mill CT15 5LA
☎ 01304 852658 & 852914
e-mail: hawthorn@keatfarm.co.uk
dir: *Signed from A258*

🚃 🚐 ⛺

Open all year (rs 18 Dec-7 Jan reception closed)

Last arrival 22.00hrs Last departure noon

This pleasant rural park set in 28 acres of beautifully-landscaped gardens is screened by young trees and hedgerows, in grounds which also include woods and a rose garden. A popular night-halt on route to and from the cross-channel ferry port, it has decent facilities including a shop/café, an excellent reception area and good hardstanding pitches. 28 acre site. 147 touring pitches. 15 hardstandings. Caravan pitches. Motorhome pitches. Tent pitches. 163 statics.

AA Pubs & Restaurants nearby: The Coastguard, ST MARGARET'S BAY, CT15 6DY, 01304 853176

Facilities: 🚿 ⊙ 💨 ♿ ☎ 🏪 [Wi-fi] 💻 ♻ ℹ

Services: 🚰 🧺 🔥 🍃 [T] 🍴 🛒

Within 3 miles: ⛳ ⛵ 🎬 🎣 ◎ 🏄 🏪 🧺 🐴

Notes: No noise after 22.00hrs. Dogs must be kept on leads.

EASTCHURCH Map 7 TQ97

Places to visit

Upnor Castle, UPNOR, ME2 4XG, 01634 718742 www.english-heritage.org.uk/daysout/properties/upnor-castle

The Historic Dockyard Chatham, CHATHAM, ME4 4TZ, 01634 823807 www.thedockyard.co.uk

74% *Warden Springs Caravan Park* *(TR019722)*

GOLD

Warden Point ME12 4HF
☎ 01795 880216
e-mail: warden.springs@park-resorts.com
web: www.park-resorts.com
dir: *M2 junct 5 (Sheerness/Sittingbourne), A249 for 8m, right onto B2231 to Eastchurch. In Eastchurch left after church, follow park signs*

🚃 🚐 ⛺

Open Apr-Oct (rs BH & peak wks)

Last arrival 22.00hrs Last departure noon

Panoramic views from the scenic cliff-top setting can be enjoyed at their best from the touring area of this holiday park. All of the many and varied leisure activities provided by the park are included in the pitch tariff, ie the heated outdoor swimming pool, adventure playground, family entertainment and a good choice of food outlets. 66 touring pitches. Caravan pitches. Motorhome pitches. Tent pitches. 198 statics.

AA Pubs & Restaurants nearby: The Ferry House Inn, LEYSDOWN-ON-SEA, ME12 4BQ, 01795 510214

Leisure: 🏊 🛝 ✋ 🎵

Facilities: 🚿 ⊙ 💨 ♿ ☎ 🏪 🧺 [Wi-fi] 💻

Services: 🧺 🍷 🍴 🛒

Within 3 miles: 🎣 🏪 🧺 🐴

Notes: No cars by caravans or tents.

FOLKESTONE
Map 7 TR23

Places to visit

Dymchurch Martello Tower, DYMCHURCH, CT16 1HU, 01304 211067 www.english-heritage.org.uk/daysout/ properties/dymchurch-martello-tower

Great for kids: Port Lympne Wild Animal Park, LYMPNE, CT21 4LR, 0844 842 4647 www.aspinallfoundation.org/portlympne

►►► 85% *Little Satmar Holiday Park* (TR260390)

Winehouse Ln, Capel Le Ferne CT18 7JF
☎ 01303 251188
e-mail: satmar@keatfarm.co.uk
dir: *Signed off B2011*

Open Mar-Nov

Last arrival 21.00hrs Last departure 12.00hrs

A quiet, well-screened site well away from the road and statics, with clean and tidy facilities. A useful base for visiting Dover and Folkestone, or as an overnight stop for the Channel Tunnel and ferry ports, and it's just a short walk from the Battle of Britain War Memorial, cliff paths with their views of the Channel, and sandy beaches below. 5 acre site. 47 touring pitches. Caravan pitches. Motorhome pitches. Tent pitches. 75 statics.

AA Pubs & Restaurants nearby: Rocksalt Rooms, FOLKESTONE, CT19 6NN, 01303 212070

Leisure:

Facilities:

Services:

Within 3 miles:

Notes: No noise after 22.00hrs. Dogs must be kept on leads.

►► 75% Little Switzerland Camping & Caravan Site (TR248380)

Wear Bay Rd CT19 6PS
☎ 01303 252168
e-mail: btony328@aol.com
dir: *M20 junct 13, A259 (Folkestone Harbour). At 2nd rdbt follow brown Country Park sign (A260). Right at next rdbt (country Park). 8th left into Swiss Way, site signed*

* £17.50-£26.50 £17.50-£26.50 £4-£9.50

Open Mar-Oct

Last arrival mdnt Last departure noon

Set on a narrow plateau below the White Cliffs and above The Warren, this unique site offers sheltered, traditional camping in secluded dells and enjoys fine views across the English Channel to the French coast - best enjoyed from the grassy alfresco area at the popular café. The toilet facilities are basic and unsuitable for disabled visitors. 3 acre site. 32 touring pitches. Caravan pitches. Motorhome pitches. Tent pitches. 13 statics.

AA Pubs & Restaurants nearby: Rocksalt Rooms, FOLKESTONE, CT19 6NN, 01303 212070

Facilities:

Services:

Within 3 miles:

Notes: No open fires. Dogs must be kept on leads.

LEYSDOWN-ON-SEA
Map 7 TR07

►►► 71% Priory Hill (TR038704)

Wing Rd ME12 4QT
☎ 01795 510267
e-mail: touringpark@prioryhill.co.uk
dir: *M2 junct 5, A249 signed Sheerness, then B2231 to Leysdown, follow brown tourist signs*

Open Mar-Oct (rs Low season shorter opening times for pool & club)

Last arrival 20.00hrs Last departure noon

A small well-maintained touring area on an established family-run holiday park close to the sea, with views of the north Kent coast. Amenities include a clubhouse and a swimming pool. The pitch price includes membership of the clubhouse with live entertainment, and use of the indoor swimming pool. 1.5 acre site. 37 touring pitches. Caravan pitches. Motorhome pitches. Tent pitches.

AA Pubs & Restaurants nearby: The Ferry House Inn, LEYSDOWN-ON-SEA, ME12 4BQ, 01795 510214

Leisure:

Facilities:

Services:

Within 3 miles:

Notes: Dogs must be kept on leads.

MARDEN
Map 6 TQ74

PREMIER PARK

►►►►► 88% Tanner Farm Touring Caravan & Camping Park (TQ732415)

Tanner Farm, Goudhurst Rd TN12 9ND
☎ 01622 832399 & 831214
e-mail: enquiries@tannerfarmpark.co.uk
dir: *From A21 or A229 onto B2079. Midway between Marden & Goudhurst*

£15.50-£25.50 £15.50-£25.50 £15-£25.50

Open 14 Feb-mid Nov

Last arrival 20.00hrs Last departure noon

At the heart of a 150-acre Wealden farm, replete with oast house, this extensive, long-established touring park is peacefully tucked away down a quiet farm drive deep in unspoilt Kent countryside, yet close to Sissinghurst Castle and within easy reach of London (Marden station 3 miles). Perfect for families, with its farm animals, two excellent play areas and recreation room (computer/TV), it offers quality toilet blocks with privacy cubicles, a good shop, spacious hardstandings (12 fully serviced), and high levels of security and customer care. 15 acre site. 100 touring pitches. 33 hardstandings. 10 seasonal pitches. Caravan pitches. Motorhome pitches. Tent pitches.

AA Pubs & Restaurants nearby: The Bull Inn, LINTON, ME17 4AW, 01622 743612

The Star & Eagle, GOUDHURST, TN17 1AL, 01580 211512

Green Cross Inn, GOUDHURST, TN17 1HA, 01580 211200

Leisure:

Facilities:

Services:

Within 3 miles:

Notes: No groups, 1 car per pitch, no commercial vehicles. Dogs must be kept on leads.

ROCHESTER Map 6 TQ76

Places to visit

Guildhall Museum, ROCHESTER, ME1 1PY, 01634 848717 www.medway.gov.uk

Upnor Castle, UPNOR, ME2 4XG, 01634 718742 www.english-heritage.org.uk/daysout/properties/upnor-castle

Great for kids: Diggerland, STROOD, ME2 2NU, 0871 227 7007 www.diggerland.com

82% Allhallows Holiday Park *(TQ841784)*

GOLD

Allhallows-on-Sea ME3 9QD
☎ 01634 270385
e-mail: allhallows@haven.com
web: www.haven.com/allhallows
dir: *M25 junct 2, A2 signed Rochester, A289 signed Gillingham. A228 signed Grain. Follow site signs*

Open Mar-Oct

Located in a peaceful country park setting close to Rochester, Allhallows is a static-only holiday park offering a wide range of sporting and leisure activities for all the family, including swimming pools, tennis courts, coarse fishing, a 9-hole golf course and fencing. Children will love the kids' club and play area, while there is a restaurant and bar with evening entertainment for adults.

Change over day: Mon, Fri, Sat **Arrival and departure times:** Please contact the site

Statics 93 Sleeps 6-8Bedrms 2-3 Bathrms 1-2 Toilets 1-2 Dishwasher Freezer TV Sky/FTV Elec inc Gas inc Grass area

Children 👪 Cots inc Highchair **Dogs** 2 on leads No dangerous dogs

Leisure: 🏊 🌊 🎾 🐴 🎣 ✋ 🛝

ST NICHOLAS AT WADE Map 7 TR26

Places to visit

Reculver Towers & Roman Fort, RECULVER, CT6 6SU, 01227 740676 www.english-heritage.org.uk/daysout/properties/reculver-towers-and-roman-fort

Great for kids: Richborough Roman Fort & Amphitheatre, RICHBOROUGH, CT13 9JW, 01304 612013 www.english-heritage.org.uk/daysout/properties/richborough-roman-fort-and-amphitheatre

►► 78% *St Nicholas Camping Site*

(TR254672)

Court Rd CT7 0NH
☎ 01843 847245
dir: *Signed from A299 & A28, site at W end of village near church*

🚐 🚌 ⛺

Open Etr-Oct

Last arrival 22.00hrs Last departure 14.00hrs

A gently-sloping field with mature hedging, on the edge of the village close to the shop. This pretty site offers good facilities, including a family/disabled room, and is conveniently located close to primary routes and the north Kent coast. 3 acre site. 75 touring pitches. 6 seasonal pitches. Caravan pitches. Motorhome pitches. Tent pitches.

Leisure: 🛝

Facilities: 🚿 ⊙ 💨 ❄ ♿ 🐕 ℹ

Services: 🚐 🔒 🍃 [T]

Within 3 miles: 🎣 [S] 🐴

Notes: 🚫 No music after 22.30hrs. Dogs must be kept on leads. Baby changing area.

WHITSTABLE Map 7 TR16

Places to visit

Royal Engineers Museum, Library & Archive, GILLINGHAM, ME4 4UG, 01634 822839 www.re-museum.co.uk

Canterbury West Gate Towers, CANTERBURY, CT1 2BQ, 01227 789576 www.canterbury-museum.co.uk

Great for kids: Howletts Wild Animal Park, BEKESBOURNE, CT4 5EL, 0844 842 4647 www.aspinallfoundation.org/howletts

►►►► 84% Homing Park

(TR095645)

SILVER

Church Ln, Seasalter CT5 4BU
☎ 01227 771777
e-mail: info@homingpark.co.uk
dir: *Exit A299 for Whitstable & Canterbury, left at brown camping-caravan sign into Church Ln. Site entrance has 2 large flag poles*

* 🚐 £19.50-£27 🚌 £19.50-£27 ⛺ £19.50-£27

Open Etr-Oct

Last arrival 20.00hrs Last departure 11.00hrs

A small touring park close to Seasalter Beach and Whitstable, which is famous for its oysters. All pitches are generously sized and fully serviced, and most are separated by hedging and shrubs. A clubhouse and swimming pool are available on site with a small cost for the use of the swimming pool. 12.6 acre site. 43 touring pitches. Caravan pitches. Motorhome pitches. Tent pitches. 195 statics.

AA Pubs & Restaurants nearby: The Sportsman, WHITSTABLE, CT5 4BP, 01227 273370

Leisure: 🌊 🛝 🎾

Facilities: 🚿 ⊙ 💨 ❄ ♿ [Wi-fi] ♻ ℹ

Services: 🚐 🧺 🍷 🔒 🍃

Within 3 miles: ⛳ 🎬 🎣 🏄 [S] 🧺 🐴

Notes: No commercial vehicles, no tents greater than 8 berth or 5mtrs, no unaccompanied minors, no cycles or scooters. Dogs must be kept on leads.

WROTHAM HEATH — Map 6 TQ65

AA CAMPING CARD SITE

►►► 80% Gate House Wood Touring Park *(TQ635585)*

Ford Ln TN15 7SD
☎ 01732 843062
e-mail: contact@gatehousewoodtouringpark.com
dir: *M26 junct 2a, A20 S towards Maidstone, through lights at Wrotham Heath. 1st left signed Trottiscliffe, left at next junct into Ford Ln. Site 100yds on left*

* 🚐 £15-£23.50 🚗 £15-£24 ⛺ £9-£23.50

Open Mar-Oct

Last arrival 21.00hrs Last departure noon

A well-sheltered and mature site in a former quarry surrounded by tall deciduous trees and gorse banks. The well-designed facilities include a reception, shop and smart toilets, and there is good entrance security and high levels of customer care. The colourful flower beds and hanging baskets are impressive and give a positive first impression. Conveniently placed for the M20 and M25 and a fast rail link to central London. 3.5 acre site. 55 touring pitches. Caravan pitches. Motorhome pitches. Tent pitches.

AA Pubs & Restaurants nearby: The Bull, WROTHAM, TN15 7RF, 01732 789800

Leisure: 🛝

Facilities: 🚿 ⊙ 🚿 ✲ ♿ ☎ $ Wi-fi ♻ ℹ

Services: 🔌 🧺 🔥 ⛽ [T] ⚓

Within 3 miles: ⛳ 🎣 🎾 ≋ $ 🐎

Notes: 💳🚫 🐕🚫 No commercial vehicles, no noise after 23.00hrs.

LANCASHIRE

See also sites under Greater Manchester & Merseyside

BLACKPOOL — Map 18 SD33

See also Lytham St Annes & Thornton

Places to visit

Blackpool Zoo, BLACKPOOL, FY3 8PP, 01253 830830 www.blackpoolzoo.org.uk

85% Marton Mere Holiday Village *(SD347349)*

Mythop Rd FY4 4XN
☎ 0871 231 0881
e-mail: martinmere@haven.com
web: www.haven.com/martonmere
dir: *M55 junct 4, A583 towards Blackpool. Right at Clifton Arms lights into Mythop Rd. Site 150yds on left*

🚐 🚗

Marton Mere Holiday Village

Open mid Mar-end Oct (rs Mar-end May & Sep-Oct reduced facilities, splash zone closed)

Last arrival 22.00hrs Last departure 10.00hrs

A very attractive holiday centre in an unusual setting on the edge of the mere, with plenty of birdlife to be spotted. The on-site entertainment is tailored for all ages, and includes a superb show bar. There's a regular bus service into Blackpool for those who want to explore further afield. The separate touring area is well equipped with hardstandings and electric pitches, and there are good quality facilities, including a superb amenities block. 30 acre site. 84 touring pitches. 84 hardstandings. Caravan pitches. Motorhome pitches. 700 statics.

Leisure: 🏊 🛝 ✋ ♫

Facilities: 🛁 🚿 ⊙ 🚿 ✲ ♿ $ 🐕 💻 ♻ ℹ

Services: 🔌 🧺 🍷 🔥 ⛽ 🍴 🍔 🍼

Within 3 miles: ⛳ 🎣 ⛳ 🎾 ◎ ≋ $ 🧺 🐎

Notes: No commercial vehicles, no bookings by persons under 21yrs unless a family booking. Max 2 dogs per booking, certain dog breeds banned. Dogs must be kept on leads.

see advert below

SERVICES: 🔌 Electric hook up 🧺 Launderette 🍷 Licensed bar 🔥 Calor Gas ⛽ Camping Gaz [T] Toilet fluid 🍴 Café/Restaurant 🍔 Fast Food/Takeaway 🔋 Battery charging 🍼 Baby care ⚓ Motorvan service point **ABBREVIATIONS:** BH/bank hols-bank holidays Etr-Easter Spring BH-Spring Bank Holiday dep-departure fr-from hrs-hours m-mile mdnt-midnight rdbt-roundabout rs-restricted service wk-week wknd-weekend x-rds-cross roads 💳🚫 No credit cards 🐕🚫 No dogs 👪 Children of all ages accepted See page 9 for details of the AA Camping Card Scheme

BLACKPOOL *continued*

►► 81% Manor House Caravan Park

(SD336318)

Kitty Ln, Marton Moss FY4 5EG
☎ 01253 764723

e-mail: info@manorhousecaravanpark.co.uk
dir: *At rdbt at end of M55 junct 4, take A5230 signed Sq Gate. At next rdbt take 3rd exit (Blackpool/Sq Gate/A5230). In 0.5m left at lights into Midgeland Rd. 500yds, straight on at x-rds. 250yds, right into Kitty Ln. 250yds site on right (NB it is advised not to follow Sat Nav)*

🚐 £20-£30 🚎 £20-£30

Open all year

Last arrival 20.00hrs Last departure 11.30hrs

A sympathetically converted former small holding close to both Lytham St Annes and Blackpool, this peacefully located adults-only park is surrounded by high neat hedges and generous sized hardstanding pitches ensure optimum privacy. A warm welcome is assured by the resident owners and although there is no shop or launderette, both services are within a ten-minute drive. There are caravan pitches and motorhome pitches. Please note that tents are not accepted. 1 acre site. 10 touring pitches. 10 hardstandings. Caravan pitches. Motorhome pitches.

Facilities: 🛏️♻️ ℹ️
Services: 🔌⛽
Within 3 miles: ⌕🎘🏕️⌖◎♨️🏪🏬🛒∪

Notes: Adults only. 🐾 No ball games or loud music. Pets accepted by prior arrangement only. Dogs must be kept on leads.

BOLTON-LE-SANDS   Map 18 SD46

Places to visit

Lancaster Maritime Museum, LANCASTER, LA1 1RB, 01524 382264
www.lancashire.gov.uk/museums

Lancaster City Museum, LANCASTER, LA1 1HT, 01524 64637 www.lancashire.gov.uk/museums

Great for kids: Lancaster Castle, LANCASTER, LA1 1YJ, 01524 64998 www.lancastercastle.com

►►►► 85% Bay View Holiday Park *(SD478683)*

GOLD

LA5 9TN
☎ 01524 701508

e-mail: info@holgatesleisureparks.co.uk
dir: *W of A6, 1m N of Bolton-le-Sands*

* 🚐 £20.50-£25.50 🚎 £20.50-£25.50
🏕️ £15.50-£18.50

Open all year

Last arrival 20.00hrs Last departure noon

A high quality, family-oriented seaside destination with fully serviced all-weather pitches, many of which have views of Morecambe Bay and the Cumbrian hills. A stylish bar/restaurant is just one of the park's amenities, and there is a wide range of activities and attractions on offer within a few miles. This makes a good choice for a family holiday by the sea. 10 acre site. 100 touring pitches. 50 hardstandings. 127 seasonal pitches. Caravan pitches. Motorhome pitches. Tent pitches. 100 statics. 2 wooden pods.

AA Pubs & Restaurants nearby: The Longlands Inn and Restaurant, CARNFORTH, LA6 1JH, 01524 781256

Hest Bank Inn, HEST BANK, LA2 6DN, 01524 824339

Leisure: 🏔️🎡🏹🖵
Facilities: 🏹◎✳️⚙️🕐🖊️🚿🏹📶♻️ℹ️
Services: 🔌⛽🍴🍽️🗑️🚽🍷🛒🏬⛟🚜
Within 3 miles: ⌕🎘🏕️⌖🏪🏬
Notes: Dogs must be kept on leads.

see advert on page 227

►►► 84% Sandside Caravan & Camping Park *(SD472681)*

The Shore LA5 8JS
☎ 01524 822311

e-mail: sandside@btconnect.com
dir: *M6 junct 35, A6 through Carnforth. Right after Far Pavillion in Bolton-le-Sands, over level crossing to site*

* 🚐 £19-£22 🚎 £19-£22 🏕️ £18

Open Mar-Oct

Last arrival 19.00hrs Last departure 13.00hrs

A well-kept family park located in a pleasant spot overlooking Morecambe Bay, with distant views of the Lake District. The site is next to a West Coast railway line with a level crossing. The shop and reception are assets to this welcoming park. Booking is advisable at peak periods. 9 acre site. 70 touring pitches. 70 hardstandings. Caravan pitches. Motorhome pitches. Tent pitches. 33 statics.

AA Pubs & Restaurants nearby: The Longlands Inn and Restaurant, CARNFORTH, LA6 1JH, 01524 781256

Hest Bank Inn, HEST BANK, LA2 6DN, 01524 824339

Facilities: 🏹◎🖊️🚿🛏️
Services: 🔌⛽
Within 3 miles: ⌕🎘🏕️⌖◎🏪🏬∪

Notes: No noise after mdnt. Dogs must be kept on leads. LPG (gas) available.

►►► 80% Red Bank Farm *(SD472681)*

LA5 8JR
☎ 01524 823196

e-mail: mark.archer@hotmail.co.uk
dir: *From Morecambe take A5015 towards Carnforth. After Hest Bank left into Pastures Ln (follow brown site sign). Over rail bridge, right (follow site sign). At T-junct left into The Shore to site at end*

* 🚎 fr £12 🏕️ fr £12

Open Mar-Oct

A gently sloping grassy field with mature hedges, close to the sea shore and a RSPB reserve. This farm site has smart toilet facilities, a superb view across Morecambe Bay to the distant Lake District hills, and is popular with tenters. Archers Café serves a good range of cooked food, including home-reared marsh lamb. 3 acre site. 60 touring pitches. Motorhome pitches. Tent pitches.

AA Pubs & Restaurants nearby: The Longlands Inn and Restaurant, CARNFORTH, LA6 1JH, 01524 781256

Hest Bank Inn, HEST BANK, LA2 6DN, 01524 824339

Facilities: ↖☉♱✳☘

Services: ♻⊡🖾

Within 3 miles: ↓✚⊟ℓ◎≚🖻🖻

Notes: No noise after 22.30hrs. Dogs must be kept on leads. Pets' corner.

CAPERNWRAY — Map 18 SD57

Places to visit

Sizergh Castle & Garden, SIZERGH, LA8 8AE, 015395 60951 www.nationaltrust.org.uk

Levens Hall, LEVENS, LA8 0PD, 015395 60321 www.levenshall.co.uk

►►►► 86% Old Hall Caravan Park (SD533716)

GOLD

LA6 1AD
☎ **01524 733276**
e-mail: info@oldhallcaravanpark.co.uk
web: www.oldhallcaravanpark.co.uk
dir: *M6 junct 35 follow signs to Over Kellet, left onto B6254, left at village green signed Capernwray. Site 1.5m on right*

🚐 £20-£26 🚍 £20-£26

Open Mar-Oct

Last departure noon

A lovely secluded park set in a clearing amongst trees at the end of a half-mile long drive. This peaceful park is home to a wide variety of wildlife, and there are marked walks in the woods. The facilities are well maintained by friendly owners, and booking is advisable. 3 acre site. 38 touring pitches. 38 hardstandings. 30 seasonal pitches. Caravan pitches. Motorhome pitches. 240 statics.

AA Pubs & Restaurants nearby: The Highwayman, BURROW, LA6 2RJ, 01524 273338

The Lunesdale Arms, TUNSTALL, LA6 2QN, 015242 74203

Leisure: ⛰

Facilities: ↖☉♱&☉♱🚾💻♻☘❶

Services: ♻⊡🖾🖾🖾🖾

Within 3 miles: ≚ℓ≚🖻🖻🖻U

Notes: No skateboards, rollerblades or roller boots. Dogs must be kept on leads.

COCKERHAM — Map 18 SD45

Places to visit

Lancaster Maritime Museum, LANCASTER, LA1 1RB, 01524 382264 www.lancashire.gov.uk/museums

Lancaster City Museum, LANCASTER, LA1 1HT, 01524 64637 www.lancashire.gov.uk/museums

Great for kids: Blackpool Zoo, BLACKPOOL, FY3 8PP, 01253 830830 www.blackpoolzoo.org.uk

►►►► 83% *Moss Wood Caravan Park* (SD456497)

GOLD

Crimbles Ln LA2 0ES
☎ **01524 791041**
e-mail: info@mosswood.co.uk
dir: *M6 junct 33, A6, approx 4m to site. From Cockerham take W A588. Left into Crimbles Lane to site*

🚐 🚍 Å

Open Mar-Oct

Last arrival 20.00hrs Last departure 16.00hrs

A tree-lined grassy park with sheltered, level pitches, located on peaceful Cockerham Moss. The modern toilet block is attractively clad in stained wood, and the facilities include cubicled washing facilities and a launderette. 25 acre site. 25 touring pitches. 25 hardstandings. Caravan pitches. Motorhome pitches. Tent pitches. 143 statics.

AA Pubs & Restaurants nearby: The Bay Horse Inn, FORTON, LA2 0HR, 01524 791204

Leisure: ⊕

Facilities: ↖☉♱&☉🖻♱🚐

Services: ♻⊡🖾🖾⊡

Within 3 miles: ↓ℓ🖻U

Notes: Dogs must be kept on leads. Woodland walks.

CROSTON — Map 15 SD41

Places to visit

Harris Museum & Art Gallery, PRESTON, PR1 2PP, 01772 258248 www.harrismuseum.org.uk

►►► 83% Royal Umpire Caravan Park (SD504190)

Southport Rd PR26 9JB
☎ **01772 600257**
e-mail: info@royalumpire.co.uk
dir: *From N M6 junct 28 (from S junct 27). Take B5209, right onto B5250*

🚐 🚍 Å

Open all year

Last arrival 20.00hrs Last departure 16.00hrs

A large park with tree- or hedge-lined bays for touring caravans and motorhomes, plus a large camping field in open countryside. There are many areas for children's activities and a several pubs and restaurants within walking distance. Four wigwam-style camping pods are available for hire. 60 acre site. 195 touring pitches. 180 hardstandings. Caravan pitches. Motorhome pitches. Tent pitches. 4 wooden pods.

AA Pubs & Restaurants nearby: Farmers Arms, HESKIN GREEN, PR7 5NP, 01257 451276

Leisure: ⛰⊕♫

Facilities: ↖☉♱✳&☉♱🚾🚾♻❶

Services: ♻⊡🖾🖾🖾🖾

Within 3 miles: ↓✚ℓ≚🖻🖻U

Notes: Dogs must be kept on leads.

FAR ARNSIDE Map 18 SD47

►►►► 87% Hollins Farm Camping & Caravanning

(SD450764)

LA5 0SL
☎ 01524 701508
e-mail: reception@holgates.co.uk
dir: *M6 junct 35, A601/Carnforth. Left in 1m at rdbt to Carnforth. Right in 1m at lights signed Silverdale. Left in 1m into Sands Ln, signed Silverdale. 2.4m over auto-crossing, 0.3m to T-junct. Right, follow signs to site, approx 3m & take 2nd left after passing Holgates*

* 🚐 fr £29 🚐 fr £29 ▲ fr £27

Open 14 Mar-7 Nov

Last arrival 20.00hrs Last departure noon

Hollins Farm is a long established park that continues to be upgraded by the owners. There are 50 fully serviced hardstanding pitches for tourers and 25 fully serviced tent pitches; the excellent amenities block provides very good facilities and privacy options. It has a traditional family camping feel and offers high standard facilities; most pitches offer views towards Morecambe Bay. The leisure and recreation facilities of the nearby, much larger, sister park (Silverdale Holiday Park) can be accessed by guests here. 30 acre site. 12 touring pitches. 12 hardstandings. 38 seasonal pitches. Caravan pitches. Motorhome pitches. Tent pitches.

Facilities: 🌂⊙✳🔧 **𝟶**
Services: 🔌🗑️ 🛢️🧹
Within 3 miles: ↓🌾 ⊙🛒🗇
Notes: No unaccompanied children. Dogs must be kept on leads.

see advert on page 227

FLEETWOOD Map 18 SD34

🏠 84% Cala Gran Holiday Park *(SD330451)*

Fleetwood Rd FY7 8JY
☎ 01253 872555
e-mail: calagran@haven.com
web: www.haven.com/calagran
dir: *M55 junct 3, A585 signed Fleetwood. At 4th rdbt (Nautical College on left) take 3rd exit. Park 250yds on left*

Open Mar-Oct

Cala Gran is a lively holiday park close to Blackpool with a range of quality holiday caravans and apartments. The park is all about fun, and the entertainment includes live music, comedy shows and resident DJs, while for children there are swimming pools and SplashZone.

Change over day: Mon, Fri, Sat **Arrival and departure times:** Please contact the site

Statics 226 Sleeps 6-8 Bedrms 2-3 Bathrms 1-2 Toilets 1-2 Freezer TV Sky/FTV Elec inc Gas inc Grass area

Children 👶 Cots Highchair **Dogs** 2 on leads No dangerous dogs

Leisure: 🏊✋🎠

GARSTANG Map 18 SD44

Places to visit

Lancaster Maritime Museum, LANCASTER, LA1 1RB, 01524 382264 www.lancashire.gov.uk/museums

Lancaster City Museum, LANCASTER, LA1 1HT, 01524 64637 www.lancashire.gov.uk/museums

Great for kids: Lancaster Castle, LANCASTER, LA1 1YJ, 01524 64998 www.lancastercastle.com

►►►► 83% Claylands Caravan Park

(SD496485)

Cabus PR3 1AJ
☎ 01524 791242
e-mail: alan@claylands.com
dir: *From M6 junct 33 S to Garstang, approx 6m past Thorpy's chipshop, left into Weavers Lane*

* 🚐 £25-£27 🚐 £25-£27 ▲ £20-£25

Open Mar-Jan

Last arrival 23.00hrs Last departure noon

Colourful seasonal floral displays create an excellent first impression. A well-maintained site with lovely river and woodland walks and good

views over the River Wyre towards the village of Scorton. This friendly park is set in delightful countryside where guests can enjoy fishing, and the atmosphere is very relaxed. The quality facilities and amenities are of a high standard, and everything is immaculately maintained. 14 acre site. 30 touring pitches. 30 hardstandings. Caravan pitches. Motorhome pitches. Tent pitches. 68 statics.

AA Pubs & Restaurants nearby: Owd Nell's Tavern, BILSBORROW, PR3 0RS, 01995 640010

Leisure: 🎠🎵
Facilities: 🌂⊙✳🔧🕐🗑️🛢️🖼️🚿📶♻️ **𝟶**
Services: 🔌🗑️🛒🍽️🛢️🍴🛒📶
Within 3 miles: ↓🌾🎣🛒🗇⛳
Notes: No roller blades or skateboards. Dogs must be kept on leads.

►►► 78% *Bridge House Marina & Caravan Park (SD483457)*

Nateby Crossing Ln, Nateby PR3 0JJ
☎ 01995 603207
e-mail: edwin@bridgehousemarina.co.uk
dir: *Exit A6 at pub & Knott End sign, immediately right into Nateby Crossing Ln, over canal bridge to site on left*

🚐🚐

Open Feb-1 Jan

Last arrival 22.00hrs Last departure 13.00hrs

A well-maintained site in attractive countryside by the Lancaster Canal, with good views towards the Trough of Bowland. The boatyard atmosphere is interesting, and there is a good children's playground. 4 acre site. 30 touring pitches. 50 hardstandings. Caravan pitches. Motorhome pitches. 40 statics.

AA Pubs & Restaurants nearby: Owd Nell's Tavern, BILSBORROW, PR3 0RS, 01995 640010

Leisure: 🎠
Facilities: 🌂⊙🛒✳🔧🕐🗑️📶 **𝟶**
Services: 🔌🗑️🛢️🧹🛒📶
Within 3 miles: ↓🌾🛒🗇
Notes: Dogs must be kept on leads.

KIRKHAM
Map 18 SD43

Places to visit

Castle Howard, MALTON, YO60 7DA,
01653 648333 www.castlehoward.co.uk

Duncombe Park, HELMSLEY, YO62 5EB,
01439 778625 www.duncombepark.com

Great for kids: Eden Camp Modern History
Theme Museum, MALTON, YO17 6RT,
01653 697777 www.edencamp.co.uk

▶▶▶ 80% Little Orchard Caravan Park (SD399355)

Shorrocks Barn, Back Ln PR4 3HN
☎ 01253 836658
e-mail: info@littleorchardcaravanpark.com
web: www.littleorchardcaravanpark.com
dir: *M55 junct 3, A585 signed Fleetwood. Left in 0.5m opposite Ashiana Tandoori restaurant into Greenhalgh Ln in 0.75m, right at T-junct, site entrance 1st left*

🚐 fr £18.50 🚐 fr £18.50 ▲ fr £15

Open 14 Feb-1 Jan

Last arrival 20.00hrs Last departure noon

Set in a quiet rural location in an orchard, this attractive park welcomes mature visitors. The toilet facilities are to a very high standard. Two excellent fisheries are within easy walking distance. The site advises that bookings should be made by phone only, not on-line. 7 acre site. 45 touring pitches. 45 hardstandings. 20 seasonal pitches. Caravan pitches. Motorhome pitches. Tent pitches.

AA Pubs & Restaurants nearby: The Ship at Elswick, ELSWICK, PR4 3ZB, 01995 672777

Facilities: 🅿️⚙️🅿️♿🍴♨️🚿 Wi-fi ♻️ 🅵

Services: 🔌🚾

Within 3 miles: 🅿️🐟🎣🚣♻️∪

Notes: 🐾 No cars by tents. No ball games or skateboards, no noise after 23.00hrs. Children must be supervised when in toilet blocks. No dangerous dog breeds. Dogs must be kept on leads.

LANCASTER
Map 18 SD46

Places to visit

Lancaster Maritime Museum, LANCASTER,
LA1 1RB, 01524 382264
www.lancashire.gov.uk/museums

Lancaster City Museum, LANCASTER, LA1 1HT,
01524 64637 www.lancashire.gov.uk/museums

Great for kids: Lancaster Castle, LANCASTER,
LA1 1YJ, 01524 64998 www.lancastercastle.com

▶▶▶ 82% New Parkside Farm Caravan Park (SD507633)

Denny Beck, Caton Rd LA2 9HH
☎ 015247 70723
e-mail: enquiries@newparksidefarm.co.uk
dir: *M6 junct 34, A683 towards Caton/Kirkby Lonsdale. Site 1m on right*

🚐🚐▲

Open Mar-Oct

Last arrival 20.00hrs Last departure 16.00hrs

Peaceful, friendly grassy park on a working farm convenient for exploring the historic City of Lancaster and the delights of the Lune Valley. 4 acre site. 40 touring pitches. 40 hardstandings. Caravan pitches. Motorhome pitches. Tent pitches. 16 statics.

AA Pubs & Restaurants nearby: The Sun Hotel and Bar, LANCASTER, LA1 1ET, 01524 66006

The White Cross, LANCASTER, LA1 4XT, 01524 33999

The Stork Inn, LANCASTER, LA2 0AN, 01524 751234

Facilities: 🅿️⚙️🅿️♿♨️♻️ 🅵

Services: 🔌🅵🔋

Within 3 miles: 🚶🏇🅿️🅵🛒

Notes: 🐾 No football. Dogs must be kept on leads.

LYTHAM ST ANNES
See also Kirkham

Places to visit

Blackpool Zoo, BLACKPOOL, FY3 8PP,
01253 830830 www.blackpoolzoo.org.uk

LYTHAM ST ANNES
Map 18 SD32

▶▶▶ 80% *Eastham Hall Caravan Park* (SD379291)

Saltcotes Rd FY8 4LS
☎ 01253 737907
e-mail: info@easthamhall.co.uk
web: www.easthamhall.co.uk
dir: *M55 junct 3. Straight over 3 rdbts onto B5259. Through Wrea Green & Moss Side, site 1m after level crossing*

🚐🚐

Open Mar-Nov (rs Nov only hardstanding pitches available)

Last arrival 21.00hrs Last departure noon

A large family-run park in a tranquil rural setting, surrounded by trees and mature shrubs. The pitch density is very good and some are fully serviced, plus the amenities blocks have been refurbished for the 2014 season. 15 acre site. 160 touring pitches. 99 hardstandings. 133 seasonal pitches. Caravan pitches. Motorhome pitches. 150 statics.

AA Pubs & Restaurants nearby: Greens Bistro, LYTHAM ST ANNES, FY8 1SX, 01253 789990

Leisure: 🎱⚽

Facilities: 🅿️⚙️🅿️☀️♿🕐🚿🚿 Wi-fi ♻️ 🅵

Services: 🔌🅵🔋🚿🅣

Within 3 miles: 🚶🏇🅿️◎🚣🛒🅵∪

Notes: No tents. Breathable groundsheets in awnings only. Dogs must be kept on leads. Football field, night touring pitches.

see advert on page 226

SERVICES: 🔌 Electric hook up 🅵 Launderette 🍺 Licensed bar 🅰️ Calor Gas 🛢️ Camping Gaz 🅣 Toilet fluid 🍽️ Café/Restaurant 🍔 Fast Food/Takeaway 🔋 Battery charging 🚼 Baby care 🔧 Motorvan service point **ABBREVIATIONS:** BH/bank hols-bank holidays Etr-Easter Spring BH-Spring Bank Holiday dep-departure fr-from hrs-hours m-mile mdnt-midnight rdbt-roundabout rs-restricted service wk-week wknd-weekend x-rds-cross roads 🐾 No credit cards 🚫 No dogs 👶 Children of all ages accepted See page 9 for details of the AA Camping Card Scheme

MORECAMBE
Map 18 SD46

Places to visit
Leighton Hall, LEIGHTON HALL, LA5 9ST, 01524 734474 www.leightonhall.co.uk

▶▶▶ 81% Venture Caravan Park
(SD436633)

Langridge Way, Westgate LA4 4TQ
☎ 01524 412986
e-mail: mark@venturecaravanpark.co.uk
dir: From M6 junct 34, A683, follow Morecambe signs. At rdbt 3rd exit, into Westgate. 1st right after fire station (site signed)

Open all year (rs Winter one toilet block open)

Last arrival 22.00hrs Last departure noon

A large family park close to the town centre, with good modern facilities, including a small indoor heated pool, a licensed clubhouse and a family room with children's entertainment. The site has many statics, some of which are for holiday hire. 17.5 acre site. 56 touring pitches. 40 hardstandings. Caravan pitches. Motorhome pitches. Tent pitches. 304 statics.

AA Pubs & Restaurants nearby: Hest Bank Inn, HEST BANK, LA2 6DN, 01524 824339

Leisure: 🏊 🎠 ⚽ 🎣
Facilities: 🛁 🚿 📶 🔌 ⚡ ☀ ♿ ⊙ 🅂 ♻
Services: 🔧 ⬛ 🍴 🍽 🚽 ⬛ 🛒 ⬇
Within 3 miles: ⚓ 🎬 🌊 🅂 🛒

Notes: Dogs must be kept on leads. Amusement arcade, off licence. Seasonal entertainment.

ORMSKIRK
Map 15 SD40

Places to visit
Astley Hall Museum & Art Gallery, CHORLEY, PR7 1NP, 01257 515555 www.chorley.gov.uk

British Commercial Vehicle Museum, LEYLAND, PR25 2LE, 01772 451011 www.bcvmt.co.uk

Great for kids: Camelot Theme Park, CHARNOCK RICHARD, PR5 5LP, 01257 452100 www.camelotthemepark.co.uk

NEW ▶▶▶▶ 82% Shaw Hall Holiday Park (SD397119)

Smithy Ln, Scarisbrick L40 8HJ
☎ 01704 840298
e-mail: shawhall@btconnect.com
dir: A570 from Ormskirk towards Southport. In Pinfold right into Smithy Lane

🚐 £25-£35 🚐 £25-£35 ⛺ £10-£20

Open all year

Last arrival 22.00hrs Last departure 10.30hrs

Ideally located between Southport and historic Ormskirk, this constantly improving holiday destination stands on open countryside and has the benefit of a waterside area, with boating holidays, in addition to well-equipped static homes and lodges. All touring pitches are fully serviced with water, waste water disposal, electric hook-up and TV connection, and future plans include a boating marina and a new serviced camping field. A well-stocked shop, stylish bar and entertainment room are additional benefits. 75 acre site. 37 touring pitches. 37

hardstandings. Caravan pitches. Motorhome pitches. Tent pitches. 247 statics.

AA Pubs & Restaurants nearby: The Eagle & Child, PARBOLD, L40 3SG, 01257 462297

Leisure: 🎠 🎣 🎮
Facilities: 🚿 ⊙ ♿ ⊙ 🅂 🛁 🐾 📶 ♻ 🛒 🚻 ℹ
Services: 🔧 ⬛ 🍴 🍽 🛒 🚽
Within 3 miles: ⚓ 🚴 🌊 ⊙ 🅂 🛒
Notes: Dogs must be kept on leads.

▶▶▶▶ 81% Abbey Farm Caravan Park (SD434098)

Dark Ln L40 5TX
☎ 01695 572686
e-mail: abbeyfarm@yahoo.com
dir: M6 junct 27, A5209 to Burscough. 4m, left onto B5240. Immediately right into Hobcross Lane. Site 1.5m on right

* 🚐 £18.20-£22.20 🚐 £18.20-£22.20 ⛺ £10.70-£24.80

Open Mar-Oct

Last arrival 21.00hrs Last departure noon

Delightful hanging baskets and flower beds brighten this garden-like rural park which is sheltered by hedging and mature trees. Modern, very clean facilities include a family bathroom, and there are suitable pitches, close to the toilet facilities, for disabled visitors. A superb recreation field caters for children of all ages, and there is an indoor games room, large library, fishing lake and dog walk. Tents have their own area with BBQ and picnic tables. 6 acre site. 56 touring pitches. 18 hardstandings. 46 seasonal pitches. Caravan

LEISURE: 🏊 Indoor swimming pool 🏊 Outdoor swimming pool 🎠 Children's playground 🧒 Kid's club 🎾 Tennis court 🎱 Games room 📺 Separate TV room 🏌 9/18 hole golf course ⛵ Boats for hire 🎬 Cinema 🎵 Entertainment 🎣 Fishing 🏌 Mini golf 🏄 Watersports 🏋 Gym 🏟 Sports field **Spa** U Stables
FACILITIES: 🛁 Bath 🚿 Shower ⊙ Electric shaver 🅿 Hairdryer ❄ Ice Pack Facility ♿ Disabled facilities 📞 Public telephone 🅂 Shop on site or within 200yds 🏪 Mobile shop (calls at least 5 days a week) 🍴 BBQ area 🪑 Picnic area 📶 Wi-fi 🖥 Internet access ♻ Recycling ℹ Tourist info 🐾 Dog exercise area

pitches. Motorhome pitches. Tent pitches. 39 statics.

AA Pubs & Restaurants nearby: The Eagle & Child, PARBOLD, L40 3SG, 01257 462297

Leisure: ⚊ ⚙ ⚘ ⚲

Facilities: ⚟ ⊙ ⚐ ⚒ ⚙ ⚙ Ⓢ 🛢 🏺 🚻 ⚙ 🅰

Services: 🔌 🧺 🛢 🚽 Ⓣ

Within 3 miles: 🚶 ⚲ 📷 🏰 🛢 ⚲

Notes: Closed for camping Oct-Mar, no camp fires, no noise after 23.00hrs. Dogs must be kept on leads. Off-licence, farm walk.

SILVERDALE

Places to visit

Leighton Hall, LEIGHTON HALL, LA5 9ST, 01524 734474 www.leightonhall.co.uk

Great for kids: RSPB Leighton Moss Nature Reserve, SILVERDALE, LA5 0SW, 01524 701601 www.rspb.org.uk/leightonmoss

SILVERDALE — Map 18 SD47

PREMIER PARK

▶▶▶▶▶ **95% Silverdale Caravan Park** *(SD455762)*

Middlebarrow Plain, Cove Rd LA5 0SH
☎ **01524 701508**
e-mail: caravan@holgates.co.uk
dir: *M6 junct 35. 5m NW of Carnforth. From Carnforth centre take unclassified Silverdale road & follow tourist signs after Warton*

* 🚐 fr £33 🚙 fr £33 ⛺ fr £33

Open all year
Last arrival 20.00hrs Last departure noon
A superb family holiday destination set in extensive wooded countryside overlooking the sea. All areas of the park are maintained in excellent condition with mature trees, shrubs and pretty, seasonal flowers creating a peaceful and relaxing atmosphere. The pitch density is generous and the spotlessly clean amenities blocks are conveniently located. An indoor swimming pool, smart bar/bistro and well-stocked shop are just a few of the additional amenities on offer. 100 acre site. 80 touring pitches. 80 hardstandings. 2 seasonal pitches. Caravan pitches. Motorhome pitches. Tent pitches. 339 statics. 3 wooden pods.

AA Pubs & Restaurants nearby: The Longlands Inn and Restaurant, CARNFORTH, LA6 1JH, 01524 781256

The Wheatsheaf at Beetham, BEETHAM, LA7 7AL, 015395 62123

Leisure: ⚊ 🏹 ⚊ ⚙ ⚲

Facilities: ⚟ ⊙ ⚐ ⚒ ⚙ ⚙ Ⓢ 🛢 🏺 🚻 ⚙ 🅰

Services: 🔌 🧺 🛢 🚽 ⚙ Ⓣ 🍴 ⚙ ⚙

Within 3 miles: 🚶 ⚲ 📷 🏰 🛢 ⚲

Notes: No unaccompanied children. Dogs must be kept on leads. Sauna, spa pool, steam room, mini-golf.

see advert below

Make the discovery
Holgates

Silverdale Caravan Park

Hard standing fully serviced 5 star pitches open all year

AA Campsite of the Year 2011

Hollins Farm

Beautiful secluded Farm site with hard standing fully serviced pitches

AA Campsite of the Year 2013 Winner for Most Improved Campsite

Bay View

Hard standing fully serviced pitches open all year round

To find out more contact us on 01524 701508 or
Email: info@holgates.co.uk   www.holgates.co.uk

THORNTON
Map 18 SD34

Places to visit

Blackpool Zoo, BLACKPOOL, FY3 8PP, 01253 830830 www.blackpoolzoo.org.uk

PREMIER PARK

►►►►► **82% Kneps Farm Holiday Park** *(SD353429)*

River Rd, Stanah FY5 5LR

☎ 01253 823632

e-mail: enquiries@knepsfarm.co.uk

web: www.knepsfarm.co.uk

dir: *Exit A585 at rdbt onto B5412 to Little Thornton. Right at mini-rdbt after school into Stanah Rd, over 2nd mini-rdbt, leading to River Rd*

* ⊞ £20-£24.50 ⊞ £20-£24.50

Open Mar-mid Nov (rs Mar & early Nov shop closed)

Last arrival 20.00hrs Last departure noon

A quality park, quietly located, adjacent to the River Wyre and the Wyre Estuary Country Park, handily placed for the attractions of Blackpool and the Fylde coast. This family-run park offers an excellent toilet block with immaculate facilities, and a mixture of hard and grass pitches (no tents), plus there are six camping pods for hire. 10 acre site. 40 touring pitches. 40 hardstandings. 5 seasonal pitches. Caravan pitches. Motorhome pitches. 40 statics. 6 wooden pods.

AA Pubs & Restaurants nearby: Twelve Restaurant and Lounge Bar, THORNTON, FY5 4JZ, 01253 821212

Leisure: ⚠

Facilities: ⊞🏕⊙🅿✳️⬇🚿⬇🚾🖥♻🛈

Services: 🔋🚽🗑🚐🅾🚰⬇

Within 3 miles: ⬇🎣🅿◎⬇🍴🛒

Notes: No commercial vehicles, max 2 dogs (chargeable) per unit. Dogs must be kept on leads.

LEICESTERSHIRE

See also Wolvey (Warwickshire)

CASTLE DONINGTON
Map 11 SK42

Places to visit

Twycross Zoo, TWYCROSS, CV9 3PX, 0844 474 1777 www.twycrosszoo.org

National Space Centre, LEICESTER, LE4 5NS, 0845 605 2001 www.spacecentre.co.uk

Great for kids: Snibston Discovery Museum, COALVILLE, LE67 3LN, 01530 278444 www.snibston.com

►►► **75% Donington Park Farmhouse** *(SK414254)*

Melbourne Rd, Isley Walton DE74 2RN

☎ 01332 862409

e-mail: info@parkfarmhouse.co.uk

dir: *M1 junct 24, pass airport to Isley Walton, right towards Melbourne. Site 0.5m on right*

* ⊞ £18-£29 ⊞ £18-£34 ▲ £14-£24

Open Jan-23 Dec (rs Winter hardstanding only)

Last arrival 21.00hrs Last departure noon

A secluded touring site, at the rear of a hotel beside Donington Park motor racing circuit, which is very popular on race days so booking is essential. Please note that both daytime and night flights from nearby East Midlands Airport may cause disturbance. 7 acre site. 60 touring pitches. 10 hardstandings. Caravan pitches. Motorhome pitches. Tent pitches.

AA Pubs & Restaurants nearby: The Priest House Hotel, CASTLE DONINGTON, DE74 2RR, 0845 072 7502

Leisure: ⚠

Facilities: 🏕⊙✳️⬇🚾🖥♻🛈

Services: 🔋🗑🚐🅾🍴⬇

Within 3 miles: ⬇🅿⬇🛒🍴U

Notes: Dogs must be kept on leads. Bread & milk sold. Hotel on site for bar & dining.

LINCOLNSHIRE

ANCASTER
Map 11 SK94

Places to visit

Belton House Park & Gardens, BELTON, NG32 2LS, 01476 566116 www.nationaltrust.org.uk

Belvoir Castle, BELVOIR, NG32 1PE, 01476 871002 www.belvoircastle.com

►►► **82% Woodland Waters** *(SK979435)*

Willoughby Rd NG32 3RT

☎ 01400 230888

e-mail: info@woodlandwaters.co.uk

web: www.woodlandwaters.co.uk

dir: *On A153 W of junct with B6403*

⊞ £16-£19.50 ⊞ £16-£19.50 ▲ £16-£19.50

Open all year

Last arrival 20.00hrs Last departure noon

Peacefully set around five impressive fishing lakes, with a few log cabins in a separate area, this is a pleasant open park. The access road is through mature woodland, and there is an excellent heated toilet block, and a pub/club house with restaurant. 72 acre site. 128 touring pitches. 5 hardstandings. Caravan pitches. Motorhome pitches. Tent pitches.

AA Pubs & Restaurants nearby: The Bustard Inn & Restaurant, SLEAFORD, NG34 8QG, 01529 488250

The Brownlow Arms, HOUGH-ON-THE-HILL, NG32 2AZ, 01400 250234

Leisure: ⚠🎣

Facilities: 🏕⊙🅿⬇🚿🚾🛈

Services: 🔋🗑🚐🚰⬇🍴🚰🛒

Within 3 miles: ⬇🅿🛒🍴U

Notes: No noise after 23.00hrs. Dogs must be kept on leads.

BOSTON

Places to visit

Battle of Britain Memorial Flight Visitor Centre, CONINGSBY, LN4 4SY, 01522 782040 www.lincolnshire.gov.uk/bbmf

Tattershall Castle, TATTERSHALL, LN4 4LR, 01526 342543 www.nationaltrust.org.uk

---

LEISURE: 🏊 Indoor swimming pool 🏊 Outdoor swimming pool ⚠ Children's playground 🧒 Kid's club 🎾 Tennis court 🎱 Games room 📺 Separate TV room ⛳ 9/18 hole golf course ⛵ Boats for hire 🎬 Cinema 🎵 Entertainment 🎣 Fishing ◎ Mini golf 🏄 Watersports 💪 Gym 🏐 Sports field U Stables

FACILITIES: 🛁 Bath 🏕 Shower ⊙ Electric shaver 🅿 Hairdryer ✳️ Ice Pack Facility ⬇ Disabled facilities 📞 Public telephone 🛒 Shop on site or within 200yds 🏪 Mobile shop (calls at least 5 days a week) 🍴 BBQ area 🌲 Picnic area 🚾 Wi-fi 🖥 Internet access ♻ Recycling 🛈 Tourist info 🐕 Dog exercise area

BOSTON Map 12 TF34

AA CAMPING CARD SITE

►►►► 83% Long Acres Touring Park
(TF384531)

Station Rd, Old Leake PE22 9RF
☎ 01205 871555
e-mail: enquiries@longacres-caravanpark.co.uk
dir: *From A16 take B1184 at Sibsey (by church); approx 1m at T-junct turn left. 1.5m, after level crossing take next right into Station Rd. Park entrance approx 0.5m on left*

🚐 🚗 ⛺

Open Mar-Oct

Last arrival 20.00hrs Last departure 11.00hrs

A small rural adults-only park in an attractive setting within easy reach of Boston, Spalding and Skegness. The park has a smart toilet block, which is very clean and has an appealing interior, with modern, upmarket fittings. Excellent shelter is provided by the high, mature boundary hedging. A holiday cottage is available to let. 2 acre site. 40 touring pitches. 40 hardstandings. Caravan pitches. Motorhome pitches. Tent pitches.

Facilities: 🚿 ⊙ 💨 ❄ ♿ 🐕 [Wi-fi] ♻ ℹ

Services: 🔌 🚰

Within 3 miles: 🎣 [S]

Notes: Adults only. Washing lines not permitted. Dogs must be kept on leads.

►►►► 81% Pilgrims Way Caravan & Camping Park *(TF358434)*

Church Green Rd, Fishtoft PE21 0QY
☎ 01205 366646 & 07973 941955
e-mail: pilgrimsway@caravanandcampingpark.com
dir: *E from Boston on A52. In 1m, after junct with A16, at Ball House pub turn right. Follow tourist signs to site*

* 🚐 fr £15 🚗 fr £15 ⛺ fr £10

Open all year

Last arrival 22.00hrs Last departure noon

A beautifully maintained and peaceful park within easy walking distance of the town centre that has many attractions. All pitches, named after birds species, are screened by well trimmed hedges to create optimum privacy; a lush tent field is also available. Regular barbecue evenings with entertainment are held during the warmer months. 2.5 acre site. 22 touring pitches. 15 hardstandings. Caravan pitches. Motorhome pitches. Tent pitches.

Leisure: 🛝 ♫

Facilities: 🚿 ⊙ 💨 ❄ ♿ ⛱ [Wi-fi] 💻 ♻ ℹ

Services: 🔌 🧺 🛢 ⛽

Within 3 miles: ⛳ 🐎 🏛 🎣 ◎ 🏊 [S] 🧺 🚴

Notes: 🚫💳 Dogs must be kept on leads. Tea house & sun terrace, day dog kennels.

►►►► 80% Orchard Park *(TF274432)*

Frampton Ln, Hubbert's Bridge PE20 3QU
☎ 01205 290328
e-mail: info@orchardpark.co.uk
dir: *On B1192 between A52 (Boston to Grantham road) & A1121 (Boston to Sleaford road)*

* 🚐 £17 🚗 £17 ⛺ £8.50-£17

Open all year (rs Dec-Feb bar, shop & café closed)

Last arrival 22.30hrs Last departure 16.00hrs

Ideally located for exploring the unique fenlands, this rapidly improving park has two lakes - one for fishing and the other set aside for conservation. The very attractive restaurant and bar prove popular with visitors, and Sandy's Café offers a delivery service to those fishing at the lakeside. 51 acre site. 87 touring pitches. 15 hardstandings. Caravan pitches. Motorhome pitches. Tent pitches. 164 statics.

Leisure: ⚽ 🔍 ♫

Facilities: 🛁 🚿 ⊙ 💨 ❄ ♿ ☎ [S] ⛱ 🐕 [Wi-fi] 💻 ♻ ℹ

Services: 🔌 🧺 🍷 🛢 ⛽ [T] 🍴 🔋 🍔

Within 3 miles: ⛳ 🎣 ◎ [S] 🧺 🚴

Notes: Adults only. 🚫💳 No washing lines. Dogs must be kept on leads.

CLEETHORPES Map 17 TA30

Places to visit

Fishing Heritage Centre, GRIMSBY, DN31 1UZ, 01472 323345 www.nelincs.gov.uk/leisure/museums

Great for kids: Pleasure Island Family Theme Park, CLEETHORPES, DN35 0PL, 01472 211511 www.pleasure-island.co.uk

83% Thorpe Park Holiday Centre *(TA321035)*

DN35 0PW
☎ 0871 231 0885
e-mail: thorpepark@haven.com
web: www.haven.com/thorpepark
dir: *From A180 at Cleethorpes take unclassified road signed Humberstone & Holiday Park*

🚐 🚗 ⛺

Open mid Mar-end Oct (rs mid Mar-May & Sep-Oct some facilities may be reduced)

Last arrival anytime Last departure 10.00hrs

A large static site, adjacent to the beach, with touring facilities, including fully serviced pitches and pitches with hardstandings. This holiday centre offers excellent recreational and leisure activities including an indoor pool with bar, bowling greens, crazy golf, 9-hole golf course, lake coarse fishing, tennis courts and a games area. Parts of the site overlook the sea. 300 acre site. 141 touring pitches. Caravan pitches. Motorhome pitches. Tent pitches. 1357 statics.

AA Pubs & Restaurants nearby: The Ship Inn, BARNOLDBY LE BECK, DN37 0BG, 01472 822308

Leisure: 🏊 🏊 🛝 ✋ 🎾 ♫

Facilities: 🚿 ⊙ 💨 ♿ ☎ [S] ⛱ [Wi-fi] 💻 ♻ ℹ

Services: 🔌 🧺 🍷 🛢 ⛽ 🍴 🍔 🍼

Within 3 miles: ⛳ 🏛 🎣 ◎ 🏊 [S] 🧺 🚴

Notes: No commercial vehicles, no bookings by persons under 21yrs unless a family booking. Max 2 dogs per booking, certain dog breeds banned. Dogs must be kept on leads.

GREAT CARLTON — Map 17 TF48

AA CAMPING CARD SITE

►►► 85% West End Farm (TF418842)

Salters Way LN11 8BF
☎ 01507 450949 & 07766 278740
e-mail: westendfarm@talktalkbusiness.net
dir: From A157 follow Great Carlton signs at Gayton Top. Follow brown sign for West End Farm in 0.5m, right into site

* ⚏ £12-£17 ⚏ £12-£17 ▲ £12-£17

Open 28 Mar-2 Oct

Last arrival 20.30hrs Last departure 14.00hrs

A neat and well-maintained four-acre touring park situated on the edge of the Lincolnshire Wolds. Surrounded by mature trees and bushes and well away from the busy main roads, yet connected by walking and cycling paths, it offers enjoyable peace and quiet close to the popular holiday resort of Mablethorpe. The site has good, clean facilities throughout and there's a passionate approach to everything 'green', with a reed bed sewage system, wild areas, bird and bat boxes and wildlife identification charts. 4 acre site. 35 touring pitches. 4 seasonal pitches. Caravan pitches. Motorhome pitches. Tent pitches.

AA Pubs & Restaurants nearby: Kings Head Inn, THEDDLETHORPE ALL SAINTS, LN12 1PB, 01507 339798

Leisure: ⚑
Facilities: ⚑⚑☀⚑⚑⚑
Services: ⚏⚏⚏
Within 3 miles: ⚑⚑⚑⚑⚑U

Notes: No fires, quiet after 22.30hrs. Dogs must be kept on leads. Fridge available.

HOLBEACH

Places to visit

Butterfly & Wildlife Park, SPALDING, PE12 9LE, 01406 363833 www.butterflyandwildlifepark.co.uk

HOLBEACH — Map 12 TF32

►►► 73% Herons Cottage Touring Park (TF364204)

Frostley Gate PE12 8SR
☎ 01406 540435
e-mail: simon@satleisure.co.uk
dir: 4m S of Holbeach on B1165 between Sutton St James & Whaplode St Catherine

⚏⚏▲

Open all year

Last arrival 20.00hrs Last departure 11.00hrs

Under the same ownership as Heron's Mead Touring Park in Orby (see entry), this park is situated in the heart of the Fens beside the Little South Holland Drain, with its extremely good coarse fishing. There's excellent supervision and 18 fully serviced pitches. 4.5 acre site. 52 touring pitches. 48 hardstandings. 40 seasonal pitches. Caravan pitches. Motorhome pitches. Tent pitches. 9 statics.

Facilities: ⚑⚑⚑⚑
Services: ⚏⚏⚏⚏⚏⚏⚏
Within 3 miles: ⚑⚑⚑

Notes: ⚑ Strictly no children under 12yrs. Dogs must be kept on leads.

MABLETHORPE — Map 17 TF58

Places to visit

The Village-Church Farm, SKEGNESS, PE25 2HF, 01754 766658 www.churchfarmvillage.org.uk

Great for kids: Skegness Natureland Seal Sanctuary, SKEGNESS, PE25 1DB, 01754 764345 www.skegnessnatureland.co.uk

84% Golden Sands Holiday Park (TF501861)

Quebec Rd LN12 1QJ
☎ 0871 231 0884
e-mail: goldensands@haven.com
web: www.haven.com/goldensands
dir: From centre of Mablethorpe turn left into Quebec Rd (seafront road). Site on left

⚏⚏▲

Open mid Mar-end Oct

Last arrival anytime Last departure 10.00hrs

A large, well-equipped seaside holiday park with many all-weather attractions and a good choice of entertainment and eating options. The large touring area is serviced by two amenities blocks and is close to the mini market and laundry. 23 acre site. 234 touring pitches. Caravan pitches. Motorhome pitches. Tent pitches. 1500 statics.

AA Pubs & Restaurants nearby: Red Lion Inn, PARTNEY, PE23 4PG, 01790 752271

Leisure: ⚑⚑⚑⚑⚑⚑
Facilities: ⚑⚑⚑⚑☀⚑⚑⚑⚑
Services: ⚏⚏⚏⚏⚏⚏⚏⚏⚏⚏
Within 3 miles: ⚑⚑⚑⚑⚑⚑

Notes: No commercial vehicles, no bookings by persons under 21yrs unless a family booking. Max 2 dogs per booking, certain dog breeds banned. Dogs must be kept on leads. Mini bowling alley, snooker/pool, indoor fun palace.

AA CAMPING CARD SITE

►►► 79% Kirkstead Holiday Park (TF509835)

North Rd, Trusthorpe LN12 2QD
☎ 01507 441483
e-mail: mark@kirkstead.co.uk
dir: From Mablethorpe town centre take A52 S towards Sutton-on-Sea. 1m, sharp right by phone box into North Rd. Site signed in 300yds

* ⚏ £16-£23 ⚏ £16-£20 ▲ £12-£18

Open Mar-Nov

Last arrival 22.00hrs Last departure 15.00hrs

A well-established family-run park catering for all age groups, just a few minutes' walk from Trusthorpe and the sandy beaches of Mablethorpe. The main touring area, which is serviced by good quality toilet facilities, has 37 fully serviced pitches on what was once the football pitch, and here portacabin toilets have been installed. The site is particularly well maintained. 12 acre site. 60 touring pitches. 3 hardstandings. 30 seasonal pitches. Caravan pitches. Motorhome pitches. Tent pitches. 70 statics.

AA Pubs & Restaurants nearby: Kings Head Inn, THEDDLETHORPE ALL SAINTS, LN12 1PB, 01507 339798

Leisure: ⚑⚑⚑⚑⚑
Facilities: ⚑⚑⚑☀⚑⚑⚑⚑⚑⚑⚑⚑ ⚑⚑
Services: ⚏⚏⚏⚏⚏⚏⚏⚏
Within 3 miles: ⚑⚑⚑⚑⚑⚑U

Notes: No dogs in tents. Dogs must be kept on leads.

LEISURE: 🏊 Indoor swimming pool 🏊 Outdoor swimming pool ⚑ Children's playground 🧒 Kid's club 🎾 Tennis court 🎱 Games room 📺 Separate TV room ⛳ 9/18 hole golf course 🚣 Boats for hire 🎬 Cinema 🎵 Entertainment 🎣 Fishing ◎ Mini golf 🏄 Watersports 💪 Gym 🏟 Sports field Spa ⚑ Stables
FACILITIES: 🛁 Bath 🚿 Shower ⚡ Electric shaver 💨 Hairdryer ❄ Ice Pack Facility 👤 Disabled facilities 📞 Public telephone 🏪 Shop on site or within 200yds 🛒 Mobile shop (calls at least 5 days a week) 🍖 BBQ area 🧺 Picnic area 📶 Wi-fi 💻 Internet access ♻ Recycling 🛈 Tourist info 🐕 Dog exercise area

MARSTON   Map 11 SK84

Places to visit

Belton House Park & Gardens, BELTON, NG32 2LS, 01476 566116 www.nationaltrust.org.uk

Newark Air Museum, NEWARK-ON-TRENT, NG24 2NY, 01636 707170 www.newarkairmuseum.org

▶▶▶▶ **84%** *Wagtail Country Park* (SK897412)

Cliff Ln NG32 2HU
☎ **01400 251955 & 07814 481088 (bookings)**
e-mail: info@wagtailcountrypark.co.uk
dir: *From A1 exit at petrol station signed Barkston & Marston, right signed Barkston into Green Ln, follow park signs*

🚐 🚎

Open all year

Last arrival 19.00hrs Last departure 16.00hrs

A peaceful site near the village of Marston, surrounded by trees and where birdsong is the only welcome distraction. The touring areas are neatly laid out and enhanced by mature shrubs and pretty seasonal flowers. There is a separate adults-only area, and coarse fishing (from dawn to dusk) is also available. 20 acre site. 49 touring pitches. 49 hardstandings. 10 seasonal pitches. Caravan pitches. Motorhome pitches.

AA Pubs & Restaurants nearby: The Brownlow Arms, HOUGH-ON-THE-HILL, NG32 2AZ, 01400 250234

Facilities: 🍴 🅿 🛁 🔥 🛒 ♻ ❗
Services: 🔌 🗒 🛢
Within 3 miles: ☂ 🎣 💷
Notes: No noise after 23.00hrs. Dogs must be kept on leads.

OLD LEAKE

Places to visit

Lincolnshire Aviation Heritage Centre, EAST KIRKBY, PE23 4DE, 01790 763207 www.lincsaviation.co.uk

Battle of Britain Memorial Flight Visitor Centre, CONINGSBY, LN4 4SY, 01522 782040 www.lincolnshire.gov.uk/bbmf

OLD LEAKE   Map 17 TF45

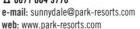
AA CAMPING CARD SITE

▶▶▶ **75% Old Leake Leisure Park** (TF415498)

Shaw Ln PE22 9LQ
☎ **01205 870121**
e-mail: oldleakeleisure@yahoo.co.uk
dir: *From Boston take A52 towards Skegness. In Old Leake right at x-rds into Shaw Lane, follow brown camping sign. At left bend turn right*

🚐 £16-£18 🚎 £16-£20 ⚑ £16-£18

Open Mar-Oct

Last arrival 22.00hrs Last departure noon

A pleasant, well-maintained small touring park set down a rural lane just off the A52, surrounded by the tranquillity of the Fenlands. It makes a peaceful base for exploring Boston and the Lincolnshire coast, and there are two holiday statics for hire. 2.5 acre site. 30 touring pitches. Caravan pitches. Motorhome pitches. Tent pitches.

Leisure: ⚽
Facilities: 🛁 📶 ♻ ❗
Services: 🔌
Within 3 miles: 🍴 🎣 💷
Notes: ⊗ No noise after 22.00hrs.

ORBY   Map 17 TF46

Places to visit

The Village-Church Farm, SKEGNESS, PE25 2HF, 01754 766658 www.churchfarmvillage.org.uk

Great for kids: Skegness Natureland Seal Sanctuary, SKEGNESS, PE25 1DB, 01754 764345 www.skegnessnatureland.co.uk

▶▶▶▶ **80% Heron's Mead Fishing Lake & Touring Park** (TF508673)

Marsh Ln PE24 5JA
☎ **01754 811340 & 07876 025369**
e-mail: mail@heronsmeadtouringpark.co.uk
dir: *From A158 (Lincoln to Skegness road) turn left at rdbt, through Orby for 0.5m*

🚐 🚎 ⚑

Open Mar-1 Nov

Last arrival 21.00hrs Last departure noon

A pleasant fishing and touring park with a carp coarse fishing lake and an eight-acre woodland

walk. The owners continue to improve the facilities, which prove particularly appealing to quiet couples and more mature visitors. 16 acre site. 21 touring pitches. 14 hardstandings. 10 seasonal pitches. Caravan pitches. Motorhome pitches. Tent pitches. 50 statics.

Facilities: 🍴 ⊙ 🅿 ✳ 🛁 ♿ 🛒 🔥 ♻ ❗
Services: 🔌 🗒 🛢 ♨
Within 3 miles: ☂ 🎣 ♨ 💷 🗒 ∪
Notes: No cars by caravans or tents. No ball games, no motorbikes.

SALTFLEET   Map 17 TF49

 83% *Sunnydale* (TF455941)

Sea Ln LN11 7RP
☎ **0871 664 9776**
e-mail: sunnydale@park-resorts.com
web: www.park-resorts.com
dir: *From A16 towards Louth take B1200 through Manby & Saltfleetby. Left into Saltfleet. Sea Lane on right. Site in approx 400mtrs*

🚐 🚎

Open Mar-Oct (rs BH & peak wks)

Last arrival noon Last departure 10.00hrs

Set in a peaceful and tranquil location in the village of Saltfleet between the seaside resorts of Cleethorpes and Mablethorpe. This park offers modern leisure facilities including an indoor pool, the tavern bar with entertainment, amusements and a coarse fishing pond. There is also direct access to the huge expanse of Saltfleet Beach. The touring facilities are incorporated into the leisure complex, and are modern and well cared for. 38 touring pitches. Caravan pitches. Motorhome pitches. 260 statics.

AA Pubs & Restaurants nearby: Kings Head Inn, THEDDLETHORPE ALL SAINTS, LN12 1PB, 01507 339798

Leisure: 🏊 🎮 🎯 🎵
Facilities: 🍴 🛁 ⊙ 💷 🔥 📶 🖥
Services: 🔌 🗒 🍺 🍽 🏪
Within 3 miles: 🎣 ♨ ♨ 💷 ∪

SERVICES: 🔌 Electric hook up 🗒 Launderette 🍺 Licensed bar 🛢 Calor Gas ⊘ Camping Gaz 🅃 Toilet fluid 🍽 Café/Restaurant 🏪 Fast Food/Takeaway 🔋 Battery charging 🍼 Baby care ♨ Motorvan service point **ABBREVIATIONS:** BH/bank hols-bank holidays Etr-Easter Spring BH-Spring Bank Holiday dep-departure fr-from hrs-hours m-mile mdnt-midnight rdbt-roundabout rs-restricted service wk-week wknd-weekend x-rds-cross roads ⊗ No credit cards ⊗ No dogs 👪 Children of all ages accepted See page 9 for details of the AA Camping Card Scheme

SKEGNESS Map 17 TF56

Places to visit

Skegness Natureland Seal Sanctuary, SKEGNESS, PE25 1DB, 01754 764345 www.skegnessnatureland.co.uk

The Village-Church Farm, SKEGNESS, PE25 2HF, 01754 766658 www.churchfarmvillage.org.uk

 **83% *Southview Leisure Park*** (TF541645) SILVER

Burgh Rd PE25 2LA
☎ 01754 896001
e-mail: southview@park-resorts.com
web: www.park-resorts.com
dir: *A158 towards Skegness. Park on left*

🚐 🚗

Open Apr-Oct

Last arrival noon Last departure 10.00hrs

A well-presented holiday and leisure park close to the resort of Skegness. The leisure and entertainment facilities are modern and well maintained, and are just a short walk from the touring area with its neat pitches and clean and tidy amenity block. The staff are friendly and efficient. 98 touring pitches. Caravan pitches. Motorhome pitches.

Leisure: 🏊‍♂️ 🏌️ 🎡 ⚽ 🎯 🎵
Facilities: 🛁 🚿 📷 ⏱️ 🔌 WiFi 💻 ♻️ 🅿️
Services: 🚐 🔄 🔧 🔨 🚽 ⊗ 🛒
Within 3 miles: ⬇️ 🎣 📋 🛍️ 🥤 🏪 🛒

TATTERSHALL Map 17 TF25

Places to visit

Tattershall Castle, TATTERSHALL, LN4 4LR, 01526 342543 www.nationaltrust.org.uk

AA CAMPING CARD SITE

▶▶▶▶ **83% Tattershall Lakes Country Park** (TF234587)

Sleaford Rd LN4 4LR
☎ 01526 348800
e-mail: tattershall.holidays@away-resorts.com
dir: *A153 to Tattershall*

* 🚐 £10-£42 🚗 £6-£42 ⛺ £6-£42

Open end Mar-end Oct (rs Off peak restricted services)

Last arrival 19.00hrs Last departure 10.00hrs

Set amongst woodlands, lakes and parkland on the edge of Tattershall in the heart of the Lincolnshire Fens, this mature country park has been created from old gravel pits and the flat, well-drained and maintained touring area offers plenty of space for campers. There's a lot to entertain the youngsters as well as the grown-ups, with good fishing on excellent lakes, an 18-hole golf course, water-ski and jet ski lakes and an indoor heated pool with spa facilities. There is a separate adults-only field. 365 acre site. 186 touring pitches. 20 hardstandings. 25 seasonal pitches. Caravan pitches. Motorhome pitches. Tent pitches. 500 statics. 3 bell tents/yurts.

AA Pubs & Restaurants nearby: The Lea Gate Inn, CONINGSBY, LN4 4RS, 01526 342370

Leisure: 🏊‍♂️ 🏌️ 🎡 ⚽ 🎯 🎣 🎱 📺 🎵 Spa
Facilities: 📷 ⊙ 🏪 👤 🚿 🔥 🚻 WiFi 💻 ♻️ 🅿️
Services: 🚐 🔄 🔧 🔒 🚽 🛒 🚗
Within 3 miles: ⬇️ 🥤 🎣 📋 🥤 🏪 🛒

Notes: No excessive noise after mdnt. Dogs must be kept on leads. Water & jet skiing, family activities.

WADDINGHAM Map 17 SK99

Places to visit

Gainsborough Old Hall, GAINSBOROUGH, DN21 2NB, 01427 612669 www.english-heritage.org.uk/daysout/properties/gainsborough-old-hall

▶▶▶ **78% Brandy Wharf Leisure Park** (TF014968)

Brandy Wharf DN21 4RT
☎ 01673 818010
e-mail: brandywharflp@freenetname.co.uk
dir: *From A15 onto B1205 through Waddingham. Site in 3m*

🚐 🚗 ⛺

Open all year (rs Nov-Etr no tents)

Last arrival dusk Last departure 17.00hrs

A delightful site in a very rural area on the banks of the River Ancholme, where fishing is available. The toilet block has unisex rooms with combined facilities as well as a more conventional ladies and gents with wash basins and toilets. All of the grassy pitches have electricity, and there's a playing and picnic area. The site attracts a lively clientele at weekends, and music around open fires is allowed until 1am. Advance booking is necessary for weekend pitches. 5 acre site. 50 touring pitches. Caravan pitches. Motorhome pitches. Tent pitches.

AA Pubs & Restaurants nearby: The George, KIRTON IN LINDSEY, DN21 4LX, 01652 640600

Leisure: 🎡
Facilities: 📷 ⊙ ❄️ 🚿 🔥 🚻 ♻️ 🅿️
Services: 🚐 🔄 🔒 🔧 🚽 🛒 🚗
Within 3 miles: ⬇️ 🥤 📋 🏪 🛒 ⛵

Notes: No disposable BBQs on grass, no music after 01.00hrs. Boat mooring & slipway, canoe hire, pedalos, pets' corner.

WOODHALL SPA
Map 17 TF16

Places to visit

Tattershall Castle, TATTERSHALL, LN4 4LR, 01526 342543 www.nationaltrust.org.uk

Battle of Britain Memorial Flight Visitor Centre, CONINGSBY, LN4 4SY, 01522 782040 www.lincolnshire.gov.uk/bbmf

---

PREMIER PARK

▶▶▶▶▶ 88% Woodhall Country Park (TF189643)

Stixwold Rd LN10 6UJ
☎ 01526 353710
e-mail: info@woodhallcountrypark.co.uk
dir: In Woodhall Spa at rdbt in High St take Stixwold Rd. 1m, site on right, just before Village Limits pub

* � £20-£24 ➤ £20-£24 ▲ £15-£17

Open Mar-Nov

Last arrival 20.00hrs Last departure noon

A peaceful and attractive touring park situated just a short walk from Woodhall Spa. The owners transformed part of the woodland area into a countryside retreat for campers who wish to escape from a hectic lifestyle. Well organised and well laid out, the park offers fishing lakes, three log cabin amenity blocks, fully serviced pitches and high levels of customer care. There's a strong ethos towards sustainability and a bio-mass boiler provides all heating and hot water supplies to the three superb amenities blocks, plus there are bird hides around the park. Six camping pods are available for hire. 80 acre site. 80 touring pitches. 80 hardstandings. Caravan pitches. Motorhome pitches. Tent pitches. 6 wooden pods.

AA Pubs & Restaurants nearby: Village Limits Country Pub, Restaurant & Motel, WOODHALL SPA, LN10 6UJ, 01526 353312

Leisure: ⚽

Facilities: 🛀⊙℘✻♿🚿🏧🎮⌂♻ ❶

Services: 🔌🗑🛢💧🔤

Within 3 miles: ↯🈵℘🏧🗑♻

Notes: No cars by tents. No fires, Chinese lanterns or fireworks, no noise between 23.00hrs-07.00hrs, BBQs must be off ground. Dogs must be kept on leads.

▶▶▶ 83% Glen Lodge Touring Park

(TF190647)

Glen Lodge, Edlington Moor LN10 6UL
☎ 01526 353523
e-mail: glenlodge1@tiscali.co.uk
dir: From Woodhall Spa take B1190 (Stixwould road) towards Bardney for 1m. At sharp left bend turn right, site on left

🚐 🚐

Open Mar-Nov

Last arrival 21.00hrs Last departure 02.00hrs

Peacefully located within a few minutes' drive of the village centre, this well-established park is surrounded by trees and colourful hedges. The spacious pitches are immaculately maintained and a warm welcome is assured. Please note, this site does not accept tents. 4 acre site. 35 touring pitches. 35 hardstandings. Caravan pitches. Motorhome pitches.

AA Pubs & Restaurants nearby: Village Limits Country Pub, Restaurant & Motel, WOODHALL SPA, LN10 6UJ, 01526 353312

Facilities: 🛀⊙✻♿♻

Services: 🔌🗑🛢

Within 3 miles: ↯🈵℘⊙🗑

Notes: 🚫 No noise after 23.00hrs. Dogs must be kept on leads.

E4 CHINGFORD
Map 6 TQ39

AA CAMPING CARD SITE

▶▶▶▶ 83% Lee Valley Campsite

(TQ381970)

Sewardstone Rd, Chingford E4 7RA
☎ 020 8529 5689
e-mail: sewardstonecampsite@leevalleypark.org.uk
dir: M25 junct 26, A112. Site signed

* � £13.50-£19.50 ➤ £13.50-£19.50 ▲ £13.50-£19.50

Open Mar-Jan

Last arrival 21.00hrs Last departure noon

Overlooking King George's Reservoir and close to Epping Forest, this popular and very peaceful park features very good modern facilities and excellent hardstanding pitches including nine that are able to accommodate larger motorhomes. This impressive park is maintained to a high standard and there are camping pods in a separate shady glade for hire, and timber cabins. A bus calls at the site hourly to take passengers to the nearest tube station, and Enfield is easily accessible. 12 acre site. 81 touring pitches. 65 hardstandings. Caravan pitches. Motorhome pitches. Tent pitches. 46 statics. 17 wooden pods.

Leisure: 🏕

Facilities: 🛀⊙℘✻♿🕐🗑🐕♻ ❶

continued

SERVICES: 🔌 Electric hook up 🗑 Launderette 🍺 Licensed bar 🛢 Calor Gas ⊘ Camping Gaz Ⓣ Toilet fluid 🍽 Café/Restaurant 🍔 Fast Food/Takeaway 🔋 Battery charging 🍼 Baby care ⛽ Motorvan service point **ABBREVIATIONS:** BH/bank hols-bank holidays Etr-Easter Spring BH-Spring Bank Holiday dep-departure fr-from hrs-hours m-mile mdnt-midnight rdbt-roundabout rs-restricted service wk-week wknd-weekend x-rds-cross roads 🚫 No credit cards 🚫 No dogs 👫 Children of all ages accepted See page 9 for details of the AA Camping Card Scheme

E4 CHINGFORD *continued*

Services: 🔌🔋🔒🪠Ⓣ🚿🚽

Within 3 miles: ⚓🎡🖊♨🎣🛒🎯⛹

Notes: Under 18s must be accompanied by an adult, no commercial vehicles. Dogs must be kept on leads.

see advert below

N9 EDMONTON	Map 6 TQ39

AA CAMPING CARD SITE

▶▶▶▶ 83% **Lee Valley Camping & Caravan Park** *(TQ360945)*

Meridian Way N9 0AR
☎ 020 8803 6900
e-mail: edmontoncampsite@leevalleypark.org.uk
dir: *M25 junct 25, A10 S, 1st left onto A1055, approx 5m to Leisure Complex. From A406 (North Circular), N on A1010, left after 0.25m, right (Pickets Lock Ln)*

* 🚐 £13.50-£19.50 🚙 £13.50-£19.50
▲ £13.50-£19.50

Open all year
Last arrival 20.00hrs Last departure noon

A pleasant, open site within easy reach of London yet peacefully located close to two large reservoirs. There are excellent gravel access roads to the camping field, good signage and lighting, and smartly refurbished toilets. The site has the advantage of being adjacent to a restaurant and bar, and a multi-screen cinema. There are also camping pods and timber cabins for hire. A convenient bus stop provides a direct service to central London. 7 acre site. 100 touring pitches. 54 hardstandings. Caravan pitches. Motorhome pitches. Tent pitches. 12 wooden pods.

Leisure: 🎠

Facilities: 🚿⊙🎣❄🔥🛒🍽🔥📶♻️ℹ️

Services: 🔌🔋🔒Ⓣ🍽🚿🚽

Within 3 miles: ⚓🎡

Notes: Under 18s must be accompanied by an adult. Dogs must be kept on leads.

see advert below

MERSEYSIDE

SOUTHPORT
Map 15 SD31

Places to visit

The British Lawnmower Museum, SOUTHPORT, PR8 5AJ, 01704 501336
www.lawnmowerworld.com

85% Riverside Holiday Park (SD405192)

BRONZE

Southport New Rd PR9 8DF
☎ 01704 228886
e-mail: reception@harrisonleisureuk.com
dir: M6 junct 27, A5209 towards Parbold/ Burscough, right onto A59. Left onto A565 at lights in Tarleton. Continue to dual carriageway. At rdbt straight across, site 1m on left

Open 14 Feb-Jan

Last arrival 17.00hrs Last departure 11.00hrs

A large popular holiday destination for couples and families, with many indoor attractions including entertainment, dancing and theme nights. A well-equipped swimming pool area also provides spa treatments; free Wi-fi is available in the attractive café . 80 acre site. 260 touring pitches. 130 hardstandings. Caravan pitches. Motorhome pitches. Tent pitches. 355 statics.

AA Pubs & Restaurants nearby: Warehouse Kitchen & Bar, SOUTHPORT, PR8 1QN, 01704 544662

Bistrot Vérité, SOUTHPORT, PR8 4AR, 01704 564199

Vincent Hotel, SOUTHPORT, PR8 1JR, 01704 883800

Leisure: 🏊 ⅄ 🦆 🎣 🎵
Facilities: 🐾 📡 ₤ ⅋ 🛁 ⛺ 🚐 ❓
Services: 🔌 🛢 🍽 🛢 🐕 🚽 🍴 🚲
Within 3 miles: 🏃 🎣 🥐 🛒 🎰 ⛳

Notes: One car per pitch. Dogs must be kept on leads.

▶▶▶ 86% Willowbank Holiday Home & Touring Park (SD305110)

GOLD

Coastal Rd, Ainsdale PR8 3ST
☎ 01704 571566
e-mail: info@willowbankcp.co.uk
web: www.willowbankcp.co.uk
dir: From A565 between Formby & Ainsdale exit at Woodvale lights onto coast road, site 150mtrs on left. From N: M6 junct 31, A59 towards Preston, A565, through Southport & Ainsdale, right at Woodvale lights

* 🚐 £14.50-£19.40 🚃 £14.50-£19.40

Open Mar-Jan

Last arrival 21.00hrs Last departure noon

Set in woodland on a nature reserve next to sand dunes, this constantly improving park is a peaceful and relaxing holiday destination with mature trees, shrubs and colourful seasonal flowers surrounding neat pitches and modern amenities blocks. 8 acre site. 87 touring pitches. 61 hardstandings. Caravan pitches. Motorhome pitches. 228 statics.

Leisure: ⅄ ☺
Facilities: 🐾 ☺ 📡 ✳ ₤ ⅋ 🚿 🚐 🅦 ♻ ❓
Services: 🔌 🛢 🐕 ↯
Within 3 miles: 🏃 ⅄ 🎣 🥐 ◎ 🛒 🎰 ⛳

Notes: Cannot site continental door entry units, no commercial vehicles. No dangerous dog breeds. Dogs must be kept on leads. Baby changing facility, bike hire.

▶▶▶ 80% Hurlston Hall Country Caravan Park (SD398107)

Southport Rd L40 8HB
☎ 01704 841064
e-mail: enquiries@hurlstonhallcaravanpark.co.uk
dir: On A570, 3m from Ormskirk towards Southport

🚐 🚃

Open Etr-Oct

Last arrival 20.30hrs (18.30hrs at wknds). Last departure 17.00hrs

A peaceful tree-lined touring park next to a static site in attractive countryside about ten minutes' drive from Southport. The park is maturing well, with growing trees and a coarse fishing lake, and the excellent on-site facilities include golf, a bistro, a well-equipped health centre, a bowling green and model boat lake. Please note that neither tents nor dogs are accepted at this site. 5 acre site. 60 touring pitches. Caravan pitches. Motorhome pitches. 68 statics.

AA Pubs & Restaurants nearby: Warehouse Kitchen & Bar, SOUTHPORT, PR8 1QN, 01704 544662

Bistrot Vérité, SOUTHPORT, PR8 4AR, 01704 564199

Vincent Hotel, SOUTHPORT, PR8 1JR, 01704 883800

Leisure: 🏊 ⅄
Facilities: 🐾 ☺ 📡 ₤ ⅋
Services: 🔌 🛢 🍽 🛢 🍴
Within 3 miles: 🏃 🥐 🎰 🛒
Notes: 🚫

Norfolk

Even today, with faster cars and improved road and rail
systems, Norfolk still seems a separate entity, as if
strangely detached from the rest of the country. There are
those who would like it to stay that way. The renowned
composer, actor and playwright, Noel Coward, famously
described Norfolk as 'very flat' and he was right.

● Horsey, Norfolk Broads National Park

Top of the list of attractions is the North
Norfolk Coast, designated an Area of
Outstanding Natural Beauty, which has
been described as a long way from anywhere,
a place of traditions and ancient secrets.
The coastline here represents a world of
lonely beaches, vast salt marshes and extensive
sand dunes stretching as far as the eye can see.
It is the same today as it has always been,
and is a stark reminder of how this area
has been vulnerable to attack and
enemy invasion.

Delightful villages

With its old harbour and quaint High Street,
Wells-next-the-Sea is a popular favourite with
regular visitors to Norfolk, as is Blakeney, famous
for its mudflats and medieval parish church,
dedicated to the patron saint of seafarers,
standing guard over the village and the estuary
of the River Glaven.

   Cromer is a classic example of a good old
fashioned seaside resort where rather grand
Victorian hotels look out to sea; the writer
and actor Stephen Fry once worked as a

▶

● Church of St Peter & St Paul, Burgh Castle

waiter at Cromer's Hotel de Paris. A pier, such a key feature of coastal towns, completes the scene.

Farther down the coast, among a string of sleepy villages, is Happisburgh, pronounced Hazeburgh. The Hill House pub here is where Sir Arthur Conan Doyle stayed at the beginning of the 20th century; the Sherlock Holmes' story *The Adventure of the Dancing Men* (1903) is set in a Norfolk where 'on every hand enormous square-towered churches bristled up from the flat, green landscape.' Explore this corner of the county today and the scene is remarkably unchanged.

The Broads and nearby area

No visit to Norfolk is complete without a tour of the popular Broads, a network of mostly navigable rivers and lakes and now a designated National Park. Located a little inland to the south of Happisburgh, the various linked rivers, streams and man-made waterways, offer about 200 miles of highly enjoyable sailing and cruising. Away from the Broads rural Norfolk stretches for miles. If you've the time, you could spend days exploring a network of quiet back roads and winding lanes, visiting en route a generous assortment of picturesque villages and quiet market towns, including Fakenham and Swaffham. Also well worth a look is Thetford, with its delightful Dad's Army Museum. The location filming for the much-loved BBC comedy series was completed in and around Thetford Forest, and fictional Walmington-on-Sea was in fact the town of Thetford.

Ideally, this itinerary should also include the village of Castle Acre, with its impressive monastic ruins, and, of course, Norwich, with its magnificent cathedral, one of the country's greatest examples of Norman cathedral architecture.

• River estuary at low tide

Walking and Cycling

The 93-mile (150km) Peddars Way and North Norfolk Coast Path is one of Britain's most popular national trails. Consisting of two paths joined together to form one continuous route, the trail begins near Thetford on the Suffolk/Norfolk border and follows ancient tracks and stretches of Roman road before reaching the coast near Hunstanton. There are also good walks around the Burnham villages, Castle Acre and the National Trust's Blickling Hall.

Cycling in Norfolk offers variety and flexibility and the chance to tie it in with a bit of train travel. You can cycle beside the Bure Valley Railway on a 9-mile (14.5km) trail running from Aylsham to Wroxham and return to the start by train. Alternatively, combine an undemanding 5 miles (8km) of mostly traffic-free cycling with a trip on the North Norfolk Railway from Sheringham to Holt, starting and finishing at Kelling Heath. There is also the North Norfolk Coast Cycleway between King's Lynn and Cromer and a series of cycle trails around the Norfolk Broads.

Festivals and Events

- The Norfolk & Norwich Festival, held in May, is a celebration of creativity, innovation, jazz, comedy, dance and classical music.
- The Sandringham Game & Country Fair in September has falconry, fishing, wildfowling and archery among many other country sports and pursuits.
- The Little Vintage Lovers Fair takes place on different dates and at different venues around the county throughout the year and includes 30 stalls with the emphasis on quality vintage fashion, textiles and accessories.

NORFOLK

BARNEY
Map 13 TF93

Places to visit

Baconsthorpe Castle, BACONSTHORPE, NR25 6LN, 01799 322399 www.english-heritage.org.uk/daysout/properties/baconsthorpe-castle

Holkham Hall & Bygones Museum, HOLKHAM, NR23 1AB, 01328 710227 www.holkham.co.uk

Great for kids: Dinosaur Adventure Park, LENWADE, NR9 5JW, 01603 876310 www.dinosauradventure.co.uk

AA CAMPING CARD SITE

PREMIER PARK

►►►►► **88% The Old Brick Kilns** (TG007328)

Best of British GOLD

Little Barney Ln NR21 0NL
☎ 01328 878305
e-mail: enquiries@old-brick-kilns.co.uk
dir: *From A148 (Fakenham to Cromer road) follow brown tourist signs to Barney, left into Little Barney Ln. Site at end of lane*

* 🚐 £17-£30 🚎 £17-£30 ▲ £17-£30

Open 15 Mar-15 Dec (rs Etr-Sep bar food & takeaway on selected nights only)

Last arrival 21.00hrs Last departure 11.00hrs

A secluded and peaceful park approached via a quiet, leafy country lane. The park is on two levels with its own boating and fishing pool and many mature trees. Excellent, well-planned toilet facilities can be found in two beautifully appointed blocks, and there is a short dog walk. Please note due to a narrow access road, no arrivals are accepted until after 1pm. There are four self-catering holiday cottages. 12.73 acre site. 65 touring pitches. 65 hardstandings. Caravan pitches. Motorhome pitches. Tent pitches.

AA Pubs & Restaurants nearby: Chequers Inn, BINHAM, NR21 0AL, 01328 830297

The Old Forge Seafood Restaurant, THURSFORD, NR21 0BD, 01328 878345

Leisure: 🎱 🕳 🖵
Facilities: 🛠 ⊙ 🗜 ✳ 🕭 ⚴ 🛎 🛱 🚻 📶 🖥 ♻ 🛈
Services: 🔌 🖴 🍴 🧺 🗑 Ⓣ 🍽 🛒 🛥 ⛟
Within 3 miles: 🚴 🛒🖸

Notes: No gazebos. Outdoor draughts, chess, family games. Massages (by appointment only).

BELTON

Places to visit

Burgh Castle, BURGH CASTLE, NR31 9PZ, 0870 333 1181 www.english-heritage.org.uk/daysout/properties/burgh-castle

Great for kids: Thrigby Hall Wildlife Gardens, FILBY, NR29 3DR, 01493 369477 www.thrigbyhall.co.uk

BELTON
Map 13 TG40

74% Wild Duck Holiday Park (TG475028)

GOLD

Howards Common NR31 9NE
☎ 0871 231 0876
e-mail: wildduck@haven.com
web: www.haven.com/wildduck
dir: *Phone for detailed directions*

🚐 🚎 ▲

Open 16 Mar-5 Nov (rs mid Mar-May & Sep-early Nov some facilities may be reduced)

Last arrival 21.00hrs Last departure 10.00hrs

This a large holiday complex with plenty to do for all ages both indoors and out. This level grassy site has well laid-out facilities and is set in a forest with small, cleared areas for tourers. Clubs for children and teenagers, sporting activities and evening shows all add to the fun of a stay here. 97 acre site. 118 touring pitches. Caravan pitches. Motorhome pitches. Tent pitches. 560 statics.

AA Pubs & Restaurants nearby: Andover House, GREAT YARMOUTH, NR30 3JB, 01493 843490

LEISURE: 🏊 Indoor swimming pool 🏊 Outdoor swimming pool 🛝 Children's playground 🙌 Kid's club 🎾 Tennis court 🎱 Games room 🖵 Separate TV room 🏌 9/18 hole golf course 🚣 Boats for hire 🎬 Cinema 🎵 Entertainment 🎣 Fishing ◉ Mini golf 🏄 Watersports 🏋 Gym 🏟 Sports field Spa ♨ Stables
FACILITIES: 🛁 Bath 🚿 Shower ⊙ Electric shaver ✂ Hairdryer ✳ Ice Pack Facility ♿ Disabled facilities 🕾 Public telephone 🛒 Shop on site or within 200yds 🚐 Mobile shop (calls at least 5 days a week) 🍖 BBQ area 🍴 Picnic area 📶 Wi-fi 🖥 Internet access ♻ Recycling 🛈 Tourist info 🐕 Dog exercise area

Leisure: N N N N N N
Facilities: N N N N N N N N N N N
Services: N N N N N N N N N N
Within 3 miles: N N N N N N N

Notes: No commercial vehicles, no bookings by persons under 21yrs unless a family booking. Max 2 dogs per booking, certain dog breeds banned. Dogs must be kept on leads.

see advert on opposite page

AA CAMPING CARD SITE

PREMIER PARK

►►►►► 85% Rose Farm Touring & Camping Park *(TG488033)*

Stepshort NR31 9JS
☎ 01493 780896
dir: *Follow signs to Belton off A143, right at lane signed Stepshort, site 1st on right*

N N N

Open all year

A former railway line is the setting for this very peaceful, beautifully presented site which enjoys rural views. It is brightened with many flower and herb beds. The refurbished toilet facilities are smart, spotlessly clean, inviting to use and include family rooms. The customer care here is truly exceptional and the quality café (open in peak season only) is very popular. 10 acre site. 145 touring pitches. 20 hardstandings. Caravan pitches. Motorhome pitches. Tent pitches.

AA Pubs & Restaurants nearby: Andover House, GREAT YARMOUTH, NR30 3JB, 01493 843490

Leisure: N N N
Facilities: N N N N N N N N N
Services: N N N N
Within 3 miles: N N N N N N N N
Notes: No dog fouling.

BURGH CASTLE   Map 13 TG40

Places to visit

Burgh Castle, BURGH CASTLE, NR31 9PZ, 0870 333 1181 www.english-heritage.org.uk/daysout/properties/burgh-castle

Thrigby Hall Wildlife Gardens, FILBY, NR29 3DR, 01493 369477 www.thrigbyhall.co.uk

Great for kids: Pettitts Animal Adventure Park, REEDHAM, NR13 3UA, 01493 700094 www.pettittsadventurepark.co.uk

77% *Breydon Water* *(TG479042)*

Butt Ln NR31 9QB
☎ 0871 664 9710
e-mail: breydon.water@park-resorts.com
web: www.park-resorts.com
dir: *From Gt Yarmouth on A12 towards Lowestoft. Right signed Diss & Beccles onto A143. Through Bradwell, right signed Burgh Castle & Belton. At mini rdbt right into Stepshort. Site on right*

N N N

Open Apr-Oct

Last arrival anytime Last departure 10.00hrs

This large park has two village areas just a short walk apart. Yare Village offers touring facilities, family fun and superb entertainment, while Bure Village, which is a quieter base, is now static caravans only. Although the villages are separated, guests are more than welcome to use facilities at both. Yare Village has modern, well maintained toilets, and tents are welcome. The park is are just a short drive from the bright lights of Great Yarmouth and the unique Norfolk Broads. 189 touring pitches. Caravan pitches. Motorhome pitches. Tent pitches. 327 statics.

AA Pubs & Restaurants nearby: Andover House, GREAT YARMOUTH, NR30 3JB, 01493 843490

Leisure: N N N N N N N
Facilities: N N N N N N N
Services: N N N N N
Within 3 miles: N N N N N N N N N

CAISTER-ON-SEA

Places to visit

Caister Roman Fort, CAISTER-ON-SEA, 0870 333 1181 www.english-heritage.org.uk/daysout/properties/caister-roman-fort

Thrigby Hall Wildlife Gardens, FILBY, NR29 3DR, 01493 369477 www.thrigbyhall.co.uk

---

CAISTER-ON-SEA   Map 13 TG51

86% Caister Holiday Park *(TG519132)*

Ormesby Rd NR30 5NQ
☎ 0871 231 0873
e-mail: caister@haven.com
web: www.haven.com/caister
dir: *A1064 signed Caister-on-Sea. At rdbt 2nd exit onto A149, at next rdbt 1st exit onto Caister by-pass, at 3rd rdbt 3rd exit to Caister-on-Sea. Park on left*

N N

Open mid Mar-end Oct

Last arrival 18.00hrs Last departure 10.00hrs

An all-action holiday park located beside the beach north of the resort of Great Yarmouth, yet close to the attractions of the Norfolk Broads. The touring area offers 46 fully serviced pitches and a modern purpose-built toilet block. Customer care is of an extremely high standard with a full time, experienced and caring warden. Please note that the park does not accept tents. 138 acre site. 46 touring pitches. Caravan pitches. Motorhome pitches. 900 statics.

AA Pubs & Restaurants nearby: Fishermans Return, WINTERTON-ON-SEA, NR29 4BN, 01493 393305

Leisure: N N N N N N N
Facilities: N N N N N N N N N N
Services: N N N N N N N N N N
Within 3 miles: N N N N N N N

Notes: No tents. No commercial vehicles, no bookings by persons under 21yrs unless a family booking, no sleeping in awnings. Max 2 dogs per booking, certain dog breeds banned. Dogs must be kept on leads.

see advert on page 242

CLIPPESBY
Map 13 TG41

Places to visit

Fairhaven Woodland & Water Garden, SOUTH WALSHAM, NR13 6DZ, 01603 270449 www.fairhavengarden.co.uk

Great for kids: Caister Roman Fort, CAISTER-ON-SEA, 0870 333 1181 www.english-heritage.org.uk/daysout/properties/caister-roman-fort

PREMIER PARK

► ► ► ► ► 93% **Clippesby Hall**

(TG423147)

Hall Ln NR29 3BL
☎ 01493 367800
e-mail: holidays@clippesby.com
web: www.clippesby.com
dir: *From A47 follow tourist signs for The Broads. At Acle rdbt take A1064, in 2m left onto B1152, 0.5m left opposite village sign, site 400yds on right*

* ☒ £16.50-£37 ☒ £16.50-£37 Å £12.50-£33

Open all year
Last arrival 17.30hrs Last departure 11.00hrs

A lovely country house estate with secluded pitches hidden among the trees or in sheltered sunny glades. The toilet facilities, appointed to a very good standard, provide a wide choice of cubicles. Amenities include a coffee shop with both Wi-fi and wired internet access, a family bar and restaurant and family golf. Excellent hardstanding pitches have been added as the park is open all year. There are pine lodges and cottages available for holiday lets. 30 acre site. 120 touring pitches. 41 hardstandings. Caravan pitches. Motorhome pitches. Tent pitches.

AA Pubs & Restaurants nearby: Fishermans Return, WINTERTON-ON-SEA, NR29 4BN, 01493 393305

The Fur & Feather Inn, WOODBASTWICK, NR13 6HQ, 01603 720003

Leisure: ⚓ 🎿 ⚽ 🔍

Facilities: 🚿 🅿 ☉ 🔩 ✳ ♿ 🕐 🚻 ♨ 🚽 ✈ Wifi 🖥 ♻ ❶

Services: 🚐 🔧 🍴 🕯 🚮 🔟 🎮 🛒 ⬇

Within 3 miles: ⬇ 🚣 🎣 ◎ 🛷 🛒 🛒 ∪

Notes: No groups, no noise after 23.00hrs, no camp fires. Dogs must be kept on leads. Bicycle hire, volley ball, table tennis, cycle trail.

CROMER
Map 13 TG24

Places to visit

RNLI Henry Blogg Museum, CROMER, NR27 9ET, 01263 511294 www.rnli.org/henryblogg

Felbrigg Hall, FELBRIGG, NR11 8PR, 01263 837444 www.nationaltrust.org.uk/main/w-felbrigghallgardenandpark

► ► ► ► 81% *Forest Park*

(TG233405)

Northrepps Rd NR27 0JR
☎ 01263 513290
e-mail: info@forest-park.co.uk
dir: *A140 from Norwich, left at T-junct signed Cromer, right signed Northrepps, right then immediately left, left at T-junct, site on right*

🚐 🚐 Å

Open 15 Mar-15 Jan

Last arrival 21.00hrs Last departure 11.00hrs

Surrounded by forest, this gently sloping park offers a wide choice of pitches. Visitors have the use of a heated indoor swimming pool, and a large clubhouse with entertainment. 100 acre site. 262 touring pitches. Caravan pitches. Motorhome pitches. Tent pitches. 420 statics.

AA Pubs & Restaurants nearby: The Wheatsheaf, WEST BECKHAM, NR25 6NX, 01263 822110

The White Horse Overstrand, CROMER, NR27 0AB, 01263 579237

Sea Marge Hotel, CROMER, NR27 0AB, 01263 579579

LEISURE: 🏊 Indoor swimming pool 🏊 Outdoor swimming pool ⚠ Children's playground 🖐 Kid's club 🎾 Tennis court 🎱 Games room 📺 Separate TV room ⛳ 9/18 hole golf course 🚣 Boats for hire 🍴 Cinema 🎭 Entertainment 🎣 Fishing ◎ Mini golf 🏄 Watersports 💪 Gym ♻ Sports field Spa ∪ Stables
FACILITIES: 🛁 Bath 🚿 Shower ☉ Electric shaver 🔩 Hairdryer ✳ Ice Pack Facility ♿ Disabled facilities 🕐 Public telephone 🛒 Shop on site or within 200yds 🚐 Mobile shop (calls at least 5 days a week) 🍴 BBQ area 🎋 Picnic area Wifi Wi-fi 🖥 Internet access ♻ Recycling ❶ Tourist info 🐕 Dog exercise area

Leisure: ☜ ⚲ 🔍

Facilities: 🏳 ⊙ 🅟 ※ ⚓ 🕔 🔥 🎾 [Wi-fi]

Services: 🔌 🅖 🍺 🔒 💧 T 🍴 🚐 ♨

Within 3 miles: ♨ ✈ 🗓 🎣 ◎ ⛷ 🅟 🅖 ∪

►►►► 79% Manor Farm Caravan & Camping Site (TG198416)

East Runton NR27 9PR
☎ 01263 512858 & 07760 324673
e-mail: stay@manorfarmcampsite.co.uk
dir: 1m W of Cromer, exit A148 or A149 (recommended towing route) at Manor Farm sign.

* 🚐 £14-£22 🚕 £14-£22 ▲ £14-£22

Open Etr-Sep

Last arrival 20.30hrs Last departure noon

A well-established family-run site on a working farm enjoying panoramic sea views. There are good modern facilities across the site, including three smart toilet blocks that include two quality family rooms and privacy cubicles, two good play areas and a large expanse of grass for games - the park is very popular with families. 17 acre site. 250 touring pitches. Caravan pitches. Motorhome pitches. Tent pitches.

AA Pubs & Restaurants nearby: The Wheatsheaf, WEST BECKHAM, NR25 6NX, 01263 822110

The White Horse Overstrand, CROMER, NR27 0AB, 01263 579237

Sea Marge Hotel, CROMER, NR27 0AB, 01263 579579

Leisure: ⚲ ⚽ ♨

Facilities: 🏳 ⊙ ※ ⚓ 🎾 ♨ 🔌 ❶

Services: 🔌 🅖 🔒 🪣 ♨

Within 3 miles: ♨ 🗓 🎣 ◎ ⛷ 🅟 🅖

Notes: ⊛ No noise after 23.00hrs, no groups. Dogs must be kept on leads. 2 dog-free fields.

DOWNHAM MARKET   Map 12 TF60

►►► 86% Lakeside Caravan Park & Fisheries (TF608013)

Sluice Rd, Denver PE38 0DZ
☎ 01366 387074 & 07790 272978
e-mail: richesflorido@aol.com
web: www.westhallfarmholidays.co.uk
dir: Exit A10 towards Denver, follow signs to Denver Windmill

🚐 🚕 ▲

Lakeside Caravan Park & Fisheries

Open Mar-Oct

Last arrival 21.00hrs Last departure noon

A peaceful, rapidly improving park set around five pretty fishing lakes. Ongoing investment has seen more electric hook-ups, a timber reception chalet and additional new toilet facilities installed in a converted office building. There are several grassy touring areas which are sheltered by mature hedging and trees, a function room, shop and laundry. 30 acre site. 100 touring pitches. Caravan pitches. Motorhome pitches. Tent pitches. 1 static.

AA Pubs & Restaurants nearby: The Hare Arms, STOW BARDOLPH, PE34 3HT, 01366 382229

Leisure: ⚲

Facilities: 🏳 ⊙ 🅟 ※ ⚓ 🅖 🎾 [Wi-fi]

Services: 🔌 🅖 🔒 🪣 T 🚐

Within 3 miles: ♨ ✈ 🗓 🎣 ⛷ 🅖 🅖

Notes: Dogs must be kept on leads. Pool table, fishing tackle/bait, caravan accessories.

FAKENHAM   Map 13 TF92

Places to visit

Houghton Hall, HOUGHTON, PE31 6UE, 01485 528569 www.houghtonhall.com

Great for kids: Pensthorpe Nature Reserve & Gardens, FAKENHAM, NR21 0LN, 01328 851465 www.pensthorpe.co.uk

►►► 83% Fakenham Campsite (TF907310)

Burnham Market Rd, Sculthorpe NR21 9SA
☎ 01328 856614
e-mail: enquiries@fakenhamcampsite.co.uk
dir: From Fakenham take A148 towards King's Lynn then right onto B1355 towards Burnham Market. Site on right in 400yds

🚐 🚕 ▲

Open all year

Last arrival 20.00hrs Last departure noon

Enthusiastic owners are running this peaceful site that is surrounded by tranquil countryside and which is part of a 9-hole, par 3 golf complex and driving range. The toilet facilities are of good quality, and there is a golf shop and licensed bar. Please note there is no laundry. 4 acre site. 50 touring pitches. 13 hardstandings. Caravan pitches. Motorhome pitches. Tent pitches.

AA Pubs & Restaurants nearby: The Blue Boar Inn, GREAT RYBURGH, NR21 0DX, 01328 829212

The Wensum Lodge Hotel, FAKENHAM, NR21 9AY, 01328 862100

Leisure: ⚲

Facilities: 🏳 ※ ⚓ 🎾 ♨ ❶

Services: 🔌

Within 3 miles: ♨ 🗓 🎣 🅖

Notes: No noise after 22.30hrs. Dogs must be kept on leads.

►►► 82% Caravan Club M.V.C. Site (TF926288)

Fakenham Racecourse NR21 7NY
☎ 01328 862388
e-mail: caravan@fakenhamracecourse.co.uk
dir: From B1146, S of Fakenham follow brown Racecourse signs (with tent & caravan symbols) leads to site entrance

🚐 🚕 ▲

Open all year

Last arrival 21.00hrs Last departure noon

A very well laid-out site set around the racecourse, with a grandstand offering smart modern toilet facilities. Tourers move to the centre of the course on race days, and enjoy free racing, and there's a wide range of sporting activities in the club house. 11.4 acre site. 120 touring pitches. 25 hardstandings. Caravan pitches. Motorhome pitches. Tent pitches.

AA Pubs & Restaurants nearby: The Blue Boar Inn, GREAT RYBURGH, NR21 0DX, 01328 829212

The Wensum Lodge Hotel, FAKENHAM, NR21 9AY, 01328 862100

Facilities: 🏳 ⊙ 🅟 ※ ⚓ 🕔 🅖 🎾 [Wi-fi] ♨ ❶

Services: 🔌 🅖 🍺 🔒 🪣 T 🍴 🔧

Within 3 miles: ♨ 🗓 🎣 ◎ 🅖 🅖 ∪

Notes: Max 2 dogs per unit. Dogs must be kept on leads. TV aerial hook-ups.

FAKENHAM ***continued***

►► 72% Crossways Caravan & Camping Park *(TF961321)*

Crossways, Holt Rd, Little Snoring NR21 0AX
☎ 01328 878335
e-mail: joyholland@live.co.uk
dir: *From Fakenham take A148 towards Cromer. After 3m pass exit for Little Snoring. Site on A148 on left behind post office*

🚐 🚙 ⛺

Open all year

Last arrival 22.00hrs Last departure noon

Set on the edge of the peaceful hamlet of Little Snoring, this level site enjoys views across the fields towards the north Norfolk coast some seven miles away. Visitors can use the health suite for a small charge, and there is a shop on site, and a good village pub. 2 acre site. 26 touring pitches. 10 hardstandings. 14 seasonal pitches. Caravan pitches. Motorhome pitches. Tent pitches. 1 static.

AA Pubs & Restaurants nearby: The Blue Boar Inn, GREAT RYBURGH, NR21 0DX, 01328 829212

The Wensum Lodge Hotel, FAKENHAM, NR21 9AY, 01328 862100

Leisure: ⚽

Facilities: 🚿 ⊙ ✲ ✆ [$] ⛩ 🐕 💻 ♻ ⓘ

Services: 🗨 🗄 🔒 🍃 [T]

Within 3 miles: ⛳ 🎬 🎣 ◎ [$] 🗄 Ʊ

Notes: Dogs must be kept on leads.

GREAT YARMOUTH **Map 13 TG50**

Places to visit

Yesterday's World Great Yarmouth, GREAT YARMOUTH, NR30 2EN, 01493 331148 www.yesterdaysworld.co.uk

Great for kids: Time and Tide Museum of Great Yarmouth Life, GREAT YARMOUTH, NR30 3BX, 01493 743930 www.museums.norfolk.gov.uk

87% Vauxhall Holiday Park *(TG520083)*

AA HOLIDAY CENTRE · DAVID BELLAMY CONSERVATION AWARD SILVER

4 Acle New Rd NR30 1TB
☎ 01493 857231
e-mail: info@vauxhallholidays.co.uk
web: www.vauxhall-holiday-park.co.uk
dir: *On A47 approaching Great Yarmouth*

🚐 🚙 ⛺

Open Etr, mid May-Sep & Oct half term

Last arrival 21.00hrs Last departure 10.00hrs

A very large holiday complex with plenty of entertainment and access to beach, river, estuary, lake and the A47. The touring pitches are laid out in four separate areas, each with its own amenity block, and all arranged around the main entertainment. 40 acre site. 220 touring pitches. Caravan pitches. Motorhome pitches. Tent pitches. 421 statics.

AA Pubs & Restaurants nearby: Andover House, GREAT YARMOUTH, NR30 3JB, 01493 843490

Vauxhall Holiday Park

Leisure: 🏊 🏖 🏋 🛝 ✋ 🎾 ⚽ ♠ 📺 🎵

Facilities: 🚿 ⊙ ✲ ♿ ✆ [$] [Wi-fi] ♻

Services: 🗨 🗄 🔌 🔒 🍃 [T] 🍴 🍳 🛍

Within 3 miles: ⛳ ⛵ 🎬 🎣 ◎ 🏄 [$] 🗄 Ʊ

Notes: No pets. Children's pool, sauna, solarium.

see advert below

LEISURE: 🏊 Indoor swimming pool 🏖 Outdoor swimming pool 🛝 Children's playground ✋ Kid's club 🎾 Tennis court ♠ Games room 📺 Separate TV room ⛳ 9/18 hole golf course ⛵ Boats for hire 🎬 Cinema 🎵 Entertainment 🎣 Fishing ◎ Mini golf 🏄 Watersports 🏋 Gym ⚽ Sports field **Spa** Ʊ Stables
FACILITIES: 🛁 Bath 🚿 Shower ⊙ Electric shaver 💨 Hairdryer ✲ Ice Pack Facility ♿ Disabled facilities ✆ Public telephone [$] Shop on site or within 200yds 🚚 Mobile shop (calls at least 5 days a week) 🍖 BBQ area ⛩ Picnic area [Wi-fi] Wi-fi 💻 Internet access ♻ Recycling ⓘ Tourist info 🐕 Dog exercise area

AA CAMPING CARD SITE

►►►► 80% The Grange Touring Park
(TG510142)

Yarmouth Rd, Ormesby St Margaret NR29 3QG
☎ 01493 730306 & 730023
e-mail: info@grangetouring.co.uk
dir: *From A419, 3m N of Great Yarmouth. Site at junct of A419 & B1159. Signed*

* ⬛ £12.50-£20 ⬛ £12.50-£20 ▲ £12.50-£20

Open Etr-Oct

Last arrival 21.00hrs Last departure 11.00hrs

A mature, ever improving park with plenty of trees, located just one mile from the sea, within easy reach of both coastal attractions and the Norfolk Broads. The level pitches have electric hook-ups and include 13 hardstanding pitches, and there are clean, modern toilets including three spacious family rooms. All pitches have Wi-fi access. 3.5 acre site. 70 touring pitches. 7 hardstandings. Caravan pitches. Motorhome pitches. Tent pitches.

AA Pubs & Restaurants nearby: Andover House, GREAT YARMOUTH, NR30 3JB, 01493 843490

Leisure: ⚠

Facilities: ⬛⬛⬛⬛⬛⬛⬛ ⬛ ⬛

Services: ⬛⬛⬛⬛⬛⬛⬛⬛

Within 3 miles: ⬛⬛⬛⬛⬛⬛

Notes: No football, no gazebos, no open fires. Dogs must be kept on leads.

85% Seashore Holiday Park (TG653103)

North Denes NR30 4HG
☎ 01493 851131
e-mail: seashore@haven.com
web: www.haven.com/seashore
dir: *A149 from Great Yarmouth to Caister. Right at 2nd lights signed seafront & racecourse. Continue to sea, turn left. Park on left*

Open Mar-Oct

Bordered by sand dunes and with direct access to a sandy beach, Seashore Holiday Park is located in Great Yarmouth yet is close enough for day trips to the peaceful Norfolk Broads. Facilities include excellent water activities and bike hire for children and lively evening entertainment for adults. There is a good range of holiday caravans and apartments.

Change over day: Mon, Fri, Sat **Arrival and departure times:** Please contact the site

Statics 285 Sleeps 6-8 Bedrms 2-3 Bathrms 1-2 Toilets 1-2 Freezer TV Sky/FTV Elec inc Gas inc

Children ⬛ Cots Highchair **Dogs** 2 on leads No dangerous dogs

Leisure: ⬛⬛⚠

HOPTON ON SEA   Map 13 TM59

Places to visit

St Olave's Priory, ST OLAVES, 0870 333 1181 www.english-heritage.org.uk/daysout/ properties/st-olaves-priory

91% Hopton Holiday Park
(TG531002)

NR31 9BW
☎ 01502 730214
e-mail: hopton@haven.com
web: www.haven.com/hopton
dir: *Site signed from A12 between Great Yarmouth & Lowestoft*

Open Mar-Oct

Located between Lowestoft and Great Yarmouth, close to beaches and the town attractions, this lively holiday park offers excellent sport activities, including golf on the 9-hole course and tennis coaching, plus popular evening entertainment in the form of shows, music and dancing. There is a good range of holiday caravans and apartments.

Change over day: Mon, Fri, Sat **Arrival and departure times:** Please contact the site

Statics 216 Sleeps 6-8 Bedrms 2-3 Bathrms 1-2 Toilets 1-2 Freezer TV Sky/FTV Elec inc Gas inc Grass area

Children ⬛ Cots Highchair **Dogs** 2 on leads No dangerous dogs

Leisure: ⬛⬛⬛⬛⚠

HUNSTANTON   Map 12 TF64

Places to visit

Lynn Museum, KING'S LYNN, PE30 1NL, 01553 775001 www.museums.norfolk.gov.uk

Norfolk Lavender, HEACHAM, PE31 7JE, 01485 570384 www.norfolk-lavender.co.uk

Great for kids: Hunstanton Sea Life Sanctuary, HUNSTANTON, PE36 5BH, 01485 533576 www.sealife.co.uk

88% Searles Leisure Resort (TF671400)

South Beach Rd PE36 5BB
☎ 01485 534211
e-mail: bookings@searles.co.uk
web: www.searles.co.uk
dir: *A149 from King's Lynn to Hunstanton. At rdbt follow signs for South Beach. Straight on at 2nd rdbt. Site on left*

⬛⬛▲

Open all year (rs Dec-Mar excl Feb half term limited facilities & use of indoor pool & country park only)

A large seaside holiday complex with well-managed facilities, adjacent to sea and beach. The tourers have their own areas, including two excellent toilet blocks, and pitches are individually marked by small maturing shrubs for privacy. The bars and entertainment, restaurant, bistro and takeaway, heated indoor and outdoor pools, golf, fishing and bowling green make this park popular throughout the year. 50 acre site. 255 touring pitches. 91 hardstandings. Caravan pitches. Motorhome pitches. Tent pitches. 158 statics.

AA Pubs & Restaurants nearby: The King William IV Country Inn & Restaurant, HUNSTANTON, PE36 5LU, 01485 571765

The Neptune Restaurant with Rooms, HUNSTANTON, PE36 6HZ, 01485 532122

The Gin Trap Inn, RINGSTEAD, PE36 5JU, 01485 525264

Marco Pierre White The Lifeboat Inn, THORNHAM, PE36 6LT, 01485 512236

Leisure: ⬛⬛⬛⚠⬛⬛⬛⬛⬛

Facilities: ⬛⬛⬛⬛⬛⬛⬛⬛ ⬛ ⬛⬛

Services: ⬛⬛⬛⬛⬛⬛⬛⬛⬛⬛⬛

Within 3 miles: ⬛⬛⬛⬛⬛⬛

Notes: Dogs must be kept on leads.

SERVICES: ⬛ Electric hook up ⬛ Launderette ⬛ Licensed bar ⬛ Calor Gas ⬛ Camping Gaz ⬛ Toilet fluid ⬛ Café/Restaurant ⬛ Fast Food/Takeaway ⬛ Battery charging ⬛ Baby care ⬛ Motorvan service point **ABBREVIATIONS:** BH/bank hols-bank holidays Etr-Easter Spring BH-Spring Bank Holiday dep-departure fr-from hrs-hours m-mile mdnt-midnight rdbt-roundabout rs-restricted service wk-week wknd-weekend x-rds-cross roads ⬛ No credit cards ⬛ No dogs ⬛ Children of all ages accepted See page 9 for details of the AA Camping Card Scheme

HUNSTANTON *continued*

80% *Manor Park Holiday Village* (TF671399)

SILVER

Manor Rd PE36 5AZ
☎ **01485 532300**
e-mail: manor.park@park-resorts.com
web: www.park-resorts.com
dir: *Take A149 (King's Lynn Rd) to Hunstanton, left onto B1161 (Oasis Way)*

🚐 🚏

Open Apr-Oct

Last arrival noon Last departure 10.00hrs

Situated just a few yards from the beach on the outskirts of the lively resort of Hunstanton, Manor Farm offers a range of leisure activities, including two heated outdoor swimming pools, children's playground, children's club, amusement arcade, restaurant, bar and cabaret. There are 64 electric, all-grass pitches set out in the heart of the park and adjacent to the leisure complex. Expect high standards of customer care. 64 touring pitches. 10 seasonal pitches. Caravan pitches. Motorhome pitches. 650 statics.

AA Pubs & Restaurants nearby: The King William IV Country Inn & Restaurant, HUNSTANTON, PE36 5LU, 01485 571765

The Neptune Restaurant with Rooms, HUNSTANTON, PE36 6HZ, 01485 532122

Leisure: 🏊 ⛰ 🛝 🔫 ▢ 🎵
Facilities: 🐾 🔌 🕐 🚿 🛏 🅆🄵 🍴 ♻ 🅑
Services: 🔧 🗑 🍴 🐕 🍴 ♨
Within 3 miles: 🔌 🛥 ⛳ ◎ 🛶 🛍 🗑 ⛺

Notes: Dogs must be kept on leads. Bicycle hire.

KING'S LYNN   Map 12 TF62

See also Stanhoe

Places to visit

Bircham Windmill, GREAT BIRCHAM, PE31 6SJ, 01485 578393 www.birchamwindmill.co.uk

African Violet Centre, KING'S LYNN, PE34 4PL, 01553 828374 www.africanvioletandgardencentre.com

Great for kids: Castle Rising Castle, CASTLE RISING, PE31 6AH, 01553 631330 www.english-heritage.org.uk/daysout/properties/castle-rising-castle

►►►► 82% *King's Lynn Caravan and Camping Park* (TF645160)

New Rd, North Runcton PE33 0RA
☎ **01553 840004**
e-mail: klcc@btconnect.com
web: www.kl-cc.co.uk
dir: *From King's Lynn take A47 signed Swaffham & Norwich, in 1.5m turn right signed North Runcton. Site 100yds on left*

🚐 🚏 ⛺

Open all year

Last arrival flexible Last departure flexible

Set in approximately ten acres of parkland, this developing camping park is situated on the edge of North Runcton, just a few miles south of the historic town of King's Lynn. There is an eco-friendly toilet block which is powered by solar panels and an air-sourced heat pump which also recycles rainwater - this in itself this proves a source of great interest. The three very extensive touring fields are equipped with 150 electric hook-ups and one field is reserved for rallies. Four high quality camping pods and four new pine lodges are for hire. 9 acre site. 150 touring pitches. 2 hardstandings. 20 seasonal pitches. Caravan pitches. Motorhome pitches. Tent pitches. 4 wooden pods.

AA Pubs & Restaurants nearby: The Stuart House Hotel, Bar & Restaurant, KING'S LYNN, PE30 5QX, 01553 772169

Bank House Hotel, KING'S LYNN, PE30 1RD, 01553 660492

Facilities: 🐾 🕐 📻 🚿 🔌 🅂 🛏 🅆🄵 ♻ 🅑
Services: 🔧 🗑 🐕 🗑 🍴 ♨
Within 3 miles: 🔌 🎿 ⛳ 🛶 🗑 🗑 ⛺

Notes: No skateboards or fires. Dogs must be kept on leads.

NORTH WALSHAM   Map 13 TG23

Places to visit

Blickling Estate, BLICKLING, NR11 6NF, 01263 738030 www.nationaltrust.org.uk/blickling

Horsey Windpump, HORSEY, NR29 4EF, 01263 740241 www.nationaltrust.co.uk

PREMIER PARK

►►►►► 85% Two Mills Touring Park (TG291286)

Best of British

Yarmouth Rd NR28 9NA
☎ **01692 405829**
e-mail: enquiries@twomills.co.uk
dir: *1m S of North Walsham on Old Yarmouth road past police station & hospital on left*

* 🚐 £17.50-£24.95 🚏 £17.50-£24.95
⛺ £17.50-£24.95

Open Mar-3 Jan

Last arrival 20.30hrs Last departure noon

An intimate, beautifully presented park set in superb countryside in a peaceful, rural spot, which is also convenient for touring. The 'Top Acre' section is maturing and features fully serviced pitches, offering panoramic views over the site, an immaculate toilet block and good planting, plus the layout of pitches and facilities is excellent. The very friendly and helpful owners keep the park in immaculate condition. Please note this park is for adults only. 7 acre site. 81 touring pitches. 81 hardstandings. Caravan pitches. Motorhome pitches. Tent pitches.

LEISURE: 🏊 Indoor swimming pool   🏊 Outdoor swimming pool   ⛰ Children's playground   🔫 Kid's club   🎾 Tennis court   🎱 Games room   ▢ Separate TV room   🏌 9/18 hole golf course   🚤 Boats for hire   🎬 Cinema   🎵 Entertainment   🎣 Fishing   ◎ Mini golf   🛶 Watersports   🏋 Gym   ⚽ Sports field   Spa   ⛺ Stables
FACILITIES: 🛁 Bath   🚿 Shower   🔌 Electric shaver   📻 Hairdryer   ✳ Ice Pack Facility   🔌 Disabled facilities   🕐 Public telephone   🅂 Shop on site or within 200yds   🏪 Mobile shop (calls at least 5 days a week)   🍴 BBQ area   🎋 Picnic area   🅆🄵 Wi-fi   🖥 Internet access   ♻ Recycling   🅑 Tourist info   🐕 Dog exercise area

AA Pubs & Restaurants nearby: The Butchers Arms, EAST RUSTON, NR12 9JG, 01692 650237

Beechwood Hotel, NORTH WALSHAM, NR28 0HD, 01692 403231

Leisure: 📺

Facilities: 🚿 ⊙ 💇 ✻ ♿ ☎ $ 🪑 🐕 [Wi-fi] 💻 ♻ ⓘ

Services: 🔌 🧺 🛢 🔥 [T] 🔋 ⚓

Within 3 miles: ⛳ $ 🧺

Notes: Adults only. Max 2 dogs per pitch. Dogs must be kept on leads. Library.

SAHAM HILLS — Map 13 TF90

Places to visit

Oxburgh Hall, OXBURGH, PE33 9PS, 01366 328258 www.nationaltrust.org.uk/main/w-oxburghhall

NEW ▶▶▶ 85% Lowe Caravan Park *(TF903034)*

Ashdale, 134 Hills Rd IP25 7EZ
☎ 01953 881051
dir: *From B1108 (High Street) in Watton follow Saham Hills sign, pass Richmond Park Golf Club on left. 2nd right into Ploughboy Ln, at T-junct right into Hills Rd. 1st drive on right*

* 🚐 £12.50-£14.50 🚚 £12.50-£14.50 ⛺ £12.50-£14.50

Open All year ex Xmas & New Year

Last arrival 21.30hrs Last departure 15.00hrs

A small, well-established adults-only touring park run by experienced and caring owners. Twenty five pitches occupy a level field behind the owners' house and there are clean, well-maintained toilets and exceptional levels of customer care and security. The site occupies a tranquil location deep in the Norfolk countryside, yet it is well-placed for visiting Norwich and the north Norfolk coast. 4 acre site. 31 touring pitches. Caravan pitches. Motorhome pitches. Tent pitches.

Notes: Adults only. [no credit cards]

ST JOHN'S FEN END — Map 12 TF51

Places to visit

African Violet Centre, KING'S LYNN, PE34 4PL, 01553 828374 www.africanvioletandgardencentre.com

Oxburgh Hall, OXBOROUGH, PE33 9PS, 01366 328258 www.nationaltrust.org.uk/main/w-oxburghhall

AA CAMPING CARD SITE

▶▶▶▶ 79% Virginia Lake Caravan Park *(TF538113)*

Smeeth Rd PE14 8JF
☎ 01945 430167 & 07757 534194
e-mail: louise@virginialake.co.uk
dir: *From A47, E of Wisbech, follow tourist signs to Terrington St John. Site on left*

* 🚐 £20-£25 🚚 £20-£25 ⛺ £15-£25

Open all year

Last arrival 21.00hrs Last departure 14.00hrs

A well-established park beside a two-acre fishing lake with good facilities for both anglers and tourers. The toilet facilities are very good and the popular clubhouse, which serves a selection of meals, now houses the excellent new reception and fishing shop. The old timber reception chalet has been converted into a camping shelter, replete with fridge, microwave, kettle and hot water for tenters. 7.5 acre site. 93 touring pitches. 6 hardstandings. 43 seasonal pitches. Caravan pitches. Motorhome pitches. Tent pitches. 3 statics. 1 wooden pod.

AA Pubs & Restaurants nearby: The Stuart House Hotel, Bar & Restaurant, KING'S LYNN, PE30 5QX, 01553 772169

Bank House Hotel, KING'S LYNN, PE30 1RD, 01553 660492

Leisure: ♠

Facilities: 🚿 ⊙ 💇 ✻ ♿ ☎ $ 🪑 [Wi-fi] 💻 ⓘ

Services: 🔌 🧺 🍷 🛢 🔥 [T]

Within 3 miles: ⛳ 🎣 $ U

Notes: No camp fires, no noise after mdnt. Dogs must be kept on leads. Clay pigeon shooting.

SCRATBY — Map 13 TG51

Places to visit

St Olave's Priory, ST OLAVES, 0870 333 1181 www.english-heritage.org.uk/daysout/properties/st-olaves-priory

Time and Tide Museum of Great Yarmouth Life, GREAT YARMOUTH, NR30 3BX, 01493 743930 www.museums.norfolk.gov.uk

Great for kids: Caister Roman Fort, CAISTER-ON-SEA, 0870 333 1181 www.english-heritage.org.uk/daysout/properties/caister-roman-fort

▶▶▶ 86% Scratby Hall Caravan Park *(TG501155)*

NR29 3SR
☎ 01493 730283
e-mail: scratbyhall@aol.com
dir: *5m N of Great Yarmouth. Exit A149 onto B1159, site signed*

🚐 🚚 ⛺

Open Etr-end Sep

Last arrival 21.00hrs Last departure noon

A neatly-maintained site with a popular children's play area, well-equipped shop and outdoor swimming pool with sun terrace. The toilets are kept very clean. The beach and the Norfolk Broads are close by. 5 acre site. 85 touring pitches. Caravan pitches. Motorhome pitches. Tent pitches.

AA Pubs & Restaurants nearby: Fishermans Return, WINTERTON-ON-SEA, NR29 4BN, 01493 393305

Leisure: 🏊 /\

Facilities: 🚿 ⊙ 💇 ✻ ♿ ☎ $ [Wi-fi] ♻ ⓘ

Services: 🔌 🧺 🛢 🔥 [T] 🔋

Within 3 miles: ⛳ 🎣 $ 🧺 U

Notes: No commercial vehicles, pool open end Jul-Aug only. Dogs must be kept on leads. Food preparation room.

STANHOE Map 13 TF83

Places to visit

Norfolk Lavender, HEACHAM, PE31 7JE, 01485 570384 www.norfolk-lavender.co.uk

Walsingham Abbey Grounds & Shirehall Museum, LITTLE WALSINGHAM, NR22 6BP, 01328 820510 www.walsinghamabbey.com

►►► 82% The Rickels Caravan & Camping Park *(TF794355)*

Bircham Rd PE31 8PU
☎ 01485 518671
dir: *A148 from King's Lynn to Hillington. B1153 to Great Bircham. B1155 to x-rds, straight over, site on left*

🚐 🚌 ⛺

Open all year

Last arrival 21.00hrs Last departure 11.00hrs

Set in three acres of grassland, with sweeping country views and a pleasant, relaxing atmosphere fostered by being for adults only. The meticulously maintained grounds and facilities are part of the attraction, and the slightly sloping land has some level areas and sheltering for tents. A field is available to hire for rallies. 3 acre site. 30 touring pitches. Caravan pitches. Motorhome pitches. Tent pitches.

AA Pubs & Restaurants nearby: The Lord Nelson, BURNHAM THORPE, PE31 8HN, 01328 738241

The Hoste, BURNHAM MARKET, PE31 8HD, 01328 738777

Leisure: 📺

Facilities: 🚿 ⊙ ✲ 🐕 ♻ ℹ

Services: ⚡ 🧺 🔒 🍃 🛁

Within 3 miles: 🎣 [$]

Notes: Adults only. 🚫 No ground sheets. Dogs must be kept on leads.

SWAFFHAM Map 13 TF80

Places to visit

Gressenhall Farm and Workhouse, GRESSENHALL, NR20 4DR, 01362 860563 www.museums.norfolk.gov.uk

Oxburgh Hall, OXBURGH, PE33 9PS, 01366 328258 www.nationaltrust.org.uk/main/w-oxburghhall

AA CAMPING CARD SITE

►►► 80% Breckland Meadows Touring Park *(TF809094)*

Lynn Rd PE37 7PT
☎ 01760 721246
e-mail: info@brecklandmeadows.co.uk
dir: *1m W of Swaffham on old A47*

🚐 £12.50-£14.50 🚌 £12.50-£14.50 ⛺ £11.50

Open all year

Last arrival 21.00hrs Last departure noon

An immaculate, well-landscaped little park on the edge of Swaffham. The impressive toilet block is well equipped, and there are hardstandings, full electricity and laundry equipment. Plentiful planting is resulting in attractive screening. 3 acre site. 45 touring pitches. 35 hardstandings. 5 seasonal pitches. Caravan pitches. Motorhome pitches. Tent pitches.

Facilities: 🚿 ⊙ ✲ ♿ [$] ⛩ 🐕 [Wi-fi] 💻 ♻ ℹ

Services: ⚡ 🧺 🔒 🍃 [T] 🛁

Within 3 miles: ⛳ 🎬 🎣 [$] 🧺 🐎

Notes: Adults only. Dogs must be kept on leads. Newspaper deliveries.

SYDERSTONE Map 13 TF83

Places to visit

Creake Abbey, NORTH CREAKE, NR21 9LF, 0870 333 1181 www.english-heritage.org.uk/daysout/properties/creake-abbey

Great for kids: Castle Rising Castle, CASTLE RISING, PE31 6AH, 01553 631330 www.english-heritage.org.uk/daysout/properties/castle-rising-castle

►►► 77% The Garden Caravan Site *(TF812337)*

Barmer Hall Farm PE31 8SR
☎ 01485 578220 & 578178
e-mail: nigel@gardencaravansite.co.uk
dir: *Signed from B1454 at Barmer between A148 & Docking, 1m W of Syderstone*

🚐 🚌 ⛺

Open Mar-Nov

Last arrival 21.00hrs Last departure noon

In the tranquil setting of a former walled garden beside a large farmhouse, with mature trees and shrubs, a secluded site surrounded by woodland. The site is run mainly on trust, with a daily notice indicating which pitches are available, and an honesty box for basic foods. An ideal site for the discerning camper, and well placed for touring north Norfolk. 3.5 acre site. 30 touring pitches. Caravan pitches. Motorhome pitches. Tent pitches.

AA Pubs & Restaurants nearby: The Lord Nelson, BURNHAM THORPE, PE31 8HN, 01328 738241

The Hoste, BURNHAM MARKET, PE31 8HD, 01328 738777

Facilities: 🚿 ⊙ 💨 ✲ ♿ 📞 🐕 ℹ

Services: ⚡ 🔒 🛁 ⚓

Within 3 miles: [$]

Notes: 🚫 Max 2 dogs per pitch. Dogs must be kept on leads. Cold drinks, ice creams & eggs available.

LEISURE: 🏊 Indoor swimming pool 🏖 Outdoor swimming pool 🛝 Children's playground 👋 Kid's club 🎾 Tennis court 🎱 Games room 📺 Separate TV room ⛳ 9/18 hole golf course ⛵ Boats for hire 🎬 Cinema 🎵 Entertainment 🎣 Fishing ◎ Mini golf 🌊 Watersports 🏋 Gym ⚽ Sports field **Spa** 🐎 Stables
FACILITIES: 🛁 Bath 🚿 Shower ⊙ Electric shaver 💨 Hairdryer ✲ Ice Pack Facility ♿ Disabled facilities 📞 Public telephone [$] Shop on site or within 200yds 🚚 Mobile shop (calls at least 5 days a week) 🍖 BBQ area ⛩ Picnic area [Wi-fi] Wi-fi 💻 Internet access ♻ Recycling ℹ Tourist info 🐕 Dog exercise area

THREE HOLES Map 12 TF50

Places to visit

African Violet Centre, KING'S LYNN, PE34 4PL, 01553 828374
www.africanvioletandgardencentre.com

Norfolk Lavender, HEACHAM, PE31 7JE, 01485 570384 www.norfolk-lavender.co.uk

►►► 77% *Lode Hall Holiday Park*

(TF529989)

Lode Hall, Silt Rd PE14 9JW
☎ 01354 638133
e-mail: dick@lode-hall.co.uk
dir: *From Wisbech take A1101 towards Downham Market. At Outwell continue on A1101 signed Littleport. Site signed from Three Holes. Right onto B1094 to site*

🚐 🚛 Å

Open Apr-Oct

Peace and tranquilly is assured at this deeply rural park in the grounds of Lode Hall. The toilet facilities are located in an imaginative restoration of a former cricket pavilion and include combined toilet/wash basin cubicles and unisex showers. Please note that this is an adults-only site. 5 acre site. 20 touring pitches. 8 hardstandings. Caravan pitches. Motorhome pitches. Tent pitches.

AA Pubs & Restaurants nearby: The Hare Arms, STOW BARDOLPH, PE34 3HT, 01366 382229

Facilities: 🚿⊙❄👶🚻🌂🔥📶

Services: 🔌🗑️💧

Within 3 miles: ✎🛒U

Notes: Adults only. 🐕

WORTWELL Map 13 TM28

Places to visit

Bressingham Steam Museum & Gardens, BRESSINGHAM, IP22 2AB, 01379 686900
www.bressingham.co.uk

Great for kids: Banham Zoo, BANHAM, NR16 2HE, 01953 887771
www.banhamzoo.co.uk

►►►► 83% Little Lakeland Caravan Park (TM279849)

IP20 0EL
☎ 01986 788646
e-mail: information@littlelakeland.co.uk
dir: *From W: exit A143 at sign for Wortwell. In village turn right 300yds past garage. From E: on A143, left onto B1062, then right. After 800yds turn left*

🚐 £15.50-£21.50 🚛 £15.50-£21.50
Å £15.50-£21.50

Open 15 Mar-Oct

Last arrival 22.00hrs Last departure noon

A well-kept and pretty site built round a fishing lake, and accessed by a lake-lined drive. The individual pitches are sited in hedged enclosures for complete privacy, and the purpose-built toilet facilities are excellent. 4.5 acre site. 38 touring pitches. 6 hardstandings. 17 seasonal pitches. Caravan pitches. Motorhome pitches. Tent pitches. 21 statics.

AA Pubs & Restaurants nearby: The Dove Restaurant with Rooms, ALBURGH, IP20 0EP, 01986 788315

Fox & Goose Inn, FRESSINGFIELD, IP21 5PB, 01379 586247

Leisure: ⚙

Facilities: 🚿⊙☂❄👶🚻📶♻🛈

Services: 🔌🗑️🔋⌀T💧

Within 3 miles: ⛴🚴✎🛒

Notes: 🐕 No noise after 22.30hrs. Dogs must be kept on leads. Library.

NORTHUMBERLAND

BAMBURGH Map 21 NU13

Places to visit

Chillingham Wild Cattle Park, CHILLINGHAM, NE66 5NP, 01668 215250
www.chillinghamwildcattle.com

Great for kids: Bamburgh Castle, BAMBURGH, NE69 7DF, 01668 214515
www.bamburghcastle.com

►►►► 81% Glororum Caravan Park

(NU166334)

Glororum Farm NE69 7AW
☎ 01670 860256
e-mail: enquiries@northumbrianleisure.co.uk
dir: *Exit A1 at junct with B1341 (Purdy's Lodge). In 3.5m left onto unclassified road. Site 300yds on left*

* 🚐 £25 🚛 £25

Open Mar-end Nov

Last arrival 18.00hrs Last departure noon

A pleasantly situated site in an open countryside setting with good views of Bamburgh Castle. A popular holiday destination where tourers have their own separate area - 42 excellent, well-spaced, fully serviced pitches have a lush grass area in addition to the hardstanding. This field also has an excellent purpose-built amenities block with a smartly clad interior and modern, efficient fittings. 6 acre site. 43 touring pitches. 43 hardstandings. 30 seasonal pitches. Caravan pitches. Motorhome pitches. 150 statics.

AA Pubs & Restaurants nearby: The Olde Ship Inn, SEAHOUSES, NE68 7RD, 01665 720200

The Bamburgh Castle Inn, SEAHOUSES, NE68 7SQ, 01665 720283

Blue Bell Hotel, BELFORD, NE70 7NE, 01668 213543

Leisure: ⚙🎡

Facilities: 🚿⊙☂❄👶🕐🚻🌂🔥🛈

Services: 🔌🗑️⌀T

Within 3 miles: ⛴🚴✎⛳🛒🎣U

Notes: No commercial vehicles, no noise after 23.00hrs. Dogs must be kept on leads.

SERVICES: 🔌 Electric hook up 🗑️ Launderette 🍺 Licensed bar 🛢 Calor Gas ⌀ Camping Gaz T Toilet fluid 🍽️ Café/Restaurant 🍟 Fast Food/Takeaway 🔋 Battery charging 🍼 Baby care 💧 Motorvan service point **ABBREVIATIONS:** BH/bank hols-bank holidays Etr-Easter Spring BH-Spring Bank Holiday dep-departure fr-from hrs-hours m-mile mdnt-midnight rdbt-roundabout rs-restricted service wk-week wknd-weekend x-rds-cross roads 🐕 No credit cards 🐕 No dogs 👨‍👩‍👧 Children of all ages accepted See page 9 for details of the AA Camping Card Scheme

BAMBURGH *continued*

►►►► 79% *Waren Caravan Park* (NU155343)

Waren Mill NE70 7EE
☎ **01668 214366**
e-mail: waren@meadowhead.co.uk
dir: *2m E of town. From A1 onto B1342 signed Bamburgh. Take unclassified road past Waren Mill, signed Budle*

Open Apr-Oct

Last arrival 20.00hrs Last departure noon

Attractive seaside site with footpath access to the beach, surrounded by a slightly sloping grassy embankment giving shelter to caravans. The park offers excellent facilities, including several family bathrooms, and the on-site restaurant serves a good breakfast. There are also wooden wigwams to rent. 4 acre site. 150 touring pitches. 24 hardstandings. Caravan pitches. Motorhome pitches. Tent pitches. 300 statics. 8 tipis.

AA Pubs & Restaurants nearby: The Olde Ship Inn, SEAHOUSES, NE68 7RD, 01665 720200

Blue Bell Hotel, BELFORD, NE70 7NE, 01668 213543

Waren House Hotel, BAMBURGH, NE70 7EE, 01668 214581

Leisure: ⚲ ⚏ ⚲

Facilities: ⚲ ⚲ ⚲ ⚲ ⚲ ⚲ ⚲ ⚲ ⚲ ⚲ ⚲ ⚲

Services: ⚲ ⚲ ⚲ ⚲ ⚲ ⚲ ⚲ ⚲ ⚲ ⚲

Within 3 miles: ⚲ ⚲ ⚲ ⚲ ⚲

Notes: Dogs must be kept on leads. 100 acres of private heathland.

BELFORD — Map 21 NU13

Places to visit

Bamburgh Castle, BAMBURGH, NE69 7DF, 01668 214515 www.bamburghcastle.com

Lindisfarne Castle, HOLY ISLAND [LINDISFARNE], TD15 2SH, 01289 389244 www.nationaltrust.org.uk

REGIONAL WINNER - NORTH EAST ENGLAND AA CAMPSITE OF THE YEAR 2014

PREMIER PARK

NEW ►►►►► 87% South Meadows Caravan Park (NU115331)

South Rd NE70 7DP
☎ **01668 213326**
e-mail: info@southmeadows.co.uk
dir: *B6349 towards Belford, site signed*

* ⚲ £19-£25.50 ⚲ £19-£25.50 ⚲ £19-£22.50

Open all year

Last departure 16.00hrs

South Meadows has been transformed in recent years and is now a top quality touring and holiday park. Set in open countryside, the park is extremely spacious and no expense has been spared in its landscaping and redevelopment. Tree planting on a grand scale has been carried out, grassy areas are expertly mown and all pitches are fully serviced. The solar heated amenity block is ultra modern, with quality fittings and smart family rooms; everywhere is spotlessly clean and fresh. There's a new adventure playground complete with a zip-wire and even dogs have two walking areas, one in a bluebell wood. 50 acre site. 120 touring pitches. 71 hardstandings. 67 seasonal pitches. Caravan pitches. Motorhome pitches. Tent pitches. 55 statics.

AA Pubs & Restaurants nearby: Blue Bell Hotel, BELFORD, NE70 7NE, 01668 213543

Leisure: ⚏ ⚲

Facilities: ⚲ ⚲ ⚲ ⚲ ⚲ ⚲ ⚲ ⚲ ⚲

Services: ⚲ ⚲ ⚲ ⚲ ⚲ ⚲

Within 3 miles: ⚲ ⚲ ⚲

Notes: Minimum noise after 23.00hrs. Under 12s must be supervised in toilet blocks. Dogs must be kept on leads.

BELLINGHAM — Map 21 NY88

Places to visit

Wallington, CAMBO, NE61 4AR, 01670 773600 www.nationaltrust.org.uk/wallington

PREMIER PARK

►►►►► 80% *Bellingham Camping & Caravanning Club Site* (NY835826)

Brown Rigg NE48 2JY
☎ **01434 220175 & 0845 130 7633**
dir: *From A69 take A6079 N to Chollerford & B6320 to Bellingham. Pass Forestry Commission land, site 0.5m S of Bellingham*

⚲ ⚲ ⚲

Open 15 Mar-3 Nov

Last arrival 20.00hrs Last departure noon

A beautiful and peaceful campsite set in the glorious Northumberland National Park. Exceptionally well managed, it continues to improve and offers high levels of customer care, maintenance and cleanliness - the excellent toilet facilities are spotlessly clean. There are four camping pods for hire. This is a perfect base for exploring this undiscovered part of England, and it is handily placed for visiting the beautiful Northumberland coast. 5 acre site. 64 touring pitches. 42 hardstandings. Caravan pitches. Motorhome pitches. Tent pitches. 4 wooden pods.

AA Pubs & Restaurants nearby: The Pheasant Inn, FALSTONE, NE48 1DD, 01434 240382

Leisure: ⚏

Facilities: ⚲ ⚲ ⚲ ⚲ ⚲ ⚲ ⚲ ⚲ ⚲ ⚲ ⚲

Services: ⚲ ⚲ ⚲ ⚲ ⚲ ⚲

Within 3 miles: ⚲ ⚲ ⚲ ⚲

Notes: Site gates closed & quiet time 23.00hrs-07.00hrs. Dogs must be kept on leads.

BERWICK-UPON-TWEED
Map 21 NT95

Places to visit

Berwick-Upon-Tweed Barracks,
BERWICK-UPON-TWEED, TD15 1DF, 01289 304493
www.english-heritage.org.uk/daysout/
properties/berwick-upon-tweed-barracks-and-
main-guard

Paxton House, Gallery & Country Park,
BERWICK-UPON-TWEED, TD15 1SZ, 01289 386291
www.paxtonhouse.com

Great for kids: Norham Castle, NORHAM,
TD15 2JY, 01289 382329 www.english-heritage.
org.uk/daysout/properties/norham-castle

80% Haggerston Castle
(NU041435)

Beal TD15 2PA
☎ 0871 231 0865 & 01289 381333
e-mail: haggerstoncastle@haven.com
web: www.haven.com/haggerstoncastle
dir: On A1, 7m S of Berwick-upon-Tweed, site
signed

🚐 🚙

Open mid Mar-end Oct (rs mid Mar-May & Sep-Oct
some facilities may be reduced)

Last arrival anytime Last departure 10.00hrs

A large holiday centre with a very well equipped
touring park, offering comprehensive holiday
activities. The entertainment complex contains
amusements for the whole family, and there are
several bars, an adventure playground, boating on
the lake, a children's club, a 9-hole golf course,
tennis courts, and various eating outlets. Please
note that this site does not accept tents. 100 acre
site. 132 touring pitches. 132 hardstandings.
Caravan pitches. Motorhome pitches. 1200 statics.

AA Pubs & Restaurants nearby: Blue Bell Hotel,
BELFORD, NE70 7NE, 01668 213543

Haggerston Castle

Leisure: 🏊 🎦 🎣 ✋ 🎮 🎵
Facilities: 🌳 ⊙ ⚡ ♿ 🚿 🛁 🚻 🚮 ⬛ ♻ ❶
Services: 🔌 🖨 🍴 🍽 ⛽ 🛒
Within 3 miles: ↯ ⚓ 🔴 🎯 🐴 ⛳

Notes: No commercial vehicles, no bookings by
persons under 21yrs unless a family booking. Max
2 dogs per booking, certain dog breeds banned.
Dogs must be kept on leads.

see advert below

PREMIER PARK

►►►►► 82% Ord House Country Park
Best of British GOLD

(NT982515)

East Ord TD15 2NS
☎ 01289 305288
e-mail: enquiries@ordhouse.co.uk
dir: At rdbt junct of A1 (Berwick bypass) &
A698 take exit signed East Ord, follow brown
camping signs

🚐 🚙 ⛺

Open all year

Last arrival 23.00hrs Last departure noon

A very well-run park set in the pleasant
grounds of an 18th-century country house.
Touring pitches are marked and well spaced,
some of them fully serviced. The very modern
toilet facilities include family bath and shower
suites, and first class disabled rooms. There is
an exceptional outdoor leisure shop with a good
range of camping and caravanning spares, as
well as clothing and equipment, and an
attractive licensed club selling bar meals. 42
acre site. 79 touring pitches. 46
hardstandings. 30 seasonal pitches. Caravan
pitches. Motorhome pitches. Tent pitches. 255
statics. 10 wooden pods.

AA Pubs & Restaurants nearby: The
Wheatsheaf at Swinton, SWINTON, TD11 3JJ,
01890 860257

continued

SERVICES: 🔌 Electric hook up 🧺 Launderette 🍺 Licensed bar 🔥 Calor Gas ⛽ Camping Gaz 🅣 Toilet fluid 🍽 Café/Restaurant 🍔 Fast Food/Takeaway
🔋 Battery charging 🍼 Baby care ⛟ Motorvan service point **ABBREVIATIONS:** BH/bank hols-bank holidays Etr-Easter Spring BH-Spring Bank Holiday dep-departure
fr-from hrs-hours m-mile mdnt-midnight rdbt-roundabout rs-restricted service wk-week wknd-weekend x-rds-cross roads 🚫 No credit cards 🚫 No dogs
👶 Children of all ages accepted See page 9 for details of the AA Camping Card Scheme

BERWICK-UPON-TWEED *continued*

Leisure:

Facilities: 🚿🍴👁️🍽️✂️♿🛒🎯🐴 WiFi ♻️ ❶

Services: 🔌🅿️🚽🛁🧺🚰🍴🛒♻️

Within 3 miles: ♨️🎣🏇🎣◎🏪🛍️

Notes: No noise after mdnt. Dogs must be kept on leads. Crazy golf, table tennis.

►► 80% Old Mill Caravan Site

(NU055401)

West Kyloe Farm, Fenwick TD15 2PG
☎ 01289 381279 & 07971 411625
e-mail: teresasmalley@westkyloe.demon.co.uk
dir: *A1 onto B6353, 9m S of Berwick-upon-Tweed. Road signed to Lowick/Fenwick. Site 1.5m signed on left*

🚐 £20 🚐 £15-£20 ▲ £15-£20

Open Apr-Oct

Last arrival 19.00hrs Last departure 11.00hrs

Small, secluded site accessed through a farm complex, and overlooking a mill pond complete with resident ducks. Some pitches are in a walled garden, and the amenity block is simple but well kept. Delightful walks can be enjoyed on the 600-acre farm. A holiday cottage is also available. 2.5 acre site. 12 touring pitches. Caravan pitches. Motorhome pitches. Tent pitches.

AA Pubs & Restaurants nearby: Blue Bell Hotel, BELFORD, NE70 7NE, 01668 213543

Facilities: 🚿👁️♿🐴♻️ ❶

Services: 🔌🛒

Within 3 miles: 🏪

Notes: ⊘ No gazebos or open fires. Dogs must be kept on leads. Wet room.

82% Berwick Holiday Park

(NT998535)

Magdalene Fields TD15 1NE
☎ 01289 307113
e-mail: berwick@haven.com
web: www.haven.com/berwick
dir: *From A1 follow Berwick-upon-Tweed signs. At Morrisons/McDonalds rdbt take 2nd exit. At mini rdbt straight on, into North Rd (pass Shell garage on left). At next mini rdbt 1st exit into Northumberland Ave. Park at end*

Open Mar-Oct

This all-happening, static-only holiday park has direct access to a beach on the edge of Berwick, and offers exciting family activities and entertainment including the FunWorks Amusement Centre and a multisports court.

Change over day: Mon, Fri, Sat **Arrival and departure times:** Please contact the site

Statics 204 Sleeps 6-8 Bedrms 2-3 Bathrms 1-2 Toilets 1-2 Freezer TV Sky/FTV Elec inc Gas inc Grass area

Children 🧒 Cots Highchair **Dogs** 2 on leads No dangerous dogs

Leisure: 〜🏊👣🏇

HEXHAM | **Map 21 NY96**

Places to visit

Vindolanda (Chesterholm), BARDON MILL, NE47 7JN, 01434 344277 www.vindolanda.com

Temple of Mithras (Hadrian's Wall), CARRAWBROUGH, 0870 333 1181 www.english-heritage.org.uk/daysout/ properties/temple-of-mithras-carrawburgh-hadrians-wall

Great for kids: Housesteads Roman Fort, HOUSESTEADS, NE47 6NN, 01434 344363 www.english-heritage.org.uk/daysout/ properties/housesteads-roman-fort-hadrians-wall

---

►►► 64% Hexham Racecourse Caravan Site *(NY919623)*

Hexham Racecourse NE46 2JP
☎ 01434 606847 & 606881
e-mail: hexrace.caravan@btconnect.com
dir: *From Hexham take B6305 signed Allendale/Alston. Left in 3m signed to racecourse. Site 1.5m on right*

🚐 🚐 ▲

Open May-Sep

Last arrival 20.00hrs Last departure noon

A part-level and part-sloping grassy site situated on a racecourse overlooking Hexhamshire Moors. The facilities, although clean, are of an older but functional type. 4 acre site. 50 touring pitches. Caravan pitches. Motorhome pitches. Tent pitches.

AA Pubs & Restaurants nearby: Miners Arms Inn, HEXHAM, NE46 4PW, 01434 603909

Dipton Mill Inn, HEXHAM, NE46 1YA, 01434 606577

Rat Inn, HEXHAM, NE46 4LN, 01434 602814

Leisure: 🎯🔍

Facilities: 🚿👁️🍽️✂️🕐🐴🐕 ❶

Services: 🔌🅿️🛁🧺🚰

Within 3 miles: ♨️🎣🏇🎣◎🏪🛍️

Notes: No noise after 23.00hrs. Dogs must be kept on leads.

LEISURE: 🏊 Indoor swimming pool 🏊 Outdoor swimming pool 🎯 Children's playground 👣 Kid's club 🎾 Tennis court 🔍 Games room 📺 Separate TV room ♨️ 9/18 hole golf course 🚣 Boats for hire 🎬 Cinema 🎵 Entertainment 🎣 Fishing ◎ Mini golf 🏊 Watersports 🏌️ Gym 🏟️ Sports field **Spa** ⛲ Stables
FACILITIES: 🚿 Bath 🚿 Shower 👁️ Electric shaver 🍴 Hairdryer ✂️ Ice Pack Facility ♿ Disabled facilities 🕐 Public telephone 🏪 Shop on site or within 200yds 🛍️ Mobile shop (calls at least 5 days a week) 🍴 BBQ area 🌲 Picnic area WiFi Wi-fi 💻 Internet access ♻️ Recycling ❶ Tourist info 🐕 Dog exercise area

NORTH SEATON
Map 21 NZ28

Places to visit

Woodhorn, ASHINGTON, NE63 9YF, 01670 624455
www.experiencewoodhorn.com

Morpeth Chantry Bagpipe Museum, MORPETH,
NE61 1PD, 01670 535163
www.experiencewoodhorn.com/morpeth-
bagpipe-museum

75% *Sandy Bay*
(NZ302858)

NE63 9YD
☎ 0871 664 9764
e-mail: sandy.bay@park-resorts.com
web: www.park-resorts.com
dir: *From A1 at Seaton Burn take A19 signed Tyne
Tunnel. Then A189 signed Ashington, approx 8m,
at rdbt right onto B1334 towards Newbiggin-by-
the-Sea. Site on right*

Open Apr-Oct

Last arrival anytime Last departure noon

A beach-side holiday park on the outskirts of the
small village of North Seaton, within easy reach of
Newcastle. The site is handily placed for exploring
the magnificent coastline and countryside of
Northumberland, but for those who do not wish to
travel, it offers the full range of holiday centre
attractions, both for parents and their children. 48
touring pitches. Caravan pitches. Motorhome
pitches. 396 statics.

Leisure: 🏊 ⛰ 🎣 🎵
Facilities: 🐾 📡 🕐 🚿 📶 🖥
Services: 🔌 🗑 🎱 🍽 🛒
Within 3 miles: 🏇 🏧 🗑
Notes: Koi carp lake.

WOOLER
Map 21 NT92

Places to visit

Chillingham Castle, CHILLINGHAM, NE66 5NJ,
01668 215359 www.chillingham-castle.com

Great for kids: Chillingham Wild Cattle Park,
CHILLINGHAM, NE66 5NP, 01668 215250
www.chillinghamwildcattle.com

▶▶▶ 78% *Riverside Leisure Park*
(NT993279)

South Rd NE71 6NJ
☎ 01668 281447
e-mail: reception@riverside-wooler.co.uk
dir: *From S: A1 to Morpeth, A697 signed Wooler
& Coldstream. In Wooler, park on left. From N:
From Berwick-upon-Tweed on A1, 1st right signed
Wooler (B6525). Through Wooler on A697. Park
on right*

🚐 🚏 ⛺

Open all year

Last departure noon

This is the sister park to Thurston Manor Leisure
Park at Dunbar in East Lothian. It is set in the
heart of stunning Northumberland countryside on
the edge of Wooler Water. Very much family
orientated, the park offers excellent leisure
facilities including swimming pools, a bar and a
restaurant, weekend entertainment and riverside
and woodland walks. Caravan pitches. Motorhome
pitches. Tent pitches.

AA Pubs & Restaurants nearby: The Red Lion Inn,
MILFIELD, NE71 6JD, 01668 216224

NOTTINGHAMSHIRE

CHURCH LANEHAM
Map 17 SK87

Places to visit

Newark Air Museum, NEWARK-ON-TRENT,
NG24 2NY, 01636 707170
www.newarkairmuseum.org

Vina Cooke Museum of Dolls & Bygone
Childhood, NEWARK-ON-TRENT, NG23 6JE,
01636 821364 www.vinasdolls.co.uk

Great for kids: Sherwood Forest Country Park
& Visitor Centre, EDWINSTOWE, NG21 9HN,
01623 823202
www.nottinghamshire.gov.uk/sherwoodforestcp

▶▶▶ 81% *Trentfield Farm* (SK815774)

DN22 0NJ
☎ 01777 228651
e-mail: post@trentfield.co.uk
dir: *A1 onto A57 towards Lincoln for 6m. Left
signed Laneham, 1.5m, through Laneham &
Church Laneham (pass Ferryboat pub on left). Site
300yds on right*

🚐 £18-£29 🚏 £18-£29 ⛺ £18-£29

Open Etr-Nov

Last arrival 20.00hrs Last departure noon

A delightfully rural and level grass park tucked
away on the banks of the River Trent. The park has
its own river frontage with free coarse fishing
available to park residents. The cosy local pub,
which serves food, is under the same ownership.
34 acre site. 45 touring pitches. 20 seasonal
pitches. Caravan pitches. Motorhome pitches. Tent
pitches.

Facilities: 🐾 ⊙ 📡 ❄ 🚿 🗑 🏕 🛒 📶 ♻ ❗
Services: 🔌 🗑 🔋 ⚡
Within 3 miles: 🎣 🏇 🏧 🗑 ⛳
Notes: Dogs must be kept on leads. 24-hour mini
shop.

SERVICES: 🔌 Electric hook up 🗑 Launderette 🍺 Licensed bar 🅱 Calor Gas 🅖 Camping Gaz 🅣 Toilet fluid 🍽 Café/Restaurant 🍟 Fast Food/Takeaway
🔋 Battery charging 🍼 Baby care ⚡ Motorvan service point **ABBREVIATIONS:** BH/bank hols-bank holidays Etr-Easter Spring BH-Spring Bank Holiday dep-departure
fr-from hrs-hours m-mile mdnt-midnight rdbt-roundabout rs-restricted service wk-week wknd-weekend x-rds-cross roads ⊗ No credit cards ⊗ No dogs
👶 Children of all ages accepted See page 9 for details of the AA Camping Card Scheme

MANSFIELD — Map 16 SK56

Places to visit

Sherwood Forest Country Park & Visitor Centre, EDWINSTOWE, NG21 9HN, 01623 823202 www.nottinghamshire.gov.uk/sherwoodforestcp

Great for kids: Vina Cooke Museum of Dolls & Bygone Childhood, NEWARK-ON-TRENT, NG23 6JE, 01636 821364 www.vinasdolls.co.uk

▶▶▶ 78% Tall Trees Touring Park (SK551626)

BRONZE

Old Mill Ln, Forest Town NG19 0JP
☎ **01623 626503 & 07770 661957**
e-mail: info@talltreestouringpark.co.uk
dir: *A60 from Mansfield towards Worksop. After 1m turn right at lights into Old Mill Lane. Site approx 0.5m on left*

🚐 £12.50-£17.50 🚐 £12.50-£17.50
⛺ £12.50-£17.50

Open all year

Last arrival anytime Last departure anytime

A very pleasant park situated just on the outskirts of Mansfield and within easy walking distance of shops and restaurants. It is surrounded on three sides by trees and shrubs, and securely set at the back of the residential park. This site has a modern amenities block, a fishing lake to the rear of the site and an extra grassed area to give more space for caravans and tents. 10 acre site. 37 touring pitches. 10 hardstandings. Caravan pitches. Motorhome pitches. Tent pitches.

AA Pubs & Restaurants nearby: Forest Lodge, EDWINSTOWE, NG21 9QA, 01623 824443

Fox & Hounds, BLIDWORTH, NG21 0NW, 01623 792383

Tall Trees Touring Park

Leisure: ⚽
Facilities: 🍴 ⊙ ℗ ♿ 🚮 🔄 ❶
Services: 🔌 🛒
Within 3 miles: ↡ ⛳ ℗ 🛒🛒

Notes: No noise after mdnt. Dogs must be kept on leads.

NEWARK

See Southwell

RADCLIFFE ON TRENT — Map 11 SK63

Places to visit

Nottingham Castle Museum & Art Gallery, NOTTINGHAM, NG1 6EL, 0115 876 3356 www.mynottingham.gov.uk/nottinghamcastle

Wollaton Hall, Gardens & Deer Park, NOTTINGHAM, NG8 2AE, 0115 915 3900 www.nottingham.gov.uk/wollatonhall

▶▶▶ 79% Thornton's Holt Camping Park (SK638377)

Stragglethorpe Rd, Stragglethorpe NG12 2JZ
☎ **0115 933 2125 & 933 4204**
e-mail: camping@thorntons-holt.co.uk
web: www.thorntons-holt.co.uk
dir: *Take A52, 3m E of Nottingham. Turn S at lights towards Cropwell Bishop. Site 0.5m on left. Or A46 SE of Nottingham. N at lights. Site 2.5m*

🚐 🚐 ⛺

Open Apr-6 Nov

Last arrival 20.00hrs Last departure noon

A well-run family site in former meadowland, with pitches located among young trees and bushes for a rural atmosphere and outlook. The toilets are housed in converted farm buildings, and an indoor swimming pool is a popular attraction. 13 acre site. 155 touring pitches. 35 hardstandings. 20 seasonal pitches. Caravan pitches. Motorhome pitches. Tent pitches.

AA Pubs & Restaurants nearby: Ye Olde Trip to Jerusalem, NOTTINGHAM, NG1 6AD, 0115 947 3171

Fellows Morton & Clayton, NOTTINGHAM, NG1 7EH, 0115 950 6795

Leisure: 🏊 🎠
Facilities: 🍴 ⊙ ℗ ✳ ♿ 🕙 🛒 🚮 🔄 ❶
Services: 🔌 🛒 🛢 ⊘ 🚽 🚐 ♨
Within 3 miles: ↡ ✚ ⛳ ℗ 🚣 🛒🛒 U

Notes: Noise curfew at 22.00hrs. Dogs must be kept on leads.

LEISURE: 🏊 Indoor swimming pool 🏊 Outdoor swimming pool 🎠 Children's playground 👶 Kid's club 🎾 Tennis court 🎱 Games room 📺 Separate TV room ⛳ 9/18 hole golf course 🚣 Boats for hire 🎬 Cinema 🎵 Entertainment 🎣 Fishing ◉ Mini golf 🏄 Watersports 🏋 Gym ⚽ Sports field Spa U Stables
FACILITIES: 🛁 Bath 🚿 Shower ⊙ Electric shaver ℗ Hairdryer ✳ Ice Pack Facility ♿ Disabled facilities 🕙 Public telephone 🛒 Shop on site or within 200yds 🛒 Mobile shop (calls at least 5 days a week) 🍖 BBQ area 🛋 Picnic area WI-FI Wi-fi 💻 Internet access 🔄 Recycling ❶ Tourist info 🚮 Dog exercise area

SOUTHWELL — Map 17 SK65

Places to visit

Galleries of Justice Museum, NOTTINGHAM, NG1 1HN, 0115 952 0555 www.galleriesofjustice.org.uk

The Workhouse, SOUTHWELL, NG25 0PT, 01636 817260 www.nationaltrust.org.uk/main/w-theworkhouse

►►► 78% *New Hall Farm Touring Park* (SK660550)

New Hall Farm, New Hall Ln NG22 8BS
☎ 01623 883041

e-mail: enquiries@newhallfarm.co.uk
dir: From A614 at White Post Modern Farm Centre, turn E signed Southwell. Immediately after Edingley turn S into New Hall Ln to site (0.5m)

Open Mar-Oct

Last arrival 21.00hrs Last departure 13.00hrs

A park on a working stock farm with the elevated pitching area enjoying outstanding panoramic views. It is within a short drive of medieval Newark and Sherwood Forest. A log cabin viewing gantry offers a place to relax and take in the spectacular scenery. 2.5 acre site. 25 touring pitches. 10 hardstandings. 7 seasonal pitches. Caravan pitches. Motorhome pitches. Tent pitches.

AA Pubs & Restaurants nearby: Tom Browns Brasserie, GUNTHORPE, NG14 7FB, 0115 966 3642

Facilities: 🐾⊙❄🎄🚐♻ **0**

Services: 🔌🗑📠

Within 3 miles: 🏇🎣🛍🗎U

Notes: Adults only. ⌨ Dogs must be kept on leads.

TEVERSAL — Map 16 SK46

Places to visit

Sherwood Forest Country Park & Visitor Centre, EDWINSTOWE, NG21 9HN, 01623 823202 www.nottinghamshire.gov.uk/sherwoodforestcp

Hardwick Hall, HARDWICK HALL, S44 5QJ, 01246 850430 www.english-heritage.org.uk/daysout/properties/hardwick-old-hall

PREMIER PARK

►►►►► 89% Teversal Camping & Caravanning Club Site (SK472615)

Silverhill Ln NG17 3JJ
☎ 01623 551838

dir: M1 junct 28, A38 towards Mansfield. Left at lights onto B6027. At top of hill straight over at lights & left at Tesco Express. Right onto B6014, left at Craven Arms, site on left

* 🚐 £7.50-£30 🚎 £7.50-£30 ⛺ £7.50-£30

Open all year

Last arrival 20.00hrs Last departure noon

A top notch park with excellent purpose-built facilities and innovative, hands-on owners. Each pitch is spacious, the excellent toilet facilities are state-of-the-art, and there are views of and access to the countryside and nearby Silverhill Community Woods. The attention to detail and all-round quality are truly exceptional - guests can even hire a car for a day and there is a special area for washing dogs and bikes. The site has an on-site shop. Buses for Sutton Ashfield and Chesterfield stop just a five-minute walk from the site. A six-berth holiday caravan, a luxury ready-erected safari tent and a log cabin are available for hire. 6 acre site. 126 touring pitches. 92 hardstandings. Caravan pitches. Motorhome pitches. Tent pitches. 1 static. 1 bell tent/yurt. 1 wooden pod.

AA Pubs & Restaurants nearby: The Shoulder at Hardstoft, HARDSTOFT, S45 8AF, 01246 850276

Leisure: 🎡⊙

Facilities: 🐾⊙🐾❄👶⊙🗎Wi-fi ♻ **0**

Services: 🔌🗑🔋⌨T📠⬆

Within 3 miles: 🏇🎣🛍🗎U

Notes: Site gates closed 23.00hrs-07.00hrs. Dogs must be kept on leads.

TUXFORD — Map 17 SK77

Places to visit

Museum of Lincolnshire Life, LINCOLN, LN1 3LY, 01522 782040 www.lincolnshire.gov.uk/museumoflincolnshirelife

Great for kids: Lincoln Castle, LINCOLN, LN1 3AA, 01522 782040 www.lincolnshire.gov.uk/lincolncastle

AA CAMPING CARD SITE

►►► 83% Orchard Park Touring Caravan & Camping Park (SK754708)

Marnham Rd NG22 0PY
☎ 01777 870228

e-mail: info@orchardcaravanpark.co.uk
dir: Exit A1 at Tuxford, follow brown camping signs for 0.5m, right into Marnham Rd. Site 0.75m on right

🚐 £19-£26 🚎 £19-£26 ⛺ £19-£26

Open mid Mar-Oct

Last arrival mdnt Last departure 18.00hrs

A rural site set in an old fruit orchard with spacious pitches arranged in small groups separated by shrubs; many of the pitches are served with water and electricity. A network of grass pathways and picnic clearings have been created in a woodland area, and there's a superb adventure playground. 7 acre site. 60 touring pitches. 30 hardstandings. Caravan pitches. Motorhome pitches. Tent pitches.

AA Pubs & Restaurants nearby: The Mussel & Crab, TUXFORD, NG22 0PJ, 01777 870491

Leisure: 🎡

Facilities: 🐾⊙🐾❄👶⊙🗎🚐🐾Wi-fi 🖥 ♻ **0**

Services: 🔌🗑🔋⌨T📠

Within 3 miles: 🎣🗎U

Notes: Dogs must be kept on leads.

SERVICES: 🔌 Electric hook up 🗑 Launderette 🍸 Licensed bar 🔋 Calor Gas ⌨ Camping Gaz T Toilet fluid 🍴 Café/Restaurant 🍔 Fast Food/Takeaway 📠 Battery charging 🚼 Baby care ⬆ Motorvan service point **ABBREVIATIONS:** BH/bank hols-bank holidays Etr-Easter Spring BH-Spring Bank Holiday dep-departure fr-from hrs-hours m-mile mdnt-midnight rdbt-roundabout rs-restricted service wk-week wknd-weekend x-rds-cross roads ⌨ No credit cards ⊗ No dogs 👫 Children of all ages accepted See page 9 for details of the AA Camping Card Scheme

OXFORDSHIRE

BANBURY — Map 11 SP44

Places to visit

Banbury Museum, BANBURY, OX16 2PQ, 01295 753752
www.cherwell.gov.uk/banburymuseum

Great for kids: Deddington Castle, DEDDINGTON, OX15 0TE, 0870 333 1181
www.english-heritage.org.uk/daysout/properties/deddington-castle

►►►► 85% Bo Peep Farm Caravan Park (SP481348)

Bo Peep Farm, Aynho Rd, Adderbury OX17 3NP
☎ 01295 810605
e-mail: warden@bo-peep.co.uk
dir: *1m E of Adderbury & A4260, on B4100 (Aynho road)*

🚐 £19-£22 🚐 £19-£22 ▲ £16-£18

Open Mar-Oct

Last arrival 20.00hrs Last departure noon

A delightful park with good views and a spacious feel. Four well laid out camping areas including two with hardstandings and a separate tent field are all planted with maturing shrubs and trees. The two facility blocks are built in attractive Cotswold stone. There is a bay where you can clean your caravan or motorhome, and the newly refurbished 'Dovecote Barn' is available for weddings/corporate events and offers on-site food at selected times. There are four miles of on-site walks through woods and on the river bank. The site is well placed for visiting Banbury and the Cotswolds. 13 acre site. 104 touring pitches. 27 seasonal pitches. Caravan pitches. Motorhome pitches. Tent pitches.

AA Pubs & Restaurants nearby: Ye Olde Reindeer Inn, BANBURY, OX16 5NA, 01295 264031

The Wykham Arms, BANBURY, OX15 5RX, 01295 788808

Saye and Sele Arms, BROUGHTON, OX15 5ED, 01295 263348

Facilities: 🅿 ⊙ 🗲 ☀ ⅄ ⓒ 🔟 ⌁ ⇥ 📶 🖳 ♻ 🎯

Services: 🔌 🔟 🚽 ⌁ 🛒 ⇵

Within 3 miles: ↨ ⌀ 🔟

AA CAMPING CARD SITE

►►►► 83% Barnstones Caravan & Camping Site (SP455454)

Great Bourton OX17 1QU
☎ 01295 750289
dir: *Take A423 from Banbury signed Southam. In 3m turn right signed Gt Bourton/Cropredy, site 100yds on right*

🚐 £13-£15 🚐 £13-£15 ▲ £8-£13

Open all year

A popular, neatly laid-out site with plenty of hardstandings, some fully serviced pitches, a smart up-to-date toilet block, and excellent rally facilities. Well run by a very personable owner, this is an excellent value park. The site is well positioned for stopovers or for visiting nearby Banbury. 3 acre site. 49 touring pitches. 44 hardstandings. Caravan pitches. Motorhome pitches. Tent pitches.

AA Pubs & Restaurants nearby: Ye Olde Reindeer Inn, BANBURY, OX16 5NA, 01295 264031

The Wykham Arms, BANBURY, OX15 5RX, 01295 788808

Saye and Sele Arms, BROUGHTON, OX15 5ED, 01295 263348

Leisure: ⌂ ⚽

Facilities: 🅿 ⊙ ☀ ⅄ ⓒ 🔟 ⌁ ⇥ ♻ 🎯

Services: 🔌 🔟 🚽 ⌁ 🛒 ⇵

Within 3 miles: ↨ ⅌ ⊟ ⌀ ◎ ⅒ 🔟 🔟 ∪

Notes: 🐕 Dogs must be kept on leads.

BLETCHINGDON

Places to visit

Rousham House, ROUSHAM, OX25 4QX, 01869 347110 www.rousham.org

Museum of the History of Science, OXFORD, OX1 3AZ, 01865 277280 www.mhs.ox.ac.uk

Great for kids: Oxford University Museum of Natural History, OXFORD, OX1 3PW, 01865 272950 www.oum.ox.ac.uk

BLETCHINGDON — Map 11 SP51

►►►► 85% Greenhill Leisure Park (SP488178)

Greenhill Farm, Station Rd OX5 3BQ
☎ 01869 351600
e-mail: info@greenhill-leisure-park.co.uk
web: www.greenhill-leisure-park.co.uk
dir: *M40 junct 9, A34 S for 3m. Take B4027 to Bletchingdon. Site 0.5m after village on left*

🚐 🚐 ▲

Open all year (rs Oct-Mar no dogs, shop & games room closed)

Last arrival 21.00 (20.00hrs winter) Last departure noon

An all-year round park set in open countryside near the village of Bletchingdon and well placed for visiting Oxford or the Cotswolds. Fishing is available in the nearby river or in the parks two well-stocked lakes. Pitches are very spacious and the park is very family orientated and in keeping with the owner's theme of 'Where fun meets the countryside'. The facilities are also very good. 7 acre site. 92 touring pitches. 33 hardstandings. 20 seasonal pitches. Caravan pitches. Motorhome pitches. Tent pitches.

AA Pubs & Restaurants nearby: Kings Arms Hotel, WOODSTOCK, OX20 1SU, 01993 813636

The Feathers Hotel, WOODSTOCK, OX20 1SX, 01993 812291

Leisure: ⌂ ⚽

Facilities: 🅿 ⊙ 🗲 ☀ ⅄ 🔟 ⌁ ⇥ 📶 🖳 ♻ 🎯

Services: 🔌 🔟 🚽 ⌁ 🔟 🛒

Within 3 miles: ↨ ⌀ 🔟

Notes: No camp fires or firepits. Dogs must be kept on leads.

LEISURE: 🏊 Indoor swimming pool ⚓ Outdoor swimming pool ⌂ Children's playground ⅄ Kid's club ⚲ Tennis court ✎ Games room ⬜ Separate TV room ⅄ 9/18 hole golf course ⚓ Boats for hire ⊟ Cinema ♫ Entertainment ⌀ Fishing ◎ Mini golf ⅒ Watersports ⅄ Gym ✿ Sports field **Spa** ∪ Stables

FACILITIES: 🛁 Bath 🅿 Shower ⊙ Electric shaver 🗲 Hairdryer ☀ Ice Pack Facility ⅄ Disabled facilities ⓒ Public telephone 🔟 Shop on site or within 200yds 🚚 Mobile shop (calls at least 5 days a week) 🍖 BBQ area ⇥ Picnic area 📶 Wi-fi 🖳 Internet access ♻ Recycling 🎯 Tourist info ⌁ Dog exercise area

►►►► 82% Diamond Farm Caravan & Camping Park (SP513170)

Islip Rd OX5 3DR
☎ 01869 350909
e-mail: warden@diamondpark.co.uk
dir: M40 junct 9, A34 S for 3m, B4027 to Bletchingdon. Site 1m on left

🚐 🚎 Å

Open Mar-Nov

Last arrival dusk Last departure 11.00hrs

A well-run, quiet rural site in good level surroundings, and ideal for touring the Cotswolds, situated seven miles north of Oxford in the heart of the Thames Valley. This popular park has excellent facilities, and offers a heated outdoor swimming pool, a games room for children and a small bar. 3 acre site. 37 touring pitches. 20 hardstandings. Caravan pitches. Motorhome pitches. Tent pitches.

AA Pubs & Restaurants nearby: Kings Arms Hotel, WOODSTOCK, OX20 1SU, 01993 813636

The Feathers Hotel, WOODSTOCK, OX20 1SX, 01993 812291

Leisure: 🏊 ⚑ ⚲

Facilities: 🚿 ☂ ⊙ ℙ ✳ 🛎 wifi ♨ ⑦

Services: 🔌 🚽 🔧 🗑 🔥 🚰 Ⓣ 🍴 🍔 ⚡

Within 3 miles: ⚓ 🏌 💲

Notes: 🚫 No gazebos or campfires, no noise after 22.30hrs. Dogs must be kept on leads.

BURFORD   Map 5 SP21

NEW ►► 85% Wysdom Touring Park

(SP248117)

Cheltenham Rd OX18 4PL
☎ 01993 823207
e-mail: geoffhayes@fsmail.net
dir: Telephone for directions

* 🚐 £12-£15 🚎 £12-£15

Open all year

Last arrival 21.00hrs Last departure noon

Owned by Burford School, this small adults' only park is very much a hidden gem being just a five-minute walk from Burford, one of prettiest towns in the Cotswolds. The pitches have good privacy; all have electric and there are many hardstandings for caravans and motorhome. The unisex toilet facilities are very clean. This makes a good base from which to explore the Cotswolds. 50 touring pitches. Caravan pitches. Motorhome pitches.

Notes: Adults only.

CHARLBURY   Map 11 SP31

Places to visit

Blenheim Palace, WOODSTOCK, OX20 1PP, 0800 849 6500 www.blenheimpalace.com

Minster Lovell Hall & Dovecote, MINSTER LOVELL, OX29 0RR, 0870 333 1181 www.english-heritage.org.uk/daysout/properties/minster-lovell-hall-and-dovecote

Great for kids: Cogges Witney, WITNEY, OX28 3LA, 01993 772602 www.cogges.org.uk

►►►► 84% Cotswold View Touring Park (SP365210)

Enstone Rd OX7 3JH
☎ 01608 810314
e-mail: bookings@gfwiddows.co.uk
dir: From A44 in Enstone take B4022 towards Charlbury. Follow site signs. Site 1m from Charlbury.

🚐 🚎 Å

Open Etr or Apr-Oct

Last arrival 21.00hrs Last departure noon

A good Cotswold site, well screened and with attractive views across the countryside. The toilet facilities include fully-equipped family rooms and bathrooms, and there are spacious, sheltered pitches, some with hardstandings. Breakfasts and takeaway food are available from the shop. The site has camping pods for hire. This is the perfect location for exploring the Cotswolds and anyone heading for the Charlbury Music Festival. 10 acre site. 125 touring pitches. Caravan pitches. Motorhome pitches. Tent pitches.

AA Pubs & Restaurants nearby: The Bull Inn, CHARLBURY, OX7 3RR, 01608 810689

The Crown Inn, CHURCH ENSTONE, OX7 4NN, 01608 677262

Leisure: ⚑ 🎱 ⚲

Facilities: 🚿 ☂ ⊙ ℙ ✳ ♿ Ⓒ 💲 🚻 🌳

Services: 🔌 🗑 🔥 🚰 Ⓣ 🍴 ⚡

Within 3 miles: 🏌 💲 🛒

Notes: Off-licence, skittle alley, chess, boules.

HENLEY-ON-THAMES   Map 5 SU78

Places to visit

Greys Court, HENLEY-ON-THAMES, RG9 4PG, 01491 628529 www.nationaltrust.org.uk

River & Rowing Museum, HENLEY-ON-THAMES, RG9 1BF, 01491 415600 www.rrm.co.uk

Great for kids: LEGOLAND Windsor Resort, WINDSOR, SL4 4AY www.legoland.co.uk

REGIONAL WINNER – SOUTH EAST ENGLAND AA CAMPSITE OF THE YEAR 2014

PREMIER PARK

►►►►► 87% Swiss Farm Touring & Camping (SU759837)

Best of British

Marlow Rd RG9 2HY
☎ 01491 573419
e-mail: enquiries@swissfarmcamping.co.uk
web: www.swissfarmcamping.co.uk
dir: From Henley-on-Thames take A4155, towards Marlow. 1st left after rugby club

* 🚐 £17-£27 🚎 £19.50-£27 Å £14-£22

Open Mar-Oct (rs Mar-May & Oct pool closed)

Last arrival 21.00hrs Last departure noon

This park enjoys an excellent location within easy walking distance of the town and is perfect for those visiting the Henley Regatta (but booking is essential at that time). Pitches are spacious and well appointed, and include some that are fully serviced. There is a tasteful bar plus a nice outdoor swimming pool. 6 acre site. 140 touring pitches. 100 hardstandings. Caravan pitches. Motorhome pitches. Tent pitches. 6 statics.

AA Pubs & Restaurants nearby: The Little Angel, HENLEY-ON-THAMES, RG9 2LS, 01491 411008

Crooked Billet, STOKE ROW, RG9 5PU, 01491 681048

The Five Horseshoes, HENLEY-ON-THAMES, RG9 6EX, 01491 641282

continued

SERVICES: 🔌 Electric hook up �▣ Launderette 🍺 Licensed bar 🅰 Calor Gas 🗘 Camping Gaz Ⓣ Toilet fluid 🍴 Café/Restaurant 🍔 Fast Food/Takeaway 🔋 Battery charging 🍼 Baby care ⚡ Motorvan service point **ABBREVIATIONS:** BH/bank hols-bank holidays Etr-Easter Spring BH-Spring Bank Holiday dep-departure fr-from hrs-hours m-mile mdnt-midnight rdbt-roundabout rs-restricted service wk-week wknd-weekend x-rds-cross roads 🚫 No credit cards 🚫 No dogs 👪 Children of all ages accepted See page 9 for details of the AA Camping Card Scheme

HENLEY-ON-THAMES *continued*

Swiss Farm Touring & Camping

Leisure: 🏊 ⛺

Facilities: 🎣 ⊙ ☂ ✳ ⟨ 🔇 🚻 ♿ 🛜 ☂ ⓘ

Services: 🔌 🗑 🍴 💧 🚰 🚽 ⎘

Within 3 miles: ⚓ ⛳ 🎏 ⊟ 🍴 🐕 🛒

Notes: No groups, no dogs during high season.

see advert below

STANDLAKE   Map 5 SP30

Places to visit

Buscot Park, BUSCOT, SN7 8BU, 01367 240786
www.buscotpark.com

Harcourt Arboretum, OXFORD, OX44 9PX,
01865 343501 www.botanic-garden.ox.ac.uk

Great for kids: Cotswold Wildlife Park and
Gardens, BURFORD, OX18 4JP, 01993 823006
www.cotswoldwildlifepark.co.uk

PREMIER PARK

▶▶▶▶▶ **96% Lincoln Farm
Park Oxfordshire** *(SP395028)*   *Best of British*

High St OX29 7RH

☎ **01865 300239**

e-mail: info@lincolnfarmpark.co.uk

web: www.lincolnfarmpark.co.uk

dir: *Exit A415 between Abingdon & Witney, 5m
SE of Witney. Follow brown campsite sign in
Standlake*

🚐 🚗 ⛺

Lincoln Farm Park Oxfordshire

Open Feb-Nov

Last arrival 20.00hrs Last departure noon

This attractively landscaped family-run park,
located in a quiet village near the River
Thames, offers a truly excellent camping or
caravanning experience. There are top class
facilities throughout the park. It has excellent
leisure facilities in the Standlake Leisure
Centre complete with two pools plus gym,
sauna etc. This is the perfect base for visiting
the many attractions in Oxfordshire and the
Cotswolds. A warm welcome is assured from
the friendly staff. 9 acre site. 90 touring
pitches. 75 hardstandings. Caravan pitches.
Motorhome pitches. Tent pitches.

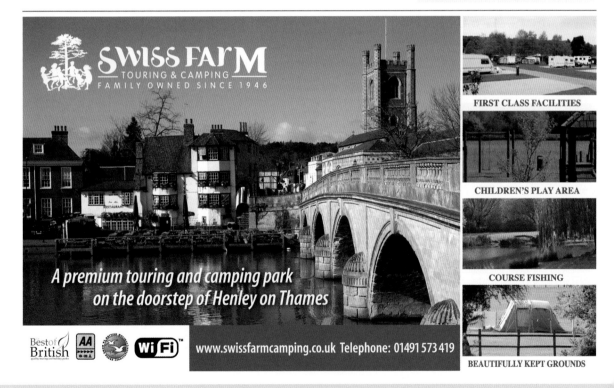

LEISURE: 🏊 Indoor swimming pool 🏊 Outdoor swimming pool 🎠 Children's playground 🙌 Kid's club 🎾 Tennis court 🎱 Games room 📺 Separate TV room
⛳ 9/18 hole golf course ⛵ Boats for hire 🎬 Cinema 🎵 Entertainment 🎣 Fishing ◉ Mini golf 🏄 Watersports 🏋 Gym ☉ Sports field **Spa** ♪ Stables
FACILITIES: 🛁 Bath 🚿 Shower ⊙ Electric shaver 🪮 Hairdryer ✳ Ice Pack Facility ♿ Disabled facilities 📞 Public telephone 🏪 Shop on site or within 200yds
🏬 Mobile shop (calls at least 5 days a week) 🍴 BBQ area 🎏 Picnic area 🛜 Wi-fi 💻 Internet access ♻ Recycling ⓘ Tourist info 🐕 Dog exercise area

AA Pubs & Restaurants nearby: Bear & Ragged Staff, CUMNOR, OX2 9QH, 01865 862329

The Vine Inn, CUMNOR, OX2 9QN, 01865 862567

Leisure: 🏊🅰️🔍

Facilities: 🛏️🖍️☉🅿️❄️&🕐💲🎠🛏️ 📶

Services: 🔌🗄️🧺🅣🔋↯

Within 3 miles: ↓🎣🦮🏊💲∪

Notes: No gazebos, no noise after 23.00hrs. Dogs must be kept on leads. Putting green, outdoor chess.

RUTLAND

GREETHAM   Map 11 SK91

Places to visit

Rutland County Museum & Visitor Centre, OAKHAM, LE15 6HW, 01572 758440 www.rutland.gov.uk/museum

Great for kids: Oakham Castle, OAKHAM, LE15 6HW, 01572 758440 www.rutland.gov.uk/castle

►►►► 83% Rutland Caravan & Camping (SK925148)

Park Ln LE15 7FN
☎ 01572 813520
e-mail: info@rutlandcaravanandcamping.co.uk
dir: From A1 onto B668 towards Greetham. Before Greetham turn right at x-rds, left to site

🚐🚍🛖

Open all year

Last arrival 20.00hrs

This pretty caravan park, built to a high specification and surrounded by well-planted banks, continues to improve due to the enthusiasm and vision of its owner. From the spacious reception and the innovative play area to the toilet block, everything is of a very high standard. The spacious grassy site is close to the Viking Way and other footpath networks, and well sited for visiting Rutland Water and the many picturesque villages in the area. 5 acre site. 130 touring pitches. 65 hardstandings. Caravan pitches. Motorhome pitches. Tent pitches.

AA Pubs & Restaurants nearby: The Wheatsheaf, GREETHAM, LE15 7NP, 01572 812325

The Olive Branch, CLIPSHAM, LE15 7SH, 01780 410355

Leisure: 🅰️🔍

Facilities: 🖍️☉🅿️❄️&🕐💲🎠🛏️ 📶 ♻️ ❗

Services: 🔌🗄️🧺🅣↯

Within 3 miles: ↓🎣🦮☉🏊💲∪

Notes: Dogs must be kept on leads. Dog shower.

OAKHAM   Map 11 SK80

Places to visit

Oakham Castle, OAKHAM, LE15 6HW, 01572 758440 www.rutland.gov.uk/castle

Rutland County Museum & Visitor Centre, OAKHAM, LE15 6HW, 01572 758440 www.rutland.gov.uk/museum

NEW ►►► 77% Ranksborough Hall Caravan and Camping (SK838110)

Ranksborough Hall Estates, Langham LE15 7JR
☎ 01572 722984 & 07794 949568
e-mail: sales@ranksboroughhall.com
dir: A606 from Oakham towards Melton Mowbray, through Langham, left at Ranksborough Hall sign

🚐 £19-£22 🚍 £19-£22 🛖 £15-£21

Open all year

Last arrival 18.00hrs Last departure anytime

This small, intimate, tranquil touring park is situated in the grounds of Ranksborough Hall. It occupies a level, secluded and mature tree fringed site with clean, well-maintained toilets, and a high priority is given to security on the site. Several attractive and historic market towns are a short drive away through rolling and unspoilt countryside, plus there are opportunities for walking, sailing and cycling at nearby Rutland Water. 1.5 acre site. 33 touring pitches. 33 hardstandings. 10 seasonal pitches. Caravan pitches. Motorhome pitches. Tent pitches.

AA Pubs & Restaurants nearby: The Grainstore Brewery, OAKHAM, LE15 6RE, 01572 770065

The Finch's Arms, OAKHAM, LE15 8TL, 01572 756575

Facilities: 🖍️☉🅿️&🕐🎠🛏️ ❗

Services: 🔌🔒

Within 3 miles: ↓🎣🦮🏊💲∪

Notes: ⊛ Quiet time after 23.00hrs, BBQs must be off the ground. Dogs must be kept on leads.

WING   Map 11 SK80

Places to visit

Lyddington Bede House, LYDDINGTON, LE15 9LZ, 01572 822438 www.english-heritage.org.uk/daysout/properties/lyddington-bede-house

Great for kids: Oakham Castle, OAKHAM, LE15 6HW, 01572 758440 www.rutland.gov.uk/castle

►►► 71% Wing Lakes Caravan & Camping (SK892031)

Wing Hall LE15 8RY
☎ 01572 737283 & 737090
e-mail: winghall1891@aol.com
dir: From A1 take A47 towards Leicester, 14m, follow Morcott signs. In Morcott follow Wing signs. 2.5m, follow site signs

🚐🚍🛖

Open all year

Last arrival 21.00hrs Last departure noon

A deeply tranquil and rural park set in the grounds of an old manor house. The four grassy fields with attractive borders of mixed, mature deciduous trees have exceptional views across the Rutland countryside and are within one mile of Rutland Water. There's a good farm shop which specialises in locally sourced produce, a licensed café, and there are high quality showers and a fully-equipped laundry. Children and tents are very welcome in what is a safe environment where there is space to roam. 11 acre site. 250 touring pitches. 4 hardstandings. Caravan pitches. Motorhome pitches. Tent pitches.

AA Pubs & Restaurants nearby: Kings Arms, WING, LE15 8SE, 01572 737634

Facilities: 🖍️🅿️❄️💲🛏️ 📶

Services: 🔌🍴🔒

Within 3 miles: ↓🎣🦮🏊💲🗄️∪

Notes: Dogs must be kept on leads. Coarse fishing.

SERVICES: 🔌 Electric hook up 🗄️ Launderette 🍴 Licensed bar 🛢️ Calor Gas ⊘ Camping Gaz 🅣 Toilet fluid 🍽️ Café/Restaurant 🍔 Fast Food/Takeaway 🔋 Battery charging 🍼 Baby care ↯ Motorvan service point **ABBREVIATIONS:** BH/bank hols-bank holidays Etr-Easter Spring BH-Spring Bank Holiday dep-departure fr-from hrs-hours m-mile mdnt-midnight rdbt-roundabout rs-restricted service wk-week wknd-weekend x-rds-cross roads ⊛ No credit cards ⊗ No dogs 👶 Children of all ages accepted See page 9 for details of the AA Camping Card Scheme

SHROPSHIRE

BRIDGNORTH   Map 10 SO79

Places to visit

Benthall Hall, BENTHALL, TF12 5RX,
01952 882159
www.nationaltrust.org.uk/main/w-benthallhall

Great for kids: Dudmaston Estate, QUATT,
WV15 6QN, 01746 780866 www.nationaltrust.
org.uk/main/w-dudmaston

PREMIER PARK

►►►►► 87% Stanmore Hall Touring Park (SO742923)

Stourbridge Rd WV15 6DT
☎ 01746 761761
e-mail: stanmore@morris-leisure
dir: 2m E of Bridgnorth on A458

🚐 🚎 Å

Open all year

Last arrival 20.00hrs Last departure noon

An excellent park in peaceful surroundings
offering outstanding facilities. The pitches,
many fully serviced (with Freeview TV), are
arranged around the lake close to Stanmore
Hall. Arboretum standard trees include some
magnificent Californian Redwoods and an oak
tree that is nearly 700 years old. The site is
handy for visiting Ironbridge, the Severn Valley
Railway and the attractive market town of
Bridgnorth. 12.5 acre site. 131 touring pitches.
53 hardstandings. Caravan pitches. Motorhome
pitches. Tent pitches.

AA Pubs & Restaurants nearby: Halfway House
Inn, BRIDGNORTH, WV16 5LS, 01746 762670

Leisure: 🄰 ⚽

Facilities: 🅿 ⊙ 🥄 ☀ ⬥ 🕓 🖥 🍴 🚻 wifi 🚳

Services: 🔌 🔲 🛢 🗑 🍴 🍺 ᵜ

Within 3 miles: ↨ ⚓ ⛳ 🍴 🛒 🍽 ∪

Notes: Max 2 dogs per pitch. Dogs must be
kept on leads.

CRAVEN ARMS   Map 9 SO48

Places to visit

Stokesay Castle, STOKESAY, SY7 9AH,
01588 672544 www.english-heritage.org.uk/
daysout/properties/stokesay-castle

Great for kids: Ludlow Castle, LUDLOW,
SY8 1AY, 01584 873355 www.ludlowcastle.com

►►► 79% Wayside Camping and Caravan Park (SO399816)

Aston on Clun SY7 8EF
☎ 01588 660218
e-mail: waysidecamping@hotmail.com
dir: From Craven Arms on A49, W onto B4368
(Clun road) towards Clun Valley. Site approx 2m on
right just before Aston-on-Clun

✳ 🚐 £12-£15 🚎 £12-£15 Å fr £7

Open Apr-Oct

A peaceful park with lovely views, close to
excellent local walks and many places of interest.
The modern toilet facilities provide a good level of
comfort, and there are several electric hook-ups.
You are assured of a warm welcome by the helpful
owner. Out of season price reductions are
available. Many places of interest are within easy
reach including Stokesay Castle, Offa's Dyke and
Ludlow. 2.5 acre site. 20 touring pitches. 7
hardstandings. Caravan pitches. Motorhome
pitches. Tent pitches. 1 static.

AA Pubs & Restaurants nearby: The Sun Inn,
CRAVEN ARMS, SY7 9DF, 01584 861239

The Crown Country Inn, MUNSLOW, SY7 9ET,
01584 841205

Facilities: 🅿 ⊙ 🥄 ☀ ⬥ 🕓 🖥 🗑 🚳 🚳

Services: 🔌 🔲 🍴 ᵜ

Within 3 miles: ↨ ⛳ 🛒 🍽

Notes: ⊚ Adults only on BHs, only 1 dog per unit.
Dogs must be kept on leads. Seasonal organic
vegetables on sale.

ELLESMERE

See Lyneal

HUGHLEY   Map 10 SO59

Places to visit

Old Oswestry Hill Fort, OSWESTRY,
0870 333 1181 www.english-heritage.org.uk/
daysout/properties/old-oswestry-hill-fort

Great for kids: Hoo Farm Animal Kingdom,
TELFORD, TF6 6DJ, 01952 677917
www.hoofarm.com

►►► 79% Mill Farm Holiday Park (SO564979)

GOLD

SY5 6NT
☎ 01746 785208
e-mail: myrtleroberts@hotmail.com
dir: On unclassified road off B4371 through
Hughley, 3m SW of Much Wenlock, 11m SW of
Church Stretton

✳ 🚐 £10-£18 🚎 £10-£18 Å £10-£18

Open all year

Last arrival 18.00hrs Last departure noon

Peacefully located within woodland, the park has
a stream running through it - the only sounds to
be heard are running water and birdsong. The
touring pitches are terraced and the lush,
screened camping area ensures peace and
relaxation. The older style amenities blocks are
spotlessly clean. Regular social events are held in
the former farm outbuildings. 20 acre site. 60
touring pitches. 6 hardstandings. 10 seasonal
pitches. Caravan pitches. Motorhome pitches. Tent
pitches. 90 statics.

AA Pubs & Restaurants nearby: The George &
Dragon, MUCH WENLOCK, TF13 6AA,
01952 727312

The Talbot Inn, MUCH WENLOCK, TF13 6AA,
01952 727077

Leisure: ⚽

Facilities: 🅿 ⊙ 🥄 ☀ 🍴 🚻 wifi 🚳 🚳

Services: 🔌 🔲 🗑 🍴 ᵜ

Within 3 miles: ⛳ 🛒 ∪

Notes: Site more suitable for adults. Dogs must
be kept on leads. Fishing.

LEISURE: 🄰 Indoor swimming pool 🄰 Outdoor swimming pool 🄰 Children's playground 🄰 Kid's club 🄰 Tennis court 🄰 Games room 🄰 Separate TV room
🄰 9/18 hole golf course 🄰 Boats for hire 🄰 Cinema 🄰 Entertainment 🄰 Fishing 🄰 Mini golf 🄰 Watersports 🄰 Gym 🄰 Sports field Spa ∪ Stables
FACILITIES: 🄰 Bath 🄰 Shower ⊙ Electric shaver 🄰 Hairdryer ☀ Ice Pack Facility ⬥ Disabled facilities 🄰 Public telephone 🄰 Shop on site or within 200yds
🄰 Mobile shop (calls at least 5 days a week) 🄰 BBQ area 🄰 Picnic area wifi Wi-fi 🄰 Internet access 🄰 Recycling 🄰 Tourist info 🄰 Dog exercise area

Places to visit

Old Oswestry Hill Fort, OSWESTRY, 0870 333 1181 www.english-heritage.org.uk/daysout/properties/old-oswestry-hill-fort

Great for kids: Hawkstone Historic Park & Follies, WESTON-UNDER-REDCASTLE, SY4 5UY, 01948 841700 www.principal-hayley.co.uk

►►►► 84% Fernwood Caravan Park (SJ445346)

SY12 0QF
☎ **01948 710221**
e-mail: enquiries@fernwoodpark.co.uk
dir: From A495 in Welshampton take B5063, over canal bridge, turn right as signed

* ⊞ £23-£27 ⊞ £23-£27

Open Mar-Nov (rs Mar & Nov shop closed)

Last arrival 21.00hrs Last departure 17.00hrs

A peaceful park set in wooded countryside, with a screened, tree-lined touring area and coarse fishing lake. The approach is past colourful flowerbeds, and the static area which is tastefully arranged around an attractive children's playing area. There is a small child-free touring area for those wanting complete relaxation, and the park has 20 acres of woodland walks. 26 acre site. 60 touring pitches. 8 hardstandings. 30 seasonal pitches. Caravan pitches. Motorhome pitches. 165 statics.

Leisure: /ᴧ
Facilities: 𝄢☉ℱ⚙☼☾⚲⚲ⓢ☜✿♻ ❼
Services: ☻⬛ 🔋Ⓣ↯
Within 3 miles: ☇ℒ🛒Ⓢ
Notes: Dogs must be kept on leads.

Places to visit

Powis Castle & Garden, WELSHPOOL, SY21 8RF, 01938 551929 www.nationaltrust.org.uk

Great for kids: Shrewsbury Castle and Shropshire Regimental Museum, SHREWSBURY, SY1 2AT, 01743 358516 www.shrewsburymuseums.com

AA CAMPING CARD SITE

►►► 86% The Old School Caravan Park (SO322977)

Shelve SY5 0JQ
☎ **01588 650410**
e-mail: t.ward425@btinternet.com
dir: 6.5m SW of Minsterley on A488, site on left 2m after village sign for Hope

⊞ ⊞ Å

Open Mar-Jan

Last arrival 21.00hrs Last departure 11.00hrs

Situated in the Shropshire Hills, an Area of Outstanding Natural Beauty, with many excellent walks starting directly from the site, and many cycle trails close by. Although a small site of just 1.5 acres it is well equipped. It is a really beautiful park, often described as 'a gem', that has excellent facilities and offers all the requirements for a relaxing countryside holiday. The friendly owners, Terry and Jan, are always on hand to help out with anything. Nearby Snailbreach Mine offers guided tours on certain days. Please note that there is no laundry at this park. 1.5 acre site. 22 touring pitches. 10 hardstandings. 6 seasonal pitches. Caravan pitches. Motorhome pitches. Tent pitches.

AA Pubs & Restaurants nearby: The Sun Inn, MARTON, SY21 8JP, 01938 561211

The Lowfield Inn, MARTON, SY21 8JX, 01743 891313

Facilities: 𝄢☉☼☾⚲✿♻ ❼
Services: ☻🔋
Within 3 miles: ℒⓈ↻
Notes: ⊘ No ball games or cycle riding. Dogs must be kept on leads. TV aerial connection.

SHREWSBURY — Map 15 SJ41

Places to visit

Attingham Park, ATCHAM, SY4 4TP, 01743 708123 www.nationaltrust.org.uk/attinghampark

AA CAMPING CARD SITE

PREMIER PARK

▶▶▶▶▶ 89% Beaconsfield Farm Caravan Park *(SJ522189)*

Best of British

Battlefield SY4 4AA
☎ 01939 210370 & 210399
e-mail: mail@beaconsfield-farm.co.uk
web: www.beaconsfield-farm.co.uk
dir: *At Hadnall, 1.5m NE of Shrewsbury. Follow sign for Astley from A49*

* ⚌ £18-£26 ⚌ £20-£26

Open all year

Last arrival 19.00hrs Last departure noon

A purpose-built family-run park on farmland in open countryside. This pleasant park offers quality in every area, including superior toilets, heated indoor swimming pool, luxury lodges for hire and attractive landscaping. Fly and coarse fishing are available from the park's own lake and The Bothy restaurant is excellent. Car hire is available directly from the site, and there's a steam room, plus free Wi-fi. 12 luxury lodges are available for hire or sale. Only adults over 21 years are accepted. 16 acre site. 60 touring pitches. 50 hardstandings. 10 seasonal pitches. Caravan pitches. Motorhome pitches. 35 statics.

AA Pubs & Restaurants nearby: The Armoury, SHREWSBURY, SY1 1HH, 01743 340525

Mytton & Mermaid Hotel, SHREWSBURY, SY5 6QG, 01743 761220

Albright Hussey Manor Hotel & Restaurant, SHREWSBURY, SY4 3AF, 01939 290571

Beaconsfield Farm Caravan Park

Leisure: 🎣
Facilities: 🏦 ⊙ 🅿 ☀ ⚒ 🔌 🔥 🚿 ⚙ 📺
🔄 ❶
Services: 🔌 📶 🛢 🍴 ↻
Within 3 miles: ⬇ 🎋 ✎ ⊚ 🛒 ⛽

Notes: Adults only. Dogs must be kept on leads. Cycle hire.

PREMIER PARK

▶▶▶▶▶ 88% Oxon Hall Touring Park *(SJ455138)*

Best of British

Welshpool Rd SY3 5FB
☎ 01743 340868
e-mail: oxon@morris-leisure.co.uk
dir: *Exit A5 (ring road) at junct with A458. Site shares entrance with 'Oxon Park & Ride'*

⚌ ⚌ ▲

Open all year

Last arrival 21.00hrs

A delightful park with quality facilities and a choice of grass and fully serviced pitches. A warm welcome is assured from the friendly staff. The adults-only section proves very popular, and there is an inviting patio area next to reception and the shop, overlooking a small lake. This site is ideally located for visiting Shrewsbury and the surrounding countryside, and the site also benefits from the Oxon Park & Ride, a short walk through the park. 15 acre site. 105 touring pitches. 72 hardstandings. Caravan pitches. Motorhome pitches. Tent pitches. 60 statics.

AA Pubs & Restaurants nearby: The Armoury, SHREWSBURY, SY1 1HH, 01743 340525

Mytton & Mermaid Hotel, SHREWSBURY, SY5 6QG, 01743 761220

Albright Hussey Manor Hotel & Restaurant, SHREWSBURY, SY4 3AF, 01939 290571

Leisure: 🎣
Facilities: 🏦 ⊙ 🅿 ☀ ⚒ 🔌 🔥 🚿 ⚙ 📺 WiFi 📺
🔄 ❶

Services: 🔌 📶 🛢 🔧 📺 ↻
Within 3 miles: ⬇ 🎋 ✎ 🛒 ⛽

Notes: Max 2 dogs per pitch. Dogs must be kept on leads.

TELFORD — Map 10 SJ60

Places to visit

Lilleshall Abbey, LILLESHALL, TF10 9HW, 0121 625 6820 www.english-heritage.org.uk/daysout/properties/lilleshall-abbey

Ironbridge Gorge Museums, IRONBRIDGE, TF8 7DQ, 01952 884391 www.ironbridge.org.uk

PREMIER PARK

▶▶▶▶▶ 81% Severn Gorge Park *(SJ705051)*

Bridgnorth Rd, Tweedale TF7 4JB
☎ 01952 684789
e-mail: info@severngorgepark.co.uk
dir: *Signed off A442, 1m S of Telford*

* ⚌ fr £18.75 ⚌ fr £18.75

Open all year

Last arrival 20.00hrs Last departure noon

A very pleasant wooded site in the heart of Telford, well-screened and well-maintained. The sanitary facilities are fresh and immaculate, and landscaping of the grounds is carefully managed. Although the touring section is small, this is a really delightful park to stay on, and it is also well positioned for visiting nearby Ironbridge and its museums. The Telford bus stops at the end of the drive. 6 acre site. 12 touring pitches. 12 hardstandings. Caravan pitches. Motorhome pitches. 120 statics.

Facilities: 🏦 ⊙ 🅿 ☀ ⚒ 🔥 ❶
Services: 🔌 📶 🛢 🔧 🛒 ↻
Within 3 miles: ⬇ 🎋 ✎ ⊚ 🛒 ⛽ U

Notes: Adults only. Well behaved dogs only. Dogs must be kept on leads.

WEM Map 15 SJ52

Places to visit

Hawkstone Historic Park & Follies, WESTON-UNDER-REDCASTLE, SY4 5UY, 01948 841700 www.principal-hayley.co.uk

Attingham Park, ATCHAM, SY4 4TP, 01743 708123 www.nationaltrust.org.uk/attinghampark

Great for kids: Shrewsbury Castle and Shropshire Regimental Museum, SHREWSBURY, SY1 2AT, 01743 358516 www.shrewsburymuseums.com

►►► 79% Lower Lacon Caravan Park
(SJ534304)

SY4 5RP
☎ 01939 232376
e-mail: info@llcp.co.uk
web: www.llcp.co.uk
dir: *A49 onto B5065. Site 3m on right*

🚐 🚙 ⛺

Open all year (rs Winter)

Last arrival anytime Last departure 16.00hrs

A large, spacious park with lively club facilities and an entertainments' barn, set safely away from the main road. The park is particularly suited to families, with an outdoor swimming pool and farm animals. 57 acre site. 270 touring pitches. 30 hardstandings. 100 seasonal pitches. Caravan pitches. Motorhome pitches. Tent pitches. 50 statics. 2 wooden pods.

AA Pubs & Restaurants nearby: The Burlton Inn, BURLTON, SY4 5TB, 01939 270284

Leisure: 🏊 ⛹ 🔍 ▭

Facilities: 🚼 🚿 ⊙ ✂ ✲ ♿ ✆ [S] 🐕 [WI-FI] ♻ ℹ

Services: 🔌 🧺 🍷 🛢 ⛽ [T] 🍴 🔋 🍔

Within 3 miles: ⛳ 🎣 ◎ [S] 🧺

Notes: No skateboards, no commercial vehicles, no sign written vehicles. Dogs must be kept on leads. Crazy golf.

WENTNOR Map 15 SO39

Places to visit

Montgomery Castle, MONTGOMERY, 01443 336000 www.cadw.wales.gov.uk

Glansevern Hall Gardens, BERRIEW, SY21 8AH, 01686 640644 www.glansevern.co.uk

►►► 81% The Green Caravan Park
(SO380932)

SY9 5EF
☎ 01588 650605
e-mail: lin@greencaravanpark.co.uk
dir: *1m NE of Bishop's Castle on A489. Right at brown tourist sign*

* 🚐 £14-£17 🚙 £14-£17 ⛺ £14-£17

Open Etr-Oct

Last arrival 21.00hrs Last departure 13.00hrs

A pleasant site in a peaceful setting convenient for visiting Ludlow or Shrewsbury. Very family orientated, with good facilities. The grassy pitches are mainly level, and some hardstandings are available. 15 acre site. 140 touring pitches. 5 hardstandings. Caravan pitches. Motorhome pitches. Tent pitches. 20 statics.

AA Pubs & Restaurants nearby: The Crown Inn, WENTNOR, SY9 5EE, 01588 650613

Leisure: ⛹

Facilities: 🚿 ⊙ ✂ ✲ [S] 🐕 ♻ ℹ

Services: 🔌 🧺 🍷 🛢 ⛽ [T] 🍴 🔋

Within 3 miles: 🎣 [S] U

Notes: Dogs must be kept on leads.

WHEATHILL Map 10 SO68

PREMIER PARK

NEW ►►►►► 81% Wheathill Touring Park *(SO603805)*

WV16 6QT
☎ 01584 823456
e-mail: info@wheathillpark.co.uk
dir: *On B4364 between Ludlow & Bridgnorth (NB Sat Nav may give directions to exit B4364, ignore this. Site entrance well signed from B4364)*

* 🚐 £25 🚙 £25 ⛺ £25

Open Mar-1 Jan

Last arrival 20.00hrs Last departure noon

Ideally located in open countryside between the historic towns of Bridgnorth and Ludlow, this development, which opened in 2013, provides spacious, fully serviced pitches, most with stunning views and a top-notch amenities block with quality fittings and good privacy options. The park is also situated adjacent to the Three Horseshoes pub serving a good range of ales and food. Please note that the on-site shop only sells caravan and camping spares but there's a licensed village shop within a 10-minute drive. 4 acre site. 25 touring pitches. 25 hardstandings. 5 seasonal pitches. Caravan pitches. Motorhome pitches. Tent pitches.

AA Pubs & Restaurants nearby: Fighting Cocks, STOTTESDON, DY14 8TZ, 01746 718270

The Crown Inn, CLEOBURY MORTIMER, DY14 0NB, 01299 270372

Facilities: 🚿 ⊙ ✂ ♿ ⛩ 🐕 [WI-FI] 💻 ℹ

Services: 🔌 🧺 🛢 ⛽ [T] 🔋 ⛛

Within 3 miles: 🎣 [S] 🧺 U

Notes: Adults only. Dogs must be kept on leads.

SERVICES: 🔌 Electric hook up 🧺 Launderette 🍷 Licensed bar 🛢 Calor Gas ⛽ Camping Gaz [T] Toilet fluid 🍴 Café/Restaurant 🍔 Fast Food/Takeaway 🔋 Battery charging 🚼 Baby care ⛛ Motorvan service point **ABBREVIATIONS:** BH/bank hols-bank holidays Etr-Easter Spring BH-Spring Bank Holiday dep-departure fr-from hrs-hours m-mile mdnt-midnight rdbt-roundabout rs-restricted service wk-week wknd-weekend x-rds-cross roads 💳 No credit cards 🚫 No dogs 👪 Children of all ages accepted See page 9 for details of the AA Camping Card Scheme

St Catherine's Church, Montacute

Somerset

South of Bristol and north-east of the West Country lies Somerset, that most English of counties. You tend to think of classic traditions and renowned honey traps when you think of Somerset – cricket and cider, the ancient and mysterious Glastonbury Tor and the deep gash that is Cheddar Gorge.

Somerset means 'summer pastures' – appropriate given that so much of this old county is rural and unspoiled. At its heart are the Mendip Hills, 25 miles (40km) long by 5 miles (8km) wide. Mainly of limestone over old red sandstone, and rising to just over 1,000 ft (303mtrs) above sea level, they have a striking character and identity and are not really like any of the other Somerset hills.

Landscape of contrasts

By contrast, to the south and south-west are the Somerset Levels, a flat fenland landscape that was the setting for the Battle of Sedgemoor in 1685, while close to the rolling acres of Exmoor National Park lie the Quantock Hills, famous for gentle slopes, heather-covered moorland stretches and red deer. From the summit, the Bristol Channel is visible where it meets the Severn Estuary; look to the east and you can see the Mendips.

The Quantocks were the haunt of several distinguished British poets. Coleridge wrote *The Ancient Mariner* and *Kubla Khan* while living in the area. Wordsworth and his sister visited on occasions and often accompanied Coleridge on his country walks.

▶

Along the coast

Somerset's fine coastline takes a lot of beating. Various old-established seaside resorts overlook Bridgwater Bay – among them Minehead, on the edge of Exmoor National Park, and classic Weston-Super-Mare, with its striking new pier (the previous one was destroyed by fire in 2008). Fans of the classic Merchant-Ivory film production of *The Remains of the Day*, starring Anthony Hopkins and Emma Thompson, will recognise the Royal Pier Hotel in Birnbeck Road as one of the locations. Weston has just about everything for the holidaymaker – including Marine Parade, which runs for 2 miles (3.2km).

Historic Wells

Inland – and not to be missed – is historic Wells, one of the smallest cities in the country, and with its period houses and superb cathedral, it is certainly one of the finest. Adorned with sculptures, Wells Cathedral's West Front is a masterpiece of medieval craftsmanship. Nearby are Vicar's Close, a delightful street of 14th-century houses, and the Bishop's Palace, which is 13th century and moated.

Walking and Cycling

The choice of walks in Somerset is plentiful, as is the range of cycle routes. One of the most attractive of long-distance trails is the 50-mile (80km) West Mendip Way, which runs from Weston to Frome. En route the trail visits Cheddar Gorge and Wells. The local tourist information centres throughout the county offer a varied mix of described walks and longer trails to suit all.

One of Somerset's most popular cycling trails is the delightfully named Strawberry Line which links Yatton railway station with Cheddar and runs for 9 miles (14.5km) along the course of a disused track bed. The trail is relatively easy and along the way are various picnic spots and various public artworks.

Festivals and Events

- The Cheddar Ales Beer Festival in June is a celebration of real ale with a range of beers from microbreweries across the country.
- The Priddy Sheep Fair in mid-August is a great occasion for country lovers and farming traditions.
- Between end of March and September there are amazing sand sculptures down on the beach at Weston-Super-Mare.
- The Autumn Steam Gala at the West Somerset Railway in Minehead during early October is a must for steam train enthusiasts.

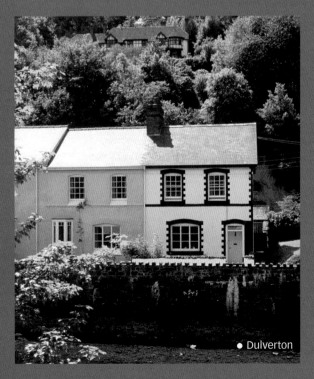

● Dulverton

● Dunkery Beacon

SOMERSET

BATH
Map 4 ST76

Places to visit

Roman Baths & Pump Room, BATH, BA1 1LZ, 01225 477785 www.romanbaths.co.uk

Bath Abbey, BATH, BA1 1LY, 01225 422462 www.bathabbey.org

Great for kids: The Herschel Museum of Astronomy, BATH, BA1 2BL, 01225 446865 www.bath-preservation-trust.org.uk

▶▶▶▶ 82% *Newton Mill Holiday Park* (ST715649)

Newton Rd BA2 9JF
☎ 08442 729503
e-mail: enquiries@newtonmillpark.co.uk
dir: *From Bath W on A4 to rdbt by Globe Inn, immediately left, site 1m on left*

Open all year (rs Wknds low season restaurant open)

Last arrival 21.30hrs Last departure 11.30hrs

An attractive, high quality park set in a sheltered valley and surrounded by woodland, with a stream running through. It offers excellent toilet facilities with private cubicles and family rooms, and there is an appealing restaurant and bar offering a wide choice of menus throughout the year. Additional hardstandings have been put in on the top area of the park. The City of Bath is easily accessible by bus or via the Bristol to Bath cycle path. 42 acre site. 106 touring pitches. 67 hardstandings. Caravan pitches. Motorhome pitches. Tent pitches.

AA Pubs & Restaurants nearby: The Marlborough Tavern, BATH, BA1 2LY, 01225 423731

King William, BATH, BA1 5NN, 01225 428096

The Hop Pole, BATH, BA1 3AR, 01225 446327

Jamie's Italian, BATH, BA1 1BZ, 01225 432340

Leisure: ⚙ ♫
Facilities: 🛁 🏕 ☉ 🗡 ✳ ♿ ⓢ 🛒 🐕 ♻ ❶
Services: 🔌 🔲 🚽 🛢 ⊘ T 🍴 ⛟
Within 3 miles: ♨ 🚲 🎯 ♨ ⓢ 🔳

Notes: No noise after 22.00hrs. Dogs must be kept on leads. Satellite TV hook-up on selected pitches.

BISHOP SUTTON
Map 4 ST55

PREMIER PARK

NEW ▶▶▶▶▶ 91% Best of British GOLD

Bath Chew Valley Caravan Park (ST586598)

Ham Ln BS39 5TZ
☎ 01275 332127
e-mail: enquiries@bathchewvalley.co.uk
dir: *A4 towards Bath, onto A39 towards Weston-Super-Mare. Right onto A368. 6m, right opposite The Red Lion into Ham Lane, site 250mtrs on left*

🚐 🚙 ▲

Open all year

Last arrival 19.00hrs Last departure 11.00hrs

This peaceful adults-only park can be described as 'a park in a garden', with caravan pitches set amidst lawns, shrubs and trees. There are excellent private facilities - rooms with showers, wash basins and toilets - all are spotlessly clean and well maintained. The park is well situated for visiting Bath, Bristol, Wells, Cheddar and Wookey Hole, and for walking in the Mendip Hills. Chew Valley Lake, noted for its top quality fishing, is close by. 4.5 acre site. 45 touring pitches. 4 seasonal pitches. Caravan pitches. Motorhome pitches. Tent pitches.

AA Pubs & Restaurants nearby: The Carpenters Arms, STANTON WICK, BS39 4BX, 01761 490202

The Bear and Swan, CHEW MAGNA, BS40 8SL, 01275 331100

The Pony and Trap, CHEW MAGNA, BS40 8TQ, 01275 332627

Facilities: 🏕 ☉ 🗡 ✳ ♿ ⓢ 🛒 🐕 🔳 📶 🖥 ♻ ❶
Services: 🔌 🔲 🚽 🛢 ⊘ T 🍴 ⛟ ⛟
Within 3 miles: 🎯 ♨ ⓢ

Notes: Adults only. No cars by caravans or tents. Dogs must be kept on leads. Lending library.

BREAN
Map 4 ST25

Places to visit

King John's Hunting Lodge, AXBRIDGE, BS26 2AP, 01934 732012 www.kingjohnshuntinglodge.co.uk

Weston-Super-Mare Museum, WESTON-SUPER-MARE, BS23 1PR, 01934 621028 www.weston-super-maretowncouncil.gov.uk

Great for kids: The Helicopter Museum, WESTON-SUPER-MARE, BS24 8PP, 01934 635227 www.helicoptermuseum.co.uk

AA CAMPING CARD SITE

91% Holiday Resort Unity (ST294539) SILVER

Coast Rd, Brean Sands TA8 2RB
☎ 01278 751235
e-mail: admin@hru.co.uk
dir: *M5 junct 22, B3140 through Burnham-on-Sea, through Berrow to Brean. Site on left just before Brean Leisure Park*

🚐 🚙 ▲

Open Feb-Nov

Last arrival 21.00hrs Last departure 10.00hrs

This is an excellent, family-run holiday park offering very good touring facilities plus a wide range of family oriented activities, including bowling, RJ's entertainment club plus good eating outlets etc. Brean Leisure Park and a swimming pool complex are available directly from the touring park at a discounted entry price. Ready erected, fully-equipped tents are also available for hire. 200 acre site. 453 touring pitches. 158 hardstandings. 168 seasonal pitches. Caravan pitches. Motorhome pitches. Tent pitches. 650 statics. 8 bell tents/yurts. 2 wooden pods.

AA Pubs & Restaurants nearby: Crossways Inn, WEST HUNTSPILL, TA9 3RA, 01278 783756

Leisure: ⚙ ♨ 🎾 ⚙ ⚙ ♻ ♫
Facilities: 🛁 🏕 ☉ 🗡 ✳ ♿ ⓢ 🛒 🐕 📶 🖥 ♻ ❶
Services: 🔲 🚽 🛢 ⊘ 🍴 🛒
Within 3 miles: 🚲 🎯 ♨ ◎ ⓢ 🔳 ∪

Notes: Family parties of 3 or more, must be over 21 (young persons' policy applies). Dogs must be kept on leads. Fishing lake.

LEISURE: 🏊 Indoor swimming pool 🏊 Outdoor swimming pool ⚙ Children's playground 🛝 Kid's club 🎾 Tennis court 🎱 Games room ▭ Separate TV room ⛳ 9/18 hole golf course 🚤 Boats for hire ⊟ Cinema ⚙ Entertainment 🎣 Fishing ⚙ Mini golf 🏄 Watersports 💪 Gym ⚙ Sports field Spa ∪ Stables
FACILITIES: 🛁 Bath 🏕 Shower ☉ Electric shaver 🗡 Hairdryer ✳ Ice Pack Facility ♿ Disabled facilities ⓢ Public telephone 🛒 Shop on site or within 200yds 🏪 Mobile shop (calls at least 5 days a week) 🍖 BBQ area 🏕 Picnic area 📶 Wi-fi 🖥 Internet access ♻ Recycling ❶ Tourist info 🐕 Dog exercise area

91% Warren Farm Holiday Centre *(ST297564)*

Brean Sands TA8 2RP
☎ 01278 751227
e-mail: enquiries@warren-farm.co.uk
dir: *M5 junct 22 , B3140 through Burnham-on-Sea to Berrow & Brean. Site 1.5m past Brean Leisure Park*

* 🚐 £8.50-£18.50 🚌 £8.50-£18.50 ⛺ £8.50-£18.50

Open Apr-Oct

Last arrival 20.00hrs Last departure noon

A large family-run holiday park just a short walk from the beach and divided up into several fields each with its own designated facilities. Pitches are spacious and level and there are some hardstandings available, and there are good panoramic views of the Mendip Hills and Brean Down. The park has its own Beachcomber Inn with bar, restaurant and entertainment area. The site is perfect for families and has a playbarn. Lake fishing is available on site and there is also a fishing tackle and bait shop. 100 acre site. 575 touring pitches. 34 hardstandings. Caravan pitches. Motorhome pitches. Tent pitches. 400 statics.

AA Pubs & Restaurants nearby: Crossways Inn, WEST HUNTSPILL, TA9 3RA, 01278 783756

Warren Farm Holiday Centre

Leisure: 🎠 ⚽ 🏓 ☐ 🎵
Facilities: 🛁 🚿 ⊙ 🪒 ✲ ♿ ☎ [$] 🪑 🐕 [Wi-fi] 💻 ℹ
Services: 🔌 🧺 🍷 🔥 🍃 [T] 🍴 🔋 🍔 ⛽
Within 3 miles: ⛳ 🎣 ◎ 🏊 [$] U
Notes: No commercial vehicles.

see advert below

BREAN *continued*

▶▶▶▶ 91% Northam Farm Caravan & Touring Park *(ST299556)*

TA8 2SE

☎ **01278 751244**

e-mail: stay@northamfarm.co.uk
dir: *M5 junct 22, B3140 to Burnham-on-Sea & Brean. Park on right 0.5m past Brean Leisure Park*

* 🚐 £9.20-£27 🚐 £11.60-£27 ▲ £9.20-£23

Open Mar-Oct (rs Mar-Oct shop, café, takeaway open limited hours)

Last arrival 20.00hrs Last departure 10.30hrs

An attractive site a short walk from the sea and a long sandy beach. This quality park also has lots of children's play areas, and also owns the Seagull Inn about 600 yards away, which includes a restaurant and entertainment. There is a fishing lake on the site, which proves very popular. Facilities on this park are excellent. A DVD of the site is available free of charge. 30 acre site. 350 touring pitches. 260 hardstandings. Caravan pitches. Motorhome pitches. Tent pitches.

AA Pubs & Restaurants nearby: Crossways Inn, WEST HUNTSPILL, TA9 3RA, 01278 783756

Leisure: ⚠ ☺
Facilities: 🛁 🏪 ⊙ 🌢 ⚙ ✳ ⚑ ⚙ 🐕 ⚙ ♻ ❶
Services: 🔌 🗑 🛢 ⊘ T 🍴 🎪 ⚙ ⚙
Within 3 miles: ♨ 🎣 ◎ 🏇 ⚙ ∪

Notes: Families & couples only, no motorcycles or commercial vehicles. Dogs must be kept on leads.

BRIDGETOWN Map 3 SS93

Places to visit

Dunster Castle, DUNSTER, TA24 6SL, 01643 821314 www.nationaltrust.org.uk

Cleeve Abbey, WASHFORD, TA23 0PS, 01984 640377 www.english-heritage.org.uk/daysout/properties/cleeve-abbey

▶▶▶▶ 90% Exe Valley Caravan Site *(SS923333)*

Mill House TA22 9JR

☎ **01643 851432**

e-mail: info@exevalleycamping.co.uk
dir: *Take A396 (Tiverton to Minehead road). Turn W in centre of Bridgetown, site 40yds on right*

🚐 £11.50-£18 🚐 £11.50-£18 ▲ £11.50-£21

Open 14 Mar-20 Oct

Last arrival 22.00hrs Last departure 11.00hrs

Set in the Exmoor National Park, this adults-only park occupies an enchanting, peaceful spot in a wooded valley alongside the River Exe. There is free fly-fishing, an abundance of wildlife and excellent walks leading directly from the park. The site has good, spotlessly clean facilities. The inn opposite serves meals at lunchtime and in the evening. 4 acre site. 48 touring pitches. 10 hardstandings. Caravan pitches. Motorhome pitches. Tent pitches.

AA Pubs & Restaurants nearby: The Rest and Be Thankful Inn, WHEDDON CROSS, TA24 7DR, 01643 841222

Facilities: 🏪 ⊙ 🌢 ✳ ⚙ ⚙ 🔔 🗑 ⚑ 🐕 WI-FI ♻ ❶
Services: 🔌 🗑 🛢 ⊘ T 🛒 ⚙
Within 3 miles: ♨ 🎣 🏇 ⚙ ∪

Notes: Adults only. ⚙ 17th-century mill, cycle hire, TV sockets & cables.

BRIDGWATER Map 4 ST23

Places to visit

Hestercombe Gardens, TAUNTON, TA2 8LG, 01823 413923 www.hestercombe.com

Coleridge Cottage, NETHER STOWEY, TA5 1NQ, 01278 732662 www.nationaltrust.org.uk/coleridgecottage

Great for kids: Tropiquaria Animal and Adventure Park, WASHFORD, TA23 0QB, 01984 640688 www.tropiquaria.co.uk

82% Mill Farm Caravan & Camping Park *(ST219410)*

Fiddington TA5 1JQ

☎ **01278 732286**

web: www.millfarm.biz
dir: *From Bridgwater take A39 W, left at Cannington rdbt, 2m, right just beyond Apple Inn towards Fiddington. Follow camping signs*

* 🚐 £15-£25 🚐 £15-£25 ▲ £15-£25

Open Mar-1 Dec

Last arrival 23.00hrs Last departure 10.00hrs

A large holiday park with plenty to interest all the family, including indoor and outdoor pools, a boating lake, a gym and horse riding. A new camping area called Hazel Park opened in 2013. There is also a clubhouse with bar, and a full entertainment programme in the main season. Although lively and busy in the main season, the park also offers a much quieter environment at other times; out of season some activities and entertainment may not be available. 6 acre site. 275 touring pitches. 40 seasonal pitches. Caravan pitches. Motorhome pitches. Tent pitches.

AA Pubs & Restaurants nearby: The Hood Arms, KILVE, TA5 1EA, 01278 741210

Leisure: ⚙ ⚙ ⚑ ⚠ ☺ ⚙ ⚙ 🎵
Facilities: 🛁 🏪 ⊙ 🌢 ✳ ⚙ ⚙ 🔔 🗑 ⚑ 🐕 WI-FI ♻ ❶
Services: 🔌 🗑 🍴 🛢 ⊘ T 🍴 🎪
Within 3 miles: ♨ 🎣 ◎ 🏇 ⚙ ∪

Notes: No noise after 23.00hrs. Dogs must be kept on leads. Canoeing, pool table, trampolines, pony rides, fitness classes, saunas.

LEISURE: ⚙ Indoor swimming pool ⚙ Outdoor swimming pool ⚠ Children's playground 🖐 Kid's club ⚙ Tennis court ⚙ Games room ⚙ Separate TV room ♨ 9/18 hole golf course 🚣 Boats for hire 🎬 Cinema 🎵 Entertainment 🎣 Fishing ◎ Mini golf ⚙ Watersports ⚙ Gym ⚙ Sports field Spa ∪ Stables
FACILITIES: 🛁 Bath 🏪 Shower ⊙ Electric shaver 🌢 Hairdryer ✳ Ice Pack Facility ⚙ Disabled facilities 🔔 Public telephone 🗑 Shop on site or within 200yds ⚙ Mobile shop (calls at least 5 days a week) 🍴 BBQ area ⚑ Picnic area WI-FI Wi-fi 🖥 Internet access ♻ Recycling ❶ Tourist info 🐕 Dog exercise area

BURNHAM-ON-SEA — Map 4 ST34

Places to visit

Glastonbury Abbey, GLASTONBURY, BA6 9EL, 01458 832267 www.glastonburyabbey.com

King John's Hunting Lodge, AXBRIDGE, BS26 2AP, 01934 732012 www.kingjohnshuntinglodge.co.uk

Great for kids: Wookey Hole Caves & Papermill, WOOKEY HOLE, BA5 1BB, 01749 672243 www.wookey.co.uk

86% Burnham-on-Sea Holiday Village (ST305485)

Marine Dr TA8 1LA
☎ 0871 231 0868
e-mail: burnhamonsea@haven.com
web: www.haven.com/burnhamonsea
dir: M5 junct 22, A38 towards Highbridge. Over mini rdbt, right onto B3139 to Burnham. After Total Garage left into Marine Drive. Park 400yds on left

Open mid Mar-end Oct (rs mid Mar-May & Sep-Oct facilities may be reduced)

Last arrival anytime Last departure 10.00hrs

A large, family-orientated holiday village complex with a separate touring park containing 43 super pitches. There is a wide range of activities, including excellent indoor and outdoor pools, plus bars, restaurants and entertainment for all the family. The coarse fishing lake is very popular, and the seafront at Burnham is only half a mile away. A wide range of well laid out holiday homes are available for hire. 94 acre site. 75 touring pitches. 44 hardstandings. Caravan pitches. Motorhome pitches. Tent pitches. 700 statics.

AA Pubs & Restaurants nearby: Crossways Inn, WEST HUNTSPILL, TA9 3RA, 01278 783756

Leisure: ♨ ⚓ ⚔ Ⓜ ⚒ ⚽ ♪ ♫

Facilities: ⚡ ⌐ ✳ ♿ ⊕ 🍴 📶

Services: 🔌 🔲 ⚙ ∅ 🍴 🛒 💧 ♨

Within 3 miles: ⚘ 🎠 🏇 ◎ 🎣 🎱 ∪

Notes: No pets, no commercial vehicles, no bookings by persons under 21yrs unless a family booking.

see advert below

CHEDDAR

Places to visit

Glastonbury Abbey, GLASTONBURY, BA6 9EL, 01458 832267 www.glastonburyabbey.com

The Helicopter Museum, WESTON-SUPER-MARE, BS24 8PP, 01934 635227 www.helicoptermuseum.co.uk

Great for kids: Wookey Hole Caves & Papermill, WOOKEY HOLE, BA5 1BB, 01749 672243 www.wookey.co.uk

---

CHEDDAR — Map 4 ST45

95% *Cheddar Woods Holiday Park* (ST448547)

Axbridge Rd BS27 3DB
☎ 01934 742610
e-mail: enquiries@cheddarwoods.co.uk
dir: From M5 junct 22 follow signs to Cheddar Gorge & Caves (8m). Site midway between Cheddar & Axbridge on A371

Nestled in the beatiful Mendip Hills, Cheddar Woods is the perfect place to relax and unwind. This state-of-the-art park is an ideal location for family holidays. Both large and smaller lodges are available for hire, all offering top quality accommodation. There are excellent leisure facilities including a gym, spa and swimming pool plus a 'Go Active' programme. In addition, there is a very tasteful bar and quality restaurant. The park is just outside the village of Cheddar with its famous Gorge and is well positioned for visiting Wells, Weston-Super-Mare and many other attractions of the area. It should be noted this a lodge-only park.

Change over day: Mon, Fri, Sat

Arrival and departure times: Please contact the site

Within 3 miles: ⚘ Spa ∪ 🎣

SERVICES: 🔌 Electric hook up 🔲 Launderette ⚙ Licensed bar 🔲 Calor Gas ∅ Camping Gaz Ⓣ Toilet fluid 🍴 Café/Restaurant 🛒 Fast Food/Takeaway 💧 Battery charging ♨ Baby care 🚐 Motorvan service point **ABBREVIATIONS:** BH/bank hols-bank holidays Etr-Easter Spring BH-Spring Bank Holiday dep-departure fr-from hrs-hours m-mile mdnt-midnight rdbt-roundabout rs-restricted service wk-week wknd-weekend x-rds-cross roads ⊘ No credit cards ⊗ No dogs ⚘ Children of all ages accepted See page 9 for details of the AA Camping Card Scheme

CHEDDAR *continued*

▶▶▶▶ 88% *Cheddar Bridge Touring Park* (ST459529)

Draycott Rd BS27 3RJ
☎ 01934 743048
e-mail: enquiries@cheddarbridge.co.uk
dir: *M5 junct 22 (Burnham-on-Sea), A38 towards Cheddar & Bristol, approx 5m. Right onto A371 at Cross, follow Cheddar signs. Through Cheddar village towards Wells, site on right just before Caravan Club site*

Open Mar-Oct

Last arrival 22.00hrs Last departure 11.00hrs

A peaceful adults-only park on the edge of the village of Cheddar, with the added attraction of the River Yeo that flows through the grounds. The site is handy for exploring Cheddar Gorge, Wookey Hole, Wells and Bath. The toilet and shower facilities are very good. There are three camping pods, a gypsy wagon, statics and two apartments for hire. 4 acre site. 45 touring pitches. 10 hardstandings. Caravan pitches. Motorhome pitches. Tent pitches. 4 statics. Wooden pods.

AA Pubs & Restaurants nearby: Wookey Hole Inn, WOOKEY HOLE, BA5 1BP, 01749 676677

Cheddar Bridge Touring Park

Facilities: ⬚⬚⬚⬚⬚⬚⬚⬚⬚
Services: ⬚⬚⬚⬚
Within 3 miles: ⬚⬚⬚⬚⬚⬚⬚⬚
Notes: Adults only. Quiet 23.00hrs-08.00hrs.

see advert below

COWSLIP GREEN

Places to visit

Clevedon Court, CLEVEDON, BS21 6QU, 01275 872257
www.nationaltrust.org.uk/clevedon-court/

Bristol Museum & Art Gallery, BRISTOL, BS8 1RL, 0117 922 3571 www.bristol.gov.uk/museums

Great for kids: HorseWorld, BRISTOL, BS14 0QJ, 01275 540173 www.horseworld.org.uk

COWSLIP GREEN — Map 4 ST46

▶▶▶ 84% *Brook Lodge Farm Camping & Caravan Park (Bristol)* (ST486620)

BS40 5RB
☎ 01934 862311
e-mail: info@brooklodgefarm.com
dir: *M5 junct 18 follow signs for Bristol Airport. Site 3m on left of A38 at bottom of hill. M5 junct 22 follow A38 to Churchill. Site 4m on right opposite Holiday Inn*

Open Mar-Oct

Last arrival 21.30hrs Last departure noon

A naturally sheltered country touring park nestling in a valley of the Mendip Hills, surrounded by trees and a historic walled garden. A friendly welcome is always assured by the family owners who are particularly keen on preserving the site's environment and have won a green tourism award. This park is particularly well placed for visiting the Bristol Balloon Festival, held in August, plus the many country walks in the area. 3.5 acre site. 29 touring pitches. 3 hardstandings. Caravan pitches. Motorhome pitches. Tent pitches.

AA Pubs & Restaurants nearby: The Langford Inn, LOWER LANGFORD, BS40 5BL, 01934 863059

Leisure: ⬚ **Facilities:** ⬚⬚⬚⬚⬚⬚⬚⬚
Services: ⬚⬚⬚⬚⬚
Within 3 miles: ⬚⬚⬚⬚
Notes: Dogs by prior arrangement. Cycle hire, walking maps available.

LEISURE: 🏊 Indoor swimming pool 🏊 Outdoor swimming pool 🎢 Children's playground 🧒 Kid's club 🎾 Tennis court 🎱 Games room 📺 Separate TV room ⛳ 9/18 hole golf course 🚣 Boats for hire 🎬 Cinema 🎭 Entertainment 🎣 Fishing ⛳ Mini golf 🏄 Watersports 💪 Gym ⚽ Sports field Spa ⛲ Stables
FACILITIES: 🛁 Bath 🚿 Shower 🔌 Electric shaver 💈 Hairdryer ❄ Ice Pack Facility ♿ Disabled facilities ☎ Public telephone 🏪 Shop on site or within 200yds 🛒 Mobile shop (calls at least 5 days a week) 🍴 BBQ area 🪑 Picnic area Wi-fi 💻 Internet access ♻ Recycling ℹ Tourist info 🐕 Dog exercise area

CREWKERNE

See Drimpton (Dorset)

CROWCOMBE   Map 3 ST13

Places to visit

Cleeve Abbey, WASHFORD, TA23 0PS, 01984 640377 www.english-heritage.org.uk/daysout/properties/cleeve-abbey

Great for kids: Dunster Castle, DUNSTER, TA24 6SL, 01643 821314 www.nationaltrust.org.uk

AA CAMPING CARD SITE

PREMIER PARK

▶▶▶▶▶ 80% **Quantock Orchard Caravan Park** *(ST138357)*

Flaxpool TA4 4AW
☎ **01984 618618**
e-mail: member@flaxpool.freeserve.co.uk
web: www.quantock-orchard.co.uk
dir: Take A358 from Taunton, signed Minehead & Williton. In 8m turn left just past Flaxpool Garage. Park immediately on left

* ⊞ £15-£27.50 ⊟ £15-£27.50 ▲ £15-£27.50

Open all year (rs 10 Sep-20 May swimming pool closed)

Last arrival 22.00hrs Last departure noon

This small family-run park is set at the foot of the beautiful Quantock Hills and makes an ideal base for touring Somerset, Exmoor and north Devon. It is also close to the West Somerset Railway. It has excellent facilities and there is a lovely heated outdoor swimming pool, plus gym and fitness centre; bike hire is also available. There are static homes for hire. 3.5 acre site. 69 touring pitches. 30 hardstandings. Caravan pitches. Motorhome pitches. Tent pitches. 8 statics.

AA Pubs & Restaurants nearby: The White Horse, STOGUMBER, TA4 3TA, 01984 656277

The Blue Ball Inn, TRISCOMBE, TA4 3HE, 01984 618242

The Rising Sun Inn, WEST BAGBOROUGH, TA4 3EF, 01823 432575

Leisure: ⚓ ⚲ ⋀ ⚡ ☐ Spa
Facilities: ⊞ ↑ ⊙ ℱ ☀ & ⊙ ⑤ ⤢ WiFi ▦ ♻ ❼
Services: ⊡ ⑤ ▮ ⬮ ⊤ ≛ ⬆
Within 3 miles: ⌀ ℱ ⑤ ⑤ ∪

Notes: Dogs must be kept on leads. Off-licence.

DULVERTON   Map 3 SS92

See also East Anstey (Devon)

Places to visit

Knightshayes, KNIGHTSHAYES, EX16 7RQ, 01884 254665 www.nationaltrust.org.uk/knightshayes

Killerton House & Garden, KILLERTON, EX5 3LE, 01392 881345 www.nationaltrust.org.uk

Great for kids: Tiverton Castle, TIVERTON, EX16 6RP, 01884 253200 www.tivertoncastle.com

AA CAMPING CARD SITE

▶▶▶ 80% **Wimbleball Lake** *(SS960300)*

Brompton Regis TA22 9NU
☎ **01398 371257 & 371460**
e-mail: wimbleball@swlakestrust.org.uk
dir: From A396 (Tiverton to Minehead road) take B3222 signed Dulverton Services, follow signs to Wimbleball Lake. Ignore 1st entry (fishing) & take 2nd entry for tea room & camping. (NB care needed due to narrow roads)

* ⊞ £13-£16 ⊟ £13-£16 ▲ £13-£16

Open Mar-Oct

Last departure 11.00hrs

A grassy site overlooking Wimbleball Lake, set high up on Exmoor National Park. The camping area is adjacent to the visitor centre and café, which also includes the camping toilets and showers. The camping field, with 14 electric hook-ups and two hardstandings, is in a quiet and peaceful setting with good views of the lake, which is nationally renowned for its trout fishing; boats can be hired with advance notice. 1.25 acre

site. 30 touring pitches. 2 hardstandings. Caravan pitches. Motorhome pitches. Tent pitches.

AA Pubs & Restaurants nearby: The Masons Arms, KNOWSTONE, EX36 4RY, 01398 341231

Leisure: ⋀ ❀
Facilities: ↑ ⊙ ℱ ☀ & ⊙ ⑤ ⤢ ▦ ♻ ❼
Services: ⊡ ⑤ ⦿
Within 3 miles: ≛ ℱ ⤢ ⑤ ⑤ ∪

Notes: No open fires. Off-ground BBQs only. No swimming in lake, no dogs in lake. Dogs must be kept on leads. Watersports & activity centre, bird watching, cycling, lakeside walks & bushcraft.

EMBOROUGH   Map 4 ST65

Places to visit

Glastonbury Abbey, GLASTONBURY, BA6 9EL, 01458 832267 www.glastonburyabbey.com

King John's Hunting Lodge, AXBRIDGE, BS26 2AP, 01934 732012 www.kingjohnshuntinglodge.co.uk

Great for kids: East Somerset Railway, CRANMORE, BA4 4QP, 01749 880417 www.eastsomersetrailway.com

▶▶▶ 83% **Old Down Touring Park** *(ST628513)*

Old Down House BA3 4SA
☎ **01761 232355**
e-mail: jsmallparkhomes@aol.com
dir: A37 from Farrington Gurney through Ston Easton. In 2m left onto B3139 to Radstock. Site opposite Old Down Inn

⊞ ⊟ ▲

Open all year

Last arrival 20.00hrs Last departure noon

A small family-run site set in open parkland, surrounded by well-established trees. The excellent toilet facilities are well maintained as is every other aspect of the park. Children are welcome. 4 acre site. 30 touring pitches. 15 hardstandings. 6 seasonal pitches. Caravan pitches. Motorhome pitches. Tent pitches.

Facilities: ↑ ⊙ ℱ ☀ ⑤ ⤢ ♻ ❼
Services: ⊡ ▮ ⬮ ⊤ ≛
Within 3 miles: ⌀ ⛴ ℱ ⑤ ⑤ ∪

Notes: Dogs must be kept on leads.

SERVICES: ⊡ Electric hook up ⑤ Launderette ⬮ Licensed bar ▮ Calor Gas ⬮ Camping Gaz ⊤ Toilet fluid ⦿ Café/Restaurant ⬛ Fast Food/Takeaway ≛ Battery charging ⬮ Baby care ⬆ Motorvan service point **ABBREVIATIONS:** BH/bank hols-bank holidays Etr-Easter Spring BH-Spring Bank Holiday dep-departure fr-from hrs-hours m-mile mdnt-midnight rdbt-roundabout rs-restricted service wk-week wknd-weekend x-rds-cross roads ⊛ No credit cards ⊗ No dogs ⬤ Children of all ages accepted See page 9 for details of the AA Camping Card Scheme

EXFORD   Map 3 SS83

Places to visit

Dunster Castle, DUNSTER, TA24 6SL,
01643 821314 www.nationaltrust.org.uk

West Somerset Railway, MINEHEAD, TA24 5BG,
01643 704996
www.west-somerset-railway.co.uk

Great for kids: Exmoor Zoological Park,
BLACKMOOR GATE, EX31 4SG, 01598 763352
www.exmoorzoo.co.uk

▶▶ 86% Westermill Farm (SS825398)

TA24 7NJ
☎ 01643 831238
e-mail: aa@westermill.com
dir: *From Exford on Porlock road. Left in 0.25m,
left to Westermill, sign on tree. Fork left (NB this is
the recommended route)*

☐ ▲

Open all year (rs Nov-May larger toilet block &
shop closed)

An idyllic site for peace and quiet, in a sheltered
valley in the heart of Exmoor, which has won
awards for conservation. Highly recommended for
traditional camping. There are four waymarked
walks over the 500-acre working farm and self-
catering accommodation is also available. Please
note that the site should only be approached from
Exford (other approaches are difficult). 6 acre site.
60 touring pitches. Motorhome pitches. Tent
pitches.

AA Pubs & Restaurants nearby: Crown Hotel,
EXFORD, TA24 7PP, 01643 831554

Facilities: � ⊙ ⏚ ✳ ◐ 🖶 ⏚ ▥ ⏍ ❖ ❶

Services: ⏚ ⏚ ⏚

Within 3 miles: ⏚ ⏚ ⏚

Notes: ⏚ No noise after 23.00hrs. Well behaved
dogs accepted. Dogs must be kept on leads.
Shallow river for fishing & bathing.

FROME   Map 4 ST74

Places to visit

Stourhead, STOURHEAD, BA12 6QD, 01747 841152
www.nationaltrust.org.uk/stourhead

Dyrham Park, DYRHAM, SN14 8ER, 0117 937 2501
www.nationaltrust.org.uk

Great for kids: Longleat Safari & Adventure
Park, LONGLEAT, BA12 7NW, 01985 844400
www.longleat.co.uk

▶▶▶ 85% Seven Acres Caravan & Camping Site (ST777444)

Seven Acres, West Woodlands BA11 5EQ
☎ 01373 464222
dir: *A361 (Frome bypass) onto B3092 at rdbt,
0.75m to site*

☐ ☐ ▲

Open Mar-Oct

A level meadowland site beside the shallow River
Frome, with a bridge across to an adjacent field,
and plenty of scope for families. The facilities are
spotless. Set on the edge of the Longleat Estate
with its stately home, wildlife safari park, and
many other attractions. 3 acre site. 16 touring
pitches. 16 hardstandings. Caravan pitches.
Motorhome pitches. Tent pitches.

AA Pubs & Restaurants nearby: The George at
Nunney, NUNNEY, BA11 4LW, 01373 836458

Vobster Inn, LOWER VOBSTER, BA3 5RJ,
01373 812920

Leisure: ⋔

Facilities: ▮ ⊙ ⏚ ✳ 🖶 ⏍ ❖

Services: ⏚

Within 3 miles: ⏚ ⊟ ⏚ ⏚ ⏚ ⏚

Notes: ⏚ Dogs must be kept on leads.

GLASTONBURY   Map 4 ST53

Places to visit

Lytes Cary Manor, KINGSDON, TA11 7HU,
01458 224471
www.nationaltrust.org.uk/lytes-cary-manor

Fleet Air Arm Museum, YEOVILTON, BA22 8HT,
01935 840565 www.fleetairarm.com

Great for kids: Haynes International Motor
Museum, SPARKFORD, BA22 7LH, 01963 440804
www.haynesmotormuseum.co.uk

PREMIER PARK

▶▶▶▶▶ 97% The Old Oaks Touring Park (ST521394)

Best of British

Wick Farm, Wick BA6 8JS
☎ 01458 831437
e-mail: info@theoldoaks.co.uk
dir: *M5 junct 23, A39 to Glastonbury. After
Street take A39 towards Wells. At 3rd rdbt
follow Wick/Brindham signs. Site 1.5m on right
(NB it is advisable to not use Sat Nav for last
part of journey)*

* ☐ £17-£32 ☐ £17-£32 ▲ £15-£26

Open mid Feb-mid Nov (rs Feb-Mar & Oct-Nov
reduced shop & reception hours)

Last arrival 20.00hrs Last departure noon

An exceptional adults-only park offering larger
than average landscaped pitches, impeccably
maintained grounds and wonderful views. The
perfect 'get away from it all' spot where you
can enjoy walking, cycling, fishing and touring
or simply relaxing amid the abundant wildlife.
The top class facilities include a well-stocked
shop selling locally-sourced produce and
home-baked cakes, a smart new shower block,
Wi-fi, free walking and cycling maps, a half-
acre fishing lake, a daily mini bus service to
nearby towns and even a hot doggy shower!
Camping cabins are available for hire. 10 acre
site. 98 touring pitches. 98 hardstandings.
Caravan pitches. Motorhome pitches. Tent
pitches. 6 wooden pods.

AA Pubs & Restaurants nearby: Ring O'Bells,
ASHCOTT, TA7 9PZ, 01458 210232

Facilities: 🛒🏠🔌⊙🗜✳⛵♿⊙§🐕📶🖥 ♻ ❸

Services: 🔌§🔋🚿⊘Ⓣ🚐⊻

Within 3 miles: 🎣§🛒

Notes: Adults only. Group or block bookings accepted only at owners' discretion. Dogs must be kept on leads. Off-licence, local produce boxes, caravan cleaning, dog owners' information pack, dog sitting.

►►►► 80% Isle of Avalon Touring Caravan Park *(ST494397)*

Godney Rd BA6 9AF
☎ **01458 833618**
dir: *M5 junct 23, A39 to outskirts of Glastonbury, 2nd exit signed Wells at B&Q rdbt, straight over next rdbt, 1st exit at 3rd rdbt (B3151), site 200yds on right*

🚐🚃🛖

Open all year

Last arrival 21.00hrs Last departure 11.00hrs

A popular site on the south side of this historic town and within easy walking distance of the town centre. This level park, with a separate tent field, offers a quiet environment in which to stay and explore the many local attractions including the Tor, Wells, Wookey Hole and Clarks Village. 8 acre site. 120 touring pitches. 70 hardstandings. Caravan pitches. Motorhome pitches. Tent pitches.

AA Pubs & Restaurants nearby: Ring O'Bells, ASHCOTT, TA7 9PZ, 01458 210232

Leisure: ⚴

Facilities: 🏠⊙🔌✳♿⊙§🐕📶 ♻ ❸

Services: 🔌§🔋🚿⊘Ⓣ🚐⛲

Within 3 miles: 🚉🎣§🛒U

Notes: Cycle hire.

LANGPORT Map 4 ST42

Places to visit
Montacute House, MONTACUTE, TA15 6XP, 01935 823289 www.nationaltrust.org.uk
Lytes Cary Manor, KINGSDON, TA11 7HU, 01458 224471 www.nationaltrust.org.uk/lytes-cary-manor

Great for kids: Fleet Air Arm Museum, YEOVILTON, BA22 8HT, 01935 840565 www.fleetairarm.com

►►► 85% Thorney Lakes Caravan Park *(ST430237)*

Thorney Lakes, Muchelney TA10 0DW
☎ **01458 250811**
e-mail: info@thorneylakes.co.uk
dir: *From A303 at Podimore rdbt take A372 to Langport. At Huish Episcopi Church turn left for Muchelney. In 100yds left (signed Muchelney & Crewkerne). Site 300yds after John Leach Pottery*

* 🚐 £10-£20 🚃 £10-£20 🛖 £10-£20

Open Etr-Oct

A small, peaceful site set in a cider apple orchard in the heart of the Somerset Levels. There are excellent coarse fishing lakes just a short stroll away from the campsite, and the good walks in the area include the Parrett Trail which is just 100 metres from the site. Excellent family facilities are available. 6 acre site. 36 touring pitches. Caravan pitches. Motorhome pitches. Tent pitches.

AA Pubs & Restaurants nearby: Rose & Crown (Eli's), HUISH EPISCOPI, TA10 9QT, 01458 250494

The Devonshire Arms, LONG SUTTON, TA10 9LP, 01458 241271

The Halfway House, PITNEY, TA10 9AB, 01458 252513

Facilities: 🏠⊙✳📶 ♻ ❸ Services: 🔌
Within 3 miles: 🚉🎣§ Notes: 🚭

MARTOCK

Places to visit
Montacute House, MONTACUTE, TA15 6XP, 01935 823289 www.nationaltrust.org.uk

Montacute House, MONTACUTE, TA15 6XP, 01935 823289 www.nationaltrust.org.uk

Great for kids: Fleet Air Arm Museum, YEOVILTON, BA22 8HT, 01935 840565 www.fleetairarm.com

---

MARTOCK Map 4 ST41

AA CAMPING CARD SITE

►►►► 82% Southfork Caravan Park *(ST448188)*

BRONZE

Parrett Works TA12 6AE
☎ **01935 825661**
e-mail: southforkcaravans@btconnect.com
dir: *8m NW of Yeovil, 2m off A303. From E, take exit after Cartgate rdbt. From W, 1st exit off rdbt signed South Petherton, follow camping signs*

* 🚐 £17-£26 🚃 £17-£26 🛖 £13-£19

Open all year

Last arrival 22.30hrs Last departure noon

A neat, level mainly grass park in a quiet rural area, just outside the pretty village of Martock. Some excellent spacious hardstandings are available. The facilities are always spotless and the whole site well cared for by the friendly owners, who will ensure your stay is a happy one, a fact borne out by the many repeat customers. The park is unique in that it also has a fully-approved caravan repair and servicing centre with accessory shop. There are also static caravans available for hire. 2 acre site. 27 touring pitches. 2 hardstandings. Caravan pitches. Motorhome pitches. Tent pitches. 3 statics.

AA Pubs & Restaurants nearby: The Nag's Head Inn, MARTOCK, TA12 6NF, 01935 823432

Ilchester Arms, ILCHESTER, BA22 8LN, 01935 840220

Leisure: ⚴
Facilities: 🏠⊙🔌✳⊙§🐕 ♻ ❸
Services: 🔌§🔋⊘Ⓣ🚐
Within 3 miles: 🚉🎣§
Notes: Dogs must be kept on leads.

MINEHEAD — Map 3 SS94

Places to visit

West Somerset Railway, MINEHEAD, TA24 5BG, 01643 704996 www.west-somerset-railway.co.uk

Dunster Castle, DUNSTER, TA24 6SL, 01643 821314 www.nationaltrust.org.uk

Great for kids: Tropiquaria Animal and Adventure Park, WASHFORD, TA23 0QB, 01984 640688 www.tropiquaria.co.uk

▶▶▶ 77% Minehead & Exmoor Caravan & Camping Park (SS950457)

Porlock Rd TA24 8SW
☎ 01643 703074
e-mail: enquiries@mineheadandexmoorcamping.co.uk
dir: 1m W of Minehead town centre, take A39 towards Porlock. Site on right

* ⊕ £12-£18 ⊕ £12-£18 Å £12-£18

Open Mar-Oct (rs Nov-Feb open certain weeks only (phone to check))

Last arrival 22.00hrs Last departure noon

A small terraced park, on the edge of Exmoor, spread over five small paddocks and screened by the mature trees that surround it. The level pitches provide a comfortable space for each unit on this family-run park. The site is very conveniently placed for visiting Minehead and the Exmoor National Park. 3 acre site. 50 touring pitches. 10 hardstandings. 10 seasonal pitches. Caravan pitches. Motorhome pitches. Tent pitches.

AA Pubs & Restaurants nearby: The Luttrell Arms, DUNSTER, TA24 6SG, 01643 821555

The Smugglers, BLUE ANCHOR, TA24 6JS, 01984 640385

Leisure: ⚞
Facilities: ⬟⊙☞✳⬥⬣⬡⬢♻ ❼
Services: ⬛⬛⬛⬛⬛
Within 3 miles: ⬥⬥⬥⬥⬥⬥⬥⬥

Notes: ⊗ No open fires or loud music. Dogs must be kept on leads. Tumble dryer.

OARE — Map 3 SS74

Places to visit

Watermouth Castle & Family Theme Park, ILFRACOMBE, EX34 9SL, 01271 863879 www.watermouthcastle.com

Marwood Hill Gardens, BARNSTAPLE, EX31 4EB, 01271 342528 www.marwoodhillgarden.co.uk

Great for kids: Exmoor Zoological Park, BLACKMOOR GATE, EX31 4SG, 01598 763352 www.exmoorzoo.co.uk

▶▶▶ 77% Cloud Farm (SS794467)

EX35 6NU
☎ 01598 741278
e-mail: stay@cloudfarmcamping.co.uk
web: www.cloudfarmcamping.com
dir: M5 junct 24, A39 towards Minehead & Porlock then Lynton. Left in 6.5m, follow signs to Oare, right, site signed

⬛ ⬛ Å

Open all year

Last arrival anytime Last departure anytime

A traditional campsite set in a stunning location in Exmoor's Doone Valley. This quiet, sheltered campsite is arranged over four riverside fields with fairly basic but modern toilet and shower facilities. It offers a good shop and a café serving food all day, including breakfasts; there is a walled Tea Garden for alfresco eating. There are also several self-catering cottages for hire. 110 acre site. 70 touring pitches. 6 hardstandings. Caravan pitches. Motorhome pitches. Tent pitches.

AA Pubs & Restaurants nearby: Rockford Inn, BRENDON, EX35 6PT, 01598 741214

Facilities: ⬟⊙☞✳⬥⬣⬡⬢☰⬟⬛ ♻ ❼
Services: ⬛⬛⬛⬛⬛⬛
Within 3 miles: ⬥⬥⬥⬥⬥

PORLOCK — Map 3 SS84

Places to visit

West Somerset Railway, MINEHEAD, TA24 5BG, 01643 704996 www.west-somerset-railway.co.uk

Dunster Castle, DUNSTER, TA24 6SL, 01643 821314 www.nationaltrust.org.uk

Great for kids: Tropiquaria Animal and Adventure Park, WASHFORD, TA23 0QB, 01984 640688 www.tropiquaria.co.uk

AA CAMPING CARD SITE

PREMIER PARK

▶▶▶▶▶ 84% Porlock Caravan Park (SS882469)

TA24 8ND
☎ 01643 862269
e-mail: info@porlockcaravanpark.co.uk
dir: Through village fork right signed Porlock Weir, site on right

⬛ ⬛ Å

Open 15 Mar-Oct

Last arrival 20.00hrs Last departure 11.00hrs

A sheltered touring park attractively laid out in the centre of lovely countryside on the edge of Porlock. The famous Porlock Hill, a few hundred yards from the site, leads to some spectacular areas of Exmoor and stunning views. The toilet facilities are superb, and there's a popular kitchen area with microwave and freezer. Seven holiday statics are available for hire. 3 acre site. 40 touring pitches. 14 hardstandings. Caravan pitches. Motorhome pitches. Tent pitches. 55 statics.

AA Pubs & Restaurants nearby: The Ship Inn, PORLOCK, TA24 8QD, 01643 862507

The Bottom Ship, PORLOCK, TA24 8PB, 01643 863288

Facilities: ⬟⊙☞✳⬥⬣⬟⬛ ♻ ❼
Services: ⬛⬛⬛⬛⬛⬛
Within 3 miles: ⬥⬥⬥⬥⬥
Notes: No fires. Dogs must be kept on leads.

►►►► 87% Burrowhayes Farm Caravan & Camping Site & Riding Stables *(SS897460)*

West Luccombe TA24 8HT
☎ 01643 862463
e-mail: info@burrowhayes.co.uk
dir: *A39 from Minehead towards Porlock for 5m. Left at Red Post to Horner & West Luccombe, site 0.25m on right, immediately before humpback bridge*

🚐 🚙 ⛺

Open 15 Mar-Oct (rs Mar-Apr caravan hire & riding only from Etr)

Last arrival 22.00hrs Last departure noon

A delightful site on the edge of Exmoor, that slopes gently down to Horner Water. The farm buildings have been converted into riding stables from where escorted rides onto the moors can be taken; the excellent toilet facilities are housed in timber-clad buildings. Hardstandings are available. There are many countryside walks that can be accessed directly from the site. 20 static holiday homes are for hire. 8 acre site. 120 touring pitches. 10 hardstandings. Caravan pitches. Motorhome pitches. Tent pitches. 20 statics.

AA Pubs & Restaurants nearby: The Ship Inn, PORLOCK, TA24 8QD, 01643 862507

The Bottom Ship, PORLOCK, TA24 8PB, 01643 863288

Facilities: 🚿 ⊙ 🚿 ✲ ♿ ✆ $ 🐕 Wi-fi 💻 ♻ ℹ

Services: 🔌 🧺 ▲ ⊘ [T] 🔋 ⚓

Within 3 miles: ⛳ 🎣 ◎ $ 🧺 U

PRIDDY Map 4 ST55

Places to visit

Glastonbury Abbey, GLASTONBURY, BA6 9EL, 01458 832267 www.glastonburyabbey.com

The Helicopter Museum, WESTON-SUPER-MARE, BS24 8PP, 01934 635227 www.helicoptermuseum.co.uk

Great for kids: Wookey Hole Caves & Papermill, WOOKEY HOLE, BA5 1BB, 01749 672243 www.wookey.co.uk

►►►► 87% Cheddar Mendip Heights Camping & Caravanning Club Site *(ST522519)*

Townsend BA5 3BP
☎ 01749 870241 & 0845 130 7633
dir: *From A39 take B3135 to Cheddar. Left in 4.5m. Site 200yds on right*

🚐 £11.60-£29.80 🚙 £11.60-£29.80 ⛺ £11.60-£29.80

Open 15 Mar-5 Nov

Last arrival 20.00hrs Last departure noon

A gently sloping site set high on the Mendip Hills and surrounded by trees. This excellent campsite offers really good facilities, including top notch family rooms and private cubicles which are spotlessly maintained. Fresh bread is baked daily and available from the well-stocked shop. The site is well positioned for visiting local attractions such as Cheddar, Wookey Hole, Wells and Glastonbury, and is popular with walkers. Self-catering caravans are now available for hire. 4.5 acre site. 90 touring pitches. 37 hardstandings. Caravan pitches. Motorhome pitches. Tent pitches. 2 statics.

AA Pubs & Restaurants nearby: Wookey Hole Inn, WOOKEY HOLE, BA5 1BP, 01749 676677

The Burcott Inn, WOOKEY, BA5 1NJ, 01749 673874

Leisure: /A\

Facilities: 🚿 ⊙ 🚿 ✲ ♿ ✆ $ 🐕 Wi-fi ♻ ℹ

Services: 🔌 🧺 ▲ ⊘ [T] 🔋 ⚓

Within 3 miles: ⛳ $ U

Notes: Site gates closed 23.00hrs-07.00hrs. Dogs must be kept on leads.

SHEPTON MALLET Map 4 ST64

Places to visit

Stourhead, STOURHEAD, BA12 6QD, 01747 841152 www.nationaltrust.org.uk/stourhead

Westwood Manor, WESTWOOD, BA15 2AF, 01225 863374 www.nationaltrust.org.uk

Great for kids: Longleat Safari & Adventure Park, LONGLEAT, BA12 7NW, 01985 844400 www.longleat.co.uk

AA SMALL CAMPSITE OF THE YEAR 2014

AA CAMPING CARD SITE

►► 96% Greenacres Camping *(ST553417)*

Barrow Ln, North Wootton BA4 4HL
☎ 01749 890497
e-mail: stay@greenacres-camping.co.uk
dir: *Approx halfway between Glastonbury & Shepton Mallet on A361 turn at Steanbow Farm signed North Wootton. Or from A39 between Upper Coxley & Wells turn at Brownes Garden Centre into Woodford Ln. Follow North Wootton & site signs*

* 🚙 ⛺ fr £8.50

Open Apr-Sep

Last arrival 21.00hrs Last departure 11.00hrs

An immaculately maintained site peacefully set within sight of Glastonbury Tor. Mainly family orientated with many thoughtful extra facilities provided, and there is plenty of space for children to play games in a very safe environment. There is even a 'glow worm safari' at certain times of the year. Facilities are exceptionally clean. 4.5 acre site. 40 touring pitches. Motorhome pitches. Tent pitches.

AA Pubs & Restaurants nearby: The Bull Terrier, CROSCOMBE, BA5 3QJ, 01749 343658

The George Inn, CROSCOMBE, BA5 3QH, 01749 342306

Leisure: /A\ ⚽

Facilities: 🚿 ⊙ 🚿 ✲ $ $ ⛩ Wi-fi ♻ ℹ

Services: 🔌 ▲ ⊘ 🔋 🍼

Within 3 miles: ⛳ ⚓ 日 🎣 $ 🧺 U

Notes: 🚫🐕 No caravans or large motorhomes. Free use of fridges & freezers, book library.

SERVICES: 🔌 Electric hook up 🧺 Launderette 🍷 Licensed bar ▲ Calor Gas ⊘ Camping Gaz [T] Toilet fluid 🍴 Café/Restaurant 🍔 Fast Food/Takeaway 🔋 Battery charging 🍼 Baby care ⚓ Motorvan service point **ABBREVIATIONS:** BH/bank hols-bank holidays Etr-Easter Spring BH-Spring Bank Holiday dep-departure fr-from hrs-hours m-mile mdnt-midnight rdbt-roundabout rs-restricted service wk-week wknd-weekend x-rds-cross roads 🚫💳 No credit cards 🚫🐕 No dogs 👪 Children of all ages accepted See page 9 for details of the AA Camping Card Scheme

SPARKFORD   Map 4 ST62

Places to visit

Lytes Cary Manor, KINGSDON, TA11 7HU,
01458 224471
www.nationaltrust.org.uk/lytes-cary-manor

Montacute House, MONTACUTE, TA15 6XP,
01935 823289 www.nationaltrust.org.uk

►►►► 82% Long Hazel Park

(ST602262)

High St BA22 7JH
☎ **01963 440002**
e-mail: longhazelpark@hotmail.com
dir: *Exit A303 at Hazlegrove rdbt, follow signs for Sparkford. Site 400yds on left*

* 🚐 £18-£22 🚎 £18-£22 ▲ £18-£22

Open all year

Last arrival 21.00hrs Last departure 11.00hrs

A very neat, adults-only park next to the village inn in the high street. This attractive park is run by friendly owners to a very good standard. Many of the spacious pitches have hardstandings. There are also luxury lodges on site for hire or purchase. 3.5 acre site. 50 touring pitches. 30 hardstandings. 21 seasonal pitches. Caravan pitches. Motorhome pitches. Tent pitches. 1 static.

AA Pubs & Restaurants nearby: The Walnut Tree, WEST CAMEL, BA22 7QW, 01935 851292

The Queens Arms, CORTON DENHAM, DT9 4LR, 01963 220317

Facilities: 🍴☺🥄🗡☀🏃🚻🚽Ⓓ📶♻ 🅹

Services: 🔌🔲🔋🚿🛢🚽↯

Within 3 miles: ↯🦋🛒

Notes: Adults only. 🐕 Dogs must be exercised off site & kept on leads. Picnic tables available, camping spares.

TAUNTON   Map 4 ST22

Places to visit

Hestercombe Gardens, TAUNTON, TA2 8LG,
01823 413923 www.hestercombe.com

Barrington Court, BARRINGTON, TA19 0NQ,
01460 241938 www.nationaltrust.org.uk

Great for kids: Sunnycroft, WELLINGTON,
TF1 2DR, 01952 242884
www.nationaltrust.org.uk/sunnycroft

AA CAMPING CARD SITE

►►►► 84% Cornish Farm Touring Park *(ST235217)*

Shoreditch TA3 7BS
☎ **01823 327746**
e-mail: info@cornishfarm.com
web: www.cornishfarm.com
dir: *M5 junct 25 towards Taunton. Left at lights. 3rd left into Ilminster Rd (follow Corfe signs). Right at rdbt, left at next rdbt. Right at T-junct, left into Killams Dr, 2nd left into Killams Ave. Over motorway bridge. Site on left, take 2nd entrance*

* 🚐 £15-£19 🚎 £15-£19 ▲ £15-£19

Open all year

Last arrival anytime Last departure 11.30hrs

This smart park provides really top quality facilities throughout. Although only two miles from Taunton, it is set in open countryside and is a very convenient base for visiting the many attractions of the area such as Clarks Village, Glastonbury and Cheddar Gorge. Also makes an excellent base for watching county cricket at the nearby Somerset County Ground. 3.5 acre site. 50 touring pitches. 25 hardstandings. Caravan pitches. Motorhome pitches. Tent pitches.

AA Pubs & Restaurants nearby: The Hatch Inn, TAUNTON, TA3 6SG, 01823 480245

The Willow Tree Restaurant, TAUNTON, TA1 4AR, 01823 352835

Facilities: 🍴☺🥄🗡☀🏃🚻🚽Ⓦ📶🖥 🅹

Services: 🔌🔲🔋🚽↯

Within 3 miles: ↯🚌☺⛳🛒🐴⛲

Notes: Dogs must be kept on leads.

►►► 83% Ashe Farm Camping & Caravan Site *(ST279229)*

Thornfalcon TA3 5NW
☎ **01823 443764 & 07891 989482**
e-mail: info@ashefarm.co.uk
dir: *M5 junct 25, A358 E for 2.5m. Right at Nags Head pub. Site 0.25m on right*

🚐 🚎 ▲

Open Apr-Oct

Last arrival 22.00hrs Last departure noon

A well-screened site surrounded by mature trees and shrubs, with two large touring fields. A modern facilities block includes toilets and showers plus a separate laundry room. Not far from the bustling market town of Taunton, and handy for both south and north coasts. Also makes a good stopover for people travelling on the nearby M5. 7 acre site. 30 touring pitches. 11 hardstandings. Caravan pitches. Motorhome pitches. Tent pitches. 3 statics.

AA Pubs & Restaurants nearby: The Hatch Inn, TAUNTON, TA3 6SG, 01823 480245

The Willow Tree Restaurant, TAUNTON, TA1 4AR, 01823 352835

Leisure: 🅰🏊

Facilities: 🍴☺🥄🗡☀🏃🚻♻ 🅹

Services: 🔌🔲

Within 3 miles: ↯🚌⛳☺🛒🐴⛲

Notes: 🐕 No camp fires, no noise after 22.00hrs. Baby changing facilities.

LEISURE: 🏊 Indoor swimming pool 🏊 Outdoor swimming pool 🅰 Children's playground 🛝 Kid's club 🎾 Tennis court 🎱 Games room 📺 Separate TV room ⛳ 9/18 hole golf course ⛵ Boats for hire 🎬 Cinema 🎵 Entertainment 🎣 Fishing ⛳ Mini golf 🚤 Watersports 🏋 Gym ⚽ Sports field Spa ⛲ Stables
FACILITIES: 🛁 Bath 🚿 Shower ☺ Electric shaver 🥄 Hairdryer ☀ Ice Pack Facility ♿ Disabled facilities 📞 Public telephone 🛒 Shop on site or within 200yds 🏪 Mobile shop (calls at least 5 days a week) 🍖 BBQ area 🏃 Picnic area 📶 Wi-fi 🖥 Internet access ♻ Recycling 🅹 Tourist info 🐕 Dog exercise area

WATCHET Map 3 ST04

Places to visit

West Somerset Railway, MINEHEAD, TA24 5BG, 01643 704996 www.west-somerset-railway.co.uk

Dunster Castle, DUNSTER, TA24 6SL, 01643 821314 www.nationaltrust.org.uk

Great for kids: Tropiquaria Animal and Adventure Park, WASHFORD, TA23 0QB, 01984 640688 www.tropiquaria.co.uk

►►► 86% Home Farm Holiday Centre *(ST106432)*

St Audries Bay TA4 4DP
☎ 01984 632487
e-mail: dib@homefarmholidaycentre.co.uk
dir: *A39 for 17m to West Quantoxhead, B3191 after garage in village (signed Doniford), 1st right in 0.25m*

🚐 £12-£27.50 🚙 £12-£27.50 ⛺ £12-£27.50

Open all year (rs Nov-1 Mar camping, shop & bar closed)

Last arrival dusk Last departure noon

In a hidden valley beneath the Quantock Hills, this park overlooks its own private beach. The atmosphere is friendly and quiet, and there are lovely sea views from the level pitches. Flowerbeds, woodland walks and the Koi carp pond all enhance this very attractive site, along with a lovely indoor swimming pool, an excellent new children's play area, and a beer garden. 45 acre site. 40 touring pitches. 35 hardstandings. Caravan pitches. Motorhome pitches. Tent pitches. 230 statics.

AA Pubs & Restaurants nearby: The Smugglers, BLUE ANCHOR, TA24 6JS, 01984 640385

Leisure: 🏊 🛝

Facilities: 🚿 ⊙ 💨 ❄ ♿ ☎ [$] 🐕 [Wi-fi] ♻ ℹ

Services: 🔌 🧺 🍷 🛢 ⌀ [T]

Within 3 miles: ⛵ [$] 🧺

Notes: No cars by caravans or tents. No noise after mdnt. Dogs must be kept on leads.

hh 89% Doniford Bay Holiday Park *(ST093432)*

David Bellamy Conservation Award GOLD

TA23 0TJ
☎ 01984 632423
e-mail: donifordbay@haven.com
web: www.haven.com/donifordbay
dir: *M5 junct 23, A38 towards Bridgwater, A39 towards Minehead. 15m, at West Quantoxhead, right after St Audries garage. Park 1m on right*

Open Mar-Oct

This well-appointed holiday park, situated adjacent to a shingle and sand beach, offers a wide range of activities for the whole family. The holiday homes are spacious and well-appointed and there is plenty to keep children (of all ages) interested, including great indoor and outdoor pools, a multi-sports centre, slides and archery. The park has good eating outlets including a nice café/restaurant. Being close to the Exmoor National Park, it offers visitors the chance to seek out some of the best scenery in the county.

Change over day: Mon, Fri, Sat **Arrival and departure times:** Please contact the site

Statics 143 Sleeps 6-8 Bedrms 2-3 Bathrms 1-2 Toilets 1-2 Freezer TV Sky/FTV Elec inc Gas inc Grass area

Children 👪 Cots Highchair **Dogs** 2 on leads No dangerous dogs

Leisure: 🏊 🏊 ✋ 🛝

WELLINGTON Map 3 ST12

Places to visit

Sunnycroft, WELLINGTON, TF1 2DR, 01952 242884 www.nationaltrust.org.uk/sunnycroft

Hestercombe Gardens, TAUNTON, TA2 8LG, 01823 413923 www.hestercombe.com

Great for kids: Diggerland, CULLOMPTON, EX15 2PE, 0871 227 7007 www.diggerland.com

►►►► 84% Greenacres Touring Park *(ST156001)*

Haywards Ln, Chelston TA21 9PH
☎ 01823 652844
e-mail: enquiries@wellington.co.uk
dir: *M5 junct 26, right at rdbt signed Wellington, approx 1.5m. At Chelston rdbt, take 1st left, signed A38 West Buckland Rd. In 500mtrs follow sign for site*

🚐 🚙

Open Apr-end Sep

Last arrival 19.00hrs Last departure 11.00hrs

This attractively landscaped adults-only park is situated close to the Somerset/Devon border in a peaceful setting with great views of the Blackdown and Quantock Hills. It is in a very convenient location for overnight stays, being just one and half miles from the M5. This park is also well positioned for visiting both the north and south coasts, and it is close to a local bus route. It has excellent facilities, which are spotlessly clean and well maintained. 2.5 acre site. 40 touring pitches. 30 hardstandings. Caravan pitches. Motorhome pitches.

Facilities: 🚿 ⊙ 💨 ♿ 🪑 ♻ ℹ

Services: 🔌

Within 3 miles: ⛳ 🎾 ⛵ [$] 🧺 🐎

Notes: Adults only. ⊘ No RVs. Dogs must be kept on leads.

►►► 81% Gamlins Farm Caravan Park *(ST083195)*

Gamlins Farm House, Greenham TA21 0LZ
☎ 01823 672859 & 07967 683738
e-mail: gamlinsfarmcaravanpark@hotmail.co.uk
dir: *M5 junct 26, A38 towards Tiverton & Exeter. 5m, right for Greenham, site 1m on right*

* 🚐 £10-£16 🚙 £10-£16 ⛺ £6-£16

Open Mar-Oct

This peaceful site (only two minutes from the A38) is set in a secluded valley with excellent views of the Quantock Hills; it is well placed for visiting both Devon and Somerset. The facilities are very good and spotlessly clean, and free coarse fishing is available. Static holiday homes for hire. 4 acre site. 35 touring pitches. 6 hardstandings. Caravan pitches. Motorhome pitches. Tent pitches. 4 statics.

Leisure: 🎣

Facilities: 🚿 ⊙ 💨 ❄ ♿ 🪑 🐕 [Wi-fi] 💻 ♻ ℹ

Services: 🔌 🧺 🛢 🔋

Within 3 miles: ⛳ ⛵ [$] 🧺 🐎

Notes: ⊘ No loud noise after 22.00hrs. Dogs must be kept on leads.

SERVICES: 🔌 Electric hook up 🧺 Launderette 🍷 Licensed bar 🛢 Calor Gas ⌀ Camping Gaz [T] Toilet fluid 🍴 Café/Restaurant 🍔 Fast Food/Takeaway 🔋 Battery charging 🍼 Baby care 🚰 Motorvan service point **ABBREVIATIONS:** BH/bank hols-bank holidays Etr-Easter Spring BH-Spring Bank Holiday dep-departure fr-from hrs-hours m-mile mdnt-midnight rdbt-roundabout rs-restricted service wk-week wknd-weekend x-rds-cross roads ⊘ No credit cards 🚫 No dogs 👪 Children of all ages accepted See page 9 for details of the AA Camping Card Scheme

WELLS
Map 4 ST54

Places to visit

Glastonbury Abbey, GLASTONBURY, BA6 9EL, 01458 832267 www.glastonburyabbey.com

PREMIER PARK

►►►►► 86% Wells Holiday Park

(ST531459)

Haybridge BA5 1AJ
☎ **01749 676869**
e-mail: jason@wellsholidaypark.co.uk
dir: *A38 then follow signs for Axbridge, Cheddar & Wells*

Open all year

Last arrival 20.00hrs Last departure noon

This well established, adults-only holiday park has first-class toilet facilities and many hardstandings, all with electricity. A restful park set in countryside on the outskirts of Wells, it is within easy walking distance of the city, with its spectacular cathedral and Bishop's Palace. Cheddar Gorge and Caves, Bath, Bristol, Weston-Super-Mare, Wookey Hole and Glastonbury are all within easy driving distance. A function room and patio is now available as well as a new beauty salon. Holiday cottages are available for hire. 7.5 acre site. 72 touring pitches. 54 hardstandings. 20 seasonal pitches. Caravan pitches. Motorhome pitches. Tent pitches. 12 statics. 20 bell tents/yurts.

AA Pubs & Restaurants nearby: The City Arms, WELLS, BA5 2AG, 01749 673916

The Fountain Inn & Boxer's Restaurant, WELLS, BA5 2UU, 01749 672317

Goodfellows, WELLS, BA5 2RR, 01749 673866

The Old Spot, WELLS, BA5 2SE, 01749 689099

Facilities: ↖ ☉ ☞ ✳ & ⓐ ⓔ ⓑ ➤ �📶 ▬ ♻ ❻

Services: ⚑ ⑤ ⬥ ⌗ Ⓣ ⚒ ⊞ ⬇

Within 3 miles: ⬇ ☰ ⌗ ◎ ⑤ ⟳

Notes: Adults only. Dogs must be kept on leads. Pètanque, beauty salon.

►► 84% Homestead Park *(ST532474)*

Wookey Hole BA5 1BW
☎ **01749 673022**
e-mail: homesteadpark@onetel.com
dir: *0.5m NW off A371 (Wells to Cheddar road). (NB weight limit on bridge into touring area now 1 tonne)*

▲

Open Etr-Sep

Last arrival 20.00hrs Last departure noon

This attractive, small site for tents only is set on a wooded hillside and meadowland with access to the river and nearby Wookey Hole. This park is for adults only and the statics are residential caravans. 2 acre site. 30 touring pitches. Tent pitches. 28 statics.

AA Pubs & Restaurants nearby: The City Arms, WELLS, BA5 2AG, 01749 673916

The Fountain Inn & Boxer's Restaurant, WELLS, BA5 2UU, 01749 672317

Goodfellows, WELLS, BA5 2RR, 01749 673866

The Old Spot, WELLS, BA5 2SE, 01749 689099

Facilities: ↖ ☉ ☞ ✳ ❻

Services: ⓐ ⬥ ➤

Within 3 miles: ☰ ⌗ ⬇ ⑤ ⑥ ⑤ ⟳

Notes: Adults only. ⊗ Dogs must be kept on leads.

WESTON-SUPER-MARE
Map 4 ST36

Places to visit

Weston-Super-Mare Museum, WESTON-SUPER-MARE, BS23 1PR, 01934 621028 www.weston-super-maretowncouncil.gov.uk

Great for kids: The Helicopter Museum, WESTON-SUPER-MARE, BS24 8PP, 01934 635227 www.helicoptermuseum.co.uk

►►►► 84% Country View Holiday Park *(ST335647)*

Sand Rd, Sand Bay BS22 9UJ
☎ **01934 627595**
e-mail: info@cvhp.co.uk
dir: *M5 junct 21, A370 towards Weston-Super-Mare. Immediately into left lane, follow Kewstoke/Sand Bay signs. Straight over 3 rdbts onto Lower Norton Ln. At Sand Bay right into Sand Rd, site on right*

* ⬛ £15-£25 ⬛ £15-£25 ▲ £15-£25

Open Mar-Jan

Last arrival 20.00hrs Last departure noon

A pleasant open site in a rural area a few hundred yards from Sandy Bay and the beach. The park is also well placed for energetic walks along the coast at either end of the beach and is only a short drive away from Weston-Super-Mare. There is now a touring section for tents, caravans and motorhomes with a toilet and shower block. There are 14 hardstanding pitches plus grass pitches all with electricity. The facilities are excellent and well maintained. 20 acre site. 190 touring pitches. 150 hardstandings. 90 seasonal pitches. Caravan pitches. Motorhome pitches. Tent pitches. 65 statics.

AA Pubs & Restaurants nearby: The Cove, WESTON-SUPER-MARE, BS23 2BX, 01934 418217

Leisure: ⬛ ⚠ ☉ ♠ ♫

Facilities: ↖ ☉ ☞ ✳ & ⓒ ➤ 📶 ▬ ♻ ❻

Services: ⚑ ⑤ ⬥ Ⓣ

Within 3 miles: ⬇ ⬆ ☰ ⌗ ◎ ⬇ ⑤ ⑤ ⟳

Notes: Dogs must be kept on leads.

LEISURE: 🏊 Indoor swimming pool 🏊 Outdoor swimming pool ⚠ Children's playground 🎣 Kid's club 🎾 Tennis court ♠ Games room ⬛ Separate TV room ⛳ 9/18 hole golf course ⛵ Boats for hire ☰ Cinema ♫ Entertainment 🎣 Fishing ◎ Mini golf 🏄 Watersports 🏋 Gym ❀ Sports field Spa ⟳ Stables
FACILITIES: 🛁 Bath ↖ Shower ☉ Electric shaver ☞ Hairdryer ✳ Ice Pack Facility & Disabled facilities ⓒ Public telephone ⑤ Shop on site or within 200yds 🏪 Mobile shop (calls at least 5 days a week) ⊞ BBQ area ➤ Picnic area 📶 Wi-fi ▬ Internet access ♻ Recycling ❻ Tourist info 🐕 Dog exercise area

▶▶▶ 82% *West End Farm Caravan & Camping Park* (ST354600)

Locking BS24 8RH

☎ 01934 822529

e-mail: robin@westendfarm.org

dir: *M5 junct 21 onto A370. Follow International Helicopter Museum signs. Right at rdbt, follow signs to site*

🚐 🚗 Å

Open all year

Last arrival 21.00hrs Last departure noon

A spacious and well laid out park bordered by hedges, with good landscaping, and well-kept facilities. Fully serviced pitches are available. It is handily located next to a helicopter museum, and offers good access to Weston-Super-Mare and the Mendips. 10 acre site. 75 touring pitches. 10 hardstandings. 30 seasonal pitches. Caravan pitches. Motorhome pitches. Tent pitches. 11 statics.

AA Pubs & Restaurants nearby: The Cove, WESTON-SUPER-MARE, BS23 2BX, 01934 418217

Leisure: ⊙

Facilities: 🍴⊙🔥♿🛁🐕🎯♻🟢

Services: 🔌🖥🔒🧺⬇

Within 3 miles: 🏇🎣🟥🌇◎🍴🛒🔥🖥🛒U

Notes: No noise after 22.00hrs. Dogs must be kept on leads.

WINSFORD

Places to visit

Dunster Castle, DUNSTER, TA24 6SL, 01643 821314 www.nationaltrust.org.uk

Cleeve Abbey, WASHFORD, TA23 0PS, 01984 640377 www.english-heritage.org.uk/daysout/properties/cleeve-abbey

Great for kids: Tropiquaria Animal and Adventure Park, WASHFORD, TA23 0QB, 01984 640688 www.tropiquaria.co.uk

---

WINSFORD Map 3 SS93

▶▶▶ 84% **Halse Farm Caravan & Camping Park** (SS894344)

TA24 7JL

☎ 01643 851259

e-mail: info@halsefarm.co.uk

web: www.halsefarm.co.uk

dir: *Signed from A396 at Bridgetown. In Winsford turn left, bear left past pub. 1m up hill, entrance on left immediately after cattle grid*

🚐 🚗 Å

Open 15 Mar-Oct

Last arrival 22.00hrs Last departure noon

A peaceful little site on Exmoor overlooking a wooded valley with glorious views. This moorland site is quite remote, but it provides good modern toilet facilities which are kept immaculately clean. This is a good base for exploring the Exmoor National Park and Minehead, Porlock and Lynton are only a short drive away. 3 acre site. 44 touring pitches. Caravan pitches. Motorhome pitches. Tent pitches.

AA Pubs & Restaurants nearby: Crown Hotel, EXFORD, TA24 7PP, 01643 831554

Royal Oak Inn, WINSFORD, TA24 7JE, 01643 851455

Leisure: ⚠

Facilities: 🍴⊙📻✳♿🕐🛏🎯📶♻🟢

Services: 🔌🖥🔒🧺

Within 3 miles: 🎣🖥U

Notes: Dogs must be kept on leads.

WIVELISCOMBE Map 3 ST02

Places to visit

Sunnycroft, WELLINGTON, TF1 2DR, 01952 242884 www.nationaltrust.org.uk/sunnycroft

Hestercombe Gardens, TAUNTON, TA2 8LG, 01823 413923 www.hestercombe.com

---

PREMIER PARK

▶▶▶▶▶ 86% **Waterrow Touring Park** (ST053251)

Best of British

TA4 2AZ

☎ 01984 623464

e-mail: info@waterrowpark.co.uk

dir: *M5 junct 25, A358 (signed Minehead) bypassing Taunton, B3227 through Wiveliscombe. Site in 3m at Waterrow, 0.25m past Rock Inn*

🚐 £16-£26 🚗 £16-£26 Å £16-£26

Open all year

Last arrival 19.00hrs Last departure 11.30hrs

This really delightful park for adults only has spotless facilities and plenty of spacious hardstandings. The River Tone runs along a valley beneath the park, accessed by steps to a nature area created by the owners, where fly-fishing is permitted. Watercolour painting workshops and other activities are available, and the local pub is a short walk away. There is also a bus stop just outside of the site. 6 acre site. 45 touring pitches. 38 hardstandings. Caravan pitches. Motorhome pitches. Tent pitches.

AA Pubs & Restaurants nearby: The Rock Inn, WATERROW, TA4 2AX, 01984 623293

Facilities: 🍴⊙📻✳♿🕐🛏🎯📶♻🟢

Services: 🔌🖥🔒🍴🛒⬇

Within 3 miles: 🎣🖥🖥

Notes: Adults only. No gazebos, max 2 dogs per unit. Dogs must be kept on leads. Caravan storage.

YEOVIL — Map 4 ST51

Places to visit

Montacute House, MONTACUTE, TA15 6XP, 01935 823289 www.nationaltrust.org.uk

Lytes Cary Manor, KINGSDON, TA11 7HU, 01458 224471 www.nationaltrust.org.uk/lytes-cary-manor

Great for kids: Fleet Air Arm Museum, YEOVILTON, BA22 8HT, 01935 840565 www.fleetairarm.com

▶▶ 82% Halfway Caravan & Camping Park (ST530195)

Trees Cottage, Halfway, Ilchester Rd BA22 8RE
☎ 01935 840342
e-mail: halfwaycaravanpark@earthlink.net
web: www.halfwaycaravanpark.com
dir: On A37 between Ilchester & Yeovil

🚐 🚫 Å

Open Apr-Oct

Last arrival 19.00hrs (21.00hrs on Fri). Last departure noon

An attractive little park near the Somerset and Dorset border, and next to the Halfway House pub and restaurant, which also has excellent AA-graded accommodation. It overlooks a fishing lake and is surrounded by attractive countryside. Dogs are welcome here. 2 acre site. 20 touring pitches. 10 hardstandings. Caravan pitches. Motorhome pitches. Tent pitches.

AA Pubs & Restaurants nearby: The Masons Arms, YEOVIL, BA22 8TX, 01935 862591

The Helyar Arms, EAST COKER, BA22 9JR, 01935 862332

Facilities: 🛁 🚿 ⚡ 🔧
Services: 🔌 🍴
Within 3 miles: 🎣 🎯 🐎 🏪 🛒
Notes: 🐕 Dogs must be kept on leads.

STAFFORDSHIRE

CHEADLE — Map 10 SK04

Places to visit

Wedgwood Visitor Centre, STOKE-ON-TRENT, ST12 9ES, 01782 282986 www.wedgwoodvisitorcentre.com

The Potteries Museum & Art Gallery, STOKE-ON-TRENT, ST1 3DW, 01782 232323 www.stoke.gov.uk/museum

Great for kids: Alton Towers Resort, ALTON, ST10 4DB, 0871 222 3330 www.altontowers.com

Etruria Industrial Museum, STOKE-ON-TRENT, ST4 7AF, 01782 233144 www.stokemuseums.org.uk

▶▶▶ 73% Quarry Walk Park (SK045405)

Coppice Ln, Croxden Common, Freehay ST10 1RQ
☎ 01538 723412
e-mail: quarry@quarrywalkpark.co.uk
dir: From A522 (Uttoxeter to Cheadle road) in Mobberley follow Freehay sign. In 1m at rdbt, 3rd exit signed Great Gate. 1.25m to site on right

Å

Open all year

Last arrival 18.00hrs Last departure 11.00hrs

A pleasant park (for tents only), close to Alton Towers, developed in an old quarry with well-screened pitches, all with water and electricity, and mature trees and shrubs which enhance the peaceful ambience of the park. There are seven glades of varying sizes used exclusively for tents, one with ten electric hook-ups. There are timber lodges for hire, each with its own hot tub. 46 acre site. Tent pitches. 1 wooden pod.

AA Pubs & Restaurants nearby: The Queens At Freehay, CHEADLE, ST10 1RF, 01538 722383

Leisure: 🅿
Facilities: 🚿 ⚡ 🔧 ❄ 🚻 🐎 📶 🖥 ♻ 🔧
Services: 🔌 🍴 🛒 🚮
Within 3 miles: 🎯 🏪 🛒 🐎
Notes: No cars by tents. No noise after 23.00hrs. Dogs must be kept on leads.

LONGNOR — Map 16 SK06

Places to visit

Poole's Cavern (Buxton Country Park), BUXTON, SK17 9DH, 01298 26978 www.poolescavern.co.uk

AA CAMPING CARD SITE

PREMIER PARK

NEW ▶▶▶▶▶ 84% Longnor Wood Holiday Park (SK072640)

Newtown SK17 0NG
☎ 01298 83648 & 07866 016567
e-mail: info@longnorwood.co.uk
dir: From A53 follow Longnor sign. Site signed from village, 1.25m

🚐 £24-£29 🚫 £24-£29 Å £10.50-£25

Open Mar-10 Jan

Last arrival 19.00hrs Last departure noon

Enjoying a secluded and very peaceful setting in the heart of the Peak District National Park, this spacious adults-only park is a hidden gem, surrounded by beautiful rolling countryside and sheltered by woodland where there is a variety of wildlife to observe. Expect a warm welcome from the O'Neill family and excellent, well-maintained facilities, including spotlessly clean modern toilets, good hardstanding pitches, high levels of security, a putting green, badminton courts, a 4-acre dog walk and super walks from the park gate. 10.5 acre site. 47 touring pitches. 47 hardstandings. 13 seasonal pitches. Caravan pitches. Motorhome pitches. Tent pitches.

AA Pubs & Restaurants nearby: The Queen Anne Inn, GREAT HUCKLOW, SK17 8RF, 01298 871246

The George, ALSTONEFIELD, DE6 2FX, 01335 310205

The Watts Russell Arms, ALSTONEFIELD, DE6 2GD, 01335 310126

Facilities: 🚿 ⚡ 🔧 ❄ 🕐 🏪 🐎 📶 ♻ 🔧
Services: 🔌 🍴 🛒 🚮 🅃 🚮 ⚡
Within 3 miles: 🎣 🏪 🐎
Notes: Adults only. No fires, no noise after 23.00hrs. Dogs must be kept on leads.

LEISURE: 🏊 Indoor swimming pool 🏊 Outdoor swimming pool 🅿 Children's playground 🧒 Kid's club 🎾 Tennis court 🎱 Games room 📺 Separate TV room 🏌 9/18 hole golf course 🚣 Boats for hire 🎬 Cinema 🎵 Entertainment 🎣 Fishing 🏌 Mini golf 🏄 Watersports 🏋 Gym 🏟 Sports field Spa 🐎 Stables
FACILITIES: 🛁 Bath 🚿 Shower ⚡ Electric shaver 🔧 Hairdryer ❄ Ice Pack Facility ♿ Disabled facilities 🕐 Public telephone 🏪 Shop on site or within 200yds 🚐 Mobile shop (calls at least 5 days a week) 🍴 BBQ area 🍴 Picnic area 📶 Wi-fi 🖥 Internet access ♻ Recycling 🔧 Tourist info 🐕 Dog exercise area

SERVICES: 🔌 Electric hook up ⬜ Launderette 🍺 Licensed bar 🔥 Calor Gas ⊘ Camping Gaz ⊤ Toilet fluid 🍽 Café/Restaurant 🏪 Fast Food/Takeaway
🔋 Battery charging 👶 Baby care ♨ Motorvan service point **ABBREVIATIONS:** BH/bank hols-bank holidays Etr-Easter Spring BH-Spring Bank Holiday dep-departure
fr-from hrs-hours m-mile mdnt-midnight rdbt-roundabout rs-restricted service wk-week wknd-weekend x-rds-cross roads 🚫 No credit cards 🚫 No dogs
👶 Children of all ages accepted See page 9 for details of the AA Camping Card Scheme

● Dunwich

Suffolk

Suffolk's superb Heritage Coast is the jewel in the county's crown. The beaches, often windswept and completely deserted, run for miles, with the waves of the North Sea breaking beside them in timeless fashion. But it is an ecologically fragile coastline with much of it claimed by the sea over the years. The poet, George Crabbe, perfectly summed up the fate of this area when he wrote: *'The ocean roar whose greedy waves devour the lessening shore.'*

With its huge skies and sense of space and solitude, Suffolk's crumbling, time-ravaged coastline is highly evocative and wonderfully atmospheric. This is where rivers wind lazily to the sea and 18th-century smugglers hid from the excise men.

Suffolk's coast

Between Felixstowe and Lowestoft the coast offers something for everyone. For example, Orford Ness is a unique visitor attraction where ecology meets military history. This internationally important nature reserve - home to many breeding birds, including the avocet – was once the setting for a highly secret military testing site. These days, Orford Ness is managed by the National Trust.

Aldeburgh is all about the arts and in particular the Aldeburgh Music Festival. Benjamin Britten lived at nearby Snape and wrote *Peter Grimes* here. The Suffolk coast is where both the sea and the natural landscape have influenced generations of writers, artists and musicians.

The charm of Southwold, further north, is undimmed and reminiscent of a fashionable, genteel seaside resort from a bygone era. ▶

Inland towns and villages

But there is much more to Suffolk than its scenic coastline. Far away to the west lies Newmarket and the world of horseracing. Apart from its equine associations, the town boasts some handsome buildings and memorable views. Palace House in Palace Street was the home of Charles II while the High Street is the setting for the National Horseracing Museum, illustrating how this great sporting tradition has evolved over the last 400 years.

Bury St Edmunds, Sudbury and Ipswich also feature prominently on the tourist trail and the county's smaller towns offer a wealth of attractions, too. With their picturesque, timber-framed houses, Lavenham, Kersey and Debenham are a reminder of Suffolk's key role in the wool industry and the vast wealth it yielded for the merchants.

Constable's legacy

It was the artist John Constable who really put Suffolk's delightful countryside on the map. Son of a wealthy miller, Constable spent much of his early life sketching in the vicinity of Dedham Vale. Situated on the River Stour at Flatford,

● Oilseed rape fields

Constable's mill is now a major tourist attraction in the area but a close look at the surroundings confirms rural Suffolk is little changed since the family lived here. Constable himself maintained that the Suffolk countryside *made me a painter and I am grateful.'*

Walking and Cycling

With 3,300 miles of rights of way, walkers in the county have plenty of choice. There are many publicised trails and waymarked routes, including the Angles Way which runs along Norfolk and Suffolk's boundary in the glorious Waveney Valley. Hard to beat is the county's famous Suffolk Coast Path which runs for 50 miles (80km) between Felixstowe and Lowestoft and is the best way to explore Suffolk's dramatic eastern extremity.

The county offers plenty of potential for cycling, too. There is the Heart of Suffolk Cycle Route, which extends for 78 miles (125km), while the National Byway, a 4,000-mile (6,436km) cycle route around Britain takes in part of Suffolk and is a highly enjoyable way to tour the county.

Festivals and Events

- The popular Aldeburgh Literary Festival takes place in early March.
- The Alde Valley Spring Festival is staged in April and May with a 4-week celebration of food, farming, landscape and the arts. The venue is Great Glemham near Saxmundham.
- There is the Lattitude Music Festival at Southwold in July.
- The 3-day Christmas Fayre at Bury St Edmunds showcases the ancient town and in recent years has attracted 70,000 visitors.

● Dunwich Beach

SUFFOLK

BUCKLESHAM — Map 13 TM24

Places to visit

Ipswich Museum, IPSWICH, IP1 3QH, 01473 433550 www.ipswich.gov.uk

Christchurch Mansion, IPSWICH, IP4 2BE, 01473 433554 www.ipswich.gov.uk

▶▶▶▶ 89% Westwood Caravan Park

(TM253411)

Old Felixstowe Rd IP10 0BN
☎ 01473 659637 & 07436 813545
e-mail: caroline.pleace@westwoodcaravanpark.co.uk
dir: *A14 towards Felixstowe, after junct 58 take 1st exit signed to Kirton. Follow road to Bucklesham for 1.5m. Site on right*

* 🚐 £18-£25 🚐 £18-£25 ▲ £18-£20

Open Mar-15 Jan

Last arrival 22.00hrs Last departure 18.00hrs

This constantly improving park is in the heart of rural Suffolk in an idyllic, peaceful setting. All buildings are of traditional Suffolk style, and the toilet facilities, improved in 2013, are of outstanding quality. The planting and landscaping is exceptional, and hardstanding pitches are generous in size. There is also a spacious room for disabled visitors, plenty of space for children to play and a new barbecue area with seating and a fire pit. 4.5 acre site. 100 touring pitches. 50 hardstandings. 45 seasonal pitches. Caravan, Motorhome and Tent pitches.

AA Pubs & Restaurants nearby: The Ship Inn, LEVINGTON, IP10 0LQ, 01473 659573

Mariners, IPSWICH, IP4 1AX, 01473 289748

Leisure: ⚠ 🔍
Facilities: 🏾 ⊙ ✳ ♿ ⓢ 🖵 🐾 ⚀ ☕ ❸
Services: 🔌 🔟 🗑 ⌀ 🕐 🚽 🚮 ⚘
Within 3 miles: ⚓ ✎ ⚓ ⓢ ⓢ
Notes: Dogs must be kept on leads.

BUNGAY — Map 13 TM38

▶▶▶ 73% Outney Meadow Caravan Park *(TM333905)*

Outney Meadow NR35 1HG
☎ 01986 892338
e-mail: c.r.hancy@ukgateway.net
dir: *At Bungay, site signed from rdbt junction of A143 & A144*

* 🚐 £14-£22 🚐 £14-£22 ▲ £14-£22

Open Mar-Oct

Last arrival 21.00hrs Last departure 16.00hrs

Three pleasant grassy areas beside the River Waveney, with screened pitches. The central toilet block offers good modern facilities, especially in the ladies, and is open at all times. The views from the site across the wide flood plain could be straight out of a Constable painting. Canoeing and boating, coarse fishing and cycling are all available here. 6 acre site. 65 touring pitches. 8 hardstandings. 8 seasonal pitches. Caravan pitches. Motorhome pitches. Tent pitches. 20 statics.

Facilities: 🏾 ⊙ ✳ 🖵 ✳ ⓢ 🐾 ⚀ ☕ ❸
Services: 🔌 🔟 🗑 ⌀ 🕐 🚽 ⚘
Within 3 miles: ⚓ ✔ ✎ ⚓ ⓢ ⓢ

Notes: Dogs must be kept on leads. Boat, canoe & cycle hire.

BURY ST EDMUNDS — Map 13 TL86

Places to visit

Moyse's Hall Museum, BURY ST EDMUNDS, IP33 1DX, 01284 757160 www.moyseshall.org

Ickworth House, Park & Gardens, HORRINGER, IP29 5QE, 01284 735270 www.nationaltrust.org.uk/ickworth

Great for kids: National Horseracing Museum and Tours, NEWMARKET, CB8 8JH, 01638 667333 www.nhrm.co.uk

▶▶▶▶ 85% Dell Touring Park

(TL928640)

Beyton Rd, Thurston IP31 3RB
☎ 01359 270121
e-mail: thedellcaravanpark@btinternet.com
dir: *A14 junct 46 follow Thurston signs & brown camping signs to site. From A143 in Great Barton at x-rds follow Thurston & brown camping signs*

🚐 £13-£21 🚐 £13-£21 ▲ £13-£30

Open Mar-Oct

Last arrival 20.00hrs Last departure noon

A small site with enthusiastic owners that has been developed to a high specification. Set in a quiet spot with lots of mature trees, the quality purpose-built toilet facilities include family rooms, dishwashing and laundry. This is an ideal base for exploring this picturesque area. 6 acre site. 50 touring pitches. 12 hardstandings. Caravan pitches. Motorhome pitches. Tent pitches.

AA Pubs & Restaurants nearby: The Old Cannon Brewery, BURY ST EDMUNDS, IP33 1JR, 01284 768769

Maison Bleue, BURY ST EDMUNDS, IP33 1RG, 01284 760623

The Leaping Hare Restaurant & Country Store, BURY ST EDMUNDS, IP31 2DW, 01359 250287

Facilities: 🚿 🏾 ⊙ 🖵 ✳ ♿ 🐾 🚾 ☕ ❸
Services: 🔌 🔟 🗑 ⚘
Within 3 miles: ✎ ⓢ

Notes: No footballs, no noise after 23.00hrs. Dogs must be kept on leads.

LEISURE: 🏊 Indoor swimming pool 🏊 Outdoor swimming pool ⚠ Children's playground 👶 Kid's club 🎾 Tennis court 🔍 Games room 🖵 Separate TV room ⛳ 9/18 hole golf course ⛵ Boats for hire 🎬 Cinema 🎵 Entertainment 🎣 Fishing ⊙ Mini golf 🏄 Watersports 💪 Gym ⚽ Sports field Spa ♨ Stables
FACILITIES: 🛁 Bath 🚿 Shower ⊙ Electric shaver 🖵 Hairdryer ✳ Ice Pack Facility ♿ Disabled facilities 📞 Public telephone ⓢ Shop on site or within 200yds 🏪 Mobile shop (calls at least 5 days a week) 🍖 BBQ area 🪑 Picnic area 🚾 Wi-fi 🖥 Internet access ☕ Recycling ❸ Tourist info 🐾 Dog exercise area

DUNWICH — Map 13 TM47

Places to visit

RSPB Nature Reserve Minsmere, WESTLETON, IP17 3BY, 01728 648281 www.rspb.org.uk/minsmere

►► 75% Haw Wood Farm Caravan Park *(TM421717)*

Hinton IP17 3QT
☎ 01986 784248
e-mail: bookings@hawwoodfarm.co.uk
dir: *Exit A12, 1.5m N of Darsham level crossing at Little Chef. Site 0.5m on right*

* ♙ £16-£19 ♙ £16-£19 ▲ £16-£19

Open Mar-14 Jan

Last arrival 21.00hrs Last departure noon

An unpretentious family-orientated park set in two large fields surrounded by low hedges. The toilets are clean and functional, and there is plenty of space for children to play. 15 acre site. 60 touring pitches. Caravan pitches. Motorhome pitches. Tent pitches. 55 statics.

AA Pubs & Restaurants nearby: The Westleton Crown, WESTLETON, IP17 3AD, 01728 648777

The Ship at Dunwich, DUNWICH, IP17 3DT, 01728 648219

The Queen's Head, HALESWORTH, IP19 9HT, 01986 784214

Leisure: ⚤
Facilities: ♙⊙⚹⑤🛒✿❶
Services: ♙🔋🚿⌔Ⓣ
Within 3 miles: ↧🏌⑤Ụ
Notes: 🐾 Dogs must be kept on leads.

FELIXSTOWE — Map 13 TM33

Places to visit

Ipswich Museum, IPSWICH, IP1 3QH, 01473 433550 www.ipswich.gov.uk

Christchurch Mansion, IPSWICH, IP4 2BE, 01473 433554 www.ipswich.gov.uk

►►► 78% Peewit Caravan Park *(TM290338)*

GOLD

Walton Av IP11 2HB
☎ 01394 284511
e-mail: peewitpark@aol.com
dir: *Signed from A14 in Felixstowe, 100mtrs past Dock Gate 1, 1st on left*

* ♙ £15-£28 ♙ £15-£28 ▲ £14-£33

Open Apr (or Etr if earlier)-Oct

Last arrival 21.00hrs Last departure 11.00hrs

A grass touring area fringed by trees, with well-maintained grounds and a colourful floral display. This handy urban site is not overlooked by houses, and the toilet and shower facilities are clean and well cared for. A function room contains a TV and library. The beach is a few minutes away by car. 13 acre site. 45 touring pitches. 4 hardstandings. Caravan pitches. Motorhome pitches. Tent pitches. 200 statics.

AA Pubs & Restaurants nearby: The Ship Inn, LEVINGTON, IP10 0LQ, 01473 659573

Leisure: ⚤
Facilities: ♙⊙⚹⚹⑤Ⓢ🛒🅆🅸🅵✿❶
Services: ♙⑤🔋🛒
Within 3 miles: ↧🏌️⊞🏌⊙🍴⑤🏌
Notes: 5mph speed restriction. Only foam footballs permitted. Dogs must be kept on leads. Boules area, bowling green, adventure trail.

HOLLESLEY

Places to visit

Woodbridge Tide Mill, WOODBRIDGE, IP12 1BY, 01394 382815 www.woodbridgetidemill.org.uk

Sutton Hoo, WOODBRIDGE, IP12 3DJ, 01394 389700 www.nationaltrust.org.uk/suttonhoo

Great for kids: Orford Castle, ORFORD, IP12 2ND, 01394 450472 www.english-heritage.org.uk/daysout/properties/orford-castle

HOLLESLEY — Map 13 TM34

►►►► 82% Run Cottage Touring Park *(TM350440)*

Alderton Rd IP12 3RQ
☎ 01394 411309
e-mail: info@run-cottage.co.uk
dir: *From A12 (Ipswich-Saxmundham) onto A1152 at Melton. 1.5m, right at rdbt onto B1083. 0.75m, left to Hollesley. In Hollesley right into The Street, through village, down hill, over bridge, site 100yds on left*

♙ £16-£18 ♙ £16-£18 ▲ £10-£18

Open all year

Last arrival 20.00hrs Last departure 11.00hrs

Located in the peaceful village of Hollesley on the Suffolk coast, this landscaped park is set behind the owners' house; for the 2014 season the site will be improved and extended. The generously-sized pitches are serviced by a well-appointed and immaculately maintained toilet block which includes two fully serviced cubicles. A newly landscaped field offers 22 extra pitches, each with an electric hook-up and TV point, and seven hardstanding pitches. This site is handy for the National Trust's Sutton Hoo, and also by travelling a little further north, the coastal centre and beach at Dunwich Heath, and the RSPB bird reserve at Minsmere. 4.25 acre site. 45 touring pitches. 14 hardstandings. 6 seasonal pitches. Caravan pitches. Motorhome pitches. Tent pitches.

AA Pubs & Restaurants nearby: The Crown at Woodbridge, WOODBRIDGE, IP12 1AD, 01394 384242

Seckford Hall Hotel, WOODBRIDGE, IP13 6NU, 01394 385678

Facilities: ♙⊙⚹⚹⑤🛒✿❶
Services: ♙🛒
Within 3 miles: ↧🏌🏌⑤Ụ
Notes: No groundsheets, ball games or cycles.

SERVICES: ♙ Electric hook up ⑤ Launderette 🍺 Licensed bar 🅰 Calor Gas 🛢 Camping Gaz Ⓣ Toilet fluid 🍴 Café/Restaurant 🍟 Fast Food/Takeaway 🔋 Battery charging 🍼 Baby care 🚐 Motorvan service point **ABBREVIATIONS:** BH/bank hols-bank holidays Etr-Easter Spring BH-Spring Bank Holiday dep-departure fr-from hrs-hours m-mile mdnt-midnight rdbt-roundabout rs-restricted service wk-week wknd-weekend x-rds-cross roads 🚫 No credit cards 🚫 No dogs 👶 Children of all ages accepted See page 9 for details of the AA Camping Card Scheme

IPSWICH

See Bucklesham

KESSINGLAND
Map 13 TM58

Places to visit

East Anglia Transport Museum, LOWESTOFT, NR33 8BL, 01502 518459 www.eatm.org.uk

Maritime Museum, LOWESTOFT, NR32 1XG, 01502 561963 www.lowestoftmaritimemuseum.org.uk

Great for kids: Africa Alive!, LOWESTOFT, NR33 7TF, 01502 740291 www.africa-alive.co.uk

  75% *Kessingland Beach Holiday Park* *(TM535852)*

Beach Rd NR33 7RN

☎ **01502 740636**

e-mail: holidaysales.kessinglandbeach@park-resorts.com

web: www.park-resorts.com

dir: *From Lowestoft take A12 S. At Kessingland take 3rd exit at rdbt towards beach. Through village. At beach follow road to right. In 400yds fork left for park*

⊕ ⊕ Å

Open Apr-Oct

Last departure 10.00hrs

A large holiday centre with direct access onto the beach, and a variety of leisure facilities. The touring area is tucked away from the statics, and served by a clean and functional toilet block. A fish and chip shop and the Boat House Restaurant are popular features. 69 acre site. 90 touring pitches. Caravan pitches. Motorhome pitches. Tent pitches. 95 statics.

Leisure: ⌂ ⌂ ⋀ ⌁ ⌁ ⌂ ⌂ ♫

Facilities: ⌂ ⌂ ⌂ ⌂ ⌂ ⌂ ⌂ ⌂ ⌂ ⌂ ⌂ ⌂

Services: ⌂ ⌂ ⌂ ⌂ ⌂

Within 3 miles: ⌂ ⌂ ⌂ ⌂ ⌂ ⌂ ⌂

Notes: Archery.

see advert below

 ►►►► **89% Heathland Beach Caravan Park** *(TM533877)*

London Rd NR33 7PJ

☎ **01502 740337**

e-mail: heathlandbeach@btinternet.com

web: www.heathlandbeach.co.uk

dir: *1m N of Kessingland exit A12 onto B1437*

⊕ ⊕ Å

Open Apr-Oct

Last arrival 21.00hrs Last departure 11.00hrs

A well-run and maintained park offering superb toilet facilities. The park is set in meadowland, with level grass pitches, and mature trees and bushes. There is direct access to the sea and beach, and good provisions for families on site with a heated swimming pool and three play areas. There is a well-stocked fishing lake, and sea fishing is also possible. 5 acre site. 63 touring pitches. Caravan pitches. Motorhome pitches. Tent pitches. 200 statics.

Leisure: ⌂ ⋀ ⌁ ⚽

Facilities: ⌂ ⌂ ⌂ ⌂ ⌂ ⌂ ⌂ ⌂ ⌂ ⌂ ⌂ ⌂ ⌂

Services: ⌂ ⌂ ⌂ ⌂ ⌂ ⌂ ⌂ ⌂ ⌂

Within 3 miles: ⌂ ⌂ ⌂ ⌂ ⌂ ⌂ ⌂ ⌂ ⌂

Notes: Only 1 dog per unit. Dogs must be kept on leads.

LEISTON

Places to visit

Long Shop Museum, LEISTON, IP16 4ES, 01728 832189 www.longshopmuseum.co.uk

Leiston Abbey, LEISTON, IP16 4TD, 01728 831354 www.english-heritage.org.uk/daysout/properties/leiston-abbey

Great for kids: Easton Farm Park, EASTON, IP13 0EQ, 01728 746475 www.eastonfarmpark.co.uk

LEISURE: 🏊 Indoor swimming pool 🏊 Outdoor swimming pool ⋀ Children's playground 👦 Kid's club ⚲ Tennis court 🎱 Games room 📺 Separate TV room ⛳ 9/18 hole golf course ⛵ Boats for hire 🎬 Cinema ♫ Entertainment 🎣 Fishing ⛳ Mini golf 🏄 Watersports 🏋 Gym ⚽ Sports field Spa ∪ Stables

FACILITIES: 🛁 Bath 🚿 Shower ⊙ Electric shaver 📍 Hairdryer ❄ Ice Pack Facility ♿ Disabled facilities 📞 Public telephone 🏪 Shop on site or within 200yds 🏪 Mobile shop (calls at least 5 days a week) 🍖 BBQ area 🪑 Picnic area 📶 Wi-fi 💻 Internet access ♻ Recycling 🛈 Tourist info 🐕 Dog exercise area

LEISTON
Map 13 TM46

►►► 86% Cakes & Ale (TM432637)

Abbey Ln, Theberton IP16 4TE
☎ 01728 831655
e-mail: reception@cakesandale.co.uk
web: www.cakesandale.co.uk
dir: *From Saxmundham E on B1119. 3m follow minor road over level crossing, turn right, in 0.5m straight on at x-rds, entrance 0.5m on left*

* ⚟ £24-£30 ⚟ £24-£30 ▲ £24-£30

Open Apr-Oct (rs Low season club, shop & reception limited hours)

Last arrival 19.00hrs Last departure 13.00hrs

A large, well spread out and beautifully maintained site, on a former Second World War airfield, with many trees and bushes. The spacious touring area includes plenty of hardstandings and super pitches, and there is a good bar. For 2014 - a new high-quality toilet block containing several fully serviced family rooms. 45 acre site. 55 touring pitches. 55 hardstandings. Caravan pitches. Motorhome pitches. Tent pitches. 200 statics.

AA Pubs & Restaurants nearby: 152 Aldeburgh, ALDEBURGH, IP15 5AX, 01728 454594

Regatta Restaurant, ALDEBURGH, IP15 5AN, 01728 452011

Cakes & Ale

Leisure: ⚐ ⚽ ✿
Facilities: ⚫🔒⊙🅿✳🚿♿⚓🕐⑤🚮 wifi 💻 ♻ ❼
Services: 🔌⑤🍺🔒💧⌀T↯
Within 3 miles: ↨⚡🏇✍⑤🛒⚲

Notes: No group bookings, no noise between 21.00hrs-08.00hrs. Dogs must be kept on leads. Practice range/net, volleyball court, boules, football nets.

see advert below

LOWESTOFT

See Kessingland

SAXMUNDHAM

Places to visit

Long Shop Museum, LEISTON, IP16 4ES, 01728 832189 www.longshopmuseum.co.uk

Leiston Abbey, LEISTON, IP16 4TD, 01728 831354 www.english-heritage.org.uk/daysout/properties/leiston-abbey

Great for kids: Museum of East Anglian Life, STOWMARKET, IP14 1DL, 01449 612229 www.eastanglianlife.org.uk

SAXMUNDHAM
Map 13 TM36

►►►► 85% Carlton Meres Country Park (TM372637)

Rendham Rd, Carlton IP17 2QP
☎ 01728 603344
e-mail: enquiries@carlton-meres.co.uk
dir: *From A12 , W of Saxmundham, take B1119 towards Framlingham (site signed)*

* ⚟ £24-£35 ⚟ £24-£35 ▲ £14-£20

Open Etr-Oct

Last arrival 17.00hrs Last departure 10.00hrs

With two large fishing lakes, a modern fitness suite, a beauty salon, sauna and steam rooms, tennis court, a bar, and a heated outdoor swimming pool, Carlton Meres offers a wealth of leisure facilities, and all for the exclusive use for

continued

SAXMUNDHAM *continued*

those staying on the site (holiday statics and lodges for hire). There is a modern heated toilet block and excellent security. This site is well-placed for all the Suffolk coast attractions. 52 acre site. 96 touring pitches. 56 hardstandings. Caravan pitches. Motorhome pitches. Tent pitches.

AA Pubs & Restaurants nearby: 152 Aldeburgh, ALDEBURGH, IP15 5AX, 01728 454594

Regatta Restaurant, ALDEBURGH, IP15 5AN, 01728 452011

Leisure: ⚓ 🎯 🎢 🧍 🎣 🎵 Spa

Facilities: 🚿 ✳ 🔌 🚾 🖥 ♻ ❶

Services: 🚐 🗑 🍴 🚰 🍴 🎡

Within 3 miles: 🎣 🏊 📅 ⛳ 🚣 🛒 🛍 ⛵

Notes: Dogs must be kept on leads.

▶▶ 82% Marsh Farm Caravan Site

(TM385608)

Sternfield IP17 1HW
☎ 01728 602168
dir: *A12 onto A1094 (Aldeburgh road), at Snape x-rds left signed Sternfield, follow signs to site*

🚐 🚃 Å

Open all year

Last arrival 21.00hrs Last departure 17.00hrs

A very pretty site overlooking reed-fringed lakes which offer excellent coarse fishing. The facilities are very well maintained, and the park truly is a peaceful haven. 30 acre site. 45 touring pitches. Caravan pitches. Motorhome pitches. Tent pitches.

AA Pubs & Restaurants nearby: 152 Aldeburgh, ALDEBURGH, IP15 5AX, 01728 454594

Regatta Restaurant, ALDEBURGH, IP15 5AN, 01728 452011

Facilities: 🚿 ✳ 🗑 🎣 🐕 ♻ ❶

Services: 🚐 🎡

Within 3 miles: 🎣 📅 ⛳ 🛍 ⛵

Notes: 🐕 Campers must report to reception on arrival. Site closed when freezing temperatures are forecast. Dogs must be kept on leads.

SUDBURY Map 13 TL84

Places to visit

Melford Hall, LONG MELFORD, CO10 9AA, 01787 379228
www.nationaltrust.org.uk/melfordhall

Kentwell Hall, LONG MELFORD, CO10 9BA, 01787 310207 www.kentwell.co.uk

Great for kids: Colne Valley Railway & Museum, CASTLE HEDINGHAM, CO9 3DZ, 01787 461174 www.colnevalleyrailway.co.uk

▶▶▶ 77% Willowmere Caravan Park

(TL886388)

Bures Rd, Little Cornard CO10 0NN
☎ 01787 310422
e-mail: awillowmere@aol.com
dir: *1.5m S of Sudbury on B1508 (Bures road)*

🚐 £13-£14 🚃 £13-£14 Å £13-£14

Open Etr-Oct

Last arrival anytime Last departure noon

A pleasant little site in a quiet location tucked away beyond a tiny residential static area, offering spotless facilities. Fishing is available on site. 3 acre site. 40 touring pitches. Caravan pitches. Motorhome pitches. Tent pitches. 9 statics.

AA Pubs & Restaurants nearby: The White Hart, GREAT YELDHAM, CO9 4HJ, 01787 237250

The Bell Inn, CASTLE HEDINGHAM, CO9 3EJ, 01787 460350

Facilities: 🚿 ⊙ ✳ 🔌 🕐 ♻ ❶

Services: 🚐 🗑 🚽

Within 3 miles: 🎣 ⛳ ◎ 🛍 ⛵

Notes: 🐕 Dogs must be kept on leads.

WOODBRIDGE

Places to visit

Sutton Hoo, WOODBRIDGE, IP12 3DJ, 01394 389700
www.nationaltrust.org.uk/suttonhoo

Orford Castle, ORFORD, IP12 2ND, 01394 450472
www.english-heritage.org.uk/daysout/properties/orford-castle

Great for kids: Easton Farm Park, EASTON, IP13 0EQ, 01728 746475
www.eastonfarmpark.co.uk

WOODBRIDGE Map 13 TM24

PREMIER PARK

▶▶▶▶▶ 92% Moon & Sixpence

(TM263454)

Newbourn Rd, Waldringfield IP12 4PP
☎ 01473 736650
e-mail: info@moonandsixpence.eu
web: www.moonandsixpence.eu
dir: *From A12 rdbt, E of Ipswich, follow brown caravan & Moon & Sixpence signs (Waldringfield). 1.5m, left at x-rds, follow signs*

* 🚐 £21-£33 🚃 £21-£33

Open Apr-Oct (rs Low season - club, shop, reception open limited hours)

Last arrival 20.00hrs Last departure noon

A well-planned site, with tourers occupying a sheltered valley position around an attractive boating lake with a sandy beach. Toilet facilities are housed in a smart Norwegian-style cabin, and there is a laundry and dish-washing area. Leisure facilities include two tennis courts, a bowling green, fishing, boating and a games room; there's also a lake, woodland trails, a cycle trail and 9-hole golf. The park has an adult-only area, and a strict 'no groups and no noise after 9pm' policy. 5 acre site. 65 touring pitches. 10 hardstandings. Caravan pitches. Motorhome pitches. 225 statics.

AA Pubs & Restaurants nearby: The Crown at Woodbridge, WOODBRIDGE, IP12 1AD, 01394 384242

Seckford Hall Hotel, WOODBRIDGE, IP13 6NU, 01394 385678

Moon & Sixpence

Leisure: ⚠ 🏊 🎯 🔍
Facilities: 🚿 📵 ⊙ 🅿 ✳ 🛁 🖊 wifi 🖥 ♻ ❶
Services: 🔌 🔟 🍴 🛢 🧺 🍽 📦 ⬇
Within 3 miles: 🛶 🎣 🏌 ⛵ 🛍 🎬

Notes: No group bookings or commercial vehicles, quiet 21.00hrs-08.00hrs. 10-acre sports area.

see advert below

►►► 85% **Moat Barn Touring Caravan Park** *(TM269530)*

Dallinghoo Rd, Bredfield IP13 6BD
☎ 01473 737520
dir: *Exit A12 at Bredfield, 1st right at village pump. Through village, 1m site on left*

🚐 🚙 ⛺

Open Mar-15 Jan

Last arrival 22.00hrs Last departure noon

An attractive small park set in idyllic Suffolk countryside, perfectly located for touring the heritage coastline and for visiting the National Trust's Sutton Hoo. The modern toilet block is well equipped and maintained. There are ten tent pitches and the park is located on the popular Hull to Harwich cycle route. Cycle hire is available, but there are no facilities for children. 2 acre site. 34 touring pitches. Caravan pitches. Motorhome pitches. Tent pitches.

AA Pubs & Restaurants nearby: The Crown at Woodbridge, WOODBRIDGE, IP12 1AD, 01394 384242

Seckford Hall Hotel, WOODBRIDGE, IP13 6NU, 01394 385678

Facilities: 🅿 ⊙ 🅿 ✳ 🛁 wifi ♻
Services: 🔌
Within 3 miles: 🛶 🎣 🛍 🎬 ⛳

Notes: Adults only. 🚫 No ball games. Breathable groundsheets only. Dogs must be kept on leads.

Sussex

Sussex, deriving its name from 'South Saxons' is divided into two - East and West - but the name is so quintessentially English that we tend to think of it as one entity. Mention its name anywhere in the world and for those who are familiar with 'Sussex by the sea', images of rolling hills, historic towns and villages and miles of spectacular chalky cliffs immediately spring to mind. Perhaps it is the bare South Downs with which Sussex is most closely associated.

● Brighton

This swathe of breezy downland represents some of the finest walking in southern England. Now a National Park, the South Downs provide country-loving locals and scores of visitors with a perfect natural playground. As well as walkers and cyclists, you'll find kite flyers, model aircraft enthusiasts and hang gliders.

Beaches and cliffs
The coast is one of the county's gems. At its western end lies sprawling Chichester harbour, with its meandering channels, creeks and sleepy inlets, and on the horizon is the imposing outline of the cathedral, small but beautiful. To the east are the seaside towns of Worthing, Brighton, Eastbourne, Bexhill and Hastings. Here, the South Downs sweep down towards the sea with two famous landmarks, Birling Gap and Beachy Head, demonstrating how nature and the elements have shaped the land over time.

The heart of the county
Inland is Arundel, with its rows of elegant Georgian and Victorian buildings standing in the shadow of the great castle, ancestral home of the Dukes of Norfolk, and the ▶

● Deck chairs on Brighton Beach

magnificent French Gothic-style Roman Catholic cathedral. Mid Sussex is the setting for a chain of attractive, typically English towns, including Midhurst, Petworth, Pulborough, Billingshurst, Uckfield and Haywards Heath.

There are grand country houses, too. Parham, built during the reign of Henry VIII, was one of the first stately homes to open its doors to the public, while the National Trust's Petworth House, in 2,000 acres of parkland, retains the 13th-century chapel of an earlier mansion and has a fine art collection including works by Rembrandt and Van Dyck.

Walking and Cycling

In terms of walking, this county is spoilt for choice. Glancing at the map reveals innumerable paths and bridleways, while there are many more demanding and adventurous long-distance paths – a perfect way to get to the heart of rural East and West Sussex. The Sussex Border Path meanders along the boundary between the two counties; the Monarch's Way broadly follows Charles II's escape route in 1651; the most famous of all of them, the South Downs Way, follows hill paths and clifftop tracks all the way from Winchester to Eastbourne; the West Sussex Literary Trail links Horsham with Chichester and recalls many literary figures associated with this area – Shelley, Tennyson and Wilde among them.

East and West Sussex offer exciting cycle rides through the High Weald, along the South Downs Way and via coastal routes between

Worthing and Rye. Brighton to Hastings via Polegate is part of the Downs and Weald Cycle Route. There is also the Forest Way through East Grinstead to Groombridge and the Cuckoo Trail from Heathfield to Eastbourne. For glorious coastal views and stiff sea breezes, the very easy ride between Chichester and West Wittering is recommended. You can vary the return by taking the Itchenor Ferry to Bosham.

Festivals and Events

- March is the month for the Pioneer Motorcycle Run from Epsom Downs to Brighton. All the participating motorcycles are pre 1915 and the event offers a fascinating insight into the early history of these machines – 300 of which are on display.
- In early May there is the Food & South Downs Fair at the Weald and Downland Open Air Museum near Chichester.
- The 15th-century moated Herstmonceux Castle hosts England's Medieval Festival on August Bank Holiday weekend, complete with minstrels, magicians, lords, ladies and serfs.
- Goodwood is the venue for the Festival of Speed in July, and the Revival Meeting in September. This is when fast cars and track legends celebrate the golden age of British motor sport from the 1940s and '50s.
- The same month – September – sees Uckfield Bonfire and Carnival Society's Annual Carnival with fancy dress and a torchlight procession.

Arundel Castle

SUSSEX, EAST

BATTLE
Map 7 TQ71

Places to visit

1066 Story in Hastings Castle, HASTINGS & ST LEONARDS, TN34 3RG, 01424 781111 www.discoverhastings.co.uk/hastings-castle-1066/

Blue Reef Aquarium, HASTINGS & ST LEONARDS, TN34 3DW, 01424 718776 www.bluereefaquarium.co.uk

Great for kids: Smugglers Adventure, HASTINGS & ST LEONARDS, TN34 3HY, 01424 422964 www.discoverhastings.co.uk

►►► 80% Brakes Coppice Park
(TQ765134)

Forewood Ln TN33 9AB
☎ 01424 830322
e-mail: brakesco@btinternet.com
web: www.brakescoppicepark.co.uk
dir: *From Battle on A2100 towards Hastings. After 2m turn right for Crowhurst. Site 1m on left*

* ⊞ £17-£21 ⇌ £17-£21 ▲ £15-£19

Open Mar-Oct

Last arrival 21.00hrs Last departure noon

A secluded farm site in a sunny meadow deep in woodland with a small stream and a coarse fishing lake. The toilet block has quality fittings and there's a good fully-serviced family/disabled room. Hardstanding pitches are neatly laid out on a terrace, and tents are pitched on grass edged by woodland. The hands-on owners offer high levels of customer care and this tucked-away gem proves a peaceful base for exploring Battle and the south coast. 3 acre site. 60 touring pitches. 10 hardstandings. Caravan pitches. Motorhome pitches. Tent pitches. 1 static.

AA Pubs & Restaurants nearby: Ash Tree Inn, ASHBURNHAM PLACE, TN33 9NX, 01424 892104

The Wild Mushroom Restaurant, WESTFIELD, TN35 4SB, 01424 751137

Leisure: ⚙

Facilities: ⚲⊙☞✳♿🕔🛁🚮📶🖥 ❂

Services: ⊞⊟🔒⊘🔩📮

Within 3 miles: ↓℘🛈∪

Notes: No fires, footballs or kite flying. Dogs must be kept on leads.

►►► 73% Senlac Wood (TQ722153)

Catsfield Rd, Catsfield TN33 9LN
☎ 01424 773969
e-mail: senlacwood@xlninternet.co.uk
dir: *A271 from Battle onto B2204 signed Bexhill. Site on left*

⊞ ⇌ ▲

Open Mar-Oct

Last arrival 22.00hrs Last departure noon

A woodland site with many secluded hardstanding bays and two peaceful grassy glades for tents. The functional toilet facilities are clean but there are plans to add new portacabin toilets in the tent area. The site is ideal for anyone looking for seclusion and shade and it is well placed for visiting nearby Battle and the south coast beaches. 20 acre site. 35 touring pitches. 16 hardstandings. Caravan pitches. Motorhome pitches. Tent pitches.

AA Pubs & Restaurants nearby: Ash Tree Inn, ASHBURNHAM PLACE, TN33 9NX, 01424 892104

The Wild Mushroom Restaurant, WESTFIELD, TN35 4SB, 01424 751137

Leisure: ⚙🔍

Facilities: ⚲⊙☞✳🕔🛁📶 ❂

Services: ⊞🔩T🔩📮

Within 3 miles: ↓℘🛈🛈∪

Notes: No camp fires, no noise after 23.00hrs. Dogs must be kept on leads. Caravan storage.

BEXHILL

Places to visit

Pevensey Castle, PEVENSEY, BN24 5LE, 01323 762604 www.english-heritage.org.uk/daysout/properties/pevensey-castle

1066 Story in Hastings Castle, HASTINGS & ST LEONARDS, TN34 3RG, 01424 781111 www.discoverhastings.co.uk/hastings-castle-1066/

Great for kids: The Observatory Science Centre, HERSTMONCEUX, BN27 1RN, 01323 832731 www.the-observatory.org

BEXHILL
Map 6 TQ70

PREMIER PARK

►►►►► 87% Kloofs Caravan Park (TQ709091)

Sandhurst Ln TN39 4RG
☎ 01424 842839
e-mail: camping@kloofs.com
dir: *NE of Bexhill exit A259 at Little Common rdbt, N into Peartree Lane, left at x-rds, site 300mtrs on left*

⊞ £26-£34 ⇌ £26-£34 ▲ £26-£34

Open all year

Last arrival anytime Last departure 11.00hrs

Hidden away down a quiet lane, just inland from Bexhill and the coast, Kloofs is a friendly, family-run park surrounded by farmland and oak woodlands, with views extending to the South Downs from hilltop pitches. Lovingly developed by the owners over the past 18 years, the site is well landscaped and thoughtfully laid out, with excellent hardstandings (some large enough for RVs), colourful flower beds, and spacious pitches, each with mini patio, bench and barbecue stand. Spotless, upmarket toilet facilities include a family shower room and a unisex block with privacy cubicles, a dog shower, a drying room and a dishwasher. 22 acre site. 50 touring pitches. 50 hardstandings. Caravan pitches. Motorhome pitches. Tent pitches. 75 statics.

AA Pubs & Restaurants nearby: Ash Tree Inn, ASHBURNHAM PLACE, TN33 9NX, 01424 892104

Leisure: ⚙♿🔍▭

Facilities: ⚲⊙☞✳♿🕔🛁📮🚮❄ ❂

Services: ⊞🔩🔒⊘T🔩🚮⛟

Within 3 miles: ↓🎿℘◎⛴🛈∪

Notes: No noise between 22.30hrs-07.00hrs. Dogs must be kept on leads. Kitchens, baby-changing facilities.

LEISURE: 🏊 Indoor swimming pool 🏊 Outdoor swimming pool ⚙ Children's playground 🪁 Kid's club 🎾 Tennis court 🎱 Games room ▭ Separate TV room ⛳ 9/18 hole golf course ⛵ Boats for hire 🎬 Cinema 🎭 Entertainment ℘ Fishing ◎ Mini golf ⛴ Watersports 🏋 Gym ⚽ Sports field **Spa** ∪ Stables
FACILITIES: 🛁 Bath 🚿 Shower ⊙ Electric shaver ☞ Hairdryer ✳ Ice Pack Facility ♿ Disabled facilities 🕔 Public telephone 🛈 Shop on site or within 200yds 🛒 Mobile shop (calls at least 5 days a week) 🍴 BBQ area 🌲 Picnic area 📶 Wi-fi 🖥 Internet access ♻ Recycling ❂ Tourist info 🐕 Dog exercise area

►►► 81% Cobbs Hill Farm Caravan & Camping Park *(TQ736102)*

Watermill Ln TN39 5JA
☎ 01424 213460 & 07708 958910
e-mail: cobbshillfarmuk@hotmail.com
dir: *Exit A269 into Watermill Ln, park 1m on left (NB it is advisable not to follow Sat Nav)*

🚐 🚌 ⛺

Open Apr-Oct

Last arrival 20.00hrs Last departure noon

A well-established farm site tucked away in pleasant rolling countryside close to Bexhill and a short drive from Battle, the South Downs and good beaches. Neat, well-maintained camping paddocks, one with eight hardstanding pitches, are sheltered by mature trees and hedging; the toilet block is clean and freshly painted. Children will love the menagerie of farm animals. 17 acre site. 55 touring pitches. 8 hardstandings. 20 seasonal pitches. Caravan pitches. Motorhome pitches. Tent pitches. 15 statics.

AA Pubs & Restaurants nearby: Ash Tree Inn, ASHBURNHAM PLACE, TN33 9NX, 01424 892104

Leisure: 🛝 ⚽

Facilities: 🚿 ⊙ 💨 ❄ ♿ 📞 [$] 🐕 [Wi-fi] ⓘ

Services: 🔌 🧺 🛢 🔥 [T] 🔋

Within 3 miles: ⛳ 🎣 🚤 [$] 🧺

Notes: No camp fires. Dogs must be kept on leads.

CAMBER — Map 7 TQ91

Places to visit

Rye Castle Museum, RYE, TN31 7JY, 01797 226728 www.ryemuseum.co.uk

Lamb House, RYE, TN31 7ES, 01580 762334 www.nationaltrust.org.uk/main/w-lambhouse

Great for kids: 1066 Story in Hastings Castle, HASTINGS & ST LEONARDS, TN34 3RG, 01424 781111 www.discoverhastings.co.uk/hastings-castle-1066/

70% Camber Sands *(TQ972184)*

AA HOLIDAY CENTRE · DAVID BELLAMY CONSERVATION AWARD GOLD

New Lydd Rd TN31 7RT
☎ 0871 664 9719 & 01797 222000
e-mail: camber.sands@park-resorts.com
web: www.park-resorts.com
dir: *M20 junct 10 (Ashford International Station), A2070 signed Brenzett. Follow Hastings & Rye signs on A259. 1m before Rye, left signed Camber. Site in 3m*

🚐 🚌 ⛺

Open Mar-Nov

Last arrival anytime Last departure 10.00hrs

Located opposite Camber's vast sandy beach, this large holiday centre offers a good range of leisure and entertainment facilities. The touring area is positioned close to the reception and entrance, and is served by a clean and functional toilet block. 110 acre site. 55 touring pitches. 6 hardstandings. Caravan pitches. Motorhome pitches. Tent pitches. 921 statics.

AA Pubs & Restaurants nearby: Mermaid Inn, RYE, TN31 7EY, 01797 223065

The Ypres Castle Inn, RYE, TN31 7HH, 01797 223248

The George in Rye, RYE, TN31 7JT, 01797 222114

Leisure: 🏊 🛝 ✋ 🎾 🔍 ♫ Spa

Facilities: 🚿 ⊙ ♿ 📞 [$] 🪑 [Wi-fi] 💻 ♻ ⓘ

Services: 🔌 🧺 🍺 🍴 🍔 🚼

Within 3 miles: ⛳ 🎣 ◎ 🚤 [$] 🧺

Notes: Quiet between 23.00hrs-07.00hrs. Dogs must be kept on leads.

FURNER'S GREEN — Map 6 TQ42

Places to visit

Sheffield Park and Garden, SHEFFIELD PARK, TN22 3QX, 01825 790231 www.nationaltrust.org.uk/sheffieldpark

Nymans, HANDCROSS, RH17 6EB, 01444 405250 www.nationaltrust.org.uk/nymans

►► 81% Heaven Farm *(TQ403264)*

TN22 3RG
☎ 01825 790226
e-mail: heavenfarmleisure@btinternet.com
dir: *On A275 between Lewes & East Grinstead, 1m N of Sheffield Park Garden*

* 🚐 £20 🚌 £20 ⛺ £20

Open all year (rs Nov-Mar no tents)

Last arrival 21.00hrs Last departure noon

A delightful, small, rural site on a popular farm complex incorporating a farm museum, craft shop, tea room and nature trail. The good, clean toilet facilities are housed in well-converted outbuildings and chickens and duck roam freely around the site. Ashdown Forest, the Bluebell Railway and Sheffield Park Garden are nearby. 1.5 acre site. 25 touring pitches. 2 hardstandings. Caravan pitches. Motorhome pitches. Tent pitches.

AA Pubs & Restaurants nearby: The Coach and Horses, DANEHILL, RH17 7JF, 01825 740369

The Griffin Inn, FLETCHING, TN22 3SS, 01825 722890

Facilities: 🚿 ⊙ ❄ ♿ [$] 🪑 🐕 ⓘ

Services: 🔌 [T] 🍴 🔋 ⛽

Within 3 miles: ⛳ 🎣 [$] 🐎

Notes: 🚫💳 Dogs must be kept on leads. Fishing.

SERVICES: 🔌 Electric hook up 🧺 Launderette 🍺 Licensed bar 🛢 Calor Gas 🔥 Camping Gaz [T] Toilet fluid 🍴 Café/Restaurant 🍔 Fast Food/Takeaway 🔋 Battery charging 🚼 Baby care ⛽ Motorvan service point **ABBREVIATIONS:** BH/bank hols-bank holidays Etr-Easter Spring BH-Spring Bank Holiday dep-departure fr-from hrs-hours m-mile mdnt-midnight rdbt-roundabout rs-restricted service wk-week wknd-weekend x-rds-cross roads 🚫💳 No credit cards 🚫🐕 No dogs 👪 Children of all ages accepted See page 9 for details of the AA Camping Card Scheme

HASTINGS Map 7 TQ80

Places to visit

Old Town Hall Museum of Local History, HASTINGS & ST LEONARDS, TN34 1EW, 01424 451052 www.hmag.org.uk

Shipwreck Museum, HASTINGS & ST LEONARDS, TN34 3DW, 01424 437452 www.shipwreck-heritage.org.uk

Great for kids: Blue Reef Aquarium, HASTINGS & ST LEONARDS, TN34 3DW, 01424 718776 www.bluereefaquarium.co.uk

Smugglers Adventure, HASTINGS & ST LEONARDS, TN34 3HY, **01424 422964** www.discoverhastings.co.uk

 87% Combe Haven Holiday Park (TQ779091)

Harley Shute Rd, St Leonards-on-Sea TN38 8BZ
☎ 01424 427891
e-mail: combehaven@haven.com
web: www.haven.com/combehaven
dir: A21 towards Hastings. In Hastings take A259 towards Bexhill. Park signed on right

Open Mar-Oct

Close to a beach and the resort attractions of Hastings, this newly upgraded holiday park has been designed with families in mind. Activities include a pirates' adventure playground, heated swimming pools and a wealth of sports and outdoor activities.

Change over day: Mon, Fri, Sat **Arrival and departure times:** Please contact the site

Statics 296 Sleeps 6-8 Bedrms 2-3 Bathrms 1-2 Toilets 1-2 Freezer TV Sky/FTV Elec inc Gas inc Grass area

Children 👶 Cots Highchair **Dogs** 2 on leads No dangerous dogs

Leisure: 🏊 🏊 ✋ 🛝

HEATHFIELD Map 6 TQ52

Places to visit

Pashley Manor Gardens, TICEHURST, TN5 7HE, 01580 200888 www.pashleymanorgardens.com

The Truggery, HERSTMONCEUX, BN27 1QL, 01323 832314 www.truggery.co.uk

Great for kids: Bentley Wildfowl & Motor Museum, HALLAND, BN8 5AF, 01825 840573 www.bentley.org.uk

▶▶ **77% Greenviews Caravan Park** (TQ605223)

Burwash Rd, Broad Oak TN21 8RT
☎ 01435 863531
dir: Through Heathfield on A265 for 1m. Site on left after Broad Oak sign

🚐 🚗 🏕

Open Apr-Oct (rs Apr & Oct bookings only, subject to weather)

Last arrival 22.00hrs Last departure 10.30hrs

A small touring area adjoining a residential park, with a smart clubhouse. The facility block includes a room for disabled visitors. The owners always offer a friendly welcome, and they take pride in the lovely flower beds which adorn the park. 3 acre site. 10 touring pitches. Caravan pitches. Motorhome pitches. Tent pitches. 51 statics.

AA Pubs & Restaurants nearby: The Middle House, MAYFIELD, TN20 6AB, 01435 872146

The Best Beech Inn, WADHURST, TN5 6JH, 01892 782046

Facilities: 🚿 ☺ ♿ 🕐
Services: 🚽 🔋 🍴 🔒 ⊘
Within 3 miles: 🔋
Notes: 🐾 🚫

PEVENSEY BAY Map 6 TQ60

Places to visit

"How We Lived Then" Museum of Shops & Social History, EASTBOURNE, BN21 4NS, 01323 737143 www.how-we-lived-then.co.uk

Alfriston Clergy House, ALFRISTON, BN26 5TL, 01323 871961 www.nationaltrust.org.uk/alfriston/

Great for kids: The Observatory Science Centre, HERSTMONCEUX, BN27 1RN, 01323 832731 www.the-observatory.org

▶▶▶ **85% Bay View Park** (TQ648028)

Old Martello Rd BN24 6DX
☎ 01323 768688
e-mail: holidays@bay-view.co.uk
web: www.bay-view.co.uk
dir: Signed from A259 W of Pevensey Bay. On seaward side of A259 take private road towards beach

＊ 🚐 £16-£25 🚗 £16-£25 🏕

Open Mar-Oct

Last arrival 20.00hrs Last departure noon

A pleasant well-run site just yards from the beach, in an area east of Eastbourne town centre known as 'The Crumbles'. The level grassy site is very well maintained and the toilet facilities feature fully-serviced cubicles. The seasonal tent field has marked pitches and improved portacabin toilet facilities with toilet and wash basins and wash basins and shower cubicles. There is now a 9-hole par 4 golf course and club house. 6 acre site. 94 touring pitches. 14 hardstandings. 15 seasonal pitches. Caravan pitches. Motorhome pitches. Tent pitches. 14 statics.

AA Pubs & Restaurants nearby: The Farm @ Friday Street, LANGNEY, BN23 8AP, 01323 766049

Leisure: 🛝
Facilities: 🚿 ☺ 🗄 ✳ ♿ 🛒 📶 ♻ ⓘ
Services: 🚽 🔋 🔒 ⊘ 🅣 🍴 ⚓
Within 3 miles: 🚣 🎏 🎣 ◎ ⚓ 🔋🔋
Notes: Families & couples only, no commercial vehicles. Dogs must be kept on leads.

LEISURE: 🏊 Indoor swimming pool 🏊 Outdoor swimming pool 🛝 Children's playground ✋ Kid's club ⚲ Tennis court 🎱 Games room 🖥 Separate TV room ⛳ 9/18 hole golf course 🚣 Boats for hire 🎬 Cinema 🎵 Entertainment ✎ Fishing ◎ Mini golf 🏄 Watersports 🏋 Gym ⚽ Sports field **Spa** ♻ Stables
FACILITIES: 🛁 Bath 🚿 Shower ☺ Electric shaver 🗄 Hairdryer ✳ Ice Pack Facility ♿ Disabled facilities ⓒ Public telephone 🛒 Shop on site or within 200yds 🚚 Mobile shop (calls at least 5 days a week) 🍴 BBQ area 🪑 Picnic area 📶 Wi-fi 🖥 Internet access ♻ Recycling ⓘ Tourist info 🐕 Dog exercise area

SUSSEX, WEST

ARUNDEL
Map 6 TQ00

Places to visit

Arundel Castle, ARUNDEL, BN18 9AB, 01903 882173 www.arundelcastle.org

Harbour Park, LITTLEHAMPTON, BN17 5LL, 01903 721200 www.harbourpark.com

Great for kids: Look & Sea! Visitor Centre, LITTLEHAMPTON, BN17 5AW, 01903 718984 www.lookandsea.co.uk

AA CAMPING CARD SITE

►► 79% Ship & Anchor Marina

(TQ002040)

Station Rd, Ford BN18 0BJ
☎ 01243 551262
e-mail: enquiries@shipandanchormarina.co.uk
dir: From A27 at Arundel take road S signed Ford. Site 2m on left after level crossing

* ⚐ £15-£21 ⚑ £15-£21 ▲ £15-£21

Open Mar-Oct

Last arrival 21.00hrs Last departure noon

Neatly maintained by the enthusiastic, hard working owner, this small, well located site has dated but spotlessly clean toilet facilities, a secluded tent area, and enjoys a pleasant position beside the Ship & Anchor pub and the tidal River Arun. There are good walks from the site to Arundel and the coast. 12 acre site. 120 touring pitches. 11 hardstandings. Caravan pitches. Motorhome pitches. Tent pitches.

AA Pubs & Restaurants nearby: The Town House, ARUNDEL, BN18 9AJ, 01903 883847

George & Dragon, BURPHAM, BN18 9RR, 01903 883131

Leisure: ⏞

Facilities: ⛟⛏☉⛿✳⛊⛱⛉⛲🔌✿

Services: ⊡⛽🚰🛢⏢Ⓣ⛌🚿

Within 3 miles: ⛷⛶⛳◎⛲🛢🛒Ụ

Notes: ⊛ No music audible to others. Dogs must be kept on leads. River fishing from site.

BARNS GREEN
Map 6 TQ12

Places to visit

Parham House & Gardens, PULBOROUGH, RH20 4HS, 01903 744888 www.parhaminsussex.co.uk

Great for kids: Bignor Roman Villa & Museum, BIGNOR, RH20 1PH, 01798 869259 www.bignorromanvilla.co.uk

►►►► 86% Sumners Ponds Fishery & Campsite (TQ125268)

Chapel Rd RH13 0PR
☎ 01403 732539
e-mail: bookings@sumnersponds.co.uk
dir: From A272 at Coolham x-rds, N towards Barns Green. In 1.5m take 1st left at small x-rds. 1m, over level crossing. Site on left just after right bend

* ⚐ £17-£26 ⚑ £17-£26 ▲ £17-£26

Open all year

Last arrival 20.00hrs Last departure noon

Diversification towards high quality camping continues at this working farm set in attractive surroundings on the edge of the quiet village of Barns Green. There are three touring areas; one continues to develop and includes camping pods and extra hardstandings, and another which has a stunning modern toilet block, has excellent pitches (and pods) on the banks of one of the well-stocked fishing lakes. There are many cycle paths on site and a woodland walk has direct access to miles of footpaths. The Café by the Lake serves meals from breakfast onwards. Horsham and Brighton are within easy reach. 40 acre site. 86 touring pitches. 45 hardstandings. Caravan pitches. Motorhome pitches. Tent pitches. 4 wooden pods.

AA Pubs & Restaurants nearby: Black Horse Inn, NUTHURST, RH13 6LH, 01403 891272

The White Horse, MAPLEHURST, RH13 6LL, 01403 891208

Leisure: ⏞

Facilities: ⛏☉⛿✳⛊⛱⛉⛲⛩🛝WiFi♻✿

Services: ⊡⛿🛢⏢Ⓣ⛌🚽🚿

Within 3 miles: ⛷⛳🛢🛒Ụ

Notes: Only one car per pitch.

BILLINGSHURST
Map 6 TQ02

Places to visit

Borde Hill Garden, HAYWARDS HEATH, RH16 1XP, 01444 450326 www.bordehill.co.uk

Petworth Cottage Museum, PETWORTH, GU28 0AU, 01798 342100 www.petworthcottagemuseum.co.uk

►► 74% Limeburners Arms Camp Site

(TQ072255)

Lordings Rd, Newbridge RH14 9JA
☎ 01403 782311
e-mail: chippy.sawyer@virgin.net
dir: From A29 take A272 towards Petworth for 1m, left onto B2133. Site 300yds on left

⚐ ⚑ ▲

Open Apr-Oct

Last arrival 22.00hrs Last departure 14.00hrs

A secluded site in rural West Sussex, at the rear of the Limeburners Arms public house, and surrounded by fields. It makes a pleasant base for touring the South Downs and the Arun Valley. The toilets are basic but very clean. 2.75 acre site. 40 touring pitches. Caravan pitches. Motorhome pitches. Tent pitches.

AA Pubs & Restaurants nearby: Black Horse Inn, NUTHURST, RH13 6LH, 01403 891272

The White Horse, MAPLEHURST, RH13 6LL, 01403 891208

Leisure: ⏞

Facilities: ⛏☉✳⛊

Services: ⊡⛿⛌🚿🚽

Within 3 miles: ⛷🛢Ụ

Notes: Dogs must be kept on leads.

SERVICES: ⊡ Electric hook up ⛿ Launderette ⛽ Licensed bar 🛢 Calor Gas ⊘ Camping Gaz Ⓣ Toilet fluid ⛌ Café/Restaurant ⛱ Fast Food/Takeaway ⛲ Battery charging 🚼 Baby care 🚽 Motorvan service point **ABBREVIATIONS:** BH/bank hols-bank holidays Etr-Easter Spring BH-Spring Bank Holiday dep-departure fr-from hrs-hours m-mile mdnt-midnight rdbt-roundabout rs-restricted service wk-week wknd-weekend x-rds-cross roads ⊛ No credit cards ⊗ No dogs ⛩ Children of all ages accepted See page 9 for details of the AA Camping Card Scheme

CHICHESTER
Map 5 SU80

Places to visit

Chichester Cathedral, CHICHESTER, PO19 1PX, 01243 782595 www.chichestercathedral.org.uk

Pallant House Gallery, CHICHESTER, PO19 1TJ, 01243 774557 www.pallant.org.uk

▶▶▶ 82% Ellscott Park (SU829995)

Sidlesham Ln, Birdham PO20 7QL
☎ 01243 512003
e-mail: camping@ellscottpark.co.uk
dir: From Chichester take A286 for approx 4m, left at Butterfly Farm sign, site 500yds right

🚐 🚙 ▲

Open Apr-3rd wk in Oct

Last arrival daylight Last departure variable

A well-kept park set in sheltered meadowland behind the owners' nursery and van storage area. The park attracts a peace-loving clientele, has spotless, well maintained toilet facilities, and is handy for the beach, Chichester, Goodwood House, the racing at Goodwood and walking on the South Downs. Home-grown produce is for sale. 2.5 acre site. 50 touring pitches. 25 seasonal pitches. Caravan pitches. Motorhome pitches. Tent pitches.

AA Pubs & Restaurants nearby: The Crab & Lobster, SIDLESHAM, PO20 7NB, 01243 641233

Leisure: 🛝 ⚽
Facilities: 🐾⊙❄🚿♨🚐🛻♻ ❶
Services: 🔌🗑 ⚗🚽🍴
Within 3 miles: ⬇🎣🚣👣🛒🏧🛍🎠U
Notes: ◉ Dogs must be kept on leads.

DIAL POST
Map 6 TQ11

Places to visit

Bignor Roman Villa & Museum, BIGNOR, RH20 1PH, 01798 869259 www.bignorromanvilla.co.uk

Great for kids: Amberley Working Museum, AMBERLEY, BN18 9LT, 01798 831370 www.amberleymuseum.co.uk

▶▶▶▶ 85% Honeybridge Park

(TQ152183)

Honeybridge Ln RH13 8NX
☎ 01403 710923
e-mail: enquiries@honeybridgepark.co.uk
dir: 10m S of Horsham, just off A24 at Dial Post. Behind Old Barn Nursery

🚐 🚙 ▲

Open all year

Last arrival 19.00hrs Last departure noon

An attractive and very popular park on gently-sloping ground surrounded by hedgerows and mature trees. A comprehensive amenities building houses upmarket toilet facilities including luxury family and disabled rooms, as well as a laundry, shop and off-licence. There are plenty of hardstandings and electric hook-ups, a games room, and an excellent children's play area. 15 acre site. 130 touring pitches. 70 hardstandings. 20 seasonal pitches. Caravan pitches. Motorhome pitches. Tent pitches. 50 statics.

AA Pubs & Restaurants nearby: The Countryman Inn, SHIPLEY, RH13 8PZ, 01403 741383

George & Dragon, SHIPLEY, RH13 8GE, 01403 741320

The Queens Head, WEST CHILTINGTON, RH20 2JN, 01798 812244

Leisure: 🛝 🎱 ⬜
Facilities: 🛒🐾⊙📻❄♨🚐 ❶
Services: 🔌🗑 🛢⚗🚽🍴🍴
Within 3 miles: 📻👣🛒🛍U
Notes: No open fires. Dogs must be kept on leads. Fridges available.

HENFIELD
Map 6 TQ21

▶▶ 72% Blacklands Farm Caravan & Camping (TQ231180)

Wheatsheaf Rd BN5 9AT
☎ 01273 493528 & 07773 792577
e-mail: info@blacklandsfarm.co.uk
dir: A23, B2118, B2116 towards Henfield. Site approx 4m on right

* 🚐 fr £18 🚙 fr £18 ▲ fr £18

Open Mar-Jan

Last arrival 20.00hrs Last departure anytime

Tucked away off the B2116, east of Henfield, and well placed for visiting Brighton and exploring the South Downs National Park, this simple, grassy site has great potential, and the owners plan positive improvements that will not spoil the traditional feel of the campsite. There are spacious pitches down by fishing lakes and the basic portaloos are clean and tidy and have been smartly clad in wood, but future plans include building a new toilet block. 5 acre site. 75 touring pitches. Caravan pitches. Motorhome pitches. Tent pitches.

AA Pubs & Restaurants nearby: The Fountain Inn, ASHURST, BN44 3AP, 01403 710219

Royal Oak, POYNINGS, BN45 7AQ, 01273 857389

Leisure: 🛝 ⚽
Facilities: 🐾📻❄♨🛍🚐🛻♻ ❶
Services: 🔌
Within 3 miles: ⬇📻🛒🛍U
Notes: No commercial vehicles. Dogs must be kept on leads. Coffee machine.

HORSHAM

See Barns Green & Dial Post

PAGHAM

Places to visit

Chichester Cathedral, CHICHESTER, PO19 1PX, 01243 782595 www.chichestercathedral.org.uk

Pallant House Gallery, CHICHESTER, PO19 1TJ, 01243 774557 www.pallant.org.uk

Great for kids: Haredown Mountain Boarding Centre, CHICHESTER, PO18 0JJ, 01243 81197 www.haredown.com

---

PAGHAM
Map 6 SZ89

90% Church Farm Holiday Park (SZ885974)

Church Ln PO21 4NR
☎ **01243 262635**
e-mail: churchfarm@haven.com
web: www.haven.com/churchfarm
dir: *At rdbt on A27 (S of Chichester) take B2145 signed Hunston & Selsey. At mini rdbt take 1st left signed North Mundham, Pagham & Bognor Regis. Site in approx 3m*

Open Mar-Oct

Close to Portsmouth, Chichester and south coast beaches, this relaxing and fun-packed holiday park is located close to Pagham Harbour Nature Reserve. On-site activities include golf on the 9-hole course, tennis coaching, shopping, kids' play areas and evening entertainment. There are a range of holiday caravans and apartments.

Change over day: Mon, Fri, Sat **Arrival and departure times:** Please contact the site

Statics 189 Sleeps 6-8 Bedrms 2-3 Bathrms 1-2 Toilets 1-2 Freezer TV Sky/FTV Elec inc Gas inc Grass area

Children 🚼 Cots Highchair **Dogs** 2 on leads No dangerous dogs

Leisure: ⌇⌇⌇⌇🏊♨️

SELSEY
Map 5 SZ89

Places to visit

Chichester Cathedral, CHICHESTER, PO19 1PX, 01243 782595 www.chichestercathedral.org.uk

Pallant House Gallery, CHICHESTER, PO19 1TJ, 01243 774557 www.pallant.org.uk

82% Warner Farm Touring Park (SZ845939)

Warner Ln, Selsey PO20 9EL
☎ **01243 604499**
e-mail: touring@bunnleisure.co.uk
web: www.warnerfarm.co.uk
dir: *From B2145 in Selsey turn right into School Lane & follow signs*

🚐🚍⛺

Open Mar-Jan

Last arrival 17.30hrs Last departure 10.00hrs

A well-screened touring site that adjoins the three static parks under the same ownership. A courtesy bus runs around the complex to entertainment areas and supermarkets. The park backs onto open grassland, and the leisure facilities with bar, amusements and bowling alley, and swimming pool/sauna complex are also accessible to tourers. 10 acre site. 250 touring pitches. 60 hardstandings. 25 seasonal pitches. Caravan pitches. Motorhome pitches. Tent pitches.

AA Pubs & Restaurants nearby: The Crab & Lobster, SIDLESHAM, PO20 7NB, 01243 641233

Warner Farm Touring Park

Leisure: ⌇⌇⌇♥️🎿🏊⚽♨️◉🎵

Facilities: 🚻⚙️🔌✳️♿🚽🛁🚿🏕️Wi-Fi 🖥️♻️ℹ️

Services: 🔌🚐🛁🔋⛽🚽🍴🏪⚰️

Within 3 miles: 🚴🚣⚓️🌳◉🚤🏪🛒🏌️⛳

Notes: Dogs must be kept on leads.

see advert below

SERVICES: 🔌 Electric hook up 🧺 Launderette 🍺 Licensed bar 🛢️ Calor Gas ⛽ Camping Gaz 🚽 Toilet fluid 🍴 Café/Restaurant 🍟 Fast Food/Takeaway 🔋 Battery charging 🍼 Baby care ⚱️ Motorvan service point **ABBREVIATIONS:** BH/bank hols-bank holidays Etr-Easter Spring BH-Spring Bank Holiday dep-departure fr-from hrs-hours m-mile mdnt-midnight rdbt-roundabout rs-restricted service wk-week wknd-weekend x-rds-cross roads 🚫 No credit cards 🚫 No dogs 🚼 Children of all ages accepted See page 9 for details of the AA Camping Card Scheme

TYNE & WEAR

SOUTH SHIELDS   Map 21 NZ36

Places to visit

Arbeia Roman Fort & Museum, SOUTH SHIELDS, NE33 2BB, 0191 456 1369 www.twmuseums.org.uk/arbeia

Tynemouth Priory and Castle, TYNEMOUTH, NE30 4BZ, 0191 257 1090 www.english-heritage.org.uk/daysout/properties/tynemouth-priory-and-castle

Great for kids: Blue Reef Aquarium, TYNEMOUTH, NE30 4JF, 0191 258 1031 www.bluereefaquarium.co.uk

AA CAMPING CARD SITE

► ► ► **80% Lizard Lane Caravan & Camping Site** (NZ399648)

Lizard Ln NE34 7AB
☎ **0191 454 4982**
e-mail: info@littlehavenhotel.com
dir: 2m S of town centre on A183 (Sunderland road)

Open Feb-28 Jan

Last arrival anytime Last departure 11.00hrs

This site is located in an elevated position with good sea views. All touring pitches are fully serviced and the modern smart amenities block is equipped with superb fixtures and fittings. A shop is also provided. Please note that tents are not accepted. 2 acre site. 47 touring pitches. Caravan pitches. Motorhome pitches. 70 statics.

Facilities: ⬡⊙🝨❄🖐🔥♻ ❶
Services: 🔌🧹🚮
Within 3 miles: 🚴🎣♻🏊🎯🛒U

Notes: Dogs must be kept on leads. 9-hole putting green.

WARWICKSHIRE

ASTON CANTLOW   Map 10 SP16

Places to visit

Mary Arden's Farm, WILMCOTE, CV37 9UN, 01789 201844 www.shakespeare.org.uk

Charlecote Park, CHARLECOTE, CV35 9ER, 01789 470277 www.nationaltrust.org.uk/charlecote-park

Great for kids: Warwick Castle, WARWICK, CV34 4QU, 0871 265 2000 www.warwick-castle.com

AA CAMPING CARD SITE

► ► ► **80% Island Meadow Caravan Park** (SP137596)

The Mill House B95 6JP
☎ **01789 488273**
e-mail: holiday@islandmeadowcaravanpark.co.uk
dir: From A46 or A3400 follow signs for Aston Cantlow. Site signed 0.25m W off Mill Lane

* 🚐 fr £22 🚐 fr £22 ▲ £15-£20

Open Mar-Oct

Last arrival 21.00hrs Last departure noon

A peacefully located site bordered by the River Alne on one side and its mill stream on the other. Surrounded by mature trees, pitch density is generous and the well-stocked shop also sells wines, beers and spirits. 7 acre site. 24 touring pitches. 14 hardstandings. Caravan pitches. Motorhome pitches. Tent pitches. 56 statics.

AA Pubs & Restaurants nearby: The Blue Boar Inn, TEMPLE GRAFTON, B49 6NR, 01789 750010

Facilities: ⬡⊙🝨❄🖐🔥♻ ❶
Services: 🔌🚽🍺🧹🚮♻
Within 3 miles: 🚴♻◎🛒

Notes: Dogs must be kept on leads.

HARBURY   Map 11 SP35

Places to visit

Warwick Castle, WARWICK, CV34 4QU, 0871 265 2000 www.warwick-castle.com

Farnborough Hall, FARNBOROUGH, OX17 1DU, 01295 690002 www.nationaltrust.org.uk

Great for kids: Stratford Butterfly Farm, STRATFORD-UPON-AVON, CV37 7LS, 01789 299288 www.butterflyfarm.co.uk

► ► ► ► **87% Harbury Fields** (SP352604)

Harbury Fields Farm CV33 9JN
☎ **01926 612457**
e-mail: rdavis@harburyfields.co.uk
dir: M40 junct 12, B4451 (signed Kineton/Gaydon). 0.75m, right signed Lightborne. 4m, right at rdbt onto B4455 (signed Harbury). 3rd right by petrol station, site in 700yds (by two cottages)

Open Feb-19 Dec

Last arrival 20.00hrs Last departure noon

This developing park is in a peaceful farm setting with lovely countryside views. All pitches have hardstandings with electric and the facilities are spotless. It is well positioned for visiting Warwick and Leamington Spa as well as the exhibition centres at NEC Birmingham and Stoneleigh Park. Stratford is just ten miles away, and Upton House (NT) and Compton Valley Art Gallery are nearby. 3 acre site. 32 touring pitches. 31 hardstandings. Caravan pitches. Motorhome pitches.

Facilities: ⬡⊙🝨🖐❶
Services: 🔌🚽⛟
Within 3 miles: 🚴♻🛒

Notes: No traffic noise mdnt-07.30hrs.

LEISURE: 🏊 Indoor swimming pool 🏊 Outdoor swimming pool 🛝 Children's playground 🖐 Kid's club 🎾 Tennis court 🎱 Games room ⬛ Separate TV room 🏌 9/18 hole golf course ⛵ Boats for hire 🎬 Cinema 🎵 Entertainment 🎣 Fishing ◎ Mini golf 🏄 Watersports 🏏 Gym 🎯 Sports field **Spa** U Stables
FACILITIES: 🛁 Bath 🝨 Shower ⊙ Electric shaver 🝨 Hairdryer ❄ Ice Pack Facility ♻ Disabled facilities 🕿 Public telephone 🛒 Shop on site or within 200yds 🏪 Mobile shop (calls at least 5 days a week) 🔥 BBQ area 🝨 Picnic area 📶 Wi-fi 🖥 Internet access ♻ Recycling ❶ Tourist info 🝨 Dog exercise area

KINGSBURY — Map 10 SP29

Places to visit

Sarehole Mill, BIRMINGHAM, B13 0BD, 0121 777 6612 www.bmag.org.uk

Museum of the Jewellery Quarter, BIRMINGHAM, B18 6HA, 0121 554 3598 www.bmag.org.uk

► 70% Tame View Caravan Site

(SP209979)

Cliff B78 2DR
☎ 01827 873853
dir: *400yds off A51 (Tamworth-Kingsbury road), 1m N of Kingsbury. Into Cliff Hall Ln (opposite pub) to site*

Open all year

Last arrival 23.00hrs Last departure 23.00hrs

A secluded spot overlooking the Tame Valley and river, sheltered by high hedges. Sanitary facilities are minimal but clean on this small park. The site is popular with many return visitors who like a peaceful, basic site. 5 acre site. 5 touring pitches. Caravan pitches. Motorhome pitches. Tent pitches.

AA Pubs & Restaurants nearby: Chapel House Restaurant With Rooms, ATHERSTONE, CV9 1EY, 01827 718949

Facilities: ☼ 🗑 🚿 🛒 ♻

Services: 🛢

Within 3 miles: ↯ ⚓ 🎡 ✒ ◎ 🗑 🛢 U

Notes: ⊘ No noise after mdnt. Dogs must be kept on leads. Fishing.

WOLVEY — Map 11 SP48

Places to visit

Arbury Hall, NUNEATON, CV10 7PT, 024 7638 2804 www.arburyestate.co.uk

Jaguar Daimler Heritage Centre, COVENTRY, CV5 9DR, 024 7640 1291 www.jdht.com

Great for kids: Lunt Roman Fort, COVENTRY, CV8 3AJ, 024 7678 6142 www.luntromanfort.org

►►► 78% Wolvey Villa Farm Caravan & Camping Site *(SP428869)*

LE10 3HF
☎ 01455 220493 & 220630
dir: *M6 junct 2, B4065 follow Wolvey signs. Or M69 junct 1 & follow Wolvey signs*

🚐 £14-£17 �"£14-£17 ▲

Open all year

Last arrival 22.00hrs Last departure noon

A level grass site surrounded by trees and shrubs, on the border of Warwickshire and Leicestershire. This quiet country site has its own popular fishing lake, and is convenient for visiting Coventry and Leicester. 7 acre site. 110 touring pitches. 24 hardstandings. Caravan pitches. Motorhome pitches. Tent pitches.

AA Pubs & Restaurants nearby: The Bell Inn, MONKS KIRBY, CV23 0QY, 01788 832352

The Pheasant, WITHYBROOK, CV7 9LT, 01455 220480

Leisure: 🎱 🎣

Facilities: 🏋 ☉ 🎠 ☼ ♿ ◐ 🗑 🚿 🛒 ❼

Services: 🔌 🗑 🛢 🧴 T 🛢

Within 3 miles: ↯ 🎡 ✒ 🗑 🛢 U

Notes: ⊘ No twin axles. Dogs must be kept on leads. Putting green, off licence.

WEST MIDLANDS

MERIDEN — Map 10 SP28

Places to visit

Blakesley Hall, BIRMINGHAM, B25 8RN, 0121 464 2193 www.bmag.org.uk

Aston Hall, BIRMINGHAM, B6 6JD, 0121 675 4722 www.bmag.org.uk/aston -hall

►►►► 92% Somers Wood Caravan Park *(SP225824)*

Best of British

Somers Rd CV7 7PL
☎ 01676 522978
e-mail: enquiries@somerswood.co.uk
dir: *M42 junct 6, A45 signed Coventry. Keep left (do not take flyover). Right onto A452 signed Meriden & Leamington. At next rdbt left onto B4102 (Hampton Lane). Site in 0.5m on left*

* 🚐 £18-£24 🚙 £18-£24

Open all year

Last arrival variable Last departure variable

A peaceful adults-only park set in the heart of England with spotless facilities. The park is well positioned for visiting the National Exhibition Centre (NEC), the NEC Arena and National Indoor Arena (NIA), and Birmingham is only 12 miles away. The park also makes an ideal touring base for Warwick, Coventry and Stratford-upon-Avon just 22 miles away. Please note that tents are not accepted. 4 acre site. 48 touring pitches. 48 hardstandings. Caravan pitches. Motorhome pitches.

AA Pubs & Restaurants nearby: The White Lion Inn, HAMPTON IN ARDEN, B92 0AA, 01675 442833

Facilities: 🏋 ☉ 🎠 ☼ ♿ ◐ WiFi ♻ ❼

Services: 🔌 🛢 🧴 T 🛢

Within 3 miles: ↯ ✒ 🗑 U

Notes: Adults only. No noise 22.30hrs-08.00hrs. Dogs must be kept on leads. Laundry service.

SERVICES: 🔌 Electric hook up 🗑 Launderette 🍷 Licensed bar 🛢 Calor Gas 🧴 Camping Gaz T Toilet fluid 🍽 Café/Restaurant 🍔 Fast Food/Takeaway
🔋 Battery charging 👶 Baby care ↯ Motorvan service point **ABBREVIATIONS:** BH/bank hols-bank holidays Etr-Easter Spring BH-Spring Bank Holiday dep-departure
fr-from hrs-hours m-mile mdnt-midnight rdbt-roundabout rs-restricted service wk-week wknd-weekend x-rds-cross roads ⊘ No credit cards ⊗ No dogs
👶 Children of all ages accepted See page 9 for details of the AA Camping Card Scheme

Isle of Wight

Generations of visitors to the Isle of Wight consistently say the same thing, that to go there is akin to stepping back to the 1950s and '60s. The pace of life is still gentle and unhurried and the place continues to exude that familiar salty tang of the sea we all remember from childhood, when bucket and spade holidays were an integral part of growing up. Small and intimate – just 23 miles by 13 miles – the Isle of Wight is just the place to get away-from-it-all.

● Coastal Path near the Needles

Being an island, it has a unique and distinctive identity. With its mild climate, long hours of sunshine and exuberant architecture, the Isle of Wight has something of a continental flavour. In the summer the place understandably gets very busy, especially during Cowes week in August – a key date in the country's sporting calendar. Elsewhere, seaside towns such as Ventnor, Shanklin and Sandown are popular during the season for their many and varied attractions.

Variety is the key on this delightful and much-loved holiday island. Queen Victoria made the place fashionable and popular when she and Prince Albert chose it as the setting for their summer home, Osborne House, and the island has never looked back. In recent years the steady increase in tourism has ushered in many new visitor attractions to meet the demands of the late 20th and early 21st centuries, but there are still the perennial old favourites. The Needles, the iconic series of chalk stacks, is a classic example, and just about everyone who has visited over the years can recall buying tubes of sand from nearby Alum Bay – a multi-coloured mix of white quartz, red iron oxide and yellow limonite.

▶

Walking and Cycling

Despite the large numbers of summer visitors, there are still plenty of places on the island where you can be alone and savour its tranquillity. The 65-mile Isle of Wight Coast Path allows walkers to appreciate the natural beauty and diversity of its coastal scenery. Much of the path in the southern half of the island is a relatively undemanding walk over sweeping chalk downs, and beyond Freshwater Bay the coast is often remote and essentially uninhabited. Completing the whole trail or just part of it is the ideal way to discover the island's coastline without the aggravation. Mostly, the route is over cliff-top paths, tracks, sea walls and esplanades. Nearly 40 miles of it is beside the coast, though the inland stretches are never far from the sea. However, beware of erosion and expect to find the path diverted in places. The Isle of Wight's hinterland may lack the sea views but the scenery is no less appealing. Here walkers can explore a vast and well publicised network of paths that reach the very heart of the island.

In all, the Isle of Wight has more than 500 miles of public rights of way and more than half the island is recognised as an Area of Outstanding Natural Beauty.

For cyclists there is also a good deal of choice. The Round the Island Cycle Route runs for 49 miles and takes advantage of quiet roads and lanes. There are starting points at Yarmouth, Cowes and Ryde and the route is waymarked with official Cycle Route blue signs.

Festivals and Events

Among a host of festivals and events held on the Isle of Wight throughout the year are:-
• The Real Ale Festival in May
• The Isle of Wight Walking Festival in May and the Isle of Wight Weekend Walking Festival held in October
• The Cycling Festival in September
• The Garlic Festival in August

For more information visit
www.islandbreaks.co.uk

• Cowes Week

● Osborne House

WIGHT, ISLE OF

BEMBRIDGE

See Whitecliff Bay

BRIGHSTONE Map 5 SZ48

NEW ►►►► 78% Grange Farm *(SZ421820)*

GOLD

Grange Chine PO30 4DA
☎ 01983 740296
e-mail: grangefarmholidays@gmail.com
dir: *From Freshwater Bay take A3055 towards Ventnor, 5m (pass Isle of Wight Pearl). Site approx 0.5m on right*

* 🚐 £13.50-£29.50 🚌 £13.50-£29.50
⛺ £13.50-£29.50

Open Mar-Oct

Last arrival noon Last departure noon

This family-run site is set in a stunning location on the south-west coast of the island in Brighstone Bay. The facilities are very good. For children there is an imaginative play area and a wide range of animals to see including llamas and water buffalo. This site is ideally located for those who like walking and cycling. There are static homes and camping pods for hire. 8 acre site. 60 touring pitches. Caravan pitches. Motorhome pitches. Tent pitches. 11 statics.

AA Pubs & Restaurants nearby: The Crown Inn, SHORWELL, PO30 3JZ, 01983 740293

COWES Map 5 SZ49

Places to visit

Osborne House, OSBORNE HOUSE, PO32 6JY, 01983 200022
www.english-heritage.org.uk/daysout/properties/osborne

Great for kids: Robin Hill Country Park, ARRETON, PO30 2NU, 01983 527352
www.robin-hill.com

84% Thorness Bay Holiday Park *(SZ448928)*

GOLD

Thorness PO31 8NJ
☎ 01983 523109
e-mail: holidaysales.thornessbay@park-resorts.com
web: www.park-resorts.com
dir: *On A3054 towards Yarmouth, 1st right after BMW garage, signed Thorness Bay*

🚐 🚌 ⛺

Open Apr-1 Nov

Last arrival anytime Last departure 10.00hrs

Splendid views of The Solent can be enjoyed from this rural park located just outside Cowes. A footpath leads directly to the coast, while on site there is an all-weather sports court, entertainment clubs for children, cabaret shows, and a bar for all the family. There are 23 serviced pitches, in the separate touring area, with TV boosters. 130 holiday homes are for hire. 148 acre site. 124 touring pitches. 21 hardstandings. 8 seasonal pitches. Caravan pitches. Motorhome pitches. Tent pitches. 560 statics.

AA Pubs & Restaurants nearby: The Fountain Inn, COWES, PO31 7AW, 01983 292397

Duke of York Inn, COWES, PO31 7BT, 01983 295171

The Folly, WHIPPINGHAM, PO32 6NB, 01983 297171

Leisure: 🏊 ⛺ ✋ ⚽ ♫

Facilities: 🛁 🚿 ⊙ 💨 ♿ 📞 [S] 🐕 Wi-fi 💻 ♻ ℹ

Services: 🔧 🧺 🍷 🔒 🌿 🍴 🛒

Within 3 miles: 🎣 🌊 [S] 🧺

Notes: Dogs must be kept on leads. Water slide.

see advert opposite

FRESHWATER Map 5 SZ38

Places to visit

Colemans Farm Park, PORCHFIELD, PO30 4LX, 01983 522831 www.colemansfarmpark.co.uk

Great for kids: Blackgang Chine Fantasy Park, BLACKGANG, PO38 2HN, 01983 730330
www.blackgangchine.com

►►►► 86% Heathfield Farm Camping *(SZ335879)*

GOLD

Heathfield Rd PO40 9SH
☎ 01983 407822
e-mail: web@heathfieldcamping.co.uk
dir: *2m W from Yarmouth ferry port on A3054, left to Heathfield Rd, entrance 200yds on right*

🚐 £13.50-£21.50 🚌 £13.50-£21.50 ⛺ £6-£8

Open May-Sep

Last arrival 20.00hrs Last departure 11.00hrs

A very good quality park with friendly and welcoming staff. There are lovely views across the Solent to Hurst Castle. The toilet facilities, the amenities, which include an excellent backpackers' area, and the very well maintained grounds, make this park amongst the best on the island. 10 acre site. 60 touring pitches. Caravan pitches. Motorhome pitches. Tent pitches.

AA Pubs & Restaurants nearby: The Red Lion, FRESHWATER, PO40 9BP, 01983 754925

The Stag at Offchurch, OFFCHURCH, CV33 9AQ, 01926 425801

The Red Lion, Hunningham, HUNNINGHAM, CV33 9DY, 01926 632715

Leisure: ⚽

Facilities: 🚿 ⊙ 💨 ❄ ♿ 📞 ⛩ 🐕 Wi-fi ♻ ℹ

Services: 🔧 🧺 🌿 ⚓

Within 3 miles: ⛳ 🚣 🎣 ◎ 🌊 [S] 🧺 Ω

Notes: Family camping only. Dogs must be kept on leads.

SERVICES: Electric hook up · Launderette · Licensed bar · Calor Gas · Camping Gaz · Toilet fluid · Café/Restaurant · Fast Food/Takeaway · Battery charging · Baby care · Motorvan service point · **ABBREVIATIONS:** BH/bank hols-bank holidays · Etr-Easter · Spring BH-Spring Bank Holiday · dep-departure · fr-from · hrs-hours · m-mile · mdnt-midnight · rdbt-roundabout · rs-restricted service · wk-week · wknd-weekend · x-rds-cross roads · No credit cards · No dogs · Children of all ages accepted · See page 9 for details of the AA Camping Card Scheme

NEWBRIDGE — Map 5 SZ48

Places to visit

Newtown Old Town Hall, NEWTOWN, PO30 4PA, 01983 531785
www.nationaltrust.org.uk/isleofwight

Brighstone Shop and Museum, BRIGHSTONE, PO30 4AX, 01983 740689
www.nationaltrust.org.uk/isleofwight

Great for kids: Yarmouth Castle, YARMOUTH, PO41 0PB, 01983 760678
www.english-heritage.org.uk/daysout/properties/yarmouth-castle

AA CAMPING CARD SITE

PREMIER PARK

▶▶▶▶▶ **92% The Orchards Holiday Caravan Park** (SZ411881)

Best of British GOLD

Main Rd PO41 0TS
☎ **01983 531331 & 531350**
e-mail: info@orchards-holiday-park.co.uk
web: www.orchards-holiday-park.co.uk
dir: A3054 from Yarmouth, right in 3m at Horse & Groom Inn. Follow signs to Newbridge. Entrance opposite post office. Or from Newport 6m via B3401

* ➡ £18-£32.50 ➡ £18-£32.50 ▲ £18-£32.50

Open 28 Mar-3 Nov

Last arrival 23.00hrs Last departure 11.00hrs

A really excellent, well-managed park set in a peaceful village location amid downs and meadowland, with glorious downland views. Pitches are terraced and offer a good provision of hardstandings, including water serviced pitches. There is a high quality facility centre offering excellent, spacious showers and family rooms, plus there is access for less able visitors to all site facilities and disabled toilets. The park has indoor and outdoor swimming pools, takeaway and licensed shop.

Static homes are available for hire and 'ferry plus stay' packages are on offer. 15 acre site. 171 touring pitches. 74 hardstandings. Caravan pitches. Motorhome pitches. Tent pitches. 65 statics.

AA Pubs & Restaurants nearby: The New Inn, SHALFLEET, PO30 4NS, 01983 531314

Leisure: 🏊🏊🎢🔍

Facilities: 🛁🚿⊙🍴☀️♿🕐🛒🔥🐕📶ℹ️

Services: 🔌🛢️🚽📞🍴🛒🏪🛗

Within 3 miles: ⚓🏪🛒

Notes: No cycling, no noise after mdnt. Dogs must be kept on leads. Table tennis room, poolside coffee shop.

NEWPORT — Map 5 SZ58

Places to visit

Carisbrooke Castle, CARISBROOKE, PO30 1XY, 01983 522107 www.english-heritage.org.uk/daysout/properties/carisbrooke-castle

Osborne House, OSBORNE HOUSE, PO32 6JY, 01983 200022 www.english-heritage.org.uk/daysout/properties/osborne

▶▶▶ **77% Riverside Paddock Camp Site** (SZ503911)

Dodnor Ln PO30 5TE
☎ **01983 821367 & 07962 400533**
e-mail: enquiries@riversidepaddock.co.uk
dir: From Newport take dual carriageway towards Cowes. At 1st rdbt take 3rd exit, immediately left at next rdbt. Follow until road meets National Cycle Route. Site on left

* ➡ fr £12 ➡ fr £12 ▲ fr £12

Open all year

Last arrival 20.00hrs Last departure 11.00hrs

Although fairly close to Newport this quiet campsite offers a really peaceful environment and has direct access to the national cycle route which runs from Newport to Cowes. The Medina River with its riverside walks is also nearby. The park's toilet facilities include two fully serviced unisex cubicles, good hardstandings many with electric plus spotless facilities. The location of the park makes it perfect for people who like to walk or to ride their bikes. 8 acre site. 28 touring pitches. 18 hardstandings. Caravan pitches. Motorhome pitches. Tent pitches. 5 tipis.

AA Pubs & Restaurants nearby: The White Lion, ARRETON, PO30 3AA, 01983 528479

Facilities: 🐕☀️♿🛒📶🖥️♻️ℹ️

Services: 📞

Within 3 miles: ⚓🎣🏊🎢🎿🛒🏪🐎

Notes: Adults only. 🚭 No loud music, no generators. Dogs must be kept on leads.

RYDE — Map 5 SZ59

Places to visit

Bembridge Windmill, BEMBRIDGE, PO35 5SQ, 01983 873945
www.nationaltrust.org.uk/isleofwight

Nunwell House & Gardens, BRADING, PO36 0JQ, 01983 407240

Great for kids: Robin Hill Country Park, ARRETON, PO30 2NU, 01983 527352
www.robin-hill.com

PREMIER PARK

▶▶▶▶▶ **92% Whitefield Forest Touring Park** (SZ604893)

GOLD

Brading Rd PO33 1QL
☎ **01983 617069**
e-mail: pat&louise@whitefieldforest.co.uk
web: www.whitefieldforest.co.uk
dir: From Ryde follow A3055 towards Brading, after Tesco rdbt site 0.5m on left

➡ ➡ ▲ fr £15

Open 28 Mar-6 Oct

Last arrival 21.00hrs Last departure 11.00hrs

This park is beautifully laid out in Whitefield Forest, and offers a wide variety of pitches, all of which have electricity. It offers excellent modern facilities, which are spotlessly clean. The park takes great care in retaining the natural beauty of the forest, and is a haven for wildlife; red squirrels can be spotted throughout the park, including on the nature walk. 23 acre site. 90 touring pitches. 38 hardstandings. Caravan pitches. Motorhome pitches. Tent pitches.

Leisure: 🎢

Facilities: 🛁⊙🍴☀️♿🛒📶♻️ℹ️

Services: 🔌🛢️🚽🛒📞🏪🛗

Within 3 miles: ⚓🎣🏊🎢🎿🛒🏪

Notes: Dogs must be kept on leads.

LEISURE: 🏊 Indoor swimming pool 🏊 Outdoor swimming pool 🎢 Children's playground 👦 Kid's club 🎾 Tennis court 🔍 Games room 📺 Separate TV room ⚓ 9/18 hole golf course ⛵ Boats for hire 🎬 Cinema 🎵 Entertainment 🎣 Fishing ◉ Mini golf 🎿 Watersports 💪 Gym 🏅 Sports field **Spa** 🐎 Stables
FACILITIES: 🛁 Bath 🚿 Shower ⊙ Electric shaver 🍴 Hairdryer ☀️ Ice Pack Facility ♿ Disabled facilities 📞 Public telephone 🛒 Shop on site or within 220yds 🏪 Mobile shop (calls at least 5 days a week) 🔥 BBQ area 🪑 Picnic area 📶 Wi-fi 🖥️ Internet access ♻️ Recycling ℹ️ Tourist info 🐕 Dog exercise area

►►► 83% *Roebeck Camping and Caravan Park* (SZ581903)

Gatehouse Rd, Upton Cross PO33 4BP
☎ **01983 611475 & 07930 992080**
e-mail: info@roebeck-farm.co.uk
dir: Right from Fishbourne ferry terminal (west of Ryde). At lights left onto A3054 towards Ryde. In outskirts straight on at 'All Through Traffic' sign. At end of Pellhurst Rd right into Upton Rd. Site 50yds beyond mini-rdbt

Open Apr-Nov

A quiet park in a country setting on the outskirts of Ryde offering very nice facilities, especially for campers, including an excellent dishwashing/kitchen cabin. The unique, ready-erected tipis, which are available for hire, add to the ambience of the site. There is also an excellent fishing lake. 4 acre site. 37 touring pitches. Caravan pitches. Tent pitches.

AA Pubs & Restaurants nearby: The Boathouse, SEAVIEW, PO34 5AW, 01983 810616

Facilities: ⛺☂☀🌳🚻🖥
Services: 🔌🗑
Within 3 miles: ↧⛵✎◎⛴🎣🎱🏌♆

ST HELENS   Map 5 SZ68

Places to visit

Brading The Experience, BRADING, PO36 0DQ, 01983 407286
www.bradingtheexperience.co.uk

Bembridge Windmill, BEMBRIDGE, PO35 5SQ, 01983 873945
www.nationaltrust.org.uk/isleofwight

Great for kids: Lilliput Antique Doll & Toy Museum, BRADING, PO36 0DJ, 01983 407231
www.lilliputmuseum.org.uk

87% *Nodes Point Holiday Park* (SZ636897)

Nodes Rd PO33 1YA
☎ **01983 872401**
e-mail: gm.nodespoint@park-resorts.com
web: www.park-resorts.com
dir: From Ryde take B3330 signed Seaview/Puckpool. At junct for Puckpool bear right. 1m past Road Side Inn in Nettlestone, site on left

Open Apr-Oct

Last arrival 21.00hrs Last departure 10.00hrs

A well-equipped holiday centre on an elevated position overlooking Bembridge Bay with direct access to the beach. The touring area is mostly sloping with some terraces. Activities are organised for youngsters, and there is entertainment for the whole family. Buses pass the main entrance road. The touring area has very well appointed, ready-erected tents for hire. Holiday homes are also available for hire or purchase. 16 acre site. 150 touring pitches. 4 hardstandings. 4 seasonal pitches. Caravan pitches. Motorhome pitches. Tent pitches. 195 statics.

AA Pubs & Restaurants nearby: The Crab & Lobster Inn, BEMBRIDGE, PO35 5TR, 01983 872244

Leisure: 🏊△🎯⚽🎵
Facilities: ➡⛺☉☂☀♿🛍🗑🌳🚻🖥
Services: 🔌🗑🍴🚿🍽♨
Within 3 miles: ↧⛵⛱✎◎⛴🎣🎱🏌♆

SANDOWN   Map 5 SZ58

Places to visit

Nunwell House & Gardens, BRADING, PO36 0JQ, 01983 407240

Bembridge Windmill, BEMBRIDGE, PO35 5SQ, 01983 873945
www.nationaltrust.org.uk/isleofwight

Great for kids: Dinosaur Isle, SANDOWN, PO36 8QA, 01983 404344 www.dinosaurisle.com

AA CAMPING CARD SITE

►►►► 79% Old Barn Touring Park (SZ571833)

Cheverton Farm, Newport Rd, Apse Heath PO36 9PJ
☎ **01983 866414**
e-mail: oldbarn@weltinet.com
dir: On A3056 from Newport, site on left after Apse Heath rdbt

⛺ £16-£25 ⛟ £16-£25 ⛺ £16-£25

Open May-Sep

Last arrival 21.00hrs Last departure noon

A terraced site with several secluded camping areas that are divided by hedges. This site is well positioned for visiting the eastern side of the island, and customers can be sure of a warm welcome from the friendly staff. Rallies are very welcome, plus there are three fully equipped tents for hire. 5 acre site. 60 touring pitches. 9 hardstandings. 6 seasonal pitches. Caravan pitches. Motorhome pitches. Tent pitches.

AA Pubs & Restaurants nearby: The Crab & Lobster Inn, BEMBRIDGE, PO35 5TR, 01983 872244

Leisure: △🎯▢
Facilities: ⛺☉☂☀♿🌳🚻🖥🖵♻🛈
Services: 🔌🗑🍴🚿🗂🍽♨
Within 3 miles: ↧⛵✎◎⛴🎣🎱🏌♆
Notes: Dogs must be kept on leads.

SANDOWN *continued*

► 78% Queenbower Dairy Caravan Park *(SZ567846)*

Alverstone Rd, Queenbower PO36 0NZ
☎ 01983 403840
e-mail: queenbowerdairy@btconnect.com
dir: *3m N of Sandown from A3056 right into Alverstone Rd, site 1m on left*

🚐 £7-£11 🚌 £7-£11 ⛺ £7-£11

Open May-Oct

A small site with basic amenities that will appeal to campers keen to escape the crowds and the busy larger sites. The enthusiastic owners keep the facilities very clean. 2.5 acre site. 20 touring pitches. Caravan pitches. Motorhome pitches. Tent pitches.

AA Pubs & Restaurants nearby: The Crab & Lobster Inn, BEMBRIDGE, PO35 5TR, 01983 872244

Facilities: ❄ 🏪

Services: 🔌 🔋

Within 3 miles: ⛳ ⛵ 🎣 ◎ 🏄 🏪 🌀

Notes: 🚫 Dogs must be exercised off site & kept on leads.

SHANKLIN — Map 5 SZ58

Places to visit

Shanklin Chine, SHANKLIN, PO37 6PF, 01983 866432 www.shanklinchine.co.uk

Ventnor Botanic Garden, VENTNOR, PO38 1UL, 01983 855397 www.botanic.co.uk

Great for kids: Dinosaur Isle, SANDOWN, PO36 8QA, 01983 404344 www.dinosaurisle.com

85% Lower Hyde Holiday Park *(SZ575819)*

Landguard Rd PO37 7LL
☎ 01983 866131
e-mail: holidaysales.lowerhyde@park-resorts.com
web: www.park-resorts.com
dir: *From Fishbourne ferry terminal follow A3055 to Shanklin. Site signed just past lake*

🚐 🚌 ⛺

Open Mar-end Oct

Last arrival 17.00hrs Last departure noon

A popular holiday park on the outskirts of Shanklin, close to the sandy beaches. There is an outdoor swimming pool and plenty of organised activities for youngsters of all ages. In the evening there is a choice of family entertainment. The touring facilities are located in a quiet area away from the main complex, with good views over the downs. Holiday homes are available for hire or purchase. 65 acre site. 151 touring pitches. 25 hardstandings. Caravan pitches. Motorhome pitches. Tent pitches.

AA Pubs & Restaurants nearby: The Bonchurch Inn, BONCHURCH, PO38 1NU, 01983 852611

The Taverners, GODSHILL, PO38 3HZ, 01983 840707

Leisure: 🏊 🌊 🛝 ✋ ⚽ 🏓 🎵

Facilities: 🛁 🚿 ❄ ♿ 📞 🏪 🪑 🐕 📶 ♻ ℹ

Services: 🔌 🌀 🍷 🧯 🍃 🍽 🔋 🛒 👶 ⬇

Within 3 miles: ⛳ ⛵ 🎬 🎣 ◎ 🏄 🏪 🌀 🐴

Notes: Dogs must be kept on leads.

see advert below

►►►► 81% Ninham Country Holidays *(SZ573825)*

Ninham PO37 7PL
☎ 01983 864243
e-mail: office@ninham-holidays.co.uk
dir: *Signed from A3056 (Newport to Sandown road)*

* 🚐 £17.25-£23.75 🚌 £17.25-£23.75 ⛺ £11.50-£21

Open May day BH-Sep

Last arrival 20.00hrs Last departure 10.00hrs

Enjoying a lofty rural position with fine country views, this delightful, spacious park occupies two separate, well-maintained areas in a country park setting near the sea and beach. An excellent new toilet and shower block opened in 2013 in The Orchards, which has a good layout of pitches, while Willow Brook is a separate camping area with more basic but adequate facilities. There is also a good outdoor pool, a games room and

LEISURE: 🏊 Indoor swimming pool 🌊 Outdoor swimming pool 🛝 Children's playground ✋ Kid's club 🎾 Tennis court 🏓 Games room 📺 Separate TV room ⛳ 9/18 hole golf course ⛵ Boats for hire 🎬 Cinema 🎵 Entertainment 🎣 Fishing ◎ Mini golf 🏄 Watersports 🏋 Gym ⚽ Sports field **Spa** 🐴 Stables
FACILITIES: 🛁 Bath 🚿 Shower 🪒 Electric shaver 💨 Hairdryer ❄ Ice Pack Facility ♿ Disabled facilities 📞 Public telephone 🏪 Shop on site or within 200yds 🚚 Mobile shop (calls at least 5 days a week) 🍖 BBQ area 🪑 Picnic area 📶 Wi-fi 💻 Internet access ♻ Recycling ℹ Tourist info 🐕 Dog exercise area

children's play area, and holiday static homes for hire. 12 acre site. 150 touring pitches. 4 hardstandings. Caravan pitches. Motorhome pitches. Tent pitches.

AA Pubs & Restaurants nearby: The Bonchurch Inn, BONCHURCH, PO38 1NU, 01983 852611

The Taverners, GODSHILL, PO38 3HZ, 01983 840707

Leisure: ⚓ ⚏ ⚙ 🔍

Facilities: 📶 ⊙ ✳ ⚐ 🕒 WiFi ♻ ℹ

Services: 🔌 🗑 🔒 ⌀ 🍽 🛒 ⚐

Within 3 miles: 🚶 ⚶ 🎣 🏌 ◎ ⚒ 🛒 🎯 U

Notes: Swimming pool & coarse fishing rules apply. Dogs must be kept on leads. Late night/ arrival area available.

►►► 80% Landguard Camping

(SZ580825)

Manor Rd PO37 7PJ
☎ **01983 863100**
e-mail: holidaysales.landguard@park-resorts.com
web: www.park-resorts.com
dir: *A3056 towards Sandown. After Morrisons on left, turn right into Whitecross Ln. Follow brown signs to site*

🚐 🚗 🅰

Open Mar-end Oct

Last arrival 17.00hrs Last departure noon

Owned by Park Resorts, this peaceful and secluded park offers good touring facilities. Customers here also have the benefit of using the swimming pool and entertainment facilities at Lower Hyde Holiday Park nearby. 142 touring pitches. 6 hardstandings. Caravan pitches. Motorhome pitches. Tent pitches.

AA Pubs & Restaurants nearby: The Bonchurch Inn, BONCHURCH, PO38 1NU, 01983 852611

The Taverners, GODSHILL, PO38 3HZ, 01983 840707

Leisure: ⚓ ⚏ ⚙ 🔍 🎵

Facilities: 📶 🍴 ✳ ⚐ 🕒 🖼 🛏 WiFi ♻ ℹ

Services: 🔌 🗑 🍴 🔒 ⌀ 🍽 🛒 🏪 🛒 ⚐

Within 3 miles: 🚶 ⚶ 🎣 🏌 ◎ ⚒ 🛒 🎯 U

Notes: Dogs must be kept on leads.

TOTLAND BAY
Map 5 SZ38

Places to visit

Dimbola Lodge Museum, FRESHWATER, PO40 9QE, 01983 756814 www.dimbola.co.uk

Mottistone Manor Garden, MOTTISTONE, PO30 4ED, 01983 741302 www.nationaltrust.org.uk/isleofwight

Great for kids: Yarmouth Castle, YARMOUTH, PO41 0PB, 01983 760678 www.english-heritage.org.uk/daysout/properties/yarmouth-castle

►►► 76% *Stoats Farm Caravan & Camping* (SZ324865)

PO39 0HE
☎ **01983 755258 & 753416**
e-mail: david@stoats-farm.co.uk
dir: *On Alum Bay road, 1.5m from Freshwater & 0.75m from Totland*

🚐 🚗 🅰

Open Apr-Oct

A friendly, personally run site in a quiet country setting close to Alum Bay, Tennyson Down and The Needles. It has good laundry and shower facilities, and the shop, although small, is well stocked. Popular with families, walkers and cyclists, it makes the perfect base for campers wishing to explore this part of the island. 10 acre site. 100 touring pitches. Caravan pitches. Motorhome pitches. Tent pitches.

AA Pubs & Restaurants nearby: The Red Lion, FRESHWATER, PO40 9BP, 01983 754925

Facilities: 📶 ⊙ 🍴 ✳ ⚐ 🕒 🛏 ℹ ⚙

Services: 🔌 🗑 🛒 ⚐

Within 3 miles: 🚶 ⚶ 🎣 ◎ ⚒ 🛒 🎯 U

Notes: No loud noise after 23.00hrs, no camp fires. Dogs must be kept on leads. Campers' fridge available.

WHITECLIFF BAY
Map 5 SZ68

84% Whitecliff Bay Holiday Park (SZ637862)

Hillway Rd, Bembridge PO35 5PL
☎ **01983 872671**
e-mail: holiday.sales@away-resorts.com
dir: *1m S of Bembridge, signed from B3395 in village*

* 🚐 £10-£49 🚗 £6-£49 🅰 £6-£49

Open Mar-end Oct (rs Off peak restricted facilities)

Last arrival 19.00hrs Last departure 10.30hrs

A large seaside complex on two sites, with camping on one and self-catering chalets and statics on the other. There is an indoor pool with flume and spa pool, and an outdoor pool with a kiddies' pool, a family entertainment club, and plenty of traditional on-site activities including crazy golf, an indoor soft play area and table tennis, plus a restaurant and a choice of bars. Activities include a 'My Active' programme for all the family in partnership with 'Fit4Life'. Access to a secluded beach from the park. The Canvas Village has 12 ready-erected tents for hire. Dogs are welcome. 49 acre site. 400 touring pitches. 50 hardstandings. Caravan pitches. Motorhome pitches. Tent pitches. 227 statics. 12 bell tents/ yurts.

AA Pubs & Restaurants nearby: The Crab & Lobster Inn, BEMBRIDGE, PO35 5TR, 01983 872244

Leisure: ⚓ ⚓ ⚏ 🔶 ⚙ 🔍 ⬜ 🎵

Facilities: 📶 ⊙ 🍴 ✳ ⚐ 🕒 🖼 🛏 WiFi 🖥 ♻ ℹ

Services: 🔌 🗑 🍴 🔒 ⌀ 🅃 🍽 🛒 🏪 🛒 ⚐

Within 3 miles: 🚶 ⚶ 🎣 ◎ ⚒ 🛒 🎯 U

Notes: Adults & families only. Dogs must be kept on leads. Sauna, sunbed, sports TV lounge.

WOOTTON BRIDGE — Map 5 SZ59

Places to visit

Osborne House, OSBORNE HOUSE, PO32 6JY, 01983 200022 www.english-heritage.org.uk/daysout/properties/osborne

Bembridge Windmill, BEMBRIDGE, PO35 5SQ, 01983 873945 www.nationaltrust.org.uk/isleofwight

Great for kids: Robin Hill Country Park, ARRETON, PO30 2NU, 01983 527352 www.robin-hill.com

►►► 83% Kite Hill Farm Caravan & Camping Park (SZ549906)

Firestone Copse Rd PO33 4LE
☎ 01983 882543 & 883261
e-mail: welcome@kitehillfarm.co.uk
dir: *Signed from A3054 at Wootton Bridge, between Ryde & Newport*

🚐 £14-£17.50 🚌 £14-£17.50 ▲ £14-£17.50

Open all year

Last arrival anytime Last departure anytime

The park, on a gently sloping field, is tucked away behind the owners' farm, just a short walk from the village and attractive river estuary. The facilities are excellent and very clean. This park provides a nice relaxing atmosphere for a stay on the island. Rallies are welcome. 12.5 acre site. 50 touring pitches. 10 hardstandings. Caravan pitches. Motorhome pitches. Tent pitches.

AA Pubs & Restaurants nearby: The Folly, WHIPPINGHAM, PO32 6NB, 01983 297171

The Fountain Inn, COWES, PO31 7AW, 01983 292397

Leisure: /A\
Facilities: 🏕⊙❄👫🐕 🤙🚜 ❼
Services: 🚐🗑⌀🚙
Within 3 miles: 🚶🎣🐴🎿◎🏊🏇🛒🗑🔄 ∪

Notes: Owners must clean up after their pets. Dogs must be kept on leads.

WROXALL — Map 5 SZ57

Places to visit

Appuldurcombe House, WROXALL, PO38 3EW, 01983 852484 www.english-heritage.org.uk/daysout/properties/appuldurcombe-house

Great for kids: Blackgang Chine Fantasy Park, BLACKGANG, PO38 2HN, 01983 730330 www.blackgangchine.com

PREMIER PARK

►►►►► 85%

Appuldurcombe Gardens Holiday Park (SZ546804)

Appuldurcombe Rd PO38 3EP
☎ 01983 852597
e-mail: info@appuldurcombegardens.co.uk
dir: *From Newport take A3020 towards Shanklin & Ventnor. Through Rookley & Godshill. Right at Whiteley Bank rdbt towards Wroxall village, then follow brown signs*

🚐🚌▲

Open Mar-Nov

Last arrival 21.00hrs Last departure 11.00hrs

This well-appointed park is set in a unique setting fairly close to the town of Ventnor. It has modern and smart facilities including a spotless toilet and shower block, and a very tasteful lounge bar and function room. There is an excellent, screened outdoor pool and paddling pool plus café and shop. The site is close to cycle routes and is only 150 yards from the bus stop making it perfect for those with a motorhome or those not wanting to use their car. Static caravans and apartments are also available for hire. 14 acre site. 130 touring pitches. 40 hardstandings. Caravan pitches. Motorhome pitches. Tent pitches. 40 statics.

AA Pubs & Restaurants nearby: The Pond Café, VENTNOR, PO38 1RG, 01983 855666

Leisure: 🏊 /A\ 🎣
Facilities: 🚿🏕⊙❄👫🐕🗑🍴 Wi-Fi 🔄 ❼
Services: 🚐🗑🚙⌀☎🍴🛒🚜🔄
Within 3 miles: 🚶🐴🎣🏊◎🏇🛒🗑🔄 ∪

Notes: No skateboards. Dogs must be kept on leads. Entertainment in high season.

YARMOUTH

See Newbridge

WILTSHIRE

AMESBURY — Map 5 SU14

Places to visit

Stonehenge, SP4 7DE, 0870 333 1181 www.english-heritage.org.uk/daysout/properties/stonehenge

Heale Gardens, MIDDLE WOODFORD, SP4 6NT, 01722 782504 www.healegarden.co.uk

Great for kids: Wilton House, WILTON [NEAR SALISBURY], SP2 0BJ, 01722 746714 www.wiltonhouse.com

►►► 82% Stonehenge Touring Park (SU061456)

Orcheston SP3 4SH
☎ 01980 620304
e-mail: stay@stonehengetouringpark.com
dir: *From A360 towards Devizes turn right, follow lane, site at bottom of village on right*

🚐 £10-£16 🚌 £10-£16 ▲ £10-£27

Open all year

Last arrival 19.00hrs Last departure 11.00hrs

A quiet site adjacent to the small village of Orcheston near the centre of Salisbury Plain and four miles from Stonehenge. There's an excellent on-site shop. 2 acre site. 30 touring pitches. 13 hardstandings. Caravan pitches. Motorhome pitches. Tent pitches.

Leisure: /A\
Facilities: 🏕⊙❄👫🗑 Wi-Fi 🔄 ❼
Services: 🚐🗑🚙⌀☎🚜⌀
Within 3 miles: 🗑🔄

Notes: No noise after 23.00hrs. Dogs must be kept on leads.

BERWICK ST JAMES
Map 5 SU03

Places to visit
Stonehenge, SP4 7DE, 0870 333 1181
www.english-heritage.org.uk/daysout/
properties/stonehenge

Heale Gardens, MIDDLE WOODFORD, SP4 6NT,
01722 782504 www.healegarden.co.uk

AA CAMPING CARD SITE

NEW ►► 86%
Stonehenge Campsite

(SU077405)

SP3 4TQ
☎ 07786 734732 & 07880 746514
e-mail: stay@stonehengecampsite.co.uk
dir: *From Stonehenge take A303 W, 3m. Through
Winterbourne Stoke. Left onto B3083 towards
Berwick St James. Site on left in 0.5m*

⊞ £13-£20 ⊞ £13-£20 ▲ £13-£22

Open all year

Last arrival 21.00hrs Last departure noon

This small site is split into three areas. The lower
area has hardstandings for caravans or
motorhomes, as well as two luxury camping pods.
The middle field is for tents, both for families and
individuals, whilst the top area is for larger
groups who can perhaps enjoy some of their
holiday time sitting around open fires or fire pits.
The site is close to Stonehenge and there are
plenty of good walks from the campsite. 4 acre
site. 35 touring pitches. 10 hardstandings.
Caravan pitches. Motorhome pitches. Tent pitches.
2 wooden pods.

Facilities: ♦♦♣❄☐⚲♦Ⱳ❤️❶
Services: ⊞⊤☐⊞
Within 3 miles: ♦⚲U

Notes: No noise after 23.00hrs. Dogs must be
kept on leads. Fire pit & mobile fire pits.

CALNE
Map 4 ST97

Places to visit
Avebury Manor & Garden, AVEBURY, SN8 1RF,
01672 539250 www.english-heritage.org.uk/
daysout/properties/avebury

Bowood House & Gardens, CALNE, SN11 0LZ,
01249 812102 www.bowood.org

Great for kids: Alexander Keiller Museum,
AVEBURY, SN8 1RF, 01672 539250
www.nationaltrust.org.uk

►►► 78% Blackland Lakes Holiday &
Leisure Centre *(ST973687)*

Stockley Ln SN11 0NQ
☎ 01249 810943
e-mail: enquiries@blacklandlakes.co.uk
web: www.blacklandlakes.co.uk
dir: *From Calne take A4 E for 1.5m, right at camp
sign. Site 1m on left*

* ⊞ £11-£20.50 ⊞ £13-£20.50 ▲ £11-£20.50

Open all year (rs 30 Oct-1 Mar pre-paid bookings
only)

Last arrival 22.00hrs Last departure noon

A rural site surrounded by the North and West
Downs. The park is divided into several paddocks
separated by hedges, trees and fences, and there
are two well-stocked carp fisheries for the angling
enthusiast. There are some excellent walks close
by, and the interesting market town of Devizes is
just a few miles away. 15 acre site. 180 touring
pitches. 16 hardstandings. 25 seasonal pitches.
Caravan pitches. Motorhome pitches. Tent pitches.

AA Pubs & Restaurants nearby: The White Horse,
CALNE, SN11 8RG, 01249 813118

Red Lion Inn, LACOCK, SN15 2LQ, 01249 730456

The George Inn, LACOCK, SN15 2LH,
01249 730263

Leisure: ⌂
Facilities: ♦☉❄⚿☐⚲♦
Services: ⊞☐♦⊘⊤⊞⚲
Within 3 miles: ⚲⚲☐⚲U

Notes: No noise after 22.30hrs, no loud music, no
groups of under 25s. Dogs must be kept on leads.
Wildfowl sanctuary, cycle trail.

LACOCK
Map 4 ST96

Places to visit
Lacock Abbey, Fox Talbot Museum & Village,
LACOCK, SN15 2LG, 01249 730459
www.nationaltrust.org.uk/lacock

Corsham Court, CORSHAM, SN13 0BZ,
01249 701610 www.corsham-court.co.uk

►►►► 82% Piccadilly Caravan Park
(ST913683)

Folly Lane West SN15 2LP
☎ 01249 730260
e-mail: piccadillylacock@aol.com
dir: *4m S of Chippenham just past Lacock. Exit
A350 signed Gastard. Site 300yds on left*

⊞ £18-£20 ⊞ £18-£20 ▲ £18-£23.50

Open Etr & Apr-Oct

Last arrival 21.00hrs Last departure noon

A peaceful, pleasant site, well established and
beautifully laid-out, close to the village of Lacock.
Both the facilities and the grounds are
immaculately maintained; there is very good
screening. A section of the park has now been
developed to provide spacious pitches especially
for tents, complete with its own toilet and shower
block. 2.5 acre site. 41 touring pitches. 12
hardstandings. Caravan pitches. Motorhome
pitches. Tent pitches.

AA Pubs & Restaurants nearby: Red Lion Inn,
LACOCK, SN15 2LQ, 01249 730456

The George Inn, LACOCK, SN15 2LH,
01249 730263

Leisure: ⌂☺
Facilities: ♦☉♣❄☉♦Ⱳ❤️❶
Services: ⊞☐♦⊘⚲
Within 3 miles: ⚲⊞⚲☐⚲U

Notes: ☺ Dogs must be kept on leads.

LANDFORD Map 5 SU21

Places to visit

Furzey Gardens, MINSTEAD, SO43 7GL,
023 8081 2464 www.furzey-gardens.org

Mottisfont Abbey & Garden, MOTTISFONT,
SO51 0LP, 01794 340757
www.nationaltrust.org.uk/mottisfontabbey

Great for kids: Paultons Park, OWER, SO51 6AL,
023 8081 4442
www.paultonspark.co.uk

►►►► 83% *Greenhill Farm Caravan & Camping Park* (SU266183)

Greenhill Farm, New Rd SP5 2AZ
☎ 01794 324117
e-mail: info@greenhillholidays.co.uk
dir: M27 junct 2, A36 towards Salisbury, approx 3m after Hampshire/Wiltshire border, (pass Shoe Inn pub on right, BP garage on left) take next left into New Rd, signed Nomansland, 0.75m on left

Open all year

Last arrival 21.30hrs Last departure 11.00hrs

A tranquil, well-landscaped park hidden away in unspoilt countryside on the edge of the New Forest National Park. Pitches overlooking the fishing lake include hardstandings and are for adults only. The other section of the park is for families and includes a play area, games room and an excellent toilet and shower block. This site is also well placed for visiting Paultons Family Theme Park at Ower. 13 acre site. 160 touring pitches. 45 hardstandings. Caravan pitches. Motorhome pitches. Tent pitches.

Leisure: ⚙ ⌕
Facilities: ⌂ ⊙ 🅿 ⚹ ⚐ ⚘ 🄵 🎿 ♻ ⓘ
Services: ⚑ 🗐 🔒 ⊘ 🎅 ⛟ 🖤
Within 3 miles: ⚲ 🅿 ⊚ 🄵 🖤 ∪

Notes: No noise after 23.00hrs. Dogs must be kept on leads. Disposable BBQs.

SALISBURY Map 5 SU12

See also Amesbury

Places to visit

Salisbury & South Wiltshire Museum, SALISBURY, SP1 2EN, 01722 332151
www.salisburymuseum.org.com

Salisbury Cathedral, SALISBURY, SP1 2EJ, 01722 555120 www.salisburycathedral.org.uk

Great for kids: The Medieval Hall, SALISBURY, SP1 2EY, 01722 412472
www.medieval-hall.co.uk

►►►► 87% **Coombe Touring Park** (SU099282)

Race Plain, Netherhampton SP2 8PN
☎ 01722 328451
e-mail: enquiries@coombecaravanpark.co.uk
dir: A36 onto A3094, 2m SW, site adjacent to Salisbury racecourse

Open 3 Jan-20 Dec (rs Oct-May shop closed)

Last arrival 21.00hrs Last departure noon

A very neat and attractive site adjacent to the racecourse with views over the downs. The park is well landscaped with shrubs and maturing trees, and the very colourful beds are stocked from the owner's greenhouse. A comfortable park with a superb luxury toilet block, and four static holiday homes for hire. 3 acre site. 50 touring pitches. 6 hardstandings. Caravan pitches. Motorhome pitches. Tent pitches. 4 statics.

AA Pubs & Restaurants nearby: The Wig and Quill, SALISBURY, SP1 2PH, 01722 335665

Leisure: ⚙
Facilities: ⌂ ⊙ 🅿 ⚹ ⚐ 🄵 ⓘ
Services: ⚑ 🗐 ⊘ 🖤
Within 3 miles: ⚲ 🄵 🖤 ∪

Notes: ⊗ No disposable BBQs or fires, no mini motorbikes, no noise between 23.00hrs-07.00hrs. Dogs must be kept on leads. Children's bathroom.

►►► 79% *Alderbury Caravan & Camping Park* (SU197259)

Southampton Rd, Whaddon SP5 3HB
☎ 01722 710125
e-mail: alderbury@aol.com
dir: Follow Whaddon signs from A36, 3m from Salisbury. Site opposite The Three Crowns pub

Open all year

Last arrival 21.00hrs Last departure 12.30hrs

A pleasant, attractive park set in the village of Whaddon not far from Salisbury. The small site is well maintained by friendly owners, and is ideally positioned near the A36 for overnight stops to and from the Southampton ferry terminals. 2 acre site. 39 touring pitches. 12 hardstandings. Caravan pitches. Motorhome pitches. Tent pitches. 1 static.

AA Pubs & Restaurants nearby: Salisbury Seafood & Steakhouse, SALISBURY, SP1 3TE, 01722 417411

Old Mill, SALISBURY, SP2 8EU, 01722 327517

The Cloisters, SALISBURY, SP1 2DH, 01722 338102

Facilities: ⌂ ⊙ ⚹ ⚐ ⓘ
Services: ⚑ 🗐 🔒 ⊘ 🖤
Within 3 miles: ⚲ ⚘ ⊟ 🅿 🄵 🖤 ∪

Notes: No open fires. Dogs must be kept on leads. Microwave & electric kettle available.

TROWBRIDGE

Places to visit

Great Chalfield Manor and Garden, BRADFORD-ON-AVON, SN12 8NH, 01225 782239
www.nationaltrust.org.uk

The Courts Garden, HOLT, BA14 6RR,
01225 782875 www.nationaltrust.org.uk

Great for kids: Longleat Safari & Adventure Park, LONGLEAT, BA12 7NW, 01985 844400
www.longleat.co.uk

TROWBRIDGE
Map 4 ST85

►► 74% Stowford Manor Farm
(ST810577)

Stowford, Wingfield BA14 9LH
☎ **01225 752253**
e-mail: stowford1@supanet.com
dir: *From Trowbridge take A366 W towards Radstock. Site on left in 3m*

* ⊞ £14-£16 ⊞ £14-£16 ▲ £14-£16

Open Etr-Oct

A very simple farm site set on the banks of the River Frome behind the farm courtyard. The owners are friendly and relaxed, and the park enjoys a similarly comfortable ambience. Farleigh & District Swimming Club, one of the few remaining river swimming clubs, is just half a mile from the site. 1.5 acre site. 15 touring pitches. Caravan pitches. Motorhome pitches. Tent pitches.

AA Pubs & Restaurants nearby: George Inn, NORTON ST PHILIP, BA2 7LH, 01373 834224

Facilities: 🏕🛒⊕❄🚿💧♻

Services: 🔌🍴📧

Within 3 miles: 🚶♨🎣♿🏊🛍🎲⛵

Notes: No open fires. Dogs must be kept on leads. Fishing, boating.

WESTBURY
Map 4 ST85

Places to visit

Great Chalfield Manor and Garden, BRADFORD-ON-AVON, SN12 8NH, 01225 782239 www.nationaltrust.org.uk

The Courts Garden, HOLT, BA14 6RR, 01225 782875 www.nationaltrust.org.uk

►►►► 83% Brokerswood
Country Park *(ST836523)*

Brokerswood BA13 4EH
☎ **01373 822238**
e-mail: info@brokerswoodcountrypark.co.uk
web: www.brokerswoodcountrypark.co.uk
dir: *M4 junct 17, S on A350. Right at Yarnbrook to Rising Sun pub at North Bradley, left at rdbt. Left on bend approaching Southwick, 2.5m, site on right*

* ⊞ £15-£30 ⊞ £15-£30 ▲ £15-£30

Brokerswood Country Park

Open Apr-4 Nov

Last arrival 21.30hrs Last departure 11.00hrs

A popular site on the edge of an 80-acre woodland park with nature trails, fishing lakes and a good range of activities including archery, tree climbing and kayaking. The adventure playground offers plenty of fun for all ages, and there is a miniature railway, an indoor play centre and a café. There are high quality toilet facilities and fully-equipped, ready-erected tents are available for hire. 5 acre site. 69 touring pitches. 21 hardstandings. Caravan pitches. Motorhome pitches. Tent pitches.

AA Pubs & Restaurants nearby: The Full Moon at Rudge, RUDGE, BA11 2QF, 01373 830936

The Bell Inn, GREAT CHEVERELL, SN10 5TH, 01380 813277

Leisure: 🎣

Facilities: 🚿🏕⊕🛒❄♿🛍🔥♻ ❓

Services: 🔌🛢🍴🍴🔌📧🍴📧🛒⛟

Within 3 miles: ♨🛍

Notes: Families only. Dogs must be kept on leads.

WORCESTERSHIRE

HONEYBOURNE

Places to visit

Kiftsgate Court Garden, MICKLETON, GL55 6LN, 01386 438777 www.kiftsgate.co.uk

Hidcote Manor Garden, MICKLETON, GL55 6LR, 01386 438333 www.nationaltrust.org.uk/hidcote

Great for kids: Anne Hathaway's Cottage, SHOTTERY, CV37 9HH, 01789 201844 www.shakespeare.org.uk

HONEYBOURNE
Map 10 SP14

PREMIER PARK

►►►►► 83% Ranch
Caravan Park *(SP113444)*

Station Rd WR11 7PR
☎ **01386 830744**
e-mail: enquiries@ranch.co.uk
dir: *From village x-rds towards Bidford, site 400mtrs on left*

* ⊞ £24-£28 ⊞ £24-£28

Open Mar-Nov (rs Mar-May & Sep-Nov swimming pool closed, shorter club hours)

Last arrival 20.00hrs Last departure noon

An attractive and well-run park set amidst farmland in the Vale of Evesham and landscaped with trees and bushes. Tourers have their own excellent facilities in two locations, and the use of an outdoor heated swimming pool in peak season. There is also a licensed club serving meals. Please note that this site does not accept tents. 12 acre site. 120 touring pitches. 46 hardstandings. 20 seasonal pitches. Caravan pitches. Motorhome pitches. 218 statics.

AA Pubs & Restaurants nearby: The Fleece Inn, BRETFORTON, WR11 7JE, 01386 831173

The Ebrington Arms, EBRINGTON, GL55 6NH, 01386 593223

Leisure: 🏊🏇🎣⚽🎱🏓🎵

Facilities: 🏕⊕🛒❄♿🛍🔥🖥♻ ❓

Services: 🔌🛢🍴🍴🔌📧🍴📧🛒⛟

Within 3 miles: 🚶♨🛍⛵

Notes: No unaccompanied minors. Dogs must be kept on leads.

WORCESTER
Map 10 SO85

Places to visit

City Museum & Art Gallery, WORCESTER, WR1 1DT,
01905 25371
www.museumsworcestershire.org.uk

The Greyfriars, WORCESTER, WR1 2LZ,
01905 23571 www.nationaltrust.org.uk

Great for kids: West Midland Safari & Leisure
Park, BEWDLEY, DY12 1LF, 01299 402114
www.wmsp.co.uk

▶▶▶ **87% Peachley Leisure
Touring Park** (SO807576)

**Peachley Ln, Lower Broadheath
WR2 6QX**
☎ **01905 641309 & 07764 540803**
e-mail: peachleyleisure@live.co.uk
dir: *M5 junct 7, A44 (Worcester ring road) towards
Leominster. Exit at sign for Elgar's Birthplace
Museum. Pass museum, at x-rds turn right. In
0.75m at T-junct turn left. Park signed on right*

* 🚐 fr £16 🚌 fr £16 ⛺ fr £12

Open all year

Last arrival 21.30hrs Last departure noon

The park is set in its own area in the grounds of
Peachley Farm. It has all hardstanding and fully
serviced pitches. There are two fishing lakes, and
a really excellent quad bike course. The park
provides a peaceful haven, and is an excellent
base from which to explore the area, which
includes the Elgar Museum, Worcester Races and
Victorian Fayre; it is also convenient for Malvern's
Three Counties Showground. 8 acre site. 82
touring pitches. 82 hardstandings. Caravan
pitches. Motorhome pitches. Tent pitches.

AA Pubs & Restaurants nearby: The Talbot,
KNIGHTWICK, WR6 5PH, 01886 821235

The Bear & Ragged Staff, BRANSFORD, WR6 5JH,
01886 833399

Leisure: ⚽ **Facilities:** 🏈☉☀♿🐕📶 🖥 ♻

Services: 🚰🔋 🛒🍽

Within 3 miles: ⚓🎏🎣♨🎱🎰🎮∪

Notes: No skateboards, no riding of motorbikes or
scooters. Dogs must be kept on leads.

SERVICES: 🔌 Electric hook up 🧺 Launderette 🍷 Licensed bar 🔋 Calor Gas ⊘ Camping Gaz T Toilet fluid 🍽 Café/Restaurant 🍔 Fast Food/Takeaway
🔋 Battery charging 🍼 Baby care ⚐ Motorvan service point **ABBREVIATIONS:** BH/bank hols-bank holidays Etr-Easter Spring BH-Spring Bank Holiday dep-departure
fr-from hrs-hours m-mile mdnt-midnight rdbt-roundabout rs-restricted service wk-week wknd-weekend x-rds-cross roads ⊗ No credit cards ⊗ No dogs
👪 Children of all ages accepted See page 9 for details of the AA Camping Card Scheme

Yorkshire

There is nowhere in the British Isles quite like Yorkshire. By far the largest county, and with such scenic and cultural diversity, it is almost a country within a country. For sheer scale, size and grandeur, there is nowhere to beat it.

● Staithes

Much of it in the spectacular Pennines, Yorkshire is a land of castles, grand houses, splendid rivers, tumbling becks and historic market towns. But it is the natural, unrivalled beauty of the Yorkshire Dales and the North York Moors that captures the heart and leaves a lasting impression. Surely no-one could fail to be charmed by the majestic landscapes of these two much-loved National Parks.

The Dales
Wherever you venture in the Yorkshire Dales, stunning scenery awaits you; remote emerald green valleys, limestone scars and timeless villages of charming stone cottages. The Dales, beautifully represented in the books of James Herriot, are characterised and complemented by their rivers – the Wharfe, Ribble, Ure, Nidd and Swale among them.

Touring this glorious region reveals the broad sweep of Wensleydale, the delights of Arkengarthdale and the charming little villages of Swaledale. There is also the spectacular limestone country of the western Dales – the land of the Three Peaks. Perhaps here, more than anywhere else in the area, ▶

there is a true sense of space and freedom. This is adventure country – a place of endless views and wild summits.

The Moors

To the east lies another sprawling landscape – the North York Moors. This is where the purple of the heather gives way to the grey expanse of

● Mausoleum at Castle Howard

the North Sea. Covering 554 square miles (1,436km) and acknowledged as an internationally important site for upland breeding birds, the North York Moors National Park is a vast, intricately-woven tapestry of heather moorland, narrow valleys, rolling dales, broad-leaved woodland and extensive conifer forests. Few places in Britain offer such variety and breadth of terrain.

Extending for 36 miles (58km), the North Yorkshire and Cleveland Heritage Coast forms the Park's eastern boundary. The popular holiday resorts of Whitby and Scarborough are the two largest settlements on this stretch of coastline, which is rich in fossils and minerals and protected for its outstanding natural beauty and historic interest.

Further south

To the south of the North York Moors is the beautiful city of York, its history stretching back 2,000 years. At its heart stands the minster, constructed between 1220 and 1470 and the largest medieval church in northern Europe. There is so much to see and do in this ancient, vibrant city that you can easily lose track of time.

Farther south, despite the relics of the county's industrial heritage, is Yorkshire's magical *Last of the Summer Wine* country. The BBC's long-running and much-loved comedy series, *Last of the Summer Wine*, ran for 37 years and was filmed in and around the town of Holmfirth, near Huddersfield.

Walking and Cycling

Not surprisingly, Yorkshire offers a myriad of circular walks and long-distance trails throughout the county. For the more ambitious walker there is the Pennine Way, which runs through Yorkshire from top to bottom, from the Scottish Borders as far south as Derbyshire. The 81-mile (130km) Dales Way, another popular route, is a perfect way to explore the magnificent scenery of Wharfedale, Ribblesdale and Dentdale, while the 50-mile (80km) Calderdale Way offers a fascinating insight into the Pennine heartland of industrial West Yorkshire.

Yorkshire also boasts a great choice of cycle routes. You can cycle to York on the track bed of the former King's Cross to Edinburgh railway line, or ride along a 20-mile (32.2km) stretch of the former Whitby to Scarborough line, looping around Robin Hood's Bay. There are also cycle routes through the Yorkshire Wolds, Dalby Forest in the North York Moors National Park and around Castle Howard, the magnificent estate near Malton where Evelyn Waugh's *Brideshead Revisited* was filmed.

Festivals and Events

- The long established Jorvik Viking Festival is held in York in February and lasts eight days. It celebrates Viking heritage with various lectures, arts and crafts and river events.
- Easter Monday is the date for Ossett's Coal Carrying Championships where competitors carry a sack of coal through the streets.
- November sees the Yorkshire Antiques and Art Fair in Harrogate. This event includes various indoor stalls, as well as displays of glass and ceramics.
- The Yorkshire Dales has numerous events and festivals throughout the year, including the Masham Arts Festival in October every two years the Lunesdale Agricultural Show in August and the Grassington Festival of Music & Arts in June.

● St Hilda's Abbey, Whitby

● Damflask Reservoir

YORKSHIRE, EAST RIDING OF

BRANDESBURTON
Map 17 TA14

Places to visit

Beverley Guildhall, BEVERLEY, HU17 9AU, 01482 392783 www.eastriding.gov.uk/museums

Burton Constable Hall, SPROATLEY, HU11 4LN, 01964 562400 www.burtonconstable.com

►►►► 82% Blue Rose Caravan Country Park *(TA110464)*

Star Carr Ln YO25 8RU
☎ **01964 543366 & 07504 026899**
e-mail: info@bluerosepark.com
dir: *From A165 at rdbt into New Rd signed Brandesburton (becomes Star Carr Ln). Approx 1m, site on left*

* 🚐 £15-£22 🚃 £15-£22

Open all year

Last arrival 20.00hrs Last departure noon

A neat and well maintained adult-only site well placed for visiting Hornsea and the Yorkshire coastline. The park is within walking distance of Brandesburton and offers an idyllic stopover for caravanners wanting a peaceful break in the countryside. 12 acre site. 58 touring pitches. 58 hardstandings. 44 seasonal pitches. Caravan pitches. Motorhome pitches. 36 statics.

Facilities: �ba ⊙ & 🎡 ⛲ ┬ 🛒 WiFi ♻ ❶

Services: 🔌 🚽 🧺 🚿 🚰 T 🔱

Within 3 miles: 🎣 🚤 🎿 ◎ 🛥 🏧 🎿 ⛵ ∪

Notes: Adults only. Dogs must be kept on leads.

►►► 82% *Dacre Lakeside Park*
(TA118468)

YO25 8RT
☎ **0800 1804556 & 01964 543704**
e-mail: dacrepark@btconnect.com
dir: *Off A165 bypass, midway between Beverley & Hornsea*

🚐 🚃 🛖

Open Mar-Oct

Last arrival 21.00hrs Last departure noon

A large lake popular with watersports enthusiasts is the focal point of this grassy site, which offers predominantly seasonal pitches - only four touring pitches are available. The clubhouse offers indoor activities; there's a fish and chip shop, a pub and a Chinese takeaway in the village, which is within

walking distance. The six-acre lake is used for windsurfing, sailing, kayaking, canoeing and fishing. Camping pods are available for hire. 8 acre site. 120 touring pitches. 110 seasonal pitches. Caravan pitches. Motorhome pitches. Tent pitches. 110 statics. 9 wooden pods.

Leisure: 🌊 ⚽ ⛱ 🎵

Facilities: �ba ⊙ ⛲ ✳ & 🎡 ┬ WiFi 🖥

Services: 🔌 🚽 🧺 🚿 🚰 T 🔱

Within 3 miles: 🎣 🚤 ◎ 🛥 🏧 🎿 ⛵ ∪

Notes: No noise 23.00hrs-08.00hrs, no craft with engines on lake.

BRIDLINGTON
Map 17 TA16

See also Rudston

Places to visit

Sewerby Hall & Gardens, BRIDLINGTON, YO15 1EA, 01262 673769 www.eastriding.gov.uk/sewerby

Hornsea Museum, HORNSEA, HU18 1AB, 01964 533443 www.hornseamuseum.com

Great for kids: Flamingo Land Theme Park & Zoo, KIRBY MISPERTON, YO17 6UX, 01653 668287 www.flamingoland.co.uk

►►► 83% Fir Tree Caravan Park
(TA195702)

Jewison Ln, Sewerby YO16 6YG
☎ **01262 676442**
e-mail: info@flowerofmay.com
dir: *1.5m from centre of Bridlington. Left onto B1255 at Marton Corner. Site 600yds on left*

🚐 £18-£24 🚃 £18-£24 🛖 £18-£24

Open Mar-Oct (rs Early & late season bar & entertainment restrictions)

Last arrival dusk Last departure noon

Fir Tree Park, a large, mainly static park, has a well laid out touring area (seasonal pitches only) with its own facilities. It has an excellent swimming pool complex and the adjacent bar-cum-conservatory serves meals. There is also a family bar, games room and outdoor children's play area. 22 acre site. 45 touring pitches. 45 hardstandings. 45 seasonal pitches. Caravan pitches. Motorhome pitches. Tent pitches. 400 statics.

AA Pubs & Restaurants nearby: The Seabirds Inn, FLAMBOROUGH, YO15 1PD, 01262 850242

Leisure: 🌊 🛝 ⛱ 🎵

Facilities: � ⊙ ✳ & 🕐 🏧 ┬ WiFi ♻ ❶

Services: 🔌 🚽 🧺 🚿 🍴 🔱

Within 3 miles: 🎣 🚤 ◎ 🛥 ∪

Notes: No noise after mdnt. Dogs accepted by prior arrangement only. Dogs must be kept on leads.

KINGSTON UPON HULL

See Sproatley

RUDSTON
Map 17 TA06

Places to visit

Sewerby Hall & Gardens, BRIDLINGTON, YO15 1EA, 01262 673769 www.eastriding.gov.uk/sewerby

►►►► 80% Thorpe Hall Caravan & Camping Site
(TA108677)

Thorpe Hall YO25 4JE
☎ **01262 420393 & 420574**
e-mail: caravansite@thorpehall.co.uk
dir: *From Bridlington take B1253 W for 5m*

* 🚐 £12.50-£25.50 🚃 £12.50-£25.50 🛖 £9-£22

Open Mar-Oct

Last arrival 22.00hrs Last departure noon

A delightful, peaceful small park within the walled gardens of Thorpe Hall yet within a few miles of the bustling seaside resort of Bridlington. The site offers a games field, its own coarse fishery, pitch and putt, and a games and TV lounge. There are numerous walks locally. 4.5 acre site. 92 touring pitches. Caravan pitches. Motorhome pitches. Tent pitches.

AA Pubs & Restaurants nearby: The Seabirds Inn, FLAMBOROUGH, YO15 1PD, 01262 850242

Leisure: 🛝 ⚽ ⛱ 🖵

Facilities: 🛁 � ⊙ ⛲ ✳ & 🕐 🍴 ┬ 🏧 WiFi ♻ ❶

Services: 🔌 🚽 🛁 🧺 T 🔱

Within 3 miles: ⛱ 🏧 🎿 ∪

Notes: No ball games (field provided), no noise 23.00hrs-08.00hrs. Well behaved dogs only. Dogs must be kept on leads. Golf practice area (4.5 acres).

LEISURE: 🌊 Indoor swimming pool 🌊 Outdoor swimming pool 🛝 Children's playground 🤚 Kid's club 🎾 Tennis court 🎱 Games room 🖵 Separate TV room 🏌 9/18 hole golf course 🚤 Boats for hire 🎬 Cinema 🎵 Entertainment 🎣 Fishing ◎ Mini golf 🎿 Watersports 🏋 Gym 🎯 Sports field Spa ∪ Stables
FACILITIES: 🛁 Bath 🚿 Shower ⊙ Electric shaver ⛲ Hairdryer ✳ Ice Pack Facility & Disabled facilities 🕐 Public telephone 🏧 Shop on site or within 200yds 🚚 Mobile shop (calls at least 5 days a week) 🍖 BBQ area 🏧 Picnic area WiFi Wi-fi 🖥 Internet access ♻ Recycling ❶ Tourist info 🎯 Dog exercise area

SKIPSEA — Map 17 TA15

Places to visit

Hornsea Museum, HORNSEA, HU18 1AB,
01964 533443 www.hornseamuseum.com

Sewerby Hall & Gardens, BRIDLINGTON, YO15 1EA,
01262 673769 www.eastriding.gov.uk/sewerby

87% Skirlington Leisure Park *(TA188528)*

YO25 8SY
☎ 01262 468213 & 468466
e-mail: info@skirlington.com
dir: *From M62 towards Beverley then Hornsea. Between Skipsea & Hornsea on B1242*

🚐 🚃

Open Mar-Oct

Last arrival 20.00hrs Last departure 11.00hrs

A large, well-run seaside park set close to the beach in partly-sloping meadowland with young trees and shrubs. The site has five newly refurbished toilet blocks, a supermarket and an amusement arcade, plus occasional entertainment in the clubhouse. The wide range of family amenities includes an indoor heated swimming pool complex with sauna, steam room and gym. A 10-pin bowling alley and indoor soft play area for children are added attractions. 24 acre site. 285 touring pitches. 15 hardstandings. 100 seasonal pitches. Caravan pitches. Motorhome pitches. 450 statics.

Leisure: 🏊 ⛳ 🎱 🐾 🎿 🎰 🎵
Facilities: 🚿 📶 ⊙ 🎯 ♿ 🔧 🕐 💲 🚽 🐕 WiFi 🖥 ♻ ❓
Services: 🔌 🔋 🍳 🍴 🛢 ⊘ 🍽 🔋 🍔
Within 3 miles: 🎣 ✈ ⛳ ◎ ⛷ 💲 🏇 🏌 ⛹

Notes: No noise after 22.00hrs. Dogs must be kept on leads. Putting green, fishing lake, Sunday market.

83% *Skipsea Sands* *(TA176563)*

Mill Ln YO25 8TZ
☎ 01262 468210
e-mail: skipsea.sands@park-resorts.com
web: www.park-resorts.com
dir: *From A165 (Bridlington to Kingston upon Hull road) 8m S of Bridlington take B1242 to Skipsea. Follow Skipsea Sands signed to left just after sharp left bend*

🚐 🚃 ▲

Open Apr-Oct

Last arrival noon Last departure 10.00hrs

A busy and popular holiday park just a stone's throw from the beach, and offering an excellent range of leisure and entertainment facilities for families and couples. There's a good, well maintained touring area with clean toilets and neat grass pitches. A dedicated team ensure that standards are high across the park. 91 touring pitches. Caravan pitches. Motorhome pitches. Tent pitches.

SPROATLEY — Map 17 TA13

Places to visit

Burton Constable Hall, SPROATLEY, HU11 4LN,
01964 562400 www.burtonconstable.com

Maritime Museum, LOWESTOFT, NR32 1XG,
01502 561963
www.lowestoftmaritimemuseum.org.uk

Great for kids: The Deep, KINGSTON UPON HULL,
HU1 4DP, 01482 381000 www.thedeep.co.uk

▶▶▶▶ 85% Burton Constable Holiday Park & Arboretum *(TA186357)*

Old Lodges HU11 4LJ
☎ 01964 562508
e-mail: info@burtonconstable.co.uk
dir: *A165 onto B1238 to Sproatley. Follow signs to site*

* 🚐 £17-£30 🚃 £17-£30 ▲ £17-£27

Open Mar-mid Feb (rs Mar-Nov tourers & tents)

Last arrival 22.00hrs Last departure 14.00hrs

Within the extensive estate of Constable Burton Hall, this large and secluded holiday destination provides a wide range of attractions including fishing and boating on the lakes, a snooker room, and a licensed bar with a designated family room. The grounds are immaculately maintained and generous pitch density offers good privacy. 90 acre site. 140 touring pitches. 20 hardstandings. 14 seasonal pitches. Caravan pitches. Motorhome pitches. Tent pitches. 350 statics.

Leisure: 🎱 🐾 🎣 🎵
Facilities: 📶 ⊙ 🎯 ♿ 🕐 💲 🏇 ♻ ❓
Services: 🔌 🔋 🍳 🛢 ⊘ 🚽 🔋 ⚡
Within 3 miles: 🎣 ⛳ 💲 🏇 ⛹

Notes: No skateboards or rollerblades. Dogs must be kept on leads. Two 10-acre fishing lakes.

SERVICES: 🔌 Electric hook up 🔋 Launderette 🍳 Licensed bar 🛢 Calor Gas ⊘ Camping Gaz T Toilet fluid 🍽 Café/Restaurant 🍔 Fast Food/Takeaway 🔋 Battery charging 👶 Baby care ⚡ Motorvan service point **ABBREVIATIONS:** BH/bank hols-bank holidays Etr-Easter Spring BH-Spring Bank Holiday dep-departure fr-from hrs-hours m-mile mdnt-midnight rdbt-roundabout rs-restricted service wk-week wknd-weekend x-rds-cross roads ⊗ No credit cards ⊗ No dogs 👪 Children of all ages accepted See page 9 for details of the AA Camping Card Scheme

TUNSTALL — Map 17 TA33

Places to visit

Burton Constable Hall, SPROATLEY, HU11 4LN, 01964 562400 www.burtonconstable.com

80% Sand le Mere Holiday Village (TA305318)

Southfield Ln HU12 0JF
☎ 01964 670403
e-mail: info@sand-le-mere.co.uk
dir: From Hull A1033 signed Withernsea, B1362 (Hull Rd) signed Hedon. In Hedon continue on B3162 towards Withernsea. Turn left signed Roos. In Roos take B1242. Turn left at brown sign for site. In Tunstall right at T-junct, right into Seaside Ln to site

Open Mar-Nov

Last arrival 23.00hrs Last departure 11.00hrs

Ideally located between Withernsea and Bridlington, this £4 million development provides first-class indoor leisure facilities with swimming pool, entertainment and a kiddies' soft ball area. The touring pitches are level and surrounded by maturing trees and shrubs. 135 acre site. 72 touring pitches. 51 hardstandings. Caravan pitches. Motorhome pitches. Tent pitches.

Leisure: Spa
Facilities:
Services:
Within 3 miles:

Notes: No noise after 23.00hrs, speed limits around site, no camp fires. Dogs must be kept on leads.

see advert below

WITHERNSEA

Places to visit

Wilberforce House, KINGSTON UPON HULL, HU1 1NE, 01482 300300 www.hullcc.gov.uk

Maister House, KINGSTON UPON HULL, HU1 1NL, 01723 879900 www.nationaltrust.org.uk

Great for kids: The Deep, KINGSTON UPON HULL, HU1 4DP, 01482 381000 www.thedeep.co.uk

WITHERNSEA — Map 17 TA32

80% Withernsea Sands (TA335289)

Waxholme Rd HU19 2BS
☎ 0871 664 9803
e-mail: withernsea.sands@park-resorts.com
web: www.park-resorts.com
dir: M62 junct 38, A63 through Hull. At end of dual carriageway, right onto A1033, follow Withernsea signs. Through village, left at mini-rdbt onto B1242. 1st right at lighthouse. Site 0.5m on left

Open Apr-Oct (rs BH & peak wknds sports available)

Last arrival 22.00hrs Last departure noon

Touring is very much at the heart of this holiday park's operation, with 100 all-electric pitches and additional space for tents. The owners, Park Resorts, continue to upgrade the facilities and attractions, and the leisure complex with its futuristic design is especially impressive. 115 touring pitches. Caravan pitches. Motorhome pitches. Tent pitches. 400 statics.

Leisure:
Facilities:
Services:
Within 3 miles:

Notes: No noise between 23.00hrs-07.00hrs. Dogs must be kept on leads. Extension leads & utilities from reception.

LEISURE: Indoor swimming pool Outdoor swimming pool Children's playground Kid's club Tennis court Games room Separate TV room 9/18 hole golf course Boats for hire Cinema Entertainment Fishing Mini golf Watersports Gym Sports field Spa Stables
FACILITIES: Bath Shower Electric shaver Hairdryer Ice Pack Facility Disabled facilities Public telephone Shop on site or within 200yds Mobile shop (calls at least 5 days a week) BBQ area Picnic area Wi-fi Internet access Recycling Tourist info Dog exercise area

YORKSHIRE, NORTH

ACASTER MALBIS   Map 16 SE54

Places to visit

Yorkshire Museum, YORK, YO1 7FR, 01904 551800 www.yorkshiremuseum.org.uk

York Art Gallery, YORK, YO1 7EW, 01904 687687 www.york.trust.museum

Great for kids: Jorvik Viking Centre, YORK, YO1 9WT, 01904 615505 www.jorvik-viking-centre.com

▶▶▶ **74% Moor End Farm** (SE589457)

YO23 2UQ
☎ **01904 706727 & 07860 405872**
e-mail: moorendfarm@acaster99.fsnet.co.uk
dir: Follow signs to Acaster Malbis from junct of A64 & A1237 at Copmanthorpe

* 🚐 £16-£20 🚐 £16-£20 ▲ £15-£22

Open Etr or Apr-Oct

Last arrival 22.00hrs Last departure 12.00hrs

A very pleasant farm site with modernised facilities including a heated family/disabled shower room. A river boat pickup to York is 150 yards from the site entrance, and the village inn and restaurant are a short stroll away. A very convenient site for visiting York Racecourse. 1 acre site. 12 touring pitches. Caravan pitches. Motorhome pitches. Tent pitches. 6 statics.

AA Pubs & Restaurants nearby: Ye Old Sun Inn, COLTON, LS24 8EP, 01904 744261

Leisure: ⚒

Facilities: 🖍☺🏳✳👶🅰♻

Services: 🔌🖭🛒

Within 3 miles: 🎣🏇🗓🎱🍴

Notes: 🐕 Dogs must be kept on leads. Use of fridge, freezer & microwave.

ALLERSTON   Map 19 SE88

Places to visit

Scarborough Castle, SCARBOROUGH, YO11 1HY, 01723 372451 www.english-heritage.org.uk/daysout/properties/scarborough-castle

Pickering Castle, PICKERING, YO6 5AB, 01751 474989 www.english-heritage.org.uk/daysout/properties/pickering-castle

Great for kids: Sea Life & Marine Sanctuary, SCARBOROUGH, YO12 6RP, 01723 373414 www.sealife.co.uk

AA CAMPING CARD SITE

PREMIER PARK

▶▶▶▶▶ **86% Vale of Pickering Caravan Park**
(SE879808)

GOLD

Carr House Farm YO18 7PQ
☎ **01723 859280**
e-mail: tony@valeofpickering.co.uk
dir: On B1415, 1.75m from A170 (Pickering-Scarborough road)

* 🚐 £16-£26 🚐 £16-£26 ▲ £13-£26

Open 5 Mar-3 Jan (rs Mar)

Last arrival 21.00hrs Last departure 11.30hrs

A well-maintained, spacious family park with excellent facilities including a well-stocked shop and immaculate toilet facilities, and an interesting woodland walk. Younger children will enjoy the attractive play area, while the large ball sports area will attract older ones. The park is set in open countryside bounded by hedges, has manicured grassland and stunning seasonal floral displays, and is handy for the North Yorkshire Moors and the attractions of Scarborough. 13 acre site. 120 touring pitches. 100 hardstandings. Caravan pitches. Motorhome pitches. Tent pitches.

AA Pubs & Restaurants nearby: The New Inn, THORNTON LE DALE, YO18 7LF, 01751 474226

The Coachman Inn, SNAINTON, YO13 9PL, 01723 859231

Leisure: ⚒☺

Facilities: 🛏🖍☺🏳✳👶🕙🅱🅰🛒♻ ❓

Services: 🔌🖭🛢🚿🕙🛒🛗

Within 3 miles: 🎣🏇🎱🍴🗓🎱

Notes: No open fires or Chinese lanterns, no noise after 23.00hrs. Microwave available.

ALNE   Map 19 SE46

Places to visit

Castle Howard, MALTON, YO60 7DA, 01653 648333 www.castlehoward.co.uk

Sutton Park, SUTTON-ON-THE-FOREST, YO61 1DP, 01347 810249 www.statelyhome.co.uk

Great for kids: National Railway Museum, YORK, YO26 4XJ, 01904 621261 www.nrm.org.uk

PREMIER PARK

▶▶▶▶▶ **80% Alders Caravan Park** (SE497654)

Home Farm YO61 1RY
☎ **01347 838722**
e-mail: enquiries@homefarmalne.co.uk
dir: From A19 exit at Alne sign, in 1.5m left at T-junct, 0.5m site on left in village centre

🚐 £20-£22 🚐 £20 ▲ fr £20

Open Mar-Oct

Last arrival 21.00hrs Last departure 14.00hrs

A tastefully developed park on a working farm with screened pitches laid out in horseshoe-shaped areas. This well-designed park offers excellent toilet facilities including a bathroom and fully-serviced washing and toilet cubicles. A woodland area and a water meadow are pleasant places to walk. 12 acre site. 87 touring pitches. 6 hardstandings. 71 seasonal pitches. Caravan pitches. Motorhome pitches. Tent pitches. 2 wooden pods.

AA Pubs & Restaurants nearby: The Black Bull Inn, BOROUGHBRIDGE, YO51 9AR, 01423 322413

The Dining Room Restaurant, BOROUGHBRIDGE, YO51 9AR, 01423 326426

continued

SERVICES: 🔌 Electric hook up 🖭 Launderette 🍷 Licensed bar 🛢 Calor Gas 🔥 Camping Gaz 🅃 Toilet fluid 🍴 Café/Restaurant 🍔 Fast Food/Takeaway 🔋 Battery charging 🍼 Baby care 🛗 Motorvan service point **ABBREVIATIONS:** BH/bank hols-bank holidays Etr-Easter Spring BH-Spring Bank Holiday dep-departure fr-from hrs-hours m-mile mdnt-midnight rdbt-roundabout rs-restricted service wk-week wknd-weekend x-rds-cross roads 🚫 No credit cards 🚫 No dogs ♿ Children of all ages accepted See page 9 for details of the AA Camping Card Scheme

ALNE *continued*

Facilities: 🛁🚿☉☂🗝✳🕐🛗🖥🚐🔌♻ ❶

Services: 🔌🗑 🛢🚮⛟

Within 3 miles: ⚓🏌🔟🛒

Notes: Max 2 dogs per pitch. Dogs must be kept on leads. Summer house. Bread, milk & other farm produce for sale.

BISHOP MONKTON — Map 19 SE36

Places to visit

Newby Hall & Gardens, RIPON, HG4 5AE, 01423 322583 www.newbyhall.com

Fountains Abbey & Studley Royal, RIPON, HG4 3DY, 01765 608888 www.english-heritage.org.uk/daysout/properties/st-marys-church-studley-royal

Great for kids: Stump Cross Caverns, PATELEY BRIDGE, HG3 5JL, 01756 752780 www.stumpcrosscaverns.co.uk

►►► 75% Church Farm Caravan Park *(SE328660)*

Knaresborough Rd HG3 3QQ

☎ 01765 676578 & 07861 770164

e-mail: churchfarmcaravan@btinternet.com

dir: *From A61 at x-rds follow Bishop Monkton signs. 1.25m to village. At x-rds right into Knaresborough Rd, site approx 500mtrs on right*

✳ 🚐 £15-£17 🚏 £15-£17 🛖 £12-£17

Open Mar-Oct

Last arrival 22.30hrs Last departure 15.30hrs

A very pleasant rural site on a working farm, on the edge of the attractive village of Bishop Monkton with its well-stocked shop and pubs. Whilst very much a place to relax, there are many attractions close by, including Fountains Abbey, Newby Hall, Ripon and Harrogate. 4 acre site. 45 touring pitches. 3 hardstandings. Caravan pitches. Motorhome pitches. Tent pitches. 3 statics.

AA Pubs & Restaurants nearby: The Black Bull Inn, BOROUGHBRIDGE, YO51 9AR, 01423 322413

The Dining Room Restaurant, BOROUGHBRIDGE, YO51 9AR, 01423 326426

Facilities: 🚿☉☂✳🕐🛗♻ ❶

Services: 🔌🖐⛟

Within 3 miles: ⚓🏌🔟🛒🕐

Notes: ⊘ No ball games. Dogs must be kept on leads.

BOLTON ABBEY — Map 19 SE05

Places to visit

RHS Garden Harlow Carr, HARROGATE, HG3 1QB, 01423 565418 www.rhs.org.uk/harlowcarr

Parcevall Hall Gardens, GRASSINGTON, BD23 6DE, 01756 720311 www.parcevallhallgardens.co.uk

Great for kids: Stump Cross Caverns, PATELEY BRIDGE, HG3 5JL, 01756 752780 www.stumpcrosscaverns.co.uk

►►►► 76% Howgill Lodge *(SE064592)*

GOLD

Barden BD23 6DJ

☎ 01756 720655

e-mail: info@howgill-lodge.co.uk

dir: *From Bolton Abbey take B6160 signed Burnsall. In 3m at Barden Tower right signed Appletreewick. 1.5m at phone box right into lane to site*

✳ 🚐 fr £20 🚏 fr £20 🛖 fr £20

Open mid Mar-Oct

Last arrival 20.00hrs Last departure noon

A beautifully-maintained and secluded site offering panoramic views of Wharfedale. The spacious hardstanding pitches are mainly terraced, and there is a separate tenting area with numerous picnic tables. There are three toilet facilities spread throughout the site, with the main block (including private, cubicled wash facilities) appointed to a high standard. There is also a well-stocked shop. 4 acre site. 40 touring pitches. 20 hardstandings. Caravan pitches. Motorhome pitches. Tent pitches.

AA Pubs & Restaurants nearby: The Devonshire Brasserie & Bar, BOLTON ABBEY, BD23 6AJ, 01756 710710

The Fleece, ADDINGHAM, LS29 0LY, 01943 830491

The Craven Arms, APPLETREEWICK, BD23 6DA, 01756 720270

CONSTABLE BURTON — Map 19 SE19

Places to visit

Middleham Castle, MIDDLEHAM, DL8 4RJ, 01969 623899 www.english-heritage.org.uk/daysout/properties/middleham-castle

Great for kids: Bedale Museum, BEDALE, DL8 1AA, 01677 427516 www.bedalemuseum.org.uk

►►►► 81% Constable Burton Hall Caravan Park *(SE158907)*

DL8 5LJ

☎ 01677 450428

e-mail: caravanpark@constableburton.com

dir: *From Leyburn on A684 towards Bedale, approx 3m site on left*

🚐 £19-£24 🚏 £19-£24

Open Apr-Oct

Last arrival 20.00hrs Last departure noon

A pretty site in the former deer park of the adjoining Constable Burton Hall, screened from the road by the park walls and surrounded by mature trees in a quiet rural location. The laundry is housed in a converted 18th-century deer barn and there is a pub and restaurant opposite; seasonal pitches are available. Please note that this site does not accept tents. 10 acre site. 120 touring pitches. Caravan pitches. Motorhome pitches.

AA Pubs & Restaurants nearby: Sandpiper Inn, LEYBURN, DL8 5AT, 01969 622206

The White Swan, MIDDLEHAM, DL8 4PE, 01969 622093

Black Swan Hotel, MIDDLEHAM, DL8 4NP, 01969 622221

The Wensleydale Heifer, WEST WITTON, DL8 4LS, 01969 622322

Facilities: 🚿☉☂✳🕐🛗🚐📶🖥♻ ❶

Services: 🔌🗑 🛢🖐

Within 3 miles: ⚓🛒

Notes: No commercial vehicles, no games. Dogs must be kept on leads.

Leisure: ✚

Facilities: 🚿☉☂✳🕐🛗🚐📶♻ ❶

Services: 🔌🗑 🛢🚮🇹🖐

Within 3 miles: 🏌🔟🛒

Notes: Dogs must be kept on leads.

LEISURE: 🏊 Indoor swimming pool 🏊 Outdoor swimming pool ⚠ Children's playground 👋 Kid's club ⚓ Tennis court 🎱 Games room 📺 Separate TV room 🏌 9/18 hole golf course 🎣 Boats for hire 🎬 Cinema 🎵 Entertainment 🎣 Fishing ◉ Mini golf 🏄 Watersports 🏋 Gym 🎯 Sports field Spa ∪ Stables
FACILITIES: 🛁 Bath 🚿 Shower ☉ Electric shaver 💈 Hairdryer ✳ Ice Pack Facility 🛗 Disabled facilities 🕐 Public telephone 🛒 Shop on site or within 200yds 🚐 Mobile shop (calls at least 5 days a week) 🍖 BBQ area 🪑 Picnic area 📶 Wi-fi 🖥 Internet access ♻ Recycling ❶ Tourist info 🐕 Dog exercise area

SERVICES: ⚡ Electric hook up ⬚ Launderette 🍸 Licensed bar 🛢 Calor Gas ⬭ Camping Gaz Ⓣ Toilet fluid 🍽 Café/Restaurant 🍟 Fast Food/Takeaway
🔋 Battery charging 🍼 Baby care ⚲ Motorvan service point **ABBREVIATIONS:** BH/bank hols-bank holidays Etr-Easter Spring BH-Spring Bank Holiday dep-departure
fr-from hrs-hours m-mile mdnt-midnight rdbt-roundabout rs-restricted service wk-week wknd-weekend x-rds-cross roads 🚫 No credit cards 🚫 No dogs
👪 Children of all ages accepted See page 9 for details of the AA Camping Card Scheme

FILEY
Map 17 TA18

Places to visit

Scarborough Castle, SCARBOROUGH, YO11 1HY, 01723 372451 www.english-heritage.org.uk/daysout/properties/scarborough-castle

Sea Life & Marine Sanctuary, SCARBOROUGH, YO12 6RP, 01723 373414 www.sealife.co.uk

90% Flower of May Holiday Park (TA085835)

Lebberston Cliff YO11 3NU
☎ 01723 584311
e-mail: info@flowerofmay.com
dir: Take A165 from Scarborough towards Filey. Site signed

⊟ £18-£24 ⊟ £18-£24 ▲ £18-£24

Open Etr-Oct (rs Early & late season restricted opening in café, shop & bars)

Last arrival dusk Last departure noon

A well-run, high quality family holiday park with top class facilities. This large landscaped park offers a full range of recreational activities, with plenty to occupy everyone. Grass and hard pitches are available, all on level ground, and arranged in avenues screened by shrubs. Enjoy the 'Scarborough Fair' museum, with its collection of restored fairground attractions, including rides, organs and vintage cars. 13 acre site. 300 touring pitches. 250 hardstandings. 100 seasonal pitches. Caravan pitches. Motorhome pitches. Tent pitches. 193 statics.

Leisure: 🏊🏊🎠⚽🎱📺🎵

Facilities: 🚿☀️✖️♿⏰🛠💲🍴🐕📶♻️ℹ️
Services: 🔌🚿🔧💧🚽📞🍴🛒🏧
Within 3 miles: ♿🎣⛳🏇⛵◎🎿💲💲🏇⛴

Notes: No noise after mdnt. 1 dog per pitch by arrangement only. Dogs must be kept on leads. Squash, bowling, basketball court, skate park.

see advert on page 331

81% Blue Dolphin Holiday Park (TA095829)

SILVER

Gristhorpe Bay YO14 9PU
☎ 0871 231 0893
e-mail: bluedolphin@haven.com
web: www.haven.com/bluedolphin
dir: On A165, 2m N of Filey

⊟ ⊟ ▲

Open mid Mar-end Oct (rs mid Mar-May & Sep-Oct some facilities may be reduced & outdoor pool closed)

Last arrival mdnt Last departure 10.00hrs

There are great cliff-top views to be enjoyed from this fun-filled holiday centre with an extensive and separate touring area. The emphasis is on non-stop entertainment, with organised sports and clubs, all-weather leisure facilities, heated swimming pools (with multi-slide), and plenty of well-planned amusements. Pitches are mainly on level or gently-sloping grass plus there are some fully serviced hardstandings. The beach is just two miles away. 85 acre site. 280 touring pitches. 20 seasonal pitches. Caravan pitches. Motorhome pitches. Tent pitches. 850 statics.

Leisure: 🏊🏊🎠⚽🎵
Facilities: 🚿◎♿⏰💲📶♻️ℹ️
Services: 🔌🚿🔧💧🚽📞🍴🏧🛒⛴
Within 3 miles: ♿⛳◎💲💲

Notes: No commercial vehicles, no bookings by persons under 21yrs unless a family booking. Max 2 dogs per booking, certain dog breeds banned. Dogs must be kept on leads.

see advert on opposite page

81% Primrose Valley Holiday Park (TA123778)

GOLD

YO14 9RF
☎ 0871 231 0892
e-mail: primrosevalley@haven.com
web: www.haven.com/primrosevalley
dir: Signed from A165 (Scarboroug to Bridlington road), 3m S of Filey

⊟ ⊟

Open mid Mar-end Oct

Last arrival anytime Last departure 10.00hrs

A large all-action holiday centre with a wide range of sports and leisure activities to suit everyone from morning until late in the evening. The touring area is completely separate from the main park with its own high quality amenity block. All touring pitches are fully serviced hardstandings with grassed awning strips. The touring area has its own reception and designated warden. 160 acre site. 50 touring pitches. 50 hardstandings. Caravan pitches. Motorhome pitches. 1514 statics.

Leisure: 🏊🏊🎠🖐⚽◎🎱🎵
Facilities: 🚿⛳♿⏰💲🍴📶💻♻️ℹ️
Services: 🔌🚿🔧💧🚽📞🍴🏧🛒
Within 3 miles: ♿🎣⛳◎💲💲

Notes: No commercial vehicles, no bookings by persons under 21yrs unless a family booking. Max 2 dogs per booking, certain dog breeds banned. Dogs must be kept on leads.

see advert on opposite page

LEISURE: 🏊 Indoor swimming pool 🏊 Outdoor swimming pool 🎠 Children's playground 🖐 Kid's club 🎾 Tennis court 🎱 Games room 📺 Separate TV room ⛳ 9/18 hole golf course 🚣 Boats for hire 🎣 Fishing ◎ Mini golf ⛵ Watersports 💪 Gym ⚽ Sports field Spa ⛴ Stables
FACILITIES: 🛁 Bath 🚿 Shower ☀️ Electric shaver ✂️ Hairdryer ✖️ Ice Pack Facility ♿ Disabled facilities ⏰ Public telephone 💲 Shop on site or within 200yds 🏪 Mobile shop (calls at least 5 days a week) 🍴 BBQ area 🌲 Picnic area 📶 Wi-fi 💻 Internet access ♻️ Recycling ℹ️ Tourist info 🐕 Dog exercise area

Blue Dolphin ★☆

Holiday Park, Filey, Yorkshire

Our favourite bits

- Heated pools with indoor multi-lane slide
- Family entertainment and kids' clubs
- Sports activities and facilities
- Sandy beach 3 miles from park
- 280 pitches on our grassy touring area
- We welcome

Save up to **50%** on 2014 holidays

Call: **0843 658 0453**   Quote: AABD   Go online at www.haventouring.com/aabd

Calls cost 5p per minute plus network extras.

Terms and conditions: Save up to 50% discount is available on selected Spring and Autumn dates in 2014. Full booking terms and conditions apply. Haven Holidays is a trading name of Bourne Leisure, registered in England and Wales, no 04011660. Registered office 1 Park Lane, Hemel Hempstead, Hertfordshire, HP2 4YL.

Primrose Valley ★☆

Holiday Park, nr. Filey, Yorkshire

Our favourite bits

- Large multi-level heated pool complex with fun pools and SplashZone
- Family entertainment and kids' clubs
- Sports activities and facilities
- Direct access to sandy bay below the park
- 50 pitches on our level and grassy touring area
- We welcome

Save up to **50%** on 2014 holidays

Call: **0843 658 0473**   Quote: AAPV   Go online at www.haventouring.com/aapv

Calls cost 5p per minute plus network extras.

Terms and conditions: Save up to 50% discount is available on selected Spring and Autumn dates in 2014. Full booking terms and conditions apply. Haven Holidays is a trading name of Bourne Leisure, registered in England and Wales, no 04011660. Registered office 1 Park Lane, Hemel Hempstead, Hertfordshire, HP2 4YL.

Reighton Sands ★☆

Holiday Park, nr. Filey, North Yorkshire

Our favourite bits

- Heated outdoor Lazy River and indoor pool
- Family entertainment and kids' clubs
- Sports activities and facilities
- 238 pitches on our grassy, gently sloping touring area
- We welcome

Save up to **50%** on 2014 holidays

Call: **0843 658 0475**   Quote: AARE   Go online at www.haventouring.com/aare

Calls cost 5p per minute plus network extras.

Terms and conditions: Save up to 50% discount is available on selected Spring and Autumn dates in 2014. Full booking terms and conditions apply. Haven Holidays is a trading name of Bourne Leisure, registered in England and Wales, no 04011660. Registered office 1 Park Lane, Hemel Hempstead, Hertfordshire, HP2 4YL.

SERVICES: 🔌 Electric hook up 🧺 Launderette 🍽 Licensed bar 🛢 Calor Gas ⛽ Camping Gaz T Toilet fluid 🍴 Café/Restaurant 🍟 Fast Food/Takeaway 🔋 Battery charging 🍼 Baby care ⚙ Motorvan service point **ABBREVIATIONS:** BH/bank hols-bank holidays Etr-Easter Spring BH-Spring Bank Holiday dep-departure fr-from hrs-hours m-mile mdnt-midnight rdbt-roundabout rs-restricted service wk-week wknd-weekend x-rds-cross roads ❌ No credit cards 🚫 No dogs 🐕 Children of all ages accepted See page 9 for details of the AA Camping Card Scheme

FILEY *continued*

79% Reighton Sands Holiday Park (TA142769)

Reighton Gap YO14 9SH
☎ 0871 231 0894
e-mail: reightonsands@haven.com
web: www.haven.com/reightonsands
dir: *On A165, 5m S of Filey at Reighton Gap, signed*

Open mid Mar-end Oct (rs mid Mar-May & Sep-Oct some facilities may be reduced)

Last arrival 22.00hrs Last departure 10.00hrs

A large, lively holiday centre with a wide range of entertainment and all-weather leisure facilities (including an indoor play area), located just a 10-minute walk from a long sandy beach. There are good all-weather pitches and a large tenting field. The site is particularly geared towards families with young children. 229 acre site. 238 touring pitches. 5 seasonal pitches. Caravan pitches. Motorhome pitches. Tent pitches. 800 statics.

Leisure: 🏊‍♀️🏊‍♀️🎠👋🎱🎵
Facilities: 🚿⊙🛁&🕐🛍🍴🅿🛎💻♻🅸
Services: 🔌🗑🔧🆃🍴🛒🚮🛒♿
Within 3 miles: ⬇🎣🏌◎🅂🛍🅂∪

Notes: No commercial vehicles, no bookings by persons under 21yrs unless a family booking. Max 2 dogs per booking, certain dog breeds banned. Dogs must be kept on leads.

see advert on page 333

►►►► 87% Lebberston Touring Park (TA077824)

Filey Rd YO11 3PE
☎ 01723 585723
e-mail: info@lebberstontouring.co.uk
dir: *Off A165 (Filey to Scarborough road). Site signed*

Open Mar-Oct

Last arrival 20.00hrs Last departure 11.00hrs

A peaceful family park in a gently-sloping rural area, where the quality facilities are maintained to a high standard of cleanliness. The keen owners are friendly and helpful, and create a relaxing atmosphere. A natural area offers views of the surrounding countryside through the shrubbery. Please note that this park does not accept tents. 7.5 acre site. 125 touring pitches. 25 hardstandings. 50 seasonal pitches. Caravan pitches. Motorhome pitches.

Facilities: 🛁🚿⊙🅿🔆&🛁🛎🐾🅆♻🅸
Services: 🔌🗑🛒🖊🆃
Within 3 miles: ⬇🎣🏌◎🅂🛍🅂∪

Notes: No noise after 22.00hrs. Dogs must be kept on leads.

►►►► 83% Crows Nest Caravan Park (TA094826)

Gristhorpe YO14 9PS
☎ 01723 582206
e-mail: enquires@crowsnestcaravanpark.com
dir: *5m S of Scarborough & 2m N of Filey. On seaward side of A165, signed from rdbt, near petrol station*

* 🚐 £15-£35 🚐 £15-£35 Å £15-£30

Open Mar-Oct

Last departure noon

A beautifully situated park on the coast between Scarborough and Filey, with excellent panoramic views. This large and mainly static park offers lively entertainment, and two bars. A small touring area is close to the attractions, and the main touring and camping section is at the top of the park overlooking the sea - this area is equipped with some excellent fully serviced pitches and a superb amenities block. 20 acre site. 49 touring pitches. 49 hardstandings. Caravan pitches. Motorhome pitches. Tent pitches. 220 statics.

Leisure: 🏊‍♀️🎠⊙🎱🎵
Facilities: 🚿⊙🅿🔆&🕐🛍🐾🅆💻♻🅸
Services: 🔌🗑🛒🖊🛁🍴🆃🚮🛒♿
Within 3 miles: ⬇🏌◎🅂🛍🅂∪

Notes: Dogs must be kept on leads.

see advert on opposite page

LEISURE: 🏊 Indoor swimming pool 🏊 Outdoor swimming pool 🎠 Children's playground 👋 Kid's club 🎾 Tennis court 🎱 Games room 📺 Separate TV room ⬇ 9/18 hole golf course 🚤 Boats for hire 🎬 Cinema 🎵 Entertainment 🎣 Fishing ◎ Mini golf 🏄 Watersports 🤸 Gym 🏟 Sports field Spa ∪ Stables
FACILITIES: 🛁 Bath 🚿 Shower ⊙ Electric shaver 🅿 Hairdryer 🔆 Ice Pack Facility & Disabled facilities 🕐 Public telephone 🛍 Shop on site or within 200yds 🅂 Mobile shop (calls at least 5 days a week) 🍴 BBQ area 🅿 Picnic area 🅆 Wi-fi 💻 Internet access ♻ Recycling 🅸 Tourist info 🐾 Dog exercise area

AA CAMPING CARD SITE

►►►► 81% Orchard Farm Holiday Village *(TA105779)*

Stonegate, Hunmanby YO14 0PU
☎ 01723 891582
e-mail: info@orchardfarmholidayvillage.co.uk
dir: *A165 from Scarborough towards Bridlington. Turn right signed Hunmanby, site on right just after rail bridge*

* 🚙 £14-£22 🚐 £14-£22 ⛺ £14-£22

Open Mar-Oct (rs Off peak some facilities restricted)

Last arrival 23.00hrs Last departure 11.00hrs

Pitches are arranged around a large coarse fishing lake at this grassy park. The enthusiastic owners are friendly, and offer a wide range of amenities including an indoor heated swimming pool and a licensed bar. 14 acre site. 91 touring pitches. 34 hardstandings. Caravan pitches. Motorhome pitches. Tent pitches. 46 statics.

Leisure: 🏊 🛝 ● □

Facilities: 🚿 ⊙ 🚿 ✱ ♿ ✆ [$] 🪑 🐕

Services: 🔌 🧺 🍷 [T] 🔋

Within 3 miles: ⛳ 🎣 ◎ 🚤 [$] 🧺

Notes: Dogs must be kept on leads. Miniature railway.

►►► 80% Centenary Way Camping & Caravan Park *(TA115798)*

Muston Grange YO14 0HU
☎ 01723 516415 & 512313
dir: *Just off A1039 near A165 junct towards Bridlington*

* 🚙 £12-£20 🚐 £12-£20 ⛺ £6-£20

Open Mar-Oct

Last arrival 21.00hrs Last departure noon

A well set-out family-owned park, with footpath access to nearby beach. Close to the seaside resort of Filey, and caravan pitches enjoy views over open countryside. 3 acre site. 75 touring pitches. 25 hardstandings. Caravan pitches. Motorhome pitches. Tent pitches.

Leisure: 🛝

Facilities: 🚿 ⊙ ✱ ♿ [$] 🐕 ♻ ℹ

Services: 🔌 🧺 🍴 🔋

Within 3 miles: ⛳ ⛵ 🎣 ◎ [$] 🧺

Notes: 💳 No group bookings in peak period, no 9-12 berth tents, no gazebos. Dogs must be kept on leads.

►►► 77% *Filey Brigg Touring Caravan & Country Park* *(TA115812)*

North Cliff YO14 9ET
☎ 01723 513852
e-mail: fileybrigg@scarborough.gov.uk
dir: *A165 from Scarborough to Filey. Left onto A1039, at rdbt into Church Cliff Dr, to site*

🚙 🚐 ⛺

Open Etr-2 Jan

Last arrival 18.00hrs Last departure noon

A municipal park overlooking Filey Brigg with splendid views along the coast, and set in a country park. The beach is just a short walk away, as is the resort of Filey. There is a good quality amenity block, and 50 all-weather pitches are available. An excellent children's adventure playground is adjacent to the touring areas. 9 acre site. 158 touring pitches. 82 hardstandings. Caravan pitches. Motorhome pitches. Tent pitches.

Leisure: 🛝 ⚽

Facilities: 🚿 ⊙ ✱ ♿ ✆ [$] 🐕 ♻ ℹ

Services: 🔌 🧺 [T] 🍴 🍔

Within 3 miles: ⛳ ⛵ 🎣 ◎ [$] 🧺 U

Notes: Dogs must be kept on leads.

SERVICES: 🔌 Electric hook up 🧺 Launderette 🍷 Licensed bar ⛽ Calor Gas 🔥 Camping Gaz [T] Toilet fluid 🍴 Café/Restaurant 🍔 Fast Food/Takeaway 🔋 Battery charging 👶 Baby care 🚐 Motorvan service point **ABBREVIATIONS:** BH/bank hols-bank holidays Etr-Easter Spring BH-Spring Bank Holiday dep-departure fr-from hrs-hours m-mile mdnt-midnight rdbt-roundabout rs-restricted service wk-week wknd-weekend x-rds-cross roads 💳 No credit cards 🚫 No dogs 👪 Children of all ages accepted See page 9 for details of the AA Camping Card Scheme

HARROGATE
Map 19 SE35

Places to visit

RHS Garden Harlow Carr, HARROGATE, HG3 1QB, 01423 565418 www.rhs.org.uk/harlowcarr

The Royal Pump Room Museum, HARROGATE, HG1 2RY, 01423 556188 www.harrogate.gov.uk/museums

Great for kids: Stump Cross Caverns, PATELEY BRIDGE, HG3 5JL, 01756 752780 www.stumpcrosscaverns.co.uk

PREMIER PARK

▶▶▶▶▶ **83% Rudding Holiday Park** *(SE333531)*

Follifoot HG3 1JH
☎ **01423 870439**
e-mail: holiday-park@ruddingpark.com
web: www.ruddingholidaypark.co.uk
dir: *From A1 take A59 to A658 signed Bradford. 4.5m, right & follow signs*

🚐 🚃 ⛺

Open Mar-Jan (rs Nov-Jan shop & Deer House Pub - limited opening, summer open times only for outdoor swimming pool)

Last arrival 23.00hrs Last departure 11.00hrs

A spacious park set in beautiful 200 acres of mature parkland and walled gardens of Rudding Park. The setting has been tastefully enhanced with terraced pitches and dry-stone walls. A separate area houses super pitches where all services are supplied including a picnic table and TV connection, and there are excellent toilets. An 18-hole golf course, a 6-hole short course, driving range, golf academy, heated outdoor swimming pool, the Deer House Family Pub, and a children's play area complete the amenities. 50 acre site. 141 touring pitches. 20 hardstandings. 50 seasonal pitches. Caravan pitches. Motorhome pitches. Tent pitches. 57 statics.

AA Pubs & Restaurants nearby: Rudding Park Hotel, Spa & Golf, HARROGATE, HG3 1JH, 01423 871350

Leisure: 🏊 ⛰ ⚽ 🎱 🎵 Spa
Facilities: 🛁 🚿 ⊙ 🌡 ✳ ⚐ ⓢ 🛒 Wi-fi 🖥 ❶
Services: 🚐 🔲 🖪 🛢 ⟢ T 🍴 🛒 🚮
Within 3 miles: 🎣 🌐 ⌂ 🛒 🐴 ⛳ U

Notes: Under 18s must be accompanied by an adult.

PREMIER PARK

▶▶▶▶▶ **77% Ripley Caravan Park** *(SE289610)*

Knaresborough Rd, Ripley HG3 3AU
☎ **01423 770050**
e-mail: ripleycaravanpark@talk21.com
web: www.ripleycaravanpark.com
dir: *3m N of Harrogate on A61. Right at rdbt onto B6165 signed Knaresborough. Site 300yds left*

✱ 🚐 £17-£21 🚃 £17-£21 ⛺ £17-£22.50

Open Etr-Oct

Last arrival 21.00hrs Last departure noon

A well-run rural site in attractive meadowland which has been landscaped with mature tree plantings. The resident owners lovingly maintain the facilities, and there is a heated swimming pool and sauna, a TV and games room, and a covered nursery playroom for small children. There is a bus every 15 minutes which gives easy access to Ripon and Leeds, and a new cycleway/walkway leads from the site directly to Harrogate, a distance of four miles. 24 acre site. 110 touring pitches. 60 hardstandings. 35 seasonal pitches. Caravan pitches. Motorhome pitches. Tent pitches. 50 statics.

AA Pubs & Restaurants nearby: van Zeller, HARROGATE, HG1 2TQ, 01423 508762

Malt Shovel Inn, BREARTON, HG3 3BX, 01423 862929

The General Tarleton Inn, KNARESBOROUGH, HG5 0PZ, 01423 340284

Leisure: 🏊 ⛰ ⚽ 🎱
Facilities: 🚿 ⊙ 🌡 ✳ ⚐ ⓢ 🛒 Wi-fi ♻ ❶
Services: 🚐 🔲 🖪 🛢 ⟢ T 🛒 🚮
Within 3 miles: 🎣 ❀ ⌂ ⌂ ◎ 🛒 🐴 U

Notes: Family camping only. No open fires, off-ground BBQs only, no skateboards or rollerblades. Dogs must be kept on leads. Football, volley ball.

▶▶▶▶ **80% High Moor Farm Park** *(SE242560)*

Skipton Rd HG3 2LT
☎ **01423 563637 & 564955**
e-mail: highmoorfarmpark@btconnect.com
dir: *4m W of Harrogate on A59 towards Skipton*

🚐 £23 🚃 £23

Open Etr or Apr-Oct

Last arrival 23.30hrs Last departure 15.00hrs

An excellent site with very good facilities, set beside a small wood and surrounded by thorn hedges. The numerous touring pitches are located in meadowland fields, each area with its own toilet block. A large heated indoor swimming pool, games room, 9-hole golf course, full-sized crown bowling green, and a bar serving meals and snacks are all popular. Please note that this park does not accept tents. 15 acre site. 320 touring pitches. 51 hardstandings. 57 seasonal pitches. Caravan pitches. Motorhome pitches. 158 statics.

AA Pubs & Restaurants nearby: van Zeller, HARROGATE, HG1 2TQ, 01423 508762

The General Tarleton Inn, KNARESBOROUGH, HG5 0PZ, 01423 340284

Leisure: 🏊 ⛰ ⚽ 🎱
Facilities: 🛁 🚿 ⊙ 🌡 ✳ ⚐ ⓢ 🛒 🐴 ♻ ❶
Services: 🚐 🔲 🖪 🛢 ⟢ T 🍴 🛒 🚮
Within 3 miles: 🎣 ⌂ 🛒 🛒 U

Notes: Dogs must be kept on leads. Coarse fishing.

LEISURE: 🏊 Indoor swimming pool 🏊 Outdoor swimming pool ⛰ Children's playground 🪁 Kid's club 🎾 Tennis court 🎱 Games room 📺 Separate TV room 🏌 9/18 hole golf course 🚣 Boats for hire 🎬 Cinema 🎭 Entertainment 🎣 Fishing ◎ Mini golf 🏄 Watersports 💪 Gym 🏐 Sports field **Spa** U Stables
FACILITIES: 🛁 Bath 🚿 Shower ⊙ Electric shaver 🌡 Hairdryer ✳ Ice Pack Facility ⚐ Disabled facilities Ⓒ Public telephone ⓢ Shop on site or within 200yds 🚐 Mobile shop (calls at least 5 days a week) 🍴 BBQ area 🏕 Picnic area Wi-fi Wi-fi 🖥 Internet access ♻ Recycling ❶ Tourist info 🐴 Dog exercise area

►► 69% Shaws Trailer Park *(SE325557)*

Knaresborough Rd HG2 7NE
☎ **01423 884432**
dir: *On A59 1m from town centre. 0.5m SW of Starbeck railway crossing*

* 🚐 £17-£20 🚍 £17-£20 ▲ £10-£16

Open all year

Last arrival 20.00hrs Last departure 14.00hrs

A long-established site just a mile from the centre of Harrogate. The all-weather pitches are arranged around a carefully kept grass area, and the toilets are basic but functional and clean. The entrance is on the bus route to Harrogate. 11 acre site. 60 touring pitches. 24 hardstandings. Caravan pitches. Motorhome pitches. Tent pitches. 146 statics.

AA Pubs & Restaurants nearby: van Zeller, HARROGATE, HG1 2TQ, 01423 508762

Malt Shovel Inn, BREARTON, HG3 3BX, 01423 862929

The General Tarleton Inn, KNARESBOROUGH, HG5 0PZ, 01423 340284

Facilities: 🛁 🚰 ☺ 🔥 ♿ 🔗
Services: 🔌 🗄 🗑
Within 3 miles: 🎣 ⛳ 🚲 🍴 💰 🛒
Notes: Adults only. ⊘ Dogs must be kept on leads.

Places to visit

Dales Countryside Museum & National Park Centre, HAWES, DL8 3NT, 01969 666210 www.yorkshiredales.org.uk/dcm

►►► 76% Bainbridge Ings Caravan & Camping Site *(SD879895)*

DL8 3NU
☎ **01969 667354**
e-mail: janet@bainbridge-ings.co.uk
dir: *Approaching Hawes from Bainbridge on A684, left at Gayle sign, site 300yds on left*

* 🚐 £18 🚍 £18 ▲ £15

Open Apr-Sep

Last arrival 22.00hrs Last departure noon

A quiet, well-organised site in open countryside close to Hawes in the heart of Upper Wensleydale, popular with ramblers. Pitches are sited around the perimeter of several fields, each bounded by traditional stone walls. 5 acre site. 70 touring pitches. 8 hardstandings. Caravan pitches. Motorhome pitches. Tent pitches. 15 statics.

AA Pubs & Restaurants nearby: The Moorcock Inn, HAWES, LA10 5PU, 01969 667488

Facilities: 🚰 ☺ 🔥 ❄ 📶 ♻ 🔗
Services: 🔌 🗄 🗑 ⛽ 🛒 🔧
Within 3 miles: 🚲 💰 🛒
Notes: ⊘ No noise after 23.00hrs. Dogs must be kept on leads.

Places to visit

Duncombe Park, HELMSLEY, YO62 5EB, 01439 778625 www.duncombepark.com

Helmsley Castle, HELMSLEY, YO62 5AB, 01439 770442 www.english-heritage.org.uk/daysout/properties/helmsley-castle

Great for kids: Flamingo Land Theme Park & Zoo, KIRBY MISPERTON, YO17 6UX, 01653 668287 www.flamingoland.co.uk

---

AA CAMPING CARD SITE

PREMIER PARK

►►►►► 83% Golden Square Touring Caravan Park *(SE604797)*

Oswaldkirk YO62 5YQ
☎ **01439 788269**
e-mail: reception@goldensquarecaravanpark.com
dir: *From York take B1363 to Oswaldkirk. Left onto B1257, 2nd left onto unclassified road signed Ampleforth, site 0.5m on right. Or A19 from Thirsk towards York. Left, follow 'Caravan Route avoiding Sutton Bank' signs, through Ampleforth to site in 1m*

* 🚐 £16.50-£20.50 🚍 £16.50-£20.50 ▲ £16.50-£20.50

Golden Square Touring Caravan Park

Open Mar-Oct

Last arrival 21.00hrs Last departure noon

An excellent, popular and spacious site with very good facilities. This friendly, immaculately maintained park is set in a quiet rural situation with lovely views over the North York Moors. Terraced on three levels and surrounded by mature trees, it caters particularly for families, with excellent play areas and space for ball games. Country walks and mountain bike trails start here and an attractive holiday home area is also available. 12 acre site. 129 touring pitches. 10 hardstandings. 50 seasonal pitches. Caravan pitches. Motorhome pitches. Tent pitches. 10 statics.

AA Pubs & Restaurants nearby: The Star Inn, HAROME, YO62 5JE, 01439 770397

Feversham Arms Hotel & Verbena Spa, HELMSLEY, YO62 5AG, 01439 770766

Leisure: ⚙ ⚽ 🎣
Facilities: 🛁 🚰 ☺ 🔥 ❄ ♿ ⏰ 💰 🚻 📻 📶 🖥 ♻ 🔗
Services: 🔌 🗄 🗑 ⛽ 🚽 🚿 🛒 🔧
Within 3 miles: 🚲 ⛳ 🚲 🍴 ◎ 💰 🛒 ⛳
Notes: No skateboards or fires. Dogs must be kept on leads. Microwave available.

SERVICES: 🔌 Electric hook up 🗄 Launderette 🍺 Licensed bar 🔋 Calor Gas ⊘ Camping Gaz ⊤ Toilet fluid 🍴 Café/Restaurant 🍟 Fast Food/Takeaway 🔋 Battery charging 🍼 Baby care 🔧 Motorvan service point **ABBREVIATIONS:** BH/bank hols-bank holidays Etr-Easter Spring BH-Spring Bank Holiday dep-departure fr-from hrs-hours m-mile mdnt-midnight rdbt-roundabout rs-restricted service wk-week wknd-weekend x-rds-cross roads ⊘ No credit cards ⊘ No dogs 👪 Children of all ages accepted See page 9 for details of the AA Camping Card Scheme

HELMSLEY *continued*

▶▶▶ 74% Foxholme Caravan Park

(SE658828)

Harome YO62 5JG
☎ 01439 771904 & 772336
dir: *A170 from Helmsley towards Scarborough, right signed Harome, left at church, through village, follow signs*

🚐 £20 🚙 £20 ▲ £20

Open Etr-Oct

Last arrival 23.00hrs Last departure noon

A quiet park set in secluded wooded countryside, with well-shaded pitches in individual clearings divided by mature trees. The facilities are well maintained, and the site is ideal as a touring base or a place to relax. Please note that caravans are prohibited on the A170 at Sutton Bank between Thirsk and Helmsley. 6 acre site. 60 touring pitches. 30 seasonal pitches. Caravan pitches. Motorhome pitches. Tent pitches.

AA Pubs & Restaurants nearby: The Star Inn, HAROME, YO62 5JE, 01439 770397

Feversham Arms Hotel & Verbena Spa, HELMSLEY, YO62 5AG, 01439 770766

Facilities: 🛁📷☉☞✳☉🚿🛝🅰
Services: 🚐🛢🔌⌀🇹📧♨
Within 3 miles: ⚓🛈🛒🔵
Notes: Adults only. 🐾

HIGH BENTHAM

Places to visit

Lancaster Maritime Museum, LANCASTER, LA1 1RB, 01524 382264
www.lancashire.gov.uk/museums

Lancaster City Museum, LANCASTER, LA1 1HT, 01524 64637 www.lancashire.gov.uk/museums

Great for kids: Lancaster Castle, LANCASTER, LA1 1YJ, 01524 64998 www.lancastercastle.com

---

HIGH BENTHAM — Map 18 SD66

PREMIER PARK

▶▶▶▶▶ 86%
Riverside Caravan Park

(SD665688)

LA2 7FJ
☎ 015242 61272
e-mail: info@riversidecaravanpark.co.uk
dir: *Exit B6480, signed from High Bentham town centre*

* £19.95-£25.75 🚙 £19.95-£25.75

Open Mar-16 Dec

Last arrival 20.00hrs Last departure noon

A well-managed riverside park developed to a high standard, with level grass pitches set in avenues separated by trees, and there are excellent facilities for children, who are made to feel as important as the adults. It has an excellent, modern amenity block, including a family bathroom, and a well-stocked shop, laundry and information room. The superb games room and adventure playground are hugely popular, and the market town of High Bentham is close by. Please note that this site does not accept tents. Bentham Golf Club (within one mile) is also under same ownership with facilities available for Riverside customers. 12 acre site. 61 touring pitches. 27 hardstandings. 50 seasonal pitches. Caravan pitches. Motorhome pitches. 206 statics.

AA Pubs & Restaurants nearby: The Traddock, AUSTWICK, LA2 8BY, 015242 51224

The Game Cock Inn, AUSTWICK, LA2 8BB, 015242 51226

Leisure: 🎢🔍
Facilities: 📷☉☞♿☉🛒🛝🔳♻🅰
Services: 🚐🛢🔌⌀🇹📧♨
Within 3 miles: ⚓🛈🛒🔵
Notes: Dogs must be kept on leads. Permits for private fishing (chargeable), discounted golf green fees.

▶ 81% Lowther Hill Caravan Park

(SD696695)

LA2 7AN
☎ 015242 61657 & 07985 478750
web: www.caravancampingsites.co.uk/northyorkshire/lowtherhill.htm
dir: *A65 at Clapham onto B6480 signed Bentham. 3m to site on right*

* 🚐 £16.50 🚙 £16.50 ▲ £10

Open Mar-Nov

Last arrival 21.00hrsLast departure 14.00hrs

A simple site with stunning panoramic views from every pitch. Peace reigns on this little park, though the tourist villages of Ingleton, Clapham and Settle are not far away. All pitches have electricity, and there is a heated toilet/washroom and dishwashing facilities. 1 acre site. 9 touring pitches. 4 hardstandings. Caravan pitches. Motorhome pitches. Tent pitches.

AA Pubs & Restaurants nearby: The Traddock, AUSTWICK, LA2 8BY, 015242 51224

The Game Cock Inn, AUSTWICK, LA2 8BB, 015242 51226

Facilities: 📷♿♻🅰
Services: 🚐
Within 3 miles: ⚓🛈🛒🔵
Notes: 🐾 Payment on arrival. Dogs must be kept on leads.

HUSTHWAITE — Map 19 SE57

NEW ▶▶▶ 79% The
Hideaway@Baxby Manor

(SE511751)

YO61 4PW
☎ 01347 666079 & 07739 666079
e-mail: info@thehideaway.org
dir: *From A19 between Thirsk & York, follow Husthwaite & Coxwold signs, 2m, left signed Baxby Manor, follow brown signs to site*

* 🚙 £18-£26 ▲ £18-£26

Open Etr-Oct

Last arrival 18.00hrs (no check-in before 14:00hrs). Last departure 11.00hrs

Located in a small five-acre field, this tranquil eco-campsite is surrounded on three sides by trees, and by a stream on the other. The site only accepts tents and motorhomes, but there are five bell tents and three camping pods for hire. Fire

---

pits are dotted around the site for 'open-fire' cooking and there is a beautiful log cabin-style building housing spotlessly clean and very modern toilet and shower facilities. 5 acre site. 32 touring pitches. Motorhome pitches. Tent pitches. 5 bell tents/yurts. 3 wooden pods.

Facilities: ⬡☺🅿☀🚿🅂🛒📶🖥♻🅰

Services: 🔌🚿🍴

Within 3 miles: 🎣✏🅂♾

Notes: No cars by tents. , no noise after 23.00hrs. Dogs must be kept on leads. Drying room.

HUTTON-LE-HOLE   Map 19 SE79

Places to visit

Nunnington Hall, NUNNINGTON, YO62 5UY, 01439 748283 www.nationaltrust.org.uk

Rievaulx Abbey, RIEVAULX, 01439 798228 www.english-heritage.org.uk/daysout/properties/rievaulx-abbey

Great for kids: Pickering Castle, PICKERING, YO6 5AB, 01751 474989 www.english-heritage.org.uk/daysout/properties/pickering-castle

▶▶▶▶ 81% *Hutton-le-Hole Caravan Park* (SE705895)

Westfield Lodge YO62 6UG
☎ **01751 417261**
e-mail: rwstrickland@farmersweekly.net
dir: *From A170 at Keldholme follow Hutton-le-Hole signs. Approx 2m, over cattle grid, left in 500yds into Park Drive, site signed*

🚐 🚗 🅰

Open Etr-Oct

Last arrival 21.00hrs Last departure noon

A small, high quality park on a working farm in the North York Moors National Park. The purpose-built toilet block offers en suite family rooms, and there is a choice of hardstanding or grass pitches within a well-tended area surrounded by hedges and shrubs. The village facilities are a 10-minute walk away. Please note that caravans are prohibited from the A170 at Sutton Bank between Thirsk and Helmsley. 5 acre site. 42 touring pitches. 36 hardstandings. Caravan pitches. Motorhome pitches. Tent pitches.

AA Pubs & Restaurants nearby: Blacksmiths Arms, LASTINGHAM, YO62 6TN, 01751 417247

The Moors Inn, APPLETON-LE-MOORS, YO62 6TF, 01751 417435

Facilities: ⬡☺🅿☀🅂🚿🍴♻🅰

Services: 🔌🚿📶🛒

Within 3 miles: 🎣◎🅂♾

Notes: Farm walks.

KNARESBOROUGH   Map 19 SE35

Places to visit

RHS Garden Harlow Carr, HARROGATE, HG3 1QB, 01423 565418 www.rhs.org.uk/harlowcarr

The Royal Pump Room Museum, HARROGATE, HG1 2RY, 01423 556188 www.harrogate.gov.uk/museums

Great for kids: Knaresborough Castle & Museum, KNARESBOROUGH, HG5 8AS, 01423 556188 www.harrogate.gov.uk/museums

---

AA CAMPING CARD SITE

▶▶▶ 78% Kingfisher Caravan Park (SE343603)

Low Moor Ln, Farnham HG5 9JB
☎ **01423 869411**
dir: *From Knaresborough take A6055. Left in 1m towards Farnham, left in village signed Scotton. Site 1m on left*

* 🚐 fr £16 🚗 fr £16 🅰 fr £18

Open Mar-Oct

Last arrival 21.00hrs Last departure 16.00hrs

A large grassy site with open spaces set in a wooded area in rural countryside. Whilst Harrogate, Fountains Abbey and York are within easy reach, anglers will want to take advantage of on-site coarse and fly fishing lakes. The park has a separate flat tenting field with electric hook-ups available. 14 acre site. 35 touring pitches. Caravan pitches. Motorhome pitches. Tent pitches. 80 statics.

AA Pubs & Restaurants nearby: The General Tarleton Inn, KNARESBOROUGH, HG5 0PZ, 01423 340284

Leisure: 🎱

Facilities: ⬡☺🅿☀🅂🚿🍴🅂🛒🅰

Services: 🔌🛒🅂🚿

Within 3 miles: 🎣🍴🚲✏🅂♾

Notes: ⊘ No football. Pets must be kept under strict adult control.

MARKINGTON   Map 19 SE26

Places to visit

Fountains Abbey & Studley Royal, RIPON, HG4 3DY, 01765 608888 www.english-heritage.org.uk/daysout/properties/st-marys-church-studley-royal

Norton Conyers, RIPON, HG4 5EQ, 01765 640333 www.weddingsatnortonconyers.co.uk

Great for kids: Stump Cross Caverns, PATELEY BRIDGE, HG3 5JL, 01756 752780 www.stumpcrosscaverns.co.uk

▶▶▶ 80% Yorkshire Hussar Inn Holiday Caravan Park (SE288650)

High St HG3 3NR
☎ **01765 677327 & 677715**
e-mail: yorkshirehussar@yahoo.co.uk
dir: *From A61 between Harrogate & Ripon at Wormald Green follow Markington signs, 1m, left past Post Office into High Street. Site signed on left behind The Yorkshire Hussar Inn*

* 🚐 £16-£22 🚗 £16-£22 🅰 £16-£22

Open Etr-Oct

Last arrival 19.00hrs Last departure noon

A terraced site behind the village inn with well-kept grass and a new toilet block in 2013. This pleasant site offers spacious pitches - hardstanding and electric hook-up pitches are available - and there are a few holiday statics for hire. Although the Yorkshire Hussar Inn does not provide food, there is a pub that does and is within walking distance. 5 acre site. 20 touring pitches. 6 hardstandings. 12 seasonal pitches. Caravan pitches. Motorhome pitches. Tent pitches. 73 statics.

AA Pubs & Restaurants nearby: Malt Shovel Inn, BREARTON, HG3 3BX, 01423 862929

Leisure: 🎱

Facilities: ⬡☺☀🅂🛒📶🖥♻🅰

Services: 🔌🛒🍴🅂🛒

Within 3 miles: ✏🅂♾

Notes: ⊘ Dogs must be kept on leads. Paddling pool.

SERVICES: 🔌 Electric hook up 🅂 Launderette 🍸 Licensed bar 🅂 Calor Gas 🅾 Camping Gaz 🅃 Toilet fluid 🍴 Café/Restaurant 🍔 Fast Food/Takeaway 🛒 Battery charging 🚼 Baby care 🚰 Motorvan service point **ABBREVIATIONS:** BH/bank hols-bank holidays Etr-Easter Spring BH-Spring Bank Holiday dep-departure fr-from hrs-hours m-mile mdnt-midnight rdbt-roundabout rs-restricted service wk-week wknd-weekend x-rds-cross roads 🅃 No credit cards ⊘ No dogs 👪 Children of all ages accepted See page 9 for details of the AA Camping Card Scheme

MASHAM — Map 19 SE28

Places to visit

Theakston Brewery & Visitor Centre, MASHAM, HG4 4YD, 01765 680000 www.theakstons.co.uk

Norton Conyers, RIPON, HG4 5EQ, 01765 640333 www.weddingsatnortonconyers.co.uk

Great for kids: Lightwater Valley Theme Park, NORTH STAINLEY, HG4 3HT, 0871 720 0011 www.lightwatervalley.co.uk

►►► 82% *Old Station Holiday Park* (SE232812)

Old Station Yard, Low Burton HG4 4DF
☎ 01765 689569
e-mail: oldstation@tiscali.co.uk
dir: *A1 onto B6267 signed Masham & Thirsk. In 8m left onto A6108. In 100yds left into site*

🚐 🚌 ⛺

Open Mar-Nov (rs Mar-Nov café closed wkdays)

Last arrival 20.00hrs Last departure noon

An interesting site on a former station. The enthusiastic and caring family owners have maintained the railway theme in creating a park with high quality facilities. The small town of Masham with its Theakston and Black Sheep breweries are within easy walking distance of the park. The reception/café in a carefully restored wagon shed provides a range of meals using local produce. 3.75 acre site. 50 touring pitches. Caravan pitches. Motorhome pitches. Tent pitches. 12 statics.

AA Pubs & Restaurants nearby: The Black Sheep Brewery, MASHAM, HG4 4EN, 01765 680101

Vennell's, MASHAM, HG4 4DX, 01765 689000

Facilities: 🚿 ⊙ 💨 ❄ ♿ ☎ 🛒 🧺 [Wi-fi] 💻 ♻ ℹ

Services: 🚽 🧼 🔒 [T] 🍴 🛏 🧺 ⬇

Within 3 miles: ⛳ 🎣 🛒 🧼 ∪

Notes: No fast cycling around site, no campfires. Dogs must be kept on leads.

NABURN — Map 16 SE54

Places to visit

Clifford's Tower, YORK, YO1 1SA, 01904 646940 www.english-heritage.org.uk/daysout/properties/cliffords-tower-york

Fairfax House, YORK, YO1 9RN, 01904 655543 www.fairfaxhouse.co.uk

Great for kids: Jorvik Viking Centre, YORK, YO1 9WT, 01904 615505 www.jorvik-viking-centre.com

►►►► 81% *Naburn Lock Caravan Park* (SE596446)

YO19 4RU
☎ 01904 728697
e-mail: wilks@naburnlock.co.uk
dir: *From A64 (McArthur Glen designer outlet) take A19 N, turn left signed Naburn on B1222, site on right 0.5m past village*

🚐 🚌 ⛺

Open Mar-6 Nov

Last arrival 20.00hrs Last departure 13.00hrs

A family park where the enthusiastic owners are steadily improving its quality. The mainly grass pitches are arranged in small groups separated by mature hedges. The park is close to the River Ouse, and the river towpath provides excellent walking and cycling opportunities. The river bus to nearby York leaves from a jetty beside the park. 7 acre site. 100 touring pitches. 22 hardstandings. Caravan pitches. Motorhome pitches. Tent pitches.

AA Pubs & Restaurants nearby: Lamb & Lion Inn, YORK, YO1 7EH, 01904 612078

Blue Bell, YORK, YO1 9TF, 01904 654904

Lysander Arms, YORK, YO30 5TZ, 01904 640845

Facilities: 🚿 ⊙ 💨 ❄ ♿ 🛒 🧺 🐕 ♻ ℹ

Services: 🚽 🧼 🔒 🌿 [T] 🛏 ⬇

Within 3 miles: 🚣 🎣 🛒 🧼 ∪

Notes: Adults only section, quiet 23.00hrs-07.00hrs. River fishing.

NORTHALLERTON — Map 19 SE39

Places to visit

Mount Grace Priory, OSMOTHERLEY, DL6 3JG, 01609 883494 www.english-heritage.org.uk/daysout/properties/mount-grace-priory

Theakston Brewery & Visitor Centre, MASHAM, HG4 4YD, 01765 680000 www.theakstons.co.uk

Great for kids: Falconry UK - Birds of Prey Centre, THIRSK, YO7 4EU, 01845 587522 www.falconrycentre.co.uk

►►►► 80% Otterington Park (SE378882)

Station Farm, South Otterington DL7 9JB
☎ 01609 780656
e-mail: info@otteringtonpark.com
dir: *From A168 midway between Northallerton & Thirsk onto unclassified road signed South Otterington. Site on right just before South Otterington*

🚐 🚌

Open Mar-Oct

Last arrival 21.00hrs Last departure 13.00hrs

A high quality park on a working farm with open vistas across the Vale of York. It enjoys a peaceful location with a lovely nature walk and on-site fishing, which is very popular. Young children will enjoy the play area. Toilet facilities are very good. The attractions of Northallerton and Thirsk are a few minutes' drive away. 6 acre site. 62 touring pitches. 62 hardstandings. Caravan pitches. Motorhome pitches. 3 wooden pods.

Leisure: 🛝 ⚽

Facilities: 🛁 🚿 ⊙ 💨 ❄ ♿ ☎ 🛒 🧺 🐕 [Wi-fi] ♻ ℹ

Services: 🚽 🧼 🔒 🛏

Within 3 miles: ⛳ 🎞 🎣 ◎ 🛒 🧼

Notes: Hot tub, fitness equipment.

LEISURE: 🏊 Indoor swimming pool 🌊 Outdoor swimming pool 🛝 Children's playground 👋 Kid's club 🎾 Tennis court 🎱 Games room 📺 Separate TV room ⛳ 9/18 hole golf course 🚣 Boats for hire 🎞 Cinema 🎵 Entertainment 🎣 Fishing ◎ Mini golf 🏄 Watersports 🏋 Gym ⚽ Sports field **Spa** ∪ Stables
FACILITIES: 🛁 Bath 🚿 Shower ⊙ Electric shaver 💨 Hairdryer ❄ Ice Pack Facility ♿ Disabled facilities ☎ Public telephone 🛒 Shop on site or within 200yds 🚚 Mobile shop (calls at least 5 days a week) 🍖 BBQ area 🧺 Picnic area [Wi-fi] Wi-fi 💻 Internet access ♻ Recycling ℹ Tourist info 🐕 Dog exercise area

NORTH STAINLEY   Map 19 SE27

Places to visit

Norton Conyers, RIPON, HG4 5EQ, 01765 640333
www.weddingsatnortonconyers.co.uk

Falconry UK - Birds of Prey Centre, THIRSK,
YO7 4EU, 01845 587522
www.falconrycentre.co.uk

Great for kids: Lightwater Valley Theme Park,
NORTH STAINLEY, HG4 3HT, 0871 720 0011
www.lightwatervalley.co.uk

▶▶▶▶ **77% Sleningford
Watermill Caravan Camping
Park** *(SE280783)*

GOLD

HG4 3HQ
☎ **01765 635201**
e-mail: bookings@sleningfordwatermill.co.uk
web: www.sleningfordwatermill.co.uk
dir: *Adjacent to A6108. 5m N of Ripon & 1m N of
North Stainley*

* 🚐 £18-£27 🚏 £18-£27 Å £18-£27

Open Etr & Apr-Oct

Last arrival 21.00hrs Last departure 12.30hrs

The old watermill and the River Ure make an
attractive setting for this touring park which is
laid out in two areas. Pitches are placed in
meadowland and close to mature woodland, and
the park has two enthusiastic managers. This is a
popular place with canoeists and seasonal fly
fishing is possible. 14 acre site. 140 touring
pitches. 8 hardstandings. 48 seasonal pitches.
Caravan pitches. Motorhome pitches. Tent pitches.

AA Pubs & Restaurants nearby: The Bruce Arms,
WEST TANFIELD, HG4 5JJ, 01677 470325

The Black Sheep Brewery, MASHAM, HG4 4EN,
01765 680101

Vennell's, MASHAM, HG4 4DX, 01765 689000

Leisure: ✪
Facilities: 🍴⊙🅿✳⚂🚿🔦🛒♻ **ℹ**
Services: 🔌🕒🛢⚗💆
Within 3 miles: 🚵🏇🛒🕒

Notes: No noise after 23.00hrs. Dogs must be
kept on leads. Newspapers can be ordered.

OSMOTHERLEY   Map 19 SE49

Places to visit

Mount Grace Priory, OSMOTHERLEY, DL6 3JG,
01609 883494 www.english-heritage.org.uk/
daysout/properties/mount-grace-priory

Gisborough Priory, GUISBOROUGH, TS14 6HG,
01287 633801 www.english-heritage.org.uk/
daysout/properties/gisborough-priory

Great for kids: Falconry UK - Birds of Prey
Centre, THIRSK, YO7 4EU, 01845 587522
www.falconrycentre.co.uk

PREMIER PARK

▶▶▶▶▶ **80% Cote Ghyll Caravan
& Camping Park** *(SE459979)*

DL6 3AH
☎ **01609 883425**
e-mail: hills@coteghyll.com
dir: *Exit A19 dual carriageway at A684
(Northallerton junct). Follow signs to
Osmotherley. Left in village centre. Site
entrance 0.5m on right*

* 🚐 fr £18 🚏 fr £18 Å fr £18

Open Mar-Oct

Last arrival 21.00hrs Last departure noon

A quiet, peaceful site in a pleasant valley on
the edge of moorland, close to the village. The
park is divided into terraces bordered by
woodland, and the extra well-appointed
amenity block is a welcome addition to this
attractive park. Mature trees, shrubs and an
abundance of seasonal floral displays create a
relaxing and peaceful atmosphere and the
whole park is immaculately maintained. There
are pubs and shops nearby and holiday statics
for hire. 7 acre site. 77 touring pitches. 22
hardstandings. Caravan pitches. Motorhome
pitches. Tent pitches. 18 statics.

AA Pubs & Restaurants nearby: The Golden
Lion, OSMOTHERLEY, DL6 3AA, 01609 883526

Leisure: ⛰
Facilities: 🛁🍴⊙🅿✳⚂🔦🛒🚿📶💻
♻ **ℹ**
Services: 🔌🕒🛢⚗🅣🍽💆🚚⚓
Within 3 miles: 🚵🏇🛒🕒↺

Notes: Quiet after 22.00hrs, no camp fires.
Dogs must be kept on leads.

PICKERING   Map 19 SE78

Places to visit

Pickering Castle, PICKERING, YO6 5AB,
01751 474989 www.english-heritage.org.uk/
daysout/properties/pickering-castle

North Yorkshire Moors Railway, PICKERING,
YO18 7AJ, 01751 472508 www.nymr.co.uk

Great for kids: Flamingo Land Theme Park &
Zoo, KIRBY MISPERTON, YO17 6UX, 01653 668287
www.flamingoland.co.uk

▶▶▶▶ **78% Wayside Holiday Park**
(SE764859)

Wrelton YO18 8PG
☎ **01751 472608 & 07940 938517**
e-mail: wrelton@waysideholidaypark.co.uk
web: www.waysideparks.co.uk
dir: *2.5m W of Pickering off A170, follow signs at
Wrelton*

Open Apr-Oct

Located in the village of Wrelton, this well-
maintained seasonal touring and holiday home
park is divided into small paddocks by mature
hedging. The amenity block has smart, modern
facilities. The village pub and restaurant are
within a few minutes' walk of the park. Please
note that caravans are prohibited from the A170
at Sutton Bank between Thirsk and Helmsley. 10
acre site. 40 seasonal pitches. 113 statics.

AA Pubs & Restaurants nearby: Fox & Hounds
Country Inn, PICKERING, YO62 6SQ, 01751 431577

The White Swan Inn, PICKERING, YO18 7AA,
01751 472288

The Fox & Rabbit Inn, PICKERING, YO18 7NQ,
01751 460213

Facilities: 🍴⊙🅿⚂🔦🛒♻ **ℹ**
Services: 🔌🕒
Within 3 miles: 🚵🎋🏇🛒🕒↺

Notes: 🚫 Dogs must be kept on leads.

RICHMOND — Map 19 NZ10

Places to visit

Green Howards Museum, RICHMOND, DL10 4QN, 01748 826561 www.greenhowards.org.uk

Bolton Castle, CASTLE BOLTON, DL8 4ET, 01969 623981 www.boltoncastle.co.uk

Great for kids: Richmond Castle, RICHMOND, DL10 4QW, 01748 822493 www.english-heritage.org.uk/daysout/properties/richmond-castle

►►►► 79% *Brompton Caravan Park*

(NZ199002)

Brompton-on-Swale DL10 7EZ
☎ 01748 824629
e-mail: brompton.caravanpark@btconnect.com
dir: *Exit A1 signed Catterick. B6271 to Brompton-on-Swale, site 1m on left*

Open mid Mar-Oct

Last arrival 21.00hrs Last departure noon

An attractive and well-managed family park where pitches have an open outlook across the River Swale. There is a good children's playground, an excellent family recreation room, a takeaway food service, and fishing is available on the river. Three river view camping pods and holiday apartments can also be hired. 14 acre site. 177 touring pitches. 2 hardstandings. Caravan pitches. Motorhome pitches. Tent pitches. 22 statics. 3 wooden pods.

AA Pubs & Restaurants nearby: The Frenchgate Restaurant and Hotel, RICHMOND, DL10 7AE, 01748 822087

Leisure: ⚠ 🎣
Facilities: 🍴 ⊙ 🌡 ☀ ⚴ 🐕 🔌 🛒 🚿 ♻ ❶
Services: 🚑 🔚 🍴 🛢 🚽 🚮 ⚙
Within 3 miles: ♨ 🎢 ⛳ ◎ 🛒 🛢 ∪

Notes: No group bookings. No motor, electric cars or scooters, gazebos, open fires or wood burners, no electricity for tents, quiet from mdnt.

RIPON

See also North Stainley

Places to visit

Fountains Abbey & Studley Royal, RIPON, HG4 3DY, 01765 608888 www.english-heritage.org.uk/daysout/properties/st-marys-church-studley-royal

Norton Conyers, RIPON, HG4 5EQ, 01765 640333 www.weddingsatnortonconyers.co.uk

Great for kids: Falconry UK - Birds of Prey Centre, THIRSK, YO7 4EU, 01845 587522 www.falconrycentre.co.uk

RIPON — Map 19 SE37

PREMIER PARK

►►►►► 76% Riverside Meadows Country Caravan Park (SE317726)

Ure Bank Top HG4 1JD
☎ 01765 602964
e-mail: info@flowerofmay.com
dir: *On A61 at N end of bridge out of Ripon, W along river (do not cross river). Site 400yds, signed*

🚐 £18-£24 🚍 £18-£24 ▲ £18-£24

Open Etr-Oct (rs Low-mid season bar open wknds only)

Last arrival dusk Last departure noon

This pleasant, well-maintained site stands on high ground overlooking the River Ure, one mile from the town centre. The site has an excellent club with family room and quiet lounge. There is no access to the river from the site. 28 acre site. 80 touring pitches. 40 hardstandings. 40 seasonal pitches. Caravan pitches. Motorhome pitches. Tent pitches. 269 statics.

Leisure: ⚠ 🎣 ⊟ 🎵
Facilities: 🍴 ⊙ ☀ ⚴ 🐕 🔌 🛒 🚿 📶 ♻ ❶
Services: 🚑 🔚 🍴 🛢 🚽 🚮 ⚙
Within 3 miles: ♨ 🎢 ⊟ ⛳ 🚤 🛒 🛢 ∪

Notes: No noise after mdnt, dogs by prior arrangement only. Dogs must be kept on leads.

see advert on page 331

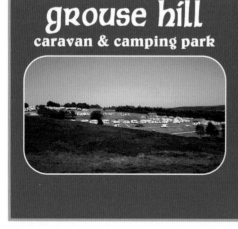
LEISURE: 🏊 Indoor swimming pool 🏊 Outdoor swimming pool ⚠ Children's playground 🧒 Kid's club 🎾 Tennis court 🎯 Games room 📺 Separate TV room ⛳ 9/18 hole golf course 🚣 Boats for hire ⊟ Cinema 🎵 Entertainment 🎣 Fishing ◎ Mini golf 🚤 Watersports 💪 Gym 🏟 Sports field Spa ∪ Stables
FACILITIES: 🛁 Bath 🚿 Shower ⊙ Electric shaver ✂ Hairdryer ☀ Ice Pack Facility ⚴ Disabled facilities 🔌 Public telephone 🛒 Shop on site or within 200yds 🏪 Mobile shop (calls at least 5 days a week) 🍴 BBQ area 🌲 Picnic area 📶 Wi-fi 🖥 Internet access ♻ Recycling ❶ Tourist info 🐕 Dog exercise area

ROBIN HOOD'S BAY

See also Whitby

Places to visit

Whitby Abbey, WHITBY, YO22 4JT, 01947 603568 www.english-heritage.org.uk/daysout/properties/whitby-abbey

Scarborough Castle, SCARBOROUGH, YO11 1HY, 01723 372451 www.english-heritage.org.uk/daysout/properties/scarborough-castle

Great for kids: Sea Life & Marine Sanctuary, SCARBOROUGH, YO12 6RP, 01723 373414 www.sealife.co.uk

ROBIN HOOD'S BAY   Map 19 NZ90

ROGER ALMOND AWARD FOR THE MOST IMPROVED CAMPSITE 2014

▶▶▶▶ **85% *Grouse Hill Caravan Park*** *(NZ928002)*

Flask Bungalow Farm, Fylingdales YO22 4QH
☎ **01947 880543 & 880560**
e-mail: info@grousehill.co.uk
dir: *Off A171 (Whitby-Scarborough road), entered via loop road at Flask Inn*

Open Mar-Oct (rs Etr-May shop & reception restricted)

Last arrival 20.30hrs Last departure noon

A spacious family park on a south-facing slope with attractive, mostly level, terraced pitches overlooking The North Yorkshire National Park. The site has quality toilet blocks, a treatment plant to ensure excellent drinking water, security barriers, CCTV, Wi-fi and camping pods. Please note that there are no hardstandings for tourers, only grass pitches. This is an ideal base for walking and touring. 14 acre site. 175 touring pitches. 30 hardstandings. Caravan pitches. Motorhome pitches. Tent pitches. 1 static. 8 wooden pods.

AA Pubs & Restaurants nearby: Laurel Inn, ROBIN HOOD'S BAY, YO22 4SE, 01947 880400

The Magpie Café, WHITBY, YO21 3PU, 01947 602058

Leisure: 🅰 🔍
Facilities: 🛁 🐾 ☉ 🏳 ✳ ♿ ◱ 🚻 🐕 🚾 ♻ ❶
Services: 🔌 🗑 🔋 🦷 🚽 🧺 ⬇
Within 3 miles: 🚴 👶 🗑 🔵 ↺
Notes: No noise after 22.30hrs. Dogs must be kept on leads.

see advert on opposite page

SERVICES: 🔌 Electric hook up   🗑 Launderette   🍷 Licensed bar   🛢 Calor Gas   🅖 Camping Gaz   🅣 Toilet fluid   🍴 Café/Restaurant   🍟 Fast Food/Takeaway   🔋 Battery charging   🍼 Baby care   ⬆ Motorvan service point   **ABBREVIATIONS:** BH/bank hols-bank holidays   Etr-Easter   Spring BH-Spring Bank Holiday   dep-departure   fr-from   hrs-hours   m-mile   mdnt-midnight   rdbt-roundabout   rs-restricted service   wk-week   wknd-weekend   x-rds-cross roads   ⊗ No credit cards   ⊗ No dogs   🧍 Children of all ages accepted   See page 9 for details of the AA Camping Card Scheme

ROBIN HOOD'S BAY continued

▶▶▶▶ 83% Middlewood Farm Holiday Park (NZ945045)

GOLD

Middlewood Ln, Fylingthorpe YO22 4UF
☎ **01947 880414**
e-mail: info@middlewoodfarm.com
dir: From A171 towards Robin Hood's Bay, into Fylingthorpe. Site signed from A171

🚐 🚐 ⛺

Open Mar-Oct

Last arrival 20.00hrs Last departure 11.00hrs

A peaceful, friendly family park enjoying panoramic views of Robin Hood's Bay in a picturesque fishing village. The park has two toilet blocks with private facilities. The village pub is a five-minute walk away, and the beach can be reached via a path leading directly from the site, which is also accessible for wheelchair users. Four 5-berth camping pods are available for hire. 7 acre site. 100 touring pitches. 19 hardstandings. Caravan pitches. Motorhome pitches. Tent pitches. 30 statics. 4 wooden pods.

AA Pubs & Restaurants nearby: Laurel Inn, ROBIN HOOD'S BAY, YO22 4SE, 01947 880400

Leisure: 🅰 **Facilities:** 🛁🚿⊙🖐✳🔥🖉🚻♻🈂❶
Services: 🚱🖾🖾🛢🖾🖾🖾🖾🖾
Within 3 miles: ↕🏇🖉🛒🖾U

Notes: No radios or noise after 23.00hrs. Dangerous dog breeds are not accepted. Dogs must be kept on leads.

see advert on page 343

ROSEDALE ABBEY — Map 19 SE79

Places to visit

Pickering Castle, PICKERING, YO6 5AB, 01751 474989 www.english-heritage.org.uk/daysout/properties/pickering-castle

North Yorkshire Moors Railway, PICKERING, YO18 7AJ, 01751 472508 www.nymr.co.uk

Great for kids: Flamingo Land Theme Park & Zoo, KIRBY MISPERTON, YO17 6UX, 01653 668287 www.flamingoland.co.uk

▶▶▶▶ 81% Rosedale Caravan & Camping Park (SE725958)

YO18 8SA
☎ **01751 417272**
e-mail: info@flowerofmay.com
dir: From Pickering take A170 towards Sinnington for 2.25m. At Wrelton right onto unclassified road signed Cropton & Rosedale, 7m. Site on left in village

🚐 £18-£24 🚐 £18-£24 ⛺ £18-£24

Open Mar-Oct

Last arrival dusk Last departure noon

Set in a sheltered valley in the centre of the North Yorkshire Moors National Park, and divided into separate areas for tents, tourers and statics. A very popular park, with well-tended grounds, and close to the pretty village of Rosedale Abbey. Two toilet blocks offer private, combined facilities. There are six camping pods situated by the river. 10 acre site. 100 touring pitches. 20 seasonal pitches. Caravan pitches. Motorhome pitches. Tent pitches. 35 statics. 6 wooden pods.

AA Pubs & Restaurants nearby: Blacksmiths Arms, LASTINGHAM, YO62 6TN, 01751 417247

The New Inn, CROPTON, YO18 8HH, 01751 417330

Leisure: 🅰
Facilities: 🖐⊙✳🔥🛢🕐🈂🚻🐾❶
Services: 🚱🖾🛢🖉🖾🖾
Within 3 miles: ↕🖉🛒🖾U

Notes: No radios or noise after 23:00hrs. No dangerous dog breeds. Dogs must be on leads.

see advert on page 331

SCARBOROUGH — Map 17 TA08

See also Filey & Wykeham

Places to visit

Scarborough Castle, SCARBOROUGH, YO11 1HY, 01723 372451 www.english-heritage.org.uk/daysout/properties/scarborough-castle

Pickering Castle, PICKERING, YO6 5AB, 01751 474989 www.english-heritage.org.uk/daysout/properties/pickering-castle

Great for kids: Sea Life & Marine Sanctuary, SCARBOROUGH, YO12 6RP, 01723 373414 www.sealife.co.uk

PREMIER PARK

▶▶▶▶▶ 78% Jacobs Mount Caravan Park (TA021868)

Jacobs Mount, Stepney Rd YO12 5NL
☎ **01723 361178**
e-mail: jacobsmount@yahoo.co.uk
dir: Direct access from A170

🚐 £12.50-£23.50 🚐 £12.50-£23.50 ⛺ £12.50-£23.50

Open Mar-Nov (rs Mar-May & Oct-Nov limited hours at shop & bar)

Last arrival 22.00hrs Last departure noon

An elevated family-run park surrounded by woodland and open countryside, yet only two miles from the beach. Touring pitches are terraced gravel stands with individual services; the toilet facilities were refurbished for 2013. The Jacobs Tavern serves a wide range of appetising meals and snacks, and there is a separate well-equipped games room for teenagers. 18 acre site. 156 touring pitches. 131 hardstandings. Caravan pitches. Motorhome pitches. Tent pitches. 60 statics.

LEISURE: 🏊 Indoor swimming pool 🏊 Outdoor swimming pool 🅰 Children's playground 🖐 Kid's club 🎾 Tennis court 🎱 Games room 📺 Separate TV room ⛳ 9/18 hole golf course 🚣 Boats for hire 🎬 Cinema 🎵 Entertainment 🎣 Fishing ⊙ Mini golf 🏄 Watersports 🏋 Gym ⚽ Sports field Spa U Stables
FACILITIES: 🛁 Bath 🚿 Shower ⊙ Electric shaver 🖉 Hairdryer ✳ Ice Pack Facility ♿ Disabled facilities ☎ Public telephone 🈂 Shop on site or within 200yds 🛒 Mobile shop (calls at least 5 days a week) 🍖 BBQ area 🪑 Picnic area 📶 Wi-fi 💻 Internet access ♻ Recycling ❶ Tourist info 🐾 Dog exercise area

AA Pubs & Restaurants nearby: The Anvil Inn, SAWDON, YO13 9DY, 01723 859896

Lanterna Ristorante, SCARBOROUGH, YO11 1HQ, 01723 363616

Leisure: ⚙ ❄ ▢ 🎵
Facilities: ⟲ ⟲ ☉ 🐾 ⚡ 🔥 🌳 🕐 🖐 📶 🖥 🛒 ❓
Services: ⚡ 🗄 🍺 🛡 ⊘ 🚽 🍽 🏪 🛒 ⚓
Within 3 miles: ⬇ ⛳ 🎣 ♫ ◎ 🏊 🎢 🗄 ∪

Notes: Dogs must be kept on leads. Food preparation area.

►►►► 83% Cayton Village Caravan Park *(TA063838)*

Mill Ln, Cayton Bay YO11 3NN
☎ 01723 583171
e-mail: info@caytontouring.co.uk
dir: *From Scarborough A64, B1261 signed Filey. In Cayton 2nd left after Blacksmiths Arms into Mill Ln. Site 150yds on left. Or from A165 from Scarborough towards Filey right at Cayton Bay rdbt into Mill Ln. Site 0.5m right. (NB it is advisable to follow guide directions not Sat Nav)*

* 🚐 £13.50-£35 🚍 £15.50-£35 ▲ £13.50-£28

Open Mar-Oct

Last arrival 18.00hrs Last departure noon

A long established, quietly located holiday destination close to all the major coastal attractions. The immaculately maintained grounds provide excellent pitch density and many areas are hedge-screened to create privacy. The latest touring field, The Laurels, is equipped with fully serviced hardstanding pitches that include TV hook-up and free Wi-fi. 30 acre site. 310 touring pitches. 239 hardstandings. 180 seasonal pitches. Caravan pitches. Motorhome pitches. Tent pitches.

AA Pubs & Restaurants nearby: Beiderbecke's Hotel, SCARBOROUGH, YO11 2PW, 01723 365766

Leisure: ⚙ ❄
Facilities: ⟲ ☉ 🐾 ❄ 🕐 🗄 🔥 🌳 📶 ❓
Services: ⚡ 🗄 🛡 ⊘ 🚽 🏪
Within 3 miles: ⬇ ⛳ 🎣 ♫ ◎ 🏊 🗄 🗄

Notes: No noise after 23.00hrs, children must be supervised, no campfires, late arrival/departure available if pre-booked (fees may apply). Dogs must be kept on leads.

►►►► 79% Scalby Close Park

(TA020925)

Burniston Rd YO13 0DA
☎ 01723 365908
e-mail: info@scalbyclosepark.co.uk
web: www.scalbyclosepark.co.uk
dir: *2m N of Scarborough on A615 (coast road), 1m from junct with A171*

🚐 🚍

Open Mar-Oct

Last arrival 22.00hrs Last departure noon

An attractive, well-landscaped park that is run by enthusiastic owners. The site has a shower block, laundry, fully serviced pitches and a new motorhome service point. Just two miles from Scarborough, this makes an ideal base from which to explore both the coast and lovely countryside. 3 acre site. 42 touring pitches. 42 hardstandings. Caravan pitches. Motorhome pitches. 5 statics.

AA Pubs & Restaurants nearby: The Anvil Inn, SAWDON, YO13 9DY, 01723 859896

Lanterna Ristorante, SCARBOROUGH, YO11 1HQ, 01723 363616

Facilities: ⟲ ☉ 🐾 ❄ 🕐 🗄
Services: ⚡ 🗄 ⊘ 🚽 🏪 ⚓
Within 3 miles: ⬇ ⛳ 🎣 ♫ 🗄 🗄 ∪
Notes: ⊗

►►► 80% Killerby Old Hall *(TA063829)*

Killerby YO11 3TW
☎ 01723 583799
e-mail: killerbyhall@btconnect.com
dir: *Direct access via B1261 at Killerby, near Cayton*

🚐 🚍

Open 14 Feb-4 Jan

Last arrival 20.00hrs Last departure noon

A small secluded park, well sheltered by mature trees and shrubs, located at the rear of the old hall. Use of the small indoor swimming pool is shared by visitors to the hall's holiday accommodation. There is a children's play area. 2 acre site. 20 touring pitches. 20 hardstandings. Caravan pitches. Motorhome pitches.

AA Pubs & Restaurants nearby: The Anvil Inn, SAWDON, YO13 9DY, 01723 859896

Lanterna Ristorante, SCARBOROUGH, YO11 1HQ, 01723 363616

Leisure: ⚙ ⚙ ❄ ❄
Facilities: ⟲ ☉ 🐾 🌳 🔥 📶 ♻ ❓
Services: ⚡ 🗄
Within 3 miles: ⬇ ♫ ◎ 🏊 🗄 🗄 ∪
Notes: Dogs must be kept on leads.

►►► 79% *Arosa Caravan & Camping Park (TA014830)*

Ratten Row, Seamer YO12 4QB
☎ 01723 862166 & 07858 694077
e-mail: info@arosacamping.co.uk
dir: *A64 towards Scarborough onto B1261. On entering village 1st left at rdbt signed Seamer. From Pickering on A171 right at Seamer rdbt. Last right in village*

🚐 🚍 ▲

Open Mar-4 Jan

Last arrival 21.00hrs Last departure by arrangement

A mature park in a secluded location, but with easy access to costal attractions. Touring areas are hedge-screened to provide privacy, and a well-stocked bar serving food is also available. Barbecues and hog roasts are a feature during the warmer months. 9 acre site. 118 touring pitches. 25 hardstandings. 40 seasonal pitches. Caravan pitches. Motorhome pitches. Tent pitches. 8 statics.

AA Pubs & Restaurants nearby: The Coachman Inn, SNAINTON, YO13 9PL, 01723 859231

Leisure: ⚙ ❄ 🎵
Facilities: ⟲ 🐾 ❄ 🕐 🗄 📶 🖥 ❓
Services: ⚡ 🗄 🍺 🛡 ⊘ 🚽 🍽 🏪 🛒
Within 3 miles: ⬇ ♫ 🗄 🗄 ∪

Notes: No noise after 23.00hrs, no generators, no powered bikes or scooters. Dogs must be kept on leads.

SERVICES: ⚡ Electric hook up ⬜ Launderette 🍺 Licensed bar 🛡 Calor Gas ⊘ Camping Gaz 🚽 Toilet fluid 🍽 Café/Restaurant 🛒 Fast Food/Takeaway
📶 Battery charging 🍼 Baby care ⚓ Motorvan service point **ABBREVIATIONS:** BH/bank hols-bank holidays Etr-Easter Spring BH-Spring Bank Holiday dep-departure
fr-from hrs-hours m-mile mdnt-midnight rdbt-roundabout rs-restricted service wk-week wknd-weekend x-rds-cross roads ⊗ No credit cards ⊗ No dogs
🚸 Children of all ages accepted See page 9 for details of the AA Camping Card Scheme

SCOTCH CORNER — Map 19 NZ20

Places to visit

Green Howards Museum, RICHMOND, DL10 4QN, 01748 826561 www.greenhowards.org.uk

Bolton Castle, CASTLE BOLTON, DL8 4ET, 01969 623981 www.boltoncastle.co.uk

Great for kids: Raby Castle, STAINDROP, DL2 3AH, 01833 660202 www.rabycastle.com

▶▶▶ 75% Scotch Corner Caravan Park *(NZ210054)*

DL10 6NS

☎ 01748 822530 & 07977 647722

e-mail: marshallleisure@aol.com

dir: *From Scotch Corner junct of A1 & A66 take A6108 towards Richmond. 250mtrs, cross central reservation, return 200mtrs to site entrance*

* ⛺ £14-£18 ⛺ £14-£20 ▲ fr £14

Open Etr or Apr-Oct

Last arrival 22.30hrs Last departure noon

A well-maintained site with good facilities, ideally situated as a stopover, and an equally good location for touring. The Vintage Hotel, which serves food, can be accessed from the rear of the site. 7 acre site. 96 touring pitches. 4 hardstandings. Caravan pitches. Motorhome pitches. Tent pitches. 1 static.

AA Pubs & Restaurants nearby: The Shoulder of Mutton Inn, KIRBY HILL, DL11 7JH, 01748 822772

Facilities: ⬛☉♟⚲☀⚷⛟☖☏⚓♻ ❼

Services: ⚡⬛⚡⬛⚑⊘Ⓣ⍭⚑⬛⬇

Within 3 miles: ⚴☷⚟⬛⬛Ⓤ

Notes: ⊛ Dogs must be kept on leads. Recreation area for children, soft ball.

SHERIFF HUTTON

Places to visit

Kirkham Priory, KIRKHAM, YO6 7JS, 01653 618768 www.english-heritage.org.uk/daysout/properties/kirkham-priory

Sutton Park, SUTTON-ON-THE-FOREST, YO61 1DP, 01347 810249 www.statelyhome.co.uk

SHERIFF HUTTON — Map 19 SE66

▶▶▶▶ 78% York Meadows Caravan Park *(SE644653)*

York Rd YO60 6QP

☎ 01439 788269 & 788236

e-mail: reception@yorkmeadowscaravanpark.com

dir: *From York take A64 towards Scarborough. Left signed Flaxton & Sheriff Hutton. At West Lilling left signed Strensall. Site opposite junct*

* ⛺ £16.50-£24.50 ⛺ £16.50-£24.50

Open Mar-Oct

Last arrival 21.00hrs Last departure noon

Peacefully located in open countryside and surrounded by mature trees, shrubs and wildlife areas, this park provides all level pitches and a modern, well-equipped amenities block. Outdoor games such as draughts and snakes and ladders have now been added. 12 acre site. 45 touring pitches. 45 hardstandings. 10 seasonal pitches. Caravan pitches. Motorhome pitches. Tent pitches. 15 statics.

AA Pubs & Restaurants nearby: The Blackwell Ox Inn, SUTTON-ON-THE-FOREST, YO61 1DT, 01347 810328

The Rose & Crown, SUTTON-ON-THE-FOREST, YO61 1DP, 01347 811333

Leisure: ⚠ ☆

Facilities: ⬛⬛☉♟☀⚷⛟☖☏⬛ ♻ ❼

Services: ⚡⬛⚑⊘⬇

Within 3 miles: ⚴☷⚟⬛⬛

Notes: No noise after 23.00hrs. Dogs must be kept on leads.

SLINGSBY — Map 19 SE67

Places to visit

Nunnington Hall, NUNNINGTON, YO62 5UY, 01439 748283 www.nationaltrust.org.uk

Castle Howard, MALTON, YO60 7DA, 01653 648333 www.castlehoward.co.uk

▶▶▶▶ 82% *Robin Hood Caravan & Camping Park (SE701748)*

Green Dyke Ln YO62 4AP

☎ 01653 628391

e-mail: info@robinhoodcaravanpark.co.uk

dir: *Access from B1257 (Malton to Helmsley road)*

⛺ ⛺ ▲

Open Mar-Oct

Last arrival 18.00hrs Last departure noon

A pleasant, well-maintained, grassy park in a good location for touring North Yorkshire. Situated on the edge of the village of Slingsby, the park has hardstandings and electricity for every pitch, and a centrally heated toilet block. There is a treasure trail and play area for children. 2 acre site. 32 touring pitches. 22 hardstandings. Caravan pitches. Motorhome pitches. Tent pitches. 35 statics.

AA Pubs & Restaurants nearby: The Worsley Arms Hotel, HOVINGHAM, YO62 4LA, 01653 628234

The Malt Shovel, HOVINGHAM, YO62 4LF, 01653 628264

The Royal Oak Inn, NUNNINGTON, YO62 5US, 01439 748271

Leisure: ⚠

Facilities: ⬛☉♟☀⚷⛟☖☏⬛⬛ ♻ ❼

Services: ⚡⬛⚑⊘Ⓣ⬇

Within 3 miles: ⚟⬛Ⓤ

Notes: No noise after 23.00hrs. Dogs must be kept on leads. Caravan hire, off-licence.

see advert on opposite page

SNAINTON — Map 17 SE98

Places to visit

Scarborough Castle, SCARBOROUGH, YO11 1HY, 01723 372451 www.english-heritage.org.uk/daysout/properties/scarborough-castle

Pickering Castle, PICKERING, YO6 5AB, 01751 474989 www.english-heritage.org.uk/daysout/properties/pickering-castle

Great for kids: Sea Life & Marine Sanctuary, SCARBOROUGH, YO12 6RP, 01723 373414 www.sealife.co.uk

▶▶▶▶ **87% Jasmine Caravan Park**

(SE928813)

Cross Ln YO13 9BE
☎ **01723 859240**
e-mail: enquiries@jasminepark.co.uk
dir: *Turn S from A170 in Snainton, then follow signs*

* 🚐 £20-£35 🚐 £20-£35 ▲ £20-£35

Open Mar-Oct

Last arrival 20.00hrs Last departure noon

A peaceful and beautifully-presented park on the edge of a pretty village, and sheltered by high hedges. The toilet block with individual wash cubicles is maintained to a very high standard, and there is a licensed shop. This picturesque park lies midway between Pickering and Scarborough on the southern edge of the North Yorkshire Moors. Please note there is no motorhome service point but super pitches for motorhomes are available. 5 acre site. 68 touring pitches. 68 hardstandings. 42 seasonal pitches. Caravan pitches. Motorhome pitches. Tent pitches. 16 statics.

AA Pubs & Restaurants nearby: The Coachman Inn, SNAINTON, YO13 9PL, 01723 859231

The New Inn, THORNTON LE DALE, YO18 7LF, 01751 474226

Leisure: 🅰 ⚙

Facilities: 🚻 🅰 ☺ 🅿 ⚒ ☀ ♿ 🕒 🛒 ⓢ 🅰 WiFi 🖥 ☁ ❂

Services: 🚽 🛢 🅿 ⊘ Ⓣ 🛒

Within 3 miles: ↓ ↗ ◎ 🛢 🛢 ∪

Notes: No noise after 23.00hrs. Dogs must be kept on leads. Baby changing unit.

STAINFORTH — Map 18 SD86

Places to visit

Brodsworth Hall & Gardens, DONCASTER, DN5 7XJ, 01302 722598 www.english-heritage.org.uk/daysout/properties/brodsworth-hall-and-gardens

Doncaster Museum & Art Gallery, DONCASTER, DN1 2AE, 01302 734293 www.doncaster.gov.uk/museums

Great for kids: The Yorkshire Waterways Museum, GOOLE, DN14 5TB, 01405 768730 www.waterwaysmuseum.org.uk

▶▶▶▶ **80% *Knight Stainforth Hall Caravan & Campsite*** *(SD816672)*

BD24 0DP
☎ **01729 822200**
e-mail: info@knightstainforth.co.uk
dir: *From W, on A65 take B6480 for Settle, left before swimming pool signed Little Stainforth. From E, through Settle on B6480, over bridge to swimming pool, turn right*

🚐 🚐 ▲

Open Mar-Oct

Last arrival 22.00hrs Last departure noon

Located near Settle and the River Ribble in the Yorkshire Dales National Park, this well-maintained family site is sheltered by mature woodland. It is an ideal base for walking or touring in the beautiful surrounding areas. The toilet block is appointed to a very high standard.

continued

Robin Hood Caravan Park

Slingsby, York YO62 4AP
Tel: 01653 628391 Fax: 01653 628392
www.robinhoodcaravanpark.co.uk

ROBIN HOOD Caravan & Camping Park is situated in the heart of picturesque Ryedale on the edge of the North Yorkshire village of Slingsby. Privately owned and operated by the Palmer family   this award winning park is a perfect base for families and couples wishing to explore the stunning countryside of North Yorkshire.

Touring Caravans, motor homes and tents are always welcome. All weather pitches complete with electric hook-up and water and waste-disposal points are available. A small shop and off-licence serves your basic requirements. Calor Gas and Camping Gaz is stocked. A Children's play area keeps the youngsters amused.

STAINFORTH *continued*

6 acre site. 100 touring pitches. 30 hardstandings. Caravan pitches. Motorhome pitches. Tent pitches. 60 statics.

AA Pubs & Restaurants nearby: Black Horse Hotel, GIGGLESWICK, BD24 0BE, 01729 822506

The Game Cock Inn, AUSTWICK, LA2 8BB, 015242 51226

The Traddock, AUSTWICK, LA2 8BY, 015242 51224

Leisure: ⚲ ⚽ ⚲ ▭

Facilities: ⚲ ⊙ ℱ ✳ ⚲ ⚲ ⑤ ☴ ⚲ ᵂᴵᶠᴵ ▤ ♲ ❶

Services: ⚲ ⑤ ⚲ ⚲ Ⓣ ⚲ ⚲

Within 3 miles: ⚲ ⚲ ⑤ ⑤ ⚲

Notes: No groups of unaccompanied minors. Dogs must be kept on leads. Fishing.

STILLINGFLEET   Map 16 SE54

Places to visit

Merchant Adventurers' Hall, YORK, YO1 9XD, 01904 654818 www.theyorkcompany.co.uk

Mansion House, YORK, YO1 9QN, 01904 613161 www.mansionhouseyork.com

Great for kids: National Railway Museum, YORK, YO26 4XJ, 01904 621261 www.nrm.org.uk

►►► 72% Home Farm Caravan & Camping *(SE595427)*

Moreby YO19 6HN
☎ **01904 728263**
e-mail: home_farm@hotmail.co.uk
dir: *6m from York on B1222, 1.5m N of Stillingfleet*

⚲ ⚲ Å

Open Feb-Dec

Last arrival 22.00hrs

A traditional meadowland site on a working farm bordered by parkland on one side and the River Ouse on another. Facilities are in converted farm buildings, and the family owners extend a friendly welcome to tourers. An excellent site for relaxing and unwinding, yet only a short distance from the attractions of York. There are four log cabins for holiday hire. 5 acre site. 25 touring pitches. Caravan pitches. Motorhome pitches. Tent pitches.

Facilities: ⚲ ⊙ ℱ ✳ ⚲ ⚲ ♲ ❶

Services: ⚲ ⑤ ⚲ ⚲ Ⓣ ⚲   **Within 3 miles:** ⚲ ⚲

Notes: ⚲ Dogs must be kept on leads. Family washroom.

SUTTON-ON-THE-FOREST   Map 19 SE56

Places to visit

Sutton Park, SUTTON-ON-THE-FOREST, YO61 1DP, 01347 810249 www.statelyhome.co.uk

Treasurer's House, YORK, YO1 7JL, 01904 624247 www.nationaltrust.org.uk

Great for kids: Jorvik Viking Centre, YORK, YO1 9WT, 01904 615505 www.jorvik-viking-centre.com

---

PREMIER PARK

►►►►► 83% Goosewood Caravan Park *(SE595636)*

YO61 1ET
☎ **01347 810829**
e-mail: enquiries@goosewood.co.uk
dir: *From A1237 take B1363. In 5m turn right. Right again in 0.5m, site on right*

⚲ £18-£24 ⚲ £18-£24

Open Mar-2 Jan (rs Low season shop, bar & pool reduced hours)

Last arrival dusk Last departure noon

A relaxing and immaculately maintained park with its own lake and seasonal fishing. It is set in attractive woodland just six miles north of York. Mature shrubs and stunning seasonal floral displays at the entrance create an excellent first impression and the well-located toilet facilities are kept spotlessly clean. The generous patio pitches, providing optimum privacy, are randomly spaced throughout the site, and in addition to an excellent outdoor children's play area, a new indoor swimming pool, club house, games room and bar/bistro opened in 2013. There are holiday homes for hire. 20 acre site. 100 touring pitches. 75 hardstandings. 50 seasonal pitches. Caravan pitches. Motorhome pitches. 35 statics.

AA Pubs & Restaurants nearby: The Blackwell Ox Inn, SUTTON-ON-THE-FOREST, YO61 1DT, 01347 810328

The Rose & Crown, SUTTON-ON-THE-FOREST, YO61 1DP, 01347 811333

Leisure: ⚲ ⚲ ⚲

Facilities: ⚲ ⊙ ℱ ✳ ⚲ ⚲ ⑤ ☴ ⚲ ᵂᴵᶠᴵ ♲ ❶

Services: ⚲ ⑤ ⚲ ⚲ Ⓣ ⚲ ⚲

Within 3 miles: ⚲ ☴ ⚲ ⑤ ⑤

Notes: No noise after mdnt, dogs by prior arrangement only. Dogs must be kept on leads.

see advert on page 331

THIRSK   Map 19 SE48

Places to visit

Monk Park Farm Visitor Centre, THIRSK, YO7 2AG, 01845 597730 www.monkparkfarm.co.uk

Norton Conyers, RIPON, HG4 5EQ, 01765 640333 www.weddingsatnortonconyers.co.uk

Great for kids: Falconry UK - Birds of Prey Centre, THIRSK, YO7 4EU, 01845 587522 www.falconrycentre.co.uk

---

AA CAMPING CARD SITE

►►►► 83% Hillside Caravan Park *(SE447889)*

Canvas Farm, Moor Rd, Knayton
YO7 4BR
☎ **01845 537349 & 07711 643652**
e-mail: info@hillsidecaravanpark.co.uk
dir: *From Thirsk take A19 N exit at Knayton sign. In 0.25m right (cross bridge over A19), through village. Site on left in approx 1.5m*

* ⚲ £19-£31 ⚲ £19-£31

Open 4 Feb-4 Jan

Last arrival 21.00hrs Last departure noon

A high quality, spacious park with first-class facilities, set in open countryside. It is an excellent base for walkers and for those wishing to explore the Thirsk area. Please note that the park does not accept tents. 9 acre site. 50 touring pitches. 50 hardstandings. Caravan pitches. Motorhome pitches.

AA Pubs & Restaurants nearby: The Black Swan at Oldstead, OLDSTEAD, YO61 4BL, 01347 868387

Leisure: ⚲ ⚽

Facilities: ⚲ ⊙ ℱ ⚲ ☴ ⚲ ᵂᴵᶠᴵ ♲ ❶

Services: ⚲ ⑤ ⚲ ⚲

Within 3 miles: ⚲ ⚲ ⑤ ⚲

Notes: ⚲ Dogs must be kept on leads.

LEISURE: 🏊 Indoor swimming pool   🏊 Outdoor swimming pool   ⚲ Children's playground   👋 Kid's club   ⚲ Tennis court   ⚲ Games room   ▭ Separate TV room   ⚲ 9/18 hole golf course   ⚲ Boats for hire   ⚲ Cinema   ♫ Entertainment   ⚲ Fishing   ⚲ Mini golf   ⚲ Watersports   ⚲ Gym   ⚲ Sports field   Spa   ⚲ Stables
FACILITIES: ⚲ Bath   ⚲ Shower   ⊙ Electric shaver   ℱ Hairdryer   ✳ Ice Pack Facility   ⚲ Disabled facilities   ⚲ Public telephone   ⑤ Shop on site or within 200yds   ⚲ Mobile shop (calls at least 5 days a week)   ⚲ BBQ area   ⚲ Picnic area   ᵂᴵᶠᴵ Wi-fi   ▤ Internet access   ♲ Recycling   ❶ Tourist info   ⚲ Dog exercise area

►►► 76% Thirkleby Hall Caravan Park (SE472794)

Thirkleby YO7 3AR
☎ **01845 501360 & 07799 641815**
e-mail: greenwood.parks@virgin.net
web: www.greenwoodparks.com
dir: *3m S of Thirsk on A19. Turn left through arched gatehouse into site*

* ⬛ £22.50-£24.50 ⬛ £22.50-£24.50
▲ £13-£24.50

Open Mar-Oct

Last arrival 17.30hrs Last departure 14.30hrs

A long-established site in the grounds of the old hall, with statics in wooded areas around a fishing lake and tourers based on slightly sloping grassy pitches. There is a quality amenities block and laundry. This well-screened park has superb views of the Hambledon Hills. 53 acre site. 50 touring pitches. 3 hardstandings. 20 seasonal pitches. Caravan pitches. Motorhome pitches. Tent pitches. 185 statics.

AA Pubs & Restaurants nearby: The Black Swan at Oldstead, OLDSTEAD, YO61 4BL, 01347 868387

Leisure: ⚲ ☼
Facilities: ⬛⊙⬛⬛⬛⬛⬛⬛⬛
Services: ⬛⬛⬛⬛⬛
Within 3 miles: ⬛⬛⬛⬛⬛

Notes: ⬛ No noise after 23.00hrs. Dogs must be kept on leads. 12-acre woods.

TOLLERTON   Map 19 SE56

Places to visit

The York Brewery Co Ltd, YORK, YO1 6JT, 01904 621162 www.york-brewery.co.uk

Yorkshire Museum, YORK, YO1 7FR, 01904 551800 www.yorkshiremuseum.org.uk

Great for kids: Jorvik Viking Centre, YORK, YO1 9WT, 01904 615505 www.jorvik-viking-centre.com

►►►► 78% Tollerton Holiday Park (SE513643)

Station Rd YO61 1RD
☎ **01347 838313**
e-mail: greenwood.parks@virgin.net
dir: *From York take A19 towards Thirsk. At Cross Lanes left towards Tollerton. 1m to Chinese restaurant just before rail bridge. Site entrance through restaurant car park*

⬛ £22-£23 ▲ £12-£23

Open Mar-Oct

Last arrival 20.00hrs Last departure 15.00hrs

Set in open countryside within a few minutes' walk of Tollerton and just a short drive from the Park & Ride for York, this is a small park. There's an amenities block of real quality, which includes a family bathroom and laundry. There is little disturbance from the East Coast mainline which passes near to the park. 5 acre site. 50 touring pitches. 17 hardstandings. 25 seasonal pitches. Caravan pitches. Motorhome pitches. Tent pitches. 75 statics.

AA Pubs & Restaurants nearby: The Blackwell Ox Inn, SUTTON-ON-THE-FOREST, YO61 1DT, 01347 810328

The Rose & Crown, SUTTON-ON-THE-FOREST, YO61 1DP, 01347 811333

Leisure: ⚲ ☼
Facilities: ⬛⬛⊙⬛⬛⬛⬛⬛⬛⬛⬛
Services: ⬛⬛⬛⬛⬛⬛
Within 3 miles: ⬛⬛⬛⬛

Notes: ⬛ No groups. Dogs must be kept on leads. Small fishing lake.

TOWTHORPE   Map 19 SE65

Places to visit

Malton Museum, MALTON, YO17 7LP, 01653 695136 www.maltonmuseum.co.uk

Wolds Way Lavender, MALTON, YO17 8HW, 01944 758641 www.woldswaylavender.co.uk

Great for kids: Eden Camp Modern History Theme Museum, MALTON, YO17 6RT, 01653 697777 www.edencamp.co.uk

►►►► 77% York Touring Caravan Site (SE648584)

Greystones Farm, Towthorpe Moor Ln YO32 9ST
☎ **01904 499275**
e-mail: info@yorkcaravansite.co.uk
web: www.yorkcaravansite.co.uk
dir: *From A64 follow Strensall & Haxby signs, site 1.5m on left*

* ⬛ £17-£22 ⬛ £17-£22 ▲ £17-£22

Open 8 Feb-3 Jan

Last arrival 21.00hrs Last departure noon

This purpose-built golf complex and caravan park is situated just over five miles from York. There is a 9-hole golf course, crazy golf, driving range and golf shop with a coffee bar/café. The generous sized, level pitches are set within well-manicured grassland with a backdrop of trees and shrubs. 6 acre site. 44 touring pitches. 12 hardstandings. Caravan pitches. Motorhome pitches. Tent pitches.

AA Pubs & Restaurants nearby: The Blackwell Ox Inn, SUTTON-ON-THE-FOREST, YO61 1DT, 01347 810328

The Rose & Crown, SUTTON-ON-THE-FOREST, YO61 1DP, 01347 811333

Leisure: ☼
Facilities: ⬛⊙⬛⬛⬛⬛⬛⬛⬛⬛⬛
Services: ⬛⬛⬛⬛⬛
Within 3 miles: ⬛⬛⊙⬛⬛

Notes: No noise after 23.00hrs, no commercial vehicles. Dogs must be kept on leads.

SERVICES: ⬛ Electric hook up ⬛ Launderette ⬛ Licensed bar ⬛ Calor Gas ⬛ Camping Gaz ⬛ Toilet fluid ⬛ Café/Restaurant ⬛ Fast Food/Takeaway ⬛ Battery charging ⬛ Baby care ⬛ Motorvan service point **ABBREVIATIONS:** BH/bank hols-bank holidays Etr-Easter Spring BH-Spring Bank Holiday dep-departure fr-from hrs-hours m-mile mdnt-midnight rdbt-roundabout rs-restricted service wk-week wknd-weekend x-rds-cross roads ⬛ No credit cards ⬛ No dogs ⬛ Children of all ages accepted See page 9 for details of the AA Camping Card Scheme

WEST KNAPTON — Map 19 SE87

Places to visit

Pickering Castle, PICKERING, YO6 5AB, 01751 474989 www.english-heritage.org.uk/daysout/properties/pickering-castle

North Yorkshire Moors Railway, PICKERING, YO18 7AJ, 01751 472508 www.nymr.co.uk

Great for kids: Eden Camp Modern History Theme Museum, MALTON, YO17 6RT, 01653 697777 www.edencamp.co.uk

▶▶▶▶ **80%** *Wolds Way Caravan and Camping* (SE896743)

West Farm YO17 8JE
☎ **01944 728463 & 728180**
dir: *Signed between Rillington & West Heslerton on A64 (Malton to Scarborough road). Site 1.5m*

Open Mar-Oct

Last arrival 22.30hrs Last departure 19.00hrs

A park on a working farm in a peaceful, high position on the Yorkshire Wolds, with magnificent views over the Vale of Pickering. This is an excellent walking area, with the Wolds Way passing the entrance to the park. A pleasant one and a half mile path leads to a lavender farm, with its first-class coffee shop. 7.5 acre site. 70 touring pitches. 5 hardstandings. Caravan pitches. Motorhome pitches. Tent pitches.

AA Pubs & Restaurants nearby: The Coachman Inn, SNAINTON, YO13 9PL, 01723 859231

The New Inn, THORNTON LE DALE, YO18 7LF, 01751 474226

Leisure: ⚠

Facilities: 🛁 📷 ☉ ✳ ♿ 🖥 🛒 🎠 Wi-Fi ♻ ❶

Services: 🖥 🖾 🚽 🅃 🛒

Within 3 miles: 𝒫 🅂

Notes: Free use of microwave, toaster & TV. Drinks machine, fridge & freezer.

WHITBY — Map 19 NZ81

See also Robin Hood's Bay

Places to visit

Whitby Abbey, WHITBY, YO22 4JT, 01947 603568 www.english-heritage.org.uk/daysout/properties/whitby-abbey

Scarborough Castle, SCARBOROUGH, YO11 1HY, 01723 372451 www.english-heritage.org.uk/daysout/properties/scarborough-castle

Great for kids: Sea Life & Marine Sanctuary, SCARBOROUGH, YO12 6RP, 01723 373414 www.sealife.co.uk

AA CAMPING CARD SITE

▶▶▶▶ **85%** Ladycross Plantation Caravan Park
(NZ821080)

GOLD

Egton YO21 1UA
☎ **01947 895502**
e-mail: enquiries@ladycrossplantation.co.uk
dir: *From A171 (Whitby to Teesside road) onto unclassified road (site signed)*

* 🚐 £19-£27.50 🚃 £19-£27.50 ⛺ £19-£22

Open Mar-Nov

Last arrival 20.00hrs Last departure noon

A unique forest setting creates an away-from-it-all feeling at this peaceful touring park set in 30 acres of woodland and under enthusiastic ownership. Pitches are sited in small groups in clearings around two smartly appointed amenity blocks, which offer excellent facilities - under-floor heating, no-touch infra-red showers, cubicles, kitchen prep areas and laundry facilities. The site is well placed for visiting Whitby and exploring the North York Moors. Children will enjoy exploring the woodland and nature walk. Oak Lodges are available for hire or sale. 30 acre site. 130 touring pitches. 33 hardstandings. 60 seasonal pitches. Caravan pitches. Motorhome pitches. Tent pitches. 2 wooden pods.

AA Pubs & Restaurants nearby: The Wheatsheaf Inn, EGTON, YO21 1TZ, 01947 895271

Horseshoe Hotel, EGTON BRIDGE, YO21 1XE, 01947 895245

The Magpie Café, WHITBY, YO21 3PU, 01947 602058

Facilities: 📷 ☉ ☎ ✳ ♿ 🅃 🖥 🛒 🎠 Wi-Fi ♻ ❶

Services: 🖥 🖾 🚽 🅃 🛒 ⅄

Within 3 miles: 𝒫 ✈ 🅂

Notes: Dogs must be kept on leads.

WYKEHAM — Map 17 SE98

Places to visit

Scarborough Castle, SCARBOROUGH, YO11 1HY, 01723 372451 www.english-heritage.org.uk/daysout/properties/scarborough-castle

Pickering Castle, PICKERING, YO6 5AB, 01751 474989 www.english-heritage.org.uk/daysout/properties/pickering-castle

Great for kids: Sea Life & Marine Sanctuary, SCARBOROUGH, YO12 6RP, 01723 373414 www.sealife.co.uk

PREMIER PARK

▶▶▶▶▶ **84%** St Helens Caravan Park (SE967836)

YO13 9QD
☎ **01723 862771**
e-mail: caravans@wykeham.co.uk
dir: *On A170 in village, 150yds on left beyond Downe Arms Hotel towards Scarborough*

* 🚐 £16.50-£25 🚃 £16.50-£25 ⛺ £11-£21

Open 15 Feb-15 Jan (rs Nov-Jan shop/laundry closed)

Last arrival 22.00hrs Last departure 17.00hrs

Set on the edge of the North York Moors National Park, this delightfully landscaped park is immaculately maintained and thoughtfully laid out; the stunning floral displays around the park are impressive. There are top quality facilities and a high level of customer care. The site is divided into terraces with tree-screening that creates smaller areas including an adults' zone. There are eight camping pods for hire (two have electricity). A cycle route leads through the surrounding Wykeham Estate and there is a short pathway to the adjoining Downe Arms Country Inn. 25 acre site. 250 touring pitches. 40

LEISURE: 🏊 Indoor swimming pool 🏊 Outdoor swimming pool ⚠ Children's playground 🎣 Kid's club 🎾 Tennis court 🎱 Games room 📺 Separate TV room ⛳ 9/18 hole golf course ⛵ Boats for hire 🎬 Cinema 🎵 Entertainment 🎣 Fishing ◎ Mini golf 🏄 Watersports 🏋 Gym 🏅 Sports field Spa ♘ Stables
FACILITIES: 🛁 Bath 📷 Shower ☉ Electric shaver ♨ Hairdryer ✳ Ice Pack Facility ♿ Disabled facilities ☎ Public telephone 🅂 Shop on site or within 200yds 🖥 Mobile shop (calls at least 5 days a week) 🍖 BBQ area 🎠 Picnic area Wi-Fi Wi-fi 🖳 Internet access ♻ Recycling ❶ Tourist info 🎯 Dog exercise area

hardstandings. Caravan pitches. Motorhome pitches. Tent pitches. 8 wooden pods.

AA Pubs & Restaurants nearby: The Coachman Inn, SNAINTON, YO13 9PL, 01723 859231

The New Inn, THORNTON LE DALE, YO18 7LF, 01751 474226

Leisure: ⛺

Facilities: 🚿 ⊙ ✲ ♿ ✆ $ ⛩ 🐕 Wi-fi ♻ ⓘ

Services: 🔌 ◙ 🛢 ⊘ [T] 🍴 🔋 🍔 ⚓

Within 3 miles: ⛳ ✦ ◎ $ ◙ ∪

Notes: No noise after 22.00hrs. Dogs must be kept on leads. Adult-only & family super pitches with water & drainage. Caravan storage.

YORK — Map 16 SE65

See also Sheriff Hutton

Places to visit

York Minster, YORK, YO1 7HH, 0844 9390016 www.yorkminster.org

National Railway Museum, YORK, YO26 4XJ, 01904 621261 www.nrm.org.uk

Great for kids: Jorvik Viking Centre, YORK, YO1 9WT, 01904 615505 www.jorvik-viking-centre.com

NEW ►►►► 79% Rawcliffe Manor Caravan Park *(SE583550)*

Manor Ln, Shipton Rd YO30 5TZ
☎ 01904 640845
e-mail: christine@lysanderarms.co.uk
dir: *From rdbt junct of A1237 & A19, take A19 signed York, Clifton, Rawcliffe. 1st left into Manor Ln, follow brown camping signs*

* 🚐 £25-£30 🚌 £25-£30

Open all year

Last arrival 18.00hrs Last departure 11.00hrs

A lovely little adults-only site tucked away behind the Lysander Arms and located only minutes from the centre of York. Each of the 13 generous-sized pithces is fully serviced with an individual chemical disposal point, and the central toilet block is very airy, modern and spotlessly clean. The grounds have been imaginatively landscaped. The pub offers good food and the York Park & Ride facility is a 10-minute walk away. 4.5 acre site. 13 touring pitches. Caravan & Motorhome pitches.

YORKSHIRE, SOUTH

WORSBROUGH — Map 16 SE30

Places to visit

Monk Bretton Priory, BARNSLEY, S71 5QD, 0870 333 1181 www.english-heritage.org.uk/daysout/properties/monk-bretton-priory

Millennium Gallery, SHEFFIELD, S1 2PP, 0114 278 2600 www.museums-sheffield.org.uk

Great for kids: Magna Science Adventure Centre, ROTHERHAM, S60 1DX, 01709 720002 www.visitmagna.co.uk

►► 79% Greensprings Touring Park *(SE330020)*

Rockley Abbey Farm, Rockley Ln S75 3DS
☎ 01226 288298
dir: *M1 junct 36, A61 to Barnsley. Left after 0.25m signed Pilley. Site 1m at bottom of hill*

* 🚐 £15 🚌 £15 ▲ £10-£12

Open Apr-30 Oct

Last arrival 21.00hrs Last departure noon

A secluded and attractive farm site set amidst woods and farmland, with access to the river and several good local walks. There are two touring areas, one gently sloping. Although not far from the M1, there is almost no traffic noise, and this site is convenient for exploring the area's industrial heritage, as well as the Peak District. 4 acre site. 65 touring pitches. 30 hardstandings. 22 seasonal pitches. Caravan pitches. Motorhome pitches. Tent pitches.

Leisure: ⚽

Facilities: 🚿 ⊙ ✲ 🐕 ⓘ

Services: 🔌 🛢

Within 3 miles: ⛳ ⛨ ◎ $ ◙ ∪

Notes: Ⓧ Dogs must be kept on leads.

YORKSHIRE, WEST

BARDSEY — Map 16 SE34

Places to visit

Bramham Park, BRAMHAM, LS23 6ND, 01937 846000 www.bramhampark.co.uk

Thackray Museum, LEEDS, LS9 7LN, 0113 244 4343 www.thackraymuseum.org

Great for kids: Leeds Industrial Museum at Armley Mills, LEEDS, LS12 2QF, 0113 263 7861 www.leeds.gov.uk/armleymills

►►►► 78% Glenfield Caravan Park *(SE351421)*

120 Blackmoor Ln LS17 9DZ
☎ 01937 574657
e-mail: glenfieldcp@aol.com
web: www.ukparks.co.uk/glenfield/
dir: *From A58 at Bardsey into Church Ln, past church, up hill. 0.5m, site on right*

* 🚐 fr £15 🚌 fr £15 ▲ £10-£20

Open all year

Last arrival 21.00hrs Last departure noon

A quiet family-owned rural site in a well-screened, tree-lined meadow. The site has an excellent toilet block complete with family room. A convenient touring base for Leeds and the surrounding area. Discounted golf and food are both available at the local golf club. 4 acre site. 30 touring pitches. 30 hardstandings. Caravan pitches. Motorhome pitches. Tent pitches. 1 static.

AA Pubs & Restaurants nearby: The Windmill Inn, LINTON, LS22 4HT, 01937 582209

Facilities: 🚿 ⊙ ✲ ♿ ✆ ⛩

Services: 🔌 ◙ 🔋 🍔

Within 3 miles: ⛳ ⛨ $ ◙ ∪

Notes: Ⓧ Children must be supervised. Dogs must be kept on leads.

LEEDS — Map 19 SE23

Places to visit

Leeds Art Gallery, LEEDS, LS1 3AA,
0113 247 8256 www.leeds.gov.uk/artgallery

Temple Newsam Estate, LEEDS, LS15 0AE,
0113 336 7460 (House)
www.leeds.gov.uk/templenewsamhouse

►►►► 79% Moor Lodge Park

(SE352423)

Blackmoor Ln, Bardsey LS17 9DZ
☎ **01937 572424**

e-mail: moorlodgecp@aol.com
dir: *From A1(M) take A659 (S of Wetherby) signed Otley. Left onto A58 towards Leeds for 5m. Right after New Inn pub (Ling Lane), right at x-rds, 1m. Site on right*

🚐 £17.50-£21 🚐 £17.50-£21

Open all year

Last arrival 20.00hrs Last departure noon

A warm welcome is assured at this well-kept site set in a peaceful and beautiful setting, close to Harewood House and only 25 minutes' drive from York and the Dales; the centre of Leeds is just 15 minutes away. The touring area is for adults only. 7 acre site. 12 touring pitches. Caravan pitches. Motorhome pitches. 60 statics.

Facilities: 🖕⊙🅿☀🕭🎄 ♻ ❶
Services: 🔌🔲🛢🏧
Within 3 miles: ↓🏌◎🛒⛳

Notes: Adults only. No large groups, no tents. Dogs must be kept on leads.

►►► 78% St Helena's Caravan Park

(SE240421)

Otley Old Rd, Horsforth LS18 5HZ
☎ **0113 284 1142**

e-mail: info@st-helenas.co.uk
dir: *From A658 follow signs for Leeds/Bradford Airport. Then follow site signs*

🚐 🚐 ⛺

Open Apr-Oct

Last arrival 19.30hrs Last departure 14.00hrs

A well-maintained parkland setting surrounded by woodland yet within easy reach of Leeds with its excellent shopping and cultural opportunities, Ilkley, and the attractive Wharfedale town of Otley. Some visitors may just want to relax in this adults-only park's spacious and pleasant surroundings. 25 acre site. 60 touring pitches. 31 hardstandings. Caravan pitches. Motorhome pitches. Tent pitches. 40 statics.

Facilities: 🖕🏧⊙🅿☀🕭🎄❶
Services: 🔌🔲🅃
Within 3 miles: ↓🏌🛒⛳
Notes: Adults only.

CHANNEL ISLANDS
GUERNSEY

CASTEL — Map 24

Places to visit

Sausmarez Manor, ST MARTIN, GY4 6SG,
01481 235571 www.sausmarezmanor.co.uk

Fort Grey Shipwreck Museum, ROCQUAINE BAY,
GY7 9BY, 01481 265036 www.museum.gov.gg

►►►► 87% Fauxquets Valley Campsite

GY5 7QL
☎ **01481 255460 & 07781 413333**

e-mail: info@fauxquets.co.uk
dir: *From pier, take 2nd exit off rdbt. At top of hill left into Queens Rd. 2m. Right into Candie Rd. Site opposite sign for German Occupation Museum*

🚐 ⛺

Open 3 May-3 Sep

A beautiful, quiet farm site in a hidden valley close to the sea. The friendly and helpful owners, who understand campers' needs, offer good quality facilities and amenities, including spacious pitches, an outdoor swimming pool, bar/restaurant (limited opening times), a nature trail and sports areas. There are pigs, sheep and chickens for the children to visit. Fully equipped tents and two lodges are available for hire. Motorhomes up to 6.9 metres are allowed on Guernsey - contact the site for details and a permit. 3 acre site. 120 touring pitches. Motorhome pitches. Tent pitches.

AA Pubs & Restaurants nearby: Fleur du Jardin, CASTEL, GY5 7JT, 01481 257996

Cobo Bay Hotel, CASTEL, GY5 7HB, 01481 257102

Leisure: 🏊🎢⚽🎣🏓
Facilities: 🖕⊙🅿☀🕭🕭🛢🎄🎄♻❶
Services: 🔌🔲🛢🅃🍽⛺🏪
Within 3 miles: ↓🎣🎡🏌◎🚤🛒⛳
Notes: Dogs must be kept on leads. Birdwatching.

ST SAMPSON — Map 24

Places to visit

Sausmarez Manor, ST MARTIN, GY4 6SG,
01481 235571 www.sausmarezmanor.co.uk

Castle Cornet, ST PETER PORT, GY1 1AU,
01481 721657 www.museums.gov.gg

►►► 85% Le Vaugrat Camp Site

Route de Vaugrat GY2 4TA
☎ 01481 257468
e-mail: enquiries@vaugratcampsite.com
web: www.vaugratcampsite.com
dir: *From main coast road on NW of island, site signed at Port Grat Bay into Route de Vaugrat, near Peninsula Hotel*

Open May-mid Sep

Overlooking the sea and set within the grounds of a lovely 17th-century house, this level grassy park is backed by woodland, and is close to the lovely sandy beaches of Port Grat and Grand Havre. It is run by a welcoming family who pride themselves on creating magnificent floral displays. The facilities here are excellent. Motorhomes up to 6.9 metres are allowed on Guernsey - contact the site for details and permit. A 'round the island' bus stops very close to the site. 6 acre site. 150 touring pitches. Motorhome pitches. Tent pitches.

AA Pubs & Restaurants nearby: The Admiral de Saumarez, ST PETER PORT, GY1 2JP, 01481 721431

The Absolute End, ST PETER PORT, GY1 2BG, 01481 723822

Mora Restaurant & Grill, ST PETER PORT, GY1 2LE, 01481 715053

Leisure: 🖵
Facilities: 🚿⊙🅿☀&🕓§🛁🚻 ♻ 🛈
Services: 🔌🗑🔋⌀🚮
Within 3 miles: 🕹🎌🅿◎⛵§🛁⛳
Notes: 🚫 No animals.

VALE — Map 24

Places to visit

Rousse Tower, VALE, 01489 726518
www.museums.gov.gg

Guernsey Museum & Art Gallery, ST PETER PORT, GY1 1UG, 01481 726518 www.museums.gov.gg

Great for kids: Castle Cornet, ST PETER PORT, GY1 1AU, 01481 721657 www.museums.gov.gg

NEW ►►► 87% La Bailloterie Camping & Leisure

Bailloterie Ln GY3 5HA
☎ 01481 243636 & 07781 103420
e-mail: info@campinginguernsey.com
dir: *3m N of St Peter Port take Vale road to Crossways, right into Rue du Braye. Site 1st left at sign*

Open 15 May-15 Sep

Last arrival 23.00hrs

A pretty rural site with one large touring field and a few small, well-screened paddocks. This delightful site has been in the same family ownership for over 30 years and offers good facilities in converted outbuildings. There are also fully-equipped tents for hire. Motorhomes up to 6.9 metres are allowed on Guernsey - contact the site for detailed instructions. 10 acre site. 100 touring pitches. Motorhome pitches. Tent pitches.

AA Pubs & Restaurants nearby: The Admiral de Saumarez, ST PETER PORT, GY1 2JP, 01481 721431

The Absolute End, ST PETER PORT, GY1 2BG, 01481 723822

Mora Restaurant & Grill, ST PETER PORT, GY1 2LE, 01481 715053

Leisure: 🅰🏊🎣🖵
Facilities: 🚿⊙🅿☀&🕓§🛁🚻🛒🖥 🛈
Services: 🔌🗑⌀🍽🚮🛒🚮
Within 3 miles: 🕹🎌🎌🅿◎⛵§🛁⛳
Notes: Dogs by prior arrangement only. Dogs must be kept on leads. Volleyball net, boules pitch.

JERSEY

ST MARTIN — Map 24

Places to visit

Mont Orgueil Castle, GOREY, JE3 6ET, 01534 853292 www.jerseyheritage.org

Maritime Museum & Occupation Tapestry Gallery, ST HELIER, JE2 3ND, 01534 811043 www.jerseyheritage.org

Great for kids: Elizabeth Castle, ST HELIER, JE2 3WU, 01534 723971 www.jerseyheritage.org

PREMIER PARK

►►►►► 84%
Beuvelande Camp Site

Beuvelande JE3 6EZ
☎ 01534 853575
e-mail: info@campingjersey.com
web: www.campingjersey.com
dir: *Take A6 from St Helier to St Martin & follow signs to site before St Martins Church*

Open Apr-Sep (rs Apr-May & Sep pool & restaurant closed, shop hours limited)

A well-established site with excellent toilet facilities, accessed via narrow lanes in peaceful countryside close to St Martin. An attractive bar/restaurant is the focal point of the park, especially in the evenings, and there is a small swimming pool and playground. Motorhomes and towed caravans will be met at the ferry and escorted to the site if requested when booking. Three fully-equipped Emperor Tents and two yurts are available for hire. 6 acre site. 150 touring pitches. Caravan pitches. Motorhome pitches. Tent pitches. 75 statics.

AA Pubs & Restaurants nearby: Royal Hotel, ST MARTIN, JE3 6UG, 01534 856289

Leisure: 🏊🅰🎣🖵
Facilities: 🚿⊙☀&🕓§🛒🚻
Services: 🔌🗑🔋🍺⌀Ⓣ🍽🛒🔋
Within 3 miles: 🕹🎌🅿⛵§🛁⛳

ST MARTIN ***continued***

►►►► 88% *Rozel Camping Park*

Summerville Farm JE3 6AX
☎ 01534 855200
e-mail: rozelcampingpark@jerseymail.co.uk
web: www.rozelcamping.co.uk
dir: *Take A6 from St Helier through Five Oaks to St Martins Church, turn right onto A38 towards Rozel, site on right*

🚐 🚙 ⛺

Open May-mid Sep

Last departure noon

Customers can be sure of a warm welcome at this delightful family-run park. Set in the north east of the island, it offers large spacious pitches, many with electric, for tents, caravans and motorhomes. The lovely Rozel Bay is just a short distance away and spectacular views of the French coast can be seen from one of the four fields on the park. The site also offers excellent facilities including a swimming pool. Motorhomes and caravans will be met at the ferry and escorted to the park if requested when booking. Fully equipped, ready-erected tents available for hire. 4 acre site. 100 touring pitches. Caravan pitches. Motorhome pitches. Tent pitches. 20 statics.

AA Pubs & Restaurants nearby: Royal Hotel, ST MARTIN, JE3 6UG, 01534 856289

Leisure: 🌊 🛝 ♠ 📺

Facilities: 🚿 ⊙ 💇 ❄ ♿ ☎ [$] [Wi-fi]

Services: 🧼 ⊡ 🔒 🍃 [T] 🛏 🛒 ⛽

Within 3 miles: ⛳ ⛵ 🎣 🏄 [$] ⊡ 🐴

Notes: Mini golf.

ISLE OF MAN

KIRK MICHAEL **MAp 24 SC39**

Places to visit

Peel Castle, PEEL, IM5 1TB, 01624 648000 www.manxnationalheritage.im

House of Manannan, PEEL, IM5 1TA, 01624 648000 www.manxnationalheritage.im

Great for kids: Curraghs Wild Life Park, BALLAUGH, IM7 5EA, 01624 897323 www.gov.im/wildlife

►►► 72% Glen Wyllin Campsite

(SC302901)

IM6 1AL
☎ 01624 878231 & 878836
e-mail: michaelcommissioners@manx.net
dir: *From Douglas take A1 to Ballacraine, right at lights onto A3 to Kirk Michael. Left onto A4 signed Peel. Site 100yds on right*

🚐 fr £8 🚙 fr £8 ⛺ £8-£55

Open mid Apr-mid Sep

Last departure noon

Set in a beautiful wooded glen with bridges over a pretty stream dividing the camping areas. A gently-sloping tarmac road gives direct access to a good beach. Hire tents are available. 9 acre site. 90 touring pitches. Caravan pitches. Motorhome pitches. Tent pitches. 18 statics.

AA Pubs & Restaurants nearby: The Creek Inn, PEEL, IM5 1AT, 01624 842216

Leisure: 🛝 📺

Facilities: 🚿 ⊙ 💇 ❄ ♿ ☎ [$] 🧺 🐕 [Wi-fi] ♻

Services: 🧼 ⊡ 🍴 🛏 🛒

Within 3 miles: 🎣 [$] ⊡ 🐴

Notes: No excess noise after mdnt, dogs must be kept on leads & under control.

LEISURE: 🏊 Indoor swimming pool 🌊 Outdoor swimming pool 🛝 Children's playground ✋ Kid's club 🎾 Tennis court ♠ Games room 📺 Separate TV room ⛳ 9/18 hole golf course ⛵ Boats for hire 🎬 Cinema 🎵 Entertainment 🎣 Fishing ◎ Mini golf 🏄 Watersports 🏋 Gym ⚽ Sports field **Spa** 🐴 Stables
FACILITIES: 🛁 Bath 🚿 Shower ⊙ Electric shaver 💇 Hairdryer ❄ Ice Pack Facility ♿ Disabled facilities ☎ Public telephone [$] Shop on site or within 200yds 🚚 Mobile shop (calls at least 5 days a week) 🍖 BBQ area 🧺 Picnic area [Wi-fi] Wi-fi 💻 Internet access ♻ Recycling ℹ Tourist info 🐕 Dog exercise area

SERVICES: 🔌 Electric hook up 🔄 Launderette 🍺 Licensed bar 🔒 Calor Gas ⊘ Camping Gaz T Toilet fluid 🍽 Café/Restaurant 🍔 Fast Food/Takeaway
🔋 Battery charging 🛒 Baby care ♨ Motorvan service point **ABBREVIATIONS:** BH/bank hols-bank holidays Etr-Easter Spring BH-Spring Bank Holiday dep-departure
fr-from hrs-hours m-mile mdnt-midnight rdbt-roundabout rs-restricted service wk-week wknd-weekend x-rds-cross roads 🚫 No credit cards 🚫 No dogs
♿ Children of all ages accepted See page 9 for details of the AA Camping Card Scheme

Scotland

Fishing boats near Old St Peter's Kirk, Thurso

WK87

Scotland

It is virtually impossible to distil the spirit and essence of
Scotland in a few short sentences. It is a country with a
particular kind of beauty and something very special to
offer. Around half the size of England but with barely one
fifth of its population, the statistics alone are enough to
make you want to rush there and savour its solitude and
sense of space.

● Eilean Donan Castle, Loch Duich

The Borders, maybe the most obvious place to begin a tour of Scotland, was for so long one of Britain's most bitterly contested frontiers. The border has survived the years of lawlessness, battle and bloodshed, though few crossing it today would probably give its long and turbulent history a second thought. Making up 1,800 square miles of dense forest, rolling hills and broad sweeps of open heather, this region includes some of the most spectacular scenery anywhere in the country. Next door is Dumfries & Galloway, where just across the English/Scottish border is

Gretna Green, famous for the 'anvil marriages' of eloping couples.

Travelling north and miles of open moorland and swathes of forest stretch to the Ayrshire coast where there are views towards the islands of Bute and Arran.

The country's two great cities, Glasgow and Edinburgh, include innumerable historic sites, popular landmarks and innovative visitor attractions. To the north lies a landscape of tranquil lochs, fishing rivers, wooded glens and the cities of Perth and Dundee. There's also the superb scenery of the Trossachs, ▶

● Dunnottar Castle, Aberdeens...

Loch Lomond and Stirling, which, with its wonderful castle perched on a rocky crag, is Scotland's heritage capital.

Further north

The country's prominent north-east shoulder is the setting for the mountain landscape of the Cairngorms and the Grampians, while Aberdeenshire and the Moray coast enjoy a pleasantly mild, dry climate with plenty of sunshine. Here, the River Spey, one of Scotland's great rivers and a mecca for salmon anglers, winds between lush pastures to the North Sea. Various famous distilleries can be found along its banks, some offering visitors the chance to sample a wee dram!

The remote far north is further from many parts of England than a good many European destinations. Names such as Pentland Firth, Sutherland, Caithness and Ross and Cromarty spring to mind, as does Cape Wrath, Britain's most northerly outpost. The stunning coast is known for its spectacular sea cliffs and deserted beaches – the haunt of some of the rarest mammals.

Highlands and Islands

The beauty of the Western Highlands and the islands has to be seen to be believed. It is, without question, one of Europe's wildest and most spectacular regions, evoking a truly breathtaking sense of adventure. There are a great many islands, as a glance at the map will reveal – Skye, Mull, Iona, Coll, Jura and Islay to name but a few; all have their own individual character and identity. The two most northerly island groups are Orkney and the Shetlands, which, incredibly, are closer to the Arctic Circle than London.

Walking and Cycling

There are numerous excellent walks in Scotland. Among the best is the 95-mile (152km) West Highland Way, Scotland's first long-distance path. The trail runs from Glasgow to Fort William. The Southern Upland Way and St Cuthbert's Way explore the best of the Scottish Borders, which is also the northerly terminus for the 250-mile (402km) Pennine Way.

Scotland's majestic landscapes are perfect for exploring by bike. There are scores of popular routes and trails – among them a ride through Dumfries & Galloway to Drumlanrig Castle and the museum where blacksmith, Kirkpatrick MacMillan, invented the bicycle. Alternatively, there's the chance to get away from the city and head for the coast along disused railway lines; perhaps the route from Edinburgh to Cramond, with good views of the Firth of Forth.

Festivals and Events

● The Viking Festival is staged at Largs on the Ayrshire coast during the August Bank Holiday week. This is where the last Viking invasion of

Britain took place in 1263. There are birds of prey displays, battle re-enactments, fireworks and the ritual burning of a longship.

- Also in August is the internationally famous Edinburgh Military Tattoo, which draws numerous visitors and participants from many parts of the world.
- The Highland Games, another classic fixture in the Scottish calendar, run from May onwards; the most famous being the Braemar gathering in September.

● Callanish Standing Stones, Isle of Lewis

● Forth Rail Bridge

ABERDEENSHIRE

ABOYNE — Map 23 NO59

Places to visit

Alford Valley Railway, ALFORD, AB33 8AD, 019755 64236 www.alfordvalleyrailway.org.uk

Crathes Castle Garden & Estate, CRATHES, AB31 5QJ, 0844 4932166 www.nts.org.uk/Property/Crathes-Castle-Garden-Estate

Great for kids: Craigievar Castle, ALFORD, AB33 8JF, 0844 493 2174 www.nts.org.uk/Property/Craigievar-Castle

▶▶▶ **72% Aboyne Loch Caravan Park** (NO538998)

AB34 5BR
☎ **013398 86244 & 82589**
e-mail: heatherreid24@yahoo.co.uk
dir: On A93, 1m E of Aboyne

* 🚐 fr £20 🚐 fr £20 ▲ fr £14

Open 31 Mar-Oct

Last arrival 20.00hrs Last departure 11.00hrs

Located on the outskirts of Aboyne on a small outcrop which is almost surrounded by Loch Aboyne, this is a mature site within scenic Royal Deeside. The facilities are well maintained, and pitches are set amongst mature trees with most having views over the loch. Boat hire and fishing (coarse and pike) are available and there is a regular bus service from the site entrance. 6 acre site. 20 touring pitches. 25 hardstandings. Caravan pitches. Motorhome pitches. Tent pitches. 100 statics.

AA Pubs & Restaurants nearby: The Milton Brasserie, CRATHES, AB31 5QH, 01330 844566

Leisure: 🎱 🔍
Facilities: 🌣 ⊙ 🏳 ✳ 🔥 ⓒ 🖈 Wi-Fi ♻ 🛈
Services: 🚽 🗑 🏮 🛁 Ⓣ 🖇
Within 3 miles: ⤮ 🛠 🥍 ◎ 🚣 Ⓢ 🗑 🐎
Notes: 🐕 Dogs must be kept on leads.

ALFORD — Map 23 NJ51

Places to visit

Alford Valley Railway, ALFORD, AB33 8AD, 019755 64236 www.alfordvalleyrailway.org.uk

Craigievar Castle, ALFORD, AB33 8JF, 0844 493 2174 www.nts.org.uk/Property/Craigievar-Castle

▶▶▶ **74% Haughton House Holiday Park** (NJ577168)

Montgarrie Rd AB33 8NA
☎ **01975 562107**
e-mail: enquiries@haughtonhouse.co.uk
web: www.haughtonhouse.co.uk
dir: Follow signs in Alford for Haughton Country House

🚐 🚐 ▲

Open 25 Mar-27 Oct

Last arrival 21.00hrs Last departure noon

Located on the outskirts of Alford this site is set within a large country park with good countryside views. Now under the same ownership as Huntly Castle Caravan Park (Huntly), this park is receiving the same attention to detail to ensure facilities are brought up to the highest standards. The existing facilities are clean and well maintained. The pitches are set amongst mature trees and the tenting area is within the old walled garden. There is plenty to do on site and within the country park which has various activities for children, including a narrow gauge railway that runs to the Grampian Transport Museum in nearby Alford. 22 acre site. 71 touring pitches. 71 hardstandings. 20 seasonal pitches. Caravan pitches. Motorhome pitches. Tent pitches. 70 statics.

Leisure: 🎱
Facilities: 🌣 ⊙ 🏳 ✳ 🔥 🖈 ♻ 🛈
Services: 🚽 🗑 🏮 Ⓣ 🛁 🖇
Within 3 miles: ⤮ 🥍 ◎ Ⓢ 🗑
Notes: No noise after 22.30hrs. Dogs must be kept on leads. Putting green, fishing permits available.

BANFF — Map 23 NJ66

Places to visit

Banff Museum, BANFF, AB45 1AE, 01771 622807 www.aberdeenshire.gov.uk/museums

Duff House, BANFF, AB45 3SX, 01261 818181 www.historic-scotland.gov.uk

NEW ▶▶▶▶ **76% Banff Links Caravan Park** (NJ668644)

Inverboyndie AB45 2JJ
☎ **01261 812228**
e-mail: banfflinkscaravanpark@btconnect.com
dir: From W: A98 onto B9038 signed Whitehills. 2nd right signed Inverboyndie. 4th left to site. From E (Banff): A98, right at brown 'Banff Links Beach' sign

* 🚐 £17-£20 🚐 £17-£20 ▲ £10-£25

Open Apr-Oct

A delightful small park set beside the award-winning sandy beach at Banff Links with magnificent views over the Moray Coast. Set at sea level, there is direct access to the beach and also a large grass esplanade and play area for children. A pleasant walk on good level paths by the sea will take you to either Banff or the small village of Whitehill, which has a leisure boat harbour. It is ideally located to explore this lovely coastline. The new family owners at the park are keen that their visitors will have an enjoyable stay. Two static caravans are for hire. 5.78 acre site. 55 touring pitches. Caravan pitches. Motorhome pitches. Tent pitches.

LEISURE: 🎱 Indoor swimming pool 🎱 Outdoor swimming pool 🎱 Children's playground 🛝 Kid's club 🎾 Tennis court 🔍 Games room 📺 Separate TV room ⤮ 9/18 hole golf course 🛥 Boats for hire 🎬 Cinema 🎵 Entertainment 🥍 Fishing ◎ Mini golf 🚣 Watersports 🏌 Gym 🎯 Sports field Spa 🐎 Stables
FACILITIES: 🛁 Bath 🌣 Shower ⊙ Electric shaver 🏳 Hairdryer ✳ Ice Pack Facility 🔥 Disabled facilities ⓒ Public telephone Ⓢ Shop on site or within 200yds 🗑 Mobile shop (calls at least 5 days a week) 🏮 BBQ area 🪑 Picnic area Wi-Fi Wi-fi 🖥 Internet access ♻ Recycling 🛈 Tourist info 🖈 Dog exercise area

FORDOUN
Map 23 NO77

Places to visit
Edzell Castle and Garden, EDZELL, DD9 7UE, 01356 648631 www.historic-scotland.gov.uk

House of Dun, MONTROSE, DD10 9LQ, 0844 493 2144 www.nts.org.uk/Property/House-Of-Dun-Montrose-Basin-Nature-Reserve

▶▶▶ 74% Brownmuir Caravan Park
(NO740772)

AB30 1SJ
☎ **01561 320786**
e-mail: brownmuircaravanpark@talk21.com
web: www.brownmuircaravanpark.co.uk
dir: *From N: A90 take B966 signed Fettercairn, site 1.5m on left. From S: A90, exit 4m N of Laurencekirk signed Fordoun, site 1m on right*

⚲ fr £20 ⚲ fr £22 **Å** fr £8

Open Apr-Oct

Last arrival 23.00hrs Last departure noon

With easy access to the A90, this peaceful site, formerly a Polish RAF base, is ideal for either a long holiday or just an overnight stop. The Howe of Mearns is a perfect area for cyclists and walkers, and there are numerous golf courses nearby. Royal Deeside and seaside towns and villages are an easy drive away; there is an award-winning farm shop and café nearby. 7 acre site. 12 touring pitches. 7 hardstandings. 7 seasonal pitches. Caravan pitches. Motorhome pitches. Tent pitches. 49 statics.

AA Pubs & Restaurants nearby: The Tolbooth Restaurant, STONEHAVEN, AB39 2JU, 01569 762287

Carron Art Deco Restaurant, STONEHAVEN, AB39 2HS, 01569 760460

Leisure: ⚙

Facilities: ⚙⊙⚲⚵⚙⚲⚙⚙ ⚙ ⚙

Services: ⚙⚙ Within 3 miles: ⚲⚲⚙

Notes: ⚙ No noise after 23.30hrs. Dogs must be kept on leads.

HUNTLY
Map 23 NJ53

Places to visit
Leith Hall, Garden & Estate, RHYNIE, AB54 4NQ, 01464 831 216 www.nts.org.uk/Property/Leith-Hall-Garden-Estate

Glenfiddich Distillery, DUFFTOWN, AB55 4DH, 01340 820373 www.glenfiddich.com

Great for kids: Archaeolink Prehistory Park, OYNE, AB52 6QP, 01464 851500 www.archaeolink.co.uk

PREMIER PARK
▶▶▶▶▶ 88% *Huntly Castle Caravan Park* (NJ525405)

The Meadow AB54 4UJ
☎ **01466 794999**
e-mail: enquiries@huntlycastle.co.uk
web: www.huntlycastle.co.uk
dir: *From Aberdeen on A96 to Huntly. 0.75m after rdbt (on outskirts of Huntly) right towards town centre, left into Riverside Drive*

⚲⚲**Å**

Open Apr-Oct (rs Wknds & school hols indoor activity centre open)

Last arrival 20.00hrs Last departure noon

A quality parkland site within striking distance of the Speyside Malt Whisky Trail, the beautiful Moray coast and the Cairngorm Mountains. The park provides exceptional toilet facilities, and there are some fully serviced pitches. The indoor activity centre provides a wide range of games; the attractive town of Huntly is only a five-minute walk away, with its ruined castle plus a wide variety of restaurants and shops. 15 acre site. 90 touring pitches. 51 hardstandings. 10 seasonal pitches. Caravan pitches. Motorhome pitches. Tent pitches. 40 statics.

Leisure: ⚙

Facilities: ⚙⊙⚲⚵⚙⚲⚙⚙ ⚙ ⚙

Services: ⚙⚙⚙⚙⚙⚙

Within 3 miles: ⚲⚲⚙⚙

Notes: Dogs must be kept on leads. Snooker table.

KINTORE
Map 23 NJ71

Places to visit
Pitmedden Garden, PITMEDDEN, AB41 7PD, 0844 493 2177 www.nts.org.uk/Property/Pitmedden-Garden

Tolquhon Castle, PITMEDDEN, AB41 7LP, 01651 851286 www.historic-scotland.gov.uk

Great for kids: Castle Fraser, KEMNAY, AB51 7LD, 0844 493 2164 www.nts.org.uk/Property/Castle-Fraser-Garden-Estate

▶▶▶▶ 77% Hillhead Caravan Park
(NJ777163)

AB51 0YX
☎ **01467 632809 & 0870 413 0870**
e-mail: enquiries@hillheadcaravan.co.uk
dir: *1m from village & A96 (Aberdeen-Inverness road). From A96 follow signs to site on B994, then unclassified road*

⚲⚲**Å**

Open all year

Last arrival 21.00hrs Last departure 13.00hrs

An attractive, nicely landscaped site, located on the outskirts of Kintore in the valley of the River Dee with excellent access to forest walks and within easy reach of the many attractions in rural Aberdeenshire. The toilet facilities are of a high standard. There are good play facilities for smaller children and a modern lodge-style games room, with TV and internet access for older teenagers. 1.5 acre site. 29 touring pitches. 14 hardstandings. Caravan pitches. Motorhome pitches. Tent pitches.

AA Pubs & Restaurants nearby: The Cock & Bull Bar & Restaurant, BALMEDIE, AB23 8XY, 01358 743249

Old Blackfriars, ABERDEEN, AB11 5BB, 01224 581922

La Stella, ABERDEEN, AB11 5BL, 01224 211414

The Silver Darling, ABERDEEN, AB11 5DQ, 01224 576229

Leisure: ⚙

Facilities: ⚙⊙⚲⚵⚙⚙⚙⚲⚙⚙

Services: ⚙⚙⚙⚙⚙⚙

Within 3 miles: ⚲⚲⚙⚙

Notes: Caravan storage, accessories shop.

SERVICES: ⚙ Electric hook up ⚙ Launderette ⚙ Licensed bar ⚙ Calor Gas ⚙ Camping Gaz ⚙ Toilet fluid ⚙ Café/Restaurant ⚙ Fast Food/Takeaway ⚙ Battery charging ⚙ Baby care ⚙ Motorvan service point **ABBREVIATIONS:** BH/bank hols-bank holidays Etr-Easter Spring BH-Spring Bank Holiday dep-departure fr-from hrs-hours m-mile mdnt-midnight rdbt-roundabout rs-restricted service wk-week wknd-weekend x-rds-cross roads ⚙ No credit cards ⚙ No dogs ⚙ Children of all ages accepted See page 9 for details of the AA Camping Card Scheme

MACDUFF — Map 23 NJ76

Places to visit

Duff House, BANFF, AB45 3SX, 01261 818181
www.historic-scotland.gov.uk

Banff Museum, BANFF, AB45 1AE, 01771 622807
www.aberdeenshire.gov.uk/museums

►► 67% Wester Bonnyton Farm Site

(NJ741638)

Gamrie AB45 3EP
☎ **01261 832470**
e-mail: westerbonnyton@fsmail.net
dir: *From A98 (1m S of Macduff) take B9031
signed Rosehearty. Site 1.25m on right*

🚐 🚍 Å

Open Mar-Oct

A spacious farm site, with level touring pitches, overlooking the Moray Firth. The small, picturesque fishing villages of Gardenstown and Crovie and the larger town of Macduff, which has a marine aquarium, are all within easy reach. All the touring pitches have good views of the coastline. Families with children are welcome, and there is a play area and play barn. 8 acre site. 8 touring pitches. 5 hardstandings. Caravan pitches. Motorhome pitches. Tent pitches. 65 statics.

Leisure: ⚠ 🔍
Facilities: 🅿 ⊙ 🎇 🖥 🚿 🚻 📶 🖳 ♲ ❶
Services: 🚰 🛢 🔋 🛒
Within 3 miles: ↧ ⚘ 🚣 🏷 🛒
Notes: Dogs must be kept on leads.

MINTLAW — Map 23 NJ94

Places to visit

Aberdeenshire Farming Museum, MINTLAW, AB42 5FQ, 01771 624590
www.aberdeenshire.gov.uk/museums

Deer Abbey, OLD DEER, 01667 460232
www.historic-scotland.gov.uk

►►► 78% Aden Caravan and Camping Park *(NJ981479)*

Aden Country Park AB42 5FQ
☎ **01771 623460**
e-mail: info@adencaravanandcamping.co.uk
dir: *From Mintlaw take A950 signed New Pitsligo &
Aden Country Park. Park on left*

🚐 🚍 Å

Open Apr-Oct

Last arrival 18.00hrs Last departure 13.00hrs

Situated in the heart of Buchan in Aberdeenshire and within Aden Country Park, this is a small tranquil site offering excellent facilities. It is ideally located for visiting the many tourist attractions in this beautiful north-east coastal area, not least of which is the 230-acre country park itself. The site is only a short drive from the busy fishing towns of Fraserburgh and Peterhead, and as it is only an hour from Aberdeen's city centre; this is an ideal spot for a short stay or a longer holiday. The country park plays host to numerous events throughout the year, including pipe band championships, horse events and various ranger-run activities. 11.1 acre site. 66 touring pitches. 31 hardstandings. 10 seasonal pitches. Caravan pitches. Motorhome pitches. Tent pitches. 17 statics.

Facilities: 🅿 ⊙ 🎇 🖥 🚿 🚻 📶 ♲
Services: 🚰 🛢 🔋 🅃
Within 3 miles: ↧ 🛒
Notes: Adults only. Dogs must be kept on leads.

NORTH WATER BRIDGE — Map 23 NO66

►►► 77% Dovecot Caravan Park *(NO648663)*

GOLD

AB30 1QL
☎ **01674 840630**
e-mail: adele@dovecotcaravanpark.co.uk
dir: *Take A90, 5m S of Laurencekirk. At Edzell
Woods sign turn left. Site 500yds on left*

* 🚐 £15-£17 🚍 £15-£17 Å £12-£20

Open Apr-Oct

Last arrival 20.00hrs Last departure noon

A level grassy site in a country area close to the A90, with mature trees screening one side and the River North Esk on the other. The immaculate toilet facilities make this a handy overnight stop in a good touring area. 6 acre site. 25 touring pitches. 8 hardstandings. 8 seasonal pitches. Caravan pitches. Motorhome pitches. Tent pitches. 44 statics.

Leisure: ⚠ 🔍
Facilities: 🅿 ⊙ 🎇 ✳ ⚙ 🕐 🚻 📶 ♲ ❶
Services: 🚰 🔋 🅃 ⛟
Notes: Dogs must be kept on leads.

PETERHEAD — Map 23 NK14

NEW ►►► 74% Lido Caravan Park

(NK123452)

South Rd AB42 2YP
☎ **01779 473358**
e-mail: admin@peterheadprojects.co.uk
dir: *Telephone for directions*

* 🚐 £20-£23 🚍 £20-£23 Å £10.50-£21.50

Open Mar-Oct

Last arrival 21.00hrs Last departure noon

This small site is located on The Lido with direct access to a small sandy beach with a nice play area and sand dunes. Each of the all-electric pitches has a view over Peterhead's busy harbour and there is always some boating activity taking place to keep you interested. The site is now under the management of the local enterprise company Peterhead Projects Limited. The Martine Heritage Centre, a few minutes' walk from the site, has an excellent café. 2 acre site. 25 touring pitches. Caravan pitches. Motorhome pitches. Tent pitches.

PORTSOY — Map 23 NJ56

Places to visit

Banff Museum, BANFF, AB45 1AE, 01771 622807
www.aberdeenshire.gov.uk/museums

Duff House, BANFF, AB45 3SX, 01261 818181
www.historic-scotland.gov.uk

Great for kids: Macduff Marine Aquarium, MACDUFF, AB44 1SL, 01261 833369
www.macduff-aquarium.org.uk

►►► 74% Portsoy Links Caravan Park *(NJ591660)*

Links Rd, Portsoy AB45 2RQ
☎ **01261 842695**
e-mail: contact@portsoylinks.co.uk
dir: *At Portsoy from A98 into Church St. 2nd right
into Institute St (follow brown camping sign). At
T-junct right, down slope to site*

* 🚐 £16.30-£17.30 🚍 £16.30-£17.30
Å £9.50-£23.70

Open 30 Mar-Oct

Last arrival 20.00hrs Last departure noon

Taken into community ownership under the auspices of the Scottish Traditional Boats Festival, this is a lovely links-type site with stunning views across the bay. There is a large, safe fenced play area for smaller children and the

LEISURE: 🏊 Indoor swimming pool 🏊 Outdoor swimming pool ⚠ Children's playground 🧒 Kid's club 🎾 Tennis court 🔍 Games room 🖳 Separate TV room ↧ 9/18 hole golf course 🚣 Boats for hire 🎬 Cinema 🎭 Entertainment 🎣 Fishing ◉ Mini golf 🏄 Watersports 🏋 Gym ⚽ Sports field Spa ♨ Stables
FACILITIES: 🛁 Bath 🚿 Shower ⊙ Electric shaver 🎇 Hairdryer ✳ Ice Pack Facility ⚙ Disabled facilities 🕐 Public telephone 🛒 Shop on site or within 200yds 🚚 Mobile shop (calls at least 5 days a week) 🍖 BBQ area 🧺 Picnic area 📶 Wi-fi 🖳 Internet access ♲ Recycling ❶ Tourist info 🐕 Dog exercise area

toilet facilities are kept clean and well maintained. Portsoy is a typical small fishing port and has various eateries and shops; it is very convenient for visiting the other small fishing villages on the North East Scotland's Coastal Trail. 0.8 acre site. 51 touring pitches. 2 hardstandings. 6 seasonal pitches. Caravan pitches. Motorhome pitches. Tent pitches. 16 statics.

Leisure: ⚙

Facilities: 🛁♿🚿🎮 ⓘ

Services: 🔌🗑🔒

Within 3 miles: ⛳🚴🛥⛵🛒

ST CYRUS — Map 23 NO76

Places to visit

House of Dun, MONTROSE, DD10 9LQ, 0844 493 2144 www.nts.org.uk/Property/ House-Of-Dun-Montrose-Basin-Nature-Reserve

Pictavia Visitor Centre, BRECHIN, DD9 6RL, 01356 626241 www.pictavia.org.uk

Great for kids: Brechin Town House Museum, BRECHIN, DD9 7AA, 01356 625536 www.angus.gov.uk/history/museum

►►►► 79% East Bowstrips Caravan Park (NO745654)

DD10 0DE
☎ **01674 850328**
e-mail: tully@bowstrips.freeserve.co.uk
web: www.caravancampingsites.co.uk/ aberdeenshire/eastbowstrips.htm
dir: From S on A92 (coast road) into St Cyrus. Pass hotel on left. 1st left then 2nd right signed

* 🚐 £16-£18 🚐 £16-£18 ⛺ £9-£10

Open Etr or Apr-Oct

Last arrival 20.00hrs Last departure noon

A quiet rural site on the edge of St Cyrus, which is a small seaside village with a large sandy beach and a National Nature Reserve. This is a well maintained site with excellent toilet facilities. The touring pitches are in two separate areas behind mature trees and hedges and some have views of the sea. 4 acre site. 32 touring pitches. 22 hardstandings. 13 seasonal pitches. Caravan pitches. Motorhome pitches. Tent pitches. 17 statics.

Facilities: 🛁☀🚿🎮♿🔥🚻📶 ⓘ

Services: 🔌🗑🔒🚐

Within 3 miles: 🛒⛴

Notes: 🚫 If camping, no dogs allowed; if touring, dogs must always be kept on leads. Separate garden with boule pitch.

STRACHAN — Map 23 NO69

Places to visit

Banchory Museum, BANCHORY, AB31 5SX, 01771 622807 www.aberdeenshire.gov.uk/museums

Crathes Castle Garden & Estate, CRATHES, AB31 5QJ, 0844 4932166 www.nts.org.uk/ Property/Crathes-Castle-Garden-Estate

Great for kids: Go Ape! Crathes Castle, CRATHES, AB31 5QJ, 0845 643 9215 www.goape.co.uk/sites/crathes-castle

AA CAMPING CARD SITE

►►►► 78% Feughside Caravan Park (NO636913)

GOLD

AB31 6NT
☎ **01330 850669**
e-mail: info@feughsidecaravanpark.co.uk
dir: From Banchory take B974 to Strachan, 3m, take B976, 2m to Feughside Inn, follow site signs

* 🚐 £20-£23 🚐 £20-£23 ⛺ £10-£20

Open Apr-Oct

Last arrival 22.00hrs Last departure noon

A small, well maintained family-run site, set amongst mature trees and hedges and located five miles from Banchory. The site is ideally suited to those wishing for a peaceful location that is within easy reach of scenic Royal Deeside. 5.5 acre site. 27 touring pitches. 10 hardstandings. 12 seasonal pitches. Caravan pitches. Motorhome pitches. Tent pitches. 54 statics.

AA Pubs & Restaurants nearby: Raemoir House Hotel, BANCHORY, AB31 4ED, 01330 824884

Leisure: ⚙

Facilities: 🛁☀🚿🎮♿🔥📶♻ ⓘ

Services: 🔌🗑🔒🚐🚰

Within 3 miles: 🚴🚲⛵🛒🗑🅿

Notes: 🚫 No cars by caravans or tents. Quiet after 22.00hrs, no open fires. Dogs to be exercised off park & kept on leads.

TURRIFF — Map 23 NJ75

Places to visit

Fyvie Castle, TURRIFF, AB53 8JS, 0844 493 2182 www.nts.org.uk/Property/Fyvie-Castle

►►► 75% Turriff Caravan Park (NJ727492)

Station Rd AB53 4ER
☎ **01888 562205**
e-mail: turriffcaravanpark@btconnect.com
dir: On A947, S of Turriff

🚐 🚐 ⛺

Open Apr-Oct

Last arrival 18.00hrs Last departure noon

Located on the outskirts of Turriff on the site of an old railway station, this site is owned by the local community. The pitches are level and the attractive landscaping is well maintained. The site also has a rally field. There is a large public park close to the site which has a boating pond and a large games park where the annual agricultural show is held. The town is only five minutes' walk through the park and has a good variety of shops to suit all tastes. This is an ideal base for touring rural Aberdeenshire and the nearby Moray coastline with its traditional fishing villages. 5 acre site. 70 touring pitches. 4 hardstandings. Caravan pitches. Motorhome pitches. Tent pitches. 14 statics.

AA Pubs & Restaurants nearby: The Redgarth, OLDMELDRUM, AB51 0DJ, 01651 872353

Leisure: ⚙✪

Facilities: 🛁🚿♿🔥📶♻ ⓘ

Services: 🔌🗑🔒🅿

Within 3 miles: 🚴🚲⛵◎⛴🗒🛒

Notes: Dogs must be kept on leads.

SERVICES: 🔌 Electric hook up 🗑 Launderette 🍷 Licensed bar 🔥 Calor Gas 🔋 Camping Gaz ⊤ Toilet fluid 🍴 Café/Restaurant 🍟 Fast Food/Takeaway 🚐 Battery charging 🍼 Baby care 🅿 Motorvan service point **ABBREVIATIONS:** BH/bank hols-bank holidays Etr-Easter Spring BH-Spring Bank Holiday dep-departure fr-from hrs-hours m-mile mdnt-midnight rdbt-roundabout rs-restricted service wk-week wknd-weekend x-rds-cross roads 🚫 No credit cards 🚫 No dogs 👶 Children of all ages accepted See page 9 for details of the AA Camping Card Scheme

ANGUS

MONIFIETH
Map 21 NO43

Places to visit

Barry Mill, BARRY, DD7 7RJ, 0844 493 2140
www.nts.org.uk/Property/Barry-Mill

HM Frigate Unicorn, DUNDEE, DD1 3BP,
01382 200900 www.frigateunicorn.org

Great for kids: Discovery Point & RRS
Discovery, DUNDEE, DD1 4XA, 01382 309060
www.rrsdiscovery.com

▶▶▶▶ 81% **Riverview
Caravan Park** (NO502322)

Best of British

Marine Dr DD5 4NN
☎ **01382 535471 & 817979**
e-mail: info@riverview.co.uk
web: www.riverview.co.uk
dir: *From Dundee on A930 follow signs to
Monifieth, past supermarket, right signed golf
course, left under rail bridge. Site signed on left*

Open Mar-Jan

Last arrival 22.00hrs Last departure 12.30hrs

A well-landscaped seaside site with individual
hedged pitches, and direct access to the beach.
The modernised toilet block has excellent facilities
which are immaculately maintained. Amenities
include a multi-gym, sauna and steam rooms. 5.5
acre site. 49 touring pitches. 45 hardstandings.
Caravan pitches. Motorhome pitches. 46 statics.

AA Pubs & Restaurants nearby: The Royal Arch
Bar, BROUGHTY FERRY, DD5 2DS, 01382 779741

Carnoustie Golf Hotel & Spa, CARNOUSTIE,
DD7 7JE, 0843 178 7109

Leisure: ✠ ⋔ ☺ ✎
Facilities: ⌐ ☉ ⋔ ✳ ⅋ ☽ ⌂ ♯ WiFi ▭ ♲ ⓘ
Services: ⚡ ⓢ ⌷ ⊤ ⌸ ⇶ ⚱
Within 3 miles: ⌕ ∐ ⌒ ◎ ⋩ ⑂ ⓢ ⓑ ∪
Notes: Dogs must be kept on leads.

MONTROSE
Map 23 NO75

Places to visit

House of Dun, MONTROSE, DD10 9LQ,
0844 493 2144
www.nts.org.uk/Property/House-Of-Dun-
Montrose-Basin-Nature-Reserve

Montrose Museum & Art Gallery, MONTROSE,
DD10 8HE, 01674 673232
www.angus.gov.uk/history/museum

NEW ▶▶▶▶ 74% **South Links
Holiday Park** (NO723576)

Trail Dr DD10 8EJ
☎ **01674 672105**
e-mail: info@southlinkspark.com
dir: *Telephone for directions*

* ⊕ £17-£19 ⊠ £17-£19 ⋀ £17-£19

Open Mar-Jan

Last arrival 20.00hrs Last departure 13.00hrs

A traditional seaside campsite set near to a Blue
Flag beach in the small coastal town of Montrose.
Previously owned by the local authority, the new
owner has upgraded facilities to a good standard
and is continuing to develop the site. Discounted
rates are available for the newly completed sports
centre which is passed on the way to the site, and
the town centre has a good range of shops and
eateries to suit all tastes. 9 acre site. 150 touring
pitches. Caravan pitches. Motorhome pitches. Tent
pitches. Wooden pods. 20 statics.

Facilities: ⓢ

ARGYLL & BUTE

CARRADALE
Map 20 NR83

▶▶▶ 87% *Carradale Bay Caravan
Park* (NR815385)

PA28 6QG
☎ **01583 431665**
e-mail: info@carradalebay.com
dir: *A83 from Tarbert towards Campbeltown, left
onto B842 (Carradale road), right onto B879. Site
0.5m*

⊕ ⊠ ⋀

Open Apr-Sep

Last arrival 22.00hrs Last departure noon

A beautiful, natural site on the sea's edge with
superb views over Kilbrannan Sound to the Isle of
Arran. Pitches are landscaped into small bays
broken up by shrubs and bushes, and backed by
dunes close to the long sandy beach. The toilet
facilities are appointed to a very high standard.
An environmentally-aware site that requires the
use of green toilet chemicals - available on the
site. Lodges and static caravans for holiday hire. 8
acre site. 74 touring pitches. Caravan pitches.
Motorhome pitches. Tent pitches. 15 statics.

Facilities: ⌐ ☉ ⋔ ✳ ⅋ ☽ ⌂ ♯ WiFi ♲ ⓘ
Services: ⚡ ⓢ
Within 3 miles: ⌕ ⋔ ⌒ ⋩ ⓢ ⓑ ∪

GLENDARUEL
Map 20 NR98

Places to visit

Benmore Botanic Garden, BENMORE, PA23 8QU,
01369 706261 www.rbge.org.uk

▶▶▶ 79% *Glendaruel Caravan Park*
(NR005865)

PA22 3AB
☎ **01369 820267**
e-mail: mail@glendaruelcaravanpark.com
web: www.glendaruelcaravanpark.com
dir: *A83 onto A815 to Strachur, 13m to site on
A886. By ferry from Gourock to Dunoon then B836,
then A886 for approx 4m N. (NB this route not
recommended for towing vehicles - 1:5 uphill
gradient on B836)*

⊕ ⊠ ⋀

Open Apr-Oct

Last arrival 22.00hrs Last departure noon

LEISURE: ⚲ Indoor swimming pool ⚲ Outdoor swimming pool ⋀ Children's playground ❉ Kid's club ⚲ Tennis court ⚲ Games room ☐ Separate TV room
⌕ 9/18 hole golf course ⚲ Boats for hire ☐ Cinema ♫ Entertainment ⌒ Fishing ◎ Mini golf ⋩ Watersports ✠ Gym ☺ Sports field Spa ∪ Stables
FACILITIES: ⚲ Bath ⌐ Shower ☉ Electric shaver ⋔ Hairdryer ✳ Ice Pack Facility ⅋ Disabled facilities ☽ Public telephone ⓢ Shop on site or within 200yds
⚲ Mobile shop (calls at least 5 days a week) ♯ BBQ area ⌂ Picnic area WiFi Wi-fi ▭ Internet access ♲ Recycling ⓘ Tourist info ♯ Dog exercise area

Glendaruel Gardens, with an arboretum, is the peaceful setting for this 22-acre, wooded site in a valley surrounded by mountains. It is set back from the main road and screened by trees so that a peaceful stay is ensured. This very pleasant, well-established site has level grass and hardstanding pitches. A regular local bus service and a ferry at Portavadie (where there are new retail outlets and eateries) make a day trip to the Mull of Kintyre a possibility. The Cowal Way, a long distance path, and a national cycle path pass the site. Static caravans and a camping lodge are available for hire. 6 acre site. 27 touring pitches. 15 hardstandings. 12 seasonal pitches. Caravan pitches. Motorhome pitches. Tent pitches. 32 statics. 1 wooden pod.

Leisure: 🛝 ⚽

Facilities: 🚿 ☉ 💨 ❄ [S] 🪑 🐕 WiFi ♻ ℹ

Services: 🔌 🧺 🛢 🔥 [T] 🔋

Within 3 miles: 🎣 [S] 🧺

Notes: Dogs must be kept on leads. Sea trout & salmon fishing, woodland walks, 24-hour emergency phone available.

OBAN — Map 20 NM82

Places to visit

Dunstaffnage Castle and Chapel, OBAN, PA37 1PZ, 01631 562465 www.historic-scotland.gov.uk

Bonawe Historic Iron Furnace, TAYNUILT, PA35 1JQ, 01866 822432 www.historic-scotland.gov.uk

►►► 75% Oban Caravan & Camping Park *(NM831277)*

Gallanachmore Farm, Gallanach Rd PA34 4QH
☎ 01631 562425
e-mail: info@obancaravanpark.com
dir: *From Oban centre follow signs for Mull Ferry. After terminal follow Gallanach signs. 2m to site*

* 🚐 £17-£20 🚌 £17-£20 ⛺ £15-£17

Open Etr & Apr-Oct

Last arrival 23.00hrs Last departure noon

A tourist park in an attractive location close to the sea and ferries. This family park is a popular base for walking, sea-based activities and for those who just want to enjoy the peace and tranquillity. There are self-catering holiday lodges for hire. 15 acre site. 120 touring pitches. 35 hardstandings. 10 seasonal pitches. Caravan pitches. Motorhome pitches. Tent pitches. 17 statics.

AA Pubs & Restaurants nearby: Coast, OBAN, PA34 5NT, 01631 569900

Leisure: 🛝 ♟ 📺

Facilities: 🚿 ☉ 💨 ❄ ☎ [S] 🪑 🐕 WiFi ℹ

Services: 🔌 🧺 🛢 🔥 [T] 🔋 ⚓

Within 3 miles: ⛳ ⛵ 🎬 🎣 🌊 [S] 🧺 🐎

Notes: No commercial vehicles, no noise after 23.00hrs. Dogs must be kept on leads. Indoor kitchen for tent campers.

TAYINLOAN — Map 20 NR64

►►► 77% Point Sands Camping & Caravan Park *(NR707484)*

Rhunahaorine PA29 6XG
☎ 01583 441263
e-mail: info@pointsands.co.uk
dir: *From A83 S of Tarbert site signed on right (opposite school) (NB Sat Nav directions cannot be guaranteed from Lochgilphead on A83)*

* 🚐 £7-£10 🚌 £7-£10 ⛺ £7-£10

Open Apr-Oct

Last departure noon

Located on the Kintyre peninsular, this peaceful site has direct access to a private sandy beach overlooking the islands of Gigha, Islay, Jura and Colonsay. It is ideally located for the ferries to these islands and also for the ferries from Campbeltown (to Ardrossan), Tarbert (to Portavadie) and Claonaig (to Lochranza on the Isle of Arran). The easy access by road and the ferries make day trips a relatively simple affair. All the pitches have sea views. The owners are continually improving facilities, and new toilets have been installed. 10 acre site. 40 touring pitches. 15 seasonal pitches. Caravan pitches. Motorhome pitches. Tent pitches. 50 statics.

Leisure: 🛝

Facilities: 🚿 ☉ 💨 ❄ [S] 🪑 🐕 WiFi ♻ ℹ

Services: 🔌 🧺 🛢 🔥 [T] 🍔 🚼 ⚓

Within 3 miles: ⛳ ⛵ 🎣 🌊 [S] 🧺 🐎

Notes: No jet skis, fireworks or Chinese lanterns.

DUMFRIES & GALLOWAY

ANNAN — Map 21 NY16

Places to visit

Ruthwell Cross, RUTHWELL, 0131 550 7612 www.historic-scotland.gov.uk

Great for kids: Caerlaverock Castle, CAERLAVEROCK, DG1 4RU, 01387 770244 www.historic-scotland.gov.uk

►► 74% Galabank Caravan & Camping Group *(NY192676)*

North St DG12 5DQ
☎ 01461 203539 & 07999 344520
e-mail: margaret.ramage@hotmail.com
dir: *Enter site via North Street*

* 🚐 fr £12.50 🚌 fr £12.50 ⛺ fr £9

Open Mar-Oct

Last departure noon

A tidy, well-maintained grassy little park with spotless facilities close to the centre of town but with pleasant rural views, and skirted by the River Annan. 1 acre site. 30 touring pitches. Caravan pitches. Motorhome pitches. Tent pitches.

AA Pubs & Restaurants nearby: Del Amitri Restaurant, ANNAN, DG12 6DJ, 01461 201999

Facilities: 🚿 ☉ 💨 [S] 🪑

Services: 🔌

Within 3 miles: ⛳ 🎬 🎣 [S] 🐎

Notes: 💳 Dogs must be kept on leads. Social club adjacent.

SERVICES: 🔌 Electric hook up 🧺 Launderette 🍷 Licensed bar 🛢 Calor Gas 🔥 Camping Gaz [T] Toilet fluid 🍴 Café/Restaurant 🍔 Fast Food/Takeaway 🔋 Battery charging 🚼 Baby care ⚓ Motorvan service point **ABBREVIATIONS:** BH/bank hols-bank holidays Etr-Easter Spring BH-Spring Bank Holiday dep-departure fr-from hrs-hours m-mile mdnt-midnight rdbt-roundabout rs-restricted service wk-week wknd-weekend x-rds-cross roads 💳 No credit cards 🚫 No dogs 👪 Children of all ages accepted See page 9 for details of the AA Camping Card Scheme

BARGRENNAN
Map 20 NX37

►►► 78% Glentrool Holiday Park
(NX350769)

DG8 6RN

☎ **01671 840280**

e-mail: enquiries@glentroolholidaypark.co.uk

dir: *Exit Newton Stewart on A714 towards Girvan, right at Bargrennan towards Glentrool. Site on left before village*

Open Mar-Oct

Last arrival 21.00hrs Last departure noon

A small park close to the village of Glentrool, and bordered by the Galloway Forest Park. Both the touring and static areas, with vans for hire, are immaculately presented and the amenity block is clean and freshly painted. The on-site shop is well stocked. The Southern Upland Way, a long distance coast to coast path, runs through the site and Galloway Forest Park Visitor Centre, providing numerous walking and cycling tracks, is one mile away. The site is within the official Dumfries & Galloway Dark Sky Zone and provides ideal star gazing opportunities. A regular bus stops at the site entrance. 6 acre site. 16 touring pitches. 13 hardstandings. 3 seasonal pitches. Caravan pitches. Motorhome pitches. Tent pitches. 26 statics.

AA Pubs & Restaurants nearby: Creebridge House Hotel, NEWTON STEWART, DG8 6NP, 01671 402121

The Galloway Arms Hotel, NEWTON STEWART, DG8 6DB, 01671 402653

Kirroughtree House, NEWTON STEWART, DG8 6AN, 01671 402141

Leisure: 🄰

Facilities: 🏕🛆⊙☂✳🔥🛟🔥🛒♻ 🌐

Services: 🚽🔅🛢🗑🚿

Within 3 miles: U

Notes: 🚫 No cars by tents. No ball games, no groups. Dogs must be kept on leads.

BRIGHOUSE BAY
Map 20 NX64

AA CAMPING CARD SITE

PREMIER PARK

►►►►► 82%
Brighouse Bay Holiday Park *(NX628453)*

DG6 4TS

☎ **01557 870267**

e-mail: info@gillespie-leisure.co.uk

dir: *From Gatehouse of Fleet take A75 towards Castle Douglas, onto B727 (signed Kirkcudbright & Borgue). Or from Kirkcudbright take A755 onto B727. Site signed*

* 🚐 £17-£22.50 � £17-£22.50 ▲ £13.50-£19

Open all year (rs Nov-Mar leisure club closed 3 days each week)

Last arrival 21.00hrs Last departure 11.30hrs

This top class park has a country club feel and enjoys a marvellous coastal setting adjacent to the beach and has superb views. Pitches have been imaginatively sculpted into the meadowland, where stone walls and hedges blend in with the site's mature trees. These features, together with the large range of leisure activities, make this an excellent park for families who enjoy an active holiday. Many of the facilities are at an extra charge. A range of self-catering units is available for hire. 120 acre site. 190 touring pitches. 100 hardstandings. 50 seasonal pitches. Caravan pitches. Motorhome pitches. Tent pitches. 285 statics.

AA Pubs & Restaurants nearby: Selkirk Arms Hotel, KIRKCUDBRIGHT, DG6 4JG, 01557 330402

Leisure: 🏊🤾🄰🎣♫

Facilities: 🛁🏕🛆⊙☂✳🔥🛟🔥🛒🛝🌊 ⬜ 🌐

Services: 🚽🔅🍴🛢🗑🚿T🍴🚿🚾🚮♿

Within 3 miles: 🚴🎣⊙🛟🛒U

Notes: No motorised scooters, jet skis or own quad bikes. Dogs must be kept on leads. Mini golf, 18-hole golf, PGA professional on site, horse riding, fishing, outdoor bowling green, jacuzzi.

CREETOWN
Map 20 NX46

Places to visit

Cardoness Castle, CARDONESS CASTLE, DG7 2EH, 01557 814427 www.historic-scotland.gov.uk

Great for kids: Creetown Gem Rock Museum, CREETOWN, DG8 7HJ, 01671 820357 www.gemrock.net

PREMIER PARK

►►►►► 83% Castle Cary Holiday Park *(NX475576)*

DG8 7DQ

☎ **01671 820264**

e-mail: enquiries@castlecarypark.f9.co.uk

web: www.castlecary-caravans.com

dir: *Signed with direct access from A75, 0.5m S of village*

Open all year (rs Oct-Mar reception/shop, no heated outdoor pool)

Last arrival anytime Last departure noon

This attractive site in the grounds of Cassencarie House is sheltered by woodlands, and faces south towards Wigtown Bay. The park is in a secluded location with beautiful landscaping and excellent facilities. The bar/restaurant is housed in part of an old castle, and enjoys extensive views over the River Cree estuary. 12 acre site. 50 touring pitches. 50 hardstandings. Caravan pitches. Motorhome pitches. Tent pitches. 26 statics. 2 bell tents/yurts.

AA Pubs & Restaurants nearby: Creebridge House Hotel, NEWTON STEWART, DG8 6NP, 01671 402121

The Galloway Arms Hotel, NEWTON STEWART, DG8 6DB, 01671 402653

Kirroughtree House, NEWTON STEWART, DG8 6AN, 01671 402141

Cally Palace Hotel, GATEHOUSE OF FLEET, DG7 2DL, 01557 814341

Leisure: 🏊🤽🄰🛟🎣⬜

Facilities: 🛁🏕⊙☂✳🔥🛟🔥🛒🛝🚾 ⬜ 🌐

Services: 🚽🔅🍴🛢🗑🚿T🍴🚿🍺

Within 3 miles: 🔱♿🎣⊙🛟🛒U

Notes: Dogs must be kept on leads. Crazy golf, coarse fishing, full size football pitch.

LEISURE: 🏊 Indoor swimming pool 🏊 Outdoor swimming pool 🄰 Children's playground 🤾 Kid's club 🎾 Tennis court 🎱 Games room ⬜ Separate TV room 🏌 9/18 hole golf course 🚣 Boats for hire 🎬 Cinema ♫ Entertainment 🎣 Fishing ⊙ Mini golf 🏄 Watersports 🤸 Gym ⚽ Sports field Spa U Stables
FACILITIES: 🛁 Bath 🏕 Shower ⊙ Electric shaver 💈 Hairdryer ✳ Ice Pack Facility ♿ Disabled facilities 🛟 Public telephone 🛒 Shop on site or within 200yds 🚐 Mobile shop (calls at least 5 days a week) 🍴 BBQ area 🛝 Picnic area 🚾 Wi-fi 🖥 Internet access ♻ Recycling 🌐 Tourist info 🐾 Dog exercise area

DALBEATTIE — Map 21 NX86

Places to visit

Threave Garden & Estate, CASTLE DOUGLAS, DG7 1RX, 0844 493 2245 www.nts.org.uk/Property/Threave-Estate

Orchardton Tower, PALNACKIE www.historic-scotland.gov.uk

▶▶▶▶ 81% Glenearly Caravan Park

(NX838628)

DG5 4NE
☎ 01556 611393
e-mail: glenearlycaravan@btconnect.com
dir: *From Dumfries take A711 towards Dalbeattie. Site entrance after Edingham Farm on right (200yds before boundary sign)*

Open all year

Last arrival 19.00hrs Last departure noon

An excellent small park set in open countryside with panoramic views of Long Fell, Maidenpap and Dalbeattie Forest. The park is located in 84 beautiful acres of farmland which visitors are invited to enjoy. The attention to detail here is of the highest standard, and this is most notable in the presentation of the amenity block. There is a regular bus service on the main road, making trips to the surrounding towns easy, and Dalbeattie is only a 10-minute walk away. The site is also convenient for visiting the Solway coast which provides good beaches and a variety of walks. Static holiday caravans are for hire. 10 acre site. 39 touring pitches. 33 hardstandings. Caravan pitches. Motorhome pitches. Tent pitches. 74 statics.

Leisure: 🅰 🎣
Facilities: 🖧 ⊙ 🌮 ✳ ♿ 🕓 🐾 🛈
Services: 🔌 🔲 🅱 🍴
Within 3 miles: 🎣 ⚘ 🎯 ◎ 🏊 🛒 🎲 ∪
Notes: No commercial vehicles. Dogs must be kept on leads.

ECCLEFECHAN — Map 21 NY17

Places to visit

Robert Burns House, DUMFRIES, DG1 2PS, 01387 255297 www.dumgal.gov.uk

Old Bridge House Museum, DUMFRIES, DG2 7BE, 01387 256904 www.dumgal.gov.uk

Great for kids: Dumfries Museum & Camera Obscura, DUMFRIES, DG2 7SW, 01387 253374 www.dumgal.gov.uk/museums

PREMIER PARK

▶▶▶▶▶ 81% Hoddom Castle Caravan Park *(NY154729)*

Hoddom DG11 1AS
☎ 01576 300251
e-mail: hoddomcastle@aol.com
dir: *M74 junct 19, follow signs to site. From A75, W of Annan, take B723 for 5m, follow signs to site*

🚐 🚍 🅰

Open Etr or Apr-Oct

Last arrival 21.00hrs Last departure 14.00hrs

The peaceful, well-equipped park can be found on the banks of the River Annan, and offers a good mix of grassy and hard pitches, beautifully landscaped and blending into the surroundings. There are signed nature trails, maintained by the park's countryside ranger, a 9-hole golf course, trout and salmon fishing, and plenty of activity ideas for children. 28 acre site. 200 touring pitches. 150 hardstandings. 100 seasonal pitches. Caravan pitches. Motorhome pitches. Tent pitches. 54 statics. 9 wooden pods.

AA Pubs & Restaurants nearby: Del Amitri Restaurant, ANNAN, DG12 6DJ, 01461 201999

Leisure: 🅰 🎣 🎵
Facilities: 🖧 🖧 ⊙ 🌮 ✳ ♿ 🕓 🐾 🖧 🖧
🖥 🛈
Services: 🔌 🔲 🅱 🧺 🅣 🍴 🛒 🚲 🔧
Within 3 miles: 🎣 🎯 ◎ 🎲 🎲
Notes: No electric scooters, no gazebos, no fires. Visitor centre.

GATEHOUSE OF FLEET — Map 20 NX55

Places to visit

MacLellan's Castle, KIRKCUDBRIGHT, DG6 4JD, 01557 331856 www.historic-scotland.gov.uk

Great for kids: Galloway Wildlife Conservation Park, KIRKCUDBRIGHT, DG6 4XX, 01557 331645 www.gallowaywildlife.co.uk

89% Auchenlarie Holiday Park

(NX536522)

DG7 2EX
☎ 01556 506200 & 206201
e-mail: enquiries@auchenlarie.co.uk
web: www.auchenlarie.co.uk
dir: *Direct access from A75, 5m W of Gatehouse of Fleet*

* 🚐 £20-£25 🚍 £20-£25 🅰 £20-£25

Open Mar-Oct

Last arrival 20.00hrs Last departure noon

A well-organised family park set on cliffs overlooking Wigtown Bay, with its own sandy beach. The tenting area, in sloping grass surrounded by mature trees, has its own sanitary facilities, while the marked caravan pitches are in paddocks, with open views and the provision of high quality toilets. The leisure centre includes a swimming pool, gym, solarium and sports hall. There are six self-catering holiday apartments for let. 32 acre site. 49 touring pitches. 52 hardstandings. Caravan pitches. Motorhome pitches. Tent pitches. 400 statics.

AA Pubs & Restaurants nearby: Cally Palace Hotel, GATEHOUSE OF FLEET, DG7 2DL, 01557 814341

Leisure: 🏊 🎾 🅰 🎿 🎣 🎵
Facilities: 🛁 🖧 ⊙ 🌮 ✳ ♿ 🕓 🐾 🖧 🖧 🖥 🛈
Services: 🔌 🔲 🧺 🅣 🍴 🛒 🔧
Within 3 miles: 🎣 🎯 ◎ 🎲 🎲 ∪
Notes: Dogs must be kept on leads. Crazy golf, teenagers' zone, baby changing facilities.

SERVICES: 🔌 Electric hook up 🔲 Launderette 🅱 Licensed bar 🅐 Calor Gas 🅖 Camping Gaz 🅣 Toilet fluid 🍴 Café/Restaurant 🛒 Fast Food/Takeaway 🔋 Battery charging 🚲 Baby care 🔧 Motorvan service point **ABBREVIATIONS:** BH/bank hols-bank holidays Etr-Easter Spring BH-Spring Bank Holiday dep-departure fr-from hrs-hours m-mile mdnt-midnight rdbt-roundabout rs-restricted service wk-week wknd-weekend x-rds-cross roads 🅐 No credit cards 🅧 No dogs 🅟 Children of all ages accepted See page 9 for details of the AA Camping Card Scheme

GATEHOUSE OF FLEET *continued*

►►►► 79% Anwoth Caravan Site

(NX595563)

DG7 2JU

☎ 01557 814333 & 01556 506200

e-mail: enquiries@auchenlarie.co.uk

dir: *From A75 into Gatehouse of Fleet, site on right towards Stranraer. Signed from town centre*

* 🚐 £20-£25 🚙 £20-£25 ⛺ £20-£25

Open Mar-Oct

Last arrival 20.00hrs Last departure noon

A very high quality park in a peaceful sheltered setting within easy walking distance of the village, ideally placed for exploring the scenic hills, valleys and coastline. Grass, hardstanding and fully serviced pitches are available and guests may use the leisure facilities at the sister site, Auchenlarie Holiday Park. 2 acre site. 28 touring pitches. 13 hardstandings. Caravan pitches. Motorhome pitches. Tent pitches. 44 statics.

AA Pubs & Restaurants nearby: Cally Palace Hotel, GATEHOUSE OF FLEET, DG7 2DL, 01557 814341

Facilities: 🛁🚿☉🌡✳♿🕙🏧 📶

Services: 🔌🗑 ⚗

Within 3 miles: 🎣🏇🛒🛍

GRETNA	Map 21 NY36

Places to visit

Carlisle Cathedral, CARLISLE, CA3 8TZ, 01228 548071 www.carlislecathedral.org.uk

Tullie House Museum & Art Gallery Trust, CARLISLE, CA3 8TP, 01228 618718 www.tulliehouse.co.uk

Great for kids: Carlisle Castle, CARLISLE, CA3 8UR, 01228 591992 www.english-heritage. org.uk/daysout/properties/carlisle-castle

►►►► 78% Braids Caravan Park

(NY313674)

Annan Rd DG16 5DQ

☎ 01461 337409

e-mail: enquiries@thebraidscaravanpark.co.uk

dir: *On B721, 0.5m from village on right, towards Annan*

* 🚐 £16-£20 🚙 £16-£20

Open all year

Last arrival 21.00hrs (20.00hrs in winter) Last departure noon

A very well-maintained park conveniently located on the outskirts of Gretna village. Within walking distance is Gretna Gateway Outlet Village, and Gretna Green with the World Famous Old Blacksmith's Shop is nearby. It proves a convenient stop-over for anyone travelling to and from both the north of Scotland, and Northern Ireland (via the ferry at Stranraer). The park has first-class toilet facilities and generous-sized all-weather pitches. Please note that tents are not accepted. A rally field and a meeting room are available. 6 acre site. 93 touring pitches. 46 hardstandings. Caravan pitches. Motorhome pitches.

AA Pubs & Restaurants nearby: Smiths at Gretna Green, GRETNA, DG16 5EA, 01461 337007

Facilities: 🔦☉🌡✳♿♻☯

Services: 🔌🗑🏧🚽↻

Within 3 miles: 🛒

Notes: Dogs must be kept on leads.

►►►► 76% King Robert the Bruce's Cave Caravan & Camping Park

(NY266705)

Cove Estate, Kirkpatrick Fleming DG11 3AT

☎ 01461 800285 & 07779 138694

e-mail: enquiries@brucescave.co.uk

web: www.brucescave.co.uk

dir: *Exit A74(M) junct 21 for Kirkpatrick Fleming, follow N through village, pass Station Inn, left at Bruce's Court. Over rail crossing to site*

🚐 🚙 ⛺

Open Apr-Nov (rs Nov shop closed, water restriction)

Last arrival 22.00hrs Last departure 16.00hrs

The lovely wooded grounds of an old castle and mansion are the setting for this pleasant park. The mature woodland is a haven for wildlife, and there is a riverside walk to Robert the Bruce's Cave. A toilet block with en suite facilities is especially useful to families. The site is convenient for the M74 and there is a good local bus service available nearby; the site is also on a National Cycle Route. 80 acre site. 75 touring pitches. 60 hardstandings. Caravan pitches. Motorhome pitches. Tent pitches. 35 statics.

AA Pubs & Restaurants nearby: Smiths at Gretna Green, GRETNA, DG16 5EA, 01461 337007

Leisure: 🛝☯🎱🖵

Facilities: 🛁🔦☉🌡✳♿🕙🏧🎍📶 🖥 ♻ℹ

Services: 🔌🗑🏧⚗🚽🎪🏪↯

Within 3 miles: 🎣🎿🏇⛵🛒🛍↻

Notes: No noise after 23.00hrs. Dogs must be kept on leads. BMX bike hire, coarse fishing, first aid available.

LEISURE: 🏊 Indoor swimming pool 🏊 Outdoor swimming pool 🛝 Children's playground 🖐 Kid's club 🎾 Tennis court 🎱 Games room 🖵 Separate TV room 🏌 9/18 hole golf course ⛵ Boats for hire 🎬 Cinema 🎵 Entertainment 🎣 Fishing 🔘 Mini golf ⛵ Watersports 🏋 Gym ☯ Sports field Spa ↻ Stables
FACILITIES: 🛁 Bath 🔦 Shower ☉ Electric shaver 🌡 Hairdryer ✳ Ice Pack Facility ♿ Disabled facilities 🕙 Public telephone 🛒 Shop on site or within 200yds 🏪 Mobile shop (calls at least 5 days a week) 🍖 BBQ area 🎍 Picnic area 📶 Wi-fi 🖥 Internet access ♻ Recycling ℹ Tourist info 🐕 Dog exercise area

KIPPFORD   Map 21 NX85

Places to visit

Orchardton Tower, PALNACKIE
www.historic-scotland.gov.uk

►►► 76% Kippford Holiday Park (NX844564)

GOLD

DG5 4LF
☎ 01556 620636
e-mail: info@kippfordholidaypark.co.uk
dir: *From Dumfries take A711 to Dalbeattie, left onto A710 (Solway coast road) for 3.5m. Park 200yds beyond Kippford turn on right*

⊕ £21-£30 ⊕ £21-£30 ▲ £16-£28

Open all year

Last arrival 21.30hrs Last departure noon

An attractively landscaped park set in hilly countryside close to the Urr Water estuary and a sand and shingle beach, and with spectacular views. The level touring pitches are on grassed hardstands with private garden areas, and many are fully serviced; and there are attractive lodges for hire. The Doon Hill and woodland walks separate the park from the lovely village of Kippford. Red squirrels can be spotted in the woods, and opportunities to fish and to play golf are very close by. 18 acre site. 45 touring pitches. 35 hardstandings. 15 seasonal pitches. Caravan pitches. Motorhome pitches. Tent pitches. 119 statics.

AA Pubs & Restaurants nearby: Balcary Bay Hotel, AUCHENCAIRN, DG7 1QZ, 01556 640217

Kippford Holiday Park

Leisure: ⚙ ☺
Facilities: ♠ ☉ ☮ ☀ & ☺ ☖ ☴ ☔ Wi-fi ▪
☻ ✪
Services: ☏ ☷ ☗ ⊘ T ☲ ☇
Within 3 miles: ↓ ✐ ☺ ☲ ☶ ☶ ∪

Notes: No camp fires. Dogs must be kept on leads. Cycle hire.

KIRKCUDBRIGHT   Map 20 NX65

Places to visit

The Stewartry Museum, KIRKCUDBRIGHT, DG6 4AQ, 01557 331643 www.dumgal.gov.uk/museums

Tolbooth Art Centre, KIRKCUDBRIGHT, DG6 4JL, 01557 331556 www.dumgal.gov.uk/museums

Great for kids: Broughton House & Garden, KIRKCUDBRIGHT, DG6 4JX, 0844 493 2246 http://www.nts.org.uk/Property/Broughton-House-Garden

►►►► 84% *Seaward Caravan Park* (NX662494)

Dhoon Bay DG6 4TJ
☎ 01557 870267 & 331079
e-mail: info@gillespie-leisure.co.uk
dir: *2m SW of Kirkcudbright off B727 (Borgue road)*

⊕ ⊕ ▲

Open Mar-Oct (rs Mar-mid May & mid Sep-Oct swimming pool closed)

Last arrival 21.30hrs Last departure 11.30hrs

An attractive park with outstanding views over Kirkcudbright Bay which forms part of the Dee Estuary. Access to a sandy cove with rock pools is just across the road. Facilities are well organised and neatly kept, and the park offers a very peaceful atmosphere. The leisure facilities at the other Gillespie Parks are available to visitors to Seaward Caravan Park. 23 acre site. 26 touring pitches. 20 hardstandings. Caravan pitches. Motorhome pitches. Tent pitches. 54 statics.

AA Pubs & Restaurants nearby: Selkirk Arms Hotel, KIRKCUDBRIGHT, DG6 4JG, 01557 330402

Leisure: ⬥ ⚙ ♦
Facilities: ♠ ♠ ☉ ☮ ☀ & ☺ ☖ ☴ ☻
Services: ☏ ☷ ☗ ⊘ T ☇
Within 3 miles: ↓ ✐ ☺ ☶ ☶ ∪

Notes: No motorised scooters or bikes (except vehicles for the disabled), no jet skis or own quad bikes. Dogs must be kept on leads. Pitch & putt, volley ball, badminton, table tennis.

LANGHOLM   Map 21 NY38

Places to visit

Hermitage Castle, HERMITAGE, TD9 0LU, 01387 376222 www.historic-scotland.gov.uk

►► 65% *Ewes Water Caravan & Camping Park* (NY365855)

Milntown DG13 0BG
☎ 013873 80386
dir: *Access directly from A7 approx 0.5m N of Langholm. Site in Langholm Rugby Club*

⊕ ⊕ ▲

Open Apr-Sep

Last departure noon

On the banks of the River Esk, this attractive park lies in a sheltered wooded valley close to an unspoilt Borders' town. 2 acre site. 24 touring pitches. Caravan pitches. Motorhome pitches. Tent pitches.

Facilities: ♠ ☉ ☀ & ☺ ☖ ☴
Services: ☏ ☗ ⊘ ☲
Within 3 miles: ↓ ✐ ☷

Notes: ☻ Large playing area.

SERVICES: ☏ Electric hook up ☷ Launderette ☵ Licensed bar ☗ Calor Gas ⊘ Camping Gaz T Toilet fluid ☉ Café/Restaurant ☴ Fast Food/Takeaway
☲ Battery charging ☇ Baby care ☖ Motorvan service point **ABBREVIATIONS:** BH/bank hols-bank holidays Etr-Easter Spring BH-Spring Bank Holiday dep-departure
fr-from hrs-hours m-mile mdnt-midnight rdbt-roundabout rs-restricted service wk-week wknd-weekend x-rds-cross roads ☻ No credit cards ⊗ No dogs
☝ Children of all ages accepted See page 9 for details of the AA Camping Card Scheme

LOCKERBIE

See Ecclefechan

NEWTON STEWART — Map 20 NX46

►►► 67% Creebridge Caravan Park

(NX415656)

Minnigaff DG8 6AJ
☎ **01671 402324 & 402432**
e-mail: john_sharples@btconnect.com
dir: *0.25m E of Newton Stewart at Minnigaff on bypass, signed off A75*

Open all year (rs Mar only one toilet block open)

Last arrival 20.00hrs Last departure 10.30hrs

A small family-owned site a short walk from the town's amenities. The site is surrounded by mature trees, and the toilet facilities are clean and functional. 5.5 acre site. 26 touring pitches. 9 hardstandings. Caravan pitches. Motorhome pitches. Tent pitches. 60 statics.

AA Pubs & Restaurants nearby: Creebridge House Hotel, NEWTON STEWART, DG8 6NP, 01671 402121

The Galloway Arms Hotel, NEWTON STEWART, DG8 6DB, 01671 402653

Kirroughtree House, NEWTON STEWART, DG8 6AN, 01671 402141

Leisure:

Facilities:

Services:

Within 3 miles:

Notes: Dogs must be kept on leads. Security lighting.

PALNACKIE — Map 21 NX85

Places to visit

Orchardton Tower, PALNACKIE
www.historic-scotland.gov.uk

►►► 79% Barlochan Caravan Park

(NX819572)

DG7 1PF
☎ **01556 600256 & 01557 870267**
dir: *On A711, N of Palnackie, signed*

✱ 🚐 £16.50-£21.50 🚐 £16.50-£21.50 ▲ £13-£18

Open Apr-Oct (rs Apr-May & Sep-Oct swimming pool closed)

Last arrival 21.30hrs Last departure 11.30hrs

A small terraced park with quiet landscaped pitches in a level area backed by rhododendron bushes. There are spectacular views over the River Urr estuary, and the park has its own coarse fishing loch nearby. The amenity block includes combined wash facilities. The leisure facilities at Brighouse Bay are available to visitors. 9 acre site. 20 touring pitches. 10 hardstandings. Caravan pitches. Motorhome pitches. Tent pitches. 65 statics.

AA Pubs & Restaurants nearby: Balcary Bay Hotel, AUCHENCAIRN, DG7 1QZ, 01556 640217

Leisure:

Facilities:

Services:

Within 3 miles:

Notes: Dogs must be kept on leads. Pitch & putt.

PARTON

Places to visit

The Rum Story, WHITEHAVEN, CA28 7DN, 01946 592933 www.rumstory.co.uk

The Beacon, WHITEHAVEN, CA28 7LY, 01946 592302 www.thebeacon-whitehaven.co.uk

LEISURE: 🏊 Indoor swimming pool 🏊 Outdoor swimming pool 🎠 Children's playground 🧒 Kid's club 🎾 Tennis court 🎱 Games room 📺 Separate TV room 🏌 9/18 hole golf course ⛵ Boats for hire 🎬 Cinema 🎵 Entertainment 🎣 Fishing ⛳ Mini golf 🏄 Watersports 🏋 Gym 🏟 Sports field Spa ⛹ Stables
FACILITIES: 🛁 Bath 🚿 Shower ⊙ Electric shaver 🪮 Hairdryer ❄ Ice Pack Facility ♿ Disabled facilities 📞 Public telephone 🏪 Shop on site or within 200yds 🏪 Mobile shop (calls at least 5 days a week) 🍖 BBQ area 🪑 Picnic area 📶 Wi-fi 💻 Internet access ♻ Recycling ❶ Tourist info 🐕 Dog exercise area

PARTON Map 20 NX67

►►►► 84% Loch Ken Holiday Park (NX687702)

DG7 3NE

☎ 01644 470282

e-mail: office@lochkenholidaypark.co.uk

web: www.lochkenholidaypark.co.uk

dir: On A713, N of Parton. (NB do not follow Sat Nav directions. Site on main road)

* ⬤ £18-£22 ⬤ £18-£22 ▲ £12-£20

Open Feb-mid Nov (rs Feb-Mar (ex Etr) & Nov restricted shop hours)

Last departure noon

Run with energy, enthusiasm and commitment by the hands-on Bryson family, this busy and popular park, with a natural emphasis on water activities, is set on the eastern shores of Loch Ken. With superb views, it is in a peaceful and beautiful spot opposite the RSPB reserve, with direct access to the loch for fishing and boat launching. The park offers a variety of watersports (canoeing, sailing, water skiing) as well as farm visits and nature trails. Static caravans are available for hire. 15 acre site. 40 touring pitches. 20 hardstandings. 15 seasonal pitches. Caravan pitches. Motorhome pitches. Tent pitches. 35 statics.

AA Pubs & Restaurants nearby: Cross Keys Hotel, NEW GALLOWAY, DG7 3RN, 01644 420494

Leisure: ⚑ ⛹ ☉ ♫

Facilities: ⬤ ⊙ ⬤ ⬤ ⬤ ⬤ ⬤ ⬤ ⬤ WiFi ♻ ✆

Services: ⬤ ⬤ ⬤ ⬤ T ⬤

Within 3 miles: ⬤ ⬤ ⬤ ⬤ ⬤

Notes: No noise after 22.00hrs. Dogs must be kept on leads. Bike, boat & canoe hire.

see advert on opposite page

PORT WILLIAM Map 20 NX34

Places to visit

Glenluce Abbey, GLENLUCE, DG8 0AF, 01581 300541 www.historic-scotland.gov.uk

►►► 78% Kings Green Caravan Site (NX340430)

South St DG8 9SG

☎ 01988 700489

dir: Direct access from A747 at junct with B7085 towards Whithorn

⬤ ⬤ ▲

Open mid Mar-Oct

Last arrival 20.00hrs Last departure noon

Located on the edge of Port William, with beautiful views across Luce Bay as far as the Isle of Man, this is a community run site which offers good facilities and large grass pitches with direct access to the pebble shore where otters have been seen. The road which runs along the coast is relatively traffic free so does not detract from the tranquillity of this small site. Two public boat launches are available. There are several good shops in the village and a local bus, with links to Whithorn, Garlieston and Newton Stewart, runs past the site. 3 acre site. 30 touring pitches. Caravan pitches. Motorhome pitches. Tent pitches.

AA Pubs & Restaurants nearby: The Steam Packet Inn, ISLE OF WHITHORN, DG8 8LL, 01988 500334

Facilities: ⬤ ⊙ ⬤ ⬤ ⬤ ⬤ ⬤ ⬤ WiFi ✆

Services: ⬤ ⬤

Within 3 miles: ⬤ ⬤ ⬤ ⬤

Notes: ⬤ No golf or fireworks permitted. Dogs must be kept on leads. Free book lending.

SANDHEAD Map 20 NX04

Places to visit

Glenwhan Gardens, STRANRAER, DG9 8PH, 01581 400222 www.glenwhangardens.co.uk

Great for kids: Castle Kennedy & Gardens, STRANRAER, DG9 8BX, 01776 702024 www.castlekennedygardens.co.uk

►►►► 80% Sands of Luce Holiday Park (NX103510)

Sands of Luce DG9 9JN

☎ 01776 830456

e-mail: info@sandsofluceholidaypark.co.uk

web: www.sandsofluceholidaypark.co.uk

dir: From S & E: left from A75 onto B7084 signed Drummore. Site signed at junct with A716. From N: A77 through Stranraer towards Portpatrick, 2m, follow A716 signed Drummore, site signed in 5m

* ⬤ £15-£25 ⬤ £15-£25 ▲ £10-£25

Open Mar-Jan

Last arrival 20.00hrs Last departure noon

This is a large, well-managed holiday park overlooking Luce Bay. The site has a private boat launch and direct access to a wide sandy beach, which is proving popular with kite surfers. There is a small café, two games rooms and a nice play area for children; adults might like to visit the Lighthouse Bar at the site's entrance. A bus stops at the site entrance so this makes an ideal base for exploring the Mull of Galloway, and Port Logan Botanical Gardens is within easy driving distance. The site is tailored mainly for statics but touring customers are well catered for. 30 acre site. 100 touring pitches. 50 seasonal pitches. Caravan pitches. Motorhome pitches. Tent pitches. 250 statics.

AA Pubs & Restaurants nearby: Tigh Na Mara Hotel, SANDHEAD, DG9 9JF, 01776 830210

Knockinaam Lodge, PORTPATRICK, DG9 9AD, 01776 810471

Leisure: ⚑ ☉ ♠ ♫

Facilities: ⬤ ⊙ ⬤ ⬤ ⬤ ⬤ ⬤ ⬤ ⬤ WiFi ▦ ♻ ✆

Services: ⬤ ⬤ ⬤ ⬤ ⬤ ⬤ ⬤

Within 3 miles: ⬤ ⬤ ⬤ ⬤ ⬤ ⬤ ↻

Notes: No quad bikes. Owners must clear up after their dogs. Dogs must be kept on leads. Boat launching & storage.

SANDYHILLS Map 21 NX85

Places to visit

Threave Garden & Estate, CASTLE DOUGLAS, DG7 1RX, 0844 493 2245 www.nts.org.uk/Property/Threave-Estate

Orchardton Tower, PALNACKIE www.historic-scotland.gov.uk

Great for kids: Threave Castle, CASTLE DOUGLAS, DG7 1TJ, 07711 223101 www.historic-scotland.gov.uk

►►►► 75% Sandyhills Bay Leisure Park *(NX892552)*

GOLD

DG5 4NY
☎ 01557 870267 & 01387 780257
e-mail: info@gillespie-leisure.co.uk
dir: *On A710, 7m from Dalbeattie, 6.5m from Kirkbean*

* 🚐 £17-£22.50 🚌 £17-£22.50 ⛺ £13.50-£19

Open Apr-Oct

Last arrival 21.30hrs Last departure 11.30hrs

A well-maintained park in a superb location beside a beach, and close to many attractive villages. The level, grassy site is sheltered by woodland, and the south-facing Sandyhills Bay and beach are a treasure trove for all the family, with their caves and rock pools. The leisure facilities at Brighouse Bay are available to visitors here. Two wigwams with TV, fridge, kettle and microwave are available for hire. 15 acre site. 24 touring pitches. Caravan pitches. Motorhome pitches. Tent pitches. 32 statics. 2 tipis.

Leisure: 🛝

Facilities: 🚿 ⊙ 💨 ❄ ✆ [S] 🧺 🐕 ⓘ

Services: 🔧 ⊡ 🛢 ⊘ [T] 🔋 🛒 ⛽

Within 3 miles: ⛳ 🎣 [S] ⊡ 🐴

Notes: No motorised scooters, jet skis or own quad bikes. Dogs must be kept on leads.

SOUTHERNESS Map 21 NX95

83% Southerness Holiday Village *(NX976545)*

AA HOLIDAY CENTRE GOLD

Off Sandy Ln DG2 8AZ
☎ 0844 335 3756
e-mail: touringandcamping@parkdeanholidays.com
web: www.parkdeantouring.com
dir: *From S: A75 from Gretna to Dumfries. From N: A74, exit at A701 to Dumfries. Take A710 (coast road), approx 16m, site easily visible*

* 🚐 £14-£35 🚌 £14-£35 ⛺ £12-£31

Open mid Mar-Oct

Last arrival 21.00hrs Last departure noon

There are stunning views across the Solway Firth from this holiday park at the foot of the Galloway Hills. A sandy beach on the Solway Firth is accessible directly from the park. The emphasis is on family entertainment, and facilities include an indoor pool, show bar, coast bar and kitchen. A very well organised park with excellent all-weather, fully serviced pitches and five 'Star Pitches' (grass or hardstanding) with electric, water supply and direct drainage system for showers and sinks. 50 acre site. 99 touring pitches. 7 seasonal pitches. Caravan pitches. Motorhome pitches. Tent pitches. 611 statics.

Leisure: 🏊 🛝 ✋ 🎱 🎵

Facilities: 🚿 ⊙ 💨 ❄ ♿ ✆ [S] [Wi-fi] ⓘ

Services: 🔧 ⊡ 🍷 🛢 ⊘ [T] 🍽 🛒

Within 3 miles: ⛳ 🎣 ◎ [S] ⊡

Notes: Dogs must be kept on leads. Amusements centre.

STRANRAER Map 20 NX06

Places to visit

Ardwell House Gardens, ARDWELL, DG9 9LY, 01776 860227

►►►► 81% Aird Donald Caravan Park *(NX075605)*

London Rd DG9 8RN
☎ 01776 702025
e-mail: enquiries@aird-donald.co.uk
dir: *From A75 left on entering Stranraer (signed). Opposite school, site 300yds*

🚐 🚌 ⛺

Open all year (rs Sep-Etr no tents)

Last departure 16.00hrs

A spacious touring site set behind mature trees and within a five-minute walk of Stranraer town centre at the head of Loch Ryan. It is an ideal base to tour the 'Rinns of Galloway', to visit Port Logan Botanical Gardens or the lighthouse at the Mull of Galloway. It provides a very convenient stopover for the Cairnryan ferry to Ireland, but there's plenty to do in the area if staying longer. A 25 pitch rally field is available. 12 acre site. 50 touring pitches. 24 hardstandings. Caravan pitches. Motorhome pitches. Tent pitches.

AA Pubs & Restaurants nearby: Knockinaam Lodge, PORTPATRICK, DG9 9AD, 01776 810471

Corsewall Lighthouse Hotel, STRANRAER, DG9 0QG, 01776 853220

Leisure: 🛝

Facilities: 🚿 ⊙ 💨 ♿ 🐕 ⓘ

Services: 🔧 ⊡ 🛢 ⊘ 🔋 ⛽

Within 3 miles: ⛳ ⛵ 🎬 🎣 [S] ⊡ 🐴

Notes: 🚫 Dogs must be kept on leads.

WIGTOWN Map 20 NX45

►►► 85% Drumroamin Farm Camping & Touring Site *(NX444512)*

1 South Balfern DG8 9DB
☎ 01988 840613 & 07752 471456
e-mail: enquiry@drumroamin.co.uk
dir: *A75 towards Newton Stewart, onto A714 for Wigtown. Left on B7005 through Bladnock, A746 through Kirkinner. Take B7004 signed Garlieston, 2nd left opposite Kilsture Forest, site 0.75m at end of lane*

🚐 £18 🚙 £18 ⛺ £15-£18

Open all year

Last arrival 21.00hrs Last departure noon

An open, spacious site overlooking Wigtown Bay and the Galloway Hills. Located near Wigtown and Newton Stewart, this is an easily accessible site for those wishing to stay in a rural location. The toilet and other facilities are maintained in an exemplary manner. There is a large and separate tent field with a well-equipped day room, while the touring pitches can easily accommodate rally events. The RSPB's Crook of Baldoon Reserve is located a 10-minute walk away. There is a good bus service at the top of the road which goes to Newton Stewart, Wigtown and Whithorn. Two of the three statics on site are for hire. 5 acre site. 48 touring pitches. Caravan pitches. Motorhome pitches. Tent pitches. 3 statics.

AA Pubs & Restaurants nearby: Creebridge House Hotel, NEWTON STEWART, DG8 6NP, 01671 402121

The Galloway Arms Hotel, NEWTON STEWART, DG8 6DB, 01671 402653

Kirroughtree House, NEWTON STEWART, DG8 6AN, 01671 402141

Leisure: ⛺ 🔍

Facilities: 🚿 ⊙ 🚽 ✲ ♿ 🪑 🐕 ♻ ℹ

Services: 🔌 🧺 🔋 ⛽

Within 3 miles: ⛳ 🏌 [S]

Notes: No fires, no noise after 22.00hrs. Dogs must be kept on leads. Ball games area.

EAST LOTHIAN

ABERLADY Map 21 NT47

Places to visit

Dirleton Castle and Gardens, DIRLETON, EH39 5ER, 01620 850330 www.historic-scotland.gov.uk

Hailes Castle, EAST LINTON www.historic-scotland.gov.uk

Great for kids: Myreton Motor Museum, ABERLADY, EH32 0PZ, 01875 870288 www.myretonmotormuseum.co.uk

►►► 77% Aberlady Caravan Park *(NT482797)*

Haddington Rd EH32 0PZ
☎ 01875 870666
e-mail: aberladycaravanpark@hotmail.co.uk
dir: *From Aberlady take A6137 towards Haddington. Right in 0.25m, site on right*

* 🚐 £19.50-£22 🚙 £19.50-£22 ⛺ £12.50-£30

Open all year (rs Nov-Feb a maximum of 5 caravans/motorhomes at any one time)

Last arrival 21.00hrs Last departure noon

A small family-run site with a new amenity block and three wooden camping pods for the 2013 season. It is peacefully located within the grounds of the old Aberlady railway station, and is pleasantly landscaped with an open outlook towards the nearby hills; it is within easy reach of many seaside towns, beaches, golf courses and attractions including the National Museum of Flight at East Fortune. The A1 is nearby, making Edinburgh easily accessible. 4.5 acre site. 22 touring pitches. 12 hardstandings. Caravan pitches. Motorhome pitches. Tent pitches. 3 wooden pods.

AA Pubs & Restaurants nearby: La Potinière, GULLANE, EH31 2AA, 01620 843214

Macdonald Marine Hotel & Spa, NORTH BERWICK, EH39 4LZ, 01620 897300

Leisure: ⛺

Facilities: 🚿 ⊙ 🚽 ✲ 🪑 🐕 [Wi-fi] ♻ ℹ

Services: 🔌 🧺 🛢 🌿 [T] 🔋 ⛽

Within 3 miles: ⛳ 🏌 ◎ ≋ [S] ∪

Notes: 💳 No ball games, no loud music. Dogs must be kept on leads.

DUNBAR Map 21 NT67

Places to visit

Preston Mill & Phantassie Doocot, EAST LINTON, EH40 3DS, 0844 493 2128 www.nts.org.uk/Property/Preston-Mill-Phantassie-Doocot

Great for kids: Tantallon Castle, NORTH BERWICK, EH39 5PN, 01620 892727 www.historic-scotland.gov.uk

PREMIER PARK

►►►►► 86% Thurston Manor Leisure Park *(NT712745)*

Innerwick EH42 1SA
☎ 01368 840643
e-mail: holidays@thurstonmanor.co.uk
dir: *4m S of Dunbar, signed from A1*

* 🚐 £12-£25.50 🚙 £12-£25.50 ⛺ £12-£25.50

Open 14 Feb-3 Jan

Last arrival 23.00hrs Last departure 10.00hrs

A pleasant park set in 250 acres of unspoilt countryside. The touring and static areas of this large park are in separate areas. The main touring area occupies an open, level position, and the toilet facilities are modern and exceptionally well maintained. The park boasts a well-stocked fishing loch, a heated indoor swimming pool, steam room, sauna, jacuzzi, mini-gym and fitness room plus seasonal entertainment. There is a superb family toilet block. 250 acre site. 120 touring pitches. 53 hardstandings. Caravan pitches. Motorhome pitches. Tent pitches. 490 statics.

AA Pubs & Restaurants nearby: Macdonald Marine Hotel & Spa, NORTH BERWICK, EH39 4LZ, 01620 897300

Leisure: ≋ 🏋 ⛺ ✋ 🔍 ▭ ♫ Spa

Facilities: 🚿 ⊙ 🚽 ✲ ♿ ☎ [S] 🪑 🐕 [Wi-fi] 🖥 ♻ ℹ

Services: 🔌 🧺 🍷 🛢 🌿 [T] 🍴 🍔 👶 ⛽

Within 3 miles: 🏌 [S] 🧺

Notes: Quiet after 23.00hrs. Dogs must be kept on leads.

DUNBAR *continued*

►►► 75% Belhaven Bay Caravan & Camping Park

(NT661781)

Belhaven Bay EH42 1TS
☎ 01368 865956
e-mail: belhaven@meadowhead.co.uk
dir: *A1 onto A1087 towards Dunbar. Site (1m) in John Muir Park*

* ⬛ £15.50-£28 ⬛ £15.50-£28 ▲ £9.75-£26.75

Open Mar-13 Oct

Last arrival 20.00hrs Last departure noon

Located on the outskirts of Dunbar, this is a sheltered park within walking distance of the beach. There is a regular bus service to Dunbar which also has an East Coast Main Line railway station. The site is convenient for the A1 and well placed to visit the area's many seaside towns and the various visitor attractions. There is a large children's play area. For 2014 - a new amenity block which will provide self-contained units. 40 acre site. 52 touring pitches. 11 hardstandings. Caravan pitches. Motorhome pitches. Tent pitches. 64 statics.

AA Pubs & Restaurants nearby: Macdonald Marine Hotel & Spa, NORTH BERWICK, EH39 4LZ, 01620 897300

Leisure: ⌂

Facilities: 🛁 🚿 ☉ ⌖ ✳ ♿ ⊙ Ⓢ ⊐ 🐕 📶 🖥 ♻ ❶

Services: 🔌 Ⓢ Ⓣ ⬇

Within 3 miles: ⚓ ✎ ☉ 🚣 ⛳ Ⓢ U

Notes: No rollerblades or skateboards, no open fires, no noise 23.00hrs-07.00hrs. Dogs must be kept on leads.

LONGNIDDRY
Map 21 NT47

Places to visit

Crichton Castle, CRICHTON, EH37 5XA, 01875 320017 www.historic-scotland.gov.uk

72% Seton Sands Holiday Village *(NT420759)*

EH32 0QF
☎ 0871 231 0867
e-mail: setonsands@haven.com
web: www.haven.com/setonsands
dir: *A1 to A198 exit, take B6371 to Cockenzie. Right onto B1348. Site 1m on right*

⬛ ⬛ ▲

Open mid Mar-end Oct (rs mid Mar-May & Sep-Oct some facilities may be reduced)

Last arrival 22.00hrs Last departure 10.00hrs

A well-equipped holiday centre with plenty of organised entertainment, clubs and bars, plus restaurants, and sports and leisure facilities. A multi-sports court, heated swimming pool and various play areas ensure that there is plenty to do, and there is lots to see and do in and around Edinburgh which is nearby; there is a regular bus service from the site entrance, which makes Edinburgh easily accessible. The touring field is in a small area to the side of the entertainment complex and has all grass pitches. 1.75 acre site. 34 touring pitches. Caravan pitches. Motorhome pitches. Tent pitches. 635 statics.

AA Pubs & Restaurants nearby: La Potinière, GULLANE, EH31 2AA, 01620 843214

The Longniddry Inn, LONGNIDDRY, EH32 0NF, 01875 852401

Leisure: 🏊 ⌂ 🤿 ⚓ 🎵

Facilities: 🚿 ☉ ⌖ ♿ Ⓢ 📶 ♻ ❶

Services: 🔌 Ⓢ 🍴 🔒 🍽 🛒 🛒

Within 3 miles: ⚓ Ⓢ U

Notes: No commercial vehicles, no bookings by persons under 21yrs unless a family booking. Max 2 dogs per booking, certain dog breeds banned. Dogs must be kept on leads.

MUSSELBURGH
Map 21 NT37

Places to visit

Dalmeny House, SOUTH QUEENSFERRY, EH30 9TQ, 0131 331 1888 www.dalmeny.co.uk

Lauriston Castle, EDINBURGH, EH4 5QD, 0131 336 2060 www.edinburghmuseums.org.uk

►►►► 82% Drum Mohr Caravan Park *(NT373734)*

Levenhall EH21 8JS
☎ 0131 665 6867
e-mail: admin@drummohr.org
web: www.drummohr.org
dir: *Exit A1 at A199 junct through Wallyford, at rdbt onto B1361 signed Prestonpans. 1st left, site 400yds*

* ⬛ £18-£32 ⬛ £18-£32 ▲ £18-£25

Open all year (rs Winter arrivals by prior arrangement)

Last arrival 18.00hrs Last departure noon

This attractive park is carefully landscaped and sheltered by mature trees on all sides. It is divided into separate areas by mature hedging, trees and ornamental shrubs. The generously sized pitches include a number of fully serviced pitches, plus there are first-class amenities. The site is ideally located for exploring East Lothian area with its numerous seaside towns, and the National Museum of Flight at East Fortune just 15 miles away. It's an easy drive on the nearby A1 to Edinburgh or alternatively, there is a regular bus service which stops near the site. There are camping pods and luxury lodges with hot tubs for hire. 9 acre site. 120 touring pitches. 50 hardstandings. Caravan pitches. Motorhome pitches. Tent pitches. 12 statics. 10 wooden pods.

AA Pubs & Restaurants nearby: The Kitchin, EDINBURGH, EH6 6LX, 0131 555 1755

Plumed Horse, EDINBURGH, EH6 6DE, 0131 554 5556

Leisure: ⌂

Facilities: 🚿 ☉ ⌖ ✳ ♿ Ⓢ ⊐ 🐕 📶 ♻ ❶

Services: 🔌 Ⓢ 🔒 ⌖ Ⓣ 🛒 ⬇

Within 3 miles: ⚓ ✎ Ⓢ

Notes: Max 2 dogs per pitch. Dogs must be kept on leads. Freshly baked bread & croissants, tea & coffee.

FIFE

ST ANDREWS   Map 21 NO51

Places to visit

St Andrews Castle, ST ANDREWS, KY16 9AR, 01334 477196 www.historic-scotland.gov.uk

British Golf Museum, ST ANDREWS, KY16 9AB, 01334 460046 www.britishgolfmuseum.co.uk

Great for kids: St Andrews Aquarium, ST ANDREWS, KY16 9AS, 01334 474786 www.standrewsaquarium.co.uk

---

AA CAMPSITE OF THE YEAR FOR SCOTLAND 2014

AA CAMPING CARD SITE

PREMIER PARK

▶▶▶▶▶ **92% Cairnsmill Holiday Park** (NO502142)

Largo Rd KY16 8NN
☎ 01334 473604
e-mail: cairnsmill@aol.com
dir: A915 from St Andrews towards Lathones. Approx 2m, site on right

🚐 fr £26.50 🚍 fr £24.50 Å fr £9

Open all year (rs Winter prior bookings only)
Last arrival flexible Last departure 11.00hrs

Hidden behind mature trees and hedging in open countryside on the outskirts of St Andrews, this top quality park is ideally placed for visiting St Andrews and exploring the Fife area. It is a family owned and run site providing high levels of customer care and excellent facilities, including a swimming pool, licensed bar and café, numerous play areas for children and a small fishing lochan, stocked annually with rainbow trout. Toilet facilities are first class, and the tent area has its own amenity block and outdoor kitchen area. Bunk house accommodation is available as well as five static homes for hire. The local bus to St Andrews stops at the site entrance. 27 acre site. 62 touring pitches. 33 hardstandings. 24 seasonal pitches. Caravan pitches. Motorhome pitches. Tent pitches. 194 statics.

AA Pubs & Restaurants nearby: The Inn at Lathones, ST ANDREWS, KY9 1JE, 01334 840494

Cairnsmill Holiday Park

Leisure: 🏊 Ⓜ 🎱 ▢ 🎵 Spa
Facilities: 🅟 ⊙ 🏳 ✳ 👣 🅲 🛁 📷 ⌂ 🆆🅵🅸 💻 ♻ ❔
Services: 🔌 🗑 🍴 🛢 🚰 🚽 🍴 🔋 🛒
Within 3 miles: ⌡ 🐾 ☰ 🎯 🏌 ◎ ⚓ 🎣 🎲 ⛳ ↺
Notes: No noise after mdnt, 1 car per pitch. Dogs must be kept on leads.

PREMIER PARK

▶▶▶▶▶ **92% Craigtoun Meadows Holiday Park** (NO482150)

Mount Melville KY16 8PQ
☎ 01334 475959
e-mail: craigtoun@aol.com
web: www.craigtounmeadows.co.uk
dir: M90 junct 8, A91 to St Andrews. Just after Guardbridge right for Strathkinness. At 2nd x-rds left for Craigtoun

🚐 🚍 Å

Open 15 Mar-Oct (rs Mar-Etr & Sep-Oct no shop & restaurant open shorter hours)

Last arrival 21.00hrs Last departure 11.00hrs

An attractive site set unobtrusively in mature woodlands, with large pitches in spacious hedged paddocks. All pitches are fully serviced, and there are also some patio pitches and a summerhouse containing picnic tables and chairs. The modern toilet block provides cubicled en suite facilities as well as spacious showers, baths, disabled facilities and baby changing areas. The licensed restaurant and coffee shop are popular, and there is a takeaway, indoor and outdoor games areas and a launderette. Located three miles from St Andrews which has sandy beaches, shops and restaurants, and being 'the home of golf', there are, of course, numerous golf courses including The Dukes, which borders the site. 32 acre site. 57 touring pitches. 57 hardstandings. 7 seasonal pitches. Caravan pitches. Motorhome pitches. Tent pitches. 199 statics.

AA Pubs & Restaurants nearby: Road Hole Restaurant, ST ANDREWS, KY16 9SP, 01334 474371

The Inn at Lathones, ST ANDREWS, KY9 1JE, 01334 840494

Leisure: Ⓜ 🎮 🎱
Facilities: 🚿 🅟 ⊙ 🏳 👣 🅲 ⌂ 🆆🅵🅸 💻 ♻ ❔
Services: 🔌 🗑 🍴 🛒 🚮 🚽
Within 3 miles: ⌡ ☰ 🏌 ◎ ⚓ 🎣 🎲 ↺
Notes: No groups of unaccompanied minors. No pets. Putting green, zip wire, all-weather football pitch.

HIGHLAND

BALMACARA
Map 22 NG82

Places to visit

Balmacara Estate & Lochalsh Woodland Garden, BALMACARA, IV40 8DN, 0844 493 2233 www.nts.org.uk/Property/Balmacara-Estate-Woodland-Walks

▶▶▶ 79% Reraig Caravan Site
(NG815272)

IV40 8DH
☎ 01599 566215
e-mail: warden@reraig.com
dir: On A87, 3.5m E of Kyle, 2m W of junct with A890

* ⬕ fr £15.90 ⬕ fr £15.90 ▲ fr £13.50

Open May-Sep

Last arrival 22.00hrs Last departure noon

A lovely site, on the saltwater Sound of Sleet, set back from the main road amongst mature trees in a garden-type environment. It is located near the Skye Bridge and very handy for exploring the surrounding area including Plockton. There is a regular bus that stops at the site entrance. 2 acre site. 40 touring pitches. 36 hardstandings. Caravan pitches. Motorhome pitches. Tent pitches.

AA Pubs & Restaurants nearby: The Waterside Seafood Restaurant, KYLE OF LOCHALSH, IV40 8AE, 01599 534813

Plockton Inn & Seafood Restaurant, PLOCKTON, IV52 8TW, 01599 544222

The Plockton Hotel, PLOCKTON, IV52 8TN, 01599 544274

Facilities: ⬕⬕⬕⬕⬕⬕⬕⬕⬕⬕
Services: ⬕⬕
Within 3 miles: ⬕

Notes: No awnings Jul & Aug, only small tents permitted. Dogs must be kept on leads. Ramp access to block.

CORPACH
Map 22 NN07

Places to visit

West Highland Museum, FORT WILLIAM, PH33 6AJ, 01397 702169 www.westhighlandmuseum.org.uk

Great for kids: Inverlochy Castle, FORT WILLIAM, PH33 6SN www.historic-scotland.gov.uk

PREMIER PARK

▶▶▶▶▶ 85% Linnhe Lochside Holidays (NN074771)

PH33 7NL
☎ 01397 772376
e-mail: relax@linnhe-lochside-holidays.co.uk
dir: On A830, 1m W of Corpach, 5m from Fort William

⬕ ⬕ ▲

Open Dec-Oct (rs Dec-Etr shop closed out of season, unisex showers during peak season only)

Last arrival 21.00hrs Last departure 11.00hrs

An excellently maintained site in a beautiful setting on the shores of Loch Eil, with Ben Nevis to the east and the mountains and Sunart to the west. The owners have worked in harmony with nature to produce an idyllic environment, where the highest standards of design and maintenance are evident. 5.5 acre site. 85 touring pitches. 63 hardstandings. 20 seasonal pitches. Caravan pitches. Motorhome pitches. Tent pitches. 20 statics.

AA Pubs & Restaurants nearby: Inverlochy Castle Hotel, FORT WILLIAM, PH33 6SN, 01397 702177

Moorings Hotel, FORT WILLIAM, PH33 7LY, 01397 772797

Lime Tree Hotel & Restaurant, FORT WILLIAM, PH33 6RQ, 01397 701806

Linnhe Lochside Holidays

Leisure: ⬕
Facilities: ⬕⬕⬕⬕⬕⬕⬕⬕⬕⬕⬕⬕⬕⬕ ⬕⬕
Services: ⬕⬕⬕⬕⬕⬕⬕
Within 3 miles: ⬕⬕⬕⬕⬕⬕⬕

Notes: No cars by tents. No large groups. Launching slipway, free fishing.

see advert on opposite page

DORNOCH
Map 23 NH78

Places to visit

Dunrobin Castle, GOLSPIE, KW10 6SF, 01408 633177 www.dunrobincastle.co.uk

81% Grannie's Heilan Hame Holiday Park
(NH818924)

Embo IV25 3QD
☎ 0844 335 3756
e-mail: touringandcamping@parkdeanholidays.com
web: www.parkdeantouring.com
dir: A949 to Dornoch, left in square. Follow Embo signs

* ⬕ £14-£32 ⬕ £14-£32 ▲ £11.50-£27

Open Mar-Nov

Last arrival 21.00hrs Last departure 10.00hrs

A 60-acre holiday park situated in Embo that has direct access to the beach on the Dornoch Firth. Within a few miles of the historic town of Dornoch and with easy access to the A9 and regular bus services, this makes an excellent touring base. There is a swimming pool, spa, sauna, solarium, mini ten-pin bowling, a children's club, a bar and restaurant and a good shop. The main amenity block provides good facilities and is well maintained. 60 acre site. 125 touring pitches. Caravan pitches. Motorhome pitches. Tent pitches. 273 statics.

AA Pubs & Restaurants nearby: Dornoch Castle Hotel, DORNOCH, IV25 3SD, 01862 810216

Leisure: 🏊 🎱 ⬇ 🎣 🎮 🎵

Facilities: 🛡 ☉ ℱ ☼ 🚿 🔥 ◷ 💷 🛂 🚻 💻 ♻ ❓

Services: 🔌 🔯 🛒 🍴 ⊘ 🚽 🍴 🍽 🔋

Within 3 miles: ⬇ ✎ ◎ 🛒 🔯

Notes: No noise after mdnt. Dogs must be kept on leads.

DUNDONNELL Map 22 NH08

NEW ▶▶▶▶ 73% Badrallach Cottage & Campsite (NH065917)

Croft 9, Badrallach IV23 2QP
☎ **01854 633281 & 07745 409130**
e-mail: mail@badrallach.com
dir: *From Inverness on A9 take A835 signed Ullapool, left onto A832 signed Gairloch. 10m, right onto single track signed Badrallach, 7m to site*

🚐 £13-£16 � £13-£16 ▲ £13-£16

Open all year

Last arrival anytime Last departure 11.00hrs

Set near the shores of Little Loch Broom, this campsite has been carefully created by the owners on a croft that has stunning scenery and an abundance of wildlife. It is a place to relax and unwind whether you use the campsite, the bothy, the cottage, the Eriba or Airstream. Kayaking, biking and kiting are available for hire, while walking in the nearby mountains directly from the campsite is possible. It's an easy drive from Inverness although the last seven miles are along a narrow single track road. To avoid disappointment pre-booking is advised; for caravans and motorhomes it is essential. Please note, there is no CDP on site and the nearest shops are 12 miles away. 2 acre site. 19 touring pitches. Caravan pitches. Motorhome pitches. Tent pitches.

Leisure: 🔍

Facilities: 🛡 ☉ ℱ ☼ 🚿 ◷ 💷 ♻ ❓

Services: 🔌

Within 3 miles: ⬇ ✎ 🛶

Notes: ⊘ Dogs must be kept on leads.

DUROR Map 22 NM95

▶▶▶▶ 78% Achindarroch Touring Park (NM997554)

PA38 4BS
☎ **01631 740329**
e-mail: stay@achindarrochtp.co.uk
dir: *A82 onto A828 at Ballachulish Bridge then towards Oban for 5.2m. In Duror site on left, signed*

🚐 � ▲

Open 24 Jan-16 Jan

Last departure 11.00hrs

A long established, well-laid out park which continues to be upgraded to a high standard by an enthusiastic and friendly family team. There is a well-appointed heated toilet block and spacious all-weather pitches and there are also 2- and 4-person camping pods for hire. The park is well placed for visits to Oban, Fort William and Glencoe. A wide variety of outdoor sports is available in the area. 5 acre site. 40 touring pitches. 21 hardstandings. 10 seasonal pitches. Caravan pitches. Motorhome pitches. Tent pitches. 2 wooden pods.

AA Pubs & Restaurants nearby: Loch Leven Hotel, NORTH BALLACHULISH, PH33 6SA, 01855 821236

Facilities: 🛡 ☉ ℱ ☼ 🚿 🔥 🛂 🚻 ♻ ❓

Services: 🔌 🔯 🛒 ⊘ 🔋 🚱

Within 3 miles: ✎ ∪

Notes: Groups by prior arrangement only. Dogs must be kept on leads. Campers' kitchen (freezer, toaster, kettle, microwave, boot dryer).

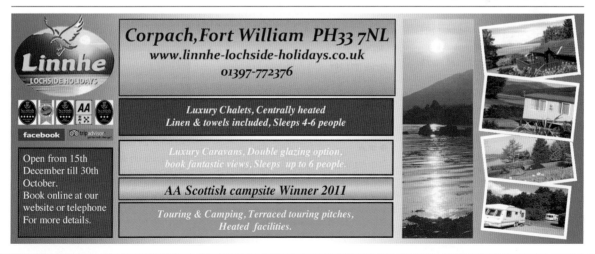

SERVICES: 🔌 Electric hook up 🔯 Launderette 🛒 Licensed bar 🔋 Calor Gas ⊘ Camping Gaz 🅣 Toilet fluid 🍴 Café/Restaurant 🍽 Fast Food/Takeaway 🔋 Battery charging 🛒 Baby care 🚱 Motorvan service point **ABBREVIATIONS:** BH/bank hols-bank holidays Etr-Easter Spring BH-Spring Bank Holiday dep-departure fr-from hrs-hours m-mile mdnt-midnight rdbt-roundabout rs-restricted service wk-week wknd-weekend x-rds-cross roads ⊘ No credit cards 🚫 No dogs ⬤ Children of all ages accepted See page 9 for details of the AA Camping Card Scheme

FORT WILLIAM — Map 22 NN17

See also Corpach

Places to visit

West Highland Museum,
FORT WILLIAM, PH33 6AJ, 01397 702169
www.westhighlandmuseum.org.uk

Great for kids: Inverlochy Castle,
FORT WILLIAM, PH33 6SN
www.historic-scotland.gov.uk

►►►► 88% Glen Nevis Caravan & Camping Park

(NN124722)

GOLD

Glen Nevis PH33 6SX
☎ 01397 702191
e-mail: holidays@glen-nevis.co.uk
web: www.glen-nevis.co.uk
dir: *On northern outskirts of Fort William follow A82 to mini-rdbt. Exit for Glen Nevis. Site 2.5m on right*

* ⊞ £12.50-£18.50 ⊞ £12.50-£18.50
▲ £11.70-£17.40

Open 15 Mar-Oct (rs Mar & Oct limited shop & restaurant facilities)

Last arrival 22.00hrs Last departure noon

A tasteful site with well-screened enclosures, at the foot of Ben Nevis in the midst of some of the most spectacular Highland scenery; an ideal area for walking and touring. The park boasts a restaurant which offers a high standard of cooking and provides good value for money. 30 acre site. 380 touring pitches. 150 hardstandings. Caravan pitches. Motorhome pitches. Tent pitches. 30 statics.

AA Pubs & Restaurants nearby: Inverlochy Castle Hotel, FORT WILLIAM, PH33 6SN, 01397 702177

Moorings Hotel, FORT WILLIAM, PH33 7LY, 01397 772797

Lime Tree Hotel & Restaurant, FORT WILLIAM, PH33 6RQ, 01397 701806

Glen Nevis Caravan & Camping Park

Leisure: /∆\
Facilities: ⬛⬛⬛⬛⬛⬛⬛⬛⬛⬛⬛
Services: ⬛⬛⬛⬛⬛⬛⬛⬛⬛⬛⬛⬛
Within 3 miles: ⬛⬛⬛⬛
Notes: Quiet 23.00hrs-08.00hrs.

see advert on opposite page

GAIRLOCH — Map 22 NG87

Places to visit

Gairloch Heritage Museum,
GAIRLOCH, IV21 2BP, 01445 712287
www.gairlochheritagemuseum.org

Inverewe Garden, POOLEWE, IV22 2LG,
0844 493 2225 www.nts.org.uk/Property/
Inverewe-Garden-Estate

AA CAMPING CARD SITE

►►► 79% Gairloch Caravan Park

(NG798773)

Strath IV21 2BX
☎ 01445 712373
e-mail: info@gairlochcaravanpark.com
dir: *From A832 take B8021 signed Melvaig towards Strath. In 0.5m turn right, just after Millcroft Hotel. Immediately right again*

⊞ ⊞ ▲

Open Apr-Oct

Last arrival 21.00hrs Last departure noon

A clean, well-maintained site on flat coastal grassland close to Loch Gairloch. The owners and managers are hard working and well organised and continued investment in recent years has

seen significant improvements around the park, including the hardstandings, good shrub and flower planting, and the building of a bunkhouse that provides accommodation for families. 6 acre site. 70 touring pitches. 13 hardstandings. 8 seasonal pitches. Caravan pitches. Motorhome pitches. Tent pitches.

AA Pubs & Restaurants nearby: The Old Inn, GAIRLOCH, IV21 2BD, 01445 712006

Facilities: ⬛⬛⬛⬛⬛⬛⬛⬛⬛⬛⬛
Services: ⬛⬛⬛⬛⬛
Within 3 miles: ⬛⬛⬛⬛⬛⬛⬛⬛
Notes: No noise after 23.00hrs. Dogs must be kept on leads.

GLENCOE — Map 22 NN15

Places to visit

Glencoe & Dalness, GLENCOE, PH49 4LA,
0844 493 2222 www.nts.org.uk/Property/
Glencoe-Dalness

Great for kids: Glencoe & North Lorn Folk Museum, GLENCOE, PH49 4HS, 01855 811664
www.glencoemuseum.com

►►►► 85% Invercoe Caravan & Camping Park (NN098594)

PH49 4HP
☎ 01855 811210
e-mail: holidays@invercoe.co.uk
web: www.invercoe.co.uk
dir: *Exit A82 at Glencoe Hotel onto B863 for 0.25m*

* ⊞ fr £22 ⊞ fr £22 ▲ fr £22

Open all year

Last departure noon

A level grass site set on the shore of Loch Leven, with excellent mountain views. The area is ideal for both walking and climbing, and also offers a choice of several freshwater and saltwater lochs. Convenient for the good shopping in Fort William. 5 acre site. 60 touring pitches. Caravan pitches.

Motorhome pitches. Tent pitches. 4 statics. 2 wooden pods.

AA Pubs & Restaurants nearby: Clachaig Inn, GLENCOE, PH49 4HX, 01855 811252

Leisure: ⚓

Facilities: ⬤⊙ℙ⋇⬤⬤⬤⬤⬤⬤

Services: ⬤⬤⬤T⬤⬤

Within 3 miles: ⬤⬤⬤⬤⬤

Notes: No large group bookings.

▶▶▶ 79% John O'Groats Caravan Site *(ND382733)*

KW1 4YR
☎ 01955 611329 & 07762 336359
e-mail: info@johnogroatscampsite.co.uk
dir: At end of A99

* ⬤ £16.50-£19.50 ⬤ £16.50-£19.50 ⬤ £13-£15

Open Apr-Sep

Last arrival 22.00hrs Last departure 11.00hrs

An attractive site in an open position above the seashore and looking out towards the Orkney Islands. Nearby is the passenger ferry that makes day trips to the Orkneys, and there are grey seals to watch, and sea angling can be organised by the site owners. 4 acre site. 90 touring pitches. 30

hardstandings. Caravan pitches. Motorhome pitches. Tent pitches.

Facilities: ⬤⊙ℙ⋇⬤⬤⬤⬤⬤⬤⬤

Services: ⬤⬤⬤⬤⬤

Within 3 miles: ⬤⬤⬤

Notes: ⊛ No noise after 22.00hrs. Dogs must be kept on leads.

LAIDE   Map 22 NG89

NEW ▶▶▶ 71% Gruinard Bay Caravan Park *(NG904919)*

IV22 2ND
☎ 01445 731225
e-mail: gruinard@ecosse.net
dir: From Inverness or Ullapool take A832 to Gairloch, follow signs to Laide. (NB on Inverness to Gairloch route there is a short stretch of single-track road with passing places just prior to Gairloch)

⬤ £15-£17 ⬤ £15-£17 ⬤ £14-£15

Open Apr-Oct

Last arrival 22.00hrs Last departure noon

With views across Gruinard Bay to the Summer Isles and the mountains, this is a lovely, small park in a particularly peaceful location. There is direct access to a small sandy beach and a small hotel nearby with a restaurant and free Wi-fi access; the small post office provides basic groceries, while larger shops can be found in Aultbuie, Poolewe, Gairloch and Ullapool, where there are ferries to the Outer Hebrides. Being beside a beach the site has no hardstandings but

the grass pitches are on well-compacted shingle. 3.5 acre site. 35 touring pitches. 2 seasonal pitches. Caravan pitches. Motorhome pitches. Tent pitches. 20 statics.

Facilities: ⬤⊙ℙ⋇⬤⬤

Services: ⬤⬤⬤⬤

Within 3 miles: ⬤⬤⬤

Notes: No noise after 22.00hrs. Dogs must be kept on leads.

LAIRG   Map 23 NC50

▶▶▶ 74% Dunroamin Caravan and Camping Park *(NC585062)*

Main St IV27 4AR
☎ 01549 402447
e-mail: enquiries@lairgcaravanpark.co.uk
dir: 300mtrs from Lairg centre on S side of A839

⬤ ⬤ ⬤

Open Apr-Oct

Last arrival 21.00hrs Last departure noon

An attractive little park with clean and functional facilities, adjacent to a licensed restaurant. The park is close to the lower end of Loch Shin. 4 acre site. 40 touring pitches. 8 hardstandings. Caravan pitches. Motorhome pitches. Tent pitches. 9 statics.

Facilities: ⬤⊙ℙ⋇⬤⬤⬤

Services: ⬤⬤⬤⬤T⬤⬤⬤⬤

Within 3 miles: ⬤⬤⬤⬤⬤

Notes: No vehicles to be driven on site between 21.00hrs-07.00hrs. Dogs must be kept on leads.

LAIRG *continued*

►►► 69% Woodend Caravan & Camping Site *(NC551127)*

Achnairn IV27 4DN
☎ 01549 402248
dir: *4m N of Lairg exit A836 onto A838, signed at Achnairn*

🚐 🚃 ⛺

Open Apr-Sep

Last arrival 23.00hrs

A clean, simple site set in hilly moors and woodland with access to Loch Shin. The area is popular with fishing and boating enthusiasts, and there is a choice of golf courses within a 30 mile radius. A spacious campers' kitchen is a useful amenity. There's also a holiday cottage to hire. 4 acre site. 55 touring pitches. 5 hardstandings. Caravan pitches. Motorhome pitches. Tent pitches.

Leisure: ⩗
Facilities: ⌁⊙☂✳
Services: 🔌🗑
Within 3 miles: ⅊🗑
Notes: 🐾

NAIRN

Places to visit

Sueno's Stone, FORRES, 01667 460232
www.historic-scotland.gov.uk

Dallas Dhu Distillery, FORRES, IV36 2RR, 01309 676548 www.historic-scotland.gov.uk

Great for kids: Brodie Castle, BRODIE CASTLE, IV36 2TE, 0844 493 2156
www.nts.org.uk/Property/Brodie-Castle

NAIRN   Map 23 NH85

76% Nairn Lochloy Holiday Park *(NH895574)*

East Beach IV12 5DE
☎ 0844 335 3756
e-mail:
touringandcamping@parkdeanholidays.com
web: www.parkdeantouring.com
dir: *From A96 (Bridge St) in Nairn follow site signs onto unclassified road at Bridgemill Direct shop*

✳ 🚐 £14-£35 🚃 £14-£35 ⛺ £12-£32.50

Open Mar-Nov

Last arrival 21.00hrs Last departure 10.00hrs

A small touring site situated within a popular holiday park with a wide range of leisure facilities including heated pool, sauna, spa bath, children's play area and clubs, toddlers' pool, crazy golf, amusements, bars, restaurant and mini supermarket. A small, well-maintained toilet block exclusively serves the touring area where all pitches have electricity. Handily placed in the centre of Nairn, only minutes from the beach and within striking distance of Inverness and the Highlands. 15 acre site. 13 touring pitches. Caravan pitches. Motorhome pitches. Tent pitches. 263 statics.

AA Pubs & Restaurants nearby: Cawdor Tavern, CAWDOR, IV12 5XP, 01667 404777

Boath House, NAIRN, IV12 5TE, 01667 454896

Newton Hotel, NAIRN, IV12 4RX, 01667 453144

The Golf View Hotel and Spa, NAIRN, IV12 4HD, 01667 452301

Leisure: 🏊⩗🛶🎣🎵
Facilities: 🛁⌁⊙☂♿⏱🛒Wi-fi
Services: 🔌🗑🍺💧🗑🍴🛒🚲
Within 3 miles: ⅊⛳🍴🛒🗑∪
Notes: Dogs must be kept on leads.

ULLAPOOL   Map 22 NH19

►►► 76% Broomfield Holiday Park *(NH123939)*

West Shore St IV26 2UT
☎ 01854 612020 & 612664
e-mail: sross@broomfieldhp.com
web: www.broomfieldhp.com
dir: *Take 2nd right past harbour*

✳ 🚐 £18-£19 🚃 £17-£18 ⛺ £16-£18

Open Etr or Apr-Sep

Last departure noon

Set right on the water's edge of Loch Broom and the open sea, with lovely views of the Summer Isles. This clean, well maintained and managed park is close to the harbour and town centre with their restaurants, bars and shops. The Ullapool ferry allows easy access to the Hebridian islands for day trips or longer visits. 12 acre site. 140 touring pitches. Caravan pitches. Motorhome pitches. Tent pitches.

Leisure: ⩗
Facilities: ⌁⊙☂✳♿🛒Wi-fi
Services: 🔌🗑💧⚡
Within 3 miles: ⅊🗑🗑
Notes: No noise at night. Dogs must be kept on leads.

LEISURE: 🏊 Indoor swimming pool 🏊 Outdoor swimming pool ⩗ Children's playground 🛶 Kid's club 🎾 Tennis court 🎱 Games room ☐ Separate TV room ⛳ 9/18 hole golf course 🚣 Boats for hire ☐ Cinema 🎵 Entertainment 🎣 Fishing ⛳ Mini golf 🏄 Watersports 🏋 Gym 🏉 Sports field **Spa** ∪ Stables
FACILITIES: 🛁 Bath 🚿 Shower ⊙ Electric shaver 🪮 Hairdryer ✳ Ice Pack Facility ♿ Disabled facilities 🕐 Public telephone 🛒 Shop on site or within 200yds 🛒 Mobile shop (calls at least 5 days a week) 🍖 BBQ area 🪑 Picnic area Wi-fi Wi-fi 🖥 Internet access ♻ Recycling 🌐 Tourist info 🐕 Dog exercise area

MORAY

ABERLOUR
Map 23 NJ24

Places to visit

Balvenie Castle, DUFFTOWN, AB55 4DH, 01340 820121 www.historic-scotland.gov.uk

▶▶▶ 80% Aberlour Gardens Caravan Park

(NJ282434)

AB38 9LD
☎ 01340 871586
e-mail: info@aberlourgardens.co.uk
dir: *Midway between Aberlour & Craigellachie on A95 turn onto unclassified road. Site signed. (NB vehicles over 10' 6" use A941 (Dufftown to Craigellachie road) where park is signed)*

* ♥ £18.75-£23.40 ♥ £18.75-£23.40
▲ £16.30-£23.40

Open Mar-27 Dec (rs Winter park opening dates weather dependant)

Last arrival 19.00hrs Last departure noon

This attractive parkland site is set in the five-acre walled garden of the Victorian Aberlour House, surrounded by the spectacular scenery of the Cairngorm National Park, through pine clad glens, to the famous Moray coastline; the park is also well placed for the world renowned Speyside Malt Whisky Trail. It offers a small, well-appointed toilet block, laundry and small licensed shop. 5 acre site. 34 touring pitches. 16 hardstandings. 10 seasonal pitches. Caravan pitches. Motorhome pitches. Tent pitches. 32 statics.

AA Pubs & Restaurants nearby: Craigellachie Hotel, CRAIGELLACHIE, AB38 9SR, 01340 881204

Leisure: ⚏
Facilities: ⚏⊙⚏✱⚏⚏⚏ ⚏ ⚏
Services: ⚏⚏⚏⚏⚏⚏
Within 3 miles: ⚏⚏⚏⚏

Notes: No ball games, max 5mph speed limit, no noise after 23.00hrs. Dogs must be kept on leads.

ALVES
Map 23 NJ16

Places to visit

Pluscarden Abbey, ELGIN, IV30 8UA, 01343 890257 www.pluscardenabbey.org

Elgin Museum, ELGIN, IV30 1EQ, 01343 543675 www.elginmuseum.org.uk

Great for kids: Duffus Castle, DUFFUS, 01667 460232 www.historic-scotland.gov.uk

▶▶▶ 67% *North Alves Caravan Park*

(NJ122633)

IV30 8XD
☎ 01343 850223
dir: *From Elgin towards Forres on A96, follow signs for site (sign in Alves), turn right onto unclassified road. Approx 1m site on right*

♥ ♥ ▲

Open Apr-Oct

Last arrival 23.00hrs Last departure noon

A quiet rural site in attractive rolling countryside within three miles of a good beach. The site is on a former farm, and the stone buildings are quite unspoilt. 10 acre site. 45 touring pitches. Caravan pitches. Motorhome pitches. Tent pitches. 45 statics.

AA Pubs & Restaurants nearby: The Old Mill Inn, FORRES, IV36 2TD, 01309 641605

Leisure: ⚏⚏⚏⚏
Facilities: ⚏⊙⚏✱⚏
Services: ⚏⚏⚏⚏⚏
Within 3 miles: ⚏⚏⚏⚏⚏⚏

Notes: ⊛ Dogs must be kept on leads.

LOSSIEMOUTH
Map 23 NJ27

Places to visit

Elgin Cathedral, ELGIN, IV30 1HU, 01343 547171 www.historic-scotland.gov.uk

NEW ▶▶▶▶ 74% Silver Sands Leisure Park *(NJ205710)*

Covesea, West Beach IV31 6SP
☎ 01343 813262
e-mail: info@richmondwight.com
dir: *B9040 from Lossiemouth, 2m to site*

* ♥ £21-£25 ♥ £20-£23 ▲ £12-£21

Open 15 Feb-15 Jan (rs 15 Feb-Jun & Oct-15 Jan shops & entertainment restricted)

Last arrival 22.00hrs Last departure noon

This is an ideal family park located on the Moray Coast two miles from the busy seaside town of Lossiemouth. There is direct access to a sandy beach and the entertainment complex has been refurbished to cater for both children and adults. There is a well-stocked shop, takeaway food and a small bistro-style café on site. With a golf course next to the park and several within easy driving distance, including the world famous Nairn Golf Course, this site makes a perfect base for touring the area. 20 static vans are available for hire. 60 acre site. 140 touring pitches. 30 hardstandings. 35 seasonal pitches. Caravan pitches. Motorhome pitches. Tent pitches. 200 statics.

Leisure: ⚏⚏⚏⚏⚏⚏
Facilities: ⚏⚏⊙⚏✱⚏⚏⚏⚏⚏⚏⚏ ⚏ ⚏
Services: ⚏⚏⚏⚏⚏⚏⚏⚏⚏⚏
Within 3 miles: ⚏⚏⚏⚏⚏⚏⚏⚏
Notes: Dogs must be kept on leads.

SERVICES: ⚏ Electric hook up ⚏ Launderette ⚏ Licensed bar ⚏ Calor Gas ⚏ Camping Gaz ⚏ Toilet fluid ⚏ Café/Restaurant ⚏ Fast Food/Takeaway ⚏ Battery charging ⚏ Baby care ⚏ Motorvan service point **ABBREVIATIONS:** BH/bank hols-bank holidays Etr-Easter Spring BH-Spring Bank Holiday dep-departure fr-from hrs-hours m-mile mdnt-midnight rdbt-roundabout rs-restricted service wk-week wknd-weekend x-rds-cross roads ⚏ No credit cards ⚏ No dogs ⚏ Children of all ages accepted See page 9 for details of the AA Camping Card Scheme

NORTH AYRSHIRE

SALTCOATS
Map 20 NS24

Places to visit

North Ayrshire Heritage Centre, SALTCOATS, KA21 5AA, 01294 464174 www.north-ayrshire.gov.uk/museums

Kelburn Castle and Country Centre, LARGS, KA29 0BE, 01475 568685 www.kelburnestate.com

Great for kids: Scottish Maritime Museum, IRVINE, KA12 8QE, 01294 278283 www.scottishmaritimemuseum.org

80% Sandylands
(NS258412)

GOLD

James Miller Crescent, Auchenharvie Park KA21 5JN
☎ 0871 664 9767 & 01294 469411
e-mail: sandylands@park-resorts.com
web: www.park-resorts.com
dir: From Glasgow take M77 & A77 to Kilmarnock, A71 towards Irvine. Follow signs for Ardrossan. Take A78 follow Stevenston signs. Through Stevenston, past Auchenharvie Leisure Centre, 1st left follow signs to site on left

⛺ 🚐 Å

Open Apr-Oct

Last arrival mdnt Last departure 10.00hrs

A holiday centre with on-site recreational and entertainment facilities for all ages, including an indoor swimming pool. With good transport links and easy access to the ferry terminal in Ardrossan, day trips to the Isle of Arran are possible. The smart amenity block provides touring customers with modern facilities. There is a links golf course nearby. 55 acre site. 20 touring pitches. 20 hardstandings. Caravan pitches. Motorhome pitches. Tent pitches. 438 statics.

Leisure: 🏊 ⛹ 🎮 🎱 🎵
Facilities: 🚿 ☺ 🚐 ♿ 🕒 🛒 🔥 🐕 WiFi 🖥 ♻ ℹ
Services: 🔌 🗑 🍴 💧 🚽
Within 3 miles: ⚓ 🎣 🛒 🏪 🛒

Notes: Dogs must be kept on leads.

PERTH & KINROSS

BLAIR ATHOLL
Map 23 NN86

Places to visit

Blair Castle, BLAIR ATHOLL, PH18 5TL, 01796 481207 www.blair-castle.co.uk

Killiecrankie Visitor Centre, KILLIECRANKIE, PH16 5LG, 0844 493 2194 www.nts.org.uk/Property/Killiecrankie

PREMIER PARK

►►►►► 88% Blair Castle Caravan Park (NN874656)

PH18 5SR
☎ 01796 481263
e-mail: mail@blaircastlecaravanpark.co.uk
dir: From A9 onto B8079 at Aldclune, follow to Blair Atholl. Site on right after crossing bridge in village

* 🚐 £23-£28 🚐 £23-£28 Å £12-£21

Open Mar-Nov

Last arrival 21.30hrs Last departure noon

An attractive site set in impressive seclusion within the Atholl Estate, surrounded by mature woodland and the River Tilt. Although a large park, the various groups of pitches are located throughout the extensive parkland, and each has its own sanitary block with all-cubicled facilities of a very high standard. There is a choice of grass pitches, hardstandings and fully serviced pitches. This park is particularly suitable for the larger type of motorhome. 32 acre site. 241 touring pitches. 155 hardstandings. 68 seasonal pitches. Caravan pitches. Motorhome pitches. Tent pitches. 107 statics.

AA Pubs & Restaurants nearby: Killiecrankie Hotel, KILLIECRANKIE, PH16 5LG, 01796 473220

Leisure: ⛰ ⛹ 🔍
Facilities: 🚿 🚽 ☺ 🚐 ✳ ♿ 🕒 🛒 🔥 🐕 WiFi 🖥 ♻ ℹ
Services: 🔌 🗑 🍴 💧 🛒 🚐 ↻
Within 3 miles: ⚓ 🎣 ◎ 🏪 🛒 ⛲

Notes: Family park, no noise after 23.00hrs. Dogs must be kept on leads.

PREMIER PARK

►►►►► 84% River Tilt Caravan Park (NN875653)

PH18 5TE
☎ 01796 481467
e-mail: stuart@rivertilt.co.uk
dir: 7m N of Pitlochry on A9, take B8079 to Blair Atholl & site at rear of Tilt Hotel

🚐 🚐 Å

Open 16 Mar-12 Nov

Last arrival 21.00hrs Last departure noon

An attractive park with magnificent views of the surrounding mountains, idyllically set in hilly woodland country on the banks of the River Tilt, adjacent to the golf course. There is also a leisure complex with heated indoor swimming pool, sun lounge area, spa pool and multi-gym, all available for an extra charge; outdoors there is a short tennis court. The toilet facilities are very good. 2 acre site. 30 touring pitches. Caravan pitches. Motorhome pitches. Tent pitches. 69 statics.

AA Pubs & Restaurants nearby: Killiecrankie Hotel, KILLIECRANKIE, PH16 5LG, 01796 473220

Leisure: 🏊 🎯 ⛲ Spa
Facilities: 🚿 ☺ 🚐 ✳ 🕒 🛒 ♻ ℹ
Services: 🔌 🗑 🍴 🛢 🍴 🚐 ↻
Within 3 miles: ⚓ 🎣 ◎ 🏪 🛒 ⛲

Notes: Sauna, solarium, steam room.

DUNKELD Map 21 N004

Places to visit

The Ell Shop & Little Houses, DUNKELD, PH8 0AN, 0844 493 2192 www.nts.org.uk/Property/Dunkeld

Castle Menzies, WEEM, PH15 2JD, 01887 820982 www.menzies.org

►►► 80% Inver Mill Farm Caravan Park (NO015422)

Inver PH8 0JR
☎ 01350 727477
e-mail: invermill@talk21.com
dir: A9 onto A822 then immediately right to Inver

🚐 🚕 ▲

Open end Mar-Oct

Last arrival 22.00hrs Last departure noon

A peaceful park on level former farmland, located on the banks of the River Braan and surrounded by mature trees and hills. The active resident owners keep the park in very good condition. 5 acre site. 65 touring pitches. Caravan pitches. Motorhome pitches. Tent pitches.

Facilities: 🏕⊙🅿☀�&🕐

Services: 🔌🖫🧺🚿 **Within 3 miles:** 🚶🎣🏪🖫

Notes: 🐾 Dogs must be kept on leads.

KINLOCH RANNOCH Map 23 NN65

► 74% *Kilvrecht Campsite* (NN623567)

PH16 5QA
☎ 01350 727284
e-mail: tay.fd@forestry.gsi.gov.uk
dir: From north shore: B846 to Kinloch Rannoch. Follow South Loch Rannoch sign. Over river bridge, 1st right signed Kilvrecht. Approach via unclassified road along loch, with Forestry Commission signs

🚐 🚕 ▲

Open Apr-Oct

Last arrival 22.00hrs Last departure 10.00hrs

Set within a large forest clearing, approximately half a mile from the road to Kinloch Rannoch which runs along the loch. This is a beautifully maintained site, with good clean facilities, for those who wish for a peaceful break. It also makes an ideal base for those who prefer the more active outdoor activities of hill walking (Schiehallion is within easy reach) or mountain biking; it is a great spot to observe the multitude of birds and wildlife in the area. Please note the site has no electricity. 17 acre site. 60 touring pitches. Caravan pitches. Motorhome pitches. Tent pitches.

Facilities: &🎡🛈

Within 3 miles: 🎣🏪🖫

Notes: 🐾 No fires. Dogs must be kept on leads.

PITLOCHRY Map 23 NN95

Places to visit

Edradour Distillery, PITLOCHRY, PH16 5JP, 01796 472095 www.edradour.co.uk

Great for kids: Scottish Hydro Electric Visitor Centre, Dam & Fish Pass, PITLOCHRY, PH16 5ND, 01796 473152

►►►► 88% Milton of Fonab Caravan Park (NN945573)

Bridge Rd PH16 5NA
☎ 01796 472882
e-mail: info@fonab.co.uk
dir: From S on A924, pass petrol station on left, next left opposite Bell's Distillery into Bridge Rd. Cross river, site on left. From N (& Pitlochry centre) on A924, under rail bridge, right opposite Bell's Distillery into Bridge Rd

* 🚐 £18-£24 🚕 £18-£24 ▲ £18-£24

Open Apr-Oct

Last arrival 21.00hrs Last departure 13.00hrs

Set on the banks of River Tummel on the outskirts of the picturesque town of Pitlochry, this is a family-owned site with excellent toilet facilities and large spacious pitches. The town, with various tourist attractions - Bells Distillery and the Pitlochry Festival Theatre to name but two - has a wide variety of shops and eateries to suit all tastes. The site makes a great base for touring beautiful rural Perthshire. 15 acre site. 154 touring pitches. Caravan pitches. Motorhome pitches. Tent pitches. 34 statics.

AA Pubs & Restaurants nearby: Moulin Hotel, PITLOCHRY, PH16 5EH, 01796 472196

Killiecrankie Hotel, KILLIECRANKIE, PH16 5LG, 01796 473220

Facilities: 🛒🏕⊙🅿☀�&🕐🖫🐎🗺📶 ♻ 🛈
Services: 🔌🖫🧴🚿
Within 3 miles: 🚶🎣🏪🖫⊙🖫

Notes: 🐾 Couples & families only, no motor cycles. Dogs must be kept on leads.

►►►► 82% *Faskally Caravan Park* (NN916603)

PH16 5LA
☎ 01796 472007
e-mail: info@faskally.co.uk
dir: 1.5m N of Pitlochry on B8019

🚐 🚕 ▲

Open 15 Mar-Oct

Last arrival 23.00hrs Last departure 11.00hrs

A large park near Pitlochry, which is divided into smaller areas by mature trees and set within well-tended grounds. This family-owned site has two large amenity blocks and an entertainment complex with a heated swimming pool, bar, restaurant and indoor games area. There are numerous walks from the site and it is ideal for either a longer stay to explore the area or as a convenient stopover. A regular bus service is available at the site entrance. 27 acre site. 300 touring pitches. Caravan pitches. Motorhome pitches. Tent pitches. 130 statics.

AA Pubs & Restaurants nearby: Moulin Hotel, PITLOCHRY, PH16 5EH, 01796 472196

Killiecrankie Hotel, KILLIECRANKIE, PH16 5LG, 01796 473220

Leisure: 🏊⚴🎱🎵 Spa
Facilities: 🏕⊙🅿☀�&🕐🖫📶 ♻
Services: 🔌🖫🍴🛒🧴🚽🍽
Within 3 miles: 🚶🎣🏪🖫🖫⛳

Notes: Dogs must be kept on leads.

SERVICES: 🔌 Electric hook up 🖫 Launderette 🍷 Licensed bar 🛒 Calor Gas 🥤 Camping Gaz 🚽 Toilet fluid 🍽 Café/Restaurant 🍟 Fast Food/Takeaway 🔋 Battery charging 🍼 Baby care 🚐 Motorvan service point **ABBREVIATIONS:** BH/bank hols-bank holidays Etr-Easter Spring BH-Spring Bank Holiday dep-departure fr-from hrs-hours m-mile mdnt-midnight rdbt-roundabout rs-restricted service wk-week wknd-weekend x-rds-cross roads 🚫 No credit cards 🚫 No dogs 👶 Children of all ages accepted See page 9 for details of the AA Camping Card Scheme

TUMMEL BRIDGE — Map 23 NN75

82% Tummel Valley Holiday Park (NN764592)

GOLD

PH16 5SA
☎ 0844 335 3756
e-mail: touringandcamping@parkdeanholidays.com
web: www.parkdeantouring.com
dir: *From Perth take A9 N to bypass Pitlochry. In 3m take B8019 signed Tummel Bridge. Site 11m on left*

* ⚏ £12-£33 ⚏ £12-£33

Open mid Mar-Oct

Last arrival 21.00hrs Last departure 10.00hrs

A well-developed site amongst mature forest in an attractive valley, beside the famous bridge on the banks of the River Tummel. Play areas and the bar are sited alongside the river, and there is an indoor pool, children's clubs and live family entertainment. This is an ideal base in which to relax. Please note that this park does not accept tents or trailer tents. 55 acre site. 26 touring pitches. 28 hardstandings. Caravan pitches. Motorhome pitches. 169 statics.

AA Pubs & Restaurants nearby: Killiecrankie Hotel, KILLIECRANKIE, PH16 5LG, 01796 473220

Leisure: ☖ ⚏ ⚏ ⚏ ♫
Facilities: ⚏ ♜ ☉ ⚏ ✳ ⚏ ⚏ ⚏ ⚏ ⚏
Services: ⚏ ⚏ ⚏ ⚏ ⚏ ⚏ ⚏
Within 3 miles: ⚏ ◎ ⚏ ⚏

Notes: Dogs must be kept on leads. Sports courts, sauna, solarium, toddlers' pool, amusements, rod hire.

SCOTTISH BORDERS

EYEMOUTH — Map 21 NT96

Places to visit
Manderston, DUNS, TD11 3PP, 01361 883450
www.manderston.co.uk

Great for kids: Eyemouth Museum, EYEMOUTH, TD14 5JE, 018907 50678

74% Eyemouth (NT941646)

SILVER

Fort Rd TD14 5BE
☎ 0871 664 9740
e-mail: eyemouth@park-resorts.com
web: www.park-resorts.com
dir: *From A1, approx 6m N of Berwick-upon-Tweed take A1107 to Eyemouth. On entering town, site signed. Right after petrol station, left at bottom of hill into Fort Rd*

⚏ ⚏

Open Apr-Oct

Last arrival mdnt Last departure 10.00hrs

A cliff-top holiday park on the outskirts of the small fishing village of Eyemouth, within easy reach of Edinburgh and Newcastle. The site is handily placed for exploring the beautiful Scottish Borders and the magnificent coastline and countryside of north Northumberland. 22 acre site. 17 touring pitches. 7 hardstandings. 17 seasonal pitches. Caravan pitches. Motorhome pitches. 276 statics.

Leisure: ⚏ ⚏ ⚏ ⚏ ♫
Facilities: ♜ ⚏ ⚏ ☉ ⚏ ⚏ ⚏ ⚏ ⚏
Services: ⚏ ⚏ ⚏ ⚏ ⚏
Within 3 miles: ⚏ ⚏ ⚏ ⚏ ⚏

Notes: Dogs must be kept on leads.

LAUDER — Map 21 NT54

Places to visit
Abbotsford, MELROSE, TD6 9BQ, 01896 752043
www.scottsabbotsford.co.uk

Harmony Garden, MELROSE, TD6 9LJ,
0844 493 2251
www.nts.org.uk/Property/Harmony-Garden

Great for kids: Thirlestane Castle, LAUDER, TD2 6RU, 01578 722430
www.thirlestanecastle.co.uk

►►► 76% Thirlestane Castle Caravan & Camping Site (NT536473)

Thirlestane Castle TD2 6RU
☎ 01578 718884 & 07976 231032
e-mail: thirlestanepark@btconnect.com
dir: *Signed from A68 & A697, just S of Lauder*

⚏ ⚏ ⚏

Open Apr-1 Oct

Last arrival 20.00hrs Last departure noon

Located on the outskirts of Lauder, close to the A68 and within the grounds of Thirlestane Castle, this is an ideal site from which to explore the many attractions in the Scottish Borders. The amenity block is immaculately maintained and the pitches are behind the estate boundary wall to provide a secluded and peaceful location. There is a regular service bus near the site entrance. 5 acre site. 60 touring pitches. 22 hardstandings. 30 seasonal pitches. Caravan pitches. Motorhome pitches. Tent pitches. 27 statics.

Facilities: ♜ ☉ ✳ ☉ ⚏ ⚏ ⚏
Services: ⚏ ⚏ ⚏
Within 3 miles: ⚏ ⚏ ⚏ ⚏

Notes: ⚏ Dogs must be kept on leads.

PEEBLES

Places to visit

Kailzie Gardens, PEEBLES, EH45 9HT,
01721 720007 www.kailziegardens.com

Robert Smail's Printing Works, INNERLEITHEN,
EH44 6HA, 0844 493 2259 www.nts.org.uk/
Property/Robert-Smails-Printing-Works

Great for kids: Culzean Castle & Country
Park, CULZEAN CASTLE, KA19 8LE, 0844 493 2149
www.nts.org.uk/Property/Culzean-Castle-
Country-Park

PEEBLES   Map 21 NT24

▶▶▶▶ 81% Crossburn Caravan Park
(NT248417)

Edinburgh Rd EH45 8ED
☎ 01721 720501
e-mail: enquiries@crossburncaravans.co.uk
web: www.crossburn-caravans.com
dir: 0.5m N of Peebles on A703

* ⊞ £24-£26 ⊟ £24-£26 ▲ £20-£24

Open Apr-Oct

Last arrival 21.00hrs Last departure 14.00hrs

A peaceful, family-run park, on the edge of
Peebles and within easy driving distance for
Edinburgh and the Scottish Borders. The park is
divided by well-maintained landscaping and
mature trees, and has good views over the
countryside. There is a regular bus service at the
site entrance and Peebles has a wide range of
shops and attractions. The facilities are
maintained to a high standard. There is also a
main caravan dealership on site and a large stock
of spares and accessories are available. 6 acre
site. 45 touring pitches. 15 hardstandings.
Caravan pitches. Motorhome pitches. Tent pitches.
85 statics. 2 wooden pods.

AA Pubs & Restaurants nearby: Cringletie House,
PEEBLES, EH45 8PL, 01721 725750

Macdonald Cardrona Hotel, Golf & Spa, PEEBLES,
EH45 8NE, 0844 879 9024

Leisure: ⚙ ⚲

Facilities: ⛟ ⚲ ⊙ ⚑ ⚲ ⚑ ♻ ❶

Services: ⚡ ⓢ ⬛ ⊘ Ⓣ ⛼ ⬇

Within 3 miles: ⚘ ⚲ ⓢ ∪

Notes: Dogs must be kept on leads.

SOUTH AYRSHIRE

AYR   Map 20 NS32

80% Craig Tara Holiday Park (NS300184)

KA7 4LB
☎ 0871 231 0866 & 01292 265141
e-mail: craigtara@haven.com
web: www.haven.com/craigtara
dir: A77 towards Stranraer, 2nd right after
Bankfield rdbt. Follow signs for A719 & to park

⊞ ⊟

Open mid Mar-end Oct (rs mid Mar-May & Sep-Oct
some facilities may be limited)

Last arrival 20.00hrs Last departure 10.00hrs

A large, well-maintained holiday centre with on-
site entertainment and sporting facilities to suit
all ages. The touring area is set apart from the
main complex at the entrance to the park, and
campers can use all the facilities, including a
water world, soft play areas, sports zone, show
bars, and supermarket with in-house bakery.
There is direct access from the park to the beach
and a bus service to Ayr. 213 acre site. 45 touring
pitches. 39 hardstandings. Caravan pitches.
Motorhome pitches. 1100 statics.

AA Pubs & Restaurants nearby: Fairfield House
Hotel, AYR, KA7 2AS, 01292 267461

The Western House Hotel, AYR, KA8 0HA,
0870 055 5510

Leisure: ⚲ ⚙ ⬇ ⊙ ⚽ ♫

Facilities: ⚲ ⊙ ⚲ ⚲ ⓢ ⛲ ℗ ♻ ❶

Services: ⚡ ⓢ ⚲ ⬛ ⌂ ⬇ ⬇

Within 3 miles: ⚘ ⊞ ⚲ ⊚ ⓢ ⓢ ∪

Notes: No commercial vehicles, no bookings by
persons under 21yrs unless a family booking. Max
2 dogs per booking, certain dog breeds banned.
Dogs must be kept on leads.

BARRHILL   Map 20 NX28

▶▶▶▶ 79% Barrhill Holiday Park
(NX216835)

KA26 0PZ
☎ 01465 821355
e-mail: barrhillholidaypark@gmail.com
dir: On A714 (Newton Stewart to Girvan road). 1m
N of Barrhill

⊞ ⊟ ▲

Open Mar-Jan

Last arrival 22.00hrs Last departure 10.00hrs

A small, friendly park in a tranquil rural location,
screened from the A714 by trees. The park is
terraced and well landscaped, and a high quality
amenity block includes disabled facilities. The
local bus to Girvan stops at the site entrance. 6
acre site. 30 touring pitches. 30 hardstandings.
Caravan pitches. Motorhome pitches. Tent pitches.
42 statics.

Leisure: ⚙

Facilities: ⚲ ⊙ ⚑ ⚲ ⓢ ⓢ ℗ ⚑ ♻ ❶

Services: ⚡ ⓢ ⊘ Ⓣ ⬇ **Within 3 miles:** ⚲ ⓢ

Notes: ⊛ No noise after 23.00hrs.

SERVICES: ⚡ Electric hook up ⓢ Launderette ⚲ Licensed bar ⬛ Calor Gas ⊘ Camping Gaz Ⓣ Toilet fluid ⌂ Café/Restaurant ⬇ Fast Food/Takeaway
⬇ Battery charging ⬇ Baby care ⬇ Motorvan service point **ABBREVIATIONS:** BH/bank hols-bank holidays Etr-Easter Spring BH-Spring Bank Holiday dep-departure
fr-from hrs-hours m-mile mdnt-midnight rdbt-roundabout rs-restricted service wk-week wknd-weekend x-rds-cross roads ⊛ No credit cards ⊗ No dogs
⚲ Children of all ages accepted See page 9 for details of the AA Camping Card Scheme

COYLTON — Map 20 NS41

82% Sundrum Castle Holiday Park (NS405208)

GOLD

KA6 5JH
☎ 0844 335 3756
e-mail: touringandcamping@parkdeanholidays.com
web: www.parkdeantouring.com
dir: *Just off A70, 4m E of Ayr near Coylton*

* ⊞ £14-£36 ⇌ £14-£36 ▲ £12-£31.50

Open mid Mar-Oct

Last arrival 21.00hrs Last departure 10.00hrs

A large family holiday park, in rolling countryside and just a 10-minute drive from the centre of Ayr, with plenty of on-site entertainment. Leisure facilities include an indoor swimming pool complex with flume, crazy golf, clubs for young children and teenagers. The touring pitch areas and amenity block have been appointed to a high standard. 30 acre site. 30 touring pitches. Caravan pitches. Motorhome pitches. Tent pitches. 247 statics.

AA Pubs & Restaurants nearby: Enterkine Country House, AYR, KA6 5AL, 01292 520580

Leisure: ≋ ⋒ ⅏ ⚑ ◖ ◻ ♫
Facilities: ⋔ ◉ ☂ ⅄ ⚤ ⓢ Wi-fi
Services: ◉ ⓢ ⬆ ⮾ ◍ ◔ ◍ ⮐
Within 3 miles: ⅃ ⅄ ⅌ ◎ ⓢ U

Notes: No cars by tents. Dogs must be kept on leads. Nature trail.

GIRVAN — Map 20 NX19

hh ☐ **NEW Turnberry Holiday Park** (NS203033)

KA26 9JW
☎ 01655 331288
e-mail: enquiries@turnberryholidaypark.co.uk
dir: *Site signed from A77 between Turnberry & Girvan. 250mtrs to site adjacent to Dowhill Farm*

Open Mar- 4 Jan

Situated in beautiful South Ayrshire with views of the Firth of Clyde and the iconic Ailsa Craig, this 26-acre park is between the busy seaside town of Ayr and the fishing town of Girvan. The many tourist attractions in the area include Turnberry Golf Course, The Burns Heritage Centre, Maidens and Culzean Castle and Country Park. The park is set in open farmland and is currently undergoing major improvements. The Ailsa Bar provides family-centred entertainment as well as a café serving good food. There is a new swimming pool, reception and sales office. There are 205 holiday homes, 9 statics, and a 3-bedroom chalet for hire.

Within 3 miles: **Spa** ≋ U

Statics 10 **Sleeps** 8 **Bedrms** 2-3 **Bathrm** 1 **Toilets** 1-2 Microwave TV Sky/FTV Modem/Wi-fi Linen included Elec included Gas included Grass area Low season £110-£197 High season £227-£546 Weekly price 169-546

Children ⅙ **Dogs** 2 on leads

Chalet 1 Microwave Freezer TV Sky/FTV Modem/Wi-fi Linen included Elec included Gas included Grass area

Leisure: ≋ ⅏ ⅌ Cycle hire

see advert below

SOUTH LANARKSHIRE

ABINGTON — Map 21 NS92

Places to visit

Moat Park Heritage Centre, BIGGAR, ML12 6DT, 01899 221050 www.biggarmuseumtrust.co.uk

Gladstone Court Museum, BIGGAR, ML12 6DT, 01899 221050 www.biggarmuseumtrust.co.uk

Great for kids: National Museum of Rural Life, EAST KILBRIDE, G76 9HR, 0300 123 6789 www.nms.ac.uk/rural

LEISURE: ≋ Indoor swimming pool ≋ Outdoor swimming pool ⋒ Children's playground ⅏ Kid's club ⅃ Tennis court ◖ Games room ◻ Separate TV room ⅃ 9/18 hole golf course ⚓ Boats for hire ⊟ Cinema ♫ Entertainment ⅌ Fishing ◎ Mini golf ≋ Watersports ⅄ Gym ◔ Sports field **Spa** U Stables
FACILITIES: ⊞ Bath ⚿ Shower ☻ Electric shaver ⚤ Hairdryer ❄ Ice Pack Facility ⅄ Disabled facilities ☏ Public telephone ⓢ Shop on site or within 200yds ⓢ Mobile shop (calls at least 5 days a week) ⧈ BBQ area ⤓ Picnic area Wi-fi Wi-fi ⊠ Internet access ♻ Recycling ⓘ Tourist info ⅏ Dog exercise area

ABINGTON   Map 21 NS92

►►► 79% Mount View Caravan Park

(NS935235)

ML12 6RW
☎ **01864 502808**
e-mail: info@mountviewcaravanpark.co.uk
dir: *M74 junct 13, A702 S into Abington. Left into Station Rd, over river & railway. Site on right*

 £16-£19 ⌂ £16-£19 ▲ £8-£24

Open Mar-Oct

Last arrival 20.45hrs Last departure 11.30hrs

A delightfully maturing family park, surrounded by the Southern Uplands and handily located between Carlisle and Glasgow. It is an excellent stopover site for those travelling between Scotland and the south, and the West Coast Railway passes beside the park. 5.5 acre site. 50 touring pitches. 50 hardstandings. Caravan pitches. Motorhome pitches. Tent pitches. 20 statics.

Leisure: ⚠ **Facilities:** ⬤⊙℗⚓☂
Services: ⬤⬤⬤ **Within 3 miles:** ⟋⬤⬤

Notes: 5mph speed limit. Dogs must be exercised outside park & kept on leads. Emergency phone.

STIRLING

ABERFOYLE   Map 20 NN50

Places to visit
Inchmahome Priory, PORT OF MENTEITH, FK8 3RA, 01877 385294 www.historic-scotland.gov.uk

PREMIER PARK

►►►►► 84% *Trossachs Holiday Park* *(NS544976)*

FK8 3SA
☎ **01877 382614**
e-mail: info@trossachsholidays.co.uk
web: www.trossachsholidays.co.uk
dir: *Access on E side of A81, 1m S of junct A821 & 3m S of Aberfoyle*

⌂ ⌂ ▲

Open Mar-Oct

Last arrival 21.00hrs Last departure noon

An attractively landscaped and peaceful park with outstanding views towards the hills, including the Munro, Ben Lomond. Set within the Loch Lomond National Park, boating, walking, cycling and beautiful drives over the Dukes Pass through the Trossachs are just some of the attractions within easy reach. Bikes can be hired from the reception and there is an internet café that sells home baked items. There are lodges for hire. 40 acre site. 66 touring pitches. 46 hardstandings. Caravan pitches. Motorhome pitches. Tent pitches. 84 statics.

AA Pubs & Restaurants nearby: The Clachan Inn, DRYMEN, G63 0BG, 01360 660824

Trossachs Holiday Park

Leisure: ⚠ ✎ ▢
Facilities: ⬤⊙℗☀⬤⬤⬤⬤ WI-FI ⬤
Services: ⬤⬤⬤⬤⬤⬤
Within 3 miles: ⬤⬤⟋⬤⬤⬤
Notes: Groups by prior arrangement only.

see advert below

SERVICES: ⬤ Electric hook up ⬤ Launderette ⬤ Licensed bar ⬤ Calor Gas ⬤ Camping Gaz Ⓣ Toilet fluid ⬤ Café/Restaurant ⬤ Fast Food/Takeaway
⬤ Battery charging ⬤ Baby care ⬤ Motorvan service point **ABBREVIATIONS:** BH/bank hols-bank holidays Etr-Easter Spring BH-Spring Bank Holiday dep-departure
fr-from hrs-hours m-mile mdnt-midnight rdbt-roundabout rs-restricted service wk-week wknd-weekend x-rds-cross roads ⬤ No credit cards ⬤ No dogs
⬤ Children of all ages accepted See page 9 for details of the AA Camping Card Scheme

BLAIRLOGIE
Map 21 NS89

Places to visit

Alloa Tower, ALLOA, FK10 1PP, 0844 493 2129
http://www.nts.org.uk/Property/Alloa-Tower/

The Regimental Museum of the Argyll &
Sutherland Highlanders, STIRLING, FK8 3PA,
01786 475165 www.argylls.co.uk

►►►► 88% Witches Craig Caravan & Camping Park

GOLD

(NS821968)

FK9 5PX
☎ 01786 474947
e-mail: info@witchescraig.co.uk
dir: *3m NE of Stirling on A91 (Hillfoots to
St Andrews road)*

* 🚐 £20.75–£23.25 🚐 £20.75–£23.25 ▲ £17–£22

Open Apr–Oct

Last arrival 20.00hrs Last departure noon

In an attractive setting with direct access to the
lower slopes of the dramatic Ochil Hills, this is a
well-maintained family-run park. It is in the
centre of 'Braveheart' country, with easy access to
historical sites and many popular attractions. 5
acre site. 60 touring pitches. 60 hardstandings. 6
seasonal pitches. Caravan pitches. Motorhome
pitches. Tent pitches.

Leisure: ⌂

Facilities: ⌂☉🅟✻♿🐕🖭♻️ℹ️

Services: 🖂🔋🛢💧🅣🛒🚮

Within 3 miles: ⚓🌭🎣◉🏪🛒⛺

Notes: Dogs must be kept on leads. Food
preparation area, baby bath & changing area.

CALLANDER
Map 20 NN60

Places to visit

Doune Castle, DOUNE, FK16 6EA, 01786 841742
www.historic-scotland.gov.uk

AA CAMPING CARD SITE

►►►► 86% Gart Caravan Park

(NN643070)

The Gart FK17 8LE
☎ 01877 330002
e-mail: enquiries@theholidaypark.co.uk
dir: *1m E of Callander on A84*

* 🚐 £23.50–£25.50 🚐 £23.50–£25.50

Open Etr or Apr–15 Oct

Last arrival 22.00hrs Last departure 11.30hrs

A very well appointed and spacious parkland site
within easy walking distance of the tourist and
outdoor activity-friendly town of Callander. The
site is in an excellent location for touring the area;
Loch Katrine where there are trips on the
SS *Sir Walter Scott*, the Trossachs and the Rob Roy
Centre are only a few of the many nearby
attractions. Free fishing is available on the River
Teith which runs along the edge of the site. The
statics vans are in a separate area. Please note
that tents are not accepted. 26 acre site. 128
touring pitches. Caravan pitches. Motorhome
pitches. 66 statics.

AA Pubs & Restaurants nearby: Roman Camp
Country House Hotel, CALLANDER, FK17 8BG,
01877 330003

Callander Meadows, CALLANDER, FK17 8BB,
01877 330181

Leisure: ⌂🌳

Facilities: ⌂☉✻♿🕙🖭🖭🖥️♻️ℹ️

Services: 🖂🔋🛢🚮

Within 3 miles: ⚓🎣🏑◉⛵🏪🛒⛺

Notes: No commercial vehicles. Dogs must be
kept on leads.

LUIB
Map 20 NN42

Places to visit

Balmacara Estate & Lochalsh Woodland
Garden, BALMACARA, IV40 8DN, 0844 493 2233
www.nts.org.uk/Property/Balmacara-Estate-
Woodland-Walks

►►►► 74% Glendochart Holiday Park
(NN477278)

FK20 8QT
☎ 01567 820637
e-mail: info@glendochart-caravanpark.co.uk
dir: *On A85 (Oban to Stirling road), midway
between Killin & Crianlarich*

* 🚐 £17.50–£19.50 🚐 £17.50–£19.50
▲ £12.50–£16

Open Mar–Nov

Last arrival 21.00hrs Last departure noon

A small site located on the A85 some eight miles
from Killin, with boating and fishing available on
Loch Tay. It is also convenient for Oban, Fort
William and Loch Lomond. Hill walkers have direct
access to numerous walks to suit all levels
including the nearby Munro of Ben More. There is a
regular bus service at the site entrance and
nearby Crianlarich provides access to the West
Highland Railway known as Britain's most scenic
rail route, and also the West Highland Way. An
ideal site as a stopover to the west coast or for a
longer holiday. 15 acre site. 35 touring pitches. 28
hardstandings. Caravan pitches. Motorhome
pitches. Tent pitches. 60 statics.

AA Pubs & Restaurants nearby: The Lade Inn,
CALLANDER, FK17 8HD, 01877 330152

Facilities: ⌂☉🅟✻♿🏪🐕ℹ️

Services: 🖂🔋🛢💧🚮

Within 3 miles: 🎣

Notes: Dogs must be kept on leads.

STIRLING

See Blairlogie

STRATHYRE   Map 20 NN51

▶▶▶ 76% Immervoulin Caravan and Camping Park (NN560164)

FK18 8NJ
☎ **01877 384285**
dir: *On A84, approx 1m S of Strathyre*

🚐 🚏 ⛺

Open Mar-Oct

Last arrival 22.00hrs

A family-run park on open meadowland beside the River Balvaig, where fishing, canoeing and other water sports can be enjoyed. A riverside walk leads to Loch Lubnaig, and the small village of Strathyre has various pubs offering food. Located on the A84, the site is ideally located for exploring this lovely area. The park has a modern well-appointed amenity block. 5 acre site. 50 touring pitches. Caravan pitches. Motorhome pitches. Tent pitches.

AA Pubs & Restaurants nearby: Creagan House, STRATHYRE, FK18 8ND, 01877 384638

Roman Camp Country House Hotel, CALLANDER, FK17 8BG, 01877 330003

Callander Meadows, CALLANDER, FK17 8BB, 01877 330181

Facilities: 🅿 ⊙ 🌊 ✳ ♿ 🕙 🚰 🚮 ♻ ❶
Services: 🔌 🗑 💧 🚿 ⓣ 🔋 ⚓
Within 3 miles: 🎣 🛒
Notes: No noise after 23.00hrs.

WEST DUNBARTONSHIRE

BALLOCH   Map 20 NS38

Places to visit

Finlaystone Country Estate, LANGBANK, PA14 6TJ, 01475 540505 www.finlaystone.co.uk

The Tall Ship at Riverside, GLASGOW, G3 8RS, 0141 357 3699 www.thetallship.com

PREMIER PARK

▶▶▶▶▶ 78% *Lomond Woods Holiday Park* (NS383816)

Old Luss Rd G83 8QP
☎ **01389 755000**
e-mail: lomondwoods@holiday-parks.co.uk
web: www.holiday-parks.co.uk
dir: *From A82, 17m N of Glasgow, take A811 (Stirling to Balloch road). Left at 1st rdbt, follow holiday park signs, 150yds on left*

🚐 🚏

Open all year

Last arrival 20.00hrs Last departure noon

This site is ideally placed on the southern end of Loch Lomond, the UK's largest inland water and a designated National Park. This site has something to suit all tastes from the most energetic visitor to those who just wish to relax. Fully serviced pitches are available. There are loch cruises and boats to hire, plus retail outlets, superstores and eateries within easy walking distance. A drive or cycle ride along Loch Lomond reveals breathtaking views. There are two large boat storage areas. Please note that this site does not accept tents. In 2014 the facilities will include three family rooms. Holiday caravans and lodges are available to let. 13 acre site. 100 touring pitches. 100 hardstandings. Caravan pitches. Motorhome pitches. 35 statics.

AA Pubs & Restaurants nearby: The Cameron Grill, BALLOCH, G83 8QZ, 01389 722582

Leisure: 🅰 🎣 ☐
Facilities: 🚿 🅿 ⊙ 🌊 ✳ ♿ 🕙 🗑 🚰 🚮 📶 ♻ ❶
Services: 🔌 🗑 💧 🚿 ⓣ 🔋 ⚓
Within 3 miles: 🚶 🎣 ⛳ 🛒 🗑 ⛷
Notes: No jet skis. Dogs must be kept on leads.

WEST LOTHIAN

EAST CALDER   Map 21 NT06

Places to visit

Suntrap Garden, GOGAR, EH12 9BY, 0131 339 7283 www.suntrap-garden.org.uk

Malleny Garden, BALERNO, EH14 7AF, 0844 493 2123 www.nts.org.uk/Property/Malleny-Garden

AA CAMPING CARD SITE

▶▶▶▶ 82% Linwater Caravan Park (NT104696)

West Clifton EH53 0HT
☎ **0131 333 3326**
e-mail: linwater@supanet.com
dir: *M9 junct 1, signed A89 & B7030 (brown Linwater sign). Or from Wilkieston on A71*

🚐 £17-£22 🚏 £17-£22 ⛺ £15-£20

Open late Mar-late Oct

Last arrival 21.00hrs Last departure noon

A farmland park in a peaceful rural area within easy reach of Edinburgh. The very good facilities are housed in a Scandinavian-style building, and are well maintained by resident owners; they are genuinely caring hosts and nothing is too much trouble. There are 'timber tents' for hire and nearby are plenty of pleasant woodland walks. 5 acre site. 60 touring pitches. 22 hardstandings. Caravan pitches. Motorhome pitches. Tent pitches. 4 wooden pods.

AA Pubs & Restaurants nearby: The Bridge Inn, RATHO, EH28 8RA, 0131 333 1320

Leisure: 🅰
Facilities: 🅿 ⊙ 🌊 ✳ ♿ 🕙 🚰 📶 ♻ ❶
Services: 🔌 🗑 💧 🚿 ⓣ 🔋
Within 3 miles: 🚶 🎣 🗑 🗑
Notes: No noise after 23.00hrs. Dogs must be kept on leads. Takeaway food can be ordered.

SERVICES: 🔌 Electric hook up 🗑 Launderette 🍸 Licensed bar 🛢 Calor Gas 🛢 Camping Gaz ⓣ Toilet fluid 🍽 Café/Restaurant 🍔 Fast Food/Takeaway 🔋 Battery charging 🍼 Baby care ⚓ Motorvan service point **ABBREVIATIONS:** BH/bank hols-bank holidays Etr-Easter Spring BH-Spring Bank Holiday dep-departure fr-from hrs-hours m-mile mdnt-midnight rdbt-roundabout rs-restricted service wk-week wknd-weekend x-rds-cross roads ⊗ No credit cards ⊗ No dogs 🚸 Children of all ages accepted See page 9 for details of the AA Camping Card Scheme

LINLITHGOW Map 21 NS97

Places to visit

Linlithgow Palace, LINLITHGOW, EH49 7AL, 01506 842896 www.historic-scotland.gov.uk

House of The Binns, LINLITHGOW, EH49 7NA, 0844 493 2127 www.nts.org.uk/Property/House-of-the-Binns

Great for kids: Blackness Castle, LINLITHGOW, EH49 7NH, 01506 834807 www.historic-scotland.gov.uk

►►►► 84% Beecraigs Caravan & Camping Site (NT006746)

Beecraigs Country Park, The Visitor Centre EH49 6PL
☎ 01506 844516 & 848943
e-mail: mail@beecraigs.com
web: www.beecraigs.com
dir: M9 junct 3 or 4, A803 from Linlithgow or Bathgate. Follow B792, signs to country park. Reception within restaurant or visitor centre

✱ ⬛ £17.60-£21.74 ⬛ £17.60-£21.74
▲ £14.49-£21.74

Open all year (rs 25-26 Dec & 1-2 Jan no new arrivals)

Last arrival 21.00hrs Last departure noon

A wildlife enthusiast's paradise where even the timber facility buildings are in keeping with the environment. Beecraigs is situated peacefully in the open countryside of the Bathgate Hills. Small bays with natural shading offer intimate pitches, and there's a restaurant serving lunch and evening meals. The smart toilet block on the main park includes en suite facilities, and there is a luxury toilet block for tenters. 6 acre site. 36 touring pitches. 36 hardstandings. Caravan pitches. Motorhome pitches. Tent pitches.

AA Pubs & Restaurants nearby: Champany Inn, LINLITHGOW, EH49 7LU, 01506 834532

Beecraigs Caravan & Camping Site

Leisure: ⚠

Facilities: 🛁 🚿 ☉ 🖐 ✳ ♿ 🔔 🛒 ⌦ 🔌 ♻ ❶

Services: 🔲 ⬛ 🛢 T 🍴 ⬇

Within 3 miles: ↓ 🎣 ⛵ ⑤ 🛒 ∪

Notes: No cars by tents. No ball games near caravans, no noise after 22.00hrs. Dogs must be kept on leads. Country park facilities including Ranger Service events. Child bath available.

KILDONAN Map 20 NS02

Places to visit

Brodick Castle, Garden & Country Park, BRODICK, KA27 8HY, 0844 493 2152 www.nts.org.uk/Property/Brodick-Castle-Garden-Country-Park

Isle of Arran Heritage Museum, BRODICK, KA27 8DP, 01770 302636 www.arranmuseum.co.uk

►►►► 79% *Sealshore Camping and Touring Site* (NS024210)

KA27 8SE
☎ 01770 820320
e-mail: enquiries@campingarran.com
dir: *From ferry terminal in Brodick turn left, 12m, through Lamlash & Whiting Bay. Left to Kildonan, site on left*

⬛ ⬛ ▲

Open Mar-Oct

Last arrival 21.00hrs Last departure noon

On the south coast of Arran and only 12 miles from the ferry at Brodick, this is a peaceful, family-run site with direct access to a sandy beach. There are fabulous views across the water to Pladda Island and Ailsa Craig, and an abundance of wildlife. The site is suited for all types of touring vehicles but caters very well for non-motorised campers. The resident owner, also a registered fisherman, sells fresh lobster and crab, and on request will give fishing lessons on a small, privately owned lochan. There is an undercover BBQ, campers' kitchen and day room with TV. A bus, which stops on request, travels around the island. 3 acre site. 43 touring pitches. 8 hardstandings. Caravan pitches. Motorhome pitches. Tent pitches.

Leisure: 🎣 🔲

Facilities: 🚿 ☉ 🖐 ✳ ♿ ⑤ ⌦ 🔌 ♻ ❶

Services: 🔲 ⬛ 🚮 T 🛒 ⬇

Within 3 miles: ↓ 🎣 ⊚ ⑤ 🛒

Notes: 🐕 No cars by tents. No fires, no noise after 22.00hrs. Dogs must be kept on leads.

LEISURE: 🏊 Indoor swimming pool 🏊 Outdoor swimming pool ⚠ Children's playground 🖐 Kid's club 🎾 Tennis court ♟ Games room 🔲 Separate TV room
↓ 9/18 hole golf course ⛵ Boats for hire 🎬 Cinema 🎵 Entertainment 🎣 Fishing ⊚ Mini golf 🏄 Watersports 🏋 Gym ⚽ Sports field Spa ∪ Stables
FACILITIES: 🛁 Bath 🚿 Shower ☉ Electric shaver 🖐 Hairdryer ✳ Ice Pack Facility ♿ Disabled facilities 🔔 Public telephone ⑤ Shop on site or within 200yds
🛒 Mobile shop (calls at least 5 days a week) 🍴 BBQ area ⌦ Picnic area WI-FI Wi-fi 🖥 Internet access ♻ Recycling ❶ Tourist info 🔌 Dog exercise area

ISLE OF MULL

CRAIGNURE
Map 20 NM73

Places to visit

Mull & West Highland Narrow Gauge Railway, CRAIGNURE, PA65 6AY, 01680 812494 (in season) www.mullrail.co.uk

▶▶▶▶ 84% *Shieling Holidays*

(NM724369)

PA65 6AY
☎ 01680 812496 & 0131 556 0068
e-mail: sales@shielingholidays.co.uk
web: www.shielingholidays.co.uk
dir: *From ferry left onto A849 to Iona. 400mtrs left at church, follow site signs towards sea*

⊞ ⊟ ⛺

Open 8 Mar-4 Nov

Last arrival 22.00hrs Last departure noon

A lovely site on the water's edge with spectacular views, and less than one mile from the ferry landing. Hardstandings and service points are provided for motorhomes, and there are astro-turf pitches for tents. The park also offers unique, en suite cottage tents for hire and bunkhouse accommodation for families. There is also a wildlife trail on site. 7 acre site. 90 touring pitches. 30 hardstandings. Caravan pitches. Motorhome pitches. Tent pitches. 15 statics.

Leisure: ⚠ ⚓ ⬜

Facilities: ➤ ♠ ☉ ☺ ⚘ ❄ ⚬ ☺ ⛱ ♨ ☵ ✧ ♻ ❶

Services: 🔌 ▣ 🛢 ⊘ Ⓣ ⛟ ♨

Within 3 miles: ⚓ 🎣 🛒 ▣

Notes: Dogs must be kept on leads. Bikes available.

ISLE OF SKYE

EDINBANE
Map 22 NG35

▶▶▶▶ 88% *Skye Camping & Caravanning Club Site* (NG345527)

Loch Greshornish, Borve, Arnisort IV51 9PS
☎ 01470 582230
e-mail: skye.site@thefriendlyclub.co.uk
dir: *Approx 12m from Portree on A850 (Dunvegan road). Site by loch shore*

⊞ ⊟ ⛺

Open Apr-Oct

Last arrival 22.00hrs Last departure noon

Situated on the beautiful Isle of Skye, this campsite stands out for its stunning waterside location and glorious views, the generous pitch density, the overall range of facilities, and the impressive ongoing improvements under enthusiastic franchisee owners. The layout maximises the beauty of the scenery and genuine customer care is very evident with an excellent tourist information room and campers' shelter being just two examples. The amenities block has that definite 'wow' factor with smart, modern fittings, including excellent showers, a generously proportioned disabled room and a family bathroom. This is a green site that uses only green toilet fluids, which are available on site. There is an on-site shop, two camping pods to let, plus car hire is available on the site. Non-members are very welcome too. 7.5 acre site. 105 touring pitches. 36 hardstandings. Caravan pitches. Motorhome pitches. Tent pitches. 2 wooden pods.

AA Pubs & Restaurants nearby: Stein Inn, STEIN, IV55 8GA, 01470 592362

Loch Bay Seafood Restaurant, STEIN, IV55 8GA, 01470 592235

The Three Chimneys, COLBOST, IV55 8ZT, 01470 511258

Facilities: ♠ ☉ ☺ ⚘ ❄ ⚬ ☺ ▣ ⛱ ♨ ☵ ♻ ❶

Services: 🔌 ▣ 🛢 ⊘ Ⓣ ⛟ ♨

Within 3 miles: 🛒 ▣

Notes: Barrier locked 23.00hrs-07.00hrs. Dogs must be kept on leads. Fish & chip van 3 nights a week (mid-high season).

STAFFIN
Map 22 NG46

▶▶▶ 79% *Staffin Camping & Caravanning* (NG492670)

IV51 9JX
☎ 01470 562213
e-mail: staffincampsite@btinternet.com
dir: *On A855, 16m N of Portree. Turn right before 40mph signs*

⊞ ⊟ ⛺

Open Apr-Oct

Last arrival 22.00hrs Last departure 11.00hrs

A large sloping grassy site with level hardstandings for motorhomes and caravans, close to the village of Staffin. The toilet block is appointed to a very good standard and the park has a laundry. Mountain bikes are available for hire. 2.5 acre site. 50 touring pitches. 18 hardstandings. Caravan pitches. Motorhome pitches. Tent pitches.

AA Pubs & Restaurants nearby: The Glenview, STAFFIN, IV51 9JH, 01470 562248

Facilities: ♠ ☉ ☺ ⚘ ❄ ⚬ ⛱ ♨ ☵ ♻ ❶

Services: 🔌 ▣ 🛢 ⊘ ♨

Within 3 miles: ⚓ 🎣 🛒 ▣

Notes: ⊘ No music after 22.00hrs. Dogs must be kept on leads. Picnic tables, kitchen area, campers' bothy.

SERVICES: 🔌 Electric hook up ▣ Launderette 🍺 Licensed bar 🛢 Calor Gas ⊘ Camping Gaz Ⓣ Toilet fluid 🍴 Café/Restaurant 🍟 Fast Food/Takeaway ⛟ Battery charging 🍼 Baby care ♨ Motorvan service point ABBREVIATIONS: BH/bank hols-bank holidays Etr-Easter Spring BH-Spring Bank Holiday dep-departure fr-from hrs-hours m-mile mdnt-midnight rdbt-roundabout rs-restricted service wk-week wknd-weekend x-rds-cross roads ⊗ No credit cards ⊗ No dogs ♦ Children of all ages accepted See page 9 for details of the AA Camping Card Scheme

Wales

The Menai Strait and suspension bridge

Llynnau Mymbyr, Capel Curig , Conwy

Wales

Wales may be small but it certainly packs a punch.
Its scenery is a matchless mix of magnificent mountains,
rolling green hills and craggy coastlines. But it is not just
the landscape that makes such a strong impression -
Wales is renowned for its prominent position in the world
of culture and the arts.

This is a land of ancient myths and traditions, of male voice choirs, exceptionally gifted singers and leading actors of stage and screen. Richard Burton hailed from the valleys in south Wales, Anthony Hopkins originates from Port Talbot and Tom Jones, born Thomas Jones Woodward, comes from Pontypridd. One man who is inextricably linked to Wales is the poet Dylan Thomas. Born in Swansea in 1914, he lived at the Boat House in Laugharne, on the Taf and Tywi estuaries, overlooking Carmarthen Bay. He is buried in the local churchyard.

The valleys

East of here are the old industrial valleys of the Rhondda, once a byword for hardship and poverty and the grime of the local coal and iron workings, it has now been transformed into a very different place. Also vastly altered and improved by the passage of time are the great cities of Swansea and Cardiff, the latter boasting a vibrant café culture, Docklands-style apartments, a science discovery centre that's fun for all the family, and the internationally renowned Wales Millennium Centre.

▶

● Aberystwyth, Ceredigion

Going west and north

Tenby in west Wales still retains the charm of a typical seaside resort while the Pembrokeshire coast, overlooking Cardigan Bay, is one of the country's scenic treasures. Lower Fishguard has a connection with Dylan Thomas. In 1971, less than 20 years after his death, some of the theatre's greatest names – Richard Burton and Peter O'Toole among them – descended on this picturesque village to film *Under Milk Wood*, which Thomas originally wrote as a radio play.

Farther north is Harlech Castle, built around 1283 by Edward I, with the peaks of Snowdonia in the distance. The formidable Caernarfon Castle, the setting for the investiture of the Prince of Wales in 1969, stands in the north-west corner of the country. Both castles are part of a string of massive strongholds built by Edward to establish a united Britain.

The mountains

With its many attractions and miles of natural beauty, the coast of Wales is an obvious draw for its many visitors but ultimately it is the country's spectacular hinterland that people make for. Snowdonia, with its towering summits and craggy peaks, is probably top of the list of adventure destinations. Heading back south reveals still more scenic landscapes – the remote country of the Welsh Borders and the stunning scenery of the dramatic Brecon Beacons among them.

Walking and Cycling

With mile upon mile of natural beauty, it's hardly surprising that Wales offers so much potential for walking. There's the Cistercian Way, which circles the country by incorporating its Cistercian abbeys; the Glyndwr's Way, named after the

15th-century warrior statesman; and the Pembrokeshire Coast Path, which is a great way to explore the Pembrokeshire National Park.

Cycling is understandably very popular here but be prepared for some tough ascents and dramatic terrain. Try the Taff Trail, which runs north from Cardiff to Caerphilly and includes three castles en route; it's a fairly easy trail, quite flat and largely free of traffic.

For something completely different, cycle from Swansea to Mumbles, enjoying memorable views of the Gower Peninsula.

Festivals and Events

- May is the month for the Royal Welsh Spring Festival, held on the Royal Welsh Showground at Llanelwedd. The event features all manner of farming and horticultural activities.
- The National Eisteddfod in Llangollen in mid July is one of the most important events on the Welsh cultural calendar and celebrates the country's long heritage of storytelling, music and poetry.
- The Abergavenny Food Festival takes place in September with more than 80 events, including masterclasses, tutored tastings, talks and debates.

South Stack Lighthouse, Isle of Anglesey

ANGLESEY, ISLE OF

BEAUMARIS   Map 14 SH67

Places to visit

Beaumaris Castle, BEAUMARIS, LL58 8AP, 01248 810361 www.cadw.wales.gov.uk

AA CAMPING CARD SITE

NEW ►►►► 82% Kingsbridge Caravan Park (SH605784)

Camp Rd, Llanfaes LL58 8LR
☎ **01248 490636 & 07774 842199**
e-mail: info@kingsbridgecaravanpark.co.uk
dir: *From either Menai Bridge or Britannia Bridge follow signs for Beaumaris & A545. In Beaumaris (castle on left) take B5109 towards Llangoed, 2m to x-rds, turn left signed Kingsbridge*

🚐 £17-£23 �“ £17-£23 ▲ £17-£23

Open Mar-Oct

Last arrival 21.00hrs Last departure noon

Peacefully located two miles from historic Beaumaris, this long-established park has been transformed by its caring owners into a must-stay destination for lovers of walking and wildlife. The generously sized pitches are located in two separate touring areas — one for families and one for adults only — each has its own modern, well-equipped amenities block that are smartly presented with quality decor and fittings. Please note that a laundry is not provided but modern facilities are available in nearby Beaumaris. 14 acre site. 90 touring pitches. 21 hardstandings. 15 seasonal pitches. Caravan pitches. Motorhome pitches. Tent pitches. 29 statics.

AA Pubs & Restaurants nearby: Ye Olde Bulls Head Inn, BEAUMARIS, LL58 8AP, 01248 810329

The Ship Inn, RED WHARF BAY, LL75 8RJ, 01248 852568

Leisure: 🅐 ⊛
Facilities: 🅚 ☉ 🍴 ✳ ⊙ 🔋 🛒 ♻ 🛈
Services: 🖂 🛢 ⊘ 🕑 🏴 ⬇
Within 3 miles: ↓ ♪ ℰ 🟰 🖉 🔵 ∪

Notes: No noise after 23.00hrs, no camp fires. Dogs must be kept on leads.

DULAS   Map 14 SH48

PREMIER PARK

►►►►► 87% Tyddyn Isaf Caravan Park (SH486873)

Lligwy Bay LL70 9PQ
☎ **01248 410203 & 410667**
e-mail: mail@tyddynisaf.co.uk
dir: *Take A5025 through Benllech to Moelfre rdbt, left towards Amlwch to Brynrefail. Turn right to Lligwy at phone box. Site 0.5m down lane on right*

🚐 �“ ▲

Open Mar-Oct (rs Mar-Jul & Sep-Oct bar & shop opening limited)

Last arrival 21.30hrs Last departure 11.00hrs

A beautifully situated, very spacious family park on rising ground adjacent to a sandy beach, with magnificent views overlooking Lligwy Bay. A private footpath leads directly to the beach and there is an excellent nature trail around the park. The site has very good toilet facilities, including a block with under-floor heating and excellent unisex privacy cubicles, a well-stocked shop, and café/bar serving meals, which are best enjoyed on the terrace with its magnificent coast and sea views. 16 acre site. 80 touring pitches. 50 hardstandings. 40 seasonal pitches. Caravan pitches. Motorhome pitches. Tent pitches. 56 statics.

AA Pubs & Restaurants nearby: The Ship Inn, RED WHARF BAY, LL75 8RJ, 01248 852568

Ye Olde Bulls Head Inn, BEAUMARIS, LL58 8AP, 01248 810329

Bishopsgate House Hotel, BEAUMARIS, LL58 8BB, 01248 810302

Leisure: 🅐 ▢
Facilities: 🅚 ☉ 🍴 ✳ ⚙ ⊙ 🔋 🛒 🛒 🛖 WiFi ♻ 🛈
Services: 🖂 🛢 🍴 🛢 ⊘ 🕑 🔌 🏴 ⬆ 🖴 ⬇
Within 3 miles: ↓ ♪ ✹ ℰ 🟰 🔵 ∪

Notes: 🐾 No groups, loud music or open fires, maximum 3 units together. Dogs must be kept on leads. Baby changing unit.

MARIAN-GLAS   Map 14 SH58

Places to visit

Bryn Celli Ddu Burial Chamber, BRYNCELLI DDU, 01443 336000 www.cadw.wales.gov.uk

PREMIER PARK

►►►►► 93% Home Farm Caravan Park (SH498850)

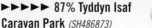

LL73 8PH
☎ **01248 410614**
e-mail: enq@homefarm-anglesey.co.uk
web: www.homefarm-anglesey.co.uk
dir: *On A5025, 2m N of Benllech. Site 300mtrs beyond church*

🚐 �“ ▲

Open Apr-Oct

Last arrival 21.00hrs Last departure noon

A first-class park run with passion and enthusiasm, set in an elevated and secluded position sheltered by trees, and with good planting and landscaping. The peaceful rural setting affords views of farmland, the sea and the mountains of Snowdonia. The modern toilet blocks are spotlessly clean and well maintained, and there are excellent play facilities for children both indoors and out. Facilities also include a visitors' parking area and a smart reception and shop. The area is blessed with sandy beaches, and the local pubs and shops cater for everyday needs. 12 acre site. 102 touring pitches. 65

LEISURE: 🅐 Indoor swimming pool ⊛ Outdoor swimming pool 🅐 Children's playground 🐤 Kid's club ♪ Tennis court 🎱 Games room ▢ Separate TV room ↓ 9/18 hole golf course ↟ Boats for hire 🎬 Cinema ♫ Entertainment ℰ Fishing ⊙ Mini golf ≋ Watersports 🏋 Gym ✹ Sports field Spa ∪ Stables
FACILITIES: 🛁 Bath 🚿 Shower ⊙ Electric shaver ✳ Hairdryer ✳ Ice Pack Facility ⚙ Disabled facilities 🕑 Public telephone 🛒 Shop on site or within 200yds 🖴 Mobile shop (calls at least 5 days a week) 🍴 BBQ area 🛖 Picnic area WiFi Wi-fi 🖥 Internet access ♻ Recycling 🛈 Tourist info 🐾 Dog exercise area

hardstandings. Caravan pitches. Motorhome pitches. Tent pitches. 84 statics.

AA Pubs & Restaurants nearby: The Ship Inn, RED WHARF BAY, LL75 8RJ, 01248 852568

Ye Olde Bulls Head Inn, BEAUMARIS, LL58 8AP, 01248 810329

Bishopsgate House Hotel, BEAUMARIS, LL58 8BB, 01248 810302

Leisure: ⚠🏊⚽🎣⌨

Facilities: ♿📶☉🅿✳⚒🕑🛉🚻🚮💻 ♻🛈

Services: 🔌🔲⊘🚰🛒🛁

Within 3 miles: ↓🚴🏊🖈🛒⛳

Notes: No roller blades, skateboards or scooters.

PENTRAETH   Map 14 SH57

Places to visit

Bryn Celli Ddu Burial Chamber, BRYNCELLI DDU, 01443 336000 www.cadw.wales.gov.uk

Plas Newydd, PLAS NEWYDD, LL61 6DQ, 01248 714795 www.nationaltrust.org.uk/main/plasnewydd

NEW ►►►► 87% St David's Park

(SH529811)

Red Wharf Bay LL75 8RJ
☎ 01248 852341 & 852702
e-mail: info@stdavidspark.com
dir: *A55 junct 8, A5025 towards Benllech. Approx 8m, right towards Red Wharf Bay, site 0.5m on left*

🚐 £25-£35 🚍 £25-£35 ▲ £25-£35

Open 15 Mar-end Sep

Last arrival 21.00hrs Last departure noon

In a stunning location with panoramic coastal and mountain views and direct access to sandy beaches, this long-established holiday village has been transformed in recent years to provide 105 pitches, 44 of which are allocated to seasonal customers. A haven for campers, the all-tent pitches have electric hook-up facilities and a stylish modern amenities block with hi-spec facilities. The Tavern Bistro and Bar offers a wide range of imaginative food and beverages. 47 acre site. 45 touring pitches. 44 seasonal pitches. Caravan pitches. Motorhome pitches. Tent pitches. 180 statics.

AA Pubs & Restaurants nearby: The Ship Inn, RED WHARF BAY, LL75 8RJ, 01248 852568

Ye Olde Bulls Head Inn, BEAUMARIS, LL58 8AP, 01248 810329

Bishopsgate House Hotel, BEAUMARIS, LL58 8BB, 01248 810302

Leisure: ⚠☉✳🚣🛒⛳

Facilities: 🛈☉✳🖈🛈

Services: 🔌🔲🛁⊘🛒

Within 3 miles: ↓🚴🖈🛒⛳↺

Notes: 🐕

Bishopsgate House Hotel, BEAUMARIS, LL58 8BB, 01248 810302

Leisure: ⚠⚽

Facilities: ♿🛈🎣✳⚒🕑🛒📶 ♻🛈

Services: 🔌🔲🚰🛁🛈🍽🚐

Within 3 miles: ↓🚴🖈🛒⛳↺

Notes: 🚫 No group bookings. No jet skis, gazebos or disposable BBQs, no noise after 23.00hrs.

►►► 78% *Rhos Caravan Park*

(SH517794)

Rhos Farm LL75 8DZ
☎ 07788 772268
web: www.rhoscaravanparkanglesey.co.uk
dir: *On A5025, 1m N of Pentraeth*

🚐🚍▲

Open Mar-Oct

Last arrival 22.00hrs Last departure 16.00hrs

A warm welcome awaits families at this spacious park on level, grassy ground with easy access to the main road to Amlwch. A 200-acre working farm that has two play areas and farm animals to keep children amused, with good beaches, pubs, restaurants and shops nearby. The two toilet blocks are kept to a good standard by enthusiastic owners who are constantly improving the facilities. 15 acre site. 98 touring pitches. Caravan pitches. Motorhome pitches. Tent pitches. 66 statics.

AA Pubs & Restaurants nearby: The Ship Inn, RED WHARF BAY, LL75 8RJ, 01248 852568

Ye Olde Bulls Head Inn, BEAUMARIS, LL58 8AP, 01248 810329

Bishopsgate House Hotel, BEAUMARIS, LL58 8BB, 01248 810302

RHOS LLIGWY   Map 14 SH48

►►► 68% Ty'n Rhos Caravan Park

(SH495867)

Lligwy Bay, Moelfre LL72 8NL
☎ 01248 852417
e-mail: robert@bodafonpark.co.uk
dir: *Take A5025 from Benllech to Moelfre rdbt, right to T-junct in Moelfre. Left, approx 2m, pass x-rds leading to beach, site 50mtrs on right*

* 🚐 £18-£25 🚍 £18-£25 ▲ £18-£25

Open Mar-Oct

Last arrival 20.00hrs Last departure noon

A family park close to the beautiful beach at Lligwy Bay, and cliff walks along the Heritage Coast. Historic Din Lligwy, and the shops at picturesque Moelfre are nearby. All the touring pitches have water, electric hook-up and TV connection. Please note that guests should register at Bodafon Caravan Park in Benllech where detailed directions will be given and pitches allocated. 10 acre site. 30 touring pitches. 4 hardstandings. 48 seasonal pitches. Caravan pitches. Motorhome pitches. Tent pitches. 80 statics. 20 bell tents/yurts.

AA Pubs & Restaurants nearby: The Ship Inn, RED WHARF BAY, LL75 8RJ, 01248 852568

Ye Olde Bulls Head Inn, BEAUMARIS, LL58 8AP, 01248 810329

Bishopsgate House Hotel, BEAUMARIS, LL58 8BB, 01248 810302

Facilities: 🛈☉✳⚒🕑🖈📶💻🛈

Services: 🔌🔲🛁

Within 3 miles: ↓🚴🖈🛒⛳↺

Notes: No campfires, no noise after 23.00hrs. Dogs must be kept on leads.

SERVICES: 🔌 Electric hook up 🔲 Launderette 🍷 Licensed bar 🔋 Calor Gas 🔥 Camping Gaz 🅣 Toilet fluid 🍽 Café/Restaurant 🍔 Fast Food/Takeaway 🛒 Battery charging 🍼 Baby care ⚓ Motorvan service point **ABBREVIATIONS:** BH/bank hols-bank holidays Etr-Easter Spring BH-Spring Bank Holiday dep-departure fr-from hrs-hours m-mile mdnt-midnight rdbt-roundabout rs-restricted service wk-week wknd-weekend x-rds-cross roads 🚫 No credit cards 🚫 No dogs ⛹ Children of all ages accepted See page 9 for details of the AA Camping Card Scheme

RHOSNEIGR — Map 14 SH37

►►► 77% Ty Hen *(SH327738)*

GOLD

Station Rd LL64 5QZ
☎ **01407 810331**
e-mail: info@tyhen.com
web: www.tyhen.com
dir: *From A55 junct 5 follow signs to Rhosneigr, at clock turn right. Entrance (red gate post) 50mtrs before Rhosneigr railway station*

Open mid Mar-Oct

Last arrival 21.00hrs Last departure noon

This site is in an attractive seaside location near a large fishing lake and riding stables. Surrounded by lovely countryside, this former working farm is close to RAF Valley, which is great for plane spotters, but expect some aircraft noise during the day. The friendly owners are always on hand. 7.5 acre site. 38 touring pitches. 5 hardstandings. 33 seasonal pitches. Caravan pitches. Motorhome pitches. Tent pitches. 42 statics.

Leisure:

Facilities:

Services:

Within 3 miles:

Notes: 1 motor vehicle per pitch, children must not be out after 22.00hrs. Dogs must be kept on leads. Fishing, family room, walks.

BRIDGEND

PORTHCAWL — Map 9 SS87

Places to visit

Newcastle, BRIDGEND, 01443 336000
www.cadw.wales.gov.uk

Coity Castle, COITY, CF35 6BG, 01443 336000
www.cadw.wales.gov.uk

►►► 79% Brodawel Camping & Caravan Park *(SS816789)*

Moor Ln, Nottage CF36 3EJ
☎ **01656 783231**
e-mail: info@brodawelcamping.co.uk
dir: *M4 junct 37, A4229 towards Porthcawl. Site on right off A4229*

* ➡ £13.50-£21 ➡ £13.50-£21 Å £13.50-£21

Open Apr-Sep

Last arrival 19.00hrs Last departure 11.00hrs

A lovely family park close to sea and other attractions, with a lush grass touring field that provides generously sized pitches; most have electric hook-up. The smart amenities block was totally refurbished to a high standard for the 2013 season, and a well-stocked shop and Wi-fi are additional benefits. 4 acre site. 100 touring pitches. 4 hardstandings. 40 seasonal pitches. Caravan pitches. Motorhome pitches. Tent pitches.

AA Pubs & Restaurants nearby: Prince of Wales Inn, KENFIG, CF33 4PR, 01656 740356

Leisure:

Facilities:

Services:

Within 3 miles:

Notes: Dogs must be kept on leads.

CARMARTHENSHIRE

LLANDOVERY — Map 9 SN73

Places to visit

Dolaucothi Gold Mines, PUMSAINT, SA19 8US, 01558 650177 www.nationaltrust.org.uk/main/w-dolaucothigoldmines

PREMIER PARK

►►►►► 83% Erwlon Caravan & Camping Park *(SN776343)*

Best of British

Brecon Rd SA20 0RD
☎ **01550 721021 & 720332**
e-mail: peter@erwlon.co.uk
dir: *0.5m E of Llandovery on A40*

Open all year

Last arrival anytime Last departure noon

A long-established, family-run site set beside a brook in the Brecon Beacons foothills. The town of Llandovery and the hills overlooking the Towy Valley are a short walk away. The superb, Scandinavian-style facilities block has cubicled washrooms, family and disabled rooms and is an impressive feature. 8 acre site. 75 touring pitches. 15 hardstandings. Caravan pitches. Motorhome pitches. Tent pitches.

AA Pubs & Restaurants nearby: The Kings Head, LLANDOVERY, SA20 0AB, 01550 720393

Leisure:

Facilities:

Services:

Within 3 miles:

Notes: Quiet after 22.30hrs. Dogs must be kept on leads. Fishing, cycle storage & hire.

►►► 77% Llandovery Caravan Park *(SN762342)*

Church Bank SA20 0DT
☎ **01550 721065 & 07970 650 606**
e-mail: llandoverycaravanpark@gmail.com
dir: *A40 from Carmarthen, over rail crossing, past junct with A483 (Builth Wells). Turn right for Llangadog, past church, 1st right signed Rugby Club & Camping*

➡ £12-£14 ➡ £12-£14 Å £8-£14

LEISURE: 🏊 Indoor swimming pool 🏊 Outdoor swimming pool Ⓐ Children's playground 🏌 Kid's club ⚴ Tennis court ✎ Games room ⬜ Separate TV room 🏌 9/18 hole golf course ⛵ Boats for hire 🎬 Cinema 🎵 Entertainment 🎣 Fishing ◎ Mini golf 🏄 Watersports 🏋 Gym ⚽ Sports field Spa ⛫ Stables
FACILITIES: 🛁 Bath 🚿 Shower ⊙ Electric shaver 🪒 Hairdryer ❄ Ice Pack Facility ⚴ Disabled facilities Ⓒ Public telephone 🏪 Shop on site or within 200yds 🚚 Mobile shop (calls at least 5 days a week) 🍖 BBQ area 🪑 Picnic area WI-FI Wi-fi 🖥 Internet access ♻ Recycling ❶ Tourist info 🐕 Dog exercise area

Open all year

Last arrival 20.00hrs Last departure 20.00hrs

Within easy walking distance of the town centre and adjacent to the notable Llandovery Dragons Rugby Club, this constantly improving park is an ideal base for touring the Brecon Beacons and many local attractions. Most pitches have both water and a hardstanding, and guests are welcome to use the popular on-site rugby club lounge bar. Please note a laundry is not provided but there is one in the town. 8 acre site. 100 touring pitches. 10 hardstandings. 40 seasonal pitches. Caravan pitches. Motorhome pitches. Tent pitches.

AA Pubs & Restaurants nearby: The Kings Head, LLANDOVERY, SA20 0AB, 01550 720393

Leisure: ⚙️🎾🏓

Facilities: 🐕☉✖🏕♻️ ❓

Services: 🔌🐾🔧🚿

Within 3 miles: ⬆️⚓️🐶

Notes: 🚫 Dogs must be kept on leads.

LLANGADOG Map 9 SN72

Places to visit

Dinefwr Park and Castle, LLANDEILO, SA19 6RT, 01558 823902 www.nationaltrust.org.uk/main/w-dinefwrpark

Carreg Cennen Castle, CARREG CENNEN CASTLE, SA19 6UA, 01558 822291 www.cadw.wales.gov.uk

►►► 77% Abermarlais Caravan Park

(SN695298)

SA19 9NG
☎ 01550 777868 & 777797
dir: On A40 midway between Llandovery & Llandeilo, 1.5m NW of Llangadog

* 🚐 £9-£11 🚙 £9-£11 ⛺ £9-£11

Open 15 Mar-15 Nov (rs Mar & Nov 1 toilet block, water point no hot water)

Last arrival 23.00hrs Last departure noon

An attractive, well-run site with a welcoming atmosphere. This part-level, part-sloping park is in a wooded valley on the edge of the Brecon Beacons National Park, beside the River Marlais. 17 acre site. 88 touring pitches. 2 hardstandings. Caravan pitches. Motorhome pitches. Tent pitches.

AA Pubs & Restaurants nearby: The Angel Hotel, LLANDEILO, SA19 6EN, 01558 822765

The Kings Head, LLANDOVERY, SA20 0AB, 01550 720393

Leisure: ⚙️

Facilities: 🐕☉✖🚿♻️🕐🔋🏕❓

Services: 🔌🐾🚿🅃🛒

Within 3 miles: ⚓️🅱️🐶

Notes: No open fires, quiet from 23.00hrs-08.00hrs. Dogs must be kept on leads. Volleyball, badminton court, softball tennis net.

LLANWRDA Map 9 SN73

►►► 88% Springwater Lakes

(SN637430)

Harford SA19 8DT
☎ 01558 650788
dir: 4m E of Lampeter on A482, entrance well signed on right

🚐 🚙 ⛺

Open Mar-Oct

Last arrival 20.00hrs Last departure 11.00hrs

In a rural setting overlooked by the Cambrian Mountains, this park is adjoined on each side by five spring-fed and well-stocked fishing lakes. All pitches (some beside one of the lakes) have hardstandings, electricity and TV hook-ups, and there is a small and very clean toilet block and a shop. 20 acre site. 30 touring pitches. 30 hardstandings. Caravan pitches. Motorhome pitches. Tent pitches.

Facilities: 🐕☉📺✖🕐🅿🏕♻️❓

Services: 🔌🐾🛒🛍🚽 **Within 3 miles:** ⚓️🅱️🐶

Notes: Children must be supervised around lakes, no cycling on site, no ball games. Dogs must be kept on leads. Bait & tackle shop, small food shop in 500yds.

NEWCASTLE EMLYN

Places to visit

Cilgerran Castle, CILGERRAN, SA43 2SF, 01239 621339 www.cadw.wales.gov.uk

Castell Henllys Iron Age Fort, CRYMYCH, SA41 3UT, 01239 891319 www.castellhenllys.com

Great for kids: Felinwynt Rainforest Centre, FELINWYNT, SA43 1RT, 01239 810882 www.butterflycentre.co.uk

---

AA CAMPING CARD SITE

PREMIER PARK

►►►►► 87% Cenarth Falls Holiday Park (SN265421)

Cenarth SA38 9JS
☎ 01239 710345
e-mail: enquiries@cenarth-holipark.co.uk
dir: From Newcastle Emlyn on A484 towards Cardigan. Through Cenarth, site on right

🚐 £17-£27 🚙 £17-£27 ⛺ £17-£27

Open Mar-Nov (rs Off peak bar & meals restricted to wknds only)

Last arrival 20.00hrs Last departure 11.00hrs

Located close to the village of Cenarth where the River Teifi, famous for its salmon and trout fishing, cascades through the Cenarth Falls Gorge. With beautifully landscaped grounds and spotless amenities, the park also benefits from an indoor heated swimming pool, sauna, fitness suite and a restaurant with bar. 2 acre site. 30 touring pitches. 30 hardstandings. Caravan pitches. Motorhome pitches. Tent pitches. 89 statics.

AA Pubs & Restaurants nearby: Nags Head Inn, ABERCYCH, SA37 0HJ, 01239 841200

Webley Waterfront Inn & Hotel, ST DOGMAELS, SA43 3LN, 01239 612085

Leisure: 🏊♨️🎾⚙️🎱🎵

Facilities: 🐕☉📺✖🕐🛜♻️❓

Services: 🔌🅱️🔧🐾🛍🅃🛒🚽

Within 3 miles: 🅷⚓️⛳🅱️🐶

Notes: No skateboards. Dogs must be kept on leads. Pool table.

SERVICES: 🔌 Electric hook up 🅱️ Launderette 🍺 Licensed bar 🅱️ Calor Gas 🛢 Camping Gaz 🅃 Toilet fluid 🍽 Café/Restaurant 🍔 Fast Food/Takeaway 🔋 Battery charging 🍼 Baby care 🚽 Motorvan service point **ABBREVIATIONS:** BH/bank hols-bank holidays Etr-Easter Spring BH-Spring Bank Holiday dep-departure fr-from hrs-hours m-mile mdnt-midnight rdbt-roundabout rs-restricted service wk-week wknd-weekend x-rds-cross roads 🚫 No credit cards 🚫 No dogs 👶 Children of all ages accepted See page 9 for details of the AA Camping Card Scheme

NEWCASTLE EMLYN *continued*

AA CAMPING CARD SITE

►►►► 82% Argoed Meadow Caravan and Camping Site *(SN268415)*

Argoed Farm SA38 9JL
☎ 01239 710690
dir: *From Newcastle Emlyn on A484 towards Cenarth, take B4332. Site 300yds on right*

Open all year

Last arrival anytime Last departure noon

A warm welcome is assured at this attractive and immaculately maintained site, situated on the banks of the River Teifi and close to Cenarth Falls Gorge. The spotlessly clean amenities block provides very good privacy options for the less able visitors. 3 acre site. 30 touring pitches. 5 hardstandings. Caravan pitches. Motorhome pitches. Tent pitches. 5 statics.

AA Pubs & Restaurants nearby: Nags Head Inn, ABERCYCH, SA37 0HJ, 01239 841200

Webley Waterfront Inn & Hotel, ST DOGMAELS, SA43 3LN, 01239 612085

Facilities: 🖡 ⊙ ℱ ⚹ ⅙ ⓢ 🛒 ♻ ❶
Services: 🕿 🖺 🛢 🧺 🚼 🛁
Within 3 miles: 🗄 🖉 🛒 ⓢ U

Notes: 🚳 No bikes or skateboards. Dogs must be kept on leads.

►►►► 79% Afon Teifi Caravan & Camping Park *(SN338405)*

Pentrecagal SA38 9HT
☎ 01559 370532
e-mail: afonteifi@btinternet.com
dir: *Signed from A484, 2m E of Newcastle Emlyn*

🏕 🚐 🅰

Open Apr-Oct

Last arrival 23.00hrs

Set on the banks of the River Teifi, a famous salmon and sea trout river, this secluded, family-owned and run park has good views. It is only two miles from the market town of Newcastle Emlyn. The smart, refurbished amenities block is appointed to a high standard. 6 acre site. 110 touring pitches. 22 hardstandings. 25 seasonal pitches. Caravan pitches. Motorhome pitches. Tent pitches. 15 statics.

AA Pubs & Restaurants nearby: Nags Head Inn, ABERCYCH, SA37 0HJ, 01239 841200

Webley Waterfront Inn & Hotel, ST DOGMAELS, SA43 3LN, 01239 612085

Leisure: 🄰 ⚽ 🎣
Facilities: 🍴 🖡 ⊙ ℱ ⚹ ⅙ ⓒ ⓢ 🎿 🛒 ♻ ❶
Services: 🕿 🖺 🛢 🧺 🆃 🛁
Within 3 miles: 🗄 🖉 🛒 ⓢ 🛢 U

Notes: 🚳 Dogs must be kept on leads. 15 acres of woodland, fields & walks.

►►► 82% Moelfryn Caravan & Camping Park *(SN321370)*

Ty-Cefn, Pant-y-Bwlch SA38 9JE
☎ 01559 371231
e-mail: moelfryn@moelfryncaravanpark.co.uk
dir: *A484 from Carmarthen towards Cynwyl Elfed. Pass Blue Bell Inn on right, 200yds take left fork onto B4333 towards Hermon. In 7m follow brown sign on left. Turn left, site on right*

* 🏕 fr £12.50 🚐 fr £12.50 🅰 fr £11

Open Mar-10 Jan

Last arrival 22.00hrs Last departure noon

A small, beautifully maintained, family-run park in a glorious elevated location overlooking the valley of the River Teifi. Pitches are level and spacious, and well screened by hedging and mature trees. Facilities are spotlessly clean and tidy, and the playing field is well away from the touring area. 3 acre site. 25 touring pitches. 16 hardstandings. 12 seasonal pitches. Caravan pitches. Motorhome pitches. Tent pitches.

AA Pubs & Restaurants nearby: Nags Head Inn, ABERCYCH, SA37 0HJ, 01239 841200

Webley Waterfront Inn & Hotel, ST DOGMAELS, SA43 3LN, 01239 612085

Leisure: 🄰
Facilities: 🖡 ⊙ ℱ ⚹ ⓢ 🆆🄸 ♻ ❶
Services: 🕿 🖺 🛢 🧺 🛁
Within 3 miles: 🗄 🎿 🗄 🖉 🛒 ⓢ 🛢 U

Notes: Games to be played in designated area only. Dogs must be kept on leads. Caravan storage.

CEREDIGION

ABERAERON   Map 8 SN46

Places to visit

Llanerchaeron, ABERAERON, SA48 8DG, 01545 570200 www.nationaltrust.org.uk

►►► 88% Aeron Coast Caravan Park *(SN460631)*

North Rd SA46 0JF
☎ 01545 570349
e-mail: enquiries@aeroncoast.co.uk
web: www.aeroncoast.co.uk
dir: *On A487 (coast road) on N outskirts of Aberaeron, signed. Filling station at entrance*

* 🏕 £17-£27 🚐 £17-£27 🅰 £17-£27

Open Mar-Oct

Last arrival 23.00hrs Last departure 11.00hrs

A well-managed family holiday park on the edge of the attractive resort of Aberaeron, with direct access to the beach. The spacious pitches are all level. On-site facilities include an extensive outdoor pool complex, a multi-activity outdoor sports area, an indoor children's play area, a small lounge bar which serves food, a games room and an entertainment suite. 22 acre site. 100 touring pitches. 30 hardstandings. Caravan pitches. Motorhome pitches. Tent pitches. 200 statics.

AA Pubs & Restaurants nearby: The Harbourmaster, ABERAERON, SA46 0BT, 01545 570755

Ty Mawr Mansion, ABERAERON, SA48 8DB, 01570 470033

Leisure: ⚓ 🅐 ♨ 🎣 ▢ 🎵

Facilities: 🏕️ ☉ 🅟 ☀ ♿ 🕔 🅢 🛒 ☂ 🕙

Services: 🔌 🅾 🍴 🍴 🍴 🚚 T🚽 🍴 🥤 ⚓

Within 3 miles: ⚓ 🚣 🅢 🅾 ∪

Notes: Families only. No motorcycles. Dogs must be kept on leads.

ABERYSTWYTH
Map 8 SN58

Places to visit

The National Library of Wales, ABERYSTWYTH, SY23 3BU, 01970 632800 www.llgc.org.uk

►►► 82% Ocean View Caravan Park
(SN592842)

North Beach, Clarach Bay SY23 3DT
☎ **01970 828425 & 623361**
e-mail: enquiries@oceanviewholidays.com
dir: Exit A487 in Bow Street. Straight on at next x-rds. Site 2nd on right

🚐 £17.50-£22 🚌 £17.50-£22 ▲ £10-£20

Open Mar-Oct

Last arrival 20.00hrs Last departure noon

This site is in a sheltered valley on gently sloping ground, with wonderful views of both the sea and the countryside. The beach of Clarach Bay is just 200 yards away, and this welcoming park is ideal for all the family. There is a children's football field and dog walking area. Campers may use the pool, gym, restaurant and bar at Clarach Bay which is within walking distance of the site. 9 acre site. 24 touring pitches. 15 hardstandings.

---

20 seasonal pitches. Caravan pitches. Motorhome pitches. Tent pitches. 56 statics.

Leisure: ⚽

Facilities: 🏕️ ☉ 🅟 ☀ 🅢 🎏 ⊓ 🖼️ 🛜 🖥️ ♻️ ❂ 🕔

Services: 🔌 🅾 ⚓ ⚓

Within 3 miles: ⚓ 🄷 🅿️ 🅾 🚣 🅢 🅾 ∪

Notes: Dogs must be kept on leads.

BORTH
Map 14 SN69

Places to visit

The National Library of Wales, ABERYSTWYTH, SY23 3BU, 01970 632800 www.llgc.org.uk

76% Brynowen Holiday Park (SN608893)

SY24 5LS
☎ **01970 871366**
e-mail: brynowen@park-resorts.com
web: www.park-resorts.com
dir: Signed from B4353, S of Borth

🚐 🚌

Open Apr-Oct

Last arrival mdnt Last departure 10.00hrs

Enjoying spectacular views across Cardigan Bay and the Cambrian Mountains, a small touring park in a large and well-equipped holiday centre. The well-run park offers a wide range of organised activities and entertainment for all the family from morning until late in the evening. A long sandy beach is a few minutes' drive away. 52 acre site. 16 touring pitches. 16 hardstandings. 4 seasonal pitches. Caravan pitches. Motorhome pitches. 480 statics.

Leisure: 🏊 🅐 🖐️ ♨ ☉ ⚓ 🎵

Facilities: 🏕️ ☉ ♿ 🕔 🅢 🎏 ⊓ 🛜 🖥️ ❂

Services: 🔌 🅾 🍴 🍴 🥤

Within 3 miles: ⚓ 🅢 🅾

Notes: No cars by caravans. Dogs must be kept on leads. Mini ten-pin bowling.

LLANON
Map 8 SN56

Places to visit

The National Library of Wales, ABERYSTWYTH, SY23 3BU, 01970 632800 www.llgc.org.uk

---

AA CAMPING CARD SITE

►►► 78% Woodlands Holiday Park
(SN509668)

SY23 5LX
☎ **01974 202342**
e-mail: info@woodlandsholidayparkllanon.co.uk
dir: Between Aberystwyth & Aberaeron (S of Llanon) follow brown camping sign onto unclassified road towards coast. Site 280yds right

🚐 £15-£20 🚌 £15-£20 ▲ £10-£20

Open Mar-Oct

Last arrival 21.30hrs Last departure noon

Located half a mile from the village centre and adjacent to the sea and a stony beach, this peacefully located park is surrounded by mature trees and meadowland. The level, mostly grass pitches are generous in size and the amenities block is very well maintained and spotlessly clean. 4 acre site. 40 touring pitches. 10 hardstandings. Caravan pitches. Motorhome pitches. Tent pitches. 59 statics.

AA Pubs & Restaurants nearby: The Harbourmaster, ABERAERON, SA46 0BT, 01545 570755

Ty Mawr Mansion, ABERAERON, SA48 8DB, 01570 470033

Facilities: 🏕️ ☉ 🅟 ❂ 🕔

Services: 🔌 🅾 ⚓ T🥤 ⚓

Within 3 miles: ⚓ 🅿️ 🅾 🅢 🅾

Notes: Dogs must be kept on leads.

NEW QUAY Map 8 SN35

Places to visit

Llanerchaeron, ABERAERON, SA48 8DG, 01545 570200 www.nationaltrust.org.uk

[hh] 86% Quay West Holiday Park *(SN397591)*

GOLD

SA45 9SE

☎ 01545 560477

e-mail: quaywest@haven.com

web: www.haven.com/quaywest

dir: *From Cardigan on A487 left onto A486 into New Quay. Or from Aberystwyth on A487 right onto B4342 into New Quay*

Open Mar-Oct

This holiday park enjoys a stunning clifftop position overlooking picturesque New Quay and Cardigan Bay. It's an easy walk to a glorious sandy beach, and the all-action on-site activities include heated swimming pools, SplashZone, football, archery and fencing (with professional tuition) and the Aqua Bar and terrace. There is a good range of holiday caravans.

Change over day: Mon, Fri, Sat **Arrival and departure times:** Please contact the site

Statics 125 Sleeps 6-8 Bedrms 2-3 Bathrms 1-2 Toilets 1-2 Freezer TV Sky/FTV Elec inc Gas inc Grass area

Children 👪 Cots Highchair **Dogs** 2 on leads No dangerous dogs

Leisure: 🏊 🏖 🎾 ✋ ⛬

CONWY

BETWS-YN-RHOS Map 14 SH97

Places to visit

Denbigh Castle, DENBIGH, LL16 3NB, 01745 813385 www.cadw.wales.gov.uk

AA CAMPING CARD SITE

►►►► 83% Plas Farm Caravan Park *(SH897744)*

GOLD

LL22 8AU

☎ 01492 680254 & 07831 482176

e-mail: info@plasfarmcaravanpark.co.uk

dir: *A547 at Abergele, right into Rhyd y Foel Rd, 3m left signed B5381, 1st farm on right*

🚐 £17.50-£27.50 🚌 £17.50-£27.50 ⛺ £10-£25

Open Mar-Oct

Last arrival 19.00hrs Last departure 11.00hrs

A quiet caravan park on a working farm which is surrounded by rolling countryside and farmland. This constantly improving park features hardstanding pitches, 45 of which are fully serviced with electricity, water and TV hook-up, plus a laundry and campers' kitchen with microwave, kettles and toasters. There's a secluded tenting field, conveniently placed for the amenities blocks. The park is close to Bodnant Garden (NT) and glorious beaches. 10 acre site. 54 touring pitches. 54 hardstandings. Caravan pitches. Motorhome pitches. Tent pitches.

AA Pubs & Restaurants nearby: The Kinmel Arms, ABERGELE, LL22 9BP, 01745 832207

Leisure: ⛬

Facilities: 🚿 ⊙ 💇 ✲ ♿ ✆ [$] ⛩ 🐕 [Wi-fi] ♻ ℹ

Services: 🔌 🧺 🔒 [T] 🍳 🛒 ⚓

Within 3 miles: ⛳ 🎬 🎣 [$] 🧺

Notes: Quiet after 23.00hrs. No campfires. Dogs must be kept on leads. Woodland walk.

►►►► 82% Hunters Hamlet Caravan Park *(SH928736)*

Sirior Goch Farm LL22 8PL

☎ 01745 832237 & 07721 552106

e-mail: huntershamlet@aol.com

web: www.huntershamlet.co.uk

dir: *From A55 W'bound, A547 junct 24 into Abergele. At 2nd lights turn left by George & Dragon pub, onto A548. 2.75m right at x-rds onto B5381. Site 0.5m on left*

* 🚐 £18-£26 🚌 £18-£26

Open Mar-Oct

Last arrival 22.00hrs Last departure noon

A warm welcome is assured at this long established, family-run working farm park next to the owners' Georgian farmhouse. Well-spaced pitches, including 15 with water, electric and TV hook-up, are within two attractive hedge-screened grassy paddocks. The well-maintained amenities block, includes unisex bathrooms. Please note that this site does not accept tents. 2 acre site. 30 touring pitches. 30 hardstandings. Caravan pitches. Motorhome pitches.

AA Pubs & Restaurants nearby: The Hawk & Buckle Inn, LLANNEFYDD, LL16 5ED, 01745 540249

The Kinmel Arms, ABERGELE, LL22 9BP, 01745 832207

Leisure: ⛬

Facilities: 🛁 🚿 ⊙ 💇 ✲ ♿ [Wi-fi] ♻ ℹ

Services: 🔌 🧺 🔒 🍳

Within 3 miles: ⛳ 🎣 [$]

Notes: No football. Dogs must not be left unattended & must be kept on leads. Baby bath & changing facilities.

LEISURE: 🏊 Indoor swimming pool 🏖 Outdoor swimming pool ⛬ Children's playground ✋ Kid's club 🎾 Tennis court ♠ Games room 📺 Separate TV room ⛳ 9/18 hole golf course ⛵ Boats for hire 🎬 Cinema 🎵 Entertainment 🎣 Fishing ◎ Mini golf 🌊 Watersports 🏋 Gym ⚽ Sports field **Spa** ∪ Stables **FACILITIES:** 🛁 Bath 🚿 Shower ⊙ Electric shaver 💇 Hairdryer ✲ Ice Pack Facility ♿ Disabled facilities ✆ Public telephone [$] Shop on site or within 200yds 🚚 Mobile shop (calls at least 5 days a week) 🍖 BBQ area ⛩ Picnic area [Wi-fi] Wi-fi 💻 Internet access ♻ Recycling ℹ Tourist info 🐕 Dog exercise area

AA CAMPING CARD SITE

▶▶▶ **78% Peniarth Bach Farm**

(SH926737)

Roadside LL22 8PL
☎ **07545 572744**
e-mail: geoff-wilson@btinternet.com
dir: *A55 junct 25, left into Abergele. Left at lights onto B5381 towards Llanfairth. Right after 3m signed Betws-yn-Rhos. Site signed on right*

🚐 fr £20 🚐 fr £20 ⛺ fr £15

Open Mar-Oct

Last arrival flexible Last departure 11.00hrs

A campsite for only a few years and part of a working farm which also offers quality stone holiday cottages for hire. Most pitches are hardstanding, with electric hook-up and water supply, and the smart purpose-built amenities block provides modern and efficient facilities. 40 acre site. 38 touring pitches. 15 hardstandings. Caravan pitches. Motorhome pitches. Tent pitches.

AA Pubs & Restaurants nearby: The Hawk & Buckle Inn, LLANNEFYDD, LL16 5ED, 01745 540249

The Kinmel Arms, ABERGELE, LL22 9BP, 01745 832207

Facilities: 🅿️⊙☂❄♿🀕📶♻️❓

Services: 🔌🗑️🚾🔋🚻

Within 3 miles: ♨️🚣🎣♪🏌️◎♨️🍴🛒🗒️⛳

Notes: 🔇 No noise after mdnt. Dogs must be kept on leads. Family room.

LLANDDULAS

Places to visit

Great Orme Bronze Age Copper Mines, LLANDUDNO, LL30 2XG, 01492 870447 www.greatormemines.info

Bodelwyddan Castle, BODELWYDDAN, LL18 5YA, 01745 584060 www.bodelwyddan-castle.co.uk

---

LLANDDULAS — Map 14 SH97

PREMIER PARK

▶▶▶▶▶ **85% Bron-Y-Wendon Caravan Park** *(SH903785)*

Wern Rd LL22 8HG
☎ **01492 512903**
e-mail: stay@northwales-holidays.co.uk
dir: *Take A55 W. Right at Llanddulas/A547 junct 23 sign, sharp right. 200yds, under A55 bridge. Park on left*

* 🚐 £20-£25 🚐 £20-£25

Open all year

Last arrival anytime Last departure 11.00hrs

A top quality site in a stunning location, with panoramic sea views from every pitch and excellent purpose-built toilet facilities including heated shower blocks. Pitch density is excellent, offering a high degree of privacy, and the grounds are beautifully landscaped and immaculately maintained. Super pitches are available. Staff are helpful and friendly, and everything from landscaping to maintenance has a stamp of excellence. An ideal seaside base for touring Snowdonia and visiting Colwyn Bay, Llandudno and Conwy. 8 acre site. 130 touring pitches. 85 hardstandings. Caravan pitches. Motorhome pitches.

AA Pubs & Restaurants nearby: Pen-y-Bryn, COLWYN BAY, LL29 6DD, 01492 533360

Leisure: 🔍

Facilities: 🐕🅿️⊙☂❄♿🕐🀕📶🖥️♻️❓

Services: 🔌🗑️🛢️🚻

Within 3 miles: ♨️🚣♪🍴🛒🗒️⛳

Notes: Dogs must be kept on leads.

LLANRWST

Places to visit

Gwydir Uchaf Chapel, LLANRWST, 01492 640578 www.cadw.wales.gov.uk

Dolwyddelan Castle, DOLWYDDELAN, LL25 0JD, 01690 750366 www.cadw.wales.gov.uk

Great for kids: Conwy Valley Railway Museum, BETWS-Y-COED, LL24 0AL, 01690 710568 www.conwyrailwaymuseum.co.uk

---

LLANRWST — Map 14 SH86

PREMIER PARK

▶▶▶▶▶ **85% Bron Derw Touring Caravan Park** *(SH798628)*

LL26 0YT
☎ **01492 640494**
e-mail: bronderw@aol.com
web: www.bronderw-wales.co.uk
dir: *A55 onto A470 for Betws-y-Coed & Llanrwst. In Llanrwst left into Parry Rd signed Llanddoged. Left at T-junct, site signed at 1st farm entrance on right*

🚐 £20-£22 🚐 £20-£22

Open Mar-Oct

Last arrival 22.00hrs Last departure 11.00hrs

Surrounded by hills and beautifully landscaped from what was once a dairy farm, Bron Derw has been built to a very high standard and is fully matured, with stunning flora and fauna displays. All pitches are fully serviced, and there is a heated, stone-built toilet block with excellent and immaculately maintained facilities. The Parc Derwen adults-only field has 28 fully serviced pitches and its own designated amenities block. CCTV security cameras cover the whole park. 4.5 acre site. 48 touring pitches. 48 hardstandings. 20 seasonal pitches. Caravan pitches. Motorhome pitches.

AA Pubs & Restaurants nearby: Ty Gwyn Inn, BETWS-Y-COED, LL24 0SG, 01690 710383

Plas Meanan Country House, LLANRWST, LL26 0YR, 01492 660232

Facilities: 🅿️⊙☂❄♿🕐🀕📶♻️❓

Services: 🔌🗑️🛢️🚻

Within 3 miles: ♪🗒️🛒

Notes: Children must be supervised, no bikes, scooters or skateboards. Dogs must be kept on leads.

LLANRWST ***continued***

►►►► 82% *Bodnant Caravan Park*

(SH805609)

Nebo Rd LL26 0SD
☎ 01492 640248
e-mail: ermin@bodnant-caravan-park.co.uk
dir: *S in Llanrwst, at lights exit A470 opposite Birmingham garage onto B5427 signed Nebo. Site 300yds on right, opposite leisure centre*

🚐 🚌 ⛺

Open Mar-end Oct

Last arrival 21.00hrs Last departure 11.00hrs

This well maintained and stunningly attractive park is filled with flower beds, and the landscape includes shrubberies and trees. The statics are unobtrusively sited and the quality, spotlessly clean toilet blocks have fully serviced private cubicles. All caravan pitches are multi-service, and the tent pitches serviced. There is a separate playing field and rally field, and there are lots of farm animals on the park to keep children entertained, and Victorian farming implements are on display around the touring fields. 5 acre site. 54 touring pitches. 20 hardstandings. Caravan pitches. Motorhome pitches. Tent pitches. 2 statics.

AA Pubs & Restaurants nearby: Ty Gwyn Inn, BETWS-Y-COED, LL24 0SG, 01690 710383

Plas Meanan Country House, LLANRWST, LL26 0YR, 01492 660232

Facilities: 🚿 ⊙ 💨 ♿ 📞 🐕 ♻ ℹ

Services: 🚐 🛢 🌿

Within 3 miles: ⛳ ⛵ 🎣 🏄 🏪 🫧

Notes: No bikes, skateboards or camp fires, main gates locked 23.00hrs-08.00hrs, no noise after 23.00hrs. Dogs must be kept on leads.

TAL-Y-BONT (NEAR CONWY) Map 14 SH76

Places to visit

Bodnant Garden, TAL-Y-CAFN, LL28 5RE, 01492 650460 www.nationaltrust.org.uk/bodnant-garden

Great for kids: Smallest House, CONWY, LL32 8BB, 01492 593484

AA CAMPING CARD SITE

► 89% Tynterfyn Touring Caravan Park *(SH768695)*

LL32 8YX
☎ 01492 660525
dir: *5m S of Conwy on B5106, signed Tal-y-Bont, 1st on left*

* 🚐 fr £12.80 🚌 fr £13.50 ⛺ fr £5

Open Mar-Oct (rs 28 days in year tent pitches only)

Last arrival 22.00hrs Last departure noon

A quiet, secluded little park set in the beautiful Conwy Valley, and run by family owners. The grounds are tended with care, and the older-style toilet facilities sparkle. There is lots of room for children and dogs to run around. 2 acre site. 15 touring pitches. 4 hardstandings. Caravan pitches. Motorhome pitches. Tent pitches.

AA Pubs & Restaurants nearby: The Old Ship, TREFRIW, LL27 0JH, 01492 640013

Leisure: 🛝 ⚽

Facilities: 🚿 ⊙ 💨 ❄ 🐕 ♻ ℹ

Services: 🚐 🛢 🌿 🔋

Within 3 miles: ⛵ 🎣 🏪

Notes: 🐕 Dogs must be kept on leads.

TOWYN (NEAR ABERGELE) Map 14 SH97

Places to visit

Rhuddlan Castle, RHUDDLAN, LL18 5AD, 01745 590777 www.cadw.wales.gov.uk

Great for kids: Welsh Mountain Zoo, COLWYN BAY, LL28 5UY, 01492 532938 www.welshmountainzoo.org

75% *Ty Mawr Holiday Park* *(SH965792)*

Towyn Rd LL22 9HG
☎ 01745 832079
e-mail: admin.tymawr@parkresorts.com
web: www.park-resorts.com
dir: *On A548, 0.25m W of Towyn*

🚐 🚌 ⛺

Open Apr-Oct (rs Apr (excluding Etr))

Last arrival mdnt Last departure 10.00hrs

Located between Chester and the Isle of Anglesey and close to many attractions including the lively resort of Rhyl. A very large coastal holiday park with extensive leisure facilities including sports and recreational amenities. Touring areas are within two level grassy fields and all amenities blocks are centrally located. The entertainment facilities are ideal for both adults and families and a choice of eating outlets is available. 18 acre site. 406 touring pitches. Caravan pitches. Motorhome pitches. Tent pitches. 464 statics.

AA Pubs & Restaurants nearby: The Kinmel Arms, ABERGELE, LL22 9BP, 01745 832207

Leisure: 🏊 🛝 ✋ ⚽ 🎱 🎵

Facilities: 🚿 ⊙ ♿ 📞 🏪 🧺 🐕 [Wi-fi] 💻

Services: 🚐 🫧 🍷 🍴 🍟

Within 3 miles: ⛳ 🎬 🎣 ◎ 🏪 🫧 🐴

see advert on opposite page

DENBIGHSHIRE

LLANDRILLO
Map 15 SJ03

Places to visit

Chirk Castle, CHIRK, LL14 5AF, 01691 777701
www.nationaltrust.org.uk/main/w-chirkcastle

Rug Chapel, CORWEN, LL21 9BT, 01490 412025
www.cadw.wales.gov.uk

►►► 80% Hendwr Country Park

(SJ042386)

LL21 0SN

☎ 01490 440210

dir: *From Corwen (A5) take B4401 for 4m. Right at Hendwr sign. Site 0.5m on right down tree-lined drive. Or follow brown signs from A5 at Corwen*

Open Apr-Oct

Last arrival 22.00hrs Last departure 16.00hrs

Surrounded by the Berwen Mountains, this well-established site has a stream meandering through it - the sound of running water and birdsong are the only distractions. A tree-lined drive welcomes visitors on to the immaculately maintained pitches. Fly fishing instruction can be arranged on the river which borders the park. Scandinavian-style lodges are available. 11 acre site. 40 touring pitches. 3 hardstandings. 30 seasonal pitches. Caravan pitches. Motorhome pitches. Tent pitches. 80 statics.

Facilities: ⬆☉✳⛴⛽⛔ WiFi ♻ 🎯
Services: 🔌🗑💷 ⃠🚽🛒⏚
Within 3 miles: 🎣 💷

Notes: No open fires. Dogs must be kept on leads. Wet weather camping facilities.

PRESTATYN
Map 15 SJ08

Places to visit

Basingwerk Abbey, HOLYWELL, CH8 7GH, 01443 336000 www.cadw.wales.gov.uk

Great for kids: Rhuddlan Castle, RHUDDLAN, LL18 5AD, 01745 590777 www.cadw.wales.gov.uk

82% Presthaven Sands Holiday Park (SJ091842)

GOLD

Gronant LL19 9TT

☎ 0871 231 0888

e-mail: presthavensands@haven.com
web: www.haven.com/presthavensands
dir: *A548 from Prestatyn towards Gronant. Site signed. (NB for Sat Nav use LL19 9ST)*

Open mid Mar-end Oct (rs mid Mar-May & Sep-Oct facilities may be reduced)

Last arrival 20.00hrs Last departure 10.00hrs

Set beside two miles of superb sandy beaches and dunes (with donkeys on site at weekends) this constantly improving holiday park provides a wide range of both indoor and outdoor attractions. The site can boast happy returning visitors. The small touring field at the park entrance offers good electric pitches - the majority are hardstandings and include five super pitches. The centrally located entertainment area includes two indoor swimming pools, excellent children's activities and a choice of eating outlets. 21 acre site. 34 touring pitches. Caravan pitches. Motorhome pitches. 1052 statics.

Leisure: 🏊🏄🎬🎪🎭🎵
Facilities: ⬆☉♿🕐💷 WiFi ♻ 🎯
Services: 🔌🗑🍴🎦🚻♻⏚
Within 3 miles: 🚴🏇🎣🏌💷🛒⛳

Notes: No commercial vehicles, no bookings by persons under 21yrs unless a family booking. Max 2 dogs per booking, certain dog breeds banned. Dogs must be kept on leads.

see advert below

SERVICES: 🔌 Electric hook up 🗑 Launderette 🍺 Licensed bar 🛢 Calor Gas 🛢 Camping Gaz 🚽 Toilet fluid 🍴 Café/Restaurant 🍟 Fast Food/Takeaway ⚡ Battery charging 🍼 Baby care ⏚ Motorvan service point **ABBREVIATIONS:** BH/bank hols-bank holidays Etr-Easter Spring BH-Spring Bank Holiday dep-departure fr-from hrs-hours m-mile mdnt-midnight rdbt-roundabout rs-restricted service wk-week wknd-weekend x-rds-cross roads ⊗ No credit cards ⊗ No dogs 👶 Children of all ages accepted See page 9 for details of the AA Camping Card Scheme

RHUALLT
Map 15 SJ07

Places to visit

Rhuddlan Castle, RHUDDLAN, LL18 5AD, 01745 590777 www.cadw.wales.gov.uk

Bodelwyddan Castle, BODELWYDDAN, LL18 5YA, 01745 584060 www.bodelwyddan-castle.co.uk

Great for kids: Denbigh Castle, DENBIGH, LL16 3NB, 01745 813385 www.cadw.wales.gov.uk

AA CAMPING CARD SITE

►►►► **89% Penisar Mynydd Caravan Park** *(SJ093770)*

Caerwys Rd LL17 0TY
☎ **01745 582227 & 07831 408017**
e-mail: contact@penisarmynydd.co.uk
web: www.penisarmynydd.co.uk
dir: *From A55 junct 29 follow Dyserth & brown caravan signs. Site 500yds on right*

* 🚐 £15-£17 🚃 £15-£17 ▲ fr £12

Open Mar-15 Jan

Last arrival 21.00hrs Last departure 21.00hrs

A very tranquil, attractively laid-out park set in three grassy paddocks with superb facilities block including a disabled room and dishwashing area. The majority of pitches are super pitches. Everything is immaculately maintained, and the amenities of the seaside resort of Rhyl are close by. 6.6 acre site. 71 touring pitches. 71 hardstandings. Caravan pitches. Motorhome pitches. Tent pitches.

AA Pubs & Restaurants nearby: The Plough Inn, ST ASAPH, LL17 0LU, 01745 585080

Leisure: ⚽

Facilities: 🏌⊙✻🅰️🅝⛑🅰️➤🚿 ⛊ ♻ ❶

Services: 🔌🔲🔒🔃↯

Within 3 miles: ⚓🍴⚲🅾️🛶🏇🔲🏰U

Notes: No cycling, no fires. Dogs must be kept on leads. Rally area.

RUABON
Map 15 SJ34

Places to visit

Plas Newydd, LLANGOLLEN, LL20 8AW, 01978 861314 www.denbighshire.gov.uk

Valle Crucis Abbey, LLANGOLLEN, LL20 8DD, 01978 860326 www.cadw.wales.gov.uk

Great for kids: Horse Drawn Boats Centre, LLANGOLLEN, LL20 8TA, 01978 860702 www.horsedrawnboats.co.uk

►►► **75% James' Caravan Park** *(SJ300434)*

LL14 6DW
☎ **01978 820148**
e-mail: ray@carastay.demon.co.uk
dir: *From Oswestry on A483 take slip road signed Llangollen & A539. At rdbt left onto A539 (Llangollen). Site 500yds on left. Or from Wrexham on A483 follow Llangollen & A539 signs. Right at rdbt onto A539, at next rdbt straight on, site on left*

🚐 🚃

Open all year

Last arrival 21.00hrs Last departure 11.00hrs

A well-landscaped park on a former farm, with modern heated toilet facilities. Old farm buildings house a collection of restored original farm machinery, and the village shop, four pubs, takeaway and launderette are a 10-minute walk away. 6 acre site. 40 touring pitches. 4 hardstandings. Caravan pitches. Motorhome pitches.

AA Pubs & Restaurants nearby: The Boat Inn, ERBISTOCK, LL13 0DL, 01978 780666

Cross Foxes, ERBISTOCK, LL13 0DR, 01978 780380

Facilities: 🏌⊙🅿️✻🅰️🅝🚿

Services: 🔌🅰️⊘🔃

Within 3 miles: ⚓🔲🔲

Notes: No fires. Dogs must be kept on leads. Chest freezer available.

GWYNEDD

ABERSOCH
Map 14 SH32

Places to visit

Plas-yn-Rhiw, PLAS YN RHIW, LL53 8AB, 01758 780219 www.nationaltrust.org.uk

Penarth Fawr, PENARTH FAWR, 01443 336000 www.cadw.wales.gov.uk

Great for kids: Criccieth Castle, CRICCIETH, LL52 0DP, 01766 522227 www.cadw.wales.gov.uk

►►►► **81% Beach View Caravan Park** *(SH316262)*

Bwlchtocyn LL53 7BT
☎ **01758 712956**
dir: *Through Abersoch & Sarn Bach. Over x-rds, next left signed Porthtocyn Hotel. Pass chapel to another Porthtocyn Hotel sign. Turn left, site on left*

🚐 🚃 ▲

Open mid Mar-mid Oct

Last arrival 19.00hrs Last departure 11.00hrs

A compact family park run by a very enthusiastic owner who makes continual improvements. Just a six-minute walk from the beach, the site's immaculately maintained grounds, good hardstanding pitches (mostly seasonal) and excellent facilities are matched by great sea and country views. 4 acre site. 47 touring pitches. 47 hardstandings. 40 seasonal pitches. Caravan pitches. Motorhome pitches. Tent pitches.

AA Pubs & Restaurants nearby: Porth Tocyn Hotel, ABERSOCH, LL53 7BU, 01758 713303

Facilities: 🏌⊙🅿️✻🅰️❶

Services: 🔌🔲⊘🔃

Within 3 miles: ⚓⚲🅿️🛶🏰U

Notes: 🐕 Dogs must be kept on leads.

LEISURE: 🏊 Indoor swimming pool 🏊 Outdoor swimming pool 🅰️ Children's playground 🧒 Kid's club 🎾 Tennis court 🎱 Games room 📺 Separate TV room ⚓ 9/18 hole golf course 🚣 Boats for hire 🎬 Cinema 🎵 Entertainment 🎣 Fishing 🅾️ Mini golf 🏄 Watersports 🏋️ Gym 🅾️ Sports field Spa U Stables
FACILITIES: 🛁 Bath 🚿 Shower ⊙ Electric shaver 🅗 Hairdryer ✻ Ice Pack Facility 🅰️ Disabled facilities 🔌 Public telephone 🔲 Shop on site or within 200yds 🔲 Mobile shop (calls at least 5 days a week) 🍴 BBQ area 🅰️ Picnic area 🅦🅘🅕🅘 Wi-fi 🔲 Internet access ♻ Recycling ❶ Tourist info 🅰️ Dog exercise area

►►►► 81% Deucoch Touring & Camping Park *(SH301269)*

Sarn Bach LL53 7LD
☎ **01758 713293 & 07740 281770**
e-mail: info@deucoch.com
dir: *From Abersoch take Sarn Bach road, at x-rds turn right, site on right in 800yds*

🚐 🚃 ⚊

Open Mar-Oct

Last arrival 22.00hrs Last departure 11.00hrs

A colourful, sheltered site with stunning views of Cardigan Bay and the mountains, and situated just a mile from Abersoch and a long sandy beach. The friendly, enthusiastic, hands-on proprietors make year-on-year improvements to enhance their visitors' experience. Facilities include outside hot showers, a superb dish washing facility, housed in an attractive log cabin, and caravan repairs. 5 acre site. 70 touring pitches. 10 hardstandings. Caravan pitches. Motorhome pitches. Tent pitches.

AA Pubs & Restaurants nearby: Porth Tocyn Hotel, ABERSOCH, LL53 7BU, 01758 713303

Leisure: 🅰 🎣

Facilities: 🛒 ⊙ 🖤 ✳ ♿ ♻ ❼

Services: 🔌 🔲 ↯

Within 3 miles: ♨ ✦ 🚲 ≋ 🛥 🎣 ∪

Notes: 🚫 Families only.

►►► 82% Tyn-y-Mur Touring & Camping *(SH304290)*

GOLD

Lon Garmon LL53 7UL
☎ **01758 712328**
e-mail: info@tyn-y-mur.co.uk
dir: *From Pwllheli into Abersoch on A499, sharp right at Land & Sea Garage. Site approx 0.5m on left*

✱ 🚐 £25 🚃 £25 ⚊ £18-£25

Open Apr-Oct

Last arrival 22.00hrs Last departure 11.00hrs

A family-only park in a glorious hill-top location overlooking a lush valley and with views extending across Abersoch to the mountains beyond Cardigan Bay. Good, clean, modern toilet facilities and spacious tent pitches in a level grassy field are on offer. There is a pathway from the site to private river fishing, and the beach at Abersoch is just a short walk away. The park offers boat storage facilities. 22 acre site. 90 touring pitches. 37 hardstandings. 37 seasonal pitches. Caravan pitches. Motorhome pitches. Tent pitches.

AA Pubs & Restaurants nearby: Porth Tocyn Hotel, ABERSOCH, LL53 7BU, 01758 713303

Tyn-y-Mur Touring & Camping

Leisure: 🅰 ⚽

Facilities: 🛒 ⊙ ✳ ♿ 🖤 ⛱ 🐕 ♻ ❼

Services: 🔌 🔲 🏷 ⊘ ⊤ 🛒 ♻

Within 3 miles: ♨ ✦ 🚲 ≋ 🛥 🎣 ∪

Notes: No open fires, no motorcycles, no noisy activity after 23.00hrs, 1 dog per unit. Dogs must be kept on leads.

►►► 80% Bryn Bach Caravan & Camping Site *(SH315258)*

Tyddyn Talgoch Uchaf, Bwlchtocyn LL53 7BT
☎ **01758 712285 & 07789 390808**
e-mail: brynbach@abersochcamping.co.uk
dir: *From Abersoch take Sarn Bach road for approx 1m, left at sign for Bwlchtocyn. Site approx 1m on left*

🚐 🚃 ⚊

Open Mar-Oct

Last arrival 20.00hrs Last departure 11.00hrs

This well-run, elevated park overlooks Abersoch Bay, with lovely sea views towards the Snowdonia mountain range. Pitches are well laid out in sheltered paddocks, with well-placed modern facilities. Fishing, watersports and golf are all nearby. The site has a private shortcut to the beach. 4 acre site. 8 touring pitches. 1 hardstanding. 30 seasonal pitches. Caravan pitches. Motorhome pitches. Tent pitches. 2 statics.

AA Pubs & Restaurants nearby: Porth Tocyn Hotel, ABERSOCH, LL53 7BU, 01758 713303

Leisure: 🅰 ⚽

Facilities: 🛒 ⊙ 🖤 ✳ ♿ ⛱ ♻ ❼

Services: 🔌 🔲 🏷 ⊘ ⊤ ↯

Within 3 miles: ♨ ✦ 🚲 ≋ 🛥 🎣 ∪

Notes: Families & couples only. Dogs must be kept on leads. Boat storage.

►►► 70% Tanrallt Farm *(SH296288)*

Tanrallt, Llangian LL53 7LN
☎ **01758 713527**
e-mail: www.abersoch-holiday.co.uk
web: www.abersoch-tanrallt.co.uk
dir: *A499 to Abersoch, right up hill, follow signs for Llangian. Site in village on left*

🚐 🚃 ⚊

Open Etr-end Oct

Last arrival 21.30hrs Last departure 10.30hrs

This site is in a secluded valley on a working farm. Friendly owners make their guests feel welcome; they provide a BBQ area, very clean and serviceable toilets, a laundry room with washer, dryer, spin dryer, iron and ironing board plus a drying area for wet clothing. There are also three bunk rooms and a kitchen. 1.5 acre site. 12 touring pitches. 12 hardstandings. Caravan pitches. Motorhome pitches. Tent pitches.

AA Pubs & Restaurants nearby: Porth Tocyn Hotel, ABERSOCH, LL53 7BU, 01758 713303

Facilities: 🛒 ⊙ 🖤 ✳ ♿ 🏠 ⛱ ♻ ❼

Services: 🔌 🔲 🏷 ↯

Within 3 miles: ♨ ✦ 🚲 ◎ ≋ 🎣 🛥 ∪

Notes: 🚫 Families & couples only, no noise after 23.00hrs.

ABERSOCH *continued*

►►► 69% Rhydolion *(SH283276)*

Llangian LL53 7LR
☎ 01758 712342
e-mail: enquiries@rhydolion.co.uk
dir: *From A499 take unclassified road to Llangian for 1m, left, through Llangian. Site 1.5m after road forks towards Hell's Mouth/Porth Neigwl*

🚐 £20-£25 🚐 £20-£25 ▲ £14-£16

Open Mar-Oct

Last arrival 22.00hrs Last departure noon

A peaceful small site with good views, on a working farm close to the long sandy surfers beach at Hell's Mouth. The simple toilet facilities are kept to a high standard by the friendly owners, and nearby Abersoch is a mecca for boat owners and water sports enthusiasts. 1.5 acre site. 28 touring pitches. Caravan pitches. Motorhome pitches. Tent pitches.

AA Pubs & Restaurants nearby: Porth Tocyn Hotel, ABERSOCH, LL53 7BU, 01758 713303

Leisure: 🅰 ✪
Facilities: 🅵 ☉ ✳ 🐕 ♻ 🄯
Services: 🄀 🄁 🄂
Within 3 miles: ⬇ ⬆ 🌊 ◎ ⬇ 🄐 🄑 U

Notes: 🄯 Families & couples only. Dogs accepted by prior arrangement only. Dogs must be kept on leads. 3 fridge freezers.

BALA Map 14 SH93

Places to visit

Bala Lake Railway, LLANUWCHLLYN, LL23 7DD, 01678 540666 www.bala-lake-railway.co.uk

Rug Chapel, CORWEN, LL21 9BT, 01490 412025 www.cadw.wales.gov.uk

Great for kids: Ewe-Phoria Sheepdog Centre, CORWEN, LL21 0PE, 01490 460369 www.ewe-phoria.co.uk

---

AA CAMPING CARD SITE

►►►► 81% Pen-y-Bont Touring Park

(SH932350)

Llangynog Rd LL23 7PH
☎ 01678 520549
e-mail: penybont-bala@btconnect.com
dir: *From A494 take B4391. Site 0.75m on right*

* 🚐 £16-£23 🚐 £16-£23 ▲ £16-£23

Open Mar-Oct

Last arrival 21.00hrs Last departure noon

A family-run, attractively landscaped park in a woodland country setting. It is set close to Bala Lake and the River Dee with plenty of opportunities for water sports including kayaking and white-water rafting. The park offers good facilities including a motorhome service point, and many pitches have water and electricity. Around the park are superb, large wood carvings of birds and mythical creatures depicting local legends. Two reproduction Romany caravans are available for hire. 6 acre site. 95 touring pitches. 47 hardstandings. 20 seasonal pitches. Caravan pitches. Motorhome pitches. Tent pitches. 1 bell tent/yurt. 2 wooden pods.

Facilities: 🅵 ☉ 🄿 ✳ ⬇ ⬅ 🄐 🄑 🄒 🄓 🄔 ♻ 🄯
Services: 🄀 🄁 🄂 🄃 🄄 🄅 🄆
Within 3 miles: ⬇ ⬆ 🄐 🌊 ⬇ 🄐 🄑 U

Notes: No camp fires, BBQs must be kept off ground, quiet after 22.30hrs. Dogs must be kept on leads.

►►►► 79% Tyn Cornel Camping & Caravan Park *(SH895400)*

Frongoch LL23 7NU
☎ 01678 520759
e-mail: tyncornel@mail.com
dir: *From Bala take A4212 (Porthmadog road) for 4m. Site on left before National White Water Centre*

* 🚐 £14-£20 🚐 £14-£20 ▲ fr £10

Open Etr-Oct

Last arrival 20.00hrs Last departure 11.00hrs

A delightful riverside park with mountain views that is popular with those seeking a base for river kayaking and canoeing - The National White Water Centre is adjacent, and there's a pleasant riverside walk to reach its café. The resident owners are always improving the already very well maintained and colourful grounds. 10 acre site. 67 touring pitches. 10 hardstandings. 14 seasonal pitches. Caravan pitches. Motorhome pitches. Tent pitches.

Leisure: ✪
Facilities: 🅵 ☉ 🄿 ✳ ⬇ ⬅ 🄐 🄑 🄒 ♻ 🄯
Services: 🄀 🄁 🄂 🄃 🄄 🄅
Within 3 miles: ⬇ ⬆ 🄐 🌊 🄐 🄑 U

Notes: Quiet after 23.00hrs, no cycling, no camp fires or wood burning. Dogs must be kept on leads. Fridge, freezer & tumble dryer available.

LEISURE: 🏊 Indoor swimming pool 🏊 Outdoor swimming pool 🅰 Children's playground 🪁 Kid's club 🎾 Tennis court 🎱 Games room 📺 Separate TV room ⛳ 9/18 hole golf course ⛵ Boats for hire 🎬 Cinema 🎵 Entertainment 🎣 Fishing ◎ Mini golf 🌊 Watersports 🏋 Gym ⚽ Sports field Spa U Stables
FACILITIES: 🛁 Bath 🅵 Shower ☉ Electric shaver 🄿 Hairdryer ✳ Ice Pack Facility ♿ Disabled facilities ☎ Public telephone 🄂 Shop on site or within 200yds 🄀 Mobile shop (calls at least 5 days a week) 🍖 BBQ area 🄐 Picnic area 🛜 Wi-fi 💻 Internet access ♻ Recycling 🄯 Tourist info 🐕 Dog exercise area

BANGOR
Map 14 SH57

Places to visit

Penrhyn Castle, BANGOR,
LL57 4HN, 01248 353084
www.nationaltrust.org.uk/penrhyncastle

Plas Newydd, PLAS NEWYDD, LL61 6DQ,
01248 714795
www.nationaltrust.org.uk/main/plasnewydd

Great for kids: Greenwood Forest Park,
Y FELINHELI, LL56 4QN, 01248 670076
www.greenwoodforestpark.co.uk

▶▶▶ 70% *Treborth Hall Farm Caravan Park* (SH554707)

The Old Barn, Treborth Hall Farm LL57 2RX
☎ 01248 364399
e-mail: enquiries@treborthleisure.co.uk
dir: A55 junct 9, 1st left at rdbt, straight over 2nd rdbt, site approx 800yds on left

🚐 🚲 Å

Open Etr-end Oct

Last arrival 22.30hrs Last departure 10.30hrs

Set in eight acres of beautiful parkland with its own trout fishing lake and golf course, this park offers serviced pitches in a sheltered, walled orchard. Tents have a separate grass area, and there is a good clean toilet block. This is a useful base for families, with easy access for the Menai Straits, Anglesey beaches, Snowdon and the Lleyn peninsula. 8 acre site. 34 touring pitches. 34 hardstandings. Caravan pitches. Motorhome pitches. Tent pitches. 4 statics.

Leisure: 🅰
Facilities: 📡 🕐 🛒 ❼
Services: 🔌
Within 3 miles: ♨ 🎣 ◎ ⛵ 🛒 🛍
Notes: Dogs must be kept on leads.

BARMOUTH
Map 14 SH61

Places to visit

Harlech Castle, HARLECH, LL46 2YH,
01766 780552 www.cadw.wales.gov.uk

Cymer Abbey, CYMER ABBEY, 01443 336000
www.cadw.wales.gov.uk

Great for kids: Fairbourne Railway,
FAIRBOURNE, LL38 2EX, 01341 250362
www.fairbournerailway.com

PREMIER PARK

▶▶▶▶▶ 92% Trawsdir Touring Caravans & Camping Park (SH596198)

Best of British

Llanaber LL42 1RR
☎ 01341 280999
e-mail: enquiries@barmouthholidays.co.uk
web: www.barmouthholidays.co.uk
dir: 3m N of Barmouth on A496, just past Wayside pub on right

* 🚐 £18-£34 🚲 £18-£34 Å £6-£30

Open Mar-Jan

Last arrival 20.00hrs Last departure noon

Well run by the owners, this quality park enjoys spectacular views to the sea and hills, and is very accessible to motor traffic. The facilities are appointed to a very high standard, and include spacious cubicles containing showers and washbasins, individual showers, smart toilets with sensor-operated flush, and under-floor heating. Tents and caravans have their own designated areas divided by dry-stone walls (both have spacious fully serviced pitches) and the site is very convenient for large recreational vehicles. There is an excellent children's play area, plus glorious seasonal floral displays and an illuminated dog walk that leads directly to the nearby pub! 15 acre site. 70 touring pitches. 70 hardstandings. Caravan pitches. Motorhome pitches. Tent pitches. 8 wooden pods.

Leisure: 🅰
Facilities: 📡 ☉ 🍴 ✳ ⛄ 🛒 🚿 🐕 📶 ♻ ❼
Services: 🔌 🗑 📦 🚿 🚽 🛒 🚐 ⛟
Within 3 miles: 🎣 ⛵ 🛒 🛍

Notes: Families & couples only. Dogs must be kept on leads. Milk/bread etc available from reception, takeaway food can be delivered from sister site.

PREMIER PARK

▶▶▶▶▶ 85% Hendre Mynach Touring Caravan & Camping Park (SH605170)

Llanaber Rd LL42 1YR
☎ 01341 280262
e-mail: mynach@lineone.net
web: www.hendremynach.co.uk
dir: 0.75m N of Barmouth on A496

🚐 🚲 Å

Open Mar-9 Jan (rs Nov-Jan shop closed)

Last arrival 22.00hrs Last departure noon

A constantly improving site where the enthusiastic owners invest year on year to enhance the customer experience. Although there is a steep decent to the arrivals' area, staff are always on hand to assist. The beautifully maintained touring areas benefit from attractive hedge screening around the large well-spaced pitches that are equipped with water and TV hook-ups. There is direct access to the seafront which leads to the town centre and its many attractions. 10 acre site. 240 touring pitches. 75 hardstandings. 23 seasonal pitches. Caravan pitches. Motorhome pitches. Tent pitches. 1 static.

Leisure: 🅰
Facilities: 📡 ☉ 🍴 ✳ ⛄ 🕐 🛒 📶 💻 ♻ ❼
Services: 🔌 🗑 📦 🚿 🚽 ⛟
Within 3 miles: 🍴 🎣 🛒 🛍 ⛳
Notes: Dogs must be kept on leads.

BETWS GARMON | Map 14 SH55

Places to visit

Snowdon Mountain Railway, LLANBERIS, LL55 4TY, 01286 870223
www.snowdonrailway.co.uk

Great for kids: Dolbadarn Castle, LLANBERIS, LL55 4UD, 01443 336000
www.cadw.wales.gov.uk

AA CAMPING CARD SITE

▶▶▶▶ **80% Bryn Gloch Caravan & Camping Park** (SH534574)

LL54 7YY
☎ **01286 650216**
e-mail: eurig@bryngloch.co.uk
web: www.campwales.co.uk
dir: On A4085, 5m SE of Caernarfon

🚐 🚐 ▲

Open all year

Last arrival 23.00hrs Last departure 17.00hrs

An excellent family-run site with immaculate modern facilities, and all level pitches in beautiful surroundings. The park offers the best of two worlds, with its bustling holiday atmosphere and the peaceful natural surroundings. The 28 acres of level fields are separated by mature hedges and trees, guaranteeing sufficient space for families wishing to spread themselves out. There are static holiday caravans for hire and plenty of walks in the area. 28 acre site. 160 touring pitches. 60 hardstandings. 50 seasonal pitches. Caravan pitches. Motorhome pitches. Tent pitches. 17 statics.

AA Pubs & Restaurants nearby: Snowdonia Parc Brewpub & Campsite, WAUNFAWR, LL55 4AQ, 01286 650409

Leisure: 🅰 🔍 🖵
Facilities: 🛁 👣 ⊙ 🗝 🌣 ⅙ 🕒 💲 🎋 🚻 Wi-fi 🖥 ♻ ⓘ
Services: 🔋 🗑 🍴 🧺 ⊥ 🛒 ⊥
Within 3 miles: ⅃ ⅄ 🎣 🌊 ◎ 🏌 🛒 U
Notes: Dogs must be kept on leads. Family bathroom, mother & baby room.

CAERNARFON | Map 14 SH46

See also Dinas Dinlle & Llandwrog

Places to visit

Segontium Roman Museum, CAERNARFON, LL55 2LN, 01286 675625 www.segontium.org.uk

Welsh Highland Railway, CAERNARFON, LL55 2YD, 01766 516024 www.festrail.co.uk

Great for kids: Caernarfon Castle, CAERNARFON, LL55 2AY, 01286 677617
www.cadw.wales.gov.uk

▶▶▶▶ **86% Llys Derwen Caravan & Camping Site** (SH539629)

Ffordd Bryngwyn, Llanrug LL55 4RD
☎ **01286 673322**
e-mail: llysderwen@aol.com
dir: A55 junct 13 (Caernarfon) onto A4086 to Llanberis, through Llanrug, turn right at pub, site 60yds on right

🚐 🚐 ▲

Open Mar-Oct

Last arrival 22.00hrs Last departure noon

On the outskirts of the village of Llanrug, three miles from Caernarfon on the way to Llanberis and Snowdon. A beautifully maintained site with enthusiastic owners who are constantly investing to improve their customers' experience. The amenities block has been refurbished to a high standard and the immaculately maintained grounds are planted with an abundance of colourful shrubs and seasonal flowers. 5 acre site. 20 touring pitches. Caravan pitches. Motorhome pitches. Tent pitches. 2 statics.

AA Pubs & Restaurants nearby: Seiont Manor Hotel, CAERNARFON, LL55 2AQ, 01286 673366

Facilities: 👣 ⊙ 🗝 🌣 ⅙ 🎋 ♻ ⓘ
Services: 🔋 🗑 🧺
Within 3 miles: ⅃ ⅄ 🎣 🌊 ◎ 🏌 🛒 U
Notes: 🚫 No open fires, no noise after 22.00hrs, no ball games. Dogs must be kept on leads.

▶▶▶▶ **85% Riverside Camping** (SH505630)

Seiont Nurseries, Pont Rug LL55 2BB
☎ **01286 678781**
e-mail: brenda@riversidecamping.co.uk
web: www.riversidecamping.co.uk
dir: 2m from Caernarfon on right of A4086 towards Llanberis, follow signs

* 🚐 £19-£25 🚐 £19-£25 ▲ £14-£22

Open Mar-end Oct

Last arrival anytime Last departure noon

Set in the grounds of a former garden centre and enjoying a superb location along the River Seiont, this park is approached by an impressive tree-lined drive. Immaculately maintained by the owners, there are a mixture of riverside grassy pitches and fully serviced pitches for caravans and motorhomes. In addition to smart amenities blocks, other facilities include an excellent café/restaurant, a volley ball court and boules pitch. River fishing permits are available. 13 hardstanding pitches have electric hook-up, water, drainage and TV connection (especially suitable for motorhomes). A haven of peace close to Caernarfon, Snowdonia and some great walking opportunities. 5 acre site. 73 touring pitches. 16 hardstandings. 10 seasonal pitches. Caravan pitches. Motorhome pitches. Tent pitches.

AA Pubs & Restaurants nearby: Seiont Manor Hotel, CAERNARFON, LL55 2AQ, 01286 673366

Leisure: 🅰
Facilities: 👣 ⊙ 🗝 🌣 ⅙ 🎋 Wi-fi 🖥 ♻ ⓘ
Services: 🔋 🗑 🍴 🧺 🛒 ⊥
Within 3 miles: ⅃ ⅄ ⅄ 🎣 ◎ 🏌 🛒 U
Notes: No fires, no loud music. Debit (not credit) cards accepted. Dogs must be kept on leads. Family shower room, baby-changing facilities.

▶▶▶ **81% Plas Gwyn Caravan & Camping Park** (SH520633)

Llanrug LL55 2AQ
☎ **01286 672619**
e-mail: info@plasgwyn.co.uk
web: www.plasgwyn.co.uk
dir: A4086, 3m E of Caernarfon, site on right. Between River Seiont & Llanrug

🚐 🚐 ▲

Open Mar-Oct

Last arrival 22.00hrs Last departure 11.30hrs

A secluded park in an ideal location for visiting the glorious nearby beaches, historic Caernarfon, the attractions of Snowdonia and for walking opportunities. The site is set within the grounds of Plas Gwyn House, a Georgian property with colonial additions, and the friendly owners constantly improve facilities to enhance their visitors' experience. A 'breakfast butty' service with fresh tea or coffee is available for delivery to individual pitches. The all-electric pitches include hardstandings and five are fully serviced. Three timber camping tents and five statics are available for hire. 3 acre site. 42 touring pitches. 8 hardstandings. 8 seasonal pitches. Caravan pitches. Motorhome pitches. Tent pitches. 18 statics. 3 wooden pods.

AA Pubs & Restaurants nearby: Seiont Manor Hotel, CAERNARFON, LL55 2AQ, 01286 673366

Facilities: 🌡️⊙🅿️✕🖥️🚾💻♻️❓

Services: 🔌🗑️🔋🚿🅣🔌⚡

Within 3 miles: 🚶🎣🎣🏊🎯🛒🎯🛒⛳

Notes: Minimal noise between 22.00hrs-mdnt, complete quiet between mdnt-08.00hrs.

►►► 80% Cwm Cadnant Valley

(SH487628)

Llanberis Rd LL55 2DF
☎ **01286 673196**
e-mail: aa@cwmcadnant.co.uk
web: www.cwmcadnant.co.uk
dir: *On outskirts of Caernarfon on A4086 towards Llanberis, adjacent to fire station*

* 🚐 £13.50-£20.50 🚙 £13.50-£20.50
🛖 £10-£20.50

Open 14 Mar-3 Nov

Last arrival 22.00hrs Last departure 11.00hrs

Set in an attractive wooded valley with a stream is this terraced site with secluded pitches, a good camping area for backpackers and clean, modernised toilet facilities. It is located on the outskirts of Caernarfon in a rural location, close to the main Caernarfon-Llanberis road and just a

10-minute walk from the castle and town centre. 4.5 acre site. 60 touring pitches. 9 hardstandings. 5 seasonal pitches. Caravan pitches. Motorhome pitches. Tent pitches.

AA Pubs & Restaurants nearby: Seiont Manor Hotel, CAERNARFON, LL55 2AQ, 01286 673366

Leisure: 🅰️

Facilities: 🌡️⊙🅿️✕👤🕐🚾♻️❓

Services: 🔌🗑️🔋🚿🅣🔋

Within 3 miles: 🚶🎣🎣🏊🎯🛒⛳

Notes: No noise after 23.00hrs, no wood fires. Dogs must be kept on leads. Family room with baby-changing facilities.

►►► 77% Ty'n yr Onnen Caravan Park *(SH533588)*

Waunfawr LL55 4AX
☎ **01286 650281 & 07976 529428**
e-mail: tynronnen.farm@btconnect.com
dir: *At Waunfawr on A4085, onto unclassified road opposite church. Site signed*

* 🚐 £15-£20 🚙 £15-£20 🛖 £12-£20

Open Apr-Oct

Last arrival 22.00hrs Last departure noon

A gently sloping site on a 200-acre sheep farm set in magnificent surroundings close to Snowdon and enjoying stunning mountain views. This secluded park is well equipped and has quality toilet facilities. Access is via a narrow, unclassified road. 3.5 acre site. 20 touring pitches. Caravan pitches. Motorhome pitches. Tent pitches.

AA Pubs & Restaurants nearby: Snowdonia Parc Brewpub & Campsite, WAUNFAWR, LL55 4AQ, 01286 650409

Leisure: 🅰️🎣⎍

Facilities: 🌡️⊙✕👤🚻🐕🚾♻️

Services: 🔌🗑️🔋

Within 3 miles: 🚶🎣🎯◎🏊🎯🛒⛳

Notes: No music after 23.00hrs. Dogs must be kept on leads. Working farm.

►►►► 82% Eisteddfa *(SH518394)*

Eisteddfa Lodge, Pentrefelin LL52 0PT
☎ **01766 522696**
e-mail: eisteddfa@criccieth.co.uk
dir: *From Porthmadog take A497 towards Criccieth. Approx 3.5m, through Pentrefelin, site signed 1st right after Plas Gwyn Nursing Home*

🚐 £15-£22 🚙 £15-£22 🛖 £13-£22

Open Mar-Oct

Last arrival 22.30hrs Last departure 11.00hrs

A quiet, secluded park on elevated ground, sheltered by the Snowdonia Mountains and with lovely views of Cardigan Bay; Criccieth is nearby. The owners are carefully improving the park whilst preserving its unspoilt beauty, and are keen to welcome families, who will appreciate the cubicled facilities. There's a field and play area, woodland walks, a cocoon pod, two tipis, six superb slate-based hardstandings, three static holiday caravans for hire, and a three-acre coarse fishing lake adjacent to the park. 24 acre site. 100 touring pitches. 17 hardstandings. Caravan pitches. Motorhome pitches. Tent pitches. 3 statics. 2 tipis. 1 wooden pod.

AA Pubs & Restaurants nearby: Bron Eifion Country House Hotel, CRICCIETH, LL52 0SA, 01766 522385

Plas Bodegroes, PWLLHELI, LL53 5TH, 01758 612363

Leisure: 🅰️🎯🎣

Facilities: 🌡️⊙🅿️✕👤🚻🐕♻️❓

Services: 🔌🗑️🔋🚿🔋

Within 3 miles: 🚶🎣🎽🎯◎🏊🎯🛒⛳

Notes: No noise after 22.30hrs. Dogs must be kept on leads. Baby bath available.

SERVICES: 🔌 Electric hook up ⬚ Launderette 🍸 Licensed bar 🛢️ Calor Gas ⬭ Camping Gaz 🅣 Toilet fluid 🍴 Café/Restaurant 🍔 Fast Food/Takeaway 🔋 Battery charging 🍼 Baby care ⬆️ Motorvan service point **ABBREVIATIONS:** BH/bank hols-bank holidays Etr-Easter Spring BH-Spring Bank Holiday dep-departure fr-from hrs-hours m-mile mdnt-midnight rdbt-roundabout rs-restricted service wk-week wknd-weekend x-rds-cross roads 🚫 No credit cards 🚫 No dogs
🚼 Children of all ages accepted See page 9 for details of the AA Camping Card Scheme

CRICCIETH *continued*

►► 82% Llwyn-Bugeilydd Caravan & Camping Site *(SH498398)*

LL52 0PN

☎ **01766 522235 & 07714 196137**

e-mail: cazzyanne1@hotmail.com

dir: From Porthmadog on A497, 1m N of Criccieth on B4411. Site 1st on right. From A55 take A487 through Caernarfon. After Bryncir right onto B4411, site on left in 3.5m

🚐 🚃 Å

Open Mar-Oct

Last arrival anytime Last departure 11.00hrs

A quiet rural site, convenient for touring Snowdonia and coastal areas. It is set amid stunning scenery and has well-tended grass pitches enhanced by shrubs and seasonal flowers. The smartly presented amenities block is kept spotlessly clean. 6 acre site. 45 touring pitches. 2 hardstandings. Caravan pitches. Motorhome pitches. Tent pitches.

AA Pubs & Restaurants nearby: Bron Eifion Country House Hotel, CRICCIETH, LL52 0SA, 01766 522385

Plas Bodegroes, PWLLHELI, LL53 5TH, 01758 612363

Leisure: 🅰 ☼

Facilities: 🏕 ☉ ℱ ☼ 🛒 ♻ 𝒊

Services: 🔌 🗄 💼

Within 3 miles: � 🚣 ℱ ◎ ≋ 🛍 🔄 ∪

Notes: ◉ No skateboards. Dogs must be kept on leads.

DINAS DINLLE Map 14 SH45

Places to visit

Snowdon Mountain Railway, LLANBERIS, LL55 4TY, 01286 870223
www.snowdonrailway.co.uk

St Cybi's Well, LLANGYBI, 01443 336000
www.cadw.wales.gov.uk

Great for kids: Dolbadarn Castle, LLANBERIS, LL55 4UD, 01443 336000
www.cadw.wales.gov.uk

►►►► 87% Dinlle Caravan Park

(SH438568)

LL54 5TW

☎ **01286 830324**

e-mail: enq@thornleyleisure.co.uk

dir: From A487 at rdbt onto A499 (signed Pwllheli). Right at sign for Caernarfon Airport (& brown camping sign)

🚐 £12-£25 🚃 £12-£25 Å £12-£25

Open Mar-Nov

Last arrival 23.00hrs Last departure noon

A very accessible, well-kept, grassy site adjacent to a sandy beach and with good views towards Snowdonia. The park is situated in acres of flat grassland that provides plenty of space for large groups. The man-made dunes offer campers additional protection from sea breezes. The lounge bar and family room are comfortable places in which to relax, and children will enjoy the exciting adventure playground. A golf club, a nature reserve and the Airworld Aviation Museum at Caernarfon Airport can all be accessed from the beach road. 20 acre site. 175 touring pitches. 20 hardstandings. Caravan pitches. Motorhome pitches. Tent pitches. 167 statics.

Leisure: ⩰ 🅰 🔍 🎵

Facilities: 🏕 ☉ ℱ ☼ ♿ 🇼 𝒊

Services: 🔌 🗄 🍽 💼 ♻ ⬇

Within 3 miles: ℱ 🛍 ∪

Notes: No skateboards. Dogs must be kept on leads.

DYFFRYN ARDUDWY Map 14 SH52

Places to visit

Cymer Abbey, CYMER ABBEY, 01443 336000
www.cadw.wales.gov.uk

Great for kids: Harlech Castle, HARLECH, LL46 2YH, 01766 780552
www.cadw.wales.gov.uk

►►► 81% *Murmur-yr-Afon Touring Park* *(SH586236)*

LL44 2BE

☎ **01341 247353**

e-mail: murmuryrafon1@btinternet.com

dir: On A496 N of village

🚐 🚃 Å

Open Mar-Oct

Last arrival 22.00hrs Last departure 11.00hrs

A pleasant family-run park alongside a wooded stream on the edge of the village, and handy for large sandy beaches. Expect good, clean facilities, and lovely views of rolling hills and mountains. 6 acre site. 77 touring pitches. 37 hardstandings. Caravan pitches. Motorhome pitches. Tent pitches.

AA Pubs & Restaurants nearby: Victoria Inn, LLANBEDR, LL45 2LD, 01341 241213

Leisure: 🅰

Facilities: 🏕 ☉ ℱ ☼ ♿ 🕐 🛍 🛒 𝒊

Services: 🔌 🗄 💼

Within 3 miles: ℱ ≋ 🛍

Notes: Dogs must be kept on leads.

LEISURE: 🏊 Indoor swimming pool ⩰ Outdoor swimming pool 🅰 Children's playground 🧒 Kid's club 🎾 Tennis court 🔍 Games room 📺 Separate TV room ⛳ 9/18 hole golf course 🚣 Boats for hire 🎬 Cinema 🎵 Entertainment ℱ Fishing ⛳ Mini golf 🏄 Watersports 🏋 Gym ⚽ Sports field Spa ∪ Stables
FACILITIES: 🛁 Bath 🚿 Shower ☉ Electric shaver ℱ Hairdryer ☼ Ice Pack Facility ♿ Disabled facilities 🕐 Public telephone 🛍 Shop on site or within 200yds 🛒 Mobile shop (calls at least 5 days a week) 🍽 BBQ area 🪑 Picnic area 🇼 Wi-fi ▬ Internet access ♻ Recycling 𝒊 Tourist info 🛒 Dog exercise area

LLANDWROG
Map 14 SH45

Places to visit

Sygun Copper Mine, BEDDGELERT, LL55 4NE, 01766 890595 www.syguncoppermine.co.uk

Great for kids: Caernarfon Castle, CAERNARFON, LL55 2AY, 01286 677617 www.cadw.wales.gov.uk

AA CAMPING CARD SITE

▶▶▶▶ **80% White Tower Caravan Park** (SH453582)

LL54 5UH

☎ 01286 830649 & 07802 562785

e-mail: whitetower@supanet.com

web: www.whitetowerpark.co.uk

dir: 1.5m from village on Tai'r Eglwys road. From Caernarfon take A487 (Porthmadog road). Cross rdbt, 1st right. Site 3m on right

🚐 £20-£28 ⛺ £20-£28 ⛺ £20-£28

Open Mar-10 Jan (rs Mar-mid May & Sep-Oct bar open wknds only)

Last arrival 23.00hrs Last departure noon

There are lovely views of Snowdonia from this park located just two miles from the nearest beach at Dinas Dinlle. A well-maintained toilet block has key access, and the hardstanding pitches have water and electricity. Popular amenities include an outdoor heated swimming pool, a lounge bar with family room, and a games and TV room. 6 acre site. 60 touring pitches. 60 hardstandings. 58 seasonal pitches. Caravan pitches. Motorhome pitches. Tent pitches. 71 statics.

Leisure: 🏊 🎱 🎯 🖥 🎵

Facilities: 🛝 ☺ 🍴 ⚡ 🔥 🕙 wifi 🖳 ♻ ✪

Services: 🔌 🛢 🍴 🥫 ♨ 🚮

Within 3 miles: ↕ 🎣 🏌 ♨ 🛒 🛢 U

Notes: Dogs must be kept on leads.

PONT-RUG

See Caernarfon

PORTHMADOG
Map 14 SH53

Places to visit

Inigo Jones Slateworks, GROESLON, LL54 7UE, 01286 830242 www.inigojones.co.uk

Great for kids: Ffestiniog Railway, PORTHMADOG, LL49 9NF, 01766 516024 www.festrail.co.uk

83% Greenacres Holiday Park (SH539374)

GOLD

Black Rock Sands, Morfa Bychan LL49 9YF

☎ 0871 231 0886

e-mail: greenacres@haven.com

web: www.haven.com/greenacres

dir: From Porthmadog High Street follow Black Rock Sands signs between The Factory Shop & Post Office. Park 2m on left at end of Morfa Bychan

🚐 ⛺

Open mid Mar-end Oct (rs mid Mar-May & Sep-Oct some facilities may be reduced)

Last arrival anytime Last departure 10.00hrs

A quality holiday park on level ground just a short walk from Black Rock Sands, and set against a backdrop of Snowdonia National Park. All touring pitches are on hardstandings surrounded by closely-mown grass, and near the entertainment complex. A full programme of entertainment, organised clubs, indoor and outdoor sports and leisure, pubs, shows and cabarets all add to a holiday experience here. A bowling alley and a large shop/bakery are useful amenities. 121 acre site. 48 touring pitches. 48 hardstandings. Caravan pitches. Motorhome pitches. 900 statics.

AA Pubs & Restaurants nearby: Royal Sportsman Hotel, PORTHMADOG, LL49 9HB, 01766 512015

The Hotel Portmeirion, PORTMEIRION, LL48 6ET, 01766 770000

Castell Deudraeth, PORTMEIRION, LL48 6ER, 01766 772400

Leisure: 🏊 🎱 🎯 🎮 🎣 🎵

Facilities: 🛝 ☺ 🍴 ⚡ 🕙 🖳 wifi ♻ ✪

Services: 🔌 🛢 🍴 🥫 ♨ 🍴 🛒 🚮

Within 3 miles: ↕ 🎯 🛢 U

Notes: No commercial vehicles, no bookings by persons under 21yrs unless a family booking. Max 2 dogs per booking, certain dog breeds banned. Dogs must be kept on leads.

PWLLHELI
Map 14 SH33

Places to visit

Penarth Fawr, PENARTH FAWR, 01443 336000 www.cadw.wales.gov.uk

Plas-yn-Rhiw, PLAS YN RHIW, LL53 8AB, 01758 780219 www.nationaltrust.org.uk

Great for kids: Criccieth Castle, CRICCIETH, LL52 0DP, 01766 522227 www.cadw.wales.gov.uk

87% Hafan Y Môr Holiday Park (SH431368)

GOLD

LL53 6HJ

☎ 0871 231 0887

e-mail: hafanymor@haven.com

web: www.haven.com/hafanymor

dir: From Caernarfon take A499 to Pwllheli. A497 to Porthmadog. Park on right, approx 3m from Pwllheli. Or from Telford, A5, A494 to Bala. Right for Porthmadog. Left at rdbt in Porthmadog signed Criccieth & Pwllheli. Park on left 3m from Criccieth

🚐 ⛺

Open mid Mar-end Oct (rs mid Mar-May & Sep-Oct reduced facilities)

Last arrival 21.00hrs Last departure 10.00hrs

Located between Pwllheli and Criccieth, and surrounded by mature trees that attract wildlife, this popular holiday centre has undergone major investment in recent years to provide a wide range of all-weather attractions. Activities include a sports hall, an ornamental boating lake, a large indoor swimming pool and show bar, to name but a few. There are also great eating options including the Mash & Barrel bar and bistro, fish & chips and a Starbucks café. The £1.1m redevelopment of the touring area includes 75 fully serviced all-weather pitches and a top notch, air-conditioned amenities block. 500 acre site. 75

continued

PWLLHELI *continued*

touring pitches. 75 hardstandings. Caravan pitches. Motorhome pitches. 800 statics.

AA Pubs & Restaurants nearby: Plas Bodegroes, PWLLHELI, LL53 5TH, 01758 612363

Leisure: 🐟 ⛰ 🏊 🎵

Facilities: 🍴 🌳 🚾 🏪

Services: 🔌 🗑 🔧 🚽 🍽 🛒

Within 3 miles: 🚶 🚣 🎣 ◎ 🛥 🏪 🛒 ⛴

Notes: No commercial vehicles, no bookings by persons under 21yrs unless a family booking. Max 2 dogs per booking, certain dog breeds banned. Dogs must be kept on leads.

see advert below

►►► 71% Abererch Sands Holiday Centre *(SH403359)*

LL53 6PJ
☎ 01758 612327
e-mail: enquiries@abererch-sands.co.uk
dir: *On A497 (Porthmadog to Pwllheli road), 1m from Pwllheli*

* 🚐 £26-£30 🚏 £25-£28 ▲ £26-£28

Open Mar-Oct

Last arrival 21.00hrs Last departure 21.00hrs

Glorious views of Snowdonia and Cardigan Bay can be enjoyed from this very secure, family-run

site adjacent to a railway station and a four-mile stretch of sandy beach. A large heated indoor swimming pool, snooker room, pool room, fitness centre and children's play area make this an ideal holiday venue. 85 acre site. 70 touring pitches. 70 hardstandings. Caravan pitches. Motorhome pitches. Tent pitches. 90 statics.

AA Pubs & Restaurants nearby: Plas Bodegroes, PWLLHELI, LL53 5TH, 01758 612363

Abererch Sands Holiday Centre

Leisure: 🐟 ⛰ 🔍

Facilities: 🍴 ☉ ❄ ⚕ 🚾 🏪 ♻

Services: 🔌 🗑 🚽 ⚡ 🛒

Within 3 miles: 🚶 🚣 ⛳ 🎣 🏪 🛒 ⛴

Notes: Dogs must be kept on leads.

TALSARNAU   Map 14 SH63

Places to visit

Portmeirion, PORTMEIRION, LL48 6ER, 01766 770000 www.portmeirion-village.com

Harlech Castle, HARLECH, LL46 2YH, 01766 780552 www.cadw.wales.gov.uk

Great for kids: Ffestiniog Railway, PORTHMADOG, LL49 9NF, 01766 516024 www.festrail.co.uk

AA CAMPING CARD SITE

►►►► 83% **Barcdy Touring Caravan & Camping Park**

(SH620375)

LL47 6YG
☎ 01766 770736
e-mail: anwen@barcdy.co.uk
dir: *From Maentwrog take A496 for Harlech. Site 4m on left*

* 🚐 £20-£24 🚏 £20-£24 ▲ £14-£22

Open Apr-Oct (rs Selected dates 2nd facility building closed (excl high season & school hols))

LEISURE: 🐟 Indoor swimming pool 🐟 Outdoor swimming pool ⛰ Children's playground 🪁 Kid's club 🎾 Tennis court 🎱 Games room 📺 Separate TV room 🏌 9/18 hole golf course 🚣 Boats for hire 🎬 Cinema 🎵 Entertainment 🎣 Fishing ◎ Mini golf 🏄 Watersports 🏋 Gym 🏈 Sports field **Spa** ⛴ Stables
FACILITIES: 🛁 Bath 🚿 Shower ☉ Electric shaver 💨 Hairdryer ❄ Ice Pack Facility ⚕ Disabled facilities 🕑 Public telephone 🏪 Shop on site or within 200yds 🚐 Mobile shop (calls at least 5 days a week) 🍖 BBQ area 🧺 Picnic area 🚾 Wi-fi 💻 Internet access ♻ Recycling ⓘ Tourist info 🐕 Dog exercise area

Last arrival 21.00hrs Last departure noon

A quiet picturesque park on the edge of the Vale of Ffestiniog near the Dwryd estuary. Two touring areas serve the park, one near the park entrance, and the other with improved and more secluded terraced pitches beside a narrow valley. The tent area is secluded and peaceful, and the toilet facilities are clean and tidy. Footpaths through adjacent woodland lead to small lakes and an established nature trail. 12 acre site. 80 touring pitches. 40 hardstandings. 15 seasonal pitches. Caravan pitches. Motorhome pitches. Tent pitches. 30 statics.

AA Pubs & Restaurants nearby: The Hotel Portmeirion, PORTMEIRION, LL48 6ET, 01766 770000

Castell Deudraeth, PORTMEIRION, LL48 6ER, 01766 772400

Facilities: ⚘ ⊙ ⚑ ☀ ♨ �📶 ♻ ✿

Services: 🔌 🅾 🅱 ⊘

Within 3 miles: 🎣 ℘ 🛥 ⛤ ∪

Notes: ⊗ No noisy parties, quiet families & couples only, no groups except Duke of Edinburgh Award participants.

TAL-Y-BONT   Map 14 SH52

Places to visit

Cymer Abbey, CYMER ABBEY, 01443 336000 www.cadw.wales.gov.uk

Great for kids: Fairbourne Railway, FAIRBOURNE, LL38 2EX, 01341 250362 www.fairbournerailway.com

AA CAMPING CARD SITE
PREMIER PARK

▶▶▶▶▶ **89% Islawrffordd Caravan Park** (SH584215)

LL43 2AQ
☎ 01341 247269
e-mail: jane@islawrffordd.co.uk
dir: *In village of Tal-y-Bont, take turn towards village railway halt, signed*

🚐 £25-£33.50 🚓 £25-£33.50 ▲ £25-£33.50

Islawrffordd Caravan Park

Open Mar-1 Nov

Last arrival 20.00hrs Last departure noon

Situated on the coast between Barmouth and Harlech, and within the Snowdonia National Park, with clear views of Cardigan Bay, the Lleyn Peninsula and the Snowdonia and Cader Idris mountain ranges, this excellent, family-run and family-friendly park has seen considerable investment over recent years. Fully matured, the touring area boasts fully serviced pitches, a superb toilet block with under-floor heating and top-quality fittings, and the park has private access to miles of sandy beach. 25 acre site. 105 touring pitches. 75 hardstandings. 50 seasonal pitches. Caravan pitches. Motorhome pitches. Tent pitches. 201 statics.

AA Pubs & Restaurants nearby: Victoria Inn, LLANBEDR, LL45 2LD, 01341 241213

Leisure: 🏊 △ 🎣 ▢

Facilities: ⚘ ⊙ ⚑ ☀ ⚒ ⊕ ⓢ 📶 ♻ ✿

Services: 🔌 🅾 🍺 🅱 ⊘ 🔧 🍽 🔋 🏪 ♨

Within 3 miles: 🎣 ℘ ⊙ ⛤ 🛥 ✇ ∪

Notes: Strictly families & couples only. Dogs must be kept on leads.

see advert on page 420

TYWYN   Map 14 SH50

Places to visit

Talyllyn Railway, TYWYN, LL36 9EY, 01654 710472 www.talyllyn.co.uk

Castell-y-Bere, LLANFIHANGEL-Y-PENNANT, 01443 336000 www.cadw.wales.gov.uk

Great for kids: King Arthur's Labyrinth, MACHYNLLETH, SY20 9RF, 01654 761584 www.kingarthurslabyrinth.co.uk

▶▶▶▶ **81% Ynysymaengwyn Caravan Park** (SH602021)

LL36 9RY
☎ 01654 710684
e-mail: rita@ynysy.co.uk
dir: *On A493, 1m N of Tywyn, towards Dolgellau*

✳ 🚐 £18-£26 🚓 £12-£17 ▲ £12-£35

Open Etr or Apr-Oct

Last arrival 23.00hrs Last departure noon

A lovely park set in the wooded grounds of a former manor house, with designated nature trails through 13 acres of wildlife-rich woodland, scenic river walks, fishing and a sandy beach nearby. The attractive stone amenity block is clean and well kept, and this smart municipal park is ideal for families. 4 acre site. 80 touring pitches. Caravan pitches. Motorhome pitches. Tent pitches. 115 statics.

Leisure: △

Facilities: ⚘ ⊙ ⚑ ☀ ⊕ ⓒ 🧺 ♨ ♻

Services: 🔌 🅾 🅱 ⊘ ♨

Within 3 miles: 🎣 🏇 ℘ ⊙ ⛤ 🛥 ✇ ∪

Notes: ⊚ Dogs must be kept on leads.

SERVICES: 🔌 Electric hook up 🅾 Launderette 🍺 Licensed bar 🅱 Calor Gas ⊘ Camping Gaz 🔧 Toilet fluid 🍽 Café/Restaurant 🏪 Fast Food/Takeaway 🔋 Battery charging 🍼 Baby care ♨ Motorvan service point **ABBREVIATIONS:** BH/bank hols-bank holidays Etr-Easter Spring BH-Spring Bank Holiday dep-departure fr-from hrs-hours m-mile mdnt-midnight rdbt-roundabout rs-restricted service wk-week wknd-weekend x-rds-cross roads ⊛ No credit cards ⊗ No dogs 👪 Children of all ages accepted See page 9 for details of the AA Camping Card Scheme

ISLAWRFFORDD CARAVAN PARK

A family owned park Est. 1957

TALYBONT, NR BARMOUTH, GWYNEDD, LL43 2AQ, NORTH WALES

01341 247269

Email: info@islawrffordd.co.uk   www.islawrffordd.co.uk

AA
▶▶▶▶▶

"AA CAMPSITE OF THE YEAR 2012"

Family owned and run since being established in 1957, Islawrffordd Caravan Park offers the very best in quality which you are immediately aware of when entering the award winning reception building now to be complimented in 2011 with similar architectural design to the laundry, bar and amusement/take-away facilities.

Situated at the southern end of the magnificent Snowdonia National Park coastline in the village of Talybont, Islawrffordd offers 201 holiday home bases, 75 touring caravan/ motorhome plots and 30 camping pitches all benefitting from the very best facilities, including a heated indoor swimming pool/sauna/ jacuzzi and tanning suite.

Nigel Mansell, O.B.E. & 1992 Formula 1 World Champion & Indy Car World Champion 1993 has a Holiday Home association with Islawrffordd that stretches back from the present day to his childhood and his opinion of the Snowdonia Coastline area and our park is still the same
"It's absolutely fantastic".

Choice of a Champion

LEISURE: 🏊 Indoor swimming pool 🏊 Outdoor swimming pool 🛝 Children's playground 🙌 Kid's club 🎾 Tennis court 🎱 Games room 📺 Separate TV room ⛳ 9/18 hole golf course 🚣 Boats for hire 🎬 Cinema 🎵 Entertainment 🎣 Fishing ⛳ Mini golf 🏄 Watersports 🏋 Gym 🏟 Sports field **Spa** ♨ Stables
FACILITIES: 🛁 Bath 🚿 Shower 💈 Electric shaver 💨 Hairdryer ❄ Ice Pack Facility ♿ Disabled facilities 📞 Public telephone 🛒 Shop on site or within 200yds 🛒 Mobile shop (calls at least 5 days a week) 🍖 BBQ area 🧺 Picnic area 📶 Wi-fi 💻 Internet access ♻ Recycling ℹ Tourist info 🐕 Dog exercise area

MONMOUTHSHIRE

ABERGAVENNY — Map 9 SO21

Places to visit

White Castle, WHITE CASTLE, NP7 8UD,
01600 780380 www.cadw.wales.gov.uk

Hen Gwrt, LLANTILIO CROSSENNY, 01443 336000
www.cadw.wales.gov.uk

Great for kids: Raglan Castle, RAGLAN,
NP15 2BT, 01291 690228
www.cadw.wales.gov.uk

NEW ►►►► 83% Wernddu Caravan Park (SO321153)

Old Ross Rd NP7 8NG
☎ 01873 856223
e-mail: info@wernddu-golf-club.co.uk
dir: From A465, N of Abergavenny, take B4521
signed Skenfrith. Site on right in 0.25m

* ⊞ ⊞ Å

Open Mar-Oct

Last arrival 21.00hrs Last departure noon

Located north of the town centre, this former fruit
farm, adjacent to a golf club and driving range, is
managed by three generations of the same family,
and has been transformed into an ideal base for
those visiting the many nearby attractions. The
well-spaced touring pitches have water, electricity
and waste water disposal, and the smart modern
amenities block provides very good privacy
options. Site guests are welcome to use the golf
club bar which also serves meals during the busy
months; they are also eligible for half-price green
fees. There is no shop on site but a daily
newspaper service is provided, and a mini-market
is less than a mile away. 6 acre site. 70 touring
pitches. 20 hardstandings. 30 seasonal pitches.
Caravan pitches. Motorhome pitches. Tent pitches.
20 statics.

AA Pubs & Restaurants nearby: Walnut Tree Inn,
ABERGAVENNY, NP7 8AW, 01873 852797

Angel Hotel, ABERGAVENNY, NP7 5EN,
01873 857121

Facilities: ⋔ & ⊼ ⊰ ㎲ ❶
Services: ⊕ 🗑 🐛 🍴 ㎲ ⬇
Within 3 miles: ⌖ ⊟ ⌀ ◎ 🖻 🖺 ∪
Notes: Adults only. Dogs must be kept on leads.

►►► 79% Pyscodlyn Farm Caravan & Camping Site (SO266155)

Llanwenarth Citra NP7 7ER
☎ 01873 853271 & 07816 447942
e-mail: pyscodlyn.farm@virgin.net
dir: From Abergavenny take A40 (Brecon road),
site 1.5m from entrance of Nevill Hall Hospital, on
left 50yds past phone box

⊞ ⊞ Å

Open Apr-Oct

With its outstanding views of the mountains, this
quiet park in the Brecon Beacons National Park
makes a pleasant venue for country lovers. The
Sugarloaf Mountain and the River Usk are within
easy walking distance and, despite being a
working farm, dogs are welcome. Please note that
credit cards are not taken on this site. 4.5 acre
site. 60 touring pitches. Caravan pitches.
Motorhome pitches. Tent pitches. 6 statics.

AA Pubs & Restaurants nearby: Angel Hotel,
ABERGAVENNY, NP7 5EN, 01873 857121

Walnut Tree Inn, ABERGAVENNY, NP7 8AW,
01873 852797

Facilities: ⋔ ⊙ ✳ & ㎲ ❂ ❶
Services: ⊕ 🗑 🐛 ⌀ ⬇
Within 3 miles: ⌖ ⊟ ⌀ ◎ 🖻 ∪
Notes: 🐕 Dogs must be kept on leads.

DINGESTOW — Map 9 SO41

Places to visit

Raglan Castle, RAGLAN, NP15 2BT, 01291 690228
www.cadw.wales.gov.uk

Tintern Abbey, TINTERN PARVA, NP16 6SE,
01291 689251 www.cadw.wales.gov.uk

Great for kids: The Nelson Museum & Local
History Centre, MONMOUTH, NP25 3XA,
01600 710630

►►► 84% Bridge Caravan Park & Camping Site (SO459104)

Bridge Farm NP25 4DY
☎ 01600 740241
e-mail: info@bridgecaravanpark.co.uk
dir: Telephone site for detailed directions

⊞ £15-£18 ⊞ £15-£18 Å £15-£18

Open Etr-Oct

Last arrival 22.00hrs Last departure 16.00hrs

The River Trothy runs along the edge of this quiet
village park, which has been owned by the same
family for many years. Touring pitches are both
grass and hardstanding, and there is a backdrop
of woodland. The quality facilities are enhanced by
good laundry equipment. River fishing is available
on site, and there is a dog walking area. The
village shop is within 100 yards and a play field
within 200 yards. 4 acre site. 94 touring pitches.
15 hardstandings. Caravan pitches. Motorhome
pitches. Tent pitches.

AA Pubs & Restaurants nearby: The Beaufort
Arms Coaching Inn & Brasserie, RAGLAN,
NP15 2DY, 01291 690412

Facilities: ⋔ ⊙ ⌀ ✳ & ◔ 🖻 ㎲ ❂ ❶
Services: ⊕ 🗑 🐛 ⌀ 🆃 ⬆ ⬇
Within 3 miles: ⌖ ⬆ ⊟ ⌀ 🖻 🖺 ∪
Notes: 🐕 Dogs must be kept on leads.

SERVICES: ⊕ Electric hook up 🗑 Launderette 🐛 Licensed bar 🐛 Calor Gas ⌀ Camping Gaz 🆃 Toilet fluid 🍴 Café/Restaurant ㎲ Fast Food/Takeaway
⬆ Battery charging ⬇ Baby care ⬇ Motorvan service point **ABBREVIATIONS:** BH/bank hols-bank holidays Etr-Easter Spring BH-Spring Bank Holiday dep-departure
fr-from hrs-hours m-mile mdnt-midnight rdbt-roundabout rs-restricted service wk-week wknd-weekend x-rds-cross roads 🐕 No credit cards 🐕 No dogs
⅋ Children of all ages accepted See page 9 for details of the AA Camping Card Scheme

USK — Map 9 SO30

Places to visit

Caerleon Roman Fortress and Baths, CAERLEON, NP18 1AE, 01663 422518 www.cadw.wales.gov.uk

Big Pit National Coal Museum, BLAENAVON, NP4 9XP, 029 20573650 www.museumwales.ac.uk

Great for kids: Greenmeadow Community Farm, CWMBRAN, NP44 5AJ, 01633 647662 www.greenmeadowcommunityfarm.org.uk

PREMIER PARK

►►►►► 85% Pont Kemys Caravan & Camping Park *(SO348058)*

Chainbridge NP7 9DS
☎ 01873 880688
e-mail: info@pontkemys.com
web: www.pontkemys.com
dir: *From Usk take B4598 towards Abergavenny. Approx 4m, over river bridge, bear right, 300yds to site. For other routes contact site for detailed directions*

* 🚐 £15-£19 🚌 £15-£19 ⛺ £15-£17

Open Mar-Oct

Last arrival 21.00hrs Last departure noon

A peaceful park next to the River Usk, offering an excellent standard of toilet facilities with family rooms. A section of the park has fully serviced pitches. The park is in a rural area with mature trees and country views, and attracts quiet visitors who enjoy the many attractions of this area. The local golf club is open during the day and serves breakfast and lunches. 8 acre site. 65 touring pitches. 29 hardstandings. 25 seasonal pitches. Caravan pitches. Motorhome pitches. Tent pitches.

AA Pubs & Restaurants nearby: Raglan Arms, USK, NP15 1DL, 01291 690800

The Nags Head Inn, USK, NP15 1BH, 01291 672820

The Three Salmons Hotel, USK, NP15 1RY, 01291 672133

Leisure: ⚽ 📺

Facilities: 🚿 ⊙ 💇 ✱ ♿ ✆ 🛒 🧺 🐕 [Wi-fi] 💻 ♻ ℹ

Services: 🔌 🫧 🔒 🍃 [T] 🛏 ⚓

Within 3 miles: ⛳ ⛵ 🎣 🛒

Notes: No music. Dogs must be kept on leads. Mother & baby room, kitchen facilities for groups.

PEMBROKESHIRE

BROAD HAVEN — Map 8 SM81

Places to visit

Pembroke Castle, PEMBROKE, SA71 4LA, 01646 681510 www.pembrokecastle.co.uk

Llawhaden Castle, LLAWHADEN, 01443 336000 www.cadw.wales.gov.uk

Great for kids: Scolton Manor Museum & Country Park, SCOLTON, SA62 5QL, 01437 731328 (Museum)

►►► 86% Creampots Touring Caravan & Camping Park *(SM882131)*

Broadway SA62 3TU
☎ 01437 781776
e-mail: creampots@btconnect.com
dir: *From Haverfordwest take B4341 to Broadway. Turn left, follow brown tourist signs to site*

🚐 🚌 ⛺

Open Mar-Nov

Last arrival 21.00hrs Last departure 11.00hrs

Set just outside the Pembrokeshire National Park, this quiet site is just one and a half miles from a safe sandy beach at Broad Haven, and the coastal footpath. The park is well laid out and carefully maintained, and the toilet block offers a good standard of facilities. The owners welcome families. 8 acre site. 72 touring pitches. 32 hardstandings. Caravan pitches. Motorhome pitches. Tent pitches. 1 static.

AA Pubs & Restaurants nearby: The Swan Inn, LITTLE HAVEN, SA62 3UL, 01437 781880

Facilities: 🚿 ⊙ 💇 ✱ ♿ 🧺 [Wi-fi] ♻ ℹ

Services: 🔌 🫧 🔒 🍃 🛏

Within 3 miles: ⛵ 🎬 🎣 🏄 🛒 🫧 🐴

Notes: Dogs must be kept on leads.

►►► 77% South Cockett Caravan & Camping Park *(SM878136)*

South Cockett SA62 3TU
☎ 01437 781296 & 781760
e-mail: esmejames@hotmail.co.uk
dir: *From Haverfordwest take B4341 to Broad Haven, at Broadway turn left, site 300yds*

🚐 🚌 ⛺

Open Etr-Oct

Last arrival 22.30hrs

A warm welcome is assured at this small site on a working farm. The touring areas are divided into neat paddocks by high, well-trimmed hedges, and there are good toilet facilities. The lovely beach at Broad Haven is only about two miles away. 6 acre site. 73 touring pitches. Caravan pitches. Motorhome pitches. Tent pitches.

AA Pubs & Restaurants nearby: The Swan Inn, LITTLE HAVEN, SA62 3UL, 01437 781880

Facilities: 🚿 ⊙ ✱ ✆ ♻

Services: 🔌 🫧 🔒 🍃 🛏

Within 3 miles: ⛵ 🎣 🏄 🛒 🫧 🐴

Notes: ⊘ Dogs must be kept on leads.

LEISURE: 🏊 Indoor swimming pool 🌊 Outdoor swimming pool 🛝 Children's playground 👋 Kid's club 🎾 Tennis court 🎱 Games room 📺 Separate TV room ⛳ 9/18 hole golf course ⛵ Boats for hire 🎬 Cinema 🎭 Entertainment 🎣 Fishing ◎ Mini golf 🏄 Watersports 🏋 Gym ⚽ Sports field **Spa** 🐴 Stables
FACILITIES: 🛁 Bath 🚿 Shower ⊙ Electric shaver 💇 Hairdryer ✱ Ice Pack Facility ♿ Disabled facilities ✆ Public telephone 🛒 Shop on site or within 200yds 🚚 Mobile shop (calls at least 5 days a week) 🍖 BBQ area 🧺 Picnic area [Wi-fi] Wi-fi 💻 Internet access ♻ Recycling ℹ Tourist info 🐕 Dog exercise area

FISHGUARD — Map 8 SM93

Places to visit

Pentre Ifan Burial Chamber, NEWPORT, 01443 336000 www.cadw.wales.gov.uk

Tredegar House & Park, NEWPORT, NP10 8YW, 01633 815880 www.newport.gov.uk

Great for kids: OceanLab, FISHGUARD, SA64 0DE, 01348 874737 www.ocean-lab.co.uk

►►► 89% Fishguard Bay Caravan & Camping Park (SM984383)

Garn Gelli SA65 9ET
☎ 01348 811415
e-mail: enquiries@fishguardbay.com
web: www.fishguardbay.com
dir: *If approaching Fishguard from Cardigan on A487 ignore Sat Nav to turn right. Turn at camp site sign onto single track road*

* ⬤ £18.50-£22.50 ⬤ £18.50-£22.50 ▲ £17.50-£25.50

Open Mar-9 Jan

Last arrival anytime Last departure noon

Set high up on cliffs with outstanding views of Fishguard Bay, this site has the Pembrokeshire Coastal Path running right through its centre, so affording many opportunities for wonderful walks. The park is extremely well kept, with a good toilet block, a common room with TV, a lounge/library, decent laundry and a well-stocked shop. 5 acre site. 50 touring pitches. 4 hardstandings. Caravan pitches. Motorhome pitches. Tent pitches. 50 statics.

AA Pubs & Restaurants nearby: The Sloop Inn, PORTHGAIN, SA62 5BN, 01348 831449

The Shed, PORTHGAIN, SA62 5BN, 01348 831518

Salutation Inn, NEWPORT, SA41 3UY, 01239 820564

Fishgard Bay Caravan & Camping Park

Leisure: ⚲ ⬤ ☐
Facilities: ⬤⊙℘✳⊙⬤⬤⚲ᴡᶠⁱ ⬤ ⬤
Services: ⬤⬤⬤⬤Ⓣ⬤
Within 3 miles: ⬤⬤℘⬤⬤⬤⬤
Notes: Dogs must be kept on leads.

►►► 78% Gwaun Vale Touring Park (SM977356)

Llanychaer SA65 9TA
☎ 01348 874698
e-mail: margaret.harries@talk21.com
dir: *B4313 from Fishguard. Site 1.5m on right*

⬤ ⬤ ▲

Open Apr-Oct

Last arrival anytime Last departure 11.00hrs

Located in the beautiful Gwaun Valley, this carefully landscaped park, with colourful, seasonal flowers, is set on the hillside with generously sized, tiered pitches on two levels that provide superb views of the surrounding countryside. 1.6 acre site. 29 touring pitches. 5 hardstandings. Caravan pitches. Motorhome pitches. Tent pitches. 1 static.

AA Pubs & Restaurants nearby: The Sloop Inn, PORTHGAIN, SA62 5BN, 01348 831449

The Shed, PORTHGAIN, SA62 5BN, 01348 831518

Salutation Inn, NEWPORT, SA41 3UY, 01239 820564

Leisure: ⚲
Facilities: ⬤⊙℘✳⊙⬤⬤⬤
Services: ⬤⬤⬤
Within 3 miles: ⬤⬤℘⬤⬤⬤
Notes: ⊛ No skateboards. Dogs must be kept on leads. Guidebooks available.

HASGUARD CROSS — Map 8 SM80

Places to visit

Pembroke Castle, PEMBROKE, SA71 4LA, 01646 681510 www.pembrokecastle.co.uk

AA CAMPING CARD SITE

►►► 83% Hasguard Cross Caravan Park (SM850108)

SA62 3SL
☎ 01437 781443
e-mail: hasguard@aol.com
dir: *From Haverfordwest take B4327 towards Dale. In 7m right at x-rds. Site 1st right*

* ⬤ £15-£19 ⬤ £15-£19 ▲ £15-£19

Open all year (rs Aug tent field for 28 days)

Last arrival 21.00hrs Last departure 10.00hrs

A very clean, efficient and well-run site in the Pembrokeshire National Park, just one and a half miles from the sea and beach at Little Haven, and with views of the surrounding hills. The toilet and shower facilities are immaculately clean, and there is a licensed bar (evenings only) serving a good choice of food. 4.5 acre site. 12 touring pitches. 3 hardstandings. Caravan pitches. Motorhome pitches. Tent pitches. 42 statics.

AA Pubs & Restaurants nearby: The Swan Inn, LITTLE HAVEN, SA62 3UL, 01437 781880

Leisure: ⚲
Facilities: ⬤⊙℘✳⬤⊙⬤⬤⬤⬤
Services: ⬤⬤⬤⬤⬤⬤⬤⬤
Within 3 miles: ⬤⬤℘⬤⬤⬤⬤
Notes: Dogs must be kept on leads.

HAVERFORDWEST Map 8 SM91

Places to visit

Llawhaden Castle, LLAWHADEN, 01443 336000 www.cadw.wales.gov.uk

Carew Castle & Tidal Mill, CAREW, SA70 8SL, 01646 651782 www.carewcastle.com

Great for kids: Oakwood Theme Park, NARBERTH, SA67 8DE, 01834 815170 www.oakwoodthemepark.co.uk

►► 81% *Nolton Cross Caravan Park* *(SM879177)*

Nolton SA62 3NP
☎ 01437 710701
e-mail: info@noltoncross-holidays.co.uk
web: www.noltoncross-holidays.co.uk
dir: *1m from A487 (Haverfordwest to St Davids road) at Simpson Cross, towards Nolton & Broadhaven*

🚐 🚙 ⛺

Open Mar-Dec

Last arrival 22.00hrs Last departure noon

High grassy banks surround the touring area of this park next to the owners' working farm. It is located on open ground above the sea and St Bride's Bay (within one and a half miles), and there is a coarse fishing lake close by - equipment for hire and reduced permit rates for campers are available. 4 acre site. 15 touring pitches. Caravan pitches. Motorhome pitches. Tent pitches. 30 statics.

AA Pubs & Restaurants nearby: The Swan Inn, LITTLE HAVEN, SA62 3UL, 01437 781880

Leisure: 🛝

Facilities: 🚿 ⊙ ❄ 📞 🛒 ⛱ 📶 ♻ ℹ

Services: 🗨 🧺 🔥 [T] 🔋

Within 3 miles: 🎣 🏄 🛒 🧺 🐴

Notes: No youth groups. Dogs must be kept on leads.

LITTLE HAVEN

See Hasguard Cross

ST DAVIDS Map 8 SM72

Places to visit

St Davids Bishop's Palace, ST DAVIDS, SA62 6PE, 01437 720517 www.cadw.wales.gov.uk

St Davids Cathedral, ST DAVID'S, SA62 6PE, 01437 720202 www.stdavidscathedral.org.uk

Great for kids: Oakwood Theme Park, NARBERTH, SA67 8DE, 01834 815170 www.oakwoodthemepark.co.uk

PREMIER PARK

►►►►► 88% Caerfai Bay Caravan & Tent Park *(SM759244)*

Caerfai Bay SA62 6QT
☎ 01437 720274
e-mail: info@caerfaibay.co.uk
web: www.caerfaibay.co.uk
dir: *In St Davids exit A487 at Visitor Centre/ Grove Hotel. Follow signs for Caerfai Bay. Right at end of road*

🚐 🚙 ⛺

Open Mar-mid Nov

Last arrival 21.00hrs Last departure 11.00hrs

Magnificent coastal scenery and an outlook over St Bride's Bay can be enjoyed from this delightful site, located just 300 yards from a bathing beach. The excellent toilet facilities include four family rooms, which are a huge asset to the park, and ongoing improvements include a second, solar-heated wet suit shower room, upgraded roadways, and modernised water points. There is an excellent farm shop just across the road. 10 acre site. 106 touring pitches. 26 hardstandings. Caravan pitches. Motorhome pitches. Tent pitches. 30 statics.

AA Pubs & Restaurants nearby: Cwtch, ST DAVIDS, SA62 6SD, 01437 720491

The Sloop Inn, PORTHGAIN, SA62 5BN, 01348 831449

The Shed, PORTHGAIN, SA62 5BN, 01348 831518

Facilities: 🚿 ⊙ 💨 ❄ ♿ 📞 🐕 📶 💻 ♻ ℹ

Services: 🗨 🧺 🛢 🔥 🔋 🍴 🍸

Within 3 miles: ⛳ ⛵ 🎣 🏄 🛒 🧺

Notes: No dogs in tent field mid Jul-Aug, no skateboards or rollerblades. Dogs must be kept on leads.

►►► 82% *Tretio Caravan & Camping Park* *(SM787292)*

SA62 6DE
☎ 01437 781600
e-mail: info@tretio.com
dir: *From St Davids take A487 towards Fishguard, left at Rugby Football Club, straight on for 3m. Site signed, left to site*

🚐 🚙 ⛺

Open Mar-Oct

Last arrival 20.00hrs Last departure 10.00hrs

An attractive site in a very rural spot with distant country views, and close to beautiful beaches; the tiny cathedral city of St Davids is only three miles away. A mobile shop calls daily at peak periods, and orienteering advice and maps are available for couples and families. 6.5 acre site. 40 touring pitches. 8 seasonal pitches. Caravan pitches. Motorhome pitches. Tent pitches. 30 statics.

AA Pubs & Restaurants nearby: Cwtch, ST DAVIDS, SA62 6SD, 01437 720491

The Sloop Inn, PORTHGAIN, SA62 5BN, 01348 831449

The Shed, PORTHGAIN, SA62 5BN, 01348 831518

Leisure: 🛝 ⚽

Facilities: 🚿 ⊙ 💨 ❄ ♿ 🚚 🐕 ♻ ℹ

Services: 🗨 🧺 🔥 [T] 🔋

Within 3 miles: ⛳ ⛵ 🎣 ◎ 🏄 🛒 🧺

Notes: Dogs must be kept on leads. Pitch & putt.

►►► 81% Hendre Eynon Camping & Caravan Site *(SM771284)*

SA62 6DB
☎ 01437 720474
e-mail: hendreeynoninfo@gmail.com
dir: *Take A487 (Fishguard road) from St Davids, left at rugby club signed Llanrhian. Site 2m on right (NB do no take turn to Whitesands)*

* ♠ £14-£20 ♠ £14-£20 Å £14-£20

Open Apr-Sep

Last arrival 21.00hrs Last departure noon

A peaceful country site on a working farm, with a modern toilet block including family rooms. Within easy reach of many lovely sandy beaches, and two miles from the cathedral city of St Davids. 7 acre site. 50 touring pitches. 20 seasonal pitches. Caravan pitches. Motorhome pitches. Tent pitches.

AA Pubs & Restaurants nearby: Cwtch, ST DAVIDS, SA62 6SD, 01437 720491

The Sloop Inn, PORTHGAIN, SA62 5BN, 01348 831449

The Shed, PORTHGAIN, SA62 5BN, 01348 831518

Facilities: ♠ ⊙ ✳ ⓒ ♠ ⑦
Services: ⌾ ⑤ ♠ ⌀ ⌷
Within 3 miles: ⌂ ⌇ ⌀ ⌇ ⑤ ⑤
Notes: ⌾ Maximum 2 dogs per unit. Dogs must be kept on leads.

TENBY   Map 8 SN10

Places to visit

Tudor Merchant's House, TENBY, SA70 7BX, 01834 842279 www.nationaltrust.org.ukmain-w-tudormerchantshouse

Great for kids: Colby Woodland Garden, AMROTH, SA67 8PP, 01834 811885 www.nationaltrust.org.uk/main

86% Kiln Park Holiday Centre *(SN119002)*

Marsh Rd SA70 7RB
☎ 0871 231 0889
e-mail: kilnpark@haven.com
web: www.haven.com/kilnpark
dir: *Follow A477, A478 to Tenby for 6m. Then follow signs to Penally, site 0.5m on left*

♠ ♠ Å

Open mid Mar-end Oct (rs mid Mar-May & Sep-Oct some facilities may be reduced)

Last arrival dusk Last departure 10.00hrs

Kiln Park Holiday Centre

A large holiday complex complete with leisure and sports facilities and lots of entertainment for all the family. There are bars and cafés and plenty of security. This touring, camping and static site is on the outskirts of town, and it's only a short walk through dunes to the sandy beach. The modern amenities block provides a stylish interior with under-floor heating and superb fixtures and fittings. 103 acre site. 130 touring pitches. Caravan pitches. Motorhome pitches. Tent pitches. 703 statics.

AA Pubs & Restaurants nearby: Hope and Anchor, TENBY, SA70 7AX, 01834 842131

Leisure: ⌾ ⌾ ⛄ ⌇ ⌾ ⚽ ⌡

Facilities: ♠ ⌾ ⌖ ⓒ ⑤ ⌾ ♣

Services: ⌾ ⑤ ⌾ ♠ ⌀ ⌾ ⌷ ♠

Within 3 miles: ⌂ ⌇ ⌗ ⌀ ⌇ ⑤ ⑤ ∪

Notes: No commercial vehicles, no bookings by persons under 21yrs unless a family booking. Max 2 dogs per booking, certain dog breeds banned. Dogs must be kept on leads. Entertainment complex, bowling & putting green.

see advert below

SERVICES: ⌾ Electric hook up ⑤ Launderette ⌾ Licensed bar ♠ Calor Gas ⌀ Camping Gaz ⑤ Toilet fluid ⌾ Café/Restaurant ⌾ Fast Food/Takeaway ⌷ Battery charging ♠ Baby care ⌦ Motorvan service point **ABBREVIATIONS:** BH/bank hols-bank holidays Etr-Easter Spring BH-Spring Bank Holiday dep-departure fr-from hrs-hours m-mile mdnt-midnight rdbt-roundabout rs-restricted service wk-week wknd-weekend x-rds-cross roads ⌾ No credit cards ⓧ No dogs ♠ Children of all ages accepted See page 9 for details of the AA Camping Card Scheme

TENBY *continued*

▶▶▶▶ 87% *Trefalun Park* (SN093027)

Devonshire Dr, St Florence SA70 8RD
☎ 01646 651514
e-mail: trefalun@aol.com
dir: *1.5m NW of St Florence & 0.5m N of B4318*

Open Etr-Oct
Last arrival 19.00hrs Last departure noon

Set within 12 acres of sheltered, well-kept grounds, this quiet country park offers well-maintained level grass pitches separated by bushes and trees, with plenty of space to relax in. Children can feed the park's friendly pets. Plenty of activities are available at the nearby Heatherton Country Sports Park, including go-karting, indoor bowls, golf and bumper boating. 12 acre site. 90 touring pitches. 54 hardstandings. 45 seasonal pitches. Caravan pitches. Motorhome pitches. Tent pitches. 10 statics.

AA Pubs & Restaurants nearby: Hope and Anchor, TENBY, SA70 7AX, 01834 842131

Trefalun Park

Leisure: ⚐
Facilities: ⚲⊙📷❄♿🕙🐕 📶 ♻ ❶
Services: ⚡🗑🛢🚮Ⓣ🛒↯
Within 3 miles: ♨✈◎♨🏇🛒🗑
Notes: No motorised scooters. Dogs must be kept on leads.

see advert below

LEISURE: 🏊 Indoor swimming pool 🏊 Outdoor swimming pool ⚐ Children's playground 🪁 Kid's club 🎾 Tennis court 🎱 Games room 📺 Separate TV room ⛳ 9/18 hole golf course ⛵ Boats for hire 🎬 Cinema 🎵 Entertainment 🎣 Fishing ◎ Mini golf 🏄 Watersports 🏋 Gym 🏟 Sports field **Spa** ♨ Stables
FACILITIES: 🛁 Bath 🚿 Shower ⊙ Electric shaver ✂ Hairdryer ❄ Ice Pack Facility ♿ Disabled facilities ☎ Public telephone 🛒 Shop on site or within 200yds 🚐 Mobile shop (calls at least 5 days a week) 🍖 BBQ area 🪑 Picnic area 📶 Wi-fi 💻 Internet access ♻ Recycling ❶ Tourist info 🐕 Dog exercise area

AA CAMPING CARD SITE

▶▶▶▶ 82% Well Park Caravan & Camping Site (SN128028)

SA70 8TL
☎ 01834 842179
e-mail: enquiries@wellparkcaravans.co.uk
dir: *A478 towards Tenby. At rdbt at Kilgetty follow Tenby/A478 signs. 3m to next rdbt, take 2nd exit, site 2nd right*

* ⊞ £14-£28 ⊞ £14-£28 ▲ £12-£19

Open Mar-Oct (rs Mar-mid Jun & mid Sep-Oct bar may be closed)

Last arrival 22.00hrs Last departure 11.00hrs

An attractive, well-maintained park with good landscaping from trees, ornamental shrubs and flower borders. The amenities include a launderette and indoor dishwashing, games room with table tennis, and an enclosed play area. The park is ideally situated between Tenby and Saundersfoot; Tenby just a 15-minute walk away, or the town can be reached via a traffic-free cycle track. 10 acre site. 100 touring pitches. 16 hardstandings. Caravan pitches. Motorhome pitches. Tent pitches. 42 statics.

AA Pubs & Restaurants nearby: Hope and Anchor, TENBY, SA70 7AX, 01834 842131

Leisure: ⋒ ⚲ ⊡
Facilities: ⋔ ⊙ ⏃ ✻ ⚲ ⓒ ⊼ ⱳ ♻ ❶
Services: ⊟ ⚐ ⛽ ⬛ ⊘ ⭒ ⭷ ⬦
Within 3 miles: ⬧ ⟓ ⌁ ⊚ ⚞ ⛻ ⊟ ↻

Notes: Family groups only. Dogs must be kept on leads. TV hook-ups.

AA CAMPING CARD SITE

▶▶▶ 78% Wood Park Caravans (SN128025)

New Hedges SA70 8TL
☎ 01834 843414 & 0844 4141464 (winter)
e-mail: info@woodpark.co.uk
dir: *At rdbt 2m N of Tenby follow A478 towards Tenby, take 2nd right & right again*

* ⊞ £15-£25 ⊞ £15-£25 ▲ £14-£19

Open Spring BH-Sep (rs May & mid-end Sep bar, laundrette & games room may not be open)

Last arrival 22.00hrs Last departure 10.00hrs

Situated in beautiful countryside between the popular seaside resorts of Tenby and Saundersfoot, and with Waterwynch Bay just a 15-minute walk away, this peaceful site provides a spacious and relaxing atmosphere for holidays. The slightly sloping touring area is divided by shrubs and hedge-screened paddocks and a licensed bar and games room are also available. 10 acre site. 60 touring pitches. 40 hardstandings. 10 seasonal pitches. Caravan pitches. Motorhome pitches. Tent pitches. 90 statics.

AA Pubs & Restaurants nearby: Hope and Anchor, TENBY, SA70 7AX, 01834 842131

Leisure: ⋒ ⚲
Facilities: ⋔ ⊙ ⏃ ✻ ⱳ ♻ ❶
Services: ⊟ ⚐ ⛽ ⬛ ⭒ ⬦
Within 3 miles: ⬧ ⟓ ⌁ ⊚ ⚞ ⊟

Notes: ⊘ No groups, 1 car per unit, only small dogs accepted, no dogs Jul-Aug & BH. Dogs must be kept on leads.

BRECON — Map 9 SO02

Places to visit
Brecknock Museum & Art Gallery, BRECON, LD3 7DS, 01874 624121
www.powys.gov.uk/breconmuseum

Regimental Museum of The Royal Welsh, BRECON, LD3 7EB, 01874 613310
www.rrw.org.uk

PREMIER PARK

▶▶▶▶▶ 88% Pencelli Castle Caravan & Camping Park (SO096248)

Pencelli LD3 7LX
☎ 01874 665451
e-mail: pencelli@tiscali.co.uk
dir: *Exit A40 2m E of Brecon onto B4558, follow signs to Pencelli*

⊞ ⊞ ▲

Open Feb-27 Nov (rs 30 Oct-Etr shop closed)

Last arrival 22.00hrs Last departure noon

Lying in the heart of the Brecon Beacons National Park, this charming park offers peace, beautiful scenery and high quality facilities. It is bordered by the Brecon and Monmouth Canal. The attention to detail is superb, and the well-equipped heated toilets with en suite cubicles are matched by a drying room for clothes and boots, full laundry, and a shop. Regular buses stop just outside the gate and go to Brecon, Abergavenny and Swansea. 10 acre site. 80 touring pitches. 40 hardstandings. Caravan pitches. Motorhome pitches. Tent pitches.

AA Pubs & Restaurants nearby: The White Swan Inn, BRECON, LD3 7BZ, 01874 665276

Leisure: ⋒ ✿
Facilities: ⋔ ⊙ ⏃ ✻ ⚲ ⓒ ⓢ ⊼ ⱳ ♻ ❶
Services: ⊟ ⚐ ⬛ ⊘ ⊤ ⬦ ⭷
Within 3 miles: ⟓ ⊟ ⌁ ⊟ ⊟ ↻

Notes: No radios, music or camp fires. Assistance dogs only. Cycle hire.

SERVICES: ⊟ Electric hook up ⛽ Launderette ⬛ Licensed bar ⬛ Calor Gas ⊘ Camping Gaz ⊤ Toilet fluid ⓣⓞⓛ Café/Restaurant ⬛ Fast Food/Takeaway ⬦ Battery charging ⭒ Baby care ⬦ Motorvan service point **ABBREVIATIONS:** BH/bank hols-bank holidays Etr-Easter Spring BH-Spring Bank Holiday dep-departure fr-from hrs-hours m-mile mdnt-midnight rdbt-roundabout rs-restricted service wk-week wknd-weekend x-rds-cross roads ⊘ No credit cards ⊗ No dogs ⬦ Children of all ages accepted See page 9 for details of the AA Camping Card Scheme

BRONLLYS Map 9 SO13

Places to visit

Brecknock Museum & Art Gallery, BRECON, LD3 7DS, 01874 624121 www.powys.gov.uk/breconmuseum

Regimental Museum of The Royal Welsh, BRECON, LD3 7EB, 01874 613310 www.rrw.org.uk

AA CAMPING CARD SITE

►►►► 80% Anchorage Caravan Park *(SO142351)*

LD3 0LD
☎ 01874 711246 & 711230
dir: *8m NE of Brecon in village centre*

🚐 fr £13 🚌 fr £13 ⛺ fr £13

Open all year (rs Nov-Mar TV room closed)

Last arrival 23.00hrs Last departure 18.00hrs

A well-maintained site with a choice of south-facing, sloping grass pitches and superb views of the Black Mountains, or a more sheltered lower area with a number of excellent super pitches. The site is a short distance from the water sports centre at Llangorse Lake. 8 acre site. 110 touring pitches. 8 hardstandings. 60 seasonal pitches. Caravan pitches. Motorhome pitches. Tent pitches. 101 statics.

AA Pubs & Restaurants nearby: Castle Inn, TALGARTH, LD3 0EP, 01874 711353

The Old Black Lion, HAY-ON-WYE, HR3 5AD, 01497 820841

Leisure: 🛝 📺

Facilities: 🚿 ⊙ 💨 ❄ ♿ ☎ [S] 🧺 🐕 ♻ ℹ

Services: 🚐 ⊡ 🔒 🔋 [T] 🍴

Within 3 miles: 🎣 [S] ⊡ 🐴

Notes: Dogs must be kept on leads. Post office, hairdresser.

BUILTH WELLS Map 9 SO05

►►►► 84% *Fforest Fields Caravan & Camping Park* *(SO100535)*

Hundred House LD1 5RT
☎ 01982 570406
e-mail: office@fforestfields.co.uk
web: www.fforestfields.co.uk
dir: *From town follow New Radnor signs on A481. 4m to signed entrance on right, 0.5m before Hundred House village*

🚐 🚌 ⛺

Open Etr & Apr-Oct

Last arrival 21.00hrs Last departure 18.00hrs

A constantly improving, sheltered park surrounded by magnificent scenery and an abundance of wildlife. The spacious pitches are well spaced to create optimum privacy, and the superb eco-friendly amenities block is fuelled by solar panels and a bio-mass boiler. The historic town of Builth Wells and The Royal Welsh Showground are just four miles away. 12 acre site. 60 touring pitches. 17 hardstandings. Caravan pitches. Motorhome pitches. Tent pitches.

AA Pubs & Restaurants nearby: The Laughing Dog, LLANDRINDOD WELLS, LD1 5PT, 01597 822406

Facilities: 🚿 ⊙ 💨 ❄ ☎ 🐕 [Wi-fi]

Services: 🚐 ⊡ 🔒 🔋 🍴

Within 3 miles: ⛳ 🎬 🎣 [S] ⊡

Notes: 🚫 No loud music or revelry. Bread, dairy produce & cured bacon available.

CHURCHSTOKE Map 15 SO29

Places to visit

Montgomery Castle, MONTGOMERY, 01443 336000 www.cadw.wales.gov.uk

PREMIER PARK

NEW ►►►►► 84% Daisy Bank Caravan Park *(SO309926)*

Snead SY15 6EB
☎ 01588 620471 & 07918 680713
e-mail: enquiries@daisy-bank.co.uk
dir: *On A489, 2m E of Churchstoke*

* 🚐 £18-£27 🚌 £18-£27 ⛺ £18-£24

Open all year

Last arrival 20.00hrs Last departure 13.00hrs

Peacefully located between Craven Arms and Churchstoke and surrounded by rolling hills, this idyllic, adults-only park offers generously sized, fully serviced pitches; all are situated in attractive hedged areas, surrounded by lush grass and pretty seasonal flowers. The immaculately maintained amenity blocks provide smart, modern fittings and excellent privacy options. Camping pods, a pitch and putt course and free Wi-fi are also available. 7 acre site. 80 touring pitches. 75 hardstandings. 30 seasonal pitches. Caravan pitches. Motorhome pitches. Tent pitches. 2 wooden pods.

Facilities: 🚿 💨 ❄ ♿ ☎ [S] 🐕 [Wi-fi] 💻 ♻ ℹ

Services: 🚐 ⊡ 🔒 🔋 [T]

Within 3 miles: ◎ [S] ⊡

Notes: Adults only. Dogs must be kept on leads. Caravan storage.

CRICKHOWELL

Places to visit

Tretower Court & Castle, TRETOWER, NP8 1RD, 01874 730279 www.cadw.wales.gov.uk

Big Pit National Coal Museum, BLAENAVON, NP4 9XP, 029 20573650 www.museumwales.ac.uk

Great for kids: Grosmont Castle, GROSMONT, 01981 240301 www.cadw.wales.gov.uk

CRICKHOWELL — Map 9 SO21

▶▶▶ 80% Riverside Caravan & Camping Park *(SO215184)*

New Rd NP8 1AY
☎ 01873 810397
dir: *On A4077, well signed from A40*

* ⌂ fr £16 ⌂ fr £16 ▲ fr £12

Open Mar-Oct

Last arrival 21.00hrs

A very well tended adults-only park in delightful countryside on the edge of the small country town of Crickhowell. The adjacent riverside park is an excellent facility for all, including dog-walkers. Crickhowell has numerous specialist shops including a first-class delicatessen. Within a few minutes' walk of the park are several friendly pubs with good restaurants. 3.5 acre site. 35 touring pitches. Caravan pitches. Motorhome pitches. Tent pitches. 20 statics.

AA Pubs & Restaurants nearby: The Bear Hotel, CRICKHOWELL, NP8 1BW, 01873 810408

Facilities: ⌂ ⊙ ℮ ✻ ⓢ ❼
Services: ☎ ⓐ ⛟
Within 3 miles: ⌂ ⛾ ⓢ ∪

Notes: Adults only. ⊗ No hang gliders or paragliders. Dogs must be kept on leads. Large canopied area for drying clothes, cooking & socialising.

LLANDRINDOD WELLS — Map 9 SO06

Places to visit
The Judge's Lodging, PRESTEIGNE, LD8 2AD, 01544 260650 www.judgeslodging.org.uk

AA CAMPING CARD SITE

▶▶▶▶ 81% Disserth Caravan & Camping Park *(SO035583)*

Disserth, Howey LD1 6NL
☎ 01597 860277
e-mail: disserthcaravan@btconnect.com
dir: *1m from A483, between Newbridge-on-Wye & Howey, by church. Follow brown signs from A483 or A470*

* ⌂ £16.50-£25 ⌂ £16.50-£25 ▲ £8.50-£35

Open Mar-Oct

Last arrival sunset Last departure noon

A delightfully secluded and predominantly adult park, by a 13th-century church, that sits in a beautiful valley on the banks of the River Ithon, a tributary of the River Wye. It has a small bar which is open at weekends and during busy periods. The amenities block and laundry have now been upgraded to a high standard and provide good privacy options. 4 acre site. 30 touring pitches. 6 hardstandings. Caravan pitches. Motorhome pitches. Tent pitches. 25 statics. 1 wooden pod.

AA Pubs & Restaurants nearby: The Laughing Dog, LLANDRINDOD WELLS, LD1 5PT, 01597 822406

The Bell Country Inn, LLANDRINDOD WELLS, LD1 6DY, 01597 823959

Facilities: ⌂ ⊙ ℮ ✻ ❤ ⓦⓘⓕⓘ ♺ ❼
Services: ☎ ⓢ ⓣⓘ ⓐ ⌁ ⊤ ⛟
Within 3 miles: ⌂ ⛘ ℮ ⓢ ⓢ ∪

Notes: ⊗ Dogs must be kept on leads. Private trout fishing.

▶▶ 82% Dalmore Camping & Caravanning Park *(SO045568)*

Howey LD1 5RG
☎ 01597 822483
dir: *3m S of Llandrindod Wells off A483. 4m N of Builth Wells, at top of hill*

⌂ ⌂ ▲

Open Mar-Oct

Last arrival 22.00hrs Last departure noon

An intimate and well laid out adults-only park. Pitches are attractively terraced to ensure that all enjoy the wonderful views from this splendidly landscaped little park. 3 acre site. 20 touring pitches. 12 hardstandings. 6 seasonal pitches. Caravan pitches. Motorhome pitches. Tent pitches. 20 statics.

AA Pubs & Restaurants nearby: The Laughing Dog, LLANDRINDOD WELLS, LD1 5PT, 01597 822406

The Bell Country Inn, LLANDRINDOD WELLS, LD1 6DY, 01597 823959

Facilities: ⌂ ⊙ ℮ ✻ ⓒ ⓛ ❼
Services: ☎ ⓐ ⌁ ⛟ ⓥ
Within 3 miles: ⌂ ⛘ ℮ ◎ ⓢ ⓢ

Notes: Adults only. ⊗ Gates closed 23.00hrs-07.00hrs, no ball games. Dogs must be kept on leads. Male & female washing areas, no cubicles.

LLANGORS — Map 9 SO12

Places to visit
Llanthony Priory, LLANTHONY, 01443 336000 www.cadw.wales.gov.uk

Great for kids: Tretower Court & Castle, TRETOWER, NP8 1RD, 01874 730279 www.cadw.wales.gov.uk

▶▶▶ 76% Lakeside Caravan Park *(SO128272)*

LD3 7TR
☎ 01874 658226
e-mail: holidays@llangorselake.co.uk
dir: *Exit A40 at Bwlch onto B4560 towards Talgarth. Site signed towards lake in Llangors centre*

* ⌂ £12.50-£14.50 ⌂ £12.50-£14.50 ▲ £12.50-£14.50

Open Etr or Apr-Oct (rs Mar-May & Oct clubhouse, restaurant, shop limited)

Last arrival 21.30hrs Last departure 10.00hrs

Surrounded by spectacular mountains and set alongside Llangors Lake, with mooring and launching facilities, this is a must-do holiday destination for lovers of outdoor pursuits - from walking to watersports and even pike fishing for which the lake is renowned. The hedge- or tree-screened touring areas provide generously sized pitches. There's a well-stocked shop, bar and café, with takeaway, under the same ownership. 2 acre site. 40 touring pitches. 8 hardstandings. Caravan pitches. Motorhome pitches. Tent pitches. 72 statics.

AA Pubs & Restaurants nearby: The Usk Inn, BRECON, LD3 7JE, 01874 676251

Star Inn, TALYBONT-ON-USK, LD3 7YX, 01874 676635

Leisure: ⚼ ❧
Facilities: ⌂ ⊙ ℮ ✻ ⓢ ⓒ ⓦⓘⓕⓘ ♺ ❼
Services: ☎ ⓢ ⓣⓘ ⓐ ⌁ ⊤ ⓘ◎ⓘ ⛀
Within 3 miles: ⛾ ℮ ⛽ ⓢ ∪

Notes: No open fires, no dogs in hire caravans. Dogs must be kept on leads. Boat hire (summer).

MIDDLETOWN Map 15 SJ31

Places to visit

Powis Castle & Garden, WELSHPOOL, SY21 8RF, 01938 551929 www.nationaltrust.org.uk

Great for kids: Old Oswestry Hill Fort, OSWESTRY, 0870 333 1181 www.english-heritage.org.uk/daysout/properties/old-oswestry-hill-fort

AA CAMPING CARD SITE

▶▶▶ **80% Bank Farm Caravan Park**

(SJ293123)

SY21 8EJ
☎ **01938 570526**
e-mail: bankfarmcaravans@yahoo.co.uk
dir: *13m W of Shrewsbury, 5m E of Welshpool on A458*

* ⊞ fr £15 ⊞ fr £15 Å fr £14

Open Mar-Oct

Last arrival 20.00hrs

An attractive park on a small farm, maintained to a high standard. There are two touring areas, one on either side of the A458, and each with its own amenity block, and immediate access to hills, mountains and woodland. A pub serving good food, and a large play area are nearby. 2 acre site. 40 touring pitches. Caravan pitches. Motorhome pitches. Tent pitches. 33 statics.

AA Pubs & Restaurants nearby: The Old Hand and Diamond Inn, COEDWAY, SY5 9AR, 01743 884379

Leisure: ⚠ ✎

Facilities: ✿ ⊙ ✳ ⅙ ⚲ ⌂ ⚲ WIFI ♻ ✿

Services: ⬜ ⬜ ⬜ ⬜

Within 3 miles: ⬜ ✎

Notes: ⊕ Dogs must be kept on leads. Coarse fishing, jacuzzi, snooker room.

RHAYADER Map 9 SN96

Places to visit

Blaenavon Ironworks, BLAENAVON, NP4 9RN, 01495 792615 www.cadw.wales.gov.uk

White Castle, WHITE CASTLE, NP7 8UD, 01600 780380 www.cadw.wales.gov.uk

Great for kids: Raglan Castle, RAGLAN, NP15 2BT, 01291 690228 www.cadw.wales.gov.uk

▶▶▶ **76% Wyeside Caravan & Camping Park** *(SO967690)*

Llangurig Rd LD6 5LB
☎ **01597 810183**
e-mail: wyesidecc@powys.gov.uk
dir: *400mtrs N of Rhayader town centre on A470*

⊞ ⊞ Å

Open Mar-Oct

Last arrival 20.00hrs Last departure noon

With direct access from the A470, the park sits on the banks of the River Wye. Situated just 400 metres from the centre of the market town of Rhayader, and next to a recreation park with tennis courts, bowling green and children's playground. There are good riverside walks from here, though the river is fast flowing and unfenced, and care is especially needed when walking with children. 6 acre site. 120 touring pitches. 22 hardstandings. 21 seasonal pitches. Caravan pitches. Motorhome pitches. Tent pitches. 39 statics.

AA Pubs & Restaurants nearby: The Bell Country Inn, LLANDRINDOD WELLS, LD1 6DY, 01597 823959

Facilities: ✿ ⊙ ✿ ✳ ⅙ ⚲ WIFI ♻ ✿

Services: ⬜ ⬜ ⬜ ⬜ T ⬜

Within 3 miles: ✎ ◎ ⬜ ⬜ ⬜ ∪

Notes: No noise after 23.00hrs. Dogs must be kept on leads.

SWANSEA

PONTARDDULAIS Map 8 SN50

Places to visit

The National Botanic Garden of Wales, LLANARTHNE, SA32 8HG, 01558 668768 www.gardenofwales.org.uk

Glynn Vivain Art Gallery, SWANSEA, SA1 5DZ, 01792 516900 www.glynnviviangallery.org

Great for kids: Plantasia, SWANSEA, SA1 2AL, 01792 474555 www.plantasia.org

PREMIER PARK

▶▶▶▶▶ **85% River View Touring Park** *(SN578086)*

The Dingle, Llanedi SA4 0FH
☎ **01269 844876**
e-mail: info@riverviewtouringpark.com
web: www.riverviewtouringpark.com
dir: *M4 junct 49, A483 signed Llandeilo. 0.5m, 1st left after lay-by, follow lane to site*

⊞ £16-£22 ⊞ £16-£22 Å £16-£20

Open Mar-mid Nov

Last arrival 20.00hrs Last departure noon

This peaceful park is set on one lower and two upper levels in a sheltered valley with an abundance of wild flowers and wildlife. The River Gwli flows around the bottom of the park where fishing for brown trout is possible. The excellent toilet facilities are an added bonus. This park is ideally situated for visiting the beaches of south Wales, The Black Mountains and the Brecon Beacons. 6 acre site. 60 touring pitches. 45 hardstandings. 19 seasonal pitches. Caravan pitches. Motorhome pitches. Tent pitches.

Leisure: ⚽

Facilities: ✿ ⊙ ✿ ✳ ⅙ ⬚ ⚲ WIFI ♻ ✿

Services: ⬜ ⬜ ⬜ ⬜ T ⬜

Within 3 miles: ⬜ 🎡 ✎ ⬜ ⬜ ∪

Notes: Reduced noise after 22.00hrs. Dogs must be kept on leads.

LEISURE: 🏊 Indoor swimming pool 🏊 Outdoor swimming pool ⚠ Children's playground 🎣 Kid's club 🎾 Tennis court ✎ Games room 📺 Separate TV room ⛳ 9/18 hole golf course ⛵ Boats for hire 🎬 Cinema 🎵 Entertainment 🎣 Fishing ◎ Mini golf 🏄 Watersports 🏋 Gym ⚽ Sports field **Spa** ∪ Stables
FACILITIES: 🛁 Bath ✿ Shower ⊙ Electric shaver ✿ Hairdryer ✳ Ice Pack Facility ⅙ Disabled facilities ⚲ Public telephone ⬚ Shop on site or within 200yds 🛒 Mobile shop (calls at least 5 days a week) 🍖 BBQ area 🪑 Picnic area WIFI Wi-fi 💻 Internet access ♻ Recycling ✿ Tourist info 🐕 Dog exercise area

PORT EYNON
Map 8 SS48

Places to visit

Weobley Castle, LLANRHIDIAN, SA3 1HB,
01792 390012 www.cadw.wales.gov.uk

Gower Heritage Centre, PARKMILL, SA3 2EH,
01792 371206 www.gowerheritagecentre.co.uk

Great for kids: Oxwich Castle, OXWICH,
SA3 1NG, 01792 390359
www.cadw.wales.gov.uk

▶▶▶▶ 80% Carreglwyd Camping & Caravan Park (SS465863)

SA3 1NL
☎ 01792 390795
dir: A4118 to Port Eynon, site adjacent to beach

🚐 🚍 Å

Open all year

Last arrival 22.00hrs Last departure 15.00hrs

Set in an unrivalled location alongside the safe sandy beach of Port Eynon on the Gower Peninsula, this popular park is an ideal family holiday spot; it is also close to an attractive village with pubs and shops. The sloping ground has been partly terraced and most pitches have sea views; the facilities are excellent. For 2014 - three new family bathrooms will be available. 12 acre site. 150 touring pitches. Caravan pitches. Motorhome pitches. Tent pitches.

AA Pubs & Restaurants nearby: Fairyhill,
REYNOLDSTON, SA3 1BS, 01792 390139

King Arthur Hotel, REYNOLDSTON, SA3 1AD,
01792 390775

Facilities: 🅿️ ⊙ 🕭 🔥 🚿 📶 ♻️ ❶
Services: 🔌 🚰 🧴 🔧 T ♻️
Within 3 miles: 🎣 🚣 🛥️ ♨️ ⛳

Notes: Dogs must be kept on leads.

RHOSSILI
Map 8 SS48

Places to visit

Weobley Castle, LLANRHIDIAN, SA3 1HB,
01792 390012 www.cadw.wales.gov.uk

Gower Heritage Centre, PARKMILL, SA3 2EH,
01792 371206 www.gowerheritagecentre.co.uk

Great for kids: Oxwich Castle, OXWICH,
SA3 1NG, 01792 390359
www.cadw.wales.gov.uk

▶▶▶ 87% Pitton Cross Caravan & Camping Park (SS434877)

SA3 1PT
☎ 01792 390593
e-mail: admin@pittoncross.co.uk
web: www.pittoncross.co.uk
dir: 2m W of Scurlage on B4247

🚐 🚍 Å

Open all year (rs Nov-Mar no bread, milk or papers)

Last arrival 20.00hrs Last departure 11.00hrs

Surrounded by farmland close to sandy Mewslade Bay, which is within walking distance across the fields, this grassy park is divided by hedging into paddocks; hardstandings for motorhomes are available. Rhossili Beach which is popular with surfers and the Wales Coastal Path are nearby. Performance kites are sold, and instruction in flying is given. Geo-caching and paragliding are possible too. 6 acre site. 100 touring pitches. 25 hardstandings. Caravan pitches. Motorhome pitches. Tent pitches.

AA Pubs & Restaurants nearby: Fairyhill,
REYNOLDSTON, SA3 1BS, 01792 390139

King Arthur Hotel, REYNOLDSTON, SA3 1AD,
01792 390775

Kings Head, LLANGENNITH, SA3 1HX,
01792 386212

Leisure: 🅐
Facilities: 🅿️ ⊙ 🅿️ 🚿 🕭 🔥 🕔 🛢️ ♻️ ❶
Services: 🔌 🚰 🧴 🔧 T
Within 3 miles: 🎣 🚣 🛢️ ♨️

Notes: Quiet at all times, charcoal BBQs must be off ground. Dogs must be kept on leads. Baby bath available.

SWANSEA
Map 9 SS69

Places to visit

Swansea Museum, SWANSEA, SA1 1SN,
01792 653763 www.swanseaheritage.net

Glynn Vivain Art Gallery, SWANSEA, SA1 5DZ,
01792 516900 www.glynnviviangallery.org

Great for kids: Plantasia, SWANSEA, SA1 2AL,
01792 474555 www.plantasia.org

75% Riverside Caravan Park (SS679991)

Ynys Forgan Farm, Morriston SA6 6QL
☎ 01792 775587
e-mail: reception@riversideswansea.com
dir: Exit M4 junct 45 towards Swansea. Left into private road signed to site

🚐 🚍 Å

Open all year (rs Winter months pool & club closed)

Last arrival mdnt Last departure noon

A large and busy park close to the M4 but in a quiet location beside the River Taw. This friendly, family orientated park has a licensed club and bar with a full high-season entertainment programme. There is a choice of eating outlets - the clubhouse restaurant, takeaway and chip shop. The park has a good indoor pool. 5 acre site. 90 touring pitches. Caravan pitches. Motorhome pitches. Tent pitches. 256 statics.

AA Pubs & Restaurants nearby: Hanson at the Chelsea Restaurant, SWANSEA, SA1 3LH, 01792 464068

Leisure: 🏊 🅐 🎣 🎱
Facilities: 🅿️ ⊙ 🅿️ 🚿 🕭 🕔 🛢️ 🔥 📶
Services: 🔌 🚰 🍴 🧴 🔧 T 🔋 🍔
Within 3 miles: 🎿 🚣 🎯 🎣 🛢️ ♨️

Notes: Dogs by prior arrangement only (no aggressive dog breeds permitted). Fishing on site by arrangement.

SERVICES: 🔌 Electric hook up 🚰 Launderette 🍺 Licensed bar 🛢️ Calor Gas 🔧 Camping Gaz T Toilet fluid 🍴 Café/Restaurant 🍔 Fast Food/Takeaway 🔋 Battery charging 🚼 Baby care 🔧 Motorvan service point **ABBREVIATIONS:** BH/bank hols-bank holidays Etr-Easter Spring BH-Spring Bank Holiday dep-departure fr-from hrs-hours m-mile mdnt-midnight rdbt-roundabout rs-restricted service wk-week wknd-weekend x-rds-cross roads 🚫 No credit cards 🚫 No dogs 🐾 Children of all ages accepted See page 9 for details of the AA Camping Card Scheme

VALE OF GLAMORGAN

LLANTWIT MAJOR   Map 9 SS96

Places to visit

Old Beaupre Castle, ST HILARY, 01443 336000
www.cadw.wales.gov.uk

Great for kids: Ogmore Castle, OGMORE,
01443 336000 www.cadw.wales.gov.uk

►►► 83% Acorn Camping & Caravan Site (SS973678)

Ham Lane South CF61 1RP
☎ 01446 794024
e-mail: info@acorncamping.co.uk
dir: *B4265 to Llantwit Major, follow camping signs. Approach site through Ham Manor residential park*

* ⚐ £16.50-£18 ⚎ £16.50-£18 ▲ £12-£15

Open Feb-Nov

Last arrival 21.00hrs Last departure 11.00hrs

A peaceful country site in level meadowland, with some individual pitches divided by hedges and shrubs. It is about one mile from the beach, which can be reached via a cliff top walk, and the same distance from the historic town of Llantwit Major. An internet station and a full-size snooker table are useful amenities. 5.5 acre site. 90 touring pitches. 10 hardstandings. Caravan pitches. Motorhome pitches. Tent pitches. 25 statics.

AA Pubs & Restaurants nearby: The Plough & Harrow, MONKNASH, CF71 7QQ, 01656 890209

Blue Anchor Inn, EAST ABERTHAW, CF62 3DD, 01446 750329

Leisure: Ⓜ ◣

Facilities: ⬤☉☂⚹ᴛ⑤ ⌨ ♻ ❸

Services: ⚐⑤ 🔒⌀Ⓣ🍴🚼⬛⚱

Within 3 miles: ↧⚑🛒📖Ⓤ

Notes: No noise 23.00hrs-07.00hrs. Dogs must be kept on leads.

WREXHAM

EYTON   Map 15 SJ34

Places to visit

Erddig, WREXHAM, LL13 0YT, 01978 355314
www.nationaltrust.org.uk

Chirk Castle, CHIRK, LL14 5AF, 01691 777701
www.nationaltrust.org.uk/main/w-chirkcastle

AA CAMPING CARD SITE

PREMIER PARK

►►►►► 93% The Plassey Leisure Park (SJ353452)

Best of British

The Plassey LL13 0SP
☎ 01978 780277
e-mail: enquiries@plassey.com
web: www.plassey.com
dir: *From A483 at Bangor-on-Dee exit onto B5426 for 2.5m. Site entrance signed on left*

⚐ £18.50-£28.90 ⚎ £18.50-£28.90
▲ £18.50-£28.90

Open Feb-Nov

Last arrival 20.30hrs Last departure noon

A lovely park set in several hundred acres of quiet farm and meadowland in the Dee Valley. The superb toilet facilities include individual cubicles for total privacy and security, while the Edwardian farm buildings have been converted into a restaurant, coffee shop, beauty studio and various craft outlets. There is plenty here to entertain the whole family, from scenic walks and a swimming pool to free fishing, and use of the 9-hole golf course. 10 acre site. 90 touring pitches. 45 hardstandings. 60 seasonal pitches. Caravan pitches. Motorhome pitches. Tent pitches. 15 statics.

AA Pubs & Restaurants nearby: The Boat Inn, ERBISTOCK, LL13 0DL, 01978 780666

Cross Foxes, ERBISTOCK, LL13 0DR, 01978 780380

Leisure: ≋ ⚐ Ⓜ ◣

Facilities: ⬤☉☂⚹⚐⑤ ⌂🐕ᴛ ♻ ❸

Services: ⚐⑤ 🔒⌀Ⓣ🍴🚼⬛⚱

Within 3 miles: ↧🍴⚑◎⑤Ⓤ

Notes: No footballs or skateboards. Dogs must be kept on leads. Sauna, badminton & table tennis.

OVERTON   Map 15 SJ34

Places to visit

Erddig, WREXHAM, LL13 0YT, 01978 355314
www.nationaltrust.org.uk

NEW ►►► 84% The Trotting Mare (SJ374396)

LL13 0LE
☎ 01978 711963
e-mail: info@thetrottingmare.co.uk
dir: *From Overton take A528 signed Ellesmere. Pub & site on right*

⚐ ⚎

Open all year

Last arrival 20.00hrs Last departure noon

Located between Overton-on-Dee and Ellesmere, this new adults-only touring park is quietly located behind The Trotting Mare pub. The majority of pitches are fully serviced, and creative landscaping and a free coarse-fishing lake are additional benefits. Please note that there is no laundry on this site but facilities are available at either Ellesmere or Overton. 4.2 acre site. 100 touring pitches. 40 hardstandings. Caravan pitches. Motorhome pitches. 11 statics. 4 tipis. 4 bell tents/yurts.

Facilities: ⬤☉⚹🐕 ⌨ ♻

Services: ⚐🔒🍴🚼⚱

Within 3 miles: ↧⚑Ⓤ

Notes: Adults only. Dogs must be kept on leads.

LEISURE: ≋ Indoor swimming pool ≋ Outdoor swimming pool Ⓜ Children's playground ⚑ Kid's club ◷ Tennis court ◣ Games room ▭ Separate TV room ↧ 9/18 hole golf course ⚑ Boats for hire ▤ Cinema ♫ Entertainment ⚑ Fishing ◎ Mini golf ≋ Watersports ⚑ Gym ☉ Sports field Spa Ⓤ Stables
FACILITIES: ⬛ Bath ⬤ Shower ☉ Electric shaver ☂ Hairdryer ⚹ Ice Pack Facility ⚐ Disabled facilities Ⓢ Public telephone ⑤ Shop on site or within 200yds ⚑ Mobile shop (calls at least 5 days a week) ⬛ BBQ area ⌂ Picnic area ⌨ Wi-fi ⬛ Internet access ♻ Recycling ❸ Tourist info ⚑ Dog exercise area

Ireland

The Mountains of Mourne

NORTHERN IRELAND

CO ANTRIM

ANTRIM   Map 1 D5

Places to visit

Antrim Round Tower, ANTRIM, BT41 1BJ, 028 9023 5000 www.discovernorthernireland.com/Antrim-Round-Tower-Antrim-P2813

Bonamargy Friary, BALLYCASTLE, 028 2076 2225 www.discovernorthernireland.com/Bonamargy-Friary-Ballycastle-P2818

Great for kids: Belfast Zoological Gardens, BELFAST, BT36 7PN, 028 9077 6277 www.belfastzoo.co.uk

▶▶▶ 83% Six Mile Water Caravan Park (J137870)

Lough Rd BT41 4DG
☎ 028 9446 4963 & 9446 3113
e-mail: sixmilewater@antrim.gov.uk
web: www.antrim.gov.uk/caravanpark
dir: From A6 (Dublin road) into Lough Rd signed Antrim Forum & Loughshore Park. Site at end of road on right

* 🚐 £18-£23 🚎 £18-£23 ▲ £15-£22

Open Mar-Oct (rs Feb & Nov wknds only)

Last arrival 21.00hrs Last departure noon

A pretty tree-lined site in a large municipal park, within walking distance of Antrim and the Antrim Forum leisure complex yet very much in the countryside. The modern toilet block is well equipped, and other facilities include a laundry and electric hook-ups. All the pitches are precisely set on generous plots. 9.61 acre site. 45 touring pitches. 37 hardstandings. Caravan pitches. Motorhome pitches. Tent pitches.

AA Pubs & Restaurants nearby: Galgorm Resort & Spa, BALLYMENA, BT42 1EA, 028 2588 1001

Leisure: ◕ ❑
Facilities: 🌣 ⊙ 🅟 ♿ 🎋 ⅢⅢ ♻ ❶
Services: 🄴 🄾 🅈 🍴 ⬛ ⬇
Within 3 miles: ⬇ ᴴ ♪ ◎ 🛶 🖺 🖥

Notes: Max stay 7 nights, no noise between 22.00hrs-08.00hrs. Dogs must be kept on leads. Watersports, angling stands.

BALLYCASTLE   Map 1 D6

Places to visit

Bonamargy Friary, BALLYCASTLE, 028 2076 2225 www.discovernorthernireland.com/Bonamargy-Friary-Ballycastle-P2818

Great for kids: Dunluce Castle, PORTBALLINTRAE, BT57 8UY, 028 2073 1938 www.doeni.gov.uk

---

AA CAMPING CARD SITE

▶▶▶ 74% Watertop Farm (D115407)

188 Cushendall Rd BT54 6RN
☎ 028 2076 2576
e-mail: watertopfarm@aol.com
dir: Take A2 from Ballycastle towards Cushendall. Site opposite Ballypatrick forest

🚐 £22 🚎 £22 ▲ £10

Open Etr-Oct (rs Etr-Jun & Sep-Oct farm activities not available)

Last departure 14.00hrs

Located on a family hill sheep farm set in the glens of Antrim, the farm offers a range of activities and attractions including pony trekking, boating, pedal go-karts, farm tours, tea room and lots more. The touring facilities consist of three individual sections, two reserved for caravans and the other for tents. The toilets are housed in a converted traditional Irish cottage, and the attached small rural museum serves as a night-time social area. 0.5 acre site. 14 touring pitches. 9 hardstandings. Caravan pitches. Motorhome pitches. Tent pitches.

Leisure: ◭ ◕
Facilities: 🌣 ⊙ ❄ 🎋 🍴 ♻
Services: 🄴 🄾 ⬛ 🅈 🍴 ⬛ ⬇
Within 3 miles: ⬇ 🖢 ♪ 🛶 🖺 🖥 ∪

Notes: No camp fires, no BBQ trays on grass. Dogs must be kept on leads.

BALLYMONEY   Map 1 C6

Places to visit

Leslie Hill Open Farm, BALLYMONEY, BT53 6QL, 028 2766 6803 www.lesliehillopenfarm.co.uk

Bonamargy Friary, BALLYCASTLE, 028 2076 2225 www.discovernorthernireland.com/Bonamargy-Friary-Ballycastle-P2818

Great for kids: Dunluce Castle, PORTBALLINTRAE, BT57 8UY, 028 2073 1938 www.doeni.gov.uk

---

PREMIER PARK

▶▶▶▶▶ 78% Drumaheglis Marina & Caravan Park (C901254)

36 Glenstall Rd BT53 7QN
☎ 028 2766 0280 & 2766 0227
e-mail: drumaheglis@ballymoney.gov.uk
dir: Signed from A26, approx 1.5m from Ballymoney towards Coleraine. Also accessed from B66, S of Ballymoney

🚐 £24-£25 🚎 £24-£25 ▲ £17

Open 17 Mar-Oct

Last arrival 20.00hrs Last departure 13.00hrs

An exceptionally well-designed and laid out park beside the Lower Bann River, with very spacious pitches (all fully serviced) and two quality toilet blocks. There's table tennis, picnic and BBQ areas, a grass volleyball court and a nature walk. This makes an ideal base for watersport enthusiasts and for those touring Antrim. 16 acre site. 55 touring pitches. 55 hardstandings. 20 seasonal pitches. Caravan pitches. Motorhome pitches. Tent pitches. 5 wooden pods.

Leisure: ◭
Facilities: 🌣 ⊙ 🅟 ❄ ♿ ◔ 🎋 🍴 ⅢⅢ ♻ ❶
Services: 🄴 🄾 ⬛ ⬇
Within 3 miles: ⬇ ♪ 🛶 🖺 🖥

Notes: Dogs must be kept on leads. Marina berths.

BUSHMILLS
Map 1 C6

Places to visit

Old Bushmills Distillery, BUSHMILLS, BT57 8XH, 028 2073 1521 www.bushmills.com

Great for kids: Belfast Zoological Gardens, BELFAST, BT36 7PN, 028 9077 6277 www.belfastzoo.co.uk

AA CAMPING CARD SITE

PREMIER PARK

▶▶▶▶▶ 88% Ballyness
Caravan Park (C944397)

40 Castlecatt Rd BT57 8TN
☎ 028 2073 2393
e-mail: info@ballynesscaravanpark.com
web: www.ballynesscaravanpark.com
dir: 0.5m S of Bushmills on B66, follow signs

🚐 fr £24 🚐 fr £24

Open 17 Mar-Oct

Last arrival 21.00hrs Last departure noon

A quality park with superb toilet and other facilities, on farmland beside St Columb's Rill, the stream that supplies the famous nearby Bushmills Distillery. The friendly owners created this park with the discerning camper in mind and they continue to improve it to ever higher standards. There is a pleasant walk around several ponds, and the park is peacefully located close to the beautiful north Antrim coast. There is a spacious play barn and

a holiday cottage to let. 16 acre site. 48 touring pitches. 48 hardstandings. Caravan pitches. Motorhome pitches. 65 statics.

AA Pubs & Restaurants nearby: Bushmills Inn Hotel, BUSHMILLS, BT57 8QG, 028 2073 3000

Leisure: ⚗ 🌞 🎣 ▢

Facilities: 🛁 🛇 ⊙ 🌣 ⚹ ⚹ 🕒 🛇 🐕 WiFi ♻ ❶

Services: 🔌 🛇 🛢 🗑 🚽 🗑 💦

Within 3 miles: 🚴 ✎ 🏪

Notes: No skateboards or rollerblades. Dogs must be kept on leads. Library.

BELFAST

DUNDONALD

Places to visit

Mount Stewart House & Gardens, NEWTOWNARDS, BT22 2AD, 028 4278 8387 www.nationaltrust.org.uk

Giant's Ring, BELFAST, 028 9023 5000 www.discovernorthernireland.com/Giants-Ring-Belfast-P2791

Great for kids: Belfast Zoological Gardens, BELFAST, BT36 7PN, 028 9077 6277 www.belfastzoo.co.uk

DUNDONALD
Map 1 D5

▶▶▶ 77% Dundonald Touring
Caravan Park (J410731)

111 Old Dundonald Rd BT16 1XT
☎ 028 9080 9123 & 9080 9129
e-mail: sales@castlereagh.gov.uk
dir: From Belfast city centre follow M3 & A20 to City Airport. Then A20 to Newtownards, follow signs to Dundonald & Ulster Hospital. At hospital right at sign for Dundonald Ice Bowl. Follow to end, turn right (Ice Bowl on left)

* 🚐 £8-£23 🚐 £8-£23 🛆 fr £15

Open 14 Mar-Oct (rs Nov-Mar Aire de Service restricted to motorhomes/caravans with own bathroom facilities)

Last arrival 23.00hrs Last departure noon

A purpose-built park in a quiet corner of Dundonald Leisure Park on the outskirts of Belfast. This peaceful park is ideally located for touring County Down and exploring the capital. In the winter it offers an 'Aire de Service' for motorhomes. 1.5 acre site. 22 touring pitches. 22

continued

SERVICES: 🔌 Electric hook up 🛇 Launderette 🍺 Licensed bar 🛢 Calor Gas 🛢 Camping Gaz 🅣 Toilet fluid 🍴 Café/Restaurant 🍔 Fast Food/Takeaway 🔋 Battery charging 👶 Baby care 🚽 Motorvan service point **ABBREVIATIONS:** BH/bank hols-bank holidays Etr-Easter Spring BH-Spring Bank Holiday dep-departure fr-from hrs-hours m-mile mdnt-midnight rdbt-roundabout rs-restricted service wk-week wknd-weekend x-rds-cross roads ㊝ No credit cards 🚫 No dogs 👪 Children of all ages accepted See page 9 for details of the AA Camping Card Scheme

DUNDONALD ***continued***

hardstandings. Caravan pitches. Motorhome pitches. Tent pitches.

Dundonald Touring Caravan Park

Facilities: 🚿 🪒 💨 ❄ ♿ ☎ 🪑 ℹ

Services: 🚐 🧺 🍽 🛒 ⬇

Within 3 miles: ⛳ 🎬 🎣 ◎ 🏪 🧺 🐎

Notes: No commercial vehicles. Dogs must be kept on leads. Bowling, indoor play area, Olympic-size ice rink (additional charges apply).

see advert on page 437

CO FERMANAGH

BELCOO Map 1 C5

PREMIER PARK

►►►►► 83% *Rushin House Caravan Park* *(H835047)*

Holywell BT93 5DY

☎ 028 6638 6519

e-mail: enquiries@rushinhousecaravanpark.com

dir: *From Enniskillen take A4 W for 13m to Belcoo. Right onto B52 towards Garrison for 1m. Site signed*

🚐 🚗 ⛺

Open mid Mar-Oct (rs Nov-Mar Aire de Service facilities available)

Last arrival 21.00hrs Last departure 13.00hrs

This park occupies a scenic location overlooking Lough MacNean, close to the picturesque village of Belcoo, and is the product of meticulous planning and execution. There are 24 very generous, fully serviced pitches standing on a terrace overlooking the lough, with additional tenting pitches below; all are accessed via well-kept, wide tarmac roads. Play facilities include a lovely well-equipped play area and a hard surface and fenced five-a-side football pitch. There is a slipway providing boat access to the lough and, of course, fishing. The excellent toilet facilities are purpose-built and include family rooms. 5 acre site. 38 touring pitches. 38 hardstandings. Caravan pitches. Motorhome pitches. Tent pitches.

Leisure: 🛝 🎾 ⚽ 📺

Facilities: 🚿 🪒 💨 ❄ ♿ ☎ 🪑 🐕 📶 ♻ ℹ

Services: 🚐 🧺 🛢 🍃 📦 ⬇

Within 3 miles: ⛳ 🚣 🏄 🏪 🧺

Notes: No cars by tents. Dogs must be kept on leads. Lakeside walk.

IRVINESTOWN Map 1 C5

Places to visit

Castle Coole, ENNISKILLEN, BT74 6JY, 028 6632 2690 www.nationaltrust.org.uk

Great for kids: Castle Balfour, LISNASKEA, 028 9023 5000 www.discovernorthernireland.com/Castle-Balfour-Lisnaskea-Enniskillen-P2901

►►►► 82% Castle Archdale Caravan Park & Camping Site *(H176588)*

Lisnarick BT94 1PP

☎ 028 6862 1333

e-mail: info@castlearchdale.com

dir: *From Irvinestown take B534 signed Lisnarick. Left onto B82 signed Enniskillen. Approx 1m right by church (site signed)*

* 🚐 £25-£30 🚗 £25-£30 ⛺ £10-£40

Open Apr-Oct (rs Apr-Jun & Sep-Oct shop, restaurant & bar open wknds only)

Last departure noon

This park is located within the grounds of Castle Archdale Country Park on the shores of Lough Erne which boasts stunning scenery, forest walks and also war and wildlife museums. The site is ideal for watersport enthusiasts with its marina and launching facilities. Also on site are a shop, licenced restaurant, takeaway and play park. There are 56 fully serviced, hardstanding pitches. 11 acre site. 158 touring pitches. 120 hardstandings. Caravan pitches. Motorhome pitches. Tent pitches. 144 statics.

AA Pubs & Restaurants nearby: Lough Erne Resort, ENNISKILLEN, BT93 7ED, 028 6632 3230

Leisure: 🛝

Facilities: 🚿 🪒 ❄ ♿ ☎ 🏪 🪑 🐕 📶 ℹ

Services: 🚐 🧺 🍸 🛢 🍃 [T] 🍽 📦 🛒 ⬇

Within 3 miles: ⛳ 🚣 🎣 🏄 🏪 🧺

Notes: No open fires. Dogs must be kept on leads.

LISNASKEA Map 1 C5

Places to visit

Castle Balfour, LISNASKEA, 028 9023 5000 www.discovernorthernireland.com/Castle-Balfour-Lisnaskea-Enniskillen-P2901

Florence Court, ENNISKILLEN, BT92 1DB, 028 6634 8249 www.nationaltrust.org.uk

Great for kids: Castle Coole, ENNISKILLEN, BT74 6JY, 028 6632 2690 www.nationaltrust.org.uk

►►► 81% Lisnaskea Caravan Park *(H297373)*

BT92 0NZ

☎ 028 6772 1040

dir: *From Lisnaskea take B514 signed Carry Bridge, site signed*

🚐 🚗 ⛺

Open Mar-Sep

Last arrival 21.00hrs Last departure 14.00hrs

A pretty riverside site set in peaceful countryside, with well-kept facilities and friendly owners. Fishing is available on the river, and this quiet area is an ideal location for touring the lakes of Fermanagh. 6 acre site. 43 touring pitches. 43 hardstandings. Caravan pitches. Motorhome pitches. Tent pitches. 8 statics.

AA Pubs & Restaurants nearby: Lough Erne Resort, ENNISKILLEN, BT93 7ED, 028 6632 3230

Leisure: 🛝

Facilities: 🚿 🪒 ❄ ♿ 🐕

Services: 🚐 🧺 🛢

Within 3 miles: ⛳ 🚣 🎣 🏪 🧺 🐎

Notes: 🚫 Dogs must be kept on leads.

LEISURE: 🏊 Indoor swimming pool ☀ Outdoor swimming pool 🛝 Children's playground 👋 Kid's club 🎾 Tennis court ♠ Games room 📺 Separate TV room ⛳ 9/18 hole golf course 🚣 Boats for hire 🎬 Cinema 🎵 Entertainment 🎣 Fishing ◎ Mini golf 🏄 Watersports 🏋 Gym ⚽ Sports field **Spa** 🐎 Stables
FACILITIES: 🛁 Bath 🚿 Shower 🪒 Electric shaver 💨 Hairdryer ❄ Ice Pack Facility ♿ Disabled facilities ☎ Public telephone 🏪 Shop on site or within 200yds 🚚 Mobile shop (calls at least 5 days a week) 🍖 BBQ area 🪑 Picnic area 📶 Wi-fi 💻 Internet access ♻ Recycling ℹ Tourist info 🐕 Dog exercise area

CO TYRONE

DUNGANNON   Map 1 C5

Places to visit

The Argory, MOY, BT71 6NA, 028 8778 4753
www.nationaltrust.org.uk

Greencastle, KILKEEL, 028 9181 1491
www.doeni.gov.uk

Great for kids: Mountjoy Castle, MOUNTJOY,
028 9023 5000 www.ehsni.gov.uk

▶▶▶ **81%** *Dungannon Park* (H805612)

Moy Rd BT71 6DY
☎ 028 8772 8690
e-mail: dpreception@dungannon.gov.uk
dir: *M1 junct 15, A29, left at 2nd lights*

* 🚐 £12-£15 🚙 £12-£15 ▲ £10

Open Mar-Oct

Last arrival 20.30hrs Last departure 14.00hrs

A modern caravan park in a quiet area of a
stunning public park with fishing lake and
excellent facilities, especially for disabled visitors.
2 acre site. 20 touring pitches. 12 hardstandings.
Caravan pitches. Motorhome pitches. Tent pitches.

Leisure: ⚗ ⚽ 🏓 ▭
Facilities: 🌳 ⊙ 🅿 ✳ 🕭 🕭 🚿 ♻ ✻
Services: 🔌 🔟 🛒
Within 3 miles: ↓ ≄ 🕭 🕭 🕭 🔟 U

Notes: Dogs must be kept on leads. Hot & cold
drinks, snacks available.

REPUBLIC OF IRELAND

CO CORK

BALLINSPITTLE   Map 1 B2

Places to visit

Cork City Gaol, CORK, 021 4305022
www.corkcitygaol.com

Blarney Castle & Rock Close, BLARNEY,
021 4385252 www.blarneycastle.ie

Great for kids: Muckross House, Gardens &
Traditional Farms, KILLARNEY, 064 6670144
www.muckross-house.ie

▶▶▶▶ **80%** *Garrettstown House
Holiday Park* (W588445)

☎ 021 4778156 & 4775286
e-mail: reception@garrettstownhouse.com
dir: *6m from Kinsale, through Ballinspittle, past
school & football pitch on main road to beach.
Beside stone estate entrance*

🚐 🚙 ▲

Open 4 May-9 Sep (rs Early season-1 Jun shop
closed)

Last arrival 22.00hrs Last departure noon

Elevated holiday park with tiered camping areas
and superb panoramic views. Plenty of on-site
amenities, and close to beach and forest park. 7
acre site. 60 touring pitches. 20 hardstandings.
Caravan pitches. Motorhome pitches. Tent pitches.
80 statics.

Leisure: ✯ ⚗ 🖐 ⚽ 🎣 ▭ 🎵
Facilities: 🌳 ⊙ 🅿 ✳ 🕭 🅂 🚿 🛒 WiFi ♻ ✻
Services: 🔌 🔟 🛒 ⏚ 🚻 ⛽ ⏚
Within 3 miles: ↓ ≄ 🕭 ◎ ≊ 🔟 U

Notes: Dogs must be kept on leads. Crazy golf,
video shows, snooker, adult reading lounge, tots'
playroom.

BALLYLICKEY   Map 1 B2

Places to visit

Muckross House, Gardens & Traditional Farms,
KILLARNEY, 064 6670144
www.muckross-house.ie

Great for kids: Fota Wildlife Park,
CARRIGTWOHILL, 021 4812678
www.fotawildlife.ie

▶▶▶▶ **85%** *Eagle Point Caravan and
Camping Park* (V995535)

☎ 027 50630
e-mail: eaglepointcamping@eircom.net
dir: *N71 to Bandon, then R586 to Bantry, then
N71, 4m to Glengarriff, opposite petrol station*

🚐 🚙 ▲

Open 19 Apr-23 Sep

Last arrival 21.00hrs Last departure noon

An immaculate park set in an idyllic position on a
headland overlooking the rugged Bantry Bay and
the mountains of West Cork. There are boat
launching facilities, small and safe pebble
beaches, a football field, tennis court, a small
playground, and TV rooms for children and adults
on the park. There is an internet café at reception
and a shop and petrol station across from the
park entrance. Nearby are two golf courses, riding
stables, a sailing centre and cycle hire facilities.
20 acre site. 125 touring pitches. 20
hardstandings. 60 seasonal pitches. Caravan
pitches. Motorhome pitches. Tent pitches.

AA Pubs & Restaurants nearby: Sea View House,
BALLYLICKEY, , 027 50073

Leisure: ⚗ ⚽ 🏓 ▭
Facilities: 🌳 ⊙ ✳ 🕭 🅂 WiFi 🖥 ♻ ✻
Services: 🔌 🔟 🛒 ⏚
Within 3 miles: ↓ 🕭 🕭 🔟

Notes: No commercial vehicles, bikes, skates,
scooters or jet skis.

SERVICES: 🔌 Electric hook up 🔟 Launderette 🍷 Licensed bar 🅂 Calor Gas ⊘ Camping Gaz 🔲 Toilet fluid 🍽 Café/Restaurant 🍔 Fast Food/Takeaway
⏚ Battery charging 🍼 Baby care ⏚ Motorvan service point **ABBREVIATIONS:** BH/bank hols-bank holidays Etr-Easter Spring BH-Spring Bank Holiday dep-departure
fr-from hrs-hours m-mile mdnt-midnight rdbt-roundabout rs-restricted service wk-week wknd-weekend x-rds-cross roads 🚫 No credit cards ✻ No dogs
♿ Children of all ages accepted See page 9 for details of the AA Camping Card Scheme

CO DUBLIN

CLONDALKIN — Map 1 D4

Places to visit

Castletown, CELBRIDGE, 01 6288252
www.heritageireland.ie

Irish Museum of Modern Art, DUBLIN,
01 6129900 www.imma.ie

Great for kids: Dublin Zoo, DUBLIN,
01 4748900 www.dublinzoo.ie

►►►► 81% Camac Valley Tourist Caravan & Camping Park (O056300)

Naas Rd, Clondalkin
☎ 01 4640644

e-mail: info@camacvalley.com
dir: M50 junct 9, N7 (South), exit 2, follow signs for Corkagh Park

🚐 €25-€30 🚐 €23-€30 ⚠ €12

Open all year

Last arrival 22.00hrs Last departure noon

A pleasant, lightly wooded park with good facilities, security and layout, situated within an hour's drive, or a bus ride, from the city centre. 15 acre site. 163 touring pitches. 113 hardstandings. Caravan pitches. Motorhome pitches. Tent pitches.

AA Pubs & Restaurants nearby: Finnstown Country House Hotel, LUCAN, , 01 6010700

Leisure: 🎠 ⚽ 📺
Facilities: 🐾 ⊙ 🖋 ✳ ✚ 🚿 🎇 WiFi ♻ ❶
Services: 🔌 🔅 🛢 🧺 📆 🚮 🛒 ⬇
Within 3 miles: ⛳ 🎏 🖊 ◎ 🏧 🛒 U

Notes: Lights out 23.00hrs. Dogs must be kept on leads.

CO MAYO

CASTLEBAR — Map 1 B4

Places to visit

King House - Georgian Mansion & Military Barracks, BOYLE, 071 9663242
www.kinghouse.ie

AA CAMPING CARD SITE

►►►► 80% Lough Lannagh Caravan Park (M140890)

Old Westport Rd
☎ 094 9027111

e-mail: info@loughlannagh.ie
web: www.loughlannagh.ie
dir: N5, N60, N84 to Castlebar. At ring road follow signs for Westport. Signs for Lough Lannagh Village on all approach roads to Westport rdbt

* 🚐 €21-€25 🚐 €21-€25 ⚠ €21-€25

Open 11 Apr-Aug

Last arrival 18.00hrs Last departure 10.00hrs

This park is part of the Lough Lannagh Village which is situated in a wooded area a short walk from Castlebar. Leisure facilities include a purpose-built fitness and relaxation centre, tennis courts, boules, children's play area and café. 2.5 acre site. 20 touring pitches. 20 hardstandings. Caravan pitches. Motorhome pitches. Tent pitches.

AA Pubs & Restaurants nearby: Knockranny House Hotel, WESTPORT, , 098 28600

Leisure: 🏌 🚣 ⚽ ✪
Facilities: 🛁 🐾 ⊙ 🖋 ✳ ✚ 🚿 WiFi 🖥 ♻ ❶
Services: 🔌 🔅 🍴 🛒
Within 3 miles: ⛳ 🏊 🎏 🖊 ◎ 🏊 🏧 🛒 U

Notes: Pets accepted by prior arrangement only, no pets in Jul & Aug. Dogs must be kept on leads.

KNOCK — Map 1 B4

Places to visit

King House - Georgian Mansion & Military Barracks, BOYLE, 071 9663242
www.kinghouse.ie

►►►► 76% Knock Caravan and Camping Park (M408828)

Claremorris Rd
☎ 094 9388100

e-mail: caravanpark@knock-shrine.ie
dir: From rdbt in Knock, through town. Site on left in 1km, opposite petrol station

🚐 €20-€22 🚐 €20-€22 ⚠ €20-€22

Open Mar-Nov

Last arrival 22.00hrs Last departure noon

A pleasant, very well maintained camping park within the grounds of Knock Shrine, offering spacious terraced pitches and excellent facilities. 10 acre site. 88 touring pitches. 88 hardstandings. Caravan pitches. Motorhome pitches. Tent pitches. 12 statics.

Leisure: 🎠 🎣 📺
Facilities: 🐾 ⊙ 🖋 ✳ ✚ 🚿 🖥 🚮 🎇 WiFi ♻ ❶
Services: 🔌 🔅 🛢 🧺 📆 🍴 🛒 ⬇
Within 3 miles: ⛳ 🖊 🏧 🛒 U

Notes: 🐾 Dogs must be kept on leads.

LEISURE: 🏊 Indoor swimming pool 🏊 Outdoor swimming pool 🎠 Children's playground 👋 Kid's club 🎾 Tennis court 🎱 Games room 📺 Separate TV room ⛳ 9/18 hole golf course 🚣 Boats for hire 🎬 Cinema 🎭 Entertainment 🎣 Fishing ◎ Mini golf 🏄 Watersports 🏌 Gym ✪ Sports field Spa U Stables
FACILITIES: 🛁 Bath 🚿 Shower ⊙ Electric shaver 🖋 Hairdryer ✳ Ice Pack Facility ✚ Disabled facilities 🖇 Public telephone 🛒 Shop on site or within 200yds 🚐 Mobile shop (calls at least 5 days a week) 🍴 BBQ area 🌳 Picnic area WiFi Wi-fi 🖥 Internet access ♻ Recycling ❶ Tourist info 🚮 Dog exercise area

CO ROSCOMMON

BOYLE
Map 1 B4

Places to visit

King House - Georgian Mansion & Military Barracks, BOYLE, 071 9663242 www.kinghouse.ie

Florence Court, ENNISKILLEN, BT92 1DB, 028 6634 8249 www.nationaltrust.org.uk

▶▶▶ 74% *Lough Key Caravan & Camping Park* (G846039)

Lough Key Forest Park
☎ 071 9662212
e-mail: info@loughkey.ie
web: www.loughkey.ie
dir: *3km E of Boyle on N4. Follow Lough Key Forest Park signs, site within grounds. Approx 0.5km from entrance*

🚐 🚍 Å

Open Apr-20 Sep

Last arrival 18.00hrs Last departure noon

Peaceful and very secluded site within the extensive grounds of a beautiful forest park. Lough Key offers boat trips and waterside walks, and there is a viewing tower. 15 acre site. 72 touring pitches. 52 hardstandings. Caravan pitches. Motorhome pitches. Tent pitches.

Leisure: ⁄Ⅱ
Facilities: 🛁 ♠ ⊙ & ⓒ 🗜 ♘
Services: 🔌 🗑
Within 3 miles: 🎣 ⌇ 🛶 🗑
Notes: 🚫 No cars by tents.

SERVICES: 🔌 Electric hook up 🗑 Launderette 🍷 Licensed bar 🔋 Calor Gas ⊘ Camping Gaz Ⓣ Toilet fluid 🍴 Café/Restaurant 🍟 Fast Food/Takeaway 🔋 Battery charging 🍼 Baby care ⚒ Motorvan service point **ABBREVIATIONS:** BH/bank hols-bank holidays Etr-Easter Spring BH-Spring Bank Holiday dep-departure fr-from hrs-hours m-mile mdnt-midnight rdbt-roundabout rs-restricted service wk-week wknd-weekend x-rds-cross roads 🚫 No credit cards 🚫 No dogs 👫 Children of all ages accepted See page 9 for details of the AA Camping Card Scheme

County Maps

The county map shown here will help you identify the counties within each country. You can look up each county in the guide using the county names at the top of each page. To find towns featured in the guide use the atlas and the index.

England

1 Bedfordshire
2 Berkshire
3 Bristol
4 Buckinghamshire
5 Cambridgeshire
6 Greater Manchester
7 Herefordshire
8 Hertfordshire
9 Leicestershire
10 Northamptonshire
11 Nottinghamshire
12 Rutland
13 Staffordshire
14 Warwickshire
15 West Midlands
16 Worcestershire

Scotland

17 City of Glasgow
18 Clackmannanshire
19 East Ayrshire
20 East Dunbartonshire
21 East Renfrewshire
22 Perth & Kinross
23 Renfrewshire
24 South Lanarkshire
25 West Dunbartonshire

Wales

26 Blaenau Gwent
27 Bridgent
28 Caerphilly
29 Denbighshire
30 Flintshire
31 Merthyr Tydfil
32 Monmouthshire
33 Neath Port Talbot
34 Newport
35 Rhondda Cynon Taff
36 Torfaen
37 Vale of Glamorgan
38 Wrexham

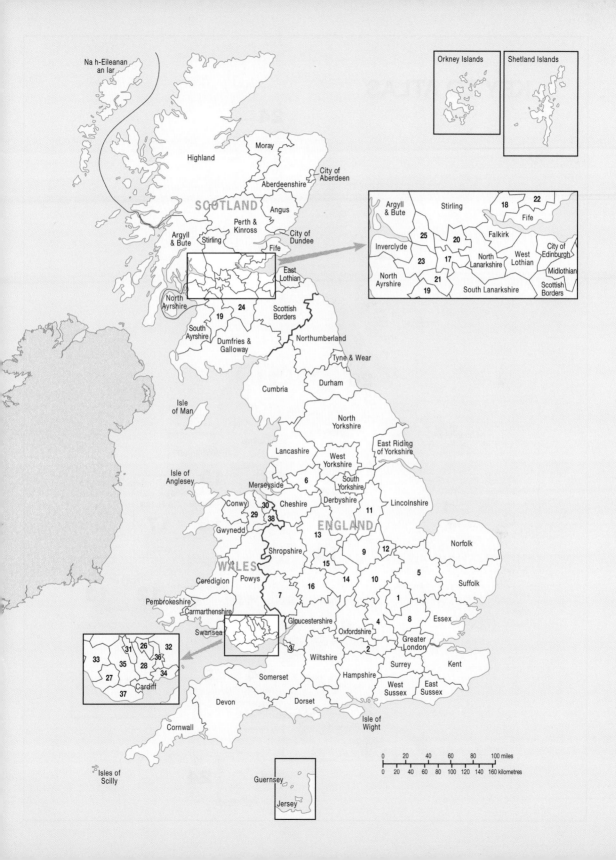

KEY TO ATLAS

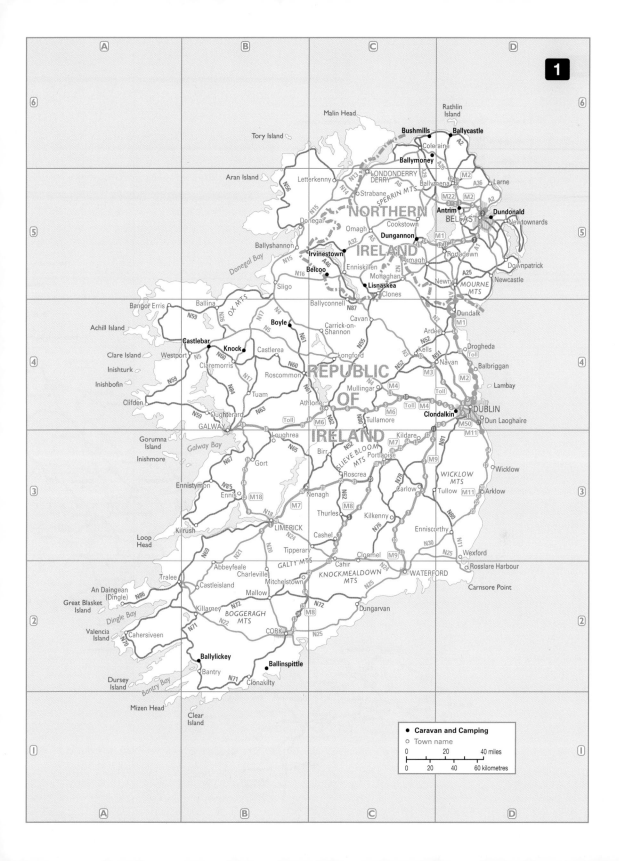

2

Legend

▭M6▭	Motorway/toll motorway
⊖⊕⊖	Motorway junction full/restricted. Service area
A30	Primary route single/dual carriageway
A34	Other A road single/dual carriageway
B3400	B road
	Unclassified road
—V—	Vehicle ferry
—C—	Fast vehicle ferry or catamaran

● Ashbourne	Caravan and Camping
● St Ives	AA Campsite Award Winner
○ Oundle	Town/Village name
	National boundary
ESSEX	English county name & boundary
CONWY	Welsh county name & boundary
MORAY	Scottish county name & boundary
	National Park

Lundy

Hartland Point
Hartland

Morwenstow

Kilkhampton

Bude
Bude
Bay
Widemouth Bay Bridge
Week
St Mary

Crackington Haven
Jacobstow

Boscastle
Tintagel ● Otterham

Delabole Camelford

Port Isaac Bolventor
Polzeath *BODMIN MOOR*
St Minver St Tudy
Harlyn Rock Blisland
St Merryn **Padstow**
Porthcothan **Wadebridge**
A389 **C O R N W A L L** St Clee
Rumford Ruthernbridge Bodmin
Mawgan St Dobwalls
Porth Mawgan Lanivet Liskeard
Watergate Bay St Columb St
Newquay Major Rochel Keyne
West Bugle Luxulyan Lostwithiel
Pentire Indian Pelynt
Holywell Cubert Queens Summercourt St Blazey St A361 Le
Bay Rejerrah Gate Blaze
Perranporth Goonhavern **St** Fowey Polperro
St Agnes Ladock **Austell** Carlyon Polruan
St Allen St Bay
Porthtowan Stephen Pentewan
Portreath **Blackwater** Grampound Mevagissey
Chacewater Gorran Gorran Haven
St Ives Bay St Day **Truro** Tregony
St Ives Gwithian **Redruth** Carnon Portloe
Zennor Camborne Downs Portscatho
Lelant Hayle A393 St Just-in- St Mawes
Leedstown Roseland Portscatho
St Just St Hilary Edgcumbe Penryn St Mawes
Penzance Marazion Ashton **Falmouth**
St Buryan Rosudgeon Praa **Helston** Constantine Mawnan Smith
Land's Newlyn Sands Porthleven Gweek
End Mousehole Manaccan
Sennen Mount's Bay St Keverne
Porthcurno Treen Mullion Coverack
Kennack
Sands
Cadgwith
Lizard
Lizard Point

Isles of Scilly inset

ISLES OF SCILLY

Bryher ○ Higher Town
New Grimsby
Hugh **St Mary's**
Town Old
Middle Town
Town

SV

SW

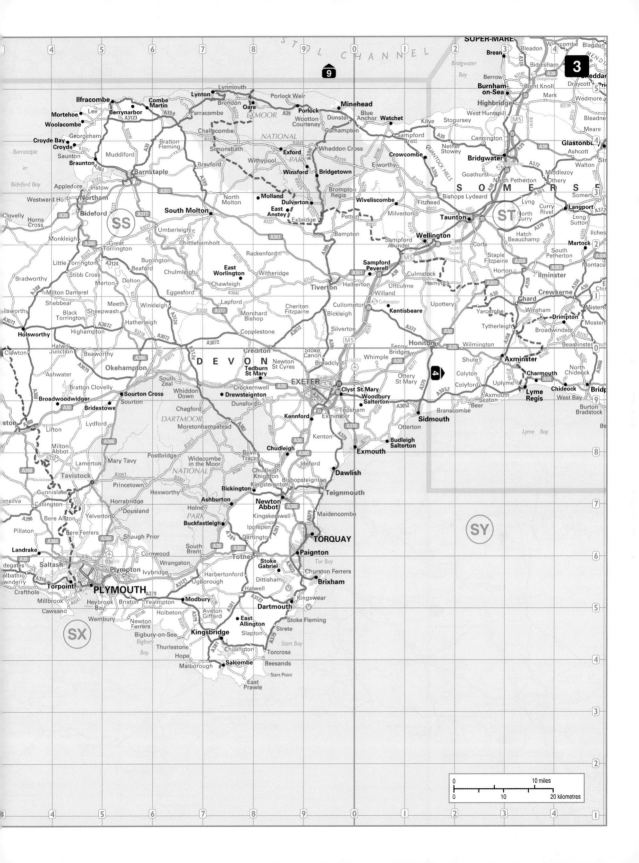

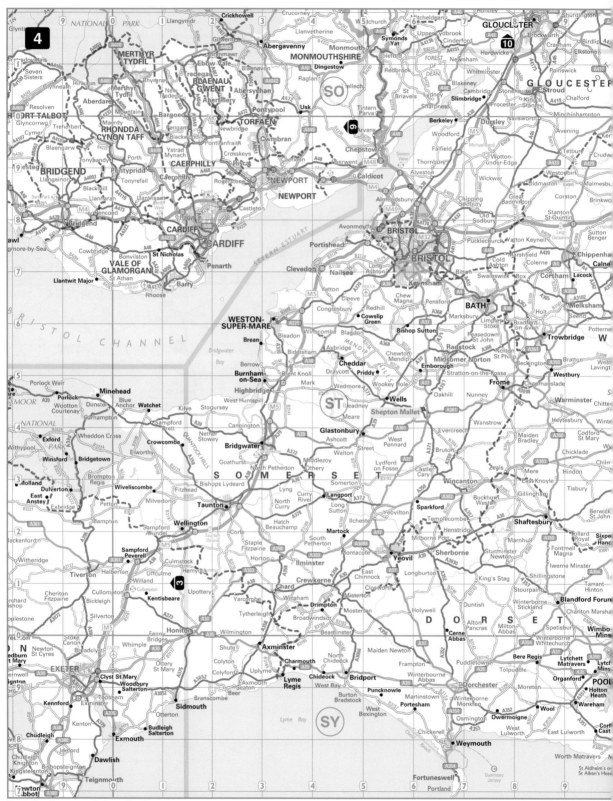

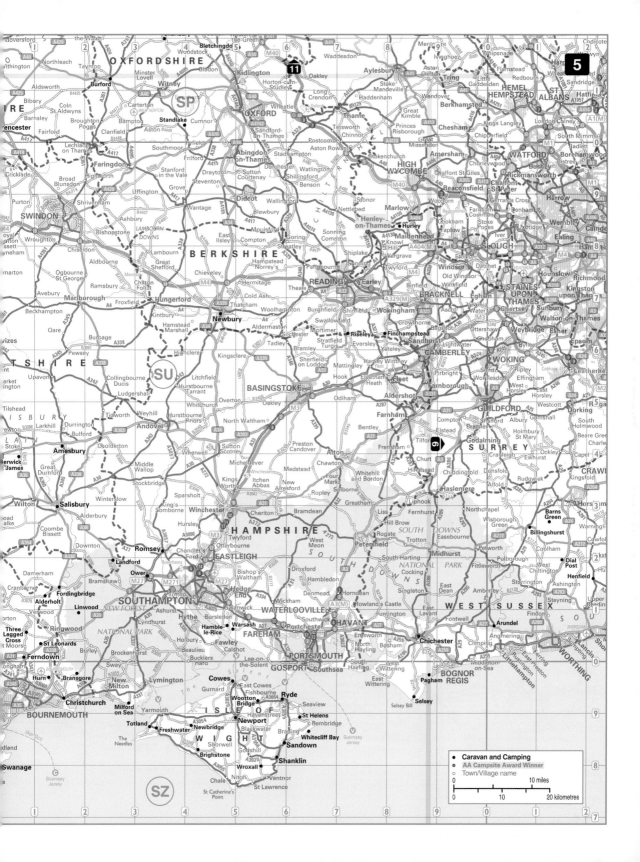

For continuation pages refer to numbered arrows

Caravan and Camping
AA Campsite Award Winner
Town/Village name

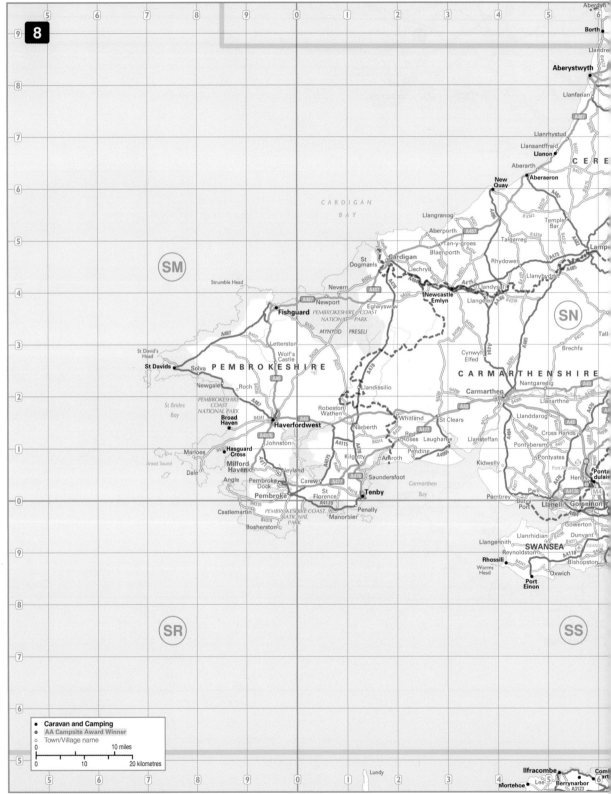

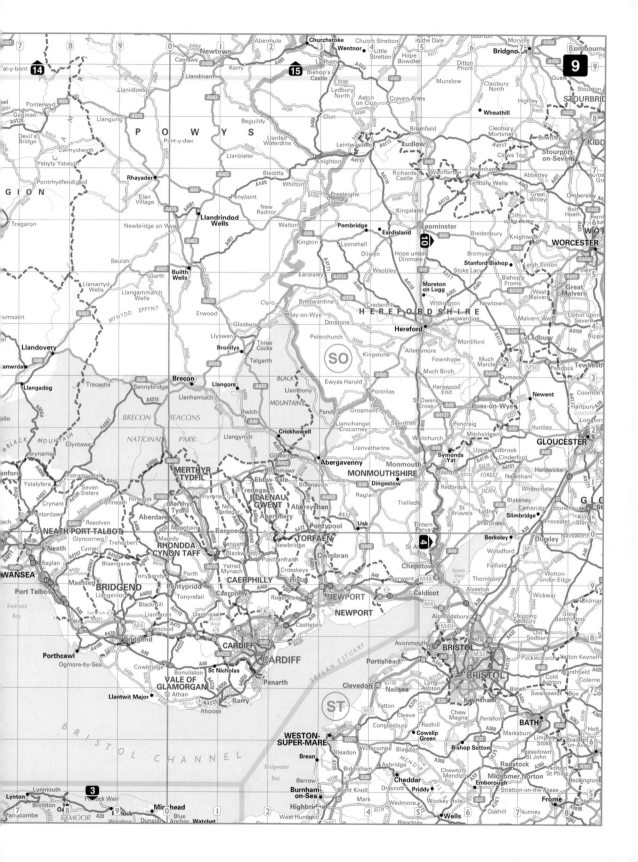

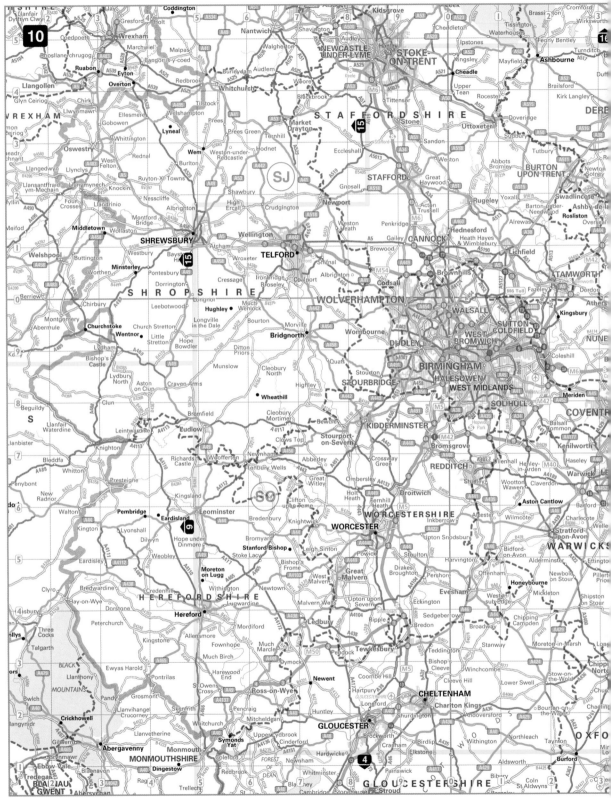

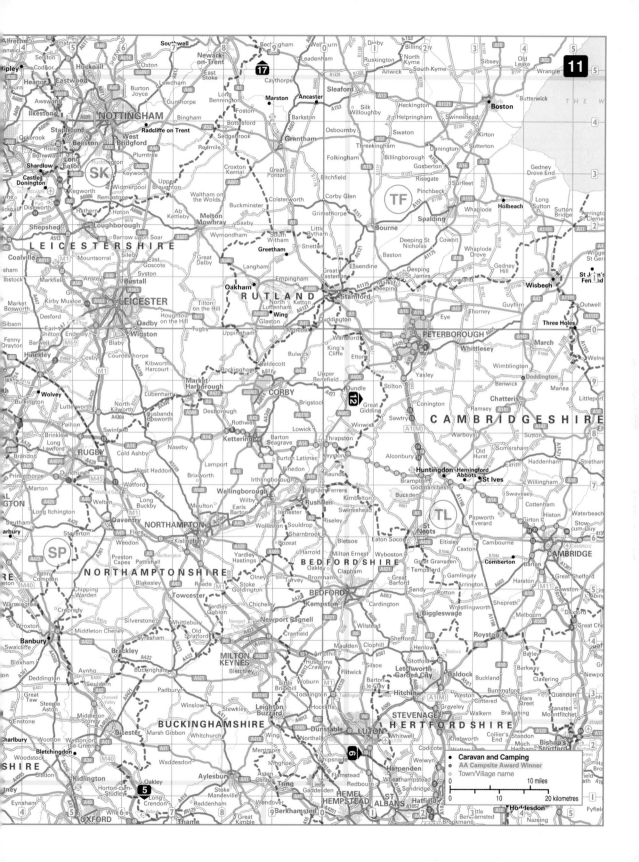

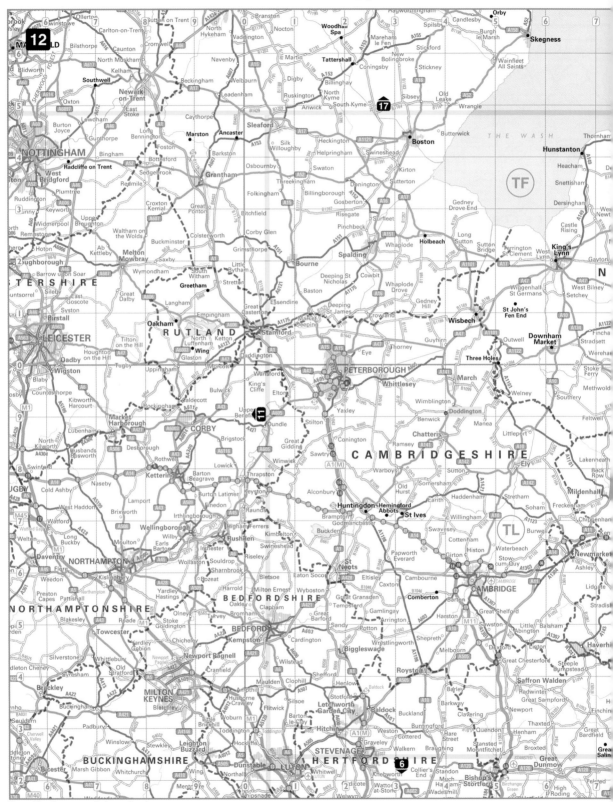

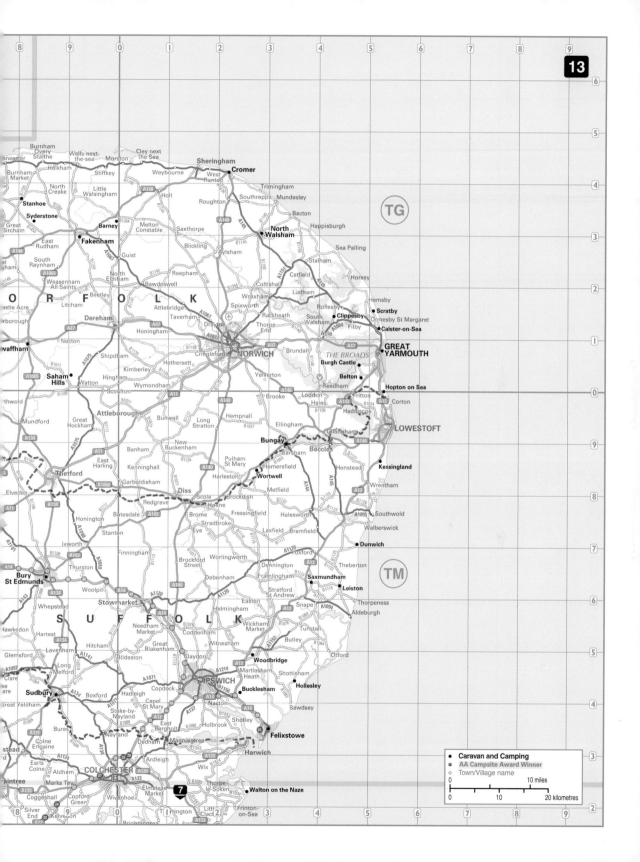

ISLE OF
ANGLESEY

Cemaes
Amlwch
Dulas
Rhôs Lligwy
Marian-Glas
Llanerchymedd
Holyhead
Llanfachraeth
Benllech
Red Wharf Bay
Pentraeth
Llangoed
Llandudno
Rhôs-on-Sea
Colwyn Bay
Towyn
Trearddur Bay
Deganwy
Conwy
Llanddulas
Abergele
Holy Island
Penmaenmawr
Beaumaris
Llanfairfechan
Betws-yn-Rhos
Llanneffy
Rhosneigr
Llangefni
Menai Bridge
Bangor
Tal-y-Cafn
Llanfair Talhaiarn
Llansanffraid Glan Conwy
Aberffraw
Llanfair P.G.
Llanllechid
Llangernyw
Llansannan
Newborough
Y Felinheli
Bethesda
Tal-y-Bont
Trefriw
Bylchau
Caernarfon
Llanrug
Llanberis
CONWY
Bontnewydd
Capel Curig
Llanrwst
Dinas Dinlle
Betws Garmon
Betws-y-Coed
Llanwnda
Llandwrog
Dolwyddelan
Pentrefoelas
Cerrigydrudion
Penygroes
Rhyd-Ddu
Penmachno
Clynnog-fawr
Penmachno
Caernarfon Bay
Beddgelert
Y Ma
Llanaelhaearn
SH
Blaenau Ffestiniog
Ffestiniog
Morfa Nefyn
Prenteg
Maentwrog
Nefyn
Tremadog
Bodfuan
Llanystumdwy
Porthmadog
Renrhyndeudraeth
Bala
PENINSULA
Criccieth
Talsarnau
Sarn
Borth-y-Gest
Trawsfynydd
LLEYN
Pwllheli
Harlech
GWYNEDD
Llanbedrog
SNOWDONIA
Llanuwchllyn
Aberdaron
Y Rhiw
Abersoch
Llanbedr
NATIONAL
Ganllwyd
PARK
Bardsey Island
Dyffryn Ardudwy
Tal-y-bont
Dolgellau
Dinas-Mawddwy
Barmouth
Llanga
Fairbourne
Mallwyd
Llwyngwril
Corris
Cemmaes Road
Llanbrynmair
Bryncrug
Llangc
Tywyn
Pennal
Machynlleth
Carno
Aberdyfi
SN
Borth
Tal-y-bont
Llanidloes
Llandre
Aberystwyth
Capel Bangor
Ponterwyd
Goginan

Caravan and Camping
AA Campsite Award Winner
Town/Village name
0   10 miles
0   10   20 kilometres

For continuation pages refer to numbered arrows

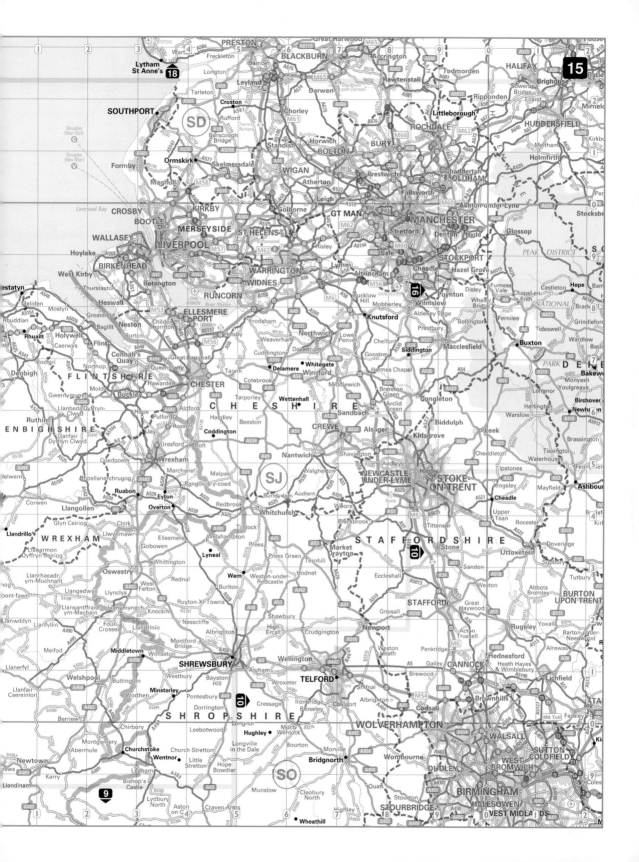

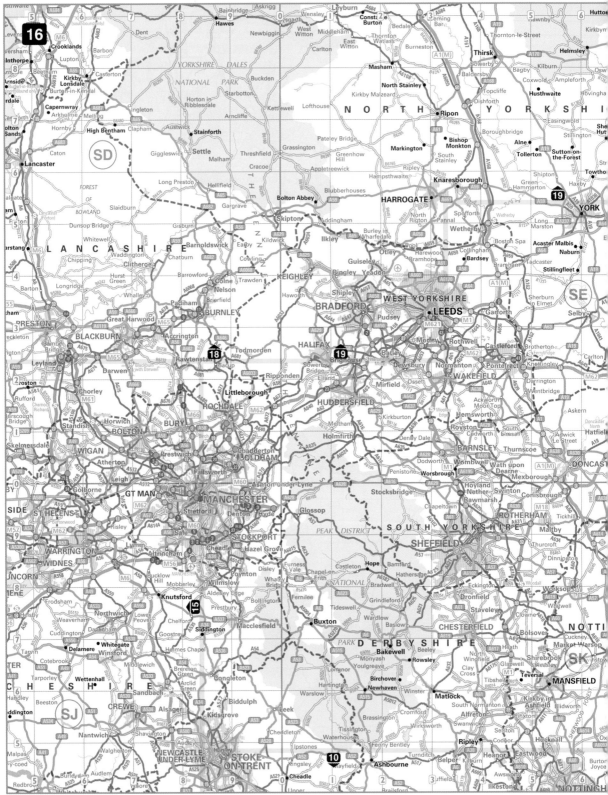

For continuation pages refer to numbered arrows

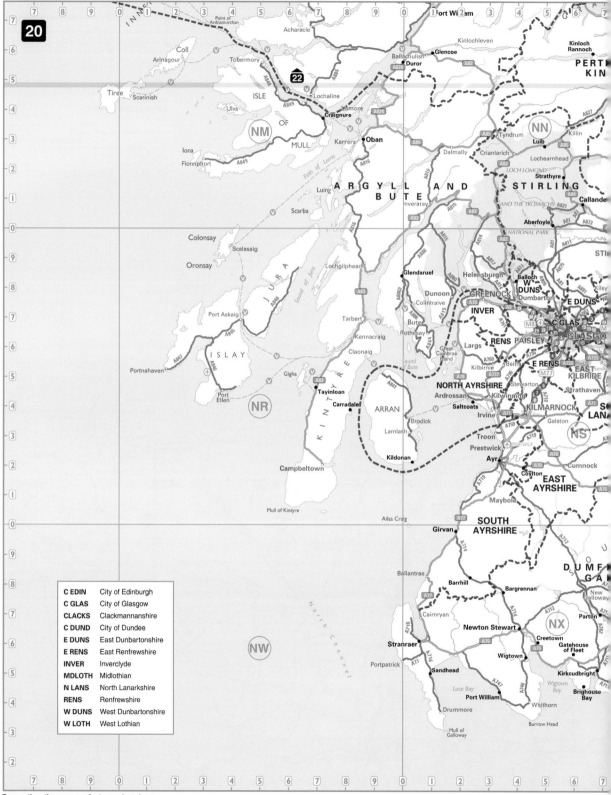

C EDIN	City of Edinburgh
C GLAS	City of Glasgow
CLACKS	Clackmannanshire
C DUND	City of Dundee
E DUNS	East Dunbartonshire
E RENS	East Renfrewshire
INVER	Inverclyde
MDLOTH	Midlothian
N LANS	North Lanarkshire
RENS	Renfrewshire
W DUNS	West Dunbartonshire
W LOTH	West Lothian

NA

NB

NA H–EILEANAN
AN IAR

Cape Wrath

Rudha Rhobhanais
(Butt of Lewis)
Port Nis
(Port of Ness)

Cellar
Head

Great
Bernera

LEWIS

Carlabhagh
(Carloway)

Scourie

A894

Lochinver

Inchnadam

A837

A858

OF

Steornabhagh
(Stornoway)

STEORNABHAGH

Tiumpan
Head

A857

A858

A859

ISLE

A857

A859

Scarp

Taransay

Tairbeart
(Tarbert)

Scalpay

Gruinard
Bay

V

A835

Laide

Ullapool

A832

Dundonnell

Pabbay

HARRIS

A859

Boreray

A858

Berneray

Gairloch

A832

V

OUTER HEBRIDES

NORTH UIST

Loch nam Madadh
(Lochmaddy)

Uig

NF

A865

A867

A865

THE LITTLE MINCH

A87

NG

Kinlochewe

A890

Achnasheen

A896

Benbecula

Ronay

A865

Dunvegan

Edinbane

ISLE

Portree

A896

A832

Wiay

A863

Raasay

Inner Sound

A890

Cannich

SOUTH
UIST

OF

Drynoch

V

Scalpay

Kyle of
Lochalsh

Balmacara

A87

A865

SKYE

A87

Loch Baghasdail
(Lochboisdale)

Soay

A851

A87

A887

Eriskay

Canna

Cuillin Sound

Ardvasar

Sound of Sleat

V

Invergarry

BARRA

V

Rúm

Mallaig

NORTH

A830

Bagh a Chaisteil
(Castlebay)

A888

Arisaig

Corpach

Spean
Bridge

Sandray

V

Eigg

A830

Fort William

Mingulay

Muck

A861

Kinlochleven

INNER HEBRIDES

Point of
Ardnamurchan

NM

Acharacle

A861

A82

Ballachulish

Glencoe

NL

Coll

V

Tobermory

A884

A82

Duror

Arinagour

A848

Tiree

Scarinish

20

ISLE

Lochaline

Lismore

Craignure

A828

A85

Ulva

A849

Kerrera

Oban

Iona

OF

A849

MULL

Dalmally

Crianlari

Fionnphort

A816

Lorne

For continuation pages refer to numbered arrows

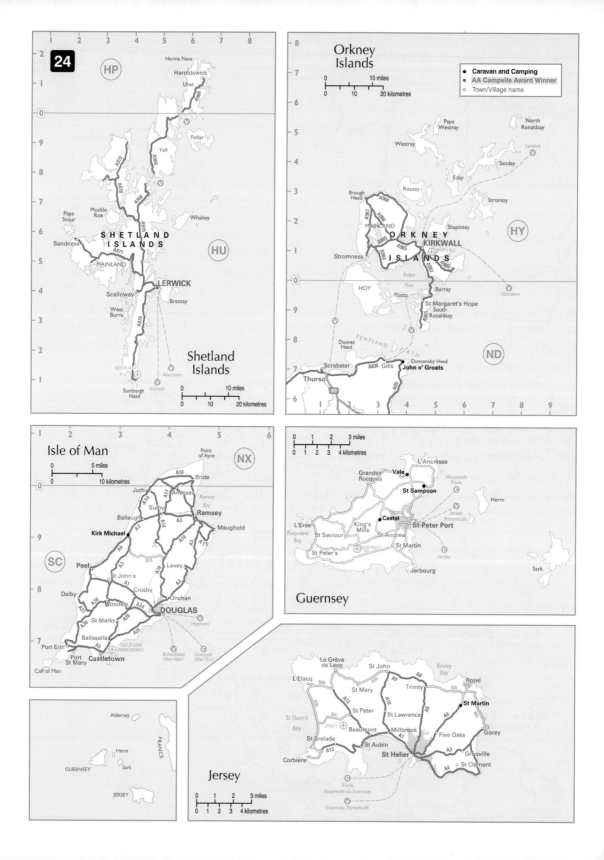

AA Camping Card Sites

The following list shows AA rated campsites that accept the AA Camping Card which is valid until 31st January 2015. See page 9 for further details of the card.

ENGLAND

CHESHIRE
DELAMERE
Fishpool Farm Caravan Park

CORNWALL
ASHTON
Boscrege Caravan & Camping Park
BUDE
Widemouth Fields Caravan & Camping Park
FALMOUTH
Pennance Mill Farm Touring Park
HELSTON
Poldown Caravan Park
LOOE
Tencreek Holiday Park
LOSTWITHIEL
Eden Valley Holiday Park
MEVAGISSEY
Seaview International Holiday Park
MULLION
Franchis Holiday Park
NEWQUAY
Treloy Touring Park
POLZEATH
Tristram Caravan & Camping Park
South Winds Caravan & Camping Park
PORTREATH
Tehidy Holiday Park
REDRUTH
Stithians Lake Country Park
SCORRIER
Wheal Rose Caravan & Camping Park
ST AGNES
Beacon Cottage Farm Touring Park
ST AUSTELL
Meadow Lakes
ST COLUMB MAJOR
Trewan Hall

ST HILARY
Wayfarers Caravan & Camping Park
ST JUST [NEAR LAND'S END]
Kelynack Caravan & Camping Park
Secret Garden Caravan & Camping Park
Roselands Caravan & Camping Park
ST MINVER
Gunvenna Caravan Park
TORPOINT
Whitsand Bay Lodge & Touring Park
WATERGATE BAY
Watergate Bay Touring Park

CUMBRIA
POOLEY BRIDGE
Park Foot Caravan & Camping Park
SILLOTH
Stanwix Park Holiday Centre
Hylton Caravan Park
WATERMILLOCK
Cove Caravan & Camping Park

DERBYSHIRE
ASHBOURNE
Carsington Fields Caravan Park
BUXTON
Lime Tree Park
NEWHAVEN
Newhaven Caravan & Camping Park

DEVON
BRIDGERULE
Hedleywood Caravan & Camping Park
CHAPMANS WELL
Chapmanswell Caravan Park
CLYST ST MARY
Crealy Meadows Caravan & Camping Park
DARTMOUTH
Woodlands Grove Caravan & Camping Park
DAWLISH
Cofton Country Holidays
Leadstone Camping
EAST ANSTEY
Zeacombe House Caravan Park

HOLSWORTHY
Tamarstone Farm
ILFRACOMBE
Hele Valley Holiday Park
KENTISBEARE
Forest Glade Holiday Park
KINGSBRIDGE
Parkland Caravan & Camping Site
MODBURY
Pennymoor Camping & Caravan Park
NEWTON ABBOT
Ross Park
PAIGNTON
Beverley Parks Caravan & Camping Park
Whitehill Country Park
SALCOMBE
Alston Camping & Caravan Site
SIDMOUTH
Salcombe Regis Caravan & Camping Park
Oakdown Country Holiday Park
SOUTH MOLTON
Riverside Caravan & Camping Park
TAVISTOCK
Woodovis Park
Langstone Manor C&C Park
TEDBURN ST MARY
Springfield Holiday Park
TORQUAY
Widdicombe Farm Touring Park
WOOLACOMBE
Woolacombe Sands Holiday Park

DORSET
BERE REGIS
Rowlands Wait Touring Park
CHARMOUTH
Manor Farm Holiday Centre
LYME REGIS
Hook Farm Caravan & Camping Park
LYTCHETT MINSTER
South Lytchett Manor C&C Park
WIMBORNE MINSTER
Charris Camping & Caravan Park

ESSEX
GREAT SALING
Golden Grove

AA Camping Card Sites *continued*

HAMPSHIRE
FORDINGBRIDGE
Sandy Balls Holiday Village

HEREFORDSHIRE
EARDISLAND
Arrow Bank Holiday Park

HERTFORDSHIRE
HODDESDON
Lee Valley Caravan Park Dobbs Weir

KENT
BIRCHINGTON
Two Chimneys Caravan Park
WROTHAM HEATH
Gate House Wood Touring Park

LINCOLNSHIRE
BOSTON
Long Acres Touring Park
GREAT CARLTON
West End Farm
MABLETHORPE
Kirkstead Holiday Park
OLD LEAKE
Old Leake Leisure Park
TATTERSHALL
Tattershall Lakes Country Park

LONDON
LONDON E4
Lee Valley Campsite
LONDON N9
Lee Valley Camping & Caravan Park

NORFOLK
BARNEY
The Old Brick Kilns
BELTON
Rose Farm Touring & Camping Park
REAT YARMOUTH
The Grange Touring Park
ST JOHN'S FEN END
Virginia Lake Caravan Park
SWAFFHAM
Breckland Meadows Touring Park

NOTTINGHAMSHIRE
TUXFORD
Orchard Park Touring C&C Park

OXFORDSHIRE
BANBURY
Barnstones Caravan & Camping Site

SHROPSHIRE
MINSTERLEY
The Old School Caravan Park
SHREWSBURY
Beaconsfield Farm Caravan Park

SOMERSET
BREAN
Holiday Resort Unity
CROWCOMBE
Quantock Orchard Caravan Park
DULVERTON
Wimbleball Lake
MARTOCK
Southfork Caravan Park
PORLOCK
Porlock Caravan Park
SHEPTON MALLET
Greenacres Camping
TAUNTON
Cornish Farm Touring Park

STAFFORDSHIRE
LONGNOR
Longnor Wood Holiday Park

SUSSEX, WEST
ARUNDEL
Ship & Anchor Marina

TYNE & WEAR
SOUTH SHIELDS
Lizard Lane Caravan & Camping Site
WARWICKSHIRE
ASTON CANTLOW
Island Meadow Caravan Park

WIGHT, ISLE OF
NEWBRIDGE
The Orchards Holiday Caravan Park

SANDOWN
Old Barn Touring Park

WILTSHIRE
BERWICK ST JAMES
Stonehenge Campsite

YORKSHIRE, NORTH
ALLERSTON
Vale of Pickering Caravan Park
FILEY
Orchard Farm Holiday Village
HELMSLEY
Golden Square Touring Caravan Park
KNARESBOROUGH
Kingfisher Caravan Park
SCARBOROUGH
Scalby Close Park
THIRSK
Hillside Caravan Park
WHITBY
Ladycross Plantation Caravan Park

SCOTLAND

ABERDEENSHIRE
STRACHAN
Feughside Caravan Park

DUMFRIES & GALLOWAY
BRIGHOUSE BAY
Brighouse Bay Holiday Park

FIFE
ST ANDREWS
Cairnsmill Holiday Park

HIGHLAND
GAIRLOCH
Gairloch Caravan Park

STIRLING
CALLANDER
Gart Caravan Park

WEST LOTHIAN
EAST CALDER
Linwater Caravan Park

WALES

ANGLESEY, ISLE OF
BEAUMARIS
Kingsbridge Caravan Park

CARMARTHENSHIRE
NEWCASTLE EMLYN
Cenarth Falls Holiday Park
Argoed Meadow Caravan & Camping Site

CEREDIGION
LLANON
Woodlands Holiday Park

CONWY
BETWS-YN-RHOS
Plas Farm Caravan Park
Peniarth Bach Farm
TAL-Y-BONT
Tynterfyn Touring Caravan Park

DENBIGHSHIRE
RHUALLT
Penisar Mynydd Caravan Park

GWYNEDD
BALA
Pen-y-Bont Touring Park
BETWS GARMON
Bryn Gloch Caravan & Camping Park
LLANDWROG
White Tower Caravan Park
TALSARNAU
Barcdy Touring Caravan & Camping Park
TAL-Y-BONT
Islawrffordd Caravan Park

PEMBROKESHIRE
HASGUARD CROSS
Hasguard Cross Caravan Park
TENBY
Well Park Caravan & Camping Site
Wood Park Caravans

POWYS
BRONLLYS
Anchorage Caravan Park
LLANDRINDOD WELLS
Disserth Caravan & Camping Park
MIDDLETOWN
Bank Farm Caravan Park

WREXHAM
EYTON
The Plassey Leisure Park

NORTHERN IRELAND

CO ANTRIM
BALLYCASTLE
Watertop Farm
BUSHMILLS
Ballyness Caravan Park

REPUBLIC OF IRELAND

CO MAYO
CASTLEBAR
Lough Lannagh Caravan Park

Acknowledgments
AA Media would like to thank the following photographers, companies and picture libraries for their assistance in the preparation of this book.

Abbreviations for the picture credits are as follows – (t) top; (b) bottom; (c) centre; (l) left; (r) right; (AA) AA World Travel Library

Interior
001 AA/Adam Burton; 002 AA/James Tims; 003 AA/Adam Burton; 004 AA/Jonathan Smith; 005 AA/Adam Burton; 010 AA/James Tims; 011 AA/Adam Burton; 013 AA/James Tims; 014 AA/James Tims; 016 AA/James Tims; 017 Beecraigs Caravan & Camping Site, Linlithgow; 021 AA/Andrew Newey; 022l AA/Tim Locke; 022r Polmanter Touring Park; 023l Cairnsmill Holiday Park; 023r Tyddyn Isaf Caravan Park; 024l Woodovis Park; 024r Swiss Farm Caravan Park; 025l Fields End Water Caravan Park; 025r Woodclose Caravan Park; 026l South Meadows Caravan Park; 026r Hafan Y Mor Holiday Park; 027l Grouse Hill Caravan Park; 027r Greenacres Camping; 028 Sumners Ponds Fishery & Campsite; 030 Sumners Ponds Fishery & Campsite; 031t Sumners Ponds Fishery & Campsite; 031b Sumners Ponds Fishery & Campsite; 032 Sumners Ponds Fishery & Campsite; 033 Sumners Ponds Fishery & Campsite; 036 AA/Adam Burton; 037 AA/James Tims; 045 AA/Michael Moody; 046 AA/Chris Coe; 050/1 AA/Malc Birkitt; 052/3 AA/Adam Burton; 54 AA/Caroline Jones; 55 AA/John Wood; 61 AA/John Wood; 79 AA/John Wood; 104 AA/Adam Burton; 110/1 AA/Adam Burton; 112/3 AA/Peter Sharpe; 114t AA/Tom Mackie; 114b AA/E A Bowness; 115 AA/Anna Mockford & Nick Bonetti; 123 AA/Anna Mockford & Nick Bonetti; 132/3 AA/Anna Mockford & Nick Bonetti; 134/5 AA/Andy Midgley; 136 AA/Andy Tryner; 137 AA/Tom Mackie; 142/3 AA/Nigel Hicks; 145 AA/Nigel Hicks; 175 AA/Guy Edwardes; 176/7 AA/Andrew Newey; 178 AA/Max Jourdan; 179 AA/Andrew Newey; 185 AA/Adam Burton; 201 Andrew Newey; 234 AA/Jonathan Smith; 236/7 AA/Tom Mackie; 238 AA/Adrian Baker; 239 AA/Derek Forss; 254 AA; 261 AA/Caroline Jones; 264/5 AA/Steve Day; 266 AA/Wyn Voysey; 267 AA/Steve Day; 283 AA/Tom Mackie; 284/5 AA/Tom Mackie; 286 AA/Clive Sawyer; 287 AA/Tom Mackie; 294/5 AA/John Miller; 296 AA/John Miller; 297 AA/Derek Forss; 306/7 AA/Andrew Newey; 308 AA/Wyn Voysey; 309 AA/Derek Forss; 313 AA/Simon McBride; 320/1 AA/Caroline Jones; 322/3 AA/Mike Kipling; 324 AA/Pete Bennett; 325t AA/Mike Kipling; 325b AA/John Morrison; 327 AA/David Clapp; 354/5 AA/Stewart Bates; 356/7 AA/Stephen Whitehorne; 358 AA/Jim Henderson; 359t AA/Stephen Whitehorne; 359b AA/Jonathan Smith; 370 AA/Jeff Beazley; 387 AA/Sue Anderson; 394/5 AA/Mark Bauer; 396 AA/Nick Jenkins; 397 AA/Graham Matthews; 426 AA/Chris Warren; 427 AA/Ian Burgum; 433 AA/Nick Jenkins; 434/5 AA/George Munday; 441 AA/Chris Hill.

Every effort has been made to trace the copyright holders, and we apologise in advance for any unintentional omissions or errors. We would be pleased to apply any corrections in a following edition of this publication.

Index

Entries are listed alphabetically by town name, then campsite name. The following abbreviations have been used: C&C – Caravan & Camping; HP – Holiday Park; CP – Caravan Park; C&C Club – Camping & Caravanning Club Site